Routledge International Encyclopedia of Women

Global Women's Issues and Knowledge

Volume 2   Education: Health—Hypertension

Editorial Board

Routledge International Encyclopedia of Women

Global Women's Issues and Knowledge

Volume 2   Education: Health—Hypertension

Cheris Kramarae and Dale Spender

General Editors

Routledge

New York • London
2000

NOTICE

Some articles in the *Routledge International Encyclopedia of Women* relate to physical and mental health; nothing in these articles, singly or collectively, is meant to replace the advice and expertise of physicians and other health professionals. Some articles relate to law and legal matters; nothing in any of these articles is meant to replace the advice and expertise of lawyers and other legal professionals.

Published in 2000 by
Routledge
29 West 35 Street
New York, NY 10001

Routledge is an imprint of the Taylor & Francis Group

Copyright © 2000 Routledge

Published in Great Britain by
Routledge
11 New Fetter Lane
London EC4P 4EE

Library of Congress Cataloging-in-Publication Data
Routledge international encyclopedia of women: global women's issues and knowledge / general editors, Cheris Kramarae, Dale Spender.

    p. cm.
    Includes bibliographical references and index.
    ISBN 0-415-92088-4 (set) — ISBN 0-415-92089-2 (v.1) —
    ISBN 0-415-92090-6 (v.2) — ISBN 0-415-92091-4 (v.3) —
    ISBN 0-415-92092-2 (v.4)
    1. Women—Encyclopedias. 2. Feminism—Encyclopedias.
I. Title: International encyclopedia of women. II. Kramarea,
Cheris. III. Spender, Dale.
HQ1115 .R69 2000
305.4′03—dc21
                                00-045792

10 9 8 7 6 5 4 3 2 1

ISBN 0-415-92088-4 (4-volume set)
ISBN 0-415-92089-2 (volume 1)
ISBN 0-415-92090-6 (volume 2)
ISBN 0-415-92091-4 (volume 3)
ISBN 0-415-92092-2 (volume 4)

Contents of Volume 2

Alphabetical List of Articles

Routledge International Encyclopedia of Women

Global Women's Issues and Knowledge

Volume 2   Education: Health—Hypertension

EDUCATION: Health

See HEALTH EDUCATION.

EDUCATION: Higher Education

Higher education refers to additional study undertaken after compulsory schooling. Universities are the oldest institutions of higher education, tracing back to Indian, Chinese, Greco-Roman, Byzantine, and Arabic societies.

Greater participation in higher education has promoted women's social and occupational positioning, particularly through increasing their representation in powerful areas of public life. It has also facilitated institutional change, including women's studies curricula, feminist scholarship, and action against sex discrimination and harassment.

Historically, women have occupied a marginal position within institutions of higher learning: universities established in the twelfth century were all-male communities attached to monasteries. Apart from some isolated instances, due mainly to individual tenacity (Lie et al., 1994: 205; Wertheim, 1997: 137–140), universities did not begin to admit women until the mid-nineteenth century, when women's colleges started to appear. Considerable scholarship exists on the merits—or disadvantages—of single-sex higher education. These debates are still current, particularly in Islamic education (Lie et al., 1994: 137–138).

Since the 1960s, international trends toward mass higher education have increased women's participation, particularly through community colleges, distance education, and special entry schemes, as well as linkages between adult, vocational, and university education. However, since the 1980s, privatization, in former communist states and elsewhere, has gradually shifted educational costs onto the individual, prompting suggestions that women's participation may now decrease. Access to higher education is closely associated with global poverty and affluence. In developing and newly industrializing countries, the female presence in higher education is small. However, civil unrest can produce contradictory outcomes, as in Iran, where labor shortages after the Iran-Iraq war led to improvements in academic women's employment (Lie et al., 1994: 206, 211).

In wealthy industrialized nations like the United States and Australia, and in parts of Europe, female university participation has matched or slightly exceeded that of men (Jacobs, 1996: 155–157). However, women have not yet attained full equality and lag well behind men at the senior faculty level and in advanced research degrees.

Globally, most women students enroll in areas traditionally regarded as "feminine"—education, health, the humanities, and the social sciences—and fewer women enter physical sciences, engineering, and technology (Thomas, 1990: 4; Wertheim, 1997: 174), except in places where sciences have lacked prestige or political influence (Lie et al., 1994: 208–209). Changes in the gender demographics of a previously "masculine" profession have sometimes been associated with a decrease in its status.

These power dynamics reflect culturally constructed hierarchies of "masculine" and "feminine," with "feminine" knowledge regarded as inferior. Access and equity policies in the late twentieth century concentrated on moving women into "nontraditional" areas like physics, law, engineering, and computer science. This raises two questions. First, does this approach adequately address all gender equity issues in higher education? Second, does it imply that areas traditionally perceived as "feminine" are less valuable?

Some earlier critiques of higher education centered on why its practices were not woman-friendly and on women's silence within masculinist, competitive, aggressive learning environments (Lewis, 1993). Extensive feminist literature has also examined the gendered construction of scientific and technological knowledge.

Contemporary projects in curriculum and pedagogy are trying to make nontraditional areas more woman-friendly, especially by changing the cultures of disciplines and fostering women's skills and confidence. Identity politics and postcolonialism influenced late-twentieth-century writing about women in higher education. This work uses personal narrative to theorize about experiences of empowerment and marginalization, while criticizing approaches that assume homogeneity among women and consider gender in isolation from cultural background, age, sexuality, disability, and class (Mintz and Rothblum, 1997; Spivak, 1993; Tokarcyzk and Fay, 1993; Wing, 1997).

There have been calls for more women—and for more women with particular experiences, such as indigenous women or women with disabilities—to act as role models for students and colleagues. These debates highlight the complexity of women's engagement with higher education, raising arguments about merit, tokenism, and essentialism. Women employed in higher education continue to grapple with issues such as denial of tenure, job security, slower promotion rates, inconsistent application of standards of "merit" to men and women, sexual harassment, and other forms of discrimination. In many countries, women academic and administrative staff are concentrated at lower levels of their institutions and form only a small minority in the most senior positions. The gendered division of labor in society is reflected, too, in women's greater share of teaching, pastoral care, and clerical roles, while men dominate in research and senior management.

Feminist activism in higher education has been crucial in developing equal opportunity policies, creating progressive networks among staff and students, and broadening university curricula, research, and teaching practices. Often, however, this has been achieved only at great personal and professional costs to individual women.

The phrase *chilly climate* (Sandler, 1986), which entered the higher education lexicon in the 1980s, reflects the range of cultural and social barriers to women's success in the academy. It refers to institutional and individual hostility to women, resistance to feminist initiatives, and the defense of masculinist privilege. In directing attention to cultural, informal, and less visible dimensions of women's experiences, chilly climate gives voice to a fuller range of concerns than those identified by a strictly quantitative focus on participation rates.

See Also

AFFIRMATIVE ACTION; CURRICULUM TRANSFORMATION MOVEMENT; DEVELOPMENT: OVERVIEW; DISCRIMINATION; EDUCATION: CHILLY CLIMATE IN THE CLASSROOM; EDUCATION: GENDERED SUBJECT CHOICE; EDUCATION: SINGLE-SEX AND COEDUCATION; EDUCATORS: HIGHER EDUCATION; EQUAL OPPORTUNITIES: EDUCATION; KNOWLEDGE; PEDAGOGY: FEMINIST; WOMEN'S STUDIES: OVERVIEW

References and Further Reading

Cohen, Dinah, et al., eds. 1999. *Winds of change: Women and the culture of universities, 13–17 July 1998, conference proceedings. 2 vols.* Sydney: Equity and Diversity Unit, University of Technology.

Jacobs, Jerry. 1996. Gender inequality and higher education. *Annual Review of Sociology* 22: 153–185.

Lewis, Magda Gere. 1993. *Without a word.* New York: Routledge.

Lie, Suzanne Stiver, Lynda Malik, and Duncan Harris, eds. 1994. *The gender gap in higher education.* London: Kogan Page.

Mintz, Beth, and Esther Rothblum, eds. 1997. *Lesbians in academia.* New York: Routledge.

Sandler, Bernice. 1986. *Campus climate revisited.* Washington, D.C.: Association of American Colleges.

Spivak, Gayatri Chakravorty. 1993. *Outside in the teaching machine.* New York: Routledge.

Thomas, Kim. 1990. *Gender and subject in higher education.* Buckingham, U.K.: SRHE and Open University Press.

Tokarcyzk, Michelle, and Elizabeth Fay. 1993. *Working-class women in the academy.* Amherst: University of Massachusetts Press.

Wertheim, Margaret. 1997. *Pythagoras' trousers.* New York: Random House.

Wing, Adrien Katherine, ed. 1997. *Critical race feminism.* New York: New York University Press.

Lici Inge
Esther Rice

EDUCATION: Mathematics

It was not until the 1970s in the United States that attention was given to differentiation in mathematics achievement by gender, led by the seminal work of Elizabeth Fennema (Fennema and Sherman, 1977, 1978). The focus of this early work, which has been the first stage of activity in many countries, was data gathering. Nel Noddings has called this the first of three generations of feminist research where women are seeking equality with men (see Hart, 1992). Researchers responded to observations of apparent gender bias in, for example, performance as well as rates of participation in mathematics course taking. Women mathematicians are well aware of the masculine bias in participation; many mathematics departments in universities have no or very few women academics. However, Fennema and her colleagues were the first to track this imbalance back into schools and begin to catalog the differences and research reasons why this should be so.

Differences in participation depend on circumstances, both educational and social. In the United States, in secondary schools, mathematics courses are optional, so who opts, why, what influences them, and what their outcomes are are all questions that have been asked. Where mathematics is a compulsory subject, participation differences might be interpreted in terms of levels of achievement and, if it exists, subsequent "streaming" or "tracking" of students, so that top streams are likely to be dominated by male achievers (see Burton, 1986, 1990, 1994). In some countries, single-sex classes or schools have provided data on differences in achievement and experiences in classrooms. Evidence suggests that such data, whether national or international and comparative, provide only a meager picture of *who* achieves at *what* mathematics under *which* assessment regime. How class, race, age, and experience, in and out of school, interact with sex to produce the recorded differences is often left unquestioned (although Reyes and Stanic, 1986, offer one, rare, analysis). The links between these differences and the mathematical diet that the learners have been offered and between this diet and societal and academic views on the nature of mathematics remain largely unexplored. Work done on the impact of different teaching, learning, and assessing strategies demonstrates that gender *is* an indicative factor for differences in performance.

Explanations for Gender Differences

The observation of these differences does not, however, provide an explanation for why they exist. Some small amount of work has been done on genetic explanations, but many scholars are critical of the assumptions and the methods used. "Mathematics anxiety" attracted attention at one stage, but interest receded, if only because of the implicit victimization that fails to account for personal, social, and cultural experiences of females and males. Researchers have offered explanatory models. For example, Laurie Reyes and George Stanic (1986) draw attention to five factors: societal influences, school mathematics curricula, teacher attitudes, student attitudes and achievement-related behaviors, and classroom processes. Gilah Leder's (1990: 15) model distinguishes environmental variables, emerging through society, the home, and the school, from learner-related variables, including cognitive development and beliefs. Elizabeth Fennema and Penny Peterson's (1985) model of autonomous learning behaviors identifies behaviors necessary to independent pursuit of high-cognitive-level activities in mathematics linked to females' perceived lower demonstration of such behaviors. Those in the developed world should not assume that because the references are mainly from the United States, the United Kingdom, and Australia, interest in gender and mathematics is outside the educational agenda of many third world countries. This is certainly not the case. Workshops to address mathematics learning from a socially just perspective have been held in Africa—for example, in Botswana and Sierra Leone. A seminar held in Sweden in 1993 had representation from 23 countries, including participants from the Middle East and the Far East.

Equity in Learning Mathematics

Fennema (1990) defines three different kinds of equity in learning mathematics: equity as equal education opportunity, equity as equal educational treatment, and equity as equal educational outcome. As she points out, in many countries the attempt to achieve equity between males and females

has provoked investigation into the issue—that is, first-generation research. This approach has been identified by Bennison et al. (1984) as a deficit approach to equity. They describe three other approaches in the literature: the assimilationist one, which asserts that learning characteristics are similar despite gender; the pluralistic one, which acknowledges diversity in learner characteristics; and the social justice one, which evokes fair treatment across similarities and differences. Some of these fit comfortably into Noddings's second generation of feminist thinking, in which female qualities are identified as particular and the impetus to be accepted as the same as males is rejected. Some of the research on classroom pedagogical experience falls into this category.

Where Next?

Noddings's third generation of feminism involves a critique of the first two, so that new approaches can be expected to take advantage of what has already been done as well as to make progress on what still needs to be done. Work in the 1990s that queries the status and derivation of knowledge and knowing in mathematics from a gender perspective seems to fall into this category (see, for example, Burton, 1995). Such epistemological inquiries are distinct from the former focus on learning and teaching.

Work in gender and mathematics has been supported and encouraged by a number of international and national networks, such as the International Organization for Women and Mathematics Education (IOWME). Some national groupings, such as Le Mouvement International pour les Femmes et l'Enseignement de la Mathématique (International Organization of Women and Mathematics Education) are affiliated with the IOWME network, and the Association of Women in Mathematics in the United States also maintains close relationships with it.

See Also

EDUCATION: ACHIEVEMENT; EDUCATION: GENDERED SUBJECT CHOICE; EQUAL OPPORTUNITIES: EDUCATION; EXAMINATIONS AND ASSESSMENT

References and Further Reading

Bennison, A., L. C. Wilkinson, E. Fennema, V. Masemann, and P. Peterson. 1984. Equity or equality: What shall it be? In E. Fennema and M. J. Ayer, eds., *Women and education: Equity or equality?* Berkeley, Calif.: McCutchan.

Burton, Leone. 1986. *Girls into maths can go.* Eastbourne, U.K.: Holt, Rinehart, and Winston.

———. 1990. *Gender and mathematics: An international perspective.* London: Cassell.

———. 1994. *Who counts? Mathematics achievement in Europe.* Stoke-on-Trent, U.K.: Trentham.

———. 1995. Moving towards a feminist epistemology of mathematics. In G. Leder, ed., *Educational Studies in Mathematics* 28(3): 1–17.

Fennema, Elizabeth. 1990. Justice, equity, and mathematics education. In G. Leder and E. Fennema eds., *Mathematics and gender.* New York: Teachers College Press.

Fennema, Elizabeth, and Penny Peterson. 1985. Autonomous learning behavior: A possible explanation of gender-related differences in mathematics. In L. C. Wilkinson and C. B. Marrett, eds., *Gender-related differences in classroom interaction.* London: Academic.

Fennema, Elizabeth, and Julia A. Sherman. 1977. Sex-related differences in mathematics achievement, spatial visualization, and affective factors. *American Educational Research Journal* 14: 51–71.

———. 1978. Sex-related differences in mathematics achievement, spatial visualization, and affective factors: A further study. *Journal for Research in Mathematics Education* 9: 189–203.

Hart, Lesley E. 1992. Two generations of feminist thinking. *Journal for Research in Mathematics Education* 23(1): 79–83.

Leder, Gilah. 1990. Gender differences in mathematics. In G. Leder and E. Fennema, eds., *Mathematics and gender.* New York: Teachers College Press.

Reyes, Laurie, and George Stanic. 1986. Race, sex, socioeconomic status, and mathematics. *Journal for Research in Mathematics Education* 19(1): 26–43.

Leone Burton

EDUCATION:
Middle East and North Africa

Educational opportunities for women in the Middle East and North Africa have, in general, advanced greatly since the 1950s, and all the Arab countries, however conservative, have formulated active policies on education, with increasing numbers of girls receiving education at least to primary level. However, there is a wide disparity of education available throughout the region, and economic and cultural factors have placed constraints on the development of girls' education. Consequently, despite gains, there is still much that needs to be achieved, particularly in the area of female illiteracy.

Traditionally the exclusion of women from public life meant that little value was placed on educating females.

Until the end of the nineteenth century, few women were educated, and no formal education systems existed for women. All the countries in the region had a predominantly Muslim population, and within Islamic culture there was a strong concern for the modesty of girls, which placed limits on their public role. Girls were expected to marry at an early age, and their horizons were strictly limited to the home and family, obviating the need for education. This is despite the high priority that Islam placed on education. The prophet Muhammad is recorded as saying, "Seeking knowledge is mandatory for every Muslim, man or woman" (al-Bayhaqi), and he did not distinguish between the right of men or women to be educated. The Qur'an repeatedly exhorts its readers, both male and female, to read, consider, and learn. Under the Prophet's social reforms, classes were set up on Islam for newly converted Muslim women. Muhammad arranged for one of his wives to be tutored by a woman and even supported the education of female slaves.

Before the nineteenth century, those few women who were educated came mainly from the most affluent families and were tutored privately at home, with their studies centering on religious texts and reading and writing. Some girls from the middle classes attended the local *kuttabs,* or Qur'anic schools. These were informal schools, usually attached to the local mosque, that offered elementary instruction in religion, reading, writing, and arithmetic and where girls and boys were taught together. However, the majority of the population did not have access to schools, and consequently illiteracy rates were extremely high for men and women.

The first formal girls' schools were established by Christian missionaries, whose activities were mainly concentrated in the Levantine countries. In 1846 a Catholic order opened the first girls' school in Egypt, which was soon followed by the first government school in the region. Egypt was also home to the early Arab feminist movement, in which a number of Egyptian women were closely involved. Notable among these were Malak Hifni Nasif, who was active in teaching and writing and who designed a ten-point plan to improve the status of Egyptian women that centered on primary- and secondary-school opportunities for women, and Huda Shirawi, who established the first secondary school for girls and was closely involved in the introduction of women to Cairo University in 1927. American missionaries had also opened schools in Beirut and Jerusalem, and in 1860 their 33 schools enrolled 1,000 students, of whom 200 were girls. However, such girls' schools were few and far between, usually in urban areas, and often charged fees, which limited the number of girls able to attend.

It was only at the end of the twentieth century that the status of basic education and literacy improved and greater educational opportunities were available for girls. These improvements can be attributed to increased national commitment to education, with all governments acknowledging the target of universal compulsory education. This commitment is most clearly seen in the increase in public expenditure on education, which rose to 6.6 percent of the region's gross national product. All countries provide free education, and almost 84 percent of all primary-age children in the region were enrolled in schools at the beginning of the twenty-first century. Twelve countries reached universal primary rates, including Bahrain, Iraq, Jordan, Kuwait, Lebanon, Oman, Qatar, Syria, Tunisia, and the United Arab Emirates.

Female enrollment has increased substantially at all levels, and from 1970 to 1984 it increased 50 percent faster than in any other developing region at primary level; significant gains have also been made at secondary level. Some countries, including Jordan, the United Arab Emirates, and Bahrain, have also managed to close or eliminate the gender gap and offer education equally to boys and girls. However, other countries in the region continued to fall short of this goal: in Egypt only 79 percent of girls were enrolled in primary school in 1987, although universal enrollment has been achieved for boys, and only 56 and 65 percent of girls were enrolled in primary schools in Morocco and Saudi Arabia, respectively.

The most startling gains in female education have been made in the six Gulf states. Historically little attention was paid to the education of girls in these extremely conservative Islamic states, but huge oil revenues have transformed the societies, and girls' education now rivals, and in many cases surpasses, that of countries like Egypt and Lebanon, where the educational systems date to the late nineteenth century. For example, Kuwait increased its female enrollment rate at secondary level from 1 percent in 1950 to 80 percent in 1987, which places it far above any other country in the region. Oman also implemented significant changes, and although its national education program started only in 1970, educational opportunities for girls had improved so significantly by 2000 that female students made up 47 percent of the student population at secondary and tertiary levels and more than 70 percent of primary-school teachers in Oman were female.

Women's participation at colleges and universities throughout the region has increased substantially, and as of 2000 female students outnumbered male students at the universities of Kuwait and Qatar, and Jordan had more women in higher education in relation to country population than the United Kingdom or Japan. This is due in part to the number of boys who go overseas to continue their education but also reflects the increased opportunities for girls and a changing cultural attitude. At both secondary and tertiary levels females have consistently achieved higher exam success than males. Although women in higher education tend to select traditionally female fields of study in the humanities and social sciences, one area where they are highly represented is medicine, because many Muslims are averse to the treatment of women by male doctors, and therefore women are encouraged to take up this profession. In Egypt women are also well represented in the field of engineering.

Vigorous literacy campaigns also were introduced throughout the region, and estimated female literacy increased from 13.2 percent in 1970 to 31.5 percent in 1985. Both government and nongovernmental organizations were tackling the problem of female illiteracy; for example, in the United Arab Emirates, Sheikha Fatima, wife of the ruler, established the Women's Federation, which champions the cause of female literacy and provides free adult education classes for women. Illiteracy among women in the United Arab Emirates had been nearly eradicated by 2000. However, throughout the region the actual number of illiterate females rose, and illiteracy was much more prevalent among females than males, thus increasing the gender disparity.

Despite the advances in female education, a number of constraints continued to limit girls' and women's educational opportunities, including economic diversity, which affects the quantity and quality of education available, and a prevailing traditional view of women.

The region exhibits extreme economic diversity, and many countries are constrained in what they can spend on their education systems. In Egypt, for example, a population of about 50 million and a low per capita income combine to hinder the progress of female education, whereas in Saudi Arabia and Kuwait large resources have been committed to education. The availability and accessibility of schools also affect the provision of education for girls. The lack of schools, teachers, and teaching materials all contribute to girls' low enrollment, particularly in rural areas, and the lower-income countries cannot afford to improve their educational facilities. The lack of qualified female teachers is also a constraint, because a direct connection has been drawn between the presence of female teachers in schools and girls' enrollment. Girls are also more likely to drop out of school, particularly in rural areas. The desirability of early marriage takes priority over a girl's education.

Throughout the region women continue to have a lower overall status, and some parents are still reluctant to have their daughters educated. Prevailing sex-role stereotypes place a lower value on educating girls than boys, and in many communities, particularly rural ones, little value is placed on the education of girls. Mixed-sex classrooms and male teachers add to the parents' distrust. Egypt, Iraq, Jordan, and Syria have all stressed the acceptability of coeducation, at least to primary level, because this avoids the expense of separate schools, but in Saudi Arabia there is a completely separate system of male and female education. The general pattern, which is coeducation at primary and tertiary levels and single-sex secondary schools, places a greater burden on educational budgets.

There is also a need for women to work together to improve their status. The limited role that women have in decision making and setting policy has not helped to advance female education. However, at the turn of the twenty-first century, increasing numbers of educated women were entering the workplace, and many education ministries had women in senior positions.

Another possible constraint on female education was the rising Islamic consciousness movement. There were fears that as states became more religiously conservative, women's education would be adversely affected.

Clearly, despite gains, there is a need to increase and improve the educational opportunities available for girls and women in the Middle East and North Africa. Most governments do recognize the problems and are trying to respond, aware that improving girls' and women's educational participation would benefit both the social and the economic development of their countries, but inadequate resources limit their options. Reforms need to be specifically aimed at girls and women, because in the past education policies were not designed to promote girls' and women's education or to lessen gender inequality. Rather, progress in female education has been a by-product of other reforms. Reforms must also be sensitive to the differing needs in the region, and governments must individually set goals and priorities for improving female education.

See Also

EDUCATION: ACHIEVEMENT; EDUCATION: SINGLE-SEX AND COEDUCATION; ISLAM

References and Further Reading

King, Elizabeth M., and Anne M. Hill. 1993. *Women's education in developing countries.* Baltimore: Johns Hopkins University Press.

Mernissi, Fatima. 1987. *Beyond the veil: Male-female dynamics in modern Muslim society.* Rev. ed. Bloomington: Indiana University Press.

Minai, Naila. 1981. *Women in Islam.* New York: Seaview.

Szyliowicz, Joseph S. 1973. *Education and modernization in the Middle East.* Ithaca, N.Y.: Cornell University Press.

UNICEF. 1994. *Strategies for female education in the Middle East and North Africa.* Paris: UNICEF.

Waddy, Charis. 1980. *Women in Muslim history.* London: Longman.

Charlotte Boyle

EDUCATION: Music

See MUSIC EDUCATION.

EDUCATION: Nonsexist

The term *nonsexist education* refers to intentional and systematic interventions to counteract sexism in society by educational means.

The unequal positions of males and females in society have often been attributed to sex-biased attitudes and practices in the educational experience of the young. Upbringing along sexist lines is based on stereotypical division between the sexes, thereby narrowing the options and autonomy of the individual. Girls in particular have been found to be harmed by expectations that assume that they will adopt conforming, feminine roles.

In a broad sense, gender-linked preconceptions counter the stated commitment of modern education to equalize access to educational resources. Equal access is viewed today as going beyond the purely technical sense of providing schools for all. In the modern and generally acknowledged sense it also aims at rendering the actual educational experience fair and equitable, in order to encourage the development of each student's abilities to the fullest extent. Consequently, nonsexist interventions, as with *antiracist policies,* must be viewed in the context of the democratic aspirations to equal educational opportunities, including gender-equitable opportunities.

The agencies for nonsexist interventions are of three major kinds.

1. *State administration:* A number of initiatives for such agencies have come from governmental sources for example, Sex Discrimination Act in Britain; Title IX in the United States; The Prime Minister's Committee on the Status of Women: Action Guide, Israel; The Commissioner for Gender Equity in Education, Ministry of Education, Israel.

2. *Private initiatives of groups or individuals:* School administrators and teachers often revise their own school practices; publishers provide guidelines for sex-equitable representation in books; feminist groups carry out investigations and suggest courses of action; parents intervene for change (AAUW, 1992).

3. *Institutions of higher learning:* These offer preservice and in-service training programs for teachers and other school personnel, as well as programs in women's studies departments that sometimes engage in intervention projects.

Examples of Nonsexist Education Programs

Creating a natural home environment. Families with children, committed to equal opportunities, often create an environment in which egalitarian values prevail on a daily basis, by personal example, consistent choices of educational material, and active, critical assessment of sexist phenomena. Although no child can be entirely shielded from the overall social climate, this kind of upbringing may constitute a sound basis for resistance to pressures of a sex-stereotypical nature.

Programs in the school environment. Most societies greatly rely on the socializing effects of formal education. Consequently, schools for all age groups sometimes become settings for nonsexist programs.

Teachers who are actively committed to the issue of sex equity might use opportunities in the course of teaching to raise and discuss it. A continuous awareness during school hours will work best if combined with a nonsexist home atmosphere. But even when teachers are the sole mediators of nonsexism, instances of the widespread unequal and stereotypical representation of women in textbooks, sexist comments and jokes among students, and media news reflecting sexism can serve as prompts for intervention.

More structured programs are often presented in a step-by-step format. They take the form of books, lesson plans, and syllabi, occasionally complete with audiovisual material and activity schemes. In terms of content, these programs can be divided as follows.

1. *Raising awareness:* Programs that identify and redress sex-biased attitudes in general and in specific social institutions: "Women's Proper Place"; "Women and the Law"

2. *Feminist aspects of school subjects:* "Women Scientists in Ancient Greece"

3. *Selected objectives and target populations:* "Girls into Technology" (written programs for students usually provide a teacher's guide)

4. *Restructuring of the physical setting:* Desegregation of seating order or of playroom corners

It has been found that programs will have little effect if the teacher is not personally committed to sex equity and is not able to convey this commitment with conviction.

A different structural intervention relates to the debate of coeducation versus single-sex schools. Historically, schools, often part of the religious system, were established for boys, with girls receiving no education or a markedly inferior one. Many countries at all levels of industrialization still maintain single-sex and coeducational schools side by side. In other countries, such as the United States and Israel, coeducation is the rule in all but the religious sectors.

In the past, coeducation has been instrumental in giving women access to equal options. New feminist research has found, however, that many coeducational classes maintain an androcentric—that is, male-centered—climate that is detrimental to girls' motivation and self-esteem. Selected examples are direct intellectual nurturing (of boys more than girls); gendered curricular channeling (boys for science, girls for the arts); teacher-student interaction (more with boys); general salience of the boys; and male-centered lessons and books. There is some evidence that more girls from single-sex schools are more motivated to choose high-level, nontraditional careers.

These findings alerted some feminist scholars to the possible advantages of single-sex schooling for girls and to the benefits of girls-only programs in math and science, areas in which girls often underachieve in coeducational settings. Although research results on the advantages of these programs are not unanimous, in the 1990s in the United States and Canada, there was some growth of single-sex schools designed for the empowerment of girls.

Nonsexist education programs belong to the affective and value domain and are best evaluated by observing long-term changes in attitudes and behavior. Consequently, testing the immediate outcomes of a program will be notably problematic. Frequently, attitudes before and after the intervention are measured. In general, girls are more affected by nonsexist interventions than are boys, who often resist changes in their position.

See Also

EDUCATION: GENDER EQUITY; EDUCATION: SINGLE-SEX AND COEDUCATION; EQUAL OPPORTUNITIES: EDUCATION; FEMININITY; GENDER CONSTRUCTIONS IN THE FAMILY; SEXISM

References and Further Reading

American Association of University Women (AAUW). 1992. *How schools shortchange girls: A study of major findings on girls and education.* Washington, D.C.: AAUW and National Education Association.

Horgan, Dianne D. 1995. *Achieving gender equity: Strategies for the classroom.* Boston: Allyn and Bacon.

Klein, Susan, et al. 1994. Continuing the journey toward gender equity. *Educational Researcher* 23(8).

Mahony, Pat. 1985. *Schools for the boys? Coeducation reassessed.* London: Hutchinson.

Sadker, Myra, and David Sadker. 1994. *Failing at fairness: How America's schools cheat girls.* New York: Charles Scribner's Sons.

Shmurak, Carole B. 1998. *Voices of hope: Adolescent girls at single sex and coeducational schools.* New York: Peter Lang.

Shoshanna Mayer-Young

EDUCATION: North America

From a feminist perspective, some aspects of education in North America have changed very little while other aspects have changed extensively since the common school movement of the 1830s and 1840s. This movement emphasized creating schools in which all children attended in common and were taught a common curriculum. Education in North America was created primarily to provide a utilitarian education and to transmit the culture required to enter the middle class (Spring, 1990: 22).

Historical Background

A system of public education was established in Canada between the 1840s and 1870s. In the United States, the first high school was established in 1821 and the first kindergarten in 1855. Such schools created a great demand for teachers. As societies grew more industrialized during the nineteenth century, opportunities for women to raise their status as employed workers outside the home were created. The construction of the role of teacher as nurturer provided a rationale for women to take up the teaching profession (Biklen, 1995). Access to teaching as a profession was not open to all groups of women, however. In the United States, for example, southern communities claimed that economic hardships prevented them from supporting black literate women, and northern organizations dedicated to encouraging education preferred to employ white teachers from the North (Biklen, 1995: 50). Subordination of women by men in the evolution of schooling emerged when schools began separating students by age into graded classrooms. Prior to this mid-nineteenth-century change, students were taught in one-room schoolhouses, where the teacher was responsible for all subjects. This model remained in rural areas until the 1920s, but in urban centers, separation by age resulted in women taking on the teaching of younger students, while men took over responsibilities for teaching the older students (Spring, 1990: 136–140). This shift resulted in hierarchical structures with men in the roles of administrators and women in the roles of elementary teachers, a structure often referred to as the pedagogical harem model (Spring, 1990: 139). Such structures resulted in men controlling the governance of the school and the regulation of the curriculum.

Curriculum and School Performance

Curriculum and classroom interaction patterns have been criticized for gender bias. Sadker and Sadker (1995) conclude that male students talk more in class and receive far more attention from their teachers. Likewise, the American Association of University Women (1998) reports a predominance of gender bias in textbooks and other curricular materials. Much attention has been focused on the underachievement of girls in math and science. There also is evidence of underparticipation among girls. In addition, the focus on math and science denies gender inequities in the other academic disciplines. For example, because girls perform well in reading, there is little attention to the language arts, and a cross-national study found that the perception of literacy as feminine shapes the ways schools teach reading (AAUW, 1998).

Legislation has been passed to ensure opportunities for all. The U.S. Civil Rights Act of 1964 introduced legislation that would withhold federal funding if institutions did not comply with its mandates. The 1972 federal law Title IX prohibited sex discrimination in education, which resulted in schools offering athletic and other extracurricular opportunities to girls equal to those available to boys. A 1987 policy statement of the Economic Council of

Canada acknowledged the need for vocational training to be flexible, adaptable, and versatile (Titley, 1990). Similarly, U.S. legislation attended to vocational preparation with the School-to-Work Opportunities Act of 1994, instituted to ensure opportunities for all to prepare for careers that may not have been traditional for their race, ethnicity, gender, or disability (AAUW, 1998). In the 1960s and 1970s, Canada increased expenditures on education to address issues of inequalities. Although legislation was put into place to provide for the education of all children in North America, increased opportunities were still denied to many.

School Structures

Structural factors inside and outside schools have a profound effect on what schools can do (Titley, 1990). Schools may be places where gendered power relations are internalized and perpetuated. For example, the role of elementary teacher as nurturer privileges helpfulness as the highest attainment for women (Walkerdine, 1990). This notion of good performance is based on middle-class, white cultural views, and the denial of different possible roles for women forces girls from other social groups to silence (Fordham, 1996). Likewise, as Fine (1991) notes, although schools welcome everyone in, those students at greatest risk of class, racial, ethnic, or gender exploitation are less likely to remain in school through graduation. According to the Canadian scholar Titley, the language, pace, and values of teachers all serve to alienate certain groups. Scholars note how the structures of schools and classrooms affect how children construct and experience gender (Cherland, 1994; Thorne, 1993; Walkerdine, 1990). Gender separation in elementary classrooms and playgrounds furthers gender dichotomies, making them seem natural (Thorne, 1993). Inattentiveness to the many possible gender roles serves to marginalize girls, especially those who do not share the racial, ethnic, socioeconomic, or cultural expectations of the school.

Initiatives and Pedagogical Approaches

Male domination in classrooms has resulted in many scholars advocating gender segregation of classrooms, especially for math and science learning. Others argue that the value of mixed-gender classrooms must not be denied and that teachers must be taught to reinforce cooperative, cross-gender activities (Thorne, 1993). Some initiatives have focused on pedagogical approaches that call for examining biases in texts, interaction patterns, and the larger culture. Scholars are calling for a pedagogy that builds on an awareness of the influence of both language and culture on students' lives. Cherland (1994), for example, calls for a critical pedagogy that explores vested interests in texts and examines how individuals are positioned to read and respond in certain ways. Gaskell and Willinsky (1995), bringing together scholars from content areas as diverse as mathematics, science, physical education, technology, and literacy, have called for a pedagogy that examines privilege and power. They suggest that across content disciplines the curriculum should have at its center attention to the processes by which patterns of participation and achievement are produced. In other words, these scholars argue that what is needed in schools is for boys and girls to examine what is taken as "natural" in any content and to investigate the politics and privileges embedded in texts, classrooms, and the larger culture.

Higher Education

College training for North American women began in 1833, when Oberlin College in Ohio opened its doors to female students. Over the next several years, the percentage of women attending college slowly increased; however, for the most part, these women majored in either education or nursing. Not until after World War II did significant numbers of women go to college to prepare for careers in the liberal arts, the sciences, or business. And until 1970 (according to some statistics) the majority of these students attended women's colleges, public or private.

Much has changed since 1970. What happened in the state of Virginia is typical of developments throughout North America. Between 1970 and 2000, the number of undergraduate women at the University of Virginia—the state's premier institute of higher learning—went from less than 5 percent to over 50 percent of the total student population. Meanwhile, the number of women's colleges in Virginia greatly decreased; approximately one-third of these schools began admitting men, and another one-third simply closed their doors. The result is that undergraduate programs have increasingly become the domain of women as well as men; in 1992, women earned 59 percent of the two-year degrees and 54 percent of the four-year degrees awarded by U.S. colleges. North American doctoral programs, however, remain predominantly male; in 1992, only 37 percent of doctoral degrees awarded in the United States were earned by women. Encouragingly, the U.S. Department of Education estimates that in the early twenty-first century this figure will rise to 50 percent. Meanwhile, women are far more likely to study than to teach at a North American college; in 1990, women constituted only 27 percent of U.S. college faculties and only 18 percent of Canadian college faculties.

See Also

DEVELOPMENT: NORTH AMERICA; EDUCATION: GENDER EQUITY; EDUCATION: GENDERED SUBJECT CHOICE; EDUCATORS: HIGHER EDUCATION; WOMEN'S STUDIES: UNITED STATES

References and Further Reading

American Association of University Women (AAUW). 1998. *Gender gaps: Where schools still fail our children.* Washington, D.C.: AAUW Educational Foundation.

Biklen, Sari. 1995. *School work: Gender and the cultural construction of teaching.* New York: Teachers College Press.

Cherland, Meredith Rogers. 1994. *Private practices: Girls reading fiction and constructing identity.* Bristol, Penn.: Taylor and Francis.

Fine, Michelle. 1991. *Framing dropouts: Notes on the politics of an urban public high school.* Albany: State University of New York.

Fordham, Signithia. 1996. *Blacked out: Dilemmas of race, identity, and success at Capital High.* Chicago: University of Chicago Press.

Gaskell, Jane, and John Willinsky. 1995. *Gender in/forms curriculum: From enrichment to transformation.* New York: Teachers College Press.

Sadker, Myra, and David Sadker. 1995. *Failing at fairness: How our schools cheat girls.* New York: Touchstone.

Schmittroth, Linda, ed. 1995. *Statistical record of women worldwide,* 2nd ed. New York: Gale Research.

Spring, Joel. 1990. *The American School, 1642–1990.* New York: Longman.

Thorne, Barrie. 1993. *Gender play: Girls and boys in school.* New Brunswick, N.J.: Rutgers University Press.

Titley, E. Brian. 1990. *Canadian education: Historical themes and contemporary issues.* Calgary, Alb.: Detselig Enterprises Limited.

United Nations. 1995. *The world's women, 1995: Trends and statistics.* New York: United Nations.

Walkerdine, Valerie. 1990. *Schoolgirl fictions.* New York: Verso.

Margaret J. Finders

EDUCATION: On-Line

Teaching and learning via computers are the latest innovations in more than a century of distance education. In places where well-organized postal services, roads, and trains made postal correspondence possible, individuals and then institutions started correspondence courses in a number of countries. By the late nineteenth century, there were, for example, correspondence studies in England, Germany, Sweden, and the United States. In 1873, Anna Ticknor founded the Society to Encourage Studies at Home, in Boston, to enable women restricted to their home to expand their education. The correspondence program in sociology at the University of Chicago, which began in 1893, had enrolled more than 30,000 students by 1923. The governments in Australia, New Zealand, and the former Soviet Union, concerned about the scarcity of schools in some rural areas, all started extensive correspondence systems to reach more students.

These early distance programs opened the door to formal education for students who had been excluded from many other educational systems because of their race, gender, occupation, location, or native-language fluency. Women have constituted the majority of correspondence students in some countries (such as Canada and the United States) and account for significant percentages of the undergraduate students in the British Open University and in the distance teaching universities in Spain, the Netherlands, and Germany.

Educators and businesspeople have promoted other technologies as promising new possibilities for the education of the many (students) by the few (teachers). For example, teachers' lessons via radio have been used as an adjunct to correspondence education, supplementing textbooks. After World War II, many educators forecast the use of television as a major educational technology that, with "master" teachers, would make classrooms and many teachers obsolete.

With increasing use of the World Wide Web, many educators and businesspeople began to talk once again about the benefits, for people with widely varied educational needs, of a new, "global" technology. Certainly, for the relatively few people of the world who have ready access to computers and the Internet, distance learning can offer new options, but in unequal ways. Overall, men have more computer access than women do, and more control of their time and finances, and thus easier access to on-line courses. Women, who often have more need for on-line education because of their many at-home caretaking responsibilities, frequently have a more difficult time obtaining the computers, time, and money needed to take the courses.

If on-line education is to offer important new options for women, the following concerns should be included in the planning by teachers, administrators, and students: learning styles (one model does not serve all students);

curriculum (courses should include the legal and social issues that particularly affect women, as well as scholarship by women); safety from harassment (mixed-sex on-line discussions are sometimes hostile); costs (scholarships and loans might be particularly important for women); outreach (notices and advertisements about on-line education should include women and the information they need and be available in places where women will see the announcements); and access to the necessary technologies and support.

Many of the old education issues and problems for women continue into the new courses and programs offered on-line, if in slightly altered forms. As feminists have pointed out regarding all technologies used in education, they are tools, not solutions.

See Also

EDUCATION: ADULT AND CONTINUING; EDUCATION: DISTANCE EDUCATION; EDUCATION: GENDER EQUITY; EDUCATION: SPECIAL NEEDS; EDUCATION: TECHNOLOGY; NETWORKS, ELECTRONIC; TECHNOLOGY

References and Further Reading

Harcourt, Wendy, ed. 1999. *Women@Internet: Creating new cultures in cyberspace.* London and New York: Zed.

Hawthorne, Susan, and Renate Klein, eds. 1999. *CyberFeminism: Connectivity, critique, and creativity.* North Melbourne: Spinifex.

Herring, Susan. 1999. The rhetorical dynamics of gender harassment online. *Information Society* 15(3): 151–167.

Jurich, Sonia. 1999. Before the e-mail there was the p-mail—Distance learning by postal correspondence. *TechKnowLogia* (Sept./Oct.).

Cheris Kramarae

EDUCATION: Physical

Much of the feminist work on girls' schooling has little direct knowledge of or involvement with physical education (PE), and few feminists working within education have a specific background in this area. The limited work in the area has focused on historical analysis and gender differentiation in the curriculum and on critical feminist analyses of girls' PE in schools and teacher education.

Although education systems differ in different countries, the legacy of British colonialism and imperialism has resulted in some commonalities. This article draws on the available literature primarily from Britain, North America, and Australasia.

History of Physical Education

PE as a distinct, coherent curricular subject developed in Britain in the pioneering girls' day schools of the late nineteenth century, which were primarily middle-class institutions for the daughters of the new bourgeoisie. The subject emerged from a radical movement, because the pioneers of girls' schooling, such as Frances Mary Buss, Dorothea Beale, and Emily Davies, were intent on demonstrating that women were fit to undertake sustained academic work and were not the frail, helpless creatures defined by the male Victorian medical and educational professions (Fletcher, 1987; Hargreaves, 1979). Although the entry of PE into the curriculum challenged the physical stereotype of the weak Victorian "lady," it was not so much a radical change to the definition as an adaptation to allow for and accommodate new educational initiatives for girls. On the one hand, the development of girls' PE in schools represented a radical and progressive challenge to dominant ideologies and commonsense assumptions that defined the female body as delicate, weak, and illness prone. On the other hand, the development occurred within the confines of sexist ideologies that delineated clear boundaries for young women's behavior and attitudes. Although PE contributed to the liberation of girls and young women in relation to dress, opportunities for physical activity and sports, and future access to a (women's) PE profession, it also reaffirmed clear physical gender differences in ability and capacity within generalized boundaries and reasserted the limitations on women's sexuality and their role in motherhood (Scraton, 1992).

Gender Differentiation in the Curriculum

Research in the 1980s in Britain, the United States, Canada, and Australia focused on identifying aspects of gender differentiation in school PE. In Australia, the Commonwealth Schools Commission (Dyer, 1986), which included empirical research evidence, identified the constraints on girls' physical activities in schools—for example, stereotyping of "feminine" activities, socialization of girls into sports, and teacher-pupil interactions within the PE lesson. Similar considerations can be found in studies in Britain (for example, Inner London Education Authority, 1984) and in the United States (for example, Greendorfer, 1983). These liberal feminist approaches to understanding girls' PE led to the emergence of policies emphasizing equal access and opportunities, supported by legislation—for example, Title IX in the United States and the Sex Discrimination Act in Britain. Despite these research findings and the development of equal opportunity legislation, there was little impact on the teaching of girls' PE other than the development of some coeducational teaching in an attempt to break down gender divisions, as well as ad hoc initiatives from committed feminist teachers.

Although it was important to identify gender differentiation in contemporary practice, later feminist work explored the ideological construction and reproduction of gender *relations* through the teaching of PE. Assumptions in relation to PE have been identified as dominant ideologies about girls' and women's physical ability and capacity, motherhood, and sexuality (Scraton, 1992). Teaching content, organization, and style are premised on assumptions of "natural" "feminine" characteristics, such as poise, grace, flexibility, control, and finesse. Although there is a divergence of opinion within PE about whether these differences are rooted in biology or culture, the emphasis remains on the *acceptance* of physical ability and capacity and the desirability of reproducing these differences through the teaching of PE (Wright, 1996).

Ideologies of motherhood and domesticity, which were central to the development of girls' PE, no longer appear to influence its content and teaching directly. However, the dominance and internalization of these ideological constructions of "woman's place" put indirect but substantial limitations on PE through restrictions on the experiences and opportunities afforded to both female staff and female students. Although PE teachers no longer identify their central objective as preparing physically fit young women for healthy motherhood, they have not directly challenged societal expectations that women's primary roles are those of wife and mother. Many female PE teachers recognize the restrictions on their time made by their domestic and child care responsibilities, which have consequences for their ability to offer comprehensive and detailed extracurricular programs, as well as for their career progression (Evans and Williams, 1989). Similarly, young women students often are restricted by domestic and child care "duties." PE does not overtly reinforce these expectations, but they persist in the attitudes and the ethos that underpin the curriculum.

The issue of physical contact and its relationship to sexuality has been identified as an important aspect of gender relations and the teaching of PE (Scraton, 1992). The acceptance of aggressive and violent physical contact

between boys and young men is open to question; yet there remains a double standard whereby only women's behavior and activity are seen to require regulation. Any demonstration of physical power and assertion between women is seen as not acceptable in relation to the social construction of female sexuality. Desirable female sexuality is a passive, responsible heterosexuality, and the engagement of girls or women in contact sports raises questions about their sexuality. An ideology of the "physical" incorporated within PE relates directly to a politics of sexuality that defines women as responsible yet vulnerable and therefore in need of protection. Ideologies of femininity and masculinity demarcate clear boundaries concerning sexuality that are reinforced by separate and different opportunities afforded to girls and boys in PE. Griffin's (1992) work in the United States shows the centrality of heterosexuality and homophobia in the culture of school PE. Appearance is also central to female sexuality. The female body is defined and portrayed in a specific form geared to an "ideal" image of femininity. PE reinforces in girls the need to be concerned with appearance, dress, and presentation of self. In Britain, maintaining "standards" of dress, appearance, discipline, and behavior is a priority for the teaching of girls' PE. The message in relation to female sexuality remains clearly articulated through PE (Clarke, 1997). Women's bodies are physically developed in order to look good and presentable (particularly to men), yet they must be protected from overdevelopment and physical contact in order to avoid "unnatural" or "unhealthy" touch and danger to delicate parts. Thus the ideological construction of the "ideal" woman is clear in PE practice in contemporary schooling.

The role of teacher education in challenging or reproducing gender relations in PE has been a focus of research (Flintoff, 1993). This research suggests that although the organization of PE initial teacher education (ITE) along coeducational lines has clearly raised important issues of physicality and sexuality, these remain unacknowledged on formal higher educational agendas. Attempts to sensitize PE students to the impact of gender on the teaching and learning process remain dependent on the initiatives of committed individuals and have not yet been systematized within the educational process.

Although PE is a central part of the curriculum, it remains marginal to feminist research and analysis. There is a lack of research into "race," ethnicity, and PE (Scraton, 1999), and there is a need for further in-depth, qualitative research into girls' and young women's experiences of PE at different stages of their education. At the turn of the twenty-first century, the emphasis was on teachers and teaching, and a greater focus on students' attitudes and ideas was necessary.

See Also

EDUCATION: CURRICULUM IN SCHOOLS; EXERCISE AND FITNESS; PHYSICAL STRENGTH; SEXUALITY: ADOLESCENT SEXUALITY; SPORT; SPORTS AND DISCRIMINATION

References and Further Reading

Clarke, G. 1997. Playing a part: The lives of lesbian physical education teachers. In G. Clarke and B. Humberstone, eds., *Researching women and sport.* London: Macmillan.

Dewar, A. 1987. The social construction of gender in physical education. *Women's Studies International Forum* 10(4): 453–465.

Dyer, K. Kenneth. 1986. *Girls' physical education and self-esteem: A review of research, resources, and strategies.* Canberra, Australia: Commonwealth Schools Commission.

Evans, John, and Trevor Williams. 1989. Moving up and getting out: The classed and gendered career opportunities of physical education teachers. In Thomas Templin and Paul Schempp, eds., *Socialization into physical education: Learning to teach,* 235–249. Carmel, Calif.: Benchmark.

Fletcher, Sheila. 1987. *Women first: The female tradition in English physical education, 1880–1980.* London: Athlone.

Flintoff, Anne. 1993. Gender, physical education, and initial teacher education. In J. Evans, ed., *Equality, education, and physical education,* 184–204. London: Falmer.

Greendorfer, Susan. 1983. Shaping the female athlete: The impact of the family. In Mary A. Boutilier and Lucinda San Giovanni, eds., *The sporting woman.* Champaign, Ill.: Human Kinetics.

Griffin, Pat. 1992. Changing the game: Homophobia, sexism, and lesbians in sport. *Quest* 44(2): 251–265.

Hargreaves, Jennifer. 1979. Playing like gentlemen whilst behaving like ladies. Master's thesis, University of London.

Inner London Education Authority. 1984. *Providing equal opportunities for girls and boys in physical education.* London: Inner London Education Authority Statistics Branch.

Scraton, S. 1999. Re-conceptualising race, gender and sport: The contribution of black feminism. In B. Carrington and I. McDonald, eds., *Racism and British Sport.* London: Routledge.

———. 1992. *Shaping up to womanhood: Gender and girls' physical education.* Milton Keynes: Open University Press.

Wright, J. 1996. The construction of complementarity in physical education. *Gender and Education* 8(1): 61–79.

Anne Flintoff
Sheila Scraton

EDUCATION: Political

The need for increased political awareness among the world's women has prompted feminist groups to promote political education as a means to gain access and ensure full participation in government. Building on the earlier successes of western nations in integrating educational systems and opening access, much of the later focus in women's education in developed nations involved efforts to narrow the gender gap in organized politics. For instance, at the turn of the twenty-first century, 36.4 percent of the members of parliament in the Nordic nations were women, but only 3.3 percent in the Arab states and 10 percent in the Caribbean and Latin America. International organizations and domestic women's groups have endeavored to increase the representation of women in politics and make women aware of their rights under their nation's laws.

In general, women's political education can be distinguished from the education of women, which can be conservative, and from the more theoretical women's studies, which tends to analyze but not necessarily engage with the subjects of study. The purpose of women's political education is to challenge the existing order. Political education serves to aid women in gaining political equality and, therefore, in overturning the male-dominated political elite in most nations.

To achieve this goal, political education for women challenges the structure and content of educational provision and, indeed, the construction of knowledge itself. The initial flowering of feminism in the late 1960s and the women's liberation movement greatly helped to propel political education. They helped reinforce the importance of drawing in new groups to adult education, of negotiating the curriculum with these groups, and of emphasizing the centrality of process and dynamics in educational provision. Women's political education identifies women's oppression and recognizes that this oppression is complex and multifaceted and includes issues of race and class as well as gender. Such education cannot be based on an assumption of the sameness of all women's experience. Not only must women's groups be recognized, but the particular dynamics of these groups must be incorporated into the broader spectrum of national politics.

Political education has been influenced by debates within the women's movement, particularly by the perspective developed by socialist feminists, radical feminists, and black feminists. Socialist feminism conceptualizes women's oppression as rooted in class and economic oppression, which institutionalize power and privilege along hierarchical lines. Many socialist feminists see their political task as being to engage with the particular oppression of women and to aid in the effort to overcome such repression. Radical feminism emphasizes gender rather than class, arguing that women are oppressed across divisions of class and race. Many radical feminists also recognize the parallels between discrimination based on gender and that based on class or race. Meanwhile, black feminists have developed an analysis of race that transcends the issues of gender and class. They have concentrated their energies in working toward structural and social change, whereas radical feminists have focused on psychological and cultural issues. Black feminists have challenged the work of both socialist and radical feminists and developed an emphasis on the complex interconnection of factors of class, race, and gender. An increasing number of feminists, however, such as Parvin Ghorayshi, from nations such as Iran and India, reject the homogeneity that attempts to transcend differences in culture and geography. Instead, they assert that individual national and cultural variations are the key factors in perpetuating oppression. In this regard, the self-titled third world feminists combine the main tenets of both radical and socialist feminism.

One of the most significant questions has been over whether to emphasize equality or difference. Socialist feminism has assumed equality as the paramount objective, whereas radical feminism has emphasized the difference between women and men, although the difference is seen as psychological and culturally constructed rather than biologically innate. Black feminist perspectives have introduced a wider analysis of oppression and of the interdependence of a number of factors in maintaining oppression. One challenge of political education is to reconcile these emphases on the inner and outer, recognizing that individual identity is constructed within a particular social context and that equality in structural and institutional terms needs to incorporate an analysis of difference.

Political education in developed nations can take the form of specific areas of study in higher education, including women's studies programs, or of efforts to introduce basic political understanding in elementary or secondary schools. Women's studies programs often serve as a base for larger efforts to educate the public. Examples of this include the Women's Campaign School (WCS) of Yale University, which offers programs to train American women to stand as candidates or run political campaigns. Some programs, including the Center for Women's Global Leadership at Douglass College, endeavor to train women from around the world in politics. Other initiatives provide education in targeted nations; for example, the Aga Khan Education Service provides teacher training in Pakistan.

Women's groups have had varying degrees of success in gaining legislation to implement political education programs. Some nations, for example, Argentina, have enacted programs to promote democracy and the understanding of minority and gender rights in early education. States with these types of programs have often passed significant legislation to promote participation. For instance, in Argentina, the *Ley de Cupos* (Law of Quotas) requires all political parties to place a minimum number of female candidates on their electoral rosters. At the time of this writing, the proportion of women in the Argentine parliament had increased from 4 percent to 28 percent; a similar law in Brazil had increased the representation of women by 40 percent.

A major component of political education is making women aware of their political rights under the law. Political education can serve as a means to familiarize women with the intricacies of legal systems and civil rights. Such efforts have encouraged women in nations such as South Africa to utilize the legal system to maintain their socioeconomic rights.

Many of the more successful political education programs have been developed and undertaken by domestic interest groups and international women's groups. In a range of both developed and lesser developed nations, domestic groups have implemented programs to make women aware of their political rights. International women's groups and international organizations such as the United Nations also have had targeted, if limited, success in supporting political education programs. There is the hope that such initiatives will increase the number of women registered to vote and ensure access to polling places.

See Also

EQUALITY; FEMINISM: BLACK BRITISH; FEMINISM: RADICAL; FEMINISM: SOCIALIST; LIBERATION MOVEMENTS; WOMEN'S MOVEMENT, *all entries*; WOMEN'S STUDIES: OVERVIEW

References and Further Reading

Afshar, Haleh. 1996. *Women and politics in the third world*. London: Routledge.

Davies, Miranda. 1983. *Third world—second sex: Women's struggles and national liberation: Third world women speak out.* Westport, Conn.: Zed.

Fisher, Jo. 1993. *Out of the shadows: Women, resistance, and politics in South America.* London: Latin American Bureau.

Grant, Rebecca, and Kathleen Newland, eds. 1991. *Gender and international relations.* Bloomington: Indiana University Press.

Jaquette, Jane S. 1994. *The women's movement in Latin America: Participation and democracy.* Boulder, Colo.: Westview.

Eileen Aird

EDUCATION: Preschool

Preschool education refers to educational provision for children who are not yet old enough to begin their primary schooling. The term *preschool* needs to be used with care, because compulsory schooling starts at different ages in different countries. Children are required to start school in Holland at the age of 4; in the United Kingdom, the United States, and New Zealand, children must start school at the age of 5; in Japan, China, Russia, and Ireland, entry to primary school must occur by the age of 6; and in many eastern European countries and Scandinavia, compulsory schooling begins at the age of 7. Children in many countries attend primary school before they reach the compulsory school age.

Preschool educational provision varies in different countries. In the United Kingdom, for example, there is a diverse range of preschool provision that includes publicly funded local authority day nurseries, nursery classes, nursery schools, and reception classes, as well as privately funded day nurseries, nursery schools, prepreparatory departments in private schools, and part-time play groups. Privately funded preschool settings may also receive government funding. In Scandinavia, children may attend publicly funded day care centers or nursery schools. In Japan, China, and many eastern European countries, kindergartens cater to 3- to 6-year-olds.

Attendance Patterns

Attendance patterns differ between forms of provision and between countries. Thus in New Zealand 3-year-olds may attend kindergartens on only three afternoons a week, whereas in China some kindergarten children are weekly boarders who return home for the weekend. In the United Kingdom a child may attend a publicly funded nursery class for two and a half hours per day with 12 weeks of vacation per year that coincide with those for children of compulsory school age, or a child may attend a private nursery for up to 12 hours a day for 52 weeks a year (Department of Education and Science, 1990). Alternatively, a child may attend a play group, although there has been debate about whether play groups are educationally comparable to nursery schools or classes. In an effort to ensure a degree of consistent provision, each early-years setting in England that receives government funding is required to demonstrate that its curriculum promotes a set of centrally determined early learning goals (Qualifications and Curriculum Authority, 1999). In France 3- to 5-year-olds may attend *écoles maternelles* for eight hours per day, with the possibility of extending these hours through utilizing school-based care facilities.

Women's Employment and Preschool Provision

Only a tiny minority of countries have embraced the ideal of women and men sharing child care to an extent that would actually facilitate adjustments in employment patterns. In the remaining countries, the funding of preschool facilities, the length of the school day, and the availability of places have a considerable impact on most women and, in particular, on working mothers or mothers who want or need paid employment. Working mothers require preschool provision for their children that is not too costly and that suits their working patterns in terms of hours and holidays.

Belgium, France, Denmark, and Italy have very high levels of publicly funded preschool provision, with places for more than 85 percent of children between the ages of 3 and compulsory school age. Greece, Spain, and many eastern European countries have achieved high levels as well, with provision for more than 70 percent of the same age group. Japan, Portugal, the United Kingdom, and the United States have relatively poor provision, with places for only 42 to 44 percent of this age group (Moss and Penn, 1996).

That low levels of publicly funded preschool provision in the United Kingdom adversely affect women is clear from statistics related to the employment patterns of single parents. The United Kingdom has the lowest number of single parents in full-time employment, at only 8 percent. The scarcity of full-time publicly funded preschool places hinders women seeking full-time employment because the alternatives are very costly or, if affordable (for example, play groups), offer only a few hours per day and have a lower standard of education than the better-resourced nurseries.

In contrast, the low level of state provision in Japan is offset by a very high number of private kindergartens that are economically accessible to the majority of Japanese parents, with the result that 85 percent of 3- to 6-year-olds attend kindergarten. The fees charged in the private kindergartens are equivalent to those charged for part-time attendance at British play groups (Lynn, 1988).

The pattern and form of preschool provision in different countries are reflections of the policy makers' views of young children and the role of women in their care and education. In eastern European countries the high levels of publicly funded full-time preschool provision have their roots in communist principles. Lenin argued that preschool institutions were the "shoots of communism" because they were a means of liberating women by enabling them to participate fully in the social life and social production of society. By way of contrast, in the United Kingdom ambivalent attitudes toward working mothers and the educational needs of very young children have resulted in a checkered history of preschool provision. Publicly funded preschool provision increased rapidly during World War II, when female labor was essential. In the 1950s and 1960s policy makers utilized the theories of John Bowlby on the damaging effects of maternal deprivation to justify the lack of publicly funded preschool education and their support of the part-time model of nursery attendance characteristic of British nurseries.

Preschool and Socialization

The role of preschool institutions in the socialization of young children is an important issue. There is an ongoing debate about the reasons for gender differences and how young children learn gender roles. The views of those who work in preschool education have important implications for the nature of the provision and the experiences of the children attending the institutions.

Western society has been heavily influenced by Freudian theories, and these have been criticized and modified. The post-Freudian Nancy Chodorow has cited the mother-child relationship as pivotal in the development of sex-role identity. She argues that mothers relate to their daughters as being "the same" and therefore "merge" more with them, which leads to girls' sense of empathy. Conversely, mothers relate to their sons as "different," and this results in boys developing a sense of separateness.

Biological determinists argue that psychological differences have a purely biological explanation. Different brain and hormonal function makes females more caring, less competitive, and less mathematically and scientifically oriented than males. Biological theories serve to support the status quo regarding women's role in society and have been criticized on a number of grounds (for example, much of

the evidence for sex differences in humans has been derived from studies of animals). It has also been argued that biologically based theories are manifestations of the theorists' own biased opinions. Despite the criticisms, many staff in preschool education promote this view and consequently make no attempts to examine the curriculum and learning resources for gender bias or to encourage children to explore a wide range of roles.

Theories that emphasize the role of environment include social learning theory and cognitive developmental theory. According to social learning theory, children learn what is gender appropriate through the process of stimulus, response, and reinforcement. Some educationists find cognitive developmental theories more persuasive. According to these theories, the child builds up an increasingly complex concept of gender through interaction with her or his environment. The concept of permanent gender identity is essential before a child is able to view gender differences as socially created.

Preschool staff who are keen to challenge assumptions about gender and who find social learning or cognitive developmental theories persuasive try to ensure that girls and boys are encouraged to play with the same toys and engage in the same sorts of activities. They work hard to ensure that adults' expectations are not gender based and are conscious of the effect that visual images have on children's developing ideas about gender (Browne, 1990).

A brief analysis of theories on how the complex concept of gender roles develops suggests that preschool educational experiences may influence the development in children of the ability and skills necessary to fulfill their potential regardless of sex and to begin to question sexism in social systems.

See Also

BIOLOGICAL DETERMINISM; CHILD CARE; CHILD DEVELOPMENT; EDUCATION: NONSEXIST; EDUCATORS: PRESCHOOL; GENDERED PLAY; GIRL CHILD; PARENTHOOD

References and Further Reading

Browne, Naima, ed. 1990. *Science and technology in the early years: An equal opportunities approach.* Milton Keynes: Open University Press.

Chodorow, Nancy. 1978. *The reproduction of mothering.* Berkeley: University of California Press.

Department of Education and Science. 1990. *Starting with quality.* London: Her Majesty's Stationery Office.

Derman-Sparks, Louise, and the A.B.C. Task Force. 1989. *Antibias curriculum: Tools for empowering young children.* Washington, D.C.: National Association for the Education of Young Children.

Lynn, Richard. 1988. *Educational achievement in Japan*. London: Macmillan.

Moss, Peter. 1990. *Childcare in the European Community, 1985–1990*. Brussels: European Commission.

——— and Helen Penn. 1996. *Transforming nursery education*. London: Paul Chapman.

Penn, Helen. 2000. *Early childhood services: Theory, policy, and practice*. Milton Keynes: Open University Press.

Qualifications and Curriculum Authority. 1999. *The early learning goals*. London: Qualifications and Curriculum Authority.

Naima Browne

EDUCATION: Religious Studies

Statistics from the British Department for Education (DFE) on girls and women in state-sector religious education (RE), primarily Christian-based, support the long-debated proposition that females are more receptive to religion than males. In 1992, 60 percent of RE teachers in England and Wales were female. In 1993, 50,000 of the 82,000 pupils who took the General Certificate in Secondary Education (GCSE) examination in religious studies were girls, and 3,500 of the 4,800 pupils who took the General Certificate of Education Advanced Level (GCE "A" Level) examination in religious studies were girls (personal communication from the DFE, October 1994). This statistical trend is reflected at all levels at which religious studies is undertaken in the United States and in Europe, except at postgraduate level.

Explanations given for this gender difference in religious interest are diverse but generally center on two opposing understandings of women's cognitive capabilities. The first of these is that women are a muted group, largely subject to authorities beyond their control. Therefore, they fit themselves into existing religious power structures, which are generally patriarchal and maintain the status quo through role fulfillment. The other, suggested by writers such as Carol Gilligan, centers on women's aptitude for "connected knowing" and intuition, which would make them more apt to accept some religious concepts. Significant variables are involved, and strict correlations between religion and gender cannot be made. Edward Thompson (1991) argues that rather than blindly accepting the axiom that women are more religious than men, researchers should look to the masculine and feminine aspects of each individual, regardless of sex, in order to chart the true relation between gender and religion. At the same time, given this unambiguously female interest in religious studies—which has, ironically, arisen in educational institutions that, on the whole, reflect and perpetuate patriarchal values—RE can undoubtedly provide a rich resource for subversion and change.

Broadly speaking, religious studies (or religious education) can be seen as conforming to one of two paradigms. The first paradigm seeks either to transmit the prevailing culture or to promote religious reform. The second is "phenomenological," and seeks to further one's understanding *without* either (1) imposing religious beliefs on its recipients or (2) imposing theories on the phenomena. Usually the promotion of tolerance and understanding and the denigration of prejudice (mainly conceived of, in this field, as racial) is emphasized.

Rita Gross (1993), however, conflated these two apparently opposing models, in the name of feminism and religious commitment, and proposed that the future of religious studies (of the phenomenological type—known in the United States as the history of religions) lay not in a neutered neutrality but in an engaged or "world-creating" approach that takes issue with social ills by utilizing the very techniques of a phenomenological approach that are usually thought to maintain that neutrality.

Religious studies of this type can be enormously effective in giving voice to groups. The nature of the subject requires that the teacher or researcher reaches the center of an individual's experience. Because of this, the subject can be inherently liberating, articulating, and empowering. Given that interest in religious studies tends to revolve around addressing prejudice and intolerance, it might be assumed that women's issues are constantly under scrutiny. Issues that do arise, at least in higher education—although perhaps not as often or to the depth they should—are feminist theology, the authority of women in religions, religious power structures, women and new religious movements, exclusive language within Scripture and liturgy, and so on. More rarely discussed but equally rich issues include the place of women in nonlogocentric or oral religions, women's spirituality, and "body-positive" spirituality.

Sadly, discussions that take place in the comparative luxury of academic circles rarely filter through to the factory floor. Female (and male) RE teachers in the United Kingdom continue to fight battles over the position and role of women in education generally. Women are still perceived as lacking in commitment, persistence, and ambition, with biological functions and maternal duties making them unfit to compete in the workplace, and there is the assumption that men are better disciplinarians. Women continue to be underrepresented in managerial positions in schools, especially as the number of single-sex schools has been reduced, and it is still presumed that women work only for "pocket money" (Measor and Sikes, 1992). There is the further assumption that female RE teachers (and Sunday school teachers) suffer from a strange variation of penis envy—dog-collar envy—and because, in general, they can't "do," they teach.

Religious Studies and Curriculum

Given these general problems, it is perhaps hardly surprising that women's spirituality, "body-positive" spirituality, and so on have not found their way into the curriculum. Some feminists, however, such as Joanmarie Smith and Maria Harris, argue that until they do, RE is not sufficiently balanced and cannot do its job properly.

Religious education for schoolchildren in the state sector in Europe, in the handful of countries in which it is taught, is designed to contribute significantly to the (culturally Christian, a problem for Muslims) personal, social, and moral education of children. In this respect, in theory it can address, perhaps more than other subjects in the curriculum, issues of ecology and world stewardship, and certainly more than other subjects it can educate and care for the "whole personhood" of the child. In doing so, it must address the religious and social experience of women and girls. Most feminist RE specialists are obviously in favor of this, but some, such as Christine Trevett, are skeptical about the extent to which the theory is put into practice: "What price exhortations to 'wholeness,' or empathy, or awareness of religions as living, changing phenomena, when so often the syllabuses are silent about *women's* distinctive contributions, their innovations, mystical experiences, heresies and lives of imposed restraint within the confines of a faith" (1989).

RE, when taught in one way, can wage war on prejudice and inequality and can give voice to muted groups; yet when taught in another way, it can be a powerful tool for the perpetuation of patriarchy. When RE is conceived of as transmitting the prevailing culture (which is, in most more developed countries, biased toward male norms and values), it can especially undermine feminism. In the United Kingdom, for example, RE, by law, has to be in the main Christian. Institutional forms of Christianity are, by nature or by historical accident, patriarchal. Although the law makes token provision for some teaching of other world religions (many of these are also patriarchal in their institutional manifestations), the ethos of RE is still that postwar cultivation of moral fiber and good Christian (by which, according to some feminists, was meant "ethnocentric and chauvinistic") values. In this atmosphere there

is little room for women's myriad voices. The question that faces feminist educators is how to rescue the religions they teach from centuries-old male control and domination without damaging them and without imposing alien structures on them.

This may perhaps be most difficult in the Muslim context. When Islam was founded, it was a religion that conferred rights on women hitherto unknown. Throughout its enormous growth and spread it has, however, merged with local cultures that tend, according to some writers, to oppress women. It is very difficult for women to see through cultural interpretations to what is seen as a liberating reading of the Qur'an, especially when many Muslim countries have high rates of illiteracy—illiteracy among women being far more common. Madrassas and Qur'anic schools are thought on the whole to perpetuate the myths of sexual inequality that are believed to come largely from Islamic cultures rather than from Islam itself. State-sector education in non-Muslim countries can do little to provide balance, although the field of Islamic studies in secular universities, which is becoming increasingly popular among Muslim women, can.

Muslim education is only available in the state sector in many European countries if Muslim children opt out of traditional RE, and boards of governors allow the community to arrange for a local imam to teach them. This situation contrasts with that of Jewish schools, which can be state funded in the United Kingdom. Many Muslim girls are sent to church schools in Christian countries because often these will be the only single-sex schools in an area. They will, however, have no opportunity to receive Muslim education, except out of school. One of the many problems that attend this situation (regardless of the wisdom or otherwise behind it) is that through the western education system, girls have imposed on them western female or feminist paradigms that are at best inappropriate and at worst destructive.

Conclusion

Given the nature both of the subject matter and of the way it has historically been mediated—through male-dominated disciplines such as anthropology, theology, philosophy, and so on—there are certain problems that feminist RE specialists face. First, there is a climate of traditionalism and conservatism that prevails over the subject. Second, there is the risk of resorting to tokenism to combat this. This has taken place on a large scale within most RE syllabi. Third, there is the danger that feminist RE specialists will develop and engender antireligious attitudes on the grounds that religions can be seen as systems of oppression. Fourth, there is the risk of imposing western feminist paradigms out of context. Finally, there is the danger of ignoring or not even perceiving as such "feminist" theories from communities that are not white or middle class.

These issues are taken up in the RE world by countless teachers and members of religious institutions inspired by the work of many scholars, among them Ursula King, Maria Harris, Mary Douglas, Mary Daly, Joanmarie Smith, Nicola Slee, Rita Gross, Judith Holland, the Christian Women's Information and Resource Centre in London, the Muslim Women's Helpline, and other comparable institutions, as well as the work done by many feminist innovators or theologians from within their traditions.

See Also

EDUCATION: ANTIRACIST; ETHNIC STUDIES I; ISLAM; RELIGION: OVERVIEW; SPIRITUALITY: OVERVIEW; THEOLOGIES: FEMINIST

References and Further Reading

British Journal of Religious Education. 1989. Issue titled "Women's studies in religious education" 12(1).

Gross, Rita. 1993. *Buddhism after patriarchy: A feminist history and reconstruction of Buddhism.* New York: State University of New York Press.

Harris, Maria. 1993. Women teaching girls: The power and the danger. *Religious Education* 88(1): 52–66.

King, Ursula. 1987. World religions, women, and education. *Comparative Education* 23(1): 35–39.

Measor, Lynda, and Patricia Sikes. 1992. *Gender and schools.* London: Cassell.

Shap Working Party. 1988. *World religions in education.* Issue titled "Women in religions."

Thompson, Edward, Jr. 1991. Beneath the status characteristics: Gender variations in religiousness. *Journal for the Scientific Study of Religion* 30(4): 381–394.

Tombs, Davis. 1990. Anti-sexism and teaching, Islam. *British Journal of Religious Education* 12(2): 869–873.

Trevett, Christine. 1989. Patriarchal structures and religious education. *British Journal of Religious Education* 12(1): 6–10.

Wendy Dossett

EDUCATION: Science

Why are there still so few young women who enjoy studying science at school and beyond? Many answers to this question have been posed that consider issues such as the masculine image of science, the way science is taught in schools, the nature of science itself, and even women's intellectual ability to study science.

Historical Background

Science was not part of the school curriculum for boys or girls until relatively recently. Before the 1920s both were offered little science, and for those who were, it was generally limited to "nature study." In industrialized countries, girls were educated to fulfill their future roles in life according to their class, and science was not seen to have a place in these girls' futures. Working-class girls in particular were offered domestic science in order to prepare them for domestic service and also to raise the standards of health in the working-class population. Even into the 1950s the curriculum offered to girls focused on their future roles as housewives and mothers (Attar, 1989).

Sex Differences

Psychological differences between the sexes have also been offered as an explanation for the smaller number of girls choosing to study science. These debates have concerned differences between males and females such as brain size, poorer spatial abilities in women, and variations in brain symmetry between women and men. Yet there is no clear evidence that any of these differences significantly affects intelligence or ability in science. Studies of random samples of the population show a great deal of overlap between women's and men's brain size, which is related to body weight, not sex. Sex differences in spatial abilities are not universal across all societies and are thought to be a function of upbringing and education rather than biology (Birke, 1992). These debates have had a powerful influence on society's view of the appropriateness of a science education for young women that still affects present-day thinking.

Other factors that influence girls' and boys' engagement with science may have their roots in psychological differences between the sexes. John Head (1985) examined personality differences between scientists and nonscientists and matched the characteristics of nonscientists to those of typical females and the characteristics of scientists to typical males. Many of the characteristics attributed to females, such as team-working skills, careful attention to detail, and good communication skills, are ones that are useful to scientists. He related the development of these characteristics to parenting, particularly the role of the mother. A girl, because of close ties to her mother, tends to take an interest in relationships and to be aware of another's perspectives, whereas a boy sees himself as different from the mother and separates. A boy is encouraged to achieve autonomy, to take risks, and not to display emotion. Head cites puberty as the crucial time for a boy's interest in science to develop. At such a time a boy looks for certainty in his life and is attracted to science because it is presented as a subject that has definite truths and is not open for debate.

Cultural Influences

Cultural influences have a major effect. The public image of science is often negative, and public understanding of science is low. Media presentations of science are few when compared with the arts. International studies have revealed that the popular stereotype of a scientist is still a white-coated, bespectacled male with wild hair—an Einstein look-alike (Kahle, 1987). This image damages science, because it discourages those who cannot, by virtue of their gender and race, and those who do not wish to aspire to this image and reduces the pool from which potential scientists might emerge. As Alison Kelly (1981) has found, this masculine image of science is pervasive across all cultures. The financial rewards of a scientific career do not compare well with those in other professions, an education in science is not highly valued by society, and funding for scientific endeavors is not given high priority.

Curriculum

In most of Europe and the United States, a common curriculum is now offered to all up to the conclusion of compulsory schooling. Boys and girls therefore have equal access to science and can, in principle, choose to study it to degree level if they wish. However, this does not mean that equal numbers of girls and boys choose to do so, because (for one reason) in actual practice the choice is often culturally restricted. The legacy of science as a masculine subject is strong, and teenage girls may not wish to be seen as clever at science if this does not fit with their developing self-image. Also, the science curriculum has typically focused on the needs and interests of the pupils for which it was first developed—boys. As far back as 1942, the Association of Women Science Teachers charged that the general science syllabus in Britain devoted a lot of time to mechanics and electricity and the way those subjects were introduced was more appropriate to boys than girls (Manthorpe, 1989).

Teachers' attitudes also play their part. Although the majority of teachers claim to treat boys and girls equally in class, observations have shown that teachers' attention is often directed more toward the boys in the class than the girls. In studies on grading students' work (Spear, 1987), science teachers were found to award higher grades if the

work carried a boy's name rather than a girl's, and the highest marks were awarded by female teachers marking work attributed to boys. The behavior of boys in science laboratory classes may also be excluding to girls, because boys often assume a dominance over laboratory equipment. It is not surprising, then, that girls have lower expectations than boys and tend to blame any failure on their lack of ability, unlike boys, who are more likely to blame failure on lack of effort or external circumstances (Dweck and Licht, 1983).

Pupils' Attitudes

Pupils' attitudes toward science are formed in the early years of schooling, and so it is crucial that girls develop a positive attitude toward science at this time. Girls should be offered opportunities to play with construction toys (and boys allowed into the "home" corner), for example (Browne, 1991; Burn, 1989). Attitudes outside school are also very influential. Studies show that girls' and boys' out-of-school activities are very different and can greatly affect their confidence and interest in science in school (Sjøberg and Imsen, 1988). Boys and girls have also been shown to have different learning styles. Girls appear to focus on the recognition of order and patterns among concepts, and their approach to understanding is greatly dependent on the task within which a science concept is set. This also has an effect on assessment outcomes. As Patricia Murphy (1989) illustrates, the use of gender-fair contexts for assessment produces an outcome that is more reliable and representative of abilities of all students, whereas context-free assessments favor a particular type of personality and training.

Since the 1960s in Europe, the United States, Asia, and Australia particularly, social influences, ideas of equality, and legislation have moved the curriculum toward equal provision for all. However, this has not necessarily resulted in the same learning experiences for boys and girls, particularly in science, where many other factors contribute to a child's view of, and hence engagement with, the subject. Students who may have been able to opt out of science before terminal examinations are now required to study and be examined in science in many European countries and in the United States. This has not led to more girls becoming scientists. The way science is presented to girls must change in order to encourage more to engage with it. Science must relate to students' lives; it is this relationship that provides motivation.

Curriculum Initiatives

Curriculum developers advocate a process-based approach to science teaching rather than the traditional content-based approach as more stimulating for all students, particularly girls (Harlen, 1993). A process-based approach involves learning about the processes of science and how these processes are put into operation rather than starting with the theories and laws of science. This approach requires a higher level of resources than more traditional teaching, and it is now more commonly used in science classes in western countries. It was introduced through a major initiative in the 1960s in Africa, but it is now largely defunct there because of lack of time and resources (Amara, 1990).

At the beginning of the 1980s, initiatives to increase the participation of girls in science focused on introducing "girl-friendly" science curricula and development of teaching methods specifically for girls; some advocated single-sex classes in science. These strategies did not have the hoped-for success. Delivering a special science for girls could reinforce the idea that girls' lack of engagement with science was a problem with the *girls* (a deficit model of girls), not a problem with science and the way it was taught. A special science curriculum for girls has been viewed as a remedial curriculum and is consequently devalued. The Girls into Science and Technology project, which took place in schools in Manchester, England, between 1979 and 1984, monitored the effectiveness of positive action programs on girls' achievements in science. The findings were disappointing. The researchers felt that the interventions took place too late; by the ages of 13 and 14 many girls had already formed negative attitudes toward science (Kelly et al., 1984).

In the 1980s many countries developed initiatives to promote change and encourage more girls to study science. Many of these are documented in the proceedings of the international Gender and Science and Technology (GASAT) conferences. In Australia the McClintock Collective (named after Barbara McClintock, the geneticist and Nobel laureate) has done much pioneering work in developing gender-inclusive science curricula and teaching methodologies. In Britain the Engineering Council initiated the Women in Science and Engineering campaign in 1984 to focus attention on the problem of girls and science and to promote initiatives to encourage girls. In the 1990s, the U.K. government commissioned a report on the position of women in science and technology, which includes recommendations for the science education of girls.

Other initiatives have focused on changing the science curriculum, teaching methodologies, and assessment strategies to make science education more appropriate for a greater diversity of students, in order to include a majority of girls, boys who have been excluded by traditional science curricula, and students from ethnic minority groups. This is known as the Science for All movement (Fensham, 1993).

See Also

EDUCATION: GENDERED SUBJECT CHOICE; EDUCATION: TECHNOLOGY; SCIENCE: OVERVIEW; SCIENCE: FEMINISM AND SCIENCE STUDIES; SCIENCE: FEMINIST PHILOSOPHY; SCIENCE: TECHNOLOGICAL AND SCIENTIFIC RESEARCH

References and Further Reading

Amara, Julia. 1990. The double dilemma of the science education of girls in developing countries: A case study of schools in Sierra Leone. Contribution to GASAT 1990 Conference, Jönköping, Sweden.

American Association of University Women. 1999. *Tech-savvy: Educating girls in the new computer age.* Washington, D.C.: American Association of University Women Educational Foundation.

Attar, Denov. 1989. Now you see it, now you don't: The history of home economics—a study in gender. In Bob Moon, Patricia Murphy, and John Raynor, eds., *Policies for the curriculum.* London: Hodder and Stoughton.

Birke, Lynda. 1992. In pursuit of difference: Scientific studies of women and men. In Gill Kirkup and Laura S. Keller, eds., *Inventing women.* Cambridge: Polity.

Browne, Naima. 1991. *Science and technology in the early years.* Milton Keynes, U.K.: Open University Press.

Burn, E. 1989. Inside the Lego house. In Christine Skelton, ed., *Whatever happens to little women?* Milton Keynes, U.K.: Open University Press.

Department of Trade and Industry. 1994. *The rising tide: A report on women in science, engineering, and technology.* London: HMSO.

Dweck, Carol, and Barbara Licht. 1983. Sex differences in achievement orientations: Consequences for academic choices and attainments. In Michael Marland, ed., *Sex differentiation and schooling.* Oxford: Heinemann.

Fensham, Peter. 1993. Reflections on science for all. In Elizabeth Whitelegg, Jeff Thomas, and Susan Tresman, eds., *Challenges and opportunities for science education.* London: Paul Chapman.

Harlen, Wynne. 1993. Education for equal opportunities in a scientifically literate society. In Elizabeth Whitelegg, Jeff Thomas, and Susan Tresman, eds., *Challenges and opportunities for science education.* London: Paul Chapman.

Head, John. 1985. *The personal response to science.* Cambridge: Cambridge University Press.

Kahle, Jane Butler. 1987. SCORES: A project for change? *International Journal of Science Education* 9(3): 325–333.

Kelly, Alison. 1981. *The missing half.* Manchester, U.K.: Manchester University Press.

Kelly, Alison, Judith Whyte, and Barbara Smail. 1984. *Girls into science and technology.* Manchester, U.K.: University of Manchester, Department of Sociology.

Manthorpe, Catherine. 1989. Reflections on the scientific education of girls. In Bob Moon, Patricia Murphy, and John Raynor, eds., *Policies for the curriculum.* London: Hodder and Stoughton.

Murphy, Patricia. 1989. Gender and assessment in science. In Patricia Murphy and Bob Moon, eds., *Developments in learning and assessment.* London: Hodder and Stoughton.

Sjøberg, Svein, and Gunn Imsen. 1988. Gender and science education I. In Peter Fensham, ed., *Development and dilemmas in science education.* London: Falmer.

Spear, Margaret G. 1987. The biasing influence of pupil sex in a science marking exercise. In Alison Kelly, ed., *Science for girls.* Milton Keynes, U.K.: Open University Press.

Elizabeth L. Whitelegg

EDUCATION: Sexuality Education

See SEX EDUCATION.

EDUCATION:
Single-Sex and Coeducation

Single-sex schools admit only females or only males or teach females and males in separate classes, with other educational facilities separated as well. The purpose is to provide an appropriate education for each sex.

Coeducational schools admit both females and males and teach both in the same classes, to create an integrated system of educating students. Coeducation is also called *mixed schooling.* Historically, the prefix *co-* ("together") meant allowing women to enter a previously male educational setting.

Single-Sex Education versus Coeducation

There are numerous issues regarding single-sex education versus coeducation for females—that is, which is the most appropriate environment for the education of girls and women. Such issues vary significantly throughout the world. Nations differ in their educational practices and philosophies, and even in whether they allow females to receive an education at all. In some countries and regions, the issue is which system will better serve female students' needs, because cross-cultural studies have found that single-sex education and coeducation have both positive and negative effects on girls' and women's educational experiences. Elsewhere, however, the basic issue remains winning equal access to education for women and girls.

Some national governments determine the educational settings for children and adults; others do not, for financial and other reasons. Worldwide, in general, rural areas tend to have coeducational schools, partly because of financial limitations but also because many girls must leave school to assist in household duties, making it difficult to maintain enrollments in female schools. Other influences on single-sex education versus coeducation include a nation's stage of industrial development; the existence of women's movements; and differences in religion, culture, societal values, and politics.

The debate over single-sex versus coeducational schooling sometimes revolves around a concern for equal educational opportunities for women and girls. Coeducation is often presented, particularly since the 1970s, as a universal cure for disparities in educational opportunities for women and girls. Coeducational schooling has been seen as crucial in places where many females are denied access to an education except in private, nonsanctioned facilities. In such contexts, females are typically taught skills needed to maintain their social position. For example, in many regions governments, educators, parents, and the public believe that if women are educated, they perform better as wives and mothers. Thus in the past, Spain sent girls to their own schools to learn domestic skills, whereas boys learned skills that would lead to jobs in nonagricultural sectors. Such differences in curricula raised questions of equal educational opportunities for women, and this concern for equality led to a trend away from single-sex schools and toward coeducational programs. Throughout the world, legislation began to be passed not only to give females access to an education but also to ensure that they would be given educational opportunities similar to those open to males.

Single-Sex Schools

The use of single-sex schooling and the rationales for it differ markedly from country to country. In some places, for instance, educators consider single-sex schools necessary because of differences in biological makeup between females and males. Religion may also be a factor; thus Muslim countries in general favor single-sex schooling because of their cultural values, in particular their religious roots. In Pakistan, to take just one example, schooling is sex-segregated at all levels, in conformance with Islamic ideology.

At the turn of the twenty-first century, in the world as a whole, most single-sex institutions were predominately secular or religious private schools or military academies. In England and Wales, for example, single-sex education was concentrated in the most prestigious and well endowed schools (Wilson, 1991). In the United States, there were few single-sex public schools. In China, schools were predominantly single-sex until a shortage of workers arose, so that more women were needed to enter the labor market. In Greece, single-sex schools and classes were abolished in the 1970s. However, many countries continued to use single-sex facilities until the level of secondary school; thus many girls would begin their education in single-sex schools. Also, many colleges and universities throughout the world remained single-sex.

Single-sex schools tend to emphasize academics significantly more than coeducational schools. They typically have same-sex teachers and administrators, and the curriculum is more narrowly focused (El-Sanabary, 1993). Such schools have several benefits for female students. One advantage is that girls and women feel less inhibited in the classroom and devote more time to academic work. Most also receive more attention and mentoring from their teachers. Another advantage is that single-sex schools foster social solidarity based on a shared gender identity. Many societies continue to have women's colleges because they provide a uniquely supportive environment in which women can develop their full potential, free from competition with men for leadership or social status. International studies have reported that when variables related to social background are controlled, girls and women excel in single-sex settings. Many girls and women themselves state that when they attend single-sex schools, they feel more confident about subjects such as the sciences, receive more encouragement from their teachers and parents, and develop a stronger academic self-concept.

However, single-sex education has certain disadvantages. The most significant problem, and the most common complaint, is that women and girls who attend single-sex schools lack the opportunities that students in coeducational schools enjoy; therefore, the women's movement has frequently urged coeducation in order to achieve educational equality. A related problem is that female schools tend to experience more financial strain, so that their students have less access to expensive programs offered in better-funded schools.

In many places, female schools are declining, because of these drawbacks and for other reasons. When some all-male colleges and universities themselves experienced financial problems, they began admitting women in order to increase their revenue from tuition. There was also a broader reason for including women: as a society develops, the labor market demands more workers, which means introducing women into this sector. This progression has meant that male educational facilities are opening their doors to women while female schools are closing theirs—or opening them to males—and that coeducation is becoming institutionalized across the world.

Coeducation

As with single-sex schooling, reasons for coeducation vary. One practical consideration is that some countries cannot afford separate facilities. In addition to economics, politics, religion, and culture influence coeducation throughout the world. Ideologically, as we have seen, coeducation has been endorsed as the optimal way to ensure equality of opportunity for women and girls.

In many societies, coeducation was the first avenue by which girls and women could gain access to an education and to the skills required to enter the labor market. However, some cultures, although they did not oppose education per se for girls and women, did oppose full coeducation at every level. Separate but equivalent settings for males and females were considered a reasonable compromise (Berkovitch and Bradley, 1999). Even in more thoroughly coeducational schools, many classes might be sex-segregated, such as home economics and "shop" (manual courses like carpentry).

Again as with single-sex education, the use of coeducation varies worldwide. In Poland, for instance, all schools are coeducational, except for theological and military academies. Islamic countries, by contrast, tend to oppose coeducation at the secondary level because of concerns about how adolescents will behave when they are together, but here too there are differences. Saudi Arabia prohibits coeducation beyond kindergarten, whereas Tunisia and Turkey have coeducation at all levels. Many colleges and universities in various places resisted coeducation because it was thought to lower a school's intellectual standing.

Worldwide, coeducation has distinct advantages for both females and males. Its advocates claim that the presence of girls in a classroom has a calming effect on the behavior of boys and that interacting with boys in the classroom helps girls become more self-reliant. The coeducational curriculum is developed to interest both sexes, and each sex thus has access to a wider range of occupational skills. Another benefit is that coeducational schools, on the whole, are committed to equal treatment of females and males. Many observers report that, as a result, each sex forms healthier, less stereotypical attitudes toward the other. This has the potential to lead to acceptance of egalitarian relationships in the world beyond school; in some countries, for instance, it is believed that healthier attitudes lead to healthier marriages. Furthermore, as coeducation began to flourish in public school systems and more females were educated, more women entered the teaching profession.

Still, there is concern about the drawbacks of coeducation. In many countries, coeducation has not succeeded in achieving equality between the sexes and has even been detrimental to girls and women. Educators and others have numerous reservations about the experiences of females in coeducational facilities. Consistently, it is found that in coeducational schools boys are treated differently from, and better than, girls; and this is true even though females have greatly increased their visibility at all levels of education. In mixed schools, teachers tend to perpetuate rivalry between the sexes. Teachers of mixed classes pay more attention to boys and give boys more praise. Some teachers design activities to meet the needs of boys and to control boys' unruly behavior in the classroom. Boys tend to monopolize physical space in school areas like classrooms and playgrounds. The premise of equal opportunities has been contradicted by hidden curricula and subtle or overt practices that reinforce the sexual hierarchy—that is, dominance by males. Patriarchal concepts transmitted in schools and universities reinforce women's subordination. In mixed schools, therefore, females are found to have diminished self-esteem. There is also a serious concern about safety: in coeducational settings at all grade levels, sexual harassment is a daily event for many girls and women. Overall, in fact, the greatest disadvantage for female students in coeducational facilities may be the behavior of male students.

Some problems, or perceived problems, of coeducation have been more specific to a given culture or a particular time. Admitting girls and women, for instance, was long thought to cause a "moral decline," because boys would not be able to focus on their studies with girls in their midst. Contact with males was thought to make girls and women hard and coarse, like males. Coeducation, though it was said to reduce homosexuality in boys and men, was also said to produce promiscuity in girls and women.

It is difficult, if not impossible, to draw any definitive conclusion about the outcomes of coeducation versus single-sex education. Multiple variables—including peer groups, parental influence, student demographics, and the quality of each school—affect these outcomes; and research often yields inconsistent results: many studies have found no significant difference between girls or women in single-sex schools and those in mixed schools. The goal of most educators is to provide a learning environment that gives girls and women every opportunity for future success in a competitive, heterogeneous world.

Researchers point out, however, that the same educational setting does not necessarily mean an equal education for all students. Thus the debate over single-sex education versus coeducation for females is likely to continue for some time.

See Also

EDUCATION: CHILLY CLIMATE IN THE CLASSROOM; EDUCATION: GENDER EQUITY; EDUCATION: GENDERED SUBJECT CHOICE; EDUCATION: NONSEXIST

References and Further Reading

Berkovitch, Nitza, and Karen Bradley. 1999. The globalization of women's status: Consensus/dissensus in the world polity. *Sociological Perspectives* 42: 481–499.

El-Sanabary, Nagat. 1993. Middle East and North Africa. In Elizabeth M. King and M. Anne Hill, eds., *Women's education in developing countries: Barriers, benefits, and policies.* Baltimore, Md.: Johns Hopkins University Press.

Wilson, Maggie. 1991. England and Wales. In Maggie Wilson, ed., *Girls and young women in education: A European perspective.* Oxford: Pergamon.

Jennifer L. Gossett

EDUCATION: South Asia

South Asia, a source of great literary and literacy traditions and a generator of great philosophies, also contains a large percentage of illiterate people, the majority of them women. South Asia includes India, Pakistan, Bhutan, Nepal, Sri Lanka, Bangladesh, Burma, and Afghanistan.

The progress of these countries is dependent on female literacy because health, hygiene, and nutrition problems can be overcome partly through educating women. "Illiteracy is closely related to underdevelopment and poverty, and the elimination of illiteracy represents an essential condition for the development and well-being of peoples and nations" (UNESCO PROAP, 1989: 11). In south Asia, women constitute nearly two-thirds of illiterate adults. There is an inherent contradiction in the region between modern amenities, modern educational systems, and advanced communications systems, on the one hand, and the high level of illiteracy and significant backwardness, on the other.

Background

Women in south Asian countries face the dual constraints of traditional views about women's education and the policy of reduced spending on women's education. The choice of educating heavily favors boys, due to the traditional division of labor and gender. This is particularly evident in rural areas, where the bulk of domestic work falls on women. Women are allotted the tasks of working in the fields and the home and maintaining routine life. This situation is aggravated by the lack of facilities. For example, projects by the United Nations Educational, Scientific, and Cultural Organization aimed at rural women have encountered highly paternalistic regional bureaucracies.

Women, Work, and Equity

Some women's education was never planned, although they "gained from education 'incidentally' or as an auxiliary development of men of their own social class" (Nayar, 1988, cited in UNESCO PROAP, 1989: 31). South Asia is a region of contrasts, with women holding positions as highly qualified professionals, such as doctors, lawyers, engineers, advocates, bankers, and teachers. There are women vice-chancellors, assembly speakers, advocates, and eminent principals. The proportion of women among the technical administrators and managers, however, is extremely low, because many women do not undertake math-based education that would enhance their technical skills. The other picture is of women who cannot read or write, with 90 percent of females in rural areas illiterate. The majority of "educated" women are found in poorly paid jobs, but these women have been instrumental in bringing educational issues to national and international notice. Some of these women are activists who have raised the issues but are yet to make a significant impact. Socialist economies such as those in India and Sri Lanka also have emphasized the need to free women from centuries of repression by providing them with special educational programs designed to bring about social reconstruction. These are highly politicized programs, however, and their impact is negligible except in isolated areas. The educational system vis-à-vis women has largely failed, because it has not prevented the mass school dropouts or "shut-outs" arising from rural or urban poverty. The struggle some women face for survival is so great that their daughters are included in the basic task of surviving; in such cases, it is not uncommon for girls to work at home, which enables their mothers to work and their brothers to attend school. Such practices explain the low female literacy rates. It may be argued that poverty and patriarchal rules combine to categorize women as housewives and mothers and fail to consider the need to reorient the gender relations within the family.

Development and literacy policies have ignored the important aspect of educating women. These dual restraints have confined women to the tasks of family, hygiene, health, and child rearing. The positive impact of education on women is reflected in better living conditions, better hygiene, and improved financial positions. Formal and informal education has focused on self-employment, cottage industries, or family planning, ignoring the issue of gender equity and thus perpetuating poor living conditions. The societies of south Asia are generally sex-discriminatory, and policy recommendations propagated by the United Nations Development Decade for Women are interpreted in ways that do not help women.

Female Illiteracy

Literacy is linked to the ideologies and cultures of the region and finds expression in severe discrimination against females in countries such as India, Pakistan, and Bangladesh, where girls are undernourished and neglected. Those that survive the malnourishment enter early marriages, with incomplete schooling contributing to a continuous cycle of oppression. In the countries where health programs have been implemented, literacy rates have increased, and women's education has helped to improve other amenities, such as child care requirements. Urbanization also has had a positive effect on women's education and related issues, with a significant narrowing of enrollment difference between girls and boys and achievement of greater gender equity. The rural population, however, has had to contend with lower resource allotment, fewer public services, and poor health conditions. The process of industrialization, which also contributes to increased literacy, is slow in the south Asian countries and has resulted in disjointed growth. Other factors working against women include the 15 to 20 hours per week of hard manual labor that many undertake in the home, discriminatory attitudes toward girls' education, a preference for boys' education, and a traditional view that sees education as superfluous for girls because educational advantages accrue to another house when the girl is married.

Female illiteracy is high in India, with an estimated 144 million women illiterate, followed by Pakistan and Bangladesh with 18 million, Nepal with 4 million, and Afghanistan with 3.3 million (UNESCO PROAP, 1989: 35). There are numerous villages in India, Pakistan, Bhutan, and Bangladesh where not a single woman is literate. Even with a significant increase in enrollment, the failure to complete primary schooling leaves the literacy level low. In an egalitarian society like Sri Lanka, the literacy level is high, supported by socially just policies of free education, health, and concessional transport, resulting in a literacy rate of almost 83 percent (UNESCO PROAP, 1989: 53).

Recent Efforts

In south Asia, adult literacy programs received attention only after the 1970s, and in India, for example, the National Literacy Mission was launched in October 1988 with a "focus on empowerment of women through functional literacy and skills development" (UNESCO PROAP, 1989). Nonformal distance education is not well attended, due to impediments such as distance, lack of child care, poor health, and malnutrition. Initiatives that would make educational programs viable for girls include a high degree of commitment from government agencies that can mobilize funds, the provision of training for female teachers, scholarships to girls, free education, curriculum structured to the needs of women, and a focus on nonformal education.

There is a major push in these countries toward educational programs that support productivity, skills training that can equip women in production techniques, and basic child care. Nongovernmental organizations, such as Shiksha Karmi in India, and strategies such as provision of free education and midday meals have attracted a great deal of attention, as have the Bangladesh Rural Advancement Committee, Cheli Beti in Nepal, and Khwendo Kor in the North-West Frontier Province of Pakistan. The emphasis is not so much on literacy skills as on health and child care issues, which also could include basic literacy skills. These countries have been formulating specific policies such as the establishment of separate education cells for women in governments, the appointment of specialists to formulate non-gender-biased curriculum, flexible school timing, and school calendars specific to an area. It is hoped that efforts made by the individual countries and international organizations will increase literacy, leading to greater equity.

See Also

DEVELOPMENT: SOUTH ASIA; EDUCATION: GENDER EQUITY; HOUSEHOLDS AND FAMILIES: SOUTH ASIA; LITERACY; WOMEN'S STUDIES: SOUTH ASIA; WORK: OCCUPATIONAL SEGREGATION

References and Further Reading

Colclough, Christopher, with Keith M. Lewin. 1993. *Educating all children.* Oxford: Clarendon.

Didi Bahini. 1996. *Toward gender fair education.* A workshop report on "Gender Perspectives in NFE Materials in Nepal." Author Kathmandu.

Duza, Asfia, et al. 1992. *Education and gender equity.* Dhaka: Women for Women.

Jafri, Ruquia. 1993. *Gender bias and female education in Pakistan.* Islamabad: Aurat Foundation.

Jahan, Roushan, and Vimala Ramachandran. 1998. *Bridging the gap between intention and action.* New Delhi: Asian–South Pacific Bureau of Adult Education UNESCO PROAP.

Krishnamurthy, Laxmi. 1996. Teacher training, school attendance, and child labor. *Alarippu.*

UNESCO PROAP. 1989. *Bulletin,* no. 30.

Radha Iyer

EDUCATION: Southeast Asia

In some countries of southeast Asia, girls are not sent to school because parents fear for their chastity. For this and other reasons—for example, poverty, dowries, cheap labor—the inequities in women's education in this area of the world continue, and although the reasons may be legitimate, they are shortsighted. The long-term results have undermined economic growth.

Concern for women's education has been so great that in October 1945 the founding charter of the United Nations addressed the issue; the UN has been instrumental in supporting a growing global movement to advance women's education ever since. In the year 2000 there were an estimated 875 million illiterate adults, two-thirds of them women. That figure is down from 1990, when the estimated illiterate population was 966 million (Women's International Network News, 1990).

Southeast Asia is only slightly ahead of Africa—the lowest-ranking of all world regions—in the status of women's education and in the disparity between male and female educational achievements. Women's education in this region progressed significantly, however, during the latter half of the twentieth century. The reasons for this are twofold. First, this area experienced western cultural imperialism, which influenced its educational system. Second, women in this region have played a strong role in the economic support of their families; therefore, they have been subjected to fewer restrictions compared with other Asian regions (Mazumdar, 1993: 17).

This is apparent in the Philippines, where educational opportunities for women first arrived in 1898 directly following the Philippine-American War, when night schools were established for working students. The motive was selfish, however: it promoted pro-American ideas. In the late

525

twentieth century, the literacy rate among females was 83 percent. There is a slight disparity in the figures from urban (97.1) to rural (89.9). What is interesting is that women in the late twentieth century accounted for the majority of undergraduate and graduate school enrollment, but they also tended toward traditional female roles of food and nutrition and nursing.

In Vietnam, there has been access to free education for all since 2 September 1945, the day President Ho Chi Minh declared Vietnam an independent nation. In the latter half of the twentieth century, Vietnam progressed from a 22.4 percent illiteracy rate among females to an 8.8 percent rate, and the trend continues in that direction. Education in this country is both universal and compulsory for children aged 6 to 11, and during the mid-1980s there were more than 80 institutions of higher learning.

In Indonesia there also is free public education, but it was not until the 1970s, during a favorable economic time, that a substantial increase in government funds targeted education. The reasons for restrictions on female school attendance are more economic than cultural in Indonesia, where the schools are coeducational. In 1971, 5.7 million girls aged 5 to 12 attended school, compared with 6.4 million boys. In 1990, 12.3 million girls attended school, while 13.0 boys attended. In addition, from 1971 to 1990 the ratios of the number of females for every 100 males attending school rose from 90 to 95 in the 7-to-12 age bracket; from 72 to 89 for 13- to 15-year-olds; from 59 to 84 for 16- to 18-year-olds; and from 41 to 69 for 19- to 24-year-olds. The conclusion, in Indonesia, is that gender bias in education is disappearing among primary-school-aged children (Oey-Gardiner and Suprapto, 1996: 98–99).

Those countries that have invested in education, particularly in women's education, also have experienced economic growth (Sadik, 1997: 147). Following the 1994 International Conference on Population and Development (ICPD), countries in Asia began investing more in education and concentrating on the education of their female population. In Malaysia, between 90 and 98 percent of girls completed their primary education, and it is to education that national development has been credited. Women, who are nearly 50 percent of Malaysia's population, also contribute significantly in the workforce, in politics, and in education. Female education has enabled women to make forays into the traditional male fields of astronomy, physics, finance, and technology.

Women's education in Malaysia closely followed its development as a nation. In the first half of the twentieth century, women's status was low, they were confined to their homes and domestic chores, and they only accounted for 15

percent of the enrollment in English schools in 1947. Then, after independence in 1957, a national education policy was established, and enrollment for girls increased significantly. By 1970, enrollment rate for girls at the primary level had reached 84.8 percent; at the lower secondary level, 43.6 percent; and at the higher secondary level, 16.1 percent, as compared with 91.6 percent, 60.6 percent, and 23.9 percent, respectively, for boys. Attendance at Malaysian universities in 1990 was 55 percent male and 45 percent female. In vocational schools, however, which the Malaysian government believes in strongly, a disparity persists: in 1987 girls were only 24 percent of the student population at vocational schools and only 35 percent at technical schools (Sidin, 1996: 122–124).

The same strides in women's education can be seen in Singapore, which was male-dominated in the nineteenth and early twentieth centuries. Female education in this country began in the mid-nineteenth century, but the goal was more to keep girls sheltered than to educate them. The girls who attended schools were mostly those of privilege. In 1941, more than one-third of the school population was female. Eleven years later, that increased to almost 50 percent for secondary school education. In 1980, that figure became 51 percent. The illiteracy rate among females aged 15 to 24 decreased from 15.5 percent in 1970 to 3.8 percent in 1990 (Low, 1996: 145, 147).

There tends to be more female illiteracy in rural areas than in urban areas of southeast Asia. Many rural people believe that money spent on a girl's education is money given to another household. One of the main causes of the continuing education bias against women, particularly in rural southeast Asia, is the fast-held conception that women are mothers and housewives; they receive little or no credit for their significant role as farmers, and it is felt that an investment in their education is throwing money away. Other parents feel that if they educate their daughters, then the girls will become unfit for labor. And yet another argument against female education is that an educated girl would demand an educated groom, and therefore the dowry price would escalate.

Tuition, books, uniforms, and transportation are prohibitively expensive for many, and parents traditionally give a higher priority to educating their sons. In addition, sending girls away to school, having them taught by male teachers, and allowing them proximity to boys go against the value placed on girls' moral chasteness (Kamimura, 1998).

In Cambodia, many girls aged 12 to 14 simply do not have access to secondary schools. There, the literacy rate in 1999 among females was 58.1 percent and among males was

81.8 percent (Kingdom of Cambodia Ministry of Education, Youth, and Sport, 1999). In 1991, there were 60 females per 100 males enrolled in second-level education. That number dropped to 19 for every 100 at the third level.

Another underlying reason for the continuing fight for women's education is the population growth and concurrent reduction in death rates in Asia. This region, as a consequence, has experienced a rapid rise in population—a rise that challenges governments' abilities to fund educational programs. One of the main factors in the persistence of high birthrates is the low status of women and their low levels of education. There is an undeniable link between eradication of poverty and education of women.

Slowly, the countries of southeast Asia have discovered that the education of women and their subsequent empowerment improve a country's socioeconomic status. In 1992, the chairman of Singapore's Economic Development Board, Philip Yeo, commented that in the next 10 years there would be no shortage of cheap labor in Asia but a serious shortage of educated, skilled people (Adler, 1994: 3). The status of Asian women in business began to change.

That change was felt as far away as U.S. graduate business programs. In 1999, the University of Chicago, Northwestern University, and the University of Illinois at Chicago all reported a significant increase in Asian women applying for admission (Littman, 1999: 15). In the last years of the twentieth century, the number of Asian-born women taking the Graduate Management Admission Test (GMAT) and enrolling in U.S. business schools increased at a rate faster than that of American women. For instance, at the University of Chicago's Graduate School of Business, applications from Asian women increased 72 percent from 1997 to 1999 (Littman, 1999: 15).

The Gender-Related Development Index (GDI), which looks at life expectancy, educational attainment, and real income, is a relatively new indicator of women's status. Singapore, Malaysia, and Thailand had a GDI index ranging from .76 to .896 in 1995. A 1.0 ranking means perfect gender equality (Son, 1995). According to the United Nation's Development Program, these countries' investments in health, education, and skills have enabled more of the population to share economic benefits.

In 1995, the Fourth World Conference on Women held in Beijing focused on the areas of education and training, the economy, power and decision making, and the environment. The report concluded that in order for a society to adapt to rampant change and increasing technology, women had to have increased access to science and technology.

On 8 March 2000, UNESCO'S International Women's Day again highlighted the disparities between men's and women's education. Although in Europe and North America only about 2 percent of the women were illiterate at the time of the conference, in southern Asia nearly three in five women, as compared with one in three men, were illiterate. And in April 2000, at the World Education Forum in Dakar, Senegal, the progress made since the World Conference on Education for All held in 1990 in Jomtien, Thailand, was assessed. For the countries of southeast Asia, documented advances are seen: the average decline in female illiteracy for the region is over 6 percent. The leading nations are the Philippines, Thailand, Singapore, Brunei Darussalam, and Vietnam.

Gender equality is generally understood as the absence of discrimination in opportunity, status, and treatment. Equal treatment encompasses the judicial, social, educational, and economic arenas. In 2000, former United Nations secretary-general Boutros Boutros-Ghali said, "Without progress in the situation of women, there can be no true social development. Human rights are not worthy of the name if they exclude the female half of humanity. The struggle for women's equality is part of the struggle for a better world for all human beings, and all societies."

Southeast Asia is slowly recognizing that educated women mean a stronger economy and a better future for the entire region.

See Also

DEVELOPMENT: OVERVIEW; EDUCATION: HIGHER EDUCATION; HOUSEHOLDS AND FAMILIES: SOUTHEAST ASIA; LITERACY; POVERTY

References and Further Reading

Adler, Nancy. 1994. Asian women in management. *International Studies of Management and Organization* 23(4).

Conway, Jill Ker, and Susan C. Bourque, eds. 1993. *The politics of women's education: Perspectives from Asia, Africa, and Latin America.* Ann Arbor: University of Michigan Press.

Kamimura, Chiharu. 1998. Global study finds girls, despite gains, trail boys. *Washington Times.*

Kingdom of Cambodia Ministry of Education, Youth, and Sport. 1999. Policies on education development. <http://www.moeys.gov.kh/profile/edu_in_cambodia/policy.htm>

Littman, Margaret. 1999. Power passport. *Crain's Chicago Business* 22(30): 15.

Low, Guat Tin. 1996. Singapore. In Grace C. L. Mak, ed., *Women, education, and development in Asia: Cross-national perspectives.* New York: Garland.

Mak, Grace C. L., ed. 1996. *Women, education, and development in Asia: Cross-national perspectives.* New York: Garland.

Mazumdar, Vina. 1993. A survey of gender issues and educational development in Asia. In Jill Ker Conway and Susan C. Bourque, eds., *The politics of women's education.* Ann Arbor: University of Michigan Press.

Oey-Gardiner, Mayling, and Riga-Adiwoso Suprapto. 1996. Indonesia. In Grace C. L. Mak, ed., *Women, education, and development in Asia: Cross-national perspectives.* New York: Garland.

Sadik, Nafis. 1997. Women, populations, and sustainable development in south Asia. *Journal of International Affairs* 51(1): 147.

Sidin, Robiah. 1996. Malaysia. In Grace C. L. Mak, ed., *Women, education, and development in Asia: Cross-national perspectives.* New York: Garland.

Son, Johanna. 1995. Women-Asia: Economic growth bring gains, but more needed. *English News Wire.*

UNESCO. 2000. News and Events. Focus on women and education.
<http://unescostat.unesco.org/en/news/news_p/news4.htm>

United Nations. The status of women. <http://www.un.org/Conferences/Women/PubInfo/Status/ TextOnly.htm>

Women's International Network News. 1990. Female illiteracy alarmingly high in Southeast Asia. *Reports from around the World: Asia and Pacific* 16(3): 60.

World Conference on Women press release. 14 March 1997. The importance of education for achieving women's equality, development, and peace stressed in status of women commission.

Sarah Cox

EDUCATION: Southern Africa

The physical and geographic differences between the southern African states—Angola, Botswana, Lesotho, Malawi, Mozambique, Namibia, South Africa, Swaziland, Zambia, and Zimbabwe—are as striking as the differences between the languages and variations in cultures. However, the countries do share some similar experiences: pertinent here are their history of colonialism and the introduction of formal schooling systems by western missionaries. These legacies remain manifest in the education systems of each country, which in turn play critical roles in the construction of gendered identities.

Education is considered a major factor in development, social change, and economic progress. However, the trans-formative potential of education is only assumed: gender discrimination and differentiation persist at all levels. In order to obtain a deeper understanding of these issues in education, it is useful to ask first how education systems treat girls and women differently from boys and men; second, what the different ways are in which males and females experience education systems; and third, how these inequalities in education systems function to maintain the divisions and inequalities of societies in general.

Most research assesses gender equity in the formal education system by quantifying the access, enrollment, and performance scores of girls and boys. Realizing that access is not the same as equity, more textured research tries to analyze qualitative aspects of the education system that discriminate against girls and women. These may include the construction of and subjects in the curricula, vocational opportunities, and the extent to which education contributes toward alleviating the societal constraints on women.

Indigenous Education

Historically, indigenous education, the learning of culture and traditions particular to a group, was a part of everyday life. Although there were variations between indigenous communities, the gendered division of labor was recognized, and the roles and skills of adult society were learned through lived experience. Initiation schools and ceremonies marked the transition to adult society, entrenched gender divisions, and stressed secrecy, solidarity, and cooperation among peers. Several of these practices are still considered desirable to safeguard and transmit the cultural heritage of each people.

Informal Education

Informal education is the lifelong process of learning from the people and resources of everyday environments. The media play a significant role in maintaining and shifting notions of gender and education through television, radio, and popular print.

Nonformal Education

Nonformal education refers to all those organized educational activities that happen outside the established formal system. Women, as primary caregivers and mediators of household relations and cultural practices, are particularly targeted by nonformal educators in health and development agencies. Issues that are seen largely as women's responsibility include potable water, AIDS, breast-feeding, and child nutrition. Nonformal learning opportunities on topics such as small business management, low-cost housing, and agriculture are offered through a variety of different media, including the radio.

Approximately 75 percent of the population of southern Africa lives in rural areas (an exception is South Africa), where illiteracy (less than five years of formal schooling) is estimated to be as high as 70 percent. It has proved difficult to resource rural areas and provide ongoing opportunities for literacy learning. Women, the majority sex in rural areas, are most affected and protest that the literacy necessary to use new technologies or to seek jobs in the cities is being learned primarily by men.

Many countries try to some extent to meet the demand for adult and continuing education through nonformal education, night schools, and distance education. The responsibilities and fears associated with being a woman usually mean that these facilities are used by more men than women.

Since 1980, the youth have often constituted the fighting forces in the civil wars in the region. Formal schooling has been frequently and severely disrupted, and because of this, it has been argued that more attention should be paid to nonformal and alternative types of schooling.

Formal Education

Formal education is usually understood to mean the education system that depends on chronological progression through a system of grades. Historically important as the first sites of formal schooling, some missionary schools offered places and opportunities to boys rather than girls. Although it is not the policy of the southern African countries to discriminate against girls, the formal schooling system remains, with the exception of South Africa, dominated by males.

However, there have been concerted efforts, such as those by the government of Mozambique, to recruit girls into the formal education system. Several smaller-scale initiatives, facilitated by donor agencies or nongovernmental organizations (NGOs), attempt to provide equivalent education for girls and young women. In Malawi the primary education bursary scheme, GLOBE, funds girls' school and book fees in a three-to-one ratio to boys'. In some areas education for girls is valued, and nursing and teaching (the two career paths most readily open to women) have considerable status. In other areas the belief that schooling is inappropriate for girls dies hard.

Preschool: The majority of children in the southern African states do not have access to preschool facilities.

Primary schooling: Free and compulsory primary education for boys and girls is, as yet, an unrealized goal in all these countries. Botswana and Zimbabwe have made the best progress in this regard. In Zimbabwe there are less than 5 percent fewer girls than boys at all levels. However, the dropout rate in rural areas and at secondary schools is higher for girls. In South Africa there are slightly more girls than boys enrolled at all school levels, and at the primary-school level the dropout rate for boys is slightly higher (53 percent) than for girls (44 percent). Elsewhere in the region at this age both girls and boys may be taken out of school to assist with domestic work, herding, or farming, but the chances are that boys will receive more schooling in their lifetime than girls.

Secondary schooling: The proportion of girls attending school decreases particularly rapidly after puberty so that only a third of school leavers are girls. Teenage pregnancies, early marriage, and the responsibility of kin and child care in both urban and rural areas are cited as reasons for girls dropping out.

In general, formal educational systems are not welcoming environments for girls and women. Girls are discriminated against in terms of the different emphases still prevalent in different subject opportunities (such as woodworking or physical science for boys and bookkeeping or domestic science for girls), the value attached to masculine knowledge in the curricula, and the different facilities and sports that are offered to girls. Female pupils and teachers are subjected to sexual harassment and discriminatory conditions of service.

Tertiary education: By the time the school population reaches tertiary levels, only about 1 percent of the original enrollment remains. Chancellors College in Malawi is fairly typical in that less than a quarter of university registrants are women, and nursing and teaching are still the predominant career choices. Throughout the southern African states there are very few women scientists, doctors, or engineers, although development funding targeted at assisting women into these careers has improved the numbers. Women are underrepresented as academic staff, especially in universities, where they usually hold junior positions. An exception is Professor Brenda Gourlay, the first woman principal and vice-chancellor of the University of Natal in South Africa.

All the countries have limited technical training facilities, with the number of university graduates greatly exceeding those technically trained. Literate and technically trained women are needed to spur economic activities, but paradoxically, technological developments being introduced are often perceived as responsible for alienating women from work that used to afford them some usefulness and economic power.

It has been argued that the formal education systems have not fulfilled the popular aspirations and goals of development and, in particular, gender equity. Nor has the crucial relationship between education and the world of work been addressed, although Namibia and Zambia have introduced educative programs that are linked to food production and user- and environmentally friendly technologies.

Throughout the southern African states, women have established national organizations such as the Organization of Mozambican Women and the Women's League of the African National Congress in South Africa, as well as networks such as the Association of African Women for Research and Development, the Forum for African Women Educationalists, and the Education Research Network for Eastern and Southern Africa to promote their educational interests. Many successful women, such as the Honorable Dr. G. K. T. Chiepe, a member of Parliament and the minister of foreign affairs in Botswana, who is herself a scientist, promote the notion of education for all and in particular science careers for girls and women.

See Also

COLONIALISM AND POSTCOLONIALISM; DEVELOPMENT: SUB-SAHARAN AND SOUTHERN AFRICA; EDUCATION: PRESCHOOL; EDUCATION: VOCATIONAL; FEMINISM: SOUTH AFRICA; POLITICS AND THE STATE: SOUTHERN AFRICA; WOMEN'S STUDIES: SOUTHERN AFRICA

References and Further Reading

Badsha, N. 1994. Equity and student access. In B. Kaplan, ed., *Changing by degrees? Equity issues in tertiary education.* Cape Town: University of Cape Town Press.

Beijing conference report: 1994 country report on the status of South African women. 1994. Cape Town: CTP Printer.

Department of National Education preliminary statistics for 1994. 1994. Pretoria, South Africa: Department of National Education.

Dorsey, B., M. Matshazi, and L. Nyaguru. 1991. *A review of education and training.* Report for the Canadian International Development Agency and the Government of Zimbabwe. Harare.

Duncan, W. 1988. School dropouts in Botswana: Gender differences at secondary level. Report no. 81. Stockholm: Institute for International Education.

Malawi government basic education statistics 1993. 1993. Planning Division, Lilongwe.

Mugomba, A., and M. Nyaggah. 1980. *Independence without freedom: The political economy of colonial education in southern Africa.* Oxford: Clio.

Truscott, K. 1994. *Gender in education.* Education Policy Unit, University of the Witwatersrand. Johannesburg: NECC.

Wendy Annecke

EDUCATION: Special Needs

Many terms are used in worldwide education systems to cover what might previously have been called handicap. The term *learning difficulties* is often used to refer to children with cognitive problems in mainstream schools, although *special educational needs* (SEN) may be used as a blanket term to cover all difficulties. In England and Scotland, a child is seen as having special educational needs if he or she has greater difficulties in learning than other children of the same age, thus requiring additional help to that normally available in the mainstream class. Until relatively recently, the child-centered approach adopted by practitioners and researchers in the area of SEN meant that gender issues tended to be neglected (Daniels et al., 1999), despite the fact that many more boys than girls are identified as having SEN (see following section for further discussion of this point). The overrepresentation of minority ethnic pupils among those identified as having SEN, by contrast, has been flagged as problematic by commentators (Diniz, 2000; ILEA, 1985; Tomlinson, 1981, 1982).

Gender Differences in the Identification of SEN

Scottish Executive statistics provide interesting background data on gender-related patterns of identification of SEN. (These patterns are broadly similar to those in England and Wales [ILEA, 1985] and other European countries.) In the academic year 1992–1993, boys in special schools outnumbered girls 2 to 1. Boys made up three-quarters of the population of independent special schools, most of which cater to children with social, emotional, and behavioral difficulties. The most marked difference was in the area of emotional and behavioral difficulties, where 81 percent of pupils were male and 19 percent were female. The smallest discrepancy in the proportion of males and females was in the area of profound learning difficulties (55 percent male, 45 percent female) and hearing difficulties (59 percent male, 41 percent female). Similar patterns were evident when comparing the nature of difficulties of girls and boys with recorded SEN placed in mainstream primary and secondary schools.

There are a number of ways in which these differences might be interpreted.

1. They represent biological differences between the sexes, reflecting male susceptibility to "germs, genes and trauma" (Abberley, 1987).

2. They reflect a tendency to construct male behavior as deviant. Hill (1994) described how the language of assessments used by teachers and psychologists in formal assessment tended to reflect gender stereotypes. Thus boys were described as aggressive, disruptive, having limited concentration, and violent, whereas girls were described as passive, socially vulnerable, and strange. Hill did not, however, discuss the extent to which these descriptions actually accorded with the pupils' classroom behavior.

3. They reflect a greater tendency among males to learning and behavioral difficulties, for social rather than physiological reasons. Willis (1977), for example, provided a vivid ethnographic account of the way in which working-class boys actively construct gender identities that are diametrically opposed to feminine identities. For instance, wherever working-class girls are relatively compliant and studious, working-class boys are ready to adopt an antieducational position.

Tomlinson (1982) distinguished between normative and nonnormative difficulties. Normative difficulties, such as profound learning difficulties and sensory impairment, she argued, are more susceptible to "objective" diagnosis, whereas nonnormative difficulties, which would include social, emotional, and behavioral difficulties and mild to moderate learning difficulties, are more dependent on subjective judgment. The statistics suggest that while boys predominate in all categories, their predominance is greatest in nonnormative areas, thus lending weight to the argument that social judgments play a large part in determining who gets labeled as having SEN, particularly with regard to social, emotional, and behavioral difficulties and moderate learning difficulties.

Gender interacts with social class in interesting ways to determine the allocation of different categories of SEN. For example, working-class boys are much more likely to be identified as having problems regarded as socially unacceptable, such as emotional and behavioral difficulties and moderate learning difficulties. Tomlinson (1988), noting this pattern, suggested that there was a growing tendency to identify this group as having social, emotional, and behavioral difficulties in order to legitimate their exclusion from a labor market in which high levels of unemployment are endemic. In relatively nonstigmatized categories, such as specific learning difficulties, middle-class boys predominate

(Riddell et al., 1994). Dyslexia is seen as a problem meriting sympathy, support, and additional resources rather than school exclusion, largely due to the efforts of voluntary organizations. The attachment of the label SEN, then, may be advantageous in terms of providing additional support or disadvantageous by raising the possibility of sanctions or school exclusion. Much depends on the social meaning of the label attached, and, as we have seen, this is highly dependent on social class as well as gender.

When pupils are referred to schools catering to emotional and behavioral difficulties, reasons for referral are often different for girls and boys. Whereas boys tend to be referred because of violent or disruptive behavior, according to Petrie (1986), girls are often referred for nonattendance, with the assumption that truancy is associated with promiscuity. Furthermore, boys are much more likely to become embroiled in the school's disciplinary system, but, as noted by Lloyd (1992) and others, teachers adhere to the belief that "a bad girl is much worse than a bad boy." There are, of course, major implications for the relatively small number of girls who are identified as experiencing social, emotional, and behavioral difficulties. They may find themselves in special schools and classrooms where they are greatly outnumbered by boys and where the atmosphere might be threatening. In addition, the curriculum on offer may be geared predominantly to male interests and values.

The School Experiences of Pupils with SEN

One might have expected that given the slower developmental rate of pupils with SEN, they would stay in school longer. This is not the case; however, Scottish Office statistics for 1993, for instance, show that 52 percent of leavers with SEN were under 16, compared with 22 percent of education authority pupils and 7 percent of independent school pupils. In all three sectors (special, mainstream, and independent), boys left school before girls. A significant proportion of pupils who leave special schools stay at home or move into the labor market. For those who progress to postschool education, it is not yet evident how successful learning support systems are in meeting the needs of pupils with SEN and particularly the needs of girls (Closs, 1993).

Lower-achieving pupils, including those with SEN, in mainstream schools were much more likely to follow a strongly sex-stereotyped curriculum. For example, in the third and fourth years of secondary education in Scotland in 1993, boys made up more than 90 percent of pupils in technological studies, more than 80 percent of pupils in craft and design, but less than 25 percent of pupils in home economics and business subjects. Croxford (1996, 2000) demonstrated the strong association between social class and sex stereotyping of option choice. (There is, of course, a strong association between social class and achievement level.) In special schools, sex stereotyping of the curriculum may be less pronounced, simply because the curriculum is likely to offer only a limited range of the subjects normally available in secondary schools (Turner et al., 1995: chap. 8).

In special schools, there is likely to be a sense of marginalization from the mainstream so that key curricular and policy developments may be resisted. Lewis and Halpin (1994) noted the opposition of special-school teachers in England to the national curriculum, despite its ostensibly democratic insistence on the right of all pupils to access the entire curriculum. The head teachers in Lewis and Halpin's study maintained that the imposition of a national curriculum undermined their goal of delivering an individualized educational package to each child. In addition, Turner et al. (1995) found that special schools in Scotland were highly unlikely to have equal opportunities policies in place and in this sense were well behind the mainstream sector. Research in one case-study school suggested that the teachers' child-centered ideology made them oblivious to the existence of gender divisions, and their awareness of structural inequality tended to focus on disability as the issue of central importance.

An interesting feature of special schools is the predominance of women within them. In Scotland 90 percent of teachers and slightly less than 80 percent of head teachers are female. These proportions are quite different from those found in primary education, where women predominate but are underrepresented at head-teacher level, and from those found in secondary education, where there are roughly equal numbers of males and females but the majority (97 percent) of head teachers are male. It would appear, then, that in career terms women do relatively well in the special sector, but nonetheless it is regarded and often experienced as a marginalized location.

There are, to date, few ethnographic studies of life in special schools and post-school destinations. There is, however, some suggestion that the management of appearance may be particularly important for girls in developing an acceptable social identity (Allan, 1999). In addition, sexuality may be especially problematic for girls. Whereas parents may acknowledge that for boys sexuality is "normal," if not to be actively encouraged, they may feel that for their daughters any expression of sexuality is dangerous because of fear of pregnancy, and they may go to great lengths to restrict girls' freedom of movement (Riddell et al., 1993).

Conclusion

There are clearly many important links between gender and SEN. This is a sphere in which boys outnumber girls even in those areas where there is greater scope for agreement over definition (for example, sensory impairment or profound learning difficulties). In areas where judgments tend to be more subjective (for example, emotional and behavioral difficulties, moderate learning difficulties), the gender divide is even more pronounced. In less stigmatized areas (for example, dyslexia), boys may benefit from being more likely to be identified, but in other areas (for example, emotional and behavioral difficulties), higher rates of identification may work against boys' interests. The child-centered focus of special-school culture may lead to gender blindness, and equal opportunities work is likely to be relatively underdeveloped.

See Also

DISABILITY AND FEMINISM; DISABILITY: QUALITY OF LIFE; EDUCATION: ACHIEVEMENT; EDUCATION: CURRICULUM IN SCHOOLS; PSYCHOLOGY: PSYCHOMETRICS; SIMULTANEOUS OPPRESSIONS

References and Further Reading

Abberley, P. 1987. The concept of oppression and the development of a social theory of disability. *Disability Handicap and Society* 2: 5–19.

Allan, J. 1999. *Actively seeking inclusion: Pupils with special needs in mainstream schools.* London: Falmer.

Closs, A., ed. 1993. *Special educational needs beyond 16.* Edinburgh: Moray House.

Croxford, L. 1996. Equal opportunities in the secondary curriculum in Scotland, 1995–1996. *British Educational Research Journal* 20(4): 371–391.

———. 2000. Gender and national curriculum. In J. Salisbury and S. Riddell, eds., *Gender, policy, and educational change: Shifting agendas in the UK and Europe.* London: Routledge.

Daniels, H., V. Hey, D. Leonard, and M. Smith. 1999. Issues of equity in special needs education from a gender perspective. *British Journal of Special Education* 26(4): 189–195.

Diniz, F. A. 2000. Race and special educational needs in the 1990s. *British Journal of Special Education* 26(4): 213–217.

Hill, J. 1994. The paradox of gender: Sex stereotyping within statementing procedure. *British Educational Research Journal* 20(3): 345–357.

Inner London Education Authority. (ILEA). 1985. *Educational opportunities for all? Report of the committee reviewing pro-*

vision to meet special educational needs (The Fish Report). London: Inner London Education Authority.

Lewis, A., and D. Halpin. 1994. A report of the perceptions of twelve headteachers of special schools. Paper presented at the annual conference of the British Educational Research Association, St. Anne's College, Oxford, 8–11 Sept.

Lloyd, G., ed. 1992. *Chosen with care? Responses to disturbing and disruptive behavior.* Edinburgh: Moray House.

Petrie, C. 1986. *The nowhere girls.* London: Gower.

Riddell, S., S. Brown, and J. Duffield. 1994. Parental power and special educational needs: The case of specific learning difficulties. *British Educational Research Journal* 20(3): 327–345.

Riddell, S., K. Ward, and G. O. B. Thomson. 1993. The significance of employment as a goal for young people with recorded special educational needs. *British Journal of Education and Work* 7(2): 57–73.

Tomlinson, S. 1981. *Educational sub-normality: A study in decision-making.* London: Routledge and Kegan Paul.

——. 1982. *The sociology of special education.* London: Routledge and Kegan Paul.

——. 1988. Why Johnny can't read: Critical theory and special education. *European Journal of Special Needs Education* 3(1): 45–58.

Turner, E., S. Riddell, and S. Brown. 1995. *The impact of recent educational reforms on gender equality in Scottish schools: A report prepared for the Equal Opportunities Commission.* Manchester: Equal Opportunities Commission.

Willis, P. 1977. *Learning to labour: How working-class kids get working-class jobs.* London: Saxon.

Sheila Riddell

EDUCATION: Sub-Saharan Africa

Conceptual and Methodological Issues

The concept of education is broad and defies definition. Practitioners in education, however, agree that it has formal, nonformal, and informal aspects and that its distinguishing characteristics differ from those of conditioning and indoctrination. At the beginning of the twenty-first century, education is regarded as a powerful lever for development. And the interplay between mother's education, child survival, and resource management is widely recognized. Even more crucial is the realization that there is a positive correlation between mother's education, school enrollment, attendance, and achievement of children (Washi et al., 1993). Consequently, the development implications of women's education have led to intensified action to promote the quantitative and qualitative aspects of formal education for all, especially girls, and of nonformal education for millions outside the formal system. In sub-Saharan Africa, nonformal education initiatives are being developed, such as cultural variations of the Bangladesh Rural Advancement Committee program.

The responsiveness of education systems to the special needs of women and girls is a human rights and a social justice issue. Historically, women's right to education as enshrined in international legal and national constitutional documents has been given second place to that of men. Education for women in sub-Saharan Africa is therefore characterized by lower levels of literacy, lower enrollment and retention, and higher levels of wastage in relation to men. *Enrollment* refers to girls' entry in school; *retention* refers to their worthwhile stay in school and progress to the final grade; and *wastage* refers to girls' dropping out of school before they complete a cycle.

When assessing the advancement of women, the concept of empowerment is used to show the extent to which women can rise above merely accessing available opportunities to break away from the cycle of submission and discrimination and to take control of issues that affect their destiny.

The Historical Background

Indigenous education in sub-Saharan Africa was a process by which all the resources of the extended family and the community contributed to the education of children. Gender roles and relationships were and still are ascribed in secret societies separate for girls and for boys. Exceptions included compound arrangements in Yorubaland, in Nigeria, where men's specialized skills were passed on within the patrilineage. Apprenticeships remain common in sub-Saharan Africa, as do Qur'anic schools mainly for boys.

In the colonial era, the assimilative and integrationist policies of the French colonial system and British institutional arrangements and Victorian values were superimposed on indigenous and Qur'anic education, in their respective spheres of influence. Education for the sons of chiefs was initially the favored policy.

Missions first brought education to coastal peoples and those along road and rail routes. Sudan was an exception in this regard. These circumstances laid the beginnings of gender and ethnic imbalances in formal, western-type education. Furthermore, precolonial and colonial values on the role of women in society and their education continue to shape attitudes on the education of women.

In the postcolonial period various interventions put in place as a result of the world economic recession had a negative impact on education generally but especially on the education of girls and women. Structural adjustment removed government subsidies to basic services, including education. Though sub-Saharan Africa is characterized by great diversity in terms of wealth, at the end of the twentieth century debt profiles were high, poverty had in general intensified, and most countries were in the low-income category. Hidden costs of education have correspondingly soared, and there is widespread use of child labor, especially girls, in the domestic and economic activities of parents. Where resources are scarce and a choice has to be made, boys are sent to school and girls are not. Rather, girls are valued for their fertility, and early marriage is the norm. When girls enroll in school, sociocultural and school factors militate against their full participation, especially in science- and technology-related programs.

Gender Differentials in Education

In most countries of the developing world, the literacy gap between women and men is an overall indicator of the degree of inequality between them. On this indicator, sub-Saharan Africa has the lowest rate of female literacy in the world. As the table shows, the adult literacy rate in sub-Saharan Africa in 1990 for the 15+ age group was 36 percent for women and 59 percent for men. For all developing countries, the rate in 1990 was 55 percent for women aged 15+. The world literacy rate for the same age group of women was 66 percent (according to these estimates). The overall figures conceal high levels of female illiteracy within countries—for instance, Niger, 83.2; Guinea, 86.6; Sierra Leone, 88.7; and Burkina Faso, 98.0. The development implications are obviously immense.

Adult Literacy Rate by Gender and Region 1990
(percentage age 15+)

	Female	Male
Sub-Saharan Africa	36	59
Arab states	38	64
Latin America and Caribbean	83	86
Eastern Asia	66	86
Southern Asia	32	59
All developing countries	55	75
Least developing countries	28	51
World	66	81

Source: UNESCO, *Compendium of Statistics on Illiteracy,* 1990.

Enrollment at first level for ages 6–11 is considerably lower than in any region except the Arab states. A few countries, such as Tanzania and Rwanda, have been relatively successful in extending access to girls, but countries in the Sahel have the lowest female enrollment at this level and the largest gaps between girls and boys. In the region, girls more often than boys drop out before they complete a school cycle, and they consequently have lower rates of transition to secondary and tertiary education. Among the reasons for wastage are the inability of households to pay fees, child labor, and pregnancies.

Except in universities for women, female enrollment at teachers colleges and universities is lower than male enrollment. Gender gaps in higher education are striking in Benin, Senegal, and Togo. Variables that constitute the grounds for unequal representation at university level are age, social class, size of community, and gender. Within some countries, such as Uganda, university enrollment is also characterized by ethnic imbalances. Where women gain access to universities, they predominate either in non-degree programs or in the humanities. Their underrepresentation in the natural sciences and engineering indicates that very few sub-Saharan women are breaking barriers into what are traditionally regarded as "male" occupations. Moreover, role models in teacher education are grossly inadequate.

This lack of training for work in national power structures means that women in sub-Saharan Africa are not equipped to participate in policy making and are mainly concentrated in less lucrative and more labor-intensive and low-status jobs. One consequence is poorer quality of life for them and their children.

Structures, Strategies, and Networks

Views on policy frameworks and strategies vary. Equal opportunities policies are regarded as inadequate to deal with underrepresentation and undervaluing of girls and women in education, because all social sectors interact. This view holds that equal opportunities policies do not challenge the power structures that perpetuate and maintain the status quo.

It follows from this argument that structures and practices of all social institutions, including schools, need radical change, change that entails going beyond reallocation of resources and tinkering with curricula processes to the removal of pervasive injustices embedded in all structures, practices, and attitudes.

Other moderate and specific strategies are documented in the African Platform for Action of the Fifth African

Regional Conference on Women held in Dakar, Senegal, in November 1994. These include calls for removing the direct and indirect costs of schooling; providing scholarships for girls, subsidies for uniforms and school meals, and free transport to schools; sensitizing teachers to gender issues in terms of teacher-pupil interaction; and providing separate schools for girls, especially for science. There is a general call for gender-positive textbooks and for revising curricula in gender-sensitive directions.

Change processes need to be timely. Problems less amenable to technical solutions have to do with teenage pregnancy, sociocultural attitudes, and poor perception of the value of education.

In the last decade of the twentieth century, relatively frequent high-level consultations and conferences for strategic planning were held: the World Conference on Education for All (EFA) by the year 2000, held in Jomtien, Thailand, 1990; the Bamaka meeting for Francophone countries in Mali, 1992; the Franco-African summit in Libreville, Gabon, 1992; and the 46th conference of Ministers of Education of Francophone African countries in Yaoundé, Cameroon, 1994. The Pan-African Conference on Girls' Education at Ouagadougou, Burkina Faso, 1993, brought Anglophone and Francophone African countries together. Major outcomes were frameworks on EFA, the Bamako initiative, and the Ouagadougou declaration.

International and regional women's networks have played strategic, catalytic roles at high-level conferences. The African Women's Development and Communication Network (FEMNET), based in Nairobi, Kenya, coordinated nongovernmental-organization (NGO) activities for the NGO Forum and the Fifth African Regional Conference on Women. It has continued to network with NGO focal points regionally. The Forum for African Women Educationalists (FAWE) has its headquarters in Nairobi, Kenya. The strength of FAWE's networking lies in its strong links of communication with its national chapters and in the policy level of its regional membership. Its members are mostly female ministers of education or vice-chancellors of universities.

FAWE's strongest networking links have been with the Donors to African Education (DAE) working groups on female participation in schooling. Its networking activities include participation at a DAE-sponsored meeting of the 44th session of the International Conference on Education for African Ministers of Education, held in Geneva, Switzerland, in October 1994. Strategically important policy and planning issues were discussed. It organized Training of Trainers seminars on girls' education for Francophone and Anglophone countries in January and May 1994 in Dakar and Nairobi, respectively. FAWE also collaborated with the government of Mauritius in organizing a ministerial consultation on school dropout and adolescent pregnancy in September 1994.

Gender and Science and Technology, an international association of female science educators, is a network for science and technology. The African region is represented on the executive board by Dr. Stella Williams of Obafemi Awolowo University, Ile-Ife, Nigeria. The proposed phase 3 of its Project 2000 is a Scientific, Technological, and Environmental Literacy and Women in the Community Project.

Other regional-level networks are the Association of African Women for Research on Development, based in Dakar, Senegal; the Education Research Network for Eastern and Southern Africa (ERNESA), with coordinating points in Nairobi and Gaborone, Botswana; and the African Academy of Sciences in Nairobi, Kenya. National networks include associations of university women and university-based women's gender research and documentation centers in Kenya, Ghana, Sierra Leone, Nigeria, and Uganda.

Several women educators in sub-Saharan Africa have played outstanding roles in education and in their countries' development. One who deserves special mention in the history of women's education is the late Agathe Uwilingiyimana (1952–1993), teacher of science, former minister of education in Rwanda, and prime minister at the time of her death. Only a full-scale survey, however, could adequately pay tribute to the women educators of sub-Saharan Africa in their struggle for justice in education.

See Also

COLONIALISM AND POSTCOLONIALISM; DEVELOPMENT: SOUTHERN AND SUB-SAHARAN AFRICA; EQUAL OPPORTUNITIES: EDUCATION; LITERACY; WOMEN'S STUDIES: SUB-SAHARAN AFRICA

References and Further Reading

Assié-Lumumba, N'Dri Thérèse. 1995. *Demand, access, and equity issues in African higher education.* Accra-North, Ghana: Association of African Universities.

Colclough, Christopher, and Keith M. Lewin. 1993. *Strategies for primary schooling in the South.* Oxford: Clarendon.

Donors to African Education. 1994. *Newsletter* 6(3, 4: Oct.–Dec.).

Economic Commission for Africa. 1994. *Summary of national reports.* Fifth African Regional Conference on Women, Dakar, Senegal, 16–23 Nov.

Forum for African Women Educationalists. 1994. *Newsletter* 2(1: May).

Hyde, Karin A. L. 1991. Sub-Saharan Africa. In Elizabeth M. King and M. Anne Hill, eds., *Women's education in developing countries: Barriers, benefits, and policy,* 79–109. Washington, D.C.: World Bank.

UNESCO. 1990. *Compendium of statistics on illiteracy.* Paris: United Nations Educational, Scientific, and Cultural Organization.

———. 1993. *Statistical yearbook.* Paris: United Nations Educational, Scientific, and Cultural Organization.

———. 1994. *Education of girls and women: Beyond access.* Contribution of UNESCO to the Fifth African Regional Conference on Women, Dakar, Senegal, 16–23 Nov.

———. 1994. *Statistical yearbook.* Paris: United Nations Educational, Scientific, and Cultural Organization.

UNICEF and ERNESA. 1992. *The girl child: Opportunities and disparities in education.* Workshop report, 6–8 July, Gaborone, Botswana, and Nairobi, Kenya.

Washi, Siddiga, et al. 1993. The impact of mothers' education on indicators of school performance of first through third grade primary school children living in low socioeconomic areas in Khartoum, Sudan. *Women and Change* 10(1): 44.

Juliette Ann Dworzak

EDUCATION: Technology

Technology is widely associated with maleness. Despite differences in educational systems, economic development, prosperity, employment patterns, and political systems, educational patterns are similar, with girls and women constituting a small percentage of technology students and practicing professionals.

It is sometimes difficult to define clearly what is meant by the term *technology* and which subjects will be included within the scope of technology education. However, the pattern of low female participation rates is similar across the fields of engineering, computing, architecture, and applied science education at post-school level, although the detailed figures vary widely between subjects and countries. School-level subjects that could be included under the heading "technology" are fairly limited and often only recent in their development and introduction, but because many post-school technology courses have science subjects and mathematics as prerequisites, these subjects are often included in any discussion of this area. Varied educational structures also often make international comparisons difficult. In 1992 in Victoria, Australia, 28 percent of physics and 38 percent of mathematics students at age 18 were female; in the United Kingdom in 1991 only 10 percent of girls studied any science subject at age 18, although this was a significant increase from 4 percent in 1974.

At university first-degree level the quoted figures are more commonly for the narrower field of engineering, with the percentage of women in these courses varying between 10 and 20 percent. Averages of 10–14 percent across engineering subjects are found in such diverse countries as Hungary, Mexico, Australia, New Zealand, the United Kingdom, and the Czech and Slovak Republics. Higher averages of 15–20 percent are found in Finland, Canada, the United States, Poland, Sri Lanka, Greece, France, Denmark, Norway, and Sweden (Carter, 1994; Committee on Women in SET, 1994; ICWES9, 1992). However, these averages mask wide variations across engineering specialties. For example, in Greece in 1993 the figures were: mechanical, 6 percent; electrical, 8 percent; civil, 15 percent; and chemical, 22 percent. In the Netherlands in 1991 only 2 percent of electrical and mechanical engineering students were female, whereas 25 percent of chemical engineering students were female. In South Africa between 1989 and 1991 polytechnic entries showed that females were 2 percent of the total in mechanical engineering, 13 percent in civil engineering, and 22 percent in design and technology. It is worth noting that the figures tend to be significantly lower for technician-level education in most subjects. These rough averages also give no indication of variations between racial, religious, cultural, or socioeconomic groups within countries, and such statistical breakdowns are rarely readily available.

Reasons for Lack of Participation

There is no simple way of explaining why these figures for women's participation in technology education are so low, and a wide variety of perspectives and theories have been presented.

Traditional arguments tended to center on the nature of technology as dirty and heavy work or on women being genetically unsuited to science and technology. Such views were then enforced and reinforced by bars against women in certain jobs, in trade unions and engineering institutions, and in science and computing clubs in schools. Equal opportunities legislation has combated such direct discrimination, but outdated cultures persist. Girls do perform well in math and science until puberty, after which the gender separation becomes notable, although those girls continuing with these subjects achieve results that are as good as boys' (Committee on Women in SET, 1994). The importance of the attitudes, behavior, and expectations of teachers is often noted, but the low numbers of primary school teachers with a science or technology background, the lack of female science and technology teachers providing positive role models, and the lack of positive training to combat gender stereotyping, although all identified as problems, have not been shown to be strong determinants of pupil choice. Unequal access to good science equipment and the packaging of the teaching with examples and illustrations taken from traditionally masculine spheres can also be identified as problems. In countries with a combination of mixed- and single-sex schools there is evidence of higher participation rates of girls in science and technology in the single-sex schools. Low participation rates have been linked to the importance of gender identity, especially in adolescents. Science and technology are also often perceived as more difficult subjects. Entry requirements for higher education lead to the perpetuation of the gender separation seen at school level.

In some countries engineering has a relatively low status, but there is little evidence of a correlation between the participation rates of women and the status of the subject. Nonfeminist approaches to tackling the low participation rates of women and girls assume that women are the problem and so attempt to develop in women traits of rationality and logic, which they are perceived to lack, but newer feminist approaches argue that the theory and practice of science and technology are the problems and need to be changed to incorporate the special characteristics of women.

Although these figures for participation rates of women in technology education are low, they rose considerably in the last decades of the twentieth century, going from less than 3 percent in New Zealand in the 1980s to 13 percent in 1993 and from 4 percent in France in 1964 to 19 percent in 1991. These increases reflect greater recognition of a problem and a concern that much potential talent is being lost at a time when technological skills are at a premium for national prosperity. Feminists have been concerned that these figures show structural discrimination limiting the career choices of women and denying them access to well-paid jobs; the most conservative have been simply concerned about perceived skills shortages in high-technology areas. Some feminists, however, question these efforts to promote technology to women and ask why, with direct and indirect discrimination and glass ceilings preventing career progression, women should be encouraged to enter this field.

Initiatives to Address the Problem

Initiatives being taken to address this issue include better recruitment, attention to the problem of women's lack of technology skills and knowledge, and examinations of the content, structure, and ethos of technology courses. Talks by women technologists to school and college students aim to provide role models and to open minds to job possibilities. The emphasis on role models has been criticized, however, for the pressure it puts on the limited number of women in the field, and mentoring schemes that place more responsibility on male colleagues are being promoted (Byrne, 1993). Women-only access and foundation courses aim to create a supportive environment where women will not be afraid to make mistakes, and conversion courses aim to interest women with proven skills but with qualifications in other subject areas. Short preparatory taster courses, which may be women only or mixed, sometimes aim to improve confidence (often a crucial factor), rather than raise levels of expertise, and to familiarize students with equipment and provide the opportunity to overcome false perceptions and stereotypes. Women-only courses and high proportions of women staff in such courses can be significant factors in attracting women, although women in traditional courses have preferred not to be singled out, for the sake of their own sense of identity and also to avoid peer antagonism (Willoughby and Carter, 1993).

Course providers have become more sensitive to their publicity material: whether it portrays a women-inclusive profile and where it is distributed. Traditional technical course titles are thought to deter women, who tend to gravitate toward more socially oriented courses, so many technology courses are now being combined with management, languages, economics, and so forth. Such shifts in direction are also motivated by changes in the skills needed by professional technologists. Course presentation is specifically addressed in some women-oriented courses, with more emphasis on collaborative projects and the use of gender-inclusive language and examples.

Although many institutions have supported such initiatives, primarily motivated by the need to increase student numbers in this area or to retain political credibility, women working from a feminist perspective highlight the inadequacy of such approaches unless they are supported by institutional change, including culture change, support networks, and a consideration of practical arrangements, such as timing of attendance, access to facilities, safe environments, and child care provision. They point out that increasing enrollments achieve little if the students are then alienated by the ensuing experience due to a culture that gives women no legitimacy or credibility.

Feminist Networks of Technology Educators

The number of conference delegates from every continent and virtually every country reporting studies and initiatives in this field indicates how widespread the problem of low participation is. Despite relative lack of funding for research, there is a thriving international community active in all aspects of this area with many national and international networks, such as the following:

Association Française des Femme-Ingenieurs Maison de l'Europe, Paris, France
Canadian Committee on Women in Engineering
GASAT (Gender and Science and Technology)
Jan Harding, Alesford, U.K.
Northern Telecon-NSERC Women in Engineering Chair, Faculty of Engineering, University of New Brunswick
SEFI (European Society for Engineering Education), Women in Engineering Working Group
Sheffield Hallam University, U.K.
Sirkka Poyry, Helsinki, Finland
SWE (Society of Women Engineers), New York, U.S.A.
WITEC (Women in Technology—Network for Women in Technology in Europe)
Women's Engineering Society, Imperial College, Department of Civil Engineering, London

See Also

CURRICULUM TRANSFORMATION MOVEMENT; EDUCATION: GENDERED SUBJECT CHOICE; TECHNOLOGY; WORK: OCCUPATIONAL SEGREGATION

References and Further Reading

Byrne, E. 1993. *Women and science: The Snark syndrome.* London: Falmer.
Carter, R. 1994. Engineering education and professional practice: Developing gender-inclusive models. Conference report, Yorkshire region, Open University, Milton Keynes, U.K.
Carter, R., and G. Kirkup. 1990. *Women in engineering: A good place to be?* London: Macmillan Education.
Committee on Women in SET. 1994. *The rising tide: A report on women in science, engineering, and technology.* London: HMSO.
ICWES9. 1992. *Demographics.* ICWES9 (Ninth International Conference of Women Engineers and Scientists), Warwick, U.K.
Rothschild, J. 1988. *Teaching technology from a feminist perspective.* Oxford: Pergamon.
Whyte, J. 1996. *Girls into science and technology.* London: Routledge and Kegan Paul.
Willoughby, L., and R. Carter. 1993. Electronics education for women: Evolving new approaches. In S. Haggerty and A. Holmes, eds., *Transforming science and technology: Our future depends on it.* GASAT7 (Gender and Science and Technology), University of Waterloo, Ontario, Canada.

Lynette Willoughby

EDUCATION: Testing

See EXAMINATIONS AND ASSESSMENT.

EDUCATION: Vocational

Vocational education prepares and trains individuals for employment in the labor market. It can be an integral part of a general education and is often an aspect of continuing education. Many people receive vocational training while employed or by attending a specialized school or program. In Nordic countries, adults receive vocational education at facilities known as "folk high schools." Vocational programs are often offered at formal schools sanctioned by the state to teach young women a specific vocational skill as part of their primary schooling, at special colleges or universities, or in industrial or commercial settings. Funding for vocational programs varies according to country, politics, economics, and available technology. Most vocational programs receive funding from the state or from private corporations or other nongovernmental agencies. Male dominance characterizes vocational education, but women are beginning to have a presence.

International Comparisons

Globally, access to vocational training varies for women and men. Females rarely study the same vocational subjects as their male peers. Men typically receive training in technical fields, specific trades, or agriculture, whereas women learn health, home economics, and office skills. Educational experiences of women vary by politics, culture, economics, and dominant social values. Research indicates that women's access to education relates directly to their access to employment outside the home. For example, in China, female employees' level of vocational training has increased, but women are unable to reach the technical competence of their male co-workers (Kun, 1996). Vocational training for women in east Asia is limited to low-paying skills such as garment making, embroidery, food and nutrition, and clerical work (Tilak, 1993). Kuwait and Saudi Arabia restrict vocational training for women to sewing, tailoring, nursing, textiles, and factory work (El-Sanabary, 1993). Japanese women begin vocational training for positions in commerce and home economics at special high schools (Matsui, 1996). In Tunisia, women's vocational training encompasses textiles, administrative positions, and crafts (Jones, 1982). In some countries, women are excluded from vocational programs altogether. Women's lack of training perpetuates their subordinate position throughout the world. A country's concern for women's vocational education directly relates to that country's level of development and the societal position of women.

Barriers to Training

Women experience a variety of barriers to vocational training. Because more than half of women worldwide are illiterate, vocational education can be difficult. Guidance into "female" occupations at the primary or secondary school level maintains women's inferior position in the sex-segregated labor market. Sex segregation, which is the distribution of sexes into specific occupations, also exists within academic realms but is more pronounced in vocational and technical programs. Women in female-dominated occupations receive minimal pay compared with men in these occupations. Gender stereotypes perpetuate women's dominance in low-paying jobs that do not require vocational training and in turn decrease their occupational mobility. Women are viewed as less stable employees because of the potential for childbirth and childbearing absences. Gender stereotypes reinforce women's traditional roles as housekeepers and caregivers. Because many women are required to exit the labor market once they become pregnant, many employers refuse to train them, because they are not perceived as permanent workers. Many training centers do not provide day care services or assistance with household duties. Further, women often feel alienated in these programs because of the lack of

relevant information, inadequate teaching methods, and language barriers. This alienation can result in their exiting these programs before completion. Women in lower socioeconomic positions often lack the financial resources needed to access vocational training programs. Rural women find it difficult to access vocational education programs located in large urban areas. In developing countries, women struggle to meet their basic needs and the needs of their children, so that vocational education tends to be a low priority.

The varieties of vocational education available to women are generally related to those occupations women monopolize and the economy of the country in question. In most societies, men participate in apprenticeships, and women are denied such training. Vocational education for many women begins in secondary school in the fields of cosmetology, nursing, and teaching. Women are typically guided into vocational schools that teach secretarial skills such as typing, filing, and dictation. Many women in factories receive training on specialized machines that evolve with advances in technology. In some developing countries, such as Kenya and those in Latin America, the vocational curriculum involves an emphasis on business and entrepreneurship to compete in a global economy (Jiggins, 1994). For women living in rural areas in developing countries, family planning is an important component of vocational training.

Throughout the world, women gain access to educational opportunities through legislated policies that promote equal access for women and men. Addressing the issue of equal access has been central to many worldwide organizations concerned with human rights and, more specifically, women's rights. For example, Ireland developed the Employment Equity Agency, which focuses on meeting the needs of women in adult educational endeavors (Roy et al., 1996). Several international organizations, including the United Nations, the International Council for Adult Education, the International Labor Organization, and the World Bank, are concerned with increasing women's access to vocational training.

The Feminization of Labor

The growing pattern of a "globalized feminization of labor"—the increase in female labor force participation and declining male involvement—has instigated change. This trend has been initiated by international competition, the growth of export manufacturing, labor deregulation, decreases in wages, and structural movements that weaken the bargaining power of workers. Studies have consistently shown that women's education plays a major role in changing the fertility patterns throughout the world. The more educated a woman becomes, the fewer children she is likely to give birth to. Better-educated women produce smaller families and, in general, healthier, better-educated children. Increasing the emphasis on educating women will bring about widespread societal changes that will affect not only their lives but the entire global community.

Access to vocational education is still a rarity for women in many parts of the world, but movements for change continue to gain momentum. Cultural values, politics, and economics complicate the matter. Access to the Internet provides some women with opportunities to receive training in nursing, journalism, automotive technology, and film, which improves their options in the labor market. Giving women access to vocational training is pivotal to achieving higher rates of employment, greater productivity, and higher financial returns for their families. Women throughout the world are discovering employment opportunities outside the home that increase their participation in and access to specialized training, which may in turn impact the inequality that women continue to experience on a daily basis.

See Also

EDUCATION: ADULT AND CONTINUING; EDUCATION: DISTANCE EDUCATION; EDUCATION: GENDER EQUITY; EDUCATION: GENDERED SUBJECT CHOICE; EDUCATION: HIGHER EDUCATION; WORK: EQUAL PAY AND CONDITIONS; WORK: OCCUPATIONAL SEGREGATION

References and Further Reading

El-Sanabary, Nagat. 1993. Middle East and North Africa. In Elizabeth M. King and M. Anne Hill, eds., *Women's education in developing countries: Barriers, benefits, and policies.* Baltimore, Md.: Johns Hopkins University Press.

Jiggins, Janice. 1994. *Changing the boundaries: Women-centered perspectives on population and the environment.* Washington, D.C.: Island.

Jones, Marie Thourson. 1982. Educating girls in Tunisia: Issues generated by the drive for universal enrollment. In Gail P. Kelly and Carolyn M. Elliott, eds., *Women's education in the third world: Comparative perspectives.* Albany: State University of New York Press.

Kun, Gao. 1996. The socioeconomic status of today's Chinese women. In Kartik Roy, Clement Tisdell, and Hans Blomqvist, eds., *Economic development and women in the world community.* Westport, Conn.: Praeger.

Matsui, Machiko. 1996. Japan. In Grace C. L. Mak, ed., *Women, education, and development in Asia: Cross-national perspectives.* New York: Garland.

Roy, Kartik, Clement Tisdell, and Hans Blomqvist. 1996. Economic development and women: An overview of issues. In Kartik Roy, Clement Tisdell, and Hans Blomqvist, eds., *Economic development and women in the world community.* Westport, Conn.: Praeger.

Tilak, Jandhyala B. 1993. East Asia. In Elizabeth M. King and M. Anne Hill, eds., *Women's education in developing countries: Barriers, benefits, and policies.* Baltimore, Md.: Johns Hopkins University Press.

Jennifer L. Gossett

EDUCATION: Western Europe

Forces for Change Since the 1960s

Within western Europe there has been a general and significant growth in enrollment by girls and women at all levels of education. The proportion of girls staying on in academic secondary education beyond compulsory school age now exceeds the proportion of boys. The ratio of male to female undergraduate university students is equal in most countries.

These positive developments have transformed the social and economic life chances of western European girls and young women, brought about by the coalescence of forces for change from within and without the education systems of Europe.

Political Forces

In a climate of liberal democratic concern for women's rights from the late 1960s onward, major international organizations, such as the United Nations and European Community, have issued a series of resolutions on equality of access to educational institutions, programs, and services. These have given a high profile to the principle of equality of educational opportunity (Sutherland, 1999).

National governments have responded to such initiatives with varying degrees of commitment, from the strong and directive policy stance of the Scandinavian countries to the more laissez-faire policies of such countries as the United Kingdom and Germany (Elgqvist-Saltzman, 1992). In the majority of countries, coeducation was introduced in the state sector of education as a panacea for old disparities (Wilson, 1991).

Pressure within the System

Pressure for change within the school system largely emanated from numerous small groups of committed women teachers and pressure groups, especially from the 1970s onward. Networks were formed within countries, and support was sought from local government authorities, particularly in metropolitan areas (Weiner and Arnot, 1987). Later, official sponsorship of such networks on a nationwide or international level, through, for example, the Insituto de la Mujer in Spain or the Women in Europe office in Brussels, was increasingly common. Links at the grassroots level continue from such bases as the European Network of Women's Studies.

Economic Forces

The period from 1975 to 1985 saw a massive influx of women into the labor force of western Europe. In 1988, 45 percent of service-sector jobs in the European Community, particularly in the state sector and in administration, were held by women, albeit with wide national variations (Eurostat, 1992; Doorne-Huiskes, van Hoof, and Roelofs, 1995). Women did not enter the labor market on equal terms with men, but many of these new opportunities required white-collar and often graduate qualifications.

In terms of enrollment patterns, differences at compulsory school level are due to differences in the birthrate of boys and girls. In countries where "underachieving" pupils are required to repeat the school year, substantially more boys do so than girls. Research from several western European countries suggests that the performance of girls in academic subjects at compulsory school age is superior on average to that of boys. More girls than boys are found to be in general upper secondary education (Eurostat, 1997a). More boys than girls also leave school without any formal qualifications, and this has sometimes been interpreted as constituting a new educational problem (Mackinnon, Elqvist-Saltzman, and Prentice, 1998).

In the majority of western European countries, girls outnumber boys in the upper levels of academic secondary education, and the great majority of these school students continue into higher education. Those who enter employment at this stage find themselves in a less favorable situation than those who opt for vocational education at a subdegree level. This sector, whether delivered under the umbrella of the school or in a separate institution, continues to be dominated by male students. In 1993–1994, 55 percent of participants in initial vocational education in the European Union (EU) were male and 45 percent female, with most member states close to this average (Eurostat, 1992).

Participation in Higher Education

Access to higher education has widened considerably since 1970, although only around 23 percent of the age group pursues it (Eurostat, 1997b). In some countries, such as the United Kingdom, a first wave of expansion largely benefit-

ing male students in the 1960s and 1970s was followed by a later expansion of new and often part-time study opportunities in the 1980s, to the advantage of female students. In others, such as Greece and Spain, accelerated reforms of education occurred relatively late and benefited male and female students at the same time. In 1984, 44.2 percent of students in higher education in the EU were female, ranging from 35.7 percent in the Netherlands to 50.2 percent in Portugal (Eurostat, 1992). In 1993–1994, the number of female undergraduate students in tertiary education in the EU was virtually equal to the number of male students, with 103 females to every 100 males. However, when higher education is organized in different institutions according to a prestige or function, more male students are found in higher status establishments, such as the French *grandes écoles,* or in technical institutes and universities. There are also significant variations among countries. In 1994–1995, for example, there were 77 females per 100 tertiary education students in Germany. More female students also tend to take short diploma courses in higher education. The ratio of male to female postgraduate students remains unequal (Eurostat, 1995).

Comparisons between national trends are problematic, particularly at the level of higher education, because of variations in subject classification. Nevertheless, broad generalizations can be made. In upper secondary education, the great majority of students of modern languages, literature, biology, and the humanities are female. Physics and chemistry remain largely male preserves. Other subjects, like mathematics, tend to attract equal numbers of both sexes.

In vocational education, the areas of study most favored by female students show a remarkable similarity across countries and can be summarized as textiles, domestic and food sciences, hairdressing, clerical and administrative work, catering, social welfare, and paramedical or nursing courses. Many courses at this level are virtually single sex (Wilson, 1991).

In higher education, the most striking absence of female students occurs in the field of engineering, where female enrollment was about 17 percent of students in 1994–1995, albeit with wide national variations (Eurostat, 1997a). The humanities and educational studies tend to be female dominated, the latter increasingly so. Law and business studies tend to be relatively gender neutral, although differences exist between subbranches, such as family case law and personnel management. Certain subjects do exhibit wide national variations at this level as a result of cultural differences in the status of such courses. Mathematics and medicine are particular examples of such national divergences.

Shifts in these patterns began in the 1980s, particularly in the number of women in the sciences. However, as women students have made inroads into some areas, there is evidence to suggest that the "feminization" of such subjects erodes their market value and social cachet (OECD, 1985).

The underrepresentation of males in other subject areas is an issue that has attracted far less concern or state funds. Programs such as the United Kingdom's Women into Science and Engineering and Girls into Science and Technology have not been matched by campaigns called Boys into Modern Languages or Boys into the Education and Caring Professions. The Scandinavian and Dutch governments have provided exceptions to this tendency, but with a mixed response from schools (Mackinnon, Elqvist-Saltzman, and Prentice, 1998; Dekkers and Wilson, 1999).

Women in Teaching

Teaching is a predominantly female profession in western Europe at the primary and secondary levels, although this trend has not been accompanied by the same rate of recruitment to management positions. Increasingly, women are university lecturers, but divisions according to subject specialty, level of teaching, and managerial status persist throughout this sector as well (Wilson, 1997).

Qualitative Research

A growing body of research into such issues as teachers' attitudes, classroom materials, and pupil interaction sheds light on the experience of girls in education. This broadens research away from the liberal equal opportunities perspective, with its emphasis on competitive achievement, to encompass a wider range of pupils, as well as presenting a fuller picture of the formation of male and female, minority and majority, identities in the education systems of western Europe.

See Also

EDUCATION: ACHIEVEMENT; EDUCATION: EASTERN EUROPE; EDUCATION: MATHEMATICS; EDUCATION: SCIENCE; EDUCATION: TECHNOLOGY; EDUCATORS: PRESCHOOL; WORK: EQUAL PAY AND CONDITIONS; WORK: PATTERNS

References and Further Reading

Buckley, M., and W. Anderson. 1988. *Women, equality, and Europe.* Basingstoke: Macmillan.

Dekkers, H., and M. Wilson. 1999. Equal opportunities initiatives: England and the Netherlands compared. In S. Erskine and M. Wilson, eds., *Gender in international education: Beyond policy.* New York: Falmer.

Doorne-Huiskes, J. van, J. van Hoof, and E. Roelofs, eds. 1995. *Women and the European labour markets.* London: Paul Chapman.

Elgqvist-Saltzman, I. 1992. Straight roads and winding tracks: Swedish educational policy from a gender equality perspective. *Gender and Education* 4(1–2).

Eurostat. 1992. *Women in the European Community.* Brussels: Commission of the European Communities.

Eurostat. 1995. *Education across the European Union: Statistics and indicators.* Luxembourg: Information Office of the CEC.

Eurostat. 1997a. *Key data on education in the European Union.* Luxembourg: Office for Official Publications of the European Community.

Eurostat. 1997b. *Eurostat yearbook.* Luxembourg: Office for Official Publications of the European Community.

Mackinnon, A., I. Elqvist-Saltzman, and A. Prentice. 1998. *Education into the 21st century: Dangerous terrain for women?* London: Falmer.

OECD. 1985. *The integration of women into the economy.* Paris: OECD.

Sutherland, M. 1999. Evaluating national policies on gender issues. In S. Erskine and M. Wilson, eds., *Gender in international education: Beyond policy.* New York: Falmer.

Weiner, G., and M. Arnot. 1987. Teachers and gender politics. In M. Arnot and G. Weiner, eds., *Gender and the politics of schooling.* London: Hutchinson/Open University.

Wilson, M., ed. 1991. *Girls and young women in education: A European perspective.* Oxford: Pergamon.

———. 1997. *Women in educational management: A European perspective.* London: Paul Chapman.

Maggie Wilson

EDUCATORS: Higher Education

Since the 1970s there has been much progress for women in higher education. However, there are many issues that still affect women's education, success, and advancement.

Struggles for Equity, Access, and Social Justice

Equal employment opportunity (EEO) and affirmative action (AA) legislation in a range of countries, including the United States, Canada, Australia, and New Zealand, have encouraged women to identify and address sources of continuing systemic discrimination in their institutions and working conditions. This has resulted in more transparent criteria and procedures for appointment and promotion in universities and in structural changes, such as ensuring that women are adequately represented on university committees. The legislation has also encouraged women to be more proactive in applying for positions at senior levels.

Although discrimination and sexual harassment have not been eliminated from universities, supportive legislation and appeal procedures, support groups, conflict resolution, and grievance mediation have all been "tools" used to attain substantial improvements in women's working conditions.

Debates around EEO and AA have led to an increasing awareness, among both male and female academics, of gendered practices within universities, which were generally thought to be gender-neutral places. There is also greater awareness of how gender bias operates in tandem with racism, classism, heterosexism, sexism, and ageism to deny equity and social justice to academic women and some men.

Valuing of Women's Knowledge

The establishment of women's studies programs has legitimated women's perspectives and women's knowledge and led to the revision of knowledge within disciplines and fields to acknowledge women's contributions. The life histories of women and their experiences in higher education (Soliman, 1998), which show their personal struggles, have empowered other women to persevere in working for change.

Increasing attention to the role of language in shaping attitudes and behavior has resulted in the development and adoption of nonsexist language policies and greater gender-sensitive and gender-inclusive policy documents and teaching materials.

There are an increasing number of publishers and scholarly journals for the publication of work on gender issues, feminism, and women's studies. Feminist scholarship and publications have critiqued masculinized forms of knowledge and power.

Communication and Networking

Communication on the Internet has enabled women to form information and support networks within their own states, countries, and around the world and across disciplines and professions. There are many interdisciplinary women's networks accessible on the Internet that also facilitate organization of women's groups to address and solve complex problems and lobby governments.

At the same time, women are increasingly organizing to come together in their own institutions and women-only professional organizations in order to gain a clearer understanding of how these can be restructured to function better in their interests. Membership in such organizations helps to reduce women's reported feelings of isolation and exclusion in male-dominated academic units. These organizations also facilitate discussion across disciplinary boundaries, which can often lead to collaborative teaching and research projects.

Economic Rationalism, Globalization, and Internationalization

The Internet also has negative implications for academic women, because the globalization and internationalization of higher education provide easier access to generic courses in higher education and require fewer providers. Decreasing the number of providers serves the agenda of governments committed to economic rationalism in education and thus to the reduction of public funding of universities. Privatization of higher education and the competition for markets is predicted to lead to a reduction of the academic workforce and the eventual loss of academic unions, which protect working conditions. The introduction of individual contracts could lead to a decline in cohesion among academics, thus increasing competition for higher-paying positions and increasing pressure for higher productivity and workloads in teaching and research (Soliman and Soliman, 1997). These changes will be felt most by those in temporary and casual positions, where women tend to be a majority, and by those without doctoral qualifications.

Mentoring

There is increasing awareness of the significance of formal and informal mentoring programs to support and induct women into the academic profession. Mentoring assists women to think and act strategically in relation to their career development. However, there are only a small number of women in senior posts who are well positioned to act as mentors. Thus there is a danger that mentoring will serve only to reproduce rather than to transform the structures and cultures that have been barriers to women's participation.

Family Responsibilities

Although there is an increasing willingness on the part of male partners to share parenting and other family responsibilities, there is still a lack of flexibility in working conditions to accommodate a better integration of academic and family demands. This is particularly acute for women in single-parent families. Without the provision of affordable, on-site child care facilities, women shoulder a greater share of family care and manage a combined workload, which can be stressful. Owing to family responsibilities, more women than men take a longer time to complete their advanced degree studies on a part-time basis. With time out for childbirth and parenting, many women's careers are discontinuous, in contrast to the more orderly progression of their male colleagues. Difficulty in maintaining continuous links with the profession may result in problems with sustaining a research program and a high output in publications. Interrupted employment also has negative implications for women's advancement to positions where they can influence policy development and decision making.

Increasing opportunities to obtain a fractional appointment on a continuing rather than a casual/temporary basis have been taken up by academic women. However, fractional positions are still regarded negatively and tend to result in contract-based research or part-time teaching rather than in a blend of the two core academic activities.

Setbacks and Systemic Discrimination

Achievements in women's studies and in the establishment of structures to monitor equity have not been without setbacks. This can be seen in Australia and elsewhere in the elimination of government funding for national agencies that monitor the implementation and maintenance of equal opportunity. Also, some universities have reduced financial support for or abolished women's studies centers.

There is still systemic discrimination in the form of lower average pay for women than men at most academic levels, a problem that must be addressed and monitored (Castleman et al., 1995; Probert et al., 1998).

The structure of women's participation in the academic profession is pyramid shaped, with women constituting between 25 and 35 percent of the academic workforce and with the majority still clustered at the entry level as lecturers or assistant professors. Women's numbers are fewer in traditionally male-dominated areas such as the sciences, economics, technology, and engineering. Relative to male colleagues, there are still few women in senior and executive positions. Women outnumber men in casual positions, and men outnumber women in tenure-track or continuing positions.

For these reasons, women do not constitute a critical mass in universities and thus cannot influence policies that affect their teaching and research interests. This reinforces the need for greater organization and communication among women.

Continuing Need for Gender Reform

The struggle to achieve gender reform and the structural and cultural transformation of universities requires ongoing commitment to analyze and challenge the place of power in sustaining gender inequalities. There is a need to critique the role that gendered social practices play in maintaining university cultures that disadvantage women and some men. By forming strategic alliances across disciplines and professions, academic women will be in a stronger position to shape university environments in ways that will allow them to forge new paths in higher education.

See Also

DISCRIMINATION; NETWORKING; NETWORKS, ELECTRONIC; PROFESSIONAL SOCIETIES; SCIENCE: TECHNOLOGICAL AND SCIENTIFIC RESEARCH; SEXUAL HARASSMENT; WOMEN'S STUDIES: OVERVIEW

References and Further Reading

Brooks, Ann. 1997. *Academic women.* Buckingham, U.K.: Society for Research into Higher Education, Open University Press.

Brown, G., and B. Irby, eds. 1988. *Women and leadership: Creating balance in life.* Commack, N.Y.: Nova Science.

Castleman, Tanya, Margaret Allen, Wendy Bastalich, and Patrick Wright. 1995. *Limited access: Women's disadvantage in higher education employment.* Melbourne: National Tertiary Education Union.

Morley, Louise. 1999. *Organising feminisms: The micropolitics of the academy.* New York: St. Martin's.

Probert, Belinda, Peter Ewer, and Kim Whiting. 1998. *Gender pay equity in Australian higher education.* Melbourne: National Tertiary Education Union.

Soliman, Izabel. 1998. *Many routes, one destination: Profiles of successful academic women.* Armidale, New South Wales, Australia: University of New England.

Soliman, Izabel, and Hani Soliman. 1997. Academic workload and quality. *Assessment and Evaluation in Higher Education* 22(2): 135–157.

Stalker, Jacqueline, and Susan Prentice, eds. 1998. *The illusion of inclusion: Women in post-secondary education.* Halifax: Fernwood.

Walton, Karen Doyle, ed. 1996. *Against the tide: Career paths of women leaders in American and British higher education.* Bloomington, Ind.: Phi Delta Kappa Educational Foundation.

Izabel Soliman

EDUCATORS: Preschool

Early childhood classrooms are workplaces that are "feminized": they are largely staffed and administered by women. The feminization of early childhood education involves a discussion of the women who work in early childhood education settings and an examination of their training, wages, and status. In this context *early childhood* is defined as the period from birth to 8 years of age.

Feminization is a term applied to an area of life in which women have (or are perceived to have) a growing or dominant influence. Thus "the feminization of early childhood education" refers to the fact that women make up the majority of workers in this field, including teachers, administrators, caregivers, and other helpers. Bailey (1996) extends this definition to describe *feminization* as an acknowledgment of women's positions within institutional situations and a movement toward nongendered debate in these sites. *Feminization* is also frequently used as a term of derision. For example, *feminization* is often coupled with *early childhood education* when referring to the perceived negative effects that being surrounded by women might have on young boys (Miller, 1992, 1996).

Implications of Feminization

The feminization of early childhood education has many implications for teachers and caregivers in this field. Some of these implications include women working with children being considered "natural," resulting in low social status, low wages, and poor working conditions; and a devaluing of the importance of training for early childhood education workers (Acker, 1989; Duncan, 1996; Miller, 1996).

The most significant of these implications is that working with young children is often considered a "natural" role for women. In becoming early childhood educators, women are simply assumed to be undertaking a natural extension of their mothering role. This assumption is problematic, however. For example, it has been argued that small children are not "worth" much and, therefore, that the teachers who work with them are not doing a "worthwhile" job (Duncan, 1996).

A study from New Zealand reports that early childhood educators have low social status compared with teachers of all other levels (Duncan, 1996). This study cites the wages of early childhood educators (in New Zealand) as about 73 percent of the wages of all other teachers. Under these conditions of low social status, early childhood educators may struggle to have their work considered teaching. This is especially so because the results of a high-quality early childhood education may not be as immediately visible as education in other sectors.

Working conditions in early childhood services are often poor, with long hours, low wages, isolation, and high staff turnover. Justification of the need for trained early childhood teachers and for better pay and working conditions is often neglected through the aforementioned "nature" argument. This is despite reports from Australia, New Zealand, and the United States that strongly indicate that quality in early childhood services is highly dependent on staff training and decent working conditions (Brennan, 1998; Duncan, 1996).

In Australia the historical basis of early childhood education and care has been one of caring for needy children. This care was lowly paid, if at all; and for caregivers, "coping against the odds" was a proud tradition (Brennan, 1998). Early childhood services are often provided in an isolated work environment. In Australia preschools are often separate from primary schools, and child care centers are often hidden among suburban streets. In the United Kingdom, nursery schools are also separate from primary schools. These workplaces are staffed according to the number of children enrolled, so staff numbers vary, as does the opportunity for professional discussion and development. As Franquet (1997) indicates, social isolation can be part of the work of early childhood teachers. This may also be a result of the fact that working with young children is undervalued and misunderstood.

Acker (1994) indicates directions for potential scholarship in gender and education that can be applied specifically to women and early childhood education. Areas identified include further examination of the characteristics of working with young children and the way in which reform affects teachers in the early childhood sector and further consideration of the gendered nature of work with young children. This potential scholarship needs to take into account the wide and varied experiences of women working with young children as well as their history, motivation, and ambition.

See Also

CHILD CARE; EDUCATION: PRESCHOOL; WORK: EQUAL PAY AND CONDITIONS

References and Further Reading

Acker, Sandra. 1994. *Gendered education: Sociological reflections on women, teaching, and feminism.* Buckingham, U.K.: Open University Press.

———, ed. 1989. *Teachers, gender, and careers.* London: Falmer.

Bailey, Lucy. 1996. The feminization of a school? Women teachers in a boys' school. *Gender and Education* 8(2): 171–184.

Brennan, Deborah. 1998. *The politics of Australian child care: Philanthropy to feminism and beyond*, 2nd ed. Cambridge: Cambridge University Press.

Duncan, Judith. 1996. "For the sake of the children" as the worth of the teacher? The gendered discourses of the New Zealand national kindergarten teachers' employment negotiations. *Gender and Education* 8(2): 159–170.

Franquet, M. 1997. R-E-S-P-E-C-T: Can I have some? Please! *Young Children* 52(5): 64.

Miller, Jane. 1992. *More has meant women: The feminization of schooling*. London: Tufnell.

———. 1996. *School for women*. London: Virago.

Young Children: The Journal of the National Association for the Education of Young Children. Washington, D.C.: National Association for the Education of Young Children.

Joanne Ailwood

ELDERLY CARE: Case Study—China

China, the world's most populous country, with 1.28 billion people, home to one-fourth of the global population, has some 126 million residents, or 10 percent of its total, over the age of 60.

According to figures released by China's State Statistical Bureau, women made up 51.8 percent of the country's aged population in 1999. The average life expectancy for Chinese females is 73, four years longer than for Chinese males.

The over-60 group in China is growing at an annual rate of 3.32 percent, and the over-80 group—which numbers nine million at present—is increasing by 5.4 percent per annum.

Greater longevity in China is attributed to better living standards and medical provisions. Growing numbers of old people, a social indicator of an industrialized country, are now causing China's leaders—the majority of whom are in their 60s and 70s themselves—to worry about the welfare of their own generation.

Despite estimates that China could have some 400 million people over 60 years of age by 2050, the country is unprepared because it does not yet possess a well-functioning social security network.

China launched its old-age pension and insurance system for retirees in 1951 within its "iron rice bowl" system, but coverage was limited to those employed by governmental institutions or state-run and collective enterprises.

At the time of this writing, 85 million workers in China were sheltered under the umbrella of the basic old-age pension social pools, accounting for 81 percent of the total. Until recently, eligibility for the pension system had two preconditions: residency in an urban area and employment in a state-owned or collective enterprise.

The practice of asking women working at government institutions and commercial enterprises in many parts of the country to retire at the age of 55, five years earlier than male employees, means that the "sunset life" years, and the challenge of adjusting to retirement, come earlier for women.

In some loss-making enterprises or over-staffed organizations, women who have worked for 30 years are encouraged to retire earlier than the official age of 55, just to ensure their receipt of a package of retirement benefits that might be difficult to deliver or even be withdrawn if redundancy strikes.

Before 1949, when the People's Republic of China was founded, 90 percent of Chinese women were illiterate. As of about the year 2000, 39.3 of China's professional and technical staff were women. In Beijing, the capital, the figure was higher—women occupied 53 percent of professional and technical jobs. Women were 46.7 percent of those working in various professions. But as far as retirement was concerned, women were still asked to bear the brunt before men.

The biggest problem area is the vast countryside, where 70.2 percent of China's aged live. Although a small number of fortunate senior farmers can receive some support from their wealthy communities, most Chinese farms, whose names have never appeared on government payrolls, get nothing. These people, the bulk of the Chinese population, have to rely entirely on their children for help when they are no longer able-bodied enough to engage in farmwork. Their futures depend on family attitudes toward them. And attitudes may vary as China itself changes.

In China there are sayings such as "Raise children for the sake of supporting yourself when you're too old to work" and "Never travel far away from your old parents." These words remain gospel for many traditionally minded people: most aged women, especially rural women, still prefer living in their own homes with three or even four generations residing under one roof.

But since 1978, when the country's opening policy was initiated, more and more young people have chosen to seek a brighter future outside their impoverished and "backward" hometowns. Some have gone abroad to study and work, leaving behind aged parents to fend for themselves.

A survey conducted in Beijing in the 1990s by Liu Ying, a senior researcher with the Sociology Institute under the Chinese Academy of Social Sciences, in cooperation with Beijing Women's Association, looked at the lives of 500 retired women over 60. It found that 36.8 percent of aged women lived only with their husbands, and that less than half of aged women lived with their children.

However, most of the aged Chinese women surveyed still expect to reap the dividend of bearing many children just like the old days, by having at least one of their offspring look after them.

In traditional Chinese society, women did household chores, served their husbands, and raised their children. They were only accorded respect and relaxation when they got "promoted" to the position of grandmother of the family. But it has become increasingly common for women over 60 years of age to live alone or be presented with a second child-raising challenge—bringing up their grandchildren.

A nationwide survey shows that about 23 percent of China's seniors over the age of 65 live by themselves. Many others are used as full-time nannies by their own children. But the "one family, one child" family planning policy in China has, to a great extent, changed this centuries-old tradition. Many young couples now send their infants to kindergartens, where they can get an early start in education. Staying at home with a grandmother means a lost opportunity of learning and interacting in the child's vital formative years, and besides, many grandmothers are poorly educated or even illiterate. For many aged women, this trend seems to be depriving them of their "great expectation" of enjoying the happiness of their senior life.

"The issue of China's aged people is actually one of aging women because women are the backbones of their families—they do the bulk of housework, spouse care, plus care of parents and in-laws. They usually find it difficult to adjust to changes around them psychologically. In addition, they generally outlive their husbands, thus their problem persists," says Liu Ying, a 71-year-old woman herself.

Although about 80 percent of those surveyed by Liu express a wish to stay at home for their old days instead of living in old folks' homes, they also say that they are in need of more enriching social activities.

In 1994, nearly 70 percent of retired people in Beijing participated in social activities. Aged women are mostly involved in public welfare, health care, self-advancement, and community services.

"Women over 60 are not looking for re-employment or money—they want to do something as a group to show their worth to themselves and society," says Liu Ying.

"Running water never goes stale and a door that's opened often never has a rusty hinge" embodies the Chinese believe that the mind and body must be kept active.

Statistics from the China National Committee on Aging (CNCA), the country's largest nongovernmental organization for elderly people, show that 28.5 percent of elders over 60 are still engaged in some sort of professional work, agricultural, scientific, or cultural.

The Beijing Retired Talent Development Center is a nongovernmental organization that promotes the idea that retiring from work does not mean retiring from life. Founded in 1986, the center had, by the end of 1999, introduced 60,000 elderly people to 10,000 enterprises in need of special knowledge and skills.

It is reported that 34.4 percent of those whose résumés are on file at the center are women between 50 and 60 years of age. However, those in the 45- to 55-year-old age group are most in demand by employers. Despite their contribution, some people complain that their employment makes job hunting by the mainstream populace even more difficult.

Zhang Wenfan, president of the CNCA, believes that the problems facing China's elderly can be solved through combined efforts by family, local community, and society as a whole. China's goal is to establish a support network for senior citizens that provides medicare, helps them avoid loneliness through study and entertainment, and encourages them to continue serving society after retirement.

To react to the issue of the "graying tide" or "silver tide," the Chinese government passed a national law in 1996 aimed at protecting its senior citizens' rights and interests. A national committee to address the "strategic issue" of aging was set up in October 1999, with Li Lanqing, a vice premier of the State Council, appointed as its director. The CNCA has also launched a comprehensive project to carry out national policy research on aging issues.

See Also

AGEISM; AGING; HEALTH CARE: EAST ASIA; HOUSEHOLDS AND FAMILIES: EAST ASIA; KINSHIP

References and Further Reading

Chen, Sheying. 1996. *Social policy of the economic state and community care in Chinese culture: Aging, family, urban change, and the socialist welfare pluralism.* Aldershot, U.K.: Avebury.

Olson, Laura Katz, ed. 1994. *Graying of the world: Who will care for the frail elderly.* New York: Haworth.

Ma Guihua

ELDERLY CARE: Case Study—India

Only in the late twentieth century did concern over the aging of populations become a worry to the governments of developing nations. This concern is well founded, because the size of older populations in these lands is growing at a rate three times that of developed countries. In 1990, for example, the elderly population—which the United Nations defines as those aged 60 and above—was 282 million in the developing world, in contrast with 206 million in the developed nations. China (101 million) and India (81 million) together accounted for over half the aged population of the developing countries (United Nations, 1995). Additionally, the United Nations predicts that the population of the elderly in developing countries will grow over 300 percent by the first quarter of the twenty-first century and that countries such as India and China will approach the demographic pyramid of more developed countries, with an increase in the proportion of elderly persons. That reversal of current trends means that a dwindling number of younger people will be responsible for supporting growing numbers of the elderly. Moreover, as the demographic pyramid begins to resemble that of developed nations, there will be more elderly women than men in the population.

Aging in India

In India, the elderly represent only a bit over 7 percent of the population. In absolute numbers, this population is large, however—about 76 million at the time of this writing, triple the number in 1960. The elderly population is often divided into the "young aged," the age group from 60 to 69; and the "old aged," those over 70.

In India, there are more men than women in every age group except the "old aged," but this is changing. Demographers expect that by 2010 women will outnumber men among all categories of the elderly in India. Therefore, the problem of care of elderly women is of prime importance.

Marital status has a strong effect on the situation of the elderly in India, where the availability of physical, financial, and emotional care for elderly women is strongly related to their marital status. Elderly women were more than three times more likely to be widowed than elderly men; about 65 percent of elderly women are widows.

Tradition and the Aged

Generally, Asian tradition demands that the younger generation respect and care for the elderly. All aspects of the cultural system, religion, mythology, folklore, and tradition reinforce this dictum. In India, there is nothing more sacred than caring for elderly parents.

Demographic and economic changes, however, have begun to eat away at the foundations of traditional systems in India as elsewhere. No longer are the elderly seen as the repositories of wisdom, nor do they have their former power to make life decisions for their children concerning marriage, education, and future occupation. It is no longer easy to ensure the loyalty of children toward them, nor is it so common or easy to train future daughters-in-law from a tender age to serve the elderly as a duty and not as a burden. Modernization has brought about changes in the size and composition of the family. Education has begun to transform the role of women through increasing both their awareness and their economic opportunities. These changes have reduced the numbers of women available to care for the elderly.

The trend toward urbanization further militates against the continuation of the extended family with its traditional roles. There is good evidence that gender disparity will continue, and women will be at an increasing disadvantage in care as the traditional family continues to decline with the increase in urbanization.

Elderly in Low-Income Households

Even when many families live together because of poverty, nuclear families are clearly marked off. This marking off signifies that separate rather than extended families are formed. The elderly, in a sense, are not the responsibility of any single family.

Some type of "pooled responsibility" develops. Those family members who work contribute toward the support of their elderly nonworking parents. The cultural ideal of caring for one's parents in their old age remains. The burden of this care now falls disproportionately on daughters and daughters-in-law rather than on sons. Women, thus, find themselves caring for their own children as well as the elderly.

Welfare and the State

In India's federal system of government, social welfare is a state responsibility. Almost all states administer schemes addressing the destitute old and widows. Under these schemes, those found eligible are entitled to a monthly pension. The coverage differs between states, however, and there are differences in the strictness and application of the eligibility criteria.

In India as elsewhere, however, as women from many different classes increasingly participate in paid employment, adequate provisions for dependency of all types—children as well as the elderly—have emerged as major social concerns. Moreover, in India, deaths from noncommunicable diseases such as heart disease, for which old people are particularly at risk, will almost double, from about 4.5 million a year in 1998 to about 8 million in 2020. Dr. Vijay Chandra, a specialist in geriatrics at the World Health Organization in New Delhi, states that geriatrics is virtually unknown in India. In fact, he notes, that there are only two geriatrics-training programs in India.

India has begun to investigate a social security pension program to ease the problem of aging. As of now, less than about 11 percent of workers are covered. Women are particularly affected, because they rarely work in industries that are covered by a pension program. One woman recounted that she had not received a pension for seven months: "I am too weak to spend three days arguing at the government offices and my son cannot go for me or he will lose his wages and we will have nothing to eat," she says. Interestingly, the government has stated that children with adequate means to care for their parents have been ignoring them. The poor often throw their parents out altogether. Therefore, there is proposed legislation requiring children with adequate means to care for their parents. The Indian government is concerned about the rise in suicides among the elderly and in demands for assisted suicide legislation on the part of many elderly Indians.

The impact of modernization on the joint family has had repercussions on the care of the elderly and in particular on the elderly woman. Traditionally, a woman received her status and validated her worth through her marriage and the production of sons. Modernization, however, has decreased the security of the joint family as economic demands and migration have given new importance to the nuclear family. In a country in which males are culturally preferred over females and in which female infanticide and the abortion of female fetuses are common, the plight of the elderly female is perilous indeed. Elderly widows, in fact, often find themselves in danger of losing their property—property that is protected by Indian law. Unfortunately, the government often does not enforce these laws and widows find that their daughters contest their property successfully in court. Moreover, the actions of agents of modernization, such as the International Monetary Fund and its Structural Adjustment Program (SAP), begun in India in 1991, have only worsened the condition of women in general and elderly women in particular. SAP has mandated an end to whatever government spending was directed toward social welfare for elderly women in the name of economic rationalization. It has aided those forces that have devalued women, while helping to fracture the joint family, the only traditional means of aid for most elderly women.

See Also

AGING; DEVELOPMENT: SOUTH ASIA; HEALTH CARE: SOUTH ASIA; HOUSEHOLDS AND FAMILIES: SOUTH ASIA; KINSHIP

References and Further Reading

Carson, Linda D., Debra Dobbs, and Phoebe Liebig. 1999. Social and political context of housing and services for elders in India. *Gerontologist* 39(1): 183.

Chen, Martha Alter, ed. 1998. *Widows in India: Social neglect and public action.* Delhi: Vedams Books International.

Cohen, Lawrence. 2000. No aging in India. *Current Anthropology* 41(2): 303–305.

Dube, Leela. 1997. *Women and kinship: Comparative perspectives on gender in south and south-east Asia.* Delhi: Vedams Books International.

Murray, E. J., and A. D. Lopez. 1996. *Global health statistics.* Cambridge, Mass.: Harvard School of Public Health in collaboration with the World Health Organization and the World Bank.

Pankaj, Mishra. 1999. They shall not grow old. *Times Literary Supplement,* May, 6–10.

Reddy, P. R., and P. Sumangala, eds. 1998. *Women in development: Perspectives from selected states of India.* Delhi: Vedams Books International.

United Nations. 1995. The world's women, 1970–1990: Trends and statistics. *Social Statistics and Indicators.* Series K, no 12. New York: United Nations.

World Health Organization. 1996. *Women, aging, and health: Achieving health across the life span.* Geneva: World Health Organization.

Leela Gulati

ELDERLY CARE: Western World

During the twentieth century western societies saw a significant increase in the number of older people and in the proportion of older people in the overall population. The United Nations estimates that by the year 2025, the elderly population of the world (age 65 and over) will reach 822 million, an increase from 6.2 percent of the population in 1990 to 9.2 percent of the population (Martin and Preston, 1994). A fall in the general birthrate, a longer life expectancy, and two world wars in which many men were killed have also meant that as the general population ages, the proportion of women to men increases. Female mortality has decreased, and women, on average, live longer than men. The large and growing number of older women in contemporary western societies, their relative poverty, and the absence of public health policy that addresses their needs have become crucial issues. For older women the combination of poverty and ill health tends to foster dependency and exploitability. The "feminization of old age" is a phenomenon that has only recently been recognized.

Gerontology

These changes have spawned a growth in the literature on aging and the development of the multidisciplinary field of gerontology. Gerontology, a field of study that emerged from North America, considers issues on aging from perspectives as diverse as anthropology, biology, economics, geography, history, politics, psychology, sociology, law, medicine, nursing, therapies, and social work.

Governments and institutions face the sociopolitical dilemma regarding the basis on which social support to older people should be provided. Pensions are the predominant form of financial assistance for older people, and they exist in some form in all western countries. A variety of financial and practical assistance is also available in the form of subsidies, discounts, and specialized provisions, especially in transport and housing. Scholars have expressed concern that the rising number of long-lived people in the population is not being matched by adequate and meaningful role opportunities or places in the social structure that can foster, protect, and reward their strengths and capacities. How do societies determine the appropriate age for retirement given the increase in life expectancy? How do we restructure the health establishment to meet the needs of geriatric patients? How do we design communities, housing, shopping centers, and roadways to meet human needs that change over the life course? Material and social inequalities experienced by older people and the poor image of the aging body mean that aging brings difficult social and personal challenges (Riley, Kahn, and Foner, 1994).

Women as Caregivers

In western societies not only do women make up the majority of elders in need of care, but women also provide most of the care for elders. Care for elders is usually provided by family members or by a largely female workforce of low-paid or volunteer carers. The social cost of community care for older people is discriminatory insofar as the family that takes care of elders is the female family. Seventy-two percent of all caregivers to the elderly are women, 77 percent of the children providing care to elderly parents are women, and nearly one-third of all caregivers to frail elderly persons are adult daughters (Stone, Cafferata, and Sangl, 1987). The expectation that women will care for aging parents and rel-

atives has to do with gender roles in western heteropatriarchal society, which attributes caring to women. Women may find themselves caring for aging parents who often have severe physical or mental decline, and the responsibility is such that they face anxiety about their ability to care for elders without neglecting or abusing them, in however mild a form.

Elder Abuse

Research into elder abuse has centered on four broad categories of abuse: physical, psychological, material, and active or passive neglect. The majority of abused older people are women, and since many of these women have only private lives in the home, their abuse goes on behind closed doors and remains unseen and undocumented. The family and the private world are still highly taboo areas for public investigation. This means that for older women, issues surrounding care and abuse become further silenced (Aitken and Griffin, 1996).

Illness and Health

With the increase in the number of female elders has come an increase in the incidence of certain chronic diseases and the greater use of sophisticated medications. Illnesses for elders are often characterized by vague symptoms, and many elders take multiple drugs at once. The Medical Research Council in the United Kingdom has found that men die at an earlier age than women from heart disease, stroke, and some cancers. Men also have a higher death rate from accidents and suicide. Women suffer higher incidence of nonfatal disabling conditions such as rheumatoid arthritis, depression, and osteoporosis (Medical Research Council, 1994).

In the twentieth century improved medical and economic conditions for older people have been accompanied by cultural disenfranchisement and by a loss of meaning and of vital social roles. The meanings surrounding old age and the ideals that older people have to live by are shaped largely by scientific definitions of the aging process. Aging has been brought under the dominion of scientific management, and society's interest in aging has been motivated by the desire to explain and control the aging process as though it were a problem to be solved. In different historical contexts, old age has been understood in alternative ways: as a spiritual coming of age; as a social identity calling for particular behaviors; and, more recently, as a medical norm focusing on the maximization of individual health and physiological function through scientific research and medical management (Cole, 1997).

Menopause

The medicalization of menopause also occurred in the twentieth century. Western medicine explains menopause as a biological condition triggered by hormonal changes. The physical symptoms associated with menopause in some women include hot flashes, weight gain, growth of facial hair, decreased size of uterus, and drying vaginal tissue. International debates in medical and popular journals discuss to what extent menopause is an illness, producing physiological distress and mental disorder.

Two divergent opinions on menopause emerged in the twentieth century: one saw it as an illness, a breakdown of body and mind, and the other saw it as initiating a time of great strength, a fresh start. Menopause has been referred to as a "dangerous age," "turn of life," "change of life," and "crisis of age forty." Positive views of menopause observed that there was nothing critical about this period. According to these views, the body's forces were no longer geared to childbirth, and therefore energy would be preserved to increase the vital forces. Menopause was seen as a form of birth control accompanied by new vigor and improved health. Negative views characterized menopause as an illness requiring medical attention and hormonal treatment. The female body during menopause was believed to experience physical and mental disequilibrium, insanity, and loss of youth and beauty (Banner, 1992).

Menopause has been regarded as the end of women's sexual function and treated as an illness rather than an experience. The medicalization of menopause has been advanced in part by negative cultural attitudes toward aging and by a characteristic medical drive to control women. And yet, despite medical attempts to define this stage of life, women's experiences of menopause are highly individualistic. Feminists have suggested new rituals to celebrate women's life-cycle transitions and have argued that menopause should be seen as a midlife experience rather than the end of one's life as a woman. Betty Friedan (1993) identifies the tendency for old people in the twentieth century to be imagined as sick, helpless, senile, incontinent, childlike, dependent, alone, and a burden on friends, family, community, and state. In interviews of older women, however, she shows the discrepancy between the dread image of old age as decline and deterioration and the vital reality of many older women's lives.

See Also

ABUSE; AGING; CAREGIVERS; LIFE EXPECTANCY; MENOPAUSE; POPULATION: OVERVIEW

References and Further Reading

Abel, Emily K. 1991. *Who cares for the elderly? Public policy and the experience of adult daughters*. Philadelphia: Temple University Press.

Aitken, Lynda, and Gabriele Griffin. 1996. *Gender issues in elder abuse*. London: Sage.

Arber, Sara, and Jay Grim, eds. 1995. *Connecting gender and ageing*. Buckingham, U.K.: Open University Press.

Banner, Lois W. 1992. *In full flower: Aging women, power, and sexuality*. New York: Knopf.

Cole, Thomas R. 1997. *The journey of life: A cultural history of ageing in America*. Cambridge: Cambridge University Press.

Friedan, Betty. 1993. *The fountain of age*. New York: Simon and Schuster.

Martin, Linda G., and Samuel H. Preston, eds. 1994. *Demography of aging*. Washington, D.C.: National Academy Press.

Medical Research Council. 1994. *The health of the UK's elderly people*. London: Medical Research Council.

Pearsall, Marilyn, ed. 1997. *The other within us: Feminist explorations of women and aging*. Boulder, Colo.: Westview.

Riley, Matilda White, Robert L. Kahn, and Anne Foner, eds. 1994. *Age and structural lag: Society's failure to provide meaningful opportunities in work, family, and leisure*. New York: Wiley.

Stone, R. I., L. Cafferata, and J. Sangl. 1987. Caregivers of the frail elderly: A natural profile. *Gerontologist* 27(5): 616–626.

Wheeler, Helen Rippier. 1997. *Women and aging: A guide to the literature*. Boulder, Colo.: Lynne Rienner.

Suzanne Goh

ELECTIONS

See POLITICAL PARTICIPATION and SUFFRAGE.

EMANCIPATION AND LIBERATION MOVEMENTS

The struggle for women's equality from the late eighteenth century to the mid-twentieth century had the goal of women's "emancipation," a word originally used for the freeing of slaves. Given the real parallels between slavery (which denied both men and women any personal rights) and the oppression of women in societies in which only men had legal rights, women's demands for legal recognition of their equality through full civil and political rights were necessary to their freedom. Emancipation also may be understood in a wider sense as freedom from barriers of custom or economic constraints.

A number of historical movements since the seventeenth century have demanded the emancipation of men from rigid social hierarchy and political domination. Liberalism emphasized individual freedom, civic equality, and constitutional limits on the power of government. By the mid-nineteenth century, when liberalism was becoming an ideology of the status quo in the more economically and politically advanced countries of the West, socialists criticized it as the ideology of the propertied classes and sought to free individuals from the domination of market forces. Anarchists often, though not always, embraced the socialist critique of capitalism, but they also emphasized the abolition of state power and all forms of authority in favor of individual autonomy and voluntary cooperation. All three ideologies embrace a belief in historical progress and a goal of universal human emancipation.

Nationalism, an ideology that also arose in the nineteenth century, called for freedom from foreign domination but not necessarily for general human emancipation. Rather, nationalism focuses on specific national history and culture, and on diversity. In practice, nevertheless, it often has been linked to liberal or socialist beliefs and has had emancipatory implications for women mobilized in national struggles.

Universalist Ideologies and the Emancipation of Women

The emancipation of women was at least implicit in the basic principles of each universalist ideology, but its explicitness varied. Liberal theory and practice effectively excluded women from civil and political rights until systematically challenged by liberal feminists. Socialists embraced women's equality in principle but (with the exception of some utopian socialists) saw women's emancipation as secondary to the emancipation of the working class and as possible only in a socialist society. Anarchism was, in general, the most favorable to women's freedom because of its attack on all forms of social and psychological oppression and its opposition to the patriarchal family.

Utopian socialists, in the early nineteenth century, were some of the strongest advocates of freeing women from male domination, including the ties of marriage and domesticity. Charles Fourier, in particular, saw the emancipation of women as intrinsic to his program for social equality and harmony based on the free play of natural human passions, including sexuality. One group of followers of another utopian socialist, Saint-Simon, also espoused freedom for women, free love, and the creation of a new religion inspired by the belief in a Woman-Messiah (Lichtheim, 1969).

These utopian socialist circles created a sympathetic milieu in which women could articulate their own aspirations, as in the case of the French women intellectuals who founded the journal *Voix des femmes* (Voice of women) after the February 1848 revolution to demand higher education, the vote, jobs, equality in marriage, and communal household arrangements (Applewhite and Levy, 1993).

Women who supported Marxism found their commitment to women's emancipation in conflict in the short term with their commitment to the struggle of the working class. Although Friedrich Engels in *The Origins of the Family, Private Property, and the State* and August Bebel in *Women under Socialism* did comment on women's long history of subordination and argue that socialism would free women, Marxists tended to condemn "bourgeois feminists" who gave priority to achieving women's rights in capitalist societies. Alexandra Kollontai, one of the few prominent women Bolsheviks, did strongly support women's equality and advocate free love and the abolition of the family, but she was the only well known Marxist to emphasize her feminism as well. Her work immediately after the Russian Revolution to promote the equality of women in the new Soviet Union was ended by the rise of Stalinism.

Marxist movements have been committed in principle to the emancipation of women—the Chinese communists, in particular, stressed the abolition of women's servitude. But the experience of women in official socialist regimes has been that despite formal commitments to equality and provision of educational and job opportunities, they were in general economically unequal, excluded from the center of political power, and still oppressed by traditional household duties and patriarchal attitudes (Scott, 1974). A very small feminist group arose in the former Soviet Union in 1979, and there was some feminist debate and writing in East Germany, but most feminist criticism of official socialism came from the West in the context of the women's liberation movement (Mitchell, 1971; Sargent, 1981).

Anarchists have attacked Marxism for its repressive tendencies ever since the disputes between Bakunin and Marx in the First International, and anarchists were among the most articulate leftist critics of the Bolshevik revolution and the subsequent regime. Emma Goldman, a Russian-born anarchist and prominent libertarian and feminist campaigner who exposed how the Bolsheviks crushed revolutionary potential in Russia, exemplified the links between anarchism and feminism (Drinnon, 1961). Anarchist ideas and groups have been so varied, however, that it is difficult to generalize about the experience of women within anarchist circles.

Women's Emancipation in Nonwestern Countries

Outside the West, women's emancipation has been shaped by diverse and sometimes conflicting trends and movements. Opponents of traditional culture and hierarchy (for example, during the Meiji Era in Japan or in the case of the Young Turks in Turkey) saw the freedom of women as central to a western model of modernization. But nationalist movements rejecting direct or indirect western imperialism also have tended to look to their own history and culture for inspiration, sometimes finding examples of freedom and equality of women in an idealized past. Egyptian reformers referred back to the queens of ancient Egypt, Iranians to a Zoroastrian tradition of respect for women (Jayarwardena, 1986). Women reformers in many developing countries also were directly influenced by western feminist writings and by feminist pioneers in countries comparable to their own. But feminist aspirations were often subordinated to movements for modernization or national independence, which frequently failed to challenge fundamental social attitudes and practices.

By the late twentieth century, both liberalism and socialism had formally emancipated women in the West and in socialist countries, respectively, but had not given them full freedom and equality. The second wave of feminism, starting in the late 1960s, called itself the women's liberation movement, implying the inadequacy of "emancipation" and demanding total freedom for women in all spheres of life, including control over their own bodies and reproduction. Women's "liberation," denoting a central concern with psychology and the freeing of women from previously defined gender roles, has extended to critiques of culture and knowledge as male-determined (Eisenstein, 1984; Tong, 1989). The women's liberation movement aspired to universal liberation of women; it soon became an international movement, involving many women in developing countries, but women in the developing world also have asserted their own cultural perspectives and priorities and rejected western formulations of what is required for liberation.

See Also

ANARCHISM; FEMINISM: LIBERAL BRITISH AND EUROPEAN; FEMINISM: LIBERAL NORTH AMERICAN; FEMINISM: SOCIALIST; MARXISM; SOCIALISM; UTOPIANISM

References and Further Reading

Afshar, Haleh, ed. 1998. *Women and empowerment: Illustrations from the third world.* Basingstoke, U.K.: Macmillan.

Applewhite, Harriet B., and Darline G. Levy. 1993. *Women and politics in the age of the democratic revolution.* Ann Arbor: University of Michigan Press.

Drinnon, Richard. 1961. *Rebel in paradise.* Chicago: University of Chicago Press.

Dunayevska, Raya. 1996. *Women's liberation and the dialectics of revolution: Reaching for the future.* Detroit, Mich.: Wayne State University Press.

Eisenstein, Hester. 1984. *Contemporary feminist thought.* London: Unwin.

Jayarwardena, Kumari. 1986. *Feminism and nationalism in the third world.* London: Zed.

Kollontai, Alexandra. 1977. *Selected writings of Alexandra Kollontai.* Trans. A. Holt. Westport, Conn.: L. Hill.

Lichtheim, George. 1969. *The origins of socialism.* London: Weidenfeld and Nicolson.

Mitchell, Juliet. 1971. *Woman's estate.* Harmondsworth: Penguin.

Sargent, Lydia, ed. 1981. *Women and revolution: A discussion of the unhappy marriage of Marxism and feminism.* London: Pluto.

Scott, Hilda. 1974. *Does socialism liberate women? Experiences in eastern Europe.* Boston: Beacon.

Tong, Rosemary. 1989. *Feminist thought: A comprehensive introduction.* Boulder, Colo.: Westview.

Women in Eastern Europe Group. 1980. *Women and Russia: First feminist samizdat.* London: Sheba.

April Carter

EMBRYO

See FETUS.

EMIGRATION

See IMMIGRATION and MIGRATION.

EMPLOYMENT: Equal Opportunities

See EQUAL OPPORTUNITIES.

EMPLOYMENT: Equal Pay and Conditions

See WORK: EQUAL PAY AND CONDITIONS.

EMPLOYMENT: Informal

See ECONOMY: INFORMAL.

EMPLOYMENT: Occupational Experiences

See WORK: OCCUPATIONAL EXPERIENCES.

EMPLOYMENT: Occupational Segregation

See WORK: OCCUPATIONAL SEGREGATION.

EMPLOYMENT: Underemployment

See UNDEREMPLOYMENT.

EMPLOYMENT: Unemployment

See UNEMPLOYMENT.

EMPLOYMENT

Empowerment is a process that aims at creating the conditions for the self-determination of a particular people or group. It is invoked to signify the potential for change and has been used successfully as a means to mobilize people to action. The openness and versatility of the idea of empowerment has meant that people have been able to give the idea their own meanings. Thus, it has been taken up by numerous peoples, groups, and organizations around the world that have sought to challenge a variety of social, economic, cultural, religious, legal, and political relations of subordination. More recently, however, the very imprecision and familiarity of the term have prompted activists to be more specific in describing and distinguishing their endeavors. Concepts such as citizenship, legal literacy, sustainable development, human rights, and education have helped to make their particular demands more effective.

The idea of women's empowerment has been central to the evolution of women's movements since the late 1960s. Early feminist theorists and activities drew from the ideas of other oppressed or excluded peoples and in particular from the idea of "conscientization" as pioneered in Latin America by Paolo Freire. Conscientization, or what women have often called consciousness-raising, involves changes in thinking, ideology, beliefs, self-image, and the definition of real-

ity. Consciousness-raising is a "coming-to-awareness" that makes explicit and is critical of the power relations that underlie and are supported by dominant ideologies, beliefs, or cultures; it is also a revaluation of the perspectives, knowledge, and contributions of members of a subordinate or "invisible" group. This notion of changing consciousness was crucial to the early feminist use of the term *empowerment*, and because it called for women to become aware of their own position and implication in structures and relations of power, it came to be understood as a process that women had to go through themselves. Women's empowerment was understood to be a process in which various people and institutions could participate or assist or for which they could provide enabling structures, but it was not something that could be benevolently bestowed on women "for their own good."

A presumed effect and extension of women's changed consciousness is the undertaking of actions informed by such critical thinking and revisioning. It has often been a challenge for women's movements to maintain these crucial links between theory and practice. On the many occasions in which critical consciousness has translated into action, women have deployed a number of strategies that range from lobbying and grassroots mobilization to education, legal reform, protest, and efforts to restructure various social institutions. A recent south Asian description, for example, defines empowerment as a far-reaching process that eventuates in the redistribution of control over resources and ideology; it involves struggle over issues of financial resources, access to information, dynamics of social relations, the role of culture and tradition in shaping people's lives, legal rights, and political representation and participation. What underlies this formulation is the idea that having control over ideology and resources enables people to make decisions that affect their own lives. It is evident, then, that the question of who participates in the process of making decisions about these issues is central to movements for women's empowerment. And as such challenges mean contesting principal decision-making processes and not simply addressing the outcomes of those decisions, women's empowerment often entails changing or broadening definitions of citizenship, of the kinds of spaces in which political action can and does take place, and of what actually constitutes politics or political actions.

Because conversations about and struggles for empowerment have direct bearing on relations between people, questions about the appropriate use of power or authority come to the fore. Many discussions of women's empowerment have revolved around the redefinition of power, focusing on changing how power is exercised in addition to changing power relations themselves. Although it is admittedly often difficult to separate the term *power* from the history of its abuse, many feminist theorists and activists have sought to reclaim the term by distinguishing "power over," understood as domination, from "power to," conceived as the ability to determine the course of one's life and actively to participate in society and culture. A fairly typical example of such an attempt is that ventured by an international feminist workshop sponsored by the Asian and Pacific Centre for Women and Development. This workshop, which aimed at influencing debates at the Second UN World Conference for Women in 1980, began by defining women's power "to control their own lives within and outside of the home" as one of the fundamental goals of the women's movement. It notes that power is used not as a mode of domination over others, but as (a) a sense of internal strength and confidence to face life; (b) the right to determine our choices in life; (c) the ability to influence the social processes that affect our lives; and (d) an influence on the direction of social change (APCWD, 1979: 27).

Of course, individual women who have gained forms of power or positions of authority have often exercised it in the traditional sense of "power over." As feminist theory and practice have grown more sophisticated, the optimistic assumptions underlying the calls for women's empowerment—including the idea that the empowerment of some people will necessarily lead to progressive change—have been examined more carefully. With the growth of feminist discourse about difference, diversity, solidarity, and community, the potential conflicts between and among groups struggling for empowerment have become a matter for serious consideration and interrogation (see, for example, Albrecht and Brewer, 1990; Yuval-Davis, 1994).

Clearly, the concept of empowerment has been of vital importance to women's efforts to improve their standing in society. It has been a critical factor enabling women to move from seeing themselves simply as victims to seeing themselves as self-conscious actors who can work, both individually and collaboratively, to change and shape the world in which they live. Nevertheless, women need to continue to reflect on and examine the assumptions that lie at the heart of calls for empowerment and to be more precise in defining the goals for which such calls aim. Empowerment will continue to be at the center of appeals for change because it has immense mobilizing power. It will continue to be useful as long as its proponents guard against the dangers of exclusion and co-optation present in any effort involving power and as long as women maintain an ongoing process of dialogue about power—for whom, by what means, and under what conditions.

See Also

CITIZENSHIP; CONSCIOUSNESS-RAISING; POWER; WOMEN'S MOVEMENT: OVERVIEW

References and Further Reading

Albrecht, Lisa, and Rose M. Brewer, eds. 1990. *Bridges of power: Women's multicultural alliances.* Philadelphia: New Society Publishers.

Asian and Pacific Centre for Women and Development (APCWD). 1979. Feminist ideology and structures in the first half of the decade for women. In *Developing strategies for the future: Feminist perspective.* Bangkok: Asian and Pacific Centre for Women and Development.

Batliwala, Srilatha. 1993. *Empowerment of women in South Asia: Concepts and practices.* New Delhi: Vision Wordtronic.

Bookman, Ann, and Sandra Morgen, eds. 1988. *Women and the politics of empowerment.* Philadelphia: Temple University Press.

Bystydzienski, Jill M., ed. 1992. *Women transforming politics: Worldwide strategies for empowerment.* Bloomington: Indiana University Press.

Collins, Patricia Hill. 1991. *Black feminist thought: Knowledge, consciousness, and the politics of empowerment.* New York: Routledge.

Freire, Paulo. 1990. *The pedagogy of the oppressed.* Trans. Myra Bergman Ramos. New York: Continuum.

Griffen, Vanessa, ed. 1989. *Women, development and empowerment: A Pacific feminist perspective.* Kuala Lumpur: Asian Pacific Development Centre.

Schuler, Margaret, ed. 1986. *Empowerment and the law: Strategies of third world women.* Washington, D.C.: OEF International.

Yuval-Davis, Nira. 1994. Women, ethnicity and empowerment. *Feminism and Psychology* 4(1).

Charlotte Bunch
Samantha Frost

ENDOCRINE DISRUPTION

Certain scientists and environmentalists have long held suspicions that widespread use of chemicals by humans may have played a significant part in the process of environmental degradation. In the 1960s, the seminal book *Silent Spring* mobilized environmental movements in many parts of the world by drawing attention to the possibility that chemicals dispersed in the environment might harm both humans and wildlife. Its author, Rachel Carson, revealed that widely used agricultural chemicals were a probable cause of several bird species' failure to reproduce normally and that exposure to these chemicals might raise the cancer risks for humans.

In the 1990s, a small interdisciplinary scientific workshop in Wingspread, Oregon, and a book published in many countries—*Our Stolen Future: Are We Threatening Our Fertility, Intelligence, and Survival?*—revived concerns that chemicals in the environment may induce changes in the reproductive organs of humans and wildlife. Scientists believe that some chemicals are interpreted by the body as estrogens or other hormones and interfere with the endocrine system. Such chemicals are called endocrine disrupters. Concern over endocrine disruption has led to legislative and regulatory action as well as to more stringent standards in international and national requirements on the testing of chemicals in the human environment.

The critical period of exposure to "foreign hormones"—endocrine-disruptive chemicals—is before birth, at the fetal stage when the reproductive and neural organs are formed. Hormones are produced naturally in the body. Also, certain plants consumed by animals and humans contain substances with hormonal action—for instance, clover, soy, and yams. Moreover, medications such as birth control pills interfere with the natural hormones in the body. Chemicals suspected to be endocrine disrupters include many substances such as pesticides, PCBs, and heavy metals, that are well-known environmental contaminants. Many of them are persistent and can be carried by winds over long distances. It has been shown that pesticides used in the tropics are transported to cold latitudes, where the substances accumulate at higher and higher concentrations in the body fat of animals at the apex of the food chain—fish, seals, polar bears, and humans. Pesticides widely used in tropical Asia and Latin America, for instance, are found in high concentrations in the breast milk of Inuit mothers, who eat fish from the lakes in northern Canada.

Scientists have pointed to disturbed reproductive functions in certain wildlife—snails, fish, birds, and alligators—as evidence that pesticides and other chemicals in the environment may disrupt hormonal functions in the developing organism. For humans, a scenario of the effects of endocrine disrupters has been provided by the widespread use of a synthetic estrogen medication, diethylstilbestrol (DES), that was erroneously believed to help pregnant women carry the pregnancy to term and deliver healthier babies. Many of the fetuses who were exposed to DES developed malformed reproductive organs, and some of the women exposed to it developed potentially lethal cancer in the vagina because of the exposure. Reports of men's declining sperm density, increasing rates of malformations of reproductive organs, and increasing rates of testicular cancer in industrialized countries have heightened the concerns over endocrine disruption.

Theo Colborn, a scientist working for the World Wildlife Fund in the United States, played a key role in raising awareness about the potential of certain chemical substances to disrupt the endocrine system. She succeeded in creating interest within the scientific community and educating the general public in many countries about this issue. She was one of the initiators of the Wingspread Workshop. Together with the science journalist Dianne Dumanoski and the biologist John Peterson Myers, she wrote the book *Our Stolen Future*. The toxicologist Retha Newbold is another woman whose work has contributed to the understanding of chemicals and endocrine disruption.

See Also

CANCER; ESTROGEN; HORMONES; THE PILL; REPRODUCTIVE HEALTH; REPRODUCTIVE PHYSIOLOGY; TOXICOLOGY

References and Further Reading

Carson, Rachel. 1994. *Silent spring.* Boston: Houghton Mifflin.

Colborn, Theo, Dianne Dumanoski, and John Peterson Myers. 1996. *Our stolen future: Are we threatening our fertility, intelligence, and survival?* New York: Dutton.

Palmlund, Ingar. 1996. Exposure to a xenoestrogen before birth: The diethylstilbestrol experience. *Journal of Psychosomatic Obstetrics and Gynecology* 17: 71–84.

Ingar Palmlund

ENERGY

Fire making and cooking have been at the heart of domestic life since time immemorial, and the energy used in these tasks remains pivotal to women in developing countries. These countries, however, consume relatively small amounts of energy, most of it in the domestic sector. Developed countries, on the other hand, consume lavish amounts of energy predominantly in the industrial, commercial, transportation, and agricultural sectors.

Across the global village daily lives are connected through an intricate web of energy-consuming activities that affect the social and natural environment. In developing countries the primary energy sources are wood, dung, and, more recently, crop waste. In the developed countries, coal, oil, hydroelectric, and nuclear power constitute the primary energy sources. Renewable energy sources, such as solar, wind, and biogas power, play only a small role in energy production. Electricity, the quintessential modern fuel, is actually an energy carrier that links energy production and consumption. Energy is seldom produced or consumed without impacting, usually negatively, the environment and therefore humans. This is the case whether the process is nuclear or geothermal or involves the burning of kerosene or wood fuel.

Traditionally women have had little control over energy sources. Their selection and purpose and the development of large-scale power-producing plants have been a male preserve, evident in the form of multinational corporations. In the late twentieth century, however, the importance of women as primary end users of domestic energy was recognized. Women thus began to play a critical role in policy debates relating, first, to access to energy sources and the impact of energy use on health and the environment and, second, to the unequal consumption of energy by the developing and developed countries.

The term *energy poverty* describes the struggle of developing countries to meet their energy needs as demands on their energy resources escalate, their populations increase, and their economies modernize. Severe pressure on natural forests has forced women to toil to meet their household energy needs and even to change their cooking patterns according to the fuel available. Under these circumstances women collect and carry up to 40 kilograms of wood over a distance of up to 20 kilometers a day with resultant damage to the spine and to childbearing capacity. In addition, women's traditional income-generating activities—for example, beer brewing, pottery, and charcoal making—are fuel-intensive and require similar exertion to accomplish.

The overcollection of fuelwood contributes to deforestation, with consequences that include severe land degradation, a situation worsened by the lack of such traditional nutrients as dung and crop waste because these too have been collected. The thin, unstable soil erodes and runs off, causing rivers and dams to silt up. Ultimately in this ripple effect, riverine ecosystems become unbalanced, and this imbalance changes the level of the water so that hydroelectric power sources become unreliable.

Women do not merely collect firewood; they have also been instrumental in conserving resources. Both women in Brazil and the Chipko movement in India have successfully resisted forest destruction. In Kenya the Green Belt movement started by the National Council of Women under the leadership of Wangari Maathai has focused on awareness raising and tree planting.

As countries develop, the relative importance of the domestic sector declines. Transport becomes the lifeblood. Arterial routes link rural and urban areas and enable mobility, particularly for men, as the industrial and commercial sectors burgeon. Rapid growth ensues in both energy consumption and environmental degradation, while women and children's transport needs are frequently neglected.

Developed countries have been charged with consuming disproportionate and wasteful amounts of energy, thereby producing some of the worst air, water, and land pollution. Technology transfer for energy usage is almost entirely from the developed North to the developing South. There are examples of appropriate technology development, including biogas projects, solar power use in rural clinics, and solar and wind power use for people living in remote areas, but as yet they remain small-scale. The Kenya Energy Non-Governmental Organization (KENGO) is one such successful structure concerned with energy supplies, tree planting, and fuel-saving stoves.

The transition from traditional to modern kitchens is a social, cultural, and economic process in which multitudes of women are engaged. But appliances, as well as the shape and form of modern kitchens, are generally designed by men in a male-dominated industry, and thus some critics think the benefits of their adoption should be weighed against the loss of cultural and traditional significance attached to cooking and food provision.

Although energy is considered an essential element for all modern and developing countries, access and availability remain dependent on one's position in society. In the developing world women hold the key to energy consumption. In the developed world they share the responsibility for its profligate use and environmental impact. Together, as primary caregivers and vigorous campaigners, they share an individual and collective ability to influence energy policy to the advantage of all.

See Also

COOKING; ENVIRONMENT: OVERVIEW; ENVIRONMENT: SOUTH ASIAN CASE STUDY—FORESTS IN INDIA; NATURAL RESOURCES; NATURE

References and Further Reading

Dankelman, Irene, and Joan Davidson. 1988. *Women and environment in the Third World: Alliance for the future.* London: Earthscan.

Fritz, M. 1982. *Future energy consumption of the Third World.* New York: Pergamon.

Ofosu-Amaah, Waafas, and Wendy Philleo, eds. 1991. Partners in life. *Proceedings of the Global Assembly of Women and the Environment* 2 (34): Energy success stories.

Wendy Jill Annecke

ENGINEERING

In the engineering profession, one utilizes knowledge of the mathematical and natural sciences and applies it to the efficient use of the materials and forces of nature. An engineer is a person who has received professional training in pure and applied science. The various branches of engineering include aeronautical and aerospace; chemical; civil; electrical and electronics; geological and mining; industrial; mechanical; military; naval or marine; nuclear; safety; and sanitary. Traditionally, men have dominated the engineering education talent pool and workforce. Women have, however, made significant progress in the field of engineering in the last three decades of the twentieth century. This progress can be seen in the increasing numbers of women earning engineering degrees at all academic levels and in the improved numbers of women in the engineering workforce. There are many issues to be addressed, nevertheless, if women are ever to be equally represented in the field of engineering. As the National Science Foundation (NSF) states in its 1997–2003 Strategic Plan, we must "strive for a diverse, globally oriented workforce of scientists and engineers" (NSF, 1999: ii).

History

As early as 1919, women engineers attempted to organize and assess the status of women in their profession. At that time, three engineering students wrote to the deans of engineering schools around the United States, asking for data on women in engineering and architecture. The responses they received ranged from small lists of women students from a handful of universities to statements such as, "We have not now, have never had, and do not expect to have... any women students registered in our engineering department" (Perusek, 2000: 19). By the 1940s, women had made little progress as engineers. In 1942, women made up 2 out of 100 engineering students enrolled in the Cooper Union for the Advancement of Science and Art, and by 1945, the Columbia School of Engineering had had only one female graduate. Although World War II provided some opportunities for all women, discrimination against women and

minorities in the engineering profession remained widespread.

Many employers felt that hiring a woman engineer was too risky because she would be likely to leave the organization to marry and have children. Female engineering students at the Drexel Institute of Technology, however, began to organize and hold monthly meetings so that they would be more effective in presenting issues they felt strongly about to the university's administration. As a result, in 1946, the Society of Women Engineers (SWE) was officially formed. In 1950, the SWE was formally incorporated as a nonprofit organization. Its mission, then and now, is to "make certain that women have the opportunity to pursue an engineering education and engineering employment" within the larger framework of "contributing to the world in a meaningful way that improves the quality of life" (Perusek, 2000: 14). The SWE provides its members with career guidance and education, gives an award for engineering excellence, produces a professional publication, holds meetings and conventions, and continuously informs the public of the availability of qualified women for engineering positions.

The SWE and its supporters have had a lot of work to do. Besides the small number of women engineering students and women in the engineering workforce, in the 1950s, high school girls were increasingly discouraged from studying mathematics and science and, without experience in these fields, were usually unable to enter engineering colleges. In the late 1960s, the Institute of Electrical and Electronic Engineers (IEEE) began actively to recruit and welcome women into their organization. In 1970, the IEEE sent a survey with each directory they mailed in order to count and keep statistics on their female members. Women made remarkable inroads into the community of scientists and engineers during the 1970s and early 1980s; however, the increase leveled off in most areas well before women achieved demographic parity and occupational equality with men (Davis et al., 1996: 29).

Education

High school students frequently choose fields that are traditional for their gender—girls typically concentrate on the social sciences, health services, and education, whereas boys gravitate toward engineering and business careers (AAUW, 1999: 115). Girls often find the subjects of science and mathematics unattractive not only because of their own interests and abilities but also because of the attitudes of their teachers, parents, and peers. In addition, girls have fewer female role models to serve as representatives for them in the field of engineering than do boys. For young girls, this often results in lower participation in math and science courses; differential treatment from teachers and counselors; a lack of knowledge of science, engineering, and math careers; and little or no peer, parental, and social support. In fact, "there is no evidence that girls are born less inclined to mathematics or mechanics than boys, but there is strong evidence that society believes this to be the case and encourages a division between boys and girls" (Davis et al., 1996: 30).

The Engineering Workforce Commission of the American Association of Engineering Societies reports that up until the 1970s, women earned less than 1 percent of all bachelor's degrees in engineering. By 1980, that number rose to 9.7 percent—the largest percentage increase in any science-related field. Another jump occurred as the number went from 15.4 percent in 1990 to 19.7 percent in 1999. A similar trend can be seen for women's progress in master's and doctorate degrees in engineering. Women earned 1.1, 6.3, 14.3, and 20.5 percent of all engineering master's degrees in 1970, 1980, 1990, and 1999, respectively. For engineering doctorate degrees, women's numbers are 0.4, 3.2, 9.1, and 14.7 percent for the same years. Because fewer individuals are entering the field of engineering and because, as can be shown from women's educational achievement patterns, the majority of female engineers have been in the workforce for 15 years or less, women clearly represent a wealth of untapped engineering talent (Catalyst, 1992: 7).

The Engineering Workforce

Women represent 46.5 percent of the total U.S. labor force, 23 percent of the science and engineering labor force, and 11 percent of the engineering labor force. In addition, women of color represent 19 percent of all women in the science and engineering labor force and 4.2 percent of all scientists and engineers in general (NSF, 1999: 113). Short-term trends show some increase in the representation of doctoral women in science and engineering employment, with women's representation advancing from 19 to 20 to 23 percent in 1991, 1993, and 1995, respectively (NSF, 1999: 100). Although full-time-employed women engineers earn less than men, these differences in salary by gender are primarily due to differences in age and field. The overall median salary for women is much lower than that for men, and with increasing age, the gap in salaries widens (NSF, 1999: 105). In addition, although the participation of women in other male-dominated professions, such as medicine and law, increased dramatically in the last 25 years of the twentieth century, the number of women in engineering has increased at a much slower rate.

Despite their low representation, a 1992 Catalyst study found that "female engineers enjoy their work and express pride in their accomplishments." In fact, these women, like their male counterparts, feel a great passion for the challenge and problem solving that engineering involves. Some of them even expressed excitement about being in a field that is relatively new for women and described how being an engineer has been extremely invigorating for them (Catalyst, 1992: 3, 14). Unfortunately, female engineers who are new to the workforce often "find that the playing field is not level for them. Their enthusiasm, therefore, is often diminished by the barriers they encounter and the lack of training and role models to help them navigate the challenges of being a female engineer" (Catalyst, 1992: 15). The main barriers to advancement for female engineers are a lack of corporate understanding of the need for and value of diversity in engineering; the perceived risk of hiring and promoting women; the exclusion from informal networks where critical information is shared; their low visibility for contributions; and the lack of role models, mentors, and sponsors. There is, however, a set of recommendations that corporations can follow to help promote the status of women in the engineering profession. Employers should:

- Encourage the formation of women's networks.
- Create greater opportunities and rewards for employees on the technical track.
- Support employees in balancing work and family responsibilities.
- Ensure that women are well represented on visible team projects.
- Build partnerships with colleges and high schools (Catalyst, 1992: 46–52).

Future Trends

The U.S. government recognizes the importance of diversity in the sciences and engineering and expressed as much on 14 October 1998, when the Commission on the Advancement of Women and Minorities in Science, Engineering, and Technology Development was established. President Bill Clinton signed H.R. 3007 into law in order to formally "research and recommend ways to improve the recruitment, retention, and representation of women, minorities, and persons with disabilities in science, engineering, and technology education and employment" (Gleiter, 1999: 26). Some private companies have recognized the need to promote and support the next generation of women in science, engineering, and technology. Some exemplary programs include AT&T's Graduate Fellowship Program, which offers educational support to women and underrepresented minorities; Procter & Gamble's Mentor-Up program, in which junior women mentor senior executives so that the latter can become aware of the issues that affect these women; and Texas Instruments' women's Professional Development Team, which was created to evaluate the environment for technical women at the company (Catalyst, 1999: 43–54). Actions to increase recruitment efforts and improve the retention of women in engineering also have been taken by many organizations, including the SWE, the Women in Engineering Programs and Advocates Network (WEPAN), and the National Academy of Engineering (NAE).

For the last 50 years of the twentieth century, the SWE conducted career-guidance programs that were usually supported by industry. In addition, they hold a combined convention and student conference each June, provide an extensive awards and recognition program that honors outstanding accomplishments of women in the engineering profession as well as those who have contributed significantly to the advancement of women in the engineering profession, and award more than $100,000 annually in scholarships. For fiscal year 2000, the SWE's goals included leveraging information technology to enhance its position as a center of information for women in engineering; developing professional programs that enhance the application of leadership skills; strengthening alliances with industry as a source of new members; increasing the number of girls participating in outreach programs; and increasing the number of members in different categories of diversity who report high satisfaction with their jobs.

WEPAN, a national nonprofit educational organization founded in 1990, also seeks to enhance the status of women in the engineering profession through its many programs. MentorNet is one such program that pairs undergraduate and graduate women studying engineering and related sciences at universities across the country with professionals in industry. This program, initiated in 1997, has thus far paired over 500 students from 26 universities with mentors representing over 250 corporations. Two more WEPAN programs are Global Alliance, which offers an opportunity for those in education, industry, government, and professional associations from different countries to share best practices, and the Program Profiles database, which provides contact information for organizations that offer programs or activities to increase enrollment or retention of women in science, engineering, and mathematics.

Finally, the NAE, founded in 1964 to provide engineering leadership in service to the nation and to work to build and articulate the implications of the rapid technological change that affects the way people work, learn, and play, conducted a Summit on Women in Engineering as part of its Celebration of Women in Engineering project. The summit's Task Committee recommended action to "increase the public's understanding of engineering as a positive force in society and as a career for women, as well as more targeted actions to assist educators and employers to attract and retain women in the engineering profession" (ASCE, 2000: 2). The committee also chose two projects for implementation: a database of women in engineering and a climate index for engineering employers. In addition, the NAE launched a new Web site (www.nae.edu/cwe) as part of a major effort to encourage young girls and women to choose engineering as a profession. The site highlights the achievements of women engineers and provides information on education, careers, and mentoring. Each week, two outstanding women engineers and their achievements are featured on the site's Gallery of Engineers, and the site provides information on financial aid, discussion rooms, and a job bank.

See Also

EDUCATION: GENDERED SUBJECT CHOICE; EDUCATION: HIGHER EDUCATION; EDUCATION: SCIENCE; EDUCATION: VOCATIONAL; SCIENCE: OVERVIEW; TECHNOLOGY; WORK: OCCUPATIONAL SEGREGATION; WORK: PATTERNS

References and Further Reading

American Association of University Women (AAUW). 1999. *Gender gaps: Where schools still fail our children.* New York: Marlow and Co.

American Society of Civil Engineers (ASCE). 2000. *Women on the move—retention and advancement of women engineers: A preliminary report.* Reston, Va.: ASCE.

Catalyst. 1992. *Women in engineering: An untapped resource.* New York: Catalyst.

———. 1999. *Women in industry: A winning formula for companies.* New York: Catalyst.

Davis, Dina-Sue, Angela B. Ginorio, and Carol S. Hollenshead, et al. 1996. *The equity equation: Fostering the advancement of women in the sciences, mathematics, and engineering.* San Francisco, Calif.: Jossey-Bass.

Gleiter, Roberta Banaszak. 1999. The congressional commission on the advancement of women and minorities in science, engineering and technology development. *SWE, Magazine of the Society of Women Engineers* (Nov./Dec.): 26–32.

McIlwee, Judith S., and J. Gregg Robinson. 1992. *Women in engineering: Gender, power, and workplace culture.* Albany: State University of New York Press.

National Science Foundation (NSF). 1999. *Women, minorities, and persons with disabilities in science and engineering: 1998.* Arlington, Va.: NSF.

Perusek, Anne M., ed. 2000. Fifty years of shaping the future and highlights of SWE's early years. *SWE, Magazine of the Society of Women Engineers.* Jan./Feb.): 14, 18–34.

Michele LaBella

ENTREPRENEURSHIP

The number of women starting and owning their own businesses has grown dramatically over the last two decades of the twentieth century in the United States and in many countries around the world. According to the National Foundation for Women Business Owners, as of 1999 there were 9.1 million women-owned businesses in the United States, employing over 27.5 million people and generating $3.6 trillion in sales. Women-owned firms accounted for 38 percent of all firms in the United States. By the end of the 1990s, one in eight (13 percent) women-owned businesses in the United States was owned by a woman of color. These 1,067,000 minority-owned firms employed 1.7 million people and generated $184.2 billion in sales. According to the same source (NFWBO, 1999), internationally women-owned firms made up from one-fourth to one-third of the business population.

Characteristics of Women Entrepreneurs

Women take many paths to business ownership. The broad classification of women business owners includes women who found, inherit, or acquire a business and women who start businesses with spouses or business partners and are at the forefront or behind the scenes; it also includes women who build fast-growing firms as well as those whose businesses are part-time or slow-growing firms (Starr and Yudkin, 1996).

According to the NFWBO (1999), women are starting businesses faster than their male counterparts. In the United States and Canada, the number of women-owned firms has increased at about twice the national rate. Early research on women entrepreneurs suggested that significant differences existed between female and male entrepreneurs. The literature to date, however, has found that there are far more similarities between women and men entrepreneurs along psychological and demographic characteristics (Birley, 1989). Some of the differences reported by the NFWBO and others are that women-owned firms are smaller in size, younger,

and more likely to be found in the service and retail industries. The growth rate of firms in less traditional fields of business is increasing, however. In the United States and Canada, the fastest growing sectors for women-owned businesses are in construction, wholesale trade, and transportation.

The early socialization of many women contributes to their perceptions and approaches to business ownership. Brush (1992) hypothesized that women view their businesses as a cooperative network of relationships rather than as a distinct profit-generating entity. This network extends beyond the business into the entrepreneur's relationships with her family and the community. In cross-cultural research, women reported that their management styles emphasize open communication and participative decision making, and their business goals reflect a concern for the community in which the business resides (Gundry and Ben-Yoseph, 1998).

Entrepreneurial Motivations: Reasons for Business Start-Up

Across cultures, there are three primary influences that draw women into entrepreneurship: lack of career advancement, job inflexibility, and economic opportunity (Chaganti, 1986; Ben-Yoseph, Gundry, and Maslyk-Musial, 1994). Women also cite layoffs, the ability to make one's own decisions, and the need for more flexible working hours to accommodate family demands as reasons for starting their own businesses. Some American women also note the desire to be helpful to others as a major reason. They believe that the world can be different and that their businesses can provide a means to change things and make a difference for other women. Results from cross-cultural studies indicate that women from eastern and central European countries often go into business ownership as a means of escaping unemployment (Lisowska, 1998; Ben-Yoseph and Gundry, 1998) and Israeli women opt for business ownership as a way of achieving economic parity, occupational segregation and wage disparities between men and women being much greater in Israel than in the United States (Lerner, Brush and Hisrich, 1997).

Key Challenges for Entrepreneurship and Business Growth

For most entrepreneurs around the world, access to capital and information are significant barriers to growing their businesses. Information needs will vary, depending on the women's professional and educational background, their location, and the type of business they are interested in launching. In addition to information, all business owners need access to financial resources and training in negotiating financial matters. Some countries have encouraged the creation of women-owned businesses through various resources that provide both loans and training. Training programs and classes range from how to get started to general business skills to how to expand a business.

American women entrepreneurs tend to rely on previous job experiences and their formal education as preparation for starting their own businesses. In Israel and other countries women are underrepresented in areas of business and engineering and lack some of the skills and experiences that could help them with business start-ups and performance, even though Israeli women have equal access to all areas of education. Eastern and central European women business owners studied have strong technical training but little business background on which to rely. They use personal contacts and their own ingenuity and creativity to prepare for business ownership (Ben-Yoseph, Gundry, and Maslyk-Musial, 1994).

Women entrepreneurs in all countries face additional challenges related to their status in society. Whether they work outside the home or not, it is still assumed that women have the primary responsibility to care for their home and family. In most societies, although both men and women ascribe a high value to family life, women are responsible for and perform most of the child care and housekeeping. Care for aging parents is still primarily the responsibility of daughters rather than sons.

Conclusions

Although factors contributing to the unprecedented growth of female entrepreneurship around the world may vary, they can be broadly characterized as "push" and "pull" elements (Turner, 1993). Unemployment, underemployment, and unsatisfactory work conditions and prospects have "pushed" a growing number of women into their own businesses. Many factors have "pulled" women into entrepreneurship, including the desire to be one's own boss, find self-actualization, reap financial benefits, and achieve a more comfortable balance between family and work responsibilities (Turner, 1993).

There are more similarities than differences between women business owners globally. Similarities can be found in reasons and circumstances for business start-up, business goals, management styles, and in most but not all challenges faced. Some differences between the various groups of women can be found in their educational background, work experience, and business skills. The major reasons for these differences is that countries have different political and economic systems, which in turn have led to different education systems, workplaces, and skill levels. Some predict that these differences will lessen with time.

It is significant that although women have still not progressed very far toward equal opportunity in the corporate world, they have been notably successful outside it (Bridges, 1994). With relevant education, experience, and better credit conditions, more women around the world will be able to create and sustain successful business ventures. This sucess will not only impact the economies of the countries in which women own their businesses but also change the status of women in these societies. The twenty-first century will be the century of the entrepreneur in general and of the woman entrepreneur in particular.

See Also

ECONOMY: HISTORY OF WOMEN'S PARTICIPATION; MANAGEMENT; WORK: PATTERNS

References and Further Reading

Ben-Yoseph, Miriam, and Lisa Gundry. 1998. The future of work: Implications for women entrepreneurs in transition economies. *Kobieta I Biznes* 3–4: 59–64.

Ben-Yoseph, Miriam, Lisa Gundry, and Ewa Maslyk-Musial. 1994. Women entrepreneurs in the United States and Poland. *Kobieta I Biznes* 2–3: 26–29.

Birley, Sue. 1989. Female entrepreneurs: Are they really different? *Journal of Small Business Management* 27 (1: Summer): 32–37.

Bridges, W. 1994. *Job shift*. Reading, Mass.: Addison Wesley.

Brush, Candida. 1992. Research on women business owners: Past trends, a new perspective and future directions. *Entrepreneurship: Theory and Practice* 16(4): 5–30.

Chaganti, R. 1986. Management in women-owned enterprises. *Journal of Small Business Management* 24(4): 18–29.

Gundry, Lisa, and Miriam Ben-Yoseph. 1998. Women entrepreneurs in Romania, Poland, and the U.S.: Cultural and family influences on strategy and growth. *Family Business Review* (Spring): 61–75.

Lerner, M., C. Brush, and R. Hisrich. 1997. Israeli women entrepreneurs: An examination of factors affecting performance. *Journal of Business Venturing* 12(4): 315–339.

Lisowska, Ewa. 1998. Entrepreneurship as a response to female unemployment and discrimination against women in the workplace. *Kobieta I Biznes* 3–4: 54–58.

National Foundation for Women Business Owners. 1999. *Facts on women-owned businesses*. Silver Spring, Md.: NFWBO.

Starr, Jennifer, and Marcia Yudkin. 1996. *Women entrepreneurs: A review of current research.* Wellesley, Mass.: Center for Research on Women.

Turner, C. 1993. Women's business in Europe: EEC initiative. In S. Allen and C. Truman, eds., *Women in business: Perspectives on women entrepreneurs,* 133–147. London: Routledge.

Miriam Ben-Yoseph
Lisa Gundry

ENVIRONMENT: Overview

Earth is a small, finite space—a planet with an average radius of 6,374 kilometers at the equator. Seen in the light from a nearby star that we call Sun, planet Earth appears blue because 71 percent of its surface is covered by an interconnected mass of water and only limited parts of its crust stick up above the water. Life has existed on Earth for around 2,600 million years. Humans with about our stature and our type of intelligence have existed on Earth for only 50,000 or 60,000 years. Life on Earth, our home, is now under threat and needs protection.

Earth is a living system, a globally pulsing web of organisms around a sphere of inanimate material. Within this biosphere, the communities of plants and animals supply the raw materials for life, using sunlight as their energy source. The chemicals of life are continually recycled by photosynthesis, respiration, and nitrogen fixation. These natural cycles can be disrupted by changes in the radiation from the sun or by the pollution of air and water by human activities.

The finite space on Earth was by year 2000 shared by some 6.2 billion human beings, all part of the intricate web of life on Earth. The world population will continue to grow during the twenty-first century until it stabilizes, probably at about 11 billion people, around 2200 (predictions vary, however). The world economy is also set to grow. At the same time, many natural resources will become scarce—fresh air, fresh water in some regions, and fertile soil. The number of species on Earth is already declining at an alarming rate, resulting in a depletion of the biodiversity that sustains the present web of life. Many ecosystems will be degraded and may disappear. Food production may not keep pace with the growth of the global population. Starvation may continue to be the lot of many who live in poor regions. In some regions and local communities, clashes between ethnic groups over scarce resources may occur again and again.

Elsewhere, there will be pockets of affluence. The economic disparities may grow between as well as within countries. The rich will become richer and the poor may become poorer as the human environment changes.

The early history of human respect for nature and the resources it provided can be traced in cave drawings and artifacts found all over the world. Hunter-gatherers as well as agriculturists through the millennia had to develop rules and practices that would allow them to sustain their use of the natural resources surrounding them, just as many governments at present are striving to create safeguards for sustainable development.

Human civilization grew around the shared utilization of natural resources, perhaps first around the sharing of river water. The settlements around the Tigris and Euphrates rivers in west Asia from about 7,000 years ago well into the 13th century, in the valley of the Nile since 5,000 years ago, and in the Indus valley between 4,500 and 3,500 years ago were prospering, complex societies with a highly organized agriculture and active commerce. With the mining of metals and coal and eventually also the exploitation of oil and gas, a different relationship evolved between humans and nature, reinforced by industrialism. Moreover, nature became the recipient of wastes from human activities. Advances in engineering, chemistry, physics, and genetics have successively added new tools to the armamentarium that humans use to further their own gains. Progress has often been accompanied by environmental deterioration as well as by hazards for human health. To nature's ever-ongoing recycling of chemicals have been added polluting chemicals emitted to air and water and contaminating the land, without regard for national frontiers. Trade in goods that in production or use harm the environment reinforce the strains on ecological resilience locally, regionally, and globally. In arid regions in the tropics and in many densely populated areas. Land degradation proceeds, accelerated by growing population pressure and by large scale modern agricultural practices that rely on the use of artificial fertilizers and chemical pesticides for the monoculture of crops. Environmental degradation often adds to poverty. It may lead to violent conflicts over scarce resources or make people seek to migrate to live better elsewhere. The unstinting use of nonrenewable natural resources and irreversible environmental degradation are threats to sustainable, peaceful development.

Other threats are the persistent toxic and radioactive chemicals that accumulate in the environment. Processed through the food webs, their concentrations increase. Some of them accumulate in the body fat of fish and mammals.

It has been shown that chemicals—both polluting emissions and intentionally distributed pesticides and herbicides—travel with the winds over large distances. The accident at the Chernobyl nuclear plant in 1986 resulted in radioactive fallout not only in Europe but also on other continents. Air pollution in North America travels to Europe. Pesticide use in tropical regions results in high concentrations of these pesticides in fish in northern Canada. The introduction into commerce of new, industrially produced chemicals during the 20th century and the persistence, transport, and bioaccumulation of such chemicals has placed humans and animals, wherever they live on Earth, under chemical exposure of a kind that never before occurred in human history. Medical scientists now are only beginning to understand the links between chemical and radiation exposure at low doses and undesirable health effects such as cancer diseases and reproductive disturbances. For instance, knowledge regarding the relationship between exposure to chemicals before birth and the development of disease during childhood and later in life is still fragmentary, but some congenital malformations and certain other diseases may be caused by chemical or radiation exposure before or shortly after birth.

Some authorities think that environmental deterioration directly and indirectly harms women more than men. Biologically, women have more sensitive immune systems. Socially, women often are the primary caretakers of the children, the sick, and the aged in the family. To the well-known poverty of women relative to men are thus added health risks, heavier work load, greater responsibilities, and lessened ability to take advantage of opportunities.

Women's Writing

Women have played a significant role in raising environmental awareness and calling attention to environmental dangers. Many have done so without, in the beginning, being specialists in their area of concern. Although their critical reports often first were met with resistance and denial and the women were branded as irrational, emotional, and hysterical, their perseverance in trying to find the sources of threatening disease and disturbed environments has inspired tremendous changes in the attention to environmental problems

In 1962, Rachel Carson, a writer and marine biologist, published her book *Silent Spring*, calling attention to the dangers of DDT, other pesticides, and chemical pollution. She described how birds and other wildlife were dying, and she called for governmental action to protect both people and the human environment against toxic hazards. In spite of initial resistance to her book, she reached a broad international public with her appeal for improved protection of human health and the environment.

Following her, many women scientists and writers have contributed to shaping a deeper understanding of the causes and effects of environmental change and the need to protect life on Earth. Helen Caldicott (1978) and Rosalie Bertell (1985) called on the world community to improve the protection against the dangers of nuclear radiation from the use of nuclear energy for civil and military purposes. Vandana Shiva (1986) drew attention to women's ability to organize effective nonviolent opposition to the commercial exploitation of natural resources in developing countries. Malin Falkenmark and Sandra Postel (1999) have raised awareness about water scarcity worldwide. Lynn Margulis played a significant role in formulating the Gaia hypothesis about Earth as a living system. Carolyn Merchant drew attention to how human civilization's break with nature is linked to the rise of scientific thought in seventeeth century Europe. Kristin Shrader-Frechette (1993) wrote on environmental ethics. Feminist writers such as Mary Daly, Susan Griffin, and Andreé Collard analyzed the exploitation and destruction of nature as another facet of the dominance and violence exerted against women in patriarchal societies.

Environmental Politics

In 1972, the United Nations organized a conference on the human environment in Stockholm that became the starting point for national and international measures to protect the human environment.

In 1987, the World Commission on Environment and Development, chaired by Gro Harlem Brundtland—several times the prime minister of Norway—published the report, "Our Common Future." This so-called Brundtland Report identified some of the major issues that linked environment and development and provided a foundation for the United Nations Conference on Environment and Development (UNCED), held in Rio de Janeiro in 1992. At UNCED, more than 154 heads of state signed the Rio Declaration on Environment and Development, stating that they recognized the integral and interdependent nature of Earth, the home of humanity. They proclaimed, among other things, that human beings are entitled to a healthy and productive life in harmony with nature and that the developmental and environmental needs of present and future generations must be met equitably. Principle 20 in the Rio Declaration is a recognition of women's contributions to raising the awareness of environmental problems and demanding solutions: "Women have a vital role in environmental management and development. Their full participation is therefore essential to achieve sustainable development." In *Agenda 21: The United Nations Program of Action from UNCED*, the principles of the Rio Declaration were translated into more concrete recommendations. A special chapter was titled "Global action for women towards sustainable and equitable development." National governments were urged to increase the proportion of women decision makers, planners, technical advisers, managers, and extension workers in environmental and developmental fields and also to strengthen and empower women's organizations and groups in enhancing capacity building for sustainable development.

All over the world, women have been among the first to respond to threats to human health and the environment. In Europe and North America, women have been a majority of the participants in peace marches and environmental and antinuclear demonstrations and protests. In northern India, the Chipko movement against the deforestation of mountain tracts was started in the mid-1970s to prevent the destruction of forests by timber contractors. In Kenya, the Green Belt movement tackled two intertwined problems—poverty and environmental degradation. The movement, involving 50,000 women, has been instrumental in planting millions of trees and has established Green Belt Training Centers to create training and employment opportunities for people in agriculture. In Latin America, several women's movements and activities to protect the environment can be traced to women's advocacy of human rights and peace in the late 1970s. Development Alternatives with Women for a New Era (DAWN) is a nongovernmental organization working across the north-south divide to protect health, the environment, and human rights.

References and Further Reading

Bertell, Rosalie. 1985. *No immediate danger: Prognosis for a radioactive Earth*. London: Women's Free Press.

Caldicott, Helen. 1978. *Nuclear madness: What can you do?* Brookline, Mass: Autumn Press.

Carson, Rachel L. 1962. *Silent Spring*. Boston: Houghton Mifflin.

Collard, Andreé, and Joyce Contrucci. 1989. *Rape of the wild: Man's violence against animals and the Earth*. Bloomington: Indiana University Press.

Daly, Mary. 1978. *Gyn/Ecology: The metaethics of radical feminism*. Boston: Beacon.

Merchant, Carolyn. 1980. *The death of nature: Women, ecology and the scientific revolution*. San Francisco: Harper and Row.

Postel, Sandra. 1999. *Pillar of sand: Can the irrigation miracle last?* Washington, D.C.: Worldwatch.

Shiva, Vandana. 1986. *Staying alive: Women, ecology and survival in India*. London: Zed.

Shrader-Frechette, Kristen S. 1993. *Environmental ethics*. 2nd ed. Pacific Grove, Calif.: Boxwood.

Ingar Palmlund

ENVIRONMENT:
Australia and New Zealand

The nations of Australia and New Zealand are linked by geography as islands in the Southern Hemisphere. They also share a dominant cultural heritage—the legacy of British colonial settlement—and similar economic bases as resource-exporting countries. Nevertheless, they are distinct in terms of geological origins, size, climate, biota, and human history. One common factor is their resource-based economies: despite well-educated populations and the recent growth of high-technology industries, they still rely heavily on exporting products of the exploitive and extractive industries established by nineteenth-century settlers under the aegis of British colonial government. These industries include pastoralism, or raising herd animals, primarily sheep and cattle; agriculture, especially grain and fruit growing; logging for timber and other wood products; and mining. Both nations are characterized by the ambivalent public attitude toward environmental issues that is common where cultural identity has been forged by a rural pioneer history. Even when the environmental harm caused by overexploitation becomes obvious, many people are reluctant to criticize traditional lifeways.

All gender and age groups must live in the same places, so it is difficult to unpick factors specific to women from the environmental tapestry, especially in developed nations where women hold equality under law. The movement known as ecofeminism comprises ideological views of environmental degradation as the result of patriarchal worldviews and legal systems, as well as the views of "pagan" and "Gaean" mystics who consider women to have a special spiritual relationship with nature. Both strains are present in Australia and New Zealand, but they exist outside the mainstream of environmental activism.

Environmental factors have indeed shaped women's lives; this situation is most apparent among indigenous peoples who have not had the technology to reshape and control their surroundings as modern Western societies do. Humans first arrived in Australia between forty and sixty thousand years ago and continued to migrate there from the north during periods of low sea levels associated with glaciation. Their descendants are the present-day Aborigines. These early peoples lived by hunting, the responsibility of men, and by gathering plants, insects, shellfish, and other foods, tasks performed mostly by women; in coastal societies, the sexes collaborated in fishing. Archaeological evidence indicates that around five thousand years ago, aborigines began to use new technologies to exploit their environment: they invented new tool types, processed toxic cycad plants for food, made fish traps and weirs, engaged in small-scale irrigated farming, and perhaps hunted with the help of the dingo, a dog subspecies brought to the continent near that time.

Early Settlers and Their Environments

Australia is the driest continent in the world (excluding Antarctica), a fact that dictates its carrying capacity for many forms of life, including humans. Aboriginal resource use was regulated by mobility—most groups were semi-nomadic—by cultural flexibility, and by social controls. Aborigines perceive themselves as part of the natural ecosystem, not as an overlay on it, and their interventions in it as a form of curatorship. Women diggers deliberately left plant parts in the ground to renew the resource, and people burned patches of vegetation to encourage useful plants and animals. They limited their population growth by means of prolonged breastfeeding, induced abortion, and sometimes infanticide.

New Zealand, in sharp contrast, has a moist maritime climate with ample water, and humans arrived there very recently. The first settlers, now known as the Moriori, arrived from Polynesia sometime before 1000 C.E., perhaps around 800 C.E. The Maori, who displaced the first settlers and were dominant when Europeans arrived, settled the islands in successive migrations from Polynesia several centuries later. The Maori had an elaborate material culture based on wood and stone and lived in permanent settlements linked by land and sea trade routes. Though they had to adapt to a much cooler climate than they had known, the Maori lived well in their new home, fishing, gathering shellfish, and hunting birds. The moa species were easy prey to humans and were hunted into extinction before Europeans first visited New Zealand. Maori women gathered and processed many native plants, but few were useful as food. They also cultivated nonnative food plants, primarily kumara (a sweet potato), yams, and taro (the tubers of *Colocasia*, a plant in the arum family), using slash-and-burn techniques, but without metal tools they could not easily clear large tracts. Their only domestic animal was the dog. Exploitation of scarce resources was controlled to some extent by the imposition of temporary prohibitions (*rahui*).

Except for destroying some prey species, the Maori did little to alter the environment.

Impact of Colonization

The European invasion and transformation of Australia began in 1788, when Great Britain established the first of its colonies destined to receive "transported" convicts, criminals sent out from England and Ireland to work under military supervision; about one-seventh of them were women. In the 1830s, communities of free immigrants began to be established. The settlers quickly dispossessed the Aborigines and founded farms and livestock "stations" (ranches). Port cities grew rapidly, their harbors polluted by sewage and the by-products of meat and hide processing. Through most of the nineteenth century, the British government encouraged population expansion, pastoralism, and other activities with severe environmental impacts, often in marginally habitable lands where only reckless exploitation could ensure subsistence.

The immigrants, men and women alike, tended to view their new land as alien, ugly, and of little utilitarian value. To make the landscape more familiar, they introduced a multitude of European and tropical plants and animals without envisioning the effects on native species. In addition to economically useful sheep, goats, cattle, horses, swine, and dogs, they released rabbits and foxes as prey for hunters; trout, salmon, and European carp as food fish; and even British songbirds. Exotic weeds, often brought in as seed with fodder or in sheep's fleece, were spread by livestock and outcompeted the grazing-stressed native vegetation. The herds stripped and trampled the land—Australian vegetation had not evolved to withstand hooved animals. Rabbits almost completed the destruction before being checked by the introduction of the disease myxomatosis. Herding and agriculture utterly transformed the face of Australia. At least half of the forests have been cleared since 1788, and logging continues. Diverse native ecosystems have been replaced by monocultures. The overuse of fertilizer has resulted in salt buildup, damage to the structure of fragile topsoils, and eutrophication (algae blooms) in critical waterways.

The first shipload of officially sanctioned European settlers arrived in New Zealand in 1840, and ten years later there were 20,000 whites there. A lower level of conflict with the Maori and the discovery of gold drew the majority of them to the South Island, which remained dominant over the North until the twentieth century. When Europeans arrived, about 70 percent of New Zealand's land was covered by trees and other woody vegetation, but clearance for timber, grazing, and farming has left only 10 to 15 percent of the land with native plant communities, mostly at higher elevations. Wool has always been a major export, and the advent of refrigerated shipping in the 1880s made it possible to ship meat and dairy products overseas. This encouraged the growth of vast herds of sheep and some cattle and led to extreme degradation of the land surface through destruction of native plant cover, soil erosion, and the introduction of exotic weeds, such as gorse and hawkweed, which have turned large areas into useless monocultures.

As in Australia, introduced species have been the bane of New Zealand's environment. In addition to domestic grazing animals, settlers brought game to hunt. Populations of two species of deer, rabbits, and European hares exploded, and despite efforts to control them through introduced disease and hunting, they still cause much damage. (Deer, rounded up from the wild, were installed in fenced pastures and are now raised for meat, hides, and antlers.) Wanting a fur-bearing animal in their new country, settlers brought in the brush-tailed opossum from Australia and initiated another biological calamity as it preyed on both native birds and plants. Weasels and stoats were even released.

Environmental Activism

By the end of the nineteenth century, New Zealanders and, perhaps to a lesser extent, Australians were becoming aware of the need to protect their adopted homelands. Interest in natural history had never been lacking; for example, Lady Jane Franklin (1791–1875), the energetic wife of an early colonial governor, traveled widely in the bush and established a botanic garden outside Hobart. Early preserves, however, were set aside in both countries more for their scenic beauty than for their ecological significance. Today there are extensive park systems administered by national and regional agencies, as well as specialized preserves for endangered species. In New Zealand, native birds are especially vulnerable to introduced predators, and some threatened populations have been relocated to predator-free offshore islands in attempts to save them from extinction.

Australian feminists often characterize their country as more sexist than most English-speaking societies, but this charge does not seem to be leveled in New Zealand. Australia's early modern history as a convict settlement under military jurisdiction is sometimes blamed as the basis for this distinction. In fact, the leadership of national Australian environmental organizations has been largely male. Women are, however, prominent in the related professional societies, many of which draw members from both Australia and New Zealand. For example, Mary Lou Morris, past president of the Environment Institute of Australia, has been her coun-

try's delegate to a number of global environmental conferences and helped to produce the Australian National Heritage Charter.

The fast-growing, economically important international tourism industry, which depends largely on these countries' natural attractions, offers many opportunities for women. There is concern, however, that overdevelopment of rural communities and the overuse of wild lands by tourists may impose a new level of damage—an issue that New Zealand, small and popular, must quickly face.

Women's activism on behalf of the environment is most prominent in smaller efforts that address specific problems. Doyle and Kellow (1995: 111–114) set up two categories of Australian environmental organizations: introspective groups devote careful planning to their own form, structure, polity, and ideology; nonintrospective groups, by contrast, turn outward to face specific tasks and are largely nondoctrinal and loosely structured. Women found and run many organizations of the second type, a role said to derive from their socialization to "philanthropic" rather than "real political" activity. The authors observe, "There is much evidence that the more 'important' an association is perceived to be by the broader community, the more men will be in positions of power" (113). Small ad hoc groups have been formed throughout Australia and New Zealand since the 1970s to promote such causes as the preservation of green spaces and natural features, pollution control, and development limitation.

See Also

DEVELOPMENT: AUSTRALIA AND NEW ZEALAND; ECOFEMINISM; ENVIRONMENT: OVERVIEW; NATURAL RESOURCES; WATER

References and Further Reading

Archer, Michael, et al. 1998. *From plesiosaurs to people: 100 million years of environmental history*. State of the Environment Technical Paper Series. Canberra: Department of Environment, Commonwealth of Australia.

Doyle, Timothy, and Aynsley Kellow. 1995. *Environmental politics and policy making in Australia*. Melbourne: Macmillan.

Hughes, Robert. 1987. *The fatal shore: The epic of Australia's founding*. New York: Knopf.

Palmer, Geoffrey. 1995. *Environment: The international challenge*. Wellington, New Zealand: Victoria University Press.

Sinclair, Keith. 1980. *A history of New Zealand*. London: Allen Lane.

Jane McGary

ENVIRONMENT: Caribbean

A high proportion of women in the Caribbean live in female-headed households. This situation is especially true of poor Afro-Caribbean women for whom poverty and family responsibilities accentuate vulnerability to environmental degradation. It is this combination of women's socioeconomic vulnerability and the physical vulnerability of small islands to both long-term environmental degradation and short-term natural disasters that provided the critical regional focus of women's engagement with the environment (Jeffery, 1982).

The Natural Environment

Most of the territories of the Caribbean region are small, densely populated islands, dependent on the natural environment for their major economic activities of agriculture, tourism, fishing, lumbering, and mining. The plantation legacy of forest clearance in order to open up land for export monoculture and the intensive development thrusts since the late 1960s based on tourism and resource exploitation have visibly altered the region's fragile natural ecosystems. In Barbados sugar cultivation was introduced around 1640 and only small pockets of forest remained by 1655. Jamaica still has a deforestation rate of 3.3 percent a year, losing 1,315 square kilometers of trees between 1981 and 1990 (Girvan and Simmons, 1991: xiii). At emancipation many of the former slaves fled the plantations to clear steep, hilly land for subsistence cultivation. Such land-use changes contribute to soil erosion, to reduced rainfall (28 percent since the 1960s in Jamaica), and to increased temperatures (annual temperatures have increased 2.3 degrees Celsius since 1947 in Jamaica, for instance) while the burning of trees releases carbon into the atmosphere (Girvan and Simmons, 1991: xiii). Streams dry up, roads, houses, and crops slide downhill, and the soil washes out to sea, suffocating coral reefs and damaging fish stocks.

Natural hazards are an ever-present danger, and modernization increases the economic cost of such disasters. Hurricanes occur during the summer months, and global warming may be causing them to become more severe. Earthquakes and volcanic eruptions are always a threat and have destroyed two cities in the region in historic times (Port Royal, Jamaica, and St. Pierre, Martinique).

Thus, long-term environmental instability has characterized the history of the countries of the region, whose open economies make them particularly vulnerable. Caribbean nations commonly depend on transnational corporations for expansion of tourism and mining, and transnationals tend to give priority to increasing earnings rather than protecting the environment. The busy shipping lanes crisscrossing the Caribbean Sea contribute to marine pollution and pose the danger of oil spills. Proximity to the industrialized nations of North American and Europe has also made the Caribbean a target for the dumping of hazardous waste. In many cases Caribbean countries do not enforce existing environmental legislation or may not have the technological and economic capabilities to assess accurately the nature of such waste. In 1986 and 1987 the Bahamas, Bermuda, and the Dominican Republic refused to allow the dumping of toxic incinerator ash from the United States, but the ash was eventually accepted in Haiti, where it was dumped on a beach (Antrobus, 1992: 22–23).

Women's Perception of the Environment

Studies (Momsen, 1993; Antrobus, 1992) have shown that gender differences in perception of environmental problems in the Caribbean are mainly a function of occupation, role, and education. In general, women give highest priority to solving problems, such as garbage disposal, beach litter, and traffic pollution, that appear directly to endanger their children, while men worry more about declining fish stocks due to marine pollution and reef damage. When only farmers are considered there are few gender differences (Momsen, 1993). In Barbados, for example, men and women farmers are equally aware of the danger of soil erosion and of the measures that can be taken to prevent it. Agricultural chemicals are seen, especially by women, as being mainly a health hazard to pregnant and nursing mothers, and so the application of pesticides and fertilizers is the most gender specific of all agricultural tasks, being virtually always undertaken by men. In poorer Caribbean countries women as household managers are affected by shortages of fuelwood, poor housing, lack of sewage services, and polluted drinking water. Women generally tend to be less aware of the causes of environmental degradation than men, although this appears to be an age-related difference reflecting a historical situation in which women had less education than men. This situation is rapidly changing as young Caribbean women now tend to be better educated than their brothers.

Feminist Understanding of the Caribbean Environment

Peggy Antrobus, former director of the third world– based NGO Development Alternatives with Women in a New Era (DAWN), was the leading feminist representative from the region at the major international environmental conferences of the 1990s (Miami in 1991 and Rio de Janeiro in 1992). She sees women's key role as being based in the perspective they bring to environmental problems. Caribbean women tend to have a more holistic view than men but have been largely excluded from decision making. Their importance to environmental policy making stems from their economic and social roles, particularly the socializing of the young and the shaping of societal values and attitudes to the environment. "We must link the experiences of women, their daily struggles to survive, with the macro economic policies which impact on every aspect of our lives," say Antrobus (1992: 12). Thus she emphasizes a direct connection between the environment and the structural adjustment policies imposed on many Caribbean governments by the International Monetary Fund. These policies affected women by reducing employment possibilities, raising prices for basic consumption goods, and introducing charges for health and education services, thus forcing women to put more pressure on the fragile island environments for fuel, food, and traditional medicinal plants (Thomas, 1997). Despite such external shocks, women are taking the lead in conservation measures such as recycling solid waste (Thomas-Hope, 1998), maintaining agrobiodiversity in dooryard gardens, and reducing use of agricultural chemicals by growing organic fruit and vegetables, which can be sold at premium prices (Commonwealth Secretariat, 1996). Thus, the new millennium opens with a heightened awareness, especially among grassroots women's groups, of the need to protect the Caribbean environment.

See Also

DAWN MOVEMENT; DEVELOPMENT: CENTRAL AND SOUTH AMERICA AND THE CARIBBEAN; ECONOMY: GLOBAL RESTRUCTURING; ENVIRONMENTAL DISASTERS; HOUSEHOLDS AND FAMILIES: CARIBBEAN; POLLUTION

References and Further Reading

Antrobus, Peggy. 1992. Why the Earth summit will be meaningless for Mother Earth—and for the mothers of the Earth. *Woman Speak! A Caribbean Journal* 28: 12–14.

Commonwealth Secretariat. 1996. *Women and natural resource management: A manual for the Caribbean region*. London: Commonwealth Secretariat.

Girvan, Norman P., and David A. Simmons, eds. 1991. *Caribbean ecology and economics*. St. Michael, Barbados: Caribbean Conservation Association.

Grossman, Lawrence S. 1998. *The political ecology of bananas. Contract farming, peasants, and agrarian change in the Eastern Caribbean*. Chapel Hill and London: University of North Carolina Press.

Jeffery, Susan E. 1982. The creation of vulnerability to natural disaster: Case studies from the Dominican Republic. *Disasters* 6 (1): 38–43.

Momsen, Janet H. 1993. Gender and environmental perception in the eastern Caribbean. In Douglas G. Lockhart, David Drakakis-Smith, and John Schembri, eds., *The development process in small island states*, 57–70. London: Routledge.

Thomas, Toni. 1997. *Traditional medicinal plants of St. Croix, St. Thomas, and St. John. A selection of 68 plants*. St. Croix, U.S.V.I.: University of the Virgin Islands Cooperative Extension Service.

Thomas-Hope, Elizabeth, ed. 1998. *Solid waste management: Critical issues for developing countries*. Barbados, Jamaica, and Trinidad and Tobago: Canoe Press, University of the West Indies.

Janet Henshall Momsen

ENVIRONMENT:
Central and Eastern Europe

Central and eastern Europe's severe problems with environmental degradation, toxic waste, and water, air, and soil pollution are a legacy of Soviet-style industrial development, although both socialist and capitalist economies have been built on the logic of "scientific development" (what Vandana Shiva calls "maldevelopment") that encourages the exploitation of resources over environmental stability. However, the Soviet goal of more actively involving women in management of the economy, cultural development, and public life has meant that, historically, women have participated in greater numbers and with greater power in the workplace. To a greater extent than in the West, eastern and central European women are well-represented in engineering fields, and work extensively in the natural sciences and medical fields giving them greater access as professionals to scientific and technical knowledge about pollution dangers and public health concerns.

At the same time, much of eastern and central European women's environmental organizing has grounded political activity in women's roles as mothers and keepers of households. Many women environmentalists have organized in the form of "'motherist groups' to protect homes and families and the resources that sustain them" (Bellows, 1996: 252); (examples include the Ukranian Mama Eighty-Six, the Czech Prague Mothers, and the Slovak South Bohemian Mothers). In addition to those cases where motherist groups publicly confronted central authoritarian states to campaign against pollution and for women's rights, motherist women were also the first to stage immediate public protests in response to the Chernobyl nuclear power plant disaster in 1986, such as by taking to the streets with baby carriages in Bulgaria, because they felt more directly responsible for children's health and because men were in control of the institutions that caused the disaster.

Drawing on their roles both as workers in the medical, scientific, and technical fields and as mothers and predominant caretakers of children and the sick, central and eastern European women's environmental activism has included a combination of home-based local and employment-based expert knowledge. Experiencing the effects of pollution on problem pregnancies, deformed fetuses, and birth defects, for example, while at the same time having access through employment to scientific data on pollutants has enabled women to make critical connections between the exploitation of the environment and the exploitation of women and has fueled women's participation in the disclosure of information in the face of government censorship.

By the 1990s, environmental work was taking place in the context of the great structural upheavals facing post-Soviet economic, political, and social life. While continuing to have a public voice as mothers concerned for family welfare, central and eastern European women also faced a post-1989 decrease in political representation and employment (the unemployment rate for women increased 25 percent more than for men), erosion of rights to reproductive control due to a resurgence of Catholic political influence, and threats to local agricultural self-sufficiency due to incursions of Western goods. In the face of these challenges, women continued to struggle on behalf of the environmentalist movement, as well as feminist, peace, nationalist, and ethnic movements.

Environmental Issues

Central and eastern European countries faced the transition into a new economic system in the context of serious environmental degradation, the inglorious legacy of Soviet development policies that ignored environmental pollution for the sake of industrial potential. The policies of communist economic development included overproduction in the most energy-consuming and environmentally hazardous industrial branches of mining and metallurgy; the construction of large industrial combines located chiefly in the most industrialized areas; and the undervaluing of mineral resources, energy, and water, which led to wasting these resources in production processes and to generating excessive amounts of wastes. These policies were reflected in a failure to take the real production costs into account in the price of products.

As the only owner of all the production plants, the communist state was not interested in introducing rigorous laws that would enforce the construction of environmental-protection installations. Investment expenditures for that purpose were at the level of 0.2–0.3 percent of gross national product (GNP). Forty years of such policies led to a catastrophic situation in all environmental components.

High levels of air pollution, exceeding air-quality standards in many places, were caused by large amounts of dust and gases emitted from power and industrial plants across central and eastern Europe. Emission levels—in relation to GNP, energy production unit, or per capita consumption—were many times higher than those in western European and North American countries, as much as eight times higher in some cases. Dramatic levels of surface-water pollution left less than 10 percent of the total length of rivers clean enough for drinking purposes, while more than 30 percent of the total length of rivers could not be used even for industrial purposes. This situation was caused by insufficient wastewater treatment before discharge to the river or by discharge of the raw wastewater directly to the river, both from municipal and industrial sources. Insufficient solid-waste management policies resulted in 1.5 to 2.5 billion tons of industrial solid wastes being deposited in dumps in Poland alone.

The effects of air and water pollution can be observed in all biotic components of the environment. Air pollution in particular has caused large areas of forest damage and decay of many flora and fauna species. The significant toxification of soils, particularly by heavy metals, makes food production impossible in the vicinity of industrial plants. Environmental degradation is obviously not without effect upon human health. Especially in the areas most exposed to pollution, significantly higher levels of mortality from cancer and circulatory diseases and very high levels of infant mortality are reported. In Poland, the number of infant deaths for every thousand births is higher in regions with high environmental degradation than in the country as a whole, despite a strong standard of health care.

Beginning in the early 1980s, a drop in production in many industrial branches caused a considerable decrease in the pressure of industry on the environment. At the same time, environmental-protection methods and instruments began to be implemented into law and adopted by industrial management; environmental-impact assessment is one of the most important of these instruments.

The Rio Conference of 1992 marked a turning point in ecological policy for eastern and central Europe, as it did for other countries. Drawing on the Rio Declaration and the recommendations from Agenda 21, strategies of sustainable development on the national level have been established, and a broad movement toward environmental education of various groups of society has been started. New laws mandating the protection of resources, particularly nonrenewable ones, have been introduced, and environmental-impact assessment is now compulsory for most development and land-use plans. Progress on the development of environmental-protection laws and policies has also been encouraged by the application of eastern and central European countries to join the European Community (EC), which requires the adoption of EC laws.

Women and the Environment

Women as a social group are particularly touched by environmental degradation, including its affect upon the availability of uncontaminated food, because the health of the environment directly influences the ability to give birth to and raise healthy children. Recognizing this fact, the Rio Declaration acknowledges the participation of women in sustainable-development activities; recommends increasing the proportion of women involved in the decision making, planning, technical advising, and managing related to environmental-protection and development policies; and supports women's rights to access to family planning.

Eastern and central European women are engaged professionally in various research, management, education, and consulting fields connected with environmental studies. Research studies in environmental science are carried out in national and private institutes; approximately 80 percent of the staff of these institutes are women. Women are involved in environmental management on all levels of administration, from the ministry down to local self-government. On the regional and local levels, more than 90 percent of the management in environmental fields is conducted by women. Women working in analytical laboratories also monitor environmental quality and carry out industry inspections. Women run wastewater treatment plants and waterworks and are very active in introducing new methods of management. These methods consist of partnerships involving various actors participating in the development process, either as environmental resource users or as groups that are exposed to environmental pollution. Women also act as mediators to solve conflicts arising over environmental recommendations.

Decision making concerning various human activities in the economic development process is connected to an analysis of the environmental consequences of the decision. Environmental impact assessment (EIA), one of the most important tools of environmental policy, is now compulsory in most eastern and central European countries. About 50

percent of EIA experts are women, who are responsible for the high quality and reliability of the EIA documents they prepare.

Environmental education is one of the most important instruments for realizing sustainable development. Environmental education in the countries of eastern and central Europe has been generally well developed, so that the subject of sustainable development is being introduced relatively easily, particularly in elementary and secondary schools. The process of ecological education includes the participation of teachers in courses training them how to introduce the subject of sustainable development in the classroom. The matter of sustainable development is so complex and interdisciplinary that it cannot be contained within any one of the existing school subjects. Thus, additional material is being developed for use in institutional lessons and by tutors. Since about 90 percent of elementary and secondary teachers are women, their participation in sustainable-development education is significant. Women are also very active participants in various pro-ecological behavior and lifestyle competitions. There are a number of such events every year, and they stimulate new ways of thinking about how everyone can contribute to improving the quality of the surrounding environment.

Sustainable-development principles point to the necessity of everyone's participation in new pro-ecological ways of living. The cultures and traditions of the countries of eastern and central Europe give an important role to women in creating the lifestyle of their families. It is generally women who decide about forms of recreation and ways of spending leisure time, who make decisions about consumption and housekeeping. Women therefore have a potentially significant amount of economic power as the predominant clients of food shops and consumers of housekeeping products. From seemingly small decisions about laundry soaps, light bulbs, and weather stripping to demands for safe and ecologically produced food to scientifically sophisticated analyses of the environmental costs of industrial production, women in eastern and central Europe are making critical contributions to improving their human and nonhuman environment.

See Also

ENERGY; ENVIRONMENT: WESTERN EUROPE; POLLUTION; RADIATION

References and Further Reading

Bellows, Anne C. 1996. Where kitchen and laboratory meet: The "Tested food for Silesia" program. In Dianne Rocheleau, Barbara Thomas-Slayter, and Esther Wangari, eds., *Femi-*

nist political ecology: Global issues and local experiences, 251–270. New York: Routledge.

Drakulic, Slavenka. 1991. How we survived communism and even laughed. New York: HarperPerennial.

Einhorn, Barbara. 1992. Where have all the women gone? Women and the women's movement in east central Europe. Feminist Review 39: 16–36.

Funk, Nanette, and Magda Mueller, eds. 1993. Gender politics and postcommunism: Reflections from eastern Europe and the former Soviet Union. New York: Routledge.

Pakszys, E., and D. Mazurczak. 1994. From totalitarianism to democracy in Poland: Women's issues in the sociopolitical transition of 1989–1993. Journal of Women's History 5: 151–155.

Peterson, D. J. 1993. Troubled lands: The legacy of Soviet environmental destruction. Boulder, Col.: Westview.

Rueschemeyer, Marilyn, ed. 1994. Women in the politics of postcommunist eastern Europe. London: Sharpe.

Scanlan, James P., ed. 1992. Technology, culture, and development: The experience of the Soviet model. London: Sharpe.

Shiva, Vandana. 1989. Staying alive: Women, ecology, and development. London: Zed.

Women and Environment. 1992–1993. Newsletter. Ed. E. Charkiewicz and J. Bucher. Amsterdam: Milieukontakt.

Anna Starzewska-Sikorska

ENVIRONMENT:
Central and South America

In Latin America global economic trends have resulted in increasing economic and ecological scarcity. Policies favoring large, commercial enterprises and privatization of land result in deforestation in the countryside and unregulated growth in cities. At the same time, shrinking state budgets result in decreased services and subsidies. Women, who are traditionally responsible for the health and welfare of their households, are disproportionately affected by environmental problems related to these trends. In rural areas these problems include degradation of agricultural lands, loss of communal resources, and shortages of both food and firewood. These ecological losses are often accompanied by a decline in status as women are displaced from their roles of subsistence providers. In urban areas problems of pollution, water quality, and occupational health, which many consider insufficiently addressed by government agencies, become the responsibility of women. As more women are drawn into low-wage "female" jobs in the formal labor market, they are also often cast in more "feminized," less powerful roles.

Environmental Degradation

A great deal of attention has been paid to the problem of deforestation in Latin America. Tropical forests once stretched contiguously from Central to South America. In Central America these forests have virtually disappeared, now existing only in small isolated "islands." The Amazon is undergoing rapid deforestation and is estimated to have lost about 20 percent of its original expanse. Given that these forests are said to contain between 50 and 90 percent of the world's species and to produce most of the world's oxygen, it is imperative that destruction be halted.

Up to this point, solutions to environmental problems have tended to follow Western constructions of the problem. Natural areas are generally viewed as needing protection from people; overpopulation of the countryside is often cited as one of the main threats to the world's forests. However, in the populated rural areas of Latin America, natural areas may be contiguous with agricultural areas and provide necessary subsistence resources for local inhabitants. In the hundreds of parks and protected areas that dot Latin America, nearby inhabitants often refuse to accept that these areas should be off-limits. In fact, park projects, whether sponsored by international development agencies, environmental groups, or local nongovernmental organizations (NGOs), have been rightly criticized for placing an undue responsibility for deforestation on local inhabitants, whose agricultural practices and subsistence activities often contribute less to deforestation than the large-scale timber practices that were permitted before the park was established. Although many parks have been established or reorganized through the efforts of Latin American environmentalists and activists who understand these dynamics, that fact does not automatically translate into quick solutions for environmental degradation, nor does it change the fact that once parks are established, poor rural dwellers are often restricted from using them for subsistence practices such as gathering firewood, felling timber, or agriculture.

This human relationship to natural areas is the factor that distinguishes third-world environmental movements from western environmental movements. Mainstream environmentalism in the West is primarily concerned with the conservation of beautiful spaces for recreational use. In contrast, "wild" areas are the sites of daily life and work. Perhaps even more important, these areas are also the points in the third world of contention between powerful groups wishing to develop natural resources or acquire land and less powerful indigenous or peasant groups that depend on those resources for daily subsistence.

Because environmental degradation in the third world has a different impact on the urban and rural poor, indigenous groups, and, most of all, women belonging to these sectors, solutions to environmental problems are inseparable from social issues such as class and gender inequality and persistent poverty. The preservation of wilderness and interest in nature for its own sake are not important driving forces behind local environmental movements in Latin America. Furthermore, analyses that view women or tribal peoples as closer to nature than "modern" industrialized peoples do not have many adherents. In general, environmental movements in Latin America are economic first and environmental second.

Two related trends contribute to the increased economic and ecological vulnerability of women in Latin America. First, the globalization of markets tends to favor large-scale businesses (in both urban and agricultural settings) at the expense of small, family-run businesses, subsistence farmers, and rural workers who supplement low wages with farming. The intensification of business and agribusiness under globalization increases urban sprawl, pollution, and the depletion of farmland and accelerates deforestation and loss of flora and fauna important for subsistence diets. In simple terms, economic growth accelerates pollution and the depletion of natural resources. Meanwhile, the benefits of this growth do not accrue to those in the poorest sectors, who continue to work for low wages but in increasingly hazardous environments and with less access to natural resources. For example, in Mexico forestry laws passed in 1997 make it possible for efficient, large-scale U.S. forestry companies to operate in Mexico. These companies will displace relatively low-impact community forestry concerns, as well as initiate monocultural forestry plantations. In the countryside policies that favor free trade and large, efficient business concerns have made communal lands—important for gathering firewood, collecting plants, and hunting—more scarce.

In Latin America a second important factor in economic and ecological impoverishment is structural adjustment. Structural adjustment is an integral part of global integration, which demands free markets and relaxed state control over economies. In boom times Latin American countries borrowed heavily to facilitate rapid industrial expansion. These debts quickly became unmanageable. Global lending institutions such as the International Monetary Fund (IMF) and the World Bank renegotiated the debts but imposed "austerity" programs, which entail greatly reduced state spending and state control over the economy. As a result, social programs such as universal health care and subsidies that once provided a cushion for the poorest sectors disappeared. Structural adjustment places increased burdens on women, who now have greater obstacles to face in order to provide for the health and well-being of their households.

Effects of Environmental Degradation

Women are disproportionately affected by economic impoverishment and ecological degradation. In Mexico structural-adjustment policies meant the end of price subsidies for staple food crops. Between 1980 and 1987, daily wages for food production in the countryside fell by an average of 40 percent. Development projects transformed communal forests into timber plantations, accelerating deforestation in southeastern Mexico. For women this translates into more work both inside and outside the domestic sphere. Low prices for staple crops means that women work virtually without pay on their family plots, are forced to supplement their incomes by entering the low-wage labor force, and may have to travel farther to gather firewood or buy fuel. This increased workload does not translate into more resources, and so poor rural families have less access to nutrition and proper healthcare.

Another trend in rural areas that affects both women and the environment adversely is displacement and colonization. In southeast Mexico during the 1970s, hydroelectric development flooded the ancestral lands of thousands of indigenous peasants. They were resettled in a lowland tropical forest zone. These lands had been recently cleared to make way for colonists. Transformed from jungle into dusty hamlets of low agricultural quality, these new communities had no economic opportunities to offer the settlers. In Brazil colonization schemes, as well as logging, ranching, and oil and mineral exploration, have brought thousands of the urban poor into the Amazon. Displaced women leave behind social networks crucial for their survival. Their new environments may be too poor for subsistence agriculture or gardening. The women may lack access to clean water for drinking or rights over resources such as timber, fish, and game.

The expansion of agribusiness in rural areas has drawn many women into the minimum-wage labor force in the countryside. Aside from long hours at low pay, a major risk of these jobs is pesticide exposure. Pesticide exposure has been reported as a hazard in the Colombian flower export business and has been well documented in agricultural concerns in Mexico. Pesticide poisoning can cause a range of illnesses, including respiratory problems, damage to the reproductive systems of both men and women, nerve damage, and death.

Latin American women identify strongly with their roles as wife and mother, and in family labor settings, women's roles and labor are not necessarily seen as less important than men's roles and labor. In urban and industrial settings, however, dominant constructions of women's roles and labor actually denigrate the economic role of women, where women's low wages are justified because women work for "lipstick money." Meanwhile, women who have been drawn into low-wage industrial jobs face daily challenges to maintain their families, which they see as their primary role. This means obtaining clean water and health care and surviving in the contaminated air of Latin America's large cities. Separated from community and family networks, women also face the challenge of either accomplishing this task alone or creating new social networks in alienating urban environments.

Responses

As women have been increasingly drawn into jobs in the city, their participation in popular movements that challenge poor environmental conditions has also increased. However, Latin American women do not specifically organize as environmentalists, nor do they necessarily express their concerns in environmental terms. Rather, they organize around their roles as workers, as mothers and wives, as indigenous or peasant women, or as poor women.

In southern Mexico, organic coffee cooperatives allow peasants to market their coffee directly to high-niche markets in Europe and the United States. Participating families receive higher prices for their goods than they would through traditional marketing venues and are able to utilize family labor, which includes men and women. Small-scale organic coffee farms utilize existing plant or forest cover to shade the coffee plants and prevent both pesticide contamination and deforestation. At the same time, women are empowered through their central economic role.

Women from rubber-tapping families in the Brazilian Amazon have been active in protests against deforestation. Although women are not generally employed as rubber tappers, they are responsible for the household, the children, collecting water, caring for small farm animals like chickens and pigs, and sharing agricultural activities with male members of the household. In the 1980s rubber tappers organized within the Xapuri Rural Workers Union to protest government policies that accelerated deforestation

in the Amazon forest. These policies favored capital-intensive agriculture and cattle ranching. Ranchers claimed large tracts of forest in which rubber tappers worked and lived. The rubber tappers fled by the thousands to neighboring Bolivia, organized themselves, and began a series of *empates*, where they and their families peacefully gathered in forest clearings to confront the hired laborers of ranchers. By doing so, they hoped to declare common cause with the ranchers and to teach them the ill effects of clearing the forest. Women and children were important participants in these *empates*. It is vital to note that policies favoring cattle ranching over agriculture cause not only physical displacement but also women's displacement from traditional agricultural work roles.

As more women have been drawn into the formal labor force, they have also become more central to popular movements that protest working and living conditions. In Colombia women and men working in the flower export business have organized for unions and against pesticide contamination. Participants emphasize the effects of this contamination on them as women: they complain of reproductive problems such as miscarriages and premature births, as well as of the possible poisoning of young children through contaminated breast milk.

In many urban areas women have organized neighborhood associations to protest the lack of basic services in their locality or to gain access to land for housing. In 1979 in Monterrey, women organized within the National Council of the Urban Popular Movement (CONAMUP) to demand running water, sewage, health centers, schools, and land for housing. These issues are intimately related both to gender roles (of caring for the household and family) and to the environment in the urban center.

These examples show that environmental activism among women in Latin America is not the result of a natural relationship between the land, womanhood, and environmental awareness. In fact, urban women of all classes and middle-class women who are removed from a direct relationship to the land tend to show more concern and awareness about environmental conservation. This may be because they are more attuned to a western or cosmopolitan construction of what constitutes an environmental problem. Interestingly, women colonists surveyed in the Lacandon forest of Mexico and in the Brazilian Amazon have stated that they are principally concerned with household survival. In the Mexican case, for example, one woman explained that although she understood why it was important to conserve the forest, the reality remained that her family had to clear the forest in order to plant crops to produce the food they needed to eat. This sentiment was echoed in

Brazil, where pioneer women were unconcerned with deforestation but worried about how their needs would be met once the forest was depleted. Participation in environmental mobilizations, for both men and women, is related to questions of land rights, economic survival, and health concerns rather than environmental concerns.

Looking Ahead

Western biases concerning both wilderness and traditional gender roles have negatively influenced the way in which environmental-development projects have been implemented. Numerous studies of park and protected areas focus on controlling the activities of rural populations that depend on these "wilderness" areas for survival. Yet little attention is paid to the colonization schemes that brought them to the forest in the first place or to the development schemes that gutted most of the resources. In the same way, urban squatters, drawn to the city by labor markets, are blamed for the unregulated, polluted squatter settlements in which they are often forced to live. National policies that promote nontraditional activities such as cattle ranching at the expense of family subsistence agriculture (which engages both men and women) empower men over women. In sum, although women may not be inherently "environmental," the same processes and trends that disadvantage them also degrade the environment. The challenge in the new millennium is to begin to work for more "global" solutions that challenge both gender inequality and environmental destruction.

See Also

DEVELOPMENT: CENTRAL AND SOUTH AMERICA AND THE
CARRIBEAN; ENVIRONMENT: OVERVIEW; HOUSEHOLDS AND
FAMILIES: CENTRAL AND SOUTH AMERICA; NATURAL
RESOURCES

References and Further Reading

Arizpe, L., F. Paz, and M. Veláquez. 1996. *Culture and global change: Social perceptions of deforestation in the Lacandona rain forest in Mexico*. Ann Arbor: University of Michigan Press.

Bose, C., and E. Acosta-Belèn. 1995. *Women in the Latin American development process*. Philadelphia: Temple University Press.

Brandon, K., K. H. Redford, and S. E. Sanderson, eds. 1998. *Parks in peril: Politics and protected areas*. Washington, D.C.: Island.

Collinson, H., ed. 1996. *Green guerrillas: Environmental conflicts and initiatives in Latin America and the Caribbean*. London: Latin America Bureau.

Guha, R. 1989. Radical American environmentalism and wilderness preservation: A third world critique. *Environmental Ethics* 11 (Spring): 71–83.

Nash, J. 1994. Global integration and subsistence insecurity. *American Anthropologist* 96 (1): 7–30.

Painter, M., and W. H. Durham, eds. 1995. *The social causes of environmental destruction in Latin America*. Ann Arbor: University of Michigan Press.

Place, S. E. 1998. Society and nature: Recent trends in the study of Latin American environments. *Latin American Research Review* 33(2): 221–236.

Rocheleau, D., B. Thomas-Slayter, and E. Wangari. 1996. *Feminist political ecology: Global issues and local experiences*. New York: Routledge.

Stephen, L. 1992. Women in Mexico's popular movements: Survival strategies against ecological and economic impoverishment. *Latin American Perspectives* 19(1): 73–96.

Molly Doane

ENVIRONMENT:
Commonwealth of Independent States

In 1986, the worst nuclear accident in history occurred at Chernobyl in Ukraine, one of the "autonomous" republics of the then Soviet Union. It essentially exposed the Soviet state to far greater scrutiny than it had ever experienced, as the radiation fallout spread beyond its political and environmental jurisdiction. By 1991, with the collapse of the Soviet Union, it was clear that economic development had been achieved, not by the introduction of modern technology and a respect for the natural environment, but with outdated equipment, labor-intensive production methods, and environmentally dangerous economic planning. This situation was nowhere more evident than in such former republics of the Soviet Union as Ukraine and the central Asian states of Uzbekistan and Kazakhstan, which were rich in resources, subject to economic experimentation, and faced with the prospect of resolving some of the worst environmental problems in the world (Malik, 1994; Marples, 1991; Rumer, 1989). Economic planning took place centrally, with no input from the regions or populations concerned. There was hardly any input from women, who were significantly underrepresented politically at this level. Yet women were the most damaged—of the adult population—by the effects of environmental degradation: air pollution, radiation, pesticide poisoning and the like.

The emancipation of women was promoted as the crowning glory of Soviet communism, whereby gender equality was claimed to have been achieved by 1930, in law if not in practice, Yet Soviet-style women's liberation was based primarily on the assumption of economic independence through the full incorporation of women into the labor force and on pronatalist policies to ensure the successful combination of work and motherhood. The ambiguities of this policy were not lost on women themselves, who continued to be the primary caregivers in the family and, as such, were caught in a classic double bind. With the advent of glasnost and perestroika, the toll of these policies on women's health and their life choices came under scrutiny. Women began to speak out at All-Union Women's Conferences and within the terms and categories of the nascent environmental movements that emerged in the 1980s right across the former Soviet Union (Buckley, 1992; Lapidus, 1993; Marples, 1991).

The Fallout of Nuclear Power

The Soviet nuclear program, with respect to energy and weaponry, was pursued rigorously from the 1950s onward. The principal regions of implementation and experimentation were not in Russia proper but in the republics of Ukraine and Kazakhstan. The nuclear energy program was important to Soviet economic planning because of the lack or expense of alternative energy supplies needed for the expansion of industrial production. At the same time, the nuclear weapons program was part of the cold war offensive in the arms race against the West. Both programs were pursued with a reckless disregard for the men, women, and children whose health might be tinged by radiation leakage or fallout. These considerations were all the more important when the coincidence between economic and geographic regions militated against population mobility.

The explosion of the Chernobyl reactor in 1986 drew attention to the lack of safety in the nuclear power industry. International attention was drawn to the plight of the population of Kiev and surrounding districts and, subsequently, to the contamination of over 12 percent of the geographical area of Ukraine. Apart from the death of 32 people in the immediate aftermath of the explosion, the tens of thousands who have died since remain the subject of medical dispute. Reliable evidence suggests that the number and range of cancers suffered by men, women, and children rose dramatically, with over half of the children in the region suffering. Women were not only residents and subsistence farmers in the region but also—a fact not often cited—workers in the plant. The legacy of Chernobyl in an independent Ukraine lies in the short- and long-term damage to women's reproductive health. In the short term, there has been a rise in the number of children born with con-

genital deformities, but much greater is the number of stillbirths and miscarriages. A similar phenomenon among livestock on the collectives also was noted. The removal of the population to the outskirts of a 30-kilometer zone surrounding Chernobyl merely relocated the problem. The contamination of food in the short term—especially that of milk, beef, and vegetables produced locally—led to the import of clean food to the region. The high cost of this imported food resulted in the consolidation of illness among women, children, and the elderly, as they continued to engage in subsistence farming to meet family needs (Bertell, 1999; Marples, 1991).

In Kazakhstan, a similar profile of radiation poisoning occurred over a period of more than 40 years in the region of Semipalatinsk, where nuclear testing was secretly carried out. Over 470 nuclear bombs were exploded between 1949 and 1989, with approximately 150 explosions occurring above ground in the years preceding 1963. The population of the region, principally indigenous Muslim nomadic and farming communities, was neither protected from the nuclear blasts nor evacuated to a safer location. By the 1980s, the effects of nuclear testing were indisputable—over 1.2 million people had been exposed to radiation poisoning, and the steppes of Semipalatinsk were contaminated with radiation dust. The Kazak government's own statistics show that one in three children born in Semipalatinsk over the period 1949–1989 were born with some mental or physical defect. Deaths from various forms of cancer were seven times the national average, and over half of the adult population suffered from damaged immune systems (Martin, 1998). Women—who, in Muslim culture, derive status from their primary role in the physical welfare and spiritual education of children—were especially affected by radiation poisoning. Some women, on discovering that they were responsible for exacerbating the debilitating and fatal illnesses suffered by their children by passing on radionuclides through their breast milk, avenged themselves by resorting to the traditional form of suicide used by central Asian women—self-immolation (Cullen, 1994).

The long-term effects of the Soviet nuclear programs have still to be accounted for in the future generation of people in Ukraine and Kazakhstan. The reproductive health of women will be the principal indicator of the long-term repercussions of radiation poisoning (Bertell, 1999).

Women, Work, and the Environment

In successive economic plans implemented by the Soviet state, the intensive development of industry and agriculture culminated in deleterious effects on the natural environment and on the health of its citizens. Women have been most vulnerable in the process, as protective labor legislation for women—instituted in the 1920s—has, for the most part, been ignored in certain sectors of the economy. By the 1970s, the number of women in the labor market had reached almost 90 percent of the total female population (this figure was approximately 10 percent lower in the Muslim republics of central Asia). In industry, women formed a high proportion of the blue-collar workforce, irrespective of training or level of education, because of the lower wage scales offered by white-collar employment. Higher pay rates and bonuses for working in poor or dangerous conditions led to women working in jobs with high levels of air and noise pollution. Until the 1980s, when new legislation was introduced, the physically debilitating nature of the work in some sectors took its toll on women's health, forcing them to abandon such work for lower-paid employment elsewhere (Illic, 1996; Shapiro, 1992).

In central Asia, where a large proportion of higly polluting heavy industry was located, the ramifications of women's blue-collar employment was disclosed in the postindependence period, when the state of women's reproductive health was blamed on the predominance of female labor in jobs with the poorest working conditions. In Uzbekistan, for example, although women did not engage in underground work in the uranium mines, they still undertook the dangerous task of washing uranium with acid, in a closed environment with few safety regulations in operation. Women would be removed from this work area only during pregnancy, not during the period of lactation, thus puting nursing infants at risk. Attempts in the postindependence period to encourage women to abandon jobs that were deleterious to their health were strongly resisted, because of the lack of alternative highly paid employment, rising inflation, and the specter of rising female unemployment. The impact of new labor laws introduced in the 1980s was substantially reduced through continued subversion of protective labor legislation by a growing private sector (Corcoran-Nantes, 2000).

The impact of agricultural development—another area that has depended heavily on female employment—has been no less damaging. The Soviet Union was one of the largest producers of cotton fiber; in fact, the economy of central Asia revolved around it. The pursuit of ever-increasing production levels destroyed entire forests and permanently damaged the ecosystem of the region. This catastrophe occurred in two ways: first, the liberal use of carcinogenic defoliants and pesticides polluted the water table and radically reduced soil fertility; and second, grandiose Soviet irrigation schemes to service cotton production led to the gradual depletion of over 60 percent of the water in the Aral Sea (which was the fourth largest inland water mass in the world). Women were engaged in most of the backbreaking work of weeding and harvesting the crop. During crop spraying, children would be sent indoors, but women continued to work in the fields as planes flew overhead, discharging a toxic defoliant similar to Agent Orange. This practice continued until 1987, and its legacy includes high levels of anemia, hepatitis, and cancer in women. The devastation of the Aral Sea is considered one of the largest environmental catastrophes of its kind and affects the populations of both Uzbekistan and Kazakhstan. The desertification of the region has destroyed the once-thriving fishing industry and created sandstorms of salt and chemical fertilizers, which are carried for hundreds of kilometers. For the four million people living in the region, the consequences of air and water pollution have produced health problems that include high rates of infant and maternal mortality, respiratory diseases, and typhoid. The continued heavy dependence of the region on cotton production in the post-Soviet era has done little to stem the environmental degradation.

Fighting for Change

Until glasnost and perestroika, popular protest was virtually unknown in the Soviet Union. By the mid-1980s, the emergence of environmental movements in Russia and, particularly, in the autonomous republics channeled popular discontent with the social and economic policies of the regime. In Ukraine and central Asia, where the destruction of entire ecosystems had reached catastrophic proportions, the environmental question was linked to Soviet economic exploitation and questions of nationalism. Large numbers of women actively engaged in a critique of the Soviet state on two fronts: first, through involvement in the environmentalist movement and, second, through participation in both existing formal women's committees and informal independent women's organizations, which grew in number in this period.

In Ukraine and Kazakhstan, the environmental movements Green World and Nevada-Semipalatinsk Anti-Nuclear Movement were founded to oppose the Soviet nuclear program and environmental degradation. Women constituted a large proportion of the participants in both social movements, but there is at present insufficient empirical information available to reveal the nature of that participation. Political action and demonstrations by Green World served to halt the nuclear program in Ukraine and place ecological issues firmly on the parliamentary agenda in the postindependence period. In Kazakhstan, the formation of the Nevada-Semipalatinsk Anti-Nuclear Movement in the late 1980s constituted the first large-scale social movement in the republic with the aim of ending nuclear testing by both the Soviet Union and the United States. The movement gathered over one million signatures, organized mass demonstrations across the country, and was instrumental in stopping nuclear tests being carried out on Kazakh soil. This political opposition succeeded in both ending nuclear testing in 1989 and gaining compensation for the victims. No similar movement emerged in Uzbekistan until after independence, when Rainbow, a nongovernmental organization that actively sought the participation of women, was formed. It was able to attract international financial support for a train equipped with medical facilities, including consulting rooms and an operating room, to carry medical personnel and material support to the Aral region to alleviate the physical suffering and economic hardship of the local population (Corcoran-Nantes, 2000; Marples, 1991; Rashid, 1994).

Perestroika also offered women the opportunity to speak out on a wide range of issues affecting them, especially the persistence of gender inequality. In the postindependence period, women's organizations emerged from within the nascent political parties. In addition, independent women's organizations arose in support of specific issues or sectors of the female population, in both Ukraine and central Asia. These organizations also were actively involved in assisting women and children affected by environmental degradation. In Ukraine, the Women's Community of Rukh (the principal opposition party) was formed initially around ecological issues, especially to draw attention to the plight of the women and children of Chernobyl. In central Asia in the immediate postindependence period, the official Soviet Women's Committees had an established network throughout the republics, making them best equipped to set up local and national support systems for women. The emphasis here was on the destruction of women's reproductive health through the total disregard of protective labor legislation in the Soviet period. It is important to note that few, if any, of the independent women's organizations were established for the purpose of ameliorating the consequences of what has been termed "ecocide" on the women and children of the former Soviet republics. The political participation of women in these organizations frequently arose, however, out of the popular protests surrounding ecological and national issues. Nevertheless, they constituted an important political forum for debate and political action around many issues—women's health, gender segregation in the workplace, women's legal rights, and changing the social division of labor among others. In an era of post-Soviet economic restructuring and rad-

ically reduced female political representation, these organizations are extremely important defenders of women's interests in the inevitable trade-off between economic growth and environmental ethics.

See Also

CANCER; ENVIRONMENT: OVERVIEW; HEALTH CARE: COMMONWEALTH OF INDEPENDENT STATES; HOUSEHOLDS AND FAMILIES: COMMONWEALTH OF INDEPENDENT STATES; OCCUPATIONAL HEALTH AND SAFETY; POLITICS AND THE STATE: COMMONWEALTH OF INDEPENDENT STATES; POLLUTION; RADIATION

References and Further Reading

Bertell, R. 1999. Victims of the nuclear age. *Ecologist* 29: 7.

Buckley, M., ed. 1992. *Perestroika and Soviet women.* New York: Cambridge University Press.

Buckley, M., ed. 1997. *Post-Soviet women: From the Baltic to central Asia.* New York: Cambridge University Press.

Corcoran-Nantes, Y. 2000. *On a broken bridge: The women of central Asia in a post-Soviet era.* London: Zed.

Cullen, R. 1994. Central Asia and the West. In Michael Mandelbaum, ed., *Central Asia and the world.* New York: Council on Foreign Relations.

Illic, M. 1996. Women workers in the Soviet mining industry: A case study of labour protection. *Europe-Asia Studies* 48(8).

Lane, D. 1992. *Soviet society under perestroika.* London and New York: Routledge.

Lapidus, G. W. 1993. Gender and restructuring: The impact of perestroika and its aftermath on Soviet women. In Valentine Moghadam, ed., *Democratic reform and the position of women in transitional economies,* 137–161. Oxford: Clarendon.

Malik, H. 1994. *Central Asia: Its strategic importance and future prospects.* New York: St. Martin's.

Marples, R. 1991. *Ukraine under perestroika: Ecology, economics and workers revolt.* London: Macmillan.

Martin, R. 1998. Cold-war death trap. *Transitions* (Oct.).

Pavlychko, S. 1992. Between feminism and nationalism: New women's groups in the Ukraine. In Mary Buckley, ed., *Perestroika and Soviet women.* New York: Cambridge University Press.

Rashid, A. 1994. *The resurgence of central Asia: Islam or nationalism.* London: Zed.

Rumer, B. Z. 1989. *Soviet central Asia: "A tragic experiment."* London: Unwin Hyman.

Shapiro, J. 1992. The industrial labour force. In Mary Buckley, ed., *Perestroika and Soviet women,* 14–39. New York: Cambridge University Press.

Yvonne Corcoran-Nantes

ENVIRONMENT: East Asia (China)

Industrialization and urbanization in China are causing increasing environmental damage. Since the 1980s, China's economy has developed rapidly, mainly in the industrial sector; moreover, because the distribution of industry in past decades was often ill considered, the majority of large and medium-size state-owned enterprises are located in cities and suburbs, posing a threat to the urban environment. This threat has also spread from cities to rural areas: since 1979, township enterprises have flourished, producing large volumes of solid, liquid, and gaseous waste.

As a result of these trends, along with increases in its population, China faces a serious problem with regard to the overall environment, which could lead to a slowing or a suspension of the country's economic growth. Environmental protection must become a factor in future development, and the Chinese people have strong reasons to promote a change from their traditional model to sustainable development.

However, significant efforts have already been made to improve the situation. Since 1972, the Chinese government has paid considerable attention to environmental issues and has formulated policies and imposed regulations. In fact, the population has been complying with rules for minimization, recycling, and decontamination for many years. For instance, to minimize industrial waste, prevent pollution, and develop cleaner production processes, traditional "end of pipe" treatment has been changed to "whole process control." China's national environmental protection agency is the main body addressing environmental issues, but many academic institutions have also been playing an important role. As a result of such efforts, the nation's capability for preventing environmental pollution has been strengthened; industrial pollution has been controlled to at least a certain extent; comprehensive reclamation of urban areas has made some progress; environmental quality in some large and medium-size cities has been improved, as have the natural environment and the ecoenvironment; research and development on environmental science and monitoring techniques have produced some good results; environmental protection capacity has been increased; pollution treatment has been expanded; and realistic methods suitable for China in particular have been identified and described.

Public awareness of environmental problems remains somewhat weak, perhaps primarily because the majority of Chinese are rural, with low educational levels and poor knowledge of environmental protection. This predicament is especially true of township enterprises, remote areas, and some small cities, and it hinders public participation throughout China. In this regard, too, though, there have been improvements during the past twenty years or so. The Chinese government, local governments, and environmental protection agencies at all levels have popularized environmental protection and disseminated information about environmental laws.

These developments in China are important for the entire world, in part because the environment has become preeminently an international issue and in part because China itself, with one-quarter of the world's population, occupies a decisive position. China's efforts to protect and improve its own environment will affect sustainable development globally.

Chinese Women and the Environment

For centuries, Chinese women, especially in remote areas, have suffered directly and swiftly from a deteriorated environment. This sad state of affairs is to some extent a legacy of China's feudal culture, in which men have been regarded as superior to women.

At the end of the twentieth century, China had more than 500 million women, about 56 million of whom were working women. In recent years, as the economy developed, women's employment has increased significantly, especially in coastal areas. Women in China still face an irrational employment structure caused by unequal job opportunities and with implications for environmental effects on their health. In rural areas, women's health is endangered by heavy use of pesticides and fertilizers and by poor sanitary conditions. The concept of the "superiority of local economies," together with the skewed employment structure and a minimal degree of environmental protection, has meant that for jobs in many areas and many industrial plants, working conditions are poor. Insufficient safeguards during production processes have caused a deterioration in the quality of women's health, which turn has affected childbearing.

In the last half century, the status of Chinese women has risen step by step as a result of economic development and social progress. Many have been gradually liberated from housework, and both the number of educated women and the amount of women's employment have greatly increased. Also, the national challenge of dealing with environmental problems has become a substantial source of employment for women. More and more women are scientists, researchers, and managers, and many women now work in environmental organizations. Women from all disciplines have significant roles in such fields as environmental management, scientific research and development, ecological protection, environmental sanitation, and pollution control. Women are especially visible in education, medical services, environmental protection, and sanitation—more than half of all working women are employed in these occupations—and they have clearly contributed much to environmental protection in the last two decades.

Technical training of women in environmental protection has accelerated. Chinese women, especially well-educated women, are teaching a new generation not only by verbal instruction but also by personal example. In education, environmental protection, and sanitation—the areas in which female personnel are mainly employed—they have set up various programs to promote environmental education and to foster young people's sense of participation.

In the future, sustainable development in China should further improve the living and working conditions of Chinese women. More women from all fields of endeavor will have a hand in enhancing environmental protection; more women will be promoted to influential decision-making levels and positions. Chinese women have progressively become initiators and agents for improving the nation's environment; thus, they are becoming a strong force for environmental protection and management not only in China but in the world.

See Also

DEVELOPMENT: CHINA; ECOFEMINISM; ECOSYSTEM; ENVIRONMENT: OVERVIEW

References and Further Reading

China Agenda 21. 1994. *White paper on China's population, environment, and development in the twenty-first century,* 177–181.

Xie Zhenhua. 1999. Women: A vital new force in environmental protection. Speech at the First Conference on China's Women and Environment.

Liu Yaoqi. 1994. Analysis and preventive options on China's industrial pollution. *China's Environment Management* 3: 13–27.

Ma Jiang

ENVIRONMENT: EAST ASIA (JAPAN)

Historical Perspectives on the Environmental Movement in Japan

The evolution of the environmental movement in Japan from the end of World War II to the present can be considered in two stages. The first stage, from the 1950s through the 1970s, revolved around local pollution issues; the subsequent stage, beginning in the mid-1980s, has revolved around global environmental issues. Japanese women have been involved in both stages of environmental activism, as individuals and as members of women's movements.

The environmental movement in Japan was born of the pollution resulting from rapid industrialization after World War II. After the war Japan was preoccupied with economic reconstruction, and little attention was paid to the increasingly serious levels of air, water, and noise pollution until they began causing severe health problems. For example, the infamous Minamata disease, caused by the release of mercury in the bay around the city of Minamata in southern Japan, appeared in 1956. In 1961 the residents of Yokkaichi in central Japan suffered a severe outbreak of asthma, later labeled Yokkaichi asthma, caused by gaseous emissions from a nearby industrial complex. The media publicized these and other health hazards. People's awareness of pollution grew, and a nationwide environmental movement emerged. In 1967 the Basic Law for Environmental Pollution Control was enacted. In 1970 the famous "Pollution Diet," a special session of the national Diet (the legislature), adopted or revised 14 laws relating to environmental problems, and the national Environment Agency was established in the following years. In addition, the 1970 oil crisis prompted dramatic improvements in the energy efficiency of industries. Thus, by the late 1970s the combined forces of the antipollution movement and the oil crisis resulted in a major improvement of the environment in Japan.

The success in solving many of Japan's environmental problems led to a decline in Japanese interest in these problems in the early 1980s. By the late 1980s, however, thanks to the emergence of global issues such as ozone depletion and climate change, a second stage in the evolution of the environmental movement was under way. The years between 1989 and 1992 are often referred to in Japan as the "environmental boom." People became interested in "environmentally friendly" ways of life, and this attitude affected Japanese government policy. Examples of Japan's new international environmental activity include its Action Programme to Arrest Global Warming (announced in 1990) and its sponsorship of international conferences, such as the Eighth Conference of the Washington Convention on international trade in endangered species in Kyoto in 1992 and the Fifth Conference of the Ramsar Convention on wetlands in Kushiro in 1993. The prominence of global issues, however, did not weaken national and local activity. In 1993 the previously existing national pollution laws were overhauled, and a more comprehensive Basic Law of the Environment was passed. At the same time, local governments started to levy fees for garbage collection, initiate recycling programs, and even distribute brochures to raise people's environmental awareness.

A variety of reasons explain the emergence of the global-issue stage in the evolution of Japan's environmental movement. First, Japan had clearly become an economic superpower by the late 1980s, and this status entailed global responsibilities. Second, the Japanese people, having achieved a high standard of living, began to acknowledge values other than economic success. And third, Japan was responding to the general worldwide environmental conservation movement.

Women and the Environmental Movement

During the two stages of the Japanese environmental movement, women played important but different roles. In the "local pollution" stage it was women's role as housewife that was most influential. Since women stayed at home, they experienced firsthand the degradation of the local environment—foul air, contaminated water, and so forth. And it was they who bore the children with birth defects, as in the case of Minamata disease. Representative of women's activity was the "soap drive" in the Lake Biwa area of central Japan. Since the 1950s water quality in this, the largest and most fabled lake in Japan, had declined dramatically. Housewives in the area organized a drive to replace high-phosphorous soaps with a nonpolluting variety, and this initiative influenced the local government to adopt a comprehensive cleanup strategy.

In the "global issues" stage of the environmental movement, women's role as professionals has become most influential. Women are now researchers, administrators, leaders of nongovernmental organizations, and even policy makers. Four women were appointed director general of the Environment Agency from 1984 through 1994, when almost all the other cabinet members were men. About 10 percent of the researchers in the National Institute for Environmental Studies are women, a high figure compared with that of other national institutes. In their new role women have begun to exert a more direct influence on environmental policy in Japan, and this trend will surely continue and become stronger in the future.

Women's Studies and the Environmental Movement in Japan

Links between women's studies and the environmental movement in Japan are weak at best. Women's studies is as yet a new field, and the environmental movement has not developed a gender consciousness. However, the links are being made. Pressure from women (and from women's stud-

ies advocates) is being exerted on men to participate more actively in the home and also in the wider environment. The rapidly changing roles (including environmental attitudes and actions) of men and women are attracting media attention and scholarly research. Internationally, interest is growing in the relation of the role of women in developing countries to high fertility rate, poverty, and environmental degradation. In 1990, the Japanese International Cooperation Agency (JICA) established a research group in the field of study known as Women in Development (WID) to assist it in its efforts to aid developing countries. It can be expected that in Japan the links between women's studies and the environmental movement will be strengthened, as they already have been in North America and Europe.

See Also

DEVELOPMENT: JAPAN; ECOFEMINISM; ECOSYSTEM; ENVIRONMENT: OVERVIEW; POLLUTION

References and Further Reading

Organization for Economic Cooperation and Development. 1994. *Environmental performance review.* Paris: Organization for Economic Cooperation and Development.

Hashimoto, Michio. 1992. *Economic development and the environment: The Japanese experience.* Tokyo: Ministry of Foreign Affairs.

Maull, Hanns. 1992. Japan's global environmental policies. In *The International Policies of the Environment,* Oxford, U.K.: Clarendon: 354–372.

Komatsu, Makiko. 1993. *Watashi no "josei-gaku" kogi* (My lectures on "women's studies"). Kyoto: Mineruva Shobo. In Japanese.

Yasuko Kawashima

ENVIRONMENT: Middle East

Contemporary Middle Eastern women involved in creating feminist approaches to environmental issues do so in the context of fluctuating nationalist, fundamentalist, and gender politics generated by waves of militarization and demilitarization, and the environmental crises reveal militaries to be the single biggest polluters of the environment (see, for example, Seager, 1993). Military expenditures and militaristic values have great influence on foreign trade, agricultural assistance, and development policies (Enloe, 1993). Feminist organizations, such as the DAWN movement, are investigating the disastrous consequences for women and the environment of militarism's effects on national and international development policies.

Feminist movements in the disparate and culturally diverse countries of the Middle East have weathered the progress and setbacks engendered by military, nationalist, and fundamentalist conflicts. All too often, the more a society is obsessed with "national security," the less likely it is to be hospitable to feminist theorizing. However, conditions during times of militaristic and nationalist fervor sometimes also encourage active public participation by women. Thus, for example, Palestinian women began to run community institutions during the Intifada; Iraqi women took on many official positions during the Iran–Iraq war; and Kuwaiti women organized a movement for suffrage and Arab women activists pushed forward nationalist feminist agendas during the Persian Gulf war. On the other hand, movements for women's rights, peace, and environmentalism have also been sacrificed to the political agenda at exactly the times when their feminist perspectives have been needed most, as governments use ideological propaganda to recall women to their traditional duties in the home during periods of postwar reconstruction.

Nevertheless, as Cynthia Enloe notes, "Middle East women are not mere symbols. First, they are diverse, distinguished by ethnicity, ideology, class, and nationality. Second, since the turn of the century, many have been active participants in their countries' freedom movements" (Enloe, 1993: 168).

The Middle East and the Environment

The designation *Middle East* refers to the area lying between southwest Asia and northeast Africa. It includes Turkey, Syria, Lebanon, Israel, Jordan, Iraq, Iran, the Saudi Arabian peninsula, and Egypt. The Middle East, as a strategically important crossroads of land and sea, has been the focus of countless wars both within and between member countries as well as with reigning powers beyond it. During the twentieth century, the Middle East gained international importance as a vast reservoir of oil and the battleground for Arab–Israeli conflict.

The Middle East includes a rich range of climates and landscapes as well as cultures, societies, and faiths. The climatic zones range from temperate to subtropical to desert conditions, the latter covering the largest area. The population density is very low, yet the rate of population increase is among the highest in the world. The social and economic characteristics of most of the region's countries lead them to be designated as part of the third world.

Desertification is the main environmental threat to the region. The combination of dry climate, massive population growth, and laxity in the regulation of water, air, and ground pollutants has led to environmental degradation. The wars that have plagued the area increase the region's susceptibility to ecological problems. The Persian Gulf war led to the burning of Kuwait's oil fields, the pollution of Persian Gulf waters by crude oil, and the bombing of Iraq's chemical plants. Wars do not simply end when the bombing stops. War continues to destroy human well-being as well as natural resources and the environment.

The impact of environmental degradation is greater on women, who represent more than 60 percent of the agricultural labor force in North Africa and the Middle East but who typically have limited access to productive resources and services. Two effects are seen: impaired health for women and their children and an increased amount of energy and time needed to carry out basic tasks like securing food, water, and fuel for the family.

Women's intimate understanding of their ecology and their traditionally acquired knowledge of natural resource management might help reverse ongoing soil and vegetation degradation in arid lands. However, women face various obstacles in their daily lives, such as low status in their families created by traditional customs and practices, that hinder their ability to effectively combat desertification.

The Middle East is also marked by environmental problems characteristic of modern affluent lifestyles. As in the West, pollution and overexploitation of nonrenewable resources are side effects of advances in technology and of the ethos of modern consumerism. Damage to natural settings, landscapes, and archaeological sites has resulted from uncontrolled development for tourist, residential, and industrial purposes.

In the majority of countries in the Middle East, protecting nature is not a high priority on either the public or the political agenda. Problems of day-to-day existence and limited economic means push general environmental concerns to the background. At present, protecting people and keeping them healthy are higher priorities than environmental protection. Although there is a recognition that certain types of development can endanger future generations, the expression of this awareness in policy statements and especially in field actions is still below the levels seen for many years in several western countries.

Environmental problems cross political borders. Their effects are, for the most part, regional and even global and require collective intervention (Shmueli and Vraneski, 1995). The peace process in the Middle East has enabled many countries of the region to join together to combat some difficult environmental problems. For example, a joint program is underway among the agrarian countries of the Gulf of Aqaba, on the Red Sea, to protect the fragile ecosystem from destruction by oil spills.

Women in the Middle East

The status of women in the Middle East represents, in general terms, deep-rooted social norms that affect women's ability to engage public issues, such as environmental protection. Because of long-standing traditions and more recent political events, women do not generally take an active part in public and political life. In many parts of the Middle East, women have little to no voice, and those who have a public voice usually have the support of their husbands and families. Women's social roles, dictated by the need to safeguard multiple pregnancies and take care of their children, are considered less important than men's.

The majority of the region's population is Muslim. Many branches of Islam demand the separation of the sexes and limit women's rights and activities, although the degree of religious observance varies from country to country and between rural and urban areas. The Middle Eastern Christian population is also characterized by the separation of men and women in their roles. The traditional Jewish approach pays respect to women as rulers in the home but also treats them unequally elsewhere. However, Jewish tradition has limited influence in Israeli public society, and in areas such as education and employment the position of women in Israel matches that of women in the West, even though the percentage of women in senior positions in business and politics is minimal.

Women and the Environment

In the Middle East, little research and few publications have dealt directly with ecofeminism. A few studies have looked at the special needs of women and children and the different sensitivities of the sexes to environmentally related diseases. Recent feminist work on gendered aspects of environmental issues has begun to address such questions as, How are women in the Middle East affected by environmental problems, and how do women work to solve these problems? Do environmental problems affect women and men differently? Do women in different areas respond differently to environmental problems?

Because women and men have more clearly defined and separated roles in the Middle East than in most western countries, it is reasonable to assume that the effects of environmental problems on women and men differ more widely than in the West. For example, remaining in or near their homes causes women and their children to be exposed to more pollution and hazards in residential areas. This problem is especially severe in poor neighborhoods, which are often found closer to polluting industries, garbage dumps, and other toxic areas.

Like their counterparts in the West, Middle Eastern women have taken the initiative in focusing public anger on damage to the environment. One case involves a 1993 report from the Egyptian newspaper *El-aharam* about women in poor neighborhoods who organized a protest about the sulfur falling on their homes from nearby refinery chimneys. Their children lick the sweet-tasting sulfur dust, which then leads to brain damage. In Haifa, Israel, in the late 1980s, a group of influential women began to lead a fight for cleaner air in the city. As a result of their battle against the proposed construction of a new power station without antipollution devices, the Israeli standard for carbon dioxide emissions was made stricter. In 1999, the Israel-Palestinian Center for Research and Information (IPCRI) sponsored the Conference on Promoting Environmental Awareness with leading Israeli and Palestinian environmentalists and representatives of the media. A special meeting for women activists followed the main conference.

Feminist analyses of environmental issues have also been influential in creating new perspectives on economic development policies. Thinking about the gendered aspects of development issues has shifted over time from "WID" (woman in development), to "WDE" (women, development, and environment) to "WED" (women, the environment, and alternatives to development). The WDE perspective is based on the assumption that there are certain characteristics that differentiate women from men and make them better suited for dealing with environmental issues. These characteristics of women include a relational view of others, an embedded view of agency, an understanding of control through empowerment, and a willingness to solve problems through dialogue. On the basis of these assumptions, WDE literature argues that women have a special and close relationship with nature and that women are therefore the "natural" constituency for conservation projects and programs. The economic and environmental realities of the Middle East underscore the necessity for suiting regulations and standards to ecological, cultural, and political conditions.

In correspondence with the WDE perspective, the number of women researchers studying environmental quality is high compared with similar areas of research in the Middle East. Also, women's involvement at senior levels in public offices and nongovernmental organizations concerned with environmental control is very high compared with their involvement in other areas of public service in similar organizations. At the beginning of the twenty-first century, three quarters of the planners and managers in Israel's Ministry of

Environment were women, including its head, Dalya Itzik. There were also many women in senior positions in the Planning Authority of the Israel Ministry of Interior. The representation of women in comparable senior positions in other countries of the Middle East demonstrates a similar trend. In Palestinian universities the number of female students studying architecture and technical professions dealing with environmental quality is high. Finally, in the working groups of the bilateral and multilateral peace talks concerned with environmental issues, women are well represented in comparison with the makeup of other working groups. If the trend continues, the influence of women in environmental issues in the countries of the Middle East may lead to a brighter future with a more benevolent attitude toward nature, women, children, and men.

See Also

DAWN MOVEMENT; DEVELOPMENT: MIDDLE EAST AND THE ARAB REGION; ENVIRONMENT: OVERVIEW; HOUSEHOLDS AND FAMILIES: MIDDLE EAST AND NORTH AFRICA; POLLUTION

References and Further Reading

Anon. 1993. *The power to change: Women in the third world redefine their environment.* London: Zed.

Antoun, R. T. 1968. On the modesty of women in Arab Muslim villages: A study in the accommodation of traditions. *American Anthropologist* 70: 671–697.

Azmon, Y., and D. N. Izraeli, eds. 1993. Women in Israel. *Studies of Israeli Society.* Vol. VI. London: Transaction.

Borges, Sugiyama N., and N. D. Bellamy. 2000. A stronger voice. *Ford Foundation Report* 31: 1.

Braidotti, R., et al. 1994. *Women, the environment and sustainable development: Towards a theoretical synthesis.* London: Zed, in association with the UN International Research and Training Institute for the Advancement of Women.

DAWN, eds. 1991. *Alternatives.* Rio de Janeiro: Editora Rosa Dos Tempos.

Enloe, Cynthia. 1993. *The morning after: Sexual politics at the end of the cold war.* Berkeley: University of California Press.

Goodwin, J. 1994. *The price of honour: Muslim women lift the veil of silence on the Islamic world.* Boston: Little, Brown.

Harcourt, W. 1994. *Feminist perspectives on sustainable development.* London: Zed, in association with the Society of International Development.

Makiya, K. 1993. *Cruelty and silence: War, tyranny, uprising and the Arab world.* New York: Norton.

Marcoux, A. 1996. *Population change: Natural resources–environment linkages in the Arab States region.* New York: United Nations Food and Agriculture Organization (FAO); Population Programme Service (SDWP), Women and Population Division. <http://www.fao.org/>

Mies, M., and V. Shiva. 1993. *Ecofeminism.* Halifax, Nova Scotia: Fernwood.

Peres, Y., and R. Katz. 1981. Stability and centrality: The nuclear family in modern Israel. *Social Forces* 59: 687–704.

Radford Ruether, R., ed. 1996. *Women healing earth: Third world women on ecology, feminism and religion.* London: SCM.

Seager, Joni. 1993. *Earth follies: Coming to feminist terms with the global environmental crisis.* New York: Routledge.

Shmueli, D., and A. Vraneski. 1995. International environmental mediation: The premises and the promises of a new approach. In J. Bercovitch ed., *Resolving international conflicts: The theory and practice of international mediation,* 191–215. Boulder, Col.: Lynne Rienner.

Women's Environment and Development Organization. 1998. *Women transform the mainstream: 18 case studies of women activists challenging industry, demanding clean water and calling for gender equality in sustainable development.* New York: Women's Environment and Development Organization.

<http://planning.pna.net/gender/index.htm>
<http://www.fao.org/desertification>
<http://www.medforum.org/informacio/mongrafics/desertificacio/english.htm> July, 1999: MedForum NGO's declaration to combat desertification in the Mediterranean.

Ariella Vraneski

ENVIRONMENT: North Africa

During the last three decades of the twentieth century, many north African nations had a difficult time balancing the relationship between humans, water, and the earth. New technologies allowed societies to transform areas of the desert and, consequently, traditional nomadic lifestyles. Meanwhile, oil and natural gas revenues provided the means to pay for these conversions. The impact on women of these transformations was dramatic. Women formed the foundation of the agricultural and pastoral systems that were most affected. As the result of oil and gas exploration and industrialization, environmental damage accumulated throughout the region. For instance, the need for water in new centers of industry resulted in poor water usage and increased desertification. As this environmental damage mounted, women emerged as a major force in the environmental movement, as they often are those most affected by ecological problems.

Industry and the Environment

Following the nationalization of the steppe lands near the desert, which had belonged collectively to some tribes and were used for grazing bovine animals, lands were attributed privately to individuals for intensive agricultural production. The main impact of this transformation was that the smaller subsistence farms, usually maintained by women, often were combined by large agricultural firms or collectivized by communities in order to produce cash export crops. Meanwhile, industrialization became located largely on the fringes of the desert. This proccess further strained the environment, increasing use of scarce water resources. One environmental consequence of such industrialization was to increase desertification as minimal water supplies were drained for purposes of development.

Furthermore, the establishment of new industries created a dislocation of people. As men moved into the new centers of industry, women faced ever more pressure to maintain and run households. There also was a growing gender gap in income. More significantly, industrial waste pollution, largely responsible for current desertification, had major impacts on women's health and reproduction. The total sum of those processes was the displacement of the collective production system and of small rural and Bedouin producers—the majority of whom are women.

In the communities of north Africa, women constitute some 60 to 80 percent of the agricultural workers. They produce most of the subsistence crops, although males often form the bulk of workers on large agricultural businesses that produce crops for export. Women often remain "invisible," however, with regard to decision-making processes and in their importance to the community. Traditional gender roles were reinforced by the colonial experiences of the nations of the region and have contributed to unwillingness to incorporate women into the infrastructure to control environmental resources.

These trends are compounded by customary laws that grant land rights to men, even though women perform the larger part of the agricultural work. Women also are usually responsible for food storage and processing. Because they often do not own land, women have a difficult time translating their views on conservation and biodiversity into practice. Another result is that the very specific information acquired or passed down among women, which forms a rich body of agro- and biodiversity knowledge, is rarely applied or taken advantage of. Women's knowledge is compounded and expanded from generation to generation, forming an extensive body of information. For example, a male agricultural worker on a large farm producing crops for export and a woman producing subsistence crops know very different things. Women often have specific knowledge of species variety and the impact of environmental stresses such as pollution or increased water usage.

The Impact of International Factors

These changing environmental patterns have been the result of the "North"-"South" partnership-based developmental model, which stresses industrialization over sustainable agricultural production. The effect of this industrialization has been enormous, as scarce agricultural and forest land, large tracts of arid and semiarid land, and huge tracts of the Sahara in their southern territories have been subject to increased deforestation and desertification. Agricultural land in north Africa is disappearing at a rate of some 8 percent per year—even 20 percent per year in some areas, including the Nile River basin. In addition, topsoil is disappearing at a rate of 16 to 300 times faster than it can be replaced (World Resources Institute, 1999). The degradation is caused by a variety of factors: poor water usage, especially with regard to irrigation; increased use of chemical fertilizers, which deplete soil nutrients; and the use of chemical pesticides, which often kill beneficial microorganisms in the soil. This combination of practices has caused traditional cultures to become increasingly prone to cyclical drought. More than 700,000 square kilometers of north Africa's arable and pasture land—which includes more than one-third of rain-fed agricultural land and one-quarter of irrigated land in the region—is endangered by desertification. Algeria, Morocco, and Tunisia have an estimated population of 90 million. Some 50 percent of the population of these nations is affected by the process (Hunter, 1991–1992). This is a significant statistic, as the mixed agrarian nomadic-bedouin economy constitutes a major portion of these nations' gross national product (GNP). Some 45 million north Africans participate in this lifestyle (Hunter, 1991–1992).

Women often are primary producers in the mixed nomadic-bedouin economy. Desert goods and products such as rugs and carpets are mainly produced by women, both younger and older. These products are a mainstay of one of the main export industries and a major source of capital (behind energy production). Although women are employed in export-oriented industries, they also are practitioners of both informal and traditional subsistence agriculture. The new industries seriously degenerate the soil structure, however, and the emerging environmental pattern affects peasant and nomadic labor conditions. It also distorts rural and bedouin socioeconomic formations and prompts the exodus of labor and migration to urban areas.

Phosphate factories in southeastern Tunisia dump water wastes containing sulfuric and phosphoric acid, phosphor gypsum, and organic matter. Consequently, wastes contaminate water some 10 to 15 kilometers from the shore. The main sources of drinkable water in Tunisia are local tipping sites, which are increasingly affected by toxic industrial wastes, agricultural inputs, fertilizers and pesticides, and nonwatertight septic tanks. In Egypt, the Nile has become one of the most polluted rivers in the world as a result of shipping and industrial discharge. In Algeria, increased water consumption has led to soil erosion and water rationing. This water penury, in the form of daily cuts, led to riots and even thirst rebellions. In several nations, including Algeria, Morocco, and Tunisia, it is predicted that water demand will exceed all available means of supply by 2020. This problem will be especially acute in rural areas, where women will face additional pressures as both the caretakers in households and as the primary workers in agriculture.

Capital scarcity in the region has prompted nations to actively seek direct foreign investment and aid. For instance, in 1999, Morocco received approximately $1 billion in foreign aid. Most of this aid was provided by international institutions such as the World Bank and the International Monetary Fund (IMF). As a result, many conditions are imposed for the aid. This aid and the so-called developmental projects—and the conditions accompanying them as incentives for attracting investment—paradoxically involve nomadic and agricultural land in development programs and upset the fragile environmental balance. They also lead to more internal and external migration. In the last decade of the twentieth century, the resource flow from north African nations decreased, while their external debts dramatically increased. Significantly, the main improvements in the economies of the region in the late 1990s occurred in the mining and fuel production industries, while manufacturing and agriculture declined. As mining produces higher pollution and environmental damage, such problems will probably be perpetuated and exacerbated.

The high birthrate among the nations of the region presents a variety of problems for women and the environment.

The birthrate is the result of the combination of increased medical care and continuing restrictions on family planning. The result has been an explosion in the youth population. For instance, in Morocco, 38 percent of the population is under the age of 15, and 22 percent live under the poverty level. Two-thirds of the poor live in rural areas. The future needs of this generation will add further stresses to the already overburdened ecosystems.

Although external aid programs may exacerbate some of the economic conditions that have expanded pollution and environmental damage, they also have provided assistance for women. UN aid programs for the region focus on four specific goals. First, the programs aim to reduce the fertility rate and improve the health of mothers. Second, they endeavor to improve water management to maintain the environment. Third, the UN initiatives seek to expand the participation of women in the economic sphere. Fourth, and finally, the programs attempt to increase the educational opportunities for women, especially rural women (UN, 1996).

Empowerment and the Environment

The empowerment of women has become a major environmental concern for the nations in the region, because the impact of population is one of the main stresses on the ecosystems of the region. By controlling birthrates, women are able to break the cycle of poverty and increase their life choices, even though traditional culture continues to constrain women. With international aid, nations in the region have seen declines in birthrates tied to increases in contraceptive use and better family planning. Furthermore, the expansion of educational opportunities reinforces these trends. Education also has proven to be a means to forestall Islamic extremism, which contributes to traditional roles that tend to limit the choices and opportunities of women.

At the national level, women and women's environmental groups have faced difficulties in translating their concerns into political action, mainly as the result of underrepresentation in politics. For instance, in Algeria, only two cabinet members are women, and only 11 of the 380 members of parliament are women. In spite of the repressive nature of the Libyan regime, women have enjoyed more opportunities for education and employment in Libya than in most of the other nations of the region. The emphasis on the export of oil and natural gas, however, in order to gain foreign currency has relegated environmental concerns to the fringes of governmental policy.

Substantial international aid also is needed to improve pollution-control mechanisms. This aid is especially important with regard to water treatment. Collaboration between the government and international aid organizations in Morocco has led to the installation of modern sewage treatment plants to serve over 450,000 people—70 percent of whom live below the nation's poverty line. Such initiatives have a ripple affect, and in Morocco, a further 225,000 people have access to much cleaner water (USAID, 1996). In 1998 an initiative by the World Bank further expanded access to drinking water to 1.3 million Moroccans. These programs are significant for women—especially young women—as a main chore of these groups has traditionally been fetching or gathering water, often from wells at great distances. Studies show a rise in school attendance and participation since the installation of running water in villages, freeing women from this mundane task (World Bank, 1998). Similar UN programs began in Egypt and Tunisia in 1998, including one intended to reduce industrial pollution in Egypt. In fact, in 1998 the Second Sector Agricultural Loan to Tunisia mandated responsible use of water in agriculture as a condition of aid (World Bank, 1998).

In these nations, there often emerges a gender gap with regard to environmental concerns, with men often favoring increased development in order to foster economic growth—despite significant ecological damage—while women and women's groups generally seek out more balanced development initiatives and resist development programs that come with heavy environmental costs. At all levels, new, cleaner technologies are needed throughout the region to reduce pollution and improve efficiency, both for new industry and for existing ventures.

As the majority of Arab women's organizations are generally founded, fostered, and funded by the state or the ruling party, most north African women's delegates to regional and international meetings represent the state. At the local levels, however, women have emerged as leaders in the environmental movement, as ecological damage often hits them first and hardest. Furthermore, as the political processes begin to open in nations such as Tunisia and Morocco, women will become more visible at the polls and thereby translate their environmental concerns into political action.

See Also

DEVELOPMENT: MIDDLE EAST AND THE ARAB REGION; ECONOMY: GLOBAL RESTRUCTURING; EDUCATION: MIDDLE EAST AND NORTH AFRICA; ENVIRONMENT: OVERVIEW; HOUSEHOLDS AND FAMILIES: MIDDLE EAST AND NORTH AFRICA; WATER

References and Further Readings

Findlay, Allan, and Richard Lawless, eds. 1986. *North Africa: Contemporary politics and economic development*. London: Croom Helm.

Hunter, Brian, ed. 1992. *The statesman's year-book: 1991–1992*. London: Macmillan.

Maes, Maria, and Vandana Shiva. 1993. *Ecofeminism*. London: Zed.

United Nations. 1996. *Fiscal year 1996 report: Morocco*. Washington, D.C.: U.S. Government Printing Office.

USAID. 1996. *Report of the ninth session of the Conference of African planners, statisticians, and population and information specialists*. New York: United Nations.

World Bank. 1998. *Annual report*. Washington, D.C.: World Bank.

World Resources Institute. 1999. *World resources 1998–1999*. Washington, D.C.: World Resources Institute.

Khadiga M. Safwat

ENVIRONMENT: North America

The dominant environmental problems of pollution and depletion of natural resources in the United States and Canada reflect the ongoing processes of urbanization, industrialization, and primary-resource extraction that characterize these nations' development. Since the late nineteenth century, women's research, teaching, governmental involvement, and grassroots organizing have had a significant influence on environmental issues in North America. Among feminist activists are many innovative leaders in environmental science and environmental politics. However, although changes are occurring, the majority of governmental organizations and major environmental groups are male dominated. Current research interests in women's studies include feminist analyses of environmental problems and the environmental movement itself, as well as examinations of the relationship between women and nature (Seager, 1993).

Diverse Problems and Their Global Impact

The United States and Canada face a broad spectrum of environmental problems. Depletion of stock and renewable resources, such as forests, fisheries, soils, groundwater, and fossil fuels are major concerns. As pressure on resources has increased, so has (1) support for the preservation of wilderness and biodiversity and (2) conflicts over land use and treaty rights. Degradation of the environment has also become a widespread problem, affecting areas under the pressure of concentrated environmental demands of urban-industrial populations and less populated areas subject to impact from agriculture and transportation activities.

These environmental problems are local, regional, and global. Ecological processes and economic relations form linkages that join local cases of environmental degradation and depletion with changes in the global environment. Along the U.S.–Canadian border, acid rain, ocean fisheries, and environmental management of the Great Lakes require cooperation between the governments. The United States also faces transboundary problems on its border with Mexico. Many U.S.-owned manufacturing firms, known as *maquiladoras,* locate on the Mexican side of this border to take advantage of lower costs of production, including low-wage female labor. This pattern of industrial location has resulted in a concentration of hazardous materials and wastes and industrial pollution in an area with limited environmental-enforcement capabilities. Many scholars believe that the environmental consequences of affluence and patterns of development in western countries have also made these nations, particularly the United States, main contributors to global problems such as energy consumption, greenhouse warming, and ozone depletion. Furthermore, the purchasing power of U.S.-Canadian markets is a component of the economic forces driving environmental degradation in less affluent countries.

These environmental problems are addressed by a wide scope of organizations, which vary from local to international, governmental to nongovernmental, and institutional to grassroots. Despite a long history of involvement, however, women's presence in leadership positions is very uneven across the range of environmental organizations. In many cases, women have pioneered new approaches and developed new understandings that brought attention to serious, neglected environmental issues. Nevertheless, in the majority of instances, women continue to work in supporting positions within organizations.

Representation of Women

As more women have joined the workforce, many have entered into environment-related occupations. Government jobs in environmental fields have increased; new regulations have created new opportunities in the private sector; and larger environmental interest groups, the "eco-establishment," have increased their professional, research, and administrative support staffs. Environmental management was described in the mid-1990s as one of the hottest careers for working women (Anzelowitz, 1993). Some of these working women have become leaders through job advancement

in government agencies, industry management, and in larger, eco-establishment groups or through grassroots volunteerism. Women participate on all sides of the numerous debates over environmental issues. For instance, in the United States, Anne Gorsuch, former head of the Environmental Protection Agency (EPA), is infamous among environmentalists and others for overseeing the dismantling of the EPA under the guidance of the Reagan administration. Ultimately, although the membership of most of the large environmental organizations is estimated at between 60 and 80 percent women, their leadership, and some would suggest their priorities, through the 1980s continued to be predominantly male (Gottlieb, 1993; Seager, 1993).

At the end of the twentieth century, increasing numbers of grassroots environmental groups had become involved in local environmental politics (CCHW, 1993; Gottlieb, 1993). As of 1991, the Canadian Environmental Network included approximately 1,300 volunteer environmental groups (Lerner, 1993), and more than 8,000 such groups existed in the United States (CCHW, 1993). Many circumstances and concerns have prompted women's involvement with environmental issues. For some women, it was their responsibility as mothers concerned for the health and the futures of their families that first motivated their involvement in environmental politics at the local level. For others, it was their experiences as employees, dealing with issues of exposure to hazardous materials and reproductive health risks in the workplace; as resource users, with their livelihoods tied to the management and sustainability of environmental practices; or as residents, considering the impoverishment of the world through the loss of wild areas and wildlife habitat. Local grassroots involvement has been a path to leadership at local, regional, and national levels.

Within the United States, there have been several focal areas for these grassroots groups, foremost of which has been the environmental justice movement, centered on issues of environmental racism and of toxins in communities generally (CCHW, 1993; Gottlieb, 1993). Women's leadership is particularly strong at this local level. The grassroots movement to address environmental racism in the United States confronts the disproportionate levels of environmental risks faced by people and communities of color. The agenda complements that of other grassroots environmental justice groups that have sprung up in response to local environmental health issues such as Superfund sites, proposed siting of landfills and incinerators, and governmental and industrial waste-management practices.

Overall, women's contributions to the environmental movement and environmental science in North America far outweigh their representation. Several women, who are introduced below, stand out as having broken a path for others. The Citizen's Clearinghouse for Hazardous Waste's Hall of Fame and the directory *Who Is Who in Service to the Earth* (Keller, 1993) acknowledge many other women deserving of greater recognition for their contributions to environmental issues (CCHW, 1993; Keller, 1993; also see Breton, 1998).

During her academic and activist career from the 1870s to 1911, Ellen Swallow pioneered the field of ecology in her holistic approach to the study of interactions in the environment; she also led the way in applying science to health concerns in living and working environments. As the first woman instructor at the Massachusetts Institute of Technology (MIT), she developed the first interdisciplinary environmental engineering and science course (Hynes, 1985; Breton, 1998).

Beginning in the early 1900s, Alice Hamilton established herself as the "first great urban/industrial environmentalist" (Gottlieb, 1993: 47). As a medical doctor in Chicago, Hamilton observed industrial and urban health problems. She campaigned for improvements in urban sanitation and environmental quality. Based on these experiences, she also gave early warnings of the impacts of industrial hazards that anticipated the formation of the federal Occupational Safety and Health Administration (OSHA) by more than 40 years. The publication of her classic text, *Industrial Poisons in the United States* (1925), and her appointment as the first professor of industrial health (and the first woman professor) at Harvard University confirmed her as the leading spokesperson in this field through the rest of her career.

Rachel Carson was heard in *Silent Spring* (1962), a compelling call for attention to the ecological damage being caused by the widespread application of pesticides. Her words altered public consciousness and shifted the course of the environmental movement within the United States. Her book met with considerable criticism, some of it gender based, from many corners of the male-dominated industries and scientific disciplines. However, by the 1960s, a national network of women concerned about the environment, such as garden clubs and the League of Women Voters, lent their support to Carson's message (Norwood, 1993). The powerful groundswell of concern ultimately led to the formation of the first comprehensive environmental agency within the United States—the federal Environmental Protection Agency (EPA)—and to congressional action on a broad range of legislation addressing hazardous materials management and pollution of the environment in general (Hynes, 1985).

Ultimately changes in environmental management practices and legislation also followed the persistence of a "hysterical housewife," Lois Gibbs, in pressing government agencies to take seriously her knowledge of the neighborhood of Love Canal, New York, and the environmental health problems confronting her community. The Superfund Law dealing with the cleanup of abandoned hazardous waste sites was the first of several legislative responses to the hazardous waste issues raised by Gibbs and the Love Canal Homeowners Association. Gibbs went on to establish the Citizen's Clearinghouse for Hazardous Waste, an organization involved in the grassroots environmental justice movement.

There are many other examples of women leading efforts on concerns ranging from wildlife and wilderness preservation to sustainable economics and occupational health. During the early 1900s, Rosalie Edge founded the Emergency Conservation Committee to push for stronger preservation efforts by the Audubon Society. Hazel Henderson, environmentalist and futurist, has published several books decrying the ecological impacts of industrialization and calling for sustainable alternatives to simple economic measures of progress. She also served on the Council of Economic Priorities under former U.S. president Jimmy Carter. Colleen McCrory, a lifelong resident of British Columbia, found her actions for forest preservation led to a national level in leadership on the issue. Margherita Howe, a Canadian environmentalist, fought to modify the plans of a U.S. company to discharge industrial wastes into the shared waters of the Niagara River. Her efforts led the way to greater involvement by Canadians in the U.S. environmental management decisions that affect them. Many women, Alice Hamilton included, have fought for improvements in environmental quality and for the assurance of health (including reproductive health) and safety in the workplace.

Thus far, feminist scholars addressing the environment have tended to concentrate on the relationship between women and nature. Other branches of feminist research have begun to apply insights gained in the study of other aspects of society to the analysis of environmental issues and the environmental movement (Seager, 1993). At this point, the agendas of women researchers and activists do not overlap significantly, although changing research interests may bring them closer (Gottlieb, 1993).

Since the earliest warnings of loss and degradation, environmental issues have continued to increase in significance. Women have played active, often pioneering roles in identifying and addressing these issues. The numbers of women involved with environmental issues is continuing to increase. Importantly, the scope of feminist research on the environment has begun to expand beyond the questions of women and nature to examine the spectrum of gender relations involved in the human causes and consequences of environmental change.

See Also

DEVELOPMENT: NORTH AMERICA; ENVIRONMENT: OVERVIEW; INDUSTRIALIZATION

References and Further Reading

Anzelowitz, Lois. 1993. Twenty-five hottest careers for women. *Working Woman* (July): 41–51.

Breton, Mary J. 1998. *Women pioneers for the environment.* Boston: Northeastern University Press.

Carson, Rachel. 1962. *Silent spring.* Boston: Houghton Mifflin.

Citizen's Clearinghouse for Hazardous Waste (CCHW). 1993. *Ten yeazrs of triumph.* Falls Church, Va.: Citizens Clearinghouse for Hazardous Waste.

Doern, G. Bruce, and Thomas Conway. 1994. *The greening of Canada.* Toronto : University of Toronto Press.

Gottlieb, Robert. 1993. *Forcing the spring.* Washington, D.C.: Island Press.

Hamilton, Alice. 1925. *Industrial poisons in the United States.* New York: Macmillan.

Hynes, P. 1985. Ellen Swallow, Lois Gibbs, and Rachel Carson: Catalysts of the American environmental movement. *Women's Studies International Forum* 8 (4): 291–298.

Keller, Hans J., ed. 1993. *Who is who in service to the Earth.* Munich: K.G. Saur Verlag.

Lerner, Sally, ed. 1993. *Environmental stewardship: Studies in active earthkeeping.* Department of Geography Publication Series no. 39. Waterloo, Ont.: University of Waterloo.

Merchant, Carolyn 1996. *Earthcare: Women and environment.* New York: Routledge.

Norwood, Vera. 1993. *Made from this Earth.* Chapel Hill: University of North Carolina Press.

Seager, Joni. 1993. *Earth follies: Coming to feminist terms with the global environmental crisis.* New York: Routledge.

Kirstin Dow

ENVIRONMENT: Pacific Islands

The countries of the South Pacific region are a fragile chain of islands in the Pacific Ocean, spread over a geographical area larger than the United States. The landscape on the islands varies from that of small coral atolls surrounded by reefs and sea to larger islands with tropical rain forests, mountains, and rushing rivers.

The population of the islands is composed of indigenous peoples who are Micronesian, Polynesian, and Melanesian, as well as Chinese, Indian, and European immigrants. Each island has its own language, traditions, customs, and historical context. The differences between countries extend to economics and issues of development, resource management, land tenure, education, and health care. Except for New Caledonia, which is still under French control, all island countries have gained political independence. Economic growth is dependent on natural resources, such as forests, and agriculture. Tourism is an important economic factor for many countries, particularly Fiji, Cook Islands, Vanuatu, and Tahiti. A customary marine and land tenure system has remained on most islands, in some cases helping to protect reef and land resources in certain areas. But environmental degradation continues because of internal and external economic factors, along with pressures from international agencies, private industry, political corruption, and government inertia.

The regional variations between countries and within cultures and subcultures means that the relationship between women and the environment across the region is also subject to cultural differences, as well as educational, political, and economic differences. Women in rural areas are the most economically vulnerable and dependent upon natural resources for their survival. Therefore, environmental degradation can have a direct impact on their overall quality of life.

Environmental Background

The island states of the Pacific have always been vulnerable to outside exploitation of resources. The rates of coral reef and mangrove loss are among the highest in the world. Large multinational companies are overharvesting the once-abundant fish stocks and timber resources. The ten-year conflict on the Papua New Guinean island of Bougainville began as a struggle for a share of profits and ownership of resources from the Australian mining company BHP. In Polynesia and Micronesia, environmental concerns include nuclear testing, and "nuclear-free Pacific" campaigns are common.

The majority of the population of these island states live in rural areas and are involved in a subsistence lifestyle, relying on the natural resources of the sea, land, and forest for their food and shelter. Traditional fishing is accomplished by hand with lines and nets from the reef. Farther out to sea, fish are caught with nets and spears from dugout canoes and fiberglass boats. Gardens consist mostly of root crops such as tarot, cassava, and sweet potato and tropical fruits such as bananas, papaya, breadfruit, and sugarcane. Houses are made from local timber, pandanus, and palm leaves. This reliance on natural resources for subsistence living is critical to the health and well-being of the general population. It also makes the islands and their inhabitants particularly vulnerable to the complex issues of resource management and environmental degradation.

Throughout the 1990s a surge of nongovernmental organization (NGO) involvement in sustainable development and environmental awareness and education took place. An emphasis was placed on community-based, smaller development projects that could be environmentally and socially sustainable on a local basis. Small-scale logging, tree planting, beekeeping, and village or family-based eco-tourism and fishing projects were initiated.

Organizations such as World Wildlife Fund, the Nature Conservancy, Greenpeace, World Heritage, South Pacific Regional Environmental Program, and the Melanesian Environmental Foundation have offices and programs throughout the South Pacific region. In Papua New Guinea, Conservation Melanesia, a community-based organization, works to preserve the rain forests of the northern province by supporting integrated community action and development (ICAD) planning. These environmental organizations attempt to balance the threat of foreign-owned, multinational corporations and national companies involved in large-scale mineral extraction, logging, and fishing.

Environment and Women's Lives

Throughout the islands, women's value and participation in society generally is based on the traditional tasks of bearing and raising children. Until recently, most of the island cultures have maintained their rules and hierarchies through a chief or "big man" system, which has excluded and oppressed women. Many cultural taboos exist for women, hindering them from participating in decision making outside the family.

While excluded from political decision making, women still bear the major responsibility of feeding and nourishing their family. Gardening, in most cases, is the work and domain of women. For this reason, the impact of large-scale logging or mining operations in rural areas is intensely felt by the local women. When a forest is clear-cut, the topsoil for gardens is washed out to sea, and the land becomes dry, unprotected, and unsuitable for gardening. The silt from the

logged forests is washed into rivers and reef areas surrounding the logged area, becoming muddy and clogged. The coral and fish populations are subsequently affected. When the trees, land, and sea resources are degraded, the daily existence of women and their families who rely on these resources is directly threatened.

When the soil is eroded and gardens can no longer be planted, locally grown food becomes scarce, and the nutritional levels of babies and young children decline. Major nutritional problems result when food imported from the West replaces the more nutritious local crops. Expensive imported goods such as white rice, sugar, tinned fish, and meat cannot supply the nutritional benefits of green cabbage, tarot, and fresh fish.

Most Pacific Islanders living in rural areas rely on subsistence agriculture to feed their families, and they, particularly women, do not have access to cash to pay for imported goods. In some cases they sell produce at local markets for cash. But when the gardens and fish resources are destroyed, they must find other ways of obtaining money to buy foreign goods. In many cases valuable and nonrenewable mining or forestry resources are sold to the lowest bidder in order to procure sought-after hard cash. Thus the cycle of dependence continues.

The traditional position of women in Pacific Island countries and their lack of rights and involvement in decision making has hindered their involvement in environmental issues that affect them. The politicians, male leaders, and men in the communities negotiate with foreign companies and local businessmen for the rights to log, fish, or mine an area. Some women, however, dare to engage issues or influence decisions about how the resources that they rely upon for their livelihood will be managed—sometimes at great personal risk. Many women actively organize around environmental problems on local, regional, and international levels. Many environmental organizations in the region are working to include women in the discussion and planning stages of resource management. Gender awareness is now included as an integral part of various projects and programs, from international agencies to grassroots, community, and nongovernment organizations. As awareness of women's inequity spreads across all sectors of society in the region and shifts in behavior and attitudes toward women slowly change, women are taking on more active public roles to preserve and protect their resources and environment.

Pacific women are represented at the NGO, community, and national levels as government ministers and at the international level as policy advisers and lawyers. For example, Hilda Keri, Minister of Environment, the only woman

591

member of parliament in the Solomon Islands (as of this writing), has introduced controversial but significant changes to government policy on logging and mining practices and rights.

Since the 1995 women's global forum in Beijing, the Pacific Women's Resource Bureau has initiated regional and national meetings to assist women in the Pacific to implement strategies from the Pacific Platform for Action. Such groups, as well as those individual women who work and mobilize in their local communities, continue to carve out a place for women in the environmental and political agendas of the Pacific Islands.

See Also

DEVELOPMENT: OVERVIEW; ENVIRONMENT: OVERVIEW; HOUSEHOLDS AND FAMILIES: MELANESIA AND ABORIGINAL AUSTRALIA; HOUSEHOLDS AND FAMILIES: MICRONESIA AND POLYNESIA; NONGOVERNMENTAL ORGANIZATIONS (NGOS); POLITICS AND THE STATE: AUSTRALIA, NEW ZEALAND, AND THE PACIFIC ISLANDS; POLLUTION

References and Further Reading

Aston, James. 1999. Experiences of coastal management in the Pacific Islands. *Ocean and Coastal Management* 42(6–7, June): 483–501.

Braidotti, Rosi. 1994. *Women, the environment and sustainable development: Towards a theoretical synthesis.* London: Zed.

Epstein, J. 1987. Indigenous attempts to protect the environment: A Pacific Island case study (Palau). *Journal of Environmental Systems* 1(17): 131–148.

International perspectives on environment, development, and health: Toward a sustainable world. 1997. A collaborative initiative of WHO, UNDP, and the Rockefeller Foundation. New York: Springer.

Pacific Concerns Resource Centre (PCRC). 1991. The new world order...What does it mean for the Pacific? *Pacific News Bulletin.* Sydney: PCRC.

Rodda, Annabel. 1991. *Women and the environment.* London: Zed.

Stromquist, Nelly, P., ed. 1998. *Women in the third world: An encyclopedia of contemporary issues.* New York: Garland.

Thistlewaite, Robert, and Gregory Votaw. 1992. *Environmental Development: A Pacific Island perspective.* Prepared by SPREP (South Pacific Regional Environmental Program), ADB Manila, Philippines.

Tongamoa, Taiamoni. 1988. *Pacific women: Roles and status of women in Pacific societies.* Suva, Fiji: Institute of Pacific Studies, University of the South Pacific.

Zohl De Ishtar. 1994. *Daughters of the Pacific.* Melbourne, Australia: Spinifex.

Zann, Leon, P. 1999. A new (old) approach to inshore resources management in Samoa. *Ocean and Coastal Management* 42(6–7): 569–590.

Pamela Harris

ENVIRONMENT: South Asia

Women in south Asia are disproportionately affected by environmental degradation as a result of existing gender inequalities. Rural women are most affected by environmental problems, and deforestation in particular often increases women's workloads and further curtails their access to independent income. However, south Asian women have not passively accepted assaults on the environment. Many major environmental movements have been initiated and largely constituted by women, and some of the most outspoken campaigners against large environmentally destructive projects, such as dams, have been women.

Environmental Degradation

Two distinct but interactive macroprocesses are severely affecting south Asia's environment: the depletion of its natural resource base and the increasing appropriation of natural resources by a few. Depletion is manifest in disappearing forests, deteriorating soil conditions, and declining water resources. In India, only one-fifth of the geographic area is forested; three-fifths of the land is suffering from environmental problems, especially water and wind erosion. Groundwater levels are falling and chemical runoffs are polluting many natural water sources, making them unfit for aquatic and human use. The rest of south Asia is similarly affected.

Along with their depletion, natural resources that were once communal have been increasingly appropriated by the state (statization) and by a minority of individuals (privatization). The British colonial state (mid-eighteenth to mid-twentieth century) established monopoly control over forests, reserved large tracts for timber extraction, severely restricted the customary rights of local populations to these resources, and encouraged commercially profitable species at the cost of locally used ones. There was also large-scale timber felling for railways, ships, tea and coffee plantations, crop cultivation, and so on (Guha, 1989). After India gained independence, state monopoly over forests persisted while local people's rights in nontimber forest produce were further curtailed.

The process of privatization has paralleled that of statization, especially of village common lands. By custom, all villages, irrespective of gender and class, have some rights of collection in the village commons. Poor households have depended on these lands for many basic items, including firewood, fodder, medicinal herbs, building materials, and wild fruits and vegetables. Until recently, in many regions of India, village commons supplied almost 90 percent of firewood and 70 percent of the grazing needs of the poor (Jodha, 1986).

In the last decades of the twentieth century, however, village common lands declined dramatically, falling by 40 to 60 percent in parts of India, partly from illegal encroachments but mostly from government distribution of land to individuals under land reform and antipoverty programs. Although the land is ostensibly distributed to benefit the poor, in fact most of the land (in some areas as much as 80 percent) has gone to the better-off (Jodha, 1986). Hence, the poor have lost collectively while gaining very little individually.

The processes of statization and privatization have not only sharpened inequalities of access to natural resources; they have also contributed to depletion of these resources by undermining traditional arrangements of communal resource use and management (including water sharing, grazing, and firewood gathering) that were typically environmentally friendly. Even in the 1990s, 75 percent of firewood for rural domestic use in northern India was gathered as twigs and fallen branches, a process that does not destroy the forest. Some religious and folk beliefs help to conserve nature, as the sacred groves still found in parts of south Asia witness.

Where community management existed, responsibility for resource management was linked to resource use. Government takeover of forests and the privatization of the commons have effectively broken this link and eroded the social base of these protective systems.

In addition, modern agricultural technology has had serious environmental costs. The technology of the green revolution, in particular, with its high dependence on chemical inputs and an assured water supply, has over time led to falling water tables following the indiscriminate sinking of tube wells, waterlogged and saline soils from large immigration schemes, declining soil fertility from excessive fertilizer use, water pollution from pesticides, the loss of genetic variety from monocultural cultivation, and the marginalization of indigenous knowledge systems.

Population growth has impinged on these processes more as an exacerbation than as a primary cause of degradation. Commercial exploitation and the appropriation of forests and village commons by a few push the vast majority of people to subsist on depleting resources and thus hasten their depletion.

Finally, the energy-intensive consumption patterns of the local elites, along with export policies that cater to Western tastes, contribute to the nature and pace of environmental degradation.

Effects of Environmental Degradation

Environmental degradation has affected landless and land-poor households most adversely, especially in environmentally high-risk areas such as hills and semiarid plains. Within poor households, these effects are borne disproportionately by women and female children. These gender-specific effects arise from preexisting inequalities: an unequal gender division of labor; gender inequalities in the distribution of household resources; women's unequal access to productive resources, such as arable land, and fewer employment opportunities for women; unequal access to modern, technological knowledge systems; and unequal access to decision-making authority.

The interaction of natural-resource depletion with preexisting gender inequalities leads to six significant effects. First, because women and female children collect most of the firewood and fodder in poor rural households, they are required to expend more time and energy when forests and village commons decline. In many areas of south Asia there has been a severalfold increase in the distances traveled and time taken for these tasks. Poor peasant women's daily work routine can total 12 to 15 hours, typically many hours more than those worked by men.

Second, the decline in forests and village commons has reduced women's incomes from gathered items and adversely affected cattle-dependent livelihoods. The extra hours needed for gathering have also cut into crop production time, thus reducing crop incomes, especially in hill communities where, with high male outmigration, women are often the primary cultivators.

Third, as the area and productivity of village commons and forests fall, so does the contribution of gathered food in the diets of poor households. In addition, fuelwood shortages can have adverse nutritional effects as people economize by shifting to less nutritious foods that need less fuel to cook or by eating cold leftovers or missing meals altogether. While these nutritional consequences impinge on the whole household, women and girls in northern south

593

ENVIRONMENT: SOUTH ASIA

Asia bear an additional burden, given the gender bias in family food distribution.

Fourth, because of the tasks poor rural women perform (fetching water, washing clothes in streams, transplanting rice), they are most directly exposed to water-borne diseases and to the pollution of rivers and ponds caused by fertilizer and pesticide runoff. The burden of ill health associated with such pollution likewise falls largely on women.

Fifth, population displacements arising from the submersion of villages by large dams and from large-scale deforestation disrupts the social support networks with kin and other villages, built up especially by women. These informal social security networks provide labor exchange as well as small loans of food and cash to tide poor families over in periods of shortage. Once disrupted, they can seldom be re-created.

Sixth, gathering food and medicinal items from forests and village commons demands an elaborate knowledge of plant species, which women who are gatherers gain through much experience. The disappearance of forests and village commons is destroying the material basis of this knowledge. Also, in many regions, peasant women have been responsible for indigenous seed selection and preservation. With the large-scale shift to hybrid seed varieties, this control has passed to laboratories. While traditional knowledge is being devalued, the women who possess and depend on this knowledge have little access to the institutions that generate what is seen as scientific knowledge and modern technology. In this sense, what we see today is not just a crisis in sustenance for the poor and for women, it is also the loss of knowledge critical for generating sustainable livelihoods.

Regional Variations

As noted, the amount by which women suffer increased burdens is a product of gender vulnerability, environmental risk, and poverty incidence in a region. Gender vulnerability is especially high in northern India, Pakistan and Bangladesh—regions characterized by high female-adverse sex ratios, low female literacy, a strong ideology of female seclusion, and women's limited effective access to property, especially arable land. In Sri Lanka and south India, in contrast, women rate better on all these indicators (Kerala, in southern India, has a female-male ratio of 104:100, similar to Europe). Environmental vulnerability, as measured by rainfall levels and forest cover, is much greater in northwest south Asia than in the northeastern belt. Regional variations in poverty are also striking: regions with the lowest poverty incidence are located largely in northwestern India, and

those with the highest incidence are mostly in eastern India and, more generally, in eastern south Asia.

Typically the three factors—gender, environment and poverty—do not coincide regionally. Taking them together, women are found to be least badly off in parts of southern south Asia, and worst off in parts of eastern south Asia. Notably, the most agriculturally prosperous regions in northwestern south Asia are also among the most gender biased, underling a highly gender-unequal distribution of benefits from economic prosperity.

Responses

The negative effects of gender inequality and environmental degradation have not gone unchallenged by those affected. Over the last two decades both women's groups and environmental groups have emerged, the former protesting the gender bias in existing patterns of development, the latter their high environmental costs. In some cases gender and environmental challenges have overlapped. Certainly women have been significant actors in major environmental movements.

One of the best known examples of this is the Chipko, or tree-hugging, movement in the Himalayas, which was sparked off in 1973, when villages saved their local forest from being axed by a sports goods manufacturer by clinging to the trees. It is notable that Chipko women have protested against the commercial exploitation of the Himalayan forests not only jointly with village men but on occasion even in opposition to them, on account of different priorities of resource use. In their choice of trees also, women have typically opted for species providing fuel and fodder and men for commercially profitable ones. In some Chipko areas women have formed vigilance teams against illegal felling and for monitoring village use of the local forest. Some also seek representation in the village councils. Elsewhere, too, women have been active in agitation against deforestation, large dams, and mining activities.

Women's involvement in movements like Chipko needs to be contextualized. Such movements have emerged primarily in hill or tribal communities where women's roles in agricultural production are visible and substantial—a context more conducive to their participation in movements than in communities practicing female seclusion. The evidence in south Asia does not support the argument (made by some ecofeminists) that women qua women are closer to nature or more conservationist than men. Rather, poor peasant women's and tribal women's responses to environmental degradation can be located in their everyday material reality—in their dependence on natural

594

resources for survival and the knowledge of nature gained in the process.

Looking Ahead

Nevertheless, environmental movements and women's involvement in them have significantly affected developmental thinking in south Asia. Resistance to the destruction of nature and nature-dependent livelihoods has created environmental awareness in policy formulation, and the demand for environmentally sustaining policies and egalitarian access to natural resources has led to shifts toward more participative program implementation. In India, for instance, in the early 1980s, tree-planting schemes initiated by the government and international agencies were characterized by monocultural plantations for commercial use, top-down implementation, and a high male bias in scheme design and implementation. Most such schemes, carried out in the face of community hostility, were unsuccessful. Recent government policy, however, seeks to involve village communities directly in forest protection and regeneration under various joint forest-management schemes.

Although women's participation in such schemes is limited, it is likely to grow as they realize that their participation could prove critical for women's empowerment and family well-being as well as for a scheme's success. Without women's cooperation, rules for protecting communal lands and forests often do not work, given their primary responsibility for collection and gathering. In the long term the challenge lies in ensuring that rural men also share equally in this responsibility.

See Also

DEVELOPMENT: SOUTH ASIA; HOUSEHOLDS AND FAMILIES: SOUTH ASIA; POVERTY

References and Further Reading

Agarwal, B. 1992. The gender and environment debate: Lessons from India. *Feminist Studies* 18(1).

Braidotti, R., et al. 1994. *Women, the environment and sustainable development.* London: Zed.

Guha, R. 1989. *The unquiet woods: Ecological change and peasant resistance in the Himalaya.* Berkeley, Calif.: Berkeley University Press.

Jodha, N. S. 1986. Common property resources and the rural poor. *Economic and Political Weekly* 21 (27).

King, Y. 1989. The ecology of feminism and the feminism of ecology. In J. Plant, ed., *Healing the wounds: The promise of ecofeminism.* Philadelphia: New Society.

Merchant, C. 1983. *The death of nature: Women, ecology and the scientific revolution.* San Francisco: Harper and Row.

Plant, J., ed. 1989. *Healing the wounds: The promise of ecofeminism.* Philadelphia: New Society.

Shiva, V. 1986. *Staying alive: Women, ecology and survival in India.* London: Zed.

Bina Agarwal

ENVIRONMENT: South Asian Case Study—Forests in India

A *forest* is a community of plants and animals, a naturally occurring ecosystem characterized by diversity of species, interacting with and sustaining each other. Thus a monoculture tree stand, cultivated to produce raw materials for the pulp and timber industry, is not a forest. Feminist analysis can be applied to forests and commercial forestry; this case study is an example.

Forests and Forestry: A Feminist Perspective

Commercial forestry, which is equated with "scientific forestry" by narrow interests exemplified by western patriarchy, is reductionist in concept and in its ecological impact, and it impoverishes many whose livelihoods and productivity depend on the forest. Commercial forestry is said to be characterized by reductionism because it sunders forestry from water management, agriculture, and animal husbandry; it reduces the diversity of life within the forest ecosystem to a dead product, wood, and wood in turn to commercially valuable wood. The object of commercial forestry is to maximize exchange value on a market by extracting valuable species; thus forest ecosystems are reduced to the timber of such species.

This commercial pattern ignores the complex relationships within the forest community and between plant life and other resources, such as soil and water; thus it creates instabilities in the ecosytem and leads to counterproductive uses of nature. Destruction of the forest ecosystem hurts the economic interests of social groups—mainly tribal peoples and particularly the women of these cultures—who depend on the multiple functions of forest resources. These functions include stabilizing soil and water and providing food, herbs, tubers, medicine, fodder, fibers, fuel, and fertilizers.

In the altenative feminine science of forestry, which has been subjugated by masculine science, a forest is not viewed as merely a stock of wood isolated from the rest of the ecosys-

595

tem, nor is its economic value reduced to the commercial value of timber. In feminine forestry, "productivity," "yield," and "economic value" are defined and measured in terms of nature and of women's work, as satisfying basic needs through an integrated ecosystem managed for multipurpose utilization. These concepts are of course entirely different from those in reductionist masculinist forestry. In fact, when ecological forestry is superseded by reductionist forestry, all scientific terms change from ecosytem-dependent to ecosytem-independent. For tribal cultures and other forest peoples and perhaps especially for their women, a complex ecosystem is productive in terms of the materials noted above (food, fuel, and so on) and also as a gene pool. For the commercial forester, these components are useless, unproductive, wasteful, or dispensable.

From a patriarchal perspective, what matters is not the diversity or ecological function of a forest but simply the volume of industrial raw materials produced; overall productivity is subordinated to industrial use, and a large biomass to profitable species. Commercially, whatever is not marketable wood is waste, or "weeds." By contrast, as far as women's survival and productivity are concerned, a natural tropical forest is a highly productive ecosystem; what industrialism calls waste is for these women a wealth of biomass that maintains nature's cycles of water and nutrients and satisfies agricultural communities' needs.

Destruction of the integrity of forest ecosystems is often experienced most vividly and concretely by peasant women, because their work, to a considerable extent, protects and conserves nature in forestry and agriculture and thereby sustains human life. For such women, forestry is closely linked to food production; the forest provides a stable, perennial supply of water for drinking and irrigation and provides fertilizers directly as "green manure" or indirectly as organic matter cycled through farm animals.

In regions like the Himalaya, women's agricultural work is largely work in and with forests, yet this work is discounted in both forestry and agriculture—the only forestry work that goes into census data is felling trees and lumbering. For the men involved in lumbering operations, cutting trees is a source of food (roti, literally a kind of bread); but for the women, food is represented by the living forest, and women's work facilitates sustainable food production.

For example, when women lop trees in an oak forest (that is, cut off branches and twigs), they enhance the forest's productivity under stable conditions and under common ownership and control. The leaves of an unlopped tree are too hard for cattle; lopping makes leaves soft and palatable, especially in early spring. Through late autumn and winter and into spring, cattle are fed oak leaves along with

a mixture of dried grasses and agricultural by-products. (During the summer monsoon season, green grass is the dominant fodder; in the early fall, fodder consists primarily of agricultural waste such as rice straw.) Lopping is actually a forest management strategy—a way to use tree produce while conserving the tree—and under appropriate conditions it can increase a forest's density and productivity as a source of fodder. Groups of women, young and old, lop trees together and develop expertise as they work; in this small, informal, decentralized "school" of forestry, they develop and transfer knowledge about maintaining living resources. By contrast, actual colleges of forestry are centralized and alienated, specializing in destruction—the transformation of a living resource into a cash commodity.

The Women of Chipko

This dispossession of local peoples has not gone unchallenged. In the early 1970s, in the Himalaya mountains, the women of the Garhwal region of Uttar Pradesh—at considerable risk to themselves—began the Chipko movement to protect their forests from commercial exploitation. Chipko comes from a word meaning "embrace," and these women literally embraced and shielded the trees—just as, three centuries earlier, members of the Bishnoi community in Rajasthan, led by a woman called Amrita Devi, had sacrificed their lives to save their sacred khejri trees by clinging to them. The philosophy and methodology of Chipko has since spread to Himachal Pradesh in the north, Karnataka in the south, Rajasthan in the west, Orissa in the east, and the central Indian highlands.

From the feminist perspective, there are two mutually incompatible paradigms of forestry in India today. One, emerging from the forest, India's ancient diverse forest culture, and the feminine principle, is life enhancing; its primary management objective is to maintain the conditions of renewability. This is the paradigm that has been revived in contemporary times through Chipko. The other paradigm, emerging from the factory and the market, is life destroying; its objective—obtainable only by destroying the conditions of renewability—is to maximize profits.

These two systems of knowledge and economics clashed in Adwani in 1977, when Chipko became explicitly an ecological and feminist movement. Women had always been the backbone of Chipko, but in the early days, when Chipko was directed against nonlocal forest contractors, the movement had also included local commercial interests. After removal of the outside private contractors, a government agency (the forest development corporation) started working through local labor contractors and forest cooperatives. The women, however, continued to oppose exploitation of the forests; they did not care whether the exploiters were outsiders or local men.

A dramatic event in this new confrontation took place when Bachni Devi of Adwani led a protest against her own husband, who had obtained a local tree-felling contract. When forest officials arrived, evidently intending to intimidate the women and the Chipko activists who had joined the protest, they found the demonstrators holding up lighted lanterns, in broad daylight. One puzzled official asked what that meant, and the women replied, "We have come to teach you forestry." The official persisted: "You foolish women, how can you who prevent felling know the value of the forest? Do you know what forests bear? They produce resin and timber and profit." The women were prepared; they sang in unison:

What do the forests bear?
Soil, water, and pure air.
Soil, water, and pure air.
Sustain the earth and all she bears.

This *satyagraha*—passive resistance—at Adwani represented a new direction for Chipko: the movement's philosophy and politics would henceforth evolve to reflect women's needs and knowledge. Peasant women openly challenged not only the reductionist commercial forestry system but also the local men who had been cognitively, economically, and politically colonized by that system.

See Also

COLONIALISM AND POSTCOLONIALISM; DEVELOPMENT: SOUTH ASIA; ECOFEMINISM; ECOSYSTEM; ENVIRONMENT: OVERVIEW; ENVIRONMENT: SOUTH ASIA

Reference and Further Reading

Bishnoi, R. S. [1948] 1987. Conservation as creed. Letter from Gandhi to Mirabehn, January 16, 1948. Dehra Dun, India: Juqual Kishore.

Guha, Ramachandra. 2000. *The unquiet woods: Ecological change and peasant resistance in the Himalaya.* Berkeley: University of California Press.

Vandana Shiva

ENVIRONMENT: Southeast Asia

The major environmental challenges facing southeast Asia are pervasive, diverse, and intricately connected. Environmental degradation is tightly bound to other regional problems, such as poverty and an uneven distribution of income, and there are various debates about these complex linkages. The environmental movement in southeast Asia is linked to these other problems in a way that differs from western environmentalism. Southeast Asian women have disproportionately borne the effects of the environment's decline in many ways. They have played vital roles at the grassroots level in responding to environmental and related problems. At the same time, their participation and representation in more formalized, urban responses has been low. There is some room for optimism that this situation might be improving; however, the reality is that advancements made in environmental care are fragile and could be subject to reversion very easily.

History of Southeast Asian Environmental Problems

The environmental challenges facing southeast Asia are numerous and vary across the countries in the region, which range from resource-poor but economically advanced Singapore to agrarian, resource-rich Laos. Environmental challenges began emerging in the broader Asian region as early as the start of the sixteenth century, when land clearing in China led to deforestation and erosion (Mackerras, 1995). More serious degradation began to take place specifically in southeast Asia when colonialism took root in the eighteenth century, but the economic boom that took off (unevenly) across the region in the 1960s—largely because of unsustainable resource depletion—exacerbated environmental problems exponentially. The American war in Vietnam, Laos, and Cambodia had a massive impact on the environments of those countries, with southern Vietnam today remaining the most dioxin-contaminated region in the world (Beresford and Fraser, 1992). Problems took a further twist in the late 1980s, when socialist countries such as Vietnam and Laos embarked on programs of market reforms. The impact on the environment of the economic crisis that hit the region and beyond in 1997 is yet to be fully determined, but generally it has exacerbated existing environmental problems while creating some new ones. It will probably not, however, change the overall environmental priorities of the region (World Bank, 1999).

Problems Today

Southeast Asia's most serious problem is deforestation. Thailand, the region's greatest consumer of forest products, was effectively logged out by the end of the 1980s, and Vietnam has lost more than half its forest cover since 1960. Laos, Burma, and—to a lesser extent—Cambodia have more significant forest resources left, yet in Cambodia, it has taken just two decades for half of its once extensive hardwood forests to disappear (*Economist,* 1999). Commercial logging, conversion to agricultural land, development projects, and demand for fuel and fodder have all contributed to regional deforestation. Indeed, although it is a major problem in its own right, the complex nature of deforestation contributes to a gamut of other environmental problems, ranging from forest fires to flash flooding, with desertification, drought, soil erosion, salinity problems, and biodiversity loss in between.

Water pollution in the region is also severe: the region's rivers are among the most polluted in the world, organic waste is a major problem, and lead in surface water due to industrial effluent is high (Asian Development Bank, 1997). Furthermore, the destruction of mangroves, pesticide usage, and topsoil runoff have polluted coastal areas, and deforestation and erosion have interfered with water supply. Domestic and industrial sewage is a major source of pollution, while pollution from agrochemicals, groundwater extraction, and saline intrusion into groundwater also are problems. Contamination of coastal and marine waters because of activities ranging from tourism to offshore mining is also occurring.

A plethora of other problems plague the region. Increasing levels of domestic waste, particularly toxic waste, challenge many countries, while intraregional transport of waste within Asia is a further twist on this problem, as the dumping of mercurial waste from Taiwan's Formosa Plastics Company in Cambodia in 1998 demonstrated. Globally, there is increasing evidence of trade in waste from richer to poorer countries, including Indonesia and the Philippines among the latter (Greenpeace, 1999). The construction of large dams has created another set of problems, and intensive shrimp farming has led to large-scale destruction of mangroves. Bangkok, Jakarta, and Manila face serious urban air pollution, which retards children's cognitive development, causes respiratory disease, and contributes to global warming. Global warming is another problem: should sea levels rise, cities such as Bangkok and Jakarta will be vulnerable to land subsidence, which has already occurred as a result of groundwater pumping.

Regional Dimension

Although the governments within the Association of Southeast Asian Nations (ASEAN) may voice regional concern over environmental issues, national governments still frequently promote the interests of companies involved in environmentally destructive industries. Domestically, too, it is not uncommon to see parliamentarians with, for instance, logging interests, concoct an official line that the chief source of forest loss is due to slash-and-burn cultivators, when their own companies are doing untold damage. Within southeast Asia, Thailand has been identified as a major culprit in exploiting the resources of its neighbors because of a combination of the depletion of its own resources, the availability of neighboring countries' resources, and the opening of their economies—and, ironically, the actions of Thailand's environmental movement (Hirsch, 1997). Malaysia's environmental movement has protested against Thai logging in Kelantan state, but other neighboring countries do not have movements significant enough to seriously resist Thailand. Within Asia, Matsui (1999) has written about Japan's exportation of pollution to southeast Asian countries, with an emphasis on its impact on women and their response to it.

Causes of Environmental Problems

Neoclassical economists cite "market failures" as being the chief cause of environmental degradation: that is, they argue that failures occur when free markets produce outcomes that fail to reflect the real social costs or benefits of an action. Solutions, therefore, lie in the realm of improving market efficiency, making the sole objective of government intervention to make markets work better, as efficient markets will provide the necessary solutions to environmental problems. Adherents to this viewpoint generally accept that development will naturally lead to environmental improvement. Some, accepting that neoclassical economics has actually failed in many instances in the region, argue that an "Asian" model of laissez-faire must be followed (Islam and Jolley, 1996), but precisely how it might differ from a model for non-Asian countries has not been clearly theorized. This rationalist model is implicitly adhered to by international organizations such as the Asian Development Bank (ADB), the World Bank, the International Monetary Fund (IMF) and the United Nations Environment Program (UNEP).

Many see free markets, certain types of development, and overseas development assistance themselves, however, as being the chief causes of environmental problems. For instance, free trade in timber and hazardous waste are seen as directly damaging the environment; in contrast, free-market advocates argue that free trade necessarily brings prosperity and with it improved environmental circumstances. The former also argue that degradation is far from a simple process; rather, a complex web of social, political, and institutional causes are to blame. These root causes, including population growth, poverty, and economic growth, are as intricately linked as the environmental problems themselves, and much debate surrounds the structure of these links. Many nongovernmental organizations (NGOs) in southeast Asia advocate working to deal with these multifarious causes in order to improve the environment, while local activists tend to focus their energy at this level as well.

Impact of Environmental Problems on Women

The effects of environmental degradation are spread unevenly, both geographically and socially, across the region and individual countries. The poorest people are typically the most adversely affected by degradation, and these usually are farmers and minority ethnic groups. Within these groups—and indeed outside of them—women tend with be disproportionately affected compared with men. In many studies focusing specifically on the alleviation of southeast Asian environmental problems (as opposed to general development), however, gender remains conspicuously absent as a tool of analysis.

The impact of environmental problems on women is complex, with one problem not simply producing one effect. For example, deforestation leads to soil erosion, which can have a severe impact on farmers in surrounding areas, with infertile land leading to poverty. A reduction in forested areas also forces women, who, unlike men, tend to forage for fuel and forest foods, to travel much greater distances to reach bountiful areas. Spoiled water supplies are also likely to affect women more directly, as their socialized roles make them more likely to be responsible for procuring clean supplies. These effects, in turn, are important factors contributing to many more indirect effects: rural-urban migration, which creates its own set of environmental problems in the urban context and sees overwhelming numbers of women working in export industries under very poor conditions; women turning to prostitution to supplement their family's income (risking HIV/AIDS); and women seeking employment abroad usually as domestic or sex industry workers, either under generally exploitative conditions (for example, from Indonesia to Saudi Arabia and from the Philippines to Hong Kong and Singapore) or by inadvertently being trafficked (particularly from Burma to Thailand and from Thailand to Japan) (Matsui, 1999).

Southeast Asian Environmentalism

Environmentalism in developing countries can be seen as being distinct from its western counterpart, although there are problems with such simplification (Hirsch and Warren, 1999). Southeast Asian environmentalism as a unit of study is problematic, as environmentalism is highly differentiated across the region and is pluralistic within countries as well.

Movements that could be considered to be the most developed are in Thailand, the Philippines, and Malaysia, whereas in Burma, Laos, and Vietnam, environmental awareness is low, and there are no coherent domestic movements and not many opportunities for independent NGO action. Other countries lie somewhere in between.

It has been suggested that for developing countries, the struggles of the rural poor, whose livelihoods are directly threatened by the destruction of their resource base, drive environmentalism. By contrast, in the West, the middle class is viewed as being the driving force. Some southeast Asian NGOs—such as Project for Ecological Recovery in Thailand, Sahabat Alam in Malaysia, and Wahana Lingkunga Hidup Indonesia, Sekretariat Kerjasama Pelestarian Hutan Indonesia, and the Green Forum in the Philippines—have become integrated into the international environmental movement, but this internationalization takes manifold forms and does not simply mean westernization (Hirsch, 1997; Hirsch and Warren, 1998).

Women in Southeast Asian Environmentalism

Feminism in southeast Asian nations as a whole is not a topic on which much academic attention has been focused (yet a 1996 reprint of a 1982 paper by Van Esterik suggests that there is a demand for this sort of research). There is, however, an ever-growing body of literature on women's issues and documenting activism by women in individual countries. As opposed to the extensive literature on gender and development in the "South," which tends to encompass environment as but one of many topics, specific links between feminism and the environment in southeast Asia is undertheorized—at least, it should be noted, in English-language publications. Similarly, academic analyses of southeast Asian women's experiences in environmentalism as a group are scant.

Nevertheless, where domestic environmental movements have developed in southeast Asia, women have played innumerable and significant roles, particularly at the local grassroots level. Just a few examples give an idea of the range of environmental issues women have been active in: Thai village women have been instrumental in protesting against fast-growth eucalyptus trees, dam building, shrimp farms, and overfishing, as well as becoming active in developing alternative income sources through work such as weaving; the indigenous women of Sarawak have mounted protests against dam building; and Filipinas have fought against losing their farming land to big agribusiness (Matsui, 1999).

There also are many vibrant groups dealing with the fallout of environmental degradation; for example, women are working toward eliminating the trafficking of women and children, improving conditions for sex workers, and providing shelter and assistance for abused migrant workers. A further positive sign is the increasing number of international links between NGOs focusing on women's issues, as broad participation in the Fourth United Nations World Conference on Women held in Beijing in 1995 demonstrated. In more formal circumstances, however, such as in urban environmental campaigns and "managerial" types of environmentalism, women's participation and representational rates are substantially lower than those of men.

The Future

Environmental problems in the region are severe enough to caution against an overoptimistic outlook for their improvement in the near future. At the governmental level, some advancements have been made in environmental management in some individual countries, but all too often the necessary accompanying action is not followed through. Nevertheless, at the grassroots level, many positive steps are being taken, both to directly alleviate environmental problems and to deal with their effects. Many of the successful results are due to significant action by women who have disproportionately borne the brunt of much of the region's environmental demise.

See Also

DEVELOPMENT: SOUTH ASIA; EDUCATION: SOUTH ASIA; ENVIRONMENTAL DISASTERS; ENVIRONMENTAL MOVEMENTS; HEALTH CARE: SOUTHEAST ASIA; HOUSEHOLDS AND FAMILIES: SOUTHEAST ASIA; POLITICS AND THE STATE: SOUTHEAST ASIA

References and Further Reading

Asian Development Bank. 1997. *Emerging Asia: Changes and challenges.* Manila: Asian Development Bank.

Beresford, Melanie, and Lyn Fraser. 1992. Political economy of the environment in Vietnam. *Journal of Contemporary Asia* 22: 1.

Brookfield, Harold, and Yvonne Byron, eds. 1993. *Southeast Asia's environmental future: The search for sustainability.* Japan: United Nations University Press.

The fight against illegal loggers. 1999. *Economist* (3 April): 24.

Greenpeace. 1999. <http://www.greenpeace.org.au/info/archives/toxic/trade/factsheet.htm>

Hirsch, Philip. 1997. *Seeing forests for trees: Environment and environmentalism in Thailand.* Chiang Mai: Silkworm.

———, and Carol Warren. 1995. Thailand and the new geopolitics of southeast asia: Resource and environmen-

tal issues. In Jonathan Rigg, ed., *Counting the costs: Economic growth and environmental change in Thailand,* 235–259. Singapore: Institute of Southeast Asian Studies.

———, and Carol Warren, eds., 1998. *The politics of environment in southeast Asia: Resources and resistance.* London: Routledge.

Islam, Sardar M. N., and Ainsley Jolley. 1996. Sustainable development in Asia: The current state and policy options. *Natural Resources Forum* 20: 4.

King, Victor T., ed. 1998. *Environmental challenges in southeast Asia.* Richmond, Surrey: Curzon.

Mackerras, Colin, ed. 1995. *Eastern Asia: An introductory history.* Melbourne: Longman Chesire.

Matsui, Yayori. 1999. *Women in the new Asia.* London: Zed.

Rush, James R. 1991. *The last tree: Reclaiming the environment in tropical Asia.* New York: Asia Society.

Van Esterik, Penny, ed. 1996. New foreword. In Northern Illinois University Monograph Series on Southeast Asia. *Women of southeast Asia.* Occasional Paper no. 17. Dekalb: Northern Illinois University.

World Bank. 1999. *Environmental implications of the economic crisis and adjustment in east Asia.* Discussion Paper Series no. 01. Washington, D.C.: World Bank.

Samantha Brown

ENVIRONMENT:
Sub-Saharan and Southern Africa

Between the Indian and Atlantic Oceans lies the vast continent of Africa: a land of diversity and contrasts, a world caught between modernization and tradition. Although much of northern Africa has joined the "modern" world of consumerism and technological growth, in the sub-Saharan and southern regions there are places not yet transformed by modern conveniences, where poverty abounds and resources are scarce and where people rely heavily on the land for survival.

Environmental problems are severe: from deforestation and pollution to desertification and depletion of natural resources. Africa has not been spared from environmental ills. Its geography is at least partially to blame: because of its soils, climate, disease ecology, and topography, the entire continent suffers from chronically low agricultural productivity, high disease incidence, and low levels of international trade. In the sub-Saharan region, widespread overgrazing, deforestation, and inappropriate farming methods erode soils and sap the land of nutrients; waterways are used as dumping grounds, and wildlife and its habitats are disappearing. And all the while, the human population—much of it living in deep poverty—is growing fast and furiously.

Of course, no two countries face all the same problems—there are great geographic and cultural differences. But what the countries do share is that each has immensely complex, multifaceted environmental and social problems for which there are no easy solutions. And one factor that seems to impact all the countries is the existence of profound social and economic inequities that divide men and women. Ironically, it is the often-silent voices of women that may be most important to improving environmental conditions in sub-Saharan Africa.

Why Women?

Women in southern Africa—as in many places—play many roles that affect and are affected by the natural environment. Their daily connection to water, food, fuel, reproduction, family, and community is almost always far stronger than that of men, yet African societies are generally patrilineal. Conventional economics fail to recognize women's substantial economic and social contributions to Africa, from Angola to Swaziland to Zambia. In reality, it is impossible to talk about the most threatening environmental problems in southern Africa—poverty, population growth, and land issues—without discussing how women's lack of access to education, reproductive health services, and agricultural resources compound them (Jiggins, 1994: 5). African girls, often illiterate and undereducated—taking on their mothers' domestic roles rather than preparing for life outside the home—grow up to be underrepresented in local and national decision-making institutions (Blackden and Bhanu, 1998). Their experience in society and on the land is invaluable, but they are generally powerless. It is a cycle that is bound to complex social policies and ingrained human attitudes, and so it is very hard to break.

Women, Population, and Poverty

African countries—once considered underpopulated—are now filling at a rapid pace. In sub-Saharan Africa, it is not uncommon for a woman to bear six children; indeed, women in this region have more children than women anywhere else in the world (Blackden and Bhanu, 1998). A large family means more workers to keep the farm and household going and is a sort of insurance where infant and childhood mortality is high. But this traditional necessity has put huge pressure on an already fragile environment. Population growth in the entire region is straining food supplies, and huge numbers of people are undernourished. Caloric intake in sub-Saharan Africa is currently the lowest in the world, with Congo, Burundi, Ethiopia, Somalia, Zambia, and Chad at the bottom (Food Security Assessment, 1997).

Many environmental and social groups insist that population growth and the accompanying resource consumption are the biggest causes of environmental degradation and human suffering and that population control is the key to a "green" revolution. But population control is more complex than just handing out contraception. Control measures target women because they are seen as being responsible for their own fertility, yet in much of southern Africa, policies are ineffective because women have little say in fertility decisions (Jiggins, 1994: 14). In addition, where childbearing is the main way to achieve status or security and education is lacking, contraception or other control measures are not likely to be willingly and immediately adopted. Women who are educated, who have access to information and family planning services, and who have reproductive choice will often exercise their freedom to have fewer children; thus, these factors are vital components of any population control measures. Demand for family planning has, in fact, increased dramatically in some countries—in Botswana, Kenya, and Zimbabwe, for example (Population Action International, 1998). Without alleviation of poverty, however, the incentive to have a large family remains strong in much of southern Africa.

Population growth without accompanying economic development leads to rapid social and environmental degradation. Where employment, housing, and social services are weak, long-term investment in preserving the environment becomes nearly impossible. In some countries, such as Botswana, the rate of economic growth is relatively high and the population still small, although there it is growing rapidly (Moyo et al. 1993: 34). But in many sub-Saharan countries, slow economic growth has been chronic, while population increase has continued to accelerate.

That economic growth is needed to help combat poverty seems obvious. Just having economic growth, however, is not the solution: although Botswana has it, it has done little to help the rural poor, whose numbers are increasing quickly on fragile lands. And such growth can be dangerous: there are limits to the amount of matter that can be converted for human use, and to the ability of the planet to assimilate the waste that is, inevitably, generated by growth. Boundaries exist that may not reveal themselves until they have been crossed. So it is vital that growth not be seen as the end-all solution. In poverty-stricken regions such as sub-Saharan Africa, there also needs to be a more equitable distribution of resources and obligations among men and women. The human costs of both poverty and a degraded environment in Africa fall most heavily on indigent women, the same group whose experience and knowledge of the land are most often ignored.

Down on the Farm and Back at the Ranch

As of the early 1990s in Africa, about 75 percent of all people still lived in rural villages (NGS, 1995). Ironically, unreliable rainfall and poor soils make rural lifestyles a challenge and farming a difficult occupation. Often, water and fuel are scarce, and there is inadequate transportation and a lack of access to "modern" farming resources. In many places, indigenous traditions of resource management have been pushed aside for large, commercial ventures. Commercial farmers and ranchers often have access to the "best" land, to good credit, and to market facilities, and they sap resources quickly with only a few (and not the neediest) benefiting from the proceeds. In semiarid Botswana, for example, drought is endemic, surface water resources are limited, and soils are poor throughout the country. With little arable land, the major occupation is cattle ranching, and ranchlands are not severely degraded because of overgrazing (Moyo et al., 1993: 33). Where there are communal grazing lands, owners of large herds (often wealthy white Africans or foreigners) tend to graze until the land is depleted, then go back to private farms where they have exclusive rights (Moyo et al., 1993: 38). Rural farmers and tribesmen (mostly black Africans) who graze small herds are at a huge disadvantage.

Namibia, similarly, has separate and unequal sectors of agriculture: the market-oriented sector and the African subsistence sector. And though agriculture is only a small part of Namibia's economy, about 70 percent of the population is in some way dependent on its fruits (Moyo et al. 1993: 164). Resource-use conflicts stem from high population growth and scarce resources, a land-tenure system that is inequitable along racial and gender lines, and the inevitable turn from food crops to cash crops in rural areas. And because family status rides on the size of livestock herds, rangelands are degraded from overstocking by people trying to climb to higher social ground.

When it comes to food in southern Africa, the farmer's wife is usually the farmer. African women produce 75 to 90 percent of the food in sub-Saharan households (Blackden and Bhanu, 1998). In many countries, they work longer days than men, transporting fuel and water, hoeing and weeding, harvesting and marketing (Blackden and Bhanu, 1998),

while being exposed to dangerous chemicals and putting themselves at risk of attack and rape in the fields (Ramphele and McDowell, 1991: 5). Yet official institutions have failed to recognize women's vital role in food production. Women often have trouble accessing the basic resources they need to improve their farming techniques, such as safe and effective fertilizers, equipment, and labor. They receive only a tiny percentage of the credit available for agriculture—in Uganda, only about 9 percent goes to women, in Kenya, only 3 percent (Blackden and Bhanu 1998). Even where policies seek to improve land management in southern Africa, land titles are typically given to men; women farmers may not have access to land or may be pushed onto lands that are marginal for cultivation (Moyo et al., 1993). This lack of support for women by national, regional, and local policies and projects has only perpetuated hunger and low food production. Only with equal opportunity can sustainable farming practices—that is, those that include safer and more efficient use of chemicals, heavier reliance on natural and renewable inputs, appropriate crop rotation and crop diversity, and better soil management—become widespread and effective.

Sustainability

The concept of "sustainable development"—defined by the United Nations Environment Programme as "development that not only generates economic growth but distributes its benefits equitably, that regenerates the environment rather than destroying it, and that empowers people rather than marginalizing them" (Earth Summit+5, 1997)—may sound too good to be true. There are those who feel it is a contradiction in terms to grow and develop and at the same time "sustain" natural resources. But the concept is getting more and more positive attention, and more people seem to be embracing it as the way to resolve many environmental problems. It means taking less and giving back more; it requires long-term thinking and planning rather than acting for short-term gain; it means moving toward a more equitable distribution of wealth and resources. Africa still has the opportunity to embrace this model before all of its natural wealth is depleted. But it requires taking on the perspective that environmental management is a worldwide necessity rather than a western luxury. It means not just bringing sustainable agriculture to rural communities but uplifting those communities through creation of wealth (MacDevette, 1995). It means that southern Africa must not follow the example of its northern neighbors, whose achievements in material assets and conditions have come with extremely unsustainable habits. It means ensuring maximum return per unit of a resource rather than maximum financial gain in the shortest time.

A focus on sustainable use of the environment may be an especially difficult sell in a country such as Angola, where war has dominated the landscape for more than 30 years. The consequences for the country's economy and social infrastructure have been massive, and environmental issues are far from high priority (Moyo et al., 1993: 5). But if the sustainability paradigm were widespread, Angola would integrate solutions for its polluted water, unsanitary conditions, lack of fuel wood, and degraded agricultural lands into the rebuilding of its society and economy. South Africa, recovering from years of human and natural-resource exploitation and unhealthy urbanization during the apartheid era (Ramphele and McDowell, 1991), has a similarly difficult road ahead. But if the environment is pushed aside rather than embraced as an integral part of the whole in these countries, the consequences could be disastrous and sustainability will remain out of reach.

Conclusion: Empowering Women

The myth that seems to drive many people's lives on earth is that resources are unlimited, that we can create something from nothing, that we can sustain ourselves without sustaining the land, the trees, the oceans and the rivers, and the other species with which we share the planet. The wealthy are often detached from the most severe environmental problems and so continue to consume more than their fair share of resources without concern. The poor must do whatever it takes to survive—their primary concern is food and family, while caring for the environment seems a luxury instead of a priority. It is a dangerous combination of extremes.

Sub-Saharan Africa is a place where a sustainable lifestyle is still possible. Many rural Africans already know the value of long-term protection of the lands, the waters, and the health of the people—better than many outside corporations that come in to deplete that value for short-term gain. A song sung by Kenyan farm women says, "Treat the earth well. It was not given to us by our parents: it was loaned to us by our children" (Jiggins, 1994: 206). Yet the same women who sing these words may be powerless to invoke change or too poor to think about sustainability day to day. They may be active in community-based environmental activism, but women remain largely absent at all levels of policy formulation and decision making related to the environment (Earth Summit+5, 1997). By narrowing the gaps between rich and poor and between men and women, there is room to think about the environment and the con-

sequences of human actions. Organizations fighting for change in Africa know that educating women will help break the cycle of poverty and that offering them equal access to goods, services, and information can help slow population growth and hunger. Some strong winds can come from the women's movement, environmental groups, and advocates of population control, but all must come together to stand behind the local African women. Their experience, wisdom, and cooperation are invaluable to bringing about a healthy, equitable Africa that can feed itself.

See Also

AGRICULTURE; DEVELOPMENT: SUB-SAHARAN AND SOUTHERN AFRICA; EDUCATION: SOUTHERN AFRICA; EDUCATION: SUB-SAHARAN AFRICA; ENVIRONMENT: OVERVIEW; POLLUTION

References and Further Reading

Blackden, M., and C. Bhanu. 1998. *Gender, growth, and poverty reduction in sub-Saharan Africa. Executive summary.* Washington, D.C.: World Bank.

Earth Summit+5. 1997. Special session of the General Assembly to review and appraise the implementation of Agenda 21. New York, 23–27 June 1997. (Accessed at www.un.org)

Food Security Assessment. 1997. *International agriculture and trade report.* Washington, D.C.: Department of Agriculture.

Jiggins, J. 1994. *Changing the boundaries.* Washington, D.C.: Island.

MacDevette, D. R. 1995. Natural resource management in sub-Saharan Africa. Empowerment for African Sustainable Development (EASD) Report 95/1. Cape Town.

Moyo, S., P. O'Keefe, and M. Sill. 1993. *The southern African environment.* London: Earthscan.

National Geographic Society (NGS). 1995. *Atlas of the world.* Rev. 6th ed. Washington, D.C.: NGS.

Population Action International. 1998. Africa's population challenge. (Accessed at www.populationaction.org)

Ramphele, M., and C. McDowell, eds. 1991. *Restoring the land.* London: Panos Institute.

Jennifer Steinberg

ENVIRONMENT: Western Europe

In the late twentieth century, western Europe saw the emergence of a growing number of women expressing gendered views on economic development, political rights, and environmental sustainability and working toward the implementation of a feminist environmentalist perspective. In response to a history of political marginalization and often drawing on women's traditionally socialized responsibility for future generations, women across western Europe began to create their own political organizations to address feminist ecological concerns. Women in a variety of grassroots environmental movements generated a critical discussion of the ecological implications of economic development, drawing attention to the idea that the environmental price paid for post–World War II economic recovery and growth was too high. Women's sometimes spontaneous acts of civil disobedience and work to gain access to mainstream politics have led many to question the basic values of modern consumer society, initiating new ways of envisioning what constitutes responsible interactions with nature and fellow human beings. Across Western Europe, "green," or environmentalist, and feminist politics and values have met with increasing success.

Environmental Issues

Environmental change and degradation in western Europe have a long history. The ancient philosopher Plato commented on the deforestation of the Greek landscape of his time, comparing it to the skeleton of a sick man. By the end of the Middle Ages only 20 percent of the original European forest cover was left. Air pollution was already known in the fourteenth century (an edict of 1307 unsuccessfully attempted to ban coal burning in London) and the ever-worsening "London smog" became notorious in 1880 when it contributed to the death of about two thousand people in three weeks.

In modern times, the European environment is affected by major problems that often have a transboundary dimension, impacting ecological systems across different western European countries, across western and eastern Europe, and at the global level. These problems include air pollution due to emissions of carbon monoxide, nitrogen monoxide, and other substances; water pollution due to the use of chemicals in agriculture and other factors; eutrophication of seas due to discharges of sewage and industrial waste; soil contamination and erosion caused by heavy metals and organic compounds as well as by improper land use; forest dieback due to acid deposition; pollution caused by industrial accidents; increase of urban and industrial waste, with the related disposal and treatment problems; and loss of biodiversity as a result of these multiple pressures on the environment (European Commission, 1992). To this list one must add the possible impacts in Europe of global climate change and ozone-layer depletion, such as desertification in southern Europe and increased flooding and soil degrada-

tion in most European countries, as well as the ecological and health risks caused by increased exposure to ultraviolet radiation.

Efforts at environmental protection began in several western European countries several decades ago, when some air-pollution and nature protection laws were enacted piecemeal. In the early 1970s, however, more comprehensive environmental protection measures and policies started to be developed. Environmental protection became a policy issue at the local and national levels and also at the European Community (EC) level. The first EC environmental action plan was adopted in 1973, and the fifth one, called "Towards Sustainability," was implemented in 1993. Besides the action plans, comprehensive environmental legislation has been formulated at the EC and national levels, and institutions specifically intended to deal with environmental protection have been established.

Environmental protection policies in western Europe have had limited success in tackling problems of pollution and of natural-resources depletion. While emissions of sulfur dioxide (a cause of acidification), some heavy metals, and chlorofluorocarbons (a cause of ozone-layer depletion) have decreased, other emissions, such as carbon dioxide (contributing to climate change), are increasing. Water pollution has decreased in some coastal areas and rivers, but groundwater pollution is becoming worse in some areas, and water-scarcity problems are emerging. Natural parks have been established and several species are now protected, but biodiversity is under increasing pressure. Soil contamination and erosion continue to raise concern. No major industrial accident caused health and environmental damage in the early 1990s, but the consequences of accidents that occurred in the 1980s are in some cases still to be dealt with, and minor accidents routinely occur. Overall, environmental quality is being pursued but is far from being achieved.

Environmental issues began to be addressed by western European women starting in the early 1970s, when the term "ecofeminism" was coined by Françoise d'Eaubonne in France. At the end of the twentieth century, women's studies scholars had begun to chronicle the development of the variety of feminist environmentalist and ecofeminist perspectives that had burgeoned since the 1970s (Baker, 1992, and Eichler, 1994, for example, offer interesting reviews of ecofeminism). While it is impossible to do justice to the diversity and complexity of perspectives on gender and the environment in western Europe, three themes in particular stand out: women, science, and the environment; reproductive choices and population issues; and lifestyles and sustainability.

Women, Science, and the Environment

Two especially significant cases where women's perspectives on science and technology meet environmental issues are nuclear accidents and biotechnology. In western Europe, women's reflections and writings on the first issue focused on the causes and consequences of the Chernobyl nuclear power plant accident that occurred in 1986 (Donini, 1990; Leonardi, 1986; Schultz and Weller, 1986). The widespread, transboundary fallout that caused long-term radioactive contamination in both eastern and western countries (in differing degrees) was taken as an example of the extent to which scientific technological development has been based on an adversarial relationship with nature marked by a will toward mastery. In her *La nube e il limite* (The Cloud and the Limit, 1990) and other writings, Elisabetta Donini points to the need for an awareness of the limits that, from both a scientific-cognitive and ethical point of view, should or do constrain human technology. She elaborates on the contribution of women's "partiality"—as opposed to men's frequent pretense of "omniscience"—in developing such awareness.

Reproductive Choices and Population Issues

Issues of what the ethical and cognitive limits of scientific and technological developments are or should be and of the risks posed by fast and often overly self-confident technological "progress" are also central to women's reflections on biotechnology, particularly reproductive technologies. The physical and symbolic consequences of invasive reproductive technologies on women's bodies and desires were emphasized, for example, during a 1988 conference in *La Nuova Ecologia* significantly entitled "Madre provetta" (Mother Test-Tube). The "double sword" of increasing the degree of reproductive choice by overcoming some cases of infertility while at the same time encouraging reproductive desire and ability to push beyond current biological thresholds is a matter of deep reflection and concern for many women in western Europe and has led to legislative proposals (only a few of which have passed) in France, Germany, Italy, the United Kingdom, and other countries.

The link between reproductive technologies, reproductive choices, and the population issue is directly relevant to environmental debate and policy and involves a consideration of the problem—and of women's varying circumstances—beyond geopolitical borders. Especially in the case of such international events as the United Nations Conference on Environment and Development of 1992 and the fourth United Nations Women's Conference of 1995, western European women have been working with women in other countries to develop gender perspectives on population issues in a way that attempts to account for the different interests and ideologies at stake. Such perspectives are by no means homogeneous. A diversity of opinions exists, for example, on whether or not addressing the issue of population within the broader environmental agenda necessarily involves addressing genocidal discourses and practices. However, broad agreement emerges around the agenda promoted by western European women on the need to guarantee women's ability and right to control and make choices regarding their own fertility and on the importance of looking at the population issue in the broader perspective of socioeconomic development, including women's health, education, and participation in decision making. This focus on women's empowerment as a key for understanding and action regarding population as an environmental issue has influenced the official policy of the European Parliament (EP)—for instance, in September 1994 the EP passed a resolution—and it has also been reflected in official documents of the European Commission, including a 1994 report that explicitly linked the problems of population, environment, and development.

Lifestyles and Sustainability

Issues surrounding the links between the environment and reproductive rights, health, consumption and production patterns, food and agriculture, employment, and peaceful conflict resolution were addressed in the sessions organized by a Europe-wide group of women at the Global Forum 1994 held in Manchester, and they are the focus of the research activities of, among others, the Institut für sozial-oekologische Forschung (Institute for Social-Ecological Research) of Frankfurt, Germany, which published a 1993 report. The relationship between women's working conditions and their preferences as consumers and producers, on the other hand, and the way these conditions and preferences have an impact on and in turn are influenced by ecological change and degradation, on the other, are matters of utmost importance that cannot be readily "solved" simply by appealing to women's partly real, partly supposed, and overemphasized closer relation with nature. The challenge ahead is to better understand these relations and to act upon them.

See Also

ECOFEMINISM; ENVIRONMENT: OVERVIEW; ENVIRONMENTAL DISASTERS; GREEN MOVEMENT; NATURAL RESOURCES; POLLUTION; TECHNOLOGY

References and Further Reading

Baker, Susan. 1992. *The principles and practice of ecofeminism: A review*. Rotterdam: Rotterdam University, Department of Public Administration.

Donini, Elisabetta. 1990. *La nube e il limite: Donne, scienza, percorsi nel tempo* (The cloud and the limit: Women, science, over the course of time). Turin: Rosenberg and Sellier.

Eichler, Margrit. 1994. "Umwelt" als soziologisches Problem ("Environment" as a sociological problem). *Das Argument*, no. 205: 359–77.

European Commission (EC). 1992. *The state of the environment in the European community*. Brussels: E.C.

Institute for Social-Ecological Research. 1993. *Forschung zur Frauen-Arbeit-Umwelt* (Gender and environment). Frankfurt: Institut für sozial-oekologische Forschung.

Leonardi, Grazia, ed. 1986. *Scienze, potere, coscienza del limite: Dopo Chernobyl, oltre l'estraneita* (Science, power, consciousness of limits: After Chernobyl, beyond the extraneous). Rome: Editori Riviste Riunite.

Marie Stopes International and Paul Harrison. 1994. *Linking population, environment, and development: A report to the European commission*. Brussels: European Commission, Directorate General for Environment, Nuclear Safety and Civil Protection.

Schultz, Irmgard, and Ines Weller. 1986. *Die Folgen von Tchernobyl* (The aftermath of Chernobyl). Frankfurt: Institut für sozial-oekologische Forschung.

Simmons, Pam, ed. 1992. *Ecologist* 22 (1). Special issue on feminism, nature, and development.

Angela Liberatore

ENVIRONMENTAL DISASTERS

Environmental hazards are threats to people and the things they value and are the products of the interaction between society, technology, and the environment (Cutter, 1993). Disasters are the realization of the hazard. The distinction is subtle and reflects the different disciplinary approaches used to study both hazards and disasters.

Causes and Impact

Environmental hazards are classified according to their origin. Extreme natural events arise from geological processes (earthquakes, volcanic eruptions, avalanches), atmospheric disturbances (hurricanes, tornadoes), or hydrologic events (flooding). Other forces of nature create more common natural events such as droughts, blizzards, and coastal erosion. Environmental hazards can originate in social events (social violence, warfare) with direct impacts on the environment (for example, the use of the Kuwaiti oil fields as a weapon during the Persian Gulf War of 1991). Large-scale industrial failures (chemical accidents or nuclear power plant failures) are another category of hazards or disaster. All of these represent single events that are frequently identified by their location—Chernobyl (nuclear accident), Pinatubo (volcanic eruption), Northridge (earthquake).

Environmental hazards also arise from chronic disturbances that aggravate the human condition just as much as these single events. The cumulative impacts of environmental degradation (pollution, tropical deforestation, climate change, desertification) are another source of hazards. They are often more difficult to study because they develop over longer periods of time, their origins are more complex, and their casualties are more difficult to assess.

Disasters effect people and places differently. Some places are more disaster-prone than others simply by location (along a floodplain or earthquake fault) or as a result of the interaction between location and societal structures (urbanization, poverty, or overpopulation). For example, there was only a slight increase in the number of disaster events since 1960 worldwide, yet the number of fatalities increased significantly during this time (Cutter, 1994). The high disaster-fatality rate disproportionately affects the developing world because of its increasing population, rendering it more vulnerable to extreme natural events. Economic losses escalated as well, topping more than U.S. $6 billion annually throughout the 1990s (IFRCRC 1999). While disaster fatalities affect the developing world more often, economic losses from disasters are more pronounced in the developed world.

Response and Resistance to Hazards

Responses to disasters are constrained by social, political, economic, and scientific institutions. Some places and societies are better able to respond to environmental hazards than others. The characteristics of the event, experience, and level of material wealth most often dictate the ability of people and places to recover from disasters (Burton, Kates, and White, 1993). In both developed and developing world contexts, women and children are among the most vulnerable to disasters.

Feminist perspectives are important in understanding how we live with environmental hazards and disasters. First, there are some clear gender differences in how hazards are identified and assessed (Cutter, 1993). Feminist critiques of science promote the position that science is just a viewpoint. Technology, the tool that is used to manipulate resources and respond to disasters, is also a product of social knowledge, practices, and products. Science and technology are not gender neutral, nor are they apolitical. Yet science and technology influence how hazards are identified, assessed, and managed, and they also influence responses to disaster. Women tend to be less tolerant of risks and hazards in the private sphere—those that affect the health and safety of themselves and their families. Women's resistance to nuclear technology and biotechnology is a good example.

Second, women tend to be more likely to resist actively those hazards, such as the chronic environmental disasters, that threaten their livelihoods and planetary stability. Local opposition to deforestation, maldevelopment (Shiva, 1988), pesticide applications, hazardous waste, and militarism (Seager, 1993) are areas where activist movements have had the greatest success. When the environment is threatened, the health and safety of women and families is equally at risk. It is not coincidental that most of the grassroots environmental movements throughout the world (Chipko in India, Green Belt in Kenya, Citizens' Clearinghouse for Hazardous Waste in the United States) were organized by women. Women often have different risk exposures than their male counterparts, largely because of sex difference and their gendered roles in societies. Exposure to heavy metals and toxins is often greatest for women and children, many of whom live and cook (without ventilation) in small, enclosed spaces (Cutter, 1995). Women commonly have more difficulty recovering from disasters (Enarson, 1999). Social norms and the division of labor along gender lines put additional pressure on women, who normally provide a major caregiving role during the disaster recovery phase. In addition to seeking shelter, food, and water, women must also contend with maintaining family stability under extremely difficult circumstances.

Finally, feminist perspectives on environmentalism help to challenge the social, cultural, and political sources of power in society. When women suffer through social discrimination and the domination of nature, the planet is also threatened. Human liberation and its relationship to nonhuman nature necessitates a new ethic about how gender intersects with culture, environmental setting, and economic and political structures. The links between poverty and environmental degradation are especially important in the developing world. There women are the stewards of natural and biological resources; when disaster strikes, they are least able to recover from it because of lack of access to economic, educational, and health resources.

Concluding Remarks

The world is becoming more vulnerable to environmental disasters. Extreme natural events may not be preventable, but people can develop mitigation measures to reduce their impact on themselves and the places they live. The UN's International Decade of Natural Disaster Reduction (1990–2000) acknowledged the importance of these natural events in the decline of the human condition and promoted global strategies for reducing disaster losses. It did not, however, focus on losses from technological failures and the more chronic environmental disturbances. These environmental hazards are more difficult to respond to because they often require a complete restructuring of social systems, including those built on the principle of economic development at any price.

See Also

DEVELOPMENT: OVERVIEW; ECOFEMINISM; ECOSYSTEM; ENVIRONMENT: OVERVIEW; POLLUTION; POVERTY

References and Further Reading

Burton, Ian, Robert W. Kates, and Gilbert F. White. 1993. *The environment as hazard.* 2nd ed. New York: Guilford.

Cutter, Susan L. 1993. The forgotten casualties: Women, children, and environmental change. *Global Environmental Change* 5 (3): 181–194.

———. 1994. "Isn't any place safe anymore?" In Susan L. Cutter, ed., *Environmental risks and hazards*, xi–xvi. Englewood Cliffs, N.J.: Prentice-Hall.

———. 1995. *Living with risk.* London: Edward Arnold.

Dankelman, Irene, and Joan Davidson. 1988. *Women and environment in the Third World.* London: Earthscan.

Enarson, Elaine. 1999. Women and housing issues in two U.S. disasters: Hurricane Andrew and the Red River Valley flood. *International Journal of Mass Emergencies and Disasters* 17 (1): 39–63.

———, and Betty Hearn Morrow. 1998. *The gendered terrain of disaster: Through women's eyes.* Westport, Conn.: Praeger.

Fothergill, Alice. 1996. Gender, risk, and disaster. *International Journal of Mass Emergencies* 14 (1): 33–56.

International Federation of Red Cross and Red Crescent Societies. 1999. *World disasters report 1999.* Oxford: Oxford University Press.

Morrow, Betty Hearn, and Elaine Enarson. 1996. Hurricane Andrew through women's eyes: Issues and recommendations. *International Journal of Mass Emergencies and Disasters* 14 (1): 5–22.

Seager, Joni. 1993. *Earth follies: Coming to feminist terms with the global environmental crisis.* New York: Routledge.

Shiva, Vandana. 1988. *Staying alive: Women, ecology, and development.* London: Zed.

Timberlake, Lloyd, and Laura Thomas. 1990. *When the bough breaks: Our children, our environment.* London: Earthscan.

Turner, Billie L., et al. 1990. *The Earth as transformed by human action.* Cambridge: Cambridge University Press.

Susan Cutter

ENVIRONMENTAL MOVEMENTS

See ECOFEMINISM; ENVIRONMENT, *specific entries;* and GREEN MOVEMENT.

EPISTEMOLOGY

Epistemology is an aspect of philosophical inquiry that asks questions about human knowledge. Philosophers have, for example, traditionally asked what constitutes "knowledge" and what sorts of things human beings can know. Can human knowledge be constructed on secure "foundations," immune from doubt or error?

The critique of some of the assumptions of traditional epistemology has been central to the feminist critique of philosophy. In particular, feminists have criticized ideals of "objectivity" that assume that it is possible to adopt a "God's-eye view" or a "view from nowhere," to which the social location of the person making knowledge claims is irrelevant. They have argued that the "God's-eye view" is in fact often a male perspective. But if all knowledge is socially located, then so too is feminist knowledge. Feminists have laid great stress on the importance, in feminist scholarship and research, of awareness of one's own social location.

Some feminist writers have argued that feminist knowledge arises directly from women's experiences and that they are the ultimate court of appeal. In some feminist writing, this view has seemed to lead to a kind of relativism: men's experiences lead to male "knowledge," women's experiences lead to female "knowledge." The problem with this kind of relativism is that it seems unable to account for the critical force of a great deal of feminist writing, in which many male claims to knowledge have been shown to be partial, not universal, motivated by male interests and concerns, not "dis-

interested" or, in a traditional sense, "objective." Feminist epistemology has tried to respond to these issues. Sometimes, in the critique of male perspectives that have masqueraded as universal, it has seemed that the goal of feminist study is simply to be *more* objective. Such a view, which is sometimes described as "feminist empiricism," does not allow for a more fundamental critique of the notion of "objectivity." Other writers have tried to develop a theory of feminist knowledge based on the idea of a "feminist standpoint," which is potentially available to women partly, although not exclusively, on the basis of their experiences of oppression. Yet others have queried the usefulness of the notion of a "standpoint," arguing, for instance, that although it lays a valuable stress on women's experiences, it cannot sufficiently recognize the fact that the experiences of women vary greatly.

Contemporary debates about feminist epistemology have centered around two particular and related groups of questions. The first is whether the notion of a "standpoint" can be reformulated in ways that meet some of the objections that have been leveled against it. The second is whether the notion of "objectivity" can be redefined in ways that do not imply a "view from nowhere." How can a theory of feminist knowledge be developed that allows for the critical force of feminist ideas and the possibility of a critical distance from one's own but that does not collapse into relativism and does not imply that the experiences of any one group of women are privileged in ways that marginalize others?

See Also

KNOWLEDGE; PHILOSOPHY; SCIENCE: FEMINIST PHILOSOPHY

References and Rurther Reading

Alcoff, Linda, and Elizabeth Potter, eds. 1993. *Feminist epistemologies.* London: Routledge.

Code, Lorraine. 1991. *What can she know?* Ithaca, N.Y.: Cornell University Press.

Harding, Sandra. 1991. *Whose science? Whose knowedge?* Ithaca, N.Y.: Cornell University Press.

Jean Grimshaw

EQUAL OPPORTUNITIES

Equal opportunity may be defined as the public policy goal of creating the conditions under which all individuals are able to develop their full potential, regardless of attributes such as race, sex, disability, class, or caste. The goal does not entail equality of outcomes but, rather, offers the equal chance to become unequal. It proposes that advancement should be solely in accordance with individual "merit" rather than determined by social attributes.

Equal opportunity policies assume that talent is distributed randomly among the population, rather than being concentrated in one race, gender, or social class, and that it is therefore important, for the sake of social utility as well as social justice, to broaden access to educational and employment opportunities.

Few governments are committed to the large-scale redistribution and social provision necessary to realize fully the goal of equal opportunity—for example, the spending on public health, housing, education, and community services that would provide to all an equal chance to develop their talents. Instead, more limited objectives are established for what are called variously affirmative action, positive action, employment equity, or equal employment opportunity programs. Indeed, such programs have been criticized for removing barriers to upward mobility for individuals from "target groups" while leaving the general structure of inequality intact. On the other hand, there has been resistance even to these programs on the grounds that they interfere with market forces or that, by their attempts to create race or gender-neutral standards, they overturn existing measures of "merit."

See Also

ANTIDISCRIMINATION; DISCRIMINATION; EQUITY; WORK: EQUAL PAY AND CONDITIONS

References and Further Reading

Burton, Clare. 1988. *Redefining merit.* Canberra, Australia: Australian Government Publishing Service.

Plantenga, Janneke, and Johan Hansen. 1999. Assessing equal opportunities in the European Union. *International Labor Review* 138(4).

Serjenian, Evelyne. 1994. Inventory of positive action in Europe. In *Women of Europe,* Supplement no. 42. Brussels: Commission of the European Communities

Marian Sawer

EQUAL OPPORTUNITIES: Education

The Concept of Equal Opportunity

Equal opportunity is fluid. It has operated as a "condensation symbol" capable of uniting a range of different political interests precisely because of its vagueness. But the concept carries within it contradictory meanings that lead to the construction of potential solutions that are themselves contra-dictory and ambiguous in relation to meeting the *actual* aims of those whose interests it is apparently intended to serve. The umbrella term *equal opportunities* is seen to cover gender, disability, minority ethnic issues, age, sexual orientation, religion, political and trade union affiliation, and marital status, with the catchall of "other unjustified differences" often being included in policy statements.

The concept of equality of opportunity in education, initially driven by socioeconomic class inequalities, has proceeded from weak versions that refer to equality of access to strong versions that call for equality of outcomes or results—from a liberal to a more radical interpretation. The liberal approach is consistent with the tenets of individualism and liberty and aims at sharing more equitably the scarce goods of society. The objective is to provide access to all levels of education on the basis of some acceptable criterion such as "ability," regardless of social class, or more recently, gender, ethnic origin or "race," disability, or sexual orientation. The radical approach is critical of these aims, which it sees as ignoring class-, gender-, and race-based power relations and structural inequalities that are built into the fabric of society and that must be addressed—for example, through antisexist and antiracist education. Equal-access approaches, particularly in relation to socioeconomic class differences, have not been particularly successful. Shavit and Blossfeld report on studies of 13 industrialized countries in which in most cases, despite a uniform trend of education expansion up to 1970, the "expansion has not entailed greater equality of educational opportunity among socio-economic strata" (1993: 15).

The legal imperative for change has been weaker in practice than might be expected. In the United States Title IX of the Education Amendment Act of 1972 was a comprehensive federal law to prohibit sex discrimination against students and employees of educational institutions receiving federal funding. Title IX was resisted by educational establishments, compliance measures were not enforced, and its scope was narrowed by challenges in the Supreme Court. Executive Order 112466, signed by President Johnson in the late 1960s, directed large federal contractors (a category that includes most colleges and universities) to establish written affirmative action programs for staff, based on extensive data collection; as a result, most have affirmative action officers. In the United Kingdom the 1975 Sex Discrimination Act and 1976 Race Discrimination Act specifically prohibit sex and racial discrimination in employment, education and training, and the provision of goods and services. In the opinion of their critics, the acts may provide the framework for the development of local policy initiatives, but they remain inadequate in scope, with weak compliance measures, and have therefore not been strong levers for change in education (Rendell, 1987).

The right to receive an equal education in terms of access has been a fundamental part of many human rights documents since World War II, including the United Nations Convention on the Elimination of All Forms of Discrimination against Women (1979). In response to the demands of the women's movement and economic and demographic change, European governments have introduced measures that have caused rapid progress in the improvement of girls' educational opportunities since the early 1970s. Despite considerable progress, however, there are disparities in enrollment in vocational education and training and particularly in patterns of subject choice at the upper secondary and higher education levels, with some areas remaining virtually single sex. An Organization for Economic Cooperation and Development study concluded that "the removal of formal barriers of access to girls and women [in education] is by no means tantamount to realizing actual equality of opportunity and results" (1986: 121).

In Europe, North America, Australia, and the United Kingdom, the impetus for gender equity in education has come from the feminist movement. Feminist research has provided the evidence of gender inequality in education (AAUW, 1992; Arnot, 1995), and feminist teachers have worked at grassroots level to change the situation for girls and women. Gender inequality and discrimination have been demonstrated in all aspects of the educational experience from nursery school to higher education, in school (and other educational institutions') organization and classroom practice, in teacher and pupil attitudes and interaction, in textbooks, in teacher training, in the curriculum and subject choice, and in the "hidden curriculum" that permeates all of these aspects. The hidden curriculum is the multitude of things pupils learn or are exposed to in education that are not part of the official curriculum but that contribute to the normative construction of gender (male and female), sexuality (femininity and masculinity), and identity. Feminists argue that it has been demonstrated, too, that in the construction of identity in the educational context, gender, race, and class are entwined, as they are in the delivery of unequal opportunities.

In the United Kingdom girls continue to do well in comparison with boys in schools, although this state of affairs has been related to gendered subject areas (girls are good in languages, boys in math) and has largely remained unremarked in the past. Their success became more visible at the start of the twenty-first century with increasing emphasis on exam results, changing methods of assessment, and girls' improved performance in areas where they tradi-

tionally did less well, namely mathematics and science. Equal opportunities for boys, to improve their comparative performance, is thus beginning to become an issue.

Researchers in the United States are investigating girls' self-esteem—what Carol Gilligan has called the "silencing of girls" as they move from elementary (primary) schools into their teenage schools. There is some evidence that girls' performance drops with this transition and that girls become more tentative and conflicted, with tensions between perceptions of their roles and the propriety of their having a voice (Rogers and Gilligan, 1988).

With some variation related to specific social, cultural, and historical contingencies, the experience of women in education is reflected in their distribution in the labor market in the countries on which this discussion is based; in short, there is strong vertical and horizontal gender differentiation. Women typically work in a limited number of areas in a narrow range of jobs and are always disproportionately represented at low levels in the occupational hierarchy. Education, a significant area of women's employment, mirrors this pattern. In the United Kingdom, for example, although most primary-school teachers are women, most primary-school head teachers are men, and although 50 percent of students in higher education are women, more than 90 percent of professional staff are male, with only a handful of women vice-chancellors.

The legal mandates described earlier provided a lever in the United States for the establishment of new policies and procedures, access programs, research studies, more resources for women's programs, and the growth of women's studies courses. Affirmative action in employment has had a high profile in the United States since the 1960s. The American Council on Education (ACE) has an Office of Women, which runs the effective National Identification Program, to increase the proportion of women presidents. There has been a good deal of work on salary equity and on data collection (Touchton and Davis, 1991). The proportion of women in undergraduate and master's programs is now more than 50 percent, with 34 percent of all doctorates received by women. Another ACE Office of Women initiative, "The New Agenda for Women," outlines the steps needed to meet the higher-education needs of women in terms of student, staff, and curriculum issues and the strategic mechanisms for achieving these needs (Pearson and Touchton, 1989).

Equal opportunities had a very low profile in U.K. higher education until the late 1980s, although there has been considerable activity since. A report from the Commission for Racial Equality on a survey of policy and practice in higher education (HE) was forthright: The research "demonstrated the current complacency of HE and the limited nature of change; that there are far more 'words than deeds'" (Williams et al, 1986). "Equal opportunities" was seen as a problematic concept for most staff in HE and, despite activists, there was a need for research, senior commitment, and resources. Further well-publicized national analyses, such as the Hansard Commission's concern about the paucity of women at senior levels in HE, spurred activity. The increase in student numbers across the sector, together with access programs, has created substantial new opportunities for women, particularly as part-time students, and the proportion of women undergraduates is now near 50 percent. This overall figure masks considerable differences between institutions and subject areas, with women continuing to be less well represented in science and technology despite many new initiatives. Staffing, curriculum and access, and student issues have often been perceived separately and tackled piecemeal.

The U.K. Committee of Vice Chancellors and Principals issued Guidance on Equal Opportunities in Employment in 1991, followed by a compendium of good practice. By 1993, more than 90 percent of universities had equal-opportunities policies, with almost 80 percent having some form of policy on dealing with sexual harassment. More than 50 percent have action plans or are drafting them, (CUCO, 1994).

Work on staff issues has focused on establishing monitoring systems, good recruitment and selection practice, and flexible working practices (including child-care arrangements), together with reviews of career development. Staff development has focused on good practice in recruitment and other areas, as well as general awareness. Some institutions have moved into the more controversial arenas of targeting and language codes. Women's studies courses at the undergraduate and graduate levels have flourished, alongside work on making the curriculum more inclusive.

Growth in active networking organizations has supported the legitimation of the issues and the spread of good practice. In the U.K. organizations specifically related to HE include Through the Glass Ceiling (for senior women in HE), Women in Higher Education (WHEN), and the Equal Opportunities Higher Education Network (EOHE). A significant proportion of universities belong to Opportunity 2000, the national campaign to increase the quantity and quality of women in work, which is based on a business case for equal opportunities.

In the United States, the ACE Office of Women, American Association of University Women, and other campus-specific or national bodies have provided strong pressure for change.

See Also

CURRICULUM: EQUALITY; EDUCATION: ACHIEVEMENT; EQUAL OPPORTUNITIES: HUMAN RIGHTS

References and Further Reading

AAUW (American Association of University Women) Educational Foundation and the Wellesley College Center for Research on Women. 1997. *How schools shortchange girls.* Washington, D.C.: AAUW.

Arnot, M. 1985. Feminism, education and the New Right. In J. Holland Dawtrey and M. Hammer (with S. Sheldon), eds., *Equality and inequality in education policy.* Cleveden, U.K.: Multilingual Matters in association with the Open University.

CUCO. 1994. *A report on universities' policies and practices on equal opportunities in employment.* London: CVCP.

Organization for Economic Cooperation and Development (OECD). 1986. *Girls and women in education.* Paris: OECD.

Pearson, C., D. Shavlik, and J. Touchton. 1989. *Educating the majority: Women challenge tradition in higher education.* Washington, DC: ACE/Macmillan.

Rendell, M. 1987. Women's equal right to equal education. In M. Buckley and M. Anderson, eds., *Women, equality and Europe.* London: Macmillan.

Rogers, A., and Carol Gilligan. 1988. *Translating girls' voices: Two languages of development.* Boston: Harvard Project on the Psychology of Women and the Development of Girls.

Shavit, Y., and H. P. Blossfeld, eds. 1993. *Persistent inequality: Changing educational attainment in thirteen countries.* Boulder, Col.: Westview.

Touchton, J., and L. Davis. 1991. *Fact book on women in higher education.* Washington, D.C.: ACE/Macmillan.

Williams, J., J. Cocking, and L. Davies. 1986. *Words or deeds— A review of equal opportunities policies in higher education.* London: Commission for Racial Equality.

Lee Taylor
Janet Holand

EQUALITY

Because women's perceived inequality and subordination to men in the family, the workplace, and the economic realm, as well as in politics, government, and law (including religious law), is historically the driving force behind feminism, equality is a concept central to feminist theory and politics. And because women's inequality is so pervasive, the concept of equality applies to issues as varied as spousal abuse, rape, sex work, reproductive health care, colonialism and imperialism, child care, pay and employment discrimination, property allocation and ownership, the sexual division of labor, and marriage law and customs.

Feminism as a worldwide organized movement emerged in the modern era from the attempt to address such inequality. Early western feminists such as Mary Wollstonecraft utilized western Enlightenment ideals of "natural" equality among men to assert women's entitlement to be recognized as human subjects with agency and intellect. Modern western feminism thus began with an emphasis on equality with men, a focus that has carried into contemporary western feminism and global feminism (Azize-Vargas, 1994; Ofei-Aboaguy, 1994).

Equity Feminism vs. Difference Feminism

There are two dominant strains within the equality debate: "equity feminism" and "difference feminism." The former holds that women are entitled to equality because they are basically the same as men in all relevant respects. Women can perform jobs traditionally held by men, such as in construction, management, and medicine, and men can hold jobs traditionally reserved for women, such as secretary, nurse, and elementary schoolteacher. By exaggerating differences between women and men, equity feminists hold, patriarchal cultures systematically exclude women from high-paying jobs and keep "women's jobs" low status and low paying (Littleton, 1993).

This "sameness" between men and women in both ability and moral status requires a standard of "procedural" equality of right, opportunity, and law. As long as procedures are fair and open to all on the the basis of ability, equality is preserved. But because current procedures do not respect women's equal abilities and deny women equal rights and opportunities, equity feminism advocates policies such as affirmative action, which would provide greater access to better-paying and higher-skilled jobs traditionally held by men, as well as "comparable worth," which maintains that jobs traditionally held by women should be granted the same status and pay as jobs typically held by men. It also advocates shared work responsibility in the home between men and women, because women's primary responsibility for the home creates a "double day" of work, which puts unfair burdens on women in competing with men in the public sphere (Hochschild, 1989).

"Difference feminists" have argued that this concept of equality in fact undermines women's equality by ignoring women's differences from men. These feminists argue that taking (white) men as the standard catches women in a double bind: either women are treated exactly the same as men,

thus denying their specific needs, such as for pregnancy leave (as in *California Federal v. Guerra,* where women lost their jobs when they took unpaid leaves from work to have babies), or else they are treated as completely different from men and in need of special protection (*Equal Employment Opportunity Commission v. Sears,* where arguments that women are more caring, nurturant, and less competitive than men justified the lack of women in higher-paying commission sales positions; Scott, 1988). Both of these approaches to difference and equality are inherently masculinist because they pass off male experience as "gender neutral."

Difference feminism gives priority to "substantive equality" over procedural equality because the latter provides only a superficial neutrality that masks a real bias against women in areas such as divorce and domestic violence (Okin, 1989). Difference feminism advocates the restructuring of social institutions and practices to bring the values and ideals historically developed and associated with women's experiences of childbearing, sexuality, and caretaking work into the public realm of politics and work. Values of care, nurturance, and relationship would need to be recognized as important and perhaps even given priority over the current liberal values of distributive justice, competitive economics, and rights and rules, all of which would seem to be central to equity feminism (Gilligan, 1982).

The Need to Acknowledge Differences among Women

Others—most notably, feminists of color, lesbians, and third world feminists—have sought to push difference feminism further by highlighting the need to acknowledge differences among women rather than between men and women. They emphasize ways in which racism, classism, ageism, and heterosexism have pervaded "the women's movement" to such an extent that the term *woman* systematically excludes the concerns and experiences of women of color, poor women, and lesbians. Some feminists have even argued that the focus on equality "with men" was mainly articulated by white middle-class feminists and is a class- and race-specific concern (hooks, 1984). They assert that difference feminism embraces a notion of "difference" based on the same white, middle-class, heterosexual model as equity feminism and systematically ignores women who do not fit the dominant class, race, and sexuality.

In abortion, for instance, while the emphasis on women's reproductive differences from men is important, white western feminism's emphasis on "the right to choose" ignores the historical use of abortion and sterilization against women of color in the West, as well as in the third world through western imperialism. By contrast, for global feminists and U.S. feminists of color, reproductive concerns center on the provision of improved health care, income, education, and physical security. They argue that a genuine feminism must address such concerns and needs if it is not to replicate the oppressive structures it claims to resist (Davis, 1981).

Equity feminists respond that difference feminism's emphasis on women's differences from men results in a perpetuation of patriarchal ideas of women being "essentially" nurturant, caring, noncompetitive, and restricted by biological or social roles in reproduction and child rearing. They also worry that women of color's emphasis on differences from white women, as well as lesbians' emphasis on differences from heterosexual women, disrupt possibilities for a unified political movement, fragment political energies and resources, and undermine possibilities for real political advancement.

Some feminists have suggested a way to bring the concerns of difference and equity feminism together by redefining equality based on particularity and context. Emphasizing the ways in which differences exist only in particular contexts of relationship and culture, such feminists urge us to recognize that difference need not be conceptualized or treated in hierarchical terms, that "similarity" rather than "sameness" can be a basis for equality without erasing the specificity of different experiences, identities, and concerns.

In such formulations, difference and equality play out a more complicated relationship. It is pointed out that women are materially different because of the way that customs, mores, and laws *define* them as different; men and women are "socially constructed" to be different, and the differential value assigned to particular characteristics generally considered male is similarly a construction. So, for instance, cultural practices where women are responsible for childcare and men for earning income will foster differences in their respective moral and epistemological frameworks, and these frameworks are valued or devalued along gender lines (Hirschmann and De Stefano, 1996).

This suggests that the relevant "difference" should be seen as inequality itself. That is, rather than focusing on supposedly gender-related differences, feminists should focus on how and in what ways such differences result in subordination and dominance. For instance, rather than asking whether women are more "caring" than men, feminists should instead attend to the fact that women perform the majority of care work, and that this work is inadequately compensated, resulting in women's greater economic vulnerability, including forced reliance on public assistance

(Fineman 1995, Kittay 1999). By analyzing the specifics of power and subordination, this "equality *through* difference" would produce greater "equity" by transcending general categories of "men" and "women" to the realization of individuals' "different" particular histories and contexts.

Though women's inequality persists in spite of such debates, these debates have indisputably advanced women's equality. Indeed, the very fact that such debates now garner so much attention may be the greatest evidence that feminism has established several powerful bases for transforming gender relations to achieve greater equality through difference.

See Also

ANTIDISCRIMINATION; DIFFERENCE, *I and II;* DISCRIMINATION; EQUAL OPPORTUNITIES; EQUITY

References and Further Reading

Azize-Vargas, Yamila. 1994. The emergence of feminism in Puerto Rico, 1897–1930. In Vicki L. Ruiz and Ellen Carol DuBois, eds., *Unequal sisters: A multicultural reader in U.S. women's history.* New York: Routledge.

Davis, Angela Y. 1981. *Women, race, and class.* New York: Random House.

Fineman, Martha Albertson. 1995. *The neutered mother, the sexual family, and other twentieth century tragedies.* New York: Routledge.

Gilligan, Carol. 1982. *In a different voice: Psychological theory and women's development.* Cambridge, Mass.: Harvard University Press.

Hirschmann, Nancy J., and Christine De Stefano, eds. 1996. *Revisioning the political: Feminist reconstructions of traditional concepts in western political theory.* Boulder, Colo.: Westview Press.

Hochschild, Arlie, with Anne Machung. 1989. *The second shift.* New York: Avon.

hooks, bell. 1984. *Feminist theory: From margin to center.* Boston: South End.

Kittay, Eva Feder. 1999. *Love's labor: Essays on women, equality, and dependency.* New York: Routledge.

Littleton, Christine A. 1993. Reconstructing sexual equality. In Patricia Smith, ed., *Feminist jurisprudence,* 110–135. Cambridge: Cambridge University Press.

MacKinnon, Catherine. 1979. *Sexual harassment of working women.* New Haven, Conn.: Yale University Press.

Ofei-Aboaguy, Rosemary Ofeibea. 1994. Altering the strands of the fabric: A preliminary look at domestic violence in

Ghana. *Signs: Journal of Women in Culture and Society* 19(2): 924–938.

Okin, Susan Mahler. 1989. *Justice, gender, and the family.* New York: Basic Books.

Scott, Joan. 1988. Deconstructing equality-versus-difference: Or, the uses of poststructuralist theory for feminism. *Feminist Studies* 14(1): 33–50.

Nancy J. Hirschmann

EQUITY

Equity is usually defined in terms of fairness and encompasses the principle that like cases should be treated alike. Debate centers on what constitutes like cases. Feminists have pointed out that to treat in the same way those disadvantaged by sex as those advantaged by sex is often to compound disadvantage. Where such equal treatment has a disparate impact and cannot be justified as a business necessity it is defined as indirect discrimination. Justice Mary Gaudron (1990) of the high court of Australia has commented that inequity arises both from the different treatment of persons who are equal and from the equal treatment of persons who are different.

Some feminists, predominantly in the United States, have feared that the "difference" principle may be used to perpetuate inequality, as with the old "protective" legislation. Conservatives have argued that gender inequalities are equitable because men have a greater willingness to work hard outside the home, to compete aggressively for advancement in bureaucratic hierarchies, or to make earning money a prime motive in their lives.

The approach adopted in the United Nations Convention on the Elimination of All Forms of Discrimination against Women is to take equal enjoyment of human rights as the benchmark for equity. Differential treatment will be judged in accordance with whether it advances or impairs women's enjoyment of human rights, including the right to work.

See Also:

ANTIDISCRIMINATION; DISCRIMINATION; EQUAL OPPORTUNITIES; EQUALITY

References and Further Reading

Gaudron, Mary. 1990. In the eye of the law: The jurisprudence of equality. The Mitchell Oration. Adelaide, Australia: Equal Opportunity Commission.

Marian Sawer

EROTICA

Anaïs Nin wrote in the preface to her collection of erotica, *Delta of Venus* (1977), that upon examining this fiction that she wrote for pay in the 1940s, she could discern through the "distortion" of writing for money a feminine point of view distinguishing it from Henry Miller's more explicit sexual descriptions: "Women are more apt to fuse sex with emotion, with love, and to single out one man rather than be promiscuous."

Nin was writing from the context of a debate spurred by second-wave feminism about the politics and possibilities of defining a specifically female language, embedded somehow in the body and thus different from dominant, phallocentric language. Women writers have used these differences to define a genre of erotica that differs from pornography, which they say targets men's sexual desires through the objectification and violation of women. In 1978, Gloria Steinem, a leader in the U.S. women's movement, wrote for *Ms.* magazine, "Erotica is rooted in eros or passionate love, and thus in the idea of positive choice, free will, the yearning for a particular person"; in contrast, in pornography, "the subject is not love at all, but domination and violence against women." The African-American writer Audre Lorde argues that "pornography and eroticism [are] two diametrically opposed uses of the sexual" (1978).

Some feminists have criticized this opposition, arguing that it establishes a hierarchy of desires that divides women; rather, they say, feminism should create spaces for the expression of diverse desires and sexual practices. The U.S. writer Gayle Rubin argues that antiporn activists use the distinction between erotica and porn to condemn certain sexual practices, such as those represented in the lesbian magazine *On Our Backs,* as "heterosexual" and pornographic (1993). Trying to define a particular female desire produces a kind of essentialism that erases differences and could support the perpetuation of certain stereotypes of women, for example, as nurturing.

The debate also has class implications; erotica is often legitimized through claims to artistic status while pornography is delegitimized as mass culture. Susan Sontag wrote in 1967 that certain works deemed pornographic by some critics, including the controversial French novel *Story of O* by Pauline Réage, qualify as serious literature because of their ability to probe human consciousness. In contrast, she argues, standard pornography has stock plots and flat characters, intended solely for immediate sexual gratification.

Despite criticisms about the dichotomy, many women continue to see aesthetic and political value in the erotica/porn distinction, a belief reflected in the growth of a popular genre of women's erotica. For example, a 1994 anthology of writings, *Pleasure in the Word: Erotic Writings by Latin American Women,* argues that the collected stories give voice to Latin American women, who are denied the right to express sexual desire due to particular sociohistorical conditions that sanction the expression of male sexuality and try to repress female sexuality. In these stories, the literary expression of a distinct female desire does not represent a belief in essential biological differences but rather a common response among women writers to common experiences of oppression.

Moreover, erotica increasingly defines the communities of women united through the genre as characterized by difference—racial, cultural, age, sexuality, and so on. The London-based Sheba Collective wrote in the introduction to their second volume of lesbian erotica, *More Serious Pleasure* (1990), "There is still no consensus about the difference, if any, between erotica and pornography, let alone what a feminist definition of pornography is."

The development of a genre of women's erotica has also occurred in the film industry; in the United States, for example, former mainstream pornography star Candida Royalle started her own company in 1984, Femme Productions, which makes erotica from a woman's point of view, emphasizing women's pleasure and featuring women and men of different ages and body types.

See Also

PORNOGRAPHY IN ART AND LITERATURE

References and Further Reading

Lorde, Audre. 1978. *Uses of the erotic: The erotic as power.* Brooklyn: Out and Out.

Nin, Anaïs. 1977. *Delta of Venus.* New York: Harcourt, Brace, Jovanovich.

Olmos, Margarite Fernandez, and Lizabeth Paravisini-Gebert, eds. 1994. *Pleasure in the word: Erotic writings by Latin American women.* New York: Plume.

Rubin, Gayle. 1993. Misguided, dangerous and wrong: An analysis of anti-pornography politics. In *Bad girls and dirty pictures.* London: Pluto.

Sheba Collective, eds. 1990. *More serious pleasure.* Pittsburgh: Cleis.

Sontag, Susan. 1967. The pornographic imagination. *Styles of radical will.* New York: Farrar, Straus and Giroux.

Steinem, Gloria. 1978. Erotica and pornography: A clear and present danger. *Ms.* (November): 53–54, 75, 78.

Jane Juffer

ESSENTIALISM

Essentialism is the view that individuals are determined by physical, intellectual, and emotional attributes. Women are said to exist as a natural category—to share, historically and cross-culturally, a set of fixed biological or psychological attributes, which are claimed to be resistant to change. Essentialism is used to justify women's current social roles and, thus, provides political justification for the subordination of women as well as "naturalizing" the sexual division of labor.

Feminists tend to see themselves as antiessentialists: they challenge the view that a woman's position in society is biologically determined and thereby justifies gender inequalities. Ann Oakley (1972), for example, describes the fluidity of gender roles both cross-culturally and historically. Other feminists have been criticized, however, for essentialism—for example, Shulamith Firestone (1971), for biological essentialism, and Luce Irigaray (1985), for psychological essentialism. Beyond this, some radical feminists have been criticized for essentializing the structure of society, suggesting that the different roles of men and women in the social system are so rigidly prescribed that there is little possibility of women being anything but passive victims, while cultural feminists argue that men and women are essentially different but argue that female biologically determined traits such as nurturance and caring are superior to masculine ones.

Jackie Stacey (1993), however, has argued that essentialism and constructionism are not two opposed categories but opposite ends of a continuum on which all theories can be inscribed.

Poststructuralists have rejected both essentialism and constructivism and have argued that sexuality and identity is multiple and fragmented (Alice et al., 1998). They resist the idea that "sexual" is an indivisible difference and suggest that there is negotiation as to what constitutes our identities at any time (Grosz, 1993).

The feminist debates surrounding essentialism are political and broadly result in three positions. First, there are those who reject essentialism and argue that differences between men and women are socially constructed; challenging the social construction of gender will enable women to achieve equality with men. Second, some accept essentialism and argue that innate feminine traits are superior to masculine-determined ones and that the roles of men and women are essentially different. Finally, there are those who argue that self is fragmented and in flux, but also that difference does not preclude equality (see Scott, 1990).

See Also

BIOLOGICAL DETERMINISM; EUGENICS; HUMANITIES AND SOCIAL SCIENCES: FEMINIST CRITIQUES; NATURE-NURTURE DEBATE; SCIENCE: FEMINIST CRITIQUES

References and Further Reading

Alice, Lynne, and Friends. 1998. Bodies, sexualities and identities: A conversation. In Rosemary DuPlessis and Lynne Alice, eds., *Feminist thought in Aotearoa New Zealand.* Auckland: Oxford University Press.

Bottler, Judith. 1993. *Bodies that matter: On the discursive limits of sex.* London: Routledge.

Firestone, Shulamith. 1971. *The dialectic of sex: The case for feminist revolution.* London: Cape.

Grosz, Elizabeth. 1993. *Volatile bodies: Towards a corporeal feminism.* Bloomington: Indiana University Press.

Irigaray, Luce. 1985. *Speculum of the other woman.* Ithaca, N.Y.: Cornell University Press.

Oakley, Ann. 1972. *Sex, gender and society.* London: Temple Smith.

Scott, Joan. 1990. Deconstructing equality-versus-difference. In Marianne Hirsch and Evelyn Foxheller, eds., *Conflicts in feminism,* 134–148. New York and London: Routledge.

Stacey, Jackie. 1993. Untangling feminist theory. In D. Richardson and V. Robinson, eds., *Introducing women's studies.* London: Macmillan.

Pamela Abbott

ESTHETICS

See AESTHETICS.

ESTROGEN

Estrogens are female sex hormones that both women and men have in their bodies. Since the mid-twentieth century, estrogens have also been used as drugs in the treatment of a variety of symptoms of illness. Some estrogen drugs are based on synthetic substances that the body interprets as if they were natural estrogens. The best known of these compounds is diethylstilbestrol (DES).

In drugs given to women, estrogens have mainly been used in the treatment and control of fertility and reproduction. Estrogen, especially ethinyloestradiol, has been an important component in oral contraceptives. Moreover, estrogens have been marketed to women during and after menopause, almost as a cure-all, to make up for the natural decline of estrogen production in the body. The list of the purported benefits of such estrogen therapy is long, although the scientific evidence on its health effects is controversial. The aggressive marketing of estrogens to millions of women around the world plays on women's fears of aging and of losing sexual attraction. With populations aging worldwide, much money is involved in reconstructing women's natural aging into an illness that requires drug treatment over many years.

Estrogen drugs are not innocuous. Some of the women who took the early oral contraceptives that were high in estrogen content died prematurely from thromboembolic (blood-clotting) disorders, and others experienced milder episodes. Estrogens have for a long time been known to have a role in the promotion of certain cancer diseases, especially breast cancer and cancer of the reproductive organs in women. DES, given to pregnant women in the erroneous belief that it would prevent miscarriage, was identified in 1971 as a cause of potentially lethal vaginal cancer in some daughters who had been exposed to DES before birth. Some of the women and men who were exposed to DES before birth have malformed reproductive organs and impaired reproductive capability. Estrogen therapy for women increases the risks of breast cancer and endometrial cancer.

In the 1990s, concerns were raised that some industrially produced and widely used chemical compounds may be interpreted by the body as estrogens or antiestrogens and disrupt reproduction in animals and humans.

The women's health movement in the 1970s and the writing of such feminists as Barbara Seaman and Germaine Greer were influential in drawing women's attention to and raising women's awareness of the risks of estrogen drugs. Many female scientists have also contributed to this awareness in the form of numerous epidemiological studies about the effects of estrogen drug usage.

See Also

ABORTION; CANCER; CONTRACEPTION; ENDOCRINE DISRUPTION; HORMONES; MENOPAUSE; PHARMACEUTICALS; REPRODUCTIVE PHYSIOLOGY

References and Further Reading

Boston Women's Health Book Collective. 1998. *Our bodies, our selves for the new century.* New York: Simon and Schuster.

Greer, Germaine. 1991. *The change: Women, aging, and the menopause.* New York: Knopf.

Palmlund, Ingar. 1991. Risk evaluation and estrogens. *International Journal of Risk and Safety in Medicine* 2 (6): 321–342.

———, Roberta Apfel, Simone Buitendijik, Anne Cabau, and John-Gunnar Forsland. 1993. Effects of DES medication during pregnancy. *Journal of Psychosomatic Obstetrics and Gynaecology* 14: 71–89.

Ingar Palmlund

ETHICS: BIOETHICS

See BIOETHICS: FEMINIST.

ETHICS: Feminist

Feminist ethics is a set of approaches to moral theory and practice that aims to challenge, supplement, and reinterpret traditional ethics so that it (1) views men and women as moral equals and, therefore, (2) values women's and men's different moral experiences, insights, modes of reasoning, virtues, and commitments equally. Although feminist approaches to ethics are as many and varied as the feminists who formulate them, most of the approaches fit comfortably under one of two rubrics: care-focused feminist approaches to ethics or power-focused feminist approaches to ethics. A care-focused feminist approach to ethics has as its primary task the rehabilitation of such culturally associated feminine values as compassion, empathy, nurturance, and kindness. A power-focused feminist approach to ethics has as its first duty the elimination or modification of any system, structure, or set of norms that contributes to women's oppression.

Care-Focused Feminist Ethics

Care-focused approaches to feminist ethics have a long history in the Anglo-American world. Nineteenth-century thinkers such as Catherine and Harriet Beecher, Elizabeth Cady Stanton, and Charlotte Perkins Gilman all praised women's morality as not only different from but also as somehow better than men's morality. The Beecher sisters argued that women's "family labor" in the private world was at least as important as men's professional work in the public world. In *The New Housekeeper's Manual,* the two sisters outlined the principle of "domestic science," stressing how mentally and physically taxing women's work as wives and mothers is and, moreover, how rapidly society would crumble if women failed to do their jobs faithfully (Beecher, 1873). They suggested that women's goodness is the stabilizing force in any well-ordered, harmonious, "Christian" society.

Adding force to the Beechers' flattering portrait of women, Stanton claimed that precisely because women pos-

sess "the diviner qualities in human nature" (Buhle, 1978) they should be permitted to enter the public world. Associating men with what she termed the "male element...a destructive force, stern, selfish, aggrandizing, loving war, violence, conquest, acquisition" (Buhle, 1978), Stanton reasoned that the world would be a better place were women in charge of it, letting mercy, love, and hope reign supreme. Agreeing with Stanton that a world ruled by women would be better than the existing world ruled by men, Gilman wrote a fictional account of an all-female society—Herland—in which women successfully cultivate the best "masculine" as well as "feminine" virtues (Gilman, 1979). The women in Herland are independent, assertive, and hardy as well as empathetic, nurturing, and compassionate; but most of all, the women in Herland are mothers, attentive to one another and their children's needs.

Twentieth-century care-focused feminist approaches to ethics had much in common with their nineteenth-century forerunners, including some of their more problematic features. Among the most widely recognized twentieth-century exponents of the ethics of care are Carol Gilligan and Nel Noddings. In her innovative book, *In a Different Voice* (1982), Gilligan offers an account of women's moral development that challenges the traditional account of human beings' moral development as described by psychologist Lawrence Kohlberg. According to Kohlberg (1971), moral development is a six-stage progressive process; on his scale, women generally reach only stage three while men routinely reach stage five, which Kohlberg says is a more highly developed morality. Gilligan hypothesized that this discrepancy in the measurements pointed to a deficiency that lies not in women but in Kohlberg's scale, which measured typical *male* moral development rather than typical *human* moral development. Gilligan (1982) concluded that for a variety of cultural reasons, women typically utilize an ethics of care that stresses relationships and responsibilities, whereas men generally employ an ethics of justice that stresses rules and rights. Therefore, Kohlberg's scale inaccurately measures the morality of women because his scale is based on a model of morality typically reflected in the decisions and actions of men. Since women's decisions and actions typically reflect a care-focused morality, they need to be measured on a scale sensitive to the rhythms of feminine ethics.

Nel Noddings's relational ethics is another example of a care-focused "feminine" approach to ethics. In any good relationship, says Noddings (1984), there is the "one-caring" and the "cared-for." The one-caring should engross herself or himself in the cared-for, focusing on her or his needs, actions, and thoughts. In return, the cared-for should gratefully welcome the one-caring's attention, willingly sharing his or her own needs, hopes, and accomplishments with the one-caring. Noddings believes that caring consists more in specific obligations to particular people than in general duties to human kind. Concrete actions, far more than abstract intentions, define real caring.

Related to feminine approaches to ethics are so-called maternal approaches to ethics. Among others, Virginia Held (1987), Sara Ruddick (1989), and Caroline Whitbeck (1984) stress that the paradigm of contractual transactions between equally informed and equally powerful autonomous men does not serve to illuminate our everyday moral transactions. Most of our relationships are between unequals: the young and the old, the client and the professional, the student and the teacher, and so on. As maternal thinkers see it, a good mother-child relationship is the best paradigm to use in assessing the moral quality of these imbalanced relationships. For example, in the course of striving to preserve, help grow, and make socially acceptable their children, mothers (or mothering persons) teach themselves as well as their children how to be responsible persons sensitive to the needs and interests of others (Ruddick, 1989).

Gilligan, Noddings, and the maternal thinkers described above have been accused of espousing a morality based on false claims about the impact of one's gender on one's moral views. This accusation is not quite fair, however. Care-focused feminist ethicists acknowledge that not all women employ a care-focused morality and that not all men employ a justice-oriented morality. They note, however, that in western culture, it is less difficult for women to embrace stereotypical "male" virtues than it is for men to embrace stereotypical "female" virtues. Suspecting that men's reluctance to be viewed as caring and compassionate stems from western culture's continuing disrespect for so-called effeminate men, Gilligan and Noddings remind their readers that a fully morally developed person is a man or woman who combines justice and care perspectives equally (Gilligan, 1982).

In addition to being faulted for mistaken claims about men's and women's respective moralities, care-focused feminist ethicists have been faulted for presenting as universal an interpretation of men's and women's separate ethics that may reflect only the moral views of a particular group of people, such as Caucasian, well-educated, socially and economically privileged U.S. citizens. In this connection, the sociologist Carol Stack (1986) has argued that, as a result of their common legacy of discrimination, African-American men and women in the United States display a markedly similar style of moral reasoning when viewing themselves in relationship to others. Using Stack's observations, feminist

approaches to ethics may be criticized for separating the moral styles of humans along gender lines, without considering the implications of other factors that may influence moral decisions. Stack inferred from her research that similar conditions of economic deprivation, for example, can have more to do with similarities in "women's and men's vocabulary of rights, morality, and the social good" than gender roles.

A variation of this criticism—that traditional, justice-based ethics is actually the traditional ethics of a particular ethnic and socioeconomic group, not humans universally—could be made by those who espouse traditional Confucian ethics, which is structured around the maintenance of an elaborate set of reciprocal relationships (Yu-Lan, 1948). Traditional Chinese men as well as traditional Chinese women measure their moral development in terms of how well they fulfill their duties to each other. A similar point could be raised by Christians, who stress Jesus Christ's self-sacrificial acts, or the Buddhists, who emulate the compassionate acts of Buddha. In many cultures, especially religious ones, the virtue of care is *the* index of moral development for everyone, not just females.

Significantly, it is this last point that leads to a very different sort of criticism directed against exponents of care-focused feminist approaches to ethics. Critics with women's best interests at heart emphasize that care-focused approaches to ethics encourage all people, but particularly women in societies characterized by male domination and female subordination, to act in a servile manner. For example, although she celebrated women's capacity for unselfish self-sacrifice, Elizabeth Cady Stanton also stressed that women have a tendency to give too much of themselves. In interpreting a New Testament passage in which Jesus praises a widow for giving her last few coins to the poor, Stanton suggested that oppressed groups (in this instance, nineteenth-century U.S. women) cannot always afford to act like Christ—not without risking their own well-being. Agreeing that the widow's gift was indeed a precious one, Stanton nonetheless cautioned nineteenth-century U.S. women that women's self-sacrifice may effectively perpetuate women's second-class status (Stanton, 1972).

Similarly, Sandra Lee Bartky points out in her book *Femininity and Domination* (1990) that women's loving care of others, particularly men, can disempower women by making them less attentive to the ways in which patriarchal society favors men and oppresses women. Sheila Mullett (1989) reinforces this idea, emphasizing that a person cannot *truly* care for someone if she is economically, socially, or psychologically pressured to do so. Mullett claims that authentic caring cannot occur under conditions characterized by male domination and female subordination. Only under conditions of sexual equality and freedom can women care for men without men diminishing or disregarding them. Therefore, women must ask themselves whether the kind of caring in which they are engaged:

1. Fulfills the one caring
2. Calls on the unique and particular individuality of the caring
3. Is not produced by a person in a role because of gender, with one gender engaging in nurturing behavior and the other engaging in instrumental behavior
4. Is reciprocated with caring and not merely with the satisfaction of seeing the ones cared for flourishing and pursuing other projects
5. Takes place within the framework of consciousness-raising practice and conversation

Care can be freely given only when the one caring is not taken for granted. As long as men demand and expect more caring from women than women demand and expect from men, both sexes will remain morally impoverished; neither men nor women will be able to care authentically.

Although care-focused feminist approaches to ethics do succeed in their goal—to rehabilitate such culturally associated feminine values as compassion, empathy, nurturance, and kindness, so that these values are seen as essential elements of human morality—these approaches, as seen above, may be criticized for putting less emphasis on the domination of women and the power structures that make feminist approaches necessary for the reinterpretation of traditional ethics. Therefore, another feminist approach to moral theory and practice exists alongside the care-focused feminist approaches described above.

Power-Focused Feminist Ethics

Unlike care-focused feminist approaches to ethics, power-focused feminist approaches to ethics ask questions about male domination and female subordination *before* they ask questions about good and evil, care and justice, or mothers and children. In an attempt to specify the kind of questions that feminist, as opposed to nonfeminist, ethicists typically ask, the philosopher Alison M. Jaggar (1991) has claimed that to qualify as feminist, an approach to ethics (whether care focused or power focused) must first critique the gender-biased character of most nonfeminist (traditional) approaches to ethics. In particular, a power-focused feminist approach to ethics must challenge nonfeminist ethicists for subordinating women to men by neglecting, trivializ-

ing, or ignoring women's moral interests, issues, insights, and identities.

Acutely aware of the ways in which nonfeminist (traditional) ethicists have tended to dismiss women's morality as "second rate," Jaggar urges feminist ethicists to develop power-focused approaches to ethics that begin "from the conviction that the subordination of women is morally wrong and that the moral experience of women is as worthy of respect as that of men." According to Jaggar (1991), regardless of what else a power-focused feminist ethicist aims to do, she or he is required "(1) to articulate moral critiques of actions and practices that perpetuate women's subordination; (2) to prescribe morally justifiable ways of resisting such actions and practices; and (3) to envision morally desirable alternatives that will promote women's emancipation." Although power-focused feminist ethicists should attend first to patterns of male domination and female subordination, Jaggar believes they should then address the immoralities caused by other patterns of human domination and subordination. Not only sexism but also classism, ethnocentrism, heterosexism, ableism, and so on, are the enemies of feminist ethics.

Among power-focused feminist approaches to ethics are lesbian approaches to ethics, which view heterosexism in particular rather than sexism in general as the primary cause of women's subordination to men. Although these power-focused feminist approaches to ethics are deliberately directed to lesbian women, they also contain valuable lessons for heterosexual women. In general, most lesbian approaches to ethics replace the traditional moral question, Is this action good? with, Does this action help my quest for freedom and self-identity? Although lesbian ethicists stress choice rather than duty, they are not relativists. As Sarah Lucia Hoagland (1989) observes, when a lesbian chooses for herself, she chooses for other lesbians, who in turn choose for her.

Ethics, in this view, is not about doing what one believes is absolutely right for everyone but about learning how to fit one's own values into a moral tapestry being woven by a diverse group of weavers. Lesbian ethicists view relationships of domination and subordination as invidious to the moral project (Hoagland, 1988). Hoagland's lesbian ethics reflects a power-focused approach to ethics, a refusal to either dominate or to be dominated by another. A power-focused feminist approach to ethics is about people making their own choices, not about some people making rules for other people to follow. Hoagland also emphasizes that power-focused feminist approaches to ethics are *not* about some people sacrificing themselves on other people's behalf.

Although care-focused and power-focused feminist approaches to ethics are likely to take several directions in the future, many feminist ethicists do agree on the desire to develop a global perspective. Charlotte Bunch (1995), for example, claims that feminists must be aware not only of gender bias in ethics but also of bias resulting from family, race, class, cultural, religious, and professional differences. If one wishes to improve women's estate worldwide, feminist ethicists will need to learn how to frame their questions "globally," not simply "locally." Feminist ethicists also must recognize that some of the so-called developed world's moral concerns are viewed as moral luxuries rather than moral necessities in much of the so-called developing world. If feminist approaches to ethics truly wish to overcome inequality and oppression, particularly gender inequality and gender-based oppression, then they must offer to all human beings the kind of thinking about care and justice that has the power to create a world in which everyone has a chance to flourish.

See Also

BIOETHICS: FEMINIST; CAREGIVERS; CHILD DEVELOPMENT; EQUALITY; ETHICS: MEDICAL; ETHICS: SCIENTIFIC; JUSTICE AND RIGHTS; PHILOSOPHY

References and Further Reading

Bartky, Sandra Lee, ed. 1990. *Femininity and domination*. New York: Routledge.

Beecher, Catherine E., and Harriet Beecher Stowe. 1873. *The new housekeeper's manual*. New York: J. B. Ford.

Buhle, Mari Jo, and Paul Buhle, eds. 1978. *The concise history of women's suffrage*. Urbana: University of Illinois Press.

Bunch, Charlotte. 1995. A global perspective on feminist ethics and diversity. In Max O. Hallman, ed., *Expanding philosophical horizons: An anthology of nontraditional writings*, 172–180. Belmont, Calif.: Wadsworth.

Gilligan, Carol. 1982. *In a different voice*. Cambridge: Harvard University Press.

Gilman, Charlotte Perkins. 1979. *Herland: A lost feminist utopian novel*. New York: Pantheon .

Held, Virginia. 1987. Feminism and moral theory. In Eva Kittay and Diana Meyers, eds., *Women and moral theory*. Savage, Md.: Rowman and Littlefield.

Hoagland, Sarah Lucia. 1989. *Lesbian ethics*. Palo Alto, Calif.: Institute of Lesbian Studies.

Jaggar, Alison M. 1991. Feminist ethics: Projects, problems, prospects. In Claudia Card, ed., *Feminist ethics*. Lawrence: University of Kansas Press.

———. 1992. Feminist ethics. In Lawrence Becker, with Charlotte Becker, eds., *Encyclopedia of ethics*, 361–364. New York: Garland.

Kohlberg, Lawrence. 1971. From is to ought: How to commit the naturalistic fallacy and get away with it in the study of moral development. In T. Mischel, ed., *Cognitive development and epistemology*. New York: Academic.

Mullett, Sheila. 1989. Shifting perspectives: A new approach to ethics. In Lorraine Code, Sheila Mullett, and Christine Overall, eds., *Feminist perspectives*. Toronto: University of Toronto Press.

Noddings, Nel. 1984. *Caring: A feminine approach to ethics and moral education*. Berkeley: University of California Press.

Ruddick, Sara. 1989. *Maternal thinking: Toward a politics of peace*. Boston: Beacon.

Stack, Carol B. 1986. The culture of gender: Women and men of color. *Signs: Journal of Women in Culture and Society* 11 (2): 321–24.

Stanton, Elizabeth Cady. 1972. *The woman's Bible*. 2 vols. New York: Arno. (Originally published 1895.)

Whitbeck, Caroline. 1984. The maternal instinct. In Joyce Trebilcot, ed., *Mothering: Essays in feminist theory*. Totowa, N.J.: Rowman and Allanheld.

Yu-Lan, Fung. 1948. *A short history of Chinese philosophy*. New York: Free Press.

Rosemarie Tong

ETHICS: Medical

The field of medical ethics is also known as bioethics, biomedical ethics, and health care ethics. Medical ethics applies a set of guiding principles to the evaluation of decisions, actions, and policies regarding health.

Principles of Medical Ethics

There are three leading principles: respect for persons, beneficence, and justice. Respect for persons requires that women and men be equally valued as autonomous persons, capable decision makers, and full participants in medical decisions. The principle of beneficence refers to practitioners' obligation to treat patients in such a way that more good than harm results from the course of treatment. Finally, the principle of justice stipulates that all members of a society should have equal access to the health care system (Macklin, 1993).

Reasonable people, feminist writers included, disagree about the relative importance of these principles in particular cases and about the best means of implementing them. Some maintain that a quest for universal guiding principles is futile; instead, a case-by-case approach, with due attention to social context, is required. One's concept of health—whether defined narrowly as the absence of disease or more broadly to encompass happiness and well-being—also conditions one's approach to medical ethics. According to the latter view, gender inequities in health care are just a reflection of women's myriad disadvantages in other spheres, such as work and the family. If one begins from this broader perspective, it follows that ethical solutions to women's health care problems must involve wider social changes in women's lives.

The ethicist Ruth Macklin, who defines health broadly, has explained why justice—"the obligation to treat like cases alike, in relevant respects"—should take precedence when principles conflict (Macklin, 1993). This core principle is violated when, for example, women are underrepresented at the highest levels of decision making concerning health care, when social and economic inequities underlie and exacerbate women's health problems, when women are excluded from research designs, or when women are defined primarily in terms of their reproductive functions. In the third world, extreme poverty and patriarchal family structures worsen the gender injustices that are found everywhere, contributing to women's excess morbidity and premature death (Koblinsky et al., 1993).

Feminism and Medical Ethics

By the end of the twentieth century, few feminist critiques of medical ethics had appeared, in part because it was a new discipline and in part because its writers have been unusually sensitive to the basic injunctions of feminism. However, in a far-reaching critique of medical ethics from a feminist perspective, the philosopher Susan Sherwin (1992) takes the discipline to task for its too-narrow focus on physicians' moral dilemmas and doctor–patient relationships. She adopts a far broader view not only of the meaning of health but of the reforms within medicine needed to achieve it. Sherwin's comprehensive treatment of ethical issues in health care ranges over topics of concern to women everywhere, including sexuality, contraception, abortion, patient autonomy, and the respective roles of gender, race, and class in the delivery of health care.

Medical technology, medical experiments, and medical practices may be enormously beneficial to women's health. But they also lend themselves to abuse if misused. Hence the growing emphasis on patients' rights, full disclosure of pertinent information, and a careful weighing of risks and benefits. Because of the centrality of reproduction in women's lives, feminist writers on medical ethics give special attention to reproductive issues, including the toll on women of inadequate access to safe and effective contra-

ception, restrictive abortion laws, a cultural preference for sons, and maternal mortality. Many take a very cautious approach to the spread of new reproductive technologies, like in vitro fertilization. These technologies are often presented by the medical establishment and the mass media as an unalloyed boon to infertile people, but critics point out that they can be considered a particular hazard to women because they help perpetuate coercive pronatalist attitudes, strengthen male control of reproduction, and threaten women's health with powerful drugs and invasive procedures (Corea et al., 1987; Sherwin, 1992).

Feminists have raised vital questions about and offered compelling insights into the proper place of medicine in society and have challenged its role in the oppression of women. The solutions they propose require change not only in medical practices but in the wider society. The ultimate goal is a more egalitarian system in which individual rights are protected, women's values are duly respected, and women are empowered to control their lives. Not just the health of individual women but the health of society as a whole will benefit from such a transformation.

See Also

BIOETHICS: FEMINIST; DISABILITY AND FEMINISM; ETHICS: SCIENTIFIC; EXPERIMENTS ON WOMEN; FERTILITY AND FERTILITY TREATMENT; GYNECOLOGY; HEALTH: OVERVIEW; MATERNAL HEALTH AND MORBIDITY; MEDICAL CONTROL OF WOMEN; REPRODUCTIVE TECHNOLOGIES

References and Further Reading

Corea, Gena, Renate Duelli Klein, Jalna Hanmer, et al. 1987. *Man-made women: How new reproductive technologies affect women.* Bloomington: Indiana University Press.

Holmes, Helen Bequaert, and Laura M. Purdy, eds. 1992. *Feminist perspectives in medical ethics.* Indianapolis: Indiana University Press.

Koblinsky, Marge, Judith Timyan, and Jill Gay, eds. 1993. *The health of women: A global perspective.* Boulder, Col.: Westview.

Macklin, Ruth. 1993. Women's health: An ethical perspective. *Journal of Law, Medicine, and Ethics* 21(2): 23–29.

Pence, Gregory. 1995. *Classic cases in medical ethics.* New York: McGraw-Hill.

Peterson, Kerry, ed. 1997. *Intersections: Women on law, medicine and technology.* Aldershot/Ashgate: Dartmouth.

Sherwin, Susan. 1992. *No longer patient: Feminist ethics and health care.* Philadelphia: Temple University Press.

Barbara Logue

ETHICS: Scientific

Science and ethics have always been closely connected, despite the fact that the dominant definition of modern science makes a sharp separation between fact and value. Recent work in feminist studies, in social and historical studies of science, and in the sociology of knowledge give a more perspicuous analysis of the relation between ethics and science. At the same time, these approaches offer a new understanding of the moral responsibility of scientific professionals and encourage new ways of practicing science.

The current, dominant definition of science is an ideological one that grew up in western nations as science became institutionalized. In this definition, ethics is the "other" to modern science, characterized in terms of what science is not. Scientific knowledge is said to be objective and controlled by data and method, while morality is subjective and open to choice; scientific knowledge is true for all times, free of culture and history, while morality is relative and culture bound. This ideology of science is supported by dividing the physical and natural sciences from the social sciences, the latter said to be polluted by value judgments. In the new feminist research, modern science as a whole is shown to be a socially and historically embedded activity, one in which scientists exercise cognitive authority in defining nature (including human nature) and in defining public problems and their solutions. This change in perspective makes it possible to show that scientific knowledge may be used as an instrument of cultural domination, despite the claims of universality and neutrality.

Some feminist historians of science have argued that modern science is based on an old, patriarchal idea of nature (including human nature) as a body that needs to be subject to rational control, an idea that also valorizes the masculine principle as active and dominating and the feminine as passive and irrational. At present, human beings themselves are being defined (for the sake of science) as biological organisms whose essential characteristics are genetically determined—thus, the human genome project. This is a representation of the world from a certain political and moral perspective, not simply a description from an "Archimedean point" outside politics, society, and morality.

In this perspective, nature and bodies are passive, scientists are active in predicting public and personal problems. The aim of science becomes prediction and rational control—flood control, population control, fertility or infertility control, control of epidemics, of pests that eat crops, of meteors that might smash the earth, of the genetic makeup of organisms, of evolution itself. Feminist historians have argued that the outcome of the patriarchal perspective, particularly in biomedical science, has been to control women. Feminist research on the "reproductive sciences" demonstrates an intimate and continual connection between morality, politics, and research, in both western and nonwestern nations.

The old ethics made scientific knowledge neutral and left moral decisions up to individual scientists—"Should I personally do this research?" Feminist epistemology has argued that making knowledge is a collective activity, so that it is essential to develop a professional ethics that allows scientists to consider broad outcomes of their collective work. The new ethics would include the outcomes of scientific work for the environment broadly considered, for human health and welfare, and for preserving or easing gross differences, as well as the ways that scientific work supports or mitigates dominance hierarchies. The outcomes affecting women would be particularly important in this new ethics.

A change in professional ethics would also bring a change in scientific practice. Dorothy Smith is one sociologist who has recommended a change in her own discipline. In her "sociology for women," she argues that the point of research is to illuminate the world from the "standpoint" of women, in the sense that women should be able to use the research to understand how their society operates. This perspective would presumably allow women themselves to define human nature and social problems and bring about their own solutions.

Ecofeminist theory as well as the feminist ethics of care would also require changing scientific ethics because research and technology would be governed by care in relationship—care by the researchers for all living things and for the planet itself. Recent work on the "precautionary principle" takes care as a component of scientific decision making. A precautionary principle requires a change in the ideological goal of science, for care is not compatible with prediction and control. Contemporary proponents of a Gandhian science also advocate care and taking the point of view of people of the community, aiming at *swaraj*—the independence of the community through the inner, moral independence of its members. The point of a professional ethics would be to offer a way for researchers to find moral independence within themselves as a community in order to serve the larger community and care for all living things.

See Also

IN SCIENCE; SCIENCE: FEMINIST PHILOSOPHY; SCIENCE: FEMINISM AND SCIENCE STUDIES

References and Further Reading

Addelson, Kathryn Pyne. 1994. *Moral passages: Toward a collectivist moral theory.* New York: Routledge.

Fonow, Mary Margaret, and J. A. Cook. 1991. *Beyond methodology.* Bloomington: Indiana University Press.

Harding, Sandra, 1998. *Is science multicultural? Postcolonialisms, feminisms, and epsitemologies.* Bloomington: Indiana University Press.

Hubbard, Ruth. 1990. *The politics of women's biology.* New Brunswick, N.J.: Rutgers University Press.

Jaggar, Alison M. 1994. *Living with contradictions: Controversies in feminist social ethics.* Boulder, Col.: Westview.

Lewontin, Richard C. 1991. *Biology as ideology: The doctrine of DNA.* New York: Harper Perennial.

Merchant, Carolyn. 1983. *The death of nature: Women, ecology, and the scientific revolution.* San Francisco: Harper and Row.

Raffenspergu, Carolyn, and Joel Tickner. 1999. Protecting public health and the environment: *Implementing the precautionary principle.* Cavela, Calif.: Island Press.

Sahasrabudhey, Sunil. n.d. *Science and politics: Essays in Gandhian perspective.* New Delhi: Ashish.

Smith, Dorothy E. 1987. *The everyday world as problematic: A feminist sociology.* Boston: Northeastern University Press.

Windt, Peter, P. C. Appleby, M. P. Battin, L. P. Francis, and B. M. Landesman, eds. 1989. *Ethical issues in the professions.* Englewood Cliffs, N.J.: Prentice Hall.

Kathryn Pyne Addelson
Mary Huggins Gamble

ETHNIC CLEANSING

"Ethnic cleansing" is a late-twentieth-century term that is often said to be a euphemism for genocide. One understanding of ethnic cleansing is the forced removal of a targeted group from a given territory. Another understanding is the extermination of a targeted group. In the first understanding of the phrase, the thing being "cleansed" would be territory. In the second understanding of the phrase, the thing being cleansed would be some assumedly ethnically "pure" population group.

Both understandings of the term "ethnic cleansing" are based on racist definitions of population groups. In addition, these racist categories of difference often suggest political or religious associations. In many instances, the political or religious associations and the categories obscure each other, so observers may perceive only one or the other as the motivating force.

Mass destruction of targeted populations has a long history. The twentieth century saw terrifyingly wide and modernized versions of genocide. These include the genocide of the Armenians in Turkey during World War I; the genocide (or Holocaust, or Shoa) perpetrated by the Nazis against Jews and other populations in Europe during World War II; and the Khmer Rouge genocide of Cambodians during the 1970s. Vast numbers of human beings have been slaughtered in these and other places. What, then, is new about ethnic cleansing?

Ethnic Cleansing—A New Concept?

If ethnic cleansing is nothing more than genocide, why has a new term for genocide come into being? This article explores that question from one perspective. Two recent developments that are significant in this regard are international law and international jurisprudence.

Bosnia is central to the notion of ethnic cleansing because the wars there in the 1990s elicited the use of the term by a superpower and because it provides a recent instance of well-documented military policy that aimed at the destruction of the enemy *civilian* population. The phrase "ethnic cleansing" itself is thought by many to have first been uttered by Lawrence Eagleburger, who served as the U.S. Secretary of State from 1992 to 1993, during the wars in Bosnia and Herzegovina and in Croatia. During these wars, military and paramilitary Serb nationalist forces associated with the Yugoslav National Army engaged in widespread, systematic attacks on non-Serb populations in the regions of the former Yugoslavia just mentioned (Bassiouni, 1994). The United States was involved with governmental leaders of the countries at war, including Slobodan Milosevic in Serbia, in negotiations that would lead to the signing of the Dayton Accord and the cessation of hostilities in late 1995. To admit that such leaders were responsible for genocide would have embarrassed and hindered U.S. foreign policy. The less harsh, vague phrase "ethnic cleansing" avoided attributing responsibility for the crime of genocide to Milosevic and others, at least for the time being.

In Bosnia, meanwhile, it has been charged, Serb nationalist forces used widespread murder, torture, rape, castration, and other means to terrorize non-Serb civilian populations and force them into flight. Major cities fell under siege for years. In rural areas, paramilitary forces often joined with Yugoslav National Army (Serb nationalist) troops to force civilians to abandon their homes and villages. The Serb nationalists then burned all the buildings except for those identified as belonging to Serbs. This wholesale destruction of property—including civil and personal records, artifacts, and even cemeteries—was a major factor in the genocide in Bosnia, as it made return of the non-Serb civilian population difficult it not impossible.

In 1994, Rwanda was the site of another genocide. Although it was associated with Hutu and Tutsi tribal identities and made use of tribal enmities, this genocide, too, was at least partly politically motivated. The international media and the official representatives of states, having become accustomed to the euphemism "ethnic cleansing" through its extensive use in policy related to the former Yugoslavia and in coverage of events there, adopted the same phrase to describe the massacres in Rwanda. Curiously, however, the term has rarely been used to describe the genocidal persecution of Kurds in Iraq or potentially genocidal aspects of the Russian war against rebel Chechnyans. Thus, "ethnic cleansing" seems to have been coined as a politically suitable way to avoid accusing those with whom one might wish or might have to negotiate of the worst crimes imaginable.

Genocide is punishable by international and national laws; ethnic cleansing is not. According to the Geneva Convention against Genocide, genocide is *any* crime committed with the intention of destroying a group. Mass murder, the crime most often associated with genocide, and forced displacement of civilian populations, a crime also commonly understood as genocide, are among the specific crimes listed. Another less commonly recognized form of genocide noted by the Geneva Convention is the prevention of reproduction in the targeted population. The realities of the recent genocides in Bosnia and in Rwanda bring to light more crimes as crimes of genocide. Foremost among these is rape.

Rape and Genetic Warfare

Rape was a secondary means (after machete attack) of mass murder in Rwanda, where women were at times tied to posts at crossroads to be raped by any and every man who came along. In Bosnia, rape was one of the primary means of genocide. There, camps were alleged to exist in which non-Serb girls and women were raped for the purpose of engendering enforced pregnancies. This was mandated by military policy, which aimed at producing not "mixed" children but, according to nationalist logic, "little Serb soldiers" who, when grown, would claim enemy territory for a legendary Greater Serbia and purportedly slaughter any non-Serbs who refused to leave that territory. Here we see the dual genocidal crimes of expulsion and mass murder—those crimes

most often referred to as "ethnic cleansing"—projected one generation into the future.

Rape "cleansed" territory and the ethnic groups in Rwanda and Bosnia by inducing terror and the flight of targeted populations and by rendering its victims physically, psychologically, or socially unsuitable for future reproduction. In Bosnia, where rape was used also to enforce pregnancy, it cleansed territory and ethnicity by producing children the perpetrators (or their commanders) considered to be purely Serb. By denying the mothers' contribution, Serb nationalist policy arrived, through warped genetic logic, at the blatant paradox of genocide by means of reproduction.

Still another consideration related to ethnic cleansing is that its relatively benign associations (with traditional identities and cleanliness) may be used to obscure the development of new methods of destruction. Mass murder—with its implications of *genetic* cleansing—and forced (by torture, enslavement, and terror) displacement—with its implications of *territorial* cleansing—are harbingers, along with genocidal rape and enforced pregnancies, of what may be the genocidal method of the new century, actual *genetic* warfare. Such warfare would enable attacking forces to engender genetic changes in targeted populations in order to induce immediate and inheritable harmful effects, such as illness, weakness, and even death, thereby debilitating and destroying the targeted population. If we call genocide ethnic cleansing now, we risk missing the mortal threat to not only local but also global populations that genetic warfare would bring.

Ethnic Cleansing and the Law

International law has recently strengthened its capacity to prosecute genocide. In particular, international jurisdiction has recently been improved by the founding of two ad hoc tribunals, the United Nations International Criminal Tribunal for the former Yugoslavia and its counterpart for Rwanda. Additionally, in a move that will likely have profound implications for life on the planet, the United Nations has established a permanent International Criminal Court to hold wide jurisdiction during times of peace as well as times of war. This International Criminal Court awaits ratification of its convention by all member countries, including the United States of America, which so far has refused to do so.

By calling it ethnic cleansing, political figures created a kinder, gentler euphemism for genocide just when they wanted to portray their negotiating partners, some of whom were responsible for genocidal policies, in a respectable light. This was also the time when the international community was acting to establish tribunals that hold war criminals and other perpetrators of genocide more accountable in a global context than ever before. These facts warn us to beware of the term "ethnic cleansing." It is dangerously deceptive.

See Also

GENOCIDE; RAPE

References and Further Reading

Allen, Beverly. 1996. *Rape warfare: The hidden genocide in Bosnia-Herzegovina and Croatia.* Minneapolis: University of Minnesota Press.

Bassiouni, M. Cherif. 1996. *Accountability for international crimes and serious violations of fundamental human rights.* Durham, N.C.: Duke University School of Law.

———, and committee. 1994. *United Nations Commission of Experts report on grave breaches of the Geneva Conventions and other violations of international humanitarian law committed in the territory of the former Yugoslavia.* New York: United Nations.

Chorbajian, Levon, and George Shirinian, eds. 1999. *Studies in comparative genocide.* New York: St. Martin's.

Des Forges, Alison. 1999. *Leave none to tell the story: Genocide in Rwanda.* New York: Human Rights Watch.

Drew, Margaret. 1988. *Facing history and ourselves: Holocaust and human behavior: Annotated bibliography.* New York: Walker.

Encyclopedia of the Holocaust. 1990. New York: Macmillan.

Horowitz, Irving Louis. 1997. *Taking lives: Genocide and state power.* New Brunswick, N.J.: Transaction.

Ratner, Steven R. 1997. *Accountability for human rights atrocities in international law: Beyond the Nuremberg legacy.* Oxford: Clarendon; New York: Oxford University Press.

Roberts, Adam, and Richard Guelff, eds. 1989. *Documents on the laws of war.* 2nd ed. Oxford: Oxford University Press.

Stiglmayer, Alexandra, ed. 1994. *Mass rape: The war against women in Bosnia-Herzegovina.* Lincoln: University of Nebraska Press.

Strozier, Charles B., and Michael Flynn, eds. 1996. *Genocide, war, and human survival.* Lanham, Md.: Rowman and Littlefield.

Beverly Allen

ETHNIC STUDIES I

Ethnic studies, the study of U.S. racialized ethnic groups, began in the 1970s with the establishment of the ethnic studies department at the University of California at Berkeley.

Ethnic studies encompasses the ethnic-specific field of black studies, African-American or Africana studies, Asian-American and Asian Pacific Islander studies, and Chicano-Chicana and Latino-Latina studies, existing as separate academic programs or departments or as ethnic-specific units within ethnic studies programs that incorporate comparative ethnic studies. American Indian studies usually stands alone or within departmental programs separate from ethnic studies because Native Americans as sovereign nations are not racialized American ethnics. However, in some instances, American Indian studies works closely with ethnic studies, intersecting with themes of colonization, slavery, and racism. The field is variously described and structured in programs and departments as interdisciplinary or multidisciplinary, comparative or ethnic specific.

Ethnic studies emerged in higher education as a result of the civil rights movement of the 1950s and 1960s. Newly arrived on predominantly white campuses in the late 1960s, black students demanded curricula reflective of African and African-American experiences and based on scholarship and writing by black Americans from the seventeenth century on. These demands evolved into demands—largely from coalitions of students of color who identified with their third world ancestry and history—for black studies, Chicano studies, Puerto Rican and Latino studies, Asian-American studies, and American Indian studies. What has come to be called ethnic studies was born. Campuses as disparate as Cornell University, the University of Massachusetts, and Smith College in the East to the College of Wooster and Earlham College in the Midwest to San Francisco State, California State at Long Beach, and the University of California at Berkeley and Santa Barbara in the West developed programs in black studies and ethnic studies that have weathered assaults on academic integrity, budget cuts, and subversive counseling of students to discourage them from majoring in these fields. During the last years of the twentieth century and the first of the twenty-first century, many colleges and universities were starting new programs and departments, while others were already celebrating thirty years of teaching and scholarship.

Goals of Ethnic Studies

Ethnic studies has major goals of correcting distorted and incorrect scholarship about U.S. racialized ethnics and advancing new knowledge about and analyses of the history, literature, politics, economics, cultures, and sociology of these groups and their relation to the larger society. This places ethnic studies in a precarious position because its scholars are often viewed as malcontents who produce "inferior" scholarship simply because it challenges mainstream interpretations of events, artistic expressions, movements, and epochs. Students often expect ethnic studies to address issues of personal identity, especially since mixed-race identity became more prominent in the latter years of the twentieth century.

The name "ethnic studies" is viewed by many as a misnomer because of the focus on the social construction of race and the ways that race and racism shape racialized ethnic American reality. In addition, many ethnic studies programs include the study of immigration and transnationalism, Africa and African diaspora, and cultural and social containment, while others focus on the more cultural manifestations of racialized American ethnics. Race in ethnic studies programs is understood to be a social construction that has real effects. Ethnicity is defined variously as cultural identification that is both U.S. American and ethnic—that is, connected by family, history, or memory to a past that is simultaneously of and not of this nation. The effort to describe and define the historical, social, cultural, political, and social dimensions of racialized ethnics in ethnic studies has been met with skepticism at best and racism at the worst. The field therefore has not received the recognition it deserves, earned by scholars of note such as Vincent Harding, Vine Deloria, Ronald Takaki, Joy James, Manning Marable, John Blassingame, Mary Francis Berry, José Saldivar, Sauling Wong, Tey Diana Rebolledo, Henry Louis Gates Jr., E. San Juan Jr., Barbara Christian, and many others.

Ethnic studies is also the academic manifestation of multiculturalism, the movement in the United States beginning in the 1970s to have U.S. American culture and life recognize and benefit from the cultural diversity of the nation. As such, it is diametrically opposed to the long-held tradition of the melting pot and advances a pluralism that goes beyond the coexistence of cultural pluralism as defined by Horace Kallen in the 1920s to a cultural pluralism constructed on the shared experiences of American citizens. Racial, ethnic, class, and gender differences however have, as one might expect, challenged the shared experience pluralism to engage power relationships and difference. Historically, however, the United States has viewed difference as a deficit, something to be ignored or eradicated. How to examine, study, and benefit from both difference and similarities is a major challenge of both multiculturalism and ethnic studies. Being both American and racialized ethnic embodies this challenge, and neither scholarship nor pedagogy has reconciled the opposition that racism engenders in this situation.

The Relationship between Ethnic Studies and Women's Studies

Gender is the most prominent difference in both ethnic-specific and comparative ethnic studies, and each of the areas of ethnic studies struggles with the incorporation of gender analyses into its scholarship and teaching. From the late 1970s through the 1980s in particular, black women scholars challenged male-centered and male-dominated scholarship in black studies, creating the field of black women studies, buttressed by works of black women writers, literary scholars, and historians extending from the nineteenth century. Chicana and Asian-American scholars soon followed suit. Seminal works such as *Sturdy Black Bridges, This Bridge Called My Back, Borderlands/La Frontera,* and *The Forbidden Stitch* not only highlighted U.S. women of color and stated their feminism but also signaled the exclusion of women's lives as a serious part of ethnic studies. The extraordinary scholarship by racialized ethnic women in the United States has affected the program, departments, scholarship, and pedagogy of ethnic studies such that, at the beginning of the twenty-first century, the challenge came to be seen as presenting the vast scholarship coherently to students within the confines of an undergraduate major.

The intersections of race, gender, class, and ethnicity have plagued women's studies and ethnic studies. How do we, in a culture that conceptualizes life in binaries, express and examine the ways that, for example race and racism are shaped, moderated, and modulated by gender, class, ethnicity, age, sexual identity, and others of the multiple identities humans claim and express? How do we express and examine the ways that, for example, gender, sexual identity, sexism, and heterosexism are shaped, moderated, and modulated by race, class, ethnicity, age, and others of the multiple identities humans claim and express?

Curriculum Transformation

The movement and the evolving field of curriculum transformation has sought since the early 1980s to address the corrective functions of women's studies and ethnic studies both within themselves and in relation to the traditional liberal arts and sciences. One goal of curriculum transformation is to incorporate the study of women into the curriculum. Since not all women are white and not all the racialized ethnics are not men, then in the U.S. context at least, curriculum transformation has to reckon with and include racialized, ethnic women. Curriculum transformation during the 1980s and early 1990s enjoyed support from major private and public foundations, and began to encourage "the difficult dialogue" between ethnic studies and women's studies. The goal of this dialogue was a more accurate body of knowledge regarding white women and racialized ethnic men and women. Faculty took part in workshops to read extensively across disciplines, to revise syllabi, and to rethink pedagogy. Feminist pedagogy attempted to address issues of authority in the classroom in order to have women's voices heard. Ethnic studies either gravitated toward the Freirian model of a pedagogy for the oppressed or ignored pedagogy and its arguments. Both fields struggled with advocates of essentialism who pursued scholarship on gender, sexual, or racial identity first and foremost; with academic conservatives who viewed solid scholarship on women and on racialized ethnics as only marginally important; and with academic bigots who preferred to see women and racialized ethnics in small numbers and mostly silent, if in the academy at all. Curriculum transformation continues, but not with the vigor and dedication that its proponents exhibited in its early years. Ethnic studies has not fully embraced it, and women studies moved on to an international or postmodern focus.

At the beginning of the twenty-first century, ethnic studies had its own professional organizations, its own faculty, and its own majors. It boasted a few strong M.A. and Ph.D. programs and a plethora of old and new undergraduate programs. Outside the United States there was growing interest in racialized American ethnic studies. In many university programs affiliated with the European American Studies Association, research interests and teaching in American ethnic literatures was particularly popular and strong. From Britain to Spain, Italy, and Germany, during the 1990s numerous conferences on African-American and Chicana-Chicano literature met with great success. Various European institutes in American studies have hosted U.S. faculty to lecture on literature, legal issues, history and politics, all reflecting primarily ethnic study content. As American studies programs proliferate in Europe, South Africa, and Asia, ethnic studies content forms much of the major interests of students and faculty; however, it is not formalized as a particular field.

Ethnic studies as a field seeks to define its distinct epistemology, to study U.S. people of color as subjects, not objects, and to "recover and reconstruct the lived historical experiences and memories of those Americans whom history has neglected, to identify and credit the contributions of these Americans to the making of U.S. society and culture, to chronicle protest and resistance, and finally, to establish alternative values and visions, institutions, and cultures" (Hu-De Hart, 701). As such, it occupies a precarious posi-

tion in higher education, offering possibilities for new knowledge and the engagement of power relationships and difference—all possibilities that challenge the status quo.

See Also

CULTURE: OVERVIEW; EDUCATORS: HIGHER EDUCATION; ETHNICITY; FEMINISM: AFRICAN AMERICAN; FEMINISM: ASIAN AMERICAN; FEMINISM: CHICANA; HIGHER EDUCATION: OVERVIEW; MULTICULTURALISM; RACE

References and Further Reading

Butler, Johnnella E. 1991. The difficult dialogue of curriculum transformation. In Johnnella E. Butler and John C. Walter, eds., *Transforming the curriculum: Ethnic studies and women's studies.* New York: State University of New York Press.

———. 1989. Difficult dialogues. *Women's Review of Books* (Feb.): 16.

Hu-De Hart, Evelyn. 1995. Ethnic studies in U.S. higher education: History, development, and goals. In James A. Banks and Cherry A. McGee Banks, eds., *Handbook of research on multicultural education,* 796–707. New York: Macmillan.

Hull, Gloria T., Patricia Bell Scott, and Barbara Smith, eds. 1982. *All the women are white, all the blacks are men, but some of us are brave.* New York: Feminist Press.

Schmitz, Betty, Johnnella E. Butler, Deborah Rosenfelt, and Beverly Guy-Sheftall. 1995. Women's studies and curriculum transformation. In James A. Banks and Cherry A. McGee Banks, eds., *Handbook of research on multicultural education,* 708–728. New York: Macmillan.

Johnnella Butler

ETHNIC STUDIES II

Feminist intellectuals analyze how ethnicity and gender simultaneously shape women who often remain invisible to patriarchal scholars and society. Since the 1960s and 1970s, when feminism attained public awareness and gained institutional credibility, efforts to demarginalize women resulted in the development of organized women's studies programs at universities. At the same time, the civil rights movement in the United States and global human rights programs—instigated because of horrific violence against specific groups of peoples, such as Khmer Rouge leader Pol Pot's directives to slaughter Cambodians—influenced some American and European colleges to offer classes about ethnicity. Students learned about the images, myths, and stereotypes of women and minorities perpetuated by society and presented in literature, popular culture, and history.

Some scholars integrated themes addressing ethnicity and women in their research and classroom lectures. Peer reception often discouraged academics from pursuing ethnic analyses of women. Because the academy at that time was dominated by white male scholars who often were not empathetic toward members of other cultural groups and women, many researchers were frustrated by limited or no funding. Others suffered professional losses, such as being denied tenure or derided publicly with unjust criticisms of their work, which was falsely described as juvenile, poorly conceived, or unimportant. In the United States, minority, Native American, and women's studies programs coexisted within established humanities and social studies departments. An interdisciplinary approach to ethnicity and gender was considered the best pedagogical method.

Early ethnicity and women's studies programs were dominated by western civilization perspectives and rarely mentioned nonwestern cultures. Scholars were restrained by administrative stipulations regarding course content. Because departmental and university leaders were primarily white males, they determined curricula according to what they considered essential for students to study. Even though they usually lacked experience with gender or ethnic scholarship, these administrators defined what scholars in the field should be familiar with in order to be considered experts and excluded aspects of global culture that they deemed insignificant. Many disdainful school executives incorrectly dismissed ethnic studies as rehashing immigrant history. Both women's studies and ethnic studies programs were often the first curricula slashed during budget cuts. Some professional organizations, such as the National Association of Scholars, claimed to support ethnic studies but criticized scholars specializing in that field for being too extreme by focusing on oppression of specific groups and accusing individuals of racism.

As more diverse students and faculty joined college communities, many academics gradually accepted research focusing on women and ethnic groups as legitimate topics for study. Still, ethnic minorities were often seen as outsiders and equated with stereotyped traits, such as being alarmingly exotic or frighteningly threatening. The first wave of ethnic studies professors were usually Anglo-Saxon males and females and represented privileged backgrounds because of their elite educations and family connections. They were biased by their own gender and ethnic experiences and tended to omit women in ethnic lectures and racial groups from women's studies discussions; their presentations were slanted by their misunderstandings of cultures dissimilar from their own. They also ignored people with sexual orientations oppositional from their heterosexual beliefs. As faculty membership expanded to include representatives of varied groups, ethnic studies changed to incorporate comprehensive international perspectives and enhance awareness of ethnic truths, such as that the term *Native American* refers to many tribes and that blacks and Asians have numerous countries of origin.

Female Foundations for Ethnicity Scholarship

A century prior to the professionalization of ethnicity studies—particularly those focusing on how cultural identities influenced women's issues—female ethnologists and anthropologists helped pioneer research methodology that formed the framework for later investigations. They were among the first people to analyze the role of women in societies. Studying scientific aspects of race, ethnologists collaborated with anthropologists to understand the relationship of humanity and culture. The behavior, beliefs, and lifestyles of groups both represented and molded their ethnic identity, which also was affected by their racial affiliation, including genetic and physical traits. European and American women, mostly from upper-class or monied families, were notable leaders in the fields of ethnology and anthropology. These women sometimes accompanied their scientist husbands or male relatives into the field or joined organized expeditions to various foreign locales. A few independently initiated and embarked on explorations, sometimes sponsored by an institutional or private patron. These adventurers lived among ethnic groups and described them in accounts that were published by scientific organizations and museums, newspapers and magazines, or as books.

Two eminent ethnologists were Erminnie Smith (1836–1886), who was a pioneering female field ethnographer, and Matilda Stevenson (1849–1915), who in 1885 founded and served as president of the Women's Anthropological Society. Daisy May Bates (1863–1951), an Irish anthropologist, read allegations that white Australians abused indigenous peoples. She lived with Aborigines and recorded information about their culture including dialects, religion, and myths. She wrote *The Passing of the Aborigines* (1938) to increase anthropologists' awareness of those tribes. Her embellished accounts caused many scientists to disregard her valid observations. The American explorer Delia Akeley (1875–1970) was the first non-African woman to cross Africa alone. She encountered indigenous peoples, particularly the Pygmies of the Ituri Forest, and stayed with them, recording her impressions of their culture and criticizing how outsiders treated natives. Akeley's observations provided anthropologists with data for future scientific research and alerted westerners to the significance of other cultures.

The French philosopher Alexandra David-Neel (1868–1969) disguised herself as a nun to infiltrate Tibet. She wrote scholarly books about Buddhism and Tibetan culture. Traveling throughout the Indian subcontinent, she chronicled her impressions, including the role of women in Oriental cultures. Marguerite Baker Harrison (1879–1967) assisted production of a documentary chronicling the Bakhtiari tribe's migration to Persia. The Swiss explorer Ella Kini Maillart (1903–1997), lived with Kirghiz and Kazakh tribes in eastern Turkestan. She hiked throughout Asia and the Middle East, writing about her experiences.

Innovative ethnic researchers included the Hungarian-born Ernestine Friedl (b. 1920), who examined gender roles in Greece, noting how women were accorded power within communities; the native Alabamian Zora Neale Hurston (1903–1960), who depicted Caribbean women in her fiction and folklore collections; and Great Britain's Phyllis Mary Kaberry (1910–1977), a pioneer in investigating the lives of women in aboriginal Australia and Papua New Guinea. Margaret Mead (1901–1978), curator of ethnology at the American Museum of Natural History in New York, was renowned for her studies of South Pacific women and how they raised children. She was one of the first anthropologists to focus on the relationship of gender roles and culture.

Elsie Clews Parsons (1874–1941) described in her book *The Old-Fashioned Woman* (1913) how women were universally restricted to some degree by sociocultural taboos and expectations, and how they were removed from public and pressured to be subordinate and passive. Numerous women immersed themselves in studies of Native American ethnicity, revealing how, in direct contrast to Parson's thesis, tribal customs assured that women were not treated as inferiors. Instead, Native American women mostly enjoyed equal political, economic, social, and religious status with men, attending meetings, supplying food, and conducting ceremonies as shamans. Native American women were represented in myths and legends as well as the etymology of native languages.

These early ethnic scholars who examined the role of women within cultures identified topics that later researchers would analyze with more sophisticated approaches and insights. Such subjects addressed women's fertility, initiation rituals, nutrition and hunger, social life, female infanticide, restrictions on activity, and language. Both early and modern ethnic investigators tend to apply proactively their findings to efforts to better the lives of their research subjects when possible. Whereas pioneering women ethnographers often were perceived as amateurs pursuing a hobby, recent scholars have been valued, for the most part, as professionals who make valid contributions to academia. During the twentieth century, however, women struggled to achieve the transition from being a minimized exception, ignored by biased colleagues who did not find their erudition and creativity meritable to becoming part of an integrated scholastic community. In between, many researchers were excluded from traditional professional features, such as university affiliation and recognition with appropriate professorial rank. Women often still are forced to seek alternative ways to secure funding and present their ethnicity studies findings at local clubs and through community activism.

The Second Wave of Ethnic Women's Studies

During the 1980s and 1990s, ethnic studies of women evolved and were reinforced as legitimate academic pursuits by respected intellectual figures who defended the significance of such research. "Ethnicity, our cultural and historical heritage, shapes our perception of race and racism, sex, sexism and heterosexism, class and classism," stated Johnnella Butler, a notable leader in establishing higher education ethnic curricula internationally. "Ethnicity as a category of analysis therefore reveals sources of identity, sources of sustenance and celebration, as well as the cultural dynamics that shape women's experiences," she said. "It makes even more apparent the necessity of viewing women pluralistically" (Butler and Walter, 1991: 7172).

A second wave of feminist scholarship profoundly affected how ethnic researchers considered research and analysis. Many of the second-wave feminists represented nonwhite minorities. Instead of European American women solely studying foreign cultures, indigenous members of those groups examined their own societies. Scholars self-critically questioned their possible ethnic biases and stereotypical perceptions of subjects that might skew their interpretations. These researchers said that the role of men should not be excluded, because males were significant to comprehend their relationships with and position of women in varying ethnic groups. They thought that the developing world should be more closely examined, and criticized mainstream feminists for focusing on patriarchy's affect on women and gender-based inequality without considering cultural differences. Stressing that gender and ethnicity should be contemplated together, second-wave scholars protested the Eurocentric theories that dominated women's studies. Researchers stated that ethnic minorities should have a voice to express their opinions and hypotheses. Often, students were assigned autobiographies of ethnically significant social activists.

Second-wave scholars also were open to new definitions of ethnicity. Ruth Frankenburg (1993) defended her thesis that white women, like members of other cultural groups, had a unique ethnic identity. These scholars wanted to understand how ethnicity empowered or weakened women by offering access to or limiting choices. They also were curious as to how women influenced cultural values and how clothing and jewelry expressed ethnicity, gender, and morality, provoking acceptance or reaction among members of similar and different groups. Religion and ethnicity were so intertwined that most scholars considered these values simultaneously.

As researchers sought to understand how individual women fit into their ethnic community, these scholars also wanted to show how women internationally were connected and unified by similar humanitarian concerns. Instead of dwelling on unfamiliar aspects of cultures, scholars stressed parallel problems and accomplishments that women encounter such as inferior health care and child care programs and environmental and business developments. By emphasizing intersections shared by women instead of gaps between ethnic identity, researchers focus on inclusion of the world's 2.8 billion women instead of excluding them ironically as they are by misogynistic social patterns.

Despite these efforts, internal academic dissension reveals disagreement about how ethnicity and gender should be addressed. Many colleges do not adequately cover those topics or present information from points of view considered incongruent with the culture. For example, some black women do not embrace the feminism constructed by white women, which the blacks believe only serves to retain white intellectual control and authority. They also resent the use of externally developed theories to evaluate and critique ethnic scholarship and creative works (often without an appreciation or awareness of cultural standards) and the dismissal of theories devised by ethnic minorities. As a result, ethnic expressions are subjugated to the dominant majority's stipulations—often deemed oppressive—that denigrate ethnic values, such as spirituality, and threaten to sever individuals from their ethnic identity by silencing them and reinforcing invalid assumptions.

Some researchers have established think tanks to work independently of universities while retaining ties with leading scholars. These institutions pursue both theoretical research and application of hypothesized solutions. The International Centre for Ethnic Studies (ICES) established at Colombo, Sri Lanka, in 1982 consists of intellectuals and political activists who investigate ethnicity's impact on social and political processes. Interested in improving human rights, particularly for women and ethnic minorities, and

securing international peace, the center hosts conferences and workshops and encourages joint efforts with other ethnic researchers to achieve goals. In addition to addressing regional ethnic concerns and promoting tolerant conflict resolution procedures, the ICES encourages international multiculturalism and amicable ethnic coexistence. The center's library focuses on sources about women, ethnicity, and violence, reflecting the fact that the former ICES director, Dr. Radhika Coomaraswamy, was named the United Nation's Special Rapporteur on Violence against Women in 1994. The ICES publishes a journal entitled *Nethra*, which features articles to educate the global community about ethnic issues by presenting case examples and comparative research that objectively discuss the realities and complexities that ethnic groups—and women—encounter in a pluralistic society polarized by ethnic identities. The center's scholars also seek to develop innovative ways to manage conflicts between cultural groups and between men and women.

Similarly, researchers at the Institute for Ethnic Studies (IES) in Slovenia examine ethnic issues, especially among minorities living in that vicinity, by using interdisciplinary methods and analysis. Concerned with ethnic minorities' legal rights, IES scholars address ways to protect those groups while encouraging peaceful coexistence of numerous ethnicities that reside within the same geographical area. The researchers compare minorities' status in Slovenia, adjacent countries, and in the former Yugoslavia. Nationalism and individual and ethnic identity and affiliations also are investigated.

Ethnic studies, whether conducted at educational facilities, institutions like ICES and IES, or independently, utilize ideas and techniques from such varied fields as law, sociology, medicine, philosophy, history, art, linguistics, and political science. As students participate in ethnic studies at schools or independent facilities, they prepare for professional careers in education, social or public service, law, and organized labor, in which they will need awareness of humanity's differences and know appropriate responses.

Global Women's Issues Concerning Ethnic Scholars

Regardless of the geographical location of researchers and their subjects, scholars who are interested in the relationship between women and ethnicity seek answers to similar questions, particularly how women contribute to society and change it as well as how public policy decisions are made regarding women. Researchers ponder how ethnicity and gender are related to autonomy, identifying obstacles that block women from becoming political participants as voters and candidates or by expressing their opinions of male-dominated governments. Such institutionally entrenched impediments include refusing to consider women's alternative ideas for implementing governmental reforms. State intervention often denies women basic freedoms. Ironically, as some countries became more open societies, especially after the 1989 revolutions, women found themselves facing new limitations such as reduced medical services and increased unemployment.

Scholars focus on familial patterns based on religion and ethnicity, which often cause women to be sequestered and isolated from the public in a form of gender apartheid. Known as *purdah,* this practice, mainly in Islamic countries, requires women to be draped in fabric to conceal their skin, hair, and faces, all of which are considered sinful enticements to men. Women metaphorically become invisible. Considered the property of their male relatives or spouses, women sometimes are victims of honor killings in which men can legally murder a female relative or wife they think is sexually impure, yet authorities overlook men who have multiple partners. Women lack basic property and inheritance rights, are forbidden to make decisions, and are forcibly married to selected mates and denied reproductive rights. Domestic violence and rape is rarely reported because of shame and male-dominated law enforcement and judicial systems. In extreme examples, Middle Eastern and Asian parents sell daughters into sexual slavery or women are kidnapped to become prostitutes in international trafficking schemes. Some girls are imprisoned at fetish shrines to atone for relatives' misdeeds.

Ethnic scholars are interested in studying these customs as well as legislators' reluctance to cease both active and passive violence directed toward women such as women being exploited for pornography or denied contraception. Gender and ethnicity impact diplomacy, for example, ignoring the violence against women at the hands of Afghanistan's Taliban warlords, in order to gain access to pipelines and oil in that country. Refugees and displaced women are also political topics, and the treatment of elderly women is of concern to ethnic researchers specializing in geriatrics. Women's freedom of speech, movement, and religion are also issues, as well as politically sanctioned abductions, torture, and extermination of targeted ethnic groups as evidenced in Bosnia. Ethnic studies scholars compare such acts with the minimal violence of Laos and Mongolia, where equality and opportunity are more available to women. They also study where and how women's advocacy groups are formed and activism occurs.

Researchers also analyze the plight of sweatshop laborers and other barbaric or unjust employment practices, such as women having to secure male permission to work or be sterilized as a hiring condition. Globally, women are underemployed and underpaid for the skills they have and the services that they provide. Although women are guaranteed equal pay by law in many nations, the reality is that they receive salaries substantially lower than male coworkers. Women endure impoverishment and inadequate child care facilities. Often temporary workers, they lack insurance and pension benefits. Ethnic researchers study the economic role of women in various countries as well as how women cope with sexual harassment, low wages, and unfair practices. Educational opportunities for women, which could help career advancement and attitudes toward women being educated and literate, also are investigated. International efforts to assist women, such as the United Nations conferences and decrees, are compared with legal rights that women purportedly have but that are seldom enforced. Women's access to modern communication forums, such as the Internet, are addressed by ethnic studies.

Medical care is a topic that ethnic studies examines, especially as it concerns women's exploitation. For example, biotechnology is occasionally tested on women in the developing world without their permission—for example, in Egypt, Norplant is implanted in women without their knowledge. Ethnic studies scholars attempt to document female genital mutilation, tracking geographical occurrences and cultural justifications for this physically and emotionally scarring practice. Women are denied health care—even in emergencies, even those who are disabled—in countries such as Afghanistan. Women lack control over the transmission of sexual diseases because of their subordinate relationship to men and unfamiliarity with facts about symptoms and causes. Depression and alcoholism plague repressed women, and scholars compare mainstream standards of beauty versus ethnic standards.

Scientists also are interested in ethnic studies, applying paradigms to medical and biological research and attempting to better understand the physiology of the female life cycle, which has been ignored in favor of medical experimentation focusing on male health concerns. In early 2000, researchers at Oxford University hypothesized that Europeans are the descendants of seven matriarchal groups identifiable by mitochondrial DNA, which can be transmitted to offspring by women only because it is destroyed in sperm during fertilization. These ancestral mother groups are known as the Seven Daughters of Eve and represent women who lived thousands of years ago. Similar common ancestors have been described for African peoples, of which one clan seems to be the progenitor of the European groups. Further investigation of Asian and Native American genetic profiles will be conducted.

Ethnicity, like biological gender, is a genetic characteristic that people are born with and cannot choose. Although some social behaviors are learned and can be altered, the fundamental essence of being a woman of a certain cultural group is not easily changed without surgery and intensive indoctrination, causing half of the worlds' population to suffer disproportionately from abuse and inequality that ethnic studies attempts to delineate and mitigate, while defining gender roles within cultures.

See Also

ANTHROPOLOGY; ETHNICITY; ETHNIC STUDIES I; MULTICULTURALISM

References and Further Reading

Abu-Lughod, Lila. 1990. Can there be a feminist ethnography? *Women and Performance: A Journal of Feminist Theory* 5. 727.

Butler, Johnnella E., and John C. Walter, eds. 1990. *Transforming the curriculum: Ethnic studies and women's studies*. Albany: State University of New York Press.

Center for the Study of Ethnicity and Gender in Appalachia. http://www.marshall.edu/csega/

Center for World Indigenous Studies. http://www.cwis.org/

Comas-Daz, Lillian, and Beverly Greene, eds. 1994. *Women of color: Integrating ethnic and gender identities in psychotherapy*. New York: Guilford.

Cultural Studies Resource Centre Ethnicity Page. http://www.routledge.com/routledge/rcenters/cultural/ethn.html

Eicher, Joanne B., ed. 1995. *Dress and ethnicity: Change across space and time*. Oxford and Washington, D.C.: Berg.

Frankenburg, Ruth. 1993. *White women, race matters: The social construction of whiteness*. Minneapolis: University of Minnesota Press.

Göçek, Fatma Müge, and Shiva Balaghi, eds. 1994. *Reconstructing gender in the Middle East: Tradition, identity, and power*. New York: Columbia University Press.

Gunew, Sneja, and Anna Yeatman, eds. 1993. *Feminism and the politics of difference*. Boulder, Col.: Westview.

hooks, bell. 1990. *Yearning: Race, gender and cultural politics*. Boston: South End.

Institute for Ethnic Studies. http://www2.arnes.si/ljinv16/indexa.htm

International Centre for Ethnic Studies. http://www.icescmb.slt.lk/

Kuper, Adam. 1982. *Wives for cattle: Bridewealth and marriage in southern Africa*. London: Routledge and Kegan Paul.

Lamphere, Louise, Helena Ragoné, and Patricia Zavella, eds. 1997. *Situated lives: Gender and culture in everyday life*. New York: Routledge.

Lanza, Carmela Delia. 1994. "Always on the brink of disappearing": Women, ethnicity, class, and autobiography. *Frontiers: A Journal of Women Studies* 15: 5168.

National Association for Ethnic Studies. http://www.ksu.edu/ameth/naes/ethnic.htm

Peterson, V. Spike, and Anne Sisson Runyan. 1999. *Global gender issues*. 2nd ed. Boulder, Col.: Westview.

Pettman, Jan. 1992. *Living in the margins: Racism, sexism and feminism in Australia*. St. Leonards: Allen and Unwin.

Spivak, Gayatri Chakravorty. 1987. *In other worlds: Essays in cultural politics*. London and New York: Methuen.

Stacey, Judith. 1988. Can there be a feminist ethnography? *Women's Studies International Forum* 11: 2127.

Stern, Steve. 1995. *The secret history of gender: Women, men, and power in late-colonial Mexico*. Chapel Hill: University of North Carolina Press.

Trinh, T. Minh-ha. 1991. *When the moon waxes red: Representation, gender and cultural politics*. London: Routledge.

Walker, Alice. 1993. *Warrior marks: Female genital mutilation and the sexual binding of women*. New York: Harcourt Brace.

Elizabeth Schafer

ETHNICITY

The term *ethnicity* has its origins in ancient Greek (*ethnos*, meaning tribe or race), which was used to describe people from regions outside the Greek polity. In the modern world, three meanings have evolved, and they are still being used today. One reading of ethnicity originated largely in the nineteenth century in the context of the rise of nation-states. Ethnicity became a positive marker that signaled a political will to statehood. Indeed, the nineteenth and twentieth centuries can be defined as periods of assertion of ethnicities, leading to pronouncements of national identity and resulting in political independence for many ethnic groups. More recently, some indigenous women also have used their ethnicity to raise nationalistic claims, insisting that the only way to identity and dignity is by reclaiming land that once was theirs. A second reading of the term uses "ethnicity" interchangeably with "race" (Ratcliffe, 1994). Many women of color have rejected the term *ethnicity*, however, to avoid being grouped with white women, since doing so would fail to recognize their specific concerns.

A third meaning, the main one to be discussed in this article, evolved slowly in the twentieth century as a consequence of increased mass migration and people's movements on a scale hitherto unknown in human history (save for the interlude in the fourth century C.E.). In the association of ethnicity with migration, the Greek term *ethos* (custom) has acquired great importance. Although all people have an ethnic identity that may or may not also be a national identity, the terms *ethnicity, ethnic group,* and *ethnic* usually (especially after World War II) came to flag "otherness" from the majority (that is, national) culture. Minority groups were thus ethnic groups, tied together by some key links, such as religion, custom, and language. Minority status or ethnic affiliation also has invited distortions and mystifications (stereotyping), and much work needs to be done to explode the myths. This has usually been achieved by a process of policy formation in the areas of human rights, focusing on equity in treatment and access to services. Ethnic or minority status may or may not be transient, that is, the children and grandchildren of immigrants may merge into the mainstream culture, unless prevented by that majority culture from doing so. There are countless studies to suggest that ethnicity matters a great deal, both in terms of treatment and in terms of expectations about life events that vary significantly with ethnicity.

Countless studies have shown that migration or ethnic status, in the modern sense of minority group, is experienced differently by women and men. Women tend to have greater difficulties than men, because a multitude of disadvantages can combine negatively with the added label of a particular ethnic marker. Quite often, such a difficulty is masked when the entire group, including males and females, has been "colonized," oppressed, or exploited by the majority culture. As has been demonstrated, for instance, in case of Chicana women (Longauex y Vasquez, 1970) and Aboriginal women of Australia (Kaplan, 1996), energies for improvements in the safety, well-being and "liberation" of the group have far outweighed concerns for one's own gender. In whichever sense the term *ethnicity* is used today, it rarely bestows honor and distinction on the wearer of the label. There are countless instances, however, in which the women, as guardians of traditions and as emotional centers of families and communities (Obbo, 1980), have mustered enormous strength and courage to uphold and support their ethnic group.

Feminism and Ethnicity

In western countries, ethnicity or migrant status was among the discoveries of the women's movements in the western world. In some western countries, the discovery of the migrant as a victim, as a poverty stricken, nonassimilated, and ill-treated group, saw immigrants graduate from labor to the migrant problem. Poverty was clustered in non-English speaking background groups. There were sociolegal barriers, and as immigrants and women they suffered from a double disadvantage. Double and triple disadvantage studies dominated the field. Work conditions for workers from non-English speaking background were described as appalling. Yet it is probably not far-fetched to say that feminists in Western Europe (Kaplan, 1992), in the United States, or in Australia (Kaplan, 1996) failed to take the opportunity for organized inclusiveness of women from different ethnic groups. Ethnic women as victims tended to maintain barriers of culture rather than forge bridges. Significantly, encyclopedias of feminism published in the 1970s and 1980s at times did not carry entries titled "ethnicity" or "migrant" or "minority" (compare Tuttle, 1987), even while women from developing countries (that is, with their own *national* identity) were increasingly welcome at international meetings. Global (or postnational) feminism acted visibly in celebration of diversity (Kaplan, 1999) but often stopped short of translating this into inclusive practices at home beyond the tokenistic. Yet it also was feminism that first discovered that women from minority groups experienced dual disempowerments (from power, wealth, influence, status, and mobility), both as exclusions within their own culture and as boundaries constructed against them from without.

Economic Factors

Across the globe, the nineteenth and twentieth centuries saw extensive programs for recruitment of labor as monocrops were set up in plantations and new industries were developed. Foreign labor often was favored, either because local resources were insufficient or because foreign labor was cheaper or both. Women were especially favored and, in some instances, there were special drives to attract women. For instance, in Malaysia of the 1920s and 1930s—and also later under Japanese occupation—special lures were employed to get Indian women recruited into the plantation sector.

The attraction worldwide for women's labor (as indeed also for child labor) has been that women's wages were and still are much lower than those of males (Ariffin, 1992). Immigrant women in the West often went into domestic service, light industry, process work, and so-called service industries (for example, cleaning). Women who were classified as foreigners and were not fluent in the language of their host country were often forced into the least attractive and most dangerous positions and paid the lowest base wage rate. Immigrants were powerless, while harnessed into the manufacturing sector of western economies. Moreover, women regularly supply unpaid labor. In certain socioeconomic contexts, being an ethnic woman exacerbates the exploitation.

Political Factors

Substantial political instability, the collapse of the former Soviet Union, and the disintegration of the former Yugoslavia unleashed two new antihumanitarian forces of the modern era. One was the growth of fundamentalism in Islamic countries, which has seen a substantial worsening of the condition of women in those countries—as, for instance, in Afghanistan. Prominent women also have been persecuted in many countries. One set of examples comes from Turkey. In 1998, the feminist writer Konca Kuris was kidnapped and later found dead (tortured and burned by a fanatical group, Hezbollah, also known as the Party of God), because she argued that women could be modern and still adhere to Islamic teachings. Another Turkish writer, Nadire Mater, was indicted for having offended the military by publishing interviews with soldiers. Behind these accusations lie not just differences of religious fervor. The women who were being persecuted in Islamic countries encountered wrath because they had seemingly adopted a false and heretical ethnicity. A modern woman in Islam, as a number of proponents argue, is not one toying with western capitalist customs, but one who voluntarily seeks a renewal of her faith and invigoration of her nation's ethnic specificity. She is meant to mobilize to achieve these goals, even if they appear to limit women's freedom of movement (Göle, 1996).

Foreign ethnicity may, on occasion, be a chief ingredient in persecution. One case, which received international attention in the year 2000, was that of Dr. Flora Brovina, a pediatrician, poet, and woman activist from Kosovo. She was found guilty of having medically treated members of the Kosovo Liberation Army and was sentenced to 12 years' imprisonment. The decisive factor in this verdict by a Serbian court was that she was Albanian (Cohen, 2000). Brovina, as an ethnic Albanian, personified the ongoing process of ethnic cleansing that had beset the former Yugoslavia but had also spread through areas of Georgia and the Middle East (Ahmed, 1995). Ethnic cleansing has been one of the many abhorrent practices of the twentieth century. Women and children were not spared in the process. Indeed, women of unacceptable ethnicity have usually endured the additional trauma of sexual abuse. In areas of the former Yugoslavia, a relatively new variant of ethnic cleansing was for men to rape and then intentionally impregnate enemy

women in captivity as if to dilute that other ethnicity. In truth, it was a variant of punishment for ethnicity. By defiling women, the entire ethnic group could be most deeply humiliated.

Class and Ethnicity

It must not be assumed that being ethnic automatically denotes being of low status. Ethnicity comes in at least three ascribed status positions: low, neutral, and high. There always have been some high-status ethnicities, such as the Germans in Russia or Hungary or the British in Australia. In the age of imperialism, high-status ethnicities were not just supremacist whites but specific national groups as part of the colonial elite. A trend toward reinventing "whiteness" also has led to a rediscovery and assertive pronouncements of European ethnic identities in New World countries (Kincheloe, 1999).

Although ethnicity may be sufficient to ascribe low status to a minority group, the members of that group may indeed be sharply divided by class and vested powers transmitted in their culture (via elders, aristocracy, the caste system, and so on). Generally speaking, women in high-status families within a minority group always tend to be much better off than their compatriots from lower classes. The relationship between ethnicity and class is a complex one.

There also are clashes and ambiguities in ethnicity when a particular minority group becomes determined to be economically and educationally successful. Ironically, the success of minority groups anywhere across the globe has rarely led to a change from low- to high-status ethnicity. Indeed, the change from invisibility to visibility of a low-status minority group often has resulted in outright hostility and hostile actions. From time to time, shops are looted and burned, discriminatory and defiling acts are committed, and, occasionally, murders are committed for reasons of ethnic difference. Women very often are the victims of these attacks, especially if they can be visibly distinguished by dress. The punishment for ethnic difference can be particularly unjust, as women are often expected to be the guardians of their ethnic traditions. In many cultures, they are asked to display this ethnicity by wearing specified clothes and cooking traditional foods. They therefore carry visible signals that may, at times, present personal risks.

Psychological Factors

Carrying the status of minority can be a reaffirming process of identity. Quite often, however, minority coupled with migration experience (from country to city and from country to country) can be an emotionally extremely unsettling process. These traumas may be experienced very differently by women and men. Partly, the gender divisions may be the result of such criteria as immigration programs, social structures, or labor-market characteristics. Typically, immigration programs tended to look to male household heads, their suitability and skills, without considering the wives of applicants—sometimes with disastrous consequences for women. If there is no infrastructure in the new country to support women's needs and, particularly, if women were not folded into the labor market, opportunities to form social networks might be minimal. It is not atypical for women in these conditions to be entirely isolated socially. This is not just a problem for women from different language backgrounds. Isolation also can occur among same-language immigrant women. Visible signs of personal isolation are reflected in mental and physical ill health; in general, women have a much higher profile of depression than men (but typically a lower rate of suicide). Women from minorities also may have a substantial psychological and sociocultural influence on the majority culture (UNESCO, 1982).

Occasionally, the experience of a low-status ethnicity is used creatively by the children of immigrants. Jhumpa Lahiri's short stories, for instance, won the Pulitzer Prize in 2000 for fiction. In them she paid tribute to the fragility of the migrant existence. Dench once called minorities "prisoners of ambivalence" (1986), but over time, at least in the western world, ethnicity also became a source of strengthened identity rather than ambiguity (Yinger, 1997).

See Also

ETHNIC STUDIES, *I and II*; ETHNIC CLEANSING

References and Further Reading

Ahmed, A. 1995. "Ethnic cleansing": A metaphor for our time. *Ethnic and Racial Studies* 18: 1–25.

Ariffin, Jamilah. 1992 *Women and development in Malaysia*. Petaling Jaya, Malaysia: Pelanduk.

Cohen, Allison. 2000. Paediatrician Flora Brovina remains imprisoned in Kosovo. *Lancet* 355: 839. (News item.)

Dench, Geoff. 1986. *Minorities in the open society*. London: Routledge and Kegan Paul.

Göle, Nilüfer. 1996. *The forbidden modern*. Ann Arbor: University of Michigan Press.

Kaplan, Gisela. 1992. *Contemporary western European feminism*. New York: University of New York Press.

———. 1996. *The meager harvest: The Australian women's movement*. Sydney: Allen and Unwin.

———. 1999. Pluralism and citizenship: The case of gender in European politics. In Philomena Murray Leslie Holmes,

ed., *Citizenship and identity in Europe,* 73–96. Aldershot, England: Ashgate.

Kincheloe, Joe L. 1999. The struggle to define and reinvent whiteness: A pedagogical analysis. *College Literature.* 26: 162–186.

Longauex y Vasquez, Enriqueta. 1970. The Mexican-American woman. In Robin Morgan, ed., *Sisterhood is powerful: An anthology of writings from the women's liberation movement.* 379–384. New York: Vintage.

Obbo, Christine. 1980. *African women: Their struggle for economic independence.* London: Zed.

Ratcliffe, Peter, ed., 1994. *"Race" ethnicity and nation: Interpersonal perspectives on social conflict.* London: UCL.

Trask, Haunani-Kay. 1997. Feminism and indigenous Hawaiian nationalism. In Lois A. West, ed., *Feminist nationalism,* 187–198. New York: Routledge.

Tuttle, Lisa. 1987. *Encyclopedia of feminism.* London: Arrow.

UNESCO. 1982. *Living in two cultures: The sociocultural situation of migrant workers and their families.* Paris, Aldershot: Gower, UNESCO Press.

Yinger, J. M. 1997. *Ethnicity: Source of strength? Source of conflict?* New Delhi: Rawat.

Gisela Kaplan

EUGENICS

The term *eugenics* refers to scientific research and social policies aimed at improving the human race through selective and discriminatory breeding.

Selecting or avoiding sexual partners on the basis of bloodlines and reproductive potential was mandated by social hierarchies and caste systems long before the modern era. In the mid-1800s, Charles Darwin's theory of evolution appeared to lend scientific credence to those practices. Under the banner of scientific improvement of the human species, eugenics was a rationalization for the social control of human sexuality and the suppression of people of color, women, the poor, and the disabled.

The English scientist Francis Galton, a cousin of Darwin, coined the term *eugenics* in 1883, basing it on the Greek root *eugenies* meaning "well born" or "noble in heredity." Galton intended the word to mean the "science" of improving human stock by giving the "more suitable races or strains of blood a better chance of prevailing speedily over the less suitable" (Kevles, 1986: ix). The term was applied to a wide set of theories and social reforms related to heredity. Galton was a biological researcher and innovator of statistical methods who theorized that almost all human characteristics (physical, intellectual, and emotional) were determined by biological inheritance. Galton's research and public policy statements consistently assumed an intellectual and moral superiority of men over women, upper classes over lower classes, Gentiles over Jews, and light-skinned people over dark-skinned people (Tucker, 1994; 43). Not all eugenicists, however, shared Galton's limited notion of biologically fixed superiority. It was not until the early twentieth century that Galton's idea of immutable biological hierarchies became the dominant theory of eugenics.

Eugenics and Social Reform Movements

Eugenic ideas had their greatest international acceptance between the 1870s and mid-1930s. In this tumultuous age of rapid industrialization, both social reformers and academicians looked hopefully to science for solutions to social problems. Early social reformers who promoted eugenics were particularly interested in environmental theories of heredity that predated Galton. There was widespread acceptance of French scientist Jean-Baptiste Lamarck's hypothesis that environmental influences could reconfigure heredity material. Lamarck's ideas were particularly popular because they seemed to support traditional folk wisdom, which held that the life experiences of parents, particularly pregnant and lactating women, influenced the personal characteristics of children. Proponents of female and African-American education, universal suffrage, access to birth control, free love, child labor laws, better working conditions, alcohol prohibition, criminal rehabilitation, and much more argued that their proposed reform would not only improve individual lives but would also have positive eugenic consequences for future generations. In the 1890s, for example, Helen Hamilton Gardener appealed to environmental eugenics in her arguments for female education, saying, "so long as the laws of heredity last, no man can give free brains to his children if their mother is the victim of superstition and priestcraft" (Gardener, 1891: 2). Some supporters of female emancipation argued that almost all the evils of society, including imperialism, could be traced to the inherited effects of female subjugation (Gordon, 1976). Historian Linda Gordon notes that the ideas of environmental eugenics were so pervasive among nineteenth-century feminists that "it would be hard to find a single piece of writing on voluntary motherhood between 1890 and 1910 that did not assert that unwanted children were likely to be morally and/or physically defective" (Gordon, 1976: 121).

Eugenic principles, however, were equally adaptable to arguments against female emancipation and other progressive reforms. After the turn of the century, Galtonian notions of immutable biological inheritance began to hold sway over Lamarckian environmental eugenics. The change was precipitated in 1900 by the reemergence of Gregor Mendel's previously ignored 1865 study of genetic pairing and continuance (which became the foundation for modern genetic science). Mendel's work appeared to give scientific support to arguments that human characteristics were a consequence of genetic material alone and environmental conditions were relevant to evolutionary success only to the extent that they affected a species' ability to reproduce and survive.

Eugenic arguments against female emancipation were further bolstered by public concerns about declining fertility. Birthrates in Great Britain fell roughly 37 percent between 1870 and 1914, and similar declines occurred in several European countries and parts of the United States and Canada. Decreases were generally thought to be greater among educated upper-class white women than among lower-class whites and minority women. Eugenic scientists initially attributed declining birthrates to environmental and evolutionary causes, but they eventually concluded that "deliberate family limitation" was the most likely culprit. Although feminists like Margaret Sanger continued to evoke eugenic arguments to support the legalization of birth control, most eugenicists blamed feminists for creating potential "race suicide." Belief in women's fundamental eugenic responsibilities led some social reformers, including some feminists, to criticize upper-class women for not having enough children and to complain that access to higher education and professional employment had led the most able women astray from the duty of motherhood (Gordon, 1976: 130–131).

The scientific development of Mendelian genetics and changing birthrates do not, however, fully explain the conservative shift in public eugenics discourse. Although eugenic scientists generally agreed that Anglo-Saxon, Nordic, and Germanic males were at least temporarily on the top of the evolutionary ladder, they were never in complete agreement about the nature of evolutionary processes nor the appropriate translation of eugenic theory into social policy. But scientific eugenic ideas were linked with the political needs that helped defined them. In the hands of white ruling-class males, eugenics became predominantly antifeminist, anti–birth control, anti-immigration, and antiminority because of the greater effectiveness of conservative organizations and the greater sympathy of the dominant classes with their point of view (Gordon, 1976: 131).

Eugenics and National Race Policies

Among the most influential advocates of conservative eugenics policies were members of national and international eugenics societies and research institutions, which arose in the decade preceding World War I. These organizations were particularly attractive to people in the fields of medicine, psychiatry, zoology, biology, biometrics, statistics, and the emerging fields of sociology, criminology, and social work. Training in eugenics allowed for professional advancement. White women constituted more than half of all students who attended the summer training programs of the influential Eugenics Record Office, a leading eugenics institute in the United States, funded by the philanthropist Mrs. E. H. Harriman (Rafter, 1988: 20).

Eugenics organizations followed Galton's earlier call for the development of both "positive" and "negative" eugenics. Positive eugenics proposals were aimed at encouraging especially "fit" young men and women to marry and procreate, early and often. The religious Oneida free love community in New York attempted the most extensive positive eugenics program between 1869 and 1879. Fifty-three young women and thirty-eight young men pledged to participate in an experiment to breed "healthy perfectionists." Participants were mated in "scientific combinations" determined by the community's founder, John Noyes, an admirer of Galton's writings. The experiment produced 58 children, at least 9 fathered by Noyes (Haller, 1963: 37–38). However, most eugenic schemes for pairing good breeding partners were never instituted, although positive eugenics arguments did help to foster family allowance policies in Germany and Great Britain during the 1930s.

Eugenicists were much more successful at developing negative eugenics programs aimed at reducing the birthrates of "unfit" members of society. In the United States, negative eugenic programs began as early as 1878, when Josephine Shaw Lowell, New York State's first female charity board commissioner, created the Newark Custodial Asylum for Feeble-minded Women. Lowell argued that feebleminded women were inherently promiscuous and inevitably gave birth to crime-prone offspring; thus, feebleminded women (particularly white women) were an evolutionary threat. The Newark Asylum institutionalized poor and socially deviant women until menopause made them "safe" to return to society (Rafter, 1997: 35). Support for Lowell's campaign to criminalize women with "bad blood" was bolstered in 1877 by the publication of Richard Dugdale's popular study, *The Jukes*, which claimed to describe a rural white and "mulatto" clan that supposedly produced 1,200 bastards, beggars, murderers, prostitutes, thieves, and syphilitics in seven generations (Rafter, 1997: 38).

More than 30 years later, the Eugenics Record Office created similar family studies to win support for compulsory sterilization. Under the direction of Charles Davenport,

the Eugenics Record Office trained hundreds of fieldworkers, primarily educated white women, to collect extensive pedigree history on "defective families." The studies were used to argue that various deviant characteristics were passed down as either recessive or dominant genes. Eugenic statisticians followed up with estimates of the economic burden society incurred from families with nonproductive and frequently institutionalized members. By 1917, 16 states had compulsory sterilization laws directed at the feebleminded, the insane, and certain classes of criminals. Superintendent Harry Laughlin of the Eugenics Record Office drafted a model for more extensive laws requiring mandatory sterilization of all potential parents of "socially inadequate" offspring. In Laughlin's proposal, the socially inadequate consisted of the feebleminded, insane, criminalistic (including the delinquent, wayward, and sexually deviant), epileptic, inebriate, diseased, blind, deaf, deformed, and dependent (including orphans, ne'er-do-wells, the homeless, tramps, and paupers) (Haller, 1963: 133). Attempts to implement Laughlin's model act were resisted by a coalition of religious organizations, some feminists, socialists, and liberal humanists. In 1927 the U.S. Supreme Court ruled that compulsory sterilization, when applied with due process, fell within the police power of the state. Justice Oliver Wendell Holmes, a supporter of eugenics, wrote the majority opinion, saying: "It is better for all the world, if instead of waiting to execute degenerate offspring for crime, or to let them starve for their imbecility, society can prevent those who are manifestly unfit from continuing their kind. The principle that sustains compulsory vaccination is broad enough to cover cutting the Fallopian tube.... Three generations of imbeciles are enough" (*Buck* v. *Bell*, 1927, cited in Smith, 1985: 149–150).

Between 1928 and 1932 Denmark, Finland, Sweden, Norway, Iceland, and parts of Canada adopted laws allowing for eugenic sterilization. In 1933 the German Nazi Party put into effect a eugenic "race hygiene" program that incorporated all of Laughlin's sterilization proposal and added the defect of "inferior race" to the list of human inadequacies to be eliminated for economic and evolutionary purposes.

Concepts of heredity and evolution have been used by white supremacists in many nations to justify racist practices, from American slavery to South African apartheid. In the late 1800s eugenic scientists lent their support to antimiscegenation laws and other government policies that kept people of color disfranchised, separate, and unequal (Tucker, 1994: 60). Organized eugenics societies, however, did not need to convince white populations that people of color were racially inferior—centuries of slave owning and imperialist ideology guaranteed such beliefs. Instead, politically active eugenicists directed their primary racial campaigns against the growing number of southern and eastern European immigrants whom they believe posed the greatest threat to Anglo-Aryan bloodlines and nations.

Building on a long history of anthropological and biological race studies, eugenic scientists such as Karl Pearson in England, Jon Mjoen in Norway, and Charles Davenport in the United States attempted to prove not only that non-Aryan people, particularly Jews, were inferior to northern Europeans but that hybridization between racial groups resulted in "disharmonic effects" and the deterioration of the Anglo-Saxon and Nordic gene pool. A coalition of anti-immigration forces in the United States was quick to adopt eugenic research to its purposes. Prescott Hall of the Immigration Restriction League explained, "The same arguments which induce us to segregate criminals and feebleminded and thus prevent their breeding apply to excluding from our borders individuals whose multiplying here is likely to lower the average of our people" (Haller, 1963: 146). The expert testimony of leading eugenicists helped to pass the U.S. Immigration Restriction Act of 1924, which selectively reduced the quota of immigrants from eastern and southern Europe. In Germany the same eugenic arguments led to the sterilization, internment, and mass killing of Jews, homosexuals, communists, the mentally ill, and others considered a threat to the social and evolutionary order.

Not all eugenicists supported movements for sterilization or anti-immigration laws. Many scientists quietly withdrew when eugenics organizations became more interested in public propaganda than scientific research. A few eugenicists vehemently objected to the unsubstantiated racial claims being made in their name. By the mid-1930s eugenics organizations had lost considerable public support. Glowing reports on Nazi sterilization and internment programs presented by prominent eugenicists prior to and even during World War II further eroded the legitimacy of eugenics institutions (Kuhl, 1994). By the end of World War II most eugenics organizations had either disbanded or been restructured into less overtly political genetic research programs. The term *eugenics* has since become virtually synonymous with scientific racism. Nonetheless, public debate over differences between human population groups has continued through the present, often reviving eugenic arguments discredited decades earlier.

See Also

BIOLOGICAL DETERMINISM; CLASS; ETHNIC CLEANSING; EUGENICS: AFRICAN-AMERICAN CASE STUDY; EUROCENTRISM; EXPERIMENTS ON WOMEN; GENETIC SCREENING; GENETICS AND GENETIC TECHNOLOGIES; GENOCIDE; SCIENTIFIC SEXISM AND RACISM; SOCIAL MOVEMENTS

References and Further Reading

Gardener, Helen H. 1891. *Pulpit, pew and cradle.* New York: Truth Seeker Library.

Gordon, Linda. 1976. *Woman's body, woman's right: A social history of birth control in America.* New York: Grossman.

Haller, Mark H. 1963. *Eugenics: Hereditarian attitudes in American thought.* Rahway, N. J.: Rutgers University Press.

Kevles, Daniel J. 1986. *In the name of eugenics: Genetics and the uses of human heredity.* Berkeley: University of California Press.

Kuhl, Stefan. 1994. *The Nazi connection: Eugenics, American racism, and German National Socialism.* New York: Oxford University Press.

Rafter, Nicole H. 1997. *Creating born criminals.* Urbana: University of Illinois Press.

————, ed. 1988. *White trash: The eugenic family studies 1877–1919.* Boston: Northeastern University Press.

Smith, J. David. 1985. *Minds made feeble.* Rockville, Md.: Aspen.

Tucker, William H. 1994. *The science and politics of racial research.* Urbana: University of Illinois Press.

Lori Blewett

EUGENICS: African-American Case Study—Eugenics and Family Planning

Eugenics is a false science (or pseudoscience) developed in the late nineteenth century and used for political purposes. It posits that the physical and moral character of human beings can and should be improved through selective breeding. Current debates over genetic causes of criminality, the validity of IQ tests, inherited intelligence, welfare reform, quotas, and affirmative action all suggest the extent to which the eugenics movement still affects public attitudes in the United States—attitudes informed, it is often charged, by a white supremacist ideology. A large portion of this debate is directed at the fertility rates of African-American women. But African-American women were never passive victims of eugenics, forced sterilization, or other medical, commercial, and state policies of reproductive control. For the past sixty years, African-American women have been at the forefront of challenges to the merger of racist pseudoscience and public policy in the United States. Many black women have historically supported birth control and abortion but, at the same time, have offered a strong critique of eugenicists. A clear sense of dual, or "paired-" values exists among African-American women: wanting individual control over their bodies while simultaneously resisting government and private depopulation policies that blur the distinction between incentives and coercion.

A History of the Eugenics Movement

There is a tendency in the African-American community to conflate family planning with eugenics and genocide, as if they were interchangeable. Evidently, the main cause of this confusion (usually articulated by men) is the eugenics movement, a set of ideas translated into public policy in the 1920s presumably to "improve" humankind through determining which sectors of the population would be allowed or encouraged to reproduce. Because of calculated attempts by the government to forcibly control blacks' fertility, confusion was created between this coercion and the right of black women to control their own reproduction.

Although the struggle for reproductive rights is not commonly perceived as being part of the civil rights movement, in fact it was part of that movement beginning in the late 1800s until after World War II. Black organizations in the early twentieth century were visible supporters of fertility control for black women, linking reproductive rights to racial advancement. The African-Americans who participated in this effort were not victims of imposed white values regarding family planning; instead, middle-class African-Americans were strongly motivated to control their fertility, and they collaborated with family planning organizations to publicly support the birth control movement, despite the racism of some of their allies.

W. E. B. Du Bois, one of the founders of the National Association for the Advancement of Colored People (NAACP), wrote in 1920 that "the future [African-American] woman...must have the right of motherhood at her own discretion." Joining him was the historian J. A. Rogers, who wrote, "I give the Negro woman credit if she endeavors to be something other than a mere breeding machine. Having children is by no means the sole reason for being." These ideas had significant consequences: from the mid–nineteenth century to the late twentieth century, the growth rate of the African-American population was more than halved.

As racism, lynchings, and poverty took a heavy toll on African-Americans in the early twentieth century, however, the fear of depopulation arose within a rising black nationalist movement and produced a pronatalist shift in the views of some African-Americans. Black nationalist leaders, such as Marcus Garvey, believed in increasing the black population in response to racial oppression. This change from relative indifference about population size to using population growth as a form of political currency presaged a conflict between the right of black women to exercise bodily self-determination and the need of the African-American community to achieve political and economic self-determination. Some opponents of family planning in the 1920s pointed to the emerging eugenics movement to strengthen their opposition.

The eugenics movement was based on the theories promoted in the late 1880s by Francis Galton (a cousin of the geneticist Charles Darwin), which alleged that social conditions like poverty and illiteracy are genetically produced and uncontrollably inherited. This notion, called social Darwinism, was based on a misconception and misapplication of Darwin's theory of evolution of species by natural selection. Eugenicists' claims were grafted onto previous economic theories by Thomas Malthus, who argued that overpopulation causes poverty and that poor people did not practice the self-control necessary to avoid poverty. (Malthus, however, was opposed to the use of contraceptives.) Blaming the poor for poverty became an enduring public policy promoted by elites in the United States. This contempt was reanimated in the 1990s when Richard Herrnstein and Charles Murray published a controversial book, *The Bell Curve*—-though there was also a strong reaction against it.

Proponents of eugenics in the United States believed that the future of native-born whites was threatened by the increasing population of people of color and whites who were not of Nordic-Teutonic descent. This belief in the dilution or corruption of a "pure" native stock by inferior strains has also existed elsewhere, including—notoriously—Nazi Germany. In the United States, the movement affected not only social Darwinist scientific circles but also public policy, receiving the endorsement of President Calvin Coolidge, who said in 1924, "America must be kept American. Biological laws show...that Nordics deteriorate when mixed with other races." To promote the reproduction of self-defined "racially superior" people, eugenicists argued for both "positive" methods, such as tax incentives and education for the desirable, and "negative" methods, such as sterilization, involuntary confinement, and immigration restrictions for the undesirable. The United States became the first nation in the world to permit mass sterilization as part of an effort to "purify the race." By the mid-1930s, about 20,000 people had been sterilized against their will, and 21 states had passed laws based on eugenics.

Supporters of eugenics included not only hatemongers such as the Ku Klux Klan but also respectable mainstream whites who were troubled by the rapid social changes that were taking place as the country became more urban and industrial. Millions of immigrants came to the United States to take advantage of the new economic opportunities. At the same time, thousands of blacks fled the South—with its Jim Crow laws that resembled apartheid—and migrated to the North. These fast-paced demographic changes alarmed many nativist whites who, while they were doubtful about birth control for themselves, saw it as a way to control the burgeoning populations of people of color and immigrants.

The Movement for Birth Control and Eugenics

When the movement for birth control began at the turn of the twentieth century, organizers such as Margaret Sanger believed that women's control of their own fertility would lead to upward social mobility for all women, regardless of race or immigrant status. Sanger's immediate effect on African-American women was to help transform their covert support for and use of family planning into visible public support by activists in the Colored Women's Club Movement. But it was African-American women who, in fact, better envisioned the concept of reproductive justice: the freedom not to have children but also to have children, a campaign that Margaret Sanger started but apparently never fully understood in terms of its effect on the activism of the black women she had encouraged to join the birth control movement.

Under the influence of eugenicists, Sanger changed her approach, moving away from a race-neutral analysis. In 1919, her American Birth Control League began to rely heavily on medical doctors and the growing eugenics movement for legitimacy. Although the eugenics movement was decidedly antifeminist and opposed women's independence, it provided the birth control movement with scientific and authoritative language that legitimated women's right to contraconception. This co-optation of the birth control movement by eugenicists resulted in racist depopulation policies and doctor-controlled birth control technology.

Sanger believed it was important to "prevent the American people from being replaced by alien or negro stock, whether it be by immigration or by overly high birth rates among others in this country." She claimed that "the mass of Negroes, particularly in the South, still breed carelessly

and disastrously, with the result that the increase among Negroes, even more than among Whites, is from that portion of the population least intelligent and fit, and least able to rear children properly." Instead of being relegated to the dustbin of history, eugenics received strong support from elites who sought to strengthen their control of society by controlling breeding.

Politicians in southern states were particularly interested in spreading birth control among African-Americans to limit black population growth that threatened their political and economic hegemony. For example, the late Leander Perez of Louisiana, who supported birth control for African-Americans, once said, "The best way to hate a nigger is to hate him before he is born."

Eugenics and birth control policies aimed at African-Americans were not the only reason blacks were concerned about eugenical subthemes in public health policies. In 1931, a pilot project to study syphilis was launched in Alabama, funded by several U.S. foundations. The program ran from 1932 to 1972, until it was exposed as an unethical research project that left syphilis untreated in poor, uneducated black farmers so that public health officials could trace the "natural course" of the disease. This program left a strong distrust among African-Americans toward public health policies and the role of private philanthropy and state funding in supplementing national research projects and programs.

African-Americans loudly protested these policies. The *Pittsburgh Courier*, a black newspaper whose editors favored family planning, said in 1936 that African-Americans should oppose depopulation programs proposed by eugenicists, because the burden would "fall upon colored people and it behooves us to watch the law and stop the spread of [eugenic sterilization]." By 1949, approximately 2.5 million African-American women were organized in social, political, and fraternal clubs and organizations that supported family planning but opposed eugenics as public policy.

Eugenics after World War II

By the end of World War II, eugenics had been discredited as a philosophy, not only on scientific grounds but also because of its association with Hitler and the Nazis. At least temporarily, the United States abandoned its explicit support of eugenics as public policy. But although the nation had contested Hitler's notions of Aryan superiority, many Euro-American whites never made a connection between their own racism and Nazism, and they retained a sense of being superior to African-Americans and other people of color. Arguably, the victories of the civil rights movement were due to the strength of the

African-American movement for social justice, not the willingness of the white majority to abandon the ideology of white supremacy, and a new rationale for controlling black fertility had to be created as white supremacy reinvented itself after the war.

The postwar global conflict between the superpowers resulted in competitive exploitation of less developed regions. The rapidly growing populations of the less developed countries and their movements against colonialism presumably threatened this balance of power. In the mid-1950s, demographers offered what might be seen as a sanitized approach to eugenics in the form of population "time bomb" theories. These theories made an ideological link between population growth in the developing world and the ability of the United States to govern world affairs. Brochures published by population control groups showed hordes of black and brown faces overwhelming a tiny earth. By the early 1960s, the U.S. government began supporting population control policies overseas and made foreign aid conditional on antinatalist depopulation programs. Some "population bomb" theorists may have believed that they were helping the poor, but they were being assisted by dictatorial governments, which feared that unchecked population growth coupled with massive human rights violations would destabilize their countries.

On a global scale, antipopulation programs were funded by the United States to forcibly curb population growth in Africa, Asia, Latin America, and the Caribbean. These programs aimed to control the insurgency of people who demanded an end to western colonialism and exploitation. At the same time, the family planning programs offered women in developing countries dubious choices about controlling their fertility, often promoting dangerous technology.

In the United States, some eugenicists argued that whites needed to be protected from the "explosiveness" of overpopulated black ghettos. These fears coincided with the growth of the civil rights movement and were perhaps a response to the militancy of the movement and its potential for sweeping social change. The political volatility of the African-American population convinced many members of the white elite and middle class that black population growth should be curbed through government intervention. Whites feared that a growing population of African-Americans concentrated in the inner cities would not only increase crime but also increase the national debt and eventually produce a political threat from urban black voting blocs.

The women targeted by these family planning programs, whether in the United States or elsewhere, were not blind to the incongruity of aggressive family planning in places that lacked basic health care. African-American, Latino, and Native American women in the United States felt that eugenics was now being marketed in new ways with new excuses. Women around the world objected to the link between these programs and women's personal decisions about controlling their own fertility. The only population problem they saw was that the elites in every country had problems with the poorer parts of the population and wanted a race- and class-directed eugenics program.

In the 1990s, saving the environment emerged as a new rationale for controlling nonwhite population growth. In addition, proposals to coercively limit the family size of poor women who received government assistance were presented as "welfare reform" in the United States. Whatever the reasoning, women have reason to be wary of government-sponsored proposals to limit their family size. Voluntary family planning is not eugenics, but coercion is eugenics; and it is urgent to distinguish between the two. That distinction has been a position held by African-American women since the 1920s.

See Also

BIOLOGICAL DETERMINISM; CLASS; ETHNIC CLEANSING; EUGENICS; EUROCENTRISM; EXPERIMENTS ON WOMEN; GENOCIDE; MEDICAL CONTROL OF WOMEN; RACISM AND XENOPHOBIA

References and Further Reading

Gordon, Linda. 1990. *Woman's body, woman's right: Birth control in America.* New York: Penguin.

Littlewood, Thomas B. 1977. *The politics of population control.* Notre Dame, Ind.: University of Notre Dame Press.

McCann, Carole R. 1994. *Birth control politics in the United States, 1916–1945.* New Haven, Conn.: Yale University Press.

Petchesky, Rosalind Pollack. 1990. *Abortion and woman's choice: The state, sexuality, and reproductive freedom.* Boston: Northeastern University Press.

Ward, Martha C. 1986. *Poor women, powerful men: America's great experiment in family planning.* Boulder, Col.: Westview.

Loretta Ross

EUROCENTRISM

Eurocentrism derives from the term *ethnocentrism*. With ethnocentrism, the social psychologist Sumner (1906) classified social groups into categories of "ingroup" and "outgroup," assuming that people differentiate between themselves and others by evaluating their own (in) group's values and manners positively while disapproving of those of others (the outgroup's). Nowadays ethnocentrism is used to characterize feelings and attitudes of superiority of one ethnic *culture* above others. An ethnocentric view or attitude is characteristic of all ethnicities to a greater or lesser extent. Ethnocentrism becomes extremely problematic where it shades off into the inferiorization of other cultures or races, as happened in the five-hundred-year history of western European hegemony, called Eurocentrism, or Europocentrism. Eurocentrism, the genesis of which is closely linked to capitalism (see Amin, 1988), is the belief (or rather the myth) that western powers had the right to annex, exploit, and colonize others on the basis of their superior "civilized" culture. Eurocentrism produced its own authorization through science and knowledge in which Europe was (and is) presented as the counterpole of barbaric others. The ideals of the Enlightenment, embracing equality of all humans, have produced contradictory notions of humanity by differentiating between civilized and human parts of the world (us) and uncivilized others (them). The distorted western notion of the Orient is one example of Eurocentrism (see Said, 1978), and others can be found in the western attitude about practically all third world countries and their peoples, viewed from a standpoint of superiority.

Since the early 1970s, the women's movement and feminist theory, evolving out of European and North American academia and therefore often conflated within the term *western,* stood accused of Eurocentrism (or even racism), as they were sustained and dominated by white (middle-class) women who had universalized their own experiences. Feminist actions had served their own needs, while black, colored, and migrant women's lives and social arrangements were excluded, misrecognized, or misinterpreted. Black women and women of color have argued that white feminism has failed to acknowledge the relationship of power and oppression between white (European and North American) women and nonwhite women. This accusation emphasized that white women had historically benefited from the exploitation of black women and women of color through colonialism and imperialism. Furthermore, white western feminists were accused of having elevated their own standards of life, including the western family, the western economy, and the western state structure, to a universal yardstick when judging others.

The writings of black and other minority feminists, as well as feminists from the third world, often criticize the basic assumptions of a Eurocentric western feminism by rewriting their own history and coming up with an alternative framework. The African-American feminist Patricia Hill Collins (1991), for example, pleads for the development of an "Afracentric" feminist epistemology, while the Indian-born feminist Chandra Talpade Mohanty (1991) calls for a rethinking of feminist praxis and theory within a cross-cultural, international framework by introducing "third world women" as a social category in feminist work. While the claim for "situationality" instead of universality is gradually incorporated into feminist thinking, other changes still have a long way to go. At the beginning of the twenty-first century Eurocentrism was still influential in determining the representation of nonwestern women and describing their lives, despite the fact that most women in the world are non-Christian and nonwhite.

References and Further Reading

Amin, Samir. 1988. *Eurocentrism.* London: Zed.

Collins, Patricia Hill. 1991. *Black feminist thought.* New York: Routledge.

Mohanty, Chandra Talpade. 1991. Cartographies of struggle: Third world women and the politics of feminism. In Chandra Talpade Mohanty, Ann Rosso, and Lourdes Torres, eds. *Third world women and the politics of feminism.* Bloomington and Indianapolis: Indiana University Press.

Sumner, William G. 1906. *Folkways: A study of the sociological importance of usages, manners, customs, mores and morals.* Boston: Ginn.

Said, Edward. 1978. *Orientalism.* New York and London: Routledge.

Helma Lutz

EUTHANASIA

Euthanasia, a Greek word meaning "easy death" or "good death," is a deliberate act, such as a lethal injection, intended to kill a patient quickly and painlessly when he or she is incurably ill and has requested it. Efforts to end useless suffering have occurred throughout history. People everywhere have preferred quality of life over mere quantity and have distinguished between good deaths and bad deaths. In fact, many nonindustrial societies devised cultural mechanisms for the timely removal of the old, the frail, and the incompetent. These mechanisms included neglect (withholding food and water, for example), abandonment, outright killing, and encouragement of suicide. The need for such practices seems to have been accepted by the recipient and his or her family, as well as the community. Likewise, many people today see a lingering death as undignified and degrading because it is so often accompanied by helplessness, dependency, senility, and pain.

Modern medicine has produced formidable life-prolonging technologies that can artificially delay death for almost everyone. Inappropriate use of these technologies can result in keeping some people alive past the point where a meaningful existence is possible, often at enormous cost to the family and the community. There are no new cultural mechanisms for coping with these problems. Hence, they have fueled debates about euthanasia around the world. Regardless of the circumstances and the wishes of the patient, euthanasia until recently was illegal everywhere, although for some time it has been tolerated and practiced openly in the Netherlands (where a further step toward legalization was taken in the year 2000). Elsewhere, it is usually carried out clandestinely; thus its true extent is unknown.

There are historical parallels between individuals' desire to control their own fertility and current efforts to give individuals more control over the timing and circumstances of death (Logue, 1993), and in both cases, public attitudes have been shifting toward greater approval. There has been a trend toward liberalization of laws to permit euthanasia under carefully controlled conditions. In 1995, when Australia's Northern Territory passed a law legalizing voluntary euthanasia, the governor general predicted that it would soon be legal nationwide. Special commissions have been set up in many nations to study the social, ethical, medical, and legal dimensions of euthanasia and make recommendations. Physicians and other health care workers are also taking a more favorable view of euthanasia, and many have become willing to speak openly on this once-taboo topic.

Women have been active on both sides of the debate. Helga Kuhse, Director of the Centre for Human Bioethics, Victoria, Australia, has served as president of the World Federation of Right-to-Die Societies; Jean Davies preceded her in the same capacity. Sheila McLean, director of the Institute of Law and Ethics in Medicine, Glasgow, Scotland, has worked to clarify euthanasia issues at home and abroad, including serving as a consultant to the World Health Organization. In the United States, the attorney Cheryl Smith cowrote the Oregon Death with Dignity Act; Smith has also spoken and written on a wide range of euthanasia issues. The ethicist Margaret Battin has advanced the debate by focusing on what different nations can learn from one another.

The long history of euthanasia is associated with an equally long history of opposition to the practice, and such opposition continues today. Some people object to euthanasia on religious and moral grounds, claiming that it interferes with God's will, devalues life, constitutes a violation of the physician's duty, or will inevitably lead to killing the helpless or needy even when they do not wish to die. Others worry that sick people who are only temporarily depressed will end their lives prematurely. Still others fear that unscrupulous doctors or greedy relatives will murder patients whose care is difficult, time-consuming, or expensive. Dame Cicely Saunders, who founded the modern hospice movement in 1967, has remained staunchly opposed to euthanasia, along with the psychiatrist Elisabeth Kübler-Ross, whose work with dying patients helped improve treatment of the terminally ill. Saunders and Kübler-Ross have maintained that pain control and good palliative care eliminate any need for deliberate killing. Rita Marker, who founded the International Anti-Euthanasia Task Force in 1987, has opposed euthanasia on religious grounds.

Proponents of euthanasia point to the suffering endured by many patients when euthanasia is forbidden; they stress the importance of patients' autonomy and the shortcomings of palliative care. They admit that risks cannot be entirely eliminated if euthanasia is permitted but contend that these risks can be minimized with good legislation. However, even proponents disagree among themselves on key issues, such as the appropriateness of euthanasia for patients who are no longer competent to request it. Should it be available only to mentally alert people who ask for it? Should it be available to severely demented people who indicated a desire for euthanasia in a legal document signed when they were still competent? Now, more than ever before in human history, the timing and circumstances of death are becoming a matter of deliberate choice. But questions regarding euthanasia are far from being resolved, and the current controversies are likely to intensify as aging populations and scarce resources make choices about death ever more salient.

See Also

DEATH; DISABILITY: QUALITY OF LIFE; ETHICS: MEDICAL; SUICIDE

References and Further Reading

Battin, Margaret. 1992. Voluntary euthanasia and the risks of abuse: Can we learn anything from the Netherlands? *Law, Medicine, and Health Care* 20(1–2): 133–143.

Logue, Barbara J. 1993. *Last rights: Death control and the elderly in America.* New York: Lexington/Macmillan.

McLean, Sheila, ed. 1995. *Death, dying, and the law.* Aldershot: Dartmouth.

Pence, Gregory. 1995. *Classic cases in medical ethics.* New York: McGraw-Hill.

Barbara J. Logue

EVOLUTION

Although it has had a variety of meanings and representations in different cultures, *evolution* has come to mean the leading contemporary theory of the development of life on Earth. This theory was first put forward by the English naturalist Charles Darwin in 1859. *The Origin of Species* sparked the "Darwinian revolution," conventionally viewed as a major episode in the history of the sciences and in the development of western intellectual thought. Darwin is popularly perceived as an almost mythical figure, one of science's so-called great men.

In the *Origin,* Darwin proposed that all existing organisms had evolved from earlier life-forms through the action of two primary processes. The chief of these was natural selection, the result of a universal "struggle for existence" in nature, whereby all organisms compete for limited food and room. Only the stronger or "better adapted" survive this struggle and reproduce. Thus, over many generations, the selective pressures of this relentless competition bring about cumulative organic changes or the gradual evolution of new life-forms.

The secondary process of sexual selection depended on a struggle for mates. Darwin recognized two aspects of this: male combat for possession of females, whereby the "most vigorous males, those which are best fitted for their places in nature," would leave most progeny; and female or aesthetic choice, whereby males compete by means of charms (brilliance of plumage, song, etc.) in their wooing of the female. Sexual selection played a vital role in Darwin's interpretation of human biological and social evolution. From the 1830s and 1840s, he argued against the orthodox Christian view of the divine origins of human mind and conscience, explaining them entirely in terms of the natural evolutionary agencies of the struggle for existence and for

mates. In 1871, Darwin published *The Descent of Man: or Selection in Relation to Sex;* here he made sexual selection primarily responsible for human racial and sexual differences, not just those that are physical but also those that are "mental"—that is, emotional, intellectual, and moral.

This insistence on the biological basis of these presumed intellectual and moral differences as the raw material on which natural and sexual selection might operate made Darwin's work vulnerable to political and ideological forces. Darwin himself took the biological "struggle for existence" from Malthusian social theory; the image of nature presented in Darwin's work was contingent on his own social context of mid-Victorian capitalist enterprise (Brown, 1995; Desmond and Moore, 1991; Young, 1985). Furthermore, the concept of sexual selection, largely dependent on Darwin's studies of the observations and activities of contemporary animal breeders, was inextricably anthropomorphic, transferring Victorian social values and racial and sexual stereotypes onto his theory. Darwinism became central to the "scientific racism" and "sexual science" that dominated late Victorian anthropological and social theory. Recent feminist scholarship thoroughly documents the significant role of leading Darwinians in imposing naturalistic, scientific limits to the claims by nineteenth-century feminists for political and social equality (Mosedale, 1978; Russett, 1989).

The Darwinian theory of evolution was accepted into science in a period of extraordinary social and economic transformation, in which preindustrial modes of legitimation, religion in particular, were giving way to a secular, naturalistic redefinition of the world. In the process, science increasingly assumed the task of defining and upholding the moral and social order. Darwinism was central to this transition. From the 1870s on, many found it expedient to look to evolution rather than religion for corroboration of social values. In this period, Britain, Germany, and the United States were expanding their imperial boundaries; mass, socialist, working-class movements were emerging all over Europe; women were beginning to demand suffrage, higher education, and entrance to middle-class professions. Thus, the origin of "man" by natural law rather than divine creation was made more palatable for its Victorian audience by Darwinian concepts of "natural" and inevitable white, middle-class male supremacy.

Darwin himself made specific contributions to this scientific ratification of Victorian values. He incorporated social opinion into *The Descent of Man* in support of his conviction that social progress could occur only through severe and sustained competitive struggle; he assumed the innate and continuing intellectual and cultural inferiority of women and the "lower races," as well as the inevitability and rightness of the sexual division of labor. By asserting the instinctively maternal and inherently modest traits of the human female and the male's innate aggressive and competitive characteristics, Darwin proffered an evolutionary justification of woman's narrow domestic role and contemporary social inequalities (Richards, 1983; Jann, 1994).

Darwin put into men's hands the modifying and shaping power of human sexual selection, thus overturning the female aesthetic choice he attributed to animals. The differing standards of beauty of the various races offered the explanation, via male aesthetic preferences, of racial and sexual differention. "Monstrous" as it was, Darwin was convinced that the "jet-blackness of the negro" had been gained through the process of male selection, just as had the "more pleasing" secondary sexual characteristics of European women—sweeter voices, long tresses, and greater beauty (Darwin, 1871: 2: 368–84).

If woman's body was pliant to male manipulation, her mind, unfortunately, was not. Her intelligence demonstrably lagged behind man's. Man attains "a higher eminence in whatever he takes up, than can woman—whether requiring deep thought, reason, or imagination, or merely the use of the senses or hands." Those aspects of intelligence conventionally attributed to women—such as intuition, rapid perception, and imitation—Darwin dismissed as "characteristic of the lower races, and therefore of a past and lower state of civilization." Male intelligence, he argued, would have been consistently sharpened through sexual selection and through hunting and other male activities such as the defense of the females and young (natural selection). "Thus," Darwin concluded, "man has ultimately become superior to woman," and the higher education of women, then furiously contested in Victorian England, could have no long-term impact on this evolutionary trend to ever increasing male intelligence (1871: 2: 326–29).

Many other evolutionists also pronounced on the "woman question." Herbert Spencer argued directly against the extension of the franchise and higher education to women on biological grounds. Thomas Henry Huxley, Darwin's "bulldog" and avowed "supporter" of women's rights, took a more insidious liberal line by conceding to women their right to the vote and higher education, but he imposed strict evolutionary limitations on the outcome. Huxley reassured threatened professionals that not even the "most skilfully conducted process of educational selection" could remove the "physical disabilities under which women have hitherto laboured in the struggle for existence with men." As its president, Huxley excluded women from the Ethnological Society, subordinating his commitment to women's issues

(such as it was) to his goal of amalgamation with the rival (and rabidly racist and sexist) Anthropological Society, thus securing Darwinian control of the key discipline of anthropology. It was primarily through the "new" evolutionary anthropology, also a vehicle for scientific racism, that the growing authority and prestige of the Darwinians were pitted against the claims by women for intellectual and social equality (Richards, 1989; Richards, 1997).

This concerted scientific refutation of feminism was all the more devastating because many feminists were deeply committed to naturalistic science and to the new Darwinism. A number of them retreated from the egalitarian ideal to claim for woman a biologically based "complementary genius" rooted in her innate maternal and womanly qualities (Alaya, 1977). Thus Antoinette Brown Blackwell (1875), a prominent U.S. feminist and evolutionist, did not dispute that the mental differences between men and women were biological and evolution based; rather, she disputed whether woman's innate mental differences could properly be called inferior to man's. She balanced man's greater strength, reasoning powers, and sexual love against woman's greater endurance, insightfulness, and parental love and argued that social progress was dependent on the full expression of these sexually divergent evolutionary traits. Such argumentation had a dangerous tendency to reinforce traditional stereotypes.

More radical dissent came from a number of socialist feminists, including Charlotte Perkins Gilman (1898), Eliza Burt Gamble (1894), and Olive Schreiner (1911). They posited a future in which women, freed from economic and social dependency, would regain their rightful power of selection, and, through their more "rational" selection of mates, advance a better, more socially just society (Love, 1983; Jann, 1997).

Such attempts to revolutionize sexual selection and give women an active and central role in evolution were crushed by dogmatic Darwinians. As sexual and natural selection went into abeyance, not to be revived until well into the twentieth century, other evolutionary based arguments continued to assert that women's nature was rooted in biology. Evolution joined a formidable body of theory purporting to show that women were inherently different from men in their anatomy, physiology, temperament, and intellect and could never expect equality (Russett, 1989).

In the twentieth century, the Darwinian theory of natural selection, since its synthesis with Mendelian genetics in the 1930s, went from strength to strength in the mainstream of biological thinking. Darwin's secondary principle of sexual selection was revived and reintegrated into contemporary evolutionary theorizing. These developments were accompanied by renewed controversy over the biological and social significance of natural and sexual selection. This conflict became most acute between sociobiologists and contemporary feminists. It gave rise to a good deal of work that has been concerned with demonstrating or rebutting the charge that the writings of Darwin and his modern-day defenders are irretrievably sexist and motivated by antifeminist purposes (e.g., Hubbard, 1990).

Other feminist scholars have attempted to develop new evolutionary models that do not relegate women to the periphery of this process. The work of Nancy Makepeace Tanner is representative of this genre. Tanner (1981) stresses the development of upright two-legged locomotion or bipedalism in her revisionist version of human prehistory. Bipedalism brought with it anatomical changes in the pelvis that led to birth at an earlier stage, prolonged the period of infant dependency, and strengthened the mother-offspring bond. Those infants who had the greatest chance of surviving were those whose mothers were the most efficient food gatherers, who habitually shared food with their young, and who exercised foresight in gathering sufficient food for their own and their offspring's needs. There were thus intense selective pressures on female intelligence and sociability. Tanner posited the critical role of females in tool innovation and use in food gathering, in group socialization, and in passing these skills and forms of knowledge on to their male and female offspring. She also reversed women's time-worn evolutionary role as passive objects of male desire and brute force by according them the initiative in sexual selection. Bipedalism, she argued, favored female selection of reproductive partners because it made male detection of female sexual receptivity more difficult and shifted the emphasis to behavioral cues that the sexually aroused female might proffer to her chosen partner. Moreover, her choice was more likely to fall on friendly, less threatening males—those who perhaps accompanied her on her gathering, sometimes shared their food, or helped in the defense of the young. So female choice of such males reinforced those traits, such as altruism and compassion, that many like to regard as uniquely human.

Such woman-centered versions of evolution have their critics. But they are no more speculative than more conventional androcentric ones. They link with other debates in primate studies, anthropology, and sociobiology to contest and reshape disciplinary understandings, offering alternative possibilities for explanation and justification of human social and economic arrangements. However, the potential of such theories to provide the foundations of a truly feminist evolutionary science or social practice is queried by Donna Haraway (1991). Her critique provokes the more fundamental question of whether feminists have anything to learn from theories about the nature of human origins and sexual difference other than the lesson that such theories are inescapably culture bound.

See Also

ANTHROPOLOGY; BIOLOGICAL DETERMINISM; BIOLOGY; CYBORG ANTHROPOLOGY; FEMINISM: NINETEENTH CENTURY; GENETICS AND GENETIC TECHNOLOGIES; PRIMATOLOGY; SCIENTIFIC SEXISM AND RACISM; SEXUAL DIFFERENCE; SOCIAL MOVEMENTS

References and Further Reading

Alaya, Flavia. 1977. Victorian science and the "genius" of woman. *Journal of the History of Ideas.* 38: 261–80.

Blackwell, Antoinette Brown. 1875. *The sexes throughout nature.* New York: Putnam.

Brown, Janet. 1995. *Charles Darwin: Voyaging.* London: Cape.

Darwin, Charles. 1871. *The descent of man; or, selection in relation to sex.* 2 vols. London: John Murray.

Desmond, Adrian, and James Moore. 1991. *Darwin.* London: Michael Joseph.

Haraway, Donna. 1991. The past is the contested zone: Human nature and theories of production and reproduction in primate behaviour studies. In *Simians, cyborgs and women,* 21–42. London: Free Association.

Hubbard, Ruth. 1990. Have only men evolved? In *The politics of women's biology,* 87–106. New Brunswick, N.J.: Rutgers University Press.

Jann, Rosemary. 1994. Darwin and the anthropologists: Sexual selection and its discontents. *Victorian Studies.* 37: 287–306.

———. 1997. Revising the descent of woman: Eliza Burt Gamble. In Barbara T. Gates and Ann B. Shteir, eds. *Natural eloquence: Women reinscribe science,* 147–63. Madison and London: University of Wisconsin Press.

Love, Rosaleen. 1983. Darwinism and feminism: The "woman question" in the life and work of Olive Schreiner and Charlotte Perkins Gilman. In David R. Oldroyd and Ian Langham, eds., *The wider domain of evolutionary thought,* 113–131. Dordrecht: Reidel.

Mosedale, Susan Sleeth. 1978. Science corrupted: Victorian biologists consider "the woman question." *Journal of the History of Biology* 11: 1–55.

Richards, Evelleen. 1983. Darwin and the descent of woman. In David R. Oldroyd and Ian Langham, eds., *The wider domain of evolutionary thought*, 57–111. Dordrecht: Reidel.

———. 1989. Huxley and woman's place in science: The "woman question" and control of Victorian anthropology. In James R. Moore, ed., *History, humanity and evolution*, 253–284. Cambridge: Cambridge University Press.

———. 1997. Redrawing the boundaries: Darwinian science and Victorian women intellectuals. In Bernard Lightman, ed., *Victorian science in context*, 119–142. Chicago and London: University of Chicago Press.

Russett, Cynthia Eagle. 1989. *Sexual science: The Victorian construction of womanhood.* Cambridge, Mass.: Harvard University Press.

Tanner, Nancy Makepeace. 1981. *On becoming human.* Cambridge: Cambridge University Press.

Young, Robert M. 1985. *Darwin's metaphor: Nature's place in Victorian culture.* Cambridge: Cambridge University Press.

Evelleen Richards

EXAMINATIONS AND ASSESSMENT

Assessment of student achievement is playing an enhanced role in education worldwide. To be useful, assessment must be *valid*—that is, equally fair and sound as a measure of achievement for all students. International surveys of achievement have consistently shown differences between males and females and between ethnic and racial groups, usually to the advantage of white males. Recently, some of these trends have reversed. This turnabout cannot be explained by changes in the innate abilities of the male and female populations, and the findings have focused concern on the assessments themselves.

Psychosocial variables in educational and assessment situations can lead to inequity either in assessment practice or in the interpretation of assessment outcomes. Parents expect different behaviors from boys and girls and encourage them to interact with the environment and people in different ways. Children absorb an idea of what constitutes appropriate gender behavior from these expectations. Boys and girls experience schooling differently and develop different perceptions of their abilities in academic disciplines; teachers' judgments and expectations vary in stereotypical ways (Wilder and Powell, 1989). The consequences of these data for assessment are considerable.

Curriculum Experiences

In most countries, girls are less likely to study math and science to an advanced level. As a result, they perform less well than boys in international surveys. However, such results are sometimes interpreted as showing that girls have less ability than boys to learn math or science. When curriculum background is controlled, the pattern of performance appears much more similar. One reason for the differential success of girls and boys in public exams in the United Kingdom is different entry patterns. Girls tend to be allocated to easier routes in math than their ability warrants because girls who do well are seen as hardworking rather than able (Walden and Walkerdine, 1985) and because teachers judge girls to be more anxious about failure than boys.

There is evidence, too, that ethnic minority pupils are allocated to lower-level exam routes (Eggleston et al., 1986; Smith and Tomlinson, 1989). British schools have admitted that they were not prepared to put Afro-Caribbean children into the academic/examination streams in case these children were disruptive or unrealistically ambitious (Eggleston, 1988). Gender differences play a role in these decisions as well.

Assessment Design

Features of assessment tasks can have differential effects on the performance of males and females. For example, the use of exclusive language (for example, *men* rather than *people*) can cause problems, as can the use of racial or gender stereotypes (for example, consistently portraying an engineer or doctor as a white male). Sensitivity review panels examine items for these face validity features and reject them on this basis.

Statistical procedures have also been used to determine if certain characteristics of items make them more or less difficult for subgroups within the population assessed. Girls and boys, for example, will react to the same item content differently if it fails to reflect their everyday experiences or if it represents an activity or experience they consider inappropriate for them. Girls and boys at ages 5, 11, and 13 are equally competent at using tables and graphs. Yet if the subject of a graph is a day in the life of a secretary, some boys will not respond, whereas some girls will respond with confidence, so that girls overall obtain a higher score. If, on the other hand, a graph is about traffic flow through a town, the reverse will happen. For some students, then, response to the items does not reflect their understanding of graphs but rather their experience of the content.

Similar differences arise if the setting or context of the task leads students to identify different features of the content as relevant to the item response. Girls more than boys value the circumstances within which the activities are presented and consider the context to give meaning to the task (Murphy, 1991). One science assessment task—to find the thermal conductivity of blanket and plastic—was set in the context of being stranded up a mountainside in cold, windy weather. The context was intended to be irrelevant to the task, but not in the view of many of the girls, who proceeded to compare thermal conductivity in dry and wet conditions and in windy and calm conditions. The girls' view of the task made it much more difficult, which affected their performance adversely.

The mode of response required in an item can also be a source of differential performance. Girls as a group choose to communicate in extended, reflective composition. Boys, responding to the same task, typically provide episodic, factual, commentative detail (White, 1988). Boys' style has been found to advantage them in science but disadvantage them in English, whereas the reverse obtains for girls (Stobart et al., 1992).

There is evidence that multiple-choice items disadvantage females and advantage males. Males are prepared to guess more than females, whereas females typically provide no response or opt for the "don't know" distractor (Anderson, 1989; Bolger and Kellaghan, 1990). Girls are more likely than boys to see ambiguity in the distractors offered, so that they fail to find a single correct response and either do not respond or check more than one box (Gipps and Murphy, 1994).

Current developments in assessment practice are aimed at ensuring that features of items do not function as barriers to certain students and at enabling assessors to distinguish between lack of achievement as an outcome of teaching and lack of achievement arising from a lack of opportunity to learn.

See Also

EDUCATION: ACHIEVEMENT; EDUCATION: MATHEMATICS; EDUCATION: SCIENCE

References and Further Reading

Anderson, J. 1989. Sex-related differences on objective tests among undergraduates. *Educational Studies in Mathematics* 20: 165–177.

Bolger, N., and T. Kellaghan. 1990. Method of measurement and gender differences in scholastic achievement. *Journal of Educational Measurement* 27: 165–174.

Eggleston, J. 1988. The new education bill and assessment: Some implications for black children. *Multicultural Teaching* 6 (Spring): 24–30.

———, D. Dunn, M. Anjali, and C. Wright. 1986. *Education for some.* Stoke-on-Trent, U.K.: Trentham.

Gipps, C., and P. Murphy. 1994. *A fair test? Assessment, achievement and equity.* Milton Keynes, U.K.: Open University Press.

Murphy, P. 1991. Gender and practical work. In B. Woolnough, ed., *Practical work in science.* Milton Keynes, U.K.: Open University Press.

Smith, D., and S. Tomlinson. 1989. *The school effect.* London: Policy Studies Institute.

Strobart, G., et al. 1992. *Differential performance at 16+: English and mathematics.* London: Schools Examination and Assessment Council.

Walden, R., and V. Walkerdine. 1985. *Girls and mathematics: From primary to secondary schooling.* Bedford Way Paper no. 24. London: University of London, Institute of Education.

White, J. 1988. *The assessment of writing: Pupils aged 11 and 15.* Windsor, U.K.: NFER-Nelson.

Wilder, G. Z., and K. Powell. 1989. *Sex differences in test performance: A survey of the literature.* College Board Report no. 88-1. New York: College Entrance Examination Board.

Patricia Murphy

EXERCISE AND FITNESS

Exercise refers to any intentional, repetitive bodily movement undertaken specifically to improve or maintain one or more components of fitness. *Fitness* relates to one's ability to perform physical activity, and *physical activity* refers to any movement performed by skeletal muscles that results in energy expenditure. In general, one performs physical activity or exercise to promote health, a dynamic state ranging from illness to optimal levels of functioning.

Benefits of Exercise

It is broadly recommended that both men and women perform aerobic exercise three or more times per week at a moderate intensity for about 30 minutes per session. This prescription will vary, however, among individuals with differing needs.

The general benefits of exercise include improved physical and psychological well-being and also a reduction in the risk of some disease. There are, however, more specific benefits for women. These include a reduction in the risk of osteoporotic fractures (due to increased bone mineral density), improved insulin sensitivity for women prone to diabetes mellitus, a reduction in the intensity of menopausal symptoms and premenstrual stress, a reduction in hypertension (due to reduced excess weight about the stomach region), and weight control or maintenance. Further increases in physical stamina and associated psychological improvements, including reduced stress and improved self-image, appear to be particularly beneficial for pregnant women. In fact, moderate exercise throughout pregnancy is generally recommended, although this should be conservative and under the guidance of a physician.

Older women who continue to participate in physical activity throughout life are more likely to maintain their physical independence and, thus, quality of life. They are less susceptible to osteoporotic fractures, and their increased muscular strength, flexibility, and aerobic capacity allow them to care for themselves more effectively and independently.

Women and Excessive Exercise

Although moderate exercise for women can be health promoting, excessive exercise produces specific concerns. A significant loss of weight due to excessive exercise, often accompanied by disordered eating, may reduce estrogen levels and, thus, bone mineral density, increasing the risk of early osteoporotic fractures. Other risks include a decreased immune system, soft tissue injuries, and menstrual irregularities that may result in amenorrhea (the cessation of the menstrual cycle).

Thus, moderation in exercise is always recommended with gradual increases in intensity as fitness improves. The goal should always be to promote health and well-being.

Women and Exercise: Historical Issues

Exercise and participation in physical activity have a history of being highly gendered. When the ancient Greek summer Olympics began in 1896, it was deemed inappropriate that women should engage in physical activity, and they were not invited to participate. By 1900, however, two events—tennis and golf—allowed women, although, overall, women's rate of inclusion in the world's most celebrated sporting event has been extremely slow. At one point, women became so frustrated about this process that they developed the Women's Olympic Games, which debuted in Paris in 1922 and ceased in 1934.

In the eighteenth and nineteenth centuries, exercise and physical activity were highly military in nature and mostly offered to boys and men in a bid to imbue masculinity. In later-nineteenth-century Europe, however, a concern with public health saw women being encouraged to undertake a little exercise to improve their constitution. Although this approach was fiercely opposed by many, women slowly began to participate in exercise from this time on but mostly in such "feminine" activities as calisthenics and ballet.

Women in Exercise: Current Issues

More recently, women have become involved in all types of physical activities (partly as a result of greater health education), although in general participation remains gendered. During adolescence particularly, girls tend to be less involved in sport and physical activity than boys. The pervasive "masculine" emphasis on competitiveness and violence runs counter to girls' concern with having fun and being social when performing physical activity, and this attitude puts future participation at risk.

More generally, women are less likely to participate in exercise if they have no history of exercise participation, if they lack family support, if the cost is too great, if they have poor body image, if leisure time is lacking, or if they see no immediate benefits of exercise. Women are more likely to participate in exercise if they have a history of participation, higher levels of education, concern for their health, and strong family support.

Internationally, these trends are similar. Women's work, family, friends, and leisure time (often centered on domestic activities) tend to take priority over exercise. This is a concern for many westernized countries, where the high level of sedentary behavior is associated with cardiovascular and other lifestyle diseases. Although many western nations have specific programs in place to address this problem, other nonwestern and poorer nations do not have the resources to focus on promoting exercise, as day-to-day living is of greater concern. (This is also an issue of race and class in western countries.) In some other nonwestern nations, however, a woman's daily activities often involve a high proportion of physical activity anyway (such as tribal and nomadic living), and intentional exercise programs are mostly unnecessary.

See Also

HEALTH: OVERVIEW; LEISURE; SPORT; SPORT AND DISCRIMINATION

References and Further Reading

Costa, D. M., and S. R. Guthrie. 1994. *Women and Sport: Interdisciplinary perspectives.* Champaign, Ill.: Human Kinetics.

Griffin, P. 1998. *Strong women, deep closets.* Champaign, Ill.: Human Kinetics.

Hall, M. A. 1996. *Feminism and sporting bodies: Essays on theory and practice.* Champaign, Ill.: Human Kinetics.

McKay, J. 1991. *No pain, no gain: Sport and Australian culture.* Englewood Cliffs, N.J.: Prentice Hall.

Messner, M. A., and D. F. Sabo. 1990. *Sport, men and the gender order: Critical feminist perspectives.* Champaign, Ill.: Human Kinetics.

Kate Connelly

EXISTENTIAL FEMINISM
SEE FEMINISM: EXISTENTIAL.

EXPERIMENTS ON WOMEN

Well before the Enlightenment, ancient cultures performed trial-and-error experiments to test their theories of the natural world. But only with the birth of modern science did experimentation and scientific research begin to supersede religion in cultural authority. For instance, nineteenth-century "craniologists" in the United States and Europe measured and compared skull sizes across race and gender in an attempt to substantiate contemporary theories of white male intellectual and moral superiority.

The previous example highlights a common thread throughout the history of experimentation: women serving as objects but not subjects of science. Cross-culturally, dominant social groups generally frame questions and conduct experiments, while less dominant or socially undesirable groups—the poor, mentally ill, elderly, prisoners, racial and ethnic minorities, and women—are relegated to study participants or play no role at all. The objectification of women by male "intellectuals" prompted Virginia Woolf to comment: "Have you any notion how many books are written about women in the course of one year? Have you any notion how many are written by men? Are you aware that you are, perhaps, the most discussed animal in the universe?" (1929: 26). Despite this apparent preoccupation with the female gender, Woolf revealed an ironic dearth of reliable information about women; contemporary feminist critiques of science have returned to this observation.

In the early twentieth century, when Woolf wrote, the practice of medicine and healing was subject to very few regulations; only a blurred line separated human experimentation and therapy. Moreover, many forms of therapy, including Freudian psychoanalysis, incorporated sexist assumptions. In addition, since manufacturers of patent medicines found women to be profitable targets, they focused especially on "embarrassing" problems "peculiar to her sex." To illustrate, at least 92 different types of douche powders and household products—for example, Lysol—were sold for feminine hygiene during the mid-1930s.

Ethical standards to guide human research emerged midcentury and only *after* revelations of gross abuse in human experimentation, in several instances involving women subjects. For example, the U.S. government did not require manufacturers to prove drug *safety* prior to market release until 1938, when elixir sulfonamide—a popular prescription drug that was tested for appearance, fragrance, and flavor but not toxicity—caused 107 deaths (mostly of children). One decade later, the Nuremberg Code—the first international policy of informed consent—was prompted by the Nazi's and Allies' abuses in human experimentation during World War II.

Responding to a history of abuse in drug testing and contraceptive research—all too often on poor women and women in developing countries—some feminists have decried all experimentation on women. However, others recognize that human research—conducted ethically and responsibly—is needed before drugs and treatments are incorporated into general medical practice. Indeed, events in the late twentieth century revealed that neglect of research may cause as much harm to women as research abuses.

U.S. federal standards requiring proof of drug *efficacy* as well as drug safety were inspired by thousands of thalidomide-induced birth defects in Europe during the 1950s. In the 1960s and 1970s, diethylstilbestrol (DES)—commonly prescribed to pregnant women during the 1940s and 1950s to prevent miscarriage—and the Dalkon Shield intrauterine device provided two further examples of unsafe drug products and devices released to the market without adequate testing, causing injury, reproductive harm, and even death. Although these tragedies resulted from the *lack* of research on women and *ignored* animal research indicating adverse reproductive effects, they prompted federal policies and ethical guidelines that restricted women's participation—especially "women of childbearing potential"—in human research.

During the 1990s, policies mandating exclusion of fertile women from research studies received renewed scientific and feminist scrutiny. While acknowledging a history of inappropriate inclusion of women and minorities in drug testing, many have concluded that the common practice of conducting large-scale clinical trials with all-male study populations—for example, Physicians Health Study and Multiple Risk Factor Intervention Trials (aptly abbreviated MR FIT)—has contributed to significant gaps in knowledge with respect to women's health. Consequently, women policy makers and women's health advocates have mobilized around the issue of research, marking a shift in both public opinion and policy development.

In response to U.S. women's demands to evaluate for themselves the relative risks and benefits inherent in research, revised federal guidelines were promulgated during the mid-1990s. The new regulations aimed at encouraging women's full participation in scientific research, ensuring informed consent, and providing adequate safeguards against reproductive harm. Beyond mere inclusion and "numerical parity," however, women and women's perspectives must be incorporated at every level of federally funded research—from policy to peer review to design and practice.

See Also

ABUSE; BIOETHICS: FEMINIST; ETHICS: MEDICAL; ETHICS: SCIENTIFIC; MEDICAL CONTROL OF WOMEN; MEDICINE: INTERNAL, *I and II*; SCIENCE, FEMINIST CRITIQUES; SCIENCE: TECHNOLOGICAL AND SCIENTIFIC RESEARCH; SCIENTIFIC: SEXISM AND RACISM

References and Further Reading

Faden, Ruth, Tom L. Beauchamp, and Nancy M. P. King. 1986. *A history and theory of informed consent.* New York: Oxford University Press.

Fee, Elizabeth, and Nancy Krieger, eds. 1994. *Women's health, politics, and power: Essays on sex/gender, medicine, and public health.* New York: Baywood.

Gordon, Linda. 1990. *Woman's body, woman's rights: Birth control in America.* New York: Penguin (originally published 1976).

Mastroianni, Anna C., Ruth Faden, and Daniel Federman, eds. 1994. *Women and health research: Ethical and legal issues of including women in clinical studies.* Vols. 1 and 2. Washington, D.C.: National Academy Press. (Vol. 1 represents the committee report; Vol. 2 consists of workshop and commissioned papers, including several feminist works.)

Woolf, Virginia. 1929. *A room of one's own.* New York: Harcourt, Brace and World.

Elizabeth Fee

F

FAIRY TALES

The realm of the fairy-story is wide and deep and high
and filled with many things.... In that realm a *man*
may, perhaps count himself fortunate to have wan-
dered.... And while he is there it is dangerous for him
to ask too many questions, lest the gates should be shut
and the keys be lost. (Tolkien, 1966: 11; emphasis
added)

Fairy tales are wonderfully evocative stories that have
shaped the fantasy world of generations of children in western Europe. Beginning in seventeenth-century France, folk-
tales were collected, rewritten, and transformed into literature
by the likes of Perrault and Grimm. Many of them were
quickly adapted for children (for example, by Marie Catherine, Comtesse d'Aulnoy, 1650–1705; and Arthur Rackham),
and others, such as Hans Christian Andersen's tales, were
written for children. Now fairy tales are read assiduously to
quite young children. Bettleheim (1997), Heuscher (1963),
Luthi (1970), and others claim that fairy tales provide children with explanations of the human behavior they observe
and experience. These stories give children an externalized
image of their feelings stage by stage as they mature. Children mediate the real world through fairy stories and emerge
richer and wiser from the experience:

> In order not to be at the mercy of the vagaries of life,
> one must develop one's inner resources, so that one's
> emotions, imagination and intellect mutually sup-
> port and enrich one another.... It is here that fairy-
> tales have unequalled value... the form and structure
> of fairytales suggest images to the child by which *he*
> can structure his daydreams and with them give a bet-
> ter direction to his life. (Bettelheim, 1977: 7; empha-
> sis added)

Jungian interpretation such as that of Marie-Louise von
Franz (1972) maintains that fairy tales also teach us about
the animus and anima, about the male and female energies
in the human subconscious.

It is true that these stories reveal and interpret social
structures, the dynamics of power, and accepted behaviors.
They also seem to have a tremendous formative influence
on the imagination of children. However, for many feminists this poses a problem: in many instances, what fairy tales
teach is not appropriate to today's society.

Many commentators who approve of fairy tales imply
that the child who will benefit is male:

> In many fairy stories a king gives his daughter in mar-
> riage to the hero and either shares his kingdom with
> him or installs him as the eventual successor. This is,
> of course, a wishful fantasy of the child. But since the
> story assures *him*... (Bettelheim, 1977: 129; emphasis
> added)

The benefit is for the male child, who is taught to see women
as objects bestowed upon him, prizes for his endeavors. And
his endeavors are exciting and interesting: travel, challenge,
success.

Girls, on the other hand, sit in trees and sew for seven
years, awaiting salvation, or sacrifice themselves to save the
men in their family. In virtually every famous tale, the heroine is systematically deprived of affection, stimulation, pleasurable activity, instruction, and even companionship. She
is a totally powerless prisoner, in turn the victim of circum-
stance, of an older woman, and of men of all ages. And when
her prince does come? "Bridebed, childbed, bed of death,"
says Hélène Cixous succinctly (Clément and Cixous, 1975:
127). Fairy tales teach girls to be powerless and teach boys to
take or win power.

Increasingly, contemporary women writers have been using fairy tale structures in ways that exploit their hold on the female imagination while changing their teaching to something more equitable or openly women-centered. In *Les Guérillères* (1969; trans. 1971) Monique Wittig "reclaimed" and rewrote "Sleeping Beauty" and "Snow White and Rose Red." (She also annexed the myths of the Golden Fleece and the Grail, and retold the story of the Garden of Eden without Adam.) She was followed in her reappropriation within the realm of French literature by Jeanne Hyvrard in *Mother Death* (1976, trans. 1988) and in Quebec by Louky Bersianik in *The Euquélionne* (1976, trans. 1981). Writers in English have made a different choice. Instead of critiquing and rewriting fairy stories within the context of another piece of fiction, several writers began writing collections of radically revised fairy tales. One of the first was Angela Carter: *The Bloody Chamber and Other Stories* (1981). Subsequently, these fairy tales have become the province of Irish feminist writers. In the 1980s, Attic Press (Dublin) published several volumes of stories written by a number of well-known authors, including Maeve Binchy, Zoé Fairbanks, and Mary Dorcey. These anthologies have titles such as *Sweeping Beauties, Cinderella on the Ball*, and *Ride on, Rapunzel* (see Stone, 1975; Zipes, 1979). It seems that new feminist fairy tales are also to be found in the futuristic fantasy of writers such as Marion Zimmer Bradley.

The original stories operate at many different levels; this is why they have been so influential for so long and also—feminists argue—why they need to be rewritten. But, although twisting the plot to create a feminist reversal may be funny and may undermine the power of the original form to some extent, it is not sufficient to ensure that the revised version will take its place in our collective imagination.

See Also

CHILDREN'S LITERATURE; MYTH

References and Further Reading

Bersianik, Louis. 1981. *The Euguélionne*. Victoria: Press Porcépic.
Bettelheim, Bruno. 1977. *The uses of enchantment: The meaning and importance of fairytales*. New York: Random House.
Bradley, Marion Zimmer. 1982. *The mists of Avalon*. New York: Knopf.
Carter, Angela. 1981. *The bloody chamber and other stories*. Harmondsworth: Penguin.
Clément, Catherine, and Hélène Cixous. 1975. *La juene néo*. Paris: Union général d'éditions.
Heuscher, Julius E. 1963. *A psychiatric study of fairy tales: Their origin, meaning and usefulness*. Springfield, Ill.: Thomas.
Hyvrard, Jeanne. 1988. *Mother Death*. Lincoln: University of Nebraska Press.
Luthi, Max. 1970. *Once upon a time: On the nature of fairy tales*. Bloomington: University of Indiana Press.
Starhawk. 1993. *The fifth sacred thing*. New York: Bantam.
Stone, Kay. 1975. The misuses of enchantment: Controversies on the significance of fairy tales. In Claire R. Farrer, ed., *Women and folklore: Images and genres*. Prospect Heights, Ill.: Waveland.
Tolkien, J. R. R. 1966. *Tree and leaf*. London: Unwin.
von Franz, Mary Louise. 1972. *The feminine in fairy tales*. Zurich: Springer.
Wittig, Monique. 1969. *Les Guérillières*. Boston: Beacon.
Zipes, Jack. 1979. *Breaking the magic spell: Radical theories of folk and fairy tales*. London: Heinemann.

Jennifer Waelti-Walters

FAITH

Faith is a term used to describe the dynamic inner character of the human response to what is perceived of as holy, sacred, or of the highest value. It is a universal and unique feature of human experience—unique because it plays an important function in making, maintaining, and transforming meaning, which only humans seek in life. All human worldviews and constructions of meaning are in some sense relative to the way in which humans try to bring clarity into their ground of being. Hence, faith is manifest in different forms and directed toward different ideas, not only toward the sacred, holy, or ultimate. Faith is relational, implying trust, reliance, and dependence as well as commitment and loyalty. It operates, therefore, within the context of human-to-human relationships as well as in relationships between humans and those things that are considered of the highest value, which in the context of religion are the holy or sacred.

Faith is usually thought of as developing on various levels. This development indicates the connection between faith and personal identity, so that faith addresses different issues at different stages of the life cycle. At a primal, prelanguage level, faith could be described as trust and loyalty. However, at the highest universalizing level, faith is grounded in the completion of a radical process that removes the self as the central reference point for constructing identification with, or participation in, the ultimate. Finally, the self is transformed and begins to love and value from a center located in the ultimate. In light of global pluralism, this is important to humanity's effort to make sense of the meaning and dynamics of faith, since it helps humanity to find a way to transcend religious differences and focus on faith as a very universal human response.

When the dimensions and developments of faith are analyzed, or the images of the objects deemed holy or sacred from any particular religion are considered, the points of divergence in the usage of the term *faith* can be clearly seen. Although the articles of faith and the role that faith plays in salvation are variously constructed in three major monotheistic religions—Judaism, Christianity, and Islam—these three converge on one major point: the object of faith is God, conceived of as a supreme male deity. Dissent from this particular concept of the object of faith has been considered heretical. However, feminist theological discourse has criticized the nature and role of gender in imagining the ultimate, contending that the perception of a masculine God, as in traditional monotheistic theological metaphors, severely limits the faithful woman's identification with the deity. The presence of a goddess or quasi goddess in a religious system has the psychological value of providing women with a more self-identifiable role model as the object of their faith, worship, and supplication.

In traditional Judaism the righteous woman was unable to effect her own salvation except through her husband and the procreation of many children. At the beginning of the twenty-first century, feminist theologians have undertaken a quest to reclaim women's stories that maintain the feminine face of God and provide more positive spiritual paradigms for women, to escape the passive "victim" awaiting salvation from the active male deity. Such stories focus on other self-motivated roles and daily actions in women's service of their redemption, such as midwife, prophet, woman of courage, and lamenting wise woman.

Shekinah, which is considered feminine and represents one way to imagine the Mystery, has always been a part of the Jewish tradition. Considering the construction of Shekinah in the language of Jewish traditional theology has become a significant way to help women recapture wholeness of being without disrupting the monotheism so essential to the integrity of Judaism.

In Islam, it is impossible to conceive of faith except through its reflection in actions, whether ritual, social, moral, political, or personal. Performing the right action is a demonstration of faith. Conversely, failure to perform the right action implies a denial of faith. Salvation awaits those who have faith, so long as they perform the prescribed right actions. Historically, Islamic law (Shari'a) was developed with the goal of giving detailed descriptions of right actions as prescribed by the Qur'an and embodied in the practices of the prophet Muhammad. However, Islamic mystics (Sufis) did not agree that the mere performance of outward ritual acts as prescribed necessarily indicated the true level of faith, which is a state of the heart.

For Muslim women, as for Muslim men, the role of faith in salvation is described in the Qur'an in exact terms. Hence, a woman who performs her prescribed deeds is guaranteed salvation. In modern times, women have come to an understanding closer to the Sufi understanding about the state of faith in the heart, especially when the prescribed deeds can be seen as reflections of a male interpretation of divine will. The Qur'an, the primary source of Islam, states that Allah is "not like any thing." It does not associate Allah with any finite or created characteristics. Since gender is a feature of created things, Allah is neither he nor she.

In Christianity, faith is the assurance of things hoped for and the conviction of things not seen. As something more than mere intellectual reasoning, faith is considered a theological virtue that is a gift of grace and involves knowledge of the right doctrine and obedience to God's commands. There is a relationship between faith and works. In Christian womanist theology, for example, faith is a miracle in the lives of ordinary black women that helps them to find some relief from the burden that their lives have often been. Faith causes them to rise above evil forces and make a way out of no way, in order to save their communities and their families. Just as faith brought slaves a new level of reality that allowed them to experience freedom while in bondage, faith can also help to inspire black women to live a life of resistance and redemption in the community, to struggle for survival, and to achieve a positive quality of life.

In the nontheistic traditions, faith is not placed in a personally defined ultimate being and therefore transcends gender hierarchy, with equally transformative potential for women and men. In nature religions, animism, and polytheism, faith is diffused throughout many things, beings, and spaces, again with a greater opportunity for women to transcend the struggle with gender inequities to attain faith.

See Also

CHRISTIANITY; CHRISTIANITY: FEMINIST CHRISTOLOGY; CREED; DEITY; HERESY; ISLAM; JUDAISM; THEOLOGIES: FEMINIST; WOMANIST THEOLOGY

References and Further Reading

Fowler, James W. 1981. *Stages of faith: The psychology of human development and the quest for meaning.* San Francisco: Harpe.

Gottlieb, Lynn. 1995. *She who dwells within: A feminist vision of renewed Judaism.* San Francisco: Harper.

Harrison, Beverly W., and Carter Heyward. 1990. Pain and pleasure: Avoiding the confusion of Christian tradition in feminist theory. In Joanne Carlson and Carole R. Brown, eds., *Patriarchy and abuse: A feminist critique*. New York: Pilgrim.

Wadud, Amina. 1999. *Qur'an and woman: Rereading the sacred text from a woman's perspective*. New York: Oxford University Press.

Williams, Delores S. 1993. *Sisters in the wilderness: The challenge of womanist God-talk*. New York: Orbis.

Amina Wadud

FAMILY: Households and Women's Roles

See HOUSEHOLDS AND FAMILIES: OVERVIEW.

FAMILY INCOME

See FAMILY WAGE.

FAMILY LAW

Because family law primarily regulates the daily lives of women, it has traditionally been seen as deeply intertwined with the moral fabric of the community, and therefore has been cordoned off from the rest of the legal system and protected from the moderating influence of uniformity. In this way, it is often argued, patriarchal systems of government replicate and reinforce an ideology of "separate spheres" that is the fulcrum of the patriarchal family.

Unlike commercial law systems, family law systems are various and individualistic. Family law has had a greater effect on the lives of most women than all other areas of law combined. Yet, "family law" is not a body of law or a single field so much as it is an amalgamation of various laws—criminal law, contract law, tort law, constitutional law, property law, and more—that converge to affect the family.

Narrowly conceived, *family law* refers to the legal requirements of marriage (or formation of a marriage) and divorce (or dissolution of a marriage), and the legal rules governing custody and support of children born within or outside marriage. These are the primary issues with which a private domestic relations law practice is concerned. But a broader concept of family law encompasses much more—the law of public benefits, the implications of marital status for tax law, laws and policies relating to adoption, inheritance law, employment law, law regarding child abuse and neglect, the recognition of intrafamily torts, and reproductive rights, among other areas.

Because describing family law systems around the world and evaluating their impact on women is a huge task, the treatment here will be organized into eight themes: (1) patriarchy and the roots of family law, (2) the internationalization of family law, (3) defining family, (4) marriage, (5) divorce, (6) children's rights, (7) intrafamily torts, (8) domestic violence.

The trend in the 1990s for family law systems worldwide was away from supporting the patriarchal model of the family in which the husband gains power and control in exchange for supporting his wife and children, and toward an egalitarian model based on marriage as a partnership. However, the transformation to gender parity remains incomplete everywhere. Radical departures from the trend exist in some Muslim countries and in the Islamic diaspora in the West, but these are not the only contexts in which family law does not serve women as well as it could. A backlash against women and a generally conservative political climate hamper progress in the West, and—as was stated at the UN Convention for Women's Rights in 1995 in Beijing—"There is no country on this Earth in which women have the same opportunities as men."

The role of law in the social construction of women and their role in the family has been well documented (Olsen, 1983). Although the West is now a place of greater opportunity for women, some scholars have noted that it was the transportation of European laws (English, French, and Dutch) to Africa and south Asia during European colonialism that completed the hegemony of a particular brand of patriarchy.

Stumbling blocks to true gender equality within the family take many forms, including economic and social. Moreover, the power of laws to structure choice has been amply documented with numerous variations in what the legal scholar Christine Littleton has called the "difference dilemma." Legal activists have not been able to construct a paradigm which takes into account the biological fact that women can bear children and men cannot and which will result in fair treatment of both genders. Because of this, formal equity against a backdrop of economic and social inequity results in disparity and in pressure on women to choose traditional roles.

Patriarchy and the Roots of Family Law

According to the noted English historian Leonard Stone, the classic patriarchal family had its apex between the 1400s and 1600s in England and has since been steadily declining in influence. To most feminist scholars the death of patriarchy has been greatly exaggerated. They argue that even a cursory examination of the role the law has played worldwide in constructing family norms demonstrates this point (Olsen, 1983). Patriarchy is an efficient way to accumulate and transmit wealth, and its presence as a building block of early society has been reinforced by biblical teachings and other literature of major world religions. Patriarchal themes run through less populous religions as well. Confucianism, for example—the building block of Korean and Chinese family law—places the father (or grandfather) at the center.

The dedication to the patriarchal family of English common law has had a tremendous impact not only in the United States but throughout the world. The imperial period caused expansion in all areas, including law, and even in postcolonial times many former colonies had a dual system of law, or a system that was essentially English law transplanted to a warm place. In English law, marriage was less a romantic arrangement than a union designed to promote the concentration of wealth and the efficient transmission of such wealth. In many contexts, such as India, Pakistan, and their diasporas, this is still seen as the primary function of marriage.

Marriage, although an elite institution, was explicitly a union in which the husband provided economic security and control, and the wife provided sex and child rearing. In common law, principles of coverture applied, and married women were essentially chattels of their husbands, had no separate legal status, and could not own property. An unmarried woman could own property, but it was more likely that she was cared for by her father or brother at the level of genteel poverty (if she was lucky) than that she was a property owner in her own right. Principles of primogeniture excluded females and all but firstborn sons from inheritance and was one of the few parts of common law in England not adopted by the United States, perhaps because of some second sons' flights to the New World.

The Married Women's Property Acts abolished coverture in the late nineteenth and the early twentieth century on both sides of the Atlantic. However, the "separate spheres" ideology, which served as a justification for women's exclusion from many professions, remained in place well into the twentieth century and still can be seen in vestigial form. Patriarchal families were by definition propertied; this placed them firmly within a tiny elite who could afford to use family law. Before the rise of the middle class few people had recourse to the law to legitimate their unions or orchestrate inheritances. The broadening of access to wealth and the legal systems available to perpetuate wealth have forced changes in family law systems worldwide.

For example, the merger of customary and civil law systems into a single constitutional democratic system in South Africa is an important point of progress for women the world over, since the former structure had kept apartheid in place. The South African constitution includes specific guarantees to women and other vulnerable groups. Black women in particular have benefited from the new constitutional regime, gaining greater access to justice. Under the dual system which still exists in most other countries in Africa, women's enforceable rights in customary-law marriages are few. Customary law, a form of law derived from a combination of tribal law and colonial views of natives, is notoriously disadvantageous to women (Obiora, 1993).

The South African legal reform, therefore, stands in stark contrast to, for instance, neighboring Zimbabwe, which retains a dual system, to the detriment of women, particularly black women. Fareda Banda, a scholar of Zimbabwean family law, describes the situation of many Zimbabwean women who, because their families have received bridewealth, or *lobolo*, from the husband, feel honor-bound to stay with abusive and adulterous husbands (1994). Marriage in customary law rather than civil law limits women's access to justice and their right to appeal for state intervention. Under the new South African constitutional system, bridewealth is treated as only a ritual, not as something affecting women's constitutional rights.

The Internationalization of Family Law

As noted earlier, family law has traditionally been viewed as closely entwined with the moral fiber of a society; therefore, it has been slow to feel the effect of globalization. The history of family law as a localized debate has had a largely negative impact on the protection of women in the family. In the United States, for instance, "family law exception" to diversity jurisdiction excludes litigants from federal court who, but for the disfavored subject matter of their cases, would have a right to a federal forum.

In the 1990s, numerous international and multilateral treaties that either directly or tangentially affect family matters have been drafted, discussed globally, and placed on the human rights agenda. Some, such as those drafted at the International Convention of Human Rights, have been signed by many countries. Others, as reported by the United Nations International Conference on Women in Beijing in 1995, are aspirational in nature and reflect gloomy reports on the position of women worldwide.

The mere existence of treaties addressing family law is an indicator of progress. The treaty from the International Convention of Human Rights was recently incorporated into the domestic law of Great Britain. It contains two provisions bearing directly on family law—Article 8, "the right to respect for a person's private and family life, his home and correspondence"; and Article 12, "the right to marry and found a family"—and separate provisions bearing on the rights of women and the rights of children, which some commentators believe clash.

Unfortunately some of the rights stated by the Convention are more illusory than real. For example, many Islamic countries, which have laws explicitly disadvantaging women, are not signatories, are not bound by the International Court of Justice in matters of incompatibility, or have reserved their signatures on the offending articles. Additionally, the International Court of Justice interprets provisions when possible so as not to conflict with a country's domestic law.

Of more practical impact is the Hague Treaty on Civil Child Abduction (echoing the U.S. Uniform Law on Parental Kidnapping), under whose provisions children who have been carried to a country not their own will be returned to their parents. Feminist scholars have noted its use (and abuse) by estranged spouses to control one another in legal battles over their children. In particular there are numerous examples of fathers using the treaty to control the actions of their children's mother.

Defining Family

The question of what constitutes a family is often debated in legal and social discourse worldwide. While the proclamation of the death of the patriarchal family, as noted above, may be premature, it is certainly true that the self-contained nuclear family has long been more misconception than reality (Clark, 1998). The law struggles to include the reality of family life in a world that is both increasingly pluralistic and globally interdependent.

Families include large numbers of single-parent households (most commonly headed by females) formed by both choice and accident. Divorced parents often arrange joint custody, equalizing the duties and importance of the roles "mother" and "father." Blended families combine children from past marriages upon remarriage. Many away from the formalities of marriage and opt for cohabitation either for life or in a serially monogamous form. Adoption (including controversial transracial and transnational adoption) is an option for singles, older people, and gay people. Reproductive technologies such as surrogacy, in vitro fertilization, and artificial insemination blur the boundaries of biology. In the United States the Family Medical Leave Act allows time off (unpaid) to care for newborns and also aging parents. The African-American family has often valued extended kinship networks that involve grandparents, relatives, and friends in the care of children. In some U.S. states, grandparents' visitation rights have been honored over the objection of parents.

Marriage

Formal marriage has only relatively recently been democratized; it was once a ritual reserved chiefly for the propertied classes. It was, and is, the most efficient way to build wealth and determine which children should inherit that wealth. Today, marriage and child rearing have been recognized in the United States as a fundamental constitutional right, and internationally as a human right. Although divorce has become easier for both men and women, its prevalence reinforces the primacy of marriage by granting the freedom to marry again. Courts are liberal in acknowledging foreign marriages, and in the United States the legal status of marriage, particularly marriage with children, brings with it numerous benefits withheld from domestic partners and single people.

At the same time, the trend worldwide is away from state-imposed requirements for marriage. Minimum eligibility requirements often consist solely of an age requirement—age sixteen is common in western countries. Western countries prohibit polygamy, and applicants must prove that they are not already married. Although some countries impose more bureaucracy than others—for example, France requires its citizens to marry in both a civil and a religious ceremony—by and large the societal preference for marriage translates into legal rules that promote it.

Controversy exists over the state's role in restricting eligibility for marriage to heterosexual men and women. Great Britain defines marriage as "a voluntary union between a man and a women," and states its purpose as "procreating." This latter justification, however, is often dropped from the formula. For this and other reasons, gay activists argue persuasively that since heterosexuals who do not plan to have children or already have children may still marry and be accorded the benefits due that status, the law is discriminatory and exclusive.

The issue of gay marriage is on the agenda in a number of countries, states, and cities, whereas it would have been unheard of in the 1970s and 1980s. Although gay marriage has yet to be tested in court, many commentators believe that the South African constitution's explicit protection against discrimination on the basis of sexual orientation guarantees the legality of gay marriage there. Several European countries—Denmark, Norway, Sweden, Finland, Iceland, Greenland, and Finland—allow for the registration of homosexual domestic partnerships. The registration confers marriage-like benefits that are explicitly different from heterosexual marriage benefits. A number of U.S. states and municipalities allow the same thing; however, legislation in Hawaii and Alaska explicitly bans such partnerships and is currently the target of constitutional challenges.

Ironically, gays and lesbians may gain the right to marry at a time when the legal benefits of marriage (as opposed to monetary benefits) have eroded to the point where the viability of the institution is being questioned. For example, in the late 1990s in Great Britain, the House of Commons was reviewing a proposal to extend legal economic rights to mistresses. The value of marriage is questionable if "second" women are awarded the same security as married wives.

Divorce

In the 1960s and 1970s, a "divorce revolution" changed the nature of the legal and social landscape with respect to dissolution of marriage. The dismantling of state-constructed barriers to divorce began when the United States, followed closely by Great Britain, adopted a "clean-break" policy which spread to Europe and the rest of the world. Even Ireland, a predominantly Catholic country, bowed to the reality that many of its married citizens had lived apart for years (Glendon, 1989).

In the United States and increasingly in Great Britain, unbridled capitalism and the dismantling of the welfare state have meant that women often must choose between poverty and stigma as a single mother, or marrying and staying married for economic reasons. This choice is particularly real for middle-class and upper-middle-class white women whose economic well-being often plunges after divorce.

Additionally, there is a fundamentalist religious backlash against women's autonomy. In the United States, "family values" campaigns have resulted in more proposals for legislation replicating the "covenant marriages," available in Louisiana. Such marriages, which are voluntary, require a higher level of commitment than more traditional modern marriage or that which the state requires.

The no-fault divorce policy, with its preference for a one-time division of marital property over alimony or support, has been criticized. Lenore Weitzman, who pioneered the equitable-distribution model adopted by most U.S. states, and by Great Britain under the credo "a clean break," argues that the model presupposes that women and men are on an equal economic playing field outside of the marriage. The result has been that many women face a greatly reduced standard of living after divorce, whereas men's standard of living increases (Weitzman, 1985). A follow-up study analyzing the international experience of divorced men and women came to the same conclusions (Weitzman and Maclean, 1992).

The dismantling of the welfare state, particularly in the United States, which has a "welfare-to-work" policy, forces poor single mothers (a group that is disproportionately though not mostly black) to leave their children in order to take minimum-wage jobs. Even for educated women from affluent backgrounds a divorced woman with children faces economic hardship. Most western countries, however, continue to move toward policies encourage a clean break at divorce. Moreover, alimony awards can be expected to continue to fall, regardless of the economic impact on women in general. On the other hand, development of laws requiring fathers to take greater economic and physical responsibility for their children may alleviate women's burden of child care.

Gender-neutral divorce statues are problematic, but the asymmetry that still exists between the genders in Muslim countries is worse. In Islamic fundamentalist regimes (and in the communities that exist in the West under their auspices), family law is governed by the "Shari'a," which purportedly derives its principles from the Qu'ran. The Qu'ran, as interpreted by those regimes, allows men (but not women) to engage in polygamy. Therefore, polygamy is not grounds for divorce initiated by the wife. Adultery on the part of women is, however, punishable by death, usually in the form of an honor killing by the women's husband or family. Men are responsible for supporting children born either in or out of wedlock, but they also exercise total legal control. For a man, divorce is an easy process; he unilaterally pronounces *talaq* ("I divorce you"), and he is free. For women, divorce is available only in cases of extreme cruelty. At divorce, the husband typically exercises all rights to custody. Usually the mother continues physical care of children under age 3, but legal control remains in the hands of the father. Concerns about child custody and the prospect of penury operate to keep many women in marriages they might otherwise want to end. Islamic feminists have been prolific and powerful in their critique of the authenticity of Islamic law systems that draw authority from the Qu'ran and in challenging the accuracy of lawmakers' conception of the Qu'ran as requiring female subordination (Yamani, 1996).

In African countries that still have a dual system of law, customary and tribal law govern the lives of women and children, whereas civil law, to the extent that it is a feasible recourse for most citizens, is merely a gender-biased replication of the concept of tribal law that colonialists and male tribal leaders had at the time of colonization (Obiora, 1997).

Children's Rights

In the 1990s, the children's rights movement became a force shaping family law reforms, sometimes in conflict with what feminists would recommend. A concern for the best interests of children was a hallmark of the twentieth century, in marked contrast to the nineteenth century and earlier, when children's suffering was viewed rather pragmatically. The modern children's rights movement has a different focus, however.

The lodestar of the children's rights movement is a belief that children are autonomous agents who must have a role in determining the terms of their upbringing. Analogies are made to the feminist movement, which deconstructed the ways in which women were categorized with criminals and the feebleminded as incapable of making decisions about themselves. The children's rights movement advocates the autonomy of children, and constructs them as free agents capable of making important decisions regarding their own lives. This autonomy is maintained even when it goes against what adults might view as a child's best interests.

Although the children's rights movement gained political recognition only in the 1990s, the theory behind it was developed much earlier (Rodham, 1979). In 1993, the Hague International Convention on the Rights of the Child served to raise awareness of children's issues worldwide. The recognition that children are separate individuals with hopes, dreams, and rights of their own underlay much of the rhetoric of the antiabortion movement in the 1960s and 1970s. In its current, more explicit conception, it recognizes both that the family can be a site of oppression and that the human rights movement, which guarantees minimum levels of dignity for all persons, can usefully be applied to prevent such oppression.

In most states in the United States, and in Great Britain, the legal category of legitimacy is now abandoned and children born in and out of wedlock have equal rights to inheritance, the father's name and so on. The question whether children have a right to be with their siblings when placed in foster care is now being litigated in the United States.

Intrafamily Torts

A bar against lawsuits for civil wrongs between spouses and between parents and their minor children was first fashioned by a court in Tennessee in 1861. As most other U.S. states fashioned similar doctrines over the years, the justi-

fications were various but all signified what many observers considered a troubling failure to distinguish between individuals within the family unit. In the 1990s, a strong trend began in the United States to abolish that peculiarly U.S. creation: intrafamily tort immunities.

Interspousal immunity, on which parent-child immunity is modeled, was initially justified on the basis of the legal unity of marriage. When the fiction of legal unity was abolished by the Married Women's Property Acts, the court's primary justifications became the "protection of family harmony and resources" and—with respect to the parent-child doctrine specifically—the need of parents to be able to discipline and control their children. Interestingly, when the Florida legislature examined a bill aimed at abolishing the parent-child immunity, it passed only with the addition of language allowing parents the right to "reasonable" corporal punishment of children (Johnson, 1993).

One criticism of abrogating the doctrine completely was that to allow minor children to sue parents is a significant step toward allowing children to sue for breaches in prenatal care. Another potential abuse of tort law is to punish marginal women, especially women of color, in the same way the criminal law has been used to punish principally women of color through "drug delivery" statues (Roberts, 1998).

Domestic Violence

The term *domestic violence* is now well known and a testament to an education and consciousness-raising campaign for what was once a hidden subject, which took place in the last two decades of the twentieth century. The fact that violence against women is often perpetrated within the family home has now been recognized and the idea of the family as a haven for women has been discredited. Restrictions on divorce and economic disparity between partners are two indicators of the likelihood of domestic violence. Therefore, the problem may be worse in Islamic countries which have failed to eradicate explicitly patriarchal laws. And yet it is likely to be a silent problem.

The fiction of marital unity has been read in Ango-American law as consisting of a blanket consent to sexual intercourse by wife to husband. Although the unities were abolished by the Married Women's Property Act, the so-called marital exception to rape law still exists in the majority of U.S. states. The exception to rape law was judicially abolished in the United Kingdom in 1991, when the House of Lords announced that the exception could no longer be said to be a part of the law of England and Wales.

Countries that still view women as family property allow honor killings of women who have been adulterous, have engaged in premarital intercourse, or have been raped. The Brazilian government, for example, did not abolish state sanctioning of honor killings until the 1990s, and the problem remains large throughout the Middle East and South America. Debate on the issue is troublesome, owing to the difficulty of most cross-cultural conversations on sensitive subjects. The level of awareness of domestic violence, to a great extent because of Lenore Walker's work in the United States on battered women's syndrome, has risen steeply, and legal reforms have taken this into account. Most U.S. states have passed legislation allowing evidence of battered women's syndrome to be adduced us homicide cases. In 1994 the U.S. federal government passed the Violence Against Women Act, recognizing the seriousness of gender-motivated crimes and the reality that much violence takes place in the private sphere. In Great Britain, the law of provocation is being rethought and slowly adopted judicially. Similarly, the law commissions of England, Wales, and Scotland have sponsored educational media campaigns on domestic violence.

The role of the law in the eradication of violence against women is still uncertain. For example, the practice of female circumcision or female genital mutilation has long been considered an important rite of passage of female adolescence in many African and Muslim countries. Because it is deeply tied to culture and is replicated from generation to generation not by law, or directly by male involvement, but as a custom encouraged by women, it has been extremely difficult to eradicate. The practice persists in spite of its condemnation by a coalition of African-American and indigenous feminist activists (Lewis, 1995; Obiora, 1997). And with our increasingly globalized and diasporic society, the practice exists as well in western countries with large minority populations. The United States has officially criminalized the practice, but Great Britain is still caught in the dilemma—often framed as a choice between a commitment to multiculturalism and respect for family autonomy and the preservation of women's future.

Scholarly attention to the field of family law should remain intense in quality and quantity well into the future. Coming after a prolonged period of marginalization within the legal academia, new material on family law is welcomed. Articles employing feminist and critical race methodology have greatly expanded our knowledge of how law operates to construct our family systems and define gender roles.

See Also

ABORTION; ADULTERY; DIVORCE; DOMESTIC VIOLENCE; FAMILY: POWER RELATIONS AND POWER STRUCTURES; FAMILY: PROPERTY RELATIONS; HOUSEHOLDS AND FAMILIES: OVERVIEW; MARRIAGE: OVERVIEW; MOTHERHOOD; PATRIARCHY: DEVELOPMENT

References and Further Reading

Bainhams, Andrew, Shelly Day Selster, and Martin Richards, eds. 1999. *What is a parent? A sociological analysis.* Oxford: Hart.

Banda, Fareda. 1994. Maintenance and support in Zimbabwe. *Cardozo Women's Law Journal* 2: 7.

Clark, Jr., Homer H. 1998. *The law of domestic relations in the United States.* St. Paul, Minn.: West.

Glendon, Mary Ann. 1989. The transformation of family law. Chicago: University of Chicago Press.

Johnson, Caroline. 1993. A cry for help: An argument for the abrogation of the parent-child doctrine in child abuse and incest. *Florida University Law Review* 21: 617.

Levit, Nancy. 1995. International family law annotated bibliography. *Journal of American Matrimonial Law* 13: 313.

Lewis, Hope. 1995. Between IRA and "female genital mutilation": Feminist human rights discourse and the cultural divide. *Human Rights Journal* 8: 1.

Minow, Martha, ed. 1993. Family matters: Readings on family lives and the law. New York: New Press.

Obiora, L. Amede. 1997. New skin, old wine: (E)ngaging nationalism, traditionalism, and gender relations. *Indiana Law Review* 28.

Olsen, Francis. 1983. The family and the market: A study of ideology and legal reform. *Harvard Law Review* 96: 1497.

Roberts, Dorothy. 1998. *Killing the black body: Race, reproduction and the meaning of liberty.* New York: Pantheon.

Rodham, Hillary. 1979. Children's rights: A legal perspective. In Patricia A. Verdin and Ilene N. Brody, eds., *Children's rights: Contemporary perspectives.* New York: Teachers College Press.

Weitzman, Lenore. 1985. *The divorce revolution: The unintended consequences of divorce for women and children.* New York: Free Press.

Weitzman, Lenore, and Mavis Maclean. 1992. *The economic consequences of divorce for women: The international perspective.* New York: Free Press.

Yamani, Mai, and Andrew Allen, eds. 1996. *Feminism and Islam: Legal and literary perspectives.* New York: New York University Press.

Mairi Morrison

FAMILY LAW: Case Study—India

Family law in south Asia is a composite area where gender discrimination and women's rights can be usefully studied. The family is integral to the fabric of Asian society, yet its boundaries and jurisdiction are said to eclipse women's individual identity. Family law has in turn institutionalized and endorsed these boundaries, and jurisdictions and been a central ground of debate for feminists in search of laws that will be just with respect to gender.

Regionally, cultural diversity and religious traditions have been preserved through complex personal laws that govern issues of marriage, inheritance, divorce, and custody. Secular laws also exist that try to homogenize rights on the basis of citizens rather than religion or community. This legal pluralism complicates the issue of women's rights, as both secular and personal laws have compromised gender equality for the sake of community and family. Feminists' attempts at legal reform have met with little success. This article surveys family laws and attempts at reform with particular reference to India.

Overview

In India, family relations are largely governed by personal laws based on religious and cultural practices even as the state has tried to establish secular laws to homogenize the rights of people according to citizenship rather than religion or community. The genesis of this political commitment to secular laws rests in the Indian Constitution: Article 44 provides that the state shall endeavor to secure for its citizens a uniform civil code (UCC). But cultural plurality was also of political concern in 1947, the date of India's independence, and the constitution underlined the right to freedom of conscience and religion as well. Hence, the state had to balance rights under personal law against the need to grant equality to all Indians. Another conceptual flaw in the original premise of the UCC was that civil laws were compartmentalized into public and private. Public law dealt with business, contracts, and property while private law was restricted to family and domestic matters. That division placed women largely in the domestic sphere, but the private sphere occasionally overlapped with civil laws such as inheritance. Even though Articles 14 and 15 of the Indian constitution granted women equality and freedom from discrimination on the basis of gender, this was compromised as a result of contradictory rights provided under the constitution itself.

Against this background of a complex legal plurality are the main religious communities—Hindu, Muslim, Christ-ian, and Parsi. Personal laws are applicable to all members of a community by virtue of birth and do not allow choice to dissenters and nonbelievers. All personal laws discriminate against women where religious tenets rather than democratic principles govern interpersonal relations and the right to autonomy and access to resources. A composite discussion of personal laws is not possible here because most personal laws are not codified and cover a vast cross-section of rights. Instead, instances of specific personal and secular laws are given.

Legal Age of Marriage and Consent

An important part of women's decision-making in marriage is governed by the legal age of marriage. In India, the Child Marriage Restraint Act, 1929 (amended 1979), increased the age of marriage to 18 for girls and to 21 for boys. The impact has been marginal, given that child marriage is largely a cultural and rural phenomenon and families marry young children off in order to save money. Personal laws like the Muslim personal law, allow the marriage of minors to be contracted by guardians; thus secular law has little impact. The Christian Marriage Act permits the marriage of a minor provided a guardian has consented to it.

While no age limit for marriage exists in Sri Lanka, the Muslim Marriage and Divorce Act requires the marriage of a girl below 12 years to be registered by a quazi (Muslim judge). Failure to do so is a punishable offense (Women's World, 1989). This provision contradicts the penal code of Sri Lanka whereby a man is said to commit rape if he has sexual intercourse with a girl below 12 years of age, even if she is his wife and he has her consent (Women's World, 1989). This contradiction is also evident in Indian rape law: if a man's wife brings a charge of rape and she is older than 12, he is not criminally liable. Child marriage across all contexts in this region reflects certain values and assumptions about women: women should defer decisions and control of their lives to male guardians, and women are transferred from owner to owner—that is, father to husband to son—like property; women's primary role is to marry and bear children; girls are an economic burden for parents.

Dowry

Dowry is primarily the commodification of females in a society that sees them as a financial burden. In India, it is the most controversial form of exploitation and violence against women. Yet the law and legal language reflect the confused stand of the state.

In 1961, the Prohibition of Dowry Act was passed in India, outlawing the practice of giving and taking dowry. The intent of this legal prohibition was to eliminate the practice of dowry, but it still upheld related behavior, that is, allowing gifts used to circumvent the law. A second change in the law (1983) criminalized cruelty toward a woman by her husband or his relatives—the first time the law acknowledged wife assault and other domestic cruelty as a criminal offense. Still, not every harassment or every type of cruelty was punishable. Further, "streedhan" (a woman's property) strictly denoted that specific property of the woman over which she possessed absolute power of disposal, which included her right to jewelry given to her in marriage. The usage of this term became focused on the jewelry and goods linked to the wedding. That approach somehow made a women's wealth peculiar and became a means of denying her any normal rights of inheritance. In Sri Lanka, for instance, the Teswalamai Code (1980) claims that dowry is a "means by which most of the girls obtain husbands, as it is not for the girls but for the property that most men marry" (Tesawalamai, Part I. s.5).

In India, despite the law, harassment and deaths related to dowry are increasing. According to the National Crime Records Bureau in 1991, one "dowry death" occurred every 1 hour and 42 minutes. In 1987, 1,912 cases of dowry murders took place compared with 5,157 cases in 1991.

The judicial process has never been able to intervene in the actual negotiating or philosophy of dowry because of a missing gender perspective—a point clearly illustrated in a judgment made in 1984:

> It is no doubt true that the girl and her family members contribute towards her oppression. Firstly the parents pay dowry to get their daughters married and each time she returns to her parents, she is sent back with a hope of reconciliation. The parents and the girl are reluctant to register cases because there is an attempt to patch up the marriage. The girl also clings to the marriage at all costs. And in the final analysis, all this goes against her making a conviction difficult in the absence of any complaint about harassment.

Hence, if a woman returned to her husband or in the absence of any complaint of harassment, there is no murder. The Indian woman is brought up to believe that to die in her husband's home is preferable to returning to her parents' home. This is her social reality and the background against which she has to take legal action against her husband and in-laws (All India Reports, 1984).

Inheritance Laws

As with other laws relating to the family, inheritance laws are also governed by the personal laws of the community. In India before the Hindu Succession Act, 1956, a daughter could not inherit the property of her father if the father was survived by a son. Similarly, in the Hindu law known as the Mitakshara, a widow could not succeed to the separate property of her husband so long as a son, his son's son, or his grandson were alive. They all had prior rights. Another means of ensuring that property stayed with the male side of the family was law or custom relating to remarriage that effectively denied widows the right to property and access to land. Widows who did remarry would forfeit their rights in the former husband's property. A customary law in Punjab still requires the widow of a deceased brother to marry one of the brothers to ensure that the property is retained within the family.

In the early 1950s there were attempts at legal reform, but conservative and reactionary forces saw to it that the changes in Hindu law resulted in separate enactments rather than a codified Hindu law. This allowed states to retain devolution of tenancy rights as well as coparcenary rights, joint heirship, in favor of males entitling a son to a share in ancestral properties equal to that of the father (Hindu Succession Act, 1956). In addition, the father's interest would pass equally to the son and daughters. Daughters would therefore receive only one-fourth of a father's share of property while a son would get three-fourths.

Indian Christians are governed by the Indian Succession Act, 1925, but many choose to follow personal laws that exclude daughters from inheriting property. Under Muslim law, a widow is entitled to one-third of the estate if the son of a descendant survives; otherwise she is entitled to one-fourth. If a man leaves behind more than one widow, they jointly take the share. Under the Hanafi law that governs most Muslims in the subcontinent, if a husband leaves behind a widow or widows and three brothers, the widows will be entitled to one-fourth share while the three brothers will inherit the balance, three-fourths.

Land reforms in these agrarian cultures have also contributed to the denial of women's access to land. Under land-ceiling legislation that attempted a fair redistribution of land, one unit of ceiling was given to a family (husband, wife, and three minor children). A son, but not a daughter, was subsequently entitled to an additional unit.

Divorce and Maintenance Rights

While law reform with respect to Hindu women has appeared more progressive than reforms of other religious personal law, such reforms have never sought to grant complete legal equality to women. For instance, the actual basis for the right to divorce was as follows: "By introducing the facility for divorce, an extraordinary remedy was being provided for the long suffering Hindu women. However it was nowhere emphasized that in view of the monogamy provision, the right to be able to ask for divorce in certain circumstances would be equally relevant for men. For instance, it was readily accepted that if a wife becomes a concubine of another man the husband should have a right to divorce. There was, however some dispute whether the wife should have a right to divorce if the husband takes a concubine. The Committee reassured men that even though it was recommending similar rights for wives, 'we are satisfied that very few Hindu wives will seek divorce where there is nothing else against the husband except that he keeps a concubine'; In the same way, the dissolution of sacramental marriages was specifically justified with the observation that there was nothing in the code to suggest that immediately after its enactment there would be a spate of divorce, especially since Hindu women were very conservative by temperament and therefore unlikely to resort to divorce except for the strongest of reasons" (Parashar, 1992: 16).

In the 1990s, statistics revealed that in Delhi courts alone, divorce had increased markedly each year—in 1990, 1,545 divorce cases were filed; in 1991, 2,153 cases; in 1992, 5,397 cases. Most of these divorces were being sought by men.

Similarly, the right to restitution of conjugal rights illustrates attitudes and perceptions that compound women's inequality under Hindu laws. When one party in the marriage has withdrawn from the other without reasonable excuse, the aggrieved party may seek a decree for restitution of conjugal rights (Hindu Marriage Act, 1956). The decree can be enforced by the attachment of property, and if the party complained against still does not comply, the Court may also punish him or her for contempt of court.

In 1984 the controversy over this provision came before the apex court (All India Reports, 1984). The supreme court held that section 9 did not violate article 14 (discrimination on the basis of sex) or article 21 (right to personal liberty) of the constitution if the purpose of the decree for restitution of conjugal rights in the act "is understood in its proper perspective and if the method of its execution in cases of disobedience is kept in view." That view was based on the following premises: (1) the conjugal right is an inherent right of the institution of marriage; (2) sufficient safeguards exist within the section to prevent exploitation; (3) the decree is enforced by attachment of property that is only a financial sanction. It serves to aid prevention of the breakup of marriage. In fact, when a court orders restitution of conjugal rights, it orders one spouse to submit to "normal" marital

life, which includes sexual intercourse. And though a court cannot enforce sexual intercourse, it is empowered to compel an unwilling spouse to provide conjugal society to her husband—a clear denial of her personal liberty.

The Politics of Legal Reform

In 1985 the well-publicized case of *Moh Ahmed Khan* v. *Shah Bano Begun* raised questions about the rights of minority women and of the way personal laws can be used to discriminate against them (All India Reports, 1985).

In 1975, Shah Bano's husband threw her out of the house with RS.200 (U.S. $5) maintenance per month, which subsequently ceased. Shah Bano applied for maintenance under the secular code that provides for up to RS.500 (U.S. $12.50) maintenance per month. While her application was pending, Bano's husband divorced her, paying her RS.3000 ($75) *mehr* (a prenuptial contract in Muslim law). The high court granted her RS.179.20 (U.S. $4.48) per month and the husband appealed to the supreme court, stating that Muslim personal law did not oblige him to maintain his wife. The Supreme Court ruled that the RS.500 provision should apply to a Muslim woman irrespective of her divorce settlement.

The decision caused a political furor as fundamentalist forces began to object to interference in their personal law. Fearful of losing the Muslim vote, the government overruled the supreme court with specific legislation that denied Muslim women the right to maintenance under secular law—a clear statement that the debate between secular and personal laws would, either way, go against women's rights. In contrast, the Hindu law has been projected as progressive because reforming minority community laws is politically inconvenient.

Spousal Violence

Violence within the family is the most controversial area of debate. Battery and harassment have only just been addressed, while rape within marriage and child sexual abuse are not acknowledged by Indian law. Legal reform extended the definition of cruelty to include physical and mental abuse. It also touched upon women's inequality by presuming that women who are beaten should be believed, yet law reform has never tallied with the asymmetry of marital relations in India. A woman's vulnerability in marriage is due to basic inequalities. Largely poor, financially dependent, and caught in the moral and religious pressures of "women's roles," women often find that violence is a way of life in marriage. In addition, a legal split, such as divorce, which is a possible outcome of a violent marriage, reveals the complete split in the lives men and women lead in a tradition-bound society. She emerges from a completely privatized existence where family determines the nature of her existence, marriage, behavior, expectations, and limitations—all of which work toward minimum development as an individual. She will forever have to justify her behavior, whether to parents, children, friends, relations, the police, or the law. On the other hand, more comforting dynamics continue to operate for the abusive husband. He will continue to enjoy the social and economic support of parents and family, work, and financial status.

That distinction has no place in the basic premise that governs the forty-year-old marriage and divorce laws and a century-old civil code that continues to maintain gender neutrality. The primary emphasis of such laws is reconciliation. When a woman files for divorce on the basis of cruelty, therefore, irrespective of the damage done to her, the fact of her abuse is secondary to preserving the marriage. In 1984, a new family courts act, rather than challenging such presumptions about marriage, reaffirmed them. What might have been a means of mediation and settlement, serving the concerns of women in the area of child custody, property, and maintenance, once again compromised women in favor of reconciliation. In other words, cruelty or harassment for dowry would be perceived as a "quarrel" between two equal partners. At best, a women in such situations would simply be told to go back home. In the Asian context, "gender-just" laws need to be reexamined in family contexts and need to redefine women's identity within the family. Otherwise they remain, at best, cosmetic.

See Also

DOWRY AND BRIDEPRICE; FAMILY LAW; HOUSEHOLDS AND FAMILIES: SOUTH ASIA; PERSONAL AND CUSTOMARY LAWS; POLITICS AND THE STATE: SOUTH ASIA, *I and II*; VIOLENCE: SOUTH ASIA

References and Further Reading

Jesudurai, Padmini. 1991. Women and the law. *Quest for Gender Justice* 37–52.

Kapur, Naina, and Kirti Singh. 1994. Practising feminist law: Some reflections. *Student Advocate* 30–36.

Marriage and divorce. 1993. *Asian and Pacific women's resource and action series: Law,* 61–92. Kuala Lumpur: Asian and Pacific Development Centre.

Narasimhan, Sakuntala. 2000. A married woman's right to live. *Ms* 10(6: Oct.-Nov.): 77–81.

Parashar, Archana. 1992. *Women and family law reform in India.* New Delhi: Sage.

Sahmsuddin, Shams, ed. 1991. Women and family law. *Women, Law, and Social Change* 1–86.

Women living under Muslim laws. 1989. *Women's World* 21–22 (December): 18.

Naina Kapur

FAMILY LIFE CYCLE AND WORK

There is no simple way to address the question of women's work in relation to the family life cycle. As Pratt and Hanson (in Katz and Monk, 1993: 7) observe, narratives on the *family* life cycle conventionally focus on women between 20 and 45—and overemphasize one life path (in which a woman marries and then bears and cares for children) and one period of the life "cycle" (intensive early child care). Such a focus leaves other phases of a woman's life "cycle" relatively unexplored in feminist literature. In particular, the working lives and economic situations of single and older women are relatively underresearched.

The focus on *life cycle* also implies that life experience is linked to relatively inevitable biological stages and ages. Yet "if we recognize that a woman's life expectancy at birth is as low as 32–33 years in Kampuchea, Sierra Leone and Afghanistan but over 78 in France, Japan and Switzerland, we can hardly assume that 'stages' will be closely linked to chronological age or be experienced in universal ways" (Katz and Monk, 1993: 5). Katz's reflections on her own research, at age 27, on Sudanese women, illustrate this point: she comments on how unnerving it was to realize that the women she felt most affinity with—young married women—were mostly 19 or 20, while a woman she regarded as a mother to herself was only 37 years old—the age when Katz herself finally began to feel "grown-up" (1993: 4).

In speaking of work and family life cycle, then, the years between 15 and 64 encompass those in which most women carry their maximum responsibility for productive and reproductive or domestic work. The balance between these two will vary according to a range of factors, among them the years spent in childbearing and the average number of children. The former ranges from 19 years in Kenya to 7 in the United States; the latter varies from fewer than two children in North America and the countries of the European Union to more than six in much of Africa and the Middle East (Seager and Olson, 1997). Younger than 15, and at whatever age each culture regards a woman as elderly, women will

FAMILY PLANNING

be less involved in "productive" labor. Their own care very probably contributes to the labor required of other women, but they may equally reciprocate by relieving their caregivers of a share of domestic work and child care, facilitating those women's involvement in "productive" work. But these two ends of a woman's place in a family life course are not well explored.

Many other factors will also shape the particular working life course of any individual woman: differences in employment structures, access to education, and cultural values concerning domestic work and aging will all have an impact. As Pratt and Hanson point out, we must remember that not only are "lives…lived through; they are also lived in place and through space" (quoted in Katz and Monk, 1993: 30).

See Also

FAMILY STRUCTURES; LIFE CYCLE

References and Further Reading

Katz, Cindi, and Janice Monk, eds. 1993. *Full circles: Geographies of women over the life course.* London: Routledge.

Seager, Joni, and Ann Olson. 1997. *Women in the world: The state of atlas.* Rev. 2nd ed. London: Penguin.

Beverly Thiele

FAMILY PLANNING

Although the term *family planning* is generally understood as being synonymous with birth control or fertility control, this was not always the case. Within the history of the evolution and the current widespread use of this term lies buried a history of the conflicting ideologies and interests that have characterized the issue of women's control over their reproduction.

History of Family Planning

From the time Malthus put forth his theory that promiscuous reproduction by the poor would cause population growth to outstrip food production (1798), two varying groups have been interested in finding the means to control fertility: those concerned with women's rights, who saw birth control as a weapon in the struggle to save women from the bondage of unwanted pregnancies, and as a means to offer them freedom, sexual satisfaction, and joyful motherhood; and those concerned with population growth, whose concern for reproduction of high fertility arose from Malthusian fears. The actions of the two groups have sometimes been similar—they have both fought conservative forces to bring knowledge and the means to control fertility within the reach of women. Their objectives, however, have always been divergent.

Malthusian concerns about rapid population growth among the poor in late eighteenth century soon came to be disregarded as British productive capacities expanded, and demand for cheap labor increased. Although concern with population growth may have abated, controlling fertility became an important concern in England in the later half of the nineteenth century. Upper- and middle-class parents had strong economic motives to limit family size as the cost of education, domestic servants, and other paraphernalia of the gentry became expensive. Diaphragms, sheaths, spermicides, and so on were already available to members of the higher social classes. In 1877, the Malthusian League was formed, with the objective of bringing birth control within the reach of the poorer mothers.

Family Planning in the Twentieth Century

The first and second decades of the twentieth century saw the emergence of the birth control movement in England. It was essentially a protest movement of women, a logical development of the suffragist movement. The term *birth control* itself was coined by the U.S. feminist Margaret Sanger in 1914 to convey to the public the social and personal significance of contraception, together with its liberating possibilities for women. In 1918, the National Union of Women's Suffrage Societies expanded its objectives to include legislative reforms in areas such as divorce and legitimacy, and also pressed for provision of both voluntary and public birth control. In 1921, the first birth control clinic was set up by Mary Stopes, one of the pioneering leaders of the movement. Many women's organizations in England, including women workers' organizations, supported the movement because they were concerned with the high rates of maternal mortality and wanted to free women from the bondage of unwanted pregnancies.

Developments in the United States did not follow the same course, but there were some early protagonists. In 1915, Emma Goldman and Margaret Sanger deliberately defied obscenity laws by distributing information on contraception. In 1916, Margaret Sanger, her sister, and some other women opened a birth control clinic in Brownsville, Brooklyn. This was the beginning of the Birth Control League. In the United States, birth control did not become popular with all classes, because birthrates among Anglo-Saxons had already begun to fall.

The decline in birthrates in England and of the Anglo-Saxon population in the United States in the early twenti-

666

eth century also led to the reemergence of concern that certain sections of the population were overreproducing. This, along with the growing influx of immigrants into the United States, led to the emergence of the eugenics movement, which became very strong after World War I. The other side of this coin was the "depopulation" scare, a fear that the white population would soon be outnumbered by "alien" races.

By the mid-1930s, the term *birth control* became suspect because of the depopulation scare. The euphemistic expression "family planning" emerged in England, placing birth control firmly within the context of family decision making. The focus thus shifted from the woman to the family. Birth control became the method for limiting the number of births—a way of ensuring that healthy children were born and that families were stable and secure—instead of a means of ensuring women's right to control over reproduction.

In the United States, there was a fusion of the eugenicists and the women protagonists of birth control. They had interests in common, and the latter had no strong antiracist tradition on which to base a critique of eugenics. Furthermore, the advocates of birth control received from the eugenicists the support that had been denied them by the socialists. Birth control came to be advocated for the poor and members of the working class.

Margaret Sanger's Birth Control League became the Planned Parenthood Federation, concerned with family planning, in 1942. In another development, there was a clash of interests between the medical profession and eugenicists. The former wanted to retain control over delivery of contraception, whereas the latter wanted it freely available to the poor. This led to the faltering and eventual demise of the clinic movement. Soon, birth control was available to middle-class people in private clinics, while the working classes had no help at all.

The rise of the feminist movement in the 1960s again brought birth control to the forefront. One of the major demands was the right to abortion, as well as ready access to contraception. The movement also fought against medical control over women's reproductive choice, and spearheaded moves to make information readily available, to set up women's clinics, and to help women learn about their bodies, sexuality, and fertility. The development of modern contraceptives greatly facilitated this process.

Family Planning in the Developing World

The scenario in most of the developing world has been entirely different. Historically, the technology of birth control did not lead but followed social demand for it. In developing countries, however, the process has been reversed, and it is concern about rapid growth of population that has brought about the promotion of family planning in the developing countries, sometimes described as the countries of the "south." Neither birth control nor women's emancipation has been the moving force.

Whereas in a small number of developing countries, such as India, state policy to restrict population growth and state-sponsored family planning programs have evolved as a result of the national leadership's concern with these issues, in most other countries these have been the result of initiatives from foundations, aid agencies, and multilateral agencies in developed countries. A pioneering role in this respect has been played by the United States.

In 1965, official endorsement for population assistance by government came in the form of Lyndon B. Johnson's statement on the occasion of the twentieth anniversary of the United Nations:

> Let us all in all our lands—including this land—face forthrightly the multiplying problems of our multiplying population and seek the answers to this most profound challenge to the future of all the world. Let us act on the fact that five dollars invested in population control is worth a hundred dollars invested in economic growth.

By 1966, official programs had been set up in twenty-five countries with USAID funds. It was the United States that persuaded the United Nations to set up a trust fund for population activities, and this fund was established in 1967–1968, with a third of its funds directly from USAID. This fund was later to become the UNFPA.

In the 1960s, developing countries were slow to accept the notion that population growth was a problem. There was a worry that focus on rapid population growth was an attempt to sidetrack important issues of power relations between the developed and the less developed world and inequitable distribution of resources across countries. Critics on the left maintained that it was not that there were too many people for the resources at hand, but that the skewed distribution of resources within and across countries, and the profit-based economic structure in place, could not support the increasing numbers of poor people. They argued that if structural changes were effected to make resource distribution more equitable, then there would no longer be a population problem. Much of this criticism eventually subsided; by the 1990s, fifty-five developing countries accounted for 80 percent of the developing world's population, and 60 percent of the world population had adopted policies to reduce their populations.

667

Even while opposition to state policies for fertility reduction was waning, the 1980s saw the emergence of yet another lobby advocating population control: environmentalists who considered population explosion to be the primary cause of environmental degradation. Concern for the planet's survival is one of the strongest arguments being made in favor for the need to implement policies and programs from the top down for effective curtailmeant of the rapid growth of population in developing countries.

The International Women's Health Movement

Given the history of population policies in developing countries, it is not surprising that they have seldom had women's well-being as their primary concern. Women's movements in developing countries and the International Women's Health Movement, which emerged in the 1970s, have, consequently, been consistent and vocal critics of state-sponsored population control policies.

"No to population control! Women decide!" was the slogan of much of the international women's health movement for the last two decades of the twentieth century. The movement opposed not only the antinatalist policies of governments of most developing countries but also the pronatalist policies of a few countries of both the developing and the developed world, as an infringement of women's reproductive rights.

The position taken by the women's health movement is that although women need contraception and, in fact, would demand that governments make contraceptive as well as abortion services available and accessible to them at affordable costs, no government has the right to dictate to women the number of children they should have or to deny them the right to terminate a pregnancy or prevent a birth. Furthermore, it is the state's responsibility not only to provide contraceptive technologies to women, but to create the enabling social and political conditions that would make it possible for women to access and use contraception.

Women's health advocates have argued that for women—and all poor people—birth control represents a major step forward only when it is combined with campaigns for equality on many fronts, between sexes and between classes and races. It has to become part of a popular cause that has as its basic principle self-determination. Otherwise, birth control is simply yet another tool to control women's lives.

Although this is the movement's broad principle, the rapid introduction during the 1970s and 1980s of population control programs in many developing countries gave rise to numerous issues of immediate concern. The international women's health movement was preoccupied with campaigns against abuses of sterilization and abuses in the conduct of clinical trials, and against the introduction of contraceptive technologies whose safety for developing countries' populations had not been established. In later years, concerns centered on the demographic targets of population policies, an orientation which leads to the introduction of those contraceptive technologies that are most effective in controlling fertility, despite a poor health service infrastructure that renders these technologies potentially hazardous. The scant attention to quality of care and contraceptive choice and the role of incentives and disincentives in manipulating women's acceptance of contraception have been other issues of contention.

Some of the most serious issues relate to the tendency of state-sponsored family planning programs to focus on limiting a woman's fertility to the exclusion of her other health problems, and the near total absence of attention to male participation in contraception. These concerns prompted women's health advocates to develop a reproductive health agenda as a comprehensive and holistic approach to women's need for control over reproduction, consistent with respect for women's reproductive rights. The reproductive health approach advocates that contraceptive services should form part of a much wider package of essential reproductive health services to women, including abortion services; prevention and control of reproductive tract infections and of HIV/AIDS; prevention, screening for, and control of women's cancers; pregnancy, delivery, and postnatal care; sex education; and sexual health care.

The reproductive health care approach calls for a radical reorientation of existing population policies and programs, with an emphasis on high-quality services, and for dispensing with the system of demographic targets with its incentives and disincentives. Women's health advocates' organization of a forceful lobby for reproductive health care at the International Conference on Population and Development, held in Cairo in 1994, together with changes in the perspectives of a number of multilateral and bilateral technical and donor agencies, has been considered a significant indicator of success. The Plan of Action that emerged from the Cairo conference upheld the reproductive health approach and called for an infusion of significant sums of money for its promotion. The first major step was taken by putting in place women-centered programs to provide women with the means to claim and defend their reproductive rights.

Whether women have, in their struggle for reproductive rights, won the war or only a battle, only the decades to come can tell.

See Also

ABORTION; CONTRACEPTIVES: DEVELOPMENT; EUGENICS; GLOBAL HEALTH MOVEMENT; HUMAN RIGHTS; MEDICAL CONTROL OF WOMEN; THE PILL; POPULATION CONTROL; PRO-CHOICE MOVEMENT; REPRODUCTIVE RIGHTS

References and Further Reading

Huston, Perdita. 1992. Motherhood by choice: *Pioneers in women's health and family planning.* New York: Feminist Press/Talman.

Ross, John A., and Frankenburg, Elizabeth. 1993. *Findings from two decades of family planning research.* New York: Population Council.

Sanger, Margaret. 1969. *My fight for birth control.* New York: Maxwell. (Originally published 1931.)

Sundari Ravindran

FAMILY: Power Relations and Power Structures

Recognition of the family as an arena of power is integral to old and new political and philosophical debates over the structuring and changeability of society and individuals. Perhaps the single most important factor in the present attention to the family as a sphere and instrument of power has been the cross-cultural exposure of domestic violence against women and children. However, power also operates more subtly.

Defining the Family Unit

The dominance of the nuclear family as a model meant that the discussions of familial power seldom focused on parents and children, spouses, and siblings. However, the universality of this model has been questioned. For example, among some groups and classes in Africa and Asia, the relation between co-wives was important. In patrilineal extended families in east and south Asia, relations between brothers are crucial, as is the power of mothers-in-law over daughters-in-law. Any study of the family, and particularly any mapping of familial power structures and relations, involves two problems.

The first pertains to definitions and boundaries: Who is a family member? Families fall between kinship relations and households and may be more or less than the domestic group. The family unit, whether conceived of as consanguineous, conjugal, or coresidential, or some combination of these, is historically specific. Spouses, parents, and young children may be considered members of different families or just live separately; adult married siblings and nonkin may be household members. In a given society, boundaries of a family or household unit are more or less flexible and strategic. People may be included or excluded (with or without consensus), depending on activities and purposes. These vary with class, caste, race, religion, ethnicity, mobility, and stages of the life cycle.

The second problem arises because familial relations and ideologies are central to gender relations. The family is the site of many themes: love, nurturance, maternalism, self-sacrifice, masculine responsibility and protectiveness, self-realization, morality, identity, culture, immortality (through one's children), and resistance as well as power. The family tends to appear as an objective, "natural," unchanging unit, consisting of long-term intensive relations; it is often represented as crucial to the security, order, and continuity of a culture—a bulwark against chaos and degeneration. Familial ideologies and relations may thus commit people to particular forms of householding, the social order, and the status quo.

Feminists have highlighted the multilayered structures and ideologies that mask power within the family. To any one family member, power can appear more or less transient and contingent. Since familial relationships intersect with and mediate each other, the conditions of power in any one relation may rest elsewhere. Wider kinship structures, societal distributions of resources, macroeconomic and political processes, and religious and educational institutions affect (and are affected by) the dynamics of familial processes and power.

Power in the Nuclear Family

Anthropologists demarcated the political-jural or public kinship domain, where power was exercised, and the domestic kinship domain, where "natural" human sentiments of love and sharing were expressed (Uberoi, 1995). This view shares elements with Parsons's model of the American (that is, modern) family, on which many contemporary analyses are based. "Normal," "functional" families are nuclear; power is absent or is exercised benevolently by the father. In the instrumental role of breadwinner, the father (man) mediates between the world and the home. The mother and homemaker (woman) plays an expressive role involving emotional and caregiving functions. This division of labor, chosen by both partners in an implicit marital or familial contract, parallels "nature" and the division between public and private, and power and love.

This description is shaped by the apparently self-evident separation of the private and the public in capitalist political ecnonomy. In what is still a prevailing view, capitalism is linked with civilization, progress, modernization, and democracy, entailing a shift from patriarchal to nuclear families and a division between public power and private affection. For women, equality demanded greater access to the public sphere, but only if they fulfilled their "natural" functions in the private sphere of heterosexual and parent-child intimacy, where love precluded power or transformed it into altruism.

The inherent equality and democracy of the nuclear family have long been contested, often in terms of interactions between intrafamilial and extrafamilial processes (Engels, 1884). It was argued that the privatized family-household subordinated women. The strengthening, relative to other ties, of the conjugal bond on which the nuclear family rests reinforced a woman's economic and emotional dependence on her husband and thence his power over her. On the other hand, this also increased a man's dependence on his wife as homemaker, so that she might gain freedom and say within the nuclear family. Similarly, the nuclear conjugal family may imply more egalitarian relations between generations, but relations which prevented the abuse of children may be erased.

Role theory is central to power in Parson's model. Society becomes a network of stereotypical behaviors; power is replaced by a theory of norms (Connell, 1987). Variations and conflict are a result of discrepancies, deviance, and dysfunctionality in roles and values. This concept of power is linked to notions of contract, right, and the autonomous self. A contract entered into freely and knowingly is fair and democratic, and the power it confers is legal authority. One critique of the last point argues that women do not enter marriage and family contracts freely and knowingly. A second critique maintains that a contract between parties with unequal power will always be unequal; this view questions the very notions of contract, choice, and the autonomous self.

The Family As a Site of Oppression

In the 1970s, feminists in Europe and North America developed two distinct but not necessarily contradictory analyses of the family. For radical feminists, especially, the family was the root and site of women's oppression, with the wife subjugated to the husband or patriarch; conjugal relations expressed unequal gender relations; inequality meant disempowerment; conjugal love and familial solidarity were myths; and domestic violence and compulsory heterosexuality were both causal factors and effects.

According to the second argument, from anthropology, the key to the universal familial and social subordination of women lay in the association of the public sphere with power and prestige, and the private, domestic sphere with powerlessness and low value; women's confinement to devalued, unpaid domestic tasks underlay males' and females' unequal power. Women were always identified with the domestic realm, but the division between public and private varied with society and culture. Where it was most marked and developed, women had the least power and value (Rosaldo and Lamphere, 1975).

This universal association of women with the home and powerlessness, and men with the public world, value, and power, has been challenged. Sanday (1981) compiled examples—the Iroquois and Cheyenne in seventeenth- and eighteenth-century America, the Lepcha and Semang in Asia, and the Mbuti and Ashanti in Africa—of cultures where the sexual division of labor and family relations were more egalitarian or women were the center of power. Others argued that not only women but many classes of men do not exercise power in the public sphere, and that male prestige and wives' deference to their husbands in public could conceal women's domestic power. In rural Greece, for instance (Friedl, 1967), women had to concur in the use and disposal of their dowries (land); supportive factors were the cultural celebration of the family and the fact that men's honor depended on women's chastity, behavior in public, and economic contribution to the household. Such arguments suggest that the dichotomy between public and private is inadequate for an understanding of familial power or gender relations; they highlight the varied sources of power and distinctions between power, authority, and prestige.

Similar issues were raised in Asia, Africa, and Latin America and by women of color in the "North" (the developed world). Their family patterns and forms of power had been described as dysfunctional by academics and marginalized by feminists. They noted that in many contexts, family solidarity has been crucial for the survival of colonized people, slaves, blacks, the poor, and other exploited groups.

These contrasting views cannot be reconciled simply as class and cultural variations in family relations. They indicate that love and power exist simultaneously in intimate relationships, making family power structures all the more difficult to comprehend (Meyer, in Davis et al., 1991). However, many of these arguments share in a concept of power as operating through conscious decision making by individuals.

Observing Family Power Structures

Two related attempts to unravel familial power structures suggest that it is the difficulty of objectively observing power which makes it elusive (Kabeer, 1994).

The family head, kinship, and power: Academics and state machineries tend to assume that a family or household has a head, who decides for it, provides for it, and represents it. Authority and headship were vested in men even in matrilineal and bilateral contexts. It was assumed that in "normal" families the de jure male head was also the de facto head, and that he was altruistic, serving the interests of the unit. These assumptions accorded with self-representations in many patrilineal societies. For instance, in northwest India and among the Kusasi of Ghana, the head of the joint family or compound claimed to act in the interests of the unit, reconciling competing claims of dependents (Palriwala, in Palriwala and Risseeuw, 1996; Whitehead, in Young et al., 1981). However, it was also assumed that this unit was primarily a group of male agnates.

Feminists also have seen headship as an indicator of power, but they have questioned earlier postulates. Leacock (1981) argues that Christian missionaries, European traders, colonial armies, and administrators imposed the authority and headship patterns of their own culture in their dealings with North American Indian societies. However, these indigenous people were relatively egalitarian societies, in which both cooperation and individual initiative were essential for survival; the family-household was not marked, and authority, leadership, and decision making were dispersed and fluid. This has also been suggested in analyses of bilateral and matrilineal societies (Dube, in Palriwala and Risseeuw, 1996).

The labels "matrilineal authority" and "patrilineal authority" do not capture the diversity, complexity, and fragmentation of a head's power. In some societies, family headship may have more to do with governance and community matters than with familial relations. Practices such as consultation and delegation may attenuate or conceal the head's power, as may absence, perceived incapability, or lack of resources. For example, in in seventeenth- and eighteenth-century Haute Provence (France), a father had to legally "free" sons to set up their own households (Collomp, in Medick and Sabean, 1984); in India a father's authority over sons weakens when a family is poor and has no inheritable property; and in Africa the father's power declines with his inability to accumulate a brideprice and thereby control the marriage of a son (Baerends, 1994).

The existence of female heads of households, even in strongly patrilineal societies, indicates that women can be independent and powerful (Maynes et al., 1996). Female headship, however, is often transitory (as when the husband is a migrant worker) and may involve little real authority, since men still hold the purse strings. Most women-headed family-households are poor and socially vulnerable. Thus the source, nature, and efficacy of the head's authority must be considered (Harris, in Young et al., 1981).

Power and intra-family consumption levels: The notion of the altruistic family head assumes that the distribution of resources within the family-household is nondiscriminatory and is based on the relative economic contributions and needs of individual members, the long-term survival interests of the unit, and love. This assumption, however, is frequently contradicted (as in south Asia) by dramatic differences between men and women in nutrition and health, reflected in morbidity rates, maternal mortality, life expectancy, and sex ratios. It is argued that these demographic patterns reflect men's and women's unequal consumption and power in and beyond the family. Class and gender biases favoring mental work, cash work, and men's work in general (which is seen as more valuable and demanding) give men a greater claim to family resources. However, numerous studies have found that women make a greater contribution to family consumption, even in standard economic terms. Familial altruism can dispossess women: a woman may spend her earnings on the family, while her husband may keep more of his income to himself. In a study in England, for instance, wives felt that when they began earning money they had less claim to their husbands' income, and thus less power within the family (Whitehead, in Young et al., 1981); in parts of sub-Saharan Africa spouses do not have a common housekeeping budget, and so they have disparate responsibilities for children and elders.

Power thus operates through values, norms, and practices regarding contributions, responsibilities, and claims. Cooperative conflict, characteristic of the family-household, affects individual members differentially (Sen, 1990). Altruism may affect decision making and the bargaining power of family members: other factors include a person's fallback position with regard to entitlements; visibility of and socially influenced perceptions of contributions, interests, and claims; the possibility of coercion; and the role of the state.

Concepts of Power

In most cultures women cook and serve food in the home and are the immediate allocators of daily consumption. This fact is sometimes cited to refute the view that the bias favoring men in familial consumption reflects male power; the bias is, rather, said to reflect self-exploitation or women's power over other women. However, in many family systems women's power is authority delegated to a subordinate group; in exercising it, women—owing to emotional investment, internalization of values and beliefs, a lack of alternatives, and a fear of sanctions—do not cross boundaries, and thereby perpetuate their own powerlessness.

Women "bargain" with patriarchy: they accept control by a loving husband or other male kin as part of being protected by them (Kandiyoti, 1988). A housewife may prefer dependence to the insecurity of being single or working outside the home. Compensation and pleasure, often based on class or race, help establish power structures. As long as the bargain is maintained, women may have an interest in current familial structures and may invest more in familial relations than men do. A crucial dimension here is the power exercised through love.

Some feminist scholars have extended into the sphere of intimacy and gender relations the works of writers such as Gramsci, Lukes, Foucault, Bourdieu, and Giddens (Risseeuw, 1991; Davis et al., 1991), who argued that power cannot be understood simply as interpersonal control, intentional action, or observable conflict, typically studied through conscious, individual decision-making. While overt disputes (and organized disputation) may be evidence of change, flexibility, or weaknesses in and challenges to norms, values, and relationships, effective power does not have to be exercised daily or explicitly; it operates through consensus, through accepted norms, or through the very terms of debate. In India, for example, arguments over a daughter's dowry and sons' shares in family property are separated, obscuring discrimination and differential power between sons and daughters. Further, agency is not the same as resistance, and large structures and collectivities act through interpersonal relations. Powerless family members—usually women, children, and the aged—comply and resist to varying degrees. Identifying their grievances can reveal issues silenced because the holders of power define the terms in which experience can be expressed and alternatives perceived. For instance, child abuse has often been concealed by children's inability to name the abuse, and their fear of losing their parents' love (and their home).

Care, Spheres of Power, and Time

Theories of maternal power have also drawn attention. Mothering is often described as a social practice which women can shape for themselves, and in which power is transformative and self-transcending rather than dominating and self-perpetuating (Trebilcot, 1983). Disputed issues include the valuation of unpaid time, the inevitability of power in a caregiving relationship, the concept of power as necessarily alienating, and the idealization of motherhood. Mothering may perpetuate or challenge unequal gender relations (Chodorow, in Rosaldo and Lamphere, 1974). Viewing power in terms of arenas and time has significant implications.

Power in one aspect of family life does not necessarily mean power in all spheres. Familial power is exercised in large part through day-to-day claims; thus the demarcation of spheres of authority within the family helps to ensure the acquiescence of the powerless. In Lagos, Nigeria, for example, men could intrude on women's activities, but many women, such as market women, had economic independence and freedom of movement (Baerends, 1994). Separate male and female spheres meant that spouses conducted many activities independently of each other, through their own networks. Also, in patrilineal extended families, within the overarching authority of senior men there may be separate lines of control: senior women have power over daughters-in-law and daughters, and elder men have power over sons.

A related matter is the cyclical character of familial power and authority, with shifts in access to resources and freedom of movement over the life cycle of family members. For example, among the Igbo (Nigeria) unmarried daughters are powerless, but after marriage women have prestige and powers of arbitration in their father's household and lineage (Amadiume, 1987). In the nuclear family, children can leave the parental home and be "released" from their parents. In a patrilineal extended family-household this is difficult, but sons and younger brothers gain in power as the balance of capabilities and responsibilities shifts with age; and young, suppressed brides become influential mothers and powerful mothers-in-law. Adulthood, responsibility, and power are linked to age, marriage, and the birth and marriage of sons.

Conditions and Sources of Power

The sources and bases of familial power lie within and without the household, family, and kinship network.

Descent and inheritance of property are crucial. In patrilineal societies, men continue the line and inherit property; women are dependent. In matrilineal and bilateral societies, where the lineage continues through women, their right to shelter, inheritance, and the products of ancestral property is recognized, and family dynamics are more egalitarian with regard to gender (Sacks, in Rosaldo and Lamphere, 1974; Dube, 1995). In many patrilineal African societies, wives had a right of access to cultivable land, and the husband's lineage could moderate power relations by overruling a man who deprived his wife of such land. This could mean that the lineage controlled wives and widows, but as lineage control of land and its members was whittled away by growing individualization, the husband's power increased. In highly stratified societies, men control property privately and thus have even more power. The effect of dowry and brideprice on women's power is a continuing debate.

In the exercise of power, property can supersede or be superseded by sex, age, and generation. The gendered matrix of power and property involves various types of property (membership in a kinship group, names, sacred beings, knowledge, land, and other productive resources) and various forms of ownership, access to property, and rights to use it or its products.

Another basis of differential power and consumption is the persistently unequal access of men and women, old and young, to *employment, markets, education, and means of livelihood.* For instance, a woman may have to choose between an abusive husband (or kinsmen) and penury; or the power of a provider or caregiver may be undermined by the obligation or the inability to perform these functions. Economic exchanges through kinship or patronage networks helped women in Morocco to circumvent male-biased rules of consumption and authority, and tended to undermine the economic and emotional importance of marriage for women (Maher, in Young et al., 1981). Economic trends may moderate tradition: among the matrilineal, caste-bound Nair in India, men's control over women's sexuality and bodies had at one time increased but was weaker in poorer families (Menon, in Maynes et al., 1996).

Patterns of residence also affect power. Patri-virilocal residence means that a young couple will start married life in an arrangement in which the woman is very dependent on her marital family. Kolenda (1967) notes that in India, women's bargaining power within the family is affected by the balance between uxorilaterality and virilaterality: the husband has more power when a married couple resides with or near, and depends on, his kin. With matrilocal or uxorilocal residence, the wife's family can provide more support, thereby reducing the power of the husband derived from his kin. Living near the wife's family can give a matrilineal character to nuclear neolocal family systems also.

Women's sexuality and fertility can be both a source of power for women and a source of sanctions against them. A basic dilemma of patrilineal descent groups is the dependence on "outsiders" (women) for reproduction. In Hindu, upper-caste Nepal, women's status changes dramatically over the life cycle (Bennett, 1983): whereas unmarried daughters and sisters are asexual and sacred, deserving of love and worship, the dangerous sexuality and power of wives must be controlled. Patrilineal inheritance usually entails the control of women's sexuality and fertility, often by limiting their relationships outside the family and even confining them to the home—thereby denying them a means to moderate familial relations. Purdah, the sexual division of labor, and patterns of production, exchange, and visitation can isolate women while giving men an extrafamilial network. Such arrangements favor older, experienced men and "insiders" over the young, women, and strangers and can be crucial to power flowing from social and cultural capital inside and outside the family. A related issue is access to and use of contraceptive methods and new reproductive technologies.

Sanday (1981) suggests that the authority relation between the sexes is linked to supernatural concepts. In some societies women have power because of a perceived reciprocal flow between their inner, reproductive, and sexual capacities and sacred natural forces; such societies are likely to be sexually integrated, with the father involved in child care. In other societies, men pursue power through activities such as hunting, war, and profit-making; here men must be prepared to control unpredictable forces, often associated with female sexuality and reproduction. Control through the family, sexual segregation, and symbols of an all-powerful male or father are likely. Sanday also suggests a third type of society, characterized by complementarity and duality in behavior, division of labor, and symbolism.

An important issue is the role of the *state* and its institutions—including religion, community structures, and the mass media—in creating, maintaining, and disrupting family power structures (Donzelot, 1979; Palriwala and Risseeuw, 1996). Women's and other movements ask whether these institutions perpetuate or change family power relations, by default or intentionally, as a result of class or other sectional interests or of organizational ignorance and inertia. In this regard, the state's response to individual and collective resistance by the powerless is significant.

Marriage is a good example. Where religious beliefs make marriage a sacrament, neither men nor women can easily terminate a bad marriage, but social values can make this even more difficult for women. Religion and law may allow men additional marriages and, along with community structures, make life after separation or divorce harder for women. Informal exit rules may also let men abandon their family obligations; this can result from ideologies regarding "good" women and wives, gender biases in access to resources and livelihoods, laws of inheritance and child custody, state economic policies and employers' practices that stereotype the male as the breadwinner, and messages in the media. Women are then locked into oppressive family situations, and their bargaining power is diminished.

See Also

DOMESTIC VIOLENCE; FAMILY LAW; FAMILY: PROPERTY RELATIONS; FAMILY: RELIGIOUS AND LEGAL SYSTEMS, *all topics;* FAMILY STRUCTURES; HOUSEHOLDS AND FAMILIES: OVERVIEW

References and Further Reading

Amadiume, I. 1987. *Male daughters, female husbands: Gender and sex in an African society.* London: Zed.

Baerends, E. A.. 1994. *Changing kinship, family and gender relations in sub-Saharan Africa.* Netherlands: Women and Autonomy Center, University of Leiden.

Barrett, M. 1980. *Women's oppression today.* London: Verso.

Bennett, L. 1983. *Dangerous wives and sacred sisters: Social and symbolic roles of high-caste women in Nepal.* New York: Columbia University Press.

Connell, R.W. 1987. *Gender and power.* Cambridge: Polity.

Davis, K., M. Leijenaar, and J. Oldersma, eds. 1991. *The gender of power.* London: Sage.

Donzelot, J. 1979. *The policing of families.* Trans. R. Hurley. London: Hutchinson.

Dube, L. 1995. *Women and kinship: Comparative perspectives on gender in south and southeast Asia.* Tokyo: United Nations University Press; Delhi: Sage.

Engels, F. 1884/1986. *The origin of the family, private property, and the state. In the light of the researches of Lewis H. Morgan.* London: Penguin.

Friedl, E. 1967. The position of women: Appearance and reality. *Anthropological Quarterly,* 210: 97–108.

Kabeer, N. 1994. *Reversed realities: Gender hierarchies in development thought.* London: Verso.

Kandiyoti, D. 1988. Bargaining with patriarchy. *Gender and Society,* 2: 274–289.

Kolenda, P. 1967. Regional differences in Indian family structure. In R.I. Crane, ed., *Regions and regionalism in south Asian studies: An exploratory study.* Durham, N.C.: Duke University Monographs and Occasional Papers Series, No. 5.

Leacock, E. 1981. *Myths of male dominance: Collected articles on women cross-culturally.* New York: Monthly Review.

Maynes, M. J., A. Waltner, B. Soland, and U. Strasser. 1996. *Gender, kinship, power.* New York: Routledge.

Medick, H., and D. W. Sabean, eds. 1984. *Interest and emotion: Essays on the study of family and kinship.* Cambridge: Cambridge University Press.

Palriwala, R., and C. Risseeuw, eds. 1996. *Shifting circles of support: Contextualising gender and kinship relations in south Asia and sub-Saharan Africa.* Sage: Delhi.

Parsons, T., and R. F. Bales. 1957. *Family, socialisation, and interaction process.* London: Routledge and Kegan Paul.

Risseeuw, C. 1991. *Gender-transformation, power, and resistance among women in Sri Lanka. The fish don't talk about the water.* Delhi: Manohar.

Rosaldo, M. Z., and L. Lamphere, eds., 1974, *Women, culture, and society.* California: Stanford University Press.

Sanday, P. 1981. *Female power and male dominance: On the origins of sexual inequality.* Cambridge: Cambridge University Press.

Sen, A. K., 1990. Gender and cooperative conflicts. In I. Tinker, ed., *Persistent inequalities.* Oxford: Oxford University Press.

Trebilcot, J., ed. 1983. *Mothering: Essays in feminist theory.* New Jersey: Rowman.

Uberoi, P. 1995. Problems with patriarchy: Conceptual issues in anthropology and feminism. *Sociological Bulletin* 44 (2):195–221.

Young, K., C. Wolkowitz, and R. McCullagh, eds. *Of marriage and the market: Women's subordination in international perspective.* London: CSE.

Rajni Palriwala

FAMILY: Property Relations

Friedrich Engels's *Origins of the Family, Private Property, and the State* (1884/1986) has been the crucial reference point for studies on the shaping of gender relations through property. Engels argued that the emergence of private property and classes created the basis for women's oppression through the privatized household economy, domestic labor, and the enforced monogamy of wives, so as to ensure heirs for patrilineal family property through the control of women's reproduction. A few empirical and cross-cultural discussions have focused on the linkages in this argument (Sacks, cited in Reiter, 1975). Many have concentrated on the rights of various family members, the modes of transmission of family property, and their implications for roles and relations within and beyond the family. Differences in ownership, control, and access to property of female family members have, in particular, been described (for example, Agarwal, 1994; Sharma, 1980). The distribution of material and productive property has been seen as crucial to systemic differences between women and men in survival, security, prosperity, and power at interpersonal and societal levels.

The Distribution of Property

Inheritance and marriage payments have been the two most frequently examined forms of transmission of family property. Inheritance transfers property over time, and marriage payments transfer it across kinship groups or space (Hirschon, 1984). Modes of property transfer affect and are affected by the formation of descent groups, patterns of post-wedding residence, and kinship networks. Rules may be flexible or there may be a systematic discrepancy between a stated rule or ideology and a practice. Sons and daughters, firstborn and later-born—but also daughters, wives, widows, mothers, and sons, sons-in-law, brothers, and fathers—are differentiated. The distribution of property among claimants is often couched in language, as of family good or family continuity, which masks discrimination between individuals, particularly by gender.

In looking at family property, inheritance and marriage must be viewed together (Goody, 1976). It has been argued that dowry turns apparently unilineal inheritance systems into systems of diverging devolution of individual rights.

Dowry creates a conjugal fund and is a daughter's "pre-mortem" inheritance. This is contrasted with the circulating social fund that bridewealth and brideprice systems embody and the greater lineage control over property, as in Africa. A comparison of the situations of women as daughters, wives, and widows has been central to this contrast and the debates about it. Given the different destinations of the various components that make it up, the analysis of dowry as a daughter's premortem inheritance in India is questionable.

Marital Property

Two aspects in particular have been reviewed with respect to marital property and the marital estate. One follows the revaluation of domestic labor and of the "economic" nature of exchanges within the household and family. Property accumulated through male earnings in the lifetime of a marriage, and often held in the husband's name, has actually been made possible by the unpaid labor of his wife. Hence, it is argued that the wife should have an equal right to such property. The second issue arises from the contemporary overshadowing of family property by individual rights and the increasing instability of marital ties. In a context in which women's access to livelihood and property depends on their familial and marital relations, women's rights in the marital estate may enable them to deal with the latter trend. This is not to be equated with earlier European systems of the marital estate, which were premised on women as legal minors under the guardianship of a father or husband, thus disadvantaging women.

Family property demonstrates most explicitly the social character of property—that property is a relation between people mediated by things. Claims and access of family members to property are differentiated by kinship link and gender. Consequent disparities in life chances are linked to more and less encompassing rights in family relationships, differences in strength and permanence of family membership, in connectedness, and assessments of value of/to individual members and/or the family unit. At the same time, the kinship idiom may permeate relations through property, as between tenant and owner (Palriwala, 1994).

Kinship and family systems, through legal and ideological practices, variously construct women's and men's capacity to act as independent subjects in relation to property objects and rights in people (Whitehead, in Hirschon, 1984). This process covers a range of rights—claims on labor or the fruits of labor, time, bodies, love, and loyalty—and can describe the gamut of family relationships. The mode of holding property shapes feelings between family members, territorializes emotion, establishes goals and ambitions, and gives to each a sense of dependence and independence

(Sabean, in Medick and Sabean, 1984). Access to property and rights in family property are central to kinship and gender identity.

Acknowledging the social character of property also questions the separation of subject and object—property owner and property owned—that has been central to the understanding of property in bourgeois capitalist economies and cultures, objectifying the "owned" persons (Strathern, in Hirschon, 1984). Take the "gifting" of a bride by her father in a Hindu wedding ritual, which entails a differential capacity to give and to be given. Rather than predicating this on the objectification of the bride, however, it may be viewed as establishing a permanent relationship between the bride-giver and the bride-receiver, as the former gives part of himself, his daughter.

The value of productive resources—land and house, education, marriage payments, names, ritual objects and other objects, time, and care—is particular to historical, cultural, and economic context. The symbolic and ritualistic value of property, however, cannot obscure its materiality. Thus, parents may be cared for in their old age only if they have property to pass on. The value of family property concerns kinship ties and citizenship—both rights and obligations. The durability of property and of family relationships—the time dimension—is also at issue (Sabean, in Medick and Sabean, 1984). In patrilineal, virilocal kinship systems one or more sons inherit the house, land, business, gold, ritual objects, and ancestors—durable possessions that symbolize and are the family line. These sons are to take care of and continue the family. However, a younger son may have to seek his fortune elsewhere, and daughters possibly marry out. The relation between a daughter and her father or ancestors demands marriage gifts but not valuable durable land. A widow's rights in her late husband's property may rest on having produced a son to continue the family.

Family property is subject to multiple claims and a complex of rights, reflecting layers of family relations. Claims are divisible, and the same object can involve various, at times contested, rights. Ownership, management rights, and usufruct rights may vest in different kin. Negotiation of family relations and property emerges particularly in the context of marriage payments, day-to-day intrafamilial distribution and consumption, and division of inheritances.

Property Rights

The larger framework of property rights—Thompson's grid of inheritance—is crucial to understanding family property and intraproperty relationships. Thus, legal separation of ownership and usufruct rights can buttress debt or dependency relationships between owner and tenant, husband and wife. Exchanges within family and kinship networks are part of a larger system of exchange. Rights in a family estate may reinforce or contradict exchanges at other economic and political levels. Legally enforceable eviction, disinheritance, or testamentary disposal affects long-term and day-to-day exchanges in families and society.

Sundry individual property rights have been recognized in a wide range of cultures and ancient law systems. Often, however, the fully acting social subject was the person who was claimed by and could claim family and thence property. The direction of legal reform has by and large been from multiple rights of individuals and groups and from rights entailing responsibilities, characteristic of family property, to individualized absolute rights. This has weakened secondary or derived rights such as those of younger sons, abandoned wives, and widows (Palriwala and Risseeuw, 1996). In many societies now, family property symbolizes a hopeful expectation rather than a right. In some countries, family property has come to be governed by a multiplicity of laws, which can offset each other and be manipulated by the "stronger." Women's claim to family property is affected by such factors, and by their lack of access to nonfamily individual income and property, education, and the law courts.

With the growing possibilities of individualized economic activity, initiative, mobility, and accumulation, and the dominance of individualism as an ideal and philosophy under capitalism, individual property has a qualitatively new significance. But people's ownership of property and economic standing continue to be largely determined by the property and economic standing of their parents and the often gendered allocations parents make through their lifetime to and among their children. Family property continues to establish demarcations within a family and society, making for gendered and discriminatory inclusions and exclusions.

See Also

DOWRY AND BRIDEPRICE; FAMILY: POWER RELATIONS AND POWER STRUCTURES; KINSHIP; MARRIAGE: REGIONAL TRADITIONS AND PRACTICES

References and Further Reading

Agarwal, B. 1994. *A field of one's own: Gender and land rights in south Asia.* Cambridge: Cambridge University Press.

Dube, L. 1997. *Women and kinship: Comparative perspectives on gender in south and southeast Asia.* Tokyo: United Nations University Press and Delhi: Sage.

Engels, F. 1884/1986. *The origin of the family, private property, and the state: In the light of the researches of Lewis H. Morgan.* London: Penguin.

Goody, J. 1976. *Production and reproduction: A comparative study of the domestic domain.* Cambridge Studies in Social Anthropology. Cambridge: Cambridge University Press.

Goody, J., J. Thirsk, and E. P. Thompson, eds. 1976. *Family and inheritance: Rural society in western Europe 1200–1800.* Cambridge: Cambridge University Press.

Hirschon, R., ed. 1984. *Women and property—women as property.* London: Croom Helm; New York: St. Martin's.

Howell, Martha C. 1998. *The marriage exchange: Property, social place, and gender in cities in the low countries, 1300–1500.* Chicago and London: University of Chicago Press.

Medick, H., and D. Sabean, eds. 1984. *Interest and emotion: Essays on the study of family and kinship.* Cambridge: University of Cambridge Press.

Palriwala, R. 1994. *Changing kinship, family, and gender relations in south Asia: Processes, trends, issues.* Leiden, Netherlands: Women and Autonomy Centre, University of Leiden.

———, and C. Risseeuw, eds. 1996. *Shifting circles of support: Contextualising gender and kinship relations in south Asia and sub-Saharan Africa.* Delhi: Sage.

Reiter, R. R., ed. 1975. *Toward an anthropology of women.* New York: Monthly Review.

Sharma, U. 1980. *Women, work, and property in northwest India.* London and New York: Tavistock.

Tambiah, S. J. 1989. Bridewealth and dowry revisited: The position of women in sub-Saharan Africa and north India. *Current Anthropology* 30(4): 413–435.

Rajni Palriwala

FAMILY: Religious and Legal Systems— Buddhist Traditions

Buddhist legal traditions are found in the countries of south and southeast Asia. In south Asia and Myanmar (formerly Burma) the impact of Hinduism has been significant. Confucianism has influenced the Buddhist legal traditions of southeast Asia. Colonial legal traditions derived from Christianity and early western laws have also transformed family laws in countries of both south and southeast Asia.

In India the norms for family law governing Buddhists have been identified with Hinduism, so that Buddhist law reflects the norms of Hindu law (Paras, 1989: 11, 149; Sampath, 1981: 43n.24; Sarkar, 1989: 91). Consequently, principles of law derived from the Dharmasastras and the laws of Manu perceive a male as the exclusive head of a household, which could be centered on a joint or nuclear family. Marriage is a sacrament, and divorce is discouraged. Legal rights regarding marital property, inheritance, and custody of minor children are determined in a context where a clear preference is shown for males. Changes introduced by postcolonial legislation, sometimes influenced by liberal western legal concepts of the twentieth century, have resulted in some changes that benefit women.

Buddhism's Influence

Remnants of a Buddhist legal tradition can be found in countries such as Vietnam, Thailand, Sri Lanka, and Myanmar. Thus, legal values concerning family relations have a core of similarity and egalitarianism regarding women that is in striking contrast to the male-centered family traditions of Hindu law, Confucianism, and local laws in these countries, which were influenced by early western laws introduced during the colonial period.

Buddhist philosophy viewed marriage as a contract rather than a religious sacrament. Buddhism recognized the equal spiritual potential of women and permitted them to be ordained into the clergy. Consequently, a woman's separate legal identity was recognized in the law on family relations. A marriage could be dissolved by mutual consent, a widow could be considered the head of the family, and women had separate contractual and property rights. Not surprisingly, the first westerners who encountered cultures influenced by Buddhism in south and southeast Asia remarked on the privileged legal position of women compared with the position of their sisters in western legal systems, which were based on early English common law or the Napoleonic codes (My-Van, 1991: 274, 281; Percival, 1803: 176).

Vietnam

Family laws in Vietnam derived from the fifteenth-century "Le Code" reflected some of these practices, before the impact of Confucianism. The nuclear family was the main unit, and kinship ties to the extended family were looser than in the case of a joint family under a patriarch. As a result, women were treated as partners with men in the exercise of family authority and in economic activity. The main occupation was rice cultivation, a labor-intensive activity that required partnership between men and women. Women's work was as important as men's work, even though men and women performed different agricultural activities connected with paddy cultivation. Their engagement in this

work as equal partners also led to social and legal recognition of their right to a common pool of economic assets and to a legal concept of equal shares in this "community of property." The legal system was familiar with a separate concept of equal individual rights in inherited property, without discrimination on the basis of sex, and shared inheritance rights in a community of property consisting of joint assets acquired after marriage.

Thailand

Similar concepts and principles in regard to economic rights in property and individual status within the family can be observed in the Civil and Commercial Code, Book V, of Thailand, which reflects concepts of traditional law (Chatsri and Varee, 1979: 197). Marriage is a contract, and the formation of a marriage does not involve the ritual and ceremony found elsewhere. One form of divorce that is recognized is a divorce by mutual consent, evidenced by an agreement to divorce recorded with an administrative authority. The concept of a woman's individual right to her separate property (sin suantua) is combined in this code with a concept of equal rights in a community of property (sin somros) acquired after marriage.

Sri Lanka

In Sri Lanka, traditional Kandyan Sinhala law, with roots in a Buddhist tradition, also recognized the individual property and contractual rights of women (Goonesekere, 1991: 193). Formalization of marriage did not include ritual, since marriage was considered a contract between spouses rather than a sacrament. Divorce was available on the basis of mutual consent or breakdown of the marriage. A divorce in either case was recorded in a simple agreement. The widow acquired the status of head of household and manager of her children's property.

Myanmar (Burma)

Available information suggests that some concepts of Burmese Buddhist law found in the Dhammathats, regarding the property rights and individual status of women before and after marriage and as widows, are almost identical to those in Sri Lanka (Gledhill, 1968: 205). Since marriage was considered nonritualistic and contractual, divorce by mutual consent was possible. The concept of equal shares in property rights was recognized, and collateral heirs, including brothers, brothers' children, or other male relatives of the deceased, did not displace women as heirs to the property of males. Burmese Buddhist law, like Kandyan Sinhala law, recognized loose extended family ties and nuclear family consisting of spouses and their children.

The agricultural environment of paddy cultivation that was found in all these countries combined with Buddhist values to produce an egalitarian approach to women. Nevertheless, significant socioeconomic changes, the different religious influences of Hinduism and Confucianism, and the impact of western colonial laws derived from English common law or the Napoleonic codes contributed to legal norms that discriminate against women and focus on male authority in the family. The Buddhist legal tradition has been transformed, and its link to the earlier egalitarian sociocultural traditions of rice-growing agricultural communities in south and southeast Asia is barely visible.

See Also

BUDDHISM; CONFUCIANISM; HINDUISM; HOUSEHOLDS AND FAMILIES: EAST ASIA; HOUSEHOLDS AND FAMILIES: SOUTH ASIA; HOUSEHOLDS AND FAMILIES: SOUTHEAST ASIA

References and Further Reading

Chatsri, Bunnag, and Nasakul Varee. 1979. Thailand. In *Law Asia: Family law series*. Vol. 1. Singapore: Law Asia.

Dhammakitti. 1999. *A manual of Buddhist traditional traditions*. Trans. Bimala Churn Law. New Delhi: Asian Educational Services.

Gledhill, Alan. 1968. Community of property in the marriage laws of Burma. In J. N. D. Anderson, ed., *Family law in Asia and Africa*. London: Allen and Unwin.

Goonesekere, Savitri. 1991. Colonial legislation and Sri Lankan family law: The legacy of history. In K. M. de Silva et al., eds., *Asian panorama*. New Delhi: Vikas.

Howland, C. W., ed. 1999. *Religious fundamentalism and the human rights of women*. New York: St. Martin's.

Huxley, Andrew, ed. 1996. *Thai law, Buddhist law: Essays on the legal history of Thailand, Laos, and Burma*. Bangkok: White Orchid.

My-Van, Tran. 1991. The position of women in traditional Vietnam: Some aspects. In K. M. de Silva et al., *Asian panorama*. New Delhi: Vikas.

Paras, Diwan. 1989. *Law of adoption minority guardianship and custody*. New Delhi: Wadhwa.

Percival, Robert. 1803. *An account of the island of Ceylon*. Colombo, Sri Lanka: Cave.

Sampath, B. N. 1981. India. In *Law Asia: Family law series*, Vol. II. Singapore: Law Asia.

Sarkar, Lothikar. 1989. Social and economic legislation dealing with the status of women. In V. Kanesalingam, ed., *Women in development in south Asia*. New Delhi: Macmillan.

Savitri Goonesekere

FAMILY: Religious and Legal Systems— Catholic and Orthodox

In the Roman Catholic faith, the family has a special dignity and sacredness because it reflects the order of God's creation. The family has its origin in the union of men and women in the sacrament of marriage. The church's involvement in the marriage of believers is a landmark in contrast to the practice of its Jewish ancestors or the Roman Empire. Ignatius of Antioch is credited with setting the precedent that a marriage should be approved by church athorities: "It befits that those marry and being given in marriage should enter upon their union with the approval of the bishop, so that their marriage may be according to the Lord and not from lust." Modestinus first stated that marriage was a sharing of religious and human rights between parties. This perspective highlights consent, rather than copulation or dowry, as the basis of marriage. This emphasis on marriage as consensual may be attributed to the growing question about whether the marriage of Mary and Joseph was valid, since, as the church teaches, they had no intercourse. As early as Roman law, it was illegal to marry "minors and the mad" because they could not fully consent. The church teaches the equality of the sexes in marriage described by Paul in his Epistle to the Corinthians (1 Cor. 7:4). Augustine of Hippo limited men's extramarital fornication to the amount that their wives engaged in; in theory, that was none at all, since the practice was entriely forbidden to women. Gregory of Nazianzen, deploring laws biased against women, argued that God made men and women in one image and placed them under the same law. Origen based his argument for equality between partners on the fact that their souls are identical. Marriage was first listed as one of the seven sacraments in 1150 C.E., in the Sentences of Peter Lombard.

The Meaning of Marriage in the Catholic Church

Some scholars of the Patristic tradition, in retrospect, were incorrect in their interpretations of marriage and family. Saint Jerome wrote, "No wise man would ever compare [married love] to the love of Christ and the Church," yet that is exactly what the church does. Throughout the history of the church, perhaps in accordance with asceticism and celibacy among the clergy, there has been some depreciation of marriage. Such heresies as Manichaeism in the early church, and Albigensianism in the medieval period, which identified the body with evil, may have subtly influenced theologians of the time, suggesting that the flesh was a lower choice than religious vows. This may be related to the growing number of celibate theologians (who were predominantly male) and to a general disdain for the body. Such a view makes it difficult to acknowledge marriage as a sacrament; but the Council of Trent affirmed this sentiment, decreeing that anyone was anathama who dared say that celibacy or virginity was not a higher state than married life. As the social, medical, political, intellectual, and spiritual climate evolved throughout the centuries, however, the concept of marriage and celibacy as equally valid has been restored in the church, as is demonstrated in the Vatican II Decree on the Church (4:35): "Husband and wife witness to each other and to their children the love that Christ has for the church."

Through his teaching Jesus honored and restored the institution of marriage. Divorce followed by remarriage, according to Jesus, in contrast to Hebrew law, is equal to adultery (Mt. 5:31–32; 19:5–10). The bond of marriage is compared to Christ's eternal bond with the church. In Vatican II, marriage is distinct from historical perceptions of its benifits—indissolubility, fidelity, and fertility. Rather, the "unitive good" of marriage is valued equally with the "procreative good" (*Gaudium et spes*, n. 48). This view reflects a significant shift in the Catholic idea of marriage; there is a renewed sense of the bond between the partners and of their mutual nurturance, and there is an emphasis on the identity between the initial spousal commitment and the subsequent parental commitment. Marriage is not instituted solely for procreation: "Marriage persists as a whole matter of life and maintains its value and indissolubility" (Decree on the Family, art. 5) even when, though procreation is attempted, there are no offspring.

Equality of the Spouses in Marriage

Concerning the equality of spouses, the pope, in the decree *Mulieres dignitatem*, deliberately states that in marriage there is a mutual "subjection of the spouses out of reverence for Christ," not merely out of wife's reverence for her husband. No longer can the church's male hierachial structure assume that "submissive wife" and "devoted mother" are a woman's exclusive indentities. The church's changing understanding of women's roles in marriage and the family is evident in Pope Pius XII: "In his early writings, he identified motherhood as the source of feminine dignity, but later he came to see that the source of feminine dignity was—notwithstanding woman's prerogatives as mother—personhood" (Butler, 1997).

According to the creation story in Genesis (1:28), God commands humanity to "be fruitful and multiply." A person who can undertake the responsibility of founding a family, has an inviolable right to marry and have children.

The church teaches that neither it nor the state should set up arbitrary obstacles, such as enforcing limits on the number of children. In giving new life, parents participate in the work of the Creator, because at the moment of conception, a soul is created by God. Parents are said to be made more perfect through parenthood because of the maternal and paternal outpouring of love. *Decree on the Apostolate of the Laity* (art. 5) states, "The family has received from God its mission to be the first and vital cell of society. Parents exercise an authority over their children that is subjective and objective, personal and *ex officio*, based on their personal superior position and their educational task." Pope Pius XII considered that it was the aim of Christian education to enable followers of Christ to embrace their goal of imitation and unity, to "cooperate with the divine grace informing the true and perfect Christian, that is, to form Christ himself in those regenerated by baptism."

Rights and Responsibilities of Parents

The duties and rights of parents extend as far as is necessary to ensure the development of their children into responsible adults. This concept includes the ability to care for a child as a human being by meeting bodily needs and by providing a religious upbringing and education. Equally, the basis of educating children must be trust and service rather than authority or obedience. A child is born of two parents; therefore, if both parents fulfill their parental functions, then they have equal duties and rights. If a parent forfeits the rights, as in the case of illegitimate children or divorce, he or she is not absolved of the duties. Parents must not delegate their educational rights without good reason. Children, however, are not the property of the parents but are equal partners with equal inalienable rights; therefore, parental rights are limited by the rights of the children. Parental rights are subject to historical change. Before schools, press, radio, and television—and now the Internet—children relied on their parents for a greater proportion of their learning. Today, parents need to be acutely aware of what influences their children. The Catholic Church stresses the care of older generations and their interaction with younger generations. Yet the older generations, in some cases, through life insurance, hospitals, savings, and social security, have become increasingly independent of the younger generations.

According to the Catholic church, a redefiniton of the role of the financial provider—the female, the male, or both parents—in a growing nuclear family needs to stress the obligation of service versus the right of precedence. In the end, in this view, a family functions best when it is alert to the need for sacrifice in the name of the family.

See Also

CHRISTIANITY; CHRISTIANITY: STATUS OF WOMEN IN THE CHURCH; FAMILY: RELIGIOUS AND LEGAL SYSTEMS—PROTESTANT; FAMILY LAW; HOUSEHOLDS AND FAMILIES: OVERVIEW; HOUSEHOLDS AND FAMILIES: CENTRAL AND EASTERN EUROPE; MARRIAGE: OVERVIEW

References and Further Reading

Butler, Sarah. 1997. Women's ordination and the development of doctrine. *Thomist* 61(4: October): 501–524.

Carmody, Denis Lardner. 1985. Marriage in Roman Catholicism. *Journal of Ecumenical Studies* 22(1): 28–40.

Davis, Thomas, and Chehan, eds. 1971. *A Catholic dictionary of theology,* Vol. 3. London: Thomas Nelson.

Gaudium et spes. 1996. In Austin Flannery, ed., *The basic sixteen documents of Vatican II: A completely revised translation in inclusive language.* New York: Costello.

Rahnier, Karl, ed. 1975. *Encyclopaedia of theology: The concise Sacramentum Mundi.* London: Burns and Oats.

Note: Following are sources on the Orthodox church.

Chirban, John T., ed. 1983. *Marriage and the family: Medicine, psychology, and religion: New directions, new integrations.* (Series on Medicine, Psychology, and Religion.) Brookline, Mass.: Holy Cross Orthodox.

Cownie, David, and Juliana Cownie. 1992. *A guide to Orthodox belief: Some beliefs, customs, and traditions of the church.* Etna, Calif.: Center for Traditionalist Orthodox Studies.

Fortescue, Adrian. 1977. *The Orthodox Eastern Church.* 3d ed. (Select Bibliographies Reprint Series.) North Stratford, N. H.: Ayer.

Zion, William Basil. 1992. *Eros and transformation: Sexuality and marriage—An Eastern Orthodox perspective.* Lanham, Md.: University Press of America.

Erin Ryan Croddick

FAMILY: Religious and Legal Systems—East Africa

The cultural, social, economic, and religious diversity in east Africa makes generalizations about the position of women problematic. Nevertheless, certain features are common to most groups in east Africa. Throughout the region, the family or kinship group is the most important social and economic unit. The role of women within family groups affects their participation in economic, religious, and legal arenas. Women do achieve status as mothers: within the household and in wider society, for example, a mother of many children is accorded respect and honor. This is particularly true in patrilineal descent systems for the mothers of boys.

Women within the Family

Within the family, women can exert considerable power and authority as sisters, wives, and mothers. They can put pressure on their male relatives in a variety of ways and can threaten to withdraw their labor and support if necessary. Organized women's protest marches are a feature throughout east Africa and are used to make demands on men. In these marches, women effectively go on strike, withdrawing from the household and their responsibilities for food production and child care, leaving men at a loss. The effectiveness of these ritual marches is rooted in the respect given to women as the moral guardians of their families and thus of the community. Among the Iraqw of Tanzania, for instance, precolonial religious beliefs held that the world was made by a female Creator who cared for the Earth and its inhabitants as a mother cares for her children. As mothers, women are viewed as having an intrinsic understanding of their children's needs, and this understanding is said to extend to the wider community. Yet the respect given to women, particularly in precolonial religious beliefs and practices, is not without ambivalence. For example, women are suspected of antisocial behavior such as witchcraft and sorcery more often than men.

While women are accorded respect for their roles as wives, mothers, and important household economic producers, they are rarely given equal decision-making rights or access to land and other economic resources such as livestock. Many east African societies have myths explaining this subordination. Usually, such a myth outlines a scenario in which women, through greed, carelessness, or some other human foible, caused the heavens and earth to be separated. Women are therefore relegated to a secondary role in public affairs.

Influence of Colonialism

In the precolonial era, many communities had rites of passage into adulthood for both boys and girls. During the colonial era, government authorities and missionaries often targeted girls' puberty rituals as practices to be eradicated. This pressure led many communities to abolish practices such as female circumcision, which was seen as an important way to transform girls into women. Group initiation ceremonies to teach girls about becoming women and to celebrate their new status were also abandoned. While most groups' celebratory rituals have been stopped, female circumcision, usually performed privately within the household, continues in several east African societies.

Marriage forms vary throughout east Africa. Polygyny was common in the precolonial era, but Christianity has successfully discouraged the practice in many communities.

Polygyny is still practiced in pastoralist societies such as the Masai or the Turkana, and in communities practicing Islam. Increasingly, however, it is becoming more difficult financially to marry multiple wives. Polygyny in the precolonial era was an important way of increasing both a man's lineage and his wealth. The more children produced, the larger the workforce—and the man's ablity to expand his economic resources. Women's attitudes toward polygyny vary: some women welcome the addition of other women who can help with household labor and child care and also provide companionship, while others feel jealous, threatened, and worried about their own children's rights and status in relation to those of their co-wives.

Influence of Religious Institutions

Many women have found avenues for participation and authority in religious institutions. Official figures on religious affiliation suggest that the population of east Africa is roughly divided in thirds among Christians, Muslims, and indigenous religions, but the intermingling of indigenous beliefs with world religions is widespread, and makes simple affiliation identification extremely difficult. In indigenous religions, women can be found in powerful roles as diviners, healers, and spirit mediums. In these positions, women, through contact with spirits and the divine, provide guidance to individuals and the community. In the Christian community, women are increasingly turning to Protestant and evangelical sects in which they can take on more significant roles than they can in the more orthodox Anglican and Catholic churches. Often, church members form voluntary associations that provide them with financial assistance for education, health, and other needs. While women have found avenues for greater participation in Christian churches, most of the officeholders and decision makers in the churches are men. The churches therefore often emphasize women's family roles and responsibilities to their families above participation in political and economic activities. In Muslim communities, Islamic law supports women's inheritance and formally recognizes their social and economic importance in kin groups. But Islam also constrains their behavior and movement outside the household, emphasizes the importance of veiling or head covering, and prevents women from suing for divorce.

Throughout east Africa, women have been prominent participants in spirit possession cults in which, they believe, they become inhabited temporarily by spirit beings who speak through them. Through spirit possession, women are often able to achieve a status and respect unavailable to them in the household or political economy. Some scholars have attributed the prevalence of women in spirit possession to their often marginal status and the stress under which they live. Many spirit possession cults focus on such female issues as infertility, childbirth, and marital problems. When women are possessed by a spirit, others, including their husbands, must listen to them and placate them, so that the spirit will also be appeased. Dorothy Hodgson reports that among the Masai, the increasing marginalization of women, resulting from modern political and economic structures that enhance male authority, has found expression in spirit possession. When women fall ill and are not cured by conventional means, for instance, Christian women will often diagnose the illness as having been caused by spirit possession. The cure for this illness is to convert to Christianity and rid the women of the spirit. As many Masai men reject Christianity, the churches become gathering places for women; participation in church activities gives women a sense of community and relief from the workload at home (Hodgson, 1997).

In conclusion, women's contributions both to their families' economic well-being and to society are crucial. However, they do not have equal access to roles involving economic and political power. Legal and social reforms are necessary to give women greater rights and access to resources and to end their marginalization. Many women find an avenue to higher status through religious activities, from spirit possession cults to membership in the Christian churches. In many communities, women are viewed as inherently more religious and often more moral than men. This view is often linked to their role as mothers, and it brings them considerable respect.

See Also

FAMILY: RELIGIOUS AND LEGAL SYSTEMS—WEST AFRICA; HOUSEHOLDS AND FAMILIES: SUB-SAHARAN AFRICA

References and Further Reading

Behrend, Heike, and Ute Luig. 1999. *Spirit possession, modernity, and power in Africa.* Madison: University of Wisconsin Press.

Caplan, Pat. 1989. Perceptions of gender stratification. *Africa* 59 (2): 196–208.

Coquery-Vidrovitch, Catherine. 1997. *African women: A modern history.* Boulder, Col.: Westview.

Grosz-Ngate, Maria, and Omari H. Kokole, eds. 1997. *Gendered encounters: Challenging cultural boundaries and social hierarchies in Africa.* New York: Routledge.

Hafkin, Nancy J., and Edna G. Bay. 1976. *Women in Africa: Studies in social and economic change.* Stanford, Calif.: Stanford University Press.

Hodgson, Dorothy. 1997. Embodying the contradictions of modernity: Gender and spirit possession among Masai in Tanzania. In Maria Grosz-Ngate and Omari H. Kokole, eds., *Gendered encounters: Challenging cultural boundaries and social hierarchies in Africa.* New York: Routledge.

Oboler, Regina Smith. 1985. *Women, power, and economic change: The Nandi of Kenya.* Stanford, Calif.: Stanford University Press.

Robertson, Claire, and Iris Berger, eds. *Women and class in Africa.* New York: Africana.

Katherine Snyder

FAMILY: Religious and Legal Systems— Islamic Traditions

The family laws of most Muslim countries remain rooted in or intermixed with Islamic systems of personal law, although most of these countries derive their general legal codes from other sources.

During the past two decades or more, there has been a move across the Muslim world to redefine or further refine personal law in religious terms. This trend has resulted from a global Islamic revival, in which the thrust of the fundamentalists has been to identify the private sphere as the essence of a common Muslim identity. Increasingly, Muslim states have succumbed to this pressure, because patriarchal and fundamentalist discourses are in harmony on the issue and because redefining personal law in religious terms is a strategy that serves to appease the fundamentalists. Even progressive, socialist, and secular Muslim states have made major concessions, and many non-Muslim states have sought to accommodate the demands of their Muslim communities. Apart from the erosion of women's personal rights, these developements are also beginning to affect women's civic, political, cultural, and economic rights.

In the Muslim family code, there are some commonalties in the overall conceptualization of the rights and responsibilities of the family members, but there is also tremendous diversity in the actual translation of these concepts into concrete laws and practices. The result—discrediting the myth of a uniform religious family code across all Muslim nations—is a widely disparate system of status and allocation of rights, which particularly affects the position of women. This diversity is a consequence of many different factors: the dominant school of thought or sect in a country; interpretations of the law by scholars or jurists; the political history of the country; and, largely, the customary laws and cultural traditions that prevail.

Family Law in Relation to Marriage and the Family

Since the family in Islam is closely interlinked to marriage, the bulk of family law concerns marriage and the relationship between husband and wife. Another large portion concerns the relationship between parents and children, and it is primarily in the areas of custody and inheritance that other relationships are specifically addressed, whether the people in these relationships are considered in economic terms (as heirs) or as persons capable of undertaking the guardianship of minor children. Although the concept of family in Islam is placed within the wider framework of the family clan, the relationships addressed in detail are those of the nuclear family.

By and large, all Islamic schools of thought, scholars, and jurists, and all Muslim nations, maintain that equality between men and women is a basic principle, but their perception of "equality" is often vastly different from the widely recognized preceptions of this concept. Within the patriarchal parameters—the male is automatically recognized as the head of the family, that is, the maintainer, protector, final decision maker, and natural guardian of the children—women are said to be equal, but with a "different" social role according to their nature and abilities; or they are said to be more than equal in that they have a right to be protected and maintained. This limiting concept of equality is justified as being necessary to a moral system for the benefit of society and future generations. Equality as widely understood is, in fact, declared as injustice to women, militating against their natural functions and denying them the care to which they are entitled.

This concept has a direct impact on the lives of women in all Muslim societies. First, women's rights are regarded as protections or favors, and this ensures women's dependent, subordinate status. Second, in the understanding and interpretation of religious texts, most of the provisions favorable to women are seen as moral injunctions, rarely translated into enforceable rights. Third, this view of equality ensures that some form of control over women is always maintained, whether directly (for example, by requiring a husband's permission for a woman to travel or work) or indirectly (by making it simple for a husband to divorce his wife at will without providing for her financial security).

Laws Affecting Women in the Muslim World

Although a detailed comparison is impossible, it is interesting to examine some of the critical issues of concern to women to get an overview of the range of interpretations across the Muslim world.

Child marriage is prevalent in many of the Muslim countries, with the legal age of marriage always being younger for girls than for boys. The variations include age of puberty, 10, 13, 16, and 18.

Consent to marriage is acknowledged as a basic requirement in what is essentially a civil contract, but whereas some countries consider a thumbprint, vocal assent, or signature an indication of consent, others consider any sign of consent (including crying) as sufficient, and a few regard the consent of the guardian as sufficient or even essential.

Polygamy has rarely been banned (Turkey being an exception), though attempts have been made to curb the practice by making it subject to conditions, permission, judicial review, or formal procedures.

The absolute, unconditional right of divorce is considered the exclusive right of men, to be exercised at will and with ease; and this remains the law in many countries. Only one or two countries have taken away this absolute right and made it conditional or delegated it to the wife, subject to agreement of the husband; but some have imposed conditions or established procedures to curb the irresponsible exercise of the right. Many countries have made it possible for a women to obtain a dissolution of a marriage, subject to some form of judicial review, on grounds ranging from narrow to very liberal.

Spousal support, or maintenance, during marriage is considered a husband's responsibility, but views on maintenance after dissolution of a marriage have varied. In most Muslim countries the right to maintenance after divorce is restricted to the period of *iddat*, the waiting period. A few have extended it beyond this period or provided for the wife's right to live in the marital home. Still others have tried to give the wife rights in common marital property.

Almost universally, the father is regarded as the natural guardian of the children,, but there are major variations in rights to custody, dependent also on the sect of the father. In principle, the mother is entitled to custody of the children in their early years, with the ages differing for boys and girls, after which custody passes to the father. In some countries the welfare of the child has been made the primary consideration, and religion is also considered within this framework. In other countries specific ages have been fixed after which the right of custody

passes to the father—for example, age 2 for boys and 7 for girls, 7 and 13, 6 and 10, 7 and until marriage, and so on.

In matters of inheritance the general principle is that females get half the share of males, with variations in terms of daughters' entitlement if there are no sons.

The Power of Custom and Tradition

Even where there are laws or codes favorable to women, customary laws and traditions usually take precedence over religions or statutory law. Moreover, inadequate safeguards and procedures, as well as prevailing social attitudes, also ensure that the laws are rarely enforced. Where plural legal systems operate, men may find it convenient to take advantage of whichever system suits them best. For example, in Pakistan customary law is used to deny women's inheritance rights, religious traditions are used to pronounce oral divorce, and codified statutory law is used to deny the divorce if the wife wants to remarry or makes financial demands. Many of the progressive interpretations of earlier decades were changing in the climate of revivalism of the late 1990s.

Nowhere in the Muslim world is there absolute equality for women, conceptually or in practice. Moves toward incorporation of Muslim personal law have been extremely detrimental to women's rights. The existing patterns are rearranging themselves kaleidoscopically; even countries with similar backgrounds are responding in very different ways, according to their own circumstances. How these pattern eventually resolve will depend on a number of factors: the political and economic stability of a country; the development of its democratic and political institutions; the strength of its women's rights and human rights movements; and the degree of the state's commitment to the issue of women's equality.

One major result of the global debates on the impact of fundamentalism is that Muslim women have begun at least to talk and learn about the issue and to question some of its premises. A fairly large number of women have become members of orthodox groups and are trying to make a space for themselves within the limited positions available to them. Some women have started the process of reinterpreting the Qur'an from a feminist perspective to establish women's equality. Some women are fighting for equality in accordance with international standards of human rights. Secular in their approach, they are fighting the hardest battle, as they challenge not only orthodoxy but all forms of patriarchal oppression.

See Also

FEMINISM: MIDDLE EAST; FEMINISM: NORTH AFRICA; FUNDAMENTALISM: RELIGIOUS; HOUSEHOLDS AND FAMILIES: MIDDLE EAST AND NORTH AFRICA; ISLAM; MARRIAGE: REGIONAL TRADITIONS AND PRACTICES; PERSONAL AND CUSTOMARY LAWS

References and Further Reading

Abul A'ala Maudoodi, Maulana. 1983. *The laws of marriage and divorce in Islam.* Kuwait: Islamic.

Al-Hibri, Azizah, ed. 1982. *Women and Islam.* New York : Pergamon.

Espito, J. L. 1982. *Women in Muslim family law.* Syracuse, N.Y.: Syracuse University Press.

Kandiyoti, Deniz. 1988–1989. Women and Islam. In *Women living under Muslim laws.* Dossier 5/6.

Lucas, M. A. Helie. 1993. The preferential symbol for Islamic identity: Women in Muslim personal laws. In *Women living under Muslim laws.* Dossier 11/12/13.

Shaheed, Farida. 1993. On laws, customs, and stereotyping. In *Women living under Muslim laws.* Dossier 11/12/13.

Shehab, Refiullah. 1986. *Rights of women in Islamic Shariah.* Lahore, Pakistan: Indus.

Shahla Zia

FAMILY: Religious and Legal Systems—Judaic Traditions

Jewish family law is based on *Halakhah,* the system of law and ritual understood by fundamentalists and orthodox Jews to apply God's will to specific life situations. *Halakhah* is itself based on sacred texts; exegitical and legal literature, including the Torah, Mishnah, and Talmud; and more recent commentaries. Laws and interpretations of spousal relations reflect changing socioeconomic and political conditions of Jewish communities and the position of women ranging from tribal pastoral nomadism 5000 years ago to diaspora communities in medieval Europe, north Africa, and the Middle East under Christian and Muslim hegemony. At the dawn of the twenty-first century, some Jewish feminists, including Orthodox feminists, challenge women's position in family law as violating universal human rights.

In the diaspora, adherence to *Halakhah* is the voluntary act of the individual who chooses to belong to a believing community and so puts himself or herself under the control of religious courts in matters of personal status. A believing community submits to the rulings of its own religious courts in matters of family law. Men control religious courts. In Israel, the state relegates personal status laws to courts of each recognized religious community: Jewish, Muslim, Christian, Druze. The fundamentalist National Rabbinic Council controls family law for all Jewish citizens. Some Israeli feminists and some Reform, Conservative and Orthodox rabbis, consider the council to be seriously misogynist. Many believe that Israel should both recognize alternative forms of Judaism and develop a civil code for personal status laws.

In Jewish tradition, an unmarried adult is incomplete. Endogamous marriage and childbearing are religious duties. Codified laws govern such social and ritual issues as acceptable marriage partners, the marriage contract, marital relations and responsibilities, divorce, widowhood, and remarriage. Duties incumbent upon parents and children are specified. Laws set patrilineal inheritance of property through fixed degrees of relationship. New religious codes have been written in Israel for adoption of children, for surrogate motherhood, and for using ovum transplant and artificial insemination technologies.

Codified law states that a child who is born of a Jewish mother is a Jew; an unmarried woman's child is illegitimate. These are the only matrilineal elements. All other laws reflect patriarchal control of the wife by the husband, her legal inferiority, and her position as property. Laws make a woman legally dependent on the husband or his family. The man write a *ketuba* (marriage contract). In the marriage ceremony under the *huppa* (canopy), the groom gives the bride a gold ring, a symbol of his acquisition.

Gender segregation and gender specific roles characterize the religiously observant. The wife is enjoined as part of her duty to sanctify the home by a cooking style which maintains *kashrut* (dietary laws). She ushers in the sacred day of rest, the Sabbath, by saying a prayer while lighting candles. Highly Orthodox and fundamentalist Jewish women observe a code of modest dress, covering the hair and wearing clothing that covers the arms and covers the legs to mid-calf. Feet must be stockinged. The observance of *nidda* is required. *Nidda* involves taboos against contact with the husband during and two weeks after menstruation and childbirth (which are considered unclean states) and rituals of purification in the *mikveh,* the ritual bath, to permit contact again. Fundamentalists prohibit birth control. Bounded communities of fundamentalists marry young and have, typically, very large families. Ideally, the husband spends his waking hours studying holy texts. To realize this cultural ideal, the wife is involved in the secular world, sometimes earning the family's living and tending to its needs.

Specific laws violate women's human rights. Married partners who want a divorce must have a *get*—a religious divorce. A divorcee cannot remarry without a *get,* which the husband alone has the right to give. With the permission of the religious court, a man can marry another woman if his wife refuses to agree to the *get;* but a woman whose husband refuses to give her the *get* can never remarry or bear legitimate children. She is an *aguna* (plural, *agunot*), chained to her husband. The husband cannot be compelled to grant a *get* against his will. For Jewish Israelis and for the diaspora communities of voluntary believers, this situation results in the chaining of thousands of women.

The *yebum* (levirate) is legal and is another violation of women's human rights. A *yevama* (childless widow) is supposed to marry her late husband's brother, the *levir.* If he is under age, she must wait until he reaches the age of 13 and undergoes the *bar mitzvah,* the ceremony that marks him as an adult for ritual purposes. If she does not want to marry him, she must undergo a *halisa* (release ceremony). She (like the divorced woman) is chained. He is, however, in control. He may refuse to undergo the ceremony, or he may demand a payment, or he may not be found. She cannot remarry unless she undergoes this ceremony.

Another violation of women's human rights occurs if the husband disappears with no physical evidence of his death and no witnesses to his death. In this case, too, his wife is chained. Among a chained woman's problems is the fact that, should she become pregnant by a man who is not her husband, her child is a *mamzer,* a bastard. A *mamzer* is not permitted to marry a Jew, nor can his or her descendants until the end of time.

The International Coalition for *Aguna* Rights and the International Jewish Women's Human Rights Watch work to free chained women. A few modern orthodox rabbis and feminist study groups and institutes in Israel and the diaspora have analyzed holy texts to develop new interpretations for men to use in rabbinic courts on behalf of chained women. Women who pass qualifying examinations are now permitted to plead on behalf of wives in a few religious courts. As long as *Halakhah* remains as it is, however, the basic disadvantage for women cannot be redressed.

In assimilating modern western culture and rejecting the notion that codified law is revealed by God and cannot be changed, the Conservative denomination interprets some codified laws liberally and drops others. Gender bias remains, however. The Reform denomination has made women equal to men by eliminating codified law. Reform customs violate Orthodox precepts, by defining a Jew as someone born of a Jewish father, and by performing interreligious and same-sex marriages. Feminism is most evolved in the Reform and Reconstructionist denominations, where newly created prayers and ceremonies celebrate female life cycle events.

See Also

FEMINISM: JEWISH; JUDAISM; MARRIAGE: REGIONAL TRADITIONS AND PRACTICES; PERSONAL AND CUSTOMARY LAWS; SACRED TEXTS

References and Further Reading

Biale, Rachel. 1984. *Women and Jewish law: An exploration of women's issues in Halakhic sources.* New York: Schocken.

International Jewish Women's Human Rights Watch. E-mail: <sshenhav@internet-zahav.net>.

Riskin, Shlomo. 1989. *Women and Jewish divorce: The rebellious wife, the Agunah, and the right of women to initiate a divorce in Jewish law: A Halakhic solution.* New York: Ktav.

Schneider, Susan Weidman. 1985. *Jewish and female: Choices and changes in our lives today.* New York: Touchstone.

Schochtman, Eliav. 1995. The status of woman in marriage and divorce judgments. In F. Raday, C. Shalev, and M. Liban-Kooby, eds., *Women's status in Israeli law and society.* (In Hebrew.)

FAMILY: Religious and Legal Systems—Native North America

In many aboriginal tribes in North America, family—in whatever form—was the nucleus around which other social institutions, such as religion and law, exsisted. It is in the family that ethical systems first surface, as children learn guideposts for acceptable social behavior. This fact is highlighted, for example, in the precontact Cheyenne native life.

In this Algonkian-speaking Plains group, children learned proper behavior in an extended family, which included many parental surrogates, both female and male, who were intent on producing competent men and women. For example, if a boy threw a rock at the lodge of a religious leader in which the sacred icons resided (Sacred Arrows or Medicine Hat), the child underwent a ceremony performed by the religious practitioner. This purified the boy and protected him from harm. It also instilled responsible behavior and made the child aware of the consequences of unacceptable behavior. Mothers and fathers, as well as other adults, explained why group harmony was so essential for a smoothly operating camp circle. In these small-scale societies, religion and "law-ways" were embedded in families with considerable female authority. Shame brought on the family also was used as a means of social control.

Legal systems were not codified but tied to supernatural sanctions and punishments. They were based on oral traditions passed from mother to daughter as well as from father to son and—more explicitly—enacted in daily life. Children were inspired to grow up to be good Cheyenne. Guidelines for proper behavior were ingrained through cultural transmission. Harmonious interpersonal relationships were a desired norm, and legally women had considerable autonomy.

In the increasingly litigatious society of twentieth-century North America, one's comprehension of unwritten legal systems may be difficult. The Cheyenne believed in a supreme being, called *Heammawihio* (Wise One Above); another supreme being lived underground. Both were beneficent. The four cardinal directions also were sacred, and pipe offerings were made to them. The powers inherent in these beings were invoked in times of trial in extracting the truth from individuals, smoking the pipe indicated truthfulness.

Individual rights were respected, but the welfare of the group was important for cultural survival. In the governance system, there was a council of 44 chiefs composed of four principal chiefs and 40 who represented a constituency of at least 12 families. Females had equal access to these men's help and intervention, and presentation to the council. The will of the people was a powerful force in the selection of these representatives. The desired personal characteristics of a leader were bravery, generosity, and compassion, as well as being a fair and just decision maker. As a Cheyenne saying goes, "He cares for the elderly, widows, and orphans." Besides being a mediator, he was expected to be able to live an exemplary life. If he transgressed in any way, he was removed by the consensus of the group, expressed through their own chiefs.

In addition, warrior societies acted as primary policing units that enforced the decisions of the council. The first duty of these societies, however, was to protect the nation from enemies. There are accounts of the warrior societies whipping braves who charged buffalo herds before the main body of hunters. This action endangered the welfare of the entire group and might deprive the entire tribe of a year's supply of protein.

The general pattern of informal law-ways was discussion of issues and careful weighing of all aspects, which resulted in a consensus. Protocol and respectful interaction were clearly enunciated. When the council reached a decision, the camp herald rode around the village to announce it.

The four major chiefs usually served for 10 years; their replacements were chosen by tribal consensus. In some rare cases, a son, if competent, might follow in his father's chiefly role. When the tribe assumed yearly nomadic travels, the sacred tribal icons in their midst all walked in reverence. Very seldom were these icons invoked in secular settlements. As in many tribal societies, this form of governance and belief system was attributed to the culture hero *Motsiiu*, the man who also brought the buffalo.

Ethnographic data on North American natives reveals the interrelatedness of legal and belief systems and social organizational features, which were functional in the lifeways of these peoples. In most cases, women's rights were encompassed within the spiritual and legal realms. Gender equity was most important in all groups. Both genders were viewed as important to group survival. Women had a definite place in rituals. Their decision making, however, was somewhat muted. In Lakota society, the culture bearer for regulating proper behavior was the White Buffalo Calf Woman, who brought the seven sacred rites, which dictated the connection between belief and moral codes. Yet the emphasis on the Lakota as a "warrior" society has diminished feminine power. Personhood—male and female—was guided by proper enactment of "law-ways." The Iroquois Confederacy, a matrilineal group, had clan mothers, who chose the sachem (political leaders)—the legal regulators. They, in turn, were guided by female elders called the Faith Keepers.

Native North America was culturally diverse. Each system of law and religion, therefore, must be seen in the context of a distinctive group. Many native belief systems persist at the beginning of the twenty-first century and are being enhanced by cultural revitalization efforts of Native North Americans.

See Also

HOUSEHOLDS AND FAMILIES: NATIVE NORTH AMERICA; MATRILINEAL SYSTEMS; TRADITIONAL HEALING: NATIVE NORTH AMERICA

References and Further Reading

Black Elk, Nicholas. 2000. *Black Elk speaks*. As told through John G. Neihardt. Lincoln: University of Nebraska Press.

Erwin, Lee. 1994. *The dream seekers*. Norman: University of Oklahoma Press.

Grinnel, George Bird. 1923, reprinted 1973. *The Cheyenne Indians*. Vols. 1 and 2. Lincoln: University of Nebraska Press.

Hall, Robert. 1998. *The archeology of the soul*. Urbana: University of Illinois Press.

Llewellyn, Karl N., and E. Adamson Hoebel. 1941. *The Cheyenne way: Conflict and case law in primitive jurisprudence*. Norman: University of Oklahoma Press.

Moore, John H. 1987. *The Cheyenne nation: A social and demographic history*. Lincoln: University of Nebraska Press.

Wallace, Anthony F. C. 1966. *Religion: An anthropological view*. New York: Random House.

Walker, James R. 1980. *Lakota belief and ritual.* Ed., Raymond J. DeMallie and Elaino A. Jahner. Lincoln: University of Nebraska Press.

Beatrice Medicine

FAMILY: Religious and Legal Systems—Protestant

Protestantism has long been closely connected with the nuclear family in which husband and wife, united by love, produce and nurture children. In the Protestant scheme there may be close ties to extended family as well, but the emphasis is on the married pair and their offspring. This "Protestant" family is explained by historical circumstances: its rise during the Reformation coincided with the growing importance of romantic love in western culture. In contrast, Roman Catholicism has never been so closely identified with the nuclear family. Most strikingly, Catholicism created alternative, valued roles for men and women as celibates living in monasteries and convents, whereas the Protestant reformers rejected the cloistered life, sometimes violently. Moreover, Roman Catholicism, already centuries old by the Reformation, had coexisted with varied concepts of marriage; for instance, the institution was often considered chiefly a contractual relationship between families.

Protestantism's close identification with the family of marriage has had both parochial and universalistic implications. Insofar as the European (and later North American) family has been a product of western culture, its transmission to minority peoples—voluntarily and otherwise—has been an instrument of cultural dominance, especially during the most intense periods of missionary activity, the nineteenth and early twentieth century. On the other hand, at times when the family has been a metaphor for divine love and caring, it has been a force for universalism: at best all peoples become brothers and sisters in a vast human family. At the least, one's neighbors and even strangers in a set geographical area become objects of concern and solicitude, members of a smaller "family."

In this same contradictory pattern, the Protestant family has had varied effects on women; it has both circumscribed them in private spheres and also opened channels by which they could enter the public arena. On the one hand, Protestantism coexisted fairly comfortably with the viewpoint, particularly strong in the nineteenth century, when the Napoleonic Code was at its most prestigious, that married women had scant legal or civil existence apart from their husbands. Property belonged to husbands, as did the right to enter into contracts; legally the man had the power of decision over the children. Among scripture-oriented Protestants, biblical texts describing the husband as head of the family reinforced this subordination. In addition, Protestant theocracies have usually legislated conservatively in regard to women. Generally, then, Protestantism supported the legal and cultural status quo, though sometimes moderating its most repressive effects.

On the other hand, Protestantism contained a stubborn streak of individualism and a recurring antiauthoritarianism that aided women's challenges to common assumptions about their civil incompetence. Women won political and civil rights in Protestant Europe, Canada, and the United States decades before achiving them in Catholic nations, though religion was hardly the only reason for this difference (Sineau, 1994). Also, the pervasive designation of "family" as a metaphor for God's love for the wider human community gave women the opening they needed to regard the whole world as their "household." Thus by the late nineteenth century, with the acquiescence of their churches, women had taken up "municipal housekeeping" and were demanding the vote, not because it was their "natural right," but because it would improve their ability to be mothers to the world. Under the guise of housekeeping, women embarked on a number of reforms both rural and urban, domestic and international.

Similar paradoxes accompanied Protestant women's efforts in foreign and home missions. Women missionaries, armed with considerable prestige, urged a largely white, middle-class, culturally determined model of marriage and child rearing on other cultures. Asian and African women sometimes took inspiration from those forms, but combined them with their own cultural ideas to come up with new social visions.

Perhaps the most complex example of the link between Protestantism and the family is found in the long history of African-Americans in the United States. Given the numerous cruelties inflicted on the black slave family, emancipated slaves had every reason to cherish marriage and their families. Black Baptists and Methodists and later Pentecostals drew upon Protestant values to build up strong middle-class black families. However, the multiple injuries of racism often made the attainment of middle-class respectability problematic. Most notoriously, unemployment and the vagaries of the welfare system have helped separate many black men from their families. Judgments of the black family in the late twentieth century varied. Some saw widespread family disintegration and a "culture of poverty," especially in the inner cities. Others celebrated poor families sustained by strong mothers and grandmothers; vibrant, supportive black churches; and all sorts of creative, extralegal family variants, such as extended families and "fictive kin," stand-in "aunts" and "grandmas" not related by blood.

The identification between Protestantism and the traditional family, though subjected to challenges through the decades since the Reformation, survived with its cultural authority relatively intact until the social revolutions of the twentieth century. It even weathered the social rebellions of the 1920s (in part by condemning them, especially in the case of the fundamentalists; in part by small concessions). The turbulence of the 1960s called for deeper soul-searching by Protestants. Families come in multiple forms, single parent, blended, multicultural, and homosexual; sexuality is no longer contained within marriage; and fewer and fewer mothers are full-time housewives. As a result there is confusion about families in Protestantism: some churches welcome single mothers but not gays or lesbians in their definitions of "family"; some wonder if judgments about sexual morality ought to be situational rather than rule-governed. Some conservative evangelicals insist upon the traditional family core (two parents, one a provider, the other a mother and housekeeper), whatever the practical contradictions involved in their ranks. In the midst of the confusion and uncertainty, the sense of the sacred in family life, however defined, becomes fainter. It may be that a new theology of the family, or of the household, is even now in the making.

See Also

FAMILY: RELIGIOUS AND LEGAL SYSTEMS—CATHOLIC AND ORTHODOX; HOUSEHOLDS AND FAMILIES: NORTH AMERICA

References and Further Reading

Airhart, Phyllis D., and Margaret Lamberts Bendroth, eds. 1996. *Faith traditions and the family*. Louisville, Ky.: Westminster/John Knox.

Ammermann, Nancy Tatom, and Wade Clark Roof, eds. 1995. *Work, family and religion in contemporary society*. New York and London: Routledge.

Higginbotham, Evelyn Brooks. 1993. *Righteous discontent: The women's movement in the black Baptist church, 1880–1920*. Cambridge, Mass.: Harvard University Press.

Hill, Patricia Ruth. 1985. *The world their household: The American foreign missions movement*. Ann Arbor: University of Michigan Press.

Lamberts Bendroth, Margaret. 1993. *Fundamentalism and gender, 1875 to the present*. New Haven: Yale University Press.

Lindley, Susan Hill. 1996. *"You have stept out of your place": A history of women and religion in America*. Louisville, Ky.: Westminster/John Knox.

Sineau, Mariette. 1994. Law and Democracy. In Francoise Thebaud, ed. 1994. *A history of women: Toward a cultural identity in the twentieth century*. Cambridge, Mass.: Harvard University Press.

Virginia Lieson Brereton

FAMILY: Religious and Legal Systems—Southern Africa

The African family today reflects changing socioeconomic structures and relations over time and space. At one extreme it is portrayed as an extended family linking indeterminate kinship groups and creating communal rights and obligations; at the other extreme lies the basic nuclear unit. Developments in Africa facilitated by state policies and religion indicate a tendency toward the hegemony of the nuclear family. However, there is no conclusive evidence that nuclear-family living is inevitable. In fact, traditionalists point to the continued importance of the extended family, while researchers studying households are coming to terms with increasing numbers of single or female-headed households.

Overview

Introduced religious and legal institutions have created multiple systems for regulating family relations. While much of north Africa and small pockets of west, east, and southern Africa are governed by Islamic law and tradition, the rest of sub-Saharan Africa is Christian. Although Christianity has largely replaced the traditional African gods, many of its teachings are not fully observed. Beliefs in witchcraft persist, and social rituals and practices such as initiation ceremonies and polygyny are common. Traditional and customary rules play a definite role in regulating private issues such as inheritance and succession, marriage, divorce, child custody, and access to and control over resources within the family. These rules, which are gendered, differ according to whether kinship and family organization follow the bilateral, matrilineal, or patrilineal system. Under the matrilineal systems commonly found in central Africa, kinship allegiance and inheritance are traced through the maternal line—for example, the maternal uncle (Hay and Stichter, 1995). Although patriarchy prevails, women in the matrilocal matrilineal system enjoy some security in that they need not move to their husband's village upon marriage; in the event of a divorce, women and their kin retain custody over their children. Under the patrilineal system, inheritance and succession from father to son is predominant, and kinship relations are traced through the male line. This is the most prevalent system in sub-Saharan Africa and is virtually the norm among southern African societies.

Southern Africa

Indigenous southern African women have a history of racial, class, and gender subordination (Walker, 1990). In the precolonial era the basic social structure revolved around a system of control over women and their productive and reproductive capacities. Through the payment of *lobola,* or brideprice, rights over women and their potential offspring were transferred from one kinship group to another. Later contacts with the settler community introduced a new set of patriarchal relations. Initially these contacts with the western gender system were instituted by missionaries who preached emancipation from traditional constraints through Christianity. Christianity discouraged polygamy, the payment of brideprice, and what it viewed as promiscuity among the African populations. Even communal rights and responsibilities were challenged by a new individualism.

Economically, women's role as subsistence agricultural producers was challenged by ideals of middle-class domesticity. This ambivalent position was intensified with the entrenchment of colonial rule, urbanization, migrant wage labor, housewifery, and domestic service. The new social structure encouraged male migration to urban mining centers but barred women. Rural women were thus propelled into the role of de facto heads of households. This situation increased their autonomy but also their burden in providing for their families. When women finally moved to urban areas, they did so as either dependents of male kin (owing to historically created gender-specific housing rights in the urban area) or as independent entrepreneurs often involved in illicit activities and generally viewed as socially inferior and far removed from the accepted Victorian image of the ideal woman. The creation of sizable numbers of independent professional women respected in their own right was a gradual process.

Women's postcolonial position in the family remains strongly patriarchal at the core. Religion, traditional norms, and formal laws governing family relations all manifest the gendered system in different ways. Women struggle with economically and socially defined roles that vary and even conflict under the different regulatory mechanisms. Introduced general law, which is based on Roman, Dutch, or English legal principles, takes formal precedence over traditional norms in some countries. Initially, colonial rule reserved introduced law for the settler communities and encouraged indigenous populations to develop their traditional system. The introduced law is now available to everyone, so that indigenous women can "choose" to be governed by either the general law or traditional norms. Social and economic constraints often determine this choice even for those who are aware of it. In addition, reinterpretations of traditional norms in response to modern developments, commonly referred to as living laws or people's practices, are widely applied in the resolution of personal issues.

Outlook

Although most formal legal structures have, in recent years, undergone reform intended to eliminate gender-based discrimination, African women's ability to challenge discrimination steeped in traditional practices and extralegal factors has not been developed to any significant level. Small groups of mainly middle-class urban women with links to international feminism have spearheaded the law reforms. However, some of the reforms have led to confusion and in some cases to the marginalization of many women who are either illiterate or unable to comprehend and identify with the theoretical conceptions of feminism.

See Also

DOWRY AND BRIDEPRICE; FAMILY: RELIGIOUS AND LEGAL SYSTEMS—EAST AFRICA; FAMILY: RELIGIOUS AND LEGAL SYSTEMS—WEST AFRICA; HOUSEHOLDS AND FAMILIES: MIDDLE EAST AND NORTH AFRICA; HOUSEHOLDS AND FAMILIES: SOUTHERN AFRICA; HOUSEHOLDS AND FAMILIES: SUB-SAHARAN AFRICA; MARRIAGE: REGIONAL TRADITIONS AND PRACTICES; POLYGYNY AND POLYANDRY

References and Further Reading

Coquery-Vidrovitch, Catherine. 1997. *African women: A modern history.* Boulder, Col: Westview.

Hay, Margaret Jean, and Marcia Wright, eds. 1992. *African women and the law: Historical perspectives.* Boston: Boston University Papers on Africa.

Hay, Margaret Jean, and Sharon Stichter, eds. 1995. *African women south of the Sahara.* 2nd ed. New York: Longman.

Mapetla, Matselitso, Anita Larsson, and Ann Schlyter. 1998. *Changing gender relations in southern Africa: Issues of urban life.* Roma, Lesotho: Institute of Southern African Studies.

Ncube, Welshman, and Julie Stewart, eds. 1995. *Widowhood, inheritance laws, customs, and practices in southern Africa*. Harare: Women and Law in Southern Africa Research Project.

Stewart, Julie, and Alice Armstrong, eds. 1990. *The legal situation of women in Southern Africa*. Harare: University of Zimbabwe Publications.

Vuyk, Trudeke. 1991. *Children of one womb: Descent, marriage and gender in central African societies*. London: Centre of Non-Western Studies, Leiden University.

Walker, Cheryl. 1990. *Women and gender in southern Africa to 1945*. Cape Town: David Philip; London: James Currey.

Maggie Mulela Munalula

FAMILY: Religious and Legal Systems— West Africa

Until the coming of colonialism in the late nineteenth century, religious and legal systems in most societies in west Africa were closely intertwined with political and social institutions. Connections existed between the sacred and the secular, and the sphere of religion was also legal and sometimes merged in one person or institution. Although men were generally preeminent, principles of gender complementarity operated and allowed each gender to manage its own affairs and to have its own gods and deities. Except in areas of northern Nigeria, Mali, Senegal, and Niger, where Islam had strongly influenced social, political, and cultural institutions and profoundly altered feminine behavior and gender roles, women could play specific and important roles in government, culture, and politics and acted to protect their interests in society.

In many societies, women married in their own right, were entitled to divorce, and could summon a husband before a tribunal where they could get a fair hearing. Women held a variety of interests in land, formed cooperative labor groups and mutual help associations, traded, and managed their own capital and profits as they saw fit. They could practice medicine in their natal villages and effectively promote order and resolve disputes.

Religion has been an important avenue through which women express themselves and where they exercise considerable power. Religious activities aim at protecting the well-being of society and deal with difficult situations such as conflict, disease, or jealousy between co-wives or marriage partners. Rites of passage mark important changes of status such as birth, puberty, and death, and women are influential as midwives, diviners, healers, and priestesses. They play sig-

nificant roles in childbirth and other rites of passage, although attempts have been made through menstruation taboos and accusations of witchcraft to curb their power. In some societies, women were required to put a curse on anyone who was deemed responsible for an epidemic, a famine, or a drought, and they paraded naked at night to curse. Men who violated the code of conduct were punished by the women's organizations (Strobel, 1984).

Women have a variety of secret societies, associations, and institutions through which they have sought to maintain their power. Among the Mende and Kpelle in Sierra Leone and Liberia, there exist Poro and Sande societies for men and women respectively that regulate social, political, legal, and economic life. These societies have been described by Sylvia Boone (1986) as "a socially consolidating force," and "religion with the power to make life good and to inspire the highest aspiration among its members." Poro and Sande societies introduce members into adulthood through initiation rituals. In the past, the Poro-Sande council was supreme and stopped village quarrels, tried and condemned social criminals, and gave permission to declare war. Poro-Sande represented law, order, and God, and its powers were derived from the association with spirits and other religious manifestations that members sought to control through ceremony, ritual, meditation, medicine, and exclusive contact.

Among the Igbo of Nigeria, women's associations exist at household, village, and clan levels, and they group women according to their social position. The Ikporo-Ani is the association of all the adult women in a village. The Inyemedi is the association of wives and includes all married women. The Umuada is the association of the daughters of the lineage and is made up of married, divorced, widowed, and unmarried women. They are active in matters pertaining to birth, marriage, and funeral ceremonies and are consulted in the family before decisions are taken. They also provide a forum for women's participation in community decision making and in public social and religious issues, as well as serving as an important communication network. In the past, these associations had recognized executive and judicial powers that were binding on every male or female member of the community. Cases affecting women were judged there, and collective decisions were taken and enforced. These associations have allowed women to organize collective public demonstrations to show their disapproval of actions unfavorable to them through group and public ostracism, ridicule, satirical songs, and dances and act as a strong deterrent to male physical and emotional abuse. Women's ultimate recourse is what is referred to as "sitting on" an offender, or going on strike, and this is considered legal by their community (Ogbomo, 1997). These tactics were utilized against the British and their warrant chiefs in what is known as the "women's war of 1929."

Other female institutions among west African peoples include the Omu among the western Igbo; the Iyalode among the Yoruba, also of Nigeria; and the Ohemaa among the matrilineal Akan of Ghana. The Omu is distinguished by her wealth, intellect, and character and is regarded as the "official mother of the society." In the past, she had her own counselors and court, had jurisdiction over women's affairs, regulated the market—the sphere of women in most of west Africa—fixed prices, and held a court of law for women. She also performed rites of propitiation and sacrifices to ensure the welfare of markets and to prevent the occurrence of epidemics and wars. Like the Omu, the Iyalode is a woman chief who is the chosen representative of women in her town. She controlled the markets, settled quarrels among women in her court, and represented women's positions to government on issues affecting women specifically and the town or nation at large. She had her council of subordinate chiefs who exercised jurisdiction over women in matters pertaining to women alone. In contrast to both the Omu and the Iyalode, the Ohemaa is a member of the royal lineage and is the actual or classificatory mother of the chief. It is her right to nominate a candidate to be chief when the position becomes vacant. She sits with the chief on all public occasions and has the constitutional duty to counsel and guide him, and she is the only person who can rebuke the chief in public. She is a member of the council of state and has to be present when important matters are discussed. She has maintained her own court where she hears cases emanating from the market, quarrels between women, and divorce cases where parties appeal to her.

At the end of the twentieth century, new opportunities arose for women through education, trade, and the professions. Some women have founded churches and others play important roles in new institutions of power and state. But for the majority of women in rural areas and towns in west Africa, it is through the associations and institutions previously discussed that they attempt to safeguard their interests in their families and to play significant roles in their communities.

See Also

FAMILY: RELIGIOUS AND LEGAL SYSTEMS—EAST AFRICA; HOUSEHOLDS AND FAMILIES: SUB-SAHARAN AFRICA; POLITICS AND THE STATE: SUB-SAHARAN AFRICA

References and Further Reading

Aidoo, Agenes Akosua. 1981. Asante Queen mothers in government and politics. In Filomina Chioma Steady, ed., *The black woman cross-culturally*, 65–78. Cambridge, Mass.: Schenkman.

Boone, Sylvia. 1986. *Radiance from the waters: Ideals of feminine beauty in Mende art*. New Haven, Conn.: Yale University Press.

Ogbomo, Onaiwu. 1997. *When men and women mattered*. Rochester, N.Y.: Rochester University Press.

Okonjo, Kamene. 1976. The dual-sex system in operation: Igbo women and community politics in midwestern Nigeria. In Nancy J. Hafkin and Edna G. Bay, eds., *Women in Africa: Studies in social and economic change*. Stanford, Calif.: Stanford University Press.

Oppong, Christine, ed. 1983. *Female and male in west Africa*. London: Unwin and Allen.

Strobel, Margaret. 1984. Women in religion and secular ideology. In Margaret J. Hay and Sharon Stitcher, eds., *African women south of the Sahara*. London: Longman.

Takyiwaa Manuh

FAMILY STRUCTURES

Family and Household

In common English parlance the word *family* is used in several different senses: (1) household, domestic group; (2) group consisting of parents and their children, whether living together or not—in a wider sense, all those who are nearly related by kinship or marriage; (3) those descended from a common ancestor—a house, kindred, lineage. However, it has become common in social science to make an analytical distinction between household and family. While the primary characteristic of the household is common residence, that of the family is kinship or genealogical relationship. Thus, families do not always form households, and households are not always composed of families. While a household may include servants and slaves, a family does not. Also, while there can be single-member households, there are no single-member families. Nevertheless, since normally the household is constituted of members having family relationships, and the domestic functions are one of the major functions of the family, the household and the family are intimately related and their studies go together.

Nuclear Family

It was long believed that the nuclear or elementary family, consisting of a man, his wife, and their own children, is a universal social grouping and the unit out of which more extensive family groups are built. It was an object of much theorizing about the family. However, cross-cultural studies have found that the nuclear family is more a feature of modern Euro-American society than a universal reality. Subsequently another view gained ground: the really universal family grouping is the mother and her children, often called the matri-central cell. While some societies add a father to this cell, recognizing the bonds between husband and wife, and father and child, other societies add a brother, without recognizing the husband-wife and father-child bonds. Lévi-Strauss (1969) and his followers have even suggested that the core of family relationships is the brother-sister unit.

The mother-child relation appears to be special because the human infant is part of its mother's body before birth and continues to be dependent on her for a considerable time. While the father-child bond can be denied, the mother-child bond cannot. It is possible that absence of a mother figure during early infancy has adverse effects on child development. However, there can also be nannies, wet nurses, and surrogate and adoptive mothers. In extended family systems child rearing is shared by several women and even men. Childbearing and child rearing practices very widely between cultures. Consequently, the cultural concept of the mother needs to be carefully distinguished from the biological relation between mother and child. Even the biological relation has begun to be less certain with the development of modern reproductive technologies. Because of these complications there is growing disagreement about considering the mother-child unit as the universal atom of family relationships. Not only that, but the entire search for the universal family grouping seems to be hopeless. A more fruitful approach is to recognize many kinds of families.

The term *nuclear family*, as it is usually defined, provides an insufficient, if not misleading, representation of concrete reality. What is really found is a complex of nuclear-family relationships: husband-wife, mother-son, mother-daughter, father-son, father-daughter, brother-sister, brother-brother, and sister-sister. These relationships are conceived differently in different societies. In particular, there are sharp differences in the concept of most of these relationships in patrilineal and matrilineal systems. Moreover, between societies following either of these systems there would be differences based on law, custom, religion, and so on. For example, in a patrilineal system there can be primogeniture, ultimogeniture, or equal division of property between sons.

Not all nuclear-family relationships will always be found together in a single family unit, for demographic as well as social reasons. Thus there are what are called incomplete, broken, or truncated nuclear families. For example, a couple may not have any child born to them, their child might have died. Either the mother or the father might die prematurely, leaving only one parent and a child or children behind. Husband and wife might separate or divorce, and this might result in a mother-child unit. The number of male and female children may differ from one nuclear family to another. Even when the nuclear family is complete, not all its members may live in a single household. All in all, the term *nuclear family* provides only a genealogical model that could be used as an analytical or taxonomic device but not as an object of theorizing about the family.

Developmental Cycle of the Family

Every family structure needs to be viewed in the context of time. Sociologists and social anthropologists have tried to deal with this temporal dimension with the help of a concept called the development cycle of the domestic group, or the family *life* cycle, or, simply, the family cycle, with its phases of expansion, dispersion (or fission), and replacement. Whether the family's developmental process is really cyclical has been a matter of debate, which has acquired additional salience in view of the emergence of historical studies of the family. It is clear, however, that the family cycle is different from, though vitally affected by, the life-cycle of the individual. The former is a social and the latter a biological process.

In the typical nuclear family system, characterizing modern Euro-American society, the family cycle is short. Normally every child of a couple sets up an independent household at marriage. In fact, the process of dispersion of the parental household might begin even before the children's marriage, because frequently children begin to live separately from parents when they go to college or begin working.

Monogamy and the nuclear family go together. In the case of polygyny or polyandry, a *compound family* is constituted. A family formed by a remarried widow or widower or a divorced person with children from a previous marriage is also called compound. Compound families can sometimes be quite large and complex, and they need not always be household groups.

Extended, Joint, and Stem Families

Large parts of the world, particularly in Asia and Africa, are characterized by the *extended family*. There is no universal agreed definition of this term, partly because of the great variety of such systems and partly because of the complex nature of each such system. Broadly speaking, the extended family is based on an extension of the nuclear family, lineally or collaterally or both. The patrilineal extended family would thus be based on an extension of the father-son or the brother-brother relationship (or both), and the matrilineal extended family on an extension of the mother-daughter or the sister-sister relationship (or both). The extension may go even further. One of the problems in the study of any extended family system is to determine the maximum limit or extension, or, to put it differently, the maximum limit of expansion of the developmental cycle of the family. This limit would also determine the distinction between the extended family and the lineage group, usually defined as the descendants of a known common ancestor through the male line in the case of the patrilineage and of the descendants of a known common ancestress through the female line in the case of matrilineage. The distinction would differ from society to society and, in a large and complex society, between one section of it and another.

The term *extended family*, whether patrilineal or matrilineal, indicates only a genealogical model. The actual extended family system in any society has many dimensions—household group, economic enterprise, ownership and inheritance of property, religious cult, power and authority, and so on. The household is crucial. Every extended-family system has its norms of household formation. For example, the patrilineal Hindus in India follow the patri-virilocal norm. That is, a woman when married leaves her parental home and joins her husband's parental home. If a couple have several sons, they would form, in time, along with their wives and children, a large, complex household. After their parents' death the married sons (brothers) might continue to form a joint household. Among the matrilineal Nayars in southwest India, during premodern times, large, complex households could be formed by a woman, her daughters and sons, and daughters' daughters and sons. The husband-wife and father-child bonds were not relevant for household formation. Husbands and fathers only visited their wives and young children.

In another matrilineal society, the Ashanti of Ghana, both husband-wife bonds and father-child bonds are relevant for household formation. These bonds conflict with the mother-child and brother-sister bonds. Attempts to reconcile this conflict are reflected in household structures:

> The household may be under a male head or a female head. If it is under a female head, it is normally a segment of a matrilineage consisting of the head and her children, her sister and her children, and perhaps her own and her sisters' uterine grandchildren. The household of a male head, on the other hand, may be either a parental family, consisting of a man and his wife or wives and their children, or it may include the head's

> sister and her children as well as his wife and his own children, with, sometimes, the children of his children or of his nieces. (Fortes, 1950 :261)

During their lifetime, individuals shift from one type of household to the other.

One of the variants of the extended family is the *stem family*. If it is patrilineal, as in China and Japan, one son and his wife remain with his parents while other sons set up separate homes. This ensures continuity of the father's line and property. A similar idea can also be found in matrilineal systems, as among the Khasi in northeastern India, where one daughter and her husband remain with her parents and inherit her property while other daughters and their husbands set up separate homes.

In much of southeast Asia, the ambilateral principle is followed. That is, an individual can choose to be a member of either the father's or the mother's birth group. Marriage is ambilocal. That is, either the wife joins her husband's home or the husband joins his wife's home. This flexibility results in extended households and families with a wide variety of members.

The term *joint family* is often used as a synonym of *extended family*, but often its use is restricted to only those extended families composed of two or more married couples. Sometimes it is also used for such a unit irrespective of whether it forms a joint household. Moreover, sometimes it is closely identified with the family systems of the Hindus, and sometimes it is used cross-culturally.

In many societies, extended-family systems are protected by codified laws, and for some systems these laws go back centuries. Nevertheless, most legal systems are concerned with the property-holding group rather than with the household group as such. Frequently, therefore, legal definitions of the word *family* differ from customary definitions. In Hindu law, for example, the term *joint family* is used in a specialized legal sense for a coparcenary or joint-heir property unit.

One complication in the study of the extended-family systems is that nuclear-family households (including the incomplete ones) are found coexisting with extended-family households as part of a single system. By and large, the formation of nuclear-family households is due to contingencies of the developmental cycle, that is, due to deaths and partitions. Moreover, such houholds continue to be part of the extended family as a unit engaged in joint economic activities, holding joint property, participating in joint ritual and ceremonial activities, helping each other in crisis situations, and so on. These nuclear households, therefore, should not be construed as signifying change from the extended-family system to the nuclear-family system, as is sometimes done, although some cases of imitation of the Euro-American nuclear-family ideology do occur.

Family Structures, Social Stratification, and Social Change

One achievement of family studies during the last four decades or so is the movement away from stereotypes to diversity of types. Apart from differences in family structures between regions, religions, and ethnic groups in large societies like China, India, Russia, or the United States, there can be significant differences even in small communities like a village or a city neighborhood. There are usually differences based on social stratification, between the rich and the poor; between landlords, tenants, and landless laborers; between upper castes and lower castes. For example, while landlords tend to live in large joint-family households, laborers tend to live in small nuclear-family households. There can also be differences between strata in the incidence of types of joint families, such as linear and collateral.

Reference has already been made to historical studies of the family. Many of these suffer from conceptual problems as well as problems of data. Nevertheless, they have succeeded in challenging, if not refuting, the widely held theory that industrialization and urbanization in Europe and Asia have led to a shift from the extended-family system to the nuclear system. The assumption of the overwhelming prevalence of the extended-family system in the past is of doubtful validity, if not false. On the other hand, modern sociological and anthropological studies have found that industrialization and urbanization do not necessarily disintegrate the extended family. In fact, such families might help the two processes and thus be strengthened. However, the extended family is increasingly coming under pressure from the modern ideology of individualism and an emphasis on the conjugal bond at the expense of the filial bond.

One function of the family, particularly the extended family, is care of the aged. In the context of the increasing population of the aged all over the world, a major debate is whether the state and other public institutions should take over this function where the family has been performing it, or whether the family should resume this function wherever it has stopped performing it.

Gender Studies and the Family

There was an upsurge in family studies from the perspective of gender over the last two decades of the twentieth century. These studies indicate women's role in the family was neglected in the observations and analyses of many previous scholars. In the study of patrilineal systems, for example, family types were often defined in terms of men alone. The head of the family was assumed to be the man, and female-headed households were ignored. The large-scale data collection systems in many countries were also male-oriented. Furthermore, male social scientists, who were preponderant, saw women mainly from a male perspective.

The extent to which the family affects women's status depends on women's roles in both familial and non-familial social structures. In no society in the world are women totally confined to the home. Nevertheless, most women at times are members of families and, therefore, their gender roles are vitally affected by the family structure. This is an aspect of family studies on which rigorous research is required. The main problem is that men and women are involved in varied relationships and roles in the family—more so in the extended family than in the nuclear family—and not all the roles are always in harmony.

Gender studies of the family have emphasized that all family structures are systems of power and authority: males exercise authority over females in all family structures, though more in some than in others. For example, matrilineal systems are more egalitarian than patrilineal systems, but even a matrilinial system vests considerable power and authority in the mother's brother. Also, it is necessary to recognize that in many family systems women are themselves carriers, if not advocates, of male authority. Whether this is due to conscious male design or to the collective consciousness of the society is a matter of perspective rather than of social scientific truth (for an elaboration of the concept of collective consciousness, see Durkheim, 1958). Moreover, in many families, particularly extended families, women have authority not only over other women but also over men. In other words, female subordination is not universal. To overlook such families would be to overlook reality in favor of ideology.

See Also

FAMILY: POWER RELATIONS AND POWER STRUCTURES; HOUSEHOLDS AND FAMILIES: OVERVIEW; HOUSEHOLDS: FEMALE-HEADED AND FEMALE-SUPPORTED; KINSHIP; MATRILINEAL SYSTEMS; REPRODUCTIVE TECHNOLOGIES; SURROGACY

References and Further Reading

Coale, A. J., L. A. Fallers, M. J. Levy, Jr., M. D. Schneider, and S. S. Tomkins. 1965. *Aspects of the analysis of family structure.* Princeton, N.J. : Princeton University Press.

Collier, Jane Fishburne, and Sylvia Junko Yanagisako, eds. 1987. *Gender and kinship: Essays toward a unified analysis.* Stanford, Calif.: Stanford University Press.

Dube, Leela. 1997. *Women and kinship: Comparative perspectives on gender in south and southeast Asia.* Tokyo: United Nations University Press; Delhi: Sage.

Durkheim, Émile. 1958. *The rules of sociological method.* Glencoe, Ill.: Free Press.

Fortes, Meyer. 1950. Kinship and marriage among the Ashanti. In A. R. Radcliffe-Brown and C. Daryll Forde, eds., *African systems of kinship and marriage.* Oxford: Oxford University Press.

Fox, Robin. 1967. *Kinship and marriage.* Harmondsworth, U.K.: Penguin.

Goode, William J. 1963. *World revolution and family patterns.* New York: Free Press.

Goody, Jack, ed. 1958. *The developmental cycle in domestic groups.* Cambridge: Cambridge University Press.

Laslett, Peter, and Richard Wall, eds. 1972. *Household and family in past time.* Cambridge: Cambridge University Press.

Lévi-Strauss, Claude. 1967. *The elementary structures of kinship.* London: Eyre and Spottiswoode.

Netting, Robert McC., Richard R. Wilk, and Eric J. Arnould, eds. 1984. *Households: Comparative and historical studies of the domestic group.* Berkeley: University of California Press.

Radcliffe-Brown, A. R., and C. Daryll Forde, eds. 1950. *African systems of kinship and marriage.* Oxford: Oxford University Press.

Schneider, David M. 1988. *American kinship: A cultural account.* Englewood Cliffs, N.J.: Prentice Hall.

———, and Kathleen Gough, eds. 1961. *Matrilineal kinship.* Berkeley: University of California Press..

Shah, A. M. 1998. *The family in India: Critical essays.* Delhi: Orient Longman.

———. 1974. *The household dimension of the family in India.* Berkeley: University of California Press; Delhi: Orient Longman.

Yanagisako, Sylvia Junko. 1979. Family and household: The analysis of domestic groups. *Annual Review of Anthropology.* 8:161–205.

A. M. Shah

FAMILY WAGE

Usually, the term *family wage* refers to a wage paid to a man. His wage is called a family wage because it is assumed to be high enough to provide financial support for both him and his family. The complementary assumption is that women earning wages support only themselves. In some countries, such as Australia, the term *family wage* has been used explicitly in wage negotiations; in many countries, however, the concept of family wage has been one of several implicit assumptions in the determination of wages.

Given that women throughout the world bear the primary responsibility for a range of domestic labor and that this labor often ties them to the household, it is not surprising that many women have supported the demand for a family wage. With financial support from a family wage, women could concentrate on their necessary household work. But many women have rejected this concept, arguing that women, too, often need to support their families and that the concept of a family wage puts men in a priviledged position in the labor force. Whatever the merits of the different arguments, it has become clear that the idea of a family wage has often been used to justify men's higher wages.

Although the family wage is often discussed as a historical reality, it seems probable that few men have ever earned enough to provide the entire support for their households. Women have contributed to the family's economic support by growing and selling food; by taking in laundry, boarders, and other people's children; by doing piecework in their homes; and by doing wage work in the market, often on a part-time and irregular basis.

Today, few men would claim that they make a family wage. Increasingly, households require at least two incomes. Indeed, it could be said that dual incomes are the new family wage.

See Also

DOMESTIC LABOR; HOUSEHOLDS: RESOURCES; WORK: EQUAL PAY AND CONDITION

References and Further Reading

Dobb, Maurice H. 1982. *Wages.* (Cambridge Economic Handbooks.) Westport, Conn.: Greenwood.

Douglas, Paul H. 1964. *Theory of wages.* (Reprints of Economic Classics Series.) New York: Kelley.

Juhn, Chinhui. 1996. *Relative wage trends, women's work, and family income.* (AEI Studies on Understanding Inequality.) Washington, D.C.: American Enterprise.

Pat Armstrong

FAMINE

See FOOD, HUNGER, AND FAMINE.

FARMING

See AGRICULTURE.

FASCISM AND NAZISM

Fascism and Nazism are totalitarian political ideologies that attempted to resolve the contradictions of the modern nation-state. Both functioned on an antidemocratic and antipluralistic principle of leadership. The first fascist regime, Benito Mussolini's government in Italy (1922–1945), and the National Socialist (Nazi) regime of Adolf Hitler in Germany (1933–1945) attempted to overcome differences between the classes, as well as those between men and women—and to unite all citizens under the single will of the nation.

Fascism and Nazism differed mainly in that the Italian fascists converged on the nationalist ideal, whereas the German Nazis were driven by fanatic anti-Semitism and the idea of an Aryan *Herrenrasse* or master race. This Aryan race considered itself superior to all other races and ethnic groups, particularly to the Jews, but also to Slavs, Sinti, Roma, and all people of color. This racism held not only these "others" in contempt, but also so-called worthless members of the Aryan race, including the psychically or physically disabled and the socially unacceptable: lesbians, gays, and prostitutes. These people were persecuted during the Third Reich (as the Nazi regime was called); hundreds of thousands were sterilized or killed. The Nazism racism and anti-semitism finally led to the most extensive, systematic mass murder in history: the Holocaust of the European Jews.

The term National "Socialism" indicates that this ideology tried to gain the support of workers and the poor with promises of employment. In fact, the movement emerged at a time when the politics of the left and the right were competing for dominance. Germany's labor movement was very strong at this time, because a high unemployment rate and widespread poverty had led to a political radicalization. At the same time, the Russian socialist revolution was seen as an enormous threat to all western countries. This is evidently one reason why the western powers tolerated the Nazis' seizure of power in Germany. The National Socialists first attacked the communists, the socialists, and the unions. National Socialism brought many workers and poor people to its side by offering jobs and economic stability, while at the same time depriving them of their rights, banning their organizations, and imprisoning and executing their leaders. In this way, National Socialism "resolved" the contradictions between the classes: it fulfilled the interests of the capitalists by destroying the labor movements and fulfilled the workers' interests by providing employ-

ment. It "reconciled" the classes by replacing the workers' anticapitalist sentiments with anti-Semitism. National Socialism drew both workers and the petit bourgeoisie as groups by offering chauvinist fanaticism and an illusion of grandeur.

A similar situation is found with regard to women. On the one hand, women were deprived of their rights to some extent: some were removed from political organizations, universities, and jobs. On the other hand, women received acknowledgment in their new roles under National Socialism. They were virtually worshiped as mothers of the family and as continuers of the race and of the nation. They acquired significance by producing as many children as possible; many women were awarded a *Mutterkreuz* (mother's cross) in gold, silver, or bronze. Women were offered the opportunity to join one of the numerous women's organizations and to devote their life to the *Volk* (the German people) and the *Führer* (the leader, that is, Hitler)—as long as they belonged to the "correct" race and conformed socially and politically. Many women of all ages were fascinated not only by the traditional image of the caring mother, but also by the image of the fighting comrade supporting the men in their struggle. As long as women accepted the "natural" hierarchy of men as leaders, National Socialism allowed them a broader range of activities; eariler, they had been restricted primarily to family affairs. In this sense, many women experienced Nazism as liberation.

Even some feminists believed that they would be emancipated within the Nazi system, by combining feminism with elitism and anti-Semitism. For example, they believed that in German prehistory, women and men were equal until the Jews introduced patriarchy. Therefore, in order to attain political equality for "Aryan" women, they organized themselves against the Jews. In the opinion of these "fascist feminists," only the best Aryan women should attain power. Not surprisingly, fascist feminists were a small group; but in any event their organization was soon prohibited.

The Nazis replaced all preexisting women's organizations with their own, which meant, first of all, that all Jewish and other non-Aryan women were stripped of membership. Some women did protest the prohibition of their organizations, but many did not object to the exclusion of Jewish and non-Aryan women, or to the oppression of women considered racially worthless (Koonz, 1986). This is quite remarkable, since until that time Jewish women had played an important role in the German women's movement. The Jüdische Frauen Bund, with Berta Pappenheim as its charismatic leader, had worked for women's rights, reproductive freedom, support systems for girls and women, and peace; it also fought against anti-Semitism. Alice Salomon, founder of the first college for women in Germany, was designated as chairwoman of the National League of Women and played an important role in international women's organizations. But she had to resign around 1920 because her pacifist and international orientation was considered scandalous by many nationalist German women. The significant differences within the women's movement before National Socialism became so unbridgeable during the Nazi regime that they destroyed all female solidarity.

The issue of gender is an enlightening example of how the Nazis and fascists dealt with the conflict between tradition and modernity. On the one hand, they relied heavily on the ideology of a traditional order—a belief in the natural hierarchy of all beings. To disturb this order was understood as a sin against nature. Thus these ideologies were basically antifeminist. On the other hand, they supported women's significance not only in the family but also for the nation. By the end of the Nazi regime, many women had built professional careers in administration or welfare organizations and many were employees in different branches of industry (Frevert, 1986).

Modernization also took place in mass communications, and in the standardization of mass culture. The fascists and Nazis also attempted to reconcile religion and modernity with a kind of secular belief in the salvation of the people through their sacrifices—analogous to Christian messianism. Here again, although the Nazis opposed the Christian churches and replaced them with a belief in nature, destiny, and the Führer, they had considerable support from the Christian churches. This contradiction can probably be explained by their shared anticommunism and anti-Semitism.

Contemporary social analysis understands these political regimes in Europe during the first decades of the twentieth century much more as a struggle toward modernization than as a throwback to premodern times. They represented, not barbarism replacing civilization, but barbarism within civilization. The Holocaust—an industrialization of murder—makes this connection clear. Baumann (1992) emphasizes that in modern bureaucracy, with its manifold division of labor, responsibility vanishes. The individual is only a tiny piece in a huge machine, and everyone is far removed from the results of his or her contribution. The banality of evil, as Hannah Arnedt put it, reflects a destruction of humanity through the breakdown of relationships between people who are governed by the principles of bureaucracy and efficiency.

A second point revealing Nazism and fascism as phenomena of modernity is the conviction that an entire society can be changed by one idea, by one will. This illusion of grandeur inherent in the modern belief in political ideology transforms systemic thinking into totalitarian thinking. In this respect—though only in this respect—Baumann finds parallels with the socialist system in the Soviet Union, especially the cruelty of Stalinist politics.

The idea that both systems were totalitarian (Arendt, 1951) has been more and more discussed since the downfall of the socialist systems in eastern Europe. We can see similarities in abuses of human rights, in antidemocracy and antipluarity, and even in racism and anti-Semitism. But many commentarors see a fundamental difference between the old fascism and the more recent communism: the socialist system claimed to emancipate the people and to diminish injustice and hierarchy, whereas facism imposed a hierarchal system of elitism based on social Darwinism and a "natural order."

Another type of fascist system was apartheid in South Africa, which can be mainly characterized by its racism against blacks and other people of color, and its failure to decolonize. It was also based on a belief in a natural hierarchal order, but in contrast to the European fascist societies, it did not emphasize the antidemocratic leader. Other fascist movements, such as those in the third world, emphasize their antiwestern and anticolonial ideology. For example, Iran's main conflict seems to be between modernization and traditionalism, particularly when modernity is understood as western supremacy. The question now at hand is, perhaps, whether the different forms of fundamentalism can be described as new forms of fascism when they attempt to solve problems of today with ideologies of yesterday.

See Also

ANTI-SEMITISM; COMMUNISM; FUNDAMENTALISM AND PUBLIC POLICY; SOCIALISM

References and Further Reading

Arendt, Hannah. 1951. *The origins of totalitarianism.* New York: Harcourt Brace.

Baumann, Zygmunt. 1989. *Modernity and the Holocaust.* Ithaca, N.Y.: Cornell University Press.

Frevert, Ute. 1986. *Frauen geschichte: Zwischen brgerlicher Verbesserung und Neuer Weiblichkeit.* Frankfurt.

Kaplan, Marion. 1981. *Die jüdische frauenbewegung in Deutschland: Organisation und Ziele des Jüdischen Frauenbundes 1904–1938.* Hamburg.

FASHION

Koonz, Claudia. 1986. *Mothers in the Fatherland*. New York: St. Martin's.

Birgit Rommelspacher

FASHION

Fashion is usually associated with styles of dress and adornment, but the term is used more generally to describe fleeting cultural changes in any field. As a term and an area of cultural scrutiny, fashion comes into being in the nineteenth and twentieth centuries, with late modernism and its logic of progress and innovation. It is part of the cultural complex of modernism, with its associated areas of print journalism (the glossy magazine), photography, new manufacturing technologies, and internationalism.

Fashion is individual display through ornamentation of the body. Clothing, accessories, hairstyles, body decoration, and textiles emphasize aspects of the body to make them culturally visible. Georg Simmel, writing in 1904, understood fashion as a way of creating a new appearance to mark a person's individuality; he also emphasized the importance of fashion in creating community identity.

Fashion and Social Meaning

Never one of the high arts, fashion was not seriously studied in the past because of its links to the interests of women, its transitory and popular nature, and its association with commercialism. Today, these associations have become its strengths, and scholars of fashion and contemporary culture see fashion as a barometer of social change and a source of social meaning. It is a huge international industry today, from haute couture and its main market in the Middle East oil states to the globalized sweatshop labor of Asia. Western fashion is thus linked to the shifting structures of contemporary capitalism and its social, economic, and aesthetic ramifications. Fashion responds both to its own industry and to a wider social world. Developments in the manufacturing and textile industry, adjacent design fields, and political movements can all influence the appearance of any given fashion. In more exciting moments, fashion's avant-garde edge can seem to reflect, or to create, a zeitgeist or "spirit of the times."

Fashion is a complicated field, because it combines individual choice with market and social restraints. Punk fashion, which appeared in the late 1970s, was partly a response by young people to a depressed economy and a conservative government in Britain (Hebdige, 1979). This subcultural style—worn, ripped T-shirts; safety pins as ornamentation, and Mohawk hairstyles; was quickly incorporated into the mainstream fashion market, initially by Vivienne Westwood.

The complex temporal logic of fashion demands that it disinherit the immediate past while aiming for an originality that can never be achieved. Punk is a good example of how fashion works, in its rejection of the ideal of originality. It shows the components of dress as appropriation of objects from other cultures and fashions.

Historical Background

Fashion differs from *dress* in the way it refers to changing styles over a given period. For example, over the past two hundred years, fashions in male attire have changed very little from the combination of trousers, shirts, and jackets. For women, fashion has been much more diverse, not only in creating new outlines and forms but also in the way clothing has emphasized particular parts of the body, such as the midriff or the back.

Few items of dress escape the vagaries of fashion. The *cheungsam* (*qupao* in Mandarin), which came out of northern China in the early twentieth century, was worn as standard formal dress by Chinese women, particularly from the 1930s to the 1960s. Although the dress changed in length and became tighter-fitting, the "soul of the dress"—the *huaniu*, the knotted button and loops fastened to the collar or lapel—always remained. The cheungsam was subject to fashion in the way it was embroidered and trimmed and in the choice of fabric. In the 1990s, the cheungsam made a reappearance on the western fashion scene.

Initially, fashion was a marker of status and wealth (social and economic) rather than an indicator of gender. From the fourteenth to the seventeenth century, there were sumptuary laws placing restrictions on dress. Throughout history, fashion has been dominated by different countries: sixteenth-century Spain as an economic power; the excess and opulence of Louis XIV's France in the seventeenth and eighteenth centuries; Britain with its industrial power in the nineteenth century. The first half of the twentieth century was dominated by Paris and the haute couture industry until the 1960s, when the British fashion industry was revived with boutiques creating and selling clothes for young people.

Fashion has always been an issue for feminists from the first wave of feminism in the late eighteenth century. Early concerns about fashion were related to the role of women and the restrictive nature of clothing such as corsets and, later, hobble skirts. Restrictive clothing once was seen as a sign that the wearer did not need to work, but today issues about such fashions include concerns about consumption, body type, dieting, and the demands of corporate capitalism. The study of fashion also has drawn attention to other aspects of the industry, such as the influence of the modeling world on the fashionable ideal of slenderness and associated medical conditions such as anorexia nervosa and bulimia.

It is now generally acknowledged that the study of fashion cannot be separated from the study of women's history. Fashion has been understood as a way of establishing identities and attracting attention to political activity. Angela McRobbie (1997) sees the fashion industry as almost wholly feminized in all its aspects, from production through advertising to consumption.

See Also

BODY; COSMETICS; CRITICAL AND CULTURAL THEORY; CULTURAL CRITICISM; CULTURE: WOMEN AS CONSUMERS OF CULTURE; FEMINISM: CULTURAL; POPULAR CULTURE; REPRESENTATION; TEXTILES

References and Further Reading

Blumer, Herbert G. 1968. Fashion. In David L. Sills, ed., *International encyclopedia of the social sciences,* Vol. 5, 341–345. New York: Macmillan/Free Press.

Brydon, Anne, and Sandra Niessen, eds. 1998. *Consuming fashion: Adorning the transnational body.* Oxford: Berg.

Breward, Christopher. 1995. *The culture of fashion: A new history of fashionable dress.* Manchester: Manchester University Press.

Hebdige, Dick. 1979. *Subculture: The meaning of style.* London: Methuen.

McRobbie, Angela. 1997. Bridging the gap: Feminism, fashion and consumption. *Feminist Review* 55 (Spring): 73–89.

Silverman, Kaja. 1986. Fragments of a fashionable discourse. In T. Modelski, ed., *Studies in entertainment: Critical approaches to mass culture,* 108–129. Bloomington: Indiana University Press.

Simmel, Georg, 1971. Fashion. In Donald N. Devine, ed., *On individuality and social forms: Selected writings.,* 294–323. Chicago: University of Chicago Press.

Steele, Valerie, and John S. Major. 1999. *China chic: East meets West.* New Haven, Conn.: Yale University Press.

Wilson, Elizabeth, and Juliet Ash, eds. 1992. *Chic thrills: A fashion reader.* London: Pandora.

Prudence Black

FEMALE CIRCUMCISION AND GENITAL MUTILATION

Female circumcision (FC) is the ritualistic cutting of parts of the external genitals of girls as a rite of passage to womanhood and in preparation for socially defined sexual and reproductive roles. Such operations have also been termed *female genital mutilation* (FGM), because they do substantial anatomical and functional damage. In 1999, an estimated 115 million girls and women in the world had undergone some form of female circumcision, and roughly 2 million women undergo FC/FGM every year.

Geographic Incidence

In modern times FC/FGM is practiced mostly in African countries: Benin, Burkina Faso, Cameroon, Central African Republic, Chad, Cote d'Ivoire, Djibouti, Egypt, Ethiopia, Eritrea, Gambia, Ghana, Guinea, Guinea Bissau, Kenya, Liberia, Mali, Mauritania, Niger, Senegal, Sierra Leone, Somalia, Sudan, Tanzania, Togo, Uganda, and Zaire. In Asia FC/FGM is practiced only by one very small ethnic group, the Bohra Daodi Muslims, in India. The practice is not currently reported in Indonesia or Malaysia, although noncutting clitoral rituals that were common in the past are still practiced by some today. Some reports from Yemen and Oman document selective tribal practice of FC/FGM, but the prevalence of the practice and the type performed in these two countries are not known. In Europe and North America today some physicians perform a male-like circumcision on women who fail to reach orgasm, with questionable outcomes. Other genital cosmetic surgery operations are performed in Europe on adult women who believe that their genitals are abnormal or ugly.

Origin and Modern Practice

In Africa FC/FGM is a cultural, not a religious, requirement. It is practiced by Muslims, by Christians (Catholics, Evangelists, and Orthodox), by one Jewish group, and by followers of indigenous African religions. Many adherents of these religions and sects do not even know about the practice. The most common mistake made about FC/FGM is that it is linked to Islam. Islam does not require FC/FGM, and the vast majority of the world's Muslims do not practice it.

The exact history and origin of FC/FGM are not known. If its current distribution, along a broad belt across central Africa and in the Nile valley, is taken to reflect tribal movement, the intersection of the two lines of prevalence would suggest a focal point of origin around southern Egypt or northern Sudan. This is the area where the practice is most severe. Some writers suggest that the practice was started by the pharaohs, but no conclusive evidence has yet substantiated this hypothesis.

Girls usually undergo circumcision between the ages of 4 and 12, but customs vary. In Uganda, girls aged 15 to 18 who are eligible for marriage display their courage by being circumcised in public. More modern families occasionally circumcise their girls in infancy, but this is very rare. A girl may be circumcised alone or with a group of her relatives or tribal peers. Historically circumcision is part of a series of initiation rituals a girl must go through to become a member of her tribe and to prepare for her role as a woman. With urbanization and increased economic pressures, most of the rituals have faded while circumcision has persisted as a stand-alone event surrounded by ceremonial celebrations.

FGM can take many forms. The most common are: *clitoridectomy*, the partial or total removal of the clitoris; *excision*, the removal of the clitoris and labia minora; and *infibulation*, removal of the labia majora to allow stitching them into a "skin hood" that covers the vagina. Rare forms of FGM involve different forms of incision or stitching around the vagina; these have been reported in Africa and among some indigenous people in other continents.

Because of the sensitive nature of the area of the genitals and its rich blood supply, FGM causes many problems, both physical and psychosexual—which are often long-lasting. Shock, bleeding, infections, cysts, ulcers, fistulae, and infertility are among the more common physical complications.

Social Controversy

African professionals have exposed and criticized the practice of FGM since the 1950s. In the late twentieth century, the growing African women's movement began raising its voice against the practice. The Inter African Committee on Traditional Practices Affecting the Health of Women and Children (IAC) was started by African women following a conference in Dakar, Senegal, in 1984. As of 2000 it had affiliates in most countries where FC/FGM is practiced.

At the same time, the immigration of Africans to Europe, Canada, and the United States extended the possibility of continuation of the practice in the host country, causing anxiety and generating much debate; the state's obligation to protect children and observe universal standards of human rights was juxtaposed against calls for cultural tolerance and acceptance of social diversity. Organizations started by immigrant women in opposition to FC/FGM include Foundation for Women's Health Research and Development and the London Black Women Health Action Project in the United Kingdom, Groupe Femmes pour l'Abolition des Mutilations Sexuelles in France, Women's Health in Women's Hands in Canada, and Research Action and Information Network for Bodily Integrity of Women in the United States. Many other women's organizations in Africa dealing with women's health and rights are becoming active in fighting against FC/FGM, as they consider it a violation of reproductive and sexual rights and a health hazard.

Because of the severe nature of this practice to control women's sexuality and reproduction and because it occurs primarily in Africa, it has generated much controversy. The way in which some western media and feminist groups have framed the practice as a "barbaric ritual" of inferior societies (rather than as a form of patriarchal control of women) is, for some comentators, at the center of the controversy. Some observers are disturbed because efforts by African women (and men) to combat this practice are not covered in the western press; they argue that western reporting is at best patronizing and in some cases verges on the pornographic.

Increased collaboration and networking among women's organizations in Africa and in the women's health and human rights movement all over the world are overcoming this rift between the women's movement in the developing "South" and the devloped "North." The view of progressive African women working on this issue is that FC/FGM is a health hazard and a human rights violation and must be stopped. They usually welcome the support and collaboration of all the people of the world if given in the spirit of equality and justice; but they will not accept aggressive threats and patronizing attitudes by conservative zealots and missionaries, least of all those offered in the name of feminism. The work toward stopping FC/FGM promises to become a test case for the international women's movement on how to develop its ethics of collaboration across racial, cultural, and national boundaries.

See Also

References and Further Reading

Toubia, Nahid F. 1993. *Female genital mutilation: A call for global action.* New York: Women Ink.

Nahid Toubia

FEMALE GAZE

See GAZE.

FEMICIDE

The term *femicide* refers specifically to the killing of women because they are women. It was first introduced at the International Tribunal on Crimes Against Women in 1976 to recognize the sexual politics of murder (Radford and Russell, 1992). The reason for the shift from the generic term *homicide* to a gender-specific term such as *femicide* was to bring attention to the misogynist killing of women. Slightly earlier, Andrea Dworkin had introduced the term *gynocide* to refer to "the systematic crippling and/or killing of women by men" in her book *Woman Hating* (1974: 16).

Although femicide is not a legal term, it is gradually being incorporated into the discourse on violence against women. This can be attributed largely to an anthology by Jill Radford and Diana Russell (1992), the first comprehensive work to give the term serious visibility, describe the pervasiveness of the problem, and address individual and collective forms of resistance. They define femicide as the "misogynous killing of women by men" and categorize it as a type of sexual violence (3).

Forms of femicide include racist femicide (murder of black women by white men); homophobic femicide or lesbicide (murder of lesbians by heterosexual men); marital and intimate femicide (murder of women by their husbands or intimate male partners); stranger femicide (murder of a woman by a stranger); religious or ritual femicide (murder based on interpretations of religious prescriptions and proscriptions); serial femicide (serial killing of a number of women, usually by a single male killer); and mass femicide (murder of a large number of women at a given time by a male or groups of males).

Although the term *femicide* is relatively new and tracing historical documentation of the practice has been problematic, there is substantial research to indicate that it has existed in various forms in different cultures for centuries and is still very prevalent. Most researchers and activists view femicide as a function of patriarchal societies, where men are culturally and structurally placed in a position of dominance over women. Men use femicide as a form of social control of women, and as a punitive measure. Although femicide cuts across race, class, religion, and sexual orientation, it affects women differently, depending on their position in the power structure in a given society as well as on the social, economic, and political contexts and circumstances.

India: Suttee

One of the oldest forms of femicide is *suttee*, or *sati*: the Indian practice of burning a woman alive on the pyre of her deceased husband. This practice can be traced as far back as 316 B.C.E. but it seems to have been most pervasive in India in the eighteenth and nineteenth centuries. Often defined as a form of suicide and glorified as the act of a woman who shows strength of character, it can be placed in the category of ritual femicide. This is because the woman may have had a choice in principle, but in practice her death was usually a result of coercion or forced choice between the normatively defined altruistic act of sharing the pyre of her deceased husband, and thus dying an honorable death, or living a life of oppression and ostracization as a widow in a community that perceived her as inauspicious.

Suttee spread from some segments of the warrior caste (Kshatriyas) to other groups, especially the priestly caste (Brahman) in Bengal, and was backed by interpretations of religious texts; but Mogul rulers such as Akbar and Aurungzeb, disapproved of it, and it was finally abolished by the British in 1829. Factors involved in suttee included control over female sexuality, specific inheritance rules, religious prescriptions, and a perception of women as property (Sharma, 1988).

Incidents of suttee occurred as recently as 1987, when of Roop Kanwar, an 18-year-old widow in Deorala, Rajasthan, was burned alive. While strongly condemned by women's rights organizations, such forms of femicide can be understood as a response to a perceived threat of loss of traditional male authority, coupled with the changing status of women.

Europe: Witch-Hunts

Another example of femicide is wich-hunting in Europe, which began in the Middle Ages. In the sixteenth and seventeenth centuries in continental Europe, Scotland, and England, thousands of people were accused of witchcraft and put to death. The majority of those accused and murdered were women, primarily older, lower-class, single, or widowed. The murder of women labeled as witches was a product of a sociohistorical period in European culture when important religious, economic, and political changes were occurring that threatened the male status quo.

The witch-hunts are often analyzed as an attempt by men, with the help of some women and a legal apparatus dominated by upper-class men, to control women who defied conventional notions of gender-appropriate behavior and who were seen as infringing on male labor and resources. Thus, this period witnessed legalized femicide. (For details see Hester, 1992; Mies, 1986: 82–87.)

Other Forms of Femicide

Examination of limited but important documentation indicates the historical practice of lesbicide, that is, the killing of women because of their lesbianism. Studies document cases of lesbicide and the existence of laws mandating the death penalty for lesbianism in various parts of Europe such as ancient Rome, Christian Rome, mid-sixteenth-century Spain, sixteenth-century France, late fifteenth-century Germany, and sixteenth-century Italy. Lesbicide took the forms of drowning, burning, starving, hanging, and mutilation of lesbians or women suspected of lesbianism (Compton, 1985, and Robson, 1992).

Although lynching of African-Americans in the United States was racially motivated and aimed primarily at males, females too were lynched. According to Radford and Russell (1992: 53–61), incidents where lynching of African-American women was combined with sexual violence can be defined as racist femicide.

One of the most prevalent forms of femicide is marital femicide, or intimate femicide—that is, the murder of women by their husbands or men with whom they have an intimate relationship. In some cases, like "dowry deaths" in India, other family members, such as the mother-in-law or members of the husband's family, may participate in the killing of the woman (Kishwar and Vanita, 1999).

In many cases of femicide, the woman is killed in her own home. The problem of such murders is compounded by the failure of the police and judicial systems to adequately protect the women. Dobash and Dobash (1979) trace the history of wife beating and wife murder from 753 B.C.E. to the mid-1970s.

Two major theoretical approaches in the study of domestic violence in the United States include the "family violence perspective" and the "feminist perspective." In the former, the family is considered the basic unit of analysis, whereas in the latter, the abused woman is taken as the unit of analysis.

Studies of motives for marital and intimate femicide include men's desire to control women's sexuality and reproductivity. It is important to note that for every murdered wife or intimate partner, there are thousands who are sexually abused, beaten, intimidated, coerced, and isolated. Battering and intimate femicide are usually exacerbated when

men perceive women as challenging their authority or betraying or leaving them. The objectification of women and the perception of women as property also exacerbate violence toward women.

In the United States domestic violence is the most pervasive crime. According to the U.S. Department of Justice, women are battered at the rate of one every 15 seconds, and each day approximately four women are murdered by an intimate male partner. Stout (1991: 483) analyzed data from *Uniform Crime Reports—Supplemental Homicide Report, 1980–1982* and found that between January 1980 and December 1982, 4,189 females age 16 or older were killed by their male intimate partners. The majority of these women were killed by their husbands. Most cases of intimate femicide are intraracial; most victims are white, (including Hispanics), followed by African-Americans.

Two highly publicized, relatively recent cases of marital femicide in the United States were those of Charles Stuart in Boston in 1989 and O. J. Simpson in 1994. Stuart, a middle-class white male, committed premeditated murder of his pregnant wife and then blamed it on a black male. Later, when the murder was traced to Stuart, he committed suicide. In 1994, Nicole Brown Simpson, the former wife of the retired football player O. J. Simpson, and her friend Ronald Goldman were found brutally murdered in her home. Simpson, who had a history of abusing her, was accused of the murders. However, after a trial that lasted more than a year and cost millions of dollars, he was acquitted.

A study of the social distribution of femicide in Toronto and Vancouver from 1921 to 1988 also indicates its intimate, domestic natures. Examining the historical nature of opportunities and motivations for femicide, the study found that despite changes in women's lives, such as greater participation in the public realm, the proportion of women killed by intimate partners had not decreased. In fact, the study found a slight increase in the number of women killed in their own homes. Intimate femicide has a distinctive character, since it occurs in what is frequently defined as the "private realm," and the home is often assumed to be a haven. Addressing intimate femicide necessitates challenging mainstream assumptions about the home and the family as a safe haven.

Another form of marital femicide in recent history is "dowry deaths." In India, arranged marriages are the prevalent form of marriage. Although the acceptance of dowry in a marriage is legally prohibited, normally the groom's parents continue to make immense material demands on the bride's family. The payment of this dowry becomes a necessary condition of marriage.

After marriage, the groom and his parents may begin to harass the bride to extract more dowry from her family. Failure to meet these continuous demands often results in the death of the bride, with the in-laws explaining it as an accident while cooking or a suicide. In most cases, the method of murder is burning. Cases registered with the police in 1976 and 1977, indicate that 5,587 women died of burns in India. In 1987, the Indian police recorded 1,786 dowry deaths. However, women's action groups maintained that this figure was a gross underrepresentation; they estimated that in a single state, such as Gujarat, there were approximately 1,000 deaths from burning (Heise, 1989: 12–21; Mies, 1986: 146–150).

Another form of femicide that has become relatively common in the last few decades is serial femicide, the torture, killing, and mutilation of a series of women by a male. A notorious example was the murder and mutilation of five prostitutes in London in 1888 by an unidentified killer called "Jack the Ripper." Highly publicized serial killers in recent decades include Ted Bundy, the "Lipstick Killer," the "Boston Strangler," "Son of Sam," the "Hillside Strangler," and the "Yorkshire Ripper," each of whom killed 6 to 20 women (Bland, 1992: 233–252; Cameron, 1992: 184–188).

A notorious incident of mass femicide in recent history was the killing of 14 women on 6 December 1989 by 25-year-old Marc Lepine at the University of Montreal. Lepine went into a classroom in the School of Engineering, ordered the men out, and opened fire on the women, calling them "fucking feminists," and finally shot himself. His suicide note blamed his failure on women.

Although there is considerable debate over the direct impact of pornography on femicide, there is evidence to show that, in many cases, males who commit misogynist killing of women were influenced by pornographic material in deciding on the nature of the murder.

Activism Against Femicide

Important collective efforts to end femicide include the Clearinghouse on Femicide in Berkeley, California, founded in 1989; the battered women's movement, which shifted domestic violence from a private problem to a public issue; the Southall Black Sisters in the United Kingdom; and Women Against Violence Against Women (WAVAW), *Manushi*, and Janwadi Mahila Samiti in India.

From the late 1970s onward, women's rights groups in the third world have been addressing the "woman question" in their countries. Various women's organizations were created to deal with issues that had an impact on women. They focused on the global and internal oppression and exploitation of third world women. Special emphasis was given to various forms of violence, such as rape, suttee, dowry deaths, female infanticide, female feticide, and marital violence, which occur in their countries (Kishwar and Vanita, 1999; Liddle and Joshi, 1986). Activists questioned normative structure and culturally prescribed values within the institution of marriage and family. Most important, they initiated legislative changes that protected the rights of women (Mies, 1986; Lawyers Collective, 1992, 1999).

Although the prevalence of femicide is extensive, it is important to note that, worldwide, women are making serious individual and collective efforts against femicide. This was articulated by women from all over the globe at the Fourth World Conference on Women in Beijing, China, in 1995.

See Also

ABUSE; BATTERY; DOMESTIC VIOLENCE; DOWRY AND BRIDEPRICE; INFANTICIDE; MISOGYNY; VIOLENCE, *specific entries*; WITCHES: WESTERN WORLD

References and Further Reading

Bart, Pauline B., and Eileen Geil Moran, eds. 1993. *Violence against women: The bloody footprints*. Thousand Oaks, Calif.: Sage.

Bland, Lucy. 1992. The case of the Yorkshire Ripper: Mad, bad, beast, or male? In Jill Radford and Diana E. H. Russell, eds., *Femicide: The politics of women killing*, 233–252. New York: Twayne.

Cameron, Deborah. 1992. "That's entertainment"? Jack the Ripper and the selling of sexual violence. In Jill Radford and Diana E. H. Russell, eds., *Femicide: The politics of woman killing*, 184–188. New York: Twayne.

Caputi, Jane. 1987. *The age of sex crime*. Bowling Green, Ohio.: Bowling Green State University Press.

Compton, L. 1985. The myth of lesbian impunity. *Journal of Homosexuality* 6 (11): 13–19.

Dobash, R.E., and R.P. Dobash. 1979. *Violence against wives: A case against the patriarchy*. New York: Free Press.

Dworkin, Andrea. 1974. *Woman hating*. New York: E. P. Dutton.

Gartner, Rosemary, and Bill McCarthy. 1991. The social distribution of femicide in urban Canada, 1921–1988. *Law and Society Review* 25 (2): 287–311.

Heise, Lori. 1989. Crimes of gender. In *World Watch* (March–April): 12–21.

Hester, Marianne. 1992. The witch-craze in sixteenth- and seventeenth-century England as social control of women. In Jill Radford and Diana E. H. Russell, eds., *Femicide: The politics of woman killing*, 27–40. New York: Twayne.

Kishwar, Madhu, and Ruth Vanita, eds. 1999. *In search of answers: Indian women's voices from "Manushi."* New Delhi: Manohar.

Lawyers Collective. 1992. *Domestic violence: Legal aid handbook 1.* New Delhi: Kali for Women.

Lawyers Collective. 1999. Domestic Violence Against Women (Prevention) Bill. Second draft by the Lawyers Collective Women's Right Initiative.

Liddle, Joanna, and Rama Joshi. 1986. *Daughters of independence: Gender, caste, and class in India.* London: Zed.

Mies, Maria. 1986. *Patriarchy and accumulation on a world scale.* London: Zed.

Radford, Jill, and Diana E. H. Russell, eds. 1992. *Femicide: The politics of woman killing.* New York: Twayne.

Robson, Ruthann. 1992. Legal lesbicide. In Jill Radford and Diana E. H. Russell, eds., *Femicide: The politics of woman killing*, 40–51. New York: Twayne.

Sharma, Arvind. 1988. *Sati: Historical and phenomenological essays.* Delhi: Motilal Banarsidas.

Stout, Karen. 1991. Intimate femicide: A national demographic overview. *Journal of Interpersonal Violence* 6(4): 476–485.

Margaret Abraham

FEMININE MYSTIQUE

The Feminine Mystique is the title of Betty Friedan's book, published in 1963, which reports on the findings of her survey of 200 women who had graduated from Smith College in the same year as she. The book reveals that these white, heterosexual, middle-class women were discontented and unhappy despite apparently living the "ideal" female life but were unable to explain why—"the problem that has no name." Indeed, the motivation for Friedan's study was her own discontent, her own mystification as to why she was not happy with what was portrayed as the ideal of womanhood. What the book argued was that middle-class women—married, supported financially by a "breadwinner," and with children—were unhappy, but that there was

no concept, no term that could be used to define and explain this discontent.

Although this work can be accused of being ethnocentric and ignoring the fact that black and working-class women in the United States were forced to take paid employment, nevertheless it is an important work in second-stage feminism. By starting from her own personal experiences as a wife and mother and rejecting biological explanations for women's discontent, Friedan was able to provide a powerful case for the political nature of women's experiences—that the personal is the political. The discontent that many white, middle-class, heterosexual women in the United States felt in the 1960s was a result, according to Friedan and many others, not of their own individual failures but of their structural position in a patriarchal society.

See Also

FEMININITY; FEMINISM: SECOND-WAVE NORTH AMERICAN; PATRIARCHY; SLOGANS: "THE PERSONAL IS THE POLITICAL"

References and Further Reading

Friedan, Betty. 1963. *The feminine mystique.* New York: Norton.
——. 1993. *The fountain of age.* New York: Simon and Shuster.

Pamela Abbott

FEMININITY

Many commentators describe femininity as the ideal of womanhood, of being female, whereby women are defined as different from and inferior to men. To be feminine, in this view, is to conform to men's images of what women should be and how women should behave. Central to this idea of femininity is the ideal of woman as the madonna. In nineteenth-century Europe and the United States, middle-class women were seen as selfless, frail, and dependent, and also as mothers. Women's supposed inherent weakness, mental and physical, was used as a justification for excluding them from higher education and paid employment. The ideal of femininity made it obligatory for women to be dependent on their husbands or fathers—male "breadwinners" who earned a "family wage." This ideology of femininity was held by many male philanthropists, politicians, and trade unionists, and by the end of the ninteeth century it was aspired to by most middle- and working-class women.

Just as domestication and dependency have been central to femininity, so also is the idea of motherhood as a woman's destiny. Implicitly, sexual attention to men is also a part of femininity—the need to be protected and supported by a man meant that one had to be attractive to men—but the madonna image limits the extent to which women are permitted to be alluring or provocative. Sexual attraction is strictly limited and defined in the patriarchal ideal of femininity. In the United States, the New Right's attack on single mothers, prostitution, and pornography, and its emphasis on "family values," can be seen as an attempt to reimpose an ideal of femininity that many women have rejected (Abbott and Wallace, 1992). Although not all feminists reject ideas of motherhood or the notion of the feminine as distinct from the masculine, they do reject the view of women as submissive and males as dominant—male as predator, female as prey. The deconstruction of "femininity" into "femininities" enables us not only to recognize difference (by class, race, and culture) but also to construct woman-defined, as opposed to male-defined, femininities.

See Also

GENDER CONSTRUCTIONS IN THE FAMILY; IMAGES OF WOMEN: OVERVIEW; MASCULINITY; MOTHER; PATRIARCHY: FEMINIST THEORY

References and Further Reading

Abbott, Pamela, and Claire Wallace. 1992. *The family and the new right.* London: Pluto.

Pamela Abbott

FEMINISM: Overview

Although many languages do not have a noun *feminism,* and *feminism* as a term for the politics of equal rights for women did not come into use in English until the 1890s, feminist history is the history of those ideas and politics that argue for sexual equality and the eradication of discrimination on the basis of sex.

Early History

Public declarations that describe "women" as a distinct social group with unequal social status date from before the eighteenth century. Feminism always appears at moments of social and political change. The French Revolution inspired the first full political argument for women's rights and individual development—Mary Wollstonecraft's *A Vindication of the Rights of Woman* in 1792. Wollstonecraft describes the psychological and economic damage done to women by their forced dependence on men and exclusion from the public sphere. Feminists championed the abolition of the slave trade and were active in food boycotts, supporting the principles of emancipation, utility, and benevolence in British Chartism and Owenism in the mid-nineteenth century, before Josephine Butler, an English reformer, campaigned against the Contagious Diseases Act and Barbara Bodichon, an advocate of women's rights, campaigned for a Married Women's Property Act. Whereas in Australia and New Zealand feminist campaigns similarly grew from social reform movements, elsewhere feminism appeared after national change—for example, the Chinese (1912) and Egyptian (1919) revolutions.

United States. The main battle of nineteenth-century feminism was for suffrage. In the United States, Elizabeth Cady Stanton and Susan B. Anthony organized the Seneca Falls Convention of 1848, and its famous Declaration of Sentiments sought to apply the principles of the American Declaration of Independence to women. When the alliance between feminism and the anti-slavery movement began to dissolve, following the nominal enfranchisement of blacks but not women after the American Civil War, Anthony and Stanton founded the National Woman Suffrage Association (1869). The suffrage movement inspired other organizations, such as the International Council of Women (1888)—one of the oldest and largest women's organizations in the world. Together with the National American Woman's Suffrage Association (NAWSA) and the support of suffragists like Alice Paul, who returned from Britain to found the separate Woman's Party, feminism made headway. There was a groundswell of socialist feminism in the settlement movement and in Charlotte Perkins Gilman's argument in *The Man-Made World* (1911) that women should be economically independent of men (Humm, 1992). NAWSA (which is now the League of Women Voters), with its suffrage trains and demonstrations, resulted in 1920 in the Nineteenth Amendment to the Constitution, which gave women the vote.

Great Britian. British Labour women, women in the arts, the Women's Cooperative Guild (1883), and other groups combined in the National Union of Women's Suffrage Societies. There were also radical working-class feminists—for example, the Women's Protective and Provident League (1874), which opposed the exploitation of women workers.

But it was the Women's Social and Political Union (WSPU), founded in 1903 by Emmeline Pankhurst and her daughters, that has become the best-known organization of first-wave feminism. By 1908 a WSPU open-air meeting in Hyde Park attracted between a quarter and a half million people, and its high public profile and militancy ensured a limited franchise for British women aged over 30 (1918) and full suffrage in 1928.

International development. First-wave feminism was a long-lasting, highly diverse, and universal phenomenon including feminists in nationalist movements (such as the Quit India Movement, 1910–1920) and Italian pacifists (dei Bonfatti). It created a new political identity for women as well as public emancipation (Humm, 1992).

From the 1920s to the 1930s

Legal advances of the 1920s and 1930s scattered the possibility of a single suffrage identity. In America "welfare feminism" was the aim of New Deal feminist antipoverty campaigns, and pacifist feminists like Jane Addams, who formed the Woman's Peace Party. In Britain feminists devoted their energies to the political education of women: the Women's Cooperative Guild, the Women's Labour League, and the Six-Point Group (1921). These decades saw divisions between "old" feminists seeking to end protective legislation and "new" feminists campaigning for the endowment of motherhood and family allowances, and pacifist and antifascist feminism. In the 1920s the National Association of Colored Women was active in political education and social welfare in the United States. The Equal Rights Amendment (ERA), first proposed to Congress in 1923 by the Woman's Party as an amendment to the Constitution— "Men and women shall have equal rights throughout the United States and every place subject to its jurisdiction"— that eventually became a focus for the new feminist movements of the late 1960s, as well as peace activism, such as the Women's Strike for Peace in 1961, which involved 50,000 women.

Second-Wave Feminism

When the women's liberation movement (WLM) emerged in the late 1960s, it was shaped both by its similarity to first-wave feminism, in the way that both grew out of their limited roles in black rights movements, and also by changes in the political order brought about by that earlier feminism. In other ways, women's liberation was radically different. Women's liberation extended the terms *politics* and the *economy* to sexuality, encapsulated in the slogan "The personal is the political." The movement created new polit-ical organizations—small antihierarchical consciousness-raising groups—and a new vocabulary, like the term *sexual politics,* the title of Kate Millett's now classic book (Millett, 1970).

The second wave in the United States. The WLM grew from radical groups such as the New York Redstockings; from concern about reproductive issues and the ubiquity of patriarchy; from the first women's studies programs, such as Naomi Weisstein's seminar at the Free University of Chicago in 1967; and from direct actions, such as the demonstration at the Miss America pageant in 1968 when bras were trashed (but not burned). Another stimulus was the publication of Betty Friedan's *The Feminine Mystique* (1963), which described the frustration of white, heterosexual, middle-class women without careers, locked into domesticity, and Friedan's founding of the National Organization for Women (NOW) in 1966.

The second wave in Great Britian. In 1968 the flurry of militant feminism that had appeared in the United States became visible in Britain. The same involvement in, and the same disenchantment with, New Left causes (in Britain, the Campaign for Nuclear Disarmament and the Vietnam Solidarity Campaign) mark the British women's liberation movement as much as its sister in the United States. An additional inspiration was the militancy of women workers in the strike against Ford (1968) for equal pay. The first Women's Liberation Conference at Ruskin College, Oxford (1970), had more than 600 participants and funneled socialist and liberation energies into demands for equal pay, 24-hour child care, free contraception, and abortion on demand. Feminists battled to defend women from sexual and domestic violence by founding the innovative battered women's refuges in Chiswick, London, in 1972 and rape crisis centers, and with campaigns such as Reclaim the Night, as well as advocating employment rights in a Working Women's Charter (1974).

The second wave internationally. Second-wave feminism has differing national histories—for example, emerging in Spain only with the death of Franco (1975) and in Turkey after the political coup of 1980. The United Nations Decade for Women (1975–1985) inspired feminists worldwide to challenge the fabric of political life with demonstrations against the veil in Egypt; rural demonstrations in India against rapists in the 1980s; and mass demonstrations for peace in Palestine and Cyprus. In 1973, 41 organizations founded the South African Black Women's Federation; and in 1949 the first feminist, Rachel Kagun, was elected to the Israeli Knesset. Major international networks include the DAWN movement (Development Alternatives with

Women for a New Era), founded in 1984, and Latin American Encounters. By the 1990s more than 100 women's peace camps were established from the pioneer Greenham Common. In Britain the Organization of Women of African and Asian Descent (OWAAD), founded in 1976, attacked racist immigration laws.

In summary: The second wave. Underlying these campaigns in Britain were important issues for all feminists regarding Eurocentrism and more diverse identities evident in the widening of feminism, which now includes—alongside black activism, the Greenham peace actions, and socialist feminists' links with the traditional left—reproductive and abortion rights campaigns and lesbian activism focused on Clause 28 (banning the public advocacy of homosexuality). Similarly, in the United States the ERA campaign, AIDS activism, and groups such as Women Against Pornography and the Women of Color Reproductive Health Rights Coalition, and in Canada the National Organization of Immigrant and Invisible Minority Women, gained support, indicating the ways in which second-wave feminism has multiple histories.

Feminist Theory

The single most important feature of second-wave feminism was, perhaps, theoretical: its challenge to traditional thinking by connecting issues of reproduction with issues of production, and the personal with the political. All variants of feminist theory share three major assumptions: gender is a social construct that oppresses women more than men (Beauvoir, 1972); patriarchy (that is, the male domination of social institutions) shapes these constructions; and women's experiential knowledge best helps us envision a future nonsexist society. These shared premises have shaped a double agenda: the task of critique (attacking gender stereotypes) and the task of construction, sometimes called feminist *praxis* (constructing new models).

Feminist theory has at least four notable characteristics. First, feminist theroy is intensely interdisciplinary, ranging across customary subject divisions including history, philosophy, anthropology, and the arts, among others. Second, certain themes recur: reproduction, representation, the sexual division of labor. Third and most striking are new concepts, such as sexism, created to address gaps in existing knowledge as well as the social discrimination these concepts describe. Fourth, women's subjective experiences are drawn on to enrich scholarship. Catharine MacKinnon (1989) argues that feminist theory is the first theory to emerge from those whose interests it affirms.

From the 1970s to 2000

While intellectual ideas rarely present themselves in neat chronological order, it may be said that in the 1970s feminists tackled the *causes* of women's oppression (such as capitalism and masculinity), describing society as a structure of oppressors (male) and oppressed (female). Feminism of this period is usually divided into *forms* (liberal, Marxist-socialist, cultural-radical). Liberal feminism argues that women's liberation will come with equal legal, political, and economic rights. More comprehensive Marxist-socialist assessments of economic gender exploitation asked: Do women form a distinct "sex class"? How far is capitalism structured by patriarchy? By widening the Marxist concept of production to include household labor and child care, feminists could highlight further sexual divisions (the debate over "domestic labor") as well as women's unequal status at work (a "reserve army of labor"). For example, Shulamith Firestone (1970) argued that the "material" of women's reproductive body was as much a source of oppression as material inequality. In opposition to a Marxist focus on *production,* cultural and radical feminists—for example, Adrienne Rich—focused on reproduction, mothering, and creativity. Although the labels "cultural" and "radical" are often misapplied, in general, radical theorists take the view that sexuality, specifically male violence, is the cause of women's oppression, condoned by the institutionalization of heterosexuality. This is the theme of Rich's milestone essay, "Compulsory Heterosexuality and Lesbian Existence" (1980), which builds on Simone de Beauvoir's premise that women are originally homosexual to propose that lesbianism can be part of every woman's cultural, if not physical, experience. This argument that "lesbianism" is shaped by ideological preference as much as by explicit practice was built on a concept of second-wave feminists: "feminism is the theory, lesbianism is the practice."

A major rethinking of symbolic and social structures of gender (*écriture féminine*), was undertaken by French feminists who claimed that cultural and gendered "binaries" such as man-woman and culture-nature always made "woman" inferior (Cixous, 1976). Binaries are said to ignore women's fluid identity and the semiotic world of mother–infant bonding. U.S. feminists drew on object-relations psychoanalysis to locate the source of male power and fear of women in men's early experience of learning to be "not the mother" (Chodorow, 1978). These accounts of gender identity and objectification greatly enriched feminist film and media studies. The notion that there is a distinctive and gendered perception (the male "gaze") is supported by the feminist standpoint theorists who challenge what they consider false notions of universalism in the social sciences.

The 1990s saw a crucial shift in feminism and feminist theory when black feminists directed attention to ethnic differences. Criticizing the three-form or three-phase typology (liberal-Marxist-cultural) as a white women's mental map that ignored the experiences of black women, they described discrimination as an *interlocking* system based on race, class, and gender (hooks, 1984). They also introduced fresh theoretical arguments suggesting, for example, that the family was not necessarily patriarchal but could be a site of resistance. Black theory derives from Afrocentric history as well as from a "both-or" reality (the act of being simultaneously inside and outside society).

These critiques of white essentialism were paralleled by feminist poststructuralist and postmodern arguments that gender structures are historically variable and are not predetermined. Italian feminists, for example, coined the term *autocoscienza* for the collective construction of new identities, and postcolonial theorists coined the term *transversed politics* for dialogue across national and other differences among women (Yuval-Davis, 1997). Many of these themes were brought together in feminist peace theory, which argues that violence stems from traditional gender socialization.

Feminist theory is pioneering in the field of international new technologies and adventurous media work across the globe and feminist challenges to mainstream thought are diverse and influential, a central claim being that *all* theory is motivated by gendered perceptions whether these are conscious or unconscious (Springer, 1996).

See Also

DAWN MOVEMENT; FEMININE MYSTIQUE; FEMINISM, *specific entries*

References and Further Reading

Beauvoir, Simone de. 1972. *The second sex.* Trans. H. M. Parshlay. Harmondsworth, U.K.: Penguin. (Originally published 1949.)

Chodorow, Nancy. 1978. *The reproduction of mothering.* Berkeley: University of California Press.

Cixous, Hélène. 1976. The laugh of the Medusa. *Signs* 1(4): 875–893.

Firestone, Shulamith. 1970. *The dialectic of sex.* New York: Morrow.

Friedan, Betty. 1963. *The feminine mystique.* New York: Norton.

Greer, Germaine. 1970. *The female eunuch.* London: MacGibbon and Kee.

hooks, bell. 1984. *Feminist theory: From margin to center.* Boston: South End.

Humm, Maggie. 1992. *Feminisms: A reader.* Hemel Hempstead, U.K.: Harvester Wheatsheaf (Published in the United States as *Modern Feminisms.* New York: Columbia University Press.)

MacKinnon, Catharine. 1989. *Toward a feminist theory of the state.* Cambridge, Mass.: Harvard University Press.

Millett, Kate. 1970. *Sexual politics.* New York: Doubleday.

Rich, Adrienne. 1980. Compulsory heterosexuality and lesbian existence. *Signs* 5(4): 631–660.

Springer, Claudia. 1996. *Electronic eros.* London: Athlone.

Wollstonecraft, Mary. 1967. *A vindication of the rights of woman.* Reprint, New York: Norton. (Originally published 1792.)

Yuval-Davis, Nira. 1997. *Gender and nation.* London: Sage.

Maggie Humm

FEMINISM: African-American

For two centuries, African-American women have struggled with the multiple realities of gender, racial, and economic or caste oppression in the United States. Their feminism has been shaped by the experience of a bourgeois democracy and a capitalist economy involving first slave labor, then Jim Crow and legal discrimination that ensured the economic and political disenfranchisement of people of African descent. Historically, the strongest motivation in the development of black feminist politics stemmed from rebellion against racism, sexism, sexual violence, and poverty. African-American feminists hold that, given the historical racism of white women's liberation and the sexism of the male-dominated civil rights and black power movements, conventional feminist and often antiracist politics obscure black women's battles and emergent feminisms.

Different ideologies shape the relationship between black feminism and dominant elites, such as state and corporate cultures. The political spectrum of black feminist progressives includes "liberal," "radical," "neoradical," and "revolutionary" politics; this diversity precludes any attempt to formulate a monolithic, homogeneous black feminism. All black feminists, including those that follow conventional ideology, to some degree share an outsider status in American culture. That marginalization is not indicative of—but is often confused with—an intrinsic or inherent radicalism. Ideological differences among African-American feminists point to the need to speak of black feminisms in their plurality. Diversity in outlook and writing, despite shared concerns for racial and gender equality—and, to a lesser degree, economic equality—gives black feminisms their complexity. Currently, the most prominent advocates for black feminism are writers and academics, although anonymous activists and educators continue to expand and redefine black feminisms. Integrative analyses of race, gender, sexuality, and class in political practice relevant to nonelite communities remain a major challenge for feminists. Central in the development of a politics and theory deal with the intersection of oppression and liberation are the historical ancestors of today's black feminisms.

Protofeminists

Historical figures such as Sojourner Truth, Maria Stewart, and Harriet Tubman in the antebellum era; Anna Julia Cooper and Ida B. Wells in the post-Reconstruction age; Amy Jacques Garvey of the pan-Africanist United Negro Improvement Association; Zora Neale Hurston of the Harlem Renaissance; and Fannie Lou Hamer, Ella Baker, and Lorraine Hansberry of the civil rights era figure prominently in contemporary black feminisms. Along with countless other black women writers, intellectuals, and political thinkers and activities, they have made significant contributions to antiracism, feminism, and democratic thought and practices.

In the antebellum years, among the abolitionists, Sojourner Truth is one of the best known, largely because of her symbolic use by white feminists, dating from the mid-nineteenth century. A contemporary of the abolitionist and profeminist Frederick Douglass and white suffragists, Truth had a profound impact on expanding notions of womanhood and gave two significant speeches: "Women's Rights" in 1861, and "When Woman Gets Her Rights Man Will Be Right" in 1860. The lesser-known Maria W. Stewart, a free black Bostonian and associate of David Walker (the black abolitionist allegedly poisoned for his antislavery radicalism), became one of the first U.S. women to give public political speeches. Merging women's rights with the rights of enslaved Africans in the United States, Stewart's fiery advocacy led her to the pulpit; she would later be ousted from the church and public speaking by African-American clergymen who found her claim of direct communion with God (as the inspiration for her liberation activism) heretical. Stewart later served in the medical corps during the American Civil War, while her contemporary, Harriet Tubman, who had escaped slavery and led thousands of people to freedom through the underground railroad before the war, fought as a soldier and officer. As the first American woman to lead black and white troops in battle, Tubman headed the Intelligence Service in the Department of the South and won the people's title of "General Tubman."

Following in the steps of Truth, Stewart, and Tubman, decades after the war and the era, the Reconstruction educator Anna Julia Cooper and anti-lynching crusader Ida B. Wells worked as protofeminists, chronicling their experiences and their understanding of justice in the nineteenth and early twentieth century in their memoirs, respectively, *A Voice from the South: By a Black Woman of the South* (1892) and *Crusade for Justice: The Autobiography of Ida B. Wells* (1970).

Tracing the trajectory of historical activists, contemporary black feminisms interpret and built on the work of their predecessors. Tubman's guerrilla foray into South Carolina's Port Royal or Combahee River region on 2 June 1863, which freed hundreds of enslaved people, provided a model for the militant black feminism of the Combahee River Collective. Formed partly in response to what it viewed as the liberal politics of the National Black Feminist Organization, Combahee's manifesto of 1977 acknowledges the influence of protofeminists or historical black women activists "who have had a shared awareness of how their sexual identity combined with their racial identity to make their whole life situation and the focus of their political struggles unique."

Contemporary African-American Feminism

Organizational and antiracist politics have been central in the development of black feminisms. In the civil rights and black liberation movements of the 1950s, 1960s, and early 1970s, black women participated in the Southern Christian Leadership Council (SCLC), the Student Nonviolent Coordinating Committee (SNCC), the Congress on Racial Equality (CORE), the Organization of Afro-American Unity (OAAU), and the Black Panther Party (BPP). In the 1950s, Ella Baker became de facto director of SCLC, an organization led by Reverend Martin Luther King, Jr., and other male clergy indifferent or hostile to black women's leadership. Baker and other leaders such as Jo Ann Robinson, Septima Clark, and Fannie Lou Hamer were pivotal in political formations that did not always acknowledge their roles, yet they created new progressive gender roles, and, although they did not use the term, feminisms.

In the 1960s and 1970s, black women helped to redefine radical praxis in America within organizations that issued cogent manifestoes for a militant black feminism. For instance, the Third World Women's Alliance grew out of SNCC to articulate a revolutionary black feminism with an international focus. Critiques of capitalism began to appear in black women's writings and speeches. Writings by Angela Y. Davis, the black feminist most associated with Marxism, on the intersections of race, class, and gender first appeared during her incarceration as a political prisoner in the early 1970s. Along with Davis, activist-writers such as Toni Cade Bambara, Audre Lorde, Sonia Sanchez, Ntozake Shange, and Alice Walker shaped antiracist and feminist concepts of liberation.

In their memoirs, black feminists describe being influenced by male revolutionary intellectuals such as Frantz Fanon, Amilcar Cabral, and Malcolm X during the movement era, from 1955 to 1975, when women found themselves politicizing and politicized by the insurgent speech and struggles of African-American males often credited as the only significant leaders of movements co-organized and co-led by African-American women. Women who initially considered themselves "antiracists"—but not necessarily "feminists" (associating the term with white women's experiences, and biases)—expanded antiracist and women's politics to constitute new forms of feminism.

Following the movement era, by the 1980s, the term *feminism* became increasingly identified with black women's struggles. Reviewing the work of black feminist writers, one can distinguish between a black feminism or womanism, one particular to women of African descent, and an antiracist feminism embraceable by all progressive women. The explorations and debates concerning what to call African-American women's gender-progressive activism and literature reflects the struggle to define the political mission of black feminisms.

Alice Walker contrasts black feminism with white or Eurocentric feminism, using the term *womanist* to render the adjective *black* superfluous for gender-progressive women of color. Exploring the experiences of black women and other women of color, Walker writes: "For white women there is apparently no felt need to preface 'feminist' with the word 'white,' since the word 'feminist' is accepted as coming out of white women culture." Walker's womanist ideology influenced the Afrocentric womanism and the womanist theology that followed (the latter would challenge male dominance in black theology and liberation theology). Patricia Hill Collins advocates Afrocentric feminism as a process of self-conscious struggle that empowers women and men to actualize a humanist vision for an emancipatory theory for black females; she notes that "the term Black feminist both highlights the contradictions underlying the assumed Whiteness of feminism and reminds White women that they are neither the only nor the normative 'feminists.' Because it challenges Black women to confront their own views on sexism and women's oppression, the term Black feminism also makes many African-American women uncomfortable." bell

hooks (1984) expands on Collins's humanist vision and Walker's cultural critique to construct feminism as opposition to white supremacy, capitalism, and patriarchy. Highlighting an antiracist feminism applicable to all women, her analysis is more political than cultural: feminism is the "struggle to eradicate the ideology of domination that permeates western culture on various levels as well as a commitment to reorganizing society so that the self-development of people can take precedence over imperialism, economic expansion, and material desires."

To various degrees, the definitions above reflect or influence feminist manifestos such as the Combahee River Collective Statement of 1977; the declaration of African American Women in Defense of Ourselves that critiques the sexual objectification and abuse of black women in media and government during the confirmation hearings when Clarence Thomas was nominated as a Supreme Court justice (hearings in which Anita Hill raised charges of sexual harassment against the nominee); and an Open Letter from the former Black Panther and political prisoner Assata Shakur in 1998, which exemplifies the revolutionary dimension of black feminism tied to black liberation politics. In addition to these manifestos, various innovative organizing and literature sought to counter racial and gender bias. Black lesbians such as Audre Lorde and Barbara Smith made significant contributions to black feminisms, to feminism in general, and to struggles against homophobia in black communities. Likewise, recent developments in theology or womanist theology, legal studies or critical race feminism, and feminist writing and activism by black men offer some of the most incisive analyses focusing on gender and racial justice.

Conclusion

African-American women continue to be visibly active with regard to health issues and economic justice: their infant mortality rate is twice that of their white counterparts; their life expectancy is lower and their poverty rates are higher than those of the general population. Combating sexual and racial violence, lobbying for child welfare, and advocating the human rights of prisoners appear central in contemporary black feminisms. With two million people in jail and prison (70 percent of them people of color), the United States has the highest incarceration rate among industrialized countries. By June 1997, 138,000 women were incarcerated in the United States—triple the number since 1985 and 10 times the number of women imprisoned in Spain, England, France, Scotland, Germany, and Italy combined (these European countries collectively have a population of

150 million women, as compared with 120 million women in the United States). Many of these women are African, Latina, or Native Americans, incarcerated for nonviolent economic crimes or drug use; 80 percent are mothers; 30 percent are poor. Racial disparities in sentencing and the death penalty, as well as social and police violence (through racial profiling, police beatings, or killings), suggest that antiviolence and antiracist movements will continue to galvanize black women's activism and feminisms. As African-American feminisms work to address repression and the internal conflicts of black communities, their impact has expanded to influence other women and cultures—Latino, African, Asian, Arab, Native American, and European—in progressive coalition politics.

See Also

BLACKNESS AND WHITENESS; CRIME AND PUNISHMENT: CASE STUDY—WOMEN IN PRISON IN THE UNITED STATES; EUROCENTRISM; FEMINISM: ASIAN AMERICAN; FEMINISM: BLACK BRITISH; FEMINISM: CHICANA; RACE; WOMANISM

References and Further Reading

Amnesty International. 1999. *Not part of my sentence: Violations of the human rights of women in custody.*

Cade, Barbara, Toni, ed. 1970. *The black woman: An anthology.* New York: New American Library.

Davis, Angela Y. 1998. *The Angela Y. Davis reader.* Oxford: Blackwell.

———. 1983. *Women, race, and class.* New York: Random House.

Giddings, Paula. 1984. *When and where I enter: The impact of black women on race and sex in America.* New York: Morrow.

Guy-Sheftall, Beverly, ed. 1995. *Words of fire: An anthology of African American feminist thought.* New York: New Press.

Hill Collins, Patricia. 1989. *Black feminist thought.* Cambridge, Mass.: Unwin Hyman.

hooks, bell. 1984. *Feminist theory: From margin to center.* Boston: South End.

James, Joy, and T. Denean Sharpley-Whiting. 2000. *The black feminist reader.* Oxford: Blackwell.

Walker, Alice. 1988. *In search of our mothers' gardens.* San Diego: Harcourt Brace Jovanovich.

Williams, Delores S. 1993. *Sisters in the wilderness: The challenge of womanist god-talk.* New York: Orbis.

Wing, Adrian K., ed. 1998. *Critical race feminism.* New York: New York University Press.

Joy James

FEMINISM: Anarchist

Anarchist feminism, also known as anarcho- or anarcha-feminism, is a term that covers a variety of perspectives. Common to these is the belief that women's liberation will be brought about not by reliance on the state or its institutions, such as the law, but only by women's self-determined activity. Social relationships based on hierarchy and dominance must be challenged, and relationships based on autonomy and mutuality fostered. Characteristically, anarchist feminists value freedom, individuality, and spontaneity, and oppose coercion and all forms of authority. They differ over how to promote such values, but most favor small-scale, locally based activities and decentralized, nonhierarchical organization. The emphasis on freedom and the critique of power in personal relationships have meant that anarchist feminists have often pioneered public discussion of sexual and reproductive freedom, as well as campaigning for birth control and against censorship of information about sexuality (Goldman, 1970, 1983; McElroy, 1982).

Anarchist feminism evolved in Europe and the United States during the late nineteenth century, drawing on liberal critiques of the emergence of the modern state, as well as contemporary feminist, socialist, and anarchist movements. Individualist forms of anarchist feminism have found most adherents in the United States, while in Europe there has been more emphasis on collectivity (Marsh, 1981).

The best known anarchist feminist is Emma Goldman (1869–1940). Although she distanced herself from the feminist organizations of her time, she was an outspoken advocate of women's sexual autonomy and the importance of a transformation in sexual as well as economic relations if women (and men) were to be truly free. Bonnie Haaland (1993) argues that Goldman's emphasis on women's sexual liberation as central to social transformation brought an important new dimension to anarchist theory while also challenging those feminists who promoted women's entry into state institutions. Anarchist feminists criticized the campaign for women's suffrage, arguing that the vote had not brought freedom for men and would not do so for women. Rather, they involved themselves in activities that had an immediate effect on women's lives, including industrial organizing, child care issues, and health and sexual education.

Anarchist feminism reemerged in the late 1960s as a part of the women's liberation movement (WLM) in North America and Europe. At first, the WLM was based on small autonomous groups that used personal experience as the starting point for analysis and action. This, together with the WLM's strong streak of antiauthoritarianism, led some to claim that it was inherently if not explicitly anarchist. As one street chant went: "Not the church and not the state: *women* must decide our fate." However, as the movement grew and fragmented, anarchist feminists rejected those campaigns that they saw as seeking to extend state power, or to acquire power for some women, rather than subverting or eliminating power relationships altogether. Many, while making international connections, chose to engage in local activism on issues such as housing, emphasizing direct action as a way of bringing about change (Ehrlich et al., 1979).

Although some anarchist feminists accept that violence may at times be necessary, the belief that means and ends are inextricably linked has led others to pacifism. A controversial argument that has gained currency in the peace and environmental movements claims that women are inclined, whether naturally or as a result of life experience, toward relationships based on interdependence and cooperation rather than domination and competition. Women, then, embody the anarchist approach necessary to bring about social transformation. Only such "female" values, rejecting "power over" in favor of "power from within" (Starhawk, 1988), can bring about a peaceful, just, and ecologically sound society.

A similar argument can be heard from those who reject all or most modern technology as inherently patriarchal and promoting inequality, as well as those who see a subversive and liberatory potential in, for instance, information technology. The latter argue that the Internet uses the kinds of communication skills and nonlinear organization (the World Wide Web) at which women excel. Some claim that the Internet could dissolve existing boundaries and hierarchies, even gender itself, in a space where humans can reimagine themselves in their encounters with one another (Bornstein, 1995; Plant, 1997).

Anarchist feminism is rarely discussed in academic journals. Possible reasons for this include institutional bias, as well as many anarchist feminists' rejection of the academy and their continuing emphasis on small-scale local activity, on practice rather than theory. "Living our politics" has been centrally important for many who have seen it as a way of trying out and spreading ideas. Mary Wollstonecraft (1759–1797) was an early heroine, for her life more than her writings, and Emma Goldman's autobiography, *Living My Life,* played a similar role in inspiring later generations. In the early twentieth century, a number of anarchist feminists had links with the new artistic movements of the time, publishing or writing for the "little magazines" that promoted political as well as cultural change.

This connection of politics and culture reappears more recently in the independent music and publications associated with the ever-changing alternative lifestyle and protest movements of the West, and the new groupings springing up in postcommunist eastern Europe. Experimentation with anarchist feminist ideas also appears increasingly often in the imaginary worlds of utopian and science fiction writers, notably Marge Piercy. Anarchist feminism, then, can be seen not as a blueprint or a goal, or even as a direction, but as a mode of travel toward diverse future worlds.

See Also

ANARCHISM; COMMUNITY POLITICS; ECOFEMINISM; NETWORKS: ELECTRONIC; PACIFISM AND PEACE ACTIVISM; REPRODUCTIVE RIGHTS; SCIENCE FICTION; UTOPIAN WRITING

References and Further Reading

Bornstein, Kate. 1995. *Gender outlaw: On men, women, and the rest of us.* New York: Vintage.

Ehrlich, Howard J.,Carol Erlich, Daniel Deleon, and Glenda Morris, eds. 1979. *Reinventing anarchy: What are anarchists thinking these days?* London: Routledge and Kegan Paul.

Goldman, Emma. 1983. *Dancing in the revolution: Selected writings and speeches.* Ed. Alix Kates Shulman. London: Virago.

———. 1970. *Living my life.* New York: Dover.

Haaland, Bonnie. 1993. *Emma Goldman: Sexuality and the impurity of the state.* Montreal: Black Rose.

Marsh, Margaret S. 1981. *Anarchist women, 1870–1920.* Philadelphia: Temple University Press.

McElroy, Wendy, ed. 1982. *Freedom, feminism, and the state: An overview of individualist feminism.* Washington, D.C.: Cato Institute.

Piercy, Marge. 1978. *Woman on the edge of time.* London: Women's Press.

Plant, Sadie, 1997. *Zeros + ones: Digital women and the new technoculture.* London: Fourth Estate.

Starhawk. 1988. *Dreaming the dark: Magic, sex and politics.* Boston: Beacon.

Judy Greenway

FEMINISM: Asian-American

The history, culture, and communities of Asian-Americans have been shaped over time by economic conditions, immigration laws, ideology, and international politics. Asian-American history began in 1820, when the U.S. Immigration Commission officially reported the arrival of the first Chinese in the United States, although the presence of Filipinos and Chinese has been reported informally in earlier years. In the mid-1850s, thriving U.S. economy and the gold rush near Sacramento, California, attracted many Chinese, most of them able-bodied men who came as low-wage, unskilled laborers to help develop the western states and Hawaii, escaping political upheavals and socioeconomic turmoil in China. The few Chinese immigrant women at that time were employed as indentured servants, prostitutes, laundresses, and laborers.

After Congress passed the U.S. Exclusion Act of 1882 forbidding further immigration—including Chinese women and families hoping to join men already in the United States—Japanese immigrants, many arriving with their "picture brides," increasingly replaced Chinese laborers. As Japan colonized Korea in the early 1900s, a small number of Koreans seeking economic opportunities and fleeing Japanese imperialism began their immigration first to Hawaii and then to the U.S. mainland to work as low-wage laborers. Asian Indians arrived in the country at about the same time. When the United States gained possession of the Philippines after the Spanish-American War, Filipinos gradually immigrated. The Exclusion Act of 1924 prohibited Asian immigration, except for the Filipinos, who were recruited to replace other Asian workers excluded by the act. When the United States granted independence to the Philippines in 1934, Filipinos also faced immigration restrictions. After World War II, racist, class-based, gender-specific repressive immigration laws were repealed, enabling many Asians from different countries to immigrate to the United States. After the collapse of South Vietnam in 1975, thousands of Vietnamese, Chinese, Laotian, and Hmong refugees arrived, changing the demographic composition and social realities of Asian-Americans.

The term *Asian-American* generally refers to Americans of Asian and Pacific Island descent, members of 29 ethnic subgroups, most of which have their own languages and cultural backgrounds. By 1998, Asian-Americans numbered 10.5 million, about 4 percent of the total U.S. population. The larger groups include the Chinese, Filipino, Japanese, Asian Indian, Korean, and Vietnamese. Currently, females constitute 51 percent of the Asian-American population.

Feminism, in its true sense, needs to address the interlocking of race, ethnicity, class, gender, sexuality, nationality, and other forms of domination and oppression embedded in a stratification system that is seen as subjugating women generally and Asian-American women specifically. The historical experience of immigration, exclusion, racism, classism, sexism, homophobia, and biases against national origins has had long-term effects on diverse Asian-Americans, especially women. Legal exclusion forced couples and families to separate and required women to make sacrifices for their families on both sides of the Pacific for more than half a century. Ill effects included a skewed sex ratio favoring males, resulting in a lack of marriageable women and forced bachelorhood for many Asian men; split households with husband and father absent in Asian homelands; and lack consequent growth of the Asian-American population.

Because many members of the white majority were unwelcoming or even hostile to Asian-Americans, community-based economies designed to provide mutual aid sprang up among the first immigrants (Chow, 1996). By consolidating their limited economic resources, using available labor sources, and integrating household members and kin, small producers and ethnic enterprises firmly established a family-based economy among Asian-Americans. For family survival, the few Asian women, along with their children, worked as unpaid laborers in the fields or in small businesses.

Denied a voice, visibility, and validity in American society and relegated to peripheral positions, Asian-American women historically lived in either marginalized ethnic colonies or isolated neighborhoods from which they were rarely invited into predominant cultural, economic, political, and social domains. Although it is unclear whether Asian-American women were active early in the U.S. women's suffrage movement, their historical struggle and cultural resistance in their everyday life implicitly demonstrated their spirit of feminism (Chow, 1996; Yung, 1986). The incorporation of more Asian-American women into the U.S. labor market as paid workers after World War II and increases in Asian female immigration since 1965 have made these women more socially and economically visible.

Asian-American women's political activism began in the wake of the civil rights movement of the early 1960s and the women's movement later that decade (Chow, 1988). They began to organize formally and informally and to address issues, problems, and needs as women of color, striving for equality and improved conditions for themselves and their ethnic communities. At first, many of them sought to establish women's caucuses within existing Asian-American organizations. Better-educated or well-to-do Asian-American women formed early women's groups such as church organizations, social service centers, and women's professional societies (Wong, 1980). These initial organizing efforts provided opportunities to acquire leadership skills and political experience.

Awareness of sexism within their ethnic communities grew as some Asian-American women activists became more conscious of their multiple disadvantaged positions as women and as members of a racial minority and of the working class (Chow, 1987; Espiritu, 1997). They began to examine the structural sources of their social inequality based on race, ethnicity, class, gender, generation, nationality, and sexual orientation within their own Asian-American communities as well as in the larger U.S. society. They also recognized the need to confront prejudice and discrimination and to solve their social problems through collective action. As they developed feminist consciousness, some Asian-Americans created their own organizations to deal with specific issues and problems and to combat racism, classism, sexism, ageism, and homophobia, while others opted to join the larger women's movement, hoping that it would meet their needs.

Over the years, a few regional organizations have evolved out of the feminist groups that these Asian-American women activists attempted to organize (Chow, 1988; Vaid, 1988). Such organizations are in the process of expanding their influence and building up their networks from the grassroots to the national level. These groups include the National Network of Asian and Pacific Women, the National Organization of Pan Asian Women, Asian American Women United of California, the Organization of Chinese American Women, the Committee on South Asian Women, the Association of Asian Indian Women in America, the Filipino American Women's Network, the Filipino Women's League, the Vietnamese Women's Association, and Cambodian Women for Progress.

These feminist organizations share the objectives of advancing the causes of women and of racial and ethnic minorities, building a strong Asian sisterhood, maximizing the social participation of Asian-American women in the larger society, and effecting changes through collective efforts and community empowerment. A majority of the members are middle-class Asian women, college students, professionals, and political activists; few working-class women are among their ranks (Asian American Women United of California, 1988; Wong, 1980).

Some problems deriving from social pressures both within and outside their own communities have hindered the growth of feminist consciousness and activism among Asian-American women. The category "Asian-American women" encompasses diverse ethnic subgroups whose issues and concerns are not always the same. (For example, the second wave of Asian-American women after World War II were designated immigrants, whereas south-

east Asian women after 1975 were designated refugees.) Thus various groups' interests have not always been equally or appropriately addressed by the women's movement. Gender subordination is compounded by ethnicity, class, caste, and generation, and women are also divided by nationality and sexual orientation, making feminist consciousness and solidarity hard to establish. In the early stages of the women's movement, Asian-American women who actively pursued feminist issues were often criticized by their male counterparts and even by some female peers who cited possible "negative" effects on Asian-American communities and their antiracism agendas. Such critics maintained that challenges to male dominance directed at Asian-American men led to possible loss of ethnic identity, weakening of Asian-American men's ego, constraints in gender relationships, destruction of work and family lives, and dilution of community efforts and resources; some also saw a struggle for "white" feminism instead of Asian-American social causes.

Fear of being accused of "separatism," of antagonizing their ethnic community, and of being co-opted by the white establishment tends to limit activism by Asian-American women against sexism in their communities and in society at large. These women also experience "double patriarchy"—an interplay between Asian and U.S. gender ideologies, which tends to subordinate women by developing racialized and sexualized images and to reinforce a gendered division of labor inside and outside the family. Social realities and standpoints for Asian-American women, then, are distinct from those of white women. Asian-American women's experience of sexism may be subverted or ignored, and the idea of feminism is contested in racial, ethnic, class, sexual, national, and cultural contexts.

Some Asian-American women who have participated actively in white feminist organizations have soon become disillusioned, though others have been at ease. Like other women of color, some Asian-American women feel alienated by racial homogeneity and insensitivity in the women's movement, which tends to be white. Some are critical of the role white women play, in partnership with their men, as defenders and perpetuators of institutional racism, classism, and homophobia that denigrate Asian women and men (Chai, 1985; Chow, 1988; Espiritu, 1997; Loo and Ong, 1982; Shad, 1997; Yamada, 1981). They find that many white women neither fully understand nor are willing to include on their agenda issues and problems central to Asian-American women (for example, racial and sexual stereotypes, Asian war brides and wives of U.S. servicemen and businessmen, exploitation of immigrant women's labor, mail-order brides, international trafficking in Asian prostitutes, domestic violence, negative media images, and hate crimes against Asians). High poverty rates among Hmong, Cambodian, and Laotian women whose families receive welfare (even higher than those of black American and Latina women) have often gone unnoticed by policymakers and the general public. The interplay between race, ethnicity, and sexuality in the life of Asian-American gays and lesbians usually remains hidden. The cry of Pacific Islander women for collective self-determination as indigenous peoples and for sovereignty over native land was not heard by white feminists (Trask, 1993). Increasingly, Asian-American women see their male counterparts as allies in the fight against racial domination and partners in the struggle for equality.

Feminism comes in different forms and colors. Asian-American feminism may be in a league of its own, sharing common bases with other women's groups but developing unique visions and perspectives. Like other women of color in the United States, Asian-American women face multiple forms of domination and oppression embedded in social institutions and dynamic processes of social life. Wrestling with multiple problems often creates dialectics for them as the forces of race, ethnicity, class, gender, sexuality, age, nationality, and physical disability may either heighten or inhibit their feminist consciousness and activism.

Despite occasional setbacks and frustrations, a growing number of Asian-American women have worked steadfastly to challenge oppression and inequality within their communities and in society. Through self-awareness, consciousness raising, community participation, feminism and other political activities, these women have begun to emerge from a culture of silence and invisibility. However, eradicating domination and inequality requires structural changes to solve systemic problems. Setting such eradication as their main goal, Asian-American women have empowered themselves from within through acts of resistance and mass political mobilization to elevate themselves out of their structural subjugation. They also are making alliances with women, Asian men, people of color, and others supportive of their struggles to change the structure of power relationships and inequality in society at large. Vision, networking, coalition building, empowerment, and feminist solidarity are essential if Asian-American feminism is to help build a just, equitable, and humane society in the United States.

Furthermore, Asian-American women are forging special links with women in Asia and in other parts of the world, especially the third world, fostering a worldview of women's struggle, solidarity, and liberation (for example, at the Fourth United Nations World Conference on Women and the NGO Forum in Beijing in 1995). This solidarity with Asian and third world women gives Asian-American women a clear vision of feminism as an international, transcending social, cultural, and national boundaries to become a momentous force for future global feminism and social change. In this effort lies their potential contribution to and linkage with the women's movement in the United States and the international women's movement.

See Also

FEMINISM: SECOND-WAVE NORTH AMERICAN

References and Further Reading

Abraham, Margaret. 2000. *Speaking the unspeakable.* New Brunswick, N.J.: Rutgers University Press.

Asian American Women United of California, ed. 1988. *Making waves: An anthology of writing by and about Asian American women.* Boston: Beacon.

Chai, Alice Yun. 1985. Toward a holistic paradigm for Asian American women's studies: A synthesis of feminist scholarship and women of color's feminist politics. *Women's Studies International Forum* 8: 62–99.

Chow, Esther Ngan-ling. 1987. The development of feminist consciousness among Asian American Women. *Gender and Society* 1: 284–299.

———. 1996. Family, economy, and the state: A legacy of struggle for Chinese American women. In Silvia Pedraza and Ruben C. Rumbaut, eds., *Origins and destinies: Immigration, race, and ethnicity in America,* 110–124. Belmont, Calif.: Wadsworth.

———. 1988. The feminist movement; Where are all the Asian American women? In Asian American Women United of California, ed., *Making waves: An anthology of writing by and about Asian American women,* 362–377. Boston: Beacon.

Espiritu, Yen Le. 1997. *Asian American women and men.* Thousand Oaks, Calif.: Sage.

Gupta, Sangeeta, ed. 1999. *Emerging voices: South Asian women redefine self, family, and community.* Thousand Oaks, Calif.: Sage.

Kim, Elaine H., Lilia V. Villaneuva, and Asian Women's United of California, eds. 1997. *Making more waves: New writing by Asian American women.* Boston: Beacon.

Loo, Chalso, and Paul Ong. 1982. Slaying demons with a sewing needle: Feminist issues for Chinatown women. *Berkeley Journal of Sociology* 27: 77–88.

Ng, Franklin, ed. 1999. *Asian American women and gender: A reader.* New York: Garland.

Sciachitano, Marian, and Linda Trinh Vo, eds. 2000. Special issues on Asian American women. *Frontiers: A Journal of Women Studies* 21 (1,2).

Shad, Sonia. 1997. *Feminists breathe fire.* Boston: South end.

Trask, Haunani Kay. 1993. *From a native daughter: Colonialism and sovereignty in Hawaii.* Monroe, Maine: Common Courage.

Vaid, Jyotsna. 1988. Seeking a voice: South Asian women's groups in North America. In Asian American Women United of California, ed., *Making waves: An anthology of writing by and about Asian American women,* 395–405. Boston: Beacon.

Wong, Germaine Q. 1980 Impediments to Asian Pacific American woman organizing. In *Conference on the educational and occupational needs of Asian Pacific American women.* Washington, D.C.: Department of Health, Education, and welfare, National Institute of Education.

Wong, Nellie, Merle Woo, and Mitsuye Yamada. 1979. *Asian American writers speak out on feminism.* San Francisco: SF Radical Women.

Yamada, Mitsuye. 1981. Asian Pacific American women and feminism. In Charrie Moraga and Gloria Anzaldua, eds. *This bridge called my back: Radical writings by women of color,* 71–75. Watertown, Mass.: Persephone.

Yung, Judy. 1986. *Chinese women of America: A pictorial history.* Seattle, Wash.: Chinese Culture Foundation of San Francisco and University of Washington Press.

Esther Ngan-ling Chow

FEMINISM: Australia and New Zealand

Feminist movements in Australia and New Zealand have distinct histories and concerns, but the dynamics of their formation have been similar, as have their achievements and vicissitudes. In both countries, there has long been a close association between feminist movements and the state; in both, the building of new societies incorporating a maternalist and civilizing mission has depended on the dispossession of indigenous women and men. It is possible to identify four phases in ongoing feminist movements. (The concept of two or three "waves," often applied to feminism, is mis-

leading here, obscuring continuities and postsuffrage experiments with citizenship.) First, there was a campaign for political rights, purity, and protection leading to women's early enfranchisement; second, there was a postsuffrage experiment with women's citizenship from the 1890s through the 1940s; third, there was a demand for revolutionary change as part of women's liberation; and, fourth, there are the contemporary challenges posed by postcoloniality, postmodernity, pluralism, and the global restructuring of markets.

The Old World in the New

Australia and New Zealand were British colonies whose settlement involved the dispossession and destruction of the lands and culture of the indigenous Aboriginal and Maori inhabitants. Nineteenth- and early twentieth-century feminism in these colonized and colonizing societies was imbued with the missionary zeal of civilizers and the moral authority that enabled the righteous agency of women. When Maori women in late nineteenth-century New Zealand objected to the idea that they should be trained as a servant class, the feminist and Women's Christian Temperance Union (WCTU) journal *White Ribbon Signal* endorsed their refusal in terms that, nevertheless, made clear the source of white women's authority: "One cannot be surprised that the Maori girls scorned the idea of becoming the servants of the Pakehas, for many of them have as much pride, and every right to have it, as their more civilized sisters" (quoted in Brookes and Tennant, 1992: 36).

Civilization, purification, and protection were the responsibilities assumed by enlightened representatives of the Old World in fashioning the New, and by the white race in the outlying posts of empire. As mothers of the race and maternal citizens of new nation-states, feminists assumed special responsibilities for the protection of women and children. As the self-conscious pioneers of a New World, feminists also shared with progressive men, with liberals and socialists, an expectation that they would and could participate in social experiments and build a new, caring society. New Zealand was specially favored, wrote Lucy Smith in *White Ribbon Signal,* because "so early in her national life she may...claim the guidance of both men and women" (quoted in Brookes, 1993: 141). One result of the convergence of the missionary impulse, the civilizing responsibility, and New World optimism was the pronounced activist impulse of feminism. A leading feminist in New Zealand, Kate Sheppard, urged branches of the WCTU to break up the "deadly calm" that sometimes characterized meetings by throwing themselves into good works in the community: "The woman who is a good citizen cannot be content with things as they are" (Sheppard, 1992: 131–32). Kate Sheppard's ethnic background was characteristic of these New World feminists. Born in Liverpool, England, she immigrated to New Zealand when she was 21. She joined the WCTU on its formation in Christchurch in 1885 and became superintendent of the New Zealand branch's Franchise and Legal Department, in which capacity she became the recognized leader of the movement for women's suffrage in that country.

An Ethical (White) State

Feminists, like other progressives in Australasia, demanded state intervention to redress social inequalities. The state was conceptualized as a benign and powerful ally of the oppressed, a force that could limit the exercise and effects of capitalist and masculine power. But social equality in this vision was reserved for white Europeans. The indigenous peoples were marginalized, consigned to separate development or, in Australia, assigned the role of a dying race. To secure the white standard of living, both countries instigated racially based immigration policies; Austrailia's rules were actually called the "white Australia policy." Feminism in these British colonies was thus shaped by social relations that were at once racist and democratic, by societies that spurned the aristocratic traditions of Europe, only to institutionalize the rights of a new aristocracy of white men. White women found themselves in a contradictory situation. As the working partners of the New World pioneers and democrats, they expected equal status with white men. The earliest of such demands were expressed in the 1860s. Yet the status of white men in these manly democracies involved an assertion of white masculine equality that rested on the subordination of women as a group—in the home, at work, in the law, and in politics.

White men (and Maori men in New Zealand) won the basic democratic right to vote in most Australasian colonies by the end of the 1850s. Four decades passed before the first women to win the vote did so—first in New Zealand (1893) and then in South Australia (1894). Feminists had to wage a long struggle to obtain woman suffrage, especially in some Australian states. As Bessie Rischbieth, president of the Australian Federation of Women Voters, was moved to reflect in 1935: "Australia was a new country, a nation forged by the pioneering spirit.... [Unfortunately] the men of the New World forgot the women standing by their side. They drew up a Constitution for their New Colonies giving Citizenship to one sex only. Consequently Australian women had a long struggle for Enfranchisement."

Feminists in nineteenth- and early twentieth-century Australia and New Zealand argued that achieving freedom for women entailed curbing the liberties of men. Petitions and campaigns were often concerned to restrict alcohol, gambling, and men's access to women's bodies. Feminists promoted temperance, purity, and restraint as values in themselves and in order to protect women and children from masculine licentiousness and violence. The WCTU was a leading player in feminist campaigns in both countries. Assuming that most women in the colonies would become wives, feminists aimed to reform marital relations, both to provide some economic security for women and to offer freedom from unwanted childbearing and venereal disease. Central to feminist thought was the importance of women's right to control their bodies. Women's economic dependence was thus always troubling, and the small measure of independence achieved with the passage of Married Women's Property Acts from the 1880s was regarded as an important victory.

Feminist analysis of the subordination of women centered on their treatment by men as "creatures of sex." Men's "animal" lusts led to women's violation and degradation. Prostitution was seen as the paradigmatic condition of women, including married women. Marriage, it was urged, should be lifted to a higher plane. Much reform effort was thus directed toward keeping girls and women out of men's hands and minimizing women's vulnerability to "seduction." Reforms included the appointment of women to a whole range of public positions—as doctors, lawyers, jail wardens, factory inspectors, and police officers. Of central importance, as well, was raising the age of consent and gaining right of entry to the education and avenues of employment that would enable women to earn a decent living. In Australia, activists in the WCTU such as Bessie Harrison Lee, Marie Kirk, and Elizabeth Nicholls were joined by feminists in secular suffrage organizations such as Vida Goldstein, organizer of the United Council for Women's Suffrage from 1899 and editor of the *Australian Women's Sphere* from 1900; Louisa Lawson, editor of *Dawn* from 1888; and Rose Scott, a founding member of the New South Wales (NSW) Womanhood Suffrage League, formed in 1891, in campaigning for women's freedom and advancement.

White Australian women were enfranchised federally in 1902, one year after the inauguration of the nation-state, and, at the same time, they became the first women in the world eligible to become candidates for their national parliament. Aboriginal women and other nonwhites were denied these rights, as they were also denied the Maternity Allowance, introduced by the Labor government in 1912 in response to lobbying by women. Feminists appropriated for themselves the significance attributed to motherhood by racist and nationalist discourse, formulating a concept of maternal citizenship, involving rights in return for duties. The feminist journal *Women Voter* (9 October 1912) was moved to protest the exclusion of Asian women from the maternity benefit. Asian women were, after all, British subjects, and "maternity was maternity whatever the race." The status of mother of the race could be used for racist and antiracist purposes.

Postsuffrage Citizenship

Feminist organizations flourished in Australia and New Zealand after the granting of suffrage, as women sought to make their new status as citizens meaningful. In New Zealand, the Society for the Protection of Women and Girls campaigned to outlaw men's sexual abuse of girls and women, within the home and outside it. In 1896 the age of consent was raised to 16 years. In Australia, the Australian Federation of Women Voters was founded in 1921, partly to lobby for citizens' rights in Australia, and partly in response to the need to have a national body represent Australian women in overseas forums such as the League of Nations and the British Commonwealth League; one of its primary aims was to achieve the establishment of an equal moral standard. In 1929, the NSW United Associations of Women was formed from three existing feminist organizations, and it campaigned ceaselessly for an independent income for mothers and, after 1932, for the repeal of NSW legislation, passed in that year, banning the employment of married women teachers and lecturers.

In the status of citizenship, feminists saw a means to escape familial and conjugal identities. The new woman of the New World was "she who has discovered herself—not relatively as mother, wife, sister, but absolutely" (Sievwright, 1992: 119). In Australian campaigns for economic independence, the right of married women to retain their nationality, and to the motherhood endowment, middle-class feminists such as Jessie Street, president of the United Associations of Women, joined with labor-oriented women such as Muriel Heagney and Jean Daley in efforts to serve women's individuality.

They were especially concerned about the situation of the married women and were drawn to the conclusion that men's and women's rights as citizens were incommensurate. Men's citizen's rights included conjugal rights, the right to women's sexual and domestic services. Feminists cam-

paigned for women's citizen's rights to control their bodies and sell their labor. To end the "sex slavery" of the married woman, feminists advocated three interrelated goals: equal pay (or the rate for the job), motherhood endowment, and childhood endowment. By World War II, some forms of maternity benefit and child endowment had been introduced in both Australia and New Zealand, but the regular income envisaged for all mothers in the claim for endowment never materialized, and women's pay rates remained at about 50 percent of men's.

Women's belief in activist citizenship also led them to run for political office, sometimes seeking endorsement from the major labor and conservative parties, but also as independent candidates. Vida Goldstein was a candidate from Victoria for the Australian senate five times but was defeated on each occasion. The first woman elected to an Australian parliament was Edith Cowan, president of the local branch of the National Council of Women, who won a seat in the Western Australian legislature as an endorsed Nationalist (conservative) candidate in 1921. Most women candidates at this time expected to speak, as Edith Cowan spoke, for women's interests, especially on issues of home and family. In New Zealand, the first woman elected to Parliament, in 1933, was a Labor canidate, Elizabeth McCombs, who declared, "I do hope that the women of New Zealand will realize that where they are concerned...I shall be their representative first" (quoted in Wallace, 1993: 188). To appeal solely to an electorate of women was, as it turned out, of dubious effectiveness. Although Australian women had been eligible to run for the federal (national) Parliament since 1902, and numerous women had run for both houses, not one had been elected by the time of the outbreak of World War II. The "right to rule," as the South Australian feminist Elizabeth Nicholls termed it, was proving more elusive then the right to vote.

The advent of war in 1939 saw a renewed push in Australia by the Council of Action for Equal Pay, which had been formed two years before at a combined meeting of unionists and feminists. The discourse on postwar reconstruction, set in motion by the war, encouraged feminists, led by Jessie Street, to formulate a charter for women's equality, which was endorsed by a conference in 1943 of representatives from 90 women's groups across Australia. In the same year the Women for Canberra movement achieved a breakthrough with the election of the first two women to the federal parliament—Dorothy Tangey (Australian Labor Party) to the Senate and Edith Lyons (United Australia Party, widow of a former prime minister, Joseph Lyons) to the House of Representatives. The year 1943 was a high point in Australian feminism.

Women's Liberation

Although the 1950s saw a new focus in social and political discourse on the "family," with women positioned as wives and mothers, feminists continued in those years to press for equal pay and opportunity in the workforce. In Australia, the left-wing Union of Australian Women was formed in 1950. As more women entered the paid workforce, drawn into new jobs opening up in professions such as teaching and nursing and in clerical and manufacturing jobs, campaigns for equal pay gained momentum, and trade union women, together with the increasing population of university students, contributed significantly to reactivation of a broad-based women's movement in the late 1960s. Local traditions converged with overseas influences. Women's liberation groups formed in the capital cities; new magazines started, such as *Mejane* and *Refractory Girl* in Sydney and *Scarlet Woman* in Melbourne; and organizations such as the Women's Action Committee and Women's Electoral Lobby demanded equal opportunities in the workforce and the right to child care, abortion on demand, and free contraception.

The more radical women's liberation groups insisted on the importance of revolutionary change defined as an end to patriarchy and dichotomous sex roles. The critique of traditional femininity that characterized women's liberation owed much to lesbian feminist analysis, which identified heterosexuality and the traditional family as key patriarchal institutions. Women's liberation was a product of and a reaction to sexual liberation. It assumed women's right to sexual pleasure, yet considered the penis irrelevant to female orgasm and critiqued dominant heterosexual relations for invariably positioning women as "sex objects." Women's rights as heterosexual subjects were usually conceptualized, as they had long been by feminists, as the right to say "no." Lesbianism was promoted as a feminist alternative to heterosexuality, but increasingly it was defined as a political position, not simply a matter of sexual desire. Just as lesbians provided feminism with radical new insights, so feminism was important in validating lesbianism and "separate" lifestyles and communities.

The resurgence of feminism in the 1970s was an important factor in the election of Australian and New Zealand Labor governments in the 1970s and 1980s, which in turn implemented a variety of reforms aimed at improving women's legal, economic, and political position. Funding for child care expanded, equal employment opportunity programs were established, and single parents' benefits and maternity leave were introduced.

In Australia, equal pay was formally granted by the Arbitration Court in December 1972, after last-minute intervention by newly elected Labor government. The traditions of state arbitration of industrial relations, pay rates, and working conditions in Australia and New Zealand have proved conducive to feminist gains in this domain. By 1990, Australian women's pay rates in full-time jobs had reached 83 percent of men's rates. The recent dismantling of state arbitration and industrial regulation in favor of enterprise bargaining, individual contracts, and the rule of the market, especially in New Zealand, where the Employment Equity Act was repealed by the National government in 1990, has had deleterious effects, especially for women workers. The more general dismantling of welfare states in which the majority of beneficiaries and employees had been women also poses particular problems for feminists today. In New Zealand, especially, strong feminist critiques of the masculinism of nonclassical economics have been developed—for example, the analysis offered by Phillipa Bunkle, whose previous work had been in the areas of women's health and women's studies. In an address to the Policy for Our Times conference in Wellington in mid-1991, Bunkle argued memorably that the "invisible hand" of neoclassical economies could actually be seen to be "white and hairy" (quoted in Du Plessis, 1992: 212).

The women's liberation movement was activated by a paradoxical combination of, on the one hand, libertarian individualism (evident in Germaine Greer's earliest work, *The Female Eunuch,* 1970), which championed personal rebellion against the social imposition of sex roles and stereotypes, and, on the other, a celebration of sisterhood and collectivism. The collectivist and egalitarian principles of the movement were antipathetic to the emergence of leaders; individual women rose to prominence only as writers (Germaine Greer, for example, and Anne Summers, whose best-selling women's history *Damned Whores and God's Police* was published in 1975) or as leading femocrats in the public service, as happened with Liz Reid, the first Australian adviser to the prime minister on women's affairs, appointed in 1973. "Femocrat" was the name given to a distinctively Australian phenomenon, the feminist bureaucrat who worked in the state and federal public service in a range of areas—education, health, child care, or labor relations, or in special sections such as the Office of the Status of Women in Canberra. The Australian and New Zealand women's movements of the 1970s and 1980s reactivated local traditions of looking to the state to redress the inequalities between the sexes and to ameliorate the effects of male power. Feminists secured state funding to support women's refuges, health centers, rape crisis centers and special projects for International Women's Year in 1975, all the while agonizing about whether such state support would lead to co-option and the negation of women's revolutionary intent of overthrowing the patriarchal system. In theoretical terms, these issues were often formulated as debates between radical, socialist, and liberal feminists. Initially most influential in the 1970s, socialist feminism was later overtaken by varieties of radical feminism and poststructuralist influences. At the same time, interventions by Maori and Aboriginal women, Asian women, and other women from non-English-speaking backgrounds challenged feminist dichotomies between women and men, the oppressed and oppressors.

Antidiscrimination legislation was introduced by a number of Australian states in the 1970s, and a requirement for affirmative action by large companies and tertiary institutions was introduced by the Australian parliament in 1984. During this decade, New Zealand and Australia institutionalized equal employment opportunity programs and outlawed sexual harassment. Universities (all, with one or two minor exceptions, state-funded) supported the rapid growth of women's studies at all levels of study and programs in nonsexist education in schools. The deep involvement of feminism with the state has become in turn a major focus for feminist research, in both New Zealand and Australia.

Contemporary Challenges

Current feminist movements in Australia and New Zealand are now tackling the challenges posed by the worlds of the "beyond"—postcoloniality, postindustrial welfare state, and postmodernity—which we now collectively inhabit. The effective mobilizations of indigenous movements during the past 40 years, asserting the importance of autonomy and self-government as well as land rights, and the simultaneous organization of ethnic minority women have at last secured acknowledgment among dominant groups of feminists of the diversity of women's interests, the plurality of women's movements, and power relations between women. Women's priorities are necessarily shaped by their different histories and current circumstances: Aboriginal women might be more concerned about infant mortality, housing, and access to land, whereas immigrant women have campaigned for access to English-language classes, culturally appropriate child care, and health services. At a theoretical and a practical level, feminist movements are coming to terms with difference and diversity, devising ways to retain the unitary and uniting category "women," while all the while remembering women's heterogeneity. To recognize the manifest differences among women and the implications of power relations between women is one challenge

faced by feminists; another is to resolve the incompatibilities between paid and unpaid work, and between careers and motherhood.

See Also

DEVELOPMENT: AUSTRALIA AND NEW ZEALAND; FEMOCRAT; IMAGES OF WOMEN: AUSTRALIA AND NEW ZEALAND; POLITICS AND THE STATE: AUSTRALIA, NEW ZEALAND, AND THE PACIFIC ISLANDS

References and Further Reading

Allen, Judith. 1994. *Rose Scott: Vision and revision in feminism.* Melbourne: Oxford University Press.

Brookes, Barbara. 1993. A weakness for strong subjects: The women's movement and sexuality. *New Zealand Journal of History* 27(2: October): 140–56.

Brookes, Barbara, and Margaret Tennant. 1992. Maori and Pakeha women: Many histories, divergent pasts? In Barbara Brookes et al., eds., *Women in History 2.* Wellington: Bridget Williams.

Bulbeck, Chilla. 1997. *Living feminism: The impact of the women's movement on three generations of Australian women.* Melbourne: Cambridge University Press.

Du Plessis, Rosemary. 1992. Stating the contradictions: The case of women's employment. In Rosemary Du Plessis et al., eds., *Feminist voices: Women's studies texts for Aotearoa/New Zealand.* Auckland: Oxford University Press.

Lake, Marilyn. 1999. *Getting equal: The history of feminism in Australia.* Sydney: Allen and Unwin.

Pettman, Jan. 1992. *Living in the Margins: Racism, sexism and feminism in Australia.* Sydney: Allen and Unwin.

Rischbieth, Bessie. 1935. Notes for an address, "Women's Work in the Empire." Canberra, Australia: Rischbieth papers, National Library 2004/4/97.

Sawyer, Marian. 1990. *Sisters in suits: Women and public policy in Australia.* Sydney: Allen and Unwin.

Sheppard, Kate. 1992. The responsibilities of women as citizens. In Margaret Lovell-Smith, ed., *The woman question: Writings by women who won the vote.* Auckland: New Women's Press.

Sievwright, Margaret. 1992. The new woman. In Margaret Lovell-Smith, ed., *The woman question: Writings by women who won the vote.* Auckland: New Women's Press.

Summers, Anne. 1999. *Ducks on the pond: An autobiography, 1945–1976.* Ringwood, Victoria: Viking Penguin.

Wallace, Sandra. 1993. Members for everywoman? The campaign promises of women parliamentary candidates. *New Zealand Journal of History* 27(2: October): 187–198.

Marilyn Lake

FEMINISM: Black British

The term *black British feminism* refers to the theory and practice of African, Asian, and Caribbean women activists in Britain. "Black" was adopted by British antiracist activists in the 1960s as a multiracial identity that indicated shared experiences of racism and imperialism. Black feminism is most commonly associated with the emergence of a black women's movement in the 1970s. Black women's concerns were marginalized in the women's liberation and antiracist movements. As a result, women established autonomous organizations such as Brixton Black Women's Group, Liverpool Black Sisters, and Awaz. These organizations campaigned on issues that affected black women in particular and developed a grassroots theory of black women's oppression (Sudbury, 1998).

Although black feminism as a phrase did not enter the political arena until the 1970s, early black women activists in Britain established a proto-black feminist agenda. This included an awareness of the intersection of race, class, and gender oppression, a focus on issues having a unique impact on black women, and the creation of black women's forms of leadership. Women leaders include Cornelia Sorabji, the first woman law student at a British university, who returned to India in 1894 to fight on behalf of women in purdah; the Jamaican Amy Garvey, who headed the Association for the Advancement of Colored People and was a member of the Pan-African Congress; and Claudia Jones, a Trinidadian deported from the United States for her communist activities, who came to Britain in 1956 and founded the Confederation of Afro-Asian-Caribbean Organizations. Black women were also active in less visible roles in a range of anti-imperialist and antiracist organizations from the beginning of the twentieth century. These include the Indian Home Rule movement, the League of Colored Peoples, and the Campaign Against Racism and Discrimination (CARD).

The Black Women's Movement

The black women's movement solidified as an autonomous political entity with the founding in 1978 of the Organisation of Women of African and Asian Descent (OWAAD). OWAAD's national campaigns were at the heart of a vigorous and politically active movement. During the key years 1978–1982, important campaigns included: (1) immigration legislation and deportation cases; (2) domestic violence; (3) school exclusions and busing of schoolchildren; (4) Depo-Provera and reproductive rights; (5) supporting industrial action by black women; and (6) policing and defense campaigns. Many of these focused on the role of the state in maintaining race, class, and gender inequalities.

Of particular interest was the campaign against the use of Depo-Provera, a long-term injectable contraceptive with potential adverse side effects. Black women argued that doctors prescribing the drug were influenced by stereotypical views of black women as sexually promiscuous. This abuse of reproductive rights was reminiscent of the forced sterilization of black and poor women in other parts of Europe, the United States, and the Caribbean. The campaign revealed the different priorities of the black women's and women's liberation movements. While white women were fighting for the right to abortion on demand, black women were fighting eugenic ideologies to protect their right to bear children (Carby, 1982). A second important campaign was against "virginity tests" carried out at Heathrow Airport by immigration officials. The tests were physically degrading and inaccurate and relied on stereotypical views of south Asian women. OWAAD picketed the airport during the summer of 1979 and succeeded in having the tests curtailed. The campaign also highlighted racist and sexist immigration legislation passed by Margaret Thatcher's Conservative government. OWAAD protested against the Immigration and Nationality Act of 1981, which withdrew the right to abode from many passport holders from former British colonies and reinforced the position of women immigrants as dependents (Brah, 1996).

In 1982, OWAAD held its annual gathering on the theme of "black feminism." Internal divisions over issues such as race, homophobia, and the terms *black* and *feminist* led to irresolvable contradictions (Brixton Black Women's Group, 1984). The demise of OWAAD fragmented the black women's movement as women focused on local struggles in their communities. However, some national campaigns continued, such as the campaign led by Southall Black Sisters on behalf of Kiranjit Ahluwahlia, who had been sentenced to life imprisonment for killing her violent husband. In 1992, Southall Black Sisters won her release, setting a new legal precedent for cases of self-defense against abusive spouses.

Black Feminist Theory

Black feminist theory emerged from the black women's movement. Early theorizing focused on challenging feminist theory that claimed to speak for all women while in fact ignoring black women. The black feminist critique of white feminism was most forcefully presented by Hazel Carby in her article "White Woman Listen!" (1982) and by Valerie Amos and Pratibha Parmar in "Challenging Imperial Fem-

721

inism" (1984). These authors argued that white feminists had generated feminist theory out of the experiences of white middle-class women, ignoring black women's struggles with racism and masking white women's participation in maintaining white privilege. In place of "imperial feminism," a feminist practice that aimed to win for white women the same privileges as white men, without dismantling racial inequality, black women created a distinct body of theory based on black women's experiences of oppression and resistance.

Carby identified three areas in which black women's experiences challenged white feminist theory: the family, reproduction, and patriarchy. While white feminists had identified the family as a primary site of oppression, Carby argued that for black women, the family was a site of resistance against racism. Reproduction was also a contested site for black women who, unlike white women, were not valued as child-rearers and homemakers. Carby also argued that black women, historically as enslaved workers and later as domestic workers, engaged in both production and reproduction of white and black labor. Finally, Carby argued that white feminists' reliance on the notion of global patriarchal dominance by men over women masked the intersection of race with gender. Black men, she argued, were not in the same relations of power and dominance as white men and could be *victims* of racism by white women as well as perpetrators of male dominance.

Difference and Heterogeneity

While in the early 1980s, black feminist theorists were concerned with identifying common struggles that unified black women, by the late 1980s, they became more concerned with issues of internal difference and heterogeneity. Black feminists in the academy were influenced by black British cultural studies, which had declared the "end of the essential black subject" (Hall, 1996). Rather than viewing black womanhood as a homogenous identity, black feminists began to map the fluidity and fragmented nature of black women's subjectivities. The move toward a postmodern sensibility was also influenced by a sense of unease about the extreme forms of identity politics that were felt to have undermined the black women's movement (Grewal et al., 1988; Parmar, 1990). Critical black feminist theory is an attempt to replace this limited essentialist vision with an acknowledgment of black women's multiple, hybrid, and complex realities (Mirza, 1997: 13).

The postmodern move in the academy has not always matched the concerns of black feminist activists outside academia. Black feminist activism continues at the local and national levels with an emphasis on creating political coalitions around issues of immigration and deportation, policing and criminal justice, schools, domestic violence, and religious conservatism. The increased entry of black women into academia in the 1990s enabled an unprecedented documentation of black women's struggles (Mirza, 1997; Brah, 1996; Sudbury, 1998). It has also created a space for black British feminism to engage in increasingly diverse theoretical perspectives and debates.

See Also

BLACKNESS AND WHITENESS; FEMINISM: BRITISH ASIAN; FEMINISM: SECOND-WAVE BRITISH; FEMINISM: POSTMODERN; RACE

References and Further Reading

Amos, Valerie, and Pratibha Parmar. 1984. Challenging imperial feminism. *Feminist Review* 17: 3–20.

Bellos, Linda. 1995. A vision back and forth. In V. Mason-John, ed. *Talking black: Lesbians of African and Asian descent speak out.* London and New York: Cassell.

Brah, Avtar. 1996. *Cartographies of diaspora: Contesting identities.* London and New York: Routledge.

Brixton Black Women's Group. 1984. Black women organising. *Many Voices, One Chant, Feminist Review* (17): Special issue.

Bryan, Beverley, Stella Dadzie, and Suzanne Scafe. 1985. *The heart of the race.* London: Virago.

Carby, Hazel. 1982. White woman listen! Black feminism and the boundaries of sisterhood. In Centre for Contemporary Cultural Studies, *The empire strikes back: Race and racism in 70s Britain.* London: Hutchinson.

Grewal, S., J. Kay, L. Landon, G. Lewis, and P. Parmar, eds. 1988. *Charting the journey: Writings by black and third world women.* London: Sheba Feminist.

Hall, Stuart. 1996. New ethnicities. In Houston Baker, Manthia Diawara, and Ruth Lindeborg, eds. *Black British cultural studies.* Chicago: University of Chicago Press.

Mirza, Heidi Safia. 1997. *Black British feminism: A reader.* London and New York: Routledge.

Parmar, Pratibha. 1990. Black feminism: The politics of articulation. In Jonathon Rutherford, ed., *Identity, community, culture, difference.* London: Lawrence and Wishart.

Sudbury, Julia. 1998. *Other kinds of dreams: Black women's organizations and the politics of transformation.* London and New York: Routledge.

Julia Sudbury

FEMINISM: British Asian

The term *British Asian feminism* refers to a significant intervention in British feminism initiated in the 1970s by women of Asian origin from India, Pakistan, and Bangladesh living in Britain.

British Asian feminists noted that their own concerns were missing from the campaigns, literature, and theory of the mainstream women's movement, which was predominantly white and focused on issues of gender and class, ignoring differences of race, culture, and ethnicity. Asian and African Caribbean women came together to protest their invisibility and their exclusion from the white women's movement (Amos and Parmar, 1984; Carby, 1982). In 1978, the book *Finding a Voice* by Amrit Wilson was one of the first attempts to identify the key areas of Asian women's experiences and oppression in Britain. Wilson focused on personal narratives of women's lives, highlighting their experiences of state discrimination through immigration practices such as "virginity testing" at airports, as well as their isolation in the home and in schools, and their struggles in the workplace.

Black was initially an umbrella term to encompass peoples originating from the Americas and people of African (including Caribbean), south Asian (including the Indian subcontinent), and southeast Asian (Chinese, Japanese, Korean, Malaysian, Singaporean, etc.) descent settled in Britain. However, the extent of discrimination in Britain has led some feminists (Anthias and Yuval-Davis, 1983) to argue that distinctions based on color do not go far enough to address the structural location of white, non-British ethnic groups, such as Turkish, Greek Cypriot, Arab, or Jewish, as a determinant of their social relations. Historically, however, the black women's movement represented the collective struggles of African, Caribbean, and Asian women.

The late 1970s and the early 1980s were crucial years of organizing and setting up autonomous campaigns and groups for women of Asian and African Caribbean descent. One significant national organization that emerged was the Organization of Women of Asian and African Descent (OWAAD), which was set up in February 1978. OWAAD acted as a national networking organization for women around the country, and between 1979 and 1982 there were national annual conferences (Amos and Parmar, 1984).

An example of the successful alliance between Asian and African Caribbean women was the protest over the use of "virginity tests" between 1978 and 1979 by British immigration officials on Asian women entering the country for marriage. The tests were carried out on the racist presumption that all Asian women would be virgins before marriage. OWAAD organized a sit-in protest and picketed at Heathrow Airport, with a demonstration in central London against state intimidation and violence organized by women from the Asian Women's Movement (AWAZ) and Brixton Black Women's Group. These protests were matched by women in India (including the All-India Women's Conference and the National Federation of Indian Women), and the Indian government delivered an official protest to the British government.

Asian feminists have been at the forefront of the campaign against domestic violence in Britain. Owing to a concerted effort in this area, a number of Asian women's refuges and advice centers have been set up around the country. Very often Asian women received little support from the predominantly white women's refuges, where their specific fear of being ostracized by their own community was not understood. Quite often they also experienced racism from the white women with whom they shared the refuge. Asian women's refuges or shelter homes have provided safe, supportive spaces for women who leave violent families.

Southall Black Sisters (SBS), founded in 1979 by a small group of Asian and African Caribbean women, has been a key group in organizing against domestic violence. SBS's high-profile public campaigns have brought it into conflict with local (male) community leaders and the antiracist left. Accused in common with other black feminists of "washing our dirty linen" at the expense of antiracist unity, SBS has countered with a spirited attack on the politics of multiculturalism, which views minority communities as homogeneous entities, disregarding class, gender, and sexual conflict.

One of the most notable causes that SBS campaigned for was the case of Kiranjit Ahluwalia. In December 1989, Kiranjit Ahluwalia, a 33-year-old Asian woman, was convicted of murdering her husband. Kiranjit had thrown petrol at him and set fire to the room after enduring ten years of humiliation and sexual abuse. At the trial, the defense failed to build a convincing case that could have broken through the prejudices of an all-white, predominantly male jury. The violence was reduced by the prosecution to being "knocked about." In fact, the night she retaliated against her husband, he had beaten her and put a hot iron against her cheek. It was argued that because she had waited for him to fall asleep, she had had time to "cool off," and a verdict of manslaughter was rejected on the grounds that she could not argue that she had been provoked.

SBS spearheaded a campaign to reopen Kiranjit's case. At the center of the new appeal was an attempt to redefine the traditional and extremely narrow interpretation of the law of provocation. This law is based on accepting as normal the male tendency to attack immediately on provocation. Instead the defense argued for the recognition of the cumulative effect that domestic violence can have. In September 1992, the courts reduced Kiranjit's conviction to manslaughter and set her free, taking into account the three years she had already spent in prison. In December, SBS was awarded the Civil Liberties Prize for 1992 for its "consistent and courageous campaigning over the years."

Asian women were pivotal in the establishment of Women Against Fundamentalism (WAF) in London in spring 1989 as a network to challenge the rise of fundamentalism of all religions, arguing that while fundamentalism appears in many different forms, the focus of all fundamentalist agendas is the control of women's minds and bodies. The impetus to establish WAF came from a public debate held on International Women's Day at the height of the furor over the *fatwa* issued against the author of *The Satanic Verses,* Salman Rushdie. Asian feminists were adamant in their defense of Rushdie, insisting that women's voices be heard over the clamor of the fundamentalists and that they would not allow themselves to be represented by the "community or religious leaders." WAF picketed a demonstration in London by orthodox Muslims who were demanding an extension of the blasphemy laws. WAF called for the abolition of the blasphemy law as it existed, an end to state involvement in all religions, and a reassertion of the right of women to dissent from religious and "multicultural" orthodoxy.

Asian lesbians have been pivotal in defining Asian feminism and raising the issue of sexuality within the Asian community. The struggle for the right to choose and to control their own bodies has made Asian lesbians more visible in the lesbian and gay movement as well as in the Asian community. Asian lesbians have helped set up counseling services and hot lines and cofounded Shakti, an Asian lesbian and gay organization.

Asian women have been active in the workplace, demanding equal pay and trade union rights. They were dominant in the Imperial Typewriters strike of 1974, and Jayabhen Desai led a group of Asian women on the picket line at the Grunwick strike in 1977. In 1991 striking Asian women at the Burnstall's factory in Smethwick, Birmingham, successfully campaigned for the right to join a trade union for health and safety and against forced overtime and low wages.

In the late 1980s and early 1990s Asian women artists became visible in all areas of cultural production. Visual artists such as Chila Kumari Burman, Sutapa Biswas, and Arina Bhimji achieved international recognition; their work often explores questions of Asian women's identities and has been exhibited at mainstream national venues such as the Tate Gallery, the Hayward Gallery, the Photographers' Gallery, and the Barbican. Zarina Bhimji was the first Asian woman to have her work in the collection of the Victoria and Albert Museum.

The filmmaker Pratibha Parmar's work has been exhibited internationally on television and at film festivals. Her films include *Khush* (1991), an award-winning documentary on Asian lesbians and gay men; *A Place of Rage* (1991), a documentary highlighting the contribution of African-American women like Angela Davis, June Jordan, and Alice Walker to the civil rights movement in the United States; and *Warrior Marks* (1993), a collaboration with the Pulitzer Prize–winning writer of *The Color Purple,* Alice Walker. This film brings to the fore the practice of female genital mutilation.

Many Asian feminists have given literary expression to their explorations of family life, relationships, fantasy, romance, and sexual love. The Asian Women Writers' Collective, set up in 1984, has been a support group instrumental in publishing many Asian women's writings.

Asian women have made important contributions to the debates, campaigns, and concepts of British feminism, and their presence has shaped the British feminist movement.

See Also

FEMINISM: SECOND-WAVE BRITISH; FEMINISM: SOUTH ASIA; FUNDAMENTALISM: RELIGIOUS; IMMIGRATION

References and Further Reading

Amos, Valerie, and Pratibha Parmar. 1984. Challenging imperial feminism. *Feminist Review* 17 (Autumn): 3–19.

Anthias, F., and N. Yuval-Davis. 1983. Contextualising feminism; gender, ethnic and class divisions. *Feminist Review* 15.

———. 1988. *Right of way.* London: Women's Press.

Asian Women Writers' Collective. 1994. *Flaming spirit.* London: Virago.

Brah, Avtar. 1993. Reframing Europe: En-Gendered racisms, ethinicities, and nationalisms in contemporary western Europe. *Feminist Review* 45 (Autumn): 9–28.

Carby, H. V. 1982. White women listen! Black feminism and the boundaries of sisterhood. In Center for Contemporary Cultural Studies, ed., *The empire strikes black: Race and racism in 70s Britain.* London: Hutchinson.

Connolly, Clara. 1991. Washing our linen: One year of women against fundamentalism. *Feminist Review* 37 (Spring): 68–77.

Sahgal, Gita, and Nira Yuval-Davis, eds. 1992. *Refusing holy orders: Women and fundamentalism in Britain.* London: Virago.

SBS Collective. 1990. *Against the grain: A celebration of survival and struggle.* London: Southall Black Sisters.

Pratibha Parmar
Rehana Kapadia

FEMINISM: Caribbean

The Caribbean region includes English-, Spanish-, French-, and Dutch-speaking territories, of which some are islands situated in the Caribbean Sea and others are located on the land masses of South and Central America. There are a wide range of spoken languages, which include not only the four major language groups just mentioned, a legacy of the colonial past, but also indigenous tongues or mixed languages such as Papiamento and Patois. The ethnic populations include African, perhaps the most dominant group, East Indian, European, Chinese, Lebanese, Syrian, and Mayan, and groups with mixed ethnicity such as mulatto and Creole.

The geographical separation between territories, together with differences in allocation of natural resources, has made for great variation in the development of these societies. However, the territories do have a shared history of colonization and decolonization. Territories such as Puerto Rico and the United States Virgin Islands are considered possessions or protectorates of the United States; some, such as Guadeloupe and Martinique, are dependencies of France and still under direct control; some are semi-dependent, such as Suriname, which has internal self-rule but functions in relation to the Netherlands; and some are fully independent, among these Trinidad and Tobago, Barbados, and Jamaica, which were former colonies of the United Kingdom. Their relatively small area, along with openness in the global economy, has made full independence and self-government virtually impossible. They remain linked by trade and foreign relations to former colonial masters or, through economic ties, to new imperialist ones.

Despite these differences, and because of similarities such as colonialism, slavery, indenture, racism, ongoing emigration, and a social structure blended from a variety of migrant cultures, the region has evolved as a geographical and social entity that is uniquely Caribbean. A distinctive feature is its high percentage of female-based households, born out of the original kinship traditions of migrants, and exacerbated by the crushing experience of slavery. This led anthropologists in the 1950s and 1960s to label Caribbean society as matrifocal or mother-centered (Clarke, 1957). Common-law marriages and visiting relationships rather than legal unions were practiced and recognized among some ethnic groups and lower-income populations. Women in these relationships were forced to take on the responsibility of chief income-earners in the household (Massiah, 1986).

As a result, the first construction of femininity in the region was a dominant stereotype—the strong, independent black woman; in control of her economic, social, and sexual life; comfortable with her familial role; and politically drawn to anticolonial and nationalist movements. This has led to another convenient stereotype for the role of men in these societies—as marginal to the home and family. These stereotypes do not fit women and men of all ethnic groups or of all classes in the Caribbean, and they misrepresent the contributions of the wider constituency of women and men in the struggle for sexual equality. The emergence and ongoing development of Caribbean feminism must be seen in the context of the region's legacy of diversity and unity.

Early Challenges for Women

Slavery, indenture, and racism most strongly influenced the challenges to women in the eighteenth and nineteenth centuries.

The history of slave revolts in many of the territories attests to the crucial roles played by women in the early anticolonial struggles of these societies. Morgan (1984) records that women were active in 1791 in the slave revolt organized by two slave leaders, Toussaint L'Overture and Henri Christophe, on Saint Dominique, now called Haiti. Among these women were Marie Jeanne à-la-Crete-à-Pierrot; Victoria, or Toya, who was a commander; and Henriette St. Marc, who was publicly executed by the French in 1802. Female slaves also participated in the slave rebellions in El Español, now called the Dominican Republic; in Martinique and Guadeloupe; and in Jamaica. In 1750 and 1795 many women were active in the Maroon rebellions of Jamaica, a slave revolt that successfully waged war against the British. Among these, Nanny, or Nana Yah, was highly regarded among the African slave population for her spiritual powers. She became a military guerrilla of the Maroons; like her sisters in Haiti, this powerful image of female spirituality and physical fortitude was an early metaphor for Caribbean womanhood (Mair, 1975). Nana Yah was named a Jamaican national heroine in 1975.

East Indian indentured laborers were brought from India from 1845 to work on the plantations. These women were numerically significant in Trinidad and British Guiana (now Guyana), but less so in the other British colonies. East Indian women had historically been viewed as passive, subservient to their menfolk, plantation masters, and overseers. More recent histories of the system of indenture have revealed that their response to unfair treatment for themselves and their families was at times militant. In their relatively free movement between one sexual partner and another in the face of abusive or unsatisfying relationships, they, like their African sisters, also posed a major challenge to the dominant patriarchy (Mohammed, 1994).

First-Wave Feminism in the Caribbean

Women's intervention in Caribbean history from the beginning of the twentieth century until 1970, and from 1970 to the present, is, for convenience, referred to as first- and second-wave feminism. The first phase benefited, in retrospect, from the English and American suffragist movements and from women's role in the Soviet revolution of 1917, as well as from foreign female visitors who advocated for women's rights. By the twentieth century more Caribbean women had been educated, while others had moved out of the agricultural sector into industrial and commercial jobs. Thus they began to articulate their political and economic rights as women in society.

In the second phase there was an intensification of "gender" consciousness, even though this was expressed differently by different ethnic groups or classes of women. An increased flow of ideas from North American and European feminism began to influence programs for equality advocated in the region.

Despite these ideological influences, the term *feminism* was not widely used in the Caribbean to describe women's responses and challenging actions, nor does it at present have positive connotations among Caribbean women themselves. The majority of women and men in the region seem to equate feminism with strident anti-male hostility, lesbianism, and separatism. Despite the continued openness of these societies to international influences

through ongoing migration, women's struggles in the twentieth century have remained ideologically rooted in the reality of Caribbean life. Their militancy is inspired by the problems encountered within the region. They maintain a dependence on other women for support, with a continued understanding of the different but serious plight of the Caribbean male. A popular notion pervasive in the region is that Caribbean women "have always been liberated." The efforts of all women who organized to improve the status of women or to assist in social reform and the political struggle are, however, seen as constituting feminist activity.

Morgan (1984) notes that in the early nineteenth century, women of European descent formed organizations aimed at literacy campaigns, social reform, legislative changes, and education for women. In 1934 women in Haiti who formed the League Féminine d'Action Sociale pressed for better marriage, family, and labor laws. They argued for the rights to be educated and edited *La Voix des Femmes,* a book about Haitian women. Women took part in oilfield strikes in Trinidad in 1937, and labor rebellions in Jamaica in 1938; both episodes prefigured the formation of recognized trade unions in the region. By the 1950s, women workers in the English- and Spanish-speaking territories began organizing for better wages and working conditions, helping to form trade unions (Chaney and Castro, 1993). Also by the 1950s, along with this more militant struggle, many women's groups were formed, attracting women from different social strata into organizations such as the Young Women's Christian Association, the Red Cross, the Soroptimist, and, as a result of the growing numbers of educated and professional women, the Business and Professional Club.

Less acknowledged in the political history of the region was the crucial importance of women in the burgeoning nationalism of these times. In Trinidad and Tobago, for instance, women provided support for the political party the People's National Movement, which came to power in 1956 and instituted democratic self-government for this country. In Jamaica, the People's National Party and the Jamaican Labour Party were launched with strong female support. In societies controlled by dictators, the struggles of women were more poignant. In 1960 in the Dominican Republic, Minerva, Patria, and Maria Teresa Mirabal were killed by paid thugs on a lonely road while returning from a visit to their jailed husbands. Their husbands, parents, and children had maintained a militant opposition to the Trujillo regime for over twenty years.

Second-Wave Caribbean Feminism

A precursor of the second wave of women's involvement in the definition of Caribbean woman was the black American struggle against racism in the 1960s. The message of civil rights and black identity filtered throughout the region, and in Trinidad it led to a black power movement, which included guerillas fighting in the hills and challenged the government. Among those killed was a young black woman, Beverly Jones. The question of national and racial identity had by now clearly emerged, but with developments in the international sphere, the murmurings of gender identity became more pronounced.

The best description of women's involvement in the struggle for sexual equality from the 1970s onward is that it developed in a mood relatively more receptive to "women's issues." Yet female activism was at first restricted to issues that society deemed acceptable as women's concerns, such as wages, consumers' rights, and legislation regarding marriage and family. In this climate both institutional and noninstitutional women's organizations flourished.

Antrobus and Gordon (1984) chronicle the launching, in 1970, of the Caribbean Women's Association (CARIWA), which served as an umbrella for a number of national women's organizations and councils already in existence in the previous decades. While many women's branches of political parties were already active, by the mid-1970s more independent women's groups with social and overtly political programs were formed. Among these were the Organization of Surinamese Women, which worked to establish crisis centers for women in need; and the United Antillean Women's Organization, which pressed for independence in Curaçao and for improved labor legislation for working women in Curaçao, Aruba, and the other Dutch-speaking islands.

The United Nations' designation of 1975 as the International Year of the Woman, and the related activities of that year, signaled another chain of developments in the Caribbean—governments' decision to establish women's desks or women's bureaus in many of the territories. In Jamaica, the Women's Bureau was established by the People's National Party in 1975. In the English-speaking societies, with the support of many of these desks, various initiatives were put into motion, such as minimum wage legislation, maternity leave benefits, and acts concerned with the legal status of children. The commitment to women in development (WID) entered the vocabulary of the territory, with numerous government and nongovernment initiatives evident in the period from 1975. In the Spanish-speaking Dominican Republic the Women's Social Movement (CIFEPAD), a government center for the integration of women in development, was created in 1975 to help women enter the agro-industrial and technical industries.

These advances signaled the beginning of what can be viewed as an undefined yet autonomous women's movement in the Caribbean. Although there were different ideological stances or programs adopted by women's groups and institutions in the various territories, they were interconnected by the international dimension of second-wave feminism and its underlying message of sisterhood. Within the various struggles for nationalism, independence, economic welfare, and socialism, women from the various territories formed internal and external alliances on the basis of gender consciousness.

In Jamaica in 1978, the theater collective SISTREN, comprising a group of working-class women, began to articulate a feminist message to women like themselves through the medium of popular theater. Formed originally as an arm of a small left-wing group, and linked closely to the labor movement in Trinidad, Concerned Women for Progress (CWP) emerged in that country in 1980 as the first women's organization openly adopting a feminist stance on issues such as abortion on demand and equal pay for equal work. Simultaneously in Jamaica, the Marxist-oriented Committee of Women for Progress was formed with similar aims and objectives. In Grenada, from 1979 until its sudden demise, the Socialist National Women's Organization had an important role in the movement to establish a popular socialist government. In Guyana the Women's Revolutionary Socialist Movement, located within the ruling party, was engaged in developing economic projects for rural women, while another group, Women Against Terrorism, was actively waging campaigns against politically motivated terror. United Antillian Women (UMA) brought together a number of women's organizations in Curaçao, some of which represented service clubs and charity organizations, to mobilize around gender issues such as housing and legal limitations for married women and unmarried mothers (Cuales, 1984). By the 1980s in all the territories, including French-speaking Guadeloupe and Martinique, there was a proliferation of small women's organizations that began to deal with issues not previously openly addressed in these societies, such as sexual violence and sexual abuse.

The growing internationalism and scope of Caribbean women's involvement in the political, social, and cultural life of the region, as well as the relative freedom of women in the expanded middle class to make autonomous choices about career, marriage, childbearing, and travel, were all contributory factors in the development of Caribbean feminism from the mid-1970s onward. Women's focus before this had been outwardly directed, to political, economic, and social development goals of the society at large, carefully preserving the notion of masculine superiority and female deference. Now the liberation struggles of women, especially women of the middle classes, became more female-centered, focusing on matters pertaining to their personal lives, including sexual and reproductive rights. They denounced practices about which they had been silent for a long time. For instance, the legacy of matrifocality and male irresponsibility in the family had led to habitual infidelity and sexual abuse. Thus the movement took a more militant stance against male disrespect of women. However, it did not adopt a self-serving or anti-male position. Colonization and racism had affected men and women alike, and the movement continued to acknowledge that the larger battle could be won only with both female and male support.

Meanwhile the institutional wheels were also rolling. By the late 1970s institutional programs reflected more commitment on the part of government and funders to dealing with issues that concerned women. In the Dominican Republic, the Centre for Investigation of Women's Action (CIPAF) and the Women's Studies Circle (CEF) were formed. In the English-speaking Caribbean the Women and Development Unit (WAND), the extramural arm of the University of the West Indies, was established as a major resource center and a catalyst for women's activities. Such institutions represented a focal point that began to bring together activists, policymakers, planners, and academics in the arena of women's struggle for recognition and improved status.

Caribbean feminism since the 1980s has been characterized by an accelerated development of nongovernmental organizations such as crisis centers, and projects for women funded by international aid agencies. The first rape crisis center in the Caribbean was established in Trinidad in 1985. The issue of sexual violence was now being openly addressed by centers such as these in other societies as well, meeting the needs of different ethnic groups and classes of women. Feminism in the region from the 1980s until the present has not been limited to social activism: immeasurable contributions have also been made by female writers and artists and male and female calypsonians and singers, some of them not residing within the region itself. What was most distinctive about the various programs in the 1980s was that women's personal lives also became an object of feminist intervention.

Three major trajectories of development can be noted by the 1990s. The first is in the introduction of women's studies and gender studies in the curricula of some secondary and tertiary teaching institutions of the region. The efforts to introduce women's studies at the University of the West Indies (UWI), which has campuses on the three islands of Trinidad, Barbados, and Jamaica, began with the establishment of WAND in Barbados and was continued in the 1980s by the Institute for Social and Economic Research (ISER) at UWI in Barbados. By 1982, utilizing researchers from throughout the region, ISER completed a large-scale project that gathered empirical data on the status of women in the English-speaking Caribbean. Funding by the Netherlands Ministry for Development Cooperation was combined with the voluntary activism of professional women at the UWI; this culminated in 1993 with the institutionalization of women's studies, now supported by the UWI at the Centre for Gender and Development Studies on the three island campuses. Similar initiatives, at different levels, were also undertaken in the Dutch-, French-, and Spanish-speaking territories.

The second development can be seen as the consolidation of a sometimes uneasy partnership between activist feminism and the institutions. In 1985 the Caribbean Association for Feminist Research and Action (CAFRA) was formed, linking academics and activists, joining government with nongovernment initiatives, and crossing language barriers in the region. The existence of this umbrella group, together with the survival of other bodies such as rape crisis centers, women's service organizations, and women's arms of various political parties, attests to a persistence of feminist consciousness that is expressed in various forms in the Caribbean. What is perhaps most evident is that the varying ideological perspectives and theoretical categories which are used to describe the developments in "first world" feminism do not fit snugly into the Caribbean feminist experience (Baksh-Soodeen, 1993).

This latter characteristic of Caribbean feminist history best introduces the third major trajectory evident in second-wave feminism in the region. With the growth and establishment of gender studies, feminists in the region have attempted to conceptualize and express the uniqueness of Caribbean feminism, and also its connection with other feminisms. This intellectual struggle is an ongoing one, alongside the persistent activism of an amorphous women's movement. Although there is general agreement that the last decades of the twentieth century were influenced by international perspectives, organizations in the region have rarely embraced the tenets of any particular perspective. On the contrary, many show signs of an eclectic mixture, adopting a socialist position on women and labor and a liberal position on women's education. As is clear from the historical construction of femininity in the Caribbean, a radical feminist concern with female spirituality, woman's strength, and female culture is indigenous to the region, yet Caribbean feminists have by and large rejected the notion that men are the ultimate enemy. The predominance of black women in the region has made the movement receptive to the struggles of their black sisters in the United States and Britain, but they recognize a different experience of racism in the region.

Viewed through a global lens, Caribbean feminism is symbiotic, a tendency consistent with the process by which these societies have emerged and are constantly developing. From within, it is a native brand of feminism, responsive to internal and external dynamics, discriminating in its choices, and firmly rooted in Caribbean soil.

See Also

HOUSEHOLDS AND FAMILIES: CARIBBEAN; IMAGES OF WOMEN: CARIBBEAN; POLITICS AND THE STATE: CARIBBEAN; VIOLENCE: CARIBBEAN; WOMEN'S STUDIES: CARIBBEAN

References and Further Reading

Antrobus, Peggy. 1988. Women in development programmes: The Caribbean experience (1975–1985). In Patricia Mohammed and Catherine Shepherd, eds., *Gender in Caribbean development*. West Indies: University of the West Indies Women and Development Studies Project.

———, and Linda Gordon. 1984. The English-speaking Caribbean: A journey in the making. In Robin Morgan, ed., *Sisterhood is global: The international women's movement anthology*. New York: Anchor Press/Doubleday.

Baksh-Soodeen, Rawwida. 1993. Is there an international feminism? *Alternative Approach.*

Barriteau-Foster, V. Eudine. 1992. The construct of a postmodernist theory for social science research. *Social and Economic Research* 41(2): June.

Brereton, Bridget. 1994. *Gendered testimony: Autobiographies, diaries, and letters by women as a source for Caribbean history.* Kingston, Jamaica: Department of History, University of the West Indies.

Bush, Barbara. 1990. *Slave women in Caribbean society 1650–1838.* Kingston, Jamaica: Heinemann (Caribbean); Bloomington: Indiana University Press; London: James Currey.

Chaney, Elsa, and Mary Garcia Castro, eds. 1993. *El trabajo de la cuarta parte: Servico domestico en America Latina y el Caribe.*

Clarke, Edith. 1957. *My mother who fathered me: A study of the family in three selected communities in Jamaica.* London: Allen and Unwin.

Cuales, Sonia. 1984. The Dutch-speaking Caribbean islands: Fighting until the end. In Robin Morgan, ed., *Sisterhood is global: The international women's movement anthology.* New York: Anchor Press/Doubleday.

Ellis, Pat, ed. 1986. *Women of the Caribbean.* London: Zed.

Green, Edward J., ed. 1993. *Race, class and gender in the future of the Caribbean.* Kingston, Jamaica: Institute of Social and Economic Research.

Latin American and Caribbean Women's Collective. 1980. *Slaves of slaves: The challenge of Latin American women.* London: Zed.

Leo-Rhynie, Elsa. 1992. Women and development studies: Moving away from the periphery? Professional address delivered at the Women and Development Studies Tenth Anniversary Symposium, Kingston, Jamaica.

Mair, Lucille. 1975. *The rebel woman in the British West Indies during slavery.* Kingston, Jamaica: Institute of Jamaica for African Caribbean Institute.

Massiah, Joycelin. 1983. *Women as heads of households in the Caribbean: Family structure and feminine status.* United Kingdom: UNESCO.

———, ed. 1986. Women in the Caribbean Project (WICP). *Social and Economic Studies* 35(2–3).

Mohammed, Patricia. 1991. Reflections on the women's movement in Trinidad: Calypsos, changes, and sexual violence. *Feminist Review* 38(Summer).

———. 1994. A social history of Indians in Trinidad 1917–1947: A gender perspective. Ph.D. dissertation, Institute of Social Studies, The Hague, Netherlands.

Robin Morgan, ed. 1984. *Sisterhood is global: The international women's movement anthology.* New York: Anchor Press/Doubleday.

Nettleford, Rex, ed. 1989. Special issue on women and Caribbean development. *Caribbean Quarterly* 35(1–2).

Reddock, Rhoda. 1994. *Women, labour, and politics in Trinidad.* London: Zed.

Patricia Mohammed

FEMINISM: Central and South America

Among Latin American feminist activists the search for equality for women was always associated with the idea of social change and justice at the national and international levels. Latin American feminism has evolved from a relatively small number of elite, educated, and economically well-off women, in what is called the first wave of feminism, to what is called the second wave of feminism, a broadly based population of women representing a range of feminisms and social movements. The second wave of feminism encompassed the various interests of women who differ by economic strata, race, ethnic group, and sexual orientation. The first wave developed during the late eighteenth century and the beginning of the nineteenth century. The second wave developed from activities surrounding the First International Conference of Women, which was held in Mexico in 1975 and was organized by the United Nations. Both waves of Latin American feminism connect their perception of women's unequal position in society to other social inequalities. Another salient characteristic of both waves was and still is the use of international forums to discuss women's issues along with other social problems. Women, in the first wave of feminism, had very few opportunities to raise topics of interest to them through participation in national politics, which was dominated by men. They found better opportunities to discuss their concerns about topics such as international peace, women's education, and civil rights in many of the international conferences held during this period.

Characteristics of Feminism in Latin America

Since Latin American countries became independent of Spain, they have been in a position of political instability and economic dependence on more developed countries. These characteristics affected the development of Latin American feminism. Even though the origins and evolution of Latin American feminism have been influenced by interaction with international feminism, it evolved in response to the specific socioeconomic and political conditions of the region, which differed from those facing feminism in Europe and in the United States. These differences affected the way Latin American feminists analyzed their specific problems as women. For them it was necessary to develop a strategy based on a combination of three levels of problems: as women, as nationals of a particular country, and as women from a particular region. This is one of the reasons that made Latin American feminists deeply concerned about national and international politics. The situation of North American feminists was different. While they were committed to social justice, they did not have to worry about development, poverty, and the sovereignty of their country. They were able to concentrate more on inequality between men and women and thus were not greatly concerned about national and international politics.

Their specific agendas and the differences between the Latin American and North American feminist movements continued to characterize these two movements during the twentieth century. The Latin American approach to women's causes has been strengthened by the cultural influence of European immigrants, in many cases exiled from their countries for their leftist ideologies. This influence was and is still reflected in the agendas of the Latin American feminisms.

Even before women in Central and South America gained their political rights and were able to vote, most educated women were aware of national and international politics, and in many cases expressed their political views. The extent to which Latin American women expressed these views is illustrated by Carrie Chapman Catt, president of the permanent Pan-American Association, in her report about the development of South American feminism in the 1900s, written after she had spent some time in South America. She states that South American women have an impressive interest in "political matters." Specifically, she notes that she heard more about the Monroe Doctrine during her trip to South America than ever before in her life (Hanner, 1976).

To repeat, then: feminism in Latin America may be characterized as evolving from an elite of educated and economically well-off women from the upper middle and upper classes—the first wave of feminism—to diverse groups of women of different economic strata, experiences, and strategies. This diversity makes it necessary to use the word *feminisms* to characterize the second wave.

Latin American Feminism at the Beginning of the Twentieth Century: First Wave of Feminism

Latin American feminism had, at the beginning of the twentieth century, more receptive audiences at the international level than at the national and regional levels. Women were excluded from political life, which was rigidly hierarchical and dominated by men. This did not bother some feminists, because they believed that politics was a corrupt, disreputable activity practiced by men, an activity in which they would rather not see women engage. Women of Latin America found that national politics did not represent their interests as women or as activists for social change and justice, because male-dominated national politics did not consider equal rights for women a concern. As a result of this exclusion from national politics, women who had more access to education and economic means were inclined to participate in international forums rather than in national politics. Their participation had two main objectives: (1) resolutions that committed signatory countries to perform social and civil reforms aimed at changing women's condition in their countries, and (2) international peace.

The experience that women gained in their participation in the Latin American scientific congresses led to the idea of discussing women's issues in international meetings. Thus, at one of the Latin American scientific congresses, supported by the Argentinean Scientific Association, the decision was made to use international conferences and congresses to propose reforms and social change. In these meetings—held in Buenos Aires, 1898; Montevideo, 1901; Rio de Janeiro, 1905; and Santiago de Chile, 1908—the participating women were largely professionals, scientists, and teachers from Uruguay, Argentina, and Chile with educational levels equivalent to their male counterparts.

Several international feminist congresses specifically related to women's issues were held during the first part of the twentieth century. At the First International Feminist Congress, held in Buenos Aires in 1910, a large majority of the participants were from Uruguay, Argentina, and Chile. The Second International Feminist Congress, held in Washington D.C., in 1919, initiated a new period in which women wanting to focus attention on issues of concern to them held an auxiliary meeting. The result of the auxiliary meeting during this feminist congress was the Pan-American Women's International Committee.

International meetings following the Washington congress in 1919 not only were concerned about women's education and social welfare but also wanted to discuss subjects related to Pan-Americanism (Miller, 1990). Over the years women added specific topics to their agendas while they continued their pursuit of social and political reform. These meetings evolved to include not only women's issues but also international issues such as support for nonintervention, resolution of conflict through arbitration, and the search for international peace, as well as their traditional concern for social and political reform.

The selection of the Pan-American meetings for discussions of women's issues was one of the most important and effective strategies of feminists from Latin America at the beginning of the twentieth century.

After women in the United States obtained the right to vote, it was clear to Latin American feminists that suffrage by itself was not the most effective way of transforming society and eliminating inequalities. Thus, there was less enthusiasm about obtaining suffrage; however, women continued their struggle for it.

The fact that Latin American women were not immediately successful in their struggle for suffrage and more equitable conditions of employment did not mean that Latin American feminist movements were lethargic between the first and second waves of feminism. In Latin America feminists were active in the 1970s, the beginning of the second wave of the movement. As Miller (1991) shows in her examination of politics in the period from 1938 to 1958, Latin American women continued their struggle by attempting to achieve two major goals: the recognition that women should participate in politics at the national level and the incorporation of women in the structure of the traditional parties.

From the end of the nineteenth and beginning of the twentieth century in Latin American countries, achievements of feminist activism were closely tied to advancing liberal and secular ideas.

Around 1950 the socioeconomic and political crises of the Latin American region resulted in a political backlash. Some of the governments were replaced by military coups d'état, beginning a period of dictatorships in Venezuela, Guatemala, Cuba, and Peru and democratic but conservative governments in Mexico, Brazil, and Chile. In this context, two important factors affected Latin American feminism: the main issues of the first wave of Latin American feminism were becoming outdated, and new social actors, men and women of the disadvantaged sectors, were trying to raise their voices. From these new political actors and their revolutionary or reformist activities, feminism in Latin America underwent several transformations and gave birth to very complex agendas in the second wave.

The Impact of Revolutionary Movements on Latin American Feminism

Women of Central and South America were strongly influenced by the Cuban revolution and the role of women in the revolutionary process. In the 1960s, after the Cuban revolution, most countries of Latin America were in some way touched by guerrilla movements (Miller, 1991). These movements differed in structure and ideology from country to country, and these differences had implications for Latin American feminist movements. Although women participated in guerrilla movements, the roles that were assigned to them were the traditional roles filled by women at the levels of family and society. Women were seen as supporters, consorts, and wives. Even when women were exposed to the same risks as men, they did not enjoy the same privileges as their male counterparts. For Cuban revolutionary leaders, as well as for leftist movements in the rest of Latin America, the subordinate position of women in society was not a separate issue from class struggle. Thus, if, for example, a communist society was established, it was assumed by these leaders that the liberation of women was obtained automatically.

Taking the same perspective, leftist political parties and the guerrilla movements in the rest of the Latin American countries ignored all concerns about women's issues that could not be solved within the framework of national and class struggle. Therefore, women who were interested in double standards, gender relations within the family, domestic violence, and other feminist issues were considered superficial members of the middle class and petit bourgeois working against revolutionary objectives. Furthermore they were suspected of being tools of U.S. imperialism and, as a result, of undermining the revolution. That was also the case in subsequent guerrilla movements in Guatemala, Brazil, Argentina, Peru, and Uruguay during the 1960s. Guerrilla women were considered "exceptions" for reasons that included their small numbers and their elitist origins. However, these women were subordinate to their male counterparts. They were isolated, so the impact of their experience was not shared with the masses of other women and, as a result, their activities and experiences had no impact on feminist movements.

Revolutionary movements emerging in the 1970s and 1980s in Nicaragua, El Salvador, and Guatemala included women in the role of soldier (Chinchilla, 1993), and compared with the revolutionary movements of the 1960s, these revolutionary movements incorporated larger numbers of women who were in combat and in command of troops. Also in contrast to the movements of the 1960s, these women soldiers were in contact with women in their neighborhood or grassroots organizations, women who were often supporters of guerrilla movements. Women's participation in these revolutionary movements was more extensive and became a total experience, particularly for young women soldiers in military activities. Soldiering was so complete a break with the traditional female roles of these women that they became aware of the subordinate conditions of women in their countries and of the need for profound changes in gender relations in both public and private, or family, life.

Feminisms and Women's Movements in Latin America: Second Wave

Most of the literature on second-wave Latin American feminisms links its origins to activities developed in the preparation for and the follow-up to the United Nations Conference on Women held in Mexico in 1975 (Alvarez,

1998). The most salient characteristics of Latin American feminisms of the second wave are (1) maintenance of the commitment to national and international politics paralleling women's interests, and (2) a change in feminists' social composition; the educated upper-and upper middle-class women feminists of the first wave were replaced by diverse groups of women with specific interests that differed by group. The different and specific interests originated in the differences in race, ethnicity, and social classes of the groups. Second-wave Latin American feminisms were more diverse than feminism in the United States or Europe. The variety of forms and projects of Latin American feminist interests included programs and shelters for battered women, women's health programs, and consciousness-raising groups. This new stage of Latin American feminisms developed in the context of economic and political crises affecting the region. In many countries military dictators were in power, and feminism began as part of the political opposition to repressive governments. Women who were interested in feminist issues were also concerned with other aspects of social injustice at both national and international levels. Different from their counterparts in Europe and the United States, Latin American feminists felt compelled to actively participate, simultaneously, in feminist movements, political parties, and revolutionary movements. Their leftist backgrounds led feminists to consider women's problems as derived from economic and social oppression. Even in the countries in which feminism broke away, organizationally, from leftist parties, feminists of the early years of the movement were loyal to their Marxist inheritance, prioritizing class struggle over gender struggle (Sternbach, et al., 1992). At the same time, economic crises impelled women of the working class and other disadvantaged sectors to find, collectively, new survival strategies. The strategies involved organizing at the neighborhood level to solve basic problems connected with their socially attributed responsibilities as mothers and wives. In all Latin American countries women of the disadvantaged sectors participated in movements to fight for services that were no longer provided by the state, to combat the rise in the cost of living, and in many cases to feed their children collectively. Latin American women also organized in the search for the disappeared. Mothers searched for missing children, grandchildren, spouses, and other relatives tortured, imprisoned, or murdered for political reasons.

Among women's movements it is possible to distinguish three types: those that are not gender-specific and are organized around specific needs that derived from women's traditional roles stemming from the sexual division of labor; those that are feminist movements and explicitly reject all justifications of women's subordination; and those in which women and men work to develop concrete strategies in regional meetings (Encuentros Regionales de Mujeres) and in their participation in women's international conferences. These interconnections and shared practices are the strongest aspects of the Latin American feminist movements and are, according to Chinchilla (1993) and Alvarez (1998), influencing feminisms around the world. Latin American feminisms reflect their uniqueness in the development of new concepts and theories. Scholars such as Chinchilla (1993) and Sternbach et al. (1992) considered contemporary Latin American feminism as being part of a large, multifaceted, socially and politically heterogeneous women's movement.

The interconnection of the three types of movements gives Latin American feminists a larger framework for analysis of women's issues and is reflected in the form and content of the feminist struggle. This framework, which always includes issues of imperialism and class oppression, had been difficult to manage in the first years of the second wave of feminism. Many women who were influenced by leftist ideas saw feminism as being divisive in the fight for social equality at the societal level and responded to this divisiveness by trying to make their two main concerns, social justice and gender equality, compatible. This was not an easy task for Latin American feminists who recognized the sexist orientation of their leftist political parties or revolutionary movements. When it became evident that equality ought to be part of their daily life and that social transformation must be accompanied by changes in gender relations as well, women decided that it was time to change the sexist way political life was conducted. They called for a new, more democratic and participatory style of politics. In different contexts this realization of the need for equality was experienced in most Latin American countries in the 1970s and 1980s. In some countries of South and Central America, women reacted to political parties or political movements. In Central America and later in the state of Chiapas (Mexico), women participated in the revolutionary movements as combatants. As soldiers, having broken with traditionally attributed roles, they became aware of their self-worth and started to combine the search for economic and social justice with the structure of gender relations.

Latin American Feminisms
Facing the New Millennium

In the 1980s Latin American countries began a process of democratization that in some cases ended military governments and resulted in democracies—Argentina, Brazil,

Uruguay, and Chile, for example. In El Salvador long and devastating internal wars gave way to negotiated peace and democratic elections in which former combatants were part of the process. In this context and mostly after the Fourth International Women's Conference in Beijing in 1995, Latin American feminists and Latin American women's movements played a major role in the changes that governments and nongovernmental organizations made to improve women's lives. In almost all these countries, committees and organizations were created for the advancement of women, and public policies incorporated gender issues. Feminisms, women's movements, and activists representing a variety of social classes, races, ethnic, and other interest groups achieved numerous social and gender objectives. Included in government agendas are topics such as unequal salaries for men and women, domestic and sexual violence, sexual harassment, and other areas in which women are disadvantaged.

It is possible that Latin American feminisms can now go beyond the analysis of specific women's topics to the reanalysis of general world problems from a gender perspective and, in so doing, make an important change in the understanding of social problems.

See Also

FEMINISM: CHICANA; HOUSEHOLDS AND FAMILIES: CENTRAL AND SOUTH AMERICA; POLITICS AND THE STATE: CENTRAL AND SOUTH AMERICA; VIOLENCE: CARIBBEAN; VIOLENCE: CENTRAL AND SOUTH AMERICA; WOMEN'S STUDIES: CENTRAL AND AND SOUTH AMERICA

References and Further Reading

Alvarez, Sonia. 1998. Los Feminismos Latinoamericanos se globalizan en los noventa: Retos para el nuevo milenio. In Maria Luisa Tarres Barraza, ed., *Genero y cultura en America Latina: Cultura y participacion politica*. Mexico City: El Colegio de Mexico.

Chinchilla, Norma. 1993. Gender and national politics: Issues and trends in women's participation in Latin American movements. In Edna Acosta-Belen and Christine E. Bosse, eds., *Researching women in Latin America and the Caribbean*. Boulder, Col.: Westview.

Hanner, June. 1976. *Women in Latin American history: Their lives and views*. Los Angeles: University of California, Latin American Center Publications.

Lavrin, Asuncion. 1995. *Women, feminism, and social change in Argentina, Chile, and Uruguay, 1890–1940*. Lincoln: University of Nebraska Press.

Miller, Francesca. 1990. Latin American feminism and the transnational arena. In Emilie Bergman, J. Greenber, G.

Kilpatrick, F. Masiello, Francisca Miller, M. Morello-Frosch, K. Newman, and M. L. Pratt, eds. *Women, culture and politics in Latin America: Seminar on feminism and culture in Latin America.* Berkeley: University of California Press.

———. 1991. *Latin American women and the search for social justice.* Hanover, N.H.: University Press of New England.

Sternbach, Nancy S., M. Navarro-Aranguren, P. Chuchryk, and Sonia Alvarez. 1992. Feminisms in Latin America: From Bogotá to San Bernardo. *Signs: Journal of Women in Culture and Society* 17 (2): 393.

Sara Poggio

FEMINISM: Chicana

The term *Chicano* originated during the 1960s, in the context of the civil rights movement in the United States. It was a politically charged self-identifier indicating Mexican-American roots and emphasizing a strong sense of pride in the indigenous. This self-labeling arose as a form of protest against the homogenizing categories for minorities used largely by government organizations. The feminine form is *Chicana.*

The roots of Chicana feminism can be traced to the expansion of the equal rights movements into the academic world. The creation of Chicano studies programs was significantly influenced by the concerns of the ethnic, working-class minority that had fueled those movements. Women were active in these new programs and soon began to voice their protests against the perpetuation of patriarchal ideology within the Chicano academy. Their attempts to make gender inequalities visible encountered considerable resistance. In an intellectual environment dominated by cultural nationalism, feminists were labeled as separatists or *vendidas*—sellouts—and accused of embracing the white, Anglo-Saxon ideology of mainstream feminism. The underlying assumption was that white feminism attempted to destroy the concept of family, which is the backbone of Mexican society and an essential element in the construction of Chicano cultural identity.

The forum sought by Chicanas, however, was not found in mainstream feminism either. In its efforts to broaden the reach of the feminist discourse, mainstream feminism constructed an ideology that erased differences while attempting to define issues common to all women. Chicanas, as well as other women of color, eventually rejected this homogenization, arguing that it did not address the singularity of their experiences.

First Writings

Frustration with a feminism that did not take race into account is eloquently articulated in the pioneering work *This Bridge Called My Back: Writings by Radical Women of Color* (Moraga and Anzaldúa, 1981). In this breakthrough anthology, prose, poetry, personal narratives, and critical analysis express a radical feminism, or bridge feminism. In this case, radical feminism is to be understood as a movement insurgent in its nature, and one that attempts to reflect oppression and resistance at the same time. The concept of bridge feminism represents the position of Chicanas as mediators inside a cultural, political, and ideological confrontation within *chicanismo* as culture and within and outside white feminism. *This Bridge* contains writings by Chicanas, as well as African-American, Asian-American and Native American women. The titles of its six sections explicitly illustrate the different levels at which the feminist struggles were being articulated during the early 1980s: "Children Passing the Streets: The Roots of Our Radicalism," "Entering the Lives of Others: Theory in the Flesh," "And When You Leave, Take Your Picture with You: Racism in the Women's Movement," "Between the Lines: On Class and Homophobia," "Speaking in Tongues: The Third World Woman Writer," and "El Mundo Zurdo: The Vision."

Feminist Agenda

While seeking an integration of cultural traditions and spiritual issues, Chicana feminism proposes a feminist agenda that encompasses issues affecting women in their everyday life (gender-specific issues) and also advances a reevaluation of the role of women in society (gender-strategic issues). Chicana feminism is proud of the Chicano cultural heritage but recognizes and acknowledges its limitations in terms of the subordinate role it assigns women. Chicanas consider themselves oppressed people on three different levels. First, they are oppressed as women, because they live in a patriarchal society that undermines the role of women. On a second level, they are also oppressed as members of a cultural and racial minority within the United States, a society that tends to silence people of different backgrounds, especially racial backgrounds. The third level of oppression is inscribed within their own Chicano culture, where the supremacy of the male and the submission of the female are institutionalized cultural values.

Critical Writing

The term *Chicana* defines a woman with a fundamental borderland quality. Chicana feminism is therefore inscribed within a *mestizaje,* that is to say within a process in which there is a combination of Anglo and Hispanic cultures. Writers' contributions reflect the reality of women living in two worlds, and it is not surprising to find creative and critical writing included in the same text. It might be said that the language of Chicanas reflects their identity as *mestizas*—daughters of the borderland—living and writing within a space and a tongue, neither definite nor exclusive. Gloria Anzaldúa's book *Borderlands/La Frontera: The New Mestiza* (1987) exemplifies this position: while different from and in resistance to U.S. literature, it is nevertheless written inside the U.S. context.

For Chicanas, language initially provided the counterpart of silence on at least two levels. Writing served as a means of breaking their historical silence as women living within the double patriarchal context created by U.S. society and Mexican culture. Chicana writing also opened up a space for their empowerment as Mexican-Americans, members of an oppressed minority within U.S. society. Having breached their silence, language then became the locus where Chicanas not only search for the appropriate words (English, Spanish, Spanglish, or Tex-Mex?) but also seek to define or find the social and political position from which they should speak (as women, as workers, as writers, as intellectuals?).

The endemic racism encountered within power-producing institutions, including academia, mainstream feminism, and policy-making organizations, is another recurrent theme in Chicana literature. Pervasive racism may be manifest through homogenizing feminist claims or as outright racial discrimination. Chicana writing addresses both, seeking to uncover and expose the subtle mechanisms that tend to perpetuate Chicanas' marginalization.

Creative Writing

These themes, the search for a proper or appropriate language and the everyday experience of racism, are invariably reflected in the creative writings of Chicanas. While an exhaustive listing of contemporary Chicana writers is beyond the scope of this article, a first approach to this seductive literature requires at least some exploration into the works of a few important authors. Poets like Lorna Dee Cervantes and Cherríe Moraga address the difficulties of expression within a language that is and, at the same time, is not the mother tongue. In her novel *The House on Mango Street* (1991), Sandra Cisneros explores the difficult process through which a young Chicana searches for her identity in a divided world. Ana Castillo's *The Mixquiahuala Letters* (1986) skillfully utilizes the letter, a commonly used vehicle for communication between women who are apart, to

uncover the reality of *chicanismo*. Other authors worth mentioning are Denise Chávez, Helena María Viramontes, and Evangelina Vigil.

The Future

Despite its confrontations with cultural *chicanismo* and white feminist ideology, Chicana feminism has been successful in delineating a space for itself. Strengthened through their experience, feminist Chicanas are nowadays in the process of building alliances with those sectors that, differences notwithstanding, might share a common cause. *Making Face, Making Soul/Haciendo Caras: Creative and Critical Perspectives by Feminists of Color* (ed. Gloria Anzaldúa, 1990), for example, resulted from approaches and conversations between Chicanas and other women of color. In many senses, this work may be considered a furthering of the efforts initiated by *This Bridge*.

Along the same lines, and despite the animosity generated by women's critique of the perpetuation of patriarchal ideology, Chicana feminists' efforts at joining forces with Chicano scholars and activists have also been somewhat successful. Since 1984 *Chicana Voices: Intersections of Class, Race, and Gender* (National Association for Chicano Studies) has provided an excellent forum as well as an opportunity to display and publish the wide range of scholarship produced by Chicanas.

Within academia, the work of Mujeres Activas en Letras y Cambio Social (MALCS), a group of working-class Chicana scholars involved in higher education at the University of California at Davis, is worth noting. In their mission statement, they clearly assert that their research tends to close the gap between the academic community and the political struggle within the Chicano communities. The volume *Chicana Critical Issues* (ed. Norma Alarcón et al., 1993) addresses the predominant themes of sexism and inequality in the university setting, in Chicano studies, and in the community. This work provides a solid perspective on social and political issues as well as updated lists of materials related to Chicana studies.

As we have seen, Chicana feminism began as a branch of the human rights movements and developed through struggles and debates within academia and the white feminist movement. Chicana feminism has evolved pragmatically and theoretically and is nowadays a feminism that seeks to link an ideological stance with grassroots militancy.

See Also

ETHNIC STUDIES, *I and II*; FEMINISM: SECOND-WAVE NORTH AMERICAN

References and Further Reading

Alarcón, Norma, eds. 1993. *Chicana critical issues.* Berkeley Calif.: Third Woman.

Anzaldúa, Gloria. 1987. *Borderlands/La frontera: The new mestiza.* San Francisco: Spinsters/Aunt Lute.

———, ed. 1990. *Making face, making soul/haciendo caras: Creative and critical perspectives by feminists of color.* San Francisco: Aunt Lute.

Castillo, Ana. 1986. *The Mixquiahuala letters.* Binghamton, N.Y.: Bilingual Review.

Cisneros, Sandra. 1983. *The house on Mango Street.* Houston, Tex.: Arte Público.

Córdova, Teresa, Norma Cantó, Gilberto Cárdenas, Juan Garná, and Christine MiSierra. 1990. *Chicana voices: Intersections of class, race, and gender.* Albuquerque: University of New Mexico Press.

De la Torre, Adela, and Beatriz M. Pesquera, eds. 1993. *Building with our hands: New directions in Chicana studies.* Berkeley: University of California Press.

Galindo, D. Letticia, and Marcia Dolores Gonzalez, eds. 1999. *Speaking Chicana: Voice, power, and identity.* Tucson: University of Arizona Press.

García, Alma M., ed. 1997. *Chicana feminist thought: The basic historical writings.* New York: Routledge.

Horno-Delgado, Asunción, Eliana Ortega, Nina M. Scottk, and Nancy Sapora Sternbach. 1989. *Breaking boundaries: Latina writing and critical readings.* Amherst: University of Massachusetts Press.

McCracken, Ellen. 1998. *New Latina narrative: The feminine space of postmodern ethnicity.* Tucson: University of Arizona Press.

Moraga, Cherríe, and Gloria Anzaldúa. 1981. *This bridge called my back: Writings by radical women of color.* Watertown, Mass.: Persephone.

Rebolledo, Tey Diana, Erlinda Gonzales-Berry, and Millie Santillanes, eds. 1992. *Nuestras mujeres: Hispanas of New Mexico: Their images and their lives, 1582–1992.* Albuquerque, N.M.: El Norte/Academia.

Saldívar-Hull, Sonia. 2000. *Feminism on the Border: Chicana gender politics and literature.* Berkeley Ill.: University of California Press.

Viviana Rangil

FEMINISM: China

Advocacy of feminism emerged in China with the rising tide of nationalism at the turn of the twentieth century. In the course of one century, feminism generated significant social changes while becoming a highly contested site in China's political transformations.

Origins of Feminism in China

After China's defeat in the Sino-Japanese War in 1895, reformers began to raise the "women problem" in their proposals for national strengthening. Reformers attacked foot-binding and campaigned for women's formal education. The most influential theme in their advocacy of women's social advancement was a utilitarian argument that women are half of China's resources. This paralleled the demand for women's equal rights that applied the western liberal concept of human rights. Inspired by international women's suffrage movements, some Chinese revolutionaries against the Qing dynasty envisioned a modern China in which women were entitled to all the rights that men enjoy. In a widely circulated pamphlet, *The Women's Bell*, published in 1903, Jin Tianhe first articulated a feminist principle for early-twentieth-century Chinese liberals: that natural rights should include women's rights. At this point the term *nüquan*, women's rights, entered public discourse.

A group of educated women from elite families were the first generation of Chinese feminist activists. They created about forty women's periodicals and newspapers between 1897 and 1912 in Shanghai, Beijing, and Tokyo, where many Chinese women went for an education. These publications advocated equality between men and women, and condemned foot-binding, arranged marriage, and the Chinese patriarchal family. Many feminists actively participated in the revolution of 1911 that toppled the Qing dynasty. Some scholars see them as nationalists rather than feminists. But women revolutionaries clearly expressed a feminist stance when they launched an organized suffrage movement in 1912 shortly after the Republic of China was founded. The rise of warlord power, however, suppressed the suffrage movement in less than a year. Many suffragists shifted their efforts to breaking gender barriers in professions.

Feminism in the New Culture May Fourth Period

In 1915, the creation of the journal *New Youth* ushered in an age of unparalleled intellectual exploration in China. Intellectuals disillusioned with the revolution turned to cultural solutions to strengthen and revitalize the nation. They believed that for China to survive as an independent nation, Chinese culture had to change. Advocates of the "New Culture" appropriated various ideologies from the West in their critique of the dominant Confucian cultural framework. Gender hierarchy as a Confucian principle was contrasted with the feminist principle of gender equality to demonstrate the backwardness of Confucian culture and the advancement of western civilization. Centuries-old practices of arranged marriage, chastity, exclusion of women from public domains, and so on, were identified as "feudal oppression of women." Women's emancipation was presented as the key to changing and modernizing China. A large number of western feminist texts were translated into Chinese and were circulated by New Culture journals and newspapers.

After a student demonstration in Beijing against an imperialist infringement of China's sovereignty on 4 May 1919, a nationwide mass movement emerged in urban China. The May Fourth movement, as it was called later, became a powerful vehicle for circulating New Culture messages. Many female students in secondary schools and women's normal schools actively participated in demonstrations, petitions, and public speaking. Young women's public actions that crossed gender boundaries were legitimized by women's patriotism and hailed as a sign of China's modernity, as young women began to demand women's emancipation. Debates on women's issues that originated in New Culture journals exploded into the mainstream media. Women's education, careers, economic independence, political participation, free social contact with men, freedom to choose a spouse, freedom to love and divorce, birth control, and so on, all became hot issues of the era. Within one year of the public debate on coeducation at the college level, Beijing University, one of the most prestigious universities in China, opened its doors to female students in 1920 after a young woman, Deng Chunlan, first requested enrollment. Other universities soon followed suit.

In the May Fourth period (1915–1925), "feminism" had several Chinese translations, including *nüzizhuyi* (female-ism), *nüxingzhuyi* (feminine-ism), *funüzhuyi* (womanism), *nüquanzhuyi* (the ism of women's rights), and *fumineishimu* (feminism). These unfixed Chinese terms reflect Chinese intellectuals' efforts to grasp the complexity of western feminism. But eventually only one version, nüquanzhuyi, remained in circulation. "The ism of women's rights" expressed the May Fourth feminist aims of women's equal rights in political, social, and economic spheres. The liberal feminist theme was popularized in several widespread Chinese phrases: "independent personhood," "women are human beings," "equality between men and women," and "pursuing women's rights." These phrases became the core of a new women's subjectivity within the May Fourth movement.

Feminism in Political Contestations

At the peak of May Fourth feminist agitation and activism in the early 1920s, the political landscape in China was going through crucial changes. The newly founded Chinese Communist Party (CCP) formed a coalition with the Nationalist Party to start a National Revolution. Its goal was to reunify a disintegrated China by destroying the power of local warlords and imperialists. The two-party alliance at once incorporated the May Fourth feminist agenda and diverted feminist energy into a nationalist cause. By 1925 the growing nationalism overshadowed May Fourth feminist voices in the public discourse. Meanwhile, a two-party women's emancipation movement was gaining momentum in the central areas of the National Revolution.

As Christina K. Gilmartin observes, the 1920s were a "period of peak influence of feminism on Communist and Nationalist revolutionaries" (1995). From its inception in 1920, the CPP incorporated gender equality and women's emancipation in its platform, which reflects both the fact that its founders were the prominent New Culture advocates of feminism and also the new party's urgent need to attract a wider constituency. The Nationalist Party also included gender equality in its platform in 1924 as a result of senior women party members' efforts. May Fourth feminism shaped the dominant political discourse to the extent that women's emancipation became a badge of modernity that both parties claimed to wear. The two parties' promotion of the women's emancipation movement in the National Revolution further consolidated feminist discourse in China.

Although the CCP actively incorporated many May Fourth feminist ideas and issues in the National Revolution, it also adopted exclusionary practice in its efforts to win followers. The CCP publications in the early 1920s began to define feminists who did not join the nationalist movement as "narrow feminists." The term *feminism, nüquanzhuyi,* in the Communist usage became increasingly negative, eventually connoting a bourgeois fantasy detached from Chinese reality and the needs of the oppressed women, and a focus on gender conflicts at the expense of national interest. "Women's emancipation movement" (*funü jiefang yundong*) was adopted by the CCP to distinguish the women's movement led by the party from the nonpartisan feminist movement. Communist theorists proposed a line of women's emancipation based on European socialist ideas and the practices of the Soviet Russian revolution. Women's emancipation, as expounded by the CCP, could come only after the success of a proletarian revolution that overthrew both the imperialist power in China and an economic system of private ownership. And economic independence through participation in social production was the top priority in the CCP's definition of women's emancipation.

The influence of the CCP's definition of feminism and women's emancipation correlates with its political power. Nüquanzhuyi retained its positive meaning, and independent feminist organizations continued to exist in urban China before the CCP rose to dominance in 1949. After the People's Republic of China was founded, the CCP completed its institutionalization of the women's movement by establishing the All-China Women's Federation. Unifying the women's movement under the leadership of the CCP, the ACWF with its subordinate local branches at provincial, municipal, and district levels soon became the only women's organization that supposedly represented all women's interests in the Mao era. In the party's texts, the party-led women's emancipation movement was presented as the only correct route to women's liberation. A history of nüquanzhuyi was erased from the public memory.

Although the social space for spontaneous feminist activism was closed in the Mao era (1949–1976), much of the May Fourth feminist agenda was incorporated in the dominant political discourse of the People's Republic of China. Under the rubric of the party-led Chinese women's liberation, many practices reflected Marxist ideas of women's participation in social production; socialist feminist visions of public kitchens, nurseries, and other social welfare facilities for women; and liberal feminist concerns for women's equal rights in all spheres. But as many scholars have pointed out, the CCP continuously subordinated gender to class issues rather than fulfilling its promise for women's emancipation.

The incessant political campaigns and overbearing Maoist class analysis left little room for women to raise gender issues. The party dismissed the gender issue by declaring that Chinese women were liberated. Many "liberated" Chinese women were more empowered than ever by a state-sponsored discourse on gender equality and the state's mobilization of women to step into the public arena. At the same time, they were subjugated to a new patriarch, the party-state, that deprived women of their own voices and their need to define their own diverse interests.

Feminism in the Post-Mao Era

In the post-Mao era, women intellectuals joined men in deconstructing Maoism. Women's challenge had a clear gender dimension. They criticized the dominance of class analysis for overriding women's issues and the Maoist line of gender equality for its masculine bias. Women were told to be like men in the public arena while continuing to play the roles of wife and mother at home. This state-mandated assimilation to the male norm was condemned by both men and women intellectuals in the 1980s for "masculinizing Chi-

nese women." A reassessment of western feminism emerged in this process as an integral part in women's critique of the CCP's definitions of women's liberation and "narrow western bourgeois feminism." Against the specific historical background of the 1980s, an essentialist version of western feminism had a strong appeal to urban educated Chinese women who were trying to justify their revolt against the dominant framework of class and a masculinist gender equality by emphasizing women's "innate, unique femaleness." To avoid invoking the negative connotations of the nüquanzhuyi and to express their understanding of feminism, Chinese women adopted a new term for feminism, nüxingzhuyi (feminine-ism).

In the mid-1980s, information on women's studies in the West aroused great interest among Chinese women intellectuals. The term women's studies suggested to them that studying women's uniqueness was a legitimate academic field in the modernized West. Women who were eager to create a forum of their own to address women's issues in post-Mao China quickly adopted "women's studies" as a legitimate site for their activism. Unlike women's studies in the United States and Europe, "women's studies" in China was located not in academia but in Women's Federations at provincial or municipal levels. Women's studies associations formed by Women's Federations provided a unique forum where Women's Federations cadres worked jointly with women academics on research projects oriented toward solving contemporary women's problems. Women's studies, or "research on women," as it is translated in Chinese, emerged as a new form of Chinese feminist activism in the reform era.

The preparation for the Fourth World Conference on Women (FWCW) in Beijing (4–15 September 1995) generated further feminist activism in China. Increasing communication between women in and outside China enhanced Chinese women's knowledge of global feminism. The FWCW directly introduced many feminist concepts and terminology to China through the Platform for Action and the Beijing Declaration, the two documents endorsed formally by participating governments at the UN conference. Because the Chinese government officially signed those documents, Chinese women activists in and outside the Women's Federation have gained new legitimacy for their goal to "merge with global women's movements." Conferences, workshops, and publications on nüxingzhuyi have become a part of Chinese women's legitimate efforts to materialize the agenda set in the Platform for Action, which called for improving gender equity and promoting women's social advancement in twelve areas. A feminist concept of gender has entered the official media and has been embraced by many women activists. Women scholars who have been active in research on women are moving toward creating a women's studies curriculum in higher education in the twenty-first century.

See Also

CONFUCIANISM; DEVELOPMENT: CHINA; EDUCATION: EAST ASIA; FEMINISM: OVERVIEW; FEMINISM: SOCIALIST; LITERATURE: CHINA; MEDIA: CHINESE CASE STUDY; POLITICS AND THE STATE: EAST ASIA; POPULATION: CHINESE CASE STUDY; WOMEN'S STUDIES: EAST ASIA

References and Further Reading

Croll, Elisabeth. 1978. *Feminism and socialism in China*. London: Routledge and Kegan Paul.

Gilmartin, Christina Kelley. 1995. *Engendering the Chinese revolution*. Berkeley: University of California Press.

———, Gail Hershatter, Lisa Rofel, and Tyrene White. 1994. *Engendering China*. Cambridge, Mass.: Harvard University Press.

Hershatter, Gail, Emily Honig, Susan Mann, and Lisa Rofel. 1998. *Guide to women's studies in China*. Berkeley: Institute of East Asian Studies, University of California.

Wang Zheng. 1999. *Women in the Chinese enlightenment*. Berkeley: University of California Press.

Wang Zheng

FEMINISM: Commonwealth of Independent States

The Commonwealth of Independent States (CIS) was formed in 1993, after the collapse of the Soviet Union. Twelve former Soviet republics, now independent states, are included in the CIS: Russia, Azerbaijan, Armenia, Belarus, Georgia, Kazakhstan, Kyrgyzstan, Moldova, Tajikistan, Turkmenistan, Ukraine, and Uzbekistan. Among these countries, some common cultural elements (even with recent strengthening of national characteristics) have developed, not only through their shared 70-year sociocultural past within the Soviet Union, but also through an even deeper history. All of these peoples were included within the Russian Empire before the socialist revolution of 1917. These circumstances allow us to single out and examine some social problems that these countries have in common—specifically regarding the status of women, the women's movement, and feminism.

Contemporary feminism exists, first, in the form of an ideology of women's equal rights; second, as a social movement, fighting for women's rights; and finally, as a counter-cultural theory—that is, as a philosophical analysis of understandings of gender and the ideas that society attributes to the biological differences between women and men.

This article will describe how, when, and in what form feminism is emerging in the countries of the CIS; what the specifics of that process are, and what prospects there are for the development of feminism in this region of the world.

The Soviet Experience of Solving the "Woman Question"

Feminism in the countries of the CIS must be examined in connection with the so-called Soviet experience of solving the woman question—a policy under which a significant gap existed between de jure and de facto equal rights.

Even the first Soviet constitution (1918) proclaimed the equal rights of women and men in all spheres of life. The actual state of affairs was contradictory. The civil-political rights of women (and of men) in the totalitarian state were fictional. These rights were merely declared; no opportunities existed for their realization, since all fundamental political and economic decisions were made by the Politburo of the Central Committee of the Communist Party of the Soviet Union (CCCPSU). The citizens of the country were obligated to submit to the CCPSU under threat of state sanctions up to and including imprisonment and physical harm.

The situation with regard to socioeconomic rights was better—women held equal rights with men to labor (on average, women were 50 percent of those employed), free schooling and higher education (women were 60 percent of specialists with higher and mid-specialized education), free medical services, free housing, and so on. However, in Soviet times the "right to labor" in fact meant identical obligations to labor, since the economic and noneconomic methods used by the state allowed people of working age no choice. Economic methods consisted of the impossibility of receiving resources for survival anywhere except by working for the state. Noneconomic methods were administrative and criminal punishment for not working (for example, the famous Russian poet Josef Brodsky was sentenced to five years in a labor camp simply for his failure to serve as an employee of a state enterprise). True, there was an exception for women with children: they could officially be located "under their husbands' support." However, only very few women, in upper Soviet party and state circles, could afford such a luxury. The main mass of women worked: the Soviet

Union characteristically maintained the highest indicator for professional employment of women—86 percent of working-age women were employed, and an additional 6 percent were students. Soviet propaganda advanced this indicator as evidence of the "emancipation" of women. At the same time, hidden discrimination always existed in the sphere of professional employment: for example, the salaries of women on average were one-third lower than those of men; and there was vertical and horizontal professional discrimination against women, as well as their professional segregation.

Even greater inequality characterized the family. Regardless of the formal legal pronouncements of equal family rights of men and women, in society the traditional ideology of women's familial destiny reigned, strongly supported by state propaganda. This brought about extra exploitation of women: working for wages 41 hours per week, they spent that much time again on household duties. Another consequence of the state ideology of woman's familial destiny was the formation of her primary personal identity as wife, mother, and housewife. The results of the Soviet experience of solving the "woman question" included such contradictory phenomena as: the proclamation in legislation of the principle of women's equality; women's alienation from policy and decision-making levels; women's mass involvement in professional employment and—simultaneously—their acquisition of economic independence from men; a high level of education among women; and the strengthening of sexist stereotypes and the formation of women's personal identity as related to family alone.

Women's Nongovernmental Organizations

Until the end of the 1980s, there existed one officially sanctioned women's nongovernmental organization (NGO)—the Committee of Soviet Women (CSW), which was financed from the state budget and controlled by the Central Committee of the CPSU. Its task was to propagandize the nation's successes in solving the woman question. Today the CSW has been renamed the Union of Women of Russia, but it has not announced a defined program of activities. The only independent organization that emerged before perestroika was the religious feminist group Maria, which worked for approximately two years and managed to publish almanacs titled *Women and Russia* and *Maria*. In 1980 the group was subjected to political repression. The leaders of that group—Tatiana Goricheva, Natalia Malakhovskaya, Yulia Voznesenskaya, and Tatiana Mamonova—were arrested and later exiled overseas.

In 1989, after the call to revive the women's movement by the general secretary of the Central Committee of the CPSU, Mikhail Gorbachev, 240,000 women's committees (*zhensovety*) were formed under the party committees of enterprises throughout the Soviet Union. These *zhensovety* did not present the state with the task of defending the rights of women, and their activity was limited to assistance to women in resolving their most urgent questions of survival (receiving food, finding places for their children in kindergartens and pioneer camps, etc.).

At the end of the 1980s several small feminist groups appeared. Valentina Konstantinova, Anastasia Posadskaya, Olga Voronina, and Natalia Zakharova formed the group LOTOS in Moscow—in Russian, this acronym stands for League for Emancipation from Social Stereotypes. Also in Moscow, Natalia Filippova, Natalia Abubikirova, and Marina Regentova formed SAFO—the Free Association of Feminist Organizations—and Olga Lipovskaya and her group represented SAFO in Saint Petersburg (then Leningrad). These groups clearly articulated themselves as being feminist, and they presented the aims of their activity as dissemination of feminist theory and practice, development of the feminist movement in Russia, and elimination of sexist stereotypes and practices of suppressing the feminine. In 1991 the Moscow Center for Gender Studies (which grew out of the group LOTOS), SAFO, and the Zhensovet of the Unified Institute for Nuclear Research organized the First Independent Women's Forum, in the city of Dubna in the Moscow region. Representatives of women's organizations independent of the state and the CSW gathered at the forum. The open declaration of a feminist agenda and the presence of lesbians at the forum brought about attempts to prevent it from taking place. However, despite the presence of representatives of the KGB (Committee for State Security) at the open forum, it did take place, and approximately 200 women attended, representing 48 organizations from different cities of the country.

In 1992, the Second Independent Women's Forum was held in Dubna, and approximately 500 women attended. The first and second forums offered a new, feminist language for discussion of women's rights. And although far from all women's nongovernmental organizations today accept feminist language or a feminist agenda, nonetheless, the idea of discrimination against women and the necessity of defending women's rights is gradually spreading in Russia and the CIS; the increase in numbers of women's organizations is testimony to this. Hence, as of the beginning of 1999, 600 women's NGOs have been registered with the Ministry of Justice of the Russian Federation, and more than 200 women's NGOs exist in various countries of the CIS.

Directions of Activity of Women's NGOs

As already noted, very few women's organizations openly declare themselves and their programs as feminist. This is connected with several circumstances. First, in the culture of the countries of the post-Soviet region, essentialism and its patriarchal (biodeterministic) variant are very widespread. Society and women themselves as a mass are deeply convinced that the "nature" of women differs strongly from the "nature" of men, and that the true destiny of women is to serve their family, husband, and children. Second, in the countries of the CIS, there is a lack of reliable information on the history and theory of feminism. Third, the mass media build an image of feminism as a theory of man-hating and a "battle of the sexes." Moreover, they characterize a feminist as an unfeminine, asexual, unsuccessful woman, who compensates for her failure in personal and family life (being unmarried and lacking children) through her social activism. Since, for the majority of women of Russia and the CIS, the primary personal identity is precisely as a wife, mother, and housewife, many women avoid any association with the "terrible" word *feminism* and the image of feminism.

Because of these circumstances, the majority of women's NGOs avoid theorizing and political activities and do not articulate the problems of discrimination against women and sexism in society as a whole. Women's NGOs in Russia and the CIS, as a rule, are oriented only toward concrete, practical tasks of women's survival in the countries undergoing economic transition. As indicated in the *Directory of Women's Nongovernmental Organizations of Russia and the CIS*, approximately 60 percent of these organizations in Russia in one way or another connect their activities with human rights in general (not only of women). Among these kinds of organizations, only one-fourth work specifically on the protection of women's rights. Such organizations include, for example, the Interregional Association of Independent Women's Organizations (including 35 Russian organizations); the Commission on Women's Legal Status of the International Nongovernmental Association "Union of Lawyers," and others. Just as many organizations work on protection of the rights of army draftees, soldiers, as well as protection of the rights of soldiers' parents—these are the so-called Committees of Soldiers' Mothers. The remaining women's NGOs are oriented toward protection of the rights of other sections of the population—children, the elderly, invalids, refugees,

and so on. Such women's NGOs organize social expertise on laws and draft legislation, present projects for new laws on observance of human rights (more successfully at the local level than on the federal level), provide legal consultation and legal assistance to the population, and appear as public defenders in the courts.

The second most widespread direction of activity of women's NGOs is education; that is, conducting various types of seminars and training, conferences, leadership schools for women, summer schools on women's and gender studies, and development of new educational courses on women's and gender studies. This area is mostly the work of various centers for gender studies (see below for more details about them).

The third direction of activity of women's NGOs is informational work; that is, the production, storage, and dissemination of various types of information. Such organizations produce newspapers; edit "women's" pages in city and oblast newspapers; release "women's" programs or film special videos; publish bulletins, newsletters, books and brochures; and spread information through electronic networks. There are women's archives and libraries. Of this type, for example, are the Women's Information Network, the Information Center of the Independent Women's Forum, the Association of Women Journalists, and the Center for Expert and Informational Support of Social Initiatives.

In recent years in large Russian cities, crisis centers for women have been developing quite actively, with the support of local administrations and western foundations. There are eleven such centers that are members of the Association of Crisis Centers of Russia. Unfortunately, there is a lack of information about such centers in other countries of the CIS.

Approximately 30 percent of women's organizations, especially in the provinces, emerged as organizations for assistance to families, in connection with the sharp worsening of the population's material situation. They work on charitable activities, locating employment for women, and pedagogical issues, and also work with children and adolescents. Also included in this area are organizations of mothers with many children, single mothers, or mothers with disabled children, which have emerged for the purpose of mutual assistance.

A small portion (no greater than 10 percent of all organizations in Russia) of women's NGOs currently work on political activity—that is, participation in elections or systematic political work. One of the largest organizations of this type is the former political bloc Women of Russia, which won seats in the elections to the State Duma in 1993. The leaders of this block were Alevtina Fedulova and Ekaterina Lakhova, who were State Duma deputies during the last session. In the elections of 1995, the bloc did not make it into the State Duma, and in fact split into two organizations: the movement "Women of Russia" is headed by Alevtina Fedulova, and the "All-Russian Socio-Political Movement of Women of Russia" is headed by Ekaterina Lakhova, a deputy of the State Duma in the current session. Both organizations are maintaining their political goals, and both speak out in support of "women, children, and family." Aside from this, participation in electoral campaigns is a goal of such organizations as the Congress of Women of the Kola Peninsula, the union "Women of the Don," and the Union of Women of Russia.

Women's NGOs in Russia and the CIS are extremely diverse in their composition and forms of existence. Several of them are formed from a few people and are not officially registered in the responsible state organs. Others are registered and consist of tens or even hundreds of people, or have affiliates in different cities. Throughout the CIS there are a few general "collections" of similar kinds of organizations: for example, the various Unions (or Councils) of Women of Azerbaijan, Armenia, Belarus, and so on (former national affiliates of the Committee of Soviet Women); Committees of Soldiers' Mothers; Associations of Women with University Education; Leagues of Women Muslims or Christians. Quite a few organizations have territorial-geographic or national characteristics—for example, the Amur Union of Women, Angara Union of Women, Women of the Caucasus, Society of Jewish Women of Azerbaijan, Union of Women of Udmurtia, and so on. These organizations work on different social problems of a particular region.

Feminist Organizations in the CIS

It is worthwhile to differentiate between women's and feminist organizations. Often any kind of association or group consisting of women is classified as being a women's organization. As already noted, a portion of such organizations do indeed fight for women's rights, while another portion defend the rights of or assist other social groups. There are also women's organizations whose activity is directed toward supporting and disseminating the traditional ideology of women's familial destiny.

Those organizations that openly call themselves feminist or gender centers study and propagandize feminist and gender theory; develop various educational programs on women's and gender research; conduct analytic research, using feminist theory; and attempt to influence policy from feminist positions. For the purpose of systematic description, it is possibly, fairly conditionally, to divide such organizations into two types. One type conducts more practical work, while the other is more oriented toward the conduct of academic research and the development and integration of courses in women's studies and gender studies in universities. This division is indeed quite conditional, as the spirit of feminism assumes a mutual enrichment of theory and practice. Precisely because of this, the practical organizations and research centers collaborate a great deal and conduct joint projects and events.

In contemporary Russia, a total of 12 organizations call themselves feminist. Among the practically oriented organizations we can name the following ones. The Information Center of the Independent Women's Forum (ICIWF, Moscow) emerged in 1994 for the purposes of obtaining information for the women's movement and disseminating feminist approaches and practical activity. The ICIWF releases informational newsletters and conducts seminars and trainings. The group FALTA—that is, the Feminist Alternative (Moscow)—has published several journals, called *FemInfo,* and conducts consultations with women and seminars for consciousness-raising among women. The club Preobrazheniye (Transformation) has released several issues of a feminist literature almanac of the same name and conducted a women's prose competition. Ariadna (Moscow) conducts seminars on women's political leadership. The Feminist Orientation Center (Moscow) assigns itself the tasks of feminist enlightenment and support for women in building strength and self-confidence. The aims of the Center for Expert and Informational Support of Social Initiatives (EPSI, Moscow) are resource support for the women's movement and activities for integrating women's interests in reform policies. The purpose of the Interregional Association of Independent Women's Organizations is to strengthen and support its member organizations and to defend their common interests in the development of independent women's initiatives.

The Association of Independent Women's Initiatives works in the city of Tver, and its tasks include protection of women's rights and the establishment of educational training programs for women. The Petersburg Center for Gender Problems conducts open seminars, translates and publishes the works of western feminists, and publishes the feminist bulletin *All People Are Sisters.* In the city of Naberezhniye Chelny (in the Republic of Tatarstan), the organization Femina has prepared a series of television programs and conducted a festival of videofilms called "Women's Theme," as well as two women's film festivals.

As for the remaining countries of the CIS, feminist organizations exist in only a few of them. Among practical feminist organizations, in Ukraine there is a feminist association, today widely renowned, called Humanitarian Initiative. In Belarus, the Association of University Women produces the *Feminist Newsletter.* In Kazakhstan, there are four organizations with a feminist orientation. Two of them work in the capital, Almaty: the Feminist League and Malvina, a noncommercial publishing house of feminist literature for girls and women, which also produces a newspaper of the same name for girls.

The Development of Research Centers for Women's and Gender Research in the CIS

We may note two peculiarities of feminism in the CIS. First of all, it is not very widespread, and even so, it is principally found in Russia. Second, feminism in Russia and the Ukraine is represented more in research and educational activities than in political activism.

Research on women and women's issues from a feminist position lacks any adequate Russian name, and is often identified using the English words *women's studies* or *research on women.* As a result of the negative associations of the word *feminism,* the term *gender* (or *gender research*) is used in the official names of such organizations, especially if they exist under universities or institutes of the Academy of Sciences. Therefore, here we shall use the words *feminist* and *gender research* interchangeably. The feminist type of research differs in its methodology (as it uses the principle of looking at problems from the position of women's experience), choice of theme (political participation and women's leadership, the image of women in the mass media, problems of violence and power over women, reproductive rights), and proposed solutions (transformation of culture and society by taking into account women's interests). As a rule, this type of research is conducted by research centers and groups that are independent of the state.

Against them stands so-called feminology—supported and sponsored by state educational courses, in which women are examined in fact from the positions of traditional resolution of the "woman question" as found in Marxism-Leninism. In the Soviet Union, quite a lot was written on the "woman question," and during the 1970s and 1980s sociological research was also conducted, mostly devoted to the problem of "women combining family and productive functions." Soviet sociology of the family, the framework within which the status and roles of women were studied, was based on the positions of Marxism-Leninism. In Marxism-Leninism, women were always

examined as a passive social object, which the party and the state must emancipate in order to do the important tasks of building socialism. The state must direct, assist, guard, and support women in their productive and reproductive functions. In this way, regardless of the formally proclaimed equality and emancipation of women, women were placed in the traditional passive position of being an object of manipulation by the state-patriarch. Contemporary feminology actually reproduces this very same schema—women continue to be examined as passive objects along with children, the elderly, and invalids. The Ministry of Higher Education approves of courses in feminology as a required program in faculties and departments that prepare workers for the social sphere.

Feminist and gender research is an intellectual paradigm that is relatively new for the CIS. The major theoretical works on this topic have been written, as a rule, in the West. However, for economic reasons, the absence of systematic academic and informational exchange, and the language barrier, familiarization with and acquisition of the intellectual baggage of feminism is quite difficult for most women. Currently in the CIS, there are really only three working research and educational centers.

Of them, the most widely known (and not only in Russia, but also overseas) is the Moscow Center for Gender Studies (MCGS, Russia), which emerged in 1990. The activities of this center, from the very beginning, had an openly feminist character and developed in several directions. Historically speaking, the first of these was to initiate the development of an independent, democratic women's and feminist movement in the country. Thus MCGS was instrumental in setting up the first (1991, Dubna) and second (1992, Dubna) women's forums, and these pushed the spread of feminist ideas and the formation of a women's movement. The second direction is the conduct of women's and gender research. The themes that MCGS examines are diverse: employment and unemployment of women, gender and culture (the symbolic meaning of gender), the image of women in the mass media, problems of violence, women migrants, and the reproductive rights of women. From 1996 to 1998, MCGS conducted a large sociological study called "The Rights of Women in an Average Russian City: Mass Consciousness and the Actual Practice of their Realization." The results of this study were published in two volumes. The next direction of MCGS's work is educational. Besides practical seminars and trainings, MCGS has conducted three Russia-wide summer schools on women's and gender research. The final direction of MCGS's work is the application of gender expertise in state social policy and legislation, and the distribution of expert materials among public policymakers, media, educators, researchers, and women's NGOs. In 1998, MCGS published four books about the effects of gender expertise on legislation regarding employment, mass media, reproductive rights, and migrants in the Russian Federation. The main research interest of MCGS is focused on analysis of concrete gender problems in Russia. As a methodological base, the center uses the theory of social construction of gender and interpretation of gender as a cultural metaphor. The results of the research are actively used by women's NGOs for public advocacy. MCGS, as initiator of the development of gender research in Russia, and by supporting close contacts with hundreds of women activists in the countries of the CIS, plays an extremely important role in the dissemination of feminist ideas throughout the post-Soviet region.

The gender program in the department of political science and sociology at the European University (Saint Petersburg, Russia) has existed since 1997. It is a program of education in gender research for graduate students in sociology and political science, for preparation of masters' and candidates' dissertations. There are courses taught on "Feminist and Gender Research" (in which emphasis is laid on acquiring the theory of social construction of gender), "Russian Gender Culture," and "Social Theory and Gender." The program has published a collection of articles, called *Gender Measurement of Social and Political Activity in the Transition Period*, as well as the first issue of the journal *Gender Notebooks*.

The Khark'iv Center for Gender Research (Ukraine) has existed since 1996. Its primary task is the preparation and presentation of lecture courses on feminist and gender research. The center has published the textbook *Theory and History of Feminism*; has released the first issue of the journal *Gender Research*, which contains both translations of western works and original articles by associates at the center; and has also begun to publish the popular feminist journal *New Image*. In theoretical terms, the center uses the theory of symbolic interpretation of gender and the language of postmodernist feminism.

Besides these centers that are well known in the CIS, several others have appeared. In the city of Karaganda (Kazakhstan), the Gender Information–Analytic Center and the Center for Gender Research have emerged. In the city of Ivanovo (Russia), there is the Ivanovo Center for Gender Research.

Unfortunately, not only on the scale of the CIS, but even in Russia, there is practically no formulated tradition of intellectual social discussion. This is even more the case as concerns feminist and gender research. Several factors aggravate this. First, until very recently, there existed practically no professional periodical in which such a discussion could take place. Second, there are extremely few people who are familiar with the theoretical problems and discussions in feminist and gender research that have taken place in the West for several years already—for example, regarding the understanding of women, women's experience, the problem of identity and difference between women and men, and other issues. Precisely because of this, even those in Russia who are familiar with such issues prefer to support one another and conduct educational work, rather than hold discussions. On the other hand, a thoroughly positive development has been the arousal of interest in gender research not only in the centers of capital cities but also in provincial universities. It is still too early to speak of the emergence of centers or gender research programs there; however, separate, albeit small, courses are being taught already in several dozen provincial universities in Russia and Ukraine. This development is conditioned not only by the search for new intellectual paradigms, but also by the sharp worsening of gender problems and the increase in gender inequality in the countries of the CIS. However, there is reason to believe that the consciousness of people in the countries of the CIS is gradually changing and that the traditional system of gender hierarchy might be eliminated.

See Also

COMMUNISM; HOUSEHOLDS AND FAMILIES: COMMONWEATH OF INDEPENDENT STATES; POLITICS AND THE STATE: COMMONWEALTH OF INDEPENDENT STATES; WOMEN'S STUDIES: COMMONWEATH OF INDEPENDENT STATES

References and Further reading

Abubikirova, N., N. Abubikirova, T. Reimenkova, E. Kotchkina, M. Regentova, and T. Troinova, eds. 1998. *Directory of Women's Non-Governmental Organizations in Russia and the NIS*. Moscow.

Holland, B., ed. 1985. *Soviet sisterhood*. Bloomington: Indiana University Press.

Posadskaya, A., ed. 1994. *Women in Russia: A new era of Russian feminism*. London: Verso.

Voronina, O. 1993. Soviet patriarchy: Past and present. *Hypathia: A journal of feminist philosophy* 8(4): 97–112.

———. 1994. Soviet women and politics: On the brink of change. In Barbara J. Nelson and Najma Chowdhury, eds.,

Women and politics worldwide, 721–737. New Haven, Conn.: Yale University Press.

Waters, E., and A. Posadskaya. 1995. Democracy without women is not democracy: Women's struggles in postcommunist Russia. In Amrita Basu, ed., *The challenge of local feminisms.* Boulder, Col: Westview.

Olga Voronina

FEMINISM: Cultural

Background: Culture and Feminism

Feminism is necessarily a cultural politics; everywhere, it involves a challenge to patriarchal cultural forms. Its view is that women and women's work and lives are to varying degrees and in more or less violent ways devalued, trivialized, and controlled in modern and traditional, dominant and dominated, secular and religious settings. Even indigenous cultures with life-affirming and holistic worldviews and balanced relations between males and females have been undermined and distorted by the hierarchical, dualistic, and androcentric impositions of colonizing powers.

Feminists in oppressed communities and groups generally selectively defend as well as critique their own cultures. In racist, colonialist, and capitalist contexts, threatened home cultures offer elements of mutual protection and can foster resistance. Victoria Tauli-Corpuz says of indigenous Igorot culture in the Philippines, for instance: "The embers of this culture need to be fanned constantly. But while there is a need to introduce and reinforce the culture which is liberating and empowering for women, there is also a need to alter those aspects which are oppressive to women" (1992: 18).

Traditional cultures are often overtly gendered in ways that support distinct, though subordinate, female subculture, organization, and identity that can be resources in feminist struggles. In an interview in 1985, for instance, Assitan Diallo from Mali and Stella Effua Graham from Ghana spoke about the ways that west African women's traditional organizations needed to be built on rather than rejected by feminists (Gevins, 1985).

Whether or not women can call on traditional resources in the process, the feminist project of transformative women-defined social change depends everywhere on women's not only naming and resisting their oppression by men in general and by the men of their own groups but also reclaiming, re-creating, and revaluing female identity and connection in their own culture and across cultures: "It is the primacy of women relating to women, of women creat-ing a new consciousness of and with each other, which is at the heart of women's liberation" (Radicalesbians, 1970: 84).

This is a revolutionary break with patriarchal cultural values. It means that, far from having to distance themselves from women-associated characteristics and activities to claim equality, feminists can claim equality in transformed societies organized around their important but currently marginalized concerns. They can develop proudly women-based general politics grounded in diverse women's particular experience of life and work. The third world feminist network DAWN (Alternative Development with Women for a New Era) asserts, for instance: "The women's movement too can have an ethic drawn from women's daily lives. At its deepest it is not an effort to play 'catch up' with the competitive, aggressive 'dog-eat-dog' spirit of the dominant system. It is, rather, an attempt to convert men and the system to the sense of responsibility, nurturance, openness, and rejection of hierarchy that are part of our vision" (Sen and Grown, 1987: 72–73).

Cultural Feminism

Learning about feminism through studying its various labeled categories is extremely problematic. This is particularly true for "cultural feminism." The term, which is largely restricted to western metropolitan settings, was coined and is still primarily used by those critical of what they call cultural feminism to refer to others. Conveying a sense of how this term is used requires not so much listing the beliefs of those who espouse the label (almost no one) as listing the political weaknesses associated with cultural feminism by those who have named it as a specific politics in order to criticize it.

The Modern Western Context

Industrialization loosens traditional family constraints on women, so it is important for ruling groups in industrial societies to disrupt women's group identity and dampen the gender-consciousness that might fuel their collective action. New opportunities for women to pursue their individual interests relatively independently of the patriarchal family must also be contained ideologically. Therefore, women in the liberal modern West, especially middle-class white women, are offered tenuous and conditional recognition as full persons in exchange for downplaying their connections with other women. Same-sex friendships and reference groups are displaced for women, though not for men, by the ideal of romantic love and partnership in supposedly equal marriages between men and women who are, ideally, each other's best friends (Rich, 1980).

In these societies, feminists have to consciously re-create women-only space. At first, they established women's political groups to escape control and undermining by men, to protect what they presumed were women's fragile capabilities, to name women's shared oppression, and to escape the limits of a "femininity" mandated and socially constructed in a binary gender system they sought to dismantle. They were concerned not only to claim power but also to transform it: "We believe in collective process and a non-hierarchical distribution of power within our own groups and in our vision of a revolutionary society" (Combahee River Collective, 1979: 372).

Feminists' experience in women's groups very soon led to deep connections with and a new appreciation of other women (Burris, 1973; Weathers, 1971). They began to meet without men, not only to escape them, but also to find one another. An amazingly rich cultural practice has developed by and for women, reflecting feminists' egalitarian and cooperative ends and their joy in one another and articulating an identification that goes beyond an acknowledgment of shared oppression to celebrate women. Feminist poetry, art, literature, dance, drama, and comedy are supported by, and in turn support, feminist publishing houses, magazines, theater groups, music festivals, art galleries, bookstores, restaurants, coffeehouses, and so forth.

This was accompanied by the emergence of new political, often women-only, family forms and collective living arrangements. The women's movement made space (often, to its shame, grudgingly and under protest) for lesbians to declare themselves and for many women to choose this sexuality and even to build separate women's communities. In the modern West, where women have been so effectively separated from one another and have lost most traditional women-defined spaces, and where there are fewer concrete constraints preventing autonomous or separate or lesbian lives when women do choose these, the contribution of lesbian feminism to building women-to-women connections and to carving out alternatives to cultural, social, sexual, and economic dependence on men has been formative. As will be clear below, the important lesbian and especially separatist component of feminist cultural expression has been particularly but not exclusively criticized. The term *cultural feminism* is often, though not always, used to refer to lesbian feminisms (Taylor and Rupp, 1993).

The Critiques

Cultural practice is antipolitical. The first systematic critique of cultural feminism was launched by the group Redstockings in the United States in the early 1970s. They argued that because feminist cultural expression often deals with personal concerns and with processes, matters not generally considered political in other social movements, it detracts from collective action and undermines the women's movement as a political movement (Brooke, 1975).

There is a real issue about where the scarce resources of a social movement can best be used, and there is a real need in western societies to guard against the individualistic undermining of political movements. However, the extreme refusal to acknowledge the political significance of feminist and women's culture imposes a traditional narrow concept of politics against the development of new holistic political forms.

Racism and ethnocentrism. Some lesbian as well as heterosexual black and third world feminists are critical of extreme forms of lesbian separatism that they call cultural feminism. They argue that the expectation that feminists break totally with their culture, community, and family of origin and seek a women-only future is ethnocentric. Many feminists struggle within their own communities as well as the wider society to shape and affirm their ethnic, class, or other identities as well as their women's identity. Ignoring the fact that these struggles are inseparable for some women is seen as just one of the many forms that racism and class bias take in the women's movement.

There is a great deal of truth in this criticism and in the more general point that ethnocentrism, racism, class prejudice, and parochialism are weaknesses in the women's movement. However, it should be recognized that not all separatist feminists would impose their personal and strategic choices on others, and that the creation of separate women-only communities and contexts brings strength to all women and must be supported. Much of the blanket rejection of cultural feminism fails to recognize this and smacks of homophobia, which is also a weakness in the women's movement.

Essentialism and puritanism. By far the broadest criticism of cultural feminism is made by those who use the term to reject all feminist claims that women share not only their oppression but also certain characteristics, structural locations, or work and life experiences that can provide positive resources in the development of feminist politics. These include, to name only a few:

- Spiritual and ecofeminisms that draw on women's particular cultural association with nature in their struggle to change the current exploitative relationship between male society and nature.
- Feminist peace activism that uses women's outsider relationship to the state, the military, and the nation, and their vulnerability to violence in the home, to develop new and broader definitions of peace and visions of change.

- Lesbian feminisms that affirm women's sexuality and connections, believing that, freed from male definition and control, they can be a major resource in creating new forms of less exploitative and objectifying human relationships.
- Black feminisms that celebrate the cultural traditions and important strengths of black women: "[A womanist] loves other women, sexually and/or nonsexually. Appreciates and prefers women's culture, women's emotional flexibility (values tears as natural counterbalance to laughter), and women's strengths" (Walker, 1983: xi).
- Quebec feminists, who are developing a body and process of writing to positively express the specific experiences and beings of women that, until now, have remained hidden and inarticulate.
- Feminisms whose transformative visions are built from the complementary affirmation of women-associated values and parallel aspects of their own indigenous, Afrocentric, or other marginalized traditional culture (Allen, 1983; Collins, 1990).
- Feminists of many different self-definitions in "first" and "two-thirds" worlds who believe women's responsibility for individual and community reproduction provides a material basis for the feminist articulation of alternative life-centered values and visions (Hartsock, 1983).

Feminists critical of these and other positions believe that affirming female characteristics, associations, experiences, work, and responsibilities is inherently antifeminist (Alcoff, 1988; Echols, 1989; Segal, 1987). They argue variously that:

- Naming any characteristics, values, and so forth as women-associated requires accepting the essential biological nature of femaleness and so, regardless of intent, entrenches dualistic hierarchical gender structure.
- Acknowledging any differences from men requires accepting that women are unequal.
- Any articulation of specific women-associated values as the basis of feminist politics betrays the aim of individual freedom by imposing a particular vision. Worse than this, holistic, cooperative, nurturing, life-centered values are old-fashioned, puritanical, and stereotypically female and reflect feminists' failure to escape from their patriarchal conditioning.

While there are essentialist elements in some feminist affirmations of women, these are not the norm. Most of the feminists criticized as "cultural feminists" on these grounds see particular female interests and insights as socially constructed and materially grounded. They affirm these as they refuse their relegation to women and struggle for a degendered society in which they are generalized.

In fact, only feminisms that refuse the false choice between speaking as women and speaking equally are able to go beyond simple pressure for women to become a full social movement addressing the whole of society and challenging all oppression. For only these feminisms can draw on women's lives to articulate the alternative, specifically feminist, values necessary to guide transformative rather than assimilationist social change.

The acknowledgment of women's specificity is most suspect in urban, white, western, middle-class circles where women are most colonized by the liberal derogation of things female and the "modern" destruction of female subcultures. Absolute rejection of women-affirming aspects of feminism can stem from a failure to hear and learn from other communities of women. On occasion it has led to the ethnocentric insistence that the only "true" or "pure" feminism is found among the relatively small group of "modern" urban western women.

See Also

BIOLOGICAL DETERMINISM; DAWN MOVEMENT; ECOFEMINISM; ÉCRITURE FÉMININE; ESSENTIALISM; FEMINISM: LESBIAN; INDUSTRIALIZATION; MODERNIZATION; LESBIAN SEXUALITY; PACIFISM AND PEACE ACTIVISM; PATRIARCHY: DEVELOPMENT; WOMANISM

References and Further Reading

Alcoff, Linda. 1988. Cultural feminism versus post-structuralism: The identity crisis in feminist theory. *Signs* 13(3: Spring): 405–436.

Allen, Paula Gunn. 1986. *The sacred hoop: Recovering the feminine in American Indian traditions.* Boston: Beacon.

Brooke. 1975. The retreat to cultural feminism. In Redstockings, ed., *Feminist revolution.* New Paltz, N.Y.: Self-published. (Abridged version with additional writings published by Random House, 1978.)

Burris, Barbara. 1973. Fourth World manifesto. In Anne Koedt, Ellen Levine, and Anita Rapone, eds., *Radical feminism,* 322–357. New York: Quadrangle.

Collins, Patricia Hill. 1990. *Black feminist thought: Knowledge, consciousness, and the politics of empowerment.* Boston: Unwin Hyman.

Combahee River Collective. 1979. A black feminist statement. In Zillah Eisenstein, ed., *Capitalist patriarchy and the case for socialist feminism,* 259–291. New York: Monthly Review.

Echols, Alice. 1989. *Daring to be bad: A history of the radical feminist movement in America.* Minneapolis: University of Minnesota Press.

Gevins, Adi. 1985. Tracking tradition: Interview with Assitan Diallo (Mali) and Stella Effua Graham (Ghana). *Connexions* 17/18 (Summer/Fall): 45–47.

Hartsock, Nancy. 1983. *Money, sex, and power: Toward a feminist historical materialism.* New York: Longman.

Radicalesbians. 1973. The woman-identified woman. In Anne Koedt, Ellen Levine, and Anita Rapone, eds., *Radical feminism,* 240–245. New York: Quadrangle.

Rich, Adrienne. 1980. Compulsory heterosexuality and lesbian experience. *Signs* 5(4: Summer): 631–60.

Segal, Lynn. 1987. *Is the future female? Troubled thoughts on contemporary feminism.* London: Virago.

Sen, Gita, and Caren Grown. 1987. *Development, crises, and alternative visions: Third world women's perspectives.* New York: Monthly Review.

Tauli-Corpuz, Victoria. 1992. Creating alternative culture against foreign domination and towards the liberation of women. *Change* 3(1: January–April): 17–20.

Taylor, Verta, and Leila J. Rupp. 1993. Women's culture and lesbian feminist activism: A reconsideration of cultural feminism. *Signs* 19(1: Fall): 32–61.

Walker, Alice. 1983. Introduction. *In search of our mothers' gardens.* New York: Harcourt Brace Jovanovich.

Weathers, Mary Ann. 1971. An argument for black women's liberation as a revolutionary force. In Leslie Tanner, ed., *Voices from women's liberation,* 306. New York: Menton.

Angela Miles

FEMINISM AND DIVINITY

See GODDESS and WOMANIST THEOLOGY.

FEMINISM: Early

See WOMEN'S MOVEMENT: EARLY INTERNATIONAL MOVEMENT.

FEMINISM: Ecological

See ECOFEMINISM and GYN/ECOLOGY.

FEMINISM: Eastern Europe

Until the early 1990s, the history of women and feminism in "Europe behind the Wall" was largely ignored by scholars in the region. Distance from not only "feminist" but also post–World War II western thinking about culture and society makes articulation of women's issues problematic. Not only are the ways of expressing the past and recent experiences of gender-related issues part of the existing signifying order examined by western feminists as "male dominated," but also most of the tools of historical feminist analyses are deeply embedded in the practices and meanings of western Europe and the United States. Feminist consciousness in eastern Europe is measured by standards of different social contexts that are often stigmatized as "less developed."

Western Interpretation of Eastern Feminism

Even the few western intellectuals who paid attention to the region tended to present ready-made, often idealized conclusions (Beauvoir, 1972) based on impressions rather than profound research. Moreover, feminist scholarship could not avoid the image of the "Iron Curtain"—the "East" as an undifferentiated region crowded with oppressed persons. As a result, eastern European women were searched for precisely at those places where they were not, blamed for not being there, and consequently accused of passivity and a lack of self-confidence often attributed to a lack of "feminist consciousness." Without serious rethinking of the role of gender-based power relations in European history, we have very little chance of understanding women's issues in eastern Europe. In this entry, without further comments on its problematic and politically biased character, the term *eastern Europe* will be used to refer to Albania, Bulgaria, Hungary, Poland, Romania, and countries of the former Czechoslovakia and Yugoslavia.

Recognition of women's issues in these countries, whether it was presented as feminist or not, was part of emancipatory efforts to build modern European nations. The question is not so much the absence or presence of feminism in this region but rather the advancement of our knowledge of women's participation in various spheres of life. As in the rest of Europe, women focused on the following areas: cultural activities and charity, access to education and to a position in the labor market, and the fight for major political rights. In many countries (Czech lands, Slovakia, Bulgaria) the first women's organizations emerged in the 1850s–1870s along with, and as a part of, nationalist movements. Despite significant differences in particular countries, this close link to nationalism made women's movements adapt their demands and goals to the "higher" aims of a struggle for national emancipation and resulted in a version of what can be called participatory feminism. Achievement of basic women's rights in order to become better mothers of the sons of these new nations was a leading strategy. Thus women's groups rarely applied aggressive "anti-male" weapons, such as bra burning. Countries of this region, relatively small in size, fought for independence from rather larger, "oppressive," multinational state units. The major oppressive "other" was thus for both men and women occupied by a nation rather than a gender—for example, for Hungarians, Czechs, and Slovaks under the Hapsburg monarchy and for Poles under Russian rule.

Furthermore, for example in Czech lands, the first small "nationalist" circles were formed by educated but rather economically weak middle-class men who were willing to negotiate a gender contract with representatives of women's movements (often their own wives or daughters), in order to further their progressive agenda. Indeed, the achievement of state independence led to the expansion of women's groups, as in Bulgaria after 1878. The Bulgarian Women's Union was established in 1901 and by 1931 had more than 8,000 members (Todorova, 1994). One quite specific situation was in the highly diversified nations of the former Yugoslavia: controversy between rural patriarchal society on the one hand, and groups of highly educated female and male advocates of women's issues, such as Draga Dejanovic or Setozar Markovic, on the other. A Jewish women's organization formed in 1874 in Belgrade and a Serbian translation of John Stuart Mill's *The Subjection of Women* two years after in its first English edition are two examples of women's activities there. In Romania a number of women's groups emerged in the mid-nineteenth century. A woman—Ana Ipatesco—helped to liberate imprisoned leaders of the revolution of 1848. A strong feminist movement for constitutional rights was led by Calipso Botez in the 1920s.

The Role of Upper-Class Women

In Poland, the first challenge to traditional women's roles did not come from middle-class circles but arose among noblewomen whose husbands and fathers were either killed or forced to emigrate after a failed uprising against Russia in 1830. They were "liberated" from dependence on their male counterparts, and also from land ownership, and thus were left with a need to take care of themselves. Around 1840 a group known as the Enthusiasts announced an ambitious program for emancipation. After nine years of cultural as well as conspiratorial activities in Warsaw—then governed by Russia—the group was uncovered by the czarist secret police, who arrested many of its leaders, including Narciza Zmichovska and Anna Skimborowicz. In the 1860s men in Warsaw—positivist writers and lawyers—supported women's emancipation despite a strong antifeminist campaign supported by the influential Catholic church, traditionally one of the major tools of Polish resistance against external oppressors. From 1880 to 1890 in all three areas of partitioned Poland women themselves started to claim their rights. Both mainstream groups of the feminist movement—bourgeois

and socialist—were led by women of landowning origins and had to develop strategies of defending women's interests within communities that were mainly occupied with a national agenda.

The Rise of Feminism in Hungary

Early initiatives by Hungarian women focused on charity as a tool of assimilation to the national emancipation battles. Their organization intensified after 1848 and resulted in the establishment of special girls' schools in 1880. Cultural and educational activities were followed by mobilizing professional women's groups. For the representation of women's economic interests the Association of Women Clerks of Hungary was formed in 1897. The opening of a women's *gymnasium* (high school) in 1895 gave Hungarian girls access to degrees necessary to enroll in universities. The first explicitly political organization, the Association of Feminists, established in 1904, developed a collaborative project with the Clerks Association in order to fight for voting rights. Leaders of this generation of liberal feminists, such as Róza Bédy-Schwimmer and Vilma Glücklich, supported the goals of equality and emancipation shared by feminists in most European countries. In the Hungarian context, however, those goals were highly dependent on sensitive ethnic, national, and social issues.

The introduction of female suffrage in 1920 (excluding illiterate women) gave birth to a second generation of the women's movement, represented by the National Association of Hungarian Women. After the parliamentary discussions about limiting enrollment for higher education in 1920, women's groups focused exclusively on this issue even when, later, the antiwomen bill was transformed into an anti-Semitic one. Ironically, the single-issue movement adapted other gender-specific concerns to antiliberal politics and in fact supported growing segregationist tendencies in Hungarian society. Despite apparent achievements, feminists lost their political influence, joining the dispersed party politics of the 1920s. Thus women's movements failed to create a tradition that could be developed by later feminists (Kovács, 1994).

Czech Feminism

The early Czech women's movement developed in Bohemia's culturally and economically advanced environment (a 90 percent literacy rate in the 1890s) and was shaped by the relatively egalitarian nature of Czech society inherited from the "revivalist" Czech movement, which women fully supported. A number of Czech women became leading figures in the national cultural and political awakening, such as Bozena Nemcová, who wrote about women's issues in the mid-nineteenth century. Under the pragmatic, nonaggressive leadership of Eliska Krásno-horská, editor of the influential journal *Zenské listy* (*Women's Gazette*, 1872) and activist of the Women's Industrial and Commercial Association, they not only achieved entrance to medical education and practice for all women in Austria, but also, in 1890, opened the first women's *gymnasium*, Minerva, in central Europe. With the support of leading male intellectuals, including the first president of the independent Czechoslovakia, T. G. Masaryk, Czech and Slovak women achieved a legal guarantee of equal rights in the constitution of 1920. Czech intellectual thought often omits the explicitly feminist philosophical tradition represented by the work of Anna Pamrová and Pavla Moudrá in the 1910s–1930s.

Slovak Feminism

Slovak women joined nationalist movements mainly through cultural activities, particularly nonprofessional theater. Their cultural and publishing project *Zivena*—established in 1869 and led by Elena Soltésová and Terézia Vansová—focused on original women's writing as well as translations and served as a center of women's initiatives. Women were more active in the small Slovak towns than in the capital, Bratislava, where social life was under Austro-Hungarian domination. Czech and Slovak women's groups were mutually supportive but remained divided along national and political lines. The distinctions between middle-class and working-class groups (strongly supported especially after the split in 1921 between Social Democrats and communists, who competed for women's attention), as well as between Czech, German, and Ukraine women, persisted through the interwar period (Garver, 1985). More than 50 women's organizations were coordinated by the National Council of Women, chaired by Senator Frantiska Plamínková and affiliated with all international women's associations. Plamínková's colleague, Milada Horáková continued her work in the Council of Czechoslovak Women from 1945 to 1948. It is one part of a tragic (however rarely mentioned) irony of Czechoslovak history that both of the leading feminists were executed—Plamínková by the Nazis in 1942 and Horáková by the communists after a show trial in 1950.

The Effect of World War II on Feminism

World War II altered women's roles all over the world. Not only did women replace missing men as breadwinners and producers, but they also joined men on the battlefield. In many eastern European countries, more dramatically than in the West, women experienced unexpected emancipation. For example, in the former Yugoslavia—a country with a rather traditional role division in rural families—the first explicitly feminist society, led by Dr. Milica Bogdanovic, appeared in 1925. The Communist Party articulated women's specific demands in 1940. The antifascist Women's Front of Yugoslavia, which brought together more than 2 million women—100,000 of whom participated in partisan units (Offen et al., 1991)—was initiated, but in 1950 it was transformed by the party into a unified, centrally controlled organization.

In Europe, exhausted by the most brutal war of the twentieth century, it was not so difficult for communist parties to offer a better future as an alternative to the fascist past. A lack of male labor as well as a need for rapid reconstruction of the devastated countries drew women into paid jobs. Images of smiling female truck drivers during the first postwar years were not just a celebration of the new regimes but an expression of deep changes in the character of work. Women helped build a new working class in overwhelmingly agrarian countries, but at the same time they were often, owing to "lower effectivity," blamed for blocking the project of "modernization." However, the rates of women's economic activity as well as their access to higher education increased more in eastern Europe than in western Europe. Consequently, women could hardly imagine themselves outside the working space.

At the time of the rise of the second wave of the feminist movement in western Europe and the United States, formal state regulation of gender relations replaced independent women's actions in eastern Europe. This specific historical situation was carefully used ideologically to advertise communist achievements. Party ideologists, following the traditions of prewar socialist and communist movements, managed to associate modernization, industrialization, and the socialization of private property with women's liberation.

Feminism in the Balkans

Nowhere was such a tendency more visible than in the Balkan countries, where one-third to one-half of the adult, mostly rural, population remained illiterate until the early 1930s. Women (the literate ones) were enfranchised only after 1945 in Romania, Albania, and Yugoslavia.

An extreme example of women's controversial role in the empowering of a communist regime can be found in Albania. Women in this former periphery of the Ottoman Empire, with a strong religious heritage, formally received the right to vote in 1946. The change in their status from a marriage commodity to holders of respected political positions indeed came with the communist regime. A massive antifascist women's movement in the final years of the war resulted in the establishment of the Union of Albanian Women, which was one of the party's most effective propagandist tools but also opened educational and occupational opportunities for women that before then were unimaginable. Its leading activists, Nexhmije Hoxha, Fiqrete Shehe, and Vito Kapo fully used their power as wives of party leaders and served as role models for a new generation of educated women who could enter equally with men the first Albanian university, established in 1957 (Kolsti, 1985). However, the unquestionable progress made by women from the 1950s to the 1970s—women formed 33 percent of deputies elected to the People's Assembly in 1976—came at the expense of both groups and individuals who resisted one of the strictest regimes in European history.

Generally, governing regimes did not allow space for independent group identity–based movements that would produce distinctive "feminist" activity, in the sense of the second wave of feminism in the United States and some western European countries. Moreover, a relative promotion of women was taking place in the historical context of the gradual decomposition of modern concepts of individuality and citizenship, within which men could exercise decision-making power based on their gender. Neither was there provided a "room of his own" for the construction of modern dominating, powerful masculinity perceived by women as a serious threat and a major source of oppression. Unified state-controlled socialist women's organizations established in the late 1940s all around the region had contradictory implications. These organizations shared a distaste for any gender-based grouping (as in Czechoslovakia), but at the same time served as a substitute for community life in the form of leisure activities, and in some countries (Bulgaria, for example) provided a floor for discussion of women's issues. To what extent the silent participation of women in such activities actually significantly contributed to maintaining the regimes or was just a way to "survive communism and even laugh" (Drakulic, 1992) will remain an open question for historians.

The Effects of Feminism

The highly controversial character of women's emancipation can be demonstrated with the case of extensive maternity benefits: while improving women's working conditions, the benefits also served as a tool to legitimize gender discrimination by both excluding men from the practice of parenthood and binding women to traditional role models. For example, in Hungary the extension of paid maternity leave in the 1960s—that is, in a time of strong echoes of the western "sexual revolution" supported by discussions about "open marriage" among Hungarian intellectuals—was followed by a dramatic increase in the divorce rate, which is now one of the highest in the world.

Pronatalist policies were implemented all over Europe beginning in the 1950s. Various regimes, however, used different techniques of fertility control. Maternal benefits were implemented by the Czechoslovak government as one of the tools to corrupt and calm the population during the "normalization" process after 1968. Pronatal actions in Romania in the mid-1960s, however, were represented by the restriction of contraception and abortion, in addition to supplementary taxes for single and childless women and only three months of paid maternity leave—the shortest in the region. Owing to constant shortages and nonprofessional abortions, Romania suffered 143.83 maternal deaths for every 100,000 live births—the highest rate in Europe (Snyder, 1992). Debates on women's issues started in the 1970s in Romania, partly owing to their most active promoter, Ecaterina Oproiu. However, women's protesting voices, such as those of Dinoea Cornea or Anna Blandiana, were brutally persecuted. A majority of women opposing the communist governments joined their male partners rather than creating gender-specific groups. Polish women were actively associated with the workers' mass oppositional movement but were underrepresented in the Solidarity hierarchy. On the other hand, women made up 20 percent of the signers of the Czechoslovak Charter 77, which was more elitist and primarily intellectual (Jancar, 1985).

After 1989, the need to reconstruct the corrupted concepts of community, social justice, and rights emerged. The concepts of social and sexual equality are being only very slowly divorced from notions of universal sisterhood. This is easier said than done for people who were suspicious of any form of ideological indoctrination and tired of centrally organized sets of beliefs and consciousness raising. There has been a strong resistance to any colonizing discourses, as well as to enthusiastic presentations of "isms" by "outsiders." The label "feminism" has joined the unwelcome "others." An ironic and cynical media representation of "feminism," along with an explicit blaming of women for the decreasing quality of education and health care, or for the high divorce rate, further complicated serious discussion about gender-related issues.

Many topics that can be defined as explicitly feminist began to be discussed in Yugoslavia in 1976. Women scholars coordinated a postgraduate seminar on women's history in 1984–1985 and organized the first postwar openly feminist meeting in Belgrade in 1978; shortly afterward, feminist groups were established in Zagreb, Ljubljana, and other cities. Teaching and research on gender issues continued even after 1991, when the war exploded in Yugoslavia. Women joined the nationalist and antinationalist camps, but those who belonged to the first feminist groups were a significant part of the antiwar initiatives.

Specific social issues, together with the opening of political space for alternative groups and discourses, mobilized women's activities such as the Polish "eFKa"—Women's Hotline Project—or one of the rare pre-1989 Czech women's groups, Prague Mothers, which focused on ecological concerns. These groups, often supported by the international academic community, contributed to uncovering socially urgent, gender-sensitive issues, starting with women's increasing unemployment and continuing with the images of naked women's bodies on advertisement billboards. Women's and gender studies centers in Belgrade, Prague, Lodz, Warsaw, Bratislava, and Sophia were established by university teachers and researchers in the early 1990s. They began with the intention of articulating gender issues within local intellectual contexts rather than with a proclaimed "feminist" agenda.

Is there room for "feminism" in Europe after the cold war? Post–World War II women's movements in the western part of Europe and the United States taught, among other things, that women can be liberated from "oppression" by recognizing that "the personal is political." Following this lesson, the present author would like to conclude personally: In the 1950s in Czechoslovakia, her mother's dream was to become a lawyer. A "recommendation" letter from the director of her student dormitory claiming that she was "not politically correct enough to represent working-class people" blocked her from entering law school. However, she pursued a successful career in agricultural research. The author's father, who was a construction engineer, was sentenced to prison for two years in a show trial in 1969 and was prevented from returning to his ongoing project in Munich. He was reinstated later, but he did not see his passport again until the late 1980s. Can one seriously ask who was "more oppressed?" Feminists who reserve for women the category of the most restricted social group may face resistance in eastern Europe.

What the author would add from the "eastern" point of view is: "The personal is historical." If the term "political" describes the individual's impact on the world he or she lives in, this is not always the case with "historical." From this point of view, complaints about the lack of "progress" in the women's movement in this part of Europe make no sense. Paradoxically enough, the communist governments,

at least formally, met a number of the demands of most "progressive" feminists. At the same time, allowing the "political" to invade the intimate "personal" generated further restrictions. That was for many people too risky an undertaking. For years, both men and women who lived in centrally organized social systems apparently underpinned by egalitarian ideals were equally "liberated" from control over their own history. But also until very recently, they were liberated from responsibility for it. This may be the only point at which the Bolshevik revolutions indeed achieved gender equality. The question remains: must the achievement of gender equality be so costly? And moreover, how will the different socioeconomical arrangements now reshape the gender contract?

See Also

DEVELOPMENT: CENTRAL AND EASTERN EUROPE; EDUCATION: EASTERN EUROPE; ENVIRONMENT: CENTRAL AND EASTERN EUROPE; FEMINISM: COMMONWEALTH OF INDEPENDENT STATES; HOUSEHOLDS AND FAMILIES: CENTRAL AND EASTERN EUROPE; LITERATURE: EASTERN EUROPE; POLITICS AND THE STATE: EASTERN EUROPE; WOMEN'S STUDIES: CENTRAL AND EASTERN EUROPE

References and Further Reading

Beauvoir, Simone de. 1972. *The second sex.* Harmondsworth, U.K.: Penguin (originally published 1949).

Corrin, Chris, ed. 1992. *Superwomen and the double burden: Women's experience of change in central and eastern Europe and the former Soviet Union.* London: Scarlet.

———. 1996. *Women in a violent world: Feminist analysis and resistance across Europe.* Edinburgh: Edinburgh University Press.

Drakulic, Slavenka. 1992. *How we survived communism and even laughed.* New York: Norton.

Einhorn, Barbara. 1993. *Cinderella goes to market: Citizenship, gender, and women's movements in east central Europe.* London: Verso.

Funk, Nanette, and Magda Mueller, eds. 1993. *Gender politics and postcommunism: Reflections from eastern Europe and the former Soviet Union.* New York: Routledge.

Garver, Bruce M. 1985. Women in the First Czechoslovak Republic. In Sharon L. Wolchik and Alfred G. Mayer, eds., *Women, state, and party in eastern Europe,* 64–81. Durham, N.C.: Duke University Press.

Heitlinger, Alena. 1979. *Women and state socialism: Sex-inequality in the Soviet Union and Czechoslovakia.* London: Macmillan.

Jancar, Barbara Wolfe. 1985. Women in the opposition in Poland and Czechoslovakia in the 1970s. In Sharon L. Wolchik and

Alfred G. Mayer, eds. *Women, state, and party in eastern Europe*, 168–185. Durham, N.C.: Duke University Press.

———. 1978. *Women under communism.* Baltimore, Md.: Johns Hopkins University Press.

Journal of Women's History. 1995. 5 (3, Winter): Special issue.

Kolsti, John. 1985. *From courtyard to cabinet: The political emergence of Albanian women.* In In Sharon L. Wolchik and Alfred G. Mayer, eds., *Women, state, and party in eastern Europe*, 138–151. Durham, N.C.: Duke University Press.

Kovács, Mária M. 1994. The politics of emancipation in Hungary. In *Women in history—Women's history: Central and Eastern European perspectives.* Central European University (CEU) History Department, Working Paper Series 1.

Mill, John Stuart. [1869] 1975. The subjection of women. In *Three Essays.* Oxford: Oxford University Press.

Offen, Karen, Ruth Roach Pierson, and Jane Rendall, eds. 1991. *Writing women's history: International perspectives.* Bloomington: Indiana University Press.

Regulska, Joanna. 1995. *Women's participation in political and public life.* Background document for European Conference on Equality and Democracy: Utopia or Challenge? Council of Europe, Strasbourg.

Scott, Hilda. 1976. *Women and socialism: Experiences from eastern Europe.* London: Allison and Busby.

Snyder, Paula. 1992. *The European women's almanac.* London: Scarlet.

Todorova, Maria. 1994. Historical tradition and transformation in Bulgaria: Women's issues or feminist issues? *Journal of Women's History,* 5(3, Winter): Special issue, 129–141.

Wolchik, Sharon L., and Alfred G. Mayer, eds. 1985. *Women, state, and party in eastern Europe.* Durham: N.C. Duke University Press.

Jirina Smejkalova

FEMINISM: Eighteenth Century

Scholars often stretch the term *eighteenth century* to designate the "long" eighteenth century running from 1660 to the early 1800s. Obvious improvements in women's position during this period (particularly in education) were offset by a strengthening of restrictive bourgeois ideologies about what was properly feminine. Progress was made toward the formulation of feminist positions on many issues, though the term *feminist* did not yet exist.

The long eighteenth century began and ended with bouts of reaction, yet even then women made certain gains. In the 1660s, when England had just abandoned its only experiment with nonmonarchical government, upper-class women were claiming new social, sexual, and cultural territory; and in the 1790s, while Europe combined against the revolutionary movement in France, radical women were newly united in movements of their own. The concepts related to feminism had a long history behind them before the term *feminism* was coined.

Roots of Feminist Cultural Tradition

Europe's cultural tradition grows from two main roots, the Greco-Roman and the Hebrew or biblical. Each of these worldviews was masculinist, yet each left some space for accounts of particular female achievements beyond the allotted female role: for tales of women as national leaders or as shapers of language. Christianity itself, the unchallenged dominant ideology during the Middle Ages, had a succession of women working at what would now be called feminist theology, pondering concepts of God as mother or of the relation between gender and spirituality. Systems of government by inheritance occasionally placed individual women in positions of power, and this encouraged the challenging of accepted ideas of women's nature and status.

With the renaissance of classical learning in Europe, men like Erasmus, Lodovicus Vicus, and Thomas More argued that women were capable of being educated. A few elite women grasped the chance to make their mark in scholarship and even publication, but, without any institutional framework to support them, they were unable to effect lasting change in educational systems. Larger numbers of women, from many social levels, were active in spreading Reformation ideas: that responsibility for religious salvation rested with the individual rather than with priest or church; and that reading the Bible, mediating language and ideas, was the business of ordinary people of both sexes. Writers and religious activists appeared from ranks below the nobility: among Englishwomen alone, Isabella Whitney wrote poems questioning and mocking male classical myths; Elizabeth Shirley wrote the biography of her convent head and spiritual "mother," Margaret Clement; Anne Askew died by torture for her right, as a woman, to engage in Protestant study and teaching; and Mary Ward worked internationally to form a women's preaching and missionary order within the Catholic church (see Beilin, 1987; Grundy, 1992; Rowlands, 1985; Wilson, 1972). For such women, engaged in various and even contrary struggles, challenge to the established gender order was integral to their goals.

The Renaissance fashion for educating girls was unhappily brief (see Warnicke, 1983). Anna Maria van Schurman in Holland and Bathsua Makin in England both reflect a sense of what their own generation had lost. Schurman in

De ingenii muliebris (1641, translated into English in 1659) and Makin in *An Essay to Revive the Antient Education of Gentlewomen in Religion, Manners, Arts, and Tongues* (1673; reprinted by the Clark Library, Los Angeles, in 1980) use old-fashioned structures (approaches through theology or formal logic, citation of eminent women of the past) to enforce forward-looking proposals for serious learning by middle-class girls. Makin (who included in her title "an answer to the objections against this way of education") was practitioner as well as publicist, with her own school at Tottenham, near London. Improving girls' education became a constant focus women in Britain and America, despite inconsistency between groups and generations about how to achieve it.

Revolution and Restoration

Many systems of dominance were broken or interrupted with the overthrow of the English monarchy in the 1640s. Printing presses, now operating freely without royal license, offered a new platform to scores of radical women, including some from the laboring classes. Among their primarily theological or religious concerns, the question of female submission was central. Indeed, the unorthodox equal status enjoyed by women in some of the radical sects was a major reason why those sects were condemned and vilified. Quaker women were as much bound as men to answer God's call as missionary preachers; they bravely defied official persecution in both Britain and America (see Hobby, 1988).

Restoration of the monarchy in 1660 brought sharp reaction against this public female voice itself, as well as against its various messages, and women of the radical sects, such as Quakers and Baptists, responded by retracting their attention from the public-political sphere into the domestic and community spheres.

But retreat on one front was balanced by advances elsewhere. As traditional church authority shrugged off Puritanism, it began to be challenged by freethinking, and by arguments from the classical pagan philosophers (such as Epicurus and Epictetus) or from the dawning of comparative religion. Court culture was influenced by the English court's years of exile in France, where women writers, most of them prominent in society, were numerous and respected long before they ceased to be oddities in England. The reopened London theaters offered women their first professional opportunities as performers (female roles had previously been taken by boys) and as dramatists. In the middle ranks, higher living standards and increased leisure time threatened women with commodification, with becoming a husband's status symbol rather than his working partner;

but at the same time they offered wider educational and social horizons.

Mary Astell

These various influences fed a complex feminist moment during the 1690s. Aphra Behn, a prolific and high-profile author, died in 1689, but a second wave of female playwrights continued to hold the stage with sex-and-violence tragedies and satirical comedies. Mary Astell, in *A Serious Proposal to the Ladies* (two parts, 1694 and 1697) and *Reflections upon Marriage* (1700), voiced seldom-articulated, unpalatable truths about women's oppression. Astell based her thinking on Descartes's high valuation of intellect: reason, she argued, was the ungendered, defining human characteristic. Custom (whose random historical accretions governed education and marriage, for instance) was open to legitimate question when it flouted the dictates of reason (see Hill, 1986; Perry, 1986).

Astell accepted many givens of patriarchal society: women should be wary of marrying, she thought, precisely because a wife owes a duty of obedience; and exercising her reason will make a woman better able to accept the demands of unreasonable "Tyrant Custom." Mary, Lady Chudleigh (an admirer of Astell), shared these beliefs, but they did not prevent her from reacting publicly and vigorously against a misogynist sermon preached at a wedding in 1699. In *The Ladies' Defence* (1701), Chudleigh makes Melissa the spokesperson for human reason, while the forces ranged against women (a brutal property-owning patriarchy, religious misogyny, and flattering sexual exploitation) are each embodied in a heavily conventional male "type": the squire, the parson, and the beau or rake. The Anglicans Astell and Chudleigh, and others like them, shared their Quaker predecessors' fondness for St. Paul's remark that in Christ there is neither male nor female. Their doctrines, centered on traditional religion, are nevertheless unmistakably feminist (see Ferguson, 1985).

Women's Investigation of the Natural World

Similar claims for women's dignity and status were made during this period in relation to new areas of knowledge. Investigation of the natural world was an Enlightenment project that is now often seen as wholly masculine, because it tended to envision nature as a female body open to the (male) scientist's gaze (see Schiebinger, 1989). But this view obscures the interest and opportunities that contemporary women found in Enlightenment inquiry. Mary Trye published *Medicatrix; or, The Woman-Physician* in 1675. Bernard le Bovier de Fontenelle cast his influential treatise on the cosmos, *Entretiens sur la pluralité des mondes* (1686), in the form of dialogues between a male scientist and a noble lady who exemplifies the female as disciple and intelligent amateur (see Phillips, 1990). Jane Barker (known today for her writings, not her medical activities) exulted when an apothecary accepted her prescription on a par with those of university-qualified doctors. Judith Drake, the most likely author of a hard-hitting *Essay in Defence of the Female Sex* (1696), practiced medicine for years among women and children and probably edited her late husband James's great work on anatomy, *Anthropologia Nova* (1707). This, remarkably, debunks antifeminist superstitions and accepts the testimony of women rather than that of doctors about the female body.

Control of women's bodies was a recurrent issue during the century, as childbirth was taken over from midwives by "man-midwives" (see Donnison, 1988). The issue was not one of simple ignorance versus improved knowledge, or of spirituality versus medicalization, or even of hands versus forceps. Midwives had been trained through practical experience and apprenticeship; the men, trained by Latin treatises and dissection of corpses, had little knowledge of the healthy female body or of normal birth. In Paris the Hôtel-Dieu, run by nuns, provided a central base for the training of midwives. In England, Elizabeth Cellier attempted in 1688 to establish a professional training and regulatory body like those for physicians and surgeons. Despite a series of vivid polemical texts (in France by Louise Bourgois, 1609; in England by Jane Sharp, 1671, Sarah Stone, 1737, and Elizabeth Nihell, 1761), women lost this battle.

Women were crucial in another medical arena, the struggle over inoculation for smallpox. Lady Mary Wortley Montagu encountered this as a folk practice in the hands of women in Turkey in 1717. Western Europeans visiting the area had already had children inoculated, and male scientists had written Latin accounts of the operation for learned societies at home; but none had transplanted the practice. Lady Mary had her daughter inoculated after returning home, and she campaigned with support on the one hand from a few medical professionals, but on the other from mostly upper-class women, led by Caroline of Anspach, Princess of Wales. Anti-inoculation pamphlets and newspaper reports mobilized sexists and orientalists who disparaged the new practice. The experience no doubt contributed to Montagu's feminist stance on marriage and the sexual double standard in many of her poems: some quickly printed, like "Written ex tempore on the Death of Mrs Bowes" (in which she says that women find no happiness in marriage after its early months); some unpublished during her lifetime, like "Epistle from Mrs Yonge to Her Husband" (in

which, more challengingly, she attacks the sexual double standard).

Feminist Arguments in Literary Form

Feminist arguments in such literary forms were far from new. Behn wrote of women's rebellious sexuality; Delarivier Manley used scandalous fiction to depict a dog-eat-dog society where the weak (generally though not always female) are ruthlessly exploited. Sarah Fyge, later Egerton, produced at the age of 15 a rousing indictment of women's exclusion (and of a misogynist text by Robert Gould) in *The Female Advocate* (1686), and Elizabeth Tollet used the ancient Alexandrian philosopher and mathematician Hypatia, in a poem titled with her name, as a mouthpiece to claim women's right to pursue both historical and scientific knowledge (*Poems on Several Occasions*, 1724).

In Britain women writers felt empowered by the reign (1702–1714) of Queen Anne, who saw herself as successor to Elizabeth I, adopting Elizabeth's personal motto (*Semper eadem*, "Ever the same"). But trends of the day were not all to women's advantage. Richard Steele and Joseph Addison were seen as raising the status and cultural level of the "fair sex" in their periodicals *The Tatler* (1709–1710) and *The Spectator* (1711–1714); but their ideal was a sharply limited female sphere that strongly enforced conformity to social norms. This ideal shifted only slightly in innumerable journals addressed to women, from *The Female Tatler* (1709–1710) and Eliza Haywood's *Female Spectator* (1744–1746) to two publications in Philadelphia, the *Columbian Magazine,* from 1786, and the *Lady's Magazine,* from 1792.

Over the eighteenth century, wives became less involved in their husbands' work, and the number of widows in business declined. Eccentricity, as displayed by court ladies like Margaret Cavendish, Duchess of Newcastle, or Montagu, became less acceptable. Domestic ideals, which were gaining ground from court ideals, set out to tame sexuality and to promote the new notion of good women as sexless. Those who hoped to see some advance in the position of women became more circumspect.

The Bluestockings

The paradigmatic grouping of eighteenth-century Englishwomen is that of the Bluestockings, ladies of the middle and gentry classes who from the 1760s and 1770s sought to create a milieu for intelligent conversation, comparable to male-only clubs and coffeehouses. Elizabeth Carter was their greatest intellect, Elizabeth Montagu their most effective patron of women writers, and Hannah More (of the second generation) the most publicly visible controversialist. Generally conservative on issues of gender, they were thrown into disarray by the second marriage of the 40-year-old Hester Thrale Piozzi, unable to defend this startling admission of sexuality in a "nice" middle-aged female. Hannah More expanded many frontiers for women: as a successful playwright in her youth, as a pioneer of education for the lower classes, and as a scourge of immorality among the upper. Yet she always maintained that she was an exception not to be imitated and saw the realm of public policy as inherently male, even while she trespassed there to such effect.

In her single, extremely popular novel, *Coelebs in Search of a Wife: Comprehending Observations on Domestic Habits and Manners, Religion and Morals* (1808), the heroine is endowed by her father with a classical education (useful for teaching her own children), with "qualities calculated to inspire attachment in persons under the dominion of reason and religion," and especially "the crowning grace of humility." She is a being formed by men to minister to them, like Milton's Eve before the Fall. She is also, however, formed by the backlash against "feminism" after the death of Mary Wollstonecraft.

More tends to assume a rhetorical stance of speaking for all right-minded people of both sexes. But it is significant that the women whose names are cited here for various feminisms were only the tiniest fraction of those who deserve citation. Women putting pen to paper, whether in familiar letters or in private diaries, or in poetry, fiction, drama, essays, or treatises, were almost bound to survey the rules of gendered behavior and to find them wanting. Until the century's last decade, most of its liveliest, most inventive feminist tracts apparently failed on publication and remain hardly known. "Sophia"'s works of 1739–1740 have attracted some attention, but not Sarah Chapone's *Hardships of the English Laws in Relation to Wives* (1735) or Lucy Hutton's *Six Sermonicles on the Punishment of Eve* (1788), or many others. Audiences for these works undoubtedly existed, but they had no communication networks, clubs, journals, or bookshops devoted to their interests. Methodist women availing themselves of John Wesley's very cautious permission to address congregations if necessary, *so long as they did not preach,* were hardly likely to mention, as earlier female preachers did, the topic of women's wrongs.

Therefore what look today like groupings were not at the time perceived as such. Proletarian women's writing is a good example. Mary Collier, washerwoman, was provoked to write *The Woman's Labour* (1739) by the anger she felt at stereotypical antifeminist jokes in the work of her class equal, the thresher poet Stephen Duck. Her portrayal of the double inequity of gender and class is matched later by Elizabeth Hands, Ann Yearsley, Janet Little, and others; but these

women, by no means homogeneous in rank or in ideological position, remained unaware of one another's work (see Landry, 1990).

Women in Social Movements

Late in the century there arose a number of related movements for social change that developed modern pressure-group tactics. Here women made an impact, finding a new, public stage for ancient influencing skills. Deaf ears met Abigail Adams's plea to her husband for women's full civic participation in the new United States; but women in the infant republic drew inspiration from the idea of the Roman matron who redeemed her civic exclusion by making her independent judgment heard. Encouragement of local manufacture by boycotting the oppressor's goods, something first heard of in an Irish setting, became a key element in the American colonists' campaign first to influence and later to resist the colonial power. Women were at the forefront here and in the English boycott of slave-grown sugar (when Elizabeth Heyrick and Susanna Watts personally canvassed every household in Leicester).

The movement for abolition of the slave trade, and later that to abolish slavery itself, took over from women's concern for ameliorating conditions for slaves. Women (less enmeshed in existing power systems than men) were not disciples but intellectual leaders here. Heyrick, for instance, championed the demand for immediate abolition at a time when William Wilberforce was still favoring gradual abolition. Susanna Strickland (later Moodie) took down from dictation the life story of the ex-slave Mary Prince, to be polished by Prince herself and the Anti-Slavery Society into a powerful opinion-shaper (see Ferguson, 1992). British and American women, notably Elizabeth Chandler, maintained close links in this struggle. Chandler is typical (no matter how unusual her force of intellect and imagination) in presenting gender as a link connecting her and her readers to their black sisters.

The campaign against slavery had its roots in a broad concern for reform of social wrongs that embraced the feminist cause along with others. Mary Wollstonecraft was a focus and leader among many radicals who wrote and worked for improved opportunities for women in education, the professions, and commercial employment; for more equitable marriage laws; and for an end to petty personal exploitation. Their message about political and cultural empowerment was promulgated by a series of voices: Catharine Macaulay, the historian, in *Letters on Education* (1790); Wollstonecraft in *A Vindication of the Rights of Woman* (1792); Mary Hays in *An Appeal to the Men of Great Britain in Behalf of the Women* (1798); Priscilla Wakefield in

Reflections on the Present Condition of the Female Sex (1798); Mary Robinson in *A Letter to the Women of England, on the Cruelties of Mental Subordination* (1799); Mary Ann Radcliffe in *The Female Advocate* (1799); and Mercy Otis Warren in the preface to her *History of the American Revolution* (1805). Despite their disparate life experiences (Wakefield was a Quaker writer on science and education, Warren a patriotic revolutionary, and Robinson an actress, royal mistress, poet, and sensational novelist), these women made common cause of their gender.

At the turn of the century, however, the climate turned against this cause. The French Revolution (or more specifically the slaughter during the Terror) made instant reactionaries of British politicians: even the most moderate reform movements were hounded by the government. A year after Wollstonecraft's death, her husband, William Godwin, published memoirs of her that, although expressing his heartfelt respect for her qualities of mind and her political effectiveness, also revealed that she had borne a daughter out of wedlock and attempted suicide. Readers were shocked by her life and eager to blame such vagaries on her advanced views. The Reverend Richard Polwhele went so far as to suggest in *The Unsex'd Females* (1799) that her death following childbirth was God's fittingly gendered rebuke. Though Wollstonecraft's life advanced the cause of feminism, reaction to her death constituted a setback for it.

Women sometimes forestalled such criticism by relating a new militancy to their traditional role as soothers and nurturers. This role was modified into tough action in the campaign against cruelty to animals (often combined with antislavery activity, as by Heyrick and Watts). Women also involved themselves in nationalist movements; in Ireland, for instance, Charlotte Brooke as reclaimer of the cultural past and Sydney Owenson, Lady Morgan, as publicist. In the United States, women were leading producers of national melting-pot novels, like Susanna Haswell Rowson's *Reuben and Rachel* (Boston, 1798) and Harriet Foster Cheney's *A Peep at the Pilgrims* (1824), which depict white and Indian, English and Spanish, masculine and feminine blending to form the new nation.

Progress

By the early nineteenth century women were well established as authors and journalists; in both capacities, they had made progress in recovery of the feminist past. Biographical studies no longer merely hold up famous women of the past as exemplars but depict the complex interaction of protofeminist women with oppressive society. Judith Sargent Murray of Massachusetts (who preceded Wollstonecraft by years in her "Essay on the Equality of the Sexes" written in 1779) uses such studies in her *Gleaner* essays (written from 1792, collected in 1798). By means of lively investigation of women's history, among other topics, and with gentle, humorous depictions of gender politics, Murray presses steadily for "a new era in female history" (*Gleaner,* no. xxxviii, 3: 189).

Britain and the United States now had respected girls' schools, female debating societies, and public lectures in big cities from which many women gained effective self-education. A tradition had taken root of middle-class women not only as social do-gooders but also as catalysts for social change. Women were prominent in expressions of antimilitaristic feeling stemming from the Napoleonic Wars. Yet many later causes—university degrees for women, a parliament with female delegates—were so little imaginable that the first references to them occur not in serious polemic but in lighthearted verse of fantasy or satire.

In Britain the death of Princess Charlotte in 1817 was mourned in print by many women who had explicitly longed for a female monarch to succeed the incapable or morally bankrupt later Georges: not an icon of wife and motherhood but a woman to be, in Margaret Croker's words, "firm when she knew she was right" (*A Monody on the Lamented Death of Her Royal Highness the Princess Charlotte-Augusta of Wales,* 1817: 23). This unfulfilled dream is not a bad emblem for the thinking of women far beyond Britain at this date: a desire to expand the sphere of women's influence without breaking the mold of society.

See Also

BLUESTOCKINGS; FEMINISM: FIRST WAVE BRITISH; FEMINISM: NINETEENTH CENTURY

References and Further Reading

Beilin, Elaine V. 1987. *Redeeming Eve: Women writers of the English Renaissance.* Princeton, N.J.: Princeton University Press.

Donnison, Jean. 1988. *Midwives and medical men.* London: Historical Publications.

Ferguson, Moira. 1985. *First feminists: British women writers, 1578–1799.* Bloomington: Indiana University Press.

———. 1992. *Subject to others: British women writers and colonial slavery, 1670–1834.* New York: Routledge.

Godineau, Dominique. 1998. *The women of Paris and their French Revolution.* Trans. Katherine Streip. Los Angeles: University of California Press.

Grundy, Isobel. 1992. Women's history? Writings by English nuns. In Isobel Grundy and Susan Wiseman, eds., *Women, writing, history 1640–1740.* London: Batsford; Athens: University of Georgia Press.

Hill, Bridget. 1986. *The first English feminist: Reflections upon marriage and other writings.* Aldershot, U.K.: Gower.

Hobby, Elaine. 1988. *Virtue of necessity: English women's writing, 1649–1688.* London: Virago.

Landry, Donna. 1990. *The muses of resistance: Laboring-class women's poetry in Britain, 1739–1796.* Cambridge: Cambridge University Press.

McDowell, Paula. 1998. *The women of Grub Street: Press, politics, and gender in the London literary marketplace.* Oxford: Clarendon.

Mendelson, Sara, and Patricia Crawford. 1998. *Women in early modern England, 1550–1720.* Oxford: Clarendon.

Perry, Ruth. 1986. *The celebrated Mary Astell: An early English feminist.* Chicago: University of Chicago Press.

Phillips, Patricia. 1990. *The scientific lady: A social history of women's scientific interests, 1520–1918.* London: Weidenfeld and Nicolson.

Rowlands, Marie B. 1985. Recusant women 1560–1640. In Mary Prior, ed., *Women in English society 1500–1800.* London: Methuen.

Schiebinger, Londa. 1989. *The mind has no sex? Women in the origins of modern science.* Cambridge, Mass.: Harvard University Press.

Smith, Hilda L., ed. 1998. *Women writers and the early modern British politcal tradition.* New York: Cambridge University Press.

Warnicke, Retha M. 1983. *Women of the English Renaissance and Reformation.* Westport, Conn.: Greenwood.

Wilson, Derek. 1972. *A Tudor tapestry: Men, women, and society in Reformation England.* London: Heinemann.

Isobel Grundy

FEMINISM: Existential

The association of existentialism with feminism is largely through the work of Simone de Beauvoir, even if the relationship is far from absolute or exclusive. The most important feature of existentialism, certainly as far as feminism is concerned, is the emphasis given to the metaphysics of freedom and the rejection of determinism. Therein, however, lies a problem for feminism, a problem most fully illustrated in the work of de Beauvoir.

The philosophy of existentialism (most often associated with de Beauvoir's lifelong companion, Jean-Paul Sartre) is grounded in the European Enlightenment tradition of philosophical thought. First and foremost, it is assumed that all individuals possess the capacity to make choices about their lives: no persons are so enslaved that they are not capable of realizing their humanity by individual choices and individual imperatives. Indeed, everyone is theoretically free to realize (or to attempt to realize) Kant's dictum that all actions should be seen in reference to a general law. Second, existentialism (at least in Sartre's case) assumes the Cartesian dualism of mind and body, a dualism in which the body is constructed as a purely physical object, separate from the mind. These two themes of existentialism are crucial to an understanding of de Beauvoir's attempt to introduce women into philosophical inquiry, a project that she attempted in *The Second Sex.*

Of all the texts that can be associated with existentialist feminism, pride of place must go to *The Second Sex,* first published in France in 1949. In this massive study of the condition of women, de Beauvoir argued that women have always occupied the place of the "other" in European philosophy, and indeed European civilization. Although her model of gender relations is not explicitly a hierarchical one, what she does suggest that women have a limited degree of agency in the world: that is, they are less free than men to fulfill the possibilities of existential freedom and choice. The reasons for this limitation on female fulfillment are defined by de Beauvoir in both social and ideological terms: conventional society (and here it has to be remembered that de Beauvoir's reference group was bourgeois France just before World War II) specifically legislates against various forms of female action, and whether or not this legislation is formal or informal, the net result is to reduce female independence and autonomy. De Beauvoir makes passing reference in *The Second Sex* to the material inequalities between the sexes, but in the main "society" is constructed as a legislative presence. In ideological terms female autonomy is equally constrained: literature and philosophy construct women as passive and as the "natural" recipients of male authority and, crucially, male choice.

What is built up in *The Second Sex* is an argument for the rejection by women of their second-class status and their position as objects of male authority. True to the traditions of existentialism, de Beauvoir argues for a realization by women of their capacity for action and freedom. As inherent in all existential thinking, if the person fails to "act" and realize her or his freedom, then the fault lies with the person rather than the world. In the late twentieth century it was impossible not to read *The Second Sex* as an exercise in blaming the victim, since the consequences of the organizing theoretical model of existentialism are to make individual women responsible for their fate. Furthermore, the body, and particularly the female body, is described in largely negative terms. Again, what can be seen is the continuation and the implicit acceptance of a philosophical tradition in which the body is separate from the mind. In de Beauvoir's view it is also clearly apparent that the female body cannot be too far away from the mind. Whatever its possibilities for sexual pleasure, the overall perception of the female body is that of an imprisoning cage.

It is thus that *The Second Sex* ends with a call to women to realize their potential for freedom and to recognize the possibilities of freedom inherent in the behavior more commonly associated with masculinity, that is, autonomy and independence. Later feminist writers have pointed out the similarity between de Beauvoir's advocacy of independence and the ethics of the capitalist entrepreneur (Walters, 1976). Yet in defense of de Beauvoir and the discussion of existentialism with feminism, it must be said that de Beauvoir's position was that once women had claimed their won freedom they would be in a better position to make real political and moral choices, among which the rejection of capitalist values might appear.

The organizing philosophy of *The Second Sex* has remained a problem for feminism, in that for many feminists an essential thesis is that which suggests women's dependence and subordination, conditions that are reversible only by the kind of collectivist action seldom associated with existentialism. Thus *The Second Sex* has long occupied an ambiguous place within feminist traditions: widely read, respected, and often revered but in many instances very much more for the descriptive account of lived subordination rather than the analysis of cause and solution. Equally, it has to be said that de Beauvoir herself recognized some absurdities of the existential belief in absolute and universal human freedom when she argued, in *The Ethics of Ambiguity* (1970), for a consideration of the historical and social roles that imprison individuals. Although published before *The Second Sex* (in 1946), this essay modifies some of the more striking assertions of the later book.

In large part, therefore, existentialism is associated with feminism through Simone de Beauvoir. Nevertheless, existentialism's impact on feminism goes beyond the work of a single author in that the belief in individual choice, freedom, and the power of the "other" has become a part of western culture. Thus even without recognizing the philosophical roots and traditions that underlie these ideas, individual women negotiate relations with others with reference to models of legitimate individual behavior fashioned within existentialism. Most crucially, the philosophy provides a means of establishing the personal independence of women, the nature of which is a complex issue within late-twentieth-century capitalism.

See Also

FEMINISM: SECOND WAVE EUROPEAN; OTHER

References and Further Reading

Bair, Deirdre. 1990. *Simone de Beauvoir: A biography.* London: Cape.

Beauvoir, Simone de. 1970. *The ethics of ambiguity.* New York: Citadel Press. (Originally published 1946.)

Evans, Mary. 1985. *Simone de Beauvoir: A feminist mandarin.* London: Tavistock.

Lundgren-Gothlin, Eva. 1996. *Sex and existence: Simone de Beauvoir's The Second Sex.* London: Athlone.

Moi, Toril. 1994. *Simone de Beauvoir: The Making of an intellectual woman.* Oxford: Blackwell.

Walters, Margaret. 1976. The rights and wrongs of women. In Juliet Mitchell and Ann Oakley, eds., *The rights and wrongs of women,* 304–379. Harmondsworth, U.K.: Penguin.

———. 1996. *Simone de Beauvoir.* London: Sage.

Mary Evans

FEMINISM: First-Wave British

It was not until 1894 that the term *feminism* entered the English language. When applied to earlier periods, it can too easily be used to correspond anachronistically to social, political, and ideological modern equivalents. In these circumstances, the term *feminisms* may be more appropriate in preserving a sense of historic specificity. First-wave feminism, which extends from the 1790s up to the 1960s, was dominated by three major texts before the advent of the suffragist or suffragette writings; Mary Wollstonecraft's *A Vindication of the Rights of Woman* (1792); William Thompson and Anna Wheeler's *Appeal of One Half the Human Race, Women, Against the Pretensions of the Other Half, Men* (1825); and John Stuart Mill's *The Subjection of Women* (1869). These landmark manifestos plot the course of campaigns from greater educational opportunities for girls through to women's rights in marriage and work, up to the demand for political equality. This last demand culminated in the enfranchisement of women, which may be traced through three separate stages. For the first, spanning 1866 to 1870, and the second, extending from 1870 to 1905, the focus was on constitutional reform. The final phase, from 1905, was marked by the rise of the militant suffrage movement.

Wollstonecraft (1759–1997) is the best known of the English female radicals who were encouraged by the progress made by women in revolutionary France. The scale of the campaign for women's rights, which formed part of a concerted political and social agenda, was more extensive than ever before and, as such, launched the first wave of feminism. From Paris, Olympe de Gouges (1748–1793) heralded the *Declaration of the Rights of Woman and the Citizen* (1791), calling attention to the lack of women's rights in the Assembly's Declaration of the Rights of Man. In her *Vindication,* Wollstonecraft attacks the feebleness of middle-class femininity by reclaiming reason for women and advocates changes in their education and conduct. Among its admirers were Mary Hayes (1760–1843), who wrote *Appeal to the Men of Great Britain on Behalf of Women* (1798); and Mary Robinson (1758–1800), the author of *Thoughts on the Condition of Women, and on the Injustice of Mental Subordination* (1798). A leading detractor was Richard Polwhele (1760–1838), who demonized both Wollstonecraft and Hays as embodiments of "The Unsex'd Female" in his misogynist poem of that title. After her death, Wollstonecraft's husband William Godwin (1756–1836) published her memoirs (1798) in unflinchingly intimate detail, with the result that her writings as well as her life were condemned. Such a response, along with the backlash against the French Revolution, meant that it was not until 1825 that Wollstonecraft's legacy was revived. This was when William Thompson (1775–1833) singled out Anna Wheeler (1785–1848) as the woman who should have "the honor of raising from the dust that neglected banner which a woman's hand nearly thirty years ago unfolded boldly, in face of the prejudices of thousands of years, and for which a woman's heart bled, and her life was all but the sacrifice" (Thompson and Wheeler, 1825).

Wheeler was more radical and broader in her outlook than Wollstonecraft, for, unlike her more inhibited predecessor, she expressed a women's right to sexual satisfaction. Thompson and Wheeler's *Appeal* was written as a reply to a paragraph by the utilitarian James Mill (1773–1836), which supported the government's exclusion of women from politics, encoded recently within the Reform Act of 1832. Although Thompson acknowledged that the text was a joint effort written with Wheeler, it was published originally under his name alone. As a result of this omission, Anna Wheeler, the most important feminist since Mary Wollstonecraft and before Emmeline Pankhurst (1858–1928), has not received her rightful recognition.

Both Wheeler and Thompson were cooperative communitarians. Their advocacy of sexual equality brought them into conflict with the narrow-minded utilitarians. Wheeler was particularly sympathetic to the theories of the French utopian socialist Charles Fourier (1772–1837),

whom she met in 1823 at her salon, which she had established in Paris. It was he who had first coined, in French, the term "feminist." Wheeler also was part of the circle in England that surrounded the socialist Robert Owen (1771–1858). Until 1983, when Barbara Taylor published *Eve and the New Jerusalem* in which she discusses pre-suffrage feminists, Owenite feminism has been treated as the Cinderella of feminisms, having been eclipsed by the radiant radicalism of the revolutionary 1790s and the momentous movement of the early twentieth-century militant suffragettes. For Owen's periodical *The Crises,* Wheeler wrote articles against marriage and other inequalities for women under the pseudonym Vlasta. Her daughter Rosina (1802–1882) suffered in a particularly unhappy marriage to Edward Bulwer-Lytton and, as a result, protested vehemently against the treatment of married and separated women.

Caroline Norton (1808–1877) is the best-known campaigner who lobbied the British parliament to change the divorce laws. The existing double standard permitted a husband to divorce his wife for infidelity, yet it did not allow her to sue him for divorce, however profligate he may have been. Because a married woman had no recognized independent legal existence, she was not allowed to make a will, sign a lease, sue, legally claim her earnings, or leave her husband's house—even though she could be forcibly removed by him from a place of refuge. Caroline Norton's campaign to protect the rights of divorced and separated wives was recognized in the Marriage and Divorce Act of 1857, which included several of her proposals. Because these measures removed the worst abuses, they put back the cause of married women's property for almost 30 years and alienated campaigners such as Frances Power Cobbe (1822–1904) and Barbara Leigh Smith Bodichon (1827–1891), who had attacked the laws that placed a wife in her husband's power. In her *A Brief Summary in Plain Language of the Most Important Laws in England Concerning Women* (1854), Bodichon campaigned for the introduction of a Married Women's Property Bill to safeguard the property and earnings of women. In 1882, wives won the right to their own property and earnings through the Married Women's Property Act.

Instead of winning points piecemeal, socialist feminists believed that women could be free only in the context of larger social change. The drawback of this doctrine was that after 1850, there was a shift toward deferring the "woman question" until "after the revolution," which meant that it was inevitably sidelined from the mainstream of socialist concerns. Within a communist–feminist ideology, female emancipation was seen as inseparable from the overthrow of capitalism and proletarian ownership of the means of production. Such radical reform was the birthright of the Marxist feminist Eleanor Marx (1855–1898), the daughter of Karl Marx, who wrote, with Edward Aveling (1851–1898), *The Woman Question: From a Socialist Point of View* (1886). Marx was a "new woman," a designation first used in 1894 by the novelist Sarah Grand (1854–1943) and "Ouida" (Marie Louise de la Ramée, 1839–1908) for the feminist activists of the *fin de siècle*. These included writers such as Olive Schreiner (1855–1920), Elizabeth Robins (1862–1952), and Mona Caird (1854–1931). Like her friend Schreiner, Marx was torn between her visionary idealism and the torments of her private life. There is no better example of this than Marx's relationship with Aveling. He blatantly betrayed the model of monogamy adhered to in their joint work by secretly marrying someone else. Disillusioned, Marx took her own life with prussic acid. Aveling's treachery even went beyond the grave, as many believed that Marx went to her death in the misguided belief that he would join her in a suicide pact.

Another partnership in which there was a clash between the agendas of gender roles was that of J. S. Mill (1806–1873) and Harriet Taylor (1807–1858). Usually remembered only as a woman who inspired Mill's powerful critique of the subordination of women, Taylor had in fact published her own essay, "The Enfranchisement of Women," in 1851, which differed with Mill in points of emphasis. Because of its anonymity, it was widely assumed to have been written by Mill, even though it was based on Taylor's own draft and contains arguments she had advanced elsewhere inveighing against the entrapment of women within marriage. Although prepared to argue for the equality of men and women in marriage, Mill was not receptive to Taylor's insistence that women should be economically independent. The publication of her essay in the *Westminster Review* appeared shortly after their wedding. In *The Subjection of Women,* and presumably in his married life, Mill upheld the traditional roles in marriage, which designated man the breadwinner and woman the dependent manager of his income. Even objectification of women as passive rather than active is condoned. It is unlikely that Taylor shared these views. Without her influence, Mill's feminist writing would probably have been much more restrained and less radical.

It is ironic that Mill's father was James Mill, who supported the first statutory act to disenfranchise and disempower women. In 1824, the father's article on government written for the annual supplement to the *Encyclopedia Britannica* gave philosophical credence to this damaging legislation. Thompson and Wheeler's reply in the *Appeal*

influenced Mill's *Subjection of Women*. Both treatises contributed to the growing pressure for female enfranchisement. In April 1886, Mill presented to the British parliament a petition for women's suffrage of 1,499 signatures, collected by the "Langham Place Ladies." These were the London-based Women's Suffrage Committee, whose members included Barbara Leigh Smith Bodichon, the educationalist Emily Davies (1830–1921)—who had founded Girton College for women—and Elizabeth Garrett Anderson (1836–1917), who established a hospital for women in London that now bears her name. Another member was Elizabeth Wolstenholme-Elmy (1834–1913), who personally collected over 300 names for the petition.

Best remembered for arguing against the sexual enslavement of women—particularly in marital rape—Wolstenholme-Elmy had also urged women to regain their rights if necessary by suspending their conjugal duties. With Josephine Butler (1828–1906), she was a member of the Ladies National Association for the Abolition of the Contagious Diseases. Butler had been instrumental in challenging the Contagious Disease Acts of the 1860s, which had encroached on the civil liberties of women. The radical feminists' slogan calling for votes for women and celibacy for men was supported by Christabel Pankhurst (1880–1958). In *The Great Scourge and How to End It* (1913), she made the alarmist estimate that 75 to 80 percent of men were infected with gonorrhea and 20 percent were likely to have contracted syphilis. Marie Carmichael Stopes (1880–1958), the doyen of the birth control movement, drew public attention to the danger of congenital syphilis, known as syphilis of the innocents. In *The Truth about Venereal Disease* (1921), she disclosed information about sexually transmitted diseases for women who as Victorian girls would have been forbidden to read medical books.

In order to regain rights over their body, it was important for women to control their reproduction. Annie Besant (1847–1933) was a powerful proselytizer in the birth-control movement, and her persistence in urging public discussion of this taboo subject aroused fierce opposition. With Charles Bradlaugh (1833–1891), she reissued in 1877 a pamphlet on birth control called *The Fruits of Philosophy*. Both were prosecuted for publishing an "obscene" book on contraception and, after a four-day trial, were found guilty. No action was taken against them, although they became the *bête noire* of feminists who were concerned that birth control could be used as a tool to sexually oppress women by encouraging husbands to make excessive conjugal demands on their wives. Christabel Pankhurst spoke out in favor of celibacy rather than contraception, which was consistent with her view that sex between men and women should take place only in a loving relationship for the purposes of procreation.

Pankhurst's main concern, however, was in securing votes for women. Her first base had been her family home in Manchester, where Lydia Becker (1827–1890) had founded *Women's Suffrage Journal*. According to Helen Blackburn (1903–1942), Becker's character and inspiration had molded the early movement for women's suffrage. The leader of the constitutional suffrage movement and president of the National Union of Women's Suffrage Societies was Millicent Fawcett (1847–1929). Insistent that eventually women would obtain the vote through reason and persuasion, Fawcett was not convinced by the militant methods of the Women's Social and Political Union (WSPU), which had been founded in 1903 by Emmeline and Christabel Pankhurst. Fawcett's belief that suffrage should be accorded to women on the same basis as men—who had to own property in order to qualify for the votes—restricted eligibility mainly to the middle class. Because working-class women were seldom property owners and, unlike men, were unlikely to be head of a household, most were excluded from the franchise. For this reason, workers in Lancashire cotton mills who were members of the North of England Society for Women's Suffrage campaigned for women over the age of 21 to be granted the vote, regardless of property ownership. In 1893, these radical suffragists found in Esther Roper (1870–1938) a leader who was eager to represent their interests.

Too often, militants and constitutionalists have been polarized as the militants (suffragettes) versus the nonmilitants (suffragists). Such oppositions can be misleading, as both groups took militant action. For the suffragists, unlike the suffragettes, militancy was not a self-defining credo—which could turn into a catalyst for inordinate self-sacrifice. An example of this is the heroic Lady Constance Lytton (1869–1923), great-granddaughter of Anna Wheeler and member of the WSPU, who, despite having a weak heart, disguised herself as a law-breaking working-class woman in order to be arrested, imprisoned, and force-fed. Her book *Prisons and Prisoners* (1914) is a moving account of the time she spent in prison and her ensuing paralysis, which may have resulted from the harsh treatment she received. The autobiographies of the Pankhurst family—Emmeline's *My Own Story* (1914) and those of her daughters Sylvia (1882–1960) and Christabel—which contain harrowing accounts of both thirst and hunger strikes provided women under siege with other sources of inspiration. Sylvia founded the East London Federation of the WSPU for working women, which became a separate organization in 1914. This secession marked Sylvia's final break with her family so that she could single-mindedly pursue the cause of international socialism.

The suffrage campaign ended in 1928, when women gained the vote. The aftermath of this triumph ushered in a period of complacency and even apathy regarding the remaining women's issues. Other victories—particularly in the workplace—had to wait until the onset of World War II, when many men left their jobs for the war effort. After the war ended in 1945, many women lost their newly won freedoms. The 1950s saw a return to domesticity and the traditional female role, the constraints of which acted as a harbinger for the women's liberation movement of the 1960s.

See Also

FEMINISM: EIGHTEENTH CENTURY; FEMINISM: FIRST-WAVE NORTH AMERICAN; FEMINISM: LIBERAL BRITISH AND EUROPEAN; FEMINISM: MILITANT; FEMINISM: NINETEENTH CENTURY; FEMINISM: OVERVIEW; FEMINISM: SECOND-WAVE BRITISH; FEMINISM: SOCIALIST; SUFFRAGE

References and Further Reading

Banks, Olive. (1981) *Becoming a feminist: The social origins of first wave feminism.* Brighton: Wheatsheaf.

Caine, Barbara. 1992. *Victorian feminists.* Oxford: Oxford University Press.

Holcombe, L. 1983. *Women and property: Reform of the married women's property law in nineteenth century England.* Toronto: Toronto University Press.

Holton, S. 1986. *Feminism and democracy: Women's suffrage and reform policies in Britain, 1897–1918.* Cambridge: Cambridge University Press.

———. 1996. *Suffrage days: Stories from the women's suffrage movement.* London: Routledge.

Kelly, Gary. 1993. *Women, writing, and revolution 1790–1827.* Oxford: Clarendon.

Lewis, Jane. 1987. *Before the vote was won: Arguments for and against women's suffrage 1864–1896.* London: Routledge and Kegan Paul.

McHugh, P. 1980. *Prostitution and Victorian social reform.* London: Croom Helm.

Purvis, June, and Sandra Stanley Holt, ed. 2000. *Votes for women.* London: Routledge.

Spender, Dale. 1988. *Women of ideas and what men have done to them.* London: Pandora.

Strachey, R. [1978], 1982. *The cause: A short history of the women's movement in Great Britain.* London: Virago.

[Taylor, Harriet.] Anon. 1995. The enfranchisement of women. *Westminster Review* 55: 284–301. Reprinted in Marie Mulvey-Robberts and Tamae Mizuta, eds., *The disenfranchised: The fight for the suffrage* in *sources of British feminism*, 7–37. Rout-ledge/Thoemmes.

Thompson, William, and Anna Wheeler. 1994. *Appeal of one half of the human race, women, against the other half, men.* Ed. Michael Foot and Marie Mulvey-Roberts. Bristol: Thoemmes. (Originally published 1825.)

Todd, Janet. 2000. *Mary Wollstonecraft: A revolutionary life.* London: Weidenfeld and Nicolson.

Marie Mulvey-Roberts

FEMINISM: First-Wave North American

In the United States, the term *feminism* gained currency in the 1910s, a few decades after its appearance in Europe. During the "first wave" of feminism (a designation for which we are indebted to Marsha Weinman Lear, who dubbed the revival of feminism in the late 1960s the "second wave"), "Feminist" (originally capitalized) defined those women and men whose concept of female liberation was more radical and comprehensive than that of the mainstream "woman movement" of the Progressive era (roughly 1890–1920). Feminists called for revolutionary changes in the economic and sexual organization of society as well as for freedom from the psychological stays of female dependency and subordination. Feminists rejected Christianity and conventional sexual respectability. Emerging from the avant-garde milieu of New York City's artistic and cultural rebellion, Feminists attacked inherited notions of female identity and experimented with new patterns in sexual relationships. Since each Feminist goal had nineteenth-century precedents, the novelty of Feminism lay less in its particular objectives than in its combination of goals and exuberance of expression. Unlike many self-defined feminists (lowercase *f*) in Europe who took traditional views of female identity in their campaigns for women's rights and societal transformation, Feminists in the United States challenged prevailing beliefs in innate gender attributes and roles.

First-Wave Feminist Organizations

Before Henrietta Rodman (1877–1923) founded the Feminist Alliance in 1914, the best-known association of Feminists was Heterodoxy, a group formed in 1913 in Greenwich Village, New York City, under the leadership of Marie Jenny Howe (1871–1934). Made up of writers, artists, labor activists, and social workers, the group met weekly and, in a spirit of mutual respect, explored unconventional and conflicting views of gender, sexuality, and social institutions. Some

members were lesbians and bisexuals; some espoused free love. Whether they were socialists, anarchists, or less radical social reformers, they shared a commitment to full female emancipation, sexual equity, and the pursuit of erotic pleasure, and to combating internalized norms of female domesticity and self-sacrifice.

The historically grounded definition of first-wave feminism, however, is not generally held. Until the relatively recent scholarship of Nancy Cott, feminist activists and scholars of women's lives applied *feminism* retrospectively as an umbrella term for the nineteenth- and early-twentieth-century "woman movement" in the United States before the emergence of Feminism *and* for the moderate and radical wings of the U.S. woman movement during the 1910s and 1920s. Although Cott (1987) recognizes the merger of the woman movement and Feminism during the second wave, she argues that ahistorical usage with regard to the first wave has blinded scholars to Feminism's distinctive agenda. This ahistorical usage, further, blurs the evolutionary phases of the woman movement, especially the vicissitudes of feminism in the 1920s and the paradoxes of twentieth-century efforts to promote women's liberation and equality. Nonetheless, because the loose retrospective use of "first-wave feminism" in the United States represented how the history of feminism was understood in the 1960s and still dominates academic and popular conceptions, and since dictionary definitions of *feminism* coincide with the woman movement as a whole, this account of first-wave feminism will encompass the entire woman movement, of the Progressive era, including its strictly Feminist aspect.

Goals and Philosophy of the Woman Movement

The primary thrust of the woman movement in the Progressive era was women's suffrage. Mainstream suffragists, most of whom understood women's rights as requiring fundamental transformations in law, education, and economic opportunities for women, believed the franchise for women to be essential to all these societal changes. For three generations, despite organizational splits from 1865 to 1890, the battle for suffrage united women of divergent political and social views and diverse racial, ethnic, and class backgrounds. Through their struggle against male domination of public life, suffragists developed a deeply shared consciousness of societal injustice against women as a category. They also learned the importance for women of securing full citizenship, not just as family members but as individuals in direct relationship to the state.

The philosophical framework for the woman movement was Enlightenment liberalism, embodied at Seneca

Falls in 1848, in the Declaration of Sentiments. This manifesto set forth, in the style of the U.S. Declaration of Independence, grievances against male privilege and resolutions for reform. Advocates of women's rights appealed to the liberal belief in the natural freedom and equality of all human beings and in a universal human capacity for critical, rational thought. They also drew on Protestant individualism, especially its faith in the sovereignty of each soul, whose first responsibility was not to the state or societal conventions but to God and truth. This combined Enlightenment and Protestant outlook emboldened abolitionist and, in turn, women's rights radicalism.

Left unclear within this liberal ideology, however, was the relationship between sexual and human identity. Whereas most women's rights advocates initially emphasized common humanity as the foundation of women's claim to freedom and sexual equality, an initially smaller group, influenced by romantic thought and evangelical Christianity, insisted that women's rights and their mission to improve public life arose from their difference from men, their moral superiority. This superiority came, these advocates asserted, from women's greater piety, tenderness, societal compassion, and sexual purity, traits derived from women's maternal instincts and destiny. Occasionally, leaders of the woman movement, including Elizabeth Cady Stanton (1815–1902) and Susan B. Anthony (1820–1906), who most often invoked the argument of common humanity, reasoned from a position opposite to the one they generally held. These self-contradictory and shifting stances have characterized the woman movement from its inception to the present day.

Joined to such intellectual traditions, another set of crosscurrents shaped first-wave ideology. Most adherents of the woman movement included within their concept of freedom the human right of private property and associated concepts of possessive individualism. But a vocal minority differed: antebellum utopian socialists and later nineteenth- and early-twentieth-century material feminists challenged liberal tenets of individualism. They regarded the private organization of the household and marriage as impediments to women's liberation and proposed communal alternatives. Like the tension over gender sameness and difference, this tension between private and collective structures of society permeated all phases of the woman movement.

Although politically the mid-nineteenth-century woman movement was defiantly radical, its ideology and strategy were gradually tempered after the American Civil War. To stem the swelling tide of antisuffragism and create a broad-based constituency, the woman movement turned conservative. When in 1890 its two branches combined to form the National American Woman Suffrage Association (NAWSA), radical voices were a distinct minority. Fearful of alienating potential supporters and frustrated by consistent failure to win state referenda for women's suffrage, NAWSA, under the leadership of Anna Howard Shaw (1847–1917) from 1904 to 1915, rejected militant strategies, shunned risky ideas (for example, attacks on patriarchal religion), and avoided close alliances with black and working-class immigrant suffrage groups. Shaw's successor from 1915 to 1920, Carrie Chapman Catt (1859–1947), though charismatic and decidedly more enterprising and effective as an organizer than Shaw, still steered a middle-of-the-road course. Determined to appeal to those who feared that woman suffrage threatened traditional family values and gender norms, NAWSA emphasized its commitment to restructuring public and private life, but without removing the major foundations of domestic and economic order. Correspondingly, how women suffragists argued for the vote shifted in balance: the argument for female moral superiority gained ascendance over the earlier dominant view of common human identity.

Social Feminists and the Reform Agenda

In the late 1960s, the historian William L. O'Neill coined the term *social feminists*—a term now much contested—to classify many of these mainstream women's rights activists. The reform agenda of social feminists included temperance; international peace; the protection of consumers, women and children; and the elimination of civic corruption and prostitution. These women championed woman suffrage as an implement of social housekeeping, a mop to assist them in expunging urban filth, ignorance, vice, and exploitation. During the Progressive era many associations advanced social feminism, most notably the General Federation of Women's Clubs (GFWC), the Women's Christian Temperance Union (the largest national women's organization in U.S. history), and the Settlement House movement. The membership of these groups consisted mainly of socially reputable, educated, white middle- and upper-class women. Because few branches of these organizations admitted black women, black women organized separately. The National Association of Colored Women formed in 1896, four years after the GFWC. Its agenda, though similar to that of white women's clubs, differed significantly by placing racial uplift and the combating of racial prejudice at the forefront.

Although these social feminists remained more conservative than the self-identified Feminists of the 1910s, their activist zeal has drawn increasing scholarly attention. The rank and file of the women's club movement not only ardently supported woman suffrage but aggressively confronted local officials and state legislatures in their efforts to salvage urban life. Even more adversarial, temperance women arguing for societal reform and female suffrage vigorously attacked on masculine traits and behavior as the cause of familial and societal woes. The Women's Trade Union League and the Settlement House movement notably shared a belief in the power of female virtue and solidarity to ameliorate the evils of public and private life. Each of the social feminist associations included harsh critics of capitalist values and structures: socialists as well as far more numerous moderate social reformers. In the Progressive era, lambasting capitalism did not necessarily undermine a woman's respectability.

The most race-, ethnic-, and class-inclusive of the social feminist organizations was the Settlement House movement, whose leaders exerted a profound influence on the course of U.S. and women's history long after the Progressive era. Spearheaded in the 1890s and federated in 1911 by Jane Addams (1860–1935), the roughly 400 Settlement Houses were administered by a female coterie of predominantly college-educated women. The houses' target population was the surrounding neighborhood's immigrant poor, who participated in Settlement House child care classes and in cultural and recreational programs. A complex mix of attitudes and policies—assimilationist Americanization programs on the one hand, and energetic efforts to preserve ethnic traditions on the other—shaped Settlement House approaches to clients. Settlement Houses also became laboratories that trained a generation of female policymakers, particularly in social welfare legislation. Two examples are seen in Edith Abbott's (1876–1957) career as a social welfare theorist and dean of the University of Chicago's School of Social Service Administration, and Florence Kelley's (1859–1932) achievements as head of the National Consumer's League and, together with Lillian Wald (1867–1940), founder of the National Child Labor Commission (culminating in the creation in 1912 of a Children's Bureau within the Department of Commerce and Labor). In their agitation for unemployment compensation, minimum-wage laws, an eight-hour day, prohibition of child labor, factory regulations and inspections, and public health programs, Settlement House workers laid the groundwork for the social welfare legislation of President Roosevelt's New Deal. Their efforts were vital, as well, to the development of social work as a profession. Moreover, in their campaigns to improve the lives of the most vulnerable, Settlement House leaders not only assumed promi-

nent positions in the temperance movement, GFWC, and NAWSA—Addams and Kelley became vice presidents of NAWSA—but also supported and collaborated with trade unions and immigrants' political associations. Their efforts were crucial to the passage of many Progressive measures, from cleaning up sewer systems to the Pure Food and Drug Act (1908).

The National Consumers' League (NCL, founded in 1899) and Women's Trade Union League (WTUL, founded in 1903) occupy a space somewhere between social feminism and explicitly socialist and anarchist efforts to promote women's liberation. Built by middle- and upper-class female social reformers, these two associations sought to bridge class differences and to improve the lives of wage-earning women. Whereas the NCL targeted the exploitation of female sales clerks and factory workers, the WTUL went beyond promoting the formation and cooperation of women's trade unions to active support of strikes. Such militance met with mixed response from mainstream suffragists. The WTUL provided crucial moral backing, publicity, and funds for the shirtwaist workers' historic strikes during 1909–1910 in New York City and Philadelphia. However, since the NCL and WTUL, like other social feminist organizations, included few black members and favored assimilation over diversity for immigrants, the distinctive needs of women who belonged to racial and ethnic minorities were subject to neglect.

Beyond Social Feminism: Socialism and Anarchism

A decided minority within the first-wave woman movement during the Progressive period were those clearly identified with radical causes. The most numerous and influential of these radical women were socialists; a smaller contingent were anarchists, some of whom spurned the woman movement, especially the woman's suffrage campaign, as a harmful diversion. Not all socialist women identified with the woman movement, but—unlike most socialist men until the Second International in 1907 rallied men and women alike to the strenuous advocacy of woman suffrage—most of the female leadership and rank and file were engaged with the woman's rights campaign. Socialists and nonsocialists joined forces, with marked impact in the West and Midwest. Indeed, socialists in California took pride in the contrast between weak support for female suffrage in wealthy districts and its solid championship in working-class neighborhoods.

Although socialist women supported many of the goals of social feminist and suffragists, they found these goals insufficient. Women's liberation, they believed, demanded the eradication of poverty and of the vast disparities in economic wealth and privilege, a move that would require revolutionary changes in the organization of labor, property, and family life. For such change, as well as in the battle for women's suffrage, they deemed working-class, not privileged, women, the appropriate leaders. At the same time, socialist women recognized an urgent need for women of all classes to form a common front against male domination.

Some socialist women also addressed the conditions women faced within their private households and the problems common to women who strove to combine family responsibilities with wage earning. Dolores Hayden (1982) has documented the nineteenth- and early twentieth-century evolution of a primarily socialist compound of collectivist perspectives on these issues, which she calls "material feminism." Material feminists reconceptualized the relationship between private household space and public space. They envisioned a variety of urban and rural communal arrangements for cooking, laundry, and child care. They viewed the isolated nuclear household as an inefficient, amateurish way to perform home and child care tasks and as detrimental to women's public roles. For married women and mothers to enter the full gamut of public occupations and to exercise the range of duties of citizenship, women must be rid of the immense burden of domestic chores. Not only did the privatized nuclear household prevent this, they contended; it also fostered a narrow, possessive spirit incompatible with the social consciousness, compassion, and cooperation of all its citizens that a nation required for progress. This said, it must be underscored that material feminists did not envision that husbands would take up the domestic weight their wives set down. Not even shared parenting by men and women figured in their proposals. The bold imaginative alternatives offered by material feminists to offset the customary barriers to women's public life involved plans for professional, expert, female managers of kitchens and day care facilities.

Charlotte Perkins Gilman, Socialist and Material Feminist

One of the most renowned early twentieth-century socialists, a material feminist, and a spokeswoman for the woman movement, Charlotte Perkins Gilman (1860–1935) also pioneered Feminism in the 1910s. The foremost theorist of emergent Feminism, she was an active member of Heterodoxy, a group that assailed cherished beliefs of woman's rights activists. Her dazzling critiques of patriarchal culture and her revolutionary alternatives seized the imagination of even the most temperate members of the woman move-

ment. Gilman's most influential treatise, *Women and Economics* (published in 1898), jettisoned both traditional constructs of female identity and prevalent views of gender differences that underpinned the idology of the woman movement during the Progressive era. Rather than leading to female moral superiority, Gilman declared, patriarchal institutions and practices had reduced women to economic and sexual parasites, stripped them of autonomy and self-esteem, crippled their social imagination, and disabled them as mothers, not to mention as effective participants in the public realm. Indeed, in her scathing analysis of the private household, *The Home* (1903), and in her many articles in women's periodicals, including her own periodical, aptly titled *The Forerunner,* Gilman described the private organization of housework and child care as institutionalizing women's arrested mental development. Gilman's radicalism had its limits: while she hoped to discredit the popular belief in women's nurturance and moral strengths, she modulated her denial of inherent female characteristics, as when she imagined woman rights activists to be representative of a vanguard of mature females who, in solidarity, could effect societal salvation. More important, she never questioned her own elitist, racist, and ethnophobic attitudes, and she failed to explore in any depth the practical implications of her loyalty to socialism. For many years she opposed the birth control movement because she feared that it heightened women's sexual objectification and vulnerability.

Margaret Sanger, Feminist, Radical, and Ex-Radical

In rejecting the legalization of contraceptives, Gilman opposed another pioneering Feminist, Margaret Sanger (1879–1966), who, no less than Gilman, represented the radical wing of the woman movement. In 1911, Sanger cut her political teeth as a salaried women's organizer for the Socialist Party, and a year later she became a paid organizer for the even more radical Industrial Workers of the World (IWW). Attracted to its direct-action tactics, Sanger joined IWW's militant textile strikes in Lawrence, Massachusetts, and Paterson, New Jersey. Sanger's brief experience as a public health nurse in New York City likewise intensified her commitment to help the poor, especially women and children. At the same time, inspired by the anarchist Emma Goldman (1869–1940), who called for reproductive freedom, Sanger increasingly addressed women's sex education and reproductive control. In issues of *Woman Rebel,* her socialist monthly that first appeared in 1914, Sanger argued for woman's freedom from wage slavery and bourgeois morality and from constraints imposed by male privilege. She stressed the magnitude of women's reproductive choice and women's right to sexual pleasure freed from anxiety about procreation. Poor women, she maintained, would especially benefit from being able to limit the number of their offspring: capitalism would have fewer children to exploit, and mothers would enjoy improved health. In her pamphlet *Family Limitation* (1915), Sanger took direct action, illegally offering advice about contraceptives and detailing methods. After her travels in England and Europe in 1914–1915, she resolved to make birth control her central mission.

Until the end of World War I, Sanger's philosophy regarding birth control remained staunchly radical. In 1916, again breaking the law, she opened the first American birth control clinic, located in Brooklyn's Brownsville, a working-class immigrant Jewish and Italian community. Imprisoned for this enterprise, she gained visibility and support for herself and her crusade. Financial help came, however, primarily from wealthy women, and as their importance to Sanger's crusade increased, her identification with labor and her attacks on capitalists dwindled. Her reliance on the support of the wealthy was the greater owing to the divisions of both the political left and the woman movement over the merits of birth control. Further accelerating the erosion of Sanger's radicalism was the demise of socialism and anarchism in 1917, when the United States' entrance into World War I, coupled with the Bolshevik Revolution, spurred government officials to raid socialist and anarchist offices and to arrest and deport those suspected of subversive activity, a prelude to an even more intense repression in 1919. By 1920 Sanger could no longer turn to radical organizations for assistance in financing her birth control campaign. Not only did she focus her search for support on the wealthy, but she also divorced her first husband and married a multimillionaire, who gladly financed her campaign. Although Sanger sustained her confrontational politics and Feminist goals, she adjusted her rationale for birth control to suit the elite class she courted. During the 1920s, along with her willingness to empower only doctors with the right to dispense contraceptives, she allowed race- and class-biased eugenics criteria of who was fit to have children to color her advocacy of birth control.

The National Women's Party

If Gilman's and Sanger's work epitomized core Feminist convictions of the 1910s, the birth in 1916 of the National Women's Party (NWP) represented Feminism's political program within the suffrage movement. Although after 1912 NAWSA became more aggressive in its strategies, it remained too tame for many suffragists. Rival suffrage associations appeared, the most significant being the NWP. Its

original members, under the leadership of Alice Paul (1885–1977) and Lucy Burns (1879–1966), labeled themselves Feminists and served under the NAWSA umbrella as the Congressional Union, a lobbying group in Washington, D.C., that formed in 1912 to revive the struggle for a federal suffrage amendment, which had been shelved since the 1890s. Disagreeing with NAWSA's nonpartisan politics, its members bolted. They attacked the Democrats, the party in power at the time, and introduced militant tactics that appealed to younger suffragists. Their most dramatic action took place in 1917: they picketed the White House during that entire year and dubbed the president "Kaiser Wilson." Periodically imprisoned, picketers, in imitation of British suffragettes, went on hunger strikes, swelling the numbers of NWP sympathizers.

The Women's Peace Party

Both Feminists and other partisans of the woman movement found political expression for their antiwar views in the Woman's Peace Party (WPP), formed in 1915 to advance social feminist and Feminist pacifist philosophy and international peace efforts. When the United States entered World War I in 1917, most women's rights activists, including Feminists, retreated from their pacifist position, but a vigorous minority, including the leadership of the NWP, persisted. Crystal Eastman (1881–1928) personified the combination of Feminism and resolute pacifism. A leader of NWP and founder in 1919 of the Feminist Congress—which demanded not only the vote but birth control, women's economic equality, and a single moral standard for both sexes—Eastman, undaunted by wartime patriotism, organized the Civil Liberties Bureau to assist conscientious objectors.

African-American Woman Movement

The NWP and WPP were no more hospitable to black women than other associations of the woman movement. Throughout the Progressive era, African-American women defined their relationship to the woman movement not only by forming their own women's clubs and suffrage associations (the National Association for the Advancement of Colored People had a female suffrage department) but also by their distinctive critique of both patriarchy and racism. Because retrospective use of the term *feminism* characterizes scholarship on black women's history no less than white women's history, various studies of the rise of black feminism in the nineteenth and early twentieth centuries focus on a pantheon of black women writers and activists, such as Frances Harper (1825–1911), Maggie Lena Walker (1867–1934), Anna Julia Cooper (1859?–1964), Pauline Hopkins (1859–1930), and Ida B. Wells (1862–1931), all of whom become identified as feminist. Although many ideas espoused by these women were akin to those held by their white Feminist contemporaries, they had a less individualistic sense of personhood. Their concept of female autonomy and equality entwined individual women's rights with gender equality and freedom with the collective black struggle, as exemplified by Ida B. Wells's linking her crusade against lynching to her campaign for women's rights as both an end in itself and a means of racial progress. Whether black women held social feminist or Feminist views on gender identity and roles, their vision of the future was radical in its rebellion against white violence and against racial hierarchy and privilege.

1920s: Feminism in the Flux

By the end of World War I and the passage in 1920 of the Constitution's Nineteenth Amendment, granting women the vote, the woman movement, including its Feminist wing, faced an uncertain future. Without the cohering battle for the vote and the Progressive era's coalition of socialists and social reformers, the first wave crashed against the rocks of repressive conservatism, dispersing into its multiple philosophical and political crosscurrents, some sustaining their vitality, others losing it. NAWSA metamorphosed into the League of Women Voters, but at a tenth of its former size. Its reshaped goals, reflecting social feminist traditions, were civic education and laws to protect women and children. The even smaller NWP seized the role of defining feminism, but it retreated from the Feminism of the 1910s and NWP's wartime openness to radical social reformers and birth control advocates, losing some of its most enthusiastic members. NWP's agenda turned strictly political and legal, focusing initially on states' ratification of the Nineteenth Amendment, the election of female candidates, and then the passage of an Equal Rights Amendment (ERA), which Alice Paul introduced to Congress in 1923. Many social feminists opposed the ERA as insensitive to women's gender-specific circumstances. Since such an amendment threatened protective labor legislation for women not accorded to men, many women reformers viewed the ERA as detrimental to women's rights. With growing acrimony and yet with increasing global concerns, the League of Women Voters and NWP competed for preeminence in the International Alliance of Women (founded, initially, as the International Woman Suffrage Alliance, in Europe in 1904), the rivalry climaxing in the alliance's rejection of NWP.

While such conflicts weakened the woman movement's political progress, and though membership in the General Federation of Women's Clubs, the National Consumers' League, and the National Women's Trade Union League plummeted, many reform-minded associations either expanded or came into being at this juncture. Among the more important were the National Congress of Parents and Teachers Associations, the Young Women's Christian Association (with its noteworthy interracial efforts and Industrial Clubs, subgroups focused on women's working conditions), the National Federation of Business and Professional Women's Clubs, and an array of peace associations—for example, the U.S. branch of the Women's International League for Peace and Freedom. Significantly, both old and new African-American women's associations remained vigorous in the 1920s. Since, however, feminism had become linked to the particular agenda of the National Woman's Party, and since social reform associations were no longer linked by the overarching cause of suffrage, the woman's movement as a broad and unified phenomenon disappeared. Most women reformers, though carrying forward many of the movement's objectives, no longer identified themselves as feminists or as participants in the woman movement . Correspondingly, while the postwar generation of women included many who responded eagerly to the earlier Feminist affirmation of sexual pleasure, they did not see the necessity of integrating sexual autonomy with women's domestic, economic, and political freedom and equality. As they extended the boundaries of respectable heterosociality and heterosexuality, condoned divorce, and promoted greater mutuality within marriage, they lost sight of the importance of same-sex friendships and solidarity. Although some women experimented with lesbian and bisexual expression, most young women, the legendary flappers, adhered to conventional notions of marriage and motherhood. The complex and comprehensive vision of the Feminism of the 1910s would not to resurge until the 1960s.

See Also

FEMINISM: ANARCHIST; FEMINISM: LIBERAL NORTH AMERICAN; FEMINISM: NINETEENTH CENTURY; FEMINISM: RADICAL; FEMINISM: SECOND-WAVE NORTH AMERICAN; SUFFRAGE

References and Further Reading

Buhle, Mari Jo. 1983. *Women and American socialism, 1870–1920.* Urbana: University of Illinois Press.

Cott, Nancy F. 1987. *The grounding of modern feminism.* New Haven, Conn.: Yale University Press.

Dubois, Ellen Carol. 1978. *Feminism and suffrage: The emergence of an independent women's movement in America 1848–1869.* Ithaca, N.Y.: Cornell University Press.

Faderman, Lillian. 1992. *Odd girls and twilight lovers.* New York: Penguin.

Giddings, Paula. 1984. *When and where I enter.* New York: Morrow.

Gordon, Ann D., et al., eds. 1997. *African-American Women and the Vote, 1837–1965.* Amherst: University of Massachusetts Press.

Gordon, Linda. 1990. *Woman's body, woman's right: Birth control in America.* New York: Penguin.

Hayden, Dolores. 1982. *The grand domestic revolution.* Cambridge, Mass.: MIT Press.

Jones, Jacqueline. 1986. *Labor of love, labor of sorrow.* New York: Basic Books.

Newman, Louise Michele. 1999. *White women's rights: The racial origins of feminism in the United States.* New York: Oxford University Press.

O'Neill, William L. 1989. *Feminism in America: A history.* New Brunswick, N.J.: Rutgers University Press.

Riley, Glenda. 1995. *Inventing the American woman: An inclusive history.* Wheeling, Ill.: Harlan Davidson.

Terborg-Penn, Rosalyn. 1998. *African American women in the struggle for the vote, 1850–1920.* Bloomington: University of Indiana Press.

Woloch, Nancy. 1999. *Women and the American experience.* New York: McGraw-Hill.

Joyce Berkman

FEMINISM: Global

See GLOBAL FEMINISM.

FEMINISM: JAPAN

In Japan, the term *feminism* is pronounced as in English, not translated; historically, it has been represented by diverse discourses. Its goals are, primarily, women's emancipation and gender equality; and, secondarily, the construction of alternative systems to accommodate differences in gender, class, race, ethnicity, and sexuality.

The feminist movement developed in two waves. The first wave, which began around 1900 and continued until the outbreak of World War II, was characterized by liberation from *ie,* the traditional household system. This wave involved reformers and suffragists who sought power for women in the private (domestic) sphere and recognition in the public sphere. The second wave began in the 1970s and continues today; it is characterized by challenges to the sexual division of labor and to the dichotomy between the public and private sphere and has expanded its goals to include

sexual liberation and greater diversity in theories, approaches, and disciplines. Feminism in Japan has been influenced by the West, particularly the United States, but western goals have often been adjusted or transformed in the Japanese context.

The First Wave of Feminism

Feminism as a modern discourse can be traced to the Meiji period (1868–1912), which followed a span of approximately 250 years when Japan was ruled by a a warrior government and secluded from the outside world. The Meiji government worked for modernization, establishing a capitalist system based on western models. Both the new imperial system and the earlier feudalistic family system were incorporated in the Meiji Constitution of 1889 and the Civil Code of 1898. *Ie,* in which men inherited all property and governed other family members, was institutionalized as the basic social unit: women were deprived of civil rights, and each woman was legally under the control of the head of her householded. Thus Japanese women were suppressed, and suffered from injustices, under a patriarchal social system based on Confucian ideology. Some male intellectuals spoke up in favor of educating women to be "good wives and wise mothers," and some women challenged convention and struggled for emancipation; but Japanese feminism dates specifically from the last quarter of the nineteenth century and the beginning of the twentieth century, when women who participated in the "popular rights" movement started to speak in their own voice and fight for their own causes.

Kishida Toshiko (1864–1901), a member of the "popular rights" movement, was the first woman to speak openly about women's rights and gender equality. She argued that the rights of the nation, its people, and women were indistinguishable. Her follower Kageyama (later Fukuda) Hideko (1865–1892) published Japan's first socialist women's magazine, *Sekai Fujin* (*Women in the World*) and started a women's social movement in 1907. Along with a liberal and socialist movement, early feminist activities included strikes by women factory workers and political agitation. Women's issues and the emerging labor movement were the impetus for female socialists to form associations. Women's demands in the "popular rights" movement are classified as domestic and socialist feminism because they were aimed at increasing women's power at home as wives and mothers and at improving their social status and securing their civil rights. The socialist feminists were hindered by a series of prohibitive laws, such as bans on assembly and public speech, from 1890 through 1900; but women continued to work for their causes in various ways, supported by humanitarianism, socialism, or Christianity. For instance, the Women's Christian Temperance Union of Japan submitted a written petition to the government urging revision of state regulation of women's political activities.

In 1911, the first liberal bourgeois feminist group, Seitosha ("Bluestocking Society"), was formed and began publishing a monthly journal, *Seito* (*Bluestocking*). This feminist literary magazine, written and edited solely by women, dealt with love, sexuality, marriage, divorce, abortion, and gender equality. Its manifesto, written by its founder, Huratsuka Raicho (1886–1971), appeared in the inaugural issue and called on women to discover their hidden power: "In ancient times, woman was the sun. An authentic person. Today, she is the moon. Living through others. We women have to regain our eclipsed sun." This issue also quoted Yosano Akiko's famous poem "When the Mountain Started Moving," which compares women to a dormant volcano about to erupt. Seitosha's emphasis on self-discipline and self-expression in gender politics, on giving a voice to middle-class women's aspirations, and on the "new woman" placed her at the center of the first wave of feminism. Its members were considered outrageous rebels because of their radicalism and their challenge to social mores, especially to conventional ideals of womanhood. Three issues of *Seito*, protesting against the family system and class hierarchies, were censored. Later, the women of Seitosha were sometimes romanticized, but they were also criticized by postwar feminists in the 1970s for having been bourgeois and not sufficiently political or radical.

Seito began to be regarded as militant a women's journal attacking the patriarchal family system and traditional sexist culture, and it became a focal point of public controversy. One of the most controversial issues concerned sexuality and reproduction. The first legal action of the Meiji government that restricted women's freedom was a prohibition of abortion in 1868. Harada Satsuki (1887–1933), a member of Seitosha, initiated a debate, proclaiming women's right to control their own reproduction and upholding choice with regard to abortion. Opposing her was Ito Noe (1895–1923), an anarchist who had been influenced by Emma Goldman and who celebrated women's right to reproduce.

Seito ceased publishing in 1917; the following year, however, various other magazines debated the issue of "protection of motherhood" and the related issue of state maternity benefits, as well as women's independence and "gender equality" of opportunities. The feminist poet Yosano Akiko, who had given birth to 13 children, initiated the debate over motherhood in 1918, when she rejected the idea that maternity warranted special protection from the state—she

argued, instead, that this was a private responsibility. She insisted on women's rights and women's economic independence, embracing individuality and gender equality. Hiratsuka criticized this position, arguing that women should be liberated as mothers and advocating maternal rights in the sense of state protection; she envisioned radical social reform—a communal world organized by the "female principle." Hiratsuka was influenced by the Swedish eugenicist Ellen Key, who believed in the biological superiority of women. Yamakawa Kikue (1890–1980) also joined this debate, taking a socialist feminist perspective; she criticized both Yosano and Hiratsuka, arguing that because housewives' work was unpaid, women's status was lowered and working-class women were underpaid; she sought a revolution in the economic system, based on anticapitalism, socialist ideology, and a classless society. She attacked the assumption of male superiority but also criticized female-centered pacifism as "bourgeois feminism" that ignored or actually encouraged class discrimination and racism. Yamakawa later joined the Sekirankai group, the first women's socialist organization, formed in 1921 to support working-class women.

In the 1930s, "maternalism" was taken up by Takamure Itsue (1894–1964), the pioneer historian of Japanese women. She challenged both Hiratsuka's ideal of "maternal protection" and Yosano's ideal of individual independence and reform of the state. Instead, she devoted herself to historical studies of a female-centered system that she recovered from prehistory. Takamure held that both capitalism and socialism overemphasized "productivity" within a modern male-centered national system; she denied that men were superior, objected to the state's power, and supported women's "reproductive power." Her theories eventually fell into essentialism—ironically, they implied the imperial system, which was characterized by maternalism. This controversy about motherhood has continued up to the turn of the twenty-first century, though with different emphases: in the 1950s it focused on the status of housewives and women's choice between motherhood and work; in the 1980s, on domestic work; in the 1990s, on working mothers.

Hiratsuka formed the New Women's Association, which took action from the position of maternal protection, in 1920, joining Ichikawa Fusae (1893–1981) and Oku Mumeo (b. 1895) to campaign for women's suffrage. Along with the cultural feminism of Seitosha, the women's suffrage movement began in the prewar period.

Ichikawa led the fight for women's suffrage by organizing the Woman's Suffrage League of Japan in 1924 (it was dissolved in 1940) and holding annual nationwide conferences on women's suffrage; her goal was not only to gain the vote as a political right, but also a commitment to world peace. However, the Fifteen-Year War began in 1931, and thereafter, under militarism, Ichikawa's group had difficulty organizing any political action. As the international crisis intensified, Ichikawa became involved in the government's war committees, although she strongly opposed Japan's withdrawal from the League of Nations in 1933. Not only Ichikawa but also Hiratsuka, Takamure, and others supported the Japanese effort in World War II, organizing patriotic associations such as the Society of Women for National Defense and helping to mobilize women for weapons factories and for domestic security. Emphasizing the responsibility of mothers to raise a superior race to serve the state, they believed that the new family-state ideology, which acknowledged women's roles outside the home, was a step toward women's transcendence of both the private and the public sphere. They also believed that Japan should save other Asian countries from western imperialism. This collaboration with fascism and with the national war mobilization terminated the suffrage movement and resulted in a decline of feminism.

Postwar Feminism

After the war, under the Allied Occupation Army (AOA), Japan began a political democratization that included gender equality. The constitution of 1947 gave women the right to vote and equal partnership in marriage; it also prohibited sex discrimination and dismantled the *ie* system. In the year when women voted for the first time, 39 women were elected to the Diet (the legislature).

It is worth noting that these women's rights had been given by the state rather than being won by women's struggle for them, and that the women activists who had supported the war did not take much responsibility for their part in the victimization of other Asian countries. The Mothers' Convention ran campaigns for peace and disarmament, presenting its members as victims who had lost loved ones; and the Housewives' Association lobbied successfully regarding such issues as pollution, waste management, price controls, and consumers' rights. These were conservative women's groups; the only women's group to take a feminist stance and seek gender equality was the Women's Democratic Club, formed with the aid of the AOA in 1946.

The Korean War in the 1950s and the expansion of the labor force in the 1960s helped Japan to reconstruct its state economy, and women started to enter the labor market. However, it was men who became "corporate warriors"; women tended to be full-time housewives or flexible workers, submitting to the sexual division of labor and even to sexual exploitation. Women's life cycle was in a sense subsumed by state policies and regulated by the system of lifetime employment with seniority, taxes and pensions based on the household unit, and a welfare format that assumed women's full participation. Nevertheless, some women were radicalized by the students' movement and by the New Left, campaigning against the Vietnam War and the Security Treaty between Japan and the United States.

"Woman Lib"

In November 1970, hundreds of women marched in the streets of Tokyo with banners proclaiming "Protesting Sexual Discrimination." This marked the beginning of the radical feminist movement, sometimes called "woman lib" or simply "lib." It was motivated in part by women's need for self-expression and in part by their disillusionment with their male comrades of the New Left, who continued to discriminate against women, treating them only as housekeepers or sexual objects and excluding them from decision making. Tanaka Mitsu, a charismatic radical feminist leader, expressed the collective concerns of women in powerful language: her manifesto was "Liberation from Toilets." She attacked heterosexism and proclaimed that "women learn that they are treated as a mother or toilet (whore), but essentially women are women, and they use their power over men" (Mizoguchi et al, 1992; Tanaka, 1972). She tried to represent women's ego, sexuality, and reproductivity through "women's logic," which, she held, was different from conventional male reasoning. This radical "lib" is considered an example of indigenous Japanese feminism, before the influence of feminism from the United Sates and Europe was felt.

The strategies of "lib," emphasizing consciousness as well as action, were (1) to focus on consciousness-raising regarding love, sex, housework, family, and power relationships in the private sphere; (2) to establish women's own identity and develop women's ego; (3) to recognize sexual politics and aim at sexual liberation; (4) to challenge cultural, psychological, and material oppression, seen as stemming from the formation of the modern family and from other forms of sexual discrimination in a male-centered society; (5) to "deconstruct" maternity; and (6) to produce a cultural revolution from the viewpoint of marginalized and oppressed groups, in order to change the patriarchal capitalistic apparatus. With regard to item 4, Tanaka argued that "we women exist for men as sexual objects, and for the state as instruments who, in the context of the *ie,* not only ensure childbearing but also indirectly serve the interests of capitalists by doing the unpaid work known as housework" (1992). "Lib" thinking about sexuality and women's identity was reflected in feminist pamphlets and journals such as *Onna Eros* (*Woman Eros*, 1992–1993).

In the 1970s, several "lib" action groups were formed: the Women's Liberation Study-Work Camp in 1971; the Shinjuku Women's Liberation Center in 1972; and the Tokyo Commune (a collective of women with children) in 1973. A controversial (and short-lived) "lib" group, Chupiren ("Pink Helmet Brigade"), demanded the legalization of oral contraceptives and was sensationalized in the mass media. Symbolically, at least, "lib" reached its peak with the issue of abortion law. In 1974, the government proposed to eliminate the economic reason for abortion in the Eugenic Protection Law, enacted in 1948 out of a need for abortion as a means of controlling the population, which had been greatly increased by the postwar baby boom. A nationwide campaign against the revision was organized by women's groups such as Fighting Women and National Meeting for the Prevention of the Revision of the Eugenic Protection Law. Not only did they succeed in retaining the economic reason for abortion; they also became an impetus for the radical women's movement.

"Lib" did not last very long; it was denigrated by the media and rejected by the majority of women. However, its radical feminist ideas were later explored by grassroots action-oriented frontline groups. The most prominent of these groups was the International Women's Year Action Group (1975–1996), which addressed discriminatory practices in employment, education, the media, and administration in order to transform social and legal institutions. The Asian Women's Association was formed in 1973 to protest against Japanese men's sex tours to other Asian countries; it was one of the few women's groups that focused on racial and ethical issues related to prostitution, trafficking in women, and migrant women workers. In 1995 it was developed into the Asian Women's Resource Center to work on broader issues in Asia, publishing journals such as *Women's Asia 21* (in Japanese) and *Voices from Japan* (in English).

The end of 1980s brought the political victory of women candidates ("Madonna Sensation") led by Doi Takako, the head the socialist party, who was later the first woman speaker of the lower house in the legislature. Diverse issue-oriented women's groups were formed as a result of an upsurge of the women's movement, a dramatic increase in women's participation in the paid workforce, the development of women's networks, and the influence of the mass media. New nongovernmental organizations (NGOs) such as Working Women's Network have focused on women's reproductive rights, child care, sexism in the media, feminist art, women's history, family law, and employment practices such as discriminatory wages.

Women's legal fight for economic independence was a factor in the enactment of the Equal Employment Opportunity Law (EEOL) in 1985, but this law had few measures addressing gender inequality in the workplace, at least in part because feminist groups had not presented a united front. In 1999, women's campaigns succeeded in having the law revised to include more provisions for enforcement, and articles prohibiting sexual harassment.

Women's Studies

Women's studies emerged in the mid-1970s as the second stage of the postwar women's movement. This was initiated by women who had started the earlier radical movement, women who had avoided the radical movement, and women who were influenced by western feminism. The term *women's studies* first appeared in 1974 as a translation from the English, implying women's education, actions, and research on and for women, with an emphasis on socioeconomic issues. Women's studies include on-campus programs, off-campus grassroots organizations, and government-sponsored programs.

Nationwide and local women's studies groups were organized in the late 1970s, including four major groups: International Group for Studies of Women, Women's Studies Association of Japan, Women's Studies Society of Japan, and Women's Study Group. They articulated feminist ideas and knowledge through workshops, symposiums, and books and periodicals such as *Yearly Report of the Women's Studies Society, Women's Studies Association Review,* and *Series of Women's Studies.* Their interdisciplinary research questioned every discipline and institution; it focused on patriarchy, housework, the modern family, motherhood, and sexism in language and media, seeking a female-centered pedagogy. One of their contributions in the 1980s was to conceptualize feminism as radical, liberal, socialist, Marxist, and ecological through debates and dialogues. A debate between Marxist feminism and ecofeminism was set off by Ivan Illich's gender theory. Ecofeminists criticized western capitalism and industrialization and celebrated maternity in premodern societies. Marxist feminists considered women's reproductive work in the context of capitalism and patriarchy; this contributed to the "housewife debate." The debate between materialist and "culturalist deconstructionist" feminists synthesized Marxist and radical feminism. Culturalists criticized Marxist feminism for reducing issues to economics and considering unpaid domestic labor on a material and class basis; they analyzed the power structure through discourse rooted in Japanese sexist traditions, which, they believe, persist in a contemporary pornographic, militaristic, postcolonial culture. The human rights debate asks whether feminism should deal with larger social and cultural structures, or only with women.

Government-sponsored off-campus women's studies programs are offered by women's bureaus and centers run by local governments to make them more acceptable to women in communities. Academic women and activists do research and lecture on local women's issues. The state-run National Women's Education Center (built in 1972) has offered seminars and research facilities and has conducted surveys of on- and off-campus women's studies. As of the year 2000, there were nearly 250 women's centers in metropolitan areas; this trend has publicized and legitimatized women's studies but has also made the field less radical.

Women's studies on campus have been aimed not only at educating students and conducting research but also at changing male-centered academia. A survey by the National Women's Education Center in 1996 found that nearly 30 percent of Japanese universities were offering at least one course in women' studies or gender studies. Dozens of universities have women's studies programs, but as of this writing only about 10 had a graduate degree program. As of 2000, state research grants became available in women's and gender studies, signifying that this field has been officially recognized as an academic discipline.

Globalization of Feminism

A third stage of Japanese feminism has been globalization: it is now crossnational and diverse, influenced by the United Nations, emerging international communties, and NGOs. The UN Decade for Women (1975–1985) and the UN women's conferences have urged governments to apply global standards in administering policies for women. Japan founded its Women's Bureau in 1975, began a Women's Action Program in 1977, and signed the Convention on the Elimination of All Forms of Discrimination Against Women (CEDAW) in 1985. To follow CEDAW's agenda, Japan had to revise its Naturalization Bill, enact EEOL, and make its educational system gender-balanced (for example, by adapting home economics courses for both sexes).

State-run policies for women, as standardized by the international community, have given the feminist movement access to government institutions and global strategies. For example, NGO forums held at UN conferences have given feminists a sense that their movement transcends borders and has common goals such as human rights,

employment rights, and the relief of poverty. Global networks of NGOs in Asia—such as the East Asian Women's Forum and Asian Pacific Women's Watch—have challenged not only sexism but also nationalism, imperialism, postcolonialism, and economic globalization by conducting discussions despite international political conflicts. Through such movements, Japanese women, as Asians, can confront their own economically privileged position, which victimizes other Asian women, and the common issues that unite them. Japanese women have also considered the domestic situation from a global perspective, to demythologize the homogeneity of Japanese culture and to work on internal issues of race, class, and ethnicity. In 1985, at the World Women's Conference in Nairobi, two Japanese women who were members of indigenous minorities—an Ainu and a buraku—said that race and ethnicity were more crucial to them than gender, although gender and race or ethnicity were often inseparable. Lesbianism, and diverse sexuality in general, emerged as a feminist issue at the Asian Lesbian Conference, held in Tokyo in 1992. Minority groups, who have been invisible "others" to many Japanese, have started to take action for their own causes.

The UN Human Rights Convention in 1993 and the Fourth UN Women's World Conference in Beijing in 1995 brought global attention to the "silenced" issue of violence against women—including domestic violence, sexual harassment, trafficking in women, sex tourism, "catalogue brides," forced domestic labor, migrant sex work, forced prostitution, and wartime sexual slavery (the use of so-called "comfort women"). Japanese human rights feminists see the use of "comfort women" as a universal form of violence against women, as sex discrimination, as a violation of women's human rights, and as related to other means of exploiting Asian women in the context of militarism, colonialism, capitalism, and Japanese patriarchy. One international NGO, Violence Against Women in War—Network Japan (VAWW-NET Japan), has organized a Women's International War Crimes Tribunal on Japan's Military Sexual Slavery (Tokyo, December 2000).

The state's "Gender-Equal Plan for the Year 2000" and "Japan NGO Alternative Report" (written by the Preparatory Committe in 1999) evaluate Japanese women's situation and suggest future policies. Responding to requests by NGOs and following the Beijing "Platform for Action," Japan enacted a Basic Law for a Gender-Equal Society in 1999—the first law for gender equality to include enforcement and to address gender-related issues such as an aging society and a decreasing birthrate. These state policies have legitimized feminist politics, but (like the state-run women's studies programs), they have tended to make the content of the feminist movement less radical.

In the 1990s, socioeconomic systems based on gender roles, subjugation of women, and commodification of women's sexuality had not been eliminated; despite women's political activism, these problems may have been insidiously worsened. A backlash against feminism was animated by conservatism and by the discourse of postfeminism in academia and the media. Postmodern scholars have tried to deconstruct gender differences, thus widening the gap between academia and activists. Nevertheless, there is still a strong movement to gain women's full independence, to extend women's global networks, and to transform gender-biased society—a movement that now involves highly developed feminist theories, new collective spaces for women, and new class, racial, and ethnic perspectives.

See Also

CONFUCIANISM; DEVELOPMENT: JAPAN; EDUCATION: EAST ASIA; FEMINISM: ASIAN AMERICAN; HOUSEHOLDS AND FAMILIES: EAST ASIA; IMPERIALISM; LIBERATION MOVEMENTS; POLITICS AND THE STATE: EAST ASIA; WOMEN'S STUDIES: EAST ASIA

References and Further Reading

AMPO-Japan Asia Quarterly Review, ed. 1996. *Voices from the Japanese women's movement.* New York: Sharpe.

Berstein, Gail Lee. 1991. *Re-creating Japanese women, 1600–1945.* Berkeley: University of California Press.

Buckley, Sandra. 1997. *Broken silence: Voices of Japanese feminism.* Berkeley: University of California Press.

Fujimura-Fanselow, Kumiko, and Atsuko Kameda. 1995. *Japanese women: New feminist perspectives on the past, present, and future.* New York: Feminist Press.

Inoue Teruko, Ueno Chizuko, Ebara Yumiko, and Amano Masako, eds. 1994. *Feminism in Japan.* 8 vols. Tokyo: Iwanami-shoten. (In Japanese.)

Kurihara, Ryoko. 1991. The Japanese woman suffrage movement. *Feminist Issues* (Fall): 81–100.

Mizoguchi Akiyo, Saeki Yoko, and Miki Soko, eds. 1992–1995. *Shiryo Nihon Uman Ribu Shi (History of Japanese Women's Lib in Documents).* 3 vols. Kyoto: Shokado. (In Japanese.)

Moore, Joe, ed. 1997. *The other Japan: Conflict, compromise, and resistance since 1945. The bulletin of concerned Asian scholars.* New York: Sharpe.

Ochiai, Emiko. 1994. *The Japanese family system in transition: A sociological analysis of family change in postwar Japan. LTCB International Library Foundation.* Tokyo: Simul.

Onna to Otoko no Jiku (Time Space of Women and Men) Editorial Board, ed. 1998. *Nenpyo: Onna to otoko no Nihonshi (Chronological table: Japanese history of women and men.* Toyko: Fujiwara-shoten. (In Japanese.)

Sievers, Sharon L. 1983. *Flowers in salt: The beginnings of feminist consciousness in modern Japan.* Stanford, Calif.: Stanford University Press.

Kazuko Watanabe

FEMINISM: Jewish

Jewish women—born of Jewish mothers or converted—are of all classes, nations, and "races"; are secular, Hasidic, Modern Orthodox, Conservative, Reform, Reconstructionist; and are diversely sexually oriented. They have been among feminism's most zealous pioneers in the United States, Israel, Canada, Australia, New Zealand, South Africa, Latin America, and Europe.

Is it good for the Jews? Jewish feminism reflects the fact that, everywhere but Israel, Jews are and have been a persecuted minority. Historically, toleration has ceded with regularity to turmoil, and most recently to the Shoah, which exterminated one-third of the Jewish people. Today, Jewish feminism, like Jewish lives, cannot be considered apart from the legacy of the Holocaust or the burden of Israeli–Palestinian relations. Even if open societies weaken appeals to corporatist sentiment, vulnerability to anti-Semitism continues, and feminists therefore balance collective obligations against efforts to increase women's individual human rights.

Two concepts inform this concern: *tikkun olam*, or repair of the world; and *tzedakah*, a concept combining charity with justice. As Fishman (1993: 48) observes of the United States: "Jewish women have absorbed feminist goals more fully than have other ethnic groups. They are more highly educated, work in higher status professions, are more sweepingly in favor of reproductive rights, and are more desirous of freedom and independence for their daughters than any other group. [Yet] the vast majority of American Jewish women remain committed to the ideals of marriage and family," structures to transmit the faith.

Israel

Secular issues: Alice Shalvi, former head of the Israel Women's Network (founded in 1984 and based in Jerusalem), holds that gender relations have been affected by Israel's fear of attack, mired in a Jewish sense of the living past. Shulamith Aloni, former minister of education and founder of the Citizens' Rights Movement (1973), concurs, deploring Israeli society's pervasive macho orientation, an aberration in Jewish history. Although Judaism as a creed elevates males, gender relations, at least in the *shtetl*, reflected the ideal of a male scholar's physical meekness and a female wage earner's strength. Aviva Cantor 1995 calls Judaism's sex-role assignment "reformed patriarchy." But militarization changed masculinity's definition, and, although the peace process may modify it once more, discrimination against women in the armed forces—two years of service to men's three, exemption for the Orthodox and for motherhood, restriction to noncombat jobs—has disempowered females in civil society as well, where an old boys' network influences political and managerial personnel choices. Excluded from public status, Israeli women find that security considerations complicate primary issues. For instance, consider abortion reform: pronatalism implies that Jewish women have a patriotic duty to replace the 1.5 million children killed by the Nazis. Battered women's shelters face similar opposition: whereas founders hoped to release the assaulted from marital bondage, the state tried to impose counseling to shore up dying unions, as women's defection from gender-differentiated roles is thought to endanger the covenant.

Nonetheless, Israel's progressive labor legislation includes three months of paid maternity leave (with nine months unpaid), nursing breaks, and subsidized day care. In 1979, the Prime Minister's Commission for the Advancement of Women published the Namir Report, and a women's issues committee formed by female members of the Knesset aims to increase women's political and financial power, strengthen men's family responsibility, and push for harsher punishments for domestic violence and rape.

Although the *chalutzot* (female pioneers) in the era before statehood allegedly served as egalitarian models—never as successful, however, as the myth suggests (see Swirski and Safir, 1993)—feminists organized again in the early 1970s. As the first book on the women's movement in Hebrew appeared—*Shichrun Ha'isha* (*Women's Liberation*) by Tchya Bat Oren—Marilyn Safir, Marcia Freedman, and others formed consciousness-raising circles in Haifa, Jerusalem, and Tel Aviv, and for many years the movement remained a network of modest issue-oriented groups criticized by some as representative of middle class Ashkenazi women and neglectful of working-class, Mizrahi concerns (see Pnina Motzafi-Haller, 1999). Yet 1998 witnessed the founding of national organizations such as the Israel Association of Feminist and Gender Studies with its E-mail list, Israel Feminist Forum (iff-l@research.haifa.ac.il). A generous grant from the Ford Foundation to five Israeli universities promises future expansion of women's studies, a response to the demand that it practice affirmative action in its own ranks.

Also in 1998, WADL-LENA (Women Against Discrimination League, or Ligat Nashim Negid Haflaya) was formed to oppose the Knesset's transfer of jurisdiction over divorce from family to rabbinic courts. Communication on such issues is ensured by *NOGA,* the world's only Hebrew feminist magazine, and *NASHIM: A Journal of Jewish Women's Studies and Gender Issues,* launched in 1998. A short-lived women's party, Mifleget Hanashim, active in 1977, has also been succeeded by Yitzug Shaveh, formed by veteran feminist activists in February 1999 to support women's campaigns for the Knesset, though minority representation remains problematic.

Issues of exclusion within Israeli feminism have been addressed by Mizrahi women organized in Hila and holding their first (separate) conference in 1996; and also by the peace movement and Isha L'Isha, the Haifa Feminist Center, which houses New Initiatives by Women, including the Haifa Women's Coalition (Rape Crisis Center, Isha L'Isha-Haifa Feminist Center, and Haifa Battered Women's Hotline), with sister nonprofit groups in Tel Aviv, Kiryat Shemona, Jerusalem, and Nazareth. Bridging differences among women due to class, national origin, language, and religion are empowerment circles for Mizrahi-Sefardi, Arab, Russian, and Ethiopian women, and single parents; and the "Army project," to train military personnel in gender sensitivity. The center's outreach program supporting Arab women's groups has achieved stunning success with its Arabic newsletter addressing victims of sexual violence, also a concern of the Women's Health and Court Watch Projects. At issue is government's leniency toward Palestinians who have killed for the sake of "family honor." Treating these criminals with the "respect" due to Arab "culture and tradition," Israeli patriarchy exploits male solidarity to tighten political control.

Naomi Graetz (1998) has reported that domestic violence, seemingly glossed over in Talmudic and Halachic passages, has also increased with the Intifada, whose influence on the movement has been considerable. Although feminists had opposed government intransigence before, 1989 witnessed the Women Go for Peace conference in Jerusalem, sponsored by the Israeli Women's Peace Movement, an umbrella for six organizations including both Jews and Palestinians. The plenary alone attracted 1,400, presaging the high profile of Women in Black, holding Friday vigils on well-traveled roads in Israel's major cities, supported by Four Mothers and Bat Shalom, a feminist peace organization which, together with Palestinians' Jerusalem Center for Women, forms the Jerusalem Link (http://www.batshalom.org). Similar vigils are now held on the last Thursday of each month by Kol Ha-Isha (kolisha@netmedia.net.il; kolisha@nedmedia.net.il); and the Israel Women's Network to commemorate women murdered during the preceding thiry days. Also at issue is trafficking, brought to public notice in May 2000 by an Amnesty International report severely criticizing the Israeli authorities' refusal to take responsibility for these human rights violations affecting between 8,000 and 10,000 women in Israel. Ironically, in 1927 Bertha Pappenheim, founder of the Jüdischer Frauenbund, or German Jewish women's movement, published *Sisyphus-Arbeit* on this very topic.

Religious issues. Nonetheless, where things seem to stay the same they also change. Blu Greenberg, president of the Jewish Orthodox Feminist Alliance, writes, "Who would have imagined 30 years ago Orthodox women studying and teaching Talmud in places like Drisha or Midreshet Lindenbaum? Who would have believed that women would serve on Israeli religious councils, or as congregational interns in Orthodox shuls?" (2000:1).

Calls for reforms in religious authorities' treatment of women continue to sound. Allied with the Labor Party at Israel's birth, the Orthodox Likud insisted that only Halachah (Jewish law) govern personal status. At least three problems for women follow. First, only males can issue a certificate of divorce (a get), this causes enormous suffering as unscrupulous husbands extort custody, money, or release from alimony before granting the coveted document without which religious women cannot remarry or have "legitimate" children permitted to marry other Jews. According to Cantor (1995), wresting this power from the rabbinical courts has known the least success of 20 years of feminist efforts. Estimated at about 10,000 in Israel, the agunot suffer so much that Rivka Haut, founder of Women's Tefillah Network, uses the term "get wars." ICAR, the International Coalition for Agunot Rights, a group of 11 Israeli women's organizations, rallied behind former minister Aloni's endorsement of the separation of synagogue and state, a precondition for improving women's status.

Yet success has met the second challenge to religious law. During the first International Jewish Feminist Conference in Jerusalem in 1988, women who tried to pray at the Western (Wailing) Wall were pelted with stones, insults, and worse, so they sued. On 22 May 2000, in a 26-page decision, the Israeli supreme court unanimously upheld the right of Women of the Wall (WoW), to daven at the Kotel with a Torah and tallit and mandated police protection, needed despite the relatively conservative nature of WoW's demands, "specifically seeking separate but equal access to the Kotel [as a] women-only, non-minyan, halachic, interdenominational prayer group . . . not asking to be integrated with men, or to abolish the mehitza, or to pray from an egalitarian siddur" (Phyllis Chesler and Rivka Haut, 22 May 2000, Email).

Third is the lesbian challenge. Active all along, lesbians (and gays) did not stage their Stonewall until 1992, as detailed in *Lesbiot: Israeli Lesbians Talk about Sexuality, Feminism, Judaism, and Their Lives* (Moore, 1995). Denial of research funds to a closeted gay professor induced him to come out to the entire country. This, and a television interview in 1992 with a lesbian couple, cleared the way for numerous gay pride events in 1994. The Community of Feminist Lesbians in Israel (www.aguanet.co.it/vip/klaf; http:// www.aguanet.co.it/vip/klaf) continues to oppose abridgement of rights.

One more provocation to the religious establishment can be felt in an Orthodox women's movement which, according to Deborah Greniman (28 March 2000, email) "has become quite strong. A first major conference, held in Jerusalem in the summer of 1999, drew hundreds of women. In Israel, it is largely an outgrowth of the tremendous upsurge of participation in Jewish studies for (and also about) women. This is now leading in two directions: efforts to increase women's participation in Jewish ritual; and attempts to rectify the status of women in rabbinic courts." In one historic step, certified Orthodox women will now be able to make halachic (legal) decisions on certain issues. Realizing that many Jewish women would prefer to consult a woman on personal issues, Nishmat Center for Women's Studies (Jerusalem) launched a program to train Orthodox women as halachic consultants. At the time of this writing, the first eight were set to rule on a number of issues, including ovulation, fertility, and miscarriage (*Jewish Week* at www.thejewish.com).

The United States

It is possible that the feminist movement, launched by U.S. women, remains relatively small in Israel because it is foreign and therefore suspect. Nonetheless, U.S./Israel Women to Women, an American organization, has been a supporter of Israeli feminist causes since 1978, helping to fund battered women's shelters, rape crisis centers, health programs, and legal counseling (www.USIsraelWomen.org or JewelB44 @aol.com.)

Part of the largest Jewish population in the world, U.S. feminists began focusing on Halachic issues such as exclusion from ritual; this led in 1971 to the proliferation of Havurot (egalitarian prayer and study groups). One of these became Ezrat Nashim, a small organization founded by Paula Hyman (1995) committed to women's equality in Judaism. Fishman (1993) chronicles other debut efforts. The North American Jewish Students' network sponsored the first national feminist conference in 1973, followed in 1974 by a second on Jewish Women and Men, out of which the short-lived Jewish Feminist Organization arose. The New York Jewish Women's

Center, active from 1975 to 1977, succeeded it. Remaining to this day is the magazine *Lilith* (founded 1976; www. lilith.org) whose editor, Susan Weidman Schneider, compiled the *Jewish Women's Networking Directory* in 1984. Up-to-date information is available from Ma'yan: The Jewish Women's Project (Barbmayan@aol.com), a national organization in New York City acting to create an environment more inclusive of and reponsive to women, with networking also encouraged by Jewish Women Leaders Online (rhondaesq@aol.com, gbdi-aspora@aol.com, or jwlegroups@ aol.com). This project of the Jewish Women's Coalition, Inc., attracts social justice activists working on issues significant to Jewish women (and men).

Secular issues: Prominent among Jewish feminist aims is a broad quest for foremothers. Diane Lichtenstein (1992) has uncovered a tradition of U.S. Jewish women writers in the nineteenth century. Sylvia Barack Fishman (1995) reviews the field of American Jewish fiction for its female images. Ann R. Shapiro (1994) has orchestrated an impressive reference work on Jewish American women writers; the entries and contributors read like a who's who of American Jewish feminist critics and literati. Paula Hyman and Deborah Dash Moore's monumental reference work *Jewish Women in America: An Historical Encyclopedia* was published in 1997.

Special concern envelops women in the Holocaust, differentiating by gender the experience in extremis. Marlene Heinemann (1986) claims that neglecting the specificity of women's treatment by the Nazis distorts the understanding of the period as a whole. Sharing this gynocritical approach is Joan Ringelheim (1993), who, however, while viewing the Shoah through the lens of gender, puts in the foreground the murderous hostility faced by both sexes, as does Cynthia Ozick. Nonetheless, analysis of women's different victimization continues in the more recent scholarship of Marion Kaplan (1998), S. Lillian Kremer (1999), and Dalia Ofer and Leonore J. Weitzman (1998).

When women are the object of anti-Semitism and Jewish self-hatred, they clearly experience gender-specific torments. In particular, the Jewish mother has been stereotyped as overbearing and invasive, and her daughter—the JAP (Jewish American princess)—as materialistic, frigid, exploitative, and pushy. Coined by (self-hating) Jewish men in part as an assimilation strategy, the term *JAP* has become an ethnic slur.

Anti-Semitism in the U.S. women's movement has been denounced by Evelyn Torton Beck (1983), Letty Cottin Pogrebin (1991), and others. For instance, Susannah Heschel (1982) criticizes a strand in both U.S. and German women's discourse that blames Jews for patriarchy and for dismissal of the Goddess. Beck's argument that "Jewish invisibility is a symptom of anti-Semitism as surely as lesbian invisibility is a symptom of homophobia" (xvii) has encouraged Jews in the women's movement to claim their ethnicity, although Joyce Antler (1997), in *The Journey Home: Jewish Women and the American Century,* seems to be among the few pointing out how significant Jewish women's influence has been in popular culture as a whole, with Jews in the vanguard on numerous issues such as birth control, trade unionism, higher education, and race relations, as well as feminism.

Religious issues. In the United States, Reform and Reconstructionists responded to feminists' demands with seeming ease, as Sally Preisand, the first female rabbi in the United States, ascended to the bima (podium) in 1972; the Conservative Rabbinate opened to women in 1983. The mehitzah (curtain) still divides the Orthodox, although even here change is occurring. Optimistically, Susannah Heschel (1983) envisions a "Copernican revolution: a new theology . . . requiring new understandings of God, revelation, halakhah, and the Jewish people in order to support and encourage change" (xxiii). In both Israel and the United States, Orthodox and Conservative women are improving women's Jewish education, reading the Talmud (Gemara and Mishnah) and the works of Jewish mysticism, Kaballah. It is generally felt that women who are learned in the law can make a more convincing case.

Contested are those Halachic issues pertaining to the female body and marital-sexual relations. Jewish jurisprudence permits only heterosexual contact within marriage. Interestingly, men, but not women, are commanded to marry, have children, and initiate coitus at stipulated intervals depending on their profession (once a week for scholars, twice for laborers, etc.); this command recognizes women's right to sexual pleasure—that is, heterosexual pleasure. Both sexes are involved in niddah—that is, abstinence for five days of menstrual bleeding followed by seven free of blood. This abstinence closes with the woman's submersion in the mikvah (a pool of fresh, circulating water). Subsequently, men desiring relations are forbidden to take their wives by force—a prohibition against marital rape—but are advised to sweet-talk them into the mood.

How have females dealt with these rules? Traditionally, the terms *pure* and *impure* have been applied, implying pollution during menstruation. Blu Greenberg (5742/1981) suggests erasing the connotations of defilement that niddah and mikvah evoke by emphasizing "the holiness of sex itself" (120), thereby concentrating on the ritual as preparation for entering into a more blissful state, like ceremonial accession to Sabbath peace. Exemplifying the growing attraction of Orthodoxy for many women, recorded by Lynn Davidman

(1991) and Debra Renee Kaufman (1991), who see in these observances an elevation of women and a spur to solidarity, Greenberg suggests "grafting" contemporary needs onto niddah, for instance, by tying it to monthly breast examination and routine Pap smears (120–121).

A second area of ritual concern is gendered language regarding the deity. Judith Plaskow (1990) argues for new ceremonies, such as Rosh Chodesh (to welcome the new moon, traditionally women's respite from the daily grind); Susan Weidman Schneider (1984) lists rituals for conceiving, giving birth, honoring daughters, weaning, puberty, and menstruation; others have proposed a comforting structure for miscarriage; and still others—such as Esther Bruner (1993)—call for revisions of the Passover Haggadah and for a female-inclusive liturgy.

Lesbians, too, in a culture so attached to heterosexual families, challenge both secular and liturgical thinking. Rachel Biale (1984) observes that "the only two references to lesbianism in the Talmud . . . agree that [it] does not constitute even an act of promiscuity." Merely "licentiousness," in the absence of any explicit any biblical prohibition and of intercourse, love between women is no "sexual transgression" (195). Moses Maimonides, however, read into lesbianism rebelliousness and disapproved of it. Celebrating this dissent is Evelyn Torton Beck in *Nice Jewish Girls: A Lesbian Anthology* (1982, 1989), followed by *The Tribe of Dina: A Jewish Women's Anthology* (1986), a special issue of *Sinister Wisdom* edited by Melanie Kaye-Kantrowitz and Irena Klepfisz, which further elevates the Jewish lesbian's profile.

Jewish women, like other minority women, clearly share the need to navigate among various identities: in this case, Jew, woman, citizen, and so on. Immense diversity within any Jewish group affects theory and tactics. *Bridges: A Magazine for Jewish Feminists and Our Friends* (biannual, founded 1989) thrives on distinctions in language, publishing in Hebrew, Yiddish, Ladino, and English; in national origins; and in economic status, giving voice to a sizable number of Jews who were or remain working-class.

Nonetheless, it is prosperity, Pogrebin claims (1991), that threatens survival of U.S. Jews as Jews. Consider the North American intermarriage rate, now surpassing 50 percent. While doubting that the United States is exceptional, Aviva Cantor (1995) recognizes an "assimilationist contract," defined as the perceived promise of safety in exchange for invisibility, which, she contends, weakens the Jewish community from within. U.S. Jewish feminists, therefore, as women who, by definition, care about a Jewish future, measure their priorities against a yardstick of ethnic survival but claim with equal vehemence that only an egalitarian Judaism will survive.

Germany and Worldwide

In *Jewish Life and Jewish Women in Germany Today* (1999), Tobe Levin (the present author) and Susanna Keval describe women as agents in the German variant of Jewish renewal. Contemporary reform activity, given a postwar impetus only in the early 1990s, has written on its banner full participation of women in synagogue life, increased relevance for Sabbath sermons, and a liturgy in German in addition to Hebrew. With its organization of egalitarian services, launched in 1994, the reform Kehillah Chadaschah in Frankfurt includes women in minyanim, integrates male and female seating, and supports women's leadership. Bea Wyler, the first postwar female rabbi in Germany, arrived in 1995 and at the time of this writing was leading communities in Oldenburg and Braunschweig. Reform groups have arisen in other cities, too, and the more than 100 individuals who attended a symposium at the Evangelische Akademie Arnoldshain an April 1997 augur well for the Reform Movement and its drive for women's egalitarian inclusion.

A revival of Jewish women's religious practice in Europe generally became evident at a Bet Devora conference for women rabbis, cantors, scholars, and all spiritually interested Jewish women and men in Berlin in May 1999. More than 150 mainly female participants answered an invitation which stated, without equivocation. "Women are standing together with men, on an egalitarian basis, on the Bima," for, "increasingly, women are exercising important ritual functions" as rabbis. The colloquium asked, "What does this mean for Jewish tradition and continuity?" Answering was the entire elite of European Jewish women's studies.

Meanwhile, activists engaged in various projects as Jews can be found in the Women's International Zionist Organization and its junior variant. Frankfurt alone has 500 members in WIZO and WIZO-Aviv who raise funds for numerous women's centers, educational institutions and hospitals in Israel. Measured against Marion Kaplan's vibrant histories of the Jewish Women's Movement (Jüdischer Frauenbund, JFB) from its inception in 1904 to its dissolution in 1938, current efforts of German Jewish women pale. The Jüdischer Frauenbund, however, has been revived, with groups in thirteen German cities and more in formation. Although the feminist aims of Bertha Pappenheim's association have not been revived, the JFB takes pride in its social services and annual symposiums. In 1997, 80 women from 19 towns discussed "Women in a History of Change" for four days at the kosher hotel Eden Park in Bad Kissingen. Among the speakers was Lea Rabin.

As welcome as participation in the new JFB is, Jewish women also appear in the broader German women's movement. For instance, the Schabbeskreis (Sabbath Circle) a group of Jewish and non-Jewish women, met Friday evenings in Berlin from 1984 to 1989 to discuss anti-Semitism in the women's movement and Jewish women in history. In 1995, Yachad—Vereinigung von Jüdischen Lesben und Schwulen (Together—Union of Jewish Lesbians and Gays) coalesced, and it presently has about eighty members, publishes a newsletter, and hosts two libertarian minyans with a female majority. Its first service in the Jewish Community Center on Fasanenstrasse in Berlin's attracted 200 people. Clearly, the postwar generation of Jews, male and female, is creating alternative institutions, including a Rosh Chodesh group meeting regularly in Berlin.

Conferences on Jewish women have included a major symposium on literature and the arts held in Essen in 1990, whose proceedings, published as *Jüdische Kultur und Weiblichkeit in der Moderne* (*Jewish Culture and Femininity in Modernism*, 1994), identifies the avant-garde in German Jewish women's studies. In 1992, a series of colloquia on "Jewish Women's Influence in Europe" attracted hundreds to Berlin. In 1997, a group called the International Working Group of Migrant, Black, and Jewish Women for Research in German-language Literature held its founding conference in Cologne, titled "Marginal Breaks—Cultural Production of Migrant, Black, and Jewish Women in Germany."

In Canada, the first collection of Jewish feminist writing was published by *Fireweed: A Feminist Quarterly* in 1992, and Toronto also hosts a significant collection of reference materials on various aspects of Jewish women, literature, and feminism (at http://www.utoronot.c/wjudaism/vın1form.htm).

Women in Judaism: A Multidisciplinary Journal, founded in 1997, the first refereed periodical solely dedicated to gender-related issues in Judaism, is available exclusively on the Internet (at http://www.utoronto.ca/wjudaism.)

The United Kingdom, having produced *Shifra,* a Jewish women's magazine, in the mid-1980s, gave birth in 1993 to the Jewish Women's Network, including all persuasions, from secular to ultra-Orthodox. It aims to promote Jewish dialogue, encourage dissenting views, improve the status and participation of Jewish women across the spectrum, and offer learning opportunities. The working committee has already run successful workshops; the group publishes a newsletter. The Association of Women against Fundamentalism unites Jews with other minority women.

In France, increased attention to anti-Semitism reveals Jewish women as victims of, but also resistors against, racist oppression. The first feminist conference at the University of Paris, in 1992, "Feminismes et Nazisme," organized by Liliane Kandel, inaugurated this strand of inquiry in that nation.

To enjoy the many contributions of Jewish women to feminism, and of feminism to Judaism, in Italy, Latin America, Iran, the former Yugoslavia, South Africa, Mexico, Lithuania, Argentina, Chile, Hungary, and Latvia, as well as Israel, Germany, France, the United Kingdom, Canada, and the United States, see Helen Epstein (1999). Because of its promise of renewal from within, feminism is good for the Jews.

See Also

ETHNICITY; FAMILY: RELIGIOUS AND LEGAL SYSTEMS—JUDAIC TRADITIONS; JUDAISM; PEACE MOVEMENTS: ISRAEL

References and Further Reading

Antler, Joyce. 1997. *The journey home: Jewish women and the American century.* New York: Free Press.
Beck, Evelyn Torton. 1989. *Nice Jewish girls: A lesbian anthology.* Boston: Beacon.
Biale, Rachel. 1984. *Women and Jewish law: An exploration of women's issues in Halakhic sources.* New York: Schocken.
Broner, E. M. 1993. *The telling: The story of a group of Jewish women who journey to spirituality through community and ceremony. Including The women's Haggadah by E.M. Broner with Naomi Nimrod.* San Francisco: HarperCollins.
Cantor, Aviva. 1995. *Jewish women, Jewish men: The legacy of patriarchy in Jewish life.* San Francisco: HarperCollins.
Davidman, Lynn. 1991. *Tradition in a rootless world: Women turn to Orthodox Judaism.* Berkeley: University of California Press.
Epstein, Helen, ed. 1999. *Jewish women 2000. Conference papers from the HRIJW International Scholarly Exchanges 1997-1998.* Working Paper 6. Waltham: Brandeis.
Fireweed: A Feminist Quarterly. 1992. Issue 35: Jewish women. Toronto, Canada.
Fishman, Sylvia Barack. 1993. *A breath of life: Feminism in the American Jewish community.* New York: Free Press.
———. 1995. *Follow my footprints: Changing images of women in American Jewish fiction.* Hanover, N.H.: University Press of New England.
Graetz, Naomi. 1998. *Silence is deadly: Judaism confronts wife-beating.* Northvale, N.J.: Jason Aaronson.
Greenberg. Blu. 1981. *On women and Judaism: A view from tradition.* Philadelphia, Pa.: Jewish Publication Society of America.
———. 2000 Orthodox feminism and the next century. *Shma,* 1-2 (Sh'vat/January). www.shma.com.
Heinemann, Marlene. 1986. *Gender and destiny: Women writers and the Holocaust.* Westport, Conn.: Greenwood.
Heschel, Susannah, ed. 1983. *On being a Jewish feminist: A reader.* New York: Schocken.

Hyman, Paula E., and Deborah Dash Moore. 1997. *Jewish women in America. An historical encyclopedia.* 2 vols. New York: Routledge.

Izraeli, Dafna N., et al. 1999. *Min migdar politica [Sex gender politics: Women in Israel].* Tel Aviv: Kibbutz Ha'meuchad.

Kaplan, Marion. 1979. *The Jewish feminist movement in Germany: The campaigns of the Jüdischer Frauenbund, 1904-1938.* Westport, Conn: Greenwood.

Kaufman, Debra Renee. 1991. *Rachel's daughters. Newly Orthodox Jewish women.* New Brunswick, N.J.: Rutgers University Press.

Kaye-Kantrowitz, Melanie, and Irena Klepfisz, eds. 1986. *The tribe of Dina: A Jewish women's anthology.* Montpelier, Vt.: Sinister Wisdom.

Kremer, S. Lillian. 1999. *Women's Holocaust writing: Memory and imagination.* Lincoln: University of Nebraska Press.

Levin, Tobe, and Susanna Keval. 2000. Jewish Life and Jewish Women in Germany today. In Helen Epstein, ed., *Jewish Women 2000, Conference Papers from the HRIJW International Scholarly Exchanges 1997–1998.* Working Paper 6, 203–231. Waltham: Brandeis.

Lichtenstein, Diane. 1992. *Writing their nations: The tradition of nineteenth-century American Jewish women writers.* Bloomington: Indiana University Press.

Moore, Tracy, ed. 1995. *Lesbiot: Isareli lesbians talk about sexuality, feminism, Judaism, and their lives.* London: Cassell.

Motzafi-Haller, Pnina. 1999. Mizrahi Women in Israel: The Double Erasure. In Helen Epstein, ed., *Jewish Women 2000, Conference Papers from the HRIJW International Scholarly Exchanges 1997-1998.* Working Paper 6, 70–96. Waltham: Brandeis.

Plaskow, Judith. 1990. *Standing again at Sinai: Judaism from a feminist perspective.* New York: HarperCollins.

Pogrebin, Letty Cottin. 1991. *Deborah, Golda, and me: Being female and Jewish in America.* New York: Crown.

Ofer, Dalia, and Leonore J. Weitzman, eds. 1998. *Women in the Holocaust.* New Haven, Conn.: Yale University Press.

Ringelheim, Joan. 1993. Women and the Holocaust: A reconsideration of research. In C. Rittner and J. Roth, eds., *Different voices: Women and the Holocaust.* New York: Paragon.

Schneider, Susan Weidman. 1984. *Jewish and female: Choices and changes in our lives today.* New York: Simon and Schuster.

Shapiro, Ann R., ed. 1994. *Jewish American women writers: A bio-bibliographical and critical sourcebook.* Westport, Conn.: Greenwood.

Stephan, Inge, Sabine Schilling, and Sigrid Weigel, eds. 1994. *Jüdische Kultur und Weiblichkeit in der Moderne.* Cologne: Buhlau.

Swirki, Barabara, and Marilyn P. Safir, eds. 1993. *Calling the equality bluff: Women in Israel.* New York: Teachers College Press.

Tobe Levin

FEMINISM: Korea

In the last 100 years, feminism in Korea has developed in two ways: one by fighting against institutionalized and culturalized patriarchy, and the other by feminists becoming a part of movements for broad social change at the national and international level. The ideological and strategical differences and conflicts between these two streams of feminism in united Korea (1900–1945) and South Korea (1945–2000) reflect a problem that many feminists have faced throughout the developing world. On the one hand, feminists have been torn between the two aspects of western feminism, which has a seemingly dual character, both liberational and imperialistic. On the other hand, Koreans and other activists in the developing world have sought to mobilize women's own gendered power and interests while simultaneously recognizing the urgency of the national independence movement, the socialist movement, the democratic movement, and the labor movement.

Korean Feminism before and during Colonization

Korean society's own patriarchy, fostered and enforced by the 500-year-old feudalistic Chosun dynasty (1392–1910), met its first major challenge in the early twentieth century in the form of western imperial modernity. From the end of nineteenth century and the early twentieth century, however, Korea experienced imperialism in not just one but two forms: the collapse of traditional feudal ideology in the face of western imperial modernity, and in 1910 the loss of land and independence in a Japanese imperialist invasion. The largely favorable view of western religion in Korea is one product of this historical sequence. In the conflict between modernity and tradition during the period from the 1880s to the 1910s, women's status was identified by many Koreans as the decisive feature that distinguished an oppressive traditional culture from an emancipatory modern culture. Early marriage, concubinage, and the prohibition of women's remarriage, in particular, became targets of the modernizing male intellectuals' criticism of Confucian patriarchy. During these years of political debate, Christianity in particular planted a seed of feminism, because some Korean women found a liberating discourse within it: men and women were equal under God. Also, Christianity—especially Protestant missions—played a key role in the rapid expansion of women's education, creating a pool of emergent Korean feminists. Some male intellectuals and upper-class women emphasized women's education, because they believed that enlightening Korea's women was crucial in building a strong national power base that could stave off the Korean nation's collapse at the hands of Japanese colonizers (Hyojae Yi, 1996). Many women across class and status boundaries participated in a broad nationalistic movement, Compensation for National Debt (1907), on the eve of formal colonization by Japan, and in what became known as the May First national independence movement (1919), the largest resistance movement against Japanese colonial government.

Yet not all Korean women activists were subsumed by nationalism. The early 1920s saw the emergence of the "New Women's Movement." The priority of this movement was to challenge the moral system of Korea's Confucian patriarchy. Korean feminists active in the New Women's Movement used a new self-identity that they crafted through modern education in Korean and journeys to and studies in Japan and Europe to demand radical reforms in Korean social and cultural practices, such as free love (love between men and women regardless of marriage), free marriage, and the destruction of the dominant Korean ideology of feminine chastity. The male contemporaries of these women, however, began to revalue patriarchy as a tool to unite colonized people, and they criticized the New Women's radical practices. They also claimed that feminist ideas were a mere imitation of imperialistic power and a degradation of the Korea's traditional culture. Ultimately, representative New Women activists were ostracized by society, and many died under miserable conditions.

In the years from 1920 to the early 1930s, there were two other groups of feminists. The first group was made up of Marxist and socialist feminists, who saw women's liberation as having to be sought through the liberation of peasants and urban workers. The second group was made up of nationalist feminists, many of whom were also Christian reformists. These feminists emphasized women's education and liberation as necessary for all Koreans' achievement of independence from Japanese colonizers. In 1927, the leftist feminists and nationalist feminists created a coalition of women's organizations, Kunwuhoe. Kunwuhoe is one of the most important women's organizations in Korean women's history in terms of its scale, ideology,

and activities. With 10,000 members organized into 64 branches, Kunwuhoe aimed to unite women in solidarity and to raise their consciousness in order to recover independence from the Japanese colonizers. However, the conflicts between the feminist nationalists and the leftist feminists, mainly due to the leftist feminists' strategically prioritizing the cultivation of peasants and workers' power, led to the dissolution of Kunwuhoe in 1931. After the onset of World War II, the feminist movement and feminism were stifled by Japanese oppression (Women's History Team, 1992).

Korean Feminism in the Divided Nation

Since its liberation from Japan in 1945, Korea has been divided into two states: South Korea and North Korea. During the years just after the liberation, the U.S. military ruled the south and the military from the Soviet Union ruled the north. In North Korea, with the support of the Soviet Union, the local Korean Communist regime undertook land reforms and advocated women's liberation, albeit in a limited version. In South Korea, the most active strand of the postwar women's movement inherited the traditions of the Marxist and socialist feminist movement created during the period of Japanese occupation. This women's movement promised that women's liberation would be gained through class and national liberation. Millions of South Korean women workers and peasants organized and engaged in class and national struggles in the late 1940s (Seunghi Yi, 1994).

The outbreak of the Korean War (1950–1953) undermined this strong tradition of leftist feminism in South Korea. Many feminists died during the war, and most of the leftist feminists went to North Korea. In North Korea, the increasingly authoritarian state's patriarchal control over women and the urgency of anti-Americanism and national unification continued to prevent North Korean feminists from developing their own agendas and voices, up to the beginning of the twenty-first century.

After the Korean War, the remaining women's group in the women's movement in South Korea was a conservative Christian group made up of the former nationalist feminists who eventually had collaborated with Japanese imperialists before and during World War II. In the years following independence from Japan, they had persisted in articulating what had become in the early 1940s a right-wing, anticommunist, privileged line of thought. Thus, they supported the pro-American government before the Korean War. Until the middle of the 1980s, some of these conservative women became token representatives of women's participation in party politics and women's political voice. In practice, though, their scope of concern was quite narrow. Although they spoke in the role of housewives for consumer rights, for example, they simultaneously supported masculinist militarist regimes of the cold war, which dominated South Korea public life from 1961 to 1992.

In South Korea in the 1970s, the dormant tradition of leftist feminists was reawakened through the newly emergent women's labor movement. The Korean "economic miracle" of the 1970s was the outcome of extremely low wages, long working hours, sexual harassment, exhaustion, and heartbreaking abuse of young women workers in factories. To first identify and then overcome these terrible conditions, many female factory workers joined new democratic labor unions and fought bravely. Female workers' courageous public protests became a sensitive political issue because the military regime under President Park Chung Hee tightly controlled and manipulated the labor movement, and it had adopted a belief that the success of the regime's economy required a brutal oppression of industrial workers. In 1979, a sit-down demonstration organized by the Y. H. trade union, one of female democratic labor unions, over the issue of the dissolution of the Y. H. Company, caused the collapse of Park's regime. The succeeding military regime, led by President Chun Doohwan, then poured more fuel on the fire by gunning down pro-democracy demonstrators in what is now known as the Kwangju massacre of 1980.

With the ascendancy of the urgent issues of democracy and class exploitation, a majority of South Korean feminists revived the leftist feminists' theory and strategies. In daily political terms, this translated into most feminists making democracy and labor movement activism their priorities. Therefore, in 1986, when a former university student activist working in a factory accused a policeman of sexually torturing her, many nationalistic leftist feminists fought for her because they saw her accusation chiefly as part of a broader charge against the militaristic regime. This then became a platform on which to mobilize other feminist factions as well as broad popular support, and to solidify their organizational power (Kyung-Ai Kim, 1995). The leftist, prolabor feminists thereafter created a united front, the Korean Women's Associations United with nationwide organizations of the progressive women's movement.

With the emphasis on women's role in the divided national situation, some of representative feminists actively participated in the movement for the unification of North Korea and South Korea. They also were engaged in the issue of prostitution on the U.S. military bases in South Korea (Kathy Moon, 1997). This nationalistic feminist tradition flourished with the "comfort women" movement in the 1990s. During World War II, the Japanese military had forced more than 100,000 women to become prostitutes for the armed forces in Asia; the majority of these women were colonized Koreans. Calling the practice sexual slavery, these women attracted attention inside South Korea, provoking nationalistic anger against Japanese imperialism and outside South Korea, provoking anger at war crimes against women.

Keeping some distance from the class-oriented and nationalistic feminist movement, one minor direction for feminists in the 1980s in South Korea was the legal reform movement. Comprising a number of women politicians and lawyers, the group focused primarily on revision of family law. Also, Alternative Culture, a group whose membership represented predominantly middle-class intellectuals, focused on creating alternatives to Korea's deeply rooted, authoritarian, homogenized patriarchal culture (Cho, 1996). In the 1980s, these themes were not always welcomed as a legitimate or politically correct version of feminism.

In the 1990s, after the collapse of many socialist countries and the military regime in South Korea, feminists' concerns and voices became even more diversified. The ideologies reflect wide and varied mobilizing impulses: peace and unification, sexual violence, sexual politics, gendered wages, employment discrimination, and extremely low political representation, as well as a very persistent Confucian patriarchal culture. Now, at the beginning of twenty-first century, with such a diversified agenda, the urgent question to be addressed is how the women's movement can achieve a collective power that can lead to deep political, economic, and cultural changes in Korea.

See Also

COLONIALISM AND POSTCOLONIALISM; FEMINISM; OVERVIEW; FEMINISM: MARXISM; FEMINISM: MILITANT; FEMINISM:SOCIALIST; NATION AND NATIONALISM

References and Further Reading

Cho, Joohyun. 1996. Gender identity politics: The case of women's liberation movement in Korea in 1980s and 1990s. *Women's Studies in Korea* 12(1):138-179.

Kim, Kyung-Ai. 1996. Nationalism: An advocate of, or a barrier to, feminism. *South Korea Women's Studies International Forum* 19: 66-74.

Moon, Katharine H. 1997. *Sex among allies: Military prostitution in U.S.-Korea relations.* New York: Columbia University Press.

Women's History Team of Korean Women Research Institution
1992. *Hankuk Yeoseongsa* [*Korean Women's History*]. Seoul:
Pulpit.

Yi Hyojae. 1996. *Hankukui yeoseong undong.* [*Women's movement
in Korea.*] Seoul: Jongwusa.

Yi Seunghi. 1994. *Hankuk hyeondae yeoseong undong.* [*Modern
Korean Women's Movement History.*] Seoul: Baesanseodang.

Insook Kwon

FEMINISM: Lesbian

The term *lesbian feminism* cannot be simply defined.
Broadly speaking, it refers to politics and practice that (1)
prioritize social, economic, political, sexual, and emotional relations between women, rather than between
women and men; and (2) offers a critique of the institution and ideology of heterosexuality as a cornerstone of
male supremacy. Largely developed by lesbians actively
involved in the women's liberation movement in the
United States, lesbian feminism first gained recognition
as a definable cultural phenomenon with an articulated
theory in 1970. Two publications of major importance in
this year were Kate Millett's *Sexual Politics* and a confrontation paper written by the New York group Radicalesbians entitled "The Woman-Identified Woman." The
former, which has since become a world best-seller,
attracted widespread media attention in Britain and the
United States, and the treatment its author received gave
many feminists with their first insight into lesbian oppression. The latter, which originated as a pamphlet and was
rapidly disseminated in feminist magazines and newsletters, is generally credited as marking the beginning of lesbian feminist consciousness.

Rita Mae Brown, one of the founding members of both
Radicalesbians and the lesbian feminist separatist collective
in Washington, D.C., the Furies, describes the anger, frustration and disappointment that led "hundreds" of lesbians,
many of whom had been extremely active in existing feminist groups, to question both the reformist, heterosexual character of the rapidly growing women's movement and their
continued involvement in it: "It's probably hard for a young
person today to realize how much pressure we were under.
The women's movement not only pushed us back in the
closet, they nailed the door shut.... Lesbians and straight
women might as well have been from another planet"
(quoted in Hoagland and Penelope, 1988: 592).

The fact that the National Organization for Women
(NOW) had been active for ten years before adding gay

rights (or, indeed, abortion rights) to its agenda in 1977 certainly supports this view. Much of the problem, as the Radicalesbians saw it, lay in the unquestioning acceptance by
many feminists of male definitions of lesbianism as a deviant
sexual practice indicative of abnormal physical or psychosexual development, and therefore of no interest whatsoever
to the majority, the "real women," whose primary attachments would always be to men. In accepting a definition
that, arguably had no natural basis and had been created by
men to support "a sexist society characterized by rigid sex
roles and dominated by male supremacy" (Radicalesbians,
1970: 17), women were not only misunderstanding lesbians
but overlooking the ways that such divisive categorizations
serve to define and reinforce notions of "appropriate" female
behavior.

Accusing a woman who in any way "challenged the terrible boundary of her sex role" of lesbianism was one of the
more overt ways of exerting male control identified by Radicalesbians (18). Another, more insidious method was the
granting or withholding of "male approval," since the very
need for such acceptability had been created through systematic conditioning beginning at an early age. While this
need remained unanalyzed and unchallenged, there could be
no women's liberation. Crucial to the Radicalesbians' argument, and to all subsequent lesbian feminist discourse, is a
redefinition of lesbianism that rejects western sexological constructions and emphasizes, instead, its potential as a powerful force in the struggle for universal women's liberation. Far
from being shameful, freaky, or inauthentic, "a lesbian is the
rage of all women condensed to the point of explosion" (Radicalesbians, 1988: 17), and lesbian feminism, with this understanding, is "a healthy *choice*...based upon self-love, the love
of other women and the rejection of male oppression" (Jeffreys, 1994: viii, emphasis added). Going against deeply
entrenched popular belief in the naturalness and the
immutability of sexual—that is, heterosexual—identity, the
operative word here is "choice." Lesbian feminists assumed
that sexuality between women would probably be one expression of this refusal of second-class gender status, but it was
no longer to be the main defining factor: any woman could
(and should) be a lesbian.

This was not an entirely new position, and numerous
earlier examples of resistance to heterosexual sex and marriage in widely differing societies might be cited here.
Members of the Women's Social and Political Union in England in the early 1900s argued that intimacy between the
sexes was an impossibility and spinsterhood a positive
choice. Women in the Chinese silkworm industry were
bribing themselves out of marriage at least a century before
that, and in the 1930s they formed "Sister Societies" to safe-

guard their economic independence from men (Grahn, 1984; Jeffreys, 1985). Ti-Grace Atkinson, the first of the second-wave western feminists to publicly question women's sexual allegiance to men and advocate celibacy (1974: 13–14), described the newly emerging definition that was to have such a radical impact on feminist politics in the 1970s like this:

> Lesbianism, for feminism, is not just "another" issue.... It is the commitment, by *choice,* full time, of one woman to others of her class, that is called lesbianism. It is this full commitment, against any and all personal considerations, if necessary, that constitutes the political significance of lesbianism.... There are other women who have never had sexual relations with other women, but who have made, and live, a total commitment to this movement. These women are "lesbians" in the political sense. (132)

In *Lesbian Nation: The Feminist Solution* (1974) Jill Johnston went further with her expression of the optimistic belief, shared by many lesbian feminists, that once women came, en masse, to an understanding of lesbianism as "a generic term signifying activism and the envisioned goal of a woman committed state" (278), the overthrow of patriarchy would inevitably follow.

The Leeds Revolutionary Feminist Group in England presented an "explosive" conference paper, "Political Lesbianism: The Case against Heterosexuality," in September 1979. (The two new terms introduced in the paper—*revolutionary feminist* and *political lesbian*—are indicative of the many variations in emphasis and approach that have contributed to the dynamics and ongoing development of lesbian feminist theory.) The paper was printed in the British feminist newsletter *WIRES* and generated unprecedented controversy. The Leeds group was unequivocal in its belief that all feminists "can and should be political lesbians" and gave a definition that in many ways echoes Ti-Grace Atkinson's call for female celibacy a decade earlier: "A political lesbian is a woman-identified woman who does not fuck men. It does not mean compulsory sexual activity with women.... Serious feminists have no choice but to abandon heterosexuality.... Giving up fucking for a feminist is about taking your politics seriously" (Onlywomen Press Collective, 1981: 5, 8).

Direct, confrontational language is characteristic of most lesbian feminist writing in the 1970s. Numerous newsletters and magazines, publishing houses, record companies, women-only events, and meeting places were set up during this time on extremely limited budgets and with a sense of excitement and urgency that left little time for considered reflection. Lesbian feminists organized and addressed conferences, attended endless meetings, and, as Carol Anne Douglas notes (1990: 167), angered "[m]any heterosexual feminists, including radical feminists," with their relentless critique of heterosexuality and their apparent assumption of the high moral ground. In their pioneering work, *Sappho Was a Right-On Woman: A Liberated View of Lesbianism* (1977; originally published 1972) Sydney Abbott and Barbara Love explain some of the impatience and forcefulness that many found objectionable: "For Lesbians, Women's Liberation is not an intellectual or emotional luxury but a personal imperative. Living without the approval or support of men, Lesbians desperately need women's rights" (135).

Though few would disagree with this, black lesbians and feminists were to point out that, with the additional burden of racial oppression, they too were working under an imperative that did not necessarily lead them to the same conclusions or sets of priorities and certainly did not provide the same conditions that allowed many white women to "make the leap" into lesbian feminism. As Barbara Smith explained in 1977 in her essay "Toward a Black Feminist Criticism": "Heterosexual privilege is usually the only privilege that Black women have. None of us have racial or sexual privilege, almost none of us have class privilege.... Being out, particularly in print, is the final renunciation of any claim to the crumbs of 'tolerance' that nonthreatening 'ladylike' Black women are sometimes fed" (in Hull et al., 1982: 171).

In 1977, too, the Combahee River Collective of black feminists and lesbians issued "A Black Feminist Statement" arguing for an "inclusive politics" and a commitment to "struggles in which race, sex, and class are simultaneous factors in oppression" (Hull et al., 1982: 21). The "logic" of lesbian feminism as *the* universal solution to the problem of women's oppression was clearly not so straightforward when tested beyond the white western context of its originators.

The number of letters and articles addressing lesbian feminism in the decade following publication of "The Woman-Identified Woman" is inestimable, because the majority of broadsheets and magazines in Australia, Canada, the United States, Britain, and many other European countries that carried them have long since disappeared or are available only in the limited number of lesbian archives that now exist. To suggest that lesbian femisism was, during this period, very much a western phenomenon is not to deny the existence of women loving women and working to undermine the institution of heterosexuality as it is variously constructed all over the world, but to make the point that very little work published by or about lesbian feminists during this time expressed any consciousness whatsoever of the cultural, political, material, or conceptual differences between women that would become central to feminist thought by the start of the 1980s. Lesbian feminists have responded to these new understandings and changes in emphasis in a number of ways.

Charlotte Bunch, another founding member of the Furies, has documented her own move toward global feminist coalitions in *Passionate Politics: Feminist Theory and Action* (1987), a collection of her essays spanning twenty years. Sheila Jeffreys, a committed lesbian feminist historian and founding member of the Leeds Revolutionary Feminist Group, draws attention to others who, "feeling exhausted and disillusioned by the struggle to persuade heterosexual feminists to take lesbians seriously into account" (1994: xiii), withdrew from confrontation at the end of the 1970s in order to allow more time and energy for constructive development within their own lesbian and woman-identified communities. Some, like the early New York Group, dropped the title *feminist* altogether, preferring to describe their politics as radical lesbian, separatist, or lesbian separatist. The French writer and theorist Monique Wittig is particularly noteworthy in this respect. Although the radical distinction that she presented in 1978 between lesbians and women was incomprehensible to many Anglo-American feminists at the time (see "The Straight Mind," "One Is Not Born a Woman," and "The Category Sex" in Wittig, 1992), her ideas were actively taken up and developed by groups of radical lesbians in France and Quebec who were more familiar with a philosophical approach.

Adrienne Rich's "Compulsory Heterosexuality and Lesbian Existence" (1987; originally published in 1980) spoke to a much wider audience and remains one of the best known and most frequently quoted lesbian feminist analyses. Many of the basic principles established in raw form in "The Woman-Identified Woman"—the need to redefine lesbianism, examine and dismantle the power of the institution of heterosexuality, and strengthen the bonds between women—are present in Rich's work, but the tone is entirely different. No less radical in many respects, "Compulsory Heterosexuality" is far more considered and scholarly than the Radicalesbians' paper and certainly more accessible and conciliatory than Wittig's. Concerned by the emerging divisions within feminism, Rich aimed to reopen constructive lesbian and feminist debate by broadening the terms of possible engagement in it. Adrienne Rich is uncompromising in her belief that the simultaneous validation of lesbian existence and challenge to the institution

of heterosexuality should be a fundamental part of feminist politics. The fact that so many women have been resistant to and, indeed, frightened by lesbian feminist theory only confirms the power of the institution and the heterosexual imperative it enforces. Rich concludes her detailed analysis of the ways in which male power over women is exercised with both a gentle challenge to women who have not analyzed their heterosexual "choice," and considerable encouragement: "To take the step of questioning heterosexuality as a 'preference' or 'choice' for women—and to do the intellectual and emotional work that follows—will call for a special quality of courage in heterosexually identified feminists, but I think the rewards will be great: a freeing-up of thinking, the exploring of new paths, the shattering of another great silence, new clarity in personal relationships" (51).

The remainder of Rich's essay concentrates on the desirability of a lesbian feminist alternative, beginning with her own controversial definitions:

> I have chosen the terms *lesbian existence* and *lesbian continuum* because the word *lesbianism* has a clinical and limiting ring. *Lesbian existence* suggests both the fact of the historical presence of lesbians and our continuing creation of the meaning of that existence. I mean the term *lesbian continuum* to include a range—through each woman's life and throughout history—of woman-identified experience, not simply the fact that a woman has had or consciously desired genital sexual experience with another woman. (51–52)

Some have objected to the way that Rich's definition seems to minimize female desire and sexuality in favor of emotion and sensuality. Others have questioned whether subsuming women's various forms of relating under one broad category is in the end very helpful. Although this essay is broader in scope than earlier lesbian feminist critiques of heterosexuality, Rich herself acknowledged its tendency to false universalism in a later essay, "Notes Toward a Politics of Location" (1984, in Rich, 1987: 210–232).

This entry began by stating that there can be no simple (or single) definition of lesbian feminism. All the variant positions noted here—political lesbian, separatist, and so forth—have developed from and contributed to this highly contested, dynamic position, and the debates within feminism that have accompanied each development are certainly notable for their intensity. To this extent, constant questioning, rethinking, and unsettling must be considered, in addition to the basic principles outlined above, a crucial part of what lesbian feminism is.

See Also

FEMINISM: RADICAL; GLOBAL FEMINISM; HETEROSEXUALITY; LESBIANISM; LESBIAN SEXUALITY

References and Further Reading

Abbott, Sydney, and Barbara Love. 1977. *Sappho was a right-on woman: A liberated view of lesbianism.* New York: Stein and Day.

Atkinson, Ti-Grace. 1974. *Amazon odyssey.* New York: Link.

Bunch, Charlotte. 1987. *Passionate politics: Feminist theory in action.* New York: St. Martin's.

Douglas, Carol Anne. 1990. *Love and politics: Radical feminist and lesbian theories.* San Francisco: Ism.

Grahn, Judy. 1984. *Another mother tongue.* Boston: Beacon.

Hoagland, Sarah Lucia, and Julia Penelope, eds. 1988. *For lesbians only: A separatist anthology.* London: Onlywomen.

Hull, Gloria T., Patricia Bell Scott, and Barbara Smith, eds. 1982. *All the women are white, al the blacks are men, but some of us are brave: Black women's studies.* Old Westbury, N.Y.: Feminist Press.

Jeffreys, Sheila. 1994. *The lesbian heresy.* London: Women's Press.
———.1985. *The spinster and her enemies: Feminism and sexuality 1880–1930.* London: Pandora.

Johnston, Jill. 1974. *Lesbian nation: The feminist solution.* New York: Simon and Schuster.

Millett, Kate. 1970. *Sexual politics.* New York: Ballantine.

Myron, Nancy, and Charlotte Bunch, eds. 1975. *Lesbianism and the women's movement.* Oakland, Calif.: Diana.

Onlywomen Press Collective. 1981. *Love your enemy? The debate between heterosexual feminism and political lesbianism.* London: Onlywomen.

Radicalesbians. 1988. *The woman identified woman.* In Sarah Lucia Hoagland and Julia Penelope, eds., *For lesbians only: A separatist anthology,* 17–22. London: Onlywomen. (Originally published 1970.)

Rich, Adrienne. 1987. *Compulsory heterosexuality and lesbian existence.* In Adrienne Rich, *Blood, bread, and poetry,* 23–75. London: Virago.

Smith, Barbara. 1982. *Toward a black feminist criticism.* In Gloria T. Hull, Patricia Bell Scott, and Barbara Smith, *All the women are white and all the blacks are men, but some of us are brave.* New York: Feminist Press.

Wittig, Monique. 1992. *The straight mind and other essays.* Hemel Hempstead, U.K.: Harvester Wheatsheaf; Boston: Beacon.

Lyndie Brimstone

FEMINISM: Liberal British and European

The Evolution of Liberal Feminism

Liberal feminism can be defined as the extension of liberal principles of individual freedom and rights to women. The roots of liberal feminism can therefore be found in seventeenth-century British liberalism and the French Enlightenment. But the formal liberal belief in the equality of all individuals had to be asserted in a specifically feminist context before women's right to be treated as autonomous individuals began to gain recognition in the nineteenth and twentieth centuries. Liberal feminists have argued for equal rights to education, equal access to all occupations, equal civic rights under the law, and equal citizenship, which meant as a minimum the right to vote and to be elected to all political bodies. Therefore, liberal feminists have protested against women's legal and customary subordination in marriage and all forms of discrimination that have treated women as appendages of their husbands or fathers. Liberal feminism has evolved from a dialogue with political liberalism and has therefore been most successful in those countries where the social, economic, and cultural conditions have been conducive to liberal institutions and attitudes.

Although some liberal thinkers were prepared to accord limited rights to women—for example, the right to education—the tendency of liberal thought until the twentieth century was to assume that women were by nature different and hence inferior. Liberalism also tended to take for granted women's subordinate role as wives and daughters. Therefore, the Enlightenment philosopher the Marquis de Condorcet, who urged at the time of the French Revolution that women should have exactly the same citizen rights as men, and John Stuart Mill, who espoused votes for women and attacked the inequality of women in Victorian England, stand out as male theorists who were feminists as well as liberals. Both argued strongly that the "nature" of women could not be deduced from their socially conditioned behavior in existing society.

The Arguments for Liberal Feminism

Liberal feminism contrasted the basic concepts of liberalism, which upheld the rights and freedom of individual men, with the servitude of women, which had been accepted as "natural." Mary Astell, for example, in her *Reflections on Marriage* at the end of the seventeenth century, used John Locke's theory of natural rights and a voluntary social con-

FEMINISM: LIBERAL BRITISH AND EUROPEAN

tract to attack the "absolute sovereignty" exercised in the family, when it had been rejected in the state. She asked: "If all Men are born free, how is it that all Women are born slaves?" since subjection to the arbitrary will of men was slavery. She also argued that the power of the husband derived from force, not from the law of nature (cited in Mitchell, 1984: 63–68). In 1791 Olympe de Gouges published her *Declaration of the Rights of Woman and Citizen* in a deliberate parallel to the Declaration of the Rights of Man and Citizen (1789), the manifesto of the French Revolution (see Arnaud and Kingdom, 1990: 99–103). Moreover, during the nineteenth century women active in the liberal antislavery campaigns were prompted to reflect on the effective slavery of women in advanced liberal societies and to call for their own emancipation.

Intellectual women in both France and Britain during the eighteenth century debated the need for women's education. Madame du Châtelet, who translated Newton's *Principles of Mathematics* from the Latin and wrote a commentary on it, declared, "I would have women participate in all human rights, especially those of the mind" (see Ehrman, 1986). Mary Wollstonecraft, in the first classic of liberal feminism, *A Vindication of the Rights of Woman,* published in 1792, laid particular emphasis on the need to educate girls and disputed the view that women's nature and role in the family required a different kind of training. She also stressed that women were encouraged by society to be frivolous and devious, but that they were as capable as men of developing reason and becoming virtuous citizens, if given the opportunity to do so. One strand of her argument was that as a result women would also be much better wives and mothers.

Wollstonecraft indicated that she believed women should have protection under the civil law, should be free to engage in well-paid work and to enter respected professions so as not to be economically dependent on marriage, and should have the right to be politically represented. She had intended to develop these ideas in a second volume but died in childbirth before she could write it. A stronger statement of the necessity for women to have the vote, to sit on juries, and to be eligible for election to Parliament was made in 1851 by Harriet Taylor (then married to John Stuart Mill) in her essay "Enfranchisement of Women." Taylor also argued that women should be able to enter the workforce and to continue to practice a profession after marriage and children, because otherwise they would be denied genuine freedom of choice. In addition she noted that a woman's economic contribution to the family would promote her status within it. Taylor makes a more radical claim than Wollstonecraft for a woman's right to a sphere outside the family. On this

issue she also went further than John Stuart Mill, who argued in *The Subjection of Women* that women should be able to enter the professions but assumed that once they married their profession would be that of wife and mother. He also assumed that once the marriage laws had been altered to ensure the equality of women, then women would not need to protect their position by earning money independently (see Rossi, 1970).

Eighteenth- and nineteenth-century liberal feminists tended to argue implicitly, and sometimes explicitly, for middle-class rather than working-class women's rights. This class bias was reflected in feminist campaigns in Britain for higher education for girls, entry to universities, and wider job opportunities for women. The Society for Promoting the Employment of Women was created in 1859, inspired by an article in *The Edinburgh Review* by the prolific author and feminist Harriet Martineau (see Weiner, 1983), and women campaigned for entry to prestigious professions such as medicine. The liberal feminist suffrage campaigns called for votes for women on the same basis as men, which could mean endorsing property qualifications that excluded poor men.

Liberal Feminist Movements

Since liberal feminism has been closely linked to the development of liberal thought and to the political and economic implementation of liberal ideas, it has been strongest in European countries that were influenced by Protestantism and engaged in early economic modernization, like the Netherlands and the Scandinavian countries. Liberal feminism has also sometimes found a voice in periods when liberal movements challenged the old regimes in Europe. Therefore the upsurge of liberal and democratic movements in Germany in 1848, in which some women participated, sparked demands by individual women for full civil rights and the vote. The novelist Luise Otto-Peters was the most prominent feminist in this period, editing a newspaper, *Equality,* and she later became president of the German Women's Association, founded in 1865 (see Robertson, 1982: 373–376). However, because the social and political climate in Germany had become more conservative after the failure of the liberal revolutions, and in Prussia women's political activity was prohibited by law, German feminism restricted its demands primarily to improving women's education and admission to the medical profession. The demand for the vote was not taken up until 1902. Socialists rather than liberals in Germany supported women's political rights, but there was strong political antagonism between socialists and middle-class women's organizations from the 1890s (see Evans, 1976).

787

France after the French Revolution was hostile to demands for women's rights; the Napoleonic Code strongly asserted the power of husband over wife. The revival of moderate liberalism in the political overthrow of the Bourbon monarchy in 1830 did not liberalize the position of women under the law. The utopian socialists rather than liberal feminists were at the forefront of feminist demands, and prominent women like George Sand advocated personal freedom from convention, not legal or political reforms. The revolution of 1848 introduced universal *male* suffrage; women had to wait until 1946 for the vote, despite a revival of liberal feminist demands with the introduction of the Third Republic and energetic suffrage campaigns in the twentieth century (see Fauré, 1991).

Women played a major part in the Italian movement for national unity, and the romantic but liberal nationalism espoused by Giuseppe Mazzini, an Italian patriot, supported women's equality. However, when a united Italy was created, the new Civil Code assigned women a clearly subordinate role. A petition for women's suffrage was promoted in 1867 by the Italian parliamentary deputy, Salvatore Morelli, author of *Woman and Science* and translator of John Stuart Mill's *Subjection of Women* into Italian. Anna Mozzoni, who also translated Mill, became the leading advocate of women's rights and wrote numerous articles and pamphlets. She attacked the new Civil Code and urged that women should have the right of guardianship over their children, as well as pressing for civil rights for single women and public education for girls. She promoted a campaign of petitions to the parliament for women's suffrage, at least in municipal elections, after a Liberal majority was elected in the mid-1870s. Mozzoni was backed by the feminist paper *La Donna*, which pressed for women's rights and established contacts with feminists in other countries. The campaign failed, and Mozzoni became increasingly committed to socialism, although she maintained her insistence on votes for women at international conferences. The Catholic church was a major barrier to women's emancipation, both because of its direct teachings and because of its perceived influence on women, which made anticlerical men hesitant to grant women the vote (see Robertson, 1982: 429–38).

Liberal feminism has usually been associated with a fairly conventional approach to the family, supporting easy divorce but not challenging the ideal of family life. Liberal feminist principles have, however, implied opposition to violent and tyrannical behavior by husbands: domestic violence was a central issue for John Stuart Mill. Liberal feminism has also in some contexts involved open support for the rights of prostitutes, as in the campaign launched in 1869 by Josephine Butler, and supported by Mill, against the Contagious Diseases Acts, which gave the police repressive powers over suspected prostitutes (see Mill, 1984: xxxvii–viii, 101–108, 349–371). Campaigns for birth control have often been pursued in the past by radicals opposed to both church and state, but since access to contraception can be seen as a necessary step to safeguard women's health and give women genuine autonomy, as well as limiting population growth, it is an issue that has united different strands of feminism, including liberal feminism.

The first wave of liberal feminism had achieved its basic goals by the 1960s in Britain and Europe. Women still suffered from various forms of legal discrimination, however, and were still significantly unequal in both economic and political terms. The second-wave feminist movements in Britain and Europe at the end of the 1960s tended to adopt socialist or radical feminist ideologies. But political parties and governments responding to the new pressure for women's equality generally reflected liberal interpretations of how to prevent discrimination or promote genuinely equal rights and opportunities through legislation. Since the 1970s many feminists have queried the adequacy of liberal feminism to explain women's continuing subordination or to remedy it, and they have examined whether liberal ideology is inherently biased against women.

See Also

FEMINISM: EIGHTEENTH-CENTURY; FEMINISM: FIRST WAVE BRITISH; FEMINISM: LIBERAL NORTH AMERICAN; FEMINISM: NINETEENTH CENTURY; SUFFRAGE

References and Further Reading

Arnaud, André-Jean, and Elizabeth Kingdom, eds. 1990. *Women's rights and the rights of man.* Aberdeen: Aberdeen University Press.

Ehrman, Esther. 1986. *Mme du Châtelet.* Leamington Spa: Berg.

Evans, Richard J. 1976. *The feminist movement in Germany 1894–1933.* London: Sage.

Fauré, Christine. 1991. *Democracy without women: Feminism and the rise of liberal individualism in France.* Bloomington: Indiana University Press.

Frazer, Elizabeth. 1996. Feminism and liberalism. In James Meadowcraft, ed., *The liberal political tradition: Contemporary reappraisals.* London: Edward Arnold.

Mill, J. S. 1984. *Essays on equality, law, and education: Collected works of John Stuart Mill.* Vol. 21. London: Routledge and Kegan Paul.

Mitchell, Juliet. 1984. Women and equality. In Juliet Mitchell, *Women: The longest revolution: Essays on feminism, literature and psychoanalysis.* London: Virago.

Robertson, Priscilla. 1982. *An experience of women: Pattern and change in nineteenth-century Europe.* Philadelphia: Temple University Press.

Rossi, Alice S., ed. 1970. *John Stuart Mill and Harriet Taylor Mill: Essays on sex equality.* Chicago: University of Chicago Press.

———. 1988. *The feminist papers.* Boston: Northeastern University Press.

Weiner, Gaby. 1983. Harriet Martineau: A reassessment (1802–1876). In Dale Spender, ed. *Feminist theories: Three centuries of key women thinkers.* New York: Pantheon.

Wollstonecraft, Mary. 1967. *A vindication of the rights of woman.* New York: Norton (Originally published 1792.)

Yeo, Elizabeth Jane, ed. 1997. *Mary Wollstonecraft and 200 years of feminism.* London: Rivers Oram.

April Carter

FEMINISM: Liberal North American

Since it ushered in the "second wave" of feminism in the early 1970s (DeCrow, 1971), liberal feminism has been a highly visible yet also highly criticized branch of feminism. Many feminists maintain that liberal feminism is inherently contradictory: its emphasis on individualism belies women's historical embeddedness in relationships; its notion of individualism is inherently masculinist; its focus on freedom and rights contradicts women's activities of care in the family; and its dedication to liberal values betrays feminist goals (Pateman, 1988).

Other feminists, however, have argued that liberalism is not only consistent with feminism but its best hope: its emphasis on individuals is a key to gaining recognition and respect for women as independent people rather than attachments to men; its emphasis on rights is a powerful tool for women to claim access to political and economic resources and to combat their oppression in the family and society; and its notion of freedom and equality can allow women to make choices that will result in control over their lives, whether they choose to pursue a career or work traditionally reserved for men, to work in traditionally "feminine" professions such as nursing, to be "full-time" mothers and housewives, or any combination thereof.

The division between these two positions is exacerbated by the fact that those opposed to liberal feminism are predominantly academic feminists, while those advocating it are predominantly activists involved in issues ranging from reproductive health and violence against women to sexual harassment and discrimination in employment. Although liberal feminism is still alive in academic circles, its advocates are a minority, possibly owing to academic feminism's origins in Marxism as well as its more recent turn to various postmodern frameworks. By contrast, those engaged in daily policy battles and activism who must confront state agencies, the courts, and the legal system are bound to work within the parameters defined by the liberal state and its capitalist economic structures.

Emerging out of the European Enlightenment, liberalism as articulated by early social contract theorists such as the seventeenth-century British theorist John Locke stressed notions of natural freedom and equality, democracy and the rejection of authoritarian government, and the notion of natural rights, such as those to life, to liberty, and property (Locke, 1964). Early liberal theories, however, generally hid the reality of power inequity behind a facade of formal freedom and equality; the "persons" who were entitled to these rights were consistently seen as propertied white males. Indeed, under the rubric of privacy rights, women often suffered abuse from husbands and fathers with little recourse to political rights of state protection.

In spite of their biased implementation, however, these Enlightenment ideals provided early eighteenth-century feminists such as Mary Wollstonecraft with the opening they needed to assert women's entitlement to be recognized as human subjects with agency and intellect (Wollstonecraft, 1985). From Abigail Adams to Sojourner Truth, early North American feminists used this new liberal vocabulary to challenge and resist patriarchy and to try to achieve greater freedom for women.

These ideals fit in closely with economic issues. Developing simultaneously with western capitalism, liberalism has accorded a central position to free enterprise, private property, and the laws of the market. This economic focus influenced U.S. and Canadian suffragists—who argued that the rights, opportunities, and liberties women should be granted included not only the vote but also equal education, equal employment opportunities, equal pay, and equal treatment (O'Neill, 1969)—as well as the "second wave" of contemporary feminism. Following Betty Friedan's classic of liberal feminism, *The Feminine Mystique* (1963), which offered a primarily economic analysis of women's social inequality deriving from women's ejection from the workplace after World War II, feminist organizations such as the National Organization for Women in the United States and the National Action Committee in Canada adopted explicitly economic liberal goals such as equal opportunity in the workplace, the end of gender segregation in employment categories, and equal pay for equal work. In the United

States, a movement for an equal rights amendment to the Constitution, seen as a focal point for such feminist goals, was revived in 1972 but defeated in 1984 (Mansbridge, 1989).

Some feminists suggest that such failure indicates the narrow and politically exclusive focus of liberal feminism. As other branches within feminism have emphasized difference—both differences among women and women's differences from men—liberal feminism has come to be seen as theoretically indebted to its racist and classist origins. Women of color and lesbians in particular criticize the mainstream liberal feminist movement in North America as one of white, middle-class, heterosexual women only.

Some feminists maintain that organizations such as the National Organization for Women (NOW) and the National Action Committee (NAC) have responded to such criticism by protesting discrimination against gays and lesbians, emphasizing the feminization of poverty, and pushing for welfare rights; in short, that liberal feminism has begun to recognize what Zillah Eisenstein (1981) once called its "radical future."

But others are left with the conclusion that this kind of feminism is no longer liberal at all. If liberal concepts such as "rights" were developed as exclusive categories for economically privileged white males—for instance, the right to black slaves and the right to white women through marriage were among the central concepts that emerged from Enlightenment property rights—then fitting feminist goals and values into a preexisting liberal framework, which liberal feminism requires, is contradictory.

Reconfiguring "liberal feminism" as "feminist liberalism," however, could help redefine liberalism by making it work within the framework assumptions of feminism (Hirschmann, 1999). For instance, Patricia J. Williams (1991) points out that despite their history of exclusiveness, rights are extremely important for those who have been historically and systematically denied them; if rights embody the voice of power, she suggests, perhaps women should not be too quick to abandon that voice. Because women of color embody an identity of multiplicity, however, their use of rights requires a transformation of the concept, just as First Nations Canadian women utilize a collective rather than an individualist notion of rights (Vickers et al., 1993). If feminists can reconstruct the concept of rights to accommodate multiplicity, particularity, relationship, and context, rights discourse could be adapted to the ends of gender equality and justice (but see Okin, 2000). Such a move would transform liberalism into a *feminist* strategy rather than the other way around.

See Also

FEMININE MYSTIQUE; FEMINISM: LIBERAL BRITISH AND EUROPEAN; LIBERALISM; LIBERATION; RACE

References and Further Reading

DeCrow, Karen. 1971. *The young woman's guide to liberation*. Indianapolis, Ind.: Bobbs-Merrill.

Eisenstein, Zillah. 1981. *The radical future of liberal feminism*. New York: Longman.

Friedan, Betty. 1963. *The feminine mystique*. New York: Norton.

Hirschmann, Nancy J. 1999. Difference as an occasion for rights: A feminist rethinking of rights, liberalism, and difference. *Critical Review of International Social and Political Philosophy* 2(1): 27–55

Locke, John. 1964. *Two treatises of government*. Ed. Peter Laslett. New York: New American Library.

Mansbridge, Jane. 1989. *Why we lost the ERA*. Chicago: University of Chicago Press.

Okin, Susan Moller. 2000. *Is multiculturalism bad for women?* Ed. Joshua Cohen, Matthew Howard, and Martha C. Nussbaum. Princeton, N.J.: Princeton University Press.

O'Neill, William L. 1969. *Everyone was brave: The rise and fall of feminism in America*. Chicago: Quadrangle.

Pateman, Carole. 1988. *The sexual contract*. Stanford: Stanford University Press.

Vickers, Jill, et al. 1993. *Politics as if women mattered: A political analysis of the National Action Committee on the status of women*. Toronto: University of Toronto Press.

Williams, Patricia J. 1991. *The alchemy of race and rights: Diary of a law professor*. Cambridge, Mass.: Harvard University Press.

Wollstonecraft, Mary. 1985. *A vindication of the rights of woman*. New York: Viking Penguin. (Originally published 1792).

Nancy Hirschmann

FEMINISM: Marxist

Marxist feminism draws on the ideas of the communist theorist Karl Marx (1818–83). It attempts to use these to develop an understanding of women's oppression and how it can be ended, linking the situation of women to class struggle and general patterns of historical development. Marxist feminism has been an important strand of feminist thought and politics since the late nineteenth century and was central to many theoretical debates within western feminism in the

1970s and 1980s. The relationship between Marxism and feminism has, however, always involved difficulties and disagreements; by the end of the twentieth century Marxism had lost much of its influence.

Early Marxist Feminism

Marx himself had very little to say about the situation of women. However, his theory claimed to be a universal one, and many have agreed with Clara Zetkin (1857–1933), a prominent German socialist, that although Marx's theory of history "has not supplied us with any ready-made formulas concerning the women's question, yet it has done something much more important: it has given us the correct unerring method to comprehend that question" (in Bryson, 1992: 129). Essentially this method argued that the key to understanding human society and history lies in the development of production—that is, in technology and the economy rather than in ideas or the actions of outstanding individuals. The family and sexual relationships are therefore, like other forms of social organization, the product of a particular stage of economic development; as such, they cannot be altered on their own; they can be altered only as a result of socioeconomic change expressed through class conflict and revolution, and leading eventually to a classless, communist society.

This understanding was developed by Frederick Engels in *The Origin of the Family, Private Property, and the State,* first published in 1884. In this work, Engels (1820–1895) argued that women's oppression has not always existed, but that it began with the first private property and class society, for it was only then that men's desire to pass property to known heirs motivated them to control women. This motive would, Engels argued, disappear with the overthrow of capitalism, when women would no longer be economically dependent on men, and the socialization of housework and child care would liberate them from domestic chores. The way forward for women, therefore, is not to campaign for their own rights, but to fight alongside working men for the revolutionary transformation of society. This position rules out any idea that the interests of working men and women might conflict, that women can have group interests cutting across class lines, or that gender relations might have independent dynamics of their own.

This "orthodox" analysis was accepted and defended by Zetkin within the German Social Democratic Party. It meant that, although she attempted to prioritize women's issues, she had no means of understanding the sexism and hostility faced by women such as herself in the socialist movement. In Russia, the Bolshevik Alexandra Kollontai (1873–1952) moved away from such crude economic reductionism. She identified power relations in the family, morality, and sexuality and argued that these would not automatically disappear with the introduction of communism, but must be tackled directly. However, although as a member of Lenin's postrevolutionary government in 1917 she was able to give women full legal rights, the resources were never available to implement her more ambitious plans (such as extensive and high-quality childcare), and she never developed any unifying theory of patriarchy as a system of domination. From the mid-1920s, Stalinist orthodoxy dominated the international communist movement, the "woman question" was officially declared solved in the Soviet Union, and the ideas of women such as Zetkin and Kollontai were silenced. It was not until the 1960s, when less rigid forms of Marxism developed in the West, that feminists were again able to draw on Marxism to develop more sophisticated analyses.

The Impact of Radical Feminism

By this time, radical feminists were developing theories claiming that patriarchy and not class is the oldest and most basic form of oppression. This analysis was in part the product of women's experience of trying to work in Marxist and other left-wing organizations, where they found that their role was expected to be that of secretary, housewife, or sex object, and where women's issues were treated as trivial, diversionary, or almost indefinitely postponable. Some radical feminists argued that Marxism and feminism are fundamentally incompatible; others attempted to adapt Marxist concepts to argue their case. For example, Shulamith Firestone (1970) attempted to rewrite the Marxist theory of history, substituting reproduction for production and biologically based "sex class" for economic class; Christine Delphy (1984) has also claimed that women constitute a sex class, but she argued that this is based not on biology but on women's common economic position as unpaid domestic workers.

Marxist Feminist Responses

Some Marxist feminists, such as the historian Sheila Rowbotham, have retained a more orthodox approach: although they insist that women's concerns are central rather than an optional extra, they reject the concept of patriarchy as ahistorical and argue that, despite the problems of working with men, feminist concerns cannot be isolated from the wider socialist movement (Rowbotham et al., 1979). Others have recognized the existence of patriarchy and argue that Marxist concepts can be used to explore its complex relationship to the capitalist economy.

Some writers have argued that this can be done by reexamining Marx's economic concepts and using these to analyze women's work both in the home and in paid employment. During the 1970s, this gave rise to the so-called domestic labor debate, which involved some very technical arguments over the precise meaning of such terms as *value*. Perhaps more important, it represented a significant attempt to make visible the work done by women in the home, to explore its relationship to the capitalist economy, and to assess the implications of this for achieving socialist or feminist change. A minority developed the analysis to demand "wages for housework" as part of a wider socialist strategy; rather more agreed that the housework done by women does not simply represent a personal service to individual men, but that it serves the interests of the capitalist economy by reproducing and maintaining the workforce in a particularly cheap and efficient way. Others have further argued that capitalism has benefited from being able to treat women as a "reserve army of labor" which can be employed or dispensed with as the economy goes through its inevitable cycles of expansion and recession, and which can constitute a "super-exploited" group at the point of production (Davis, 1995).

The above arguments are based on economic analysis. Other writers such as Juliet Mitchell have used Marxist ideas to explore spheres of life traditionally considered "private" or nonpolitical. In her pioneering *Women, the Longest Revolution,* first published in 1966, Mitchell argued that although earlier Marxists were correct in seeing women's relation to production as of key importance, their analysis ignored the crucial ways in which women's subordination is maintained within the family. This led her to an analysis of the ways in which subordination is internalized and consent engineered, which in turn involved an examination of the workings of the unconscious, drawing on psychoanalytic theory. Therefore, while she retained the orthodox Marxist insistence that economic factors are the most basic, Mitchell rejected any kind of crude economic reductionism and has been able to argue that, because there will be no automatic dissolution of patriarchy without a feminist struggle, women can organize autonomously when working for their liberation.

The idea that gender issues may have a degree of independence from class has also been explored by Michele Barrett. In *Women's Oppression Today* (first published in 1980), she argues that although women's oppression has become almost inseparably entangled with the capitalist economy, it

was not simply caused by capitalism; rather, it was also the product of an earlier gender ideology. Since then, her rejection of crude materialism has led her further from Marxism and toward postmodernism (Barrett, 1988).

"Dual Systems" versus Capitalist Patriarchy

Even the loosest forms of Marxism have seemed to insist that "in the last analysis" class and capitalism are more fundamental than gender and patriarchy, and frequently have seemed to contrast feminist ideological struggle with economic class struggle, with the success of the former ultimately being dependent on the latter. Such relegation to secondary status has been resisted by many feminists, who have agree with Heidi Hartmann's critique of the "unhappy marriage" of Marxism and feminism: she claimed that this was based on the same kind of subordination as the marriage of husband and wife in English common law, through which the wife loses her independent legal position, which is incorporated into that of her husband. To avoid this secondary status for feminism, she argued, "either we need a healthier marriage or we need a divorce" (Hartmann, 1986: 2). For Hartmann, there are two dynamic forces at work in history, which must be understood in terms of both class and gender struggle. Although modern society is both capitalist and patriarchal, neither of these "dual systems" can, she says, be reduced to the other, and although at times they are mutually reinforcing, they may also come into conflict. Marxist analysis, she says, forgets that men as well as capitalism benefit from present arrangements, so that women's oppression both predates capitalism and may continue beyond it.

Other writers have rejected such "dual system" approaches and argue that what we now have is a unified system of capitalist patriarchy; from this perspective, gender relations are central, rather than the kind of optional extra that traditional Marxist analysis implied (Young, 1986). Some have argued that the Marxist concept of production should be expanded to include human reproduction, which is therefore understood as part of the material basis of society (Bryson, 1995; Jaggar, 1983; Vogel, 1983). This approach retains the Marxist idea that women's oppression has a material base, but includes in this the biological processes involved in procreation and sexuality, arguing that these are not constant and unchanging but historically produced. It also enables the Marxist concept of alienation to be extended to personal relationships and family life, seeing here the same kind of loss of control and denial of human needs that Marx had identified in the workplace.

Marxist Feminism Today

Today, all forms of Marxism are very much on the defensive, and many feminists reject the idea of turning to a Victorian patriarch for inspiration. Nevertheless, the basic idea that gender relations are bound up with economic development, and that women can be liberated only in the context of a socialist society based on the fulfillment of human needs rather than the pursuit of profit, remains powerful at the level both of feminist theory and of feminist politics.

See Also

DOMESTIC LABOR; FEMINISM: POSTMODERN; FEMINISM: RADICAL; FEMINISM: SOCIALIST; SOCIALISM; MARXISM

References and Further Reading

Barrett, Michele. 1988. *Women's oppression today: The Marxist/feminist encounter.* London: Verso.

Bryson, Valerie. 1995. Adjusting the lenses: Feminist analyses and Marxism at the end of the twentieth century. *Contemporary Politics* 1(1).

———. 1992. *Feminist political theory.* Basingstoke, England: Macmillan.

Collins, Patricia Hill. 1990. *Black feminist thought.* London: Routledge.

Davis, M. 1995. Towards a theory of Marxism and oppression. *Contemporary Politics* 1(2).

Delphy, Christine. 1984. *Close to home: A materialist analysis of women's oppression.* London: Hutchinson.

Firestone, Shulamith. 1970. *The dialectic of sex.* London: Women's Press.

Hartmann, Heidi. 1986. The unhappy marriage of Marxism and feminism. In Lydia Sargent, ed. *The unhappy marriage of Marxism and feminism,* 1–41. London: Pluto.

Jaggar, Alison. 1983. *Feminist politics and human nature.* Brighton, England: Harvester.

Mirza, Heidi Safia, ed. 1997. *Black British feminism: A reader.* London: Routledge.

Mitchell, Juliet. 1971. *Woman's estate.* Harmondsworth: Penguin.

———. 1984. *Women, the longest revolution.* London: Virago.

Rowbotham, Sheila, Lynne Segal, and Hilary Wainwright. 1979. *Beyond the fragments.* London: Merlin.

Segal, Lynne. 1999. *Why feminism?* Cambridge: Polity Press.

Vogel, Lise. 1983. *Marxism and the oppression of women.* London: Pluto.

Young, Iris. 1986. Beyond the unhappy marriage: A critique of the dual systems theory. In Lydia Sargent, ed., *The unhappy marriage of Marxism and feminism,* 43–69. London: Pluto.

Valerie Bryson

FEMINISM: Middle East

Arab feminists, as well as western feminists studying Arab societies, deeply disagree about the impact on Arab women of modernity brought about by the expansion of the post-Renaissance, post–French Revolution west. Many women claim that without modernization women would still be enslaved; their opponents claim that the only thing modernity achieved was to take away from women a traditional means of defense without making their lives easier or happier. The first group blames the traditionalists and the reactionaries, with their brutal and sometimes even fatal attacks on women; but others point to the growing numbers of Arab women who are choosing to adopt traditional modes of behavior, to veil as a means of regaining their own respectability and their traditional cultural identity.

No single program would respond to the demands of a peasant woman from upper Egypt and those of a secretary in Beirut, a lawyer in Tunisia, or a housewife in Yemen. Modernization has brought the recognition of women's education throughout the Arab countries, but also a war of symbols in which the wearing of the veil is just the most obvious—some would say the least important and the shallowest—issue in the fight to define cultural identity, as well as the adoption of new family codes and the design of new architectural spaces.

The Place of Women in the Arab-Muslim Family

Strict sexual boundaries are essential to true Islam. What is called the *seclusion* of women is not a very exact term. Islamic sexual politics are very frankly stated in Islamic theology and codified in the Shari'a (Muslim laws). According to authoritative Islamic texts, women as well as men need and should lead sexually satisfying lives. It is the duty of both sexes to act according to the call of the libido, and the prophet Muhammad himself preached and praised the care of the body. Signs of femininity are also encouraged, but these have to be hidden behind a veil and exhibited only within narrowly defined spaces.

Islam promoted a sophisticated integration of sacred and sexual politics. To accept the faith in the Prophet and his *umma* (nation) is to behave according to the demands of sexuality within any societal organization that regulates this.

It is almost inconceivable in Islam not to marry, for this disrupts the sophisticated sexual and social organization. But the *nikah*, the consummated marriage, if based on mutual consent according to the original religious texts, is also based on the idea that a man can marry up to four wives provided he treats them equally.

If Islam established itself as a religion and a social contract in an age of growing patriarchism, how did this total vision of the sacred and the sexual-societal affect on women? There is no doubt that sexual segregation is not experienced equally by men and women.

If the boundaries between the sexes are not to be trespassed, it is the woman who is going to be confined to the home (the *haram*, meaning both women and taboo). Clara Makhlouf (1979) observes this mutual form of segregation in her descriptions of afternoon gatherings of women to chew *qat* (a nonaddictive drug; *qat* leaves are a stimulant). Although this respect of secluded spaces is manageable within the wall of a private home, it becomes more difficult in public spaces.

Islam has always recognized women's intellect. It has always recognized that men and women alike should pursue knowledge (knowledge and religious knowledge were never conceived as separate in early Islam). These factors should place women in a very strong position. In reality, the sacred, now civil, law (its interpretation as well as its implementation) is used to inhibit women from realizing their potential.

Hence the necessity of the veil, preferably black, to erase individuality. Hence the laws that allow the man to divorce automatically on a whim (provided he can pay the promised sum—*muakhar*—agreed on before the marriage). Hence limitations of child custody, when children are taken away by the husband once they reach a certain age (generally 9 for boys and 11 for girls—this age may vary from one Arab country to another, but the principle is almost general). Women's rights and spaces are limited by laws that men have established, with a severity equal to their fear.

The Women's Movement and the Birth of Feminism

Many feminist studies find that women often use wit and influence to turn things to their advantage within the family. For instance, divorce is in the hands of men in the Shari'a (unless the man ignores his wife's bed for some months or disappears for more than a year), but a wife can make life unbearable for a husband until he repudiates her.

These defense strategies were initially seen as individual. The first women's publication reported by feminists and historians appeared in 1799 in Egypt and was to have no consequence for almost a century afterward: in a *hammam* (public bath where women meet regularly) in Rashid village in Egypt, the women wrote a letter addressed to Napoleon asking the French authorities to oblige their husbands to treat women with gallantry the way French men do their wives.

In 1892, the first women's journal in Arabic, *Al Fatat* (*Miss*), appeared in Egypt, edited by Hind Nawfal, a Lebanese woman. She called for women's education and for a public declaration of women's rights and duties. During the same period Rifaa Rifaat al-Tahtawi, who was deeply influenced by the ideas of the Enlightenment, wrote the first *plaidoyer*, or plea, still referred to today, arguing for women's education. Tahrir al-Maraa of Qassem Amin, like al-Tahtawi, supported women's emancipation for the sake of the renaissance of their country, although this concept is still far from modern feminism, which argues for women's well-being for the sake of women themselves.

The woman's issue has stood at the center of change and Arab identity since the beginning of the twentieth century. Between 1892 and 1940 more than 40 different women's magazines were published either in Arab countries or in centers of immigration (New York and São Paulo). These were directed at women and were often published by women, and they aimed at women's emancipation but also in some cases promoted the traditional role of women and opposed their right to vote, or to go unveiled—which would be an attempt to ape their western counterparts. Currently there are more than 50 women's magazines.

The place of women in Arab societies is indeed very central, either negatively or positively. From 1917 in Palestine and 1919 in Egypt, women took their demands to the streets for the first time. Women asked for the right to vote, a right inspired by western parliamentary democracy, and did so by first acting publicly in support of antiwestern nationalist movements. Huda Sha'rawi, an aristocrat, led the movement in Egypt and is remembered today as the most prominent Arab feminist. She saw the national struggle for independence and the struggle for women's emancipation as inseparable and interdependent (see Sha'rawi, 1986). For example, in writing to Lady Brunyate, the wife of Sir William Brunyate, the judicial and financial adviser to the Egyptian government, in March 1919, Sha'rawi asked her to explain why Britain acted contrary to all the beautiful values she had described as being British values, involving the defense of freedom and peace. Words like *justice* and *humanity* had nothing in common with what the British government and its soldiers were doing on the streets of Cairo. In her letter, Sha'rawi assumes the role of a woman speaking to a woman as well as an Egyptian active nationalist sending a message to the authorities.

Since 1919, when the first union of Arab women was founded in Egypt, women have combined demands for emancipation with those of the national struggle. Yet if independence has been achieved in all countries of the Arab world, the same cannot be said for women's demands and status.

Since the 1920s women have challenged the unequal treatment given to them by the law. The law, inspired by the Shari'a, is based on a system of values dating from the first centuries of Islam. For example, since 1919, women have asked for the abolition of male polygamy, but this has not yet been granted, nor is the testimony of a woman in a court still worth that of a man (two women witnesses equal one male witness in a courtroom).

These inequalities still stand as the basis of all civil codes in almost all of the 22 countries that are members of the Arab League. The exceptions include Tunisia and countries (such as Lebanon) where different civil codes are applied to other religious communities.

In most Arab countries, women have, since the 1950s, won the right to vote, in advance of some European countries, especially Switzerland. In Egypt, despite many attempts during Nasserism, and during the rule of Sadat (mainly through the efforts of Gihane al-Sadat), the Shari'a law had repelled any attack, although Egypt, like many other Arab countries, has aimed for a legal minimum age for marriage, as well as encouraging family planning.

The "Gihane Law" (after Mrs. Sadat), in 1979, limited the exercise of polygamy and repudiation (when a husband tells his wife he is divorcing her) in Egypt, but it was declared anticonstitutional by the High Court, which in 1985 abolished the law altogether and returned the legal status of women to that of the 1920s.

In Algeria the situation is even more dramatic. After the victory against colonialism, to which Algerian women made a great contribution, the situation of women saw no improvement. For example, slogans like "Women are not equal to men," and "Our labor masses are profoundly Muslim, traditionalists, and conservative; otherwise where would our religion stand?" were often printed in the official daily newspaper *Al Mujahid*.

The situation of Palestinian women suffers from all the complications brought about by a very radical colonization and the status of communities in the diaspora. The result is that the question of women is unclear. In Israel, women are subject both to Ottoman-inherited laws and to those of the Israeli state. In the Occupied Territories, many laws still apply, bequeathed by the Egyptians, the Jordanians, and the old Ottoman system.

In the Palestinian liberation movement, women mainly support the national struggle. Nonetheless, some voices have raised women's specific interests, and, occasionally, others challenge the male-dominated leadership and masculine mentality of the movement: Liana Badr, a Palestinian novelist, complains that the Palestinian liberation movement perpetuated traditional roles of women (see Shaaban, 1988). She attacks the Palestinian Women's Union for its similarity to other Arab women's unions—unions that are established by one-party regimes, which adopt official propaganda. The peace, if successful, may help to normalize Palestinian society and put the "woman question" on the social and legal agenda.

In Tunisia during the early years of the Bourguiba regime, more daring and radical changes in family law were introduced. Polygamy was strictly forbidden in 1956 and girls' education became available. The laws of 1958 and 1964 stipulate that a man can be sentenced to one year in jail for taking a second wife. In 1959, a law introduced equal inheritance for both daughters and sons (no other Arab country had changed the Shari'a inheritance law), but under the pressure of the traditionalists, Bourguiba abandoned this last reform. In Tunisia abortion is legal and free during the first three months of pregnancy, but, with the fading of Bourguiba's prestige, these rights are not secure.

Although countries like Syria and Iraq call for women's education, none touches the fundamental inequality of the Shari'a law. In Syria and Iraq, polygamy is not outlawed; a woman cannot travel without her husband's consent; and even her right to work is subject to her husband's authorization. A few years ago, Iraq decriminalized the "honor killing." A man who kills his wife, sister, or daughter because her sexual behavior has "shamed" him is not legally considered to have committed a crime.

The "honor killing," like the clitoridectomy in countries like Sudan, is not of Muslim origin. Clitoridectomy is contrary to the whole spirit of Islamic sexual politics and is found only in African Arab countries. In Sudan, and to a lesser degree in Egypt, it is unfortunately often women who have suffered this physical mutilation themselves who still believe in its "necessity" in order to keep their daughters fit for marriage and for them to be "respected."

Nothing has proved more difficult, more frightening, than the balance between tradition and emancipation. The result is that whatever the nature of a regime or government, including royal Saudi Arabia, Jordan, revolutionary ex-South

Yemen, and parliamentary (pre–civil war) Lebanon, women's status is at odds with the contradictory wishes of different sectors of society.

The dilemma of the women's movements in the Arab world lies here, in the problem created by the fact that women's demands for emancipation seem western but rose alongside (and often in the shade of) nationalist movements. For Arab nationalism itself oscillated between a need to modernize according to the western model and a need to reject this model as that of the colonizer and a powerful threat to local identity.

Women and Education

As far as education is concerned, women's access has improved enormously. Before World War II the great majority of Arab women were illiterate, but today compulsory schooling of both boys and girls is dictated by law in all Arab countries. A high level of education is not always accompanied by a change in the laws that discriminate against women. Some of the countries that have the highest level of women's education are also those that have retained the most archaic family laws. It is as if education were disconnected from the other spheres of life. In many Arab countries today, a woman can be the head of a university but would still need the consent of her husband to leave the country for a conference.

In Saudi Arabia, a woman cannot leave the country without a legal authorization given by her male next of kin, or without her husband, her father, or even her younger brother accompanying her to the airport and informing the passport officer of his consent to her traveling.

This discrepancy between the now accepted right of women to education and the fact that women do not, whatever the level of their education, enjoy free movement, is perhaps one way in which modernization clashes with tradition. Women's education is not a modern phenomenon. What *is* new is that education is public, in the sense that male and female spaces are not strictly exclusive. As we saw earlier, knowledge was never the domain only of men in Islam. Prominent families taught the Qur'an, the *hadiths* (traditions), and the highly praised art of poetry to their daughters.

Many women slaves played important roles in the life of Arab societies with their knowledge of the arts, sciences, and literature. A bibliographical dictionary of the elite and other leading figures of the ninth Hijra century (fifteenth century) lists 411 women among the names of 1,075 people who were definitely educated (*Addwa'a Allamaa Li Ahl al Qarn attasaa*). Although women never went to the Madrassa (an early version of boarding schools for men),

Sukaina, a granddaughter of the Imam Ali, had the equivalent of a literary salon.

If the right to education for women is a fait accompli in almost all Arab countries, the results are not always encouraging, and studies often reveal widespread illiteracy in certain countries, like Algeria, Egypt, Morocco, Yemen, and Sudan. Literacy levels do not, however, correspond to political rights. For example, the highest level of literacy is in Kuwait, where women are still fighting for the right to vote. In Saudi Arabia, where women are still secluded, 32 percent of the university teaching staff is female. In Egypt, where illiteracy persists, women constitute 28 percent of the university staff, and a great number of doctors are women.

In the midst of these contradictions, some women are active feminists. Others support fundamentalist movements, segregation, and the obligatory veiling of women, as well as a return to the Shari'a law. This phenomenon, called backlash in other parts of the world, is described by the sociologist Maxine Molyneux (writing in the context of Nicaragua) as a change that could threaten the short-term practical interest of some women or entail a cost in the loss of forms of protection that are not then compensated for in some way.

Long gone is the time when women were just secluded in their homes, with a marriage contracted by the woman's family. But the present is not clear, and the future is likely to be tumultuous. Many Arab women are standing bravely against the current, defending their notion of dignity, their professions, and their share of independence.

See Also

FAMILY: RELIGIONS AND LEGAL SYSTEMS: ISLAMIC TRADITION; FEMINISM: NORTH AFRICAN; IMAGES OF WOMEN: MIDDLE EAST; ISLAM; LITERATURE: ARABIC; POLITICS AND THE STATE: MIDDLE EAST; ISLAM; VIOLENCE: MIDDLE EAST AND THE ARAB WORLD; WOMEN'S STUDIES: MIDDLE EAST AND NORTH AFRICA

References and Further Reading

Ahmed, Leila. 1992. *Women and gender in Islam.* New Haven, Conn.: Yale University Press.

Al-Hawrani, A. 1994. *Les ruses femmes.* Paris: Phebus.

Altorki, Suraya. 1986. *Women in Saudi Arabia.* New York: Columbia University Press.

Beck, Lois. 1978. *Women in the Muslim world.* Cambridge, Mass.: Harvard University Press.

Bouhdiba, A. 1988. *Sexuality in Islam.* London: Routledge.

Esoposito, John. 1989. *Women in Muslim family law.* Syracuse, N.Y.: Syracuse University Press.

Fernea, Elizabeth, ed. 1985. *Women and family in the Middle East.* Austin: University of Texas Press.

Haeri, Shahla. 1989. *Law of desire: Temporary marriage.* London: Tauris.

Hijab, Nadia. 1988. *Womenpower: The Arab debate.* Cambridge: Cambridge University Press.

Kandiyoti, Denise. 1991. *Women, Islam, and the state.* London: Macmillan.

Keddie, Nikki, and Beth Baron, eds. 1992. *Women in Middle Eastern history: Shifting boundaries in sex and gender.* New Haven, Conn.: Yale University Press.

Khalifa, Ijlal. 1975. *Qissat Al Maara, Ala Ard Misr* [*The story of women in the land of Egypt*]. Cairo: General Egyptian Book Organization.

Makhlouf, Clara. 1979. *Changing veils.* London: Croom Helm.

Mernissi, Fatima. 1985. *Beyond the veil: Male-female dynamics in Muslim societies,* (rev. ed.). London: Al-Saqi.

———. 1991. *Women and Islam.* Oxford: Basil Blackwell.

Mudawanat Assahafa Al Arabiya. 1985. (Arab press records.) 2 vols. Beirut: Maahad Al Inmaa.

Saadawi, Nawal El. 1980. *The hidden face of Eve.* London: Zed.

Shaaban, Bulthaina. 1988. *Both right- and left-handed.* London: Women's Press.

Sha'rawi, Huda. 1986. *Harem years.* London: Virago.

Tillion, Germaine. 1986. *The republic of cousins.* London: Al-Saqi.

Tuker, Judith. 1985. *Women in nineteenth-century Egypt.* Cambridge: Cambridge University Press.

———, ed. 1993. *Arab women: Old boundaries, new frontiers.* Indianapolis: Indiana University Press.

Waddy, C. 1980. *Women in Muslim history.* London: Longman.

Walther, W. 1993. *Women in Islam.* Princeton, N.J.: Markus Wiener.

Mai Ghoussoub

FEMINISM: Militant

Feminists today are often viewed as "militant," especially when they engage in public protests. However, the term *militant feminism* is commonly applied to the political activities of those first-wave feminists who were members of the Women's Social and Political Union (WSPU) founded in Manchester, England, on 10 October 1903 by Emmeline Pankhurst and her eldest daughter, Christabel. As a women-only organization, free from affiliation with any of the male-dominated and male-centered political parties, the WSPU campaigned for the granting of the vote to women on equal terms with men, as well as for a more equal society for women generally. "Deeds, not words" was its famous slogan.

The strategies of the WSPU are often contrasted with the "constitutional," law-abiding methods of the National Union of Women's Suffrage Societies (NUWSS), led by Millicent Garrett Fawcett. The constitutional suffragists used old methods: petitions and pressure group activity, including memorials to members of Parliament, deputations, and the occasional large public meeting. However, the dividing line between "constitutional" and "militant" methods is not clear. Similarly, in terms of friendships and practical feminist politics, the divisions between the WSPU, the NUWSS, and other women's suffrage organizations, such as the United Suffragists (US) and the East London Federation of Suffragettes (ELF), were often blurred.

It is impossible to give exact figures for the membership of the WSPU at any one point, since the necessary records do not exist. The circulation of *Votes for Women,* for example, the first official newspaper of the WSPU, was reputed to have reached a peak of about 50,000 and was undoubtedly read by many more.

Although members were united in their belief in "the cause" and in the common bonds of all womanhood, the WSPU was a loose coalition of different groupings of women who differed in what they considered the best means to attain their goal. In particular, there was a small core of "militants" who engaged in a range of activities different from those of other WSPU members, such as arson and smashing windows, although the term *militant* is usually applied to all.

From 1905 until the eve of World War I in August 1914, about 1,000 women (and about 40 men) were imprisoned as a result of suffrage activity. Many, although not all, of these women were members of the WSPU, spanning the early stage of what Christabel Pankhurst termed "mild militancy" to a second, more aggressive, militant phase. Mild militancy involved peaceful means of protest that had been commonly used by other dissenting groups—such as open-air rallies, marches, demonstrations, deputations to Parliament, and heckling male politicians at major political meetings. When the government refused to yield on women's suffrage or to recognize WSPU protesters as political offenders who should be placed in the more privileged first division rather than the second or third division in prison, new and more aggressive militant tactics were adopted. In July 1909, Marion Wallace Dunlop, protesting because she was not recognized as a political prisoner, went on a hunger strike—a political weapon that soon became common among the "suffragettes," as they became known. The government responded in October of the same year by introducing forcible feeding for all women prisoners refusing to take food. The ordeal of forcible feeding became especially cruel and hazardous under the Prisoners' Temporary Discharge for Ill-Health Act of April 1913, which allowed a prisoner who was weak through hunger striking to be released into the community in order to regain her health sufficiently to be rearrested and to continue her sentence. Under the "Cat and Mouse Act," as it became known, "mice" (suffragettes) were often released in an emaciated condition only to be clawed back by the "cat" (the state) as many times as necessary.

By 1913, the second, more aggressive stage of militancy included such deeds as smashing windows, setting fire to and planting bombs in empty buildings, destroying art treasures, pouring acid on golf courses and cricket pitches, and pouring jam and syrup into state-owned mailboxes. The aim throughout was never to endanger life but to damage property. In a speech in 1912, Mrs. Pankhurst, the much-loved leader of the WSPU, justified such actions on the grounds that other, more peaceful methods had failed. Even when women had been physically battered and insulted in making their protests, it had all been to no avail. Furthermore, she emphasized that every advance of men's political freedom had been marked with violence and the destruction of property.

On the eve of the outbreak of World War I, Mrs. Pankhurst called an end to all militancy. In 1918 a partial victory for the women's suffrage campaign was won when women over 30 years of age were given the vote, provided they were householders or the wives of householders, graduates of British universities, or occupiers of property with an annual rent of £5 or more. It was not until 2 July 1928 that women could vote on equal terms with men, that is, on attaining the age of 21. Sadly, Mrs. Pankhurst had died some weeks before this, on 14 June.

See Also

FEMINISM: FIRST-WAVE BRITISH; SUFFRAGE

References and Further Reading

Holton, Sandra Stanley. 1990. "In sorrowful wrath": Suffrage militancy and the romantic feminism of Emmeline Pankhurst. In Harold L. Smith, ed., *British feminism in the twentieth century.* Aldershot, U.K..: Edward Elgar.

Jorgensen-Earp, Cheryl R., ed. 1999. *Speeches and trails of the militant suffragettes: The Women's Social and Political Union, 1903–1918.* London: Associated University Presses.

Marcus, Jane, ed. 1987. *Suffrage and the Pankhursts.* London and New York: Routledge.

Pankhurst, Emmeline. 1914. *My own story.* London: Eveleigh Nash.

Purvis, June. 1995a. "Deeds, not words": The daily lives of militant WSPU suffragettes in Edwardian Britain. *Women's Studies International Forum* 18(2): 91–101.

———. 1995b. The prison experiences of the suffragettes in Edwardian Britain. *Women's History Review* 4(1): 103–133.

Purvis, June. 1998. Christabel Pankhurst and the Women's Social and Political Union. In Maroula Joannou and June Purvis, eds., *The women's suffrage movement: New feminist perspectives.* Manchester: Manchester University Press.

Purvis, June. 2000. Emmeline Pankhurst (1858–1928) and votes for women. In June Purvis and Sandra Stanley Holton, eds., *Votes for women.* London and New York: Routledge.

Rosen, Andrew. 1974. *Rise up women! The militant campaign of the Women's Social and Political Union 1903–1914.* London: Routledge and Kegan Paul.

Stanley, Liz, with Ann Morley. 1988. *The life and death of Emily Wilding Davison: A biographical detective story.* London: Women's Press.

Vicinus, Martha. 1985. Male space and women's bodies: The suffragette movement. In Martha Vicinus, *Independent women: Work and community for single women 1850–1920,* chap. 7. London: Virago.

June Purvis

FEMINISM: Nineteenth Century

Scope and Definition

The term *feminism* was not used throughout most of the nineteenth century. It first came into usage in England and the rest of Europe in the 1890s and in the United States only early in the twentieth century. Nineteenth-century feminism, broadly defined, encompasses arguments, organizations, and activities that focused on examining and redefining ideas about women, critiquing oppression based on sex, and advocating changes in women's situations. In nineteenth-century Britain and the United States, these would most commonly have been identified as debates about the "woman question" or as activities of the "woman movement." The definition or redefinition of womanhood was a central social question of the nineteenth century. "The true history of the Women's Movement is the whole history of the nineteenth-century" Ray Strachey wrote in *The Cause,* a history of the suffrage movement (1928:5).

Early in the century, industrialization and urbanization destabilized the arrangements of work and gender roles within the family, essentially creating the middle-class family and reshaping the working-class family, formerly a collaborative productive economic unit. In this transition, the family became in ideological terms the "private sphere," a domestic refuge from the stresses of the working worlds presided over by "the angel in the house." This ideology of separate spheres joined with the social and customary subordination of women to produce a set of social values in which the roles, privileges, duties, and obligations of men and women were sharply distinguished. This narrowed definition of women's role solidified at the same time that enlightenment liberalism was articulating the rights of man and revolutions in the United States and France were demanding that these rights be embodied in political institutions and practices. The ironies and tensions of these simultaneous developments contributed to producing an environment in which the woman movement developed and grounded its analyses.

Neither the people nor the movement designated by the phrase "woman movement," however, can be seen as monolithic, coherent, or unified. The class, race, and gender composition of the woman movement shifted within time periods and over time. Debates arose within the movement—about the theoretical analysis of women's situation, and also about preferred strategies of change and the priority to be given to particular issues or campaigns. Women and men came to work on the woman question from prior involvement in a range of movements and issues, among them revolutionary and nationalist, anti-slavery and abolitionist, progressive social reform, and labor organizing. They brought with them divergent and often conflicting social values and models of political and social change. Feminists also worked in several movements at once, so exchange between other movements and the woman movement continued throughout the century.

Focal issues and arguments also changed over the course of the century, so what came to be called feminism by 1899 and the "woman movement" of earlier in the century had some commonalities but also many differences. As the century progressed, some issues, particularly those of property ownership and equal access to education and the professions for middle-class women, were addressed through legislation and social change, so the focus shifted to other issues. New groups of women—immigrants, laborers, women of color—entered the movement and brought new issues with them. In examining the span of nineteenth-century feminism, one might best begin from its Enlightenment roots in the political thought that drove the French and American revolutions of the late eighteenth century and grounded British liberalism, and follow it through transformation into twentieth-century movements and

arguments with World War I and the granting of suffrage to women in much of northern Europe, the United States, New Zealand, and Australia in the first two decades of the twentieth century.

The woman movement was practically and self-consciously international in two ways. First, there were nineteenth-century movements for changes in women's situation (most often for access to education and reform of property, inheritance law, and marriage practices) in many parts of the world—not just in the United States, Britain, and France but throughout Europe and in India, China, Russia, much of Latin America, and North Africa. In many of these countries, organizing for change began as part of revolutionary, nationalist, or independence struggles. For example, as in the United States and France, women who fought in early nineteenth-century struggles for independence in such South American countries as Columbia, Venezuela, Argentina, and Brazil attempted to demand legal reform and enfranchisement for women, but saw post-independence legal codes established that enfranchised only men. Here and elsewhere, these struggles produced various kinds of feminist activities and institutions, even though it was not until the middle of the twentieth century that Latin American women, like women in France and other predominantly Catholic countries of southern Europe, gained suffrage.

Second, the woman movement was international in that these local, regional, and national efforts were linked through formal and informal networks, strengthened by improvements through the century in international travel and communication. As Maggie Mcfadden has documented in *Golden Cables of Sympathy*, a strong transatlantic feminist community existed throughout the century. Activists in the United States and Europe communicated regularly, met in international meetings and personal visits, and formed intentionally international organizations. Thinking and strategies were shared across national boundaries and oceans; support for local efforts was sought from activists in other countries. International abolitionist and suffrage organizing offers good examples of such transatlantic networks, but examples can also be found elsewhere, as in the First International Feminist Congress, which gathered suffrage organizers from around Latin America in Buenos Aires in 1910.

Intellectual Foundations and Influences

Two veins of argument run through nineteenth-century feminism and inform its arguments for change. One argument asserted women's similarity to men, deemphasizing biological differences and claiming "women's rights."

According to this argument, women's intellects, talents, and capacities are equal to men's and women are as fully "human" as men; they should therefore have access, as humans and citizens, to all spheres of public and civic life open to men. This argument underpins demands for suffrage and for women's admission to higher education, professional training and employment, and public and municipal offices. These were also most likely to be the arguments made by organizations in which men were welcomed as collaborators.

The other vein of feminist argument asserted that "women's nature" is fundamentally different from men's and emphasized "women's duties." Women were seen as more nurturing, compassionate, altruistic, peace-loving, and fundamentally moral, their motherhood being their essential and defining difference. From this perspective, women are a social group with a natural inclination to affiliate in women-only institutions and organizations. This argument was a basis of women's work in temperance and moral reform societies, in settlement houses, in sanitation and public health campaigns, and in campaigns against prostitution; and of women's entry into nursing, social work, and teaching. It advanced reasons for women's entry into the public sphere on the basis of the special capacities a woman will bring with her, and it grounds demands for the protection of women workers (ironically, often grouped with children) from long hours and workplace hazards. By invoking qualities recognizably associated with traditional womanhood, these arguments from "women's nature" appear to have been functional particularly for middle-class feminists, because they allowed women to act publicly to change women's situations without appearing "unwomanly."

The tension between "similarity" arguments and "difference" arguments is at the core of nineteenth-century feminism. Both arguments were used to justify suffrage and other demands, and they were used by the same people at different times. In fact, Nancy Cott (1987) argues, this tension at the heart of feminism was never resolved, but it remains a "functional ambiguity" rather than a "debilitating tension." It provided a "double-lensed view" with considerable strategic and theoretical advantages for the movement and the women who worked within it.

Particularly early in the century, woman movement activists brought to their arguments conceptual tools honed by late eighteenth-century Enlightenment liberalism and radical and evangelical Protestantism. Enlightenment liberalism, the grounding political theory of the U.S. Constitution, the French Revolution, and the British Liberal Party, argued for the right of all humans to life, liberty, property, and full citizenship. Nevertheless, the relationship between nineteenth-century feminist thought and liberal arguments and institutions was complicated. Unquestionably, these arguments were useful to feminism and could be extended to the rights of women, as they were by Mary Wollstonecraft in *A Vindication of the Rights of Woman* (1792), by John Stuart Mill in *The Subjection of Women* (1869), and by Elizabeth Cady Stanton, whose "Declaration of Sentiments" (1848), borrowed and revised the very language of the U.S. Constitution. By asserting the natural rights of all humans, liberal political arguments made visible to women their exclusion from rights they should be able to claim as human beings and also the ways in which femaleness itself was defined as less than human by that exclusion. Liberalism, however, was also criticized by many nineteenth-century feminists. While it provided theoretical frameworks within which women could make arguments for their rights, it did not produce institutions that acknowledged women's full citizenship and personhood. As Abigail Adams observed in a letter to John Adams (May 1776), "whilst you are proclaiming peace and goodwill to all men, emancipating all nations, you insist on retaining absolute power over wives" (Schneir, 1987: 4). Ironically, in the consolidation of the political gains of Enlightenment liberalism in the U.S. Constitution and in Britain and France, citizens were explicitly defined as men, and women were overtly excluded by their gender from political participation.

Evangelical Protestantism and the Quaker movement were also influences on the early nineteenth-century woman movement, particularly in the United States, with the "Great Awakening," but also to some extent in Britain. Their doctrines of individual conversion and the importance of the relationship between the individual soul and God validated women's action on the basis of individual conscience. More important perhaps, evangelical Protestantism set about eradicating sin, in the form of slavery, vice, drunkenness, and prostitution, and organized moral reform societies and missionary societies to accomplish that goal. Many of these organizations were overwhelmingly composed of women, who learned organizational and political skills as well as social reform arguments which they took with them into later activities on behalf of women. Quakerism, well known for its early moral opposition to slavery and as a training ground for abolitionist and suffrage activists, was particularly important as one of few religious traditions which allowed women leadership in preaching and ministry. The legacy of evangelical Protestantism and the Quaker movement is complex, however, for, as Olive Banks as argued, "[T]he philanthropic and humanitarian zeal of the Quakers and Evangelicals clearly provided a fruitful background from which feminist ideas emerge, but it is clear that even a deep involvement in such issues did not necessarily lead women to question their traditional role" (1981: 26). These influences contributed most to "difference" arguments for bringing women's moral influence into public reform. Late in the century, Elizabeth Cady Stanton in *The Women's Bible*, and Matilda Jocelyn Gage in *Woman, Church, and State* were strongly critical of the ways in which Christian doctrine and institutions continued to reinforce the subordination of women.

The abolitionist and antislavery movements were important to the formation of the nineteenth-century woman movement in similarly complex ways. As in many nationalist movements and liberal reforms, abolitionist women found that, ironically, when legal reforms to end slavery were implemented, as in the Fourteenth Amendment to the U.S. Constitution, not only were black and white women not included, but "manhood," although expanded to include black men, was an explicit qualification for voting. However, the U.S. abolitionist movement and the British antislavery movement were a political training ground for many feminists. Many of the women involved in the American and British woman movements came to feminist activism from the abolitionist movement in the United States and the antislavery societies in Britain. Among U.S. women were Elizabeth Cady Stanton, Lucy Stone, Lucretia Mott, Sojourner Truth, and Susan B. Anthony; among British women were Josephine Butler and Harriet Martineau.

Through involvement in abolitionism, they learned both political organizing tactics and the moral and intellectual rationales—largely liberal and evangelical Protestant—that could be applied to the woman question. Within this framework, feminist arguments that link race and gender in important ways were articulated for the first time. In her *Letters on the Equality of the Sexes*, Angeline Grimké, a white U.S. southern woman, argued that slave women experienced slavery *as* women, because they were subjected to sexual exploitation in ways that male slaves were not. In her speech at a suffrage convention in 1851, Sojourner Truth, a freed black slave, asking "ain't I a woman?" asserted her common womanhood with white women in spite of her racial difference and the very different material conditions in which she had lived and worked.

The suffrage and antislavery movements also provided women with opportunities for contact with women from outside their own countries. One notable instance was the World Anti-Slavery Convention in London in 1840 at which the male leadership of the British Anti-Slavery Society refused to seat the women in the U.S. delegation. This moment was important for the outrage it produced in different ways in both British and U.S. feminists, heightening their awareness of the inequality and mistreatment of women within their own movement and of the failure of some of their male colleagues to link women's emancipation with that of the slaves. It also initiated a transatlantic feminist discussion about these insights that continued throughout the century.

Both early in the century (1820s and 1830s) and at the end of the century (1880s and 1890s), socialism had a significant influence on the thought of women involved in the woman movement, particularly regarding issues of sexuality and the sexual division of labor. Early in the century, the major socialist influences on feminism came from the utopian socialism of Robert Owen in Britain and from the French socialist Charles Fourier (1772–1837), both of whom also influenced various U.S. utopian communities in the 1840s. Major early feminist proponents of socialism included Frances Wright, a Scottish feminist and abolitionist who attempted to found an interracial utopian community in Tennessee based on her free love and abolitionist principles; and Anna Wheeler, who introduced French socialism in Britain and arranged visits of the French feminist socialist Flora Tristan to London in the 1820s. From socialists in Britain, France, and the United States, feminists absorbed radical views of marriage and sexuality. Most utopian socialists in the 1820s and 1830s either saw bourgeois marriage as the equivalent of legalized prostitution and advocated only marriages of affection and easy divorce, as the Owenites did, or, following Fourier, rejected marriage altogether and advocated free love and sexual autonomy for women. Owenites also opposed the family as the bastion of private property, advocating communitarian values and proposing the centralization of domestic labor in communal dining rooms, kitchens, and nurseries, an idea proposed again at the end of the century by the American socialist Charlotte Perkins Gilman in her *Women and Economics* (1898).

Again, as with other intellectual and social movements of the period, the relationship between feminism and socialism was conflicted. Socialism provided certain intellectual and political resources but at the same time failed to incorporate the woman question in its agendas. For example, Chartism, a working-class political movement that evolved out of British socialism in the 1830s and 1840s and demanded a variety of electoral reforms, engaged the support of many radical and working-class women, but then failed them by demanding only universal "manhood" suffrage in its "People's Charter." Socialist ideas also caused dissension within the woman movement. Particularly later in the century, many socialist women—Eleanor Marx, for example—saw the goals of the mainstream women's suffrage

801

movement as far too limited and individualistic to fully change women's situation. Women suffragists, on the other hand, considered the views of many socialist feminists far too radical and unwomanly; they disassociated themselves from these women, fearing that affiliating themselves with socialist women's open discussion of sexuality in particular would undermine their middle-class respectability and thus also the suffrage cause.

Analyzing and Changing Women's Lives

Much of the intellectual work of nineteenth-century feminism was focused on explicating the conditions of women's lives and the legal structures, customs, and practices that constructed and perpetuated those conditions. Attempts to understand women's lives within the family—their subordination through marriage, motherhood, sexuality and inheritance—was one focus of analysis, while a related argument focused on women's exclusion from education, professional training, and employment, as well as from political enfranchisement.

Analysis and transformation of the institution of marriage was one of the earliest projects of nineteenth-century feminism, and remained a central concern throughout the 1830s, 1840s, and 1850s. Stanton and the midcentury British feminists Frances Power Cobbe ("Wife Torture in England," 1878; "Celibacy vs. Marriage," 1862) and Barbara Leigh Bodichon ("A Brief Summary, in Plain Language, of the Most Important Laws Concerning Women," 1854) explicated the areas in which the situation of married women desperately needed redress. "A man and a wife are one person in law," wrote Bodichon, "he is civilly responsible for her acts; she lives under his protection or cover, and her condition is called coverture....A woman's body belongs to her husband; she is in his custody" (Lacey, 1987:25). Bodichon's description of a wife's status under English law fairly accurately represents what was also true for women in the United States and northern Europe and largely parallels the view of marriage embodied in the Napoleonic code in France and canon law in Catholic countries. Midcentury organizing focused on gaining three essential rights for a married woman: the right to the property she has brought into a marriage and to her own earnings during marriage; the right to divorce violent, alcoholic, insane, or brutal husbands; and the right to retain custody of her children in cases of separation or divorce. The last issue was brought to the fore in Britain in the late 1840s by Caroline Norton's very public fight for custody of her children. The first attempts to address property issues through legislation came in the 1830s in the United States and in 1870 in Britain. Many feminists who later joined the strug-

gle for women's suffrage learned organizing skills in the relative safety of U.S. and British campaigns for married women's property rights.

These arguments for reform of women's rights within the family were increasingly linked, as the century progressed, to demands for women's suffrage, education, and employment. The British feminist Mona Caird, for example, argued in her essay "Marriage" (1888) that the only way for women to achieve equality in the home was to achieve economic and political independence in the public world. If women do not marry by choice and are unable to survive apart from marriage, she argued, they will never be other than subordinates to men.

In the latter half of the century, female "redundancy," or the overabundance of adult women in the population as a result of the deaths of men in midcentury (the Crimean War, the U.S. Civil War) and the departure of men for the West and for colonial service, made alternatives to marriage an even more pressing social need. In her essay "What Shall We Do With Our Old Maids?" (1862), Cobbe writes, "The old assumption that marriage was the sole destiny of women, and that it was the business of her husband to support her, is brought up short by the statement that one in four is certain not to marry and that three millions of women earn their own living at this moment in England" (Hamilton, 1995: 86). The number and situation of these "redundant" women made still more visible the inadequate and ill-paid employment available for women, with middle-class women working as governesses and working-class women as household servants, factory laborers, or prostitutes. Women who had begun by organizing to improve women's condition within families expanded their efforts to focus on the need for improved education, training, and employment for all girls and women, and these issues moved into mainstream feminism.

As educational, training, and employment opportunities expanded, independent life and the choice not to marry were increasingly seen as a real and desirable option for middle-class women. Among the first generations of college-educated women, marriage rates were as low as 50 percent in the United States. In "Celibacy vs. Marriage" (1862) Cobbe asserts that one might well prefer "true and tender" friendships with women to subordination within traditional marriage. Although negative stereotypes of spinsters and "new women" persisted, single women increasingly made lives for themselves with other women in social reform organizations, settlement houses, women's schools and colleges, religious organizations, and hospitals, and formed the core of many feminist organizations and institutions (Vicinus, 1985).

Discussion of women's sexuality and sexual autonomy became more central to feminist thinking in the latter half of the century. Despite early utopian socialist discussions of sexuality and "free love," women were for the most part constructed ideologically as sexless; a woman's sexual ignorance was in part a mark of her true womanliness and most women of the woman movement endorsed, at least publicly, those ideological prescriptions. Female moral reform societies in the United States began to campaign against prostitution as early as the 1840s under the banner of "social purity." In Britain, from the mid-1860s on, feminists organized to repeal the Contagious Diseases Acts, which gave police the power to pick up prostitutes and subject them to examination for venereal disease. Through these campaigns against the Contagious Diseases Acts and the social purity campaigns, feminists developed a nuanced critique of a sexual double standard, which condoned promiscuity and adultery for men but enjoined chastity and abstinence for women. Christabel Pankhurst's slogan "Votes for Women! Chastity for Men" in "The Scourge," her essay on the evils of prostitution, articulates succinctly the linkage between private and public emancipation that feminists increasingly understand and name as the century progresses. As Susan Kent argues, "the vote became both the symbol of the free, sexually autonomous woman and the means by which the goals of a feminist sexual culture were to be attained" (1987: 13).

In the last three or four decades of the century, the work of the early decades bore some fruit in legal reform of divorce, child custody, and property law; in the admission of women to municipal voting rights and some local public offices; in the founding of women's schools and colleges; in the admission of women to medical schools; and in the opening of some professions to women. While many of these successes were partial and work remained to be done in all areas, they made material differences in the lives and situation particularly of middle-class women. Late in the century, much of the energy that had gone into achieving such reforms recentered on suffrage organizing. Although only New Zealand (1893) granted women full suffrage in the nineteenth century, the suffrage gains of the early twentieth century (Australia, 1902; Finland, 1906; Norway, 1913; Denmark, 1915; Britain, 1918 for women over 30, and 1928 for all women; Sweden, 1919; The Netherlands, 1919; United States, 1920) were the clear outcomes of nineteenth-century feminist organizing.

See Also

DIFFERENCE, *I and II*; FEMINISM: FIRST-WAVE BRITISH *and* NORTH AMERICAN; SUFFRAGE; WOMEN'S MOVEMENT, UNITED STATES

References and Further Reading

Banks, Olive. 1981. *Faces of feminism: A study of feminism as a social movement.* New York: St. Martin's.

Caine, Barbara. 1992. *Victorian feminists.* Oxford: Oxford University Press.

Cott, Nancy. 1987. *The grounding of modern feminism.* New Haven, Conn.: Yale University Press.

Fraisse, Geneviève, and Michelle Perrot. 1993. *A history of women: IV. Emerging feminism from revolution to world war.* Cambridge, Mass.: Harvard University Press.

Hamilton, Susan, ed. 1995. *Criminals, idiots, women, and minors: Nineteenth century writing on women by women.* Peterborough, Ontario: Broadview.

Jeffreys, Sheila. 1987. *The sexuality debates.* London: Routledge.

Kent, Susan. 1987. *Sex and suffrage in Britain: 1860–1914.* Princeton, N.J.: Princeton University Press.

Kerber, Linda. 1998. *No constitutional right to be ladies: Women and the obligations of citizenship.* New York: Hill and Wang.

Lacey, Candida Ann. 1987. *Barbara Leigh Smith Bodichon and the Langham Place group.* London: Routledge.

Levine, Phillippa. 1990. *Feminist lives in Victorian England.* Oxford: Blackwell.

Lerner, Gerda. 1993. *The creation of feminist consciousness: From the Middle Ages to 1870.* Oxford: Oxford University Press.

Mcfadden, Maggie. 1999. *Golden cables of sympathy: The transatlantic sources of nineteenth century feminism.* Lexington: University of Kentucky Press.

Morgan, Robin, ed. 1996. *Sisterhood is global.* New York: Feminist Press.

Rossi, Alice. 1987. *The feminist papers: From Adams to de Beauvoir.* 2nd ed. Boston: Northeastern University Press.

Schneir, Miriam. 1987. *The Vintage book of historical feminism.* London: Vintage.

Strachey, Ray. 1928. *The cause.* London: Bell.

Vicinus, Martha. 1985. *Independent women: Work and community for single women, 1850–1920.* Chicago: University of Chicago Press.

Wheeler, Marjorie S. 1995. *One woman, one vote: Rediscovering the woman suffrage movement.* Troutdale, Ore.: New Sage.

Wendy Kolmar

FEMINISM: North Africa

The term *feminism* is often applied to a variety of issues including women's rights, liberation, and emancipation. In this sense, north African feminism represents the collective efforts of the women from these regions (Morocco, Algeria, Tunisia, Egypt, and so on) to fight for their rights and liberation. Even though feminist ideology is a worldwide phenomenon, it is often conditioned and characterized by cultural, historical, traditional, political, social, and even economic factors. The uniqueness of north African feminism is mainly due to two particular factors: the existence of the Arab tradition and culture on the one hand, and Islamic fundamentalism, conservatism, or integralism on the other. In the final analysis, these two factors could be reduced to the all-penetrating influence of the Islamic religion.

History and Development of North African Feminism

Generally, the history of north African feminism and the active role and contributions of women to the social, economic, and political development of north Africa could be divided into two periods: preindependence and postindependence. It goes without saying that the participation of women in the economy cannot be traced to any particular period, since they have been a strong producing force throughout history.

The development of feminism in preindependent north Africa can broadly be seen as the participation of women in the various movements of nationalism, reform, and resistance to imperialism, such as the Wafdist Women's Central Committee (WWCC) of Egypt, formed in 1920 as the women's wing of the Wafdist Nationalist Party. During these years women's particular needs did not actually come to the fore, since the more apparent need was the liberation struggle against colonialism. Naturally, all available forces, including women's, were mobilized and directed toward the reconstruction of a national identity. These years therefore witnessed the identification of women and their interests with "the nation" or "the people"; women belonged to "the masses" without any class differentiation or conflicting aims, attitudes, and interests.

The situation did bring to women of north Africa a sort of self-awakening as women with specific needs, not identified and not identifiable with those of "the people." Their participation in the struggles for independence paved the way for their consciousness of the need for another liberation struggle—this time concerning women, as women and for women.

North African feminism, which took roots in the years before independence, did not become solidified until the years after independence. Since north African feminism is strictly linked to Islamic religion and culture, the first areas of women's lives to be reconsidered in reform efforts and legislation were marriage and veiling.

North African Women in Politics

Feminists in the developed world have been fighting to make domestic work matter, to receive financial remuneration for their never-ending jobs in the home, and to bring men back to the home as collaborators.

This situation is unheard of in third world countries, especially in north Africa, where the traditional place of the woman still remains the home. The situation of north African women is all the more aggravated by the existence of Islamic laws and customs, which often act as a strong rationale for the restriction of women. Hence there is a dichotomy between the private and public lives of north African women, the latter meaning active or passive participation in politics.

The most politically active and organized of all north African women are, without doubt, Egyptian women. Apart from the fact that Egypt is one of the few countries to have been ruled by many queens (like Nefertiti, Hatshepsut, and Cleopatra), the participation of Egyptian women in politics dates to 1919, when they gathered in the streets to demonstrate with men against colonialism and British imperialism. Thereafter, women took an active role in politics and were educated and recruited into political parties, especially after World War I. Their presence was particularly felt in both the old and the new Wafd parties, and they were leaders and prominent members of the antifascist movements of the 1930s.

The conservative and traditional nature of Egyptian women's lives as wives and mothers was not a total block to the activities of some of these women, especially in leading opposition groups and political parties. Perhaps not surprisingly, they were often attracted to and identified with the left and its Marxist philosophy. Women in the political front functioned as both political activists and feminists. As Marxists, they believed that the freedom of society at large means the liberation of each individual, not vice versa, and so they dedicated themselves in the first instance to the needs of society.

Women who took part in the political life of Egypt were not only feminists and leftists but also intellectuals, such as Inge Aflatum, Latifa al Zayat, and Soraya Adham. Since Egyptian women were marginalized by their educational backwardness, the only way to bridge the gap created by educational and intellectual inequality was to get an education. It is no wonder, then, that the first feminist political activists were also intellectuals, a necessary precondition, without which they would have simply been "mobilized." Of equally great importance in the intellectual activity of these women was the creation of the League of Women Students and University Graduates, formed between 1944 and 1945, which provided a strong forum for a new evaluation of women and their role in revolutionizing society.

The accomplishments of women in the political arena of Egypt's public life can be described as "consciousness-raising" and "organizational creation or innovation" (Sullivan, 1986). Their most important achievement in the 1980s was the passage of the Personal Status Law of July 1985, which introduced norms proposed by Egyptian political leaders, including women.

As has been said above, north African women, especially Egyptian women, were faced with the double function of liberating society and then liberating themselves as women. This latter task calls for a specific consideration of what women were able to do for themselves.

Key Campaigns and Feminist Movements

The first areas for which north African women sought legislative consideration were marriage and the veil. What constituted a real revolution of women was to reject the veil and the harem. Woman campaigned for improvement of the condition of women, which they believed was a prerequisite for the general well-being of society. Women advocated the abolition of polygamy, decried prostitution, and fought for the education of young women, to whom the doors of education remained closed. The main aim was to bring the "woman question" to the level of political consciousness.

One of the earliest feminist movements dedicated specifically to feminist issues was the Egyptian Feminist Union (EFU), founded in 1923 by Huda Sha'rawi. The EFU launched one of the first feminist journals in the French language, *L'Egyptienne,* in 1925 and its Arabic edition in 1927. It is important to note that there is no direct translation in Arabic for the term *feministe;* the EFU women used the French term, French being the language of the upper class. Feminism thereafter came to stand for many arguments concerning the social, political, and legal rights of women. Feminists first demanded women's education, and women were first admitted to the University of Cairo between 1929 and 1930.

North African feminism cannot be fully discussed without the mention of Nawal Al Saadawi, a medical doctor dedicated to the physical and psychological health of women, and founder of the Arab Women's Solidarity Association (ASWA). Al Saadawi is best known for exposing delicate issues regarding the sexual oppression and exploitation of women and for bringing to public attention issues such as female circumcision, virginity, and incest. Her ideas were considered threatening and dangerously ahead of her time, her books were censored, and she incurred exile.

ASWA has been a member of the nongovernmental organizations (NGOs) with the United Nations since 1985. Its guiding principle is best expressed in the words, "We know that the liberation of the people as a whole cannot take place without the liberation of women, and this could not take place without the liberation of the land, economy, culture, information" (Badran and Cooke, 1990).

Another feminist union worth mentioning, though less radical, is the Union Nationale des Femmes de Tunisie (National Union of Tunisian Women, UNFT, 1956). It is generally recognized that the juridical position of Tunisian women is the best in the Arab world. Tunisia is the only north African country that immediately after independence recognized juridical equality between the sexes, with its revolutionary code of civil rights of 1956. Despite a wave of integralism, the UNFT continued to struggle for a more prominent role for women in society. Thanks to its efforts, Tunisia was one of the first north African nations to adhere to the United Nation's women's decade (1975–1985), whose main objective was equal job opportunities and treatment for women.

The most important accomplishment of Tunisian women is, without doubt, the introduction of the Personal Status Code (CSP) in August 1956. Key issues resolved include the regulation of marriage (the minimum marriageable age for girls is 15 years), the abolition of polygamy, and the possibility of choosing one's spouse. Most important, women could now take the initiative in divorce. To the outside world, the most revolutionary aspect of the code is the contraction of marriage by civil rites, so that a marriage does not necessarily have to be valid in religious terms.

Another feminist movement is Women Living under Muslim Laws, created in the 1980s as an information and solidarity network for women and groups from various Islamic countries, including north Africa.

North African Feminism and Other Feminisms

The network of Women Living under Muslim Laws is one feminist association, along with many others, that works for solidarity among women in Islamic countries.

This network can therefore be seen as one of the main ways in which north African feminism bears a relation to other feminisms. Untied by the same circumstances of living under Muslim laws, women meet on common ground to discuss the various cultural contexts separating them and making their experiences more or less rigid, liberal, or conservative.

The need of north African feminism to open itself and have a dialogue with other feminisms cannot be overemphasized. If north African women suffer one injustice, it is precisely isolation from the outside world.

One of the factors that accelerated the growth of north African feminism, and especially the EFU, was the relationship these women established with other women through journeys and conferences. For example, Huda Sha'rawi of Egypt will not be forgotten for her heroic act of casting her veil into the sea on her return from Rome in 1924 after having attended an international conference on women.

North African feminists are in debt to western international feminists who, in the 1970s, started inviting women from the third world to international feminist gatherings, granting them the privilege of being in contact with the feminist movement at large, as well as meeting other third world women. It is through international gatherings that they came to know one another and later founded associations at the regional, continental, and international levels.

Present-Day Situation of North African Feminism

The present-day situation of north African women can best be explained in terms of antagonism, hanging in the balance between traditionalism or Islamic fundamentalism and modernity. While throwing off the veil was a symbol of women's emancipation in the wake of feminism, today a return to the veil is often considered an indispensable means of protest against neocolonialism.

The most radical and politically active women are the Egyptians, while the most emancipated are the Tunisians. Even though Tunisian women are well represented in the parliament and constitute half the population, they continue to remain a "minority race," because traces of discrimination are still evident in Tunisia.

The women of Algeria, after having played a key role in the liberation of their country, are still fighting for their own liberation. Part of the problem could be the fact that they were simply "mobilized" and led in the liberation struggle instead of seeking to occupy decision-making positions in politics. The Family Code does not favor women; in fact, it puts them at the mercy of men. Polygamy is still widely practiced, and women are heavily discriminated against in cases of marriage dissolution, while men have unlimited rights.

One of the main achievements of Algerian women is the abolition of a husband's right to vote in place of his wife.

This is a result of the relentless efforts of many feminist associations operating in Algeria. The presence of women on the political scene continues to remain minimal and marginal, but women continue to struggle for their rights, even at the cost of their lives.

Moroccan women are the most discriminated against. They are at the margins of the political life; Morocco is one of the few countries of the world with no female representative in parliament. Despite this, women are actively present in the economic sphere, constituting, near the end of the twentieth century, more than 85 percent of the urban workforce. On the other hand, the rate of female illiteracy is very high, and this may, in part, be responsible for women's backwardness. The only possible way to a change for women remains education.

That education is the answer applies not only to the women of north Africa but also to women in the third world generally. Today, the majority of third world women are illiterate, and until the problem of mass female illiteracy is resolved, "feminism," "liberation," and "emancipation" will continue to remain more elitist issues.

See Also

EDUCATION: MIDDLE EAST AND NORTH AFRICA; FEMINISM: MIDDLE EAST; HOUSEHOLDS AND FAMILIES: MIDDLE EAST AND NORTH AFRICA; LITERATURE: ARABIC; POLITICS AND THE STATE: MIDDLE EAST AND NORTH AFRICA; WOMEN'S STUDIES: MIDDLE EAST AND NORTH AFRICA

References and Further Reading

Badran, Margot, and Miriam Cooke, eds. 1990. *Opening the gates: A century of Arab feminist writing*. London: Virago; and Bloomington: University of Indiana Press.

Hijab, Nadia. 1988. *Womanpower: The Arab debate on women at work*. Cambridge: Cambridge University Press.

Kandiyoti, Deniz, ed. 1991. *Women, Islam, and the state*. London: Macmillan.

Kumari, Jayawardena. 1987. *Feminism and nationalism in the third world*. London: Zed.

Mernissi, Fatima. 1988. Women and fundamentalism. *Middle East Reports* (July–August): 8–11.

Merriam, Kathleen Howard. 1979. Women, education, and the professions in Egypt. *Comparative Education Review*. 23: 256–271.

Salem, Norma. 1984. Islam and the status of women in Tunisia. In Freida Hussain, ed., *Muslim women*. London: Croom Helm.

Sha'rawi, Huda. 1986. *Harem years: The memoirs of an Egyptian feminist*. London: Virago.

Smith, Jane. 1984. Islam, women, and revolution in twentieth-century Arab thought. *Muslim World* 124 (3–4, July–August): 137–160.

Stowasser, Barbara Freyer. 1987. *The Islamic impulse.* London: Croom Helm.

Sullivan, Earl. 1986. *Women in Egyptian public life.* Syracuse, N.Y.: Syracuse University Press.

Zèniè, Wedad Ziegler. 1988. *In search of shadows: Conversation with Egyptian women.* London: Zed.

Pauline Ogho Aweto

FEMINISM: Postmodern

Postmodern feminism was assumed to be a contradiction in terms as recently as the early 1980s; by 1990, however, the notion was at the forefront of serious debates within feminist theory. Jean-François Lyotard's *The Postmodern Condition,* translated into English in 1984, seemed to lay the foundations for this development in the history of ideas. Lyotard started with an assumption that the metanarrative or critique of the Enlightenment—the belief, arising in the eighteenth century, in the capacity of reason to free human beings from servitude to internal and external forces of irrationality—was now exhausted, and that history could no longer be seen as continuous progress tending toward a final condition of absolute justice and equality. The commitment of post-Enlightenment political thinkers to the instrumental uses of science and technology in the cause of social justice and to the pursuit of objective knowledge as the foundation of social progress was deemed to be no longer viable or, indeed, even desirable. For example, from a postmodern perspective there can no longer be belief in nature, history, spirit, or pure reason as universal principles that transcend local and contingent conditions. What follows from this is that gender, like class or race or ethnicity, can no longer be regarded as an essential or even stable category, nor can it be used cross-culturally to explain the practices of human societies. Formerly conceived by feminists as the necessary "other" constructed through the universalist but actually exclusivist and masculinist claims of Enlightenment discourse, the category "woman" must now itself be regarded as a repressive enactment of metaphysical authority, coming to stand for all that is excluded by the Enlightenment understanding of rationality. Therefore, it is simply no longer legitimate to seize the category as the ground for a metanarrative of political practice or social ethics, even of a revisionary or emancipatory nature.

Hence the continued adherence to metanarratives of gender must necessarily blind feminist theorists to the ethnoheterocentric and oppressive perspectivism lurking in all essentialist claims about the nature of woman or of feminine experience. Thus any claim to be using the category "woman" as a universal one is either blind to or deliberately screening the particularity or difference that is the historical experience of femininity in the world. Moreover, Lyotard's argument implied that any recourse to transhistorical structures as a means of explaining political oppression would simply reenact those forms of oppression in reverse. For example, political communities founded on the solidarity of shared experience might exist legitimately only in local, provisional, and attenuated forms. The feminist commitment to "difference," furthermore, must entail the deconstruction of feminist difference itself as the next logical step in its development. It would seem impossible for any one constellation of identity to represent or speak for any other. Indeed, the very notion of representative democracy might now be viewed as the theft of another's voice, position, or (decentered) subjectivity.

Identity Politics

The publication of Lyotard's book coincided with a shift within feminism itself to the concept of "identity politics," an assault on essentialist views, and a reexamination of the notion of difference. Compatible with a postmodern position was Julia Kristeva's argument for the existence of the feminine as an impulse of transgression within the dominant codes of the "symbolic" and incidentally, if not ironically, more apparent in the avant-gardist writings of Joyce or Mallarmé than in the measured certainties or rational skepticism of, say, George Eliot or Mary Wollstonecraft. Alice Jardine's "Gynesis" (1985) too would claim as feminine any mode of "alterity" (otherness) struggling to exist as a space outside the totalizing logic of modernity and defying or attempting to ignore its structures. Yet neither of these disembodying versions of femininity actually stepped out of the dualisms of Enlightenment thought or avoided the essentialism within such logic. Each, however, indicated an increasingly self-conscious interpretative perspective within feminist theory in its recognition of a basic dilemma arising from the attempt to articulate a feminist theory of knowledge: that women seek equality and value for a gendered identity that has been constructed through the very cultural institutions and discourses of modernity that feminism had dismantled and challenged throughout the 1970s.

The resulting crisis of legitimation exposed the sense in which feminism had always, in effect, been postmodern in its voicing of experience excluded from the domain of the rational Enlightenment subject, but had equally always required the assumption of a modern position in order to function as an effective political discourse that might empower actual selves in the world. Feminism had always assumed its own modernist project as a collective and progressive movement committed to the moral and intellectual realization of free and equal selves through the faculty of reason and the overcoming of prejudiced views and irrational impulses. Now postmodernists and protopostmodernists such as Lyotard, Foucault, Baudrillard, and Deleuze had exposed the Enlightenment will-to-truth as a will-to-power and, without reference to feminism per se, articulated doubts about the project of modernity that were always implicitly present in feminist theory. The crucial question, however, was whether feminism as a political practice would be fatally wounded by the acknowledgment of some of the modes and arguments of postmodern theory. How could the adoption of local or "little" narratives avoid collapse into a cacophony of competing claims and voices? How might irony, subversion, pastiche, and self-conscious mimicry allow for the articulation of an effective political or ethical identity that would not collapse representation into simulation, depth into surface, justice into rhetorical persuasiveness? Can there ever be an ethics or a politics without a subject?

Opinion remains divided. For commentators such as the literary critic Linda Hutcheon, the fragmentariness, disruption, and destabilizing effects of postmodern art and thought as practiced by writers such as Angela Carter, Margaret Atwood, and Salman Rushdie constitute the only viable form of critique within a late capitalist culture that has disabled the possibility of a Kantian, that is to say, purely transcendent, critique. For others, like the Marxist critic Fredric Jameson, however, postmodernism is simply one more depressing reminder of the complicity of all forms of art and knowledge with the devouring thrust of capitalism in its final and most imperialistic phase: the subsumption of a commodified culture entirely into economics. Postmodern art, like postmodern thought, is simply a reflection of the depthless and soulless surfaces of an atomized, anomic (purposeless), and fragmented world.

The Value of Postmodern Theory

Even feminists skeptics, however, might agree that one value of postmodern theory has been its explicit exposure of the universalism and essentialism in earlier feminist invocations of feminine difference or in conspiracy versions of the theorization of patriarchy. Feminists and postmodernists have always shared an aestheticist understanding of subjectivity: just as Foucault's late dandified self is continuously refash-

ioned and reshaped, so de Beauvoir's woman was always made and not born. Is it really such a leap from this argument to Judith Butler's (1990) openly postmodern rejection of the search for an essential gender identity as a myth generated within a "hetero-reality" that has no more existential substance than the pantomimic impersonation of an impersonation that she sees flaunted in the act of the drag queen? And from there, what is the distance to Haraway's (1990) posthumanist cyborg, a hybrid and unstable constellation of human and machine, fact and fiction, mind and body? For the cyborg denies any privileged epistemological status to biologism and seems to offer a tantalizing escape route from the sometimes disabling and often dangerous nostalgia for and entanglement in all those seductive cultural myths of unity that seem to persist in the postmodern as much as in so-called rational modernity. And yet, would such a cybernetic utopia be a desirable place to live? Without cultural myths of unity, would human beings continue to write, dream, love, or commit themselves to any form of collective belief or politics whatsoever?

See Also

CRITICAL AND CULTURAL THEORY; CYBORG ANTHROPOLOGY; DIFFERENCE, *I and II*; GENDER; IDENTITY POLITICS; POSTMODERNISM: FEMINIST CRITIQUES; POSTMODERNISM: LITERARY THEORY

References and Further Reading

Butler, Judith. 1990. *Gender trouble: Feminisims and the subversion of identity.* New York: Routledge.

Flax, Jane. 1990. *Thinking fragments: Psychoanalysis, feminism and postmodernism in the contemporary West.* Berkeley: University of California Press.

Haraway, Donna. 1990. A manifesto for cyborgs: Science, technology, and socialist feminism in the 1980s. In Linda J. Nicholson, ed., *Feminism/postmodernism*, 190–234. New York: Routledge.

Heckman, Susan J. 1990. *Gender and knowledge: Elements of a postmodern feminism.* Oxford: Polity.

Hutcheon, Linda. 1989. *The politics of postmodernism.* London: Routledge.

Jameson, Fredric. 1984. Postmodernism, or the cultural logic of late capitalism. *New Left Review* 146: 53–93.

Jardine, Alice. 1985. *Gynesis.* Ithaca, N.Y.: Cornell University Press.

Lyotard, Jean-François. 1985. *The postmodern condition.* Manchester, UK.: Manchester University Press.

Nicholson, Linda. 1998. *The play of reason: From the modern to the postmodern.* Ithaca, N.Y.: Cornell University Press.

Patricia Waugh

FEMINISM: Psychoanalytic

See PSYCHOANALYSIS.

FEMINISM: Radical

Radical feminism is in a sense redundant, for all varieties of feminism are radical in that they work for fundamental social and political change. Usually the term is associated with a particular set of ideas and political practices as set out in typologies of feminism that define different versions in contrast with each other, emphasizing disagreements rather than areas of agreement. However, what the ideas and practices of radical feminism are has been fiercely debated, as proponents and critics frequently see its defining features very differently indeed.

In general, its proponents have associated radical feminism with an analysis of the links between the micropolitics of everyday life and the macropolitical analysis of capitalist patriarchy, seeing the explanatory link here as men's oppressive behaviors, by which men's stereotypical characterizations are enforced on women. Its critics, in contrast, have associated radical feminism variously with: (1) cultural feminism (the notion that women are essentially—biologically, morally, emotionally, behaviorally—different from and better than men), and thus with women's culture as a kind of universalism; (2) lesbian separatism; and also (3) psychological explanations of women's subordination based on the essential characteristics of men.

Much of the debate and counterdebate here has arisen because of a focus on typologies rather than what feminism "on the ground" is actually like. This in turn is because the typologies operate as simple academic constructions of "types of feminism" that divide up feminist ideas and assign them to different and fixed groupings. The most usual typology is radical, Marxist-socialist, and liberal feminisms; only the relatively complex typologies even mention lesbian and black feminisms. However, it is interesting to note that very little comparable countercritique of Marxist-socialist feminism has taken place: the critique of radical feminism can be read as a concerted attempt to discredit one variant of feminism by others, based more on misunderstanding than, perhaps, on fundamental disagreement.

As always with feminist ideas, radical feminist thinking and analysis produced over a now nearly 30-year period cannot and should not be reduced to the writings of a few "theorists" whose work is then taken to stand on behalf of this position. Indeed, radical feminism has provided a major critique of this basically male mainstream approach of creating elite groups of feminists who are seen as theorizing on behalf of the rest. Some of the key ideas associated with radical feminism across a very broad spectrum of political practice and writing have been identified as follows.

1. The unity of theory and practice. This is the insistence that "theorizing" must not be seen as separate from thinking and behaving in everyday life; indeed, that feminist theorizing must begin with the everyday and center its analysis there, "where women are." This is radical feminism defined as "praxis," that is, the enactment of "small revolutions" in the here-and-now—Gail Chester has described this by arguing that "our theory is that practising our practise is our theory" (1979: 13). This is an approach that situates theory, not as a special expertise "owned" by only a very few, but instead as an everyday practice that underpins everybody's thinking and behavior. Thus this precept of radical feminist thinking threatens the conventional hierarchical division between theorists and their followers, and therefore challenges divisions of power within academia.

2. The centrality of "the personal is the political." This is not a form of psychological or any other kind of reductionism, but rather the bringing together of micropolitical and macropolitical analysis and action, along with the recognition that "the personal" is central to understanding the dynamics of women's subordination. Chester describes this as follows: "To bring revolutionary change within the realm of the possible is one of the most important attitudes I have learned from radical feminism.... The small advances I have contributed will have made life better for some people, and most importantly, myself" (1979: 15). This constitutes a very different idea of "social change," one that perceives a continuum between changing macropolitical systems and structures and the small changes that can be effected in everyday life.

3. The importance of "women's oppression." This is the view that oppression—the use of force and the threat of force—is central to the maintenance of male supremacy, rather than only women's inequality (in relation to civil and legal rights) or exploitation (in relation to economic profiteering). Here the critique of phallocentrism has been crucial. Male use of force, rather than any supposedly "internalized" psychological characteristics or roles, constrains many of the possibilities in women's lives. The emphasis on sexual and other forms of male violence also links these to sexism and heterosexism. Although there has been often fierce resistance to linking male violence

and heterosexuality, in the 1990s the very large amount of research and theory about violence toward women and children showed that this has been one of the most influential of radical feminist ideas.

4. The fundamental nature of women's subordination. Women's subordination is seen as fundamental in the sense that other oppressions are "engendered" at their basis, for gender is not only a "binary" opposition between masculinities and feminities, but also a worldview that specifies and justifies a wide range of social relations, hierarchies, and social injustices. For example, racism and heterosexism position nonwhites and nonheterosexuals as "other" relative to a gendered, white, and masculinist subject, who is seen not only as constituting "the norm" but also as possessing the only fully human characteristics. It was on such grounds that early varieties of lesbian feminism theorized about links between the oppression of gay men and that of lesbian women before more fundamental differences between gay men and lesbian feminist women were recognized. This centrality of gender to structures of thinking as much as to forms of categorization has, perhaps paradoxically, been taken up and reworked within Lacanian-influenced ideas about the structures of language.

While newer labels exist to categorize—and divide—feminism (including poststructuralist, deconstructionist, and even postfeminist), the basic ideas represented in these precepts of radical feminist analysis are still fundamental to current debate. Thus notions of epistemology, speaking positions, and the politics of location are the heirs of radical feminist theorizing about the relationship between theory and practice; thinking about difference, the everyday, and political change can be associated with radical feminist ideas about "the personal is the political"; theorizing about the social construction of sexualities and masculinities is prefigured in the radical feminist analysis of the forms of male violence; and questioning binary ways of thinking, including thinking about gender, and theorizing about the links between women's oppression and all other forms of oppression, are to be found in radical feminist analysis of the basis of women's subordination.

In practice typologies are not a good guide to feminist ideas or to feminists' lives. "On the ground," feminists have taken ideas drawn from many "types" of feminism, as well as from elsewhere, not least because over time women's ideas shift and change along with the political practices associated with them. Thus, for instance, Robin Morgan (1978) chronicles her move from Leninism through Mao-

ism to Marxist feminism to radical feminism; and, while other feminists' "journeys" through feminist ideas may not take this route, it is nonetheless true that people's ideas and political analyses change over time as these are used and modified in practical circumstances. One result is that its critics are likely to share many of the ideas and analyses associated with radical feminism even while fiercely disavowing the label—and also of course vice versa. This is because over time variants on some of the most fundamental ideas associated with radical feminism have come to be taken for granted; these include the need to move beyond binary conceptualizations of the public and private, the importance of organization against sexual violence, acceptance of lesbianism, the "gendering" of the "other," and recognition of the role of "race" and sexuality in marking gender. Another result is that the ideas and practices of "radical feminism" have been subject to considerable change over the last twenty to thirty years; however, this has occurred with all varieties of feminist thought, most dramatically with Marxist-socialist feminism since the changes in eastern Europe.

See Also

FEMINISM: LESBIAN; FEMINISM: SOCIALIST; SLOGANS: "THE PERSONAL IS THE POLITICAL"

References and Further Reading

Atkinson, Ti-Grace. 1974. *Amazon odyssey.* New York: Links.

Chester, Gail. 1979. *I call myself a radical feminist: Notes from the 10th year.* London: Theory Press. (Reprinted in Feminist Anthology Collective, ed. 1983. *No turning back: Writings from the women's liberation movement 1975–1980.* London: Women's Press.)

Morgan, Robin. 1978. *Going too far: The personal chronicle of a feminist.* New York: Vintage.

Koedt, Anne, Ellen Levine, and Anita Rapone, eds. 1973. *Radical feminism.* New York: Quadrangle.

Liz Stanley

FEMINISM: Second-Wave British

Pinpointing when the second wave of feminism began in the United Kingdom is difficult. Even the women's liberation movement (WLM) of 1960–1978, comprising small local groups meeting at an annual conference, and working almost entirely outside of conventional political institutions, never entirely represented the second wave. The second wave could be called "feminism's radical wing," its "reformists" constituting groups working mainly within trade unions and political parties (Gelb, 1986). The reason for focusing on the WLM is its new feminist politics, stemming, as in the United States, partly from student and other radical groups, but inspired also by radical feminist writing. The second wave can be dated either from 1968, from the separate and spontaneous founding of small, informal local groups, or from the first national Women's Liberation Conference in 1970. No date can be given for the "reformists," working within the Labour Party, for example, for equal opportunities and equal pay. Their existence makes it difficult to characterize the politics of the second wave because these wings varied in their beliefs.

Origins of the Women's Liberation Movement

The first known WLM groups were formed by young mothers in south London, students in Essex, women striking for equal pay at the Ford plant in Dagenham, and a fisherman's wife, campaigning for safer working conditions for trawlermen, in Hull. Other groups followed; by late 1969 the London Women's Liberation Workshop coordinated about 70 groups. As in the United States, "veterans" of student movements and the left formed or joined early groups, some linking locally with "housewives." Some groups focused on consciousness raising or reading texts, others campaigned locally for better welfare, easier access to abortion, and free contraception, and others joined trade union women on picket lines. This variety and overlap continued—though groups worked mainly in parallel, not together—as trade union women campaigned for equal opportunities, and 1969 saw a demonstration against the London Miss World Contest and a march for equal pay.

Most WLM members aimed to ally with working-class women. Among the latter was a new militancy, prior to and independent of the movement: the strike at Ford was an example. The union campaign of women night cleaners of 1970–1971, however, sprang from direct cooperation between the cleaners and the Dalston Women's Liberation Workshop.

Campaigns

In February 1970 the first national Women's Liberation Conference, held in Oxford, agreed to the WLM's first "manifesto": equal pay, equal education and opportunity, 24-hour nurseries, free contraception, and abortion on demand. The campaign for the availability of contracep-

tion predated the movement, as did the Abortion Act of 1967. So the items were not, with the partial exception of the last, new. It was their wording that suggested a demand for greater change. This "manifesto" could not cover the range of the politics of those attending the conference, nor could it encompass the views of those who distrusted or opposed reform. Issues of race and sexual preference were omitted. At the Edinburgh Conference in 1974 women's legal and financial independence and an end to discrimination against lesbians were added to the list of aims. But the WLM remained split, particularly between separatist radical feminists and socialist feminists who were prepared to work with existing organizations and institutions. The movement opposed central direction and control; this may have been the reason that the coordinating committee, alleged to have been taken over by one faction, fell, and no replacement was formed.

At the beginning of the 1970s many WLM members, especially socialist feminists, were community activists—like radical feminists but with different targets. By the mid-1970s these women asked local councils for funding, and projects like nurseries and women's centers became bases for distribution of resources and information. Both radical and socialist feminists addressed violence against women, including violence within marriage. In 1972 Erin Pizzey set up the first battered women's center in Chiswick, drawing attention to this form of violence and to the unwillingness of the police to intervene in what they called "domestics." Media coverage followed, and by 1980 the Women's Aid Federation had set up 200 (though still not enough) refuges for battered women and their children.

Other campaigns, successful at least on a case-by-case basis, included protests against convicting battered wives of murder. A different kind of "provocation" defense was developed, taking into account women's slowness to anger and to act, and women's and men's comparative physical strength. Premenstrual syndrome (PMS) was also a new defense. Both ideas, although their emphasis on female "difference" troubled certain feminists, made some gains possible. The first rape crisis center was opened in London in 1976; the first "Reclaim the Night" marches were held in Leeds, London, and Edinburgh in 1977. (Such marches continue to be held in the United Kingdom, and the United States.) The marches addressed many women's fear of walking alone in cities but also raised disputes concerning men's participation in the marches and highlighted the tendency of some feminists to see violence as inherent in relationships between women and men. The notion of men's essential violence split the WLM conference in 1978;

as a result of this and previous disputes, no one would organize another national conference.

The movement benefited to some extent from the sexual and cultural freedom of the 1960s, and it took the initiative in the 1970s in seeking protection of women in a number of key areas such as rape, sexual assault, and domestic violence. These problems affected women of all ages and classes and were issues on which new women's groups could link with established and more conventional groups and gain the sympathy of many men. At the same time, violence against women highlighted the radical feminist critique of existing society, because violence was often hidden or ignored, and when it was brought to light women were often blamed.

By the 1970s WLM and its views had made an impact on health and social services and local government, and feminists were raising issues such as child care and family welfare at the national level through pressure groups like the Child Poverty Action Group. Defending the abortion laws had also brought feminists closer to women Labour members of Parliament (some of whom were feminists themselves). For WLM, abortion was a key issue regarding the right of women to control their own bodies. But in practice the movement worked with others less committed to that view. The National Abortion Campaign was formed in 1975 to defend the law and mobilized opposition to bills that aimed to restrict abortion. The "pro-abortion" coalition held firm, defeating an attempt to limit abortion in 1987.

The Issue of "Race"

"Race" had not emerged as an issue within the WLM in its first decade, even though it had become an important factor in trade unions and trade union activity, and African Caribbean and Asian women had become an important new force. In 1978 the first black women's organization in the United Kingdom, the Organisation of Women of Asian and African Descent, campaigned against immigration laws, opposing, especially, the virginity tests imposed on black women joining men in the United Kingdom. Black women also took part in campaigns against racist violence; Southall Black Sisters, for example, was formed in 1979 after a demonstration against a National Front meeting held in Southall. The first black women's conference was held in the same year. Because there were no more WLM conferences, the issue of the movement's ignoring questions of ethnicity and race was discussed in articles and letters in the only nationally available feminist magazine, *Spare Rib*. The questions remained, as Ann Phoenix (1990) said, mostly or entirely unconsidered. Where they were dis-

cussed, they were presented as issues of "black" and "white" alone, diversity being largely ignored (Anthias and Yuval-Davis, 1990).

Sexuality

The WLM's view of sexuality was mainly libertarian—its early refusal to endorse equality of sexual preference was a stark exception to this—in its support for free birth control and freely available abortion. The WLM viewed the "sexual liberation" of the 1960s as part of a larger struggle for freedom but protested, for example, the exploitation of women in advertising. Many of its members were concerned about pornography but would not ally with conservatives who wanted to ban it. By 1974 the movement supported lesbians' challenge to the idea that women's sexuality is necessarily directed toward men. Lesbians themselves had various perspectives. For example, some lesbians were members of the WLM, living with other women they loved, but the Leeds Revolutionary Feminists and others argued in the late 1970s that heterosexual women were collaborators and in 1979 that political lesbianism was the only alternative. Prostitutes' campaigns also caused a split because some WLM feminists supported decriminalization of prostitution, but others attacked prostitutes for servicing men.

Protest Campaigns

The conference of 1978 might seem a sign that the WLM would, despite its gains, not simply break up but fade. And in large part it did, perhaps affected by the general political pessimism left in the United Kingdom. However, many feminists, "new" and "old," were invigorated, even if the WLM was not, by the events at the Greenham Common cruise missile base. A massive and sustained peace campaign began when, in August 1981, 30 people, mainly women and children, set out on a march from Wales to Greenham. Ignored by the national media, they appealed to women and were joined by thousands of all ages and of varied political views. A well-publicized and enduring campaign was born, novel in its emphasis on "womanly" and "motherly" attributes, and mainly separatist. The protest was remarkably long-lived, even as the number of protestors fell; the last demonstrator left in 2000. The campaign attracted many women unconnected with either separatist or cultural feminist politics, but it was strongly opposed by certain radical feminists who disliked both the Greenham women's "motherly" tactics and the notion that ending warfare as conventionally understood would bring women "peace." For them, "Greenham" was not a feminist cause.

A very different kind of action took place during the miners' strike of 1984–1985, when miners' wives mobilized on a large scale. After their communities' defeat, some helped other women set up support groups during strikes. Elsewhere, in very different forums and under very different conditions, women's studies groups and courses were being set up. Throughout the 1980s, the case for equal opportunities continued to be advanced, and gains were made, aided by rulings of the European Court. No movement existed, but feminist ideas spread.

The 1990s

The 1990s saw a continuation of previous work. In 1991 rape in marriage was, finally, declared a crime. During the first half of the 1990s Southall Black Sisters and Justice for Women took up the cases of several women imprisoned for killing violent husbands. The Women's Institute, formerly a conservative and apolitical group, but now radicalized by the political marginality of rural women, was a crucial ally. In 1995 wives of striking dockers in Liverpool formed their own group, like the miners' wives in 1984, but they received less publicity and support. Lynne Segal (1999) reflects on feminists' knowledge of and support for the women strikers at Grunwick, West London, in 1976–1977 and the lack of such solidarity, and even of awareness, at the end of the twentieth century.

The 1990s also saw a shift within political parties to national politics and an aim of electing more women to Parliament. In the general election, 1997, 119 women were elected to Parliament, and 5 government ministers were women; this election appeared to bring the issue of women's inequality to the fore. But no major ministry was held by a woman, and most of the newly elected women had won their seats because the Labour Party's victory was a landslide. Current centralized control of the parliamentary party aside, many women lacked the political experience to make the most of their posts. A minister for women was, in effect, demoted and ignored; "dress codes," formal or informal, were put forward, and inadequate mixed-family policies (which at least pay tribute to some feminist arguments and to the notion that a single-parent family is still a family) suggested that at the top level of politics feminist influence was fairly weak.

One concern at this time was Clause 28, forbidding local authorities to present homosexuality "positively." The government wanted to repeal it but—after the defeat of initial attempts at repeal—intended to have teachers promote the heterosexual nuclear family as the "approved" way to live. The rationale was that this would gain the established

church's support for change; however, the situation was an issue not only for homosexual men, lesbians, and black women (who were more likely to be single parents) but for many other women and probably for all feminists. A reactionary measure such as this was a cause for concern despite the political rhetoric—and even the reality—of equal opportunities.

Sheila Rowbotham (1999) comments that second-wave feminist politics in the United Kingdom center on the results of women's paid work, and on a general failure of the nation to support the needs of parents and children. For her, this situation largely explains why women claim both public equality with men and improvement of their own conditions at home, and why feminism is torn between equal rights and measures based on female "difference." Statutory maternity leave with pay is well established in the United Kingdom, has been enhanced by European Union rules, and is indeed taken for granted; this suggests that the division in feminism may always have existed, but perhaps the contradiction was not clear to feminists. If that is true, living with the resulting dilemma may have been easier in the United Kingdom than, for example, in the United States, where there is a similar duality of aims.

Current Trends

The WLM of the late 1960s and early 1970s tried to avoid focusing on external reform. That strategy was part of what "The personal is political" meant. But during the 1970s, feminism, at least in its theoretical form, turned too much inward (Segal, 1987). In the 1980s this trend continued until sexuality became not simply a political act but a political aim. Alongside this, however, there was always an emphasis on external politics. The problem may be to join the two.

The WLM's national meetings are long gone, and there remains no broadly feminist organization in the United Kingdom. But more specific national groups have been formed, and feminist activities continue. An optimistic assessment of the situation in the United Kingdom is that the ideas of the WLM, at least as encapsulated in its conferences, and the ideas of second-wave "reformists," have spread widely. Opinion polls provide some evidence of this. But even minimal ideas have not spread completely, and where they have spread at all, they have not always been translated into political or social change. Thus there is still a need for books like Kate Figes's *Because of Her Sex* (1985), there is still talk of "postfeminism," and there are still statements beginning, "I'm not a feminist, but . . . ," and there are still popular antifeminist books like John Gray's *Men Are from Mars, Women Are from Venus*. Despite ties to the Labor

Party and trade unions by members of the WLM and women in more "reformist" groupings, feminists in the United Kingdom have been far less inclined to engage in networking, lobbying, and legal change than U.S. feminists (Gelb, 1986). Some similarities were concealed by the "hidden" activities of women before the WLM's founding, and similarities may be greater now, given an emphasis on national politics in the past decade. But Britain has never had an umbrella group like the National Organization for Women in the United States. That is not the only reason why Britain has, despite notable exceptions like abortion, achieved less than U.S. feminism, but it may well be an important one. Because lack of success has had less to do with legal gains than with the laws' implementation, it is difficult to tell whether the increased influence of the European Union will bring the success that feminists in the United Kingdom have not yet achieved.

See Also

ACTIVISM; EMANCIPATION AND LIBERATION MOVEMENTS; FEMINISM: BLACK BRITISH; FEMINISM: BRITISH ASIAN; FEMINISM: FIRST-WAVE BRITISH; FEMINIST PHILOSOPHIES; LIBERATION MOVEMENTS; SOCIAL MOVEMENTS

References and Further Reading

Anthias, Floya, and Nira Yuval-Davis. 1990. Contextualizing feminism—Gender, ethnic, and class divisions. In Terry Lovell, ed., *British feminist thought: A reader,* 103–118. Oxford: Blackwell.

Figes, Kate. 1995. *Because of her sex: The myth of equality for women in Britain.* London: Pan.

Gelb, Joyce. 1986. Feminism in Britain: Politics without power. In Drude Dahlerup, ed., *The new women's movement,* 103–121. London: Sage.

Gray, John. 1997. *Men are from Mars, Women are from Venus: A practical guide for improving communication and getting what you want in your relationships.* London: Thorsons.

Mitchell, Juliet. 1966. The longest revolution. *New Left Review* 40(Nov./Dec.).

Phoenix, Ann. 1990. Theories of gender and black families. In Terry Lovell, ed., *British feminist thought: A reader,* 119–133. Oxford: Blackwell.

Rowbotham, Sheila. 1999. *A century of women: The history of women in Britain and the United States.* Harmondsworth: Penguin.

———. 1989. *The past is before us: Feminism in action since the 1960s.* London: Pandora.

Segal, Lynne. 1987. *Is the future female? Troubled thoughts on contemporary feminism.* London: Virago.

———. 1999. *Why feminism? Gender, psychology, politics.* Cambridge: Polity.

Wandor, Michelene, ed. 1990. *Once a feminist: Stories of a generation.* London: Virago.

Judith Evans

FEMINISM: Second-Wave European

Historical Strands

Despite a number of common concerns, there is no single concept that can be described as European feminism. Different historical traditions of feminism, combined with different sociopolitical situations, have resulted in a plurality of voices. Changes in eastern Europe in the 1990s added a new dimension to questions of feminist politics.

The English-speaking world has tended to distinguish trends in feminist thinking in broadly two ways, defined by Toril Moi as the Anglo-American and the French (1985). These are perceived as "binary" opposites—French feminism is said to be predominantly theoretical, concerned with questions of cultural politics, psychoanalysis, and history; Anglo-American feminism takes a more pragmatic approach and is more concerned with questions of sexual politics, gender identity, race, and class. A great many Anglo-American feminists have drawn extensively on French theorists such as Hélène Cixous, Luce Irigaray, and Julia Kristeva, but European feminist work outside the French tradition has tended to receive little attention, perhaps because of a lack of translations into English, and perhaps also because of the culture-specific nature of some of the principal aspects of feminism in countries such as Italy, Spain, Germany, and Poland.

Western European feminism developed parallel to the feminist resurgence in the English-speaking world in the late 1960s and early 1970s. There were numerous translations, and texts by Shulamith Firestone, Betty Freidan, Germaine Greer, Kate Millett, and a host of others rapidly appeared in several European languages, along with translations of works by earlier feminist writers such as Virginia Woolf, Charlotte Perkins Gilman, and Mary Wollstonecraft. A network of women's bookshops emerged in the 1970s, offering a wide range of writings by women from many different countries. This cosmopolitan dimension of European feminism, which reflected publishing policy and demand in many countries, ensured the spread of ideas across cultural and linguistic boundaries, even as individual women's movements developed in their own way and at their own speed.

European and Anglo-American Feminism

European feminist activity can therefore be said to be autonomous, with its own diverse history and culture-specific developments, and should not be seen as either a derivative of Anglo-American feminism or a range of minor branches of French feminist thought, despite the obvious influence of Simone de Beauvoir in many countries.

Nevertheless, it is probably fair to say that academic feminism in a number of European countries was heavily influenced by writing in English, and a number of early courses introduced into universities came in the form of courses on women's writing, often taught within English and American Literature departments. This does not support the contention that Europe imported its feminism from the English-speaking world; rather, the explanation may be seen in terms of the institutional constraints within which teachers interested in questions of gender have had to operate. Since many European systems require proposed university courses to pass through ministries of education for approval, which is often a time-consuming process, the introduction of feminist work under a heading such as "literature" or "language" is often the only way of initiating work in gender studies quickly. As feminist literary criticism has become more established internationally, and women's studies has developed as a discipline in its own right, institutional barriers have been more easily overcome, and the initial dominance of English-language work has diminished.

In her introduction to one of the few collections of essays on European feminist writing, *Textual Liberation,* Helena Forsas-Scott (1991) notes that the history of Europe between 1919 and 1939 (the end of World War I and the start of World War II) was largely a history of the emergence of dictatorships. The legacy of that period lasted a long time, and it is possible to see the history of Europe since 1945 as one of refashioning cultures in the aftermath of war and the gradual crumbling of dictatorships, which happened in several waves.

European Feminism after World War II

The first stage, that of reconstruction, literally and psychologically, runs from the late 1940s to 1968, the year of student protests across western and eastern Europe. The late 1960s also saw the beginnings of separate women's groups in the oppositional parties of the left. Often ad hoc and disorganized, the early women's groups formed as a way of registering women's dissatisfaction with the masculinist

attitudes of their male comrades. The Italian pamphlet *Sputiamo su Hegel* (*We Spit on Hegel*) was the manifesto of a feminist group that emerged in Rome and Milan in 1970 and deliberately rejected the Marxist view of the primacy of the class struggle over other forms of social protest (Bassnett, 1986). Given the strength of Marxist thought in alternative politics in western Europe in general at this time, the decision of some feminists to challenge that supremacy was very radical indeed. By now a second stage had begun.

The problem of reconciling feminism and Marxism dominated feminist discussion in Europe in the early 1970s. Since many European feminist movements could trace their origins to nineteenth-century socialist feminism, the process of unraveling second-wave feminism from patriarchal Marxism was a painful one. Women's groups looked for support from male colleagues on the left, but at the same time were struggling to redefine the political agenda in ways that gave gender priority over class. The way forward initially was through large-scale campaigns concerning such issues as divorce and abortion, to change established social structures and conventions.

The 1970s finally saw the collapse of the old fascist dictatorships in Spain and Portugal and the development of feminism on a massive scale across Europe. There were huge rallies demanding reforms in patriarchal legal systems that denied women the right to divorce and discriminated openly in favor of husbands in family law, and equally large-scale protests demanding the right to contraception and abortion and an end to violence against women. A pamphlet published in 1970 by the Italian Movimento di Liberazione della Donna (Women's Liberation Movement) pointed out that being a woman in Italy meant sooner or later becoming a criminal, since both abortion and contraception were illegal, and yet millions of women practiced both (Bono and Kemp, 1991). Significantly, by the mid-1990s Italy and Spain, both traditionally Catholic countries, had the lowest birthrates in Europe, and the declining birthrate in Ireland, another state opposed to contraception and abortion, but with an active feminist movement, is further evidence of a radical change in attitude to the role of women in the family despite the continuation of state policies dominated by the church.

Feminist mass meetings in many parts of Europe in the early 1970s involved tens of thousands of women from all walks of life, and pressure groups were set up to bring about reform. The effect of this period of mass protest was to raise the consciousness of society as a whole and to place feminism in the public eye. By the early 1980s, feminist infrastructures were beginning to develop in many countries, and the large-scale protests subsided as grassroots movements expanded. Feminist publishing had developed into a substantial industry, with journals, books, and entire publishing houses, like Frauenoffensive in Germany, Virago and Women's Press in Britain, and Des Femmes in France.

The 1980s marked the start of the third stage, in which feminist politics reflected a tendency in Europe away from the mass demonstration and toward a more private form of social protest. This in turn reflects a growing uneasiness across western Europe that can be perceived as a combination of identity crisis and economic crisis. The boom years of the 1960s and 1970s, with fast-growing economies and rising standards of living in urban areas in particular, contrasted ever more sharply with the emergence of a new underclass, often comprising immigrant populations from former colonies, Turkey, North Africa, and increasingly eastern Europe. Countries such as Italy, which had prided itself on a history of antiracism, now found racist politics high on the agenda, as the success of neo-Nazi groups and organized neofascist political parties was to show throughout the 1980s and 1990s. Anti-Semitism and overt racism gained ground in Germany, France, and the Low Countries. In Britain, the government of a woman prime minister committed to radical right-wing politics (Margaret Thatcher was elected for the first time in 1979 and held office throughout the 1980s) exposed the shallowness of the idealistic belief of early feminism that society would improve if only women held power.

The End of the Cold War

In 1989, the collapse of the Berlin Wall and the end of the cold war opened the borders between western and eastern Europe. This change of direction for Europe had particular implications for feminism. Former eastern European states such as Poland, Hungary, Czechoslovakia (soon to divide into the Czech Republic and Slovakia), and the German Democratic Republic (East Germany) had applied a policy of socialist feminism, which placed great stress on institutionalized welfare services, such as nurseries, to enable women to join the labor force. In the 1980s in the German Democratic Republic (GDR), for example, about 87 percent of all women of working age were either employed or in some form of further education. Whereas in western Europe the early women's liberation movements had been calling for improved maternity leave, nurseries, and abortion on demand, in many eastern European states such provisions were routine. But at the same time, there was nothing like the western concept of patriarchy, which meant that feminism did not develop in the same way in eastern Europe. Slavenca Drakulic (1987), in her collection of essays,

How We Survived Communism and Even Laughed, contrasts the world of her feminist friends in western Europe and the United States with the world she inhabited in the former Yugoslavia. She recalls the time she went to the first international feminist conference in Belgrade, "Comrade Woman," where she met women like Christine Delphy, Dacia Maraini, and Alice Schwarzer, and compares their view of the world she inhabited with her own and her colleagues' view: "We thought they were too radical when they told us they were harassed by men on our streets. We don't even notice it, we said. Or when they talked about wearing high-heeled shoes as a sign of women's subordination. We didn't see it quite like that; we wore such shoes and even loved them."

Drakulic argues that the history of a culture affects the development of feminist consciousness, and cites the question of "femininity" as a crucial area of difference between western feminist thinking and that of eastern European women. She suggested that eastern European women, deprived of the trappings of the beauty industry for decades, chose to collude with the development of that industry in the postcommunist period—hence their interest in clothes, makeup, beauty contests, and so forth, and their toleration of strip shows and pornography generally. Given that the beauty industry was a prime target for western European feminists in the late 1960s and early 1970s, as it was for feminists in the United States, Canada, and Australia, the attitude of eastern European women to the same phenomenon appeared to be a direct contrast.

The key to understanding the difference in attitude lies in the different histories of the new enlarged Europe, and the different emphasis on consumerism on either side of the Iron Curtain. Whereas western European feminists initially had to address their own relationship to Marxist politics, seeking to reconcile class consciousness with the struggles for racial and gender equality, in eastern Europe women had to come to terms with their suspicion of the very term *feminism* as adopted in the West, which many saw as referring to a bourgeois movement. At the same time, they were eager to reject the version of socialist feminism with which they had been living, which reinforced above all else the link between woman and the family and continued to disregard the wider debates on sexuality and gender in the rest of the world. Despite the ostensibly prowomen policies of the socialist countries, the lack of access to contraception (or its prohibition, as in Romania) all too often meant abortion and unwanted pregnancies, and too many children brought up in cramped living spaces. The material conditions of many women's lives in eastern Europe were drab at best, deprived at worst, and the prospect of material improvements has been viewed by many as a priority. The abolition of welfare services with the advent of free market economies has exacerbated the situation for women further, as has the deterioration in political stability in many parts of the former Soviet Union, the Balkans, and former Yugoslavia.

In the 1990s, the differences between eastern and western European feminism became increasingly apparent. The unification of the two Germanies meant large-scale unemployment for women from the former GDR, along with diminished maternity leave and less access to abortion. In strongly Catholic Poland, abortion was abolished altogether. On the other hand, the high priority given to national identity and culture, and the growing specter of racism and anti-Semitism across Europe meant that feminist issues had to be subsumed into other debates. The 1990s were a decade for reflection rather than direct feminist action, and the joining of the two Europes at a moment in time when the post-colonial world began to assert itself, and when black and Muslim feminists set their own agendas, meant that there was considerable divergence between the different versions of feminist thinking operating between the two poles of Lisbon and Moscow.

The impact of feminism in European political life has been mixed. More women have entered political life, and the European Parliament has provided opportunities for women beyond the boundaries of their own nation-states. Both Iceland and Ireland elected women as presidents, and Britain, Poland, and Norway elected women prime ministers. Germany appointed its first woman president of the Federal Constitutional Prime Court, and France appointed Yvette Roudy minister for women's rights in 1981. However, not all women appointed to positions of power have been feminists, and some, such as Margaret Thatcher, actively discriminated against women; there was a decline in women in positions of power during the years of Thatcher's government. Many women were involved in far-right political activity in Europe. The difference between the women of Greenham Common in the 1970s, living in tents outside a U.S. air base to protests against nuclear weapons and the Serbian women refusing to allow humanitarian aid convoys to relieve starving Muslim villages in former Yugoslavia showed the gap between feminist idealism of the 1970s and the harsh realities of life in Europe in the 1990s.

While there has been considerable divergence in feminist aims and organizations, there is greater consistency in feminist cultural production. The radical voices of antiauthoritarianism in eastern and western Europe in times of political oppression were frequently women's voices, speak-

ing through poetry, the novel, theater, and cinema. If there was no feminist movement as such in Poland or Romania, for example, there have been a great number of gifted writers. Wislawa Szymborska and Nina Cassian stand out as two examples of poets who write about their experiences as women and about the lives of women (Bassnett and Kuhiwczak, 1988; Cassian, 1988). The role of the writer in a totalitarian system is inevitably different from the role of the writer in a system of free-market economics, and significantly, for many eastern European women writers, as for Spanish and Portuguese women, their art offered a means both of communicating with others, and hence breaking silence, and of sharing experiences. The publication of *New Portuguese Letters* by the Three Marias in 1972 was a landmark in feminist consciousness-raising in a society struggling out of decades of fascist oppression (Barreno, Horta, and Da Costa, 1975).

In western Europe, likewise, feminist writing has been crucially important. In Germany, Verena Stefan's influential *Häutingen* (*Shedding*, 1979) dealt with the problem of how to set down the burden of a borrowed skin, a borrowed language, and how to explore oneself as a woman, through the discovery of lesbian sexuality. Escape from the past and the need to move beyond the mistakes of history is a powerful theme in much European women's fiction. Hélène Cixous's collaboration with Ariane Mnouchkine in Paris and Pina Bausch's intercultural dance-theater in Wuppertal have similarly explored the question of escaping from history and from the oppressive power of patriarchal systems. In 1986, the establishment of the Magdalena Project in Cardiff brought together women theater practitioners from all over Europe, along with some from the United States and Latin America, to share their experiences and to explore the question of women's language in theater. The success of the project, which went from strength to strength, inspiring performances and workshops, showed the strong interest in women's creativity that arose out of the early feminist explorations of the late 1960s.

The Magdalena Project was essentially a network for international alternative theater practitioners, and probably the most significant success stories of European feminism have involved the establishment of networks—in academic life, in the creative arts, in business, in publishing, in politics. The European Union (EU) has been useful for women in enabling the establishment of such networks and ensures that the question of sexual politics remains on the international agenda, despite the decline of organized women's liberation movements as such.

It is possible to see a progression over three decades from the 1960s to the 1990s through the gradual shedding of terms that changed their meaning over the years as the political context altered across Europe. The word *liberation* was profoundly significant in the years immediately following 1968—the revolutionary phase—and the struggle for the liberation of women, from their past oppression and present constraints, was a key aspect of feminist discourse. The sense of being a militant group was strongly felt in the 1970s, the period of mass action, coordinated campaigns, and public demonstrations. But as women made inroads into cultural and political life in many countries, and as the impact of feminism was felt throughout society, including especially a younger generation growing up with the terminology of feminism as their norm, the sense of struggle declined and the emphasis on liberating women shifted in favor of greater public prominence for women and on the achievements of women, rather than on their absence or marginalization.

By the 1980s, the word *movement* was used less and less, as grassroots politics replaced larger-scale organization. Women's movements organized on a national level had been transformed into smaller, locally based groups or into special interest groups and networks. Writing in *Die Zeit* in October 1994, Margrit Gerste noted that: "The wild curiosity of the 1970s has gone. The theme of the 1980s, with its stress on inner experience, has not quite faded. . . . But feminism has not lost its explosiveness—whether it is about the value of housework, or about the radical criticism of society."

Gerste's article, in which she interviews a number of leading German feminist politicians and academics, noted that the expected deterioration of conditions for women with the election of Helmut Kohl in the 1980s did not happen, largely because the inroads women had made into politics and public life in general enabled them to block more repressive legislation. This is an interesting theory and a hopeful one, because it suggests that the success of feminism is the impact women are having in all aspects of social organization, despite the disappearance of the women's liberation movement as such. The German situation was reflected in other European countries, where equal opportunity policies were laid down by government and reinforced by the European Parliament.

Women in Europe in the 1970s shouted their protests in the streets. Their rage, expressed through violent slogans and angry demonstrations, brought feminism out of the margins and onto the public stage. By the 1980s the rage was being channeled into productive action, gender issues were being analyzed in a highly sophisticated manner, feminists were setting up networks, and sexual politics were being taken seriously. The changes that brought eastern Europe out from behind the Iron Curtain threw into the melting pot some of the more facile assumptions about feminist goals and expectations, as did the emergence of other forms of feminism that challenged the eurocentricity of many of the earlier assumptions. These alternative voices made themselves heard, and the 1990s were a time of greater listening, resulting in more reflection. From the cries of rage of the early 1970s, through the gradual discovery of a range of voices that have enabled more and more women to become empowered, feminist activity in Europe has steadily increased. There is not and never has been one European feminism, and the many voices of European feminists today reflect the rich variety of cultural heritages of the continent that now stretches from Iceland to the shores of the Caspian Sea.

See Also

FEMINISM: EASTERN EUROPE; FEMINISM: SECOND-WAVE BRITISH; FEMINISM: SECOND-WAVE NORTH AMERICAN; WOMEN'S STUDIES: CENTRAL AND EASTERN EUROPE; WOMEN'S STUDIES: WESTERN EUROPE

References and Further Reading

Altbach, E. Hoskino, J. Clausen, D. Schultz, and N. Stephan, eds. 1984. *German feminism: Readings in politics and literature.* Albany: State University of New York Press.

Barreno, Maria Isabel, Maria Teresa Horta, and Maria Velho da Costa. 1975. *New Portuguese letters.* Trans. Helen Lane and Faith Gillespie. London: Golancz.

Bassnett, Susan. 1992. Crossing cultural boundaries, or how I became an expert on east European women overnight. *Women's Studies International Forum* 15(1): 11–15.

———. 1986. *Feminist experiences: The women's movement in four cultures.* London: Allen and Unwin.

———, and Piotr Kuhiwczak, trans. 1988. *Ariadne's thread: Polish women's poetry.* London: Forest.

Bono, Paola, and Sandra Kemp, eds. 1991. *Italian feminist thought.* Oxford: Blackwell.

Cassian, Nina. 1988. *Call yourself alive: The love poems of Nina Cassian.* Trans. Andrea Deletant and Brenda Walker. London: Forest.

Dahlerup, D., ed. 1986. *The new women's movement: Feminism and political power in Europe and the U.S.A.* London: Sage.

Drakulic, Slavenka. 1987. *How we survived communism and even laughed.* London: Hutchinson.

Duchen. Claire. 1986. *Feminism in France from May '68 to Mitterand.* London: Routledge.

———. 1987. *French connections: Voices from the women's movement in France.* London: Hutchinson.

Forsas-Scott, Helena. 1991. *Textual liberation: European feminist writing in the twentieth century.* London: Routledge.

Moi, Toril. 1985. *Sexual/textual politics.* London: Routledge.

Michielson, Magda, and Mary Evans, eds. 1994. *The European journal of women's studies.* London: Sage.

Slaughter, J., and R. Kern, eds. 1981. *European women on the Left.* Westport, Conn.: Greenwood.

Stefan, Verena. 1979. *Häutungen (Shedding).* Trans. J. Moore and B. Weckmiller. London: Women's Press. (Originally published 1975.)

Ward-Jouve, Nicole. 1991. *White woman speaks with forked tongue.* London: Routledge.

Susan Bassnett

FEMINISM:
Second-Wave North American

Feminists in North America, beginning in the mid-1960s, both continued and departed from the activities and accomplishments of first-wave feminists. The earlier movement had secured voting rights and opened educational and employment opportunities for women, but did not achieve gender equality or transform women's sexual and family roles. The second wave has challenged male domination not only in politics, education, and employment, but also in the "private" realm of family and sexual relations. However, there has not been a united women's movement in North America; rather, there have been a variety of feminisms with diverse and even clashing views about "gender issues." Feminist consciousness and activism are based not only on gender but also on class, race, nationality, age, and sexual orientation. Canadian feminists have criticized the domination of the United States, and within Canada the "two solitudes," or the movements of English Canadians and francophone Québec women, have distinct histories and priorities.

The Roots of Second-Wave Feminism

The three factors largely responsible for the revival of feminism are women's organizations that bridge the first and second waves, postwar demographic and economic changes in North America, and social movements of the 1960s. The period between the two waves was relatively short in Québec, as women did not obtain the vote or the right to hold political office until 1940. Women in the United States and English Canada had won suffrage by 1920, but their organizations did not disappear.

In the United States, the National Woman's Party (NWP), led by Alice Paul, focused on removing all forms of legal discrimination based on sex through an Equal Rights Amendment (ERA) to the Constitution. However, the NWP was outnumbered by women trade unionists and the League of Women Voters, who opposed the ERA because it would threaten gender-specific protective labor legislation. Unlike the NWP, the League showed a healthy growth rate in the 1950s among middle-class, suburban women and served as an important training ground for women to enter both conventional electoral politics and social-change movements, such as civil rights and feminism, in the 1960s.

The National Council of Women of Canada (NCWC) forms one bridge for English Canadians between the first and second waves. Established in 1893 as a nonpartisan umbrella organization of national women's organizations, it encouraged women to extend their domestic roles into larger social reform issues. The NCWC also educated women about their political responsibilities and supported such issues as equal pay for equal work.

The Federation of Business and Professional Women's Clubs, with members in both countries, was especially active in Canada after World War II. Under the leadership of Margaret Hyndman, it assumed a key role in the campaign to legislate equal pay for equal work; such laws were enacted first by Ontario in 1952, and by all the other provinces except Québec and Newfoundland by the end of the decade. The rural Women's Institutes and the Young Women's Christian Association (YWCA) were also active in the equal pay campaigns and in working for other laws concerning antidiscrimination in employment.

In the United States, the YWCA (or "Y") was in the forefront of the struggle for racial justice, especially after the Interracial Charter of 1946 committed the organization to desegregating itself. The Y became an essential bridge to both the civil rights movement and second-wave feminism through intergenerational and cross-racial mentoring (Lynn, 1992). White women, such as Sandra Cason (later known as Casey Hayden) and Mary King, who joined the civil rights movement in its early years, typically came from the student Y.

New women's peace organizations, which sprang up in the early 1960s, were both forerunners of the second wave and a link between older and younger activists. The Voice of Women (La Voix des Femmes), founded in Toronto in 1960, and Women Strike for Peace, organized in the United States in 1961, were the most important. Thérèse Casgrain, a leader of Québec's suffrage movement, started La Voix des Femmes and was a founder of the Fédération des Femmes du Québec (FFQ) in 1966, the first of Canada's second-wave organizations.

Labor unions provided another route to feminism, as working women sought equal wages and seniority rights with men. Before the beginning of the second wave, the efforts of U.S. union women had resulted in the passage of equal pay laws, first on the state level, and, finally, in coalition with middle-class groups, on the national level, with the Federal Equal Pay Act of 1963. Female labor leaders were also important participants in what Cynthia Harrison calls the "Women's Bureau coalition," or women's organizations allied with the Women's Bureau in the U.S. Department of Labor. This coalition was largely responsible for establishing the President's Commission on the Status of Women in 1961 (Harrison, 1988).

In addition to ongoing organizational activity, the increasing participation of women in the labor force, smaller-sized families, rising divorce rates, and the increase in women's college enrollments laid the basis for the revival of feminism.

While the media in the United States and Canada emphasized women's domestic roles and government policies favored men for employment and educational subsidies, many women either remained in the workforce or returned after a short absence. The ideology of consumerism was partly responsible, because the desired standard of suburban living required more than one paycheck per family. Less privileged women, who had worked before and during the war out of economic necessity, had no choice but to continue working. When they lost their high-wage manufacturing jobs, they sought lower-paying service and clerical employment. The nadir for women's employment in the United States was reached in 1947, when 29 percent of women were working, but by 1960, 37.7 percent of all women aged 16 and over were employed, constituting one-third of the U.S. workforce. In Canada, women aged 15 and over who were in the labor force climbed from 24 percent in 1952 to 37 percent by 1971.

More important than the overall increase was the marital status of women workers. In Canada only slightly more than 10 percent of all employed women were married in 1941, but by 1961 this figure had climbed to nearly 50 percent. By the early 1960s, 41.5 percent of married women with children between ages 6 and 17 were working in the United States, and married women constituted 60 percent of the female workforce.

Women were generally employed in those occupations where they had been the majority of workers even before World War II. From 75 to 98 percent of all nurses, telephone operators, clerical workers, and elementary school teachers were women. Although women's choices were relatively narrow, their occupations were in growing sectors of the economy. In both countries women were marrying at younger ages and completing their childbearing earlier; they were able to return to work by their late twenties or early thirties, and after the mid-1950s the high postwar fertility rate started to decline.

In spite of the ideology of family "togetherness," young women began to live outside the family, divorce rates climbed, and the number of widows increased, owing to the widening gap between male and female life expectancy. While the postwar ideal of domesticity did not keep women at home, it did reinforce their responsibility for housework and child care. More women were experiencing the "double day." By the early 1960s, Betty Friedan in the United States and Doris Anderson and June Callwood in Canada were publishing articles about sex-role stereotyping and criticizing notions of femininity that limited women's activities.

Although U.S. women's college attendance had dropped compared with that of men's after the war, it began to pick up as the demand increased for college-educated workers. Between 1950 and 1974, college enrollments grew by 234 percent for men, but by 456 percent for women, and the ratio of women to men in college went from a low of 0.48 in 1950 to 0.79 in 1974. In Canada, women represented only 21 percent of university undergraduates in 1945, but they accounted for 37 percent by 1970.

In Québec, economic, demographic, and educational changes occurred so quickly that they have been called the "quiet revolution." One result of rapid urbanization, agricultural mechanization, and a decline in the social and moral authority of the Roman Catholic church was that between 1959 and 1969 Québec's birthrate was cut in half. Another was the increase in women's university attendance. By 1970, women accounted for one-third of all full-time undergraduates in the province and for nearly half of all part-time students.

College students in both countries became a politically active segment of the population in the 1960s, and the rebirth of feminism was partly an outgrowth of women's experiences in the student New Left, as well as in peace, civil rights, and Native rights movements. Women claimed the ideals of these movements for themselves and began to criticize the gap between a rhetoric of equality and the practice of sexism, in much the same way that the movements themselves had judged the dominant society.

In the United States, the civil rights movement, initiated by southern African-Americans, was the catalyst and model for other movements, including women's liberation. African-American women had taken the lead in breaking down racial segregation after the Supreme Court's decision in *Brown* v. *Topeka Board of Education* in 1954. A bus boycott in Montgomery, Alabama, which began after Rosa Parks was arrested for purposely violating a bus segregation ordinance, had been planned for almost a decade by Jo Ann Robinson and the Women's Political Council. Young women and girls were in the front lines of desegregation efforts at Central High School in Little Rock, Arkansas (1957), and at elementary schools in New Orleans and Atlanta.

After southern black students launched a "sit-in" movement across the South in early 1960, they were encouraged by Ella Baker, an older activist, to form their own organization, the Student Nonviolent Coordinating Committee (SNCC). In spite of the physical dangers involved in protests against segregated facilities and in voter registration work, almost half of the early black activists were women. Diane Nash and Ruby Doris Smith (Robinson) were early leaders, and older women, such as Fannie Lou Hamer, Amelia Boynton, and Carolyn Daniels, sheltered younger civil rights workers in their homes and arranged community support. Both the younger and the older women became role models for the less numerous white women, such as Casey Hayden and Mary King, who joined the movement in its early years.

Disparities between men's and women's positions in the civil rights organizations and the different treatment given to black and white women surfaced during the Freedom Summers of 1964 and 1965, when a large number of northern white women were recruited into the southern movement. Although black women had criticized male chauvinism, the first feminist position paper was written by Casey Hayden and Mary King in 1964. With the rise of "black power" in the mid-1960s, white activists were no longer welcome in SNCC. Black women remained committed to the struggle for racial justice, while white women began to focus more on gender relations, especially in the New Left.

Women in Students for a Democratic Society (SDS), one of the most important of the U.S. New Left organizations, were effective organizers. They pioneered an early form of consciousness-raising while working with poor women on such "women's issues" as welfare, housing, and sanitation. However, as community work was downgraded in favor of antiwar protests, women found themselves relegated to auxiliary roles. They were expected to support draft-resisting men in every way, including sexually, as was suggested in the widespread slogan "Girls say yes to guys who say no!" When a women's liberation workshop presented an analysis and a set of demands to the SDS national convention in July 1967, it was ridiculed in the organization's newsletter. The following month, at the National Conference for New Politics, the chair continually refused to allow women to speak. One of them was Shulamith Firestone, who would later write in *The Dialectic of Sex* (1971: 37) that the "sexual class system" is "the model for all other exploitative systems."

In 1967 and 1968, North American women began to form their own "women's liberation" groups. Unlike their U.S. counterparts, Canadian feminists also continued their strong presence in mixed-sex organizations. Canadian nationalism and the greater strength of Canadian democratic socialism are partly responsible for the difference in the two countries. The two nations converge, however, in their discriminatory treatment of racial and ethnic minorities. The independence movement in Québec, which dominated politics in the late 1960s, was analogous to the black power struggle in the United States in that neither *Québéçoises* nor African-American women could make common cause with English Canadian or white U.S. women as long as the latter resisted making racism and nationalism integrally feminist issues. Racial and national divisions would remain among the greatest problems and limitations of second-wave feminism.

Feminist Ideas, Issues, and Organizations

By 1970, white feminists in the United States and anglophones in Canada were developing into two main branches: liberal and radical. Liberal feminists are reformers who want women included in the existing political economy and society on the same terms as men. Their model is a gender-integrated society, with all individuals having equal rights. Especially in the United States, liberals have minimized gender differences, believing that "difference" would perpetuate unequal treatment. Yet there is an inherent paradox because women must organize collectively as a "class" and win such gender-based measures as reproductive rights, child care services, and an end to sexual harassment. Simply trying to include women in existing institutions may lead to changing those institutions.

In both Canada and the United States, government commissions initiated or strengthened liberal feminism. The President's Commission on the Status of Women issued its report in 1963, the year Betty Friedan's best-seller *The Feminine Mystique* was published. Although both addressed white, highly educated women and neglected the problems of poor women and women of color, they helped to make sex discrimination a subject of serious political discussion. Hundreds of readers wrote to Friedan, telling their stories of stifled ambition and calling for a revival of women's political activism (May, 1988: 208–226). The immediate impact of the President's Commission was less dramatic. It had been put together in 1961 by the Women's Bureau Coalition partly to derail the National Woman's Party's work for the ERA, and therefore did not heal the old split among feminists. The NWP did manage to insert the word *sex* into Title VII of the 1964 Civil Rights Act, which had been designed to end racial discrimination in employment. The lack of enforcement of Title VII galvanized Betty Friedan and others to form the National Organization for Women (NOW) in 1966, the first of the liberal second-wave organizations. NOW's Bill of Rights in 1968 supported a broad range of reforms: the ERA, publicly funded child care, and reproductive rights, including abortion.

The President's Commission and the Civil Rights Act of 1964 preceded the revival of feminism in the United States, but Canada's Royal Commission on the Status of Women, initiated in 1967, held its meetings simultaneously with the onset of the radical women's liberation movement. However, the commission itself reflected the views of the more moderate wing of the movement. In 1966, Laura Sabia, then president of the Canadian Federation of University Women, had called together representatives from 32 national women's organizations, including the National Council of Women of Canada, the YWCA, and the Voice of Women. After forming the Committee on Equality for Women, they lobbied for a royal commission. Although the Fédération des Femmes du Québec did not officially join the committee, the delegates who went to Ottawa to petition the prime minister included Thérèse Casgrain and Réjane Laberge-Colas, FFQ's first president. Public hearings held in all ten provinces gave the commission's members an education about women's issues, and the final report in 1970, with 167 recommendations, provided a feminist agenda for Canadian society.

By 1972, the Committee on Equality for Women had evolved into the National Action Committee on the Status of Women (NAC). Unlike NOW, NAC is a government-funded umbrella organization that includes representatives from hundreds of women's groups—radical and socialist as well as liberal. While radical feminists in the United States have formed coalitions with liberals, especially for reproductive rights, there is no one organization that brings U.S. feminists together to the same degree as Canada's NAC. Canadian feminists generally have a closer relationship with the state and expect government funding for their projects.

In both countries, radical feminism (initially called women's liberation) came out of the student New Left,

with splits then occurring between women who wished to synthesize socialism and feminism and others who rejected all leftist ideology as an expression of "male" thinking and values. The latter tendency was stronger in the United States, where radicals insisted that "patriarchy," instead of "capitalism," was the primary cause of women's oppression. Kate Millett's *Sexual Politics* and Shulamith Firestone's *The Dialectic of Sex,* both initially published in 1970, were two important early works that provided a framework for feminist theories of patriarchy and a critique of all aspects of "male" culture and institutions. Unlike liberals or socialists, radicals emphasized gender differences and insisted that women's values and experience could be a basis for creating totally new institutions and forms of knowledge.

The process to accomplish this was *consciousness-raising* (CR), a term coined by Kathie Sarachild, an early member of Redstockings, a group founded in New York City in 1969 by Ellen Willis and Shulamith Firestone. Adopting the premise that the personal is the political, women in small discussion groups became aware that their problems were not unique or due to individual inadequacies; rather, such problems were caused by a social order that could be changed.

Radicals also incorporated the "participatory democracy" of the New Left, replacing formal hierarchical structures with rotating or shared leadership. The results were mixed; more women became active participants, but the distrust of "elitism" also led to attacks on individuals with leadership abilities or strong personalities. Intragroup relations and conflicts sometimes overshadowed community outreach and political organizing. Organizational splits were common, with dissatisfied women forming new groups. Most radical feminist organizations were small and locally based. Political organizing was often combined with providing essential information and services through a range of alternative institutions, such as health care collectives, rape crisis centers, shelters for battered women, bookstores, and publishing companies.

Feminist education has been disseminated not only through community-based services and cultural centers, but also in academic women's studies programs, beginning in the late 1960s with a few courses taught by radical feminists. A decade later approximately half of American institutions of higher education had courses on women and women's studies programs. These programs and organizations, such as the Canadian Research Institute for the Advancement of Women (1976) and the National Women's Studies Association (1977), try to bridge the academic and activist worlds and encourage both academic scholarship and applied or action-based research. Feminists have identified sexist biases in textbooks and research and have developed new epistemologies and theories. They have made gender an accepted analytical category in the social sciences, history, and humanities. Women's caucuses and committees within professional associations, such as the Canadian Sociology and Anthropology Association, the American Historical Association, and the Modern Language Association, work to eliminate sex discrimination in hiring, promotion, and publication. Despite conservatives' criticism and problems with funding, women's studies programs, research on women and gender, and feminist publications continue to flourish.

In addition to new forms of knowledge, radical feminists expanded "politics" to include issues that had been formerly regarded as "private" or "natural," especially sexuality and reproduction. In 1968, Anne Koedt wrote "The Myth of the Vaginal Orgasm," an early critique of male-defined sexuality. After presenting the facts of female anatomy, she explained why sexual pleasure was a political issue. Once women realized that orgasm could be obtained without male penetration, not only male supremacy, but also the institution of heterosexuality, was threatened (Koedt, 1970/1973).

Lesbians, however, did not initially meet with unqualified acceptance. Betty Friedan even attempted to purge them from NOW, but the organization did not succumb to homophobia, and by 1971 it acknowledged sexual orientation as a feminist issue. Most lesbian feminists were more inclined toward the radical wing of the movement, but here, too, conflicts occurred over how much to emphasize sexual relations and whether lesbianism was central to feminism. While some lesbians chose separation, many more worked with nonlesbians and convinced them that all women's choices are limited by heterosexism.

The politics of reproduction, especially abortion, have been a top priority for feminists from the beginning of the second wave until today. One of the first national actions in Canada was the Abortion Caravan of 1970 to protest the inadequate revisions in the criminal code regarding abortion. Not until January 1988 did the Canadian Supreme Court, in the *Morgentaler* case, remove the legal obstacles to abortion. The U.S. Supreme Court had acted 15 years earlier in *Roe* v. *Wade* (1973), but since then the pro-choice position has lost ground to adverse court rulings and a vocal pro-life movement. The right to abortion in the United States has been generally limited to women who can afford it, since the Court ruled in 1977 that the state does not have to pay for the abortions of low-income

women in medical assistance programs. That white middle-class feminists in the United States were slow to remobilize until their own "right" to abortion was threatened in the late 1980s is indicative of class and race divisions among women.

Women of color and white working-class women have felt excluded from the middle-class women's movement even when they have supported its goals. Women's organizations have engaged in overt and subtle forms of racism and classism, and feminist theory has been white and middle-class without acknowledging these limitations. Although early socialist feminists contributed historical and economic dimensions to theories of patriarchy, they did not sufficiently analyze racism. Many were students or young professionals rather than working-class. Autonomous Canadian socialist feminist groups, such as Saskatoon Women's Liberation and the International Women's Day Committee (Toronto), became involved in organizing workplaces and supporting strikes by immigrant working women. Socialist feminists in the United States were less successful in building coalitions with working women or with trade unions. They devoted much time and energy in the early 1970s to developing a "correct" theory. Their audience was more the New Left than the women's movement, but by the mid-1970s the left was a dwindling force in U.S. politics (Hansen, 1990). As individuals, however, socialist feminists have been important theoreticians and teachers in women's studies programs, as well as activists in the reproductive rights and peace movements and in antiracism work.

Working-class women's politics in the 1970s were not ideologically driven and included aspects of liberal, radical, and socialist feminism. U.S. trade union women were found both in the Coalition of Labor Union Women (CLUW), formed in 1974 to act as a women's pressure group within the trade union "establishment," and in independent or left-leaning groups outside the American Federation of Labor and Congress of Industrial Organizations (AFL-CIO), such as Union WAGE (Women's Alliance to Gain Equality). Freestanding organizations of U.S. clerical workers, such as Women Organized for Employment (San Francisco), Nine to Five (Boston), and Women Employed (Chicago), focused on practical workplace issues, especially ending sex discrimination in pay and promotions. The Service, Office, and Retail Workers' Union of Canada tried to organize clerical, restaurant, and retail workers into an independent feminist union. These and other organizations of working women helped to reshape feminist movements as they entered their second decade.

The Conservative 1980s and Prospects for a Third Wave

By the late 1970s, white radical feminists were becoming less distinguishable from liberal feminists. The partial acceptance and institutionalization of feminism gave the liberals legitimate, almost hegemonic, status, while the increasingly conservative political climate in the 1980s limited ideological debate. Feminists concentrated on defending what they had already gained. English Canadians were successful in having equality provisions included in the Charter of Rights and Freedoms in 1982, although women in Québec were divided over the new Canadian constitution. The same year, the ERA in the United States was defeated when it fell three states short of ratification.

In both countries women have increased their percentage of elected and appointed public officials. They are growing more visible as scientists, legal and medical professionals, corporate executives, and trade union leaders. The growing salience of employment issues is not, however, a reflection of women's occupational success, but rather a result of overall increases in women's workforce participation within a changing North American economy.

Sixty percent of all women are in the labor force, and the rate is more than 70 percent for those between the ages of 24 and 50. Women are no longer leaving their jobs for extended periods of unpaid family work. Despite their continuous employment, working-class women are as occupationally segregated as they were in 1960. Antidiscrimination laws and affirmative action programs have primarily benefited university-educated middle-class women, and deindustrialization, coupled with renewed male resistance, has hindered women's entry into better-paying skilled trades.

Gender segregation in the labor force is directly related to women's lower wages. Although the wage gap has narrowed, women in 1998 still earned 75 cents for every dollar men earned. Efforts to move beyond equal pay for equal work and to implement "pay equity," or equal pay for work of comparable value, have encountered serious political and corporate resistance. Additionally, women and people of color are more likely to work in the "secondary sector" or in "casualized" forms of work, where wages are lower and there are few, if any, opportunities for promotion or work-related benefits.

Finally, the sexual division of labor keeps women subordinate in the household, as well as in the paid workforce. Although men are beginning to share household tasks and spend more time with their children, women remain largely responsible for housework and child care. This "double day" leaves them with fewer hours than men for leisure, study, or political activity.

While most women rely on individual strategies or informal workplace networks, others have formed organizations or joined labor unions. Women's share of labor union membership has increased dramatically since 1960: from 18.3 percent to 37 percent in the United States, and from 16.4 percent to 39.5 percent in Canada by the early 1990s. However, the U.S. labor movement is far weaker than it was in 1960, and less than 12 percent of U.S. employed women belonged to a union, compared with 28 percent in Canada, at the end of the twentieth century. Backed by CLUW in the AFL-CIO and the Women's Department of the Canadian Labour Council, unions are training more women organizers and including parental leave, child care, and other "family issues" in their negotiations. In Canada, but not the United States, it is legal and politically acceptable to set aside seats or positions for women and other underrepresented groups in order to achieve more diversity in union leadership.

For women of color, class and gender issues are always inseparable from issues of race and nationality. According to Alma Garcia, Chicanas (Mexican-Americans) and other women of color must first find a relationship between feminism and racial pride or cultural nationalism. This usually involves both a feminist critique of cultural traditions that reinforce male supremacy and an analysis that stresses the interconnections of race, gender, and class. A second, related issue involves challenging the notion that feminism is an ideology from the white (alien) culture and, therefore, irrelevant or threatening to cultural or racial unity. Lesbians, in particular, have been accused of "selling out" or "going over" to the "white movement," and all feminists risk being labeled as lesbians. Third, and most important, is the issue of racism and the middle-class orientation of the white women's movement (Garcia, 1989).

As feminists, women of color and Québécoises have generally worked within already existing organizations for racial and national justice or have created their own women's groups. The Ontario Native Women's Association, formed in 1972, was one of many native women's groups that worked to change sexist components of Canada's Indian Act and in 1985 succeeded in restoring to Native women full Indian status, rights, and identity. During International Women's Year in 1975, immigrant women merged as a vocal pressure group in Canada and have since formed numerous local organizations. In 1986, the National Organization of Immigrant and Visible Minority Women of Canada began to coordinate immigrant women's concerns and organizations at the national level.

Since the mid-1980s, many new community-based and national coalitions have appeared in the United States to fill gaps in the white liberal feminist agenda and to create structures that could survive cutbacks in public funding for education, health, and other services. The National Black Women's Health Project, National Latina Health Organization, Asian Women's Health Organization, and others joined forces in 1992 to form the Women of Color Reproductive Health Rights Coalition. On the local level, Asian Women's Shelter (San Francisco), Every Woman's Shelter (Los Angeles), and the New York Women's Center address the needs of physically assaulted immigrant women. Asian Immigrant Women Advocates, based in the San Francisco area, and Fuerza Unida in San Antonio, Texas, support women workers who earn wages below the legal minimum and face the loss of jobs as industries move operations to third world countries (Louie, 1994).

Repeated cases of corporate "flexibility" and flight have turned feminists' attention to economic restructuring. Women's employment opportunities and standards of living are jeopardized by the privatization or "downsizing" of publicly owned enterprises, cutbacks in social services, and free trade agreements. In 1988, Canadian feminists made strong but ultimately unsuccessful efforts to stop the Canada-U.S. Free Trade Agreement. The more recent North American Free Trade Agreement (NAFTA), which includes Mexico, had adversely affected larger proportions of North American women workers by transferring jobs to areas with low wages and low safety standards.

In addition to effective coalitions across national lines, white feminists in the United States and Canada must expand their agenda to include the "gender issues" of women of color. Among these, for Chicanas and African-Americans, are welfare, housing, the racist criminal justice system, and adolescents at risk of drug addiction, early pregnancy, and leaving school. Bilingual education and the legal and economic problems of undocumented immigrants are growing concerns for Latinas and Asian women. Native Americans struggle with alcoholism, disease, and an assimilationist educational system that ignores Native traditions. Reproductive health care means not only access to safe contraceptives and abortions but also improved prenatal and infant care and an end to involuntary sterilization.

The possibility of a third wave depends on a critical rethinking of work, family, sexuality, community, knowledge, and power, much as in second-wave feminism, but this time based on the assumption that race, class, and gender are interconnected and part of every issue.

See Also

CONSCIOUSNESS-RAISING; FEMININE MYSTIQUE, FEMINISM: AFRICAN-AMERICAN; FEMINISM: ASIAN-AMERICAN; FEMINISM: CHICANA; FEMINISM: FIRST WAVE NORTH AMERICAN; FEMINISM: LESBIAN; FEMINISM: LIBERAL NORTH AMERICAN; FEMINISM: RADICAL; FEMINISM: SOCIALIST; LIBERATION; WOMEN'S STUDIES: UNITED STATES

References and Further Reading

Adamson, Nancy, Linda Briskin, and Margaret McPhail. 1988. *Feminist organizing for change: The contemporary women's movement in Canada.* Toronto: Oxford University Press.

Backhouse, Constance, and David H. Flaherty, eds. 1992. *Challenging times: The women's movement in Canada and the United States.* Montreal: McGill-Queen's University Press.

Cobble, Dorothy Sue, ed. 1993. *Women and unions: Forging a partnership.* Ithaca, N.Y.: ILR.

Du Plesis, Rachel Blau and Ann Snitow, ed. 1998. *The feminist memoir project: Voices from women's liberation.* New York: Three Rivers.

Echols, Alice. 1989. *Daring to be bad: Radical feminism in America, 1967–1975.* Minneapolis: University of Minnesota Press.

Evans, Sara. 1979. *Personal politics: The roots of women's liberation in the civil rights movement and the New Left.* New York: Knopf.

Firestone, Shulamith. 1971. *The dialectic of sex: The case for feminist revolution.* New York: Bantam.

Garcia, Alma M. 1989. The development of Chicana feminist discourse, 1970–1980. *Gender and Society* 3(2): 217–38.

Gatlin, Rochelle. 1987. *American women since 1945.* Basingstoke: Macmillan Education.

Hansen, Karen V. 1990. Women's unions and the search for a political identity. In Karen V. Hansen and Ilene J. Philipson, eds., *Women, class, and the feminist imagination: A socialist-feminist reader,* 213–238. Philadephia, Pa.: Temple University Press.

Harrison, Cynthia. 1988. *On account of sex: The politics of women's issues, 1945–1968.* Berkeley: University of California Press.

Hartmann, Susan M. 1998. *The other feminists: Activists in the liberal establishment.* New Haven and London: Yale University Press.

Horowitz, Daniel. 1998. *Betty Friedan and the making of* The Feminine Mystique: *The American left, the cold war, and modern feminism.* Amherst: University of Massachusetts Press.

Koedt, Anne. 1970/1973. The myth of the vaginal orgasm. In Anne Koedt, Ellen Levine, and Anita Rapone, eds., *Radical feminism,* 198–207. New York: Quadrangle/New York Times.

Louie, Miriam Ching. 1994. Grassroots women organize. *Cross-roads*, 39: 10–14.

Lynn, Susan. 1992. *Progressive women in conservative times: Racial justice, peace, and feminism, 1945 to the 1960s.* New Brunswick, N.J.: Rutgers University Press.

May, Elaine Tyler. 1988. *Homeward bound: American families in the cold war era.* New York: Basic Books.

Millett, Kate. 1970. *Sexual politics.* New York: Aron/Hearst.

Prentice, Alison, Paula Bourne, Gail Cuthbert Brandt, Beth Light, Wendy Mitchinson, and Naomi Black. 1988. *Canadian women: A history.* Toronto: Harcourt Brace Jovanovich.

Rosen, Ruth. 2000. *The world split open: How the modern women's movement changed America.* New York: Viking/Penguin Putnam.

Rochelle Gatlin

FEMINISM: Socialist

Socialist feminism appeared as an organized current of feminism in most western capitals in the mid-1970s. It expressed the outlook and many of the early assumptions of women's liberation, a self-conscious movement of women that first emerged in the closing years of the civil rights and student movements of the 1960s. Typically, Marge Piercy (1970) in the United States had complained: "The Movement is supposed to be for human liberation; how come the position of women in it is no better than outside?" In Great Britain, as elsewhere, the clenched fist inside the women's sign, symbolizing women's liberation, was testimony to its birth within the militant left. The emphasis on "prefigurative" politics or the creation of alternative institutions and lifestyles in the opening years of women's liberation—with the setting up of nurseries, play groups, self-help and resource centers, alongside collective households, women's publications, and a strong emphasis on participatory democracy—was a continuation of New Left strategies and perspectives.

A Rhetoric of Revolution

A rhetoric of social revolution thus accompanied the birth of women's liberation. Its goals, as drawn up in a manifesto for the first national women's liberation conference in Britain in March 1970, were to enable women to come together "to further our part in the struggle for social change and the transformation of society," to provide solidarity with women's struggles for a better life everywhere, and to enable women to control their "own lives." Social transformation was thus to accompany women's search for personal growth and happiness, most persuasively presented in all of the writing of Sheila Rowbotham—from her pioneering pamphlet "Women's Liberation and the New Politics," written in 1969 before there was any women's liberation movement in Britain, to her internationally successful *Woman's Consciousness, Man's World* (1973). The goal of social transformation was as central in the United States as it was in Britain in these years, although the former was distinctive in the presence of a strong liberal or reformist wing of the movement, organized through the National Organization for Women (NOW). Then led by Betty Friedan, it sought to strengthen women's civil rights through alliances with mainstream political groups.

Although some form of radical left politics was shared by many feminists in the early 1970s, a distinction between "radical feminism" and socialist feminism soon emerged as feminists sought the causes of the global subordination of women to men. Some internationally influential feminist voices, such as Robin Morgan in the United States, represented a radical feminism according to which women's oppression is fundamental or primary and underlies all other forms of oppression. Others, like Morgan's compatriot Barbara Ehrenreich, provided a similarly influential account of socialist feminism, arguing that women's oppression is interconnected with other equally basic forms of hierarchy and oppression in capitalist class society. Some socialist feminists, emphasizing the interconnected significance of class relations and sexual hierarchy, introduced the notion of "capitalist patriarchy" (Eisenstein, 1979).

Many early women's liberationists hoped to avoid divisive labels, but within a few years women who were part of strong socialist feminist currents were holding their own national and regional conferences and preparing their own publications, from *Red Rag* in Britain to *Scarlet Woman* in Australia. (The color coding of socialist feminist productions was broken only by the New York *radical* feminist group Redstockings.) These socialists wanted to explore the practical and theoretical connections between women's continuing subordination and the structural underpinning and daily routines of contemporary capitalist societies, in search of the best strategies for change. As the most comprehensive analysis of capitalist societies, socialist feminists drew on the classical and contemporary work of theoretical Marxism, while stressing its inability, so far, to offer an adequate explanation of the situation of women or how to change it.

Squabbles over Marx and Grassroots Activism

Although socialist feminism flourished within the wider movement in the 1970s, its conferences often became bogged down in abstract debate about some of the least creative areas of Marxist thought. There could be no smooth or easy reapplication of such theorizing, focused traditionally on labor power, production, and profit, to the new feminist issues of personal life, reproduction, and the social and cultural marginalization of women, oppressed by images of themselves as powerless, passive, and inferior. For example, the feminist critique of women's major responsibility for housework and child care reappeared as the "domestic labor debate" in early socialist feminist polemic discussing whether women's unpaid housework created "surplus value," thereby increasing capitalist profits. This seemed to marginalize the more challenging feminist critique of men's power over women in the home (and the exposure of how abusively some men were using it). It also illustrated the socialist feminist tendency to locate women's oppression first and foremost in "their imprisonment in the home as wives and mothers—still their basic role under capitalism as in all other societies" (Red Rag Collective, 1973).

Any such focus on one basic cause of women's subordinate status, however, always entailed a blindness to the complexity of issues involved in its maintenance—as socialist feminists themselves were pointing out a few years later. (Indeed, they criticized radical feminists for their single emphasis on men's desire for power as the fundamental cause of women's oppression, but at times displayed a not dissimilar search for original causes themselves—at least at first.) Other socialist feminists, like Juliet Mitchell, turned to psychoanalysis as a way of assessing the limitations of Marxism for understanding the situation of women. When it came to explaining the depth of patriarchy and the difficulty of eroding it, there seemed to be some absolute difference—more entrenched than any other social division—that only psychoanalysis could address through its account of the unconscious construction of sexual difference (Mitchell, 1974). Although always contentious, in its prioritizing of sexual difference over all other forms of difference, this strand of psychoanalytic feminism has become more influential in the decades since its appearance. (Segal, 1987).

If attempts to explain the origins of women's oppression often created dissent, however, it proved harder for socialist feminists to avoid the more destructive strategic interventions of some existing Marxist groups. Although the bulk of socialist feminists were nonaligned libertarian socialists, suspicious of leadership and eager to reach agreement only through democratic consensus, they frequently had to fend off sectarian attempts to hijack their conferences by women hostile to their shared principles and practices (in Britain, primarily from Trotskyist grouplets; in the United States, from Marxist-Leninist and Maoist factions). The women from these groups tended to dismiss the rich diversity of socialist feminist activities and their attempts to make changes in their own lives, demanding instead support for some single anticapitalist "transitional" program or strategy. Those interventions proved so tedious and debilitating for other participants that few national conferences were held in either the United Kingdom or the United States after the mid-1970s, later causing Barbara Ehrenreich (1984) to wonder just why so many successful socialist feminist gatherings and organizations had "crumbled in the face of so much bullshit."

Despite its theoretical and organizational problems—which are hardly unusual in political life (whatever the sentimental hopes for a conflict-free sisterhood)—self-identified socialist feminists remained prominent in most feminist activities throughout the 1970s. These ranged from work in community resource centers, campaigns, and self-help activities for women's health, reproductive needs, and welfare rights to trade union activism and engagement in women's refuges; rape crisis centers; antiracist, antifascist, and antimilitarist politics; and campaigns for policy and legal reform. In Britain the diversity of all this grassroots activism was celebrated in a socialist feminist book by Sheila Rowbotham, Lynne Segal and Hilary Wainwright, *Beyond the Fragments: Feminism and the Making of Socialism,* which began as a pamphlet in 1979 and would soon become an influential, widely translated book, in the early 1980s (Rowbotham et al., 1980). Its aim of asserting the validity and potential of the social movements, and of the role of feminism within them, as a basis for strengthening the creative links with more traditional labor movement and socialist perspectives proved, briefly, so popular that a conference of 1,600 people met in 1980 to plan new ways forward for a feminist-inspired socialism. But this apparent high point, ironically, would mark the beginning of a decline of both feminist and socialist activism, whether united or separate. The confidence of grassroots struggles for change faded fast as far-right governments came to power in both Britain and the United States, rolling back the hopes of the previous decade. Any loose alliance of all the "fragments" proved organizationally unworkable.

Growing Conflict and Divisions

Tied in with a new mood of pessimism eroding collective action in the generally more individualistic and conservative climate of the 1980s, three further forces played a part in the decline of socialist feminism as an organized feminist current and a self-conscious political identification. All contributed, at the same time, to the fragmentation of the women's movement more generally as any type of coherent political entity, although most certainly not to the disappearance of feminism as a significant, if highly diversified, political influence.

With the spread of feminist activism beyond its largely white ex-student origins, the differences between groups of women became more conflictual. Tearing apart notions of "sisterhood," feminists spoke of their specific oppression by other women—along lines of race, ethnicity, class, age, sexual orientation, disability, or religion—creating struggles over the hierarchy of oppression. In particular, the rise of a confident and organized black feminism in the early 1980s left many white feminists feeling guilty, as accused, of developing exclusionary white, eurocentric perspectives. Socialist feminists, in particular, were troubled by criticism from black women that their theorizing and strategies concerning "women's" situation in the family and the workplace, and on welfare rights, men, motherhood, and sexuality, had distorted the circumstances of black women, contributing only to "an improvement in the material situation of white middle class women often at the expense of their Black and working class 'sisters'" (Amos and Parmar, 1984). If socialist feminists had found it hard to make theoretical connections between sex and class, it proved harder to theorize about sex, class, *and* race from within any overall feminist framework.

It was not race, however, but sexuality that would produce the definitive rupture within feminism, paving the way for the "sex wars" of the 1980s. These wars began and became most entrenched in the United States, as the work of polemicists like Andrea Dworkin was taken up and turned into legislative strategy by theoreticians like Catharine MacKinnon. They introduced a critique of heterosexuality as the root of women's oppression, linked, inevitably, to rape, pornography, and male violence against women (MacKinnon, 1989). In Britain proponents of this analysis called themselves revolutionary feminists, practicing "political lesbianism." The anger triggered by this debate not only made broad-based feminist gatherings places to be avoided but, in emphasizing the primacy of sexuality and male violence in women's lives, tended to marginalize the earlier debates and activities of socialist feminists. The focus on male sexuality and its abuses had come to dominate the public stage of feminism in the 1980s, however, partly because other currents of feminism, like

socialist feminism, were already fragmented and demoralized by the recognition of hierarchies and divisions between women and the decline of leftist optimism.

Poststructuralist Critique

Finally, and in the end perhaps most significantly, the move away from any confident assertion of a socialist feminist identity accompanied the growth of a new era of feminist theory now distancing itself from what it saw as the old "Anglo-American orthodoxies" of the feminism of the 1970s. It became known as *feminist postmodernism*—although the term is both conceptually confused and confusing and has been rejected by many placed under its banner. With the spread of women's studies and feminist scholarship within academic institutions in the 1980s, women sought to find a place for themselves and to critique male-centered theorizing and research across disciplinary boundaries. By the mid-1980s this had produced a growing academization of theory calling on the contemporary prestige and authority of French poststructuralism and deconstruction. These new approaches ranged from a critique of the notion of women as unified individuals sharing personal experiences to gain autonomous selfhood (as in "consciousness-raising") to a rejection of all universalizing thought, loosely drawing on the quite distinctive positions of three French theorists: Lacan, Derrida, and Foucault.

Poststructuralist theory moved academic feminism a long way from the confident hopes with which women's liberation movements once took to the streets. Feminism of the 1970s, like socialist feminism, is scorned both for its false certainties about women's shared interests and its search for structural causes of women's oppression (Barrett and Phillips, 1992). "Postmodern feminism" replaces the "naive" search for social causation with abstract elaborations of the discursive constitution of an array of key concepts: "female difference" in particular and "binary oppositions" in general. Those stressing "difference" have drawn on post-Lacanian psychoanalysis (like that of Luce Irigaray) to marginalize the many social "differences" dividing women and stress the silenced and repressed "feminine" side of the spurious unity of the western "subject" (man). The more rigorous Derridian strand of deconstructing (like that of Donna Haraway) rejects all unitary patternings of the self, including "woman." While the former project marginalizes all social differences between women, such as race, in search of a highly disputed female "difference," the latter endorses an indeterminacy that threatens to undermine political solidarity. Broad-based strategic projects also tend to disappear in the anonymous analysis of power in the Foucauldian strand of poststructuralist feminism, recently explored by Judith Butler and others (see Nicholson, 1990).

The influence of socialist thought has shrunk in feminist writing, as elsewhere. Yet some feminists remain convinced of the need to strengthen democratic socialist forces wherever they can, if the most oppressed women today are to share in the successes that feminism has been able to bring to the lives of some women (Ehrenreich, 1990; Segal, 1999). While it is crucial for feminists to claim a space to theorize and act regarding their differing interests as women, those who describe themselves as socialist feminists today still believe that feminist voices alone can never protect the fortunes of the bulk of women without working in solidarity with other forces for progressive change (see Du Plessis and Snitow, 1998).

See Also

FEMINISM: BLACK BRITISH; FEMINISM: LESBIAN; FEMINISM: MARXIST; FEMINISM: POSTMODERN; FEMINISM: RADICAL; GLOBAL FEMINISM; LIBERATION; MARXISM; SOCIALISM

References and Further Reading

Amos, Valerie, and Pratibha Parmar. 1984. Challenging imperialist feminism. *Feminist Review* 17: 3–20.

Barrett, Michèle, and Anne Phillips. 1988. Introduction. *Destabilizing theory: Contemporary feminist debates*, 1–9. Cambridge: Polity.

Du Plessis, Rachel Blau, and Ann Snitow, eds. 1998. *The feminist memoir project: Voices from women's liberation.* New York: Three Rivers.

Ehrenreich, Barbara. 1984. Life without father. *Socialist Review* 14(1: January–February): 43–49.

———. 1990. *The worst years of our lives.* New York: Doubleday.

Eisenstein, Zillah, ed. 1979. *Capitalist patriarchy and the case for socialist feminism.* New York: Monthly Review.

MacKinnon, Catharine. 1989. *Feminism unmodified: Discourses on life and law.* 1989. Cambridge, Mass.: Harvard University Press.

Mitchell, Juliet. 1974. *Psychoanalysis and feminism.* London: Allen Lane.

Nicholson, Linda, ed. 1990. *Feminism/postmodernism.* London: Routledge.

Piercy, Marge. 1970. The Grand Coolie damn. In Robin Morgan, ed., *Sisterhood is powerful: An anthology of writings from the women's liberation movement*, 421–23. New York: Vintage.

Red Rag Collective. 1973. Editorial. *Red Rag* 5: 2.

Rowbotham, Sheila. 1973. *Woman's consciousness, man's world.* Harmondsworth, U.K.: Penguin.

———, Lynne Segal, and Hilary Wainwright. 1980. *Beyond the fragments: Feminism and the making of socialism.* London: Merlin.

Segal, Lynne. 1987. *Is the future female? Troubled thoughts on contemporary feminism.* London: Virago.

———. 1999. *Why feminism? Gender, psychology, politics.* Cambridge: Polity.

Lynne Segal

FEMINISM: South Africa

In South Africa, all women suffer some form of discrimination on the basis of their sex. Black women in particular carry the burden of a triple oppression of race, class, and gender. Bozzoli (1983: 139) refers to South Africa as a "patchwork quilt of patriarchies," pointing to the complexity and diversity of women's experience of oppression in this country.

As Walker (1990: 2) points out, however, "there is considerable disagreement, not to mention confusion, about how to explain women's oppression in contemporary South Africa, as well as how to analyse the intricate interrelationships of gender, race and class and their differential impact on women."

A statement of the National Executive Committee of the African National Congress (ANC) on the emancipation of women in South Africa (2 May 1990) acknowledges that "the experience of other societies has shown that the emancipation of women is not a by-product of a struggle for democracy, national liberation or socialism. It has to be addressed in its own right within our organisation the mass democratic movement and in the society as a whole" (ANC, 1990).

The difficulty lies in translating this rhetoric into practice. As Walker (1991) observes, in this document lurks the familiar tension between instrumentalist reasons for emancipating women as a means to an end—the strengthening of the liberation movement against apartheid—and a feminist commitment to gender equality at all levels of society.

The Problematic View of Feminism

Although the term *feminism* no longer bears the stigma it once carried, feminism and the relevance of a feminist theoretical debate in southern and South Africa are still in question. Historically, feminism and feminist theory have been regarded with much skepticism and suspicion, and have consequently been largely rejected. There has, therefore, since the early 1990s, been a marked absence of feminist theoretical debate in South Africa. Moreover, there is little or no indigenous scholarship on the role of women in South African society and, as Walker (1991) notes, no historical record of women's lives. The tendency to subsume the experience of women under that of the family in general or abstractions such as reproduction, "oppression," or "gender" has obscured the complexity of women's lives. This may be attributed to a number of factors.

First, it has been argued that feminism and feminist theory are irrelevant and misplaced in a society torn apart by racial and structural inequalities. The women's movement and the struggle for women's rights has, thus, been regarded as subordinate to the more important struggle for national liberation and social reconstruction. Feminism in South Africa has been dismissed as a white, middle-class, western, bourgeois import offering little of benefit to African women. This view has virtually become a cliché in discussions on feminism in southern and South Africa.

Second, women who have been relatively privileged by the existing power relations have tended not to oppose gender oppression. That is, economic and other forms of privilege have tended to foster acquiescence in gender oppression among women in certain social positions (Hansson, 1994: 41).

Third, the relative disadvantage of black men has made it more difficult for black and white women to recognize their specific and common oppression as women. Inequalities on the basis of gender have been obscured by the more visible system of racially and ethnically informed class relations (Hansson, 1994; Walker, 1990).

Fourth, existing debates often have been stifled by what Walker (1991) describes as "an over-concern with the correctness of one's theoretical position" with regard to the debates on race and class. She argues that this has perhaps been one of the most insidious constraints on the development of women's studies in southern Africa. A general preoccupation with political correctness and a perceived need for unity among women, with an associated tendency to avoid conflict on sensitive issues such as race, class, and sexual preference, among others, has had a dampening effect on a broader feminist debate.

These factors combined have adversely affected and inhibited the development of a local feminist theoretical perspective and hampered the formation of a nationally organized women's movement (Hansson, 1994: 41). The apparent lack of unity among South African women and

their failure to identify and struggle together against a patriarchal order has led to a perception that they lack a feminist consciousness (Kemp et al., 1995: 133). However, this view presents only one perspective—a rather narrow perspective—on a continuing debate as to what constitutes South African feminism. This is particularly true given the prominent role played by powerful black women in the antiapartheid struggle.

Although there has been little feminist debate and consequently little theory, this does not mean that South Africa has not had a women's movement. On the contrary, women in South Africa have always been actively involved as a powerful force in the struggle for national liberation. By their very presence, women challenge unequal gender relations in the liberation movement and associated organizations.

Feminism and the Rising Women's Movement

With the dawn of a new democratic social, cultural, and political dispensation in South Africa in 1994, there was a remarkable growth of gender-consciousness in South Africa. Women and issues of gender are finally on the agenda (Bazilli, 1991; Walker, 1991). Several conferences have been held since 1990, which highlight women's subordination and identify contexts where issues of gender inequality in a postapartheid society need to be addressed. *Gender* is now an acceptable term and *feminism* is no longer received quite as negatively as it was in the past. There is a growing recognition of the need to examine gender relations more closely and to analyze the relationship between women's oppression and the struggle against national and racial oppression in South Africa. There also is a growing recognition of the need for an autonomous women's movement to challenge patriarchal assumptions (Kemp et al., 1995: 131). Moreover, women's studies and gender studies as academic disciplines are themselves becoming subjects of analysis and debate (Walker, 1991).

Increasingly, South African women realized that if any real change in the position of women is to occur, women themselves need to attain real economic, political, and social power. It is recognized that women must gain access to and participate in decision-making structures at all levels of society. To this end, women have begun to organize, forming local, regional, and national organizations and coalitions. Probably one of the most important developments has been the formation of the Women's National Coalition (WNC), the first nationally organized women's movement in South Africa. On the initiative of the ANC Women's League, the WNC was launched in April 1992.

The coalition, representing over 90 women's organizations—more than two million women in all—from all regions of South Africa, is the largest and most diverse grouping of women in South Africa. It was formed with the mandate to draft the first *Women's Charter for Effective Equality*, to be used as a political mobilizing document to inform the constitution-making process of the new government, and as a consciousness-raising exercise for women in South Africa.

The coalition was formed at a time of intense political activity in the history of South Africa in a society deeply divided by race, class, and gender. The coalition was regarded by many as a most ambitious project that would probably not live beyond its inception. However, on the basis of the findings of what is believed to be the largest and most comprehensive research campaign on women's demands, the first draft *Women's Charter for Effective Equality* was unanimously adopted in February 1994. The charter contains 12 articles dealing with equality, including "the law and the administration of justice; the economy; education and training; development, infrastructure, and the environment; social services; political and civic life; family life and partnerships; custom, culture, and religion; violence against women; health; and the media."

The WNC, which was launched in 1991, is probably the most powerful symbol of the movement for women's equality in South Africa. Its mandate was extended and its objectives focus on the mobilization and empowerment of all women and women's organizations to secure the objectives of the charter, as well as popularization of the charter and continued research on women's issues and demands in South Africa.

Critical issues that face the WNC and the women's movement in South Africa concern the problem of dealing with diversity, unity, and disunity; ensuring the continued existence of a strong women's movement; the development and promotion of strong regional representation; the need for a continued theoretical feminist debate; funding; and education and training. Threats to the advancement of women's equality in South Africa lie in the possibility of fragmentation and division, the dangers of co-optation and subsequent marginalization, the ghettoization of women's issues in women's desks and ministries in government, and token appointments and the probability of an antifeminist backlash.

Feminist Theory in South Africa: Theoretical Points of Departure

Until 1991, when debates began to be more focused, self-identified feminist writing and discussion in South Africa

drew mostly on western European or North American feminist though, which regards women's primary struggle as the one against patriarchy. The "prescriptive, Western-centric, middle class and white orientation" alienated many black women from feminist debates and discussions (Hendricks and Lewis, 1994: 64). As Kemp et al. (1995: 141) point out, patriarchy is differentiated. Power is not shared equally among men. The related notions of public and private spheres cannot simply be transplanted from European and North American discourses to South Africa. "Theorizing a single patriarchy without regard to the multiplicity of experiences created by race, class privilege, and oppression has effectively caused feminist discourse to marginalize Black women's resistance.... The key challenge for South African women through this century has been to negotiate successfully how and when these contradictions are confronted" (Kemp et al., 1995: 142).

One significant and distinctive feature of feminism in South Africa is the apparent conservatism of women and feminist thought. For example, a distinctive feature of feminism in South Africa is the importance attached to the role of the mother and motherhood, leading to the development of what Wells (in Walker, 1991: xix) identifies as "motherism"—"a women's politics of resistance [which] affirms obligations traditionally assigned to women and calls on the community to respect them." The debate has centered on two related issues: (1) the way in which motherhood has been perceived and utilized by political organizations, and (2) the way in which African women have themselves organized politically around the notion of motherhood.

As Walker (1991: xix) points out, the identification with motherhood has generally been interpreted as evidence of conservatism among women and their defence of, and hence support for, patriarchal values and institutions. Because of the complex factors of racial, class, and gender oppression in South Africa (that is, apartheid), however, women have often found themselves in a conservative defence of traditional institutions such as the chieftainship, the patriarchal family, and established sex roles.

Under apartheid, black women in South Africa came to understand that it was the white state, not the family unit, that was the primary locus of their oppression. The stresses on family life resulting from migrant labor, forced removals, influx control, and poverty meant that the establishment and maintenance of a family unit that included fathers and sons at home were, in fact, among the rights for which black women had to fight (compare Kemp et al., 1995: 133).

The legacy of apartheid has meant that feminism in South Africa often focuses on seemingly more "conservative" aims and objectives—on "bread and butter" issues such as the provision of basic services, for example, clean water and sanitation; the provision of adequate and affordable housing; education; and the provision of health services, among others—issues that have not necessarily traditionally been defined as feminist. Against this background, is clear that more intricate attempts must be made to understand the apparent paradox of women's militancy in protest coupled with their apparent conservatism in formulating their goals. For example, women's defence of their maternal roles does not necessarily constitute a negation of their rights as women (Walker, 1991). Clearly, black women have a dual interest—in national liberation and in women's emancipation—and have had to make strategic decisions over the years in this regard. Feminism in South Africa, like feminism and feminist theory elsewhere in the world, is not one but many theories or perspectives. Feminism is largely defined as a political practice aimed at the "redefinition and redistribution of power" (Riano, 1994: 282). Feminism in this context is both a social theory and a political framework that recognizes the oppression of women and has a commitment to end such oppression. Feminist principles advocate the defence of women's rights and the need to build alternative paradigms for social theory and research (Walker, 1991). Cardinal to this process is the accumulation of indigenous knowledge—that is, specific knowledge accumulated by a community, including the concepts, belief structures, explanatory systems, and analytical perspectives peculiar to it.

Conclusion

Feminism in South Africa may be seen as having three points of departure.

First, women's identities as women are shaped by race, class and gender, and these identities have molded women's particular experience of gender oppression. As Mohanty (1991: 12) writes,

> To define feminism purely in gendered terms assumes our consciousness (or identity) of being "women" has nothing to do with race, class, nation, or sexuality, just gender. But no-one becomes a woman purely because she is female. Ideologies of womanhood have as much to do with class and race as they have to do with sex.

Second, women's struggles as feminists encompass the struggle for national liberation. The liberation of black people as a whole is therefore also a feminist issue. Third, even though black men have been allies in the fight for national liberation, black patriarchies—the "patchwork of patriarchies"—must be challenged and transformed (Bozzoli, 1983; Kemp et al., 1995: 133).

See Also

APARTHEID, SEGREGATION, AND GHETTOIZATION; FEMINISM: SUB-SAHARAN AFRICA; HOUSEHOLDS AND FAMILIES: SOUTHERN AFRICA; LITERATURE: SOUTHERN AFRICA RACE; WOMEN'S STUDIES: SOUTHERN AFRICA

References and Further Reading

Agenda. *Empowering women for gender equity.* <http://www.agenda.org.za/>

Basu, A., ed. 1995. *The challenge of local feminisms: Women's movements in global perspective.* Boulder, Col.: Westview.

Bazilli, S. 1991. *Putting women on the agenda.* Johannesburg: Ravan.

Bozzoli, B. 1983. Marxism, feminism, and South African studies. *Journal of Southern African Studies* 9: 139–171.

Gender relations in South Africa <http://www.womensnet.org.za/links/genderpr.htm>

Hansson, D. 1994. South African feminism and the patchwork quilt of power relations. *Women's Studies* 6: 40–54.

Hendricks, C., and D. Lewis. 1994. Voices from the margins. *Agenda* 20: 64.

Kemp, A., N. Madlala, A. Moodley, and E. Salo. 1995. The dawn of a new day: Redefining South African feminism. In A. Basu, ed., *The challenge of local feminisms: Women's movements in global perspective, 131–162.* Boulder, Col.: Westview.

Klugman, B. 1994. Women in politics under apartheid: A challenge to the New South Africa. In B. Nelson and N. Chowdhury, eds., *Women and politics worldwide.* New Haven, Conn.: Yale University.

Mohanty, C., ed. 1991. *Third world women and feminism.* Bloomington: Indiana University.

Mzamane, M. V. 1994. Gender politics and the unfolding culture of liberation in South Africa. *Women's Studies* 6: 1–25.

Nelson, B. J., and N. Chowdhury, eds. 1994. *Women and politics worldwide.* New Haven, Conn.: Yale University Press.

Nnaemeka, O., ed. 1998. *Sisterhood, feminisms, and power: From Africa to the diaspora.* Eritrea: Africa World.

Riano, Pilar, ed. 1994. *Women in grassroots communication: Furthering social change.* London: Sage.

Sadie, Y., and Y. van Aardt. 1995. Women's issues in South Africa: 1990–1994. *Africa Insight* 25(2): 80–90.

Unisa. 1991. *Conferences on women and gender in southern Africa.* Collected papers. Praetoria, S.A.: Unisa.

Walker, C. 1991. *Women and resistance in South Africa.* Cape Town: David Philips.

———, ed. 1990. *Women and gender in southern Africa to 1945.* Cape Town: David Philips.

Walters, S., and L. Manicom, eds. 1996. *Gender in popular education.* London: Zed.

Jennifer Lemon

FEMINISM: South Asia

Feminism in south Asia is as diverse as the region itself, and although certain themes are similar across regional boundaries, others are unique to a location. Historically, too, some issues have been constant whereas others have changed. A significant aspect of south Asian feminist movements is their relationship to nationalist struggles for independence, and to national religious fundamentalism; implications of this relationship can be seen in an intensification of self-criticism within feminism. Other important facets of feminism in south Asia include efforts to reform constitutional and personal laws; the issue of sectarian extremism; and the question of ideals such as justice, equality, and human rights in the light of postmodernist theory that considers these "enlightenment" concepts retrogressive.

Pakistan

Pakistan was created in 1947 as a nation-state with a Muslim majority, and the social, economic, and political status of Pakistani women can be understood only in the context of this history and past and present Islamic law. The national constitution established a relatively autocratic patriarchal rule; and women are positioned in society as religiously inferior, economically dependent, and politically naive—a status which implies that they must be shielded within the private domain (purdah) and defended by men (honor). Islamic structures and religious interpretations affect laws governing the family, women's property rights, women's attire, divorce, rape, and so on. In terms of redressing inequities faced by women, religious injunctions can supersede legal injunctions; as a result, fundamental issues of human rights and gender equality are often ambiguous.

Culturally, women may be categorized on the one hand as traditional, religious, good, submissive, and accepting of the patriarchal order; or, on the other hand, as western, liberal, and loose—and thus deserving of sexual assault. Here, class is influential, since elite, urban, educated women may, for example, conform less with dress laws and thus be placed in the second category. This dichotomy not only constricts women's lives in general but impinges on laws affecting women. Striking examples are criminal laws related to property, prohibition, rape, adultery, abduction, and fornication; in particular, the laws involving sex reflect a concept of female sexuality as putting masculinity at risk of chaos (*fitna*).

In this intersection of state and religion, the body of the nation-state comes to be identified with the female body; accordingly, patriarchal laws are framed to protect the honor of the "state-woman" against violation by modernity or by any immoral behavior on the part of women themselves. Progressive legislation has later been counteracted by conservative laws; thus the Muslim Family Laws Ordinance of 1961 was replaced around 1980, under a religiously controlled legislature, by more repressive rules: the Shariat Laws and the Hadood Ordinances; the Law of Evidence, which quantified a woman's testimony as equivalent to half of a man's; and religiously sanctioned punishments such as stoning and death for misdemeanors. Rape is a case in point: before the Hadood Ordinances, it was punishable as a crime; under the Hadood Ordinances it was in effect equated with adultery, since the onus of proof was on the victim, and the criterion of "proof" was extremely high (four male witnesses provided by the victim).

The Pakistani feminist movement had its origin within the Muslim Women's League, a branch of the nationalist Muslim League that had been instrumental in the partitioning of India and the formation of Pakistan as a separate state. A parliamentary women's division was established by President Mohammad Zia ul-Haq with the preparation of a Report on the Status of Women, subsequently released by his successor Benazir Bhutto. In her second term, Bhutto established a women's bank, a ministry for women's development, and various committees and literacy programs for women. However, these developments are often seen as tokenism, given the prevailing autocratic disempowerment of women, the pervasive illiteracy among women, and women's limited representation in the parliament.

Zia's Hadood Ordinances were an impetus for the formation of the Women's Action Front, which later became affiliated with Women Living Under Muslim Law, an international group. An ongoing examination of Islamic texts on the position of women in scripture has some potential for an eventual revision of the personal laws. At present, different interpretations of the Qur'an (the "divine word of Allah") and the sunna (exemplary deeds of the Prophet Muhammad) provide a basis for framing personal laws. However, there has been a well-documented backlash against militant feminist groups, so future changes may be possible only by feminist scholars working within the traditions.

Bangladesh

The Bangladeshi feminist movement is part of a longer tradition, an indigenous "subaltern," or grassroots, women's movement in the Greater Bengal region whose critique has not been structured by a western framework. Bangladesh is a prominent example of resurgent Islamic fundamentalism and sectarian extremism—a trend that was highlighted by antiwoman sentiments expressed about the subversive writer Taslima Nasreem.

Nasreem is the author of *Lajja* ("Shame"), a fictional account of atrocities committed by Muslims against a Hindu family. In 1993 the government banned the book and issued a warrant for her arrest, and she became the object of a *fatwa*, or death threat. One aim of the sensitive responses to the *fatwa* from within the indigenous movement was to disentangle the polemics of the discourse and re-create a space for a more effective continuing debate about women's role and rights in Bangladeshi society. The issue of empowerment concerns not merely Nasreem's individual voice but a larger movement that spans gender, class, and religious groups and has had a history of achievement in Bangladesh. Nasreem herself, however, did not work with the grassroots feminists and therefore was somewhat alienated from this possible source of support. Also, the fear that the *fatwa* could lead to the death of systematic dissent by indigenous women's groups was not well understood by the media in India (where secular Hindu intellectuals and fundamentalists took up Nasreem's cause) or in the west; the media tended instead to see Nasreem as an isolated case of resistance to Muslim law. In 1994, this issue was discussed by south Asian feminists at the International Conference on Women, Power, and Cultural Difference: Negotiating Gender in South Asia.

Women's work is also a crucial feminist issue. There has been a steep rise in the number of women entering the workforce, and Gitiara Nasreen (1995) has analyzed the situation of Bangladeshi working women in the context of a relatively new global market that relies significantly on third world women as cheap labor; Bangladesh, in particular, draws heavily on women in the garment and jute industries. Factors affecting women's work in the Bangladeshi context include the distinction between private and public spaces, the role of purdah and other traditional customs, and a unique fusion of Hindu and Muslim practices that makes women dependents within the family. Generalizations about oppression may not account for economic and educational differences; for instance, western clothing is worn by a large percentage of urban middle-class women. Moreover, the postcolonial economy of Bangladesh depended on external aid, which was accompanied by western concepts of gender and reproduction, methods of birth control, and medicines.

Islam is the state religion, and there are marked contradictions between economic liberalization and the return to Muslim legal practices and cultural mores—contradictions that have far-reaching implications for the feminist movement. Nasreen (1995) has argued that modified forms of purdah symbolize upward mobility and allow movement into the workforce within the confines of traditional space, bypassing misogyny, harassment, and stigmatization. The climate of rapid economic change has also encouraged trade unions, which counter the myth of subservience (Rock, 1995).

The emancipation of women may be seen as starting with the pioneering educator Begum Rokeya Sakhawat Hossain, who was born in 1880 (Haque, 1995). Hossain's achievements include the first publication by a Bengali Muslim woman, *The Innocent Bengali*, issued in 1904; the first Muslim girls' school, established in Calcutta in 1911; and the first Muslim Women's Association, formed in 1916. Her activism led to noticeable increases in the number of women involved in education. In 1880, the year Hossain was born, the Indian Education Commission reported that there were only 1,500 girls in school; by 1936 there were 400,000. There were also, by then, numerous visible women activists; and in 1937 two Muslim women were elected to the legislature.

Since then, the indigenous women's movement has made many achievements. The journal *Begum* was established in 1947; voting rights were won in 1950; the Begum Club, a writers' organization, was formed in 1953; the Bangladesh Women Writers' association was formed in 1973; and the first assembly of women freedom fighters was organized by Narigrantha Prabartana in 1991. However, this activism has faced considerable adversity—for example, members of the Muslim Women's League were massacred in 1952 during a protest against the imposition of Urdu as the state language, and current efforts are confronting a rising tide of fundamentalism.

Sri Lanka

Historically, Sri Lanka is unique in South Asia for its emphasis on the education of women; and this fact has been reflected in its women's movement, which has gained one of the highest rates of female literacy in the region. Sri Lankan feminism has also been characterized by a strong elite movement, which produced the world's first woman prime minister (Sirimavo Bandaranaike, elected in 1959, when Sri Lanka was still Ceylon). However, this elitist structure has maintained a class distinction; and in the absence of strong oppression, the movement has retained connections to major religious and nationalist groups. Thus it may not heed some fundamental issues facing less privileged women in Sri Lanka, a country torn by fierce civil conflict.

Family law affecting women in Sri Lanka reflects complex colonial influences—Portuguese, Dutch, and British. Under colonial rule, there was a gradual shift from agrarian practices such as polyandry, inheritance in *binna* (contract) marriages, and the traditional dowry *(diga)* to a more westernized system.

Sri Lanka has several religions, the most prominent being Buddhism, Hinduism, and Christianity. The origins of Buddhism in India as a anticaste religion had implications for the status of women: Sri Lankan women were able to enter monastic orders in premodern times, and this influenced not only women's participation in religious rituals but also women's education. Under the more egalitarian Buddhist system, popular religious culture also moved away from suttee, dowries, and child marriages—practices prevalent in India.

Early women's writings were a product of monastic learning in Sankrit and Sinhalese; a school of woman poets flourished in the eighteenth century. Dutch coeducational parish schools, along with the monastic traditions emphasizing education for women and also along with educational efforts by Christian missionaries, continued into the twentieth century. As early as 1869, the Morgan Report recommended establishing subsidized girls' schools. A complex system of private and public schools for various socioeconomic categories developed. An additional stimulus for education came from the founders of the mystical, pantheistic theosophical movement, Annie Besant (1847–1933) and Helena Blavatsky (1831–1891), who lived and traveled in this region. A Women's Education Society, which joined forces with wealthy, aristocratic Buddhist women, was formed in the 1880s. This interplay between western theosophists and Sri Lankans left a lasting impression on the education of Buddhist women.

Not surprisingly, considering its strong historical drive for literacy, Sri Lanka was one of the first countries to achieve women' suffrage, in 1931. The Mallika Kulanga Samitiya (Women's Organization), a wing of the congress, had begun working toward this in 1925, and the Women's Franchise Union was founded in 1927. After 1931, several subgroups were formed, including the Lanka Mahila Samita (Women's Political Union) and the Tamil Women's Union. The All-Ceylon Women's Conference was established in 1944.

By the early nineteenth century women were joining largely middle-class nationalistic and religious anticolonial movements. Against the background of achievement by elite women's groups, struggles by other classes focused on the rights of share farmworkers and unskilled workers on tea and coffee plantations, who were vulnerable to exploitation. Later, A. E. Goonaesinha was influential in women's participation in labor and trade unions—first under the aegis of the Ceylon Labor Party and later in nationalist, socialist union movements.

Somewhat ironically, feminism in Sri Lanka today faces impasses deriving from women's relative freedom from religious oppression, the achievement of independence by negotiation rather than civil strife, and liberal, class-based educational institutions that accept rather than criticize patriarchal values regarding family and sexuality (Jayawardena, 1986).

India

Far more has been written about women and feminism in India than in other Asian nations; there is a long history of writing in English and an even earlier philosophical tradition that called attention to Indian women. However, much of this commentary can be seen as western "orientalism," and a more useful perspective can be gained through the writings of women who come from within the tradition.

A compilation by Tharu and Lalita (1993) draws on a plethora of writings by Indian women from 600 B.C.E. to the early twentieth century. Women who wrote in the ancient period invoked gender-related ideals that are still relevant today, and probably the main reason why so much of their work did not survive is simply that male-dominated Sanskrit texts rather than women's regional dialects—an oral tradition—entered the canon. Sanskrit texts (as registered at the Ninth World Sanskrit Conference in Melbourne in 1994) are often misogynist; but some women did write in Sanskrit, forthrightly addressing perennial issues: concubinage; property and maintenance rights of mistresses and wives; *niyogas,* a premodern form of surrogacy whereby, in the absence of progeny, children could be begotten by sanctioned permissiveness; prayers for the welfare of illegitimate children; and questions involving secret lovers *(jara).*

The nineteenth and twentieth centuries were largely concerned with the formation of India as a nation-state. The modern Indian women's movement begain with nineteenth-century social reforms, which, as part of their anticolonialism, redefined concepts of gender, class, and caste. Orientalism—a view that contained certain colonial standards—tended to see a falling-off from a glorious Aryan Vedic past of brahmanic asceticsm to an inchoate, ungovernable India; the reformers undertook to prove the worth of their own attitudes toward women, caste, and orthodox practices. Later, Gandhi opposed Hindu practices such as child marriage, discrimination against women, and women's low social status, attempting to put into place a new ideal of women that would counteract brahmanical British imperialism.

The nineteenth-century reformers were mostly men (such as Ram Mohan Roy, Tilak, and Phule), but they did include some women. Pandita Ramabai, for example, was a progressive freedom-fighter who focused solely on the plight of women. In 1917, the Women's India Association (WIA) was formed by Sarojini Naidu, Annie Besant, Begam Hasrat Mohani, and others; in 1927, WIA organized the All India Women's Conference (AIWC). Important legislative measures related to the status of women included human rights and opportunities for legal redress (Mies, 1980).

Modernist feminism is also closely connected with the Indian nationalists, who took up the cause of women; thus the women's struggle was linked to the struggle for freedom. The WIA, for instance, was aligned with the nationalist movement and remained so until the 1970s. Women were mobilized in great numbers during the nationist struggle that coalesced around Gandhi and led to independence in 1945. Women's part in the freedom movement is still imprinted on the memory of the Indian middle class—women had moved from being objects of social and religious reform to being active participants in political and social processes.

However, in India as elsewhere there has been tension between feminism and nationalism. Nationalists tended to identify the state with the mother and to conflate woman, goddess, mother, and state, seeing "mother India" as wronged and her honor despoiled by colonial rule; this merged corporeality of the state and "woman" was an essential part of the vocabulary of male nationalist leaders. Although that concept gave women a role in the public sphere of resistance, a corollary was the relegation of women to certain positions within the movement. Figures such as Pandita Ranabai were problematic and controversial because they eluded the nationalistic definition of womanhood—and the definition itself has been controversial.

Philosophically, what this nationalist definition has meant is that the women's movement in India was born in a prescriptive way, shaped by an emerging ideal of womanhood. The idea was, at base, internalized orientalism: western and Victorian, with an added component of moral superiority derived from traditional Indian myths of purity, though its subordination of women was carefully presented so as not to diminish the honor of the "woman-state" in the eyes of the oppressor. One result has been that

the modern Indian women's movement was, from the beginning, set in opposition not only to men and to the colonizer but also to western women, so that it still has difficulties in finding correspondences with western feminism. Today, there are echoes of this past in Hindu fundamentalist movements such as Vishwas Hindu Parishad (VHP) and the Bharatiya Janaka, or Indian People's, Party (BJP), which define masculinity as saving women from the "other," Islam. This situation is complicated by issues facing Indian Muslim women—health, divorce (talaq), and education—because any statements of support from Indian feminist groups are seized on by anti-Muslim Hindu extremists. The Muslim Intelligensia meetings (organized by Imtiaz Ahmed of Delhi after the anti-Muslim riots of 1984) have tried to develop consensus on such issues within the female community.

In the decades after independence, when India was governed by Nehru and then Indira Gandhi, there was a realization that the socioeconomic experiments had not succeeded in many respects, especially in relation to women's needs and rights. In 1975, widely seen as a watershed year, many women activists regrouped, and there was a refocusing on women's issues by women involved in other spheres of life, such as trade unions. Partition—the division of British India into India and Pakistan in 1947—remains a tremendous undercurrent, but the forced repatriation of Hindu and Muslim women across the new borders is still largely undocumented.

The South Asian Diaspora

The south Asian diaspora is emerging as a significant economic force. During the early 1990s, there were 20 million Indians working overseas; they constituted one of the world's best-educated and most affluent migrant group. Other diaspora groups include Sindhis from Pakistan, Jains, Muslim Ismalis, the Gujerati, Afghans, and Sikhs.

Although the overall impression of this diaspora is one of achievement, a number of issues affecting women have emerged. For instance, first-generation women often bear the brunt of resettlement, because they must raise their families without their traditional support networks and because their own qualifications may be unrecognized. One contentious issue is the care of the aged—in the country of origin such care is provided by the extended family, but in the new setting it is left to the limited resources of the nuclear family. Other issues are the problems facing elderly single women and second-generation adolescents; adolescent girls in particular experience conflicts between the new culture and traditions such as arranged marriages and parental authority.

Organizations formed to address some of these issues include Apna Ghar (in Chicago), Sakhi (New York), South Asian Women's Study and Support Group (Australia), and Southall Black Sisters (Great Britain), These groups also provide a forum for discussing the experience of migration, women's identity, and women's future needs.

A new genre of feminist writing has also developed to examine these issues. For example, Mohanty (1991) and Grewal and Kaplan (1994) consider identity formation and displacement; and Bhattacharjee (1992), from the standpoint of an Asian women's shelter, has looked at the stress of resettlement as related to religion and identity. But much research remains to be done on apsects of the south Asian diaspora, such as the exchange of social capital between nonresident Indians and the state in the context of arranged marriages; and the sociological, psychological, and economic implications of the "green card" or imported spouse. The diaspora is a complex interweaving of gender, culture, and migratory factors, and important trends will become apparent as studies in this field continue.

See Also

BUDDHISM; COLONIALISM AND POSTCOLONIALISM; ELDERLY CARE: CASE STUDY—INDIA; FAMILY LAW: CASE STUDY—INDIA; HINDUISM; ISLAM; POLITICS AND THE STATE: SOUTH ASIA, *I and II*

References and Further Reading

Bhattacharjee, Anannya. 1992. The habit of ex-nomination: Nation, woman and the Indian migrant bourgeoisie. *Public Culture: Bulletin of the Society for Transnational Cultural Studies* 5 (1: Fall): 19–44.

Chattopadhyay, Kamaladevi. 1983. *Indian women's battle for freedom.* Delhi: Abhinav.

Grewal, Inderpal, and Caren Kaplan. 1994. *Scattered hegemonies: Postmodernity and transnational feminist practices.* London and Minneapolis: University of Minnesota Press.

Haque, Roshan, Ara. 1995. *Muslim women in Bengal: 1880–1937.* (NARI: Series in Gender Studies Vol. 3.) Delhi: Indian Book Centre.

Jayasinghe, Vinitha. 1995. The impact of the Women's Decade for women in Sri Lanka. In Renuka Sharma, ed. *Representations of gender and identity politics in relation to south Asia.* (NARI: Series in Gender Studies Vol. 2.) Delhi: Indian Book Centre.

Jayawardena, Kumari. 1986. *Feminism and nationalism in the third world.* London: Zed.

———, and S. Jayaweera. 1986. *A profile on Sri Lanka: A study of the integration of women in development planning.* (Education Series No. 13.) Colombo: Women's Education Centre.

Kotkin, Joel. 1993. *Tribes: How race, religion, and identity determine success in the new global economy.* New York: Random House.

Mernissi, Fatima. 1985. *Beyond the veil: Male-female dynamics in Musli society.* Rev. ed. London: Al-Saqi.

Mies, Maria. 1980. *Indian women and patriarchy.* Delhi: Concept.

Mohanty, Chandra Talpade, Anna Russo, and Lourdes Torres, eds. 1991. *Third world women and the politics of feminism.* Bloomington and Indianapolis: Indiana University Press.

Nasreen, Gitiara. 1995. (Ad)dressing change: Working women and the resurgence of purdah in Bangladesh. In Renuka Sharma, ed., *Representations of gender and identity politics in relation to south Asia.* (NARI: Series in Gender Studies Vol. 2.) Delhi: Indian Book Centre.

Rock, Marilyn. 1995. South Asian women in export-orientated production: The garment industry in Bangladesh. In Renuka Sharma, ed., *Women, power, and cultural difference: Negotiating gender in south Asia.* (NARI: Series in Gender Studies Vol. 4.) Delhi: Indian Book Centre.

Sharma, Renuka. 1995. *Women, power and cultural difference: Negotiating gender in south Asia.* (NARI: Series in Gender Studies Vol. 4.) Delhi: Indian Book Centre.

Tharu, Susie, and K. Lalita. 1993. *Women writing in India, 600 B.C. to the present:* Vol. 1 *600 B.C. to the early twentieth century.* Vol. 2: *The twentieth century.* London: Pandora.

Yasmin, Samina. 1995. The history of the women's movement in Pakistan. In Renuka Sharma, ed., *Women, power and cultural difference: Negotiating gender in south Asia.* (NARI: Series in gender Studies Vol. 4.) Delhi: Indian Book Centre.

Zafar, Afreeha. 1995. Ideology, gender, and the state: The Pakistan experience. In Renuka Sharma, ed., *Representations of gender and identity politics in relation to south Asia.* (NARI: Series in Gender Studies Vol. 2.) Delhi: Indian Book Centre.

Zia, Afiya Shenrbano. 1994. *Sex in the Islamic context: Rape, class, and gender in Pakistan.* Lahore: ASR.

Renuka Sharma

FEMINISM: Southeast Asia

There is no single strand of feminism in southeast Asia, since this region is very diverse. It includes conditions characteristic of developed ("northern") nations, as in Singapore, as well as developing ("southern" or third world) nations, as in Kampuchea. It includes both capitalist systems (the Philippines, Indonesia, Singapore, Malaysia, Brunei, and Thailand) and socialist systems (Laos, Kampuchea, Vietnam, and Burma, now Myanmar). Governance also differs: for example, southeast Asia has seen autocracy in Brunei, a military dictatorship in Indonesia, a socialist republic in Vietnam, and a liberal democracy in the Philippines. Each southeast Asian country is multiethnic; Brunei, for instance, has Malays, Chinese, Indians, and other groups. Religions also vary; they include Islam, Buddhism, Hinduism, and Christianity.

In general, though, the oldest and most widely held form of feminism here is an inversion of Shulamith Firestone's western radical feminist theory (1972). Firestone held that gender oppression is primary and is the model for other kinds of oppression; inverting this would produce a view of gender oppression as stemming from, for example, oppression of the third world by the developed world, the propertyless by the propertied, and nonwhite by whites. Why southeast Asian women would tend to subscribe to this may be related to the region's geography, its egalitarian kinship systems, the high status of women in its precolonial societies, and its experience of oppressive colonialism.

Geography

Southeast Asia includes the geographical areas bounded by Myanmar (Burma), Thailand, Malaysia, Singapore, Brunei, Indonesia, Laos, Kampuchea (Cambodia), Vietnam, and the Philippines. Its strategic location connecting East and West has attracted the French, Dutch, British, Portuguese, and Americans as colonizers, and the superpowers during the cold war. The region experiences frequent natural disasters—floods, typhoons, monsoons, earthquakes, tsunamis, and volcanos. Both colonization and natural disasters have had effects on feminism: women, culturally defined as preservers and nurturers of life, often find rampaging nature a more urgent threat than gender oppression; and they may place the gender struggle in the background because national poverty and underdevelopment—increasingly seen by politicized feminists as a product of colonialism and neocolonialism—loom much larger.

Cultural geography is also manifested as ethnicity and tribalism, related in part to the fact that some states are archipelagoes (Indonesia has over 13,000 islands and the Philippines has about 7,000; and there are more than 100 ethnic groups), and as competing religions. This fact was exploited by the colonizers' divide-and-rule tactics; and the fragility of a multiethnic nation-state, which challenges the concept of unity in diversity, has not been lost on women. Secessionist movements like the Karens in Burma and the Muslims in Mindanao dramatize the primacy of nationalistic struggles.

Egalitarian Kinship Structures

Egalitarian kinship systems in southeast Asia have evidently contributed to the primacy of nationalism by mitigating patriarchy. For instance, the matrilineal, matrilocal kinship structure in Thailand is one of the most egalitarian in the world, despite the existence of patriarchal institutions; thus Thai women are not as oppressed as the women of India, where kinship is generally patrilineal and patrilocal (Omvedt, 1988). Similarly, Burmese and Filipino women—whose kinship systems are matrilineal and bilateral—are less oppressed than Japanese women (Matsui, 1989, Khaing, 1984). Kampuchea, Laos, Vietnam, Malaysia, and Indonesia also have matrilineal or bilateral systems. Western legal codes and patriarchal ideologies such as Confucianism, Hinduism, Islam, and Christianity have made inroads in southeast Asia; but in this region Confucian women have not experienced footbinding, Muslim women have not worn the veil, Hindu women have not been subjected to sutee, and women living under western legal systems have not become civil nonentities.

Women's Status in Precolonial Societies

During precolonial times, southeast Asian women enjoyed a relatively high status. Throughout the region, they could inherit, own, and manage property; divorce their husbands; engage in economic activities outside the household; become chieftains; and become priestesses (such as the *babaylanes* in the Philippines). Significantly, the brideprice, not the dowry, prevailed: the groom's family paid the bride's family, in recognition of the bride's worth. At the village level, women's work was far more important than men's (and remains so today). While bearing and rearing children and doing household chores, women also engaged in farmwork, batik-making, weaving, trading, food processing, and so on. They also held the purse strings and were thus considered partners, not slaves, of men. In Vietnam, women are called "ministers of the interior"; in the Philippines, they are called "the best men"; in Thailand, they are described as "the hind legs that push the forelegs of the elephant."

To some extent the effects of women's precolonial status can still be felt. However, capitalism has to a considerable degree diminished their role: women's work is regarded as supplemental to men's even when a woman is her family's only source of income; women farmworkers are marginized by modern technology; and women who migrate to cities are likely to become mail-order brides, exploited industrial or domestic workers, or prostitutes.

Colonialism and Nationalistic Struggles

Women in southeast Asia have been disproportionately affected by ethnic rivalry and western invasion and colonization. During wars between ethnic groups (such as the Burmese and the Karens, the Malays and the Chinese, the Chinese and the Vietnamese, or the Vietnamese and the Khmers), women had to support their families and were also subjected to rape and maltreatment by male combatants; moreover, bereaved women had to carry on the task of reconstruction for peace without the help of men.

Western colonizers represented a strong challenge for nation-building. Colonial governments were not only undemocratic and racist but also sexist—through law and religion, they transplanted to southeast Asia a more developed form of patriarchy—and southeast Asian women became active participants in the struggle for nationhood. Examples of women who fought side by side with men against foreign invaders are Gabriela Silang, Trinidad Tecson, and Agueda Cahabagan in the Philippines; Dayang Bandang in Sabah; Cut Nyak Dien and Cut Meutia in northern Sumatra; Ror Gusik in Java; Martha Tiahua in the Moluccas; Emmy Saelan in south Sulawesi; and Bang Rachan, Thanphuying Mo, and queens Chamadevi, Suriyothai, and Saowapa in Burma—as well as innumerable women in Vietnam.

Concepts of Feminism in Southeast Asia

The relatively high status of southeast Asian women in precolonial times was eroded by western colonization, which introduced the highly defined patriarchal state and other social institutions and also increasingly pauperized large numbers of people, at least in comparison with the colonialists and their native collaborators. For these reasons, both women and men have different concepts of feminism.

For those who are not feminists, feminism is another threat from the exploitative, "decadent" West. Rightists perceive feminists as bra-burning man-haters, home wreckers, proponents of abortion and free sex, disrupters of tradition, and destroyers of religious beliefs and practices. Centrists see feminism as a threat to social stability because feminists are driving a wedge between women and men at a time when the immediate need is national sovereignty and economic development. Leftists see feminism as a bourgeois ideology and a bourgeois movement—and they, like the centrists, see feminism as divisive at a time when consolidation is essential for postcolonial nation-building, victory in the class struggle, and the implementation of socialism.

Conscious feminists in southeast Asia hold—individually or together—that:

1. Feminism, though identified with the West, is not a western imposition on southeast Asia but was born and bred there, preceding "first wave" feminism.
2. Southeast Asian feminism should not mimic western feminism, because the contexts are different.
3. Women should not consider men the enemy; rather, the enemy is injustice between nations and people that leads to poverty for some and wealth for others.
4. Women should respect the need for nation-building and avoid separatism.
5. Both men and women are victims of oppression, and the liberation of one sex depends on the liberation of the other; thus women should struggle to liberate both.
6. Strategies for liberation must suit the needs of a particular society at a particular time.
7. Women have always been a vital force in development; thus their integration into development need no longer be a goal of feminism.
8. Fighting on the "gender front" without fighting on other fronts is counterproductive; all fronts intersect.
9. Women of developed nations oppress southeast Asian women in various ways—as purchasers of cheap goods produced by low-paid southeast Asians, as employers of low-paid southeast Asian domestic workers, and as women safe from assault by their own men because southeast Asians are available as cheap prostitutes.
10. Global sisterhood is imperiled because western feminists tend to "colonize" southeast Asian women through orientalism—seeing Asia through occidental eyes—and tend to assume a privileged position in the feminist movement.
11. Feminism was born not in academia or in women's centers but in the struggle itself; it is pointless to try to separate theory from practice.

Nationalism and Feminism in Southeast Asia

The "woman question" came to the fore during the nationalist movements of the late nineteenth century; both women and men focused on this issue. For example, José Rizal, a national hero of the Philippines, said that the enslavement of the Philippine people was a result of enslavement of Filipino women. Women, Rizal argued, were kept blind by friars, who used Catholicism to maintain the colonial order; thus women could only teach their children how to be blind, so to redeem the country, its women needed to seek education and address the "national question." In the twentieth century, Ho Chi Minh in Vietnam and Sukarno in Indonesia argued similarly; indeed, there was a "gentlemen's agreement" that emancipation of a people could not take place without the emancipation of women (Eisen, 1984; Jayawardena, 1988; Wieringa, 1985).

Among the earliest females who took up the "woman question" are the women of Malolos in the Philippines around 1888 and Radeng Agang Kartini (1879–1904) in Indonesia. The women of Malolos—twenty-one daughters of well-off families—fought the Spanish curate because he would not allow them to set up a night school where they and their mothers could learn Spanish, a language they needed in order to have access to modern European ideas. They wrote a letter (December 12, 1988) to the governor general, arguing their case, and it was published in Madrid, creating a sensation because, as Rizal put it, "women are at last awakening" (Fernandez, 1990–1991: 10–33).

Kartini also sought an education so that she could have access to modern ideas. Her father, the regent of Japan, had not allowed her to study in the Netherlands; but from her "gilded cage" (as she called her upper-class home) she wrote letters to a Dutch pen friend, the socialist feminist Stella Zeehandelaar. This woman, along with another Dutch feminist, Ovink-Soer (the wife of a colonial administrator in Java), and J. H. Abendanon, director of education of the colonial government, befriended Kartini and made her famous. Kartini's letters, published in a magazine in the Netherlands called *The Echo* (Zainu'ddin, 1986), inspired women to look at themselves as caught between traditionalism and modernism. Her feminist agenda included education for women (since women were pivotal in nation-building), professional training, and the abolition of polygyny; and she built a school for girls in 1904. Kartini died in childbirth at age 25. Two contemporaries who pursued similar ideas were Dewi Sartika in western Java and Rohana Kudus in western Sumatra (Wieringa, 1985).

Education for women, polygyny, child marriage, and divorce were issues that divided women along class, ethnic, and religious lines. Indonesia and Malaya, where reformed Islam was considered a uniting force against western imperialism, are examples. In Indonesia, there was tension over coeducation and abolishing polygyny between Islamic, nationalist, and Christian women's organizations during the first women's congress, held in Jogjakarta in 1928, and at succeeding congresses before World War II. In 1939, a council was formed to investigate women's matrimonial rights according to custom (*adat*), Islamic law (*fikh*), and European law, but the war had broken out before Islamic and non-Islamic women's groups were able to reach a compromise.

Women's organizations in Malaya divided on the same issues, which also divided Malays, Chinese, and Indians (Ng and Yong, 1991). Women's wings of the major political parties and organizations outside the party system took up these questions. The foremost party wing, Kaum Ibu United Malays National Organization (KI UMNO), later became Wanita UMNO. During its 30-year history (1946–1976), each leader (*ketua*) saw to it that a resolution was passed each year on marriage and divorce reform. One *ketua*, the fiery orator Khadijah Sidek, confronted UMNO on women's issues and women's role in the party; she was expelled in 1956. Another *ketua*, Ibu Zain, emphasized independence and fund-raising for the party more than women's issues. At present reform of family law does not seem imminent, since resurgent Muslim fundamentalism calls for women to return to their traditional roles.

The same issue preoccupied women in Burma (now Myanmar), where the dominant religion is Buddhism. Ideologically, Buddhism is egalitarian, but in practice it favors men and has been a basis for a sexist division of labor. Only men are allowed to leave home and purify themselves by becoming monks, and monastic communities educate men in various disciplines. Women stay home and support their families, and while this gave them independence, it also precluded women's education (Omvedt, 1988). During the Thakin movement of the 1930s women asked for, and received, the right to an education. After Burma gained independence, its new constitution abolished polygyny and recognized women's right to vote and to run for office; but to this day, women in Burma cannot become monks (Khaing, 1984).

In Thailand, women's education was encouraged during the reign of King Chulalungkorn (1865–1912), who favored westernization, but women had to fight to abolish polygyny. The Monogamy Law of 1935 ended men's right to punish their wives and to kill adulterous wives; however, it put men in charge of conjugal property, and a wife could not engage in business without her husband's permission.

Spain ceded the Philippines to the United States in 1898. Whereas the Spaniards had denied Filipinos the right to an education, the Americans brought education; but feminists (among others) often argue that the United States used education here to further colonization—that by extending American education to Filipinos, it produced brown Americans. To the present, feminists have had to fight the *querida* system—the system concerning men's extramarital affairs—which in a sense was worse than polygyny, because a man's *queridas* had no legal rights until the Family Code was amended in 1988. (Under Islamic law, by contrast, multiple wives are protected.) Because of the influence of the Roman Catholic church, divorce is illegal in the Philippines, and reproductive rights for women are frowned upon.

Upper- and Middle-Class Women and the Feminist Movement

In southeast Asia, the first challenges to gender oppression came from middle- and upper-class women, who were, compared with the lower classes, more oppressed by men. Lower-class women were busy not only as childbearers but as production workers, and so they had economic power that translated itself into other forms of power; also, western values left them relatively untouched, so that they continued their traditional lifestyle. Elite women, on the other hand, were used to display their husband's social rank—kept idle, dressed up, bejeweled, and relegated to reproduction. Under western legal systems, elite women were "civilly dead"; they could not vote or receive higher education, and religion discriminated against them.

Upper-class women remain in the forefront of feminism in Malaysia, Thailand, and Indonesia. Although there are some grassroots women's organizations, they are fewer in number; in general, they were initially led by upper- and middle-class intellectuals; and some continue to take directions from above. In Thailand, this may be explained in terms of pragmatism of the part of lower-class women, who realize that the elite women have better resources and more influence (Tantiwiramond and Pandey, 1991). However, in the Philippines the dominance of upper-class women ended when politicized middle-class and grassroots women established organizations (De Dios, 1989; Subido, 1955). There, the oldest grassroots feminist organization is Katipunan ng Bagong Pilipina (KaBaPa), founded by rural women in 1976.

Women and the Class Struggle

Southeast Asian women have recognized the intersection of national, class, racial, and gender oppression. In Indonesia, for instance, two women's organization—Isteri Sedar and the women of Sarekat Rakyat—moved beyond questions of polygyny and divorce to other issues, which many groups feared to touch. They criticized the Dutch colonial government and called attention to the plight of proletarian women (Wieringa, 1985). Indonesia was the first country in this region to welcome socialist ideas, though socialism would be crushed by communism in 1965. The largest and most influential socialist women's organization was Gerakan Wanita Indonesia (GERWANI), founded in 1950.

In Malaysia, Parti Sosyalis Rakyat Malaya (PSRM) and the Labor Party had women's wings, which brought into public life women like P. G. Lim (who was appointed ambassador to Yugoslavia) and Ganga Nayar (a major opposition figure in parliament). In 1957 the two parties formed an alliance emphasizing the "class question" and the "woman question." As early as 1959 the Labor Party had a women's charter providing equal pay for equal work, monogamy for non-Muslims, and an International Women's Day (March 8). But such initiatives did not survive the government ban on leftist activities in the late 1960s (Dancz, 1987).

In Thailand, leftist women's groups formed during the democratic Philbun administration of 1972–1976, but they could not operate openly after that government was toppled by a military coup which banned communism. In the Philippines, leftist women's groups, notably Makibaka and Gabriela, formed during the Marcos regime.

Women in Indochina addressed the "national question" and the "class question" simultaneously. Nguyen Thi Minh, in a speech at the Seventh Communist International in Moscow in 1935, said that in the revolution, Vietnamese women were "ridding themselves of the feudalist codes of conduct and behaviour" and "struggling for equal pay for equal work," "against the colonialists," and "for the complete independence of our country" (Mai Thi Tu, 1978: 122–123). Vietnamese women tend not to use terms such as "male power"—they see their oppressors as "the fuedalists, the colonialists, and the imperialists" (Eisen, 1984: 8).

Conclusion

Today, there are at least two strands of feminism in southeast Asia. Some feminists give primacy to the "national question," believing that only an emancipated nation can liberate its people. Others argue that unless its women are emancipated, a nation can never be free of its oppressors, asking, "How can women hold half of the sky if their hands are tied behind their backs?" In this latter group, first-wave feminists have sought equality with men in a framework of patriarchy, working for the vote, access to education and professions, and reforms in family law, welfare, and social benefits. Second-wave feminists, mostly of the politicized middle and lower classes, consider that approach limited; they analyze women's oppression in terms of male-dominated social, cultural, economic, and political systems and thus advocate and mobilize for radical change—not only in gender relations but in all hierarchical structures that produces war and injustice. Their battle cry is, "Fight on all fronts," and they assert that on these fronts women must not exclude men but must make them allies.

See Also

References and Further Reading

Dancz, Virginia H. 1987. *Women and party politics in peninsular Malaysia.* Oxford: Oxford University Press.

De Dios, Aurora J. 1889. Participation of women's groups in the anti-dictatorship struggle: Genesis of a movement. In Prosperpina Tapales and Priscila Manalang, eds., *The role of women in Philippine History.* Quezon City: Center for Women's Studies, University of the Philippines.

Eisen, Arlene. 1984. *Women and revolution in Vietnam.* London: Zed.

Fernandez, Albina Peczon. 1990–1991. Rizal on women and children in the struggle for nationhood. *Review of Women's Studies* (2).

Firestone, Shulamith. 1972. *The dialectic of sex.* New York: Bantam.

Jayawardena, Kumari. 1994. *Feminism and nationalism in the third world.* Lahore, Pakistan: ASR.

Khaing, Mi Mi. 1984. *The world of Burmese Women.* London: Zed.

Mai Thi Tu. 1978. *Women in Vietnam.* Hanoi: Foreign Languages Publications.

Matsui, Yayori. 1989. *Women's Asia.* London: Zed.

Ng, Cecilia, and Carol Yong. 1991. Malaysian women at the crossroads. In *Women in Action.* Quezon City, Philippines: ISIS International.

Omvedt, Gail. 1988. *Women in popular movements: India and Thailand during the decade of women.* Geneva: UN Research Institute for Social development.

Subido, Tarrosa. 1955. *The feminist movement in the Philippines 1905–1955.* Manila: National Federation of Women's Clubs of the Philippines.

Tantiwiramond, Darunee, and Shaski Ranjan Pandey. 1991. *By women, for women: A study of women's organizations in Thailand.* Singapore: Institute of Southeast Asian Studies.

Wieringa, Saskia. 1985. *The perfumed nightmare: Some notes on the Indonesian women's movement.* Working Paper. The Hague, Netherlands: Institute of Social Studies.

Zainu'ddin, Ailsa G. Thomson. 1986. *What should a girl become? Further reflections on the letters of R. A. Kartini.* In David P. Chandler and M. C. Ricklef, eds., *Nineteenth and twentieth century Indonesia.* Clayton, Victoria: Centre of Southeast Asian Studies, Monash University.

Albina Peczon Fernandez

FEMINISM:
Sub-Saharan Africa

Throughout Africa, no less in the sub-Saharan region than in other parts of the continent, women were engaged in prolonged struggles of resistance against the onslaught of various European powers that invaded the continent in the late nineteenth century in a process that has sometimes been described as the "scramble for Africa." The new phase of imperialist expansion in the 1880s coincided with a global depression and a major rivalry for markets for consumer goods and products, because industrial capitalism had entered a new phase in its search for markets for these goods and products. Industrial capitalism had also entered a new phase in its search for cheap raw materials and safe havens for the investment of surplus capital. African people's resistance took a variety of forms and included a wide range of militant and nonmilitant strategies. These included the use of diplomatic channels; mass migration of entire villages from west to east and south to north; in many cases, selective suicide; guerrilla warfare, as in the case of the movement associated with Samory Toure of the western Sudanic region; pitched battles; hand-to-hand combat and various other forms of conventional and nonconventional warfare that in some contexts lasted for as long as thirty years. Dahomey's female soldiers, for example, became legendary for their courage and expertise in the struggle against the French.

Female leaders, such as Yaa Asantewaa of the Asante Empire and Nehanda of Zimbabwe, often operated more as nationalist than feminist activists, but they set the precedent for the participation of women in various movements in the twentieth century, in activities ranging from the Igbo Women's Wars of the 1920s in eastern Nigeria to more decidedly feminist and female-conscious organizations such as the National Council of Women's Societies of Nigeria and the Women's National Coalition, based in Marshalltown, South Africa. Some of these organizations were also directly inspired by the second wave of nationalist activism of the postwar period, or the struggle against apartheid, in the case of South Africa.

Many of the postwar women's organizations on the continent eventually became associated with the prevailing ideological offensive of "modernization," an ideological orientation that associated the liberation of women with exposure to formal education, easier access to credit facilities, the offer of elective posts, exposure to technical innovations and the fundamentals of entrepreneurship, and the organization of women into cooperatives in the context of land reform. These were all viewed as positive signs in the direction of female liberation. These organizations had in some cases assimilated the intellectual baggage of neoclassical and monetarist theory and had assumed that it was the sluggishness with which some of these principles had been implemented that led to the predicament of women and their marked disempowerment. Such arguments and perspectives have been reflected in multiple organizations throughout Africa in what seems a dominant strain in the feminist literature and activity in this continent, where feminism is defined as a philosophy and a perspective advocating social and political rights for women on a platform of equality with men.

Several such organizations have emerged in South Africa. Vukani Makhosikazi and Black Sash, based in the Cape, focus on legal aspects and paralegal training aimed at alerting women to their legal rights. In Natal and Kwa-Zulu the emphasis of Women for Peaceful Change Now (WPCN) and the Natal and Kwazulu Zenzele Women's Association has been on mobilizing women in the context of an improved quality of life and egalitarianism, granted that the latter seems to be more radically feminist in approach than the former. The Christian Women Enrichment Programme, the National Council of Women of South Africa, and Women for Peace, based in Johannesburg, tend to emphasize the promotion of cooperation, self-reliance, and equality, and in general they seem to be natural allies of other organizations such as the Itoseng Women's Self-Help Project, based in Odendaalsrus, the National Keyboards Skills and Development Project of Braamfontein, and Kontak, Johannesburg. Under the leadership of Lulu Xingawana, the Malibongwe National Women's Institute, like the Women's Informal Training Institute of Roodepoost, directed by Lindiwe Myeza, focuses on training and the development of skills. This is also true of their counterparts in other parts of the South African region.

In Africa's most populous state, Nigeria, the liberal reformist model has been a dominant one for women. It is the major orientation of organizational activity. Initially influenced by the postwar nationalist struggle for independence and change and the strategy of piecemeal reform, organizations such as the National Council for Women's Societies—which at the time of this writing had recently been headed by the northerner Hajiya Laila Dogonyaro—sought to usher in a new era of opportunity and change for women in an environment that was for the most part historically patriarchal and chauvinistic.

One of the major developments associated with the liberal reformist model is the incremental growth of female representatives at the level of state power, at the local and regional level, in several African states. The trend toward increased representation has also manifested itself in the academic field and administratively, although few of the organizations that have clamored for such representation would express total satisfaction with the pace of change: for many, the change is as yet too slow. The implementation of the demands of female-conscious and feminist activists is a task yet to be fully accomplished, granted that the gains made are not ignored. Among prominent female achievers in Ethiopia have been Genet Zewdie, minister of education; and Adanech Mariam, minister of public health. As in the case of Nigeria, a women's desk has also been created; Tadellech Mikael was the minister initally associated with this activity. In several areas prominent female activists associated with women's organizations occupy commanding heights in the hierarchy of state officials. In the new postapartheid South Africa, for example, Frene Ginwale, Speaker of the parliament, has played a major role in the Women's National Coalition, an umbrella organization centered in Marshalltown, South Africa. In Namibia it is interesting to note that in the 1992 regional and local authority council elections women constituted 31.49 percent of elected local councilors, although out of the 72-member chamber there were only five women members of parliament. The trend suggests that women have a higher rate of success at the lower local levels. Generally, in Namibia, as in South Africa, Ethiopia, and Nigeria, there have been substantial gains.

Several criticisms have been leveled against the liberal reformist feminists, in spite of their gains. Some of the epistemological assumptions underlying their mode of activity have been challenged and so, too, the overall conceptual framework and the long-established myths and assumptions that underlie them. The improvement of amenities and the creation of a suitable infrastructure for development are considered important for bettering the condition of women in Africa. The patriarchal and chauvinistic structures in various parts of the continent are challenged, however. The exploitation of women in household duties, the power relations dominant in family life, and the existing pattern of patriarchal relations are seen as part of a network of dependent relations and socialization that kept African woman subordinate in the past and continue to do so in contemporary Africa. The critics of the liberal reformist feminists attempt to uncover some of the various chauvinistic tendencies inherent in the entire process of learning and language formation in various regions. There is a challenge to the societal structures that makes it possible for children to be used as pawns in the power struggle between husbands and wives, and to the socialization process that seems to deny women their humanity from time to time. Few organizations on the continent have addressed this issue, an exception being Women in Nigeria, which emerged in 1982, having grown from a conference attended by a group of dedicated women and men from all over that state. Among its several objectives are the promotion of the study of the condition of women in Nigeria with the aim of combating discriminatory and sexist practices in the family, the workplace, and society; the defense of the rights of women under the Nigerian Constitution and the United Nations Human Rights Convention; the struggle against sexual harassment and abuse of females in the family; the combating of sexist stereotypes in literature, the media, and educational materials; and the struggle against class and sex oppression.

By the end of the twentieth century the organization had been quite active, hosting a series of conferences in various parts of the Nigeria such as Zaria, Port Harcourt, Ilorin, Calabar, Bauchi, and Kano. Thematically the conferences dealt with issues appropriate to the stated aims of the organization, including child abuse, women and democratization, women and the family, and, more recently, wife abuse. Like the liberal reformist organizations, Women in Nigeria also provides legal aid, engages in community projects aimed at generating income for women, and pays attention to education. However, in this organization, unlike some liberal reformist groups, a major aim has been to view the liberation of women as integrally related to the liberation of the oppressed and poor of Nigeria, and to view the process of liberation as fundamentally structural, recognizing that sexist stereotypes and hostility to women pervade the ideological apparatus of the state and the educational and intellectual arena in general. Well-known feminist activists of this persuasion, such as Ayesha Imam, Bene Madunagu, and Clara Ejembi, recognize that the struggle for the rights of Nigerian women is also a struggle against all forms of colonialism, whether internally or externally derived.

The radical feminists on the continent are outnumbered by the liberal reformists, but in South Africa, for example, organizations such as the Black Women's Research and Development Network, based in Johannesburg, are ideologically affiliated with organizations and movements such as Women in Nigeria, their major aim being the restructuring of power relations and gender research, rather than piecemeal reform.

On the whole, we may see these two major tendencies as comprising subtle gradations and variations. Some radical feminists are more socialistic than others, ideologically speaking, while the liberal reformist spectrum includes ideals and propositions that are decidedly neoclassical and involve "modernization," in juxtaposition with more theological orientations.

It is important to note that in the eastern and western regions of the continent, Islam is a major factor and that sub-Saharan feminism is influenced by it in regions such as the Somali-speaking area, northern Sudan, and Kenya in east Africa; and Senegal, Mali, Chad, and Nigeria in the west. In the case of either the Somali-speaking region or Senegal, we are actually dealing with populations that are more than 90 percent Muslim in a context of overall regional expansion due to the relatively uncomplicated mode of conversion, Islamic accommodation of a largely polygynous indigenous marital system, and a historic trend whereby most Muslim missionaries in the pioneering years of conversion were indigenous Africans. The implication for African feminism in the region is that the preexisting norms and values have been displaced by new propositions about the world in some cases, while in others a complex network of syncretic ideals has taken root, with distinct implications for the "woman question" and the struggle of women for equal rights and political and economic empowerment. Islam has been specific about the rights of women in several areas, among which are the question of equitable treatment of co-wives in the polygamous household; the grounds for divorce for women and the subsequent attitude toward the divorcee; and inheritance rights, whereby daughters became entitled to 50 percent of the property of the deceased. Moreover, Islam encourages women to recognize their rights in the context of various Qu'ranic injunctions and a framework of reference that may be properly identified as liberal reformist in overall orientation. African feminism has undoubtedly been affected and influenced by the latter in various ways, whether at the level of jurisprudence or in terms of ideals and values. There are four Sunni Muslim schools of jurisprudence, namely, Maliki, Shafi'i, Hanbali, and Hanafi, with the Maliki school being the dominant one in the case of Nigeria. More significant for the nature of feminist thought is the distinction between the Tijaniyya brotherhood—founded by Abu al-Abbas Ahmad al-Tijani in north Africa during the second half of the eighteenth century and reinforced by the activities of the Senegalese cleric Al Hajj Tall in the nineteenth century—and the Qadriyya brotherhood, with its roots in Baghdad. The Tijaniyya brotherhood encourages the appointment of women to positions of power and is less committed to the principle of seclusion (purdah) for women, a principle that few feminists can logically accommodate.

Throughout Africa's 56 states a variety of feminist thought has emerged, but two basic schools of thought hold sway, namely the liberal reformist and the radical feminist. Gradations exist—more so, given Africa's rich multireligious tradition and the expanding Islamic system of thought. Conflict and contradictions within and between the various orientations have served to make feminist thought on the continent complex, fascinating, and attractive to researchers, some of whom have challenged mainstream western analysis and perceptions in recent discourse.

See Also

DEVELOPMENT: SUB-SAHARAN AND SOUTHERN AFRICA; FEMINISM: NORTH AFRICA; FEMINISM: SOUTH AFRICA; HOUSEHOLDS AND FAMILIES: SUB-SAHARAN AFRICA; VIOLENCE: SUB-SAHARAN AND SOUTHERN AFRICA; WOMEN'S STUDIES: SUB-SAHARAN AFRICA

References and Further Reading

Bappa, S., et al. 1985. *Women in Nigeria today.* London: Zed.

Boahen, A. A., ed. 1991. *Africa under foreign domination.* Harlow, U.K.: Longman.

Callaway, B., and L. Creevy. 1994. *The heritage of islam: Women, religion, and politics in west Africa.* Boulder, Col.: Lynne Rienner.

Emeagwali, G.T. In press. *Challenging hegemonic discourses on Africa.* New Jersey: African World.

———. 1995. *Women pay the price: Structural adjustment in Africa and the Caribbean.* New Jersey: Africa World.

Kolawole, M. 1997. *Womanism and African consciousness.* New Jersey: Africa World.

Hay, M., and Stichter, S. 1995. *African women south of the Sahara.* New York: Addison-Wesley.

Imam, A., et al. 1986. *Women and the family.* Dakar, Senegal: CODESRIA.

Nnaemeka, O., ed. 1998. *Sisterhood, feminisms, and power—From Africa to the diaspora.* New Jersey: Africa World.

Ogundipe, Leslie, M. 1994. *Recreating ourselves: African women and critical transformations.* New Jersey: Africa World.

Oyewumi, O. 1998. *The invention of women: Making an African sense of western gender discours.* Minneapolis: University of Minnesota Press.

———, ed. In press. *African women and feminism: Reflections on the politics of sisterhood.* New Jersey: Africa World.

Vera, Y., ed. 1999. *Opening spaces—An anthology of contemporary African women's writing.* Zimbabwe: Baobb Books, Meinemann.

Gloria Emeagwali

FEMINISM: Third-Wave

The first generation of feminists struggles for crucial structural changes, a struggle to bring to consciousness new terms and new conditions in a climate both ready for, but resistant to, their efforts. The second generation inherits a new set of terms and social relationships, experiencing the freedoms created by the first generation as well as the limits of their work. The third generation takes the freedoms for granted and consequently finds the limits unacceptable, generating the conditions for a rebirth of feminism in yet another first generation's efforts. In each case the demands for change arise from women's experience. (Schneider, 1987: 12)

Throughout history, feminists have agreed to disagree about a definition of feminism and about who and what a feminist is and can be. Taking an international perspective, in the bulk of the feminist literature the term *feminist* remains strongly contested, even though there have been all kinds of feminists (Rupp and Taylor, 1999). Feminists have been differentiated by race, color, and ethnicity, socioeconomic status and class, sexual orientation, nationality and geography, ideology, physical disability, and, of course, by generation. It is the latter category that defines the framework for third-wave feminism, although all the other issues remain important.

Although *third-wave feminism* was a term first heard sometime in the 1980s, it was only in the latter part of the 1990s that the term came to imply any new type of feminism or feminist. Primarily relevant to western industrialized countries, third-wave feminism does, however, span countries and continents. In Britain, for example, third-wave feminism is known as the "new feminism." In Australia, it is known as DIY feminism (Bail, 1994) or generation X feminism (Stewart, forthcoming). What does this third wave mean, and how is it different from the second and first waves?

Discussions of third-wave feminism can be found in a number of important books and articles. These writings address a range of issues, including victim and power feminism, pornography, the media, alternative music, aerobics, the politics of color, motherhood, marriage, living as a dyke, women's bodies, spirituality, and religion. These issues also are central to the public debate that creates an understanding of third-wave feminism.

Third-wave feminism, however, can also be defined in other ways. As a way of "seeing, doing and being," it can be understood as the feminism of women born between 1963 and 1974 (Heywood and Drake, 1997). According to Natasha Walter, author of *New Feminism,* it is a feminism that is in "the air that they [younger women] breathe." Although it may have fragmented and splintered, third-wave feminists experience this feminism as "lodged in the[ir] hearts and minds" (Walter, 1999: 43, 32). These features of third-wave feminism notwithstanding, it seems to be only when one tries to define what the third wave actually is that problems of classification become truly apparent. As Barbara Findlen (1995: xiii) has said of third-wave feminism more broadly, "One of the characteristics we're known for is our disunity. Maybe we're not as unified as the generation that preceded us. Maybe we're just not as categorizable." Although third-wave feminism may be known for a broad agenda of concerns, it is also know for its inability to be neatly categorized—there is no one type of third-wave feminist.

Third-wave feminism is also a feminism that seeks to differentiate itself from its predecessor—second-wave feminism, which grew out of the women's liberation movement of the 1970s. In this respect, those that write about the third wave go to some length to ensure that what they have to say is one step on from the agendas of their mothers. Often accused of lacking knowledge about the history of twentieth-century women's movements, third-wavers tread the fine line between taking the gains of the second wave as their own, or failing to acknowledge such gains at all. As Gloria Steinem warned in her foreward to Rebeca Walker's collection *To Be Real* (1995): "I want to remind readers . . . that some tactical and theoretical wheels don't have to be reinvented. You may want to make them a different size or color . . . but many already exist."

In addition to the variety of ways in which third-wavers seek to define themselves, there are other feminists whom they also seek not to emulate. This other school of feminists or "postfeminists" includes Kate Roiphe, Rene Denfield, and Naomi Wolf (although Wolf contributed to *To Be Real*). In this respect, prominent third-wavers shy away from the rampant individualism that characterizes such "postfeminists," choosing instead to emphasize women's collective interests, at least inasmuch as there is common ground among women of this generation in English-speaking western countries. This is perhaps not surprising, given that the term *third wave* also

identifies the Third Wave Direct Action Corporation, founded by Rebecca Walker, a national nonprofit organization devoted to cultivating young women's leadership and activism (Findlen, 1995: 264). But, you say, you've told me what third-wave feminism is not; why don't you tell me what it is?

First, there is a general belief among third-wavers that second-wave feminism hit a dead end because it relied on a rigid ideology that alienated and divided women who were working toward the same end (see Walter, 1999). This rigidity applies also to who is and who is not a feminist. As Jennifer Drake notes, "Young women struggle with the feminist label because rigid definitions of 'a good feminist' entrap women as much as sexist definitions of womanhood ever did" (Drake, 1997: 103).

The second characteristic that can be used to summarize third-wave feminism is the sense of entitlement that third-wave writings exude. According to Catherine Orr (1997), it is this sense of entitlement that defines much of what is written under the guise of the new and third-wave feminisms. However, as Ellen Neuborne points out in "Imagine My Surprise"—her chapter in *Listen Up*—"It is a dangerous thing to assume that just because we were raised in a feminist era, we are safe. We are not." The safety that Neuborne is referring to here is not so much women's physical safety but younger women's access to a world that offers equal and fair treatment.

Finally, and almost regardless of the topic under discussion, third-wave feminism is about speaking out. It is about young women drawing on their own life experiences. In this sense, third-wave feminism can be seen as young women's reaction to being "spoken for and spoken at, but not heard" (Detloff, 1997: 77).

In all its apparent contradictions, third-wave feminism is a hybrid of much that has gone before (Drake, 1997: 102), along with new ideas and new voices.

See Also

References and Further Reading

Bail, K., ed. 1994. *DIY feminism.* St. Leonards, New South Wales: Allen and Unwin.

Bauer Maglin, N., and D. Perry, eds. 1994. *Bad girls good girls: Women, sex, and power in the nineties.* New Brunswick, N.J.: Rutgers University Press.

Detloff, M. 1997. Mean spirits: The politics of contempt between feminist generations. *Hypatia* 12(3): 76–101.

Drake, J. 1997. Third wave feminism. *Feminist Studies* 23(1): 97–108.

Findlen, B., ed. 1995. *Listen up: Voices from the next feminist generation.* Seattle, Wash.: Seal.

Heywood, L., and J. Drake, eds. 1997. *Third wave agenda: Being feminist, doing feminism.* Minneapolis: University of Minnesota Press.

Neuborne, E. 1999. Imagine my surprise. In B. Findlen, ed., *Listen up: Voices from the next feminist generation.* Seattle, Wash.: Seal.

Orr, C. 1997. Charting the currents of the third wave. *Hypatia* 12(3): 29–44.

Rupp, L., and Taylor, V. 1999. Forging feminist identity in an international movement: A collective identity approach to twentieth century feminism. *Signs* 24(2): 363–385.

Schneider, B. 1987. Political generations and the contemporary women's movement. *Sociological Inquiry* 58(1): 4–21.

Stewart, F. Forthcoming. *Return to sender, generation x returns the baby boom.*

Walker, R., ed. 1995. *To be real: Telling the truth and changing the face of feminism.* New York: Anchor.

Walter, N., ed. 1999. *On the move: Feminism for a new generation.* London: Virago.

Walter, N. 1999. *The new feminism.* London: Virago.

Note: Readers interested in reading original writings on the third wave and new feminism should seek out: *Listen up: Voices from the next feminist generation,* edited by Barbara Findlen; *To be real: Telling the truth and changing the face of feminism,* edited by Rebecca Walker with a foreword by Gloria Steinem and an afterword by Angela Davis; *Bad Girls/Good Girls: Women, sex, and power in the nineties,* edited by Nan Bauer Maglin and Donna Perry, *Third wave agenda: Being feminist, doing feminism,* edited by Leslie Heywood and Jennifer Drake; *The new feminism* by Natasha Walter, *On the move: Feminism for a new generation,* edited by Natasha Walter; *DIY feminism,* edited by Kathy Bail; and *Return to sender: Generation X returns the baby boom letter,* by Fiona Stewart. Feminist academic journals such as *Hypatia, Signs* and *Feminist Studies* have published articles in this area.

Fiona Stewart

FEMME/BUTCH

See BUTCH/FEMME.

FEMOCRAT

The term *femocrat* refers to feminists working in state government bureaucracies, especially but not only in sections or programs dealing with "women's issues." The term was first coined and is still mainly used in Australia, where feminists have a comparatively close relationship with the state (Watson, 1992; Sawyer, 1998), but it has gained some currency referring to "state feminists" elsewhere, who might or might not have links with feminist organizations outside the state.

Feminist research internationally has traced women's often difficult relations with the state, including as beneficiaries and consumers of state services, and as employees, especially in welfare and support roles at lower levels (Rai and Lievesley, 1996). There is much debate, too, about seeking to use the masculinist state for women's rights, given the perceived involvement of states in perpetuating gender inequalities and patriarchal power.

Women's movements and feminists' demands within states have been reinforced by transnational alliances, international conferences, and information gathering associated with the United Nations Decade for Women. By the 1990s, more than 140 states had "women's machinery" in government, although in many cases this was associated with welfare issues and focused on women primarily as mothers. In some states, governments have undertaken equal employment opportunity and other gender equity policies, and set up women's bureaus to monitor and implement these. Whereas liberal feminists point to such developments as evidence that the state can be mobilized in women's interests, other feminists are more critical, suggesting that states still favor women who are members of the dominant group, and that these programs come at the cost of co-option and intensified surveillance and control in return for meager benefits or funding.

Femocrat does not refer to all women working in bureaucracies, or even in women's units; rather, it connotes state workers who identify themselves as feminists or are appointed to administer gender equity units or policies. *Femocrat* can be a term of abuse, and it suggests tension between femocrats' professional and feminist political responsibilities. Femocrats also carry the burden of representation, if they are expected to speak for all women; or, alternatively, they are dismissed as unrepresentative of "ordinary" women and so not entitled to speak for them. There can be conflicts between femocrats and feminist academics and activists, although individual women move between these roles, and there are coalitions across the lines with regard to particular issues like equal pay and child care.

In Australia, femocrats thrived under Labour governments but were marginalized under conservative coalition governments. They were influential in winning funding for women's and child's services, as well as developing innovative equal employment opportunity legislation. Most significant, perhaps, has been the implementation of the Women's Budget Program, which required all governmental departments and agencies to assess the impact of their proposals on women. This model has recently been taken up internationally, including by the Commonwealth Secretariat (Sawer, 1998). However, the defeat of the Australian Labour government in 1996, combined with the dominance of neoliberal policies, substantially reduced femocrats' effect.

In developing, transition, and liberal democratic states, global restructuring and "rolling back the state" have meant hardwon feminist gains are under attack internationally. The state may now seem less hostile to women than new globalized market relations are.

See Also

BUREAUCRACY; POLITICS AND THE STATE: OVERVIEW; WOMEN'S STUDIES: AUSTRALIA

References and Further Readings

Australian Feminist Policy Network (AUSFEM-POLNET). E-mail network for policy activists, analysts, and practitioners. Subscribe to: majordomo.

Rai, Shirin, and Geraldine Lievesley. 1996. *Women and the state: International perspectives.* London: Francis and Taylor.

Sawyer, Marian. 1998. Political institutions. In Barbara Caine and Moira Gatens, *Australian feminism: A companion.* Melbourne: Oxford University Press.

United Nations Division for the Advancement of Women. *National machineries for gender equality: Report of expert group meeting.* Santiago, Chile: UNDAW.

Watson, Sophie, ed. 1992. *Playing the state: Australian feminist interventions.* Sydney: Allen and Unwin.

Jan Jindy Pettman

FERTILITY AND FERTILITY TREATMENT

Fertility is one of the most important natural capabilities of human beings. Having children has been widely regarded as a "matter of course." Furthermore, bearing children is often considered a "woman's duty," as childbearing is seen as women's contribution to the labor force and to society. Therefore, every culture has rituals centered on fertility and reproduction.

Although fertility is sometimes expressed as a fertility rate—the rate of reproduction—this illustrates only one aspect of fertility. Ironically, studying infertility leads us to a more comprehensive understanding of fertility. The social ostracism that infertile couples often undergo reflects the importance of fertility in a traditional society whose economy is based on crops or livestock. Infertility—that is, the inability to bear children—has been associated with an image of barrenness and poverty. Infertility often threatens women's identity because society glorifies maternity and motherhood. Inability to procreate can also bring men to an identity crisis. In addition, many cultures and societies have considered infertility to be a deviation from "normality." Methods to heal infertility and restore normality have been developed in every culture. These methods include white magic, prayer, faith healing, and the consumption of medicinal plants.

In patriarchal societies, being unable to bear children can mean a crisis of succession in the family line, the family name, or the family's vested rights. This has been a major issue, especially for the propertied class. For this reason, infertility was considered a justifiable reason to divorce one's wife, and having both a wife and a concubine was tolerated in many male-dominant societies. These practices were intended to avoid childlessness even in the case of male infertility, because the concept of male infertility was not generally considered, or even known. The practice of adopting children also was established, although it varied widely among cultures, in both concept and significance.

Infertility is often defined medically as the inability of a couple to conceive after 24 months of intercourse without contraception. However, the defining time period has been changed as new reproductive technology develops; thus 1 year is now a common criterion. The medical professions involved in fertility treatments estimate that about 10 percent of all (de facto) married couples are infertile. Exact statistics on infertility are almost impossible to obtain, however, even in technologically advanced countries.

Causes of infertility among women include problems of ovulation, blocked or scarred fallopian tubes, and miscarriages. Most infertility among men is related to the quantity or quality of semen. There are many cases in which the cause is unknown.

Preventing infertility in women is sometimes difficult, because of factors such as pelvic inflammatory diseases, sexually transmitted diseases, endometriosis, pelvic infection after a delivery, abortion, surgery, or invasive diagnostic testing. Improper contraceptive methods and abortion also can cause infertility. Environmental toxins, drugs, smoking, stress, poor nutrition, and lack of exercise can be causes in both females and males. A serious problem is that medical professionals tend to have more interest in applying advanced technologies than in prevention.

Most methods of treating infertility are directed at women. Technologies such as artificial insemination (AI) and in vitro fertilization (IVF, the so-called "test tube baby" method) do not cure the physical condition, for the woman or her partner remains infertile even after a child is born by these methods. Infertility treatment itself often entails physical discomfort and mental stress. Diagnosis and treatment of infertility are diverse. Some of the diagnostic and treatment methods, especially for women, are invasive and risky. For example, side effects of ovulation-inducing drugs, which are frequently used, include hyperstimulation accompanied by superovulation, the formation of cysts, rupture of ovaries, and abdominal dropping.

The first human pregnancy resulting from artificial insemination sperm with the husband's sperm (AIH) was reported in the late eighteenth century. Artificial insemination with donor sperm (AID) succeeded in the late nineteenth century. As western medical practitioners gradually gained anatomical knowledge of reproductive organs, they also acquired a better understanding of the function of reproductive hormones in the later twentieth century. Oral contraceptive medication also was developed at that time. The first IVF baby was born in London in 1978. The IVF method opened the door to a new era, which made it possible to manipulate human gametes and embryos in the laboratory. Infertility came to be treated as a "medical disorder" in some cultures and societies in which western medicine was dominant. Considering infertility as a medical problem often seemed to have the effect of giving doctors, through their medical treatments, control over women's bodies.

Feminists see clinical tests conducted during the developmental phases of the new reproductive technology as human experiments. They have demanded that medical professionals provide a woman patient with sufficient information concerning the tests so that her consent may be truly informed. This information should include, for example, the fact that only about 15 percent of all the women who enter an IVF program will have a successful pregnancy. In addition to the low success rate, women should be well informed as to the risks accompanying these advanced fertility treatments, such as the side effects of hormonal drugs, risks caused by anesthesia, and risks associated with gametes intrafallopian tube transfer (GIFT), microinjection with IVF, and so on.

The donation of gametes, surrogacy, and other new reproductive technologies involving a third party are in use in several countries. These methods, originally developed as a means of treating infertility, have also come to be used by some single women and lesbian couples, even though they are, in fact, able to become pregnant. Sometimes, single men and gay couples make use of surrogacy so that they can become parents. Furthermore, there are sperm banks in the United States established from the eugenic point of view. Theoretically at least, it is possible to perform AID utilizing the sperm of men with high IQs, superior athletic abilities, or other desirable attributes.

Some counties, for example the United States and Australia, have enacted laws to regulate infertility treatments and other new reproductive technologies. Some countries have guidelines for medical specialists necessitated by the increasing diversification and expansion of infertility treatments and technologies. Some regulations confine treatment to heterosexual married couples.

Feminists often object to "social conformity" as a condition of IVF and other reproductive technologies. They say that providing such treatment only to legally married heterosexual couples is actually a stipulation of "qualifications to become parents." Some feminists view egg donation and surrogacy negatively because these practices may create a situation in which socially and economically disadvantaged women are induced to offer their bodies to advantaged women in exchange for money. However, some feminists see IVF, artificial insemination, and other such advanced reproductive technologies as having the potential to free women from pregnancies and deliveries, thus making it possible for women to conceive and give birth when they choose.

As noted above, reproductive technologies have created the possibility of fertility being controlled by doctors; this technology also creates the possibility of control by other powers. In some nations today, the government imposes compulsory or semicompulsory birth control by using hormonal drugs, contraceptive vaccines, or abortion "health" control policies, and prenatal diagnosis, which is called a fetus test. Control can also be less direct. As long as the development and application of technologies for "infertility treatment" are made available through delivery systems based on class, economic, and gender biases, future technologies will not necessarily be welcome news for women. There is a strong possibility that advanced reproductive technologies will perpetuate a view of women as bearers of children with an inherent desire for motherhood and little else.

Fertility has, in fact, been controlled politically, economically, and socially. It should be emphasized that every woman, disabled or not disabled, poor or not poor, ought to have the right to determine for herself whether or not she wishes to have a child. She also should have the right to decide when to have a child and how many children she wishes to bear. It goes without saying that she has the right to bear a baby regardless of its gender. Furthermore, women who are involuntarily childless should not be encouraged or forced to undergo infertility treatment against their wishes. No power should intervene in the process of a woman's decision making concerning her body.

See Also

ADOPTION; CHILDBIRTH; CLONING; ETHICS: MEDICAL; GYNECOLOGY; INFERTILITY; PREGNANCY AND BIRTH; REPRODUCTIVE HEALTH; REPRODUCTIVE PHYSIOLOGY; REPRODUCTIVE TECHNOLOGIES; SURROGACY

References and Further Reading

Congress of the United States, Office of Technology Assessment, ed. 1998. *Infertility: Medical and social choices.* Washington, D.C.: U.S. Government Printing Office.

Interpreting infertility: Medical anthropological perspectives. 1994. *Social science and medicine* 39(4): Special issue.

Issues in Reproductive and Genetic Engineering: Journal of International Feminist Analysis. New York: Pergamon.

Klein, Renate D., ed. 1989. *Infertility—Women speak out about their experiences of reproductive medicine.* London: Pandora.

Azumi Tsuge

FETUS

The fetus, a cultural icon of the 1980s, emerged in the 1990s as an object of feminist inquiry. Although feminist scholars have long been interested in various aspects of reproduction, analysis has focused primarily on women. Attention has centered on the ways in which women's embodied reproductive experiences have been configured by science, medicine, and politics. The fetus has been peripheral to these examinations, subsumed within a liberatory emphasis on women's rights, autonomy, and bodily integrity—despite the fact that in the United States and other western nations, the fetus has become a major figure in abortion politics and is highly sig-

nificant to conservative forces. While "pro-life" groups exalted the fetus, feminist scholars remained largely silent on questions of fetal ontology and instead continued to work toward expanded reproductive rights for all women. Indeed, given the elevation of the fetus in antiabortion discourses, feminists *strategically* avoided drawing attention to the womb's occupant for fear of participating in the construction of fetal personhood.

The situation in feminist research has changed significantly. No longer wishing to cede the cultural terrain of reproductive polities to fetocentric forces, scholars from a variety of disciplines in the 1990s began to focus on the social construction of the fetus itself (Morgan and Michaels, 1999). Feminist scholarship on the fetus explicitly disrupts and challenges scientific, medical, legal, ethical, cultural, and political constructions of a monolithic, universal, "naturalized" fetus whose rights are often assumed to supersede those of women. Feminists have worked instead to resituate the free-floating public fetus within the social conditions of its origin and to draw attention to the ways in which fetal iconography sustains and reproduces social hierarchies. Feminists have analyzed fetal rights, fetal personhood, fetal patienthood, fetal icons, fetal images, fetal politics, maternal-fetal relationships, globalization of fetuses, fetal practices in science and medicine, and other topics related directly to fetal status.

Historically, fetal status and ontology have been the province of philosophers, theologians, and ethicists. These authorities wrestled with questions of ontological status, agency, rights and benefits, and the moral value of the fetus. A burning question has been: Is the fetus a person? Answers range from defining the fetus as a full person, with all the rights afforded members of the human community, to defining a fetus as a potential human being with limited rights to viewing it as a nonsentient form of life without rights. In other words, while there is general agreement that a fetus is some form of human life, contestation centers around what moral status to accord that life. In most of these discussions, the pregnant woman has been largely invisible, or ethical conundrums have been framed as "maternal-fetal conflict" (Macklin, 1990). With the exception of some feminist ethicists who view fetal status in relation to that of pregnant women, most philosophers and ethicists have attempted to define fetal status as if the fetus did not inhabit a living woman's body.

With the advent of modern science and medicine, questions of fetal ontology have taken on added significance. Indeed, biomedicine has given rise to supposed conflicts between maternal and fetal patients that have spurred ontological deliberations. Biomedical practices have contributed to the notion of the fetus as a natural, universal entity that can be known by science. In scientific frameworks, fetuses are represented as potential human beings passing through stages of development. Fetal physiology has given us trimesters in pregnancy as well as the notions of neural substrate of individuality, human genome, brain integration, and organogenesis as markers of human life. Western medicine has begun to identify and treat the "unborn patient" (Casper, 1998), while also developing visual tools such as ultrasound that have contributed to the proliferation of cultural images of the fetus. For clinicians, whose ways of seeing are shaped by the historical biases of western science, ultrasound images represent an objectification of the fetus that simultaneously personifies it. The power of such images is evidenced in the wide popularity of Lennart Nilsson's intricate fetal photographs (1990) and their subsequent appropriation by pro-life movements.

Feminist scholars and activists have responded to the emergence of the "public fetus" in a number of ways. Some have considered the *social* dimensions of fetal personhood, such as a woman's relationship with her own fetus (Layne, 1997; Rothman, 1986). Others have situated fetal personhood historically, offering evidence that the current public fetus is a product of its time (Duden, 1993; Newman, 1996). Anthropologists have brought a much needed relativism, reporting that fetuses and infants are given meaning and importance differently depending on culture and geopolitical context (Morgan, 1989, 1997 Oaks, 1999; Ortiz, 1997; Scheper-Hughes, 1992). Feminist ethicists and social scientists have challenged traditional bioethics by grounding questions of fetal personhood in actual social and political practices, suggesting that the fetal person acquires meaning locally rather than universally (Franklin, 1991). Fetal images have been deconstructed and resituated by feminist scholars who have drawn attention to their cultural, political, and economic foundations (Hartouni, 1997; Mitchell and Georges, 1997; Petchesky, 1987; Stabile, 1992; Taylor, 1993). Another line of research has addressed the gender, race, and class dimensions of reproduction, including fetal status (Rapp, 1999; Roberts, 1997) and international systems of "stratified reproduction" (Ginsburg and Rapp, 1995). Abortion politics and the contemporary centrality of the fetus have provided a further line of questioning (Petchesky, 1990; Solinger, 1998). Scholars have addressed the historical emergence of the fetal patient and the politics of western medicine's attention to the contents of the womb (Casper, 1998). Finally, some western feminist artists such as Helen Chadwick and Kathy High

have begun refiguring fetal imagery in explicitly political ways.

In sum, this body of feminist scholarship has illustrated that there is no "natural" or ahistorical fetus. History and context matter in how meanings are attributed to individual and public fetuses. Any workable feminist theory of fetuses must start with an assumption that fetuses are socially, culturally, politically, and geographically constructed. Fetal ontology, like any other social category, is produced within social interactions rather than biologically or naturally given. Fetuses are social objects, made into human beings through various social practices rather than found in nature. Locating fetuses in both material and symbolic realms has enabled feminist theorists to examine how meanings and practices accrue around fetuses and are disseminated throughout cultures. Countering the notion of the fetus as a "silent subject" (Stetson, 1996), feminists have instead articulated the presence of multiple, heterogeneous fetuses shaped and given meaning through a variety of local, national, and global practices in which race, class, and gender matter a great deal. Through deconstructing the monolithic fetus, feminists have offered a valuable tool in the *social* fetus that can tell us much about women's embodied experiences, reproductive politics, and national and global inequities.

See Also

ABORTION; BIOETHICS: FEMINIST; BODY; GENETIC SCREENING; GENETICS AND GENETIC TECHNOLOGIES; OBSTETRICS; PREGNANCY AND BIRTH; PRO-CHOICE MOVEMENT; REPRODUCTION: OVERVIEW; REPRODUCTIVE PHYSIOLOGY; REPRODUCTIVE TECHNOLOGIES

References and Further Reading

Casper, Monica J. 1998. *The making of the unborn patient: A social anatomy of fetal surgery.* New Brunswick, N.J.: Rutgers University Press.

Duden, Barbara, 1993. *Disembodying women: Perspectives on pregnancy and the unborn.* Cambridge, Mass.: Harvard University Press.

Franklin, Sarah. 1991. Fetal fascinations: New dimensions to the medical-scientific construction of personhood. In Sarah Franklin, Celia Lury, and Jackie Stacey, eds., *Off-centre: Feminism and cultural studies,* 190–205. London: HarperCollins.

Ginsburg, Faye, D., and Rayna Rapp, eds. 1995. *Conceiving the new world order: The global politics of reproduction.* Berkeley: University of California Press.

Hartouni, Valerie. 1997. *Cultural conceptions: On reproductive technologies and the remaking of life*. Minneapolis: University of Minnesota Press.

Layne, Linda. 1997. Breaking the silence: An agenda for a feminist discourse on pregnancy loss. *Feminist Studies* 23(2): 289–316.

Macklin, Ruth. 1990. Maternal-fetal conflict: An ethical analysis. *Women's Health Issues* 1: 28–30.

Mitchell, Lisa M., and Eugenia Georges. 1997. Cross-cultural cyborgs: Greek and Canadian women's discourses on fetal ultrasound. *Feminist Studies* 23(2): 373–402.

Morgan, Lynn M. 1997. Imagining the unborn in the Ecuadoran Andes. *Feminist Studies* 23(2): 323–50.

———. 1989. When does life begin? A cross-cultural perspective on the personhood of fetuses and young children. In Ed Doerr and James W. Prescott, eds., *Abortion rights and fetal personhood*, 97–114. Long Beach, Calif.: Centerline Press.

———, and Meredith W. Michaels, eds. 1999. *Fetal subjects, feminist positions*. Philadelphia: University of Pennsylvania Press.

Newman, Karen. 1996. *Fetal positions: Individualism, science, visuality*. Stanford, Calif.: Stanford University Press.

Nilsson, Lennart. 1990. *A child is born*. New York: Delta-Seymour Lawrence.

Oaks, Laury. 1999. Irish trans/national politics and locating fetuses. In Lynn M. Morgan and Meredith W. Michaels, eds., *Fetal subjects, feminist positions*. Philadelphia: University of Pennsylvania Press.

Ortiz, Ana Teresa. 1997. "Bare-handed" medicine and its elusive patients: The unstable construction of pregnant women and fetuses in Dominican obstetrics discourse. *Feminist Studies* 23(2): 263–288.

Perchesky, Rosalind Pollack. 1990. *Abortion and woman's choice: The state, sexuality, and reproductive freedom*. Boston: Northeastern University Press.

Rapp, Rayna. 1999. *Testing women, testing the fetus: The social impact of amniocentesis in America*. New York: Routledge.

Roberts, Dorothy. 1997. *Killing the black body: Race, reproduction, and the meaning of liberty*. New York: Vintage.

Rothman, Barbara Katz. 1986. *The tentative pregnancy: Prenatal diagnosis and the future of motherhood*. New York: Penguin.

Scheper-Hughes, Nancy. 1992. *Death without weeping: The violence of everyday life in Brazil*. Berkeley: University of California Press.

Solinger, Rickie, ed. 1998. *Abortion wars: A half century of struggle, 1950–2000*. Berkeley: University of California Press.

Stabile, Carol. 1992. Shooting the mother: Fetal photography and the politics of disappearance. *Camera Obscura* 28: 179–206.

Stetson, Brad, ed. 1996. *The silent subject: Reflections on the unborn in American culture*. Westport, Conn.: Greenwood.

Taylor, Janelle Sue. 1993. The public fetus and the family car: From abortion politics to a Volvo advertisement. *Science As Culture* 3: 601–618.

Monica Casper

FICTION

At the beginning of the twenty-first century enormous changes are occurring in the construction of knowledge and culture, including how it is produced and whose work is taken seriously. Although it has not yet come to full term, a revolution is occurring among some writers of fiction.

Women have historically played a central role in developing the genre of fiction. In the twelfth century, Lady Murasaki Shikibu of the Heian court in Japan wrote *The Tale of the Genji*, which is often said to be the world's first novel. The rise of the novel in England in the seventeenth century has been documented by Dale Spender (1986). Women have also been literary innovators. Dorothy Richardson's use of stream of consciousness for her multivolume work *Pilgrimage* (1915), for instance, predated James Joyce's use of the technique by well over a decade. Virginia Woolf took the novel form to new heights, and Gertrude Stein made radical use of language. The modernists challenged the idea that women could write only about romance and domestic themes, and contemporary feminist writers continue this tradition of resistance, creating new possibilities and forms.

Exciting and innovative work is coming from writers who dig deeply and broadly into the traditions of their cultures, in a sense becoming archaeologists. Many are creating previously unknown histories. Keri Hulme's and Leslie Marmon Silko's personal and cultural renditions open up to modern readers—whether members of the culture described or outsiders—a new range of knowledge. Hulme and Silko draw on Maori and Native American traditions.

The traditions unearthed in these and similar works are, on the whole, best exemplified by writers who do not locate themselves within the dominant tradition of a particular culture. Cultural traditions include discourses framed by ethnicity, sexuality, ability, mobility, class, and ideology. Themes are wide-ranging, but many focus on political conflict and war, re-creating traditions (particularly evident among lesbian writers), unearthing suppressed cultural histories (particularly evident in the work of indigenous and minority writers), or reclaiming histories (particularly in the work of displaced people by migration, imprisonment, or exile). Whatever the "surface" of the text, enrichment, through a knowledge of the tradition within which the writer is working, is integral to the success of fiction.

War and Political Conflict

As war and political conflict have moved into the civilian arena over the past century, women have sometimes found themselves imprisoned for their beliefs, or witnesses to violence perpetrated against friends and relatives. Women's exposure to political conflict has resulted in many extraordinary works of fiction. In North America, Lee Maracle, Leslie Marmon Silko, and Louise Erdich are among many indigenous writers who focus on the dual nature of resistance and capitulation. Hyllus Maris and Sonia Borg's *Daughters of the Sun* (1985), Toni Morrison's *Beloved* (1988), and Tsi Tsi Dangarembga's *Nervous Conditions* (1988) explore the mental colonization that accompanies wars of invasion. Jeanne Hyvrard in *Mother Death* (1988) explores the invasion of women's minds and bodies through madness, as Charlotte Perkin's Gilman did a century earlier in *The Yellow Wallpaper* (1973).

Civil war has been a catalyst for many powerful works of fiction by women. Andrée Chedid's *The Return to Beirut*, (1989), Bapsi Sidhwa's *Cracking India* (1991, made into the film *Earth* by Deepa Mehta), and Rose Zwi's *Another Year in Africa* (1995) depict the bewilderment of young girls confronted with political violence. Taking up the codes of magical realism, which is prevalent in Latin American fiction, Luisa Valenzuela, Isabelle Allende, and Marta Traba depict the absurdity and horror of war. Christa Wolf, Ninotchka Rosca, and Duong Thu Huong contextualize war by offering an understanding of the interaction between the historical and the personal.

Joy Kogawa's *Obasan* (1983) attempts to explain the internment of "enemy aliens" in Canada during World War II. The interminable war against women is exposed by Li Ang in *The Butcher's Wife* (1990) and Andrea Dworkin in *Mercy* (1990). Both writers draw the reader into the madness of violence.

Suppressed Cultural Traditions

Like war, colonization has had a profound effect on women, many of whom have been dispossessed of land, culture, and sometimes their children. The cultural traditions of the vanquished, the colonized, the enslaved, and the overlooked are being nurtured by many fiction writers. Some are traditions with a long history; others are emerging from new identities and political definitions.

The African tradition is well represented in Africa and in the diaspora. Toni Morrison's *Beloved* (1988) is perhaps the most thoroughgoing example of tradition unearthed (the slave tradition)—this is evident in her radical use of language and in the structure of the work. Toni Cade Bambara's *The Salt Eaters* (1980) is also a strong exhumation of women's traditions. Bessie Head, Flora Nwapa, Ama Ata Aidoo, Buchi Emecheta, Tsi Tsi Dangarembga, and Jane Tapsubei Creider are among African writers whose work draws on the history of women. Flora Nwapa and Buchi Emecheta explore the history of the Ibu of Nigeria; Ama Ata Aidoo, Tsi Tsi Dangarembga, and Bessie Head examine the effects of colonization; Jane Tapsubei Creider depicts an entire community (the Nandi in Kenya) and its relationships. In the United States, Audre Lorde, Alice Walker, Michelle Cliff, and Jamaica Kincaid draw on the history of black resistance, linking it with their personal resistance as black women.

Cultural erosion complicates the process of discovering the thread of women's tradition, particularly for indigenous writers from the Pacific region. Patricia Grace, Ngahula Te Awekotuku, and Keri Hulme from Aotearoa-New Zealand have been important in putting Maori culture on the international map. All use their cultural traditions in their fiction, showing the spiritual strength of the culture and the difficulties caused by cultural breakdown. Faith Bandler, a descendant of the Kanaks, who were brought as slaves to Australia in the nineteenth century, writes about the little-known history of women who resisted slavery and colonial domination. Similar themes can be found in the work of the Canadian writers Darlene Barry Quaife and Jovette Marchessault.

New Identities

Gillian Hanscombe writes: "No one is proud of dykes (not families not neighbours not workmates not bosses not teachers not mentors not universities not literature societies not any nation not any ruler not any benefactor not any priest not any healer not any advocate). Only other dykes are proud of dykes" (1987: 7). Lesbians therefore, have recreated their own tradition. Judy Grahn and Paula Gunn Allen paved the way for reassessing the lesbian tradition; and most of the fiction writers mentioned here have also written critical or theoretical works, thus creating a body of theoretical work alongside the imaginative. Monique

Wittig's *The Lesbian Body* (1975), Suniti Namjoshi's *Feminist Fables* (1981, 1993), and Nicole Brossard's *These Our Mothers* (1983) were early examples. Wittig and Brossard examine the possibilities of the body; Namjoshi examines the lesbian's actions from a social and ethical perspective. These strands have continued in subsequent works of literature. Jeanette Winterson celebrates the body in *The Passion* (1987) and *Written on the Body* (1993), as does Mary Fallon in *Working Hot* (1989, 2000). Cathie Dunsford, in *Cowrie* (1993), celebrates the fat body, and Susan Hawthorne explores the mind-body connection through a character who suffers from epilepsy. Helen Hodgman in *Broken Words* (1988) and Finola Moorhead in *Darkness More Visible* (2000) explore the development of lesbian culture in a self-consciously international context. Monique Wittig's later work *Across the Acheron* (1989) reinterprets an icon of western culture in Dante's underworld, exploring, as Namjoshi does, ethical issues. Michelle Cliff, Ngahuia Te Awekotuku, Jovette Marchessault, Paula Gunn Allen, and Audre Lorde alter and expand the ways lesbians from all cultures see themselves, as does recent lesbian crime fiction, particularly Gillian Hanscombe's *Figments of a Murder* (1995) and Dorothy Porter's verse novel, *The Monkey's Mask* (1994).

Invention and tradition are central to all art. Within lesbian culture the creation of imaginary histories is an integral part in this process. Virginia Woolf's *Orlando* is a notable precursor to this tradition, which is reflected in Jeannette Winterson's *Art and Lies* (1994). Gertrude Stein too, offered a model for late twentieth-century lesbian writers that can be seen in the short fiction and monologues of Sandra Shotlander.

A. S. Byatt, in *Possession* (1991), following the trail of women's friendships and scholarship, pursues a comparable unearthing, as do actual scholars researching the life of Emily Dickinson and other foremothers. Leonora Carrington, working in a different tradition, creates an imaginary history in her occult novel about old age, *The Hearing Trumpet* (1977). New shapes in fiction are suggested by a shift toward hypertext and virtual cultures within fictional worlds. Both developments can be seen in works such as Suniti Namjoshi's allegorical *Building Babel* (1996) and Finola Moorhead's cyber conspiracy and maze in *Darkness More Visible* (2000).

Contemporary feminist fiction showcases a rich array of traditional motifs as well as new ways of interpreting the strata of women's lives. The twenty-first century promises an extraordinary diversity of women's voices in fiction writing: resisting, reclaiming, and inventing traditions.

See Also

References and Further Readings

Agosin, Marjorie, ed. 1998. *A map of hope: Women's writing on human rights.* New Brunswick, N.J.: Rutgers University Press.

Badran, Margot, and Miriam Cooke, eds. 1990. *Opening the gates: A century of Arab feminist writing.* London: Virago.

Busby, Margaret, ed. 1993. *Daughters of Africa.* London: Vintage.

Christian, Barbara. 1985. *Black feminist criticism: Perspectives on black women writers.* New York: Pergamon, Athene Series.

Garfield, Evelyn Picon, ed. 1988. *Women's fiction from Latin America.* Detroit, Mich.: Wayne State University Press.

Hanscombe, Gillian, and Virginia L. Smyers. 1987. *Writing or their lives: The modernist woman 1910–1940.* London: Women's Press.

Hawthorne, Susan, Cathie Dunsford, and Susan Sayer, eds. 1987. *Car maintenance, explosives and love and other contemporary lesbian writings.* Melbourne: Spinifex.

Hobby, Elaine, and Chris White, eds. 1991. *What lesbians do in books.* London: Women's Press.

Hung, Eva, ed. 1990. *Contemporary women writers: Hong Kong and Taiwan.* Hong Kong: Renditions Paperbacks.

Sistren with Honor Ford Smith, eds. 1987. *Lionheart gal: Life stories of Jamaican women.* Toronto: Sister Vision.

Spender, Dale. 1986. *Mothers of the novel: 100 good women writers before Jane Austen.* London and New York: Pandora.

Thadani, Giti. 1996. *Sakhiyani: Lesbian desire in ancient and modern India.* London: Cassell.

Tharu, Susie, and K. Lalita, eds. 1993. *Women writing in India,* Vol. 1, *The twentieth century.* New York: Feminist Press.

Susan Hawthorne

FILM

Since the beginning of film history, in the late nineteenth century, women have been instrumental in the making of films. They have directed, acted, edited, produced, written, and photographed a diverse collection of work. Women from all over the globe have distinguished themselves in this artistic medium.

In 1896, the very first fictional film *(The Cabbage Fairy)* was made by Alice Guy Blache in France. Blache was a young woman working for Leon Gaumont, who patented a motion picture camera in 1895. Blache's film was one and one-half minutes long and was based on a fairy story. Compared with the street scenes and "slice of life" images that had been the mainstay of film, Blache's work was revelatory. Blache and her husband went on to set up the most professional film studio of the time, in the United States, the Solax Company. This studio became the model of all films studios to follow.

A large number of women participated in the beginnings of the film industry. It was a new and exciting industry that had yet to become exclusively a male domain. There were over 100 female film directors working around the globe during the silent film era (1895–1927). Lois Weber, who began her career as an actress, went on to become the first female American director. From 1911 to 1920, Weber's career progressed so far that she had a five-picture deal with Paramount Studios, and Universal Studios financed her own production unit. She had complete control over her work, and her name, above the studio's, was stamped on it.

With so many women working in the field during this era, it was a golden age for women in film. Some screen actresses in the United States, such as Gloria Swanson and Mary Pickford, also had their own production companies; and some, such as Lillian Gish, directed movies. The industry was far more accepting of this collaborative way of working before the Hollywood studio system became entrenched. In the late twentieth century, actresses in Hollywood again formed their own production companies and branched out into directing. Actresses such as Jodie Foster reestablished the tradition, although they still remain a clear minority.

In the beginnings of the western film industry, movies were made independently, but as the industry became more established and developed, the means of production became increasingly compartmentalized and hierarchical. Movies became big business. From the formation of the MGM studio in 1924, production became extremely controlled. From script development through distribution, the studio had an autocratic hold.

Films have always been extremely expensive to produce, and by housing the means of production in one place, the studios were able to regulate production through economics of scale. As soon as filmmaking became big business— through the development of the studios—the positions of power and control that previously included women became almost exclusively a male domain. Women who had been directing, writing, editing, and producing films now found themselves out of the loop.

Women writers and directors were finding that they could no longer compete making independent films, and they were not getting hired by the male studio executives. They were shuffled into the "feminine" areas of makeup, hair, and wardrobe.

However, there were a few notable exceptions, such as Julia Crawford Ivers, who was the first female general manager of a Hollywood studio (Bosworth) in 1915; and Mary Pickford, who in 1919 joined forces with D. W Griffith, Charlie Chaplin, and Douglas Fairbanks, Sr., to form United Artists. These exceptions took place in the very early days of Hollywood, when the studios were being set up, and before the "factory environment" took over.

The history of women's involvement in the film industry included significant periods when women were denied access to the means of filmmaking. Yet, despite these obstacles, some women, such as Dorothy Arzner, managed to break through the male stranglehold on the industry. Arzner was the only female director working for a studio in the period from 1927 to 1943. In 1936 she was the only woman to become a member of the Directors Guild of America.

Arzner was able to use her influence to give other women an entrée into the industry, and she is credited with giving several stars, including Katharine Hepburn, Lucille Ball, Clara Bow, and Rosalind Russell their first big break in film.

Although women were effectively shut out of the production arena, many women made vital and important contributions to film in postproduction, as editors. Viola Lawrence, who began her career in 1915, is considered the first female film editor. Lawrence was the first editor to work on a studio sound picture, in 1929.

Many well-regarded male film directors of the twentieth century had strong associations with female editors. Alfred Hitchcock's editor was his wife, Alma Reville; Cecil B. de Mille worked with Anne Bauchens; Martin Scorsese worked with Thelma Shoonmaker; and Woody Allen worked with Susan E. Morse.

With the advent of "talkies" (the introduction of sound to films) and the outbreak of World War II during the 1930s and the 1940s, women were able to break into the studio system in greater numbers, particularly as writers. Studio executives needed to have good dialogue writers on board, and so they attempted to attract playwrights and authors to Hollywood. Gender suddenly did not matter quite as much. And because the war took a significant percentage of men away from their jobs, women were needed to fill the gap.

The writer Dorothy Parker was seduced away from New York to write for Hollywood. Among the scripts she penned was *A Star Is Born*. The Writer's Guild had its first female president, Mary McCall, Jr., in 1942.

During the 1930s and 1940s, melodramas, or "women's films," had their heyday. These were films that had a female protagonist and dealt with social issues. This was another golden age for women in film, and for the studios. At this time, Edith Head became the first woman to run a studio design department. During her long career, Head was nominated for 34 Academy Awards, more than any other artist in the history of film.

At this time, one of the most revered and reviled women filmmakers of all time was working in Germany. Leni Riefenstahl began her career as an actress and gradually moved into directing. Her first film, *The Blue Light,* drew the attention of Adolf Hitler, who subsequently commissioned her to film the Nuremberg Rally in 1934. *Triumph of the Will* was the result. Despite its subject matter, it is considered the most powerful propaganda film ever made. Riefenstahl went on to make *Olympia,* about the Olympic Games in Berlin in 1936. Many consider this to be one of the greatest films ever made. Riefenstahl pioneered new uses of the camera, inventing moving shots and many other innovations, which allowed her to capture the human form in a way no one did before, or since. After the defeat of the Nazis, Riefenstahl ceased to make films.

The popularity of "women's films" began to decline by the 1950s, and with the end of the war in 1945, a new phase in film production had begun. Men regained their jobs as writers and directors, and women were encouraged to go back home and leave the workplace open for the men. With the exception of the director Ida Lupino, there were very few women working in positions other than on camera. Lupino was the only female director to work in the Hollywood studio system from 1949 to 1966.

In France, however, one director was pioneering an entirely new style of cinema. Agnès Varda directed commercial feature films from World War II through the 1960s and was known as the "mother of the new wave." The "new wave" was a film movement typified by the work of such figures as François Truffaut, Jean-Luc Godard, Claude Chabrol, and Varda.

In Russia, two women were writing, directing, and acting in films. Vera Chytilova directed *Villa in the Suburbs* in 1959, and Larisa Shepitko directed *The Blind Cook* in 1956. Shepitko's film *Farewell* was made in 1983.

The 1950s also brought the introduction of television. This medium was seen as the greatest threat to films, but for a long time it was considered inferior to film production. It also was a male-dominated industry, although some actresses created and produced their own shows, as well as starring in them (for example, Lucille Ball).

Feminist film studies arose in the 1960s, alongside the women's movement, and researchers began to explore women's involvement in the production of films. Cultural studies about the meaning of women's films and women's representations in films have been another area of research since the 1960s.

It was not until the 1980s that women began to gain a foothold in executive positions within Hollywood studios. In the 1990s, women worked in increasing numbers as writer-directors and producers. The percentage of films written, directed, or produced by women is still far less than that produced by men, however. Organizations such as Women in Film (United States) and Women in Film and Television (Australia) have been established to monitor statistics and to actively encourage the employment of women in the film industry. There are many female directors from all over the globe whose films have succeeded at the box office and with the critics. The Indian writer-directors Deepa Mehta (*Fire,* 1996; and *Earth,* 1998) and Mira Nair (*Salaam Bombay!* 1988; *Mississippi Masala,* 1991; and *Karma Sutra: A Tale of Love,* 1996) have achieved international success, and have also created controversy. The Chinese actress-writer-director-producer Joan Chen, who attended the prominent Shanghai Film Academy, has appeared in a numerous films both in China and in the West. In Hong Kong, Ann Hui has been working as a director and producer since the 1970s. In Japan, the filmmaker Naomi Kawasi wrote and directed *Suzaku* in 1997.

From art house directors such as Jane Campion *(The Piano),* to the popular director Penelope Spheeris *(Wayne's World),* women directors, writers, and producers across the globe have distinguished themselves. The statistics remain heavily male-dominated, but considering the breakthroughs that have been made by women in film in recent times, and the increasing number of women who are studying at film schools around the globe, those figures could soon become more equal.

See Also

FILM CRITICISM; FILM THEORY; FILM: LESBIAN; PHOTOGRAPHY

References and Further Reading

Acker, Ally. 1991. *Reel women: Pioneers of the cinema, 1896 to the present.* New York: Continuum.

Cook, Pam, and Philip Dodd. 1993. *Women and film: A sight and sound reader.* Philadelphia, Pa.: Temple University Press.

Kuhn, Annette, with Susannah Radstone. 1990. *The women's companion to international film.* Berkeley and Los Angeles: University of California Press.

Seger, Linda. 1996. *When women call the shots.* New York: Holt.

Web Sites

Annotated bibliography of feminist aesthetics in the literary, performing, and visual arts, 1970–1990. Compiled by Linda Krumholz and Estella Lauter: <www.inform.umd.edu>

Selected women's studies bibliographies published in periodicals 1989–1992: <www.inform.umd.edu>

Women Film Pioneers Project Duke University: <http://www.duke.edu/web/film/pioneers.html>

Women in cinema: A reference guide. Compiled by Philip McEldowney: <http://www.people.virginia.edu/~pm9k/libsci/womFilm.html>

Sarah Neal

FILM CRITICISM

Film criticism is the analysis and study of film that goes beyond mere review. Film criticism deconstructs the entire cinematic apparatus, from the making of films to questions about audiences and spectators. At the heart of film criticism is a quest to understand the meanings created by film as a medium of cultural production and representation. Film criticism is used by critical theorists in areas such as film theory, feminist theory, cultural studies, black studies, and postcolonial discourses.

The Practice of Film Criticism

Central to the tasks of film criticism are questions about the meanings that are consciously and unconsciously reproduced and represented in film; the language of film and its symbolic significance; the constructions of film; who is included as subject or spectator and who is excluded and why; and what dominant cultural representations are being reproduced or challenged. Film criticism can also be seen as a tool that allows different interpretations of film and film discourse which then, for example, allow for negotiated readings (Doane, 1990; Hall, 1988; Stacey, 1992).

Questions are the basis of film criticism as a theoretical pursuit. For this reason film criticism has particular appeal to those who apply critical analyses of society. Film criticism can, therefore, be used as a political tool and as a form of resistance to the dominant production and reception of film. In this latter case film criticism deconstructs film in order to challenge conscious and unconscious social constructions, for example, those based on gender, race, sexuality, and

nationality. It can be seen as part of the cultural politics that Stuart Hall argued must "challenge, resist and, where possible,... transform the dominant regimes of representation" (1988: 27). Implicit in this argument is an understanding that film criticism is an integral part of counterhegemonic cultural production (hooks, 1991) that empowers those involved in film production as well as spectators, and offers a critical resistance to the culture of dominant film production. Film criticism then becomes a theory that allows for the questioning of cinematic discourse.

Feminism and Film Criticism

Feminist film criticism questions not only the gendered nature of dominant film and film production but also the gendered nature of spectatorship. At its center are questions not only about what films portray, but also about what the basis is for such portrayal. In particular it asks about the place of women in film production, as writers, directors, producers, and so on, and the place of women as spectators. An important issue is the way that female subjects and spectators are treated. One of the earliest arguments offered by feminist film criticism, put forward in "Visual Pleasure and Narrative Cinema" (Mulvey, 1992), is that film puts men and their pleasures in a privileged position; the "visual pleasure" that film offers is created for the male gaze. Using psychoanalytic theory, Mulvey argued that film

> reflects, reveals and even plays on straight, socially established interpretations of sexual difference which controls images, erotic ways of looking and spectacle.... Psychoanalytic theory is thus appropriated... as a political weapon, demonstrating the way the unconscious of patriarchal society has structured film. (1992: 22)

This argument, however, does not address the nature of female subjectivity. For example, can all women, regardless of class, race, sexuality, and other categories, be treated as autonomous psychological subjects? Are all women excluded equally from the visual pleasure of film? Some feminist critics have considered this. A number of lesbian film critics, for example, argue that women's pleasure can be derived either from the homoerotic pleasure of looking at other women (Stacey, 1992) or through a perspective shift—or masculinization—by female spectators that allows women to see film "as men" (Doane, 1990).

Stacey offers a more flexible way of analyzing film that takes into account not only the idea that "film text can be read and enjoyed from different gendered positions," but also that "women's pleasure in narrative cinema [is] based on different processes of spectatorship, according to sexual difference" (1992).

Feminist film criticism, however, has tended to focus on sexual difference in cinematic discourse at the expense of class, racial, and other differences (Gaines, 1990: 98). Black and postcolonial film criticism, on the other hand, asserts that since the dominant global cinematic apparatus is white and western, white western women are better able to see film "as men," since the visual pleasure of dominant film is for a white (male) spectator. Those who are considered "others" not only because of their gender but also because of race, color, nationality, and so on, have to transcend more boundaries to consume film. bell hooks (1991), for example, argues for film criticism to become a theory that both questions cinematic discourse and is part of an oppositional politics of counterhegemonic cultural production that offers a critical resistance to dominant film. Black film criticism, therefore, emphasizes the need to position film criticism within a historical and contemporary context, which also requires an explicit analysis of racial difference in film discourse (Reid, 1993).

In conclusion, film criticism as critical theory investigates cinematic discourse. This not only means that cinematic discourse is transformed by it, but also holds out a promise of emancipating filmmakers and their audiences.

See Also

FILM: LESBIAN; FILM THEORY

References and Further Reading

Doane, Mary Ann. 1990. Film and the masquerade: Theorizing the female spectator. In Patricia Erens, ed., *Issues in feminist film criticism*. Bloomington: Indiana University Press.

Gaines, Jane. 1990. White privilege and looking relations: Race and gender in feminist film theory. In Patricia Erens, ed. *Issues in feminist film criticism*. Bloomington: Indiana University Press.

Hall, Stuart. 1988. New ethnicities. In ICA Documents 7, *Black Film British Cinema*. London: Institute of Contemporary Arts/BFI.

hooks, bell. 1991. *Yearning: Race, gender, and cultural politics*. London: Turnaround.

Mulvey, Laura. 1992. Visual pleasure and narrative cinema. In *The sexual subject: A screen reader in sexuality*. London: Routledge.

Reid, Mark A. 1993. *Redefining black film*. Berkeley: University of California Press.

Stacey, Jackie. 1992. Desperately seeking difference. In Screen, ed., *The sexual subject: A screen reader in sexuality*. London: Routledge.

Felly Nkweto Simmonds

FILM: Lesbian

What is "lesbian film"? Is a film "lesbian" if it is about lesbians, is made by lesbians, features lesbian actresses, or is intended for lesbian audiences? The relationship between lesbians and film is complex, as such questions suggest. Understanding this complexity is important for feminists, because cinema is so influential. For millions of people, from the most privileged to some of the most deprived, film is both a treasured fantasy, offering momentary escape from daily life, and a significant influence on the way they perceive the world. Politically, it is important that we understand the relationship between lesbians and film because, in almost every part of the world, lesbians face hostility and discrimination. The way in which lesbians are represented in film can either contribute to this hostility or challenge it. Psychologically, it is important to understand the relationship because film, in common with other mass media, is overwhelmingly heterosexist; it generally presents heterosexuality as the norm and assumes it to be right and proper. It is psychologically damaging for lesbians to see distorted reflections of themselves on the cinema screen, as it is for other marginalized groups.

Film Studies

Film studies also tend to be heterosexist. Psychoanalytic theories of film developed by writers such as Laura Mulvey (1975) assume that the pleasure of watching film is structured around heterosexual dynamics. The "gaze" of the spectator is gendered masculine, and the object of that gaze is gendered feminine. Such theories fail to recognize that men may look with desire on other men or (importantly) that women may look with desire on other women. A lesbian looking at a woman on the cinema screen may both desire her and identify with her, thus occupying both subject-position and object-position at the same time. This "lesbian gaze" tends to destabilize the assumptions on which psychoanalytic film theories are founded (Wilton, 1995). A recognition of lesbian desire thus adds an important new element to film studies.

Films about Lesbians

Until very recently the film industry has been as male-dominated as any other. Most films about lesbians have therefore been made by men and reflect dominant patriarchal ideas about lesbianism. Such films—for example, *The Children's Hour* (U.S., 1961) and *The Killing of Sister George* (U.S., 1968)—typically depict lesbians as unhappy, destructive, and pathological. The lesbian characters generally meet an unhappy end: suicides abound, relationships founder, and "conversion" to heterosexuality is common. It is not hard to imagine the destructive effect of all this on lesbian spectators. The liberalization of social attitudes toward lesbians in western industrialized nations is reflected in mainstream films such as *Personal Best* (U.S., 1982) *Lianna* (U.S., 1983), and *Bound* (U.S., 1997). However, although they are less melodramatic, such films generally continue to represent lesbianism as flawed and inadequate. For example, the lesbian affair in *Personal Best* founders when one of the women falls in love with a man.

If Hollywood has produced distorted representations of lesbians, other filmmaking traditions have, if anything, excluded lesbians still more determinedly. Until very recently, the substantial film industries of Europe, Japan, and India, with the exception of a few films in the European art-house genre, ignored lesbians entirely.

Films by Lesbians

The handful of lesbians working in the cinema since its earliest days were seldom able to be "out" in their professional lives and rarely touched on explicitly lesbian subject matter in their films. The struggles of the "second wave" of the women's movement and of the lesbian and gay liberation movement have begun to change this.

The film that led the way in its treatment of a lesbian story was Donna Deitch's *Desert Hearts* (U.S., 1985), based on the lesbian writer Jane Rule's novel *Desert of the Heart*. This was the first commercially released lesbian romance film to provide a happy ending and was enormously popular with English-speaking lesbian audiences. Yet it took Deitch four years to raise money for the film by collecting small amounts from sympathetic individuals. Many commentators (Howes, 1993; Stacey, 1995), have noted, with surprise, that *Desert Hearts* has not been followed by other mainstream lesbian romances. However, the advent of the new queer cinema, although dominated by gay men (Rich, 1992), heralded an increase in independent lesbian film and video production, and independent lesbian-made feature-length films such as *Go Fish* (U.S., 1994), although generally released on the art cinema circuit rather than in the mainstream commercial cinema chains, are more accessible to lesbian audiences than ever before. An important feature of the new wave of independent lesbian-made film and video is that for the first time, filmmakers such as Pratibha Parmar, Michelle Parkerson, and Cheryl Dunye are producing work from a black lesbian perspective.

The growth of international lesbian and gay film festivals and of video technology has been important for lesbian film. Making a feature-length film requires enormous material resources that are simply beyond the reach of most lesbians, especially those from disadvantaged or minority communities. Video is a relatively cheap and accessible technology, and many lesbians are producing innovative work in this medium, ranging from the most basic watch-and-wipe magazine format, such as the British video-mag *Pout*, to sophisticated experimental pieces. Some works have been funded by institutions such as the British Film Institute and Channel 4 television (in the United Kingdom) or the National Endowment for the Arts (in the United States), although the resurgence of the political and religious right in many western nations means that such funding is increasingly vulnerable. Moreover, it remains extremely difficult for lesbians in most third world countries to gain access to film or video of any kind written by lesbians.

"Race," Colonialism, and Lesbian Film

In the wake of colonialism, black sexuality has often been exploited by white filmmakers, who represent it as exotic, uncontained, and perverse. As Michelle Parkerson comments, "The litany of black gay and lesbian characters in Hollywood films and network television reads like its own form of blackface" (in Gever et al., 1993). White lesbian and gay filmmakers may also racially exploit black lesbian and gay characters. And the very notion "a lesbian" or "a gay man" that exists in western industrial nations is specific to those cultures; there may be no counterpart in other cultures, or there may be other social roles—such as the hijras in Hindu India or the kotoi in Thailand—that, although they may be adopted by people who would be called lesbian or gay in the West, are in fact very different. Sunil Gupta writes, "*Gay* is a word that does not appear to exist in the vernacular languages of India" (in Gever et al., 1993). To speak about third world "lesbian film" is to impose western language and concepts in what may be an inappropriate context, and third world lesbians are increasingly speaking for themselves in film and video.

Questions for Lesbian Film

Lesbian film in the West is often a subject of debate and contention in lesbian communities. For example, does filming lesbian sex constitute pornography or the assertion and celebration of autonomous lesbian sexuality? Sheila McLaughlin's brilliant *She Must Be Seeing Things* (U.S., 1987) caused furious debate over this question.

Some lesbian filmmakers suggest that, since mainstream cinema is structured around heterosexuality, lesbian film should break away from such traditional structures. Lesbian filmmakers such as Barbara Hammer, Jan Oxenburg, Cheryl Dunye, and Clara Van Gool have experimented with alternatives to "straight" (in both senses of the word) narrative structures, producing work that does not conform to standard cinematic conventions. The problem with such innovative work is that, since most lesbians are comfortable with familiar cinematic structures, experimental work is all too often dismissed as elitist or exclusive. There is no obvious resolution to this conflict.

One more problem for lesbian film is its scarcity. Because lesbian audiences are so starved of films that reflect lesbian realities, there is a demand that every lesbian film will accurately represent the experience of every lesbian who watches it. Clearly, such representativeness is an unrealistic demand, but it is one that will fade as lesbian film proliferates and accurate reflections of lesbian life become commonplace in the cinema.

See Also

FILM; FILM CRITICISM; FILM THEORY

References and Further Reading

Bad Object-Choices, eds. 1991. *How do I look? Queer film and video.* Seattle, Wash.: Bay.

Dyer, Richard. 1990. *Now you see it: Studies on lesbian and gay film.* London: Routledge.

Gever, Martha, John Greyson, and Pratibha Parmar, eds. 1993. *Queer looks: Perspectives on lesbian and gay film and video.* London: Routledge. See the following articles: Sunil Gupta's Indian Postcard, or Why I make work in a racist, homophobic society (340–347); Kobena Mercer's Dark and lovely too: Black gay men in independent film (238–256); Michelle Parkerson's Birth of a nation: Towards black gay and lesbian imagery in film and video (234–237).

Hadleigh, Boze. 1993. *The lavender screen: The gay and lesbian films: Their stars, makers, characters, and critics.* New York: Citadel.

Howes, Keith. 1993. *Broadcasting it: An encyclopedia of homosexuality on film, radio, and TV in the U.K. 1923–1993.* London: Cassell.

Mulvey, Laura. 1975. Visual pleasure and narrative cinema. *Screen* (3: Autumn): 6–18.

Rich, B. Ruby. 1992. New queer cinema. *Sight and Sound* (September): 31–34.

Russo, Vito. 1981. *The celluloid closet: Homosexuality in the movies.* New York: Harper and Row.

Weiss, Andrea. 1992. *Vampires and violets: Lesbians in the cinema.* London: Jonathan Cape.

Wilton, Tamsin, ed. 1995. *Immortal, invisible: Lesbians and the moving image.* London: Routledge. See Jackie Stacy's If you don't play, you can't win: *Desert Hearts* and the lesbian romance film (92–114).

Tamsin Wilton

FILM THEORY

The aim of *film theory* is to explain how the visual and audial elements of film create meanings for viewers, and to what aesthetic, psychological, and sociopolitical effects. Although film theory is different from *film criticism* (which attempts to interpret individual movies, often as an audience guide), these two approaches to film have extensively cross-fertilized in some periods and publications. Contemporary film theorists practicing "cultural studies" methods, such as Richard Dyer (United Kingdom), Barbara Klinger (United States), and Rosie Thomas (India), often examine popular movie criticism as a facet of their analysis. And theories about cinema's workings have helped shape film criticism and also some aspects of production, particularly through the work of critics and moviemakers who have attended film schools.

Feminist film theory, criticism, and production, all of which flowered with second-wave feminist movements, have developed as sometimes overlapping, sometimes oppositional practices and perspectives on the analysis of gender difference.

An overview of early and contemporary film theory provides a context for understanding key issues in feminist film theory, which emerged in the early 1970s in western Europe and North America. Central tenets of feminist film theory have gradually entered popular media criticism, and also have influenced the study of art and art history, literature, and theater.

Film Theory from Its Beginnings to the Early 1970s

Film theory originated by about 1910 in philosophical and sociological discussions of moving pictures, particularly in France and Germany, and a decade later in the Soviet Union. Film historians have begun researching these earliest film analyses as an "archaeological project" (Abel, 1988; Hake, 1993). Film theory in the United States is often dated to a book by the Harvard philosopher and psychologist Hugo Munsterberg published in 1916.

Film theorists have mostly analyzed fictional feature movies. Since the 1920s, many theorists have taken the works of a single director or national movement (such as Sergei Eisenstein on D. W. Griffith, Siegfried Kracauer on Weimar film dramas, and Gaylyn Studlar on Josef von Sternberg and Marlene Dietrich) as exemplars of cinematic workings. The feminist film theorists Claire Johnston, Pam Cook, Annette Kuhn, and Judith Mayne have explored "auteurist" concepts (a theoretical approach of the 1960s and 1970s appraising thematic similarities in the work of some directors) in relation to gender issues.

Pioneering film theorists have proposed models for understanding specific genres, such as the gangster film, the melodrama, the western, the musical, film and TV comedy, pornography, and the horror movie. Other media scholars have also addressed documentary work and avant-garde films. Recent film theory analyzes the incidence and impact of combined documentary, experimental, and conventional fictional modes of representation.

In North America and much of Europe, *film theory* refers to a discrete set of analytical approaches to cinema that arose in the 1960s and 1970s, initially in France. Via scholarly exchange and translation, these approaches soon came into discussion in Great Britain, the United States, and Canada. The U.S. film scholar Kaja Silverman has described ensuing developments as a "potent synthesis" of feminist, semiotic, Marxist, and psychoanalytic perspectives that focused on how films engage viewers through their "spectatorship" and influence their self-perceptions, their "subjectivity" (foreward to Burnett, 1991).

An important film theorist is Christian Metz, who posited that movies communicate meanings in part through systematic sequences of images, which create a visual language. Metz combined his work in this vein—a "semiotic" approach—with an original psychoanalytic approach, to argue that a film projected in a dark theater may evoke for viewers a sense of infantile pleasures such as feeling securely connected to their mother. Other influential French film theorists of the 1960s and 1970s include Jean-Louis Baudry, Jean-Louis Comolli, and other contributors to the film journal *Cahiers du Cinéma* based in Paris.

These analysts drew on the writings of the French psychoanalyst Jacques Lacan and the political philosopher Louis Althusser to examine how films appealed to viewers' desires to escape mundane social reality. This was a change from "realist" theories, which constituted the bulk of film theory at that time. Instead of being seen as analogous to a "window on the world," cinema resembled a dream or a mirror, through which viewers could momentarily experience powerful childhood fantasies.

The most provocative theoretical works of this period combined semiotic, psychoanalytic, and materialist approaches to analyze the historical impact of films or to explore how the "cinematic apparatus" (the combined technologies in the production and consumption of film) engages and holds spectators' attention.

Feminist Film Theory

In 1973 British feminist film scholars like Johnston, Laura Mulvey, Christine Gledhill, Kuhn, and E. Ann Kaplan began examining new ideas from the French theorists, primarily through the British journal *Screen*. Mulvey's essay "Visual Pleasure and Narrative Cinema" (1975) significantly revised Metz's psychoanalytic approach by arguing that movies predominantly situate men as active central characters and use mostly passive and idealized female figures only to invoke male viewers' fantasies. Mulvey maintained that Hollywood cinema perpetuates patriarchal social structures and exhorted female filmgoers to reject the self-negating pleasures it offers, and to seek instead alternative cinema techniques that make audiences aware of their construction as illusion.

The enduring interest of Mulvey's groundbreaking essay lies in its effectively requiring film theorists to address gender difference. Especially influential is Mulvey's succinct analysis of three cinematic "looks": the camera's (filming), the audience's (watching), and the characters' (at each other). Filmic conventions usually efface the first two looks and engage the spectator, positioned as a voyeur, through the third look, a (usually male) character's perspective.

Silverman's summary of feminist film theory (1988) highlighted two concepts: subjectivity and spectatorship. Most discussions of subjectivity draw on psychoanalytic theory. "Spectatorship" has attracted debate regarding gender, race, and class differences in viewers' perceptions. B. Ruby Rich and Julia Lesage were among the first to question Lacanian theory as a model accounting for women's experiences. Mayne, Teresa de Lauretis, and Chris Straayer argued that lesbian spectators offer a challenge to dominant theories, by eluding conventional gender presumptions. Among those who treat racial difference as a factor in spectatorship are Andrea Stuart, Jacqueline Bobo, bell hooks, and Michele Wallace.

Ongoing Controversies

A rough division has developed between two tendencies: to focus on a film's power over the viewer or to attribute a given film's impact to viewers' diverse responses, due to their differing social positioning and personal experiences. Most feminist theorists through the late 1980s took the former approach; feminist-inflected cultural studies have influenced the latter trend in film theory and recently contributed to the emergence of "theorized film history," in which scholars such as Janet Staiger, Heide Schlüpmann, Kuhn, and Thomas Elsaesser are leading practitioners.

Fundamentally at issue in contemporary feminist debates about the media are the potential dangers and pleasures of popular culture, as well as women's roles in media, both in front of and behind the camera and as critics and consumers. Assessments of these issues remain contested, as do their implications for personal or collective political action; varying feminist stances regarding film pornography are one case in point.

A further point of contention concerns the connections between political and academic feminist media theory. This issue crystallized in the United States with the founding, in 1974, of *Camera Obscura,* a journal spin-off of the first explicitly feminist film publication *Women and Film,* which brought out seven issues in its two-year existence. Both publications offered detailed analyses of films, but the editors of *Camera Obscura* applied psychoanalytic theory and explicitly dismissed a perspective which comparatively catalogues various "images of women" over a range of films, thereby treating representations as real and ignoring how filmic techniques constructed and deployed a particular image across a film. Changes in format and style around 1982 in the West German feminist journal *Frauen und Film* (also founded in 1974) marked a similar shift in theoretical emphases. Editors' professional and political aims—to legitimate feminist film theory as a career, contrasted with a commitment to film production, and intelligent analysis as an accessible practice—also played a role in these developments.

Over the last decade many U.S. and British feminist film theorists have attempted to write for broader audiences and to incorporate into their analyses consideration of women's film practices outside Europe and North America. Feminist scholars have introduced "postcolonialist" approaches to film theory by explicitly addressing the potential of films (also influential documentaries) and television to rectify or exacerbate the effects of racism and sexism on previously colonized societies. Among scholars who have written books or edited anthologies that take these approaches are Trinh T. Minh-ha, Elia Shohat, Robert Stam, Fatimah Tobing-Rony, Ana Maria López, and Purnima Mankekar.

Feminist methodologies have profoundly influenced long-established perspectives on film such as genre theory (which now usually addresses gender representation and class issues in relation to conventional film styles and types), although they have had impact on other traditional approaches such as the formalist (analyzing how cinematic forms of storytelling create an illusion of time and space) and the phenomenological (exploring how an audience perceives film images and sounds in relation to other lived experiences).

Some media scholars who reject psychoanalytic theory are reviving empirical or cognitive psychological approaches that focus on how audiences make sense of films and respond to particular cinematic effects such as suspense. While such revisions may offer paths around intellectual impasses in psychoanalytic film theory, the empiricist response has arguably arisen in part as a backlash against feminism and the professional influence of many feminist film theorists. However, most strands of film theory now either explicitly incorporate fundamental feminist theoretical precepts or implicitly consider gender a crucial factor in the analysis of cinema and its audiences.

See Also

CRITICAL AND CULTURAL THEORY; CULTURAL STUDIES; FILM CRITICISM; FILM: LESBIAN; FILM; GAZE; PSYCHOANALYSIS

References and Further Reading

Abel, Richard. 1988. *French film theory and criticism: 1907–1939.* Princeton, N.J.: Princeton University Press.

Burnett, Ron, ed. 1991. *Explorations in film theory: Selected essays from Cine-Tracts.* Bloomington: Indiana University Press.

Curry, Ramona. 1993. "Frauen und Film—Then and now," in Sandra Frieden, Rick McCormick, Vibeke Petersen, and Melissa Vogelsang, eds., *Gender and German cinema: Feminist interventions.* Providence, R.I., and Oxford: Berg.

de Lauretis, Teresa, and Stephen Heath, eds. 1978. *The cinematic apparatus.* New York: St. Martin's.

Dyer, Richard. 1977. Entertainment and utopia. *Movie* 24.

———. 1992. *Only entertainment*. London: Routledge.

Gledhill, Christine. 1988. Pleasurable negotiations. In E. Deirde Pribham, ed., *Female spectators: Looking at film and television*, 64–79, London: Verso.

Hake, Sabine. 1993. *The cinema's third machine: Writing on film in Germany, 1907–1933*. Lincoln: University of Nebraska Press.

hooks, bell. 1996. *Reel to real : Race, sex, and class at the movies*. New York: Routledge.

Mankekar, Purnima. 1999. *Screening culture, viewing politics: An ethnography of television, womanhood, and nation in postcolonial India*. Durham, N.C.: Duke University Press.

Mayne, Judith. 1993. *Cinema and spectatorship*. London: Routledge.

Mulvey, Laura. 1975. Visual pleasure and narrative cinema. *Screen* 16 (3).

Rony, Fatimah Tobing. 1996. *The third eye: race, cinema. and ethnographic spectacle*. Durham, N.C.: Duke University Press.

Screen editors. 1992. *The sexual subject: A Screen reader in sexuality*. London: Routledge.

Shohat, Ella, and Robert Stam. 1994. *Unthinking Eurocentrism, multiculturalism, and the media*. London: Routledge.

Silverman, Kaja. 1988. *The acoustic mirror: The female voice in psychoanalysis and cinema*. Bloomington: Indiana University Press.

Thomas, Rosie, and Behroze Gandhy. 1991. Three Indian film stars. In Christine Gledhill, ed., *Stardom: Industry of desire*, 107–131. London: Routledge.

Ramona Curry

FINANCE

The term *finance* is used in economics to cover the workings of the savings, credit, and capital markets. Women undertake transactions in financial markets when they make or accept deposits, provide or apply for personal and business loans, purchase shares, and invest in long-term savings options. This article focuses on the various ways in which women engage in financial market activity and examines the barriers women may encounter when attempting to gain access to funds in credit markets.

Markets and Intermediaries

Women's financial market activity centers on the saving, borrowing, and lending of money. Women apply for credit in order to fulfill consumption and investment plans in the present that may not be otherwise achievable given their current income and wealth. Lenders and savers are concerned with earning interest income over time, ensuring a safe haven for their wealth, or supporting borrowers to achieve economic advancement. Financial market transactions undertaken either in formal markets regulated or supervised by central banks or in informal markets, and with commercially or noncommercially oriented financial intermediaries. A financial intermediary is any institution (such as a bank or credit union) or individual (a moneylender) that accepts deposits from savers and provides credit to borrowers.

Marguerite Berger (1989) argues that women may face barriers to gaining access to funds from commercially oriented financial intermediaries in formal financial markets and may therefore seek funds in the informal credit market, establish their own financial networks, or use financial intermediaries in the formal credit market who are supportive of women. Examples of financial intermediaries owned and run by women and focusing entirely on lending to women include the Self-Employed Women's Association (SEWA) and the Working Women's Forum (WWF) of India (Egger, 1986; Tendler, 1989). SEWA is a trade union organization that developed a banking arm in 1974 because of the difficulties its members had with existing financial intermediaries. WWF followed a similar route, establishing a Working Women's Credit Society in 1981. In Zimbabwe, rural women have developed an organized network of savings associations run by and for women that provides sources of finance to meet individual or collective capital and social demands. Such networks are also common in other countries and are often linked to larger financial intermediaries or to umbrella nongovernmental organizations (NGOs) such as Women's World Banking, the foundation for International Community Assistance, and Acción International. These organizations act as intermediaries between groups of women and financial institutions in the formal credit market.

Focusing on Poverty

Women have gained from the establishment of financial intermediaries that focus on alleviating poverty. The Grameen Bank of Bangladesh is the best known of these financial intermediaries, providing credit to the very poor and particularly targeting women. After starting operations as a pilot project in 1976, the Grameen Bank had provided loans to more than 2.4 million borrowers by August 1998. More than 90 percent of these members were women. The Grameen Bank provides credit on a group liability basis and without an emphasis on collateral requirements. It has consistently achieved high loan recovery rates (Wahid, 1994). Pitt and Khandker (1998) argue that credit provided to women by the Grameen Bank and similar group-based and micro-credit programs has led to increases in children's school enrollments, women's labor supply and assets holdings, and consumption levels. The success of the Grameen Bank has promoted the development of many other similarly focused financial intermediaries, a recent example being the Women's Development Bank in South Africa.

Barriers to Access

Women may face a range of barriers to accessing funds from commercially oriented financial intermediaries. Barriers to access result either from the interaction of commercial lending criteria with social influences that reduce women's market income or from discriminatory practices in credit markets themselves. Commercial criteria can restrict women's access to credit as a result of the undervaluation of women's work and the spillover effects of discrimination in education and labor markets. Women's unpaid household work, reproductive and caring labor, and voluntary labor are not recognized directly "in the market" in terms of cash payments. A national accounting framework that discounts the value of women's work underpins and finds its counterpart in commercial lending policies that discount the value of women's "full income" (Waring, 1988).

Women who are discriminated against in terms of educational opportunities or in labor markets are more likely to face difficulties in applying for credit in the formal market, more likely to have broken employment records, and more likely to receive lower wages than men with similar educational qualifications and labor market experience. Broken employment records and low income reduce creditworthiness and the maximum loan value a financial intermediary will offer.

Access problems also occur in the area of savings. For example, one concern in Australia in recent years has been an increasing emphasis on occupational superannuation—as opposed to state-provided pensions—as a means of funding retirement incomes. If women spend more time outside the formal labor market and receive lower wages when in it, then employee and employer superannuation contributions will be lower for women than men. The consequence is that women will have smaller long-term savings funds to draw on in retirement. Moreover, they will not have benefited from the tax concessions that have applied to superannuation contributions.

Direct and Indirect Discrimination

Direct discrimination in financial markets occurs when gender, marital position, and childbearing status are explicitly incorporated in deposit and lending guidelines (blatant discrimination) or when women are consciously treated differently from men in the processes of decision making. Blatant discrimination in the mortgage market arises when lending guidelines specify that women's cash incomes are to be discounted in determining household income for loan purposes or when loan fees are raised as a result of gender-specific characteristics. Indirect discrimination results not from the targeting of gender-specific characteristics but because general rules are applied that adversely affect women more than men. If, for example, government benefits and child support income are excluded from eligible income for purposes of loan applications, then sole-parent women in particular will be adversely affected.

The issue of discrimination against women in formal credit markets has been examined in relation both to the availability of business loans and to mortgage finance. Most studies of business loans focus on evidence from surveys of women's perceptions of the loan application process. Women consistently report difficulties in obtaining venture capital and list discriminatory behavior as a major concern. Evidence from controlled experiments in which the experience of men and women in the loan application process can be compared and from the examination of data provides mixed results, possibly reflecting differences between countries in legislation, culture, and politics; differences in sample selection; outdated studies; or nuances in the design of the experimental situation. In one study, Michael Fay and Lesley Williams (1993) adopted correspondence-testing techniques to determine whether women seeking loans to establish business ventures in New Zealand were discriminated against. Applications for loan finance differing only in terms of gender and education level were mailed to banks for examination and approval. For university-educated applicants, women and men had an equal probability of obtaining a business loan, but education was given greater prominence in the case of women. For those with high school qualification, significant bias against women was observed. On the other hand, Baydas et al. (1994), using loan application data and applying econometric techniques, found no evidence of discrimination against women by loan officers in Ecuador.

Despite the increased focus on racial and ethnic discrimination in the mortgage market, particularly in the United States with the availability of comprehensive data from the Home Mortgage Disclosure Act, few studies have examined gender discrimination. Robert Schafer and Helen Ladd (1981), who analyzed lending behavior and appraisal patterns in New York and California in the late 1970s using indirect statistical techniques, did not find strong evidence of lenders discriminating against women or of women's incomes being discounted. Cavalluzzo and Cavalluzzo (1998) report similar findings in regard to lending to small businesses owned by women in the United States.

Targeted Investment

While women's financial market activity is centered on saving and borrowing through banks and other financial intermediaries, women also invest their savings in the share market. One issue that is gaining increasing attention in terms of women and the share market is the question of targeted investments. Some equity funds, including funds managed by women, provide advice on making investments in companies that support women or are women-owned and managed. This allows investors to steer away from firms that have a poor track record in terms of their employment practices with regard to women.

See Also

DISCRIMINATION; POVERTY

References and Further Reading

Baydas, Mayada M., Richard L. Meyer, and Nelson Aguilera-Alfred. 1994. Discrimination against women in formal credit markets: Reality or rhetoric? *World Development* 22(7): 1073–1082.

Berger, Marguerite. 1989. Giving women credit: The strengths and limitations of credit as a tool for alleviating poverty. *World Development* 17(7): 1017–1082.

Cavalluzzo, Ken S., and Linda C. Cavalluzzo. 1998. Market structure and discrimination—The case of small business. *Journal of Money, Credit, and Banking* 30(4): 771–792.

Egger, Philippe. 1986. Banking for the rural poor: Lessons from some innovative savings and credit schemes. *International Labor Review* 125(4): 447–462.

Fay, Michael, and Lesley Williams. 1993. Gender bias and the availability of business loans. *Journal of Business Venturing* 8: 363–376.

Pitt, Mark M., and Shahidur R. Khandker. 1998. The impact of group-based credit programs on poor households in Bangladesh: Does the gender of participants matter? *Journal of Political Economy* 106(5): 958–996.

Schafer, Robert, and Helen F. Ladd. 1981. *Discrimination in mortgage lending.* Cambridge, Mass.: MIT Press.

Tendler, Judith. 1989. Whatever happened to poverty alleviation? *World Development* 17(7): 1033–1044.

Wahid, Abu N. M. 1994. The Grameen Bank and poverty alleviation in Bangladesh: Theory, evidence, and limitations. *American Journal of Economics and Sociology* 53(1): 1–15.

Waring, Marilyn. 1988. *Counting for nothing: What men value and what women are worth.* Wellington, New Zealand: Allen and Unwin.

Jane Harrison

FINE ARTS: Overview

Over the last 30 years of the twentieth century, the art world became increasingly aware of the work of women artists throughout history. Moreover, the interdisciplinarity of contemporary western art history encouraged many art historians to look beyond traditional definitions of fine arts to examine cultural productions and methodological approaches once considered the domain of anthropologists or literary critics. The blurring of disciplines and expanding fields of study have made the work of both artist and art historian challenging in ways never before imagined. Nevertheless, the fact that an essay might focus on the "fine arts" is an indication that conventional boundaries continue to order the way art is evaluated. This article will focus on traditions established in the early modern period, when the notion of fine arts began to be articulated within western philosophical and political systems, systems that continue to exert power and influence over how the visual arts are created and perceived in the West and beyond.

Writing in the second half of the sixteenth century, Giorgio Vasari, an artist and biographer of artists, described the citizens of Bologna as saddened by the death of the sculptor Properzia de' Rossi (c. 1490–1530), because "while she lived they had regarded her as one of the greatest miracles of nature in our times" (1991: 341). The artistic, accomplished, creative woman in the West has often been regarded as a curiosity—or worse. Indeed, in the few pages devoted to women artists from antiquity to his own time (and these few pages in a voluminous work on art from c. 1200 to c. 1550), Vasari writes of the ancient poet Sappho, "if Sappho really was a woman..." (1991: 339).

Vasari continues his comments on Properzia de' Rossi by informing his readers that she was "not only skillful in household duties like other women, but in countless fields of knowledge, so that not only the women but all the men were envious of her" (1991: 340). Vasari's brief commentary on de'Rossi's life and work is introduced with this passage aimed at reassuring his readers that this artist did, indeed, fulfill what his society required of women. He then describes one of de'Rossi's major works for the cathedral of San Petronio, Bologna—a marble relief of Joseph and Potiphar's wife, a story from the Book of Genesis about the love of a woman for a man who failed to return her desires. "This sculpture was deemed most beautiful by everyone, and it gave [the artist] great satisfaction, since with this figure from the Old Testament she felt she had expressed in part her own most burning passion" (1991: 341). Vasari could not forget the romantic and personal aspect of a woman artist's work, and he refers to de'Rossi's own experience of unrequited love. "In the end, the poor enamored girl succeeded in everything except her most unhappy love." (1991: 341)

Vasari's biography of Properzia de'Rossi focuses on themes that have followed women artists as they have been interpreted by male viewers and critics: their extraordinary, even unnatural talent (it is easier to describe them as unnatural than to see them as competitors), the degree to which they conform to contemporary standards of femininity, their works as illustrations of their presumed romantic aspirations, and their ability to work within the unstated but patriarchal system—although this system was never regarded as patriarchal until feminist viewers began looking for the evidence of women artists in history. Earlier in the sixteenth century, in 1520, Albrecht Dürer remarked about a contemporary painter, Susan Hornebout, "It is a great marvel that a woman can do so much." (Chadwick, 1990) Dürer and Vasari were not alone among their contemporaries in holding this attitude toward women artists, or women in general. Indeed, it would be nearly 500 years before women artists would begin to approach the opportunities, recognition, and acceptance their male colleagues had taken for granted for centuries.

In the early modern period, women artists in the West often received their training and developed something of a professional career within their own artistic families as daughters, sisters, or wives of artists. For example, Marietta Robusti (c. 1552–1590), daughter of the Venetian painter Tintoretto, was praised by her contemporaries for her portraits and her contributions to her father's work; there was also the portraitist Lavinia Fontana (1552–1614), daughter of Prospero Fontana, a painter of Bologna, who was highly regarded by her noble Bolognese patrons; and the still-life painter, Maria Sibylla Merian (1647–1717), daughter of the German printer-publisher Matthäus Merian the Elder, and stepdaughter of the still-life painter Jacob Marell. The work produced by these artists, and many other women in similar situations, has been difficult to identify, because contemporaries often accepted their work as productions by the workshop master, and therefore their individual contributions were merged with those of others in the studio. While attributions were sometimes secure during their lives, their ouevre was often taken from them entirely after their death by collectors who found it more advantageous to own a work by a male painter. This occurred after the death of the Dutch genre painter Judith Leyster (1609–1660), wife of the Dutch painter Jan Miense Molenaer. Many of Leyster's portraits and genre paintings were attributed to her contemporary Frans Hals. Moreover, later scholars often refused to recognize the work of the daughter as equal to that of the father, as happened with early assessments of the work of Artemisia Gentileschi (1593–1652), whose representations of violence in paintings depicting Judith decapitating Holofernes were considered too powerful and dramatic for a woman and, hence, were attributed to her father, Orazio Gentileschi, a painter in Rome.

Women artists in the West also came to their profession through their faith as well as their responsibilities within the religious communities in which they were living. Herrad, Abbess of Hohenbourg (c. 1178–c. 1196), is closely associated with an illuminated manuscript, known only in nineteenth-century copies, the *Hortus Deliciarum (Garden of Delights)*, which recounts the biblical story of salvation from the fall of Lucifer to the Last Judgment. The texts were selected by Herrad from earlier writers and combined with images that interpret and reassert the meaning of the words. Herrad states in the preface to this work that she was responsible for the text; her role in the design of the manuscript has not been determined, although scholars believe she must have been closely involved with the imagery and its production. Like Herrad, Suora Plautilla Nelli (1523–1588) entered a religious community as a child. In 1537, Nelli became a member of the convent of Santa Caterina di Siena in Florence, and she was elected prioress by 1568. At the time this Dominican convent was established in the late fifteenth century, the leader of the Dominican community in Florence, Fra Girolamo Savonarola, urged religious women to dedicate themselves to painting and sculpture as a way to sustain their community and to encourage charitable gifts. The young Plautilla entered an environment in which she was expected to contribute according to her talents. Among her works is a monumental frescoed *Last Supper* for the refectory of her convent, which suggests the artist's knowledge of earlier representations of this significant theme, including Leonardo da Vinci's fresco of c. 1495–1498 in Milan. Nelli produced other works for her community, including large altarpieces, in which she placed

Dominican nuns as if to identify the work with her community, as well as paintings that were sold to the public.

Secular women artists in the early modern period excelled in portraiture and still-life painting, in part because limitations were placed on what women artists could represent. Women were excluded from studios and classrooms where the male nude was the subject of study, so it was nearly impossible for them to succeed in the celebrated genre of history painting that had as its focus the grand achievements of ancient and contemporary male heroes. Without the opportunity to study the male nude, early modern women turned to their own domestic surroundings, as in the early portraits of her own family by Sofonisba Anguissola (c. 1532–1625), innovative in their representation of intimacy and the personality of her subjects. Women also looked to their own bodies as a source for study, as in the heroines of the Hebrew Bible painted by Artemisia Gentileschi (1593–1652). Clara Peters (active 1611–1621), Maria Sibylla Merian (1647–1717), and Rachel Ruysch (1664–1750) were women painters of northern Europe whose significant contributions to the art of still-life painting were critical to the development of this new genre. Portraiture and still-life painting were considered imitative of nature and, therefore, not requiring the genius of a creative, imaginative, and male artist. It was, no doubt, out of necessity that women turned to these subjects. Within religious communities, however, portrait and still-life painting were probably considered less appropriate subjects for women artists because of their focus on physical reality over spiritual learning. Moreover, religious communities needed representations of religious narratives and figures; women artists within these communities, therefore, probably had greater opportunities to express their artistic talents.

In his *Book of the Courtier* (1528), Baldassare Castiglione urged families to offer instruction in painting and music to daughters because of the value of these endeavors. It is surprising, however, to discover that any noblewomen would make a professional career as an artist. Sofonisba Anguissola, of a minor noble northern Italian family, is one of these exceptions. Approximately 50 works, mostly portraits, have been attributed to Anguissola. Some of these were attributed to other artists after her death, including Titian—this is an indication that her paintings were considered of high quality; but, again, there attribution point up the resistance of collectors and writers to the possibility that a woman could paint such work. Anguissola's fame as a portraitist was so great that she was invited to join the court of Philip II, the Hapsburg king of Spain, in 1559; she became lady-in-waiting to Queen Isabella and tutor to the Infanta Isabella Clara Eugenia. As court painter, she was responsible for making portraits of the royal family.

Women artists continued to work at European courts and were influential in establishing professional environments for the education of young artists. The neoclassical painter Angelica Kauffman (1741–1807), daughter and wife of artists, spent several years in Italy, which brought her fame and election to the prestigious art academies in Bologna and Florence. Kauffman arrived in England in 1766 in search of patronage for her portraits and history paintings and was well received by such influential individuals as Sir Joshua Reynolds. In 1768, Kauffman joined other artists to establish the Royal Academy of Arts. Portraits of Kauffman and Mary Moser, the only other female member of this elite society, are shown in a painting by Johann Zoffany, *The Academicians of the Royal Academy* (1771–1772); the presence of these women artists is marked by portraits because the focus of the academicians is on the nude male model at the center of the work, the study of which was central to the Academy's teaching, but the viewing of which remained problematic for women artists in the minds of male viewers. Elisabeth Vigée-Lebrun (1755–1842), daughter of a painter and wife of a painter and art dealer, became the favorite artist of Marie-Antoinette. Vigée-Lebrun's secured her postion at court with her portrait of the queen (Vienna, Kunsthistorisches Museum, c. 1779), although the French Academy continued to place obstacles to her membership; she was finally elected as member in 1783. Her alliance with the queen brought the artist under the scrutiny of French revolutionaries, and she spent the years 1789 to 1801 in exile. In 1801, however, over 250 artists petitioned the government to allow her to return to France, an indication of the respect and honor finally given to her by her colleagues. One result of the French Revolution was the opening of the French Academy to many new artists, and this included an increase in the number of women receiving artistic training as well as exhibiting at the annual salon throughout the nineteenth century. Among them were Marguérite Gérard (1761–1837) and Constance Mayer (1775–1821), both who continued to be portraitists and painters of domestic scenes.

In spite of a certain, although limited, institutional support for women artists in the nineteenth century, many of these women were better known during their lives and well into the twentieth century as models and muses to their more celebrated male peers and companions. Such was the case for the Pre-Raphaelite painter Elizabeth Siddal (1829–1862), model to several of the Pre-Raphaelite painters and wife of the painter and poet Dante Gabriel Rossetti. The consideration of a woman artist in relation to her male companion plagued women artists throughout the twentieth century. Such working pairs include Sonia Delaunay (1885–1979) and Robert Delaunay, Frida Kahlo (1907–1954) and Diego Rivera, Lee Krasner (1908–1984) and Jackson Pollock, and Elaine de Kooning (1919–1989) and Willem de Kooning. In these cases, critics and historians have focused on issues of originality and influence, and until the 1970s looked at the work of the wife or female partner as a reflection or shadow of the work of her male mentor and master-artist. In the case of Georgia O'Keeffe (1887–1986) and Alfred Stieglitz, however, the critical reception of O'Keeffe's work has been seen not as a reflection of that of Stieglitz, but as a reflection of her own sexuality, again, a recurring theme for the woman artist who challenges accepted norms of behavior and production.

The art produced during the women's movement of the 1960s and 1970s explored, among other things, the idea of women's work as a collaborative project, artistically and politically. In 1970, Judy Chicago (b. 1939) established the first feminist art program at California State University, Fresno, believing that women artists must work together to develop means for changing traditional patriarchal institutions. In 1971, Chicago, with her collaborator Miriam Schapiro (b. 1923), moved the feminist art program to the California Institute of the Arts in Valencia, where they were joined by others, as well as students who became the next important group of feminist artists and activists, including Faith Wilding and Suzanne Lacy.

Many of these feminist women artists laid claim to their sexuality and bodies in remarkable ways, exploring the essentialist vocabulary that identified the productions of women with the biology of woman. Perhaps the most important example here is *Dinner Party* (begun 1974), designed by Judy Chicago as a triangular table for which 39 place settings were made to honor the contributions of 39 women (with 999 other women's names placed on tiles at the center of the triangle). Each place setting includes an elaborate textile with imagery related to the woman's achievements, and a ceramic plate, most of which are three-dimensional colorful designs with circular imagery abstractly patterned after female genitalia. Essentialists claim that a different set of criteria are essential to women's creativity, criteria based on a woman's body and a woman's experience of her body. Countering the essentialist approach are those artists, critics, and historians who argue that essentialism plays into the male patriarchal hierarchy by insisting that women's art remain gender-defined.

In addition to issues of collaboration and a focus on media traditionally associated with women, such as textiles and ceramics, feminist artists have taken to performance art

as activists and advocates for women's rights. In 1977, Suzanne Lacy and Leslie Labowitz performed *In Mourning and In Rage* outside Los Angeles City Hall to protest the media's coverage of a series of murders, and to address the spread of violence against women. From the 1980s, the "guerrilla girls" have claimed to be the conscience of the art world by bringing attention to the fact that so few works by women and people of color have been introduced into major museums and exhibitions. Playing on a pun—the image of the gorilla and the strategies of the guerrilla—these nonviolent protestors protect their anonymity by wearing gorilla masks; their anonymity, moreover, is part of their strength because their public appearances suggest the power of an all-seeing observer who is carefully watching for sexual and racial discrimination.

Western women artists' renewed focus on techniques and media traditionally produced by women finds a parallel in the work of Magdalene Odundo (b. 1950), a Kenyan ceramicist who teaches and exhibits internationally. Odundo creates her works using a traditional coiling technique with designs from both African and non-African sources. Deborah (Kepola) U. Kakalia, a Hawaiian textile artist, reflects in her work on the cultural and political interactions between her native Hawaiian cultures and those of the European colonizers. Her textiles evoke the history of quiltmaking in the Hawaiian Islands, a craft introduced in the early nineteenth century by missionaries; Kakalia's works are layered with an imagery that is both native Hawaiian and European-inspired.

The movement among artists in the 1990s toward exploring issues of cultural diversity has led women artists to examine personal histories as members of a larger group. Jaune Quick-to-See Smith (b. 1940) is a Native American artist raised on the Flatrock Reservation in Montana. She identifies her own heritage within the Salish of the northwest coast, the Shoshone of southern California, and the Cree, a northern woodlands and plateau people. Quick-to-See Smith has worked to combine the complex traditions of Native Americans, with non-Native traditions in inspired mixed media works that question identity, history, and the meaning of cultural exchanges.

Feminist artists and scholars have developed side by side, often exploring similar issues in their work. The generation of the 1970s—including Linda Nochlin, Anne Sutherland Harris, and others—saw as their task the recovery of the woman artist from a history in which she seemed not to exist. In some respects, their work may be compared to that of an archaeologist who uncovers from the earth evidence of a hidden, even unknown, culture or civilization. Indeed, these scholars literally dug deep into archives, sifting through centuries of dust to discover names, works, lives, academies, and workshops of women artists of the past. Following the lead of Nochlin and Harris, Norma Broude, Mary Garrard, Griselda Pollock, Lisa Tickner, and many others have begun to focus on the status of women in society—legal, religious, political, familial, philosophical, and sexual. Such an approach, it is believed, leads to a better understanding and interpretation of women's responsibilities and opportunities, or lack of these, within particular societies.

Throughout the development of feminist art history, scholars have debated how to deal with the evidence of a history of women artists. Is this material to be incorporated into the existing history of art, based as it is on established definitions of quality, originality, and genius—notions that are themselves enshrined within a patriarchal system? Research by feminist scholars, however, indicates that women's artistic productions have often been different from those of men for many reasons, only one of which is the fact that women have been socialized differently. The alternative might be to write a history of women artists that places them apart from traditional art history. This suggests, though, that there were no interactions between the two worlds of male and female artists, and that the dichotomy is as simple as male and female. Perhaps as artists, critics, historians, and viewers, we should consider the parallels that may exist between the artistic productions of women and men, all the while recognizing the individual contributions of what must remain individual talents.

See Also

AESTHETICS: FEMINIST; FINE ARTS: CRITICISM AND ART HISTORY; FINE ARTS: PAINTING; FINE ARTS: POLITICS OF REPRESENTATION; FINE ARTS: SCULPTURE AND INSTALLATION

References and Further Readings

Broude, Norma, and Mary Garrard. 1989. An exchange on the feminist critique of art history. *Art Bulletin* 71: 124–126.

Chadwick, Whitney. 1990, 1994. *Women, art, and society.* London: Thames and Hudson.

Garrard, Mary. 1989. *Artemesia Gentileschi: The image of the female hero in Italian baroque art.* Princeton, N.J.: Princeton University Press.

Gouma-Peterson, Thelma, and Patricia Mathews. 1987. The feminist critique of art history. *Art Bulletin* 69: 326–357.

———. 1989. The feminist critique of art history. *Art Bulletin* 71: 126–127.

Hamburger, Jeffrey F. 1977. *Nuns as artists: The visual culture of a medieval convent.* Berkeley: University of California Press.

hooks, bell. 1995. *Art on my mind: Visual politics.* New York: New Press.

Jones, Amelia, ed. 1996. *Sexual politics: Judy Chicago's "Dinner Party" in feminist art history.* Los Angeles: University of California Press.

Nochlin, Linda. 1971. Why have there been no great women artists? *Art News* 69(9): 22–39, 67–71.

———, and Anne Sutherland Harris. 1977. *Women artists, 1550–1950.* Exhibition catalogue. Los Angeles, Calif.: Los Angeles County Museum of Art.

Pollock, Griselda. 1988. *Vision and difference: Femininity, feminism, and the histories of art.* London: Routledge.

Vasari, Giorgio. 1991. *The lives of the artists (1550, 1568).* Trans. Julia Conaway Bondanella and Peter Bondanella. Oxford: Oxford University Press. (Originally published 1550, 1568.)

Marjorie Och

FINE ARTS: Criticism and Art History

To some extent, women have been actively writing about art for decades—art history has been seen as an "acceptable" academic subject for women—but since the late 1960s, women writers have become more prominent, and their work has been more evidently influenced or informed by feminism. Today there is a sophisticated body of writing and an extensive forum for debate. This article will chart the development of art writing through, and influenced by, the women's movement.

Areas of Art Writing

Writing about fine art in the late twentieth century can generally be placed in one of four categories: art history, criticism, reviewing, or theory. These categories are not watertight and frequently overlap—reviews can include historical material, theory can develop in a piece of criticism, and so on. Feminist writing, in particular, crosses borders between forms of art writing and often is broadly interdisciplinary. At the outset, however, certain generalizations can usefully describe each area:

1. Reviews are short pieces of writing about contemporary or recent exhibitions. They are found in newspapers and other publications for a general audience, and in review sections of art magazines. Reviewers come to the work via other arttistic interests, or through a journalistic background.

2. Art history as we know it today is an academic discipline developed in universities (initially in central

Europe) during the nineteenth century. Still based in the universities, it is an academic, text-based subject, with all the surrounding academic paraphernalia, and has entered the secondary-school curriculum. Its main task is establishing the origin and provenance of artworks—their artists, the influences on them, their position in the canon of artworks, and their general history—and their conditions of production and reception. Art history is developed and disseminated through specialist journals, books, and conferences.

3. Art theory could be described as the philosophy of fine art. It explores conceptual meanings and functions of artworks and practices. In addition to traditional areas such as aesthetics (the study and evaluation of beauty in art), recent theory has developed in an interdisciplinary way, drawing on, inter alia, literary criticism, psychoanalysis, semiotics, and Marxist and feminist philosophy. It is usually disseminated through books, academic journals, and conferences.

4. Criticism can be seen as containing aspects of all the other areas. Often inspired by recent exhibitions, the writer will generally build up a particular argument about art practices, frequently in a professional magazine aimed at artists and art workers rather than academics.

Distribution of Debate

The development of feminist thought about art practices has been highly dependent, first, on the spoken word for local discussion (in groups, meetings, and conferences), and, second, on access to publishing for wider circulation and debate. The broader international debate has, therefore, generally been in English, deemed by publishers to be the most widely understood language. Few texts have been translated. This situation has been compounded by a third dependency: a "critical mass" of women artists and art writers to generate debate. The numbers necessary to develop thinking and writing about feminist art practices are most obviously found in undergraduate and postgraduate fine art and art history departments and their graduates—which are most concentrated in English-speaking countries (such as the United States, the United Kingdom, Australia, and Ireland) and in a few others such as Germany. This means that the debate has taken on a distinctly United States and United Kingdom centrism.

The 1970s: Art History

The essay often cited as the beginning of feminist art history is Linda Nochlin's "Why Have There Been No Great Women Artists?" (1989, originally published in 1971). This

developed from a seminar Nochlin taught at Vassar College in the United States in 1970. Even now, its radical, wide-reaching arguments are clear; it indicated many of the areas (if not the developments in feminist scholarship, methodologies, and politics) still occupying women art writers. Nochlin outlined the need to research the history of women artists, as most standard art histories mention no women. But she also warned that this alone would be far from sufficient—the assumptions of art history would need to be questioned. Among these assumptions were race (the assumption that white people produce art); art education (including the exclusion of women from the academies); and notions of "genius" and "femininity." Throughout her essay, she argues that the construction of the "great artist" is embedded in social practices. Subsequently, art historians (including Elsa Honig Fine, Mary Garrard, Anne Sutherland Harris, and Lorna Tufts) produced books revising art history, reclaiming women "lost" from it. But the work of revision was soon seen to be heading in two differing directions: on the one hand, reinserting women artists into art history, in order to rewrite it; and, on the other hand, questioning the whole premise, structure, and value system of the discipline.

The 1970s: Criticism

Women critics writing about contemporary work without academic constraints found it more appropriate to question the whole structure of the art world—as did many of the artists about whom they wrote. Lucy Lippard was one of the most prolific, principled, and radical critics. She questioned why women artists should want part of the "rotten pie" of the art world; she explored the possibility of recognizing a female sensibility in women's work, analyzing its construction (1976). Others, such as Arlene Raven, also took up and developed this latter debate, making it a major focus of their work through to the 1990s. Artists and critics alike adopted interdisciplinary approaches; the film theorist Laura Mulvey helped develop theories of representation in art and the male gaze.

Periodicals

Magazines and journals have been crucial in developing debate. *The Feminist Art Journal* (1972–1977), *Chrysalis* (1977–1980), *Heresies* (1977 on), *Women Artist's News* (1978 on), *Woman's Art Journal* (1980 on), *FAN: Feminist Art News* (1983–1993), and *Women's Art Magazine*) have been the most prominent, representing a broad spectrum of political and artistic positions. Mainstream journals producing "special issues" on women's art include *Artnews* (January 1971), *Art Journal* (Summer 1976, Summer 1991), and *Studio Interna-*

tional (no. 3, 1977). Journals including some feminist discussion are *Block, Art History, Parachute, Performance, Artforum, ArtMonthly,* and *Third Text.* Cultural coverage in academic feminist journals (such as *Signs* and *Feminist Review)* is weighted toward literary theory; and activist magazines *(*such as *Spare Rib*) often share the left's distrust of fine art, while covering other art forms.

Into the 1980s: Anthologies

In the 1980s, the anthology came into its own. Women's writing, spread through magazines, was variously collected (including Broude and Garrard, 1982; Parker and Pollock, 1987; Robinson, 1987 and 1988). Key articles and areas of debate, published in diverse journals, were collated, usually with informative bibliographies. Journal articles by individuals such as Lippard, Nochlin, and Griselda Pollock were also anthologized.

Art History: United Kingdom

Rozsika Parker and Griselda Pollock's *Old Mistresses: Women, Art, and Ideology* (1981) had as much impact as Nochlin's paper a decade earlier. As art historians, Parkas and Pollock were not content simply to excavate women artists and reinsert them into art history; instead, they questioned the ideology and language of art, exploring women's strategies to negotiate these structures. They saw art as a result of interrelating practices rather than a hermetically sealed product. Parker went on to apply these methodologies to craft, embroidery in particular; Pollock, drawing on Marxist and deconstruction theory, became the most prolifically published feminist art historian.

Debates and Methodologies

When writing about contemporary work, Pollock stressed deconstructive photo-text art practices and a refusal to "image" the body of woman, not commenting on other contemporary practices, particularly painting and performance. This indicated a major debate of the 1980s. In the United Kingdom, many art writers followed deconstructive and psychoanalytic methodology, which found favor in academic publishing and threatened to become a new orthodoxy. The art historian Lisa Tickner broadened terms of debate when writing about contemporary art, incorporating the French writers Luce Irigaray and Hélène Cixous in theories of bodily representation. Younger historians, such as Tamar Garb, often stayed within art history, deconstructing the representation of women by male artists, or writing on neglected women artists. A broadside to photo-text work came from Katy Deepwell, who edited a "painting issue" of *Feminist Art News* (no. 2, 1987)

and kept the debate alive in *Women Artist's Slide Library Magazine* and *Women's Art Magazine.* Sometimes the arguments remained superficial—were some techniques intrinsically more politically correct than others?—but this belied the serious discussion of how women artists best create meaning through visual languages. In the meantime, other writers developed other positions: among them, Sarah Kent was a prominent populist, pro-woman critic; and the artist Maud Sulter (1990) and other black and Asian women developed debates on black women's art practices.

Differences in the United States

In the United States, the debate centred on differences between so-called constructionists (such as Kate Linker), who believe that femininity and women's art practices are social constructions; and so-called essentialists, who believe in a feminine essence, and related purity within women's art. The term *essentialist* was often extended disparagingly to writers who highlighted a community of women, prioritizing woman-centered work and terminology; Cassandra Langer termed this "gynergenic criticism" (Raven, Langer, and Fruch, 1988). Echoes of this were found in Europe (Ecker, 1985). Beyond these two ideological wings, Whitney Chadwick (1985, 1989) was the first historian to combine the methodologies and feminist politics of the 1980s with the need for exhaustive histories of women's work; the critic Moira Roth charted women's performance art; and various artists published journal articles on practice. Feminism informed a broad spectrum of debates. Lucy Lippard, who in the 1970s had written only about women, now expanded her focus. Her writing about land art, primitivism, and artists of differing ethnicities was informed by her feminism. The mainstream art theorist Suzi Gablik incorporated feminist approaches in writing that addressed ethics and ecology. More divisively, the gay male critic Craig Owens wrote supportively of feminist photo-text strategies and was much anthologized—often at the expense of women writers. Similarly, critical theory and postmodernist anthologies included token "feminist" essays but left patriarchal academic structures unaltered.

Into the 1990s

Developments in women's more recent research can be exemplified by two widely differing books. The philosopher Christine Battersby's study of "genius" (1989) argues that the concept has shifted but has always excluded women. The art historian Lynda Nead (1992) combines rigorous historical and feminist methodologies with an inclusive approach to recent women's art in her exploration of the female nude. In the mid-1990s, *Heresies, Woman's Art Journal,* and *Women's Art Magazine* flourished, and publishers' lists, art historians' organizations, and art magazines had varying space for feminist debates. The most urgent debates concerned cultural identity, the body, and ecology; women's art writing is highly diversified, developed, and able to make substantial use of and contribution to these debates.

See Also

FINE ARTS: OVERVIEW; FINE ARTS: PAINTING; FINE ARTS: POLITICS OF REPRESENTATION; FINE ARTS: SCULPTURE AND INSTALLATION; PERFORMANCE ART; PHOTOGRAPHY

References and Further Reading

Battersby, Christine. 1989. *Gender and genius: Towards a feminist aesthetics.* London: Women's Press.

Broude, Norma, and Mary D. Garrard, eds. 1982. *Feminism and art history: Questioning the litany.* New York: Harper and Row.

———. 1989. *Women, art and society.* London: Thames and Hudson.

Chadwick, Whitney. 1985. *Women artists and the surrealist movement.* London: Thames and Hudson.

Deepwell, Katy, ed. 1995. *New feminist art criticism: Critical strategies.* Manchester: Manchester University Press.

Ecker, Gisela, ed. 1985. *Feminist aesthetics.* London: Women's Press.

Gouma-Peterson, Thalia, and Patricia Mathews. 1987. The feminist critique of art history. *Art Bulletin* 69(3): 326–357.

Lippard, Lucy. 1976. *From the center: Feminist essays on women's art.* New York: Dutton.

Nead, Lynda. 1992. *The female nude: Art, obscenity and sexuality.* London: Routledge.

Nochlin, Linda. 1989. *Women, art, and power and other essays.* London: Thames and Hudson.

Parker, Rozsika, and Griselda Pollock. 1987. *Framing feminism art and the women's movement 1970–1985.* London and New York: Pandora.

———. 1981. *Old mistresses: Women, art, and ideology.* London: Routledge.

Raven, Arlene, Cassandra Langer, and Joanna Frueh, eds. 1988. *Feminist art criticism: An anthology.* London: UMI Research Press.

Robinson, Hilary, ed. 1987 and 1988. *Visibly female: Feminism and art today.* London: Camden Press; New York: Universe.

Sulter, Maud Passion, ed. 1990. *Discourses on black women's creativity.* Hebden Bridge: Urban Fox.

Hilary Robinson

FINE ARTS: Painting

Throughout history and all over the world, women have painted. From the *parfleches* (hideskin containers) painted with vivid abstract designs by Native American women to the watercolor sketches produced by upper-class European women as a sign of feminine accomplishment and the painted bark cloth produced by Mbuti women in Africa, women have always been involved in the activity of painting. Women's access to painting as a fine art—and to the training, cultural prestige, and financial privilege it implies—has been far more limited. As a result, a historically documented tradition of individual women painters is rare before the early modern period, and the records that do exist tend to be incomplete. Even when there is historical evidence of women painters, scholars have often omitted them from histories of art, as (arguably) standards of artistic achievement and identity historically have been defined in terms that exclude women.

"Women Artists": Obstacles and Assumptions

The very label "women artists" suggests the gendered nature of artistic terminology; there is no equivalent term "men artists." The position of being an artist—a painter, a sculptor, and so on—is assumed to be inherently male, and the woman who practices such activities is an exception. This assumption reveals a long history of institutional bias and exclusion in the practices of art and art history. Challenging this tradition, feminist scholars have focused attention on the social nature of art, as a sphere of human activity influenced by cultural beliefs, practices, and assumptions about gender, as well as race, class, ethnicity, and other categories of social identity. In addition, they have questioned the reasons for this bias, arguing that masculine definitions of the "great artist" and "high art" are dependent for their meaning and status on the devaluation of the woman artist, the feminine, and the decorative arts (Parker and Pollock, 1981).

Recognizing painting as a social practice calls attention to the impact of institutional and social factors on women painters. One example is the history of western women's access to drawing the human figure. The European tradition of oil painting was historically based on the study of the nude, as history paintings telling stories of human virtue and heroism were considered the highest genre of painting. Male artists underwent long years of training to acquire an understanding of human anatomy and form, culminating in drawing from the nude model. Women, however, were not allowed to have access to these life-drawing classes, as it was considered improper for "respectable" women to see the nude model (often a working-class woman). In practice, this meant that women were denied the opportunity to learn how to draw the human figure, and, thus, were hindered in their attempts at history painting. In contrast, the scholar-amateur tradition of Chinese painting created very different opportunities for women of the gentry classes. The high value placed on "amateur" art and a tradition of individual tutoring rather than academic instruction meant that some women of the gentry had access to training in brushwork and that their artistic efforts were accorded high cultural value. The work of women artists such as the bamboo painter Kuan Tao-sheng (1262–1319) was recorded alongside-that of their male peers and became a valued and imitated part of artistic tradition.

Women's social roles and cultural ideals of femininity have also affected their access to professional training and careers. Women have most often been associated with the private sphere of home and family and assigned primary responsibility for domestic work and the care of children. Such responsibilities often prevented women from devoting significant amounts of time to art, as did the social expectation that after marriage a woman would give up her career. Perhaps even more important, cultural beliefs about femininity and about the nature of creative achievement have also been used as a justification for keeping women out of the fine arts and as a means of devaluing their work. For example, art critics have often described women's paintings as "soft" "delicate" and "weak," terms whose critical subtext is made clear when they are juxtaposed with terms of praise such as "virile," "strong," and "masculine" applied to paintings made by men.

Such critical evaluations raise an often debated question: is women's painting different from men's? Although some twentieth-century artists consciously tried to create a feminine aesthetic, most scholars agree that the work of women painters in general does not reveal any essential similarities. Indeed, there are many examples of critical evaluations of a work of art suddenly changing for the worse when the artist is revealed to be a woman. Whereas most scholars agree that there is no natural or essential feminine style, there is debate about the possibility of a particularly feminine aesthetic. In addition, many scholars hold that the social experience of being a woman often affects an artist's choice of subject and treatment.

Women and Painting in History

Despite the often daunting barriers, many women did become successful painters. Feminist art historians have worked to recover the histories, biographies, and paintings of the women artists of the past. Although most of the scholarship in English has focused on the western tradition, more recent scholarship has uncovered histories of women painters working in various traditions around the world (for example, Fister, 1988; Weidner, 1990). An international history of women painters is further complicated by the fact that the history of women's access to painting is not a linear narrative of progress, as different social, political, and artistic traditions offered women different possibilities. Not surprisingly, at times when women had more opportunities politically and intellectually, there are larger numbers of recorded female painters. For example, the importance of matrilineal descent in the Fujiwara political system gave Japanese women at court during the Heian period (794–1185) increased power and corresponded with a unique flowering of women's predominance in the cultural sphere (Weidner, 1990).

Notwithstanding some periods of sustained female success in the arts, the history of women's achievements in painting before the modern era looks more like a mosaic than the succession of "great masters" common to narratives of male artists. Even a short list of examples reveals the richness and variety of women's contributions to painting. The Italian baroque artist Artemisia Gentileschi (1593–1652/3) supported herself as a professional artist and became famous for her dramatic pictures of "female heroes" such as the biblical figures Judith and Susanna. Ch'en Shu (1660–1736), a Chinese painter of landscape, figures, and flowers, achieved renown in her lifetime and began an artistic lineage that extended into several generations. Elisabeth Vigée-Lebrun (1755–1842) became a favorite portraitist of the French queen Marie Antoinette and a member of the prestigious Académie Royale in the late eighteenth century. Each of these exceptional women was celebrated and recognized in her lifetime and has been a subject of important contemporary scholarship.

Although women artists have worked in a wide variety of historical circumstances, it is possible to see that women who achieved success as painters tended to have certain characteristics in common. Most consistently, a large number of women painters came from (or married into) artistic families and thus had access to training and opportunities not available to most women. For example, the success of Angelica Kauffman (1741–1807) as a neoclassical artist stems in part from the fact that her artist father took her to Rome, where she met the influential theorist Johann Winckelmann, copied from the old masters, and became immersed in the classical tradition. Another common theme in histories of women painters is their frequent specialization in the so-called lesser genres: still life and flower painting. The Dutch artist Rachel Ruysch (1664–1750) became internationally famous for her flower paintings, and well into the nineteenth century the genre was still considered particularly appropriate for women. Although in China the hierarchy of genres took a different form, flower painting was still a common subject for female artists. For example, Liu Yin (1618–1664) painted primarily narcissus, bamboo, and orchids, a choice that James Cahill points out was a common one for Chinese courtesan-artists, as such subjects required less technical training than landscape or figure painting (Cahill in Weidner, 1990).

The Nineteenth and Twentieth Centuries

In late nineteenth and early twentieth century—under the influence of the struggle for women's equal rights and in tandem with the expansion of educational opportunities for women—there was an explosion in the number of women painters. One of main areas of struggle was the fight for access to formal artistic training. In the fairly typical case of the British Royal Academy schools, limited numbers of women were admitted by 1862, but it took another 40 years until there were mixed classes of men and women. Aspiring women artists traveled far from home to find art schools that would accept them. One example is artist Annie Walker (1855–1929), who was rejected by the Corcoran Gallery of Art schools in Washington, D.C., when the instructor learned that she was an African-American. Walker later traveled to Paris to study at the Académie Julian. As this example makes clear, access to artistic training was dependent not only on the social status of women in a given culture; other historical factors also shaped the possibilities available to women artists. For example, the history of western imperialism meant that many colonized countries' traditional art forms and heritage were abandoned in favor of western models of training.

The fight for equal access to artistic training and professional standing resulted in substantial numbers of women painters in the twentieth century, a list that includes participants in most of the famous artistic movements of the century. Ironically, however, the twentieth century also witnessed an almost complete erasure of women artists from art-historical accounts and an increasing identification of artistic creativity with masculinity. Modernist accounts of the history of art have tended to emphasize the heroic figure of the artist working in isolation, to mythologize creative genius as synonymous with masculine sexual desire, and to recount artistic progress as succeeding generations of fathers and sons.

The women's liberation movement of the late twentieth century radically reshaped the artistic landscape for women, opening up new opportunities for training, exhibition, and community. In addition, the feminist adage that "the personal is political" helped to establish issues of gender, race, and class as valid aspects of artistic expression. Although some contemporary female painters downplay the importance of gender in their work, others specifically engage with issues of female identity. For example, one important theme in contemporary women's painting is challenging the ways women have been represented in traditional male-dominated painting. Joan Semmel, Jenny Saville, and Alice Neel rework the idealized representation of the white female nude that has held such sway in western art since the Renaissance in their paintings of aging, pregnant, decidedly unidealized female bodies. The Indian artist Gogi Saroj' Pal's paintings appropriate images of the ideal *nayika* (heroines) from Persian miniatures into a feminist critique. Faith Ringgold and Betye Saar have reimagined stereotypes of African-American women, transforming them into symbols of power. Together, these artists and others working around the world have mounted a powerful challenge to the traditions and exclusiveness of the art of the past.

Despite their successes, however, women painters—and especially women of color—remain underrepresented in museum exhibitions, art galleries, and art history textbooks and classes. Women painters continue to challenge the sexism of the art world, protesting against exclusionary exhibition tactics and working to change the gendered dynamics of contemporary life-drawing classes. Others focus on creating new opportunities for women, establishing new forms of art education, exhibition opportunities, and critical and academic writing.

See Also

AESTHETICS; FINE ARTS: OVERVIEW; FINE ARTS: CRITICISM AND ART HISTORY; FINE ARTS: POLITICS OF REPRESENTATION; GENRES: GENDERED; HISTORY

References and Further Reading

Broude, Norma, and Mary D. Garrard, 1992. *The expanding discourse: Feminism and art history.* New York: HarperCollins.

Fister, Patricia. 1988. *Japanese women artists, 1600–1900.* Kansas: Spencer Museum of Art.

Harris, Ann Sutherland, and Linda Nochlin. 1976. *Women artists: 1550–1950.* Los Angeles: Los Angeles County Museum of Art.

Nashashibi, Salwa Mikdadi. 1994. *Forces of change: Artists of the Arab world.* Washington, D.C.: National Museum of Women in the Arts.

Nochlin, Linda. 1988. *Women, art, and power and other essays.* New York: Harper and Row.

Parker, Rozsika, and Griselda Pollock. 1981. *Old mistresses: Women, art, and ideology.* New York: Pantheon.

Robinson, Jontyle Theresa. 1996. *Bearing witness: Contemporary works by African-American women artists.* New York: Spelman College and Rizzoli.

Weidner, Marsha, ed. 1990. *Flowering in the shadows: Women in the history of Chinese and Japanese painting.* Honolulu: University of Hawaii Press.

Pamela Fletcher

FINE ARTS: Politics of Representation

In English, the word *representation* has two distinct but related meanings. In its most familiar usage, it refers to the images, texts, and symbols that interpret and represent the world around us—what we might call *cultural representations.* Simultaneously, the term refers to the political process of representation, whereby one person speaks for—represents—a group of people. This double meaning calls attention to the political nature of all forms of representation. Representations—paintings, photographs, novels, movies, and the mass media—are always interpretations and, as such, are always open to debate. Scholars, activists, and politicians from all sides of the political spectrum argue over cultural representations: Who (or what) is represented, how, and by and for whom? Feminist scholars and activists have participated in and shaped these debates in many ways, analyzing the role of representations in sustaining and challenging political relations of dominance and subordination.

Theories of Representation

The cultural studies scholar Stuart Hall (1997) has summarized three main approaches to understanding representation: the reflective, the intentional, and the constructionist. The *reflective* theory of representation holds that things and events have a true, essential meaning that is transparently mirrored in representation. The *intentional* theory of representation gives the person who creates a particular representation ultimate control over its meaning. The *constructionist* theory of representation, by contrast, posits that meaning is created within the cultural systems of representation themselves. In this view, representations do not just passively reflect the world or our inner selves, but actively produce our understanding and knowledge of the world. In the process, they shape us as socially identified individuals, or "subjects." This third theory has become the dominant model for understanding representation in most contemporary scholarship. Although it incorporates elements of each of the other approaches—acknowledging the role of producers and paying attention to the relationship between representations and the real world of people and events—a constructionist approach shifts the focus to the politics of representation, asking questions about the role of cultural representations in producing ideologies and relations of power.

Feminist scholars of visual representation have generally adopted a constructionist approach, as it has important implications for thinking about representations of women. To begin with, such an approach implies that there is not necessarily a direct correlation between the images of women produced by a culture and any actual historical women. Whereas early feminist critiques of representation focused on identifying "good" and "bad" images of women, most scholars have rejected such an approach as too limited. In order to understand how visual images are related to a given cultural and historical moment, it is necessary to ask instead what kinds of meanings they produce, for what kinds of viewers. Images of women shape and contest cultural definitions of femininity (and masculinity) and, thus, affect the lives, choices, and pleasures of historical women and men in complicated ways.

The Politics of Representing the Female Body

Images of the female body in film, high art, advertisements, and pornography have been one of the most important subjects of a feminist analysis of representation. As John Berger pointed out in his book *Ways of Seeing* (1972), there are important similarities between images of the (white) female body in high art, in advertisements, and in pornography. Berger argues that most images in western culture are shaped by a fundamental division along the lines of sexual difference: whereas men are represented as active subjects, women are represented as objects to be looked at. The term "objectification" is frequently used to describe this mode of representing the female body as a thing to be possessed rather than as a person. Berger interprets this phenomenon from a Marxist perspective, arguing that the real economic and political inequities of power between men and women are reproduced in visual images. Other critics, drawing on the film critic Laura Mulvey's notion of the "male gaze," argue that the very act of looking is gendered. Mulvey (1989) applied psychoanalytic theory to argue that the structure of classic Hollywood cinema supports and creates a gendered imbalance in looking, identifying active looking as masculine and passive "to-be-looked-at-ness" as feminine. Mulvey's concept of the "male gaze" has been used as a tool in investigating many other forms of representing the female body, from the high art tradition of the female nude to the commodification of women's bodies in advertising.

In such analyses, images of the female body are understood to actively produce masculine subjects, confirming for the male viewer his right to be *the* subject—the one who looks, knows, and defines. This position of masculine superiority is established and confirmed by the availability of women (both represented and real) for his erotic pleasure and possession. But what happens when women look at such images of the female body? One possibility is that women absorb the same messages that men do, as they either identify with a (white) male position or enter into a masochistic identification with the (white) woman. Either way, a female viewer learns that to be a woman is to be judged on her appearance, to be passive, to be the object of knowledge rather than the subject. Through this process of identification, such representations shape women's sense of pleasure and sexuality as well as men's. But this view of representation, although powerful, is ultimately incomplete. Focusing solely on the power of representations carries with it the danger of erasing any possibility of human agency or resistance. In addition, it omits other aspects of identity that affect the experience of viewing, such as race, class, sexuality, and ethnicity.

Addressing such questions, the cultural critic bell hooks (1992) talks about the possibilities of an "oppositional gaze," a refusal to identify with the ideological representation (of blackness, femininity, heterosexuality, and so on) presented to the viewer. Instead, the bearer of an oppositional gaze resists and critiques the representation and the subject positions it offers. hooks's analysis also calls attention to another function of the plethora of representations of the white female body in the western cultural field. In the fetishization of the white female body and the exclusion (or vilification) of the black female body, high art and classical cinematic representations produce a racialized sexual difference, in which whiteness is the "norm" and white dominance is reinforced.

Another resistant form of viewing involves identifying "against the grain," as, for example, when a lesbian viewer identifies with and appropriates the desiring "male" gaze. The artist Deborah Bright's photographic series *Dream Girls* makes this resisting gaze explicit. Bright alters film stills from classic Hollywood films by putting herself in the position of admiring and being admired by the film heroines, wittily rewriting a narrative of lesbian desire within the heterosexual romance of the film.

Stereotype and Difference: Representing the "Other"

As the discussion above begins to suggest, representation works to define and maintain difference. One common strategy for producing difference is the stereotype. Stereotyping is a representational practice based on limiting representation of the members of a group to a small number of fixed, exaggerated types. For example, representations of African-American women have traditionally fallen into two distinct stereotypes: the oversexed Jezebel figure and the domestic Mammy figure, happily taking care of the white man's home and children. These stereotypes—along with other stereotypes of black men and women as childlike, foolish, and unable to take care of themselves—have their roots in the American system of slavery. Such stereotypes were used to define and naturalize a difference between blacks and whites, thus functioning as an ideological justification for the ownership of black people by white people. As this example makes clear, a stereotype often has a political purpose. Its function is to draw a firm boundary between "us" and "them"—or, as is often said, between "self" and "other"—presenting political or social inequity as "natural."

How can stereotypes be resisted? One strategy is to appropriate the stereotype, questioning and altering its meaning. The artist Betye Saar's work *The Liberation of Aunt Jemima* (1972) take the Mammy stereotype as its starting point, but dramatically alters it by adding a rifle, a revolver, some cotton, and a "black power" fist to the image. The effect is to explode the meaning of the stereotype, invoking the history of enslavement as the context for contemporary resistance. Another strategy is to create alternative representations of social groups and identities through the process of self-representation.

Identity and Self-Representation

Representation produces our understanding not only of "others" but also of ourselves. For example, when white men and women in United States and Europe see "themselves" reflected in art, on television, and in the mass media, it confirms a sense of whiteness as the "norm." When people of color look at these same sources and do not see themselves represented, they are denied this affirmation of self and group identity. One direct form of challenge to this erasure is making visible the identities and selves excluded from or stereotyped in dominant ideology. For example, Laura Aguilar's photographic series of portraits, *Latina Lesbians* (1987–1990), brings powerful images of the traditionally excluded into the realm of representation. Yolanda López's *Portrait of the Artist as Virgin of Guadalupe* (1978) casts the artist in the role of an important symbol of Mexican identity, but makes the image of femininity it presents more active by adding running shoes and an active forward stride. Alice Neel's *Nude Self-Portrait* (1980) shows the artist as an older woman, naked and seated in a chair with her paintbrush in hand, challenging both the traditional identification of the "great artist" as masculine and the female body as idealized. Other artists such as Adrian Piper, Carrie Mae Weems, and Mary Kelly address question of identity and self-representation from another stance, laying bare the mechanisms and structures that produce "gender" and "race" as social categories.

See Also

FINE ARTS: OVERVIEW; FINE ARTS: CRITICISM AND ART HISTORY; GAZE; IMAGES OF WOMEN: OVERVIEW

References and Further Reading

Berger, John. 1972. *Ways of seeing.* London: British Broadcasting Corporation.

Bloom, Lisa, ed. 1999. *With other eyes: Looking at race and gender in visual culture.* Minneapolis: University of Minnesota Press.

Broude, Norma, and Mary D. Garrard. 1994. *The power of feminist art.* New York: Abrams.

Hall Stuart, ed. 1997. *Representation.* London: Sage and Open University.

hooks, bell. 1992. *Black looks: Race and representation.* Boston: South End.

Mulvey, Laura. 1989. *Visual and other pleasures.* Bloomington: Indiana University Press.

Nead, Lynda. 1992. *The female nude: Art, obscenity, and sexuality.* London: Routledge.

Neumaier, Diane, ed. 1995. *Reframings: New American feminist photographies.* Philadelphia, Pa: Temple University Press.

Pollock, Griselda. 1988. *Vision and difference: Femininity, feminism, and the history of art.* London: Routledge.

Pamela Fletcher

FINE ARTS: Sculpture and Installation

Both sculpture and installation fall within the broader area of the fine arts. For centuries, sculpture was male-dominated and structurally excluded women. By contrast, installation is an aspect of sculptural practice developed since the 1970s, which, given the institutionalized sexism of the fine arts, has a relatively large proportion of women practitioners. Both sculpture and installation are three-dimensional; but whereas sculpture is freestanding and, at least in theory, movable, an installation depends on the architectural particularity of its specific site and cannot be exactly replicated elsewhere.

Background

If sculpture and installation are both described as three-dimensional (3D) fine art, it might appear that the difference between them and other practices is a matter of choosing materials on aesthetic grounds. However, the realities surrounding women's choices in the fine arts are more complex, informed by wider significations of materials, the accessibility of artworks to women viewers, issues of cultural diversity, and political activism. During the twentieth century, mainstream concepts of sculpture underwent enormous change. Formerly, sculpture was generally made by modeling materials like clay or wax (which were often then cast in bronze) or carving materials like stone or wood. In the early twentieth century, some movements—dada and surrealism in Europe, including women like Meret Oppenheim (1913–1985) and Eileen Agar (1899–1991) and constructivism in the Soviet Union, including Alexandra Exter (1884–1949) and Varvara Stepanova (1894–1958)—began to democratize art practices. Notions of the permanence and timelessness of the artwork and the unique skill and genius of the artist were challenged. Artists used "found objects"—everyday materials and items, often of little intrinsic value—as art materials. The market-oriented art establishment, however, continued to consider genius, skill, and the unique object of central importance. A few women sculptors such as Louise Nevelson (1899–1988), Barbara Hepworth (1903–1975), Germaine Richier (1904–1959), and Elizabeth Frink (1930–1993) were recognized on these terms, though often only late in their lives.

The Impact of the Women's Movement

Women have contributed notably to the development of sculpture and installation since the 1960s. With the rise of the liberation movements of the 1960s—civil rights, black power, and the women's movement—many artists sought ways of bringing together their practices and political commitment. In this effort, women drew from earlier democratizing art movements and from feminist activism. Some followed patterns of consciousness-raising, whereby personal experience was politicized and deemed valid for discussion, which art could facilitate. Feminist activist art developed, linking political and cultural activities. In both cases, art materials—and the concept of the "artist"—underwent fundamental challenges from within a feminist framework. The result was a burgeoning of 3D work using personal mementos, domestic and other found objects, "feminine" crafts such as stitching and knitting, and activist strategies. Prime considerations were the concepts of the work and political redefinitions of "art" and "artist." Women worked on the streets, in their homes, through the postal system; they worked collectively, anonymously, with or without considering themselves artists (Lippard, 1984; Parker and Pollock, 1987). Some aspects of these strategies were developed by women in the encampment at Greenham Common and elsewhere, in radical demonstrations, decorated bases, and symbolic structures,

By the 1980s, even mainstream 3D art practices had been comprehensively altered by feminist strategies as well as by postmodernism; some male critics even identified feminist art as a subsection of postmodernism. For a feminist artist, however, the choice and use of materials and imagery, and the interaction between work and audience, will always have a political dimension beyond aesthetics or style. Thus, when Janine Antoni (b. 1964) exhibits one large cube of chocolate and one of lard, which she has partly gnawed away (using the chewed bits to make chocolate boxes and lipsticks), provocative questions are raised about women, consumption, and consumerism.

Diversity of Practices and Strategies

The following artists are cited not as representatives of particular strands, but to demonstrate the diversity of practices, politics, and strategies within contemporary sculpture and installation. Louise Bourgeois (b. 1911) juxtaposes traditionally carved marble pieces with rusty mirrors and windows from derelict houses. By her use of both beauty and dereliction to evoke the experience of emotional abuse as a child, she shows the complexity of remembering. Judy Chicago's (b. 1939) vast undertaking *The Dinner Party* (1974–1977), made with four hundred assistants, was criticized by diverse women but remains one of the most substantial works instigated by a woman. In this work, which uses traditional female arts of embroidery and china painting, 39 plates, each with a symbolized vaginal image representing a particular well-known woman, rest on embroidered runners on a 48-foot triangular table. The work of Mary Kelly (b. 1941) suggests that feminist theories develop from women's lived experiences and can deconstruct western art's prescriptive icon of mother and child. *Post Partum Document* (1976–1980) analyzes mother–child relationships using feminist readings of the psychoanalyst Jacques Lacan. Its materials include slates, early presents from Kelly's son, and washed diaper lin-

ers. Adrian Piper (b. 1948) uses video installations, media photographs superimposed with text, and other means to confront white gallery audiences with their own perhaps unacknowledged racism. Because it focuses on the privileged position of the viewer and poses direct questions to the audience, Piper's work cannot be passively absorbed but, instead, finds meaning in audiences' reactions. Ana Mendieta's (1948–1985) temporary female figures made in a landscape with natural materials articulate complex relationships between women and land, actual women and the Goddess, meaning and permanence.

The diversity of women's positions and the strategies they choose are directly related to the diversity of production and presentation of 3D artwork by women artists.

See Also

FINE ARTS: OVERVIEW; FINE ARTS: CRITICISM AND ART HISTORY; FINE ARTS: PAINTING; FINE ARTS: POLITICS OF REPRESENTATION; GODDESS; IMAGES OF WOMEN: OVERVIEW; PACIFISM AND PEACE ACTIVISM; PERFORMANCE ART; PHOTOGRAPHY; POSTMODERNISM: FEMINIST CRITIQUES; PSYCHOANALYSIS; RACISM AND XENOPHOBIA; TEXTILES

References and Further Reading

Chadwick, Whitney. 1989. *Women, art, and society.* London: Thames and Hudson.

de Olivera, Nicolas, et al. 1994. *Installation art.* London: Thames and Hudson.

Lippard, Lucy. 1984. *Get the message? A decade of art for social change.* New York: Dutton.

Parker, Rozsika, and Griselda Pollock, eds. 1987. *Framing feminism: Art and the women's movement 1970–1985.* London: Pandora.

Robinson, Hilary, ed. 1987 and 1988. *Visibly female: Feminism and art today.* London: Camden; New York: Universe.

Rosen, Randy, and Catherine C. Brawer, compilers. 1989. *Making their mark: Women artists move into the mainstream.* New York: Abbeville.

Hilary Robinson

FIRST-WAVE FEMINISM

See FEMINISM: FIRST-WAVE BRITISH and FEMINISM: FIRST-WAVE NORTH AMERICAN.

FITNESS: Physical

See EXERCISE AND FITNESS.

FOLK MEDICINE

See TRADITIONAL HEALING.

FOLKTALES

See FAIRY TALES and ORAL TRADITION.

FOOD AND CULTURE

The field of food and culture looks at "foodways"—beliefs and behaviors surrounding the production, distribution, and consumption of food. Anthropologists have always looked at foodways because of their centrality in the precapitalist societies first studied by ethnographers and because anthropology's holistic approach is ideal for critically examining the interconnected economic, political, social, symbolic, and biological significance of food across cultures. Audrey Richard's (1932) pioneering work in southern Africa in the 1930s and Margaret Mead's (1964) work in the United States in the 1960s established women's centrality in ethnographic foodways research and have been followed by several other studies in New Guinea (Kahn, 1986), Ecuador (Weismantel, 1988), Fiji (Becker, 1995), Italy (Counihan, 1999), Canada (Reiter, 1991), and the United States (Paules, 1991). Because of women's central role in foodways, they are an ideal focus for feminist research across many disciplines. In the last decades of the twentieth century, feminist influences have strengthened in food and culture studies in anthropology, history, literature, memoirs, philosophy, psychology, and sociology.

Food, Gender Roles, and Sexual Relations

Foodways symbolize gender and sexuality in many cultures. Food often stands for sex, eating for copulation. Among the Wamira of Papua New Guineas, for example, women's fear of and desire to eat *mota*—snakes and eels—represents their ambivalence about sexual relations with men (Kahn, 1986). Male and female are often defined through association with foods and rules about consumption. The Hua of Papua New Guinea classify foods as *koroko,* female; and *hakeri'a,* male (Meigs, 1984). Their belief that women and men can become more alike by consuming each other's foods affirms a vision of gender as malleable. In the United States, by contrast, college students believe in rules that promote distinct and hierarchical concepts of gender: for example, that men should eat a lot of heavy foods such as beef whereas women should eat sparingly of light foods such as salad (Counihan,

1999). Carol Adams (1990) argues that meat-eating upholds patriarchal dominance by linking and objectifying women and animals.

Feeding the Family

In many cultures, men's and women's economic relationships are played out in food-centered roles where men and women may share production but where women almost universally are responsible for cooking and feeding. Women's hard work to produce, preserve, prepare, serve, and clean up after food can bring value and respect, as among Ecuadorean peasants (Weismantel, 1988); but under conditions of capitalist economic development, women's food roles become highly conflicted. In Italy, women struggle to balance traditional expectations regarding cooking while they also work outside the home (Counihan, 1999). In Canada and the United States, many women end up in low-paying, low-status roles in the food service sector (Paules, 1991; Reiter, 1991). In England and the United States, women's food roles in the home sometimes reveal deference and conflict, where wives are obligated by custom to cook and please their husbands while subordinating their own desires (Charles and Kerr, 1988; DeVault, 1991).

On the other hand, some women can use their culinary skills as a creative form of self-expression and a way to give pleasure and gain influence in the family. In Laura Esquivel's Mexican novel *Like Water for Chocolate* (1992), the protagonist Tita infuses her rapturous dishes with her emotions to connect with her lover Pedro and challenge the oppression inflicted by her mother and sister. In Arlene Avakian's *Through the Kitchen Window* (1997), women address in poetry and prose whether cooking is creativity or servitude. They write about women forging ties with each other across generations and preserving cultural memory by passing down recipes and food traditions.

Food as Women's Voice

Many women communicate by cooking and feeding while others find a voice by writing about food. M. F. K. Fisher's stunning opus of memoirs and essays (1954) centers on descriptions of human communion through cooking, feeding, and eating. Other women fast, eat compulsively, or use appetite and hunger as metaphors for their longings—to find the self, to exercise control, to have meaningful relationships, and to combat oppression (Thompson, 1994). Kim Chernin (1985) writes about women's hunger from a psychoanalytic perspective while Margaret Randall (1997) uses poems, many of which are recipes, to evoke the multiple ways women use food and hunger to struggle for recognition and power. The historian Caroline Bynum (1987) explores how medieval women used fasting, food gifts, and miraculous emissions of breast milk as forms of self-expression; while Joan Jacobs Brumberg (1988) examines how bourgeois girls in the Victorian era used "appetite as voice" to speak their need for personhood.

Food, Body, and Identity

Struggles over control of eating have led many women in western cultures into a highly conflicted relationship with their body, which can symbolize the imperfect self always in need of improvement, shaping, and reduction (Bordo, 1993). Yet women from many cultures have relationships with their bodies that defy their own worthlessness and celebrate diverse corporeal beauty. In cultures as disparate as Fiji, Florence, Jamaica, Puerto Rico, and African-America, people eschew a too-thin body as evidence of social neglect and celebrate women's amplitude as a reflection of contentment, fertility, and family heritage (Becker, 1995; Counihan, 1999; Hughes; 1997; Massara, 1997; Sobo, 1997). Feminist research in studies of body, like studies of women's role in food and culture, have shown ways to challenge women's oppression and to affirm women's agency and power.

See Also

BODY; BREAST FEEDING; COOKING; DOMESTIC LABOR; EATING DISORDERS; FOOD, HUNGER, AND FAMINE; NUTRITION AND HOME ECONOMICS; VEGETARIANISM

References and Further Reading

Adams, Carol J. 1990. *The sexual politics of meat: A feminist-vegetarian critical theory.* New York: Continuum.

Avakian, Arlene Voski, ed. 1997. *Through the kitchen window: Women explore the intimate meanings of food and cooking.* Boston: Beacon.

Becker, Anne. 1995. *Body, self, and society: The view from Fiji.* Philadelphia: University of Pennsylvania Press.

Bordo, Susan. 1993. *Unbearable weight: Feminism, western culture, and the body.* Berkeley: University of California Press.

Brumberg, Joan Jacobs. 1988. *Fasting girls: The emergence of anorexia nervosa as a modern disease.* Cambridge, Mass.: Harvard University Press.

Bynum, Caroline Walker. 1987. *Holy feast and holy fast: The religious significance of food to medieval women.* Berkeley: University of California Press.

Charles, Nickie, and Marion Kerr. 1988. *Women, food, and families.* Manchester, U.K.: Manchester University Press.

Chernin, Kim. 1985. *The hungry self: Women, eating, and identity.* New York: Times Books.

Counihan, Carole. 1999. *The anthropology of food and body: Gender, meaning, and power.* New York: Routledge.

DeVault, Marjorie L. 1991. *Feeding the family: The social organization of caring as gendered work.* Chicago: University of Chicago Press.

Esquivel, Laura. 1992. *Like water for chocolate.* New York: Doubleday. (Originally published as *Como agua para chocolate,* 1988.)

Fisher, M. F. K. 1954. *The art of eating.* Cleveland, Ohio: World.

Hughes, Marvalene,. 1997. Soul, black women, and food. In Carole Counihan and Penny Van Esterik, eds., *Food and culture: A reader,* 272–280. New York: Routledge.

Kahn, Miriam. 1986. *Always hungry, never greedy: Food and the expression of gender in a Melanesian society.* New York: Cambridge University Press.

Massara, Emily. 1997. Que gordita. In Carole Counihan and Penny Van Esterik, eds., *Food and culture: A reader,* 251–255. New York: Routledge.

Mead, Margaret. 1964. *Food habits research: Problems of the 1960s.* Washington, D.C.: National Academy of Science.

Meigs, Anna S. 1984. *Food, sex, and pollution: A New Guinea religion.* New Brunswick, N.J.: Rutgers University Press.

Paules, Greta Foff. 1991. *Power and resistance among waitresses in a New Jersey restaurant.* Philadelphia, Pa.: Temple University Press.

Randall, Margaret. 1997. *Hunger's table: Women, food, and politics.* Watsonville, Calif.: Papier-Mâché.

Reiter, Ester. 1991. *Making fast food: From the frying pan into the fryer.* Montreal: McGill-Queens University Press.

Richards, Audrey I. 1932. *Hunger and work in a savage tribe.* London: Routledge.

Sobo, Elisa J. 1997. The sweetness of fat: Health, procreation, and sociability in rural Jamaica. In Carole Counihan and Penny Van Esterik, eds., *Food and culture: A reader.* 256–271. New York: Routledge.

Thompson, Becky. 1994. *A hunger so wide and so deep: American women speak out on eating problems.* Minneapolis: University of Minnesota Press.

Wesimantel, M. J. 1988. *Food, gender, and poverty in the Ecuadorian Andes.* Philadelphia: University of Pennsylvania Press.

Carole Counihan

FOOD, HUNGER, AND FAMINE

Hunger is an everyday reality for 800 million people. Hunger is not just the stereotyped images of bony, barefoot children in Somalia, now familiar to all with a television. It is a pernicious, even deadly affliction that kills 12 million children under the age of 5 every year. Hunger is not just a hardship of the "poor" countries in Africa or southeast Asia; 36 million people in the United States do not have adequate access to food, and of them 20 million are women. This is an international problem of epidemic proportions, and its primary victims are women and children.

In a world that is so technologically and socially advanced, how is it possible that so many people, specifically women, are still unable to get enough food, one of the most basic necessities of life?

Overpopulation and the Green Revolution

Overpopulation is often blamed for spreading our resources too thin and causing hunger. It is true that the Earth's capacity to produce is limited, and if our numbers outstrip our capacity, hunger is a possible result. Subscribers to this explanation of hunger believe that policies of population reduction in the form of stringent birth control, and increased agricultural yields, are the solution to the hunger problem. Women have requently borne the brunt of these policies, especially in the nations of the developing "South", because they are perceived to have high birthrates and low productivity.

Programs designed to limit population almost always blamed women for having too many children. They ignored the factors that are commonly known to contribute to large families such as lack of education and opportunities for women. Instead, many international programs began forcibly imposing birth control policies. In Brazil, thousands of poor women were sterilized without their knowledge or consent in order to lower birthrates. Rather than empowering women, this often plunged them deeper into poverty. Many women depend on their children to care for them as they age. Fewer children mean less security and a greater likelihood of extreme poverty.

Some believed that people in the "South" were hungry because they relied on inefficient traditional agricultural systems. This philosophy spawned the green revolution of the 1970s: scientists, primarily from the developed "North," created new seed varieties that worked in concert with pesticides and fertilizers to increase the yield per acre of numerous staple crops. These seeds were exported to farmers across the world, and have been massively cultivated in much of the "South," where hunger is most severe.

Technologies of the green revolution did succeed in increasing yields; world food production has increased 16 percent faster than population over the last 35 years. Enough food is now produced to provide every human being with 3,500

calories a day in grains alone, and when vegetables, meats, and fish are included there is more than enough food to keep everyone well fed. Yet hunger has increased in areas targeted by the green revolution, especially among women and children. In fact, 78 percent of all malnourished children live in countries with food surpluses.

Obviously hunger is not caused merely by overpopulation or shortages; otherwise, yield increases would have succeeded in reducing hunger. We must look beyond these simplistic explanations to see how the structures of global food economics and politics neglected the poor and pushed women further out of the systems of production and profit.

Food Exports and Farm Consolidation

The green revolution failed to benefit the poor, women, and children, because it encourages food production for export. Most of the countries with a large number of hungry people are actually net exporters of food. The industrialized countries of the "North" are responsible for 71.2 percent of the world's total food imports; their consumers have more money and greater purchasing power, which motivates farmers in the "South" to grow cash crops specifically for export.

The export economy favors wealthy, male farmers. It is a pattern established in colonial times when colonists expropriated the most fertile lands, while indigenous populations tried to feed themselves on the marginal lands. Women often controlled traditional agriculture, and they were marginalized along with their agricultural system.

The same structures remain in place today and were actually furthered by the green revolution. High-yield seeds require expensive farm inputs such as chemical fertilizers and pesticides. Farmers rely on loans, often from international institutions such as the World Bank or the International Monetary Fund (IMF). These loans are given almost exclusively to men with larger farms. Therefore, small farms and farms owned by women could not compete, and many lost their land. This phenomenon is already familiar to farmers in the United States, where the number of farms has decreased by two-thirds since World War II, and the size of the average farm has grown by more than 50 percent.

The impoverishing effects of farm consolidation could have been offset in part if the larger farms had generated jobs for those they had displaced. The green revolution technologies, however, lead to mechanization in order to avoid the labor issues and unions that a large workforce may invite. The few remaining jobs greatly favor men. The displaced are then without jobs to earn money to buy food, or land on which to cultivate it. They are at serious risk of hunger. Many men are forced to migrate in search of work, leaving women to care for their families. Although some men do send remittances, many do not, and women often work extra hours and still go hungry to feed their children. For women who migrate to urban areas, jobs are scarce; and pay is poor for "women's work."

There are those who claim that farm consolidation is necessary for efficiency. Numerous studies have found, however, that the opposite is true; small farms have more than twice the output and profit per acre of large farms. Large farms, often with absentee landowners, are not as well supervised and do not have as much accountability. Historically as well as today, when women and families control the land, they make greater use of available resources and utilize the land more completely, while caring for it to ensure its future productivity.

Nevertheless, farm size continues to grow all over the world. When input costs increase and agricultural prices drop because of the larger harvests, only the larger farms can survive. Furthermore, many large farms are owned by corporations which not only grow but also process and distribute their products, and have a great deal more control of the prices fetched by their goods than a small, individual farmer. These corporations have the economic and political influence to depress wages, avoid environmental regulations, and work around import-export taxes in order to maximize their profits. Small farmers, particularly women, do not have the political clout necessary to enact policies that would aid and support them.

Hunger and Environmental Degradation

Environmental factors also contribute to hunger, but again it is political and economic structures and not natural phenomena that determine who eats and who does not eat. When drought hits Ethiopia, a hurricane tears through India, or floods ravage the Mississippi delta, food crops and livelihoods can be destroyed. Food is almost always available for those who can afford it; only the poorest are plunged into famine. Their lives are already unstable, and they have no savings to help them in hard times, so any kind of disruption can cause hunger.

Even without natural disasters, extensive studies have found that green revolution technologies are not sustainable. The high-yield seeds lack the biodiversity usually found in traditionally planted fields. Without this biodiversity, crops are more susceptible to insects and diseases and, therefore, need more pesticides. Studies around the world have proved that more and more pesticides are required over time, because the natural predators of pests are killed off, and because insects build up a resistance to pesticides. The same cycle is found with chemical fertilizers. Numerous scientific studies show that intensive cultivation using chemical fer-

tilizers and heavy irrigation causes soil to lose its organic content, and its quality degrades. Yields climb for a while, but then they begin to decline and only increased fertilizer can extend cultivation.

This degradation of land can affect hunger in a number of ways. First, it makes the farmers themselves more indebted to the agrochemical corporations that supply the needed inputs. Debt incurred by individual farmers and governments increased the need for revenue from exports to service those debts, and more food leaves the country. Also, as good farmland becomes unusable, the wealthier farms find it less expensive to expand onto the land occupied by small farmers than to rehabilitate their own soil, displacing more farmers from the land. The landless, desperate for jobs, also can be directly affected by environmental contamination because they work at jobs in which they are exposed to dangerous pesticides without adequate protection. This is especially true for women, who are not educated about the risks posed by agrochemicals and often experience health and reproductive problems due to overexposure.

Failure of Foreign Aid

The United States gives $12 billion per year in bilateral aid. Unfortunately, most foreign aid is actually harmful to the poor. Although aid may be couched in the rhetoric of alleviating hunger, the true goal is to expand markets for domestic producers and to support U.S. foreign policy. Aid levels reached an all-time high in 1985, with U.S. aid at $20.2 billion, when the cold war motivated both sides to collect as many allies as it could.

There are two types of aid. The first, Title I aid, takes the form of low-interest loans to the governments of allies in order to purchase the United States grain surpluses. The grain is then resold to domestic markets, usually to large-scale processors, doing nothing to alleviate hunger. Title II aid is called "humanitarian aid," and accounts for less than a third of total aid. It involves direct donation of food, primarily from private voluntary organizations and intergovernmental organizations. By flooding the markets with cheap grains, it discourages local production—instead of increasing local production, which could provide a stable food supply. It has a Band-Aid effect in the short term but destroys long-term self-reliance.

Many U.S. and World Bank aid programs are conditional on policies of austerity and structural adjustment. Countries must enact these policies in order to receive the aid. The theory behind these policies is to open domestic economies to international trade, thus creating more government revenue, but they also devalue currency and slash domestic spending on programs designed to promote health and education and allieviate poverty. Many of the programs that are cut provide support to women, children, and families. The same families that are impoverished by farm consolidation and lack of decent jobs are then neglected by government programs. This is also true in the United States, where the minimum wage has not kept up with the increasing cost of living and welfare reform has taken away the safety net for the working poor.

Food Security and Human Rights

Hunger is not a production problem; it is a problem of power. Enough food exists, yet many people are unable to access it or obtain the means to produce it themselves. Hunger is a result of an uneven and unjust distribution of resources that denies food security to millions of people. *Food security* means the existence of safe, reliable, and sustainable food sources. Even if people do not suffer from daily hunger, they are at risk if their food supply is dependent on outside forces beyond their control. Food insecurity means that any disruption—be it job loss, illness, migration, or even international market fluctuations—can cause hunger.

Women tend to be most susceptible to food insecurity and instability. Half of the women on public assistance in the United States are fleeing situations of domestic violence. Across the world, women must shoulder more responsibility with fewer resources, less access to education and employment, and restricted social and political freedoms. Women have less money, and therefore less food. In a free market, food is available only to those with the means to pay for it. The Universal Declaration of Human Rights, adopted by the United Nations General Assembly in 1948, guarantees everyone an adequate standard of living. Food, clothing, housing, health care, and security are defined as basic human rights. It is not until we begin to look at hunger as a human rights issue that women, children, and the poor will achieve food security.

Some areas in the world that have taken this approach to food production and distribution, and levels of hunger there have dropped dramatically. The southern Indian state of Kerala has decreased hunger by allowing renters to own the land that they farm and by keeping food affordable in "fair-price" shops. In Sweden, all farmland is owned by the farmers who work it, and farm size is carefully monitored. The sale prices of agricultural goods are determined by agreements between government, producers, and consumers. Cuba responded to a severe food shortage in the early 1990s brought about by the collapse of the Soviet Union and the intensification of the United States' embargo by redesign-

ing its entire agricultural system. The monolithic state farms have been largely broken up and distributed to small individual farmers or cooperatives, and sustainable, low-input technologies have been utilized. These measures, among others, have greatly increased national food security in a time of crisis.

All these approaches stress the importance of democratic decision making in terms of resource allocation. Responsibility for hunger cannot be foisted on the "South," and the problem of hunger cannot be solved by token gestures and short-term remedies. The elimination of hunger is possible, but only through a profound change in the global structures that create gross economic and political inequalities.

See Also

AGRICULTURE; ECONOMY: OVERVIEW; ECONOMY: GLOBAL RESTRUCTURING; ENVIRONMENT: OVERVIEW; POPULATION CONTROL; POVERTY

References and Further Reading

Boucher, Douglas H. ed. 1999. *The paradox of plenty.* Oakland, Calif.: Institute for Food and Development Policy.

Lappé, Frances Moore, Joseph Collins, and Peter Rosset. 1998. *World hunger: 12 myths.* New York: Grove.

Mittal, Anuradha and Peter Rosset, eds. 1999. *American needs human rights.* Oakland, Calif: Institute for Food and Development Policy.

Kristina Canizares

FOSTERING: Case Study—Oceania

Fostering refers to rearing or having children through social rather than biological relationships. *Oceania* refers to the island societies of the Pacific and includes Papua New Guinea and Irian Jaya. "Oceania" fostering is a continuum of child sharing and giving arrangements that reflect behavioral aspects of kinship, including kindness and love. Fostering demonstrates mutual generosity, where, ideally, all participants benefit and community harmony is ensured. In this culture, unlike European, American, and Canadian societies, sharing a child is not a sign of parental inadequacy or a result of tragedy.

While western societies separate fostering from adoption, in Oceania the distinction is often irrelevant. For analytical purposed, fosterage has been differentiated from adoption by how permanent the arrangement was intended to be. When arrangements are intended to be permanent, jural rights, including access to land, food, titles, and other heritable assets, are formally transferred and the arrangement is called adoption. Less formalized or temporary situations where transfer of rights is not automatic are fostering. This distinction is useful mostly for western audiences; it does not reflect categories in Oceania. Regardless of the permanence of the arrangement, both sets of parents retain interests in the welfare of the fostered child and acknowledge their relationship to each other and the child.

Sharing children among kin is a long-standing cultural practice that predates Christian and colonial influences. Even as economic and ecological circumstances create urbanized and wage-labor populations, fostering persists. Explanations for the prevalence and persistence of fostering include social and environmental adaptations; Liliuokalani, the late queen of Hawai'i, explained: "Alliance by adoption cemented the ties of friendship . . . and has doubtless fostered a community of interest and harmony." Others have noted that fostering protects against community destruction after natural and political disasters such as droughts and colonization. In normal times, sharing helps redistribute children from large families, and ensures community survival.

The majority of fosterage relationships are organized between people who are related, either by blood or by a previous fosterage. Legal or state involvement in fosterage is infrequent. Current statistics for all Oceania are unavailable, but ethnographic literature indicates that between 20 percent and 100 percent of households samples (depending on location) have at least one adopted or fostered child, a rate far higher than in western societies. On the Polynesian island of Taku'u, for example, "everyone is adopted at birth, and individuals are under great pressure to honor adoptive relationships over natural ones" (B. Moir in Howard and Kirkpatrick, 1989: 77). The most common form of fosterage is probably the fostering of infants or toddlers by their grandparents; the next is the sharing of children between siblings. Fosterage of one sibling by another appears in the historical literature, but less in contemporary practice. Children or young adults may precipitate a fosterage themselves in Tahiti and other Polynesian societies. Tongans commonly ask toddlers, "Would you like to sleep at my house?"—a teasing question that indicates the option of fosterage.

Recent data for the entirety of Oceania on gender of the fostering adult or child are not available. Usually, gender is considered a less important factor than kinship relationships as they are prioritized in the particular Oceania community. In Tonga, for example, where sisters rank over brothers, and fathers rank over mothers, a sister has prior-

ity over her brothers and her brothers' children. A sister, and especially a father's sister, is therefore free to request a child for a fosterage, and very difficult (emotionally) to refuse. However, grandparents are most likely to foster a child. Again, kinship may influence the choice of a grandchild for fosterage: because the father's side of the family has authority, and the mother's side is associated with nurturance, maternal grandparents may be more likely to end up fostering a child. In North American settings, adoption is often considered traumatic for the birth mother, and hence a women's issue, but in Oceania kinship and about care expectations about care mean that both fathers and mothers miss the child who is fostered out. They will, however, take comfort in the extension of their kinship bonds through the sharing of a child. Thus, for Oceania in general, gender is not likely to be a prime factor in fostering, except in cases where there is a desire to balance gender ratios in a household, or, in keeping with local principles of kinship, to ensure the continuation of a matrilineage or patrilineage.

Throughout Oceania, feeding constructs and signifies kinship identity. "Feeding" is a euphemism for adoption in both Tahiti and Tuamotu. People who intend to foster an unborn child may provide a pregnant women with food. This ensures her well-being but also establishes a kinship connection between unborn infant and fostering parents. Birth parents often continue to provide food to both child and fostering adults, partly to maintain their own relationship with that child.

Increasingly, as Oceanic peoples search for education, work, and experience overseas, children may be fostered in the home village while parents travel. This is thought to provide children with an environment that is culturally familiar, safer, and kinder. Political-economic and racial factors are also considered in these cases: brown-skinned children who do not speak English are likely to be marked as racially different in western societies. Migrants often work long hours or odd shifts, or stay in inferior housing, making it difficult to give children adequate attention. Sending children home allows the parents to work, study, or travel without the restrictions of child care, and saves the child the stigma of racism. It also helps perpetuate kin relations, so that the fostered child becomes the tie that binds migrants to their home and (sometimes) financially dependent kin. Fostering adults hope to prevent the loss of culture and identity in the next generation.

Fosterage can lead to its own set of problems. Children sent "home" while parents work overseas may suffer from anxiety associated with separation and culture shock. An increased financial burden can result when fostering is taken for granted because of ideologies linking kinship with generosity. While high levels of fostering mean that there are multiple sources of kin and caring, and that lost individuals are replaceable, the psychological message of fostering may also be that relationships are contingent and interchangeable.

Research on fostering in Oceania would probably benefit from an explicitly feminist perspective. Contemporary Oceanic societies are subject to economic, political, and social pressures that threaten the ideology of kinship, gender roles, and the practice of kin-based generosity. These influences are likely to precipitate changes in patterns and styles of child sharing.

See Also

ADOPTION; HOUSEHOLDS AND FAMILIES: MELANESIA AND ABORIGINAL AUSTRALIA; HOUSEHOLDS AND FAMILIES: MICRONESIA AND POLYNESIA

References and Further Reading

Brady, Ivan. 1976. *Transactions in kinship: Adoption and fosterage in Oceania.* Honolulu: University of Hawaii Press.

Carroll, Vem, ed. 1970. *Adoption in eastern Oceania.* Honolulu: University of Hawaii Press.

Howard, Alan, and John Kirkpatrick. 1989. Social organization. In Alan Howard and Robert Borofsky, eds., *Developments in Polynesian ethnology.* Honolulu: University of Hawaii Press.

Liliuokalani. 1974. *Hawaii's story by Hawaii's queen.* Rutland, Vt.: Tuttle.

Linnekin, Jocelyn, and Lin Poyer. 1990. *Cultural identity and ethnicity in the pacific.* Honolulu: University of Hawaii Press.

Morton, Helen. 1996. *Becoming Tongan: An ethnography of childhood.* Honolulu: University of Hawaii Press.

Terrell, John, and Judith Modell. 1994. Anthropology and adoption. *American Anthropologist* 96: 155–161.

Heather Young Leslie

FREE SPEECH AND FREE PRESS

See CENSORSHIP.

FRIENDSHIP

The word *friendship* takes on different meanings both across and within cultures and in different historical times. Most often implying some level of intimacy between non-kin members of a social network, friendship is a relationship between people that varies in duration, intensity, and meaning. It is shaped in both form and meaning by socially marked categories such as gender, race, economic class, sexual orientation, ethnicity, religion, physical ability, and age. For example, in their description of white, middle-class women in the United States, Helen Gouldner and Mary Strong (1987) argue that friendships are formed on the basis of automatically excluding those who do not meet very specific qualifications of race, class, and sexual orientation.

Friendship takes many forms, reflecting the resources within a network: economic (with people in given social classes and occupational groups), social (with people whose cultural practices either segregate or integrate the sexes in voluntary associations), psychological (with people who are in certain developmental stages of life), and physical (with some elderly or disabled people whose mobility is limited). Friendships serve many functions, providing partners in activity, listeners in discussions of shared concerns, continuity of human contact for long periods, education, psychological support in times of crisis, monetary and other forms of forms of reciprocity, child care, and intellectual exchange. In her study of white women's friendships in Great Britain, Pat O'Connor (1992) found parallel functions, again shaped by the socially marked categories of class, age, sexual orientation, and social standing.

Not all friendships are endogamous, however; that is, not all friends share demographic characteristics. Research on women in various cultures indicates that some friendships include partners from different racial, class, ethnic, religious, and other groups. Minrose Gwin (1985) traces friendships between African slave women and white slave-owning women in the nineteenth-century United States. Maria Lugones (1990), Marsha Houston (1994), and Althea Smith and Stephanie Nickerson (1986) describe friendships across Latina and African-American racial and ethnic boundaries in the twentieth century. Mary McCullough's work on cross-race friendships between black and white working-class and middle-class women (1998) describes the barriers and challenges women face in sustaining such relationships in cultures that value only the endogamous and give high priority to men's friendships while ignoring or devaluing those between women.

Friendships between women and those between men have received different kinds of research attention, evidently reflecting patriarchal bias. There is some evidence that friendships between men are based on activity, whereas women's friendships are based both on activity and on lengthy and involved discussion over time. For this reason, women's friendships are often described as more intimate than men's.

Feminist scholars have encouraged women to reach across cultures to create friendships that will enhance both broader cultural understanding between routinely segregated groups and, ultimately, social change. Fern Johnson (1995) and Ruth Frankenberg (1993) write of the challenge of doing this work as white women. Victoria Chen (1994), Marsha Houston (1994), Tamar Katriel (1986), and Lynet Uttal (1990) describe the challenges of keeping friendships as Chinese-American, African-American, Israeli, and Japanese–Russian–Jewish American women, respectively.

Friendship provides a way to extend a chosen family and to obtain support for one's sense of self and psychological growth, as well as a way to work for political and social change. Feminist friendships tend to integrate the two, making the personal political and vice versa.

See Also

COMMUNITY; CONVERSATION; HOUSEHOLDS AND FAMILIES: OVERVIEW; NETWORKING; ROMANTIC FRIENDSHIP; SISTERHOOD

References and Further Reading

Allen, Brenda J. 2000. Sapphire and Sappho: Allies in authenticity. In *Our voices: Essays in culture, ethnicity, and communication.* Los Angeles: Roxbury.

Chen, Victoria. 1994. Feminist politics of racial difference. Paper presented at the meeting of the Speech Communication Association, New Orleans, La., (November).

Cole, Johnetta B. 1993. Between a rock and a hard place. In *Conversation: Straight talk with America's Sister President.* New York: Doubleday.

Frankenberg, Ruth. 1993. *White women, race matters: The social construction of whiteness.* Minneapolis: University of Minnesota Press.

Goodman, Ellen, and Patricia O'Brien. 2000. *I know just what you mean: The power of friendship in women's lives.* New York: Simon and Schuster.

Gouldner, Helen, and Mary Strong. 1987. *Speaking of friendship: Middle-class women and their friends.* New York: Greenwood.

Gwin, Minrose. 1985. *Black and white women of the old South: The peculiar sisterhood in American literature.* Knoxville: University of Tennessee Press.

Houston, Marsha. 1994. When black women talk with white women. In Alberto Gonzales, Marsha Houston, and Victoria Chen, eds. *Our voices: Essays in culture, ethnicity, and communication,* 133–140. Los Angeles: Roxbury.

Johnson, Fern. 1995. Friendships among women: Closeness in dialogue. In Julia T. Wood, ed., *Gendered relationships,* 79–94. Mountain View, Calif.: Mayfield.

Katriel, Tamar. 1986. *Talking straight: Dugri speech in Israeli Sabra culture.* New York: Cambridge University Press.

Lugones, Maria. 1990. Playfulness, "world"-traveling, and loving perception. In Gloria Anzaldúa, ed., *Making face, making soul haciendo caras: Creative and critical perspectives by women of color,* 390–402. San Francisco: Aunt Lute Foundation.

McCullough, Mary. 1998. *Black and white women as friends: Building cross-race friendships.* Cresskill, N.J.: Hampton.

O'Connor, Pat, 1992. *Friendships between women: A critical review.* New York: Guilford.

Smith Althea, and Stephanie Nickerson. 1986. Women's interracial friendships. *Women's Studies Quarterly* 14 (1 and 2: Spring/Summer): 13–14.

Uttal, Lynet. 1990. Nods that silence. In Gloria Anzaldúa, ed., *Making face, making soul haciendo caras: Creative and critical perspectives by women of color,* 317–320. San Francisco: Aunt Lute Foundation.

Mary McCullough

FUNDAMENTALISM: Religious

Although the term *religious fundamentalism* is widely used to describe conservative religious movements that seek to restrict women's rights, there is no consensus among scholars of religion as to what fundamentalism is or how it affects women. As the media describe it, *fundamentalism* refers to any religion that aggressively promotes traditionalist beliefs and practices, including patriarchal gender roles. In the United States, opposition to abortion and to the proposed Equal Rights Amendment to the Constitution was led by "Christian fundamentalists." In Iran, a "fundamentalist Muslim" government outlawed abortion, reinstated child marriage, and segregated the workplace. In Israel, "fundamentalist Jews" threw rocks at women who came to pray at the Wailing Wall. Fundamentalism, according to such reports, oppresses women because it asserts that they should restrict their lives to the care of home and children and must always submit to male rule. Fundamentalism is the enemy of feminists because it insists that patriarchy is God-given and should not be challenged. For those with secular or liberal religious inclinations, it seems obvious that women who live in fundamentalist communities would not do so if they had a choice. This image of fundamentalism, however, is oversimplified.

Definitions of Fundamentalism

Fundamentalism originated in the early twentieth century when conservative Protestants in the United States chose this term as a positive label to distinguish their own beliefs from what they saw as the watered-down doctrine of liberal Christians. Although some scholars see fundamentalism as a "patriarchal protest movement" (Riesebrodt, 1990), opposition to women's rights was not central to the early fundamentalist agenda. Most historians argue that Protestant fundamentalism was a response to modernization, including intellectual innovations (for example, theories of evolution, higher criticism of the Bible), as well as socioeconomic changes and demographic shifts (for example, greater religious pluralism in industrialized urban areas). While most Protestants adapted to these changes (for example, by rejecting a literal interpretation of the Bible and by promoting ecumenism), others resisted, insisting on biblical inerrancy and publishing a list of "fundamentals" in which true Christians must believe. The doctrinal battle was fought within Protestant denominations, all across the United States, for several decades. Following their public humiliation in the Scopes trial, fundamentalists realized that they could not stem the rising tide of modernism, and they left their denominations to form independent churches that withdrew from active participation in society. It was not until the 1970s and the rise of the religious right that fundamentalist once again became visibly involved in politics, this time in opposition to many feminist issues. By then the popular use of *fundamentalism* had acquired mostly negative connotations and was being broadly applied to many religious, especially Islam.

Given its Protestant origins and its negative slant, scholars have long debated whether it is appropriate to use *fundamentalism* as a comparative term. Those who defend its use (for example, Marty and Appleby, 1991–1995) argue that certain family resemblances that define fundamentalist movements worldwide: for example, the belief that Scripture is inerrant and should be interpreted literally; militant opposition to the values, though not the technology, of modernity (especially pluralism, relativism, and individualism); and a perception of themselves as victims. Others (Harris, 1994) point out that some of the religions labeled as fundamentalist lack these characteristics, while other religions that do exhibit these traits are not so labeled. So-called fundamentalist Muslims do believe the Qur'an is inerrant—but so do liberal Muslims. Catholics who subscribe to liberation theology and mobilize the poor in Latin America are in militant opposition to some of the values of modernity (corporate capitalism), but they are never called fundamentalists. The common factor in all applications of the term *fundamentalism* is, arguably, its pejorative use by liberal educated elites to designate challenges to modern western society as "other," nonmainstream, extreme, and therefore not to be taken seriously. Applying fundamentalism to anything other than conservative Protestantism, then, amounts to cultural imperialism.

This charge has important implications for research, as well as for international policy on women's rights. Delegates to the United Nations convention on women have sought to include sexual rights as part of the United Nations Charter on Human Rights. If this proposal were accepted, African or Asian countries that practice female circumcision or arranged marriage could be subject to United Nations sanctions for violating human rights. Westerners often assume that opposition to sexual rights is mobilized by religious fundamentalists. But third world women have long complained that western feminists indiscriminately impose their understanding of women's liberation on other cultures. Gilliam (1991), for example, has argued that women in developing countries are more concerned about economic than sexual liberation. Their oppression arises more from exploitation by western export capitalism than from modesty rules or prohibition of abortion or divorce imposed by religion.

Fundamentalism's Impact on Women

Even if we could agree on what fundamentalism is, it is not at all clear what impact it has on women. Three questions are commonly raised. First, do fundamentalist movements have a characteristic gender ideology? Virtually all fundamentalist religions are led by men, and most endorse patriarchal gender roles. Fundamentalist Christians, Jews, Muslims, and Hindus all teach that a woman's primary role is to be a wife and mother and that she should submit to her husband. They all emphasize female virginity, prohibit contraception, condemn homosexuality, and limit divorce. They all exclude women from ordination as religious leaders and limit their participation in worship services. In short, all of them insist that patriarchal structures outlined centuries ago in the Bible, Talmud, Qur'an, or Laws of Manu are eternally valid.

Yet these differences do not necessarily amount to a unified ideology. For one thing, there are important differences in the restrictions these religions place on women. Fundamentalist Hindus, Muslims, and Jews segregate men and women during worship, while Christians do not. Hindus and Muslims encourage female seclusion, veiling, and the segregation of public space, while Jews and Christians do not. Abortion and divorce are permissible in Orthodox Judaism but not in fundamentalist Christianity. Only Muslim law allows polygamy, and only Hindu law encourages a woman to worship her husband as lord.

Moreover, restrictions are enforced for different reasons. Fundamentalist Christians do not allow women pastors because women should not have authority over men. By contrast, an Orthodox Jewish woman cannot become a rabbi because women are exempted from all positive time-bound commandments including the requirement to attend synagogue. In biblical and Qur'anic theology, woman (like Eve) must be controlled because she is weak and more liable to deception. In the Upanishads, by contrast, woman must be controlled because (like the goddess Kali) when the feminine is independent, it is dangerous. And while fundamentalist Christians legitimate patriarchy in a literal reading of the Bible, Hindus, Jews, and Muslims build on long traditions of legal interpretation that exist precisely because scripture must be adapted to changing times.

Finally, patriarchal gender ideology is by no means unique to fundamentalism. The Roman Catholic church, for example, is clearly a patriarchy but is rarely labeled fundamentalist. What is different about so-called fundamentalist religions is that they dare to impose their patriarchal views (or at least attempt to do so) on the rest of society.

A second question frequently asked is why control of women is so important to fundamentalists. Reflecting on a variety of fundamentalisms, Karen Brown (1994) asserts that the inability of fundamentalist men to control the "external other" (the secular society they oppose) leads them to seek control over women, the "internal other." Her thesis is supported by Margaret Bendroth's research (1993), which suggests that evangelical Christian antifeminism is rooted in conservative Protestants' loss of mainstream status in U.S. society. In the past, much of what we today associate with fundamentalism (for example, a literal interpretation of the Bible) was the norm among Protestants. It was the simultaneous secularization of society and feminization of religion in the late nineteenth century that led fundamentalist men to reestablish a more masculine Christianity. Brown's thesis is challenged, however, by Nayereh Tohidi's study of Iran (1991), where fundamentalists moved to restrict women's rights only after the secular government had been replaced by a religious one.

Last but not least we must ask about the experience of fundamentalist women. Does fundamentalism oppress women? Or, put differently, how effective are fundamentalists in controlling women? In some cases it is clear that patriarchal rule is forced on women against their will. In Afghanistan, for example, women were forced by funda-mentalist Muslim rebels to give up positions of employment or education and prohibited from moving freely in public. In the United States, some fundamentalist Christian women suffer domestic abuse and are told by their pastor that submission and love will save them. In Saudi Arabia, a group of women staged a protest by driving unescorted in their car and were promptly arrested. (It is significant that Saudi Arabia is almost never labeled "fundamentalist" by western societies, while Iran consistently is—might this have something to do with the West's political relationships with these nations?) In cases where fundamentalist gender roles are imposed—often aided by armed force—many women feel oppressed.

In other cases, women seem to embrace fundamentalism. Tohidi (1991) has pointed out that millions of Iranian women voluntarily joined Ayatollah Khomeini's Islamic revolution. In the formerly secular country, the shah had implemented many legal reforms that by western standards would seem to liberate women (for example, abolition of the veil and desegregation of the workplace). Yet these changes were imposed by an undemocratic government and were part of a larger plan of capitalist development and westernization that was harmful to the lower classes. Thus many Iranian women donned the veil not as a sign of submission but as an expression of national pride and cultural identity.

There is a growing literature on American women who choose Orthodox Judaism or fundamentalist Christianity and who do not feel oppressed (see Brasher, 1998; Kaufman, 1991; Manning, 1999). Some of these women were raised fundamentalist and remain somewhat isolated from society. Others come from secular or liberal, sometimes even feminist, backgrounds and convert to fundamentalism as adults. Many are disillusioned with the feminist movement, either blaming it for society's failure to eliminate sexism or arguing that feminists have pushed change too far. Feminism, some fundamentalist women argue, has opened the doors for women to compete with men on male terms, but it has ignored many women's desire to be mothers and has allowed men to abdicate their responsibility to care for the family. Fundamentalist religion, by contrast, values and rewards women for motherhood and encourages men to keep their promises. Some fundamentalist women, then, are bargaining with patriarchy, trading freedom for security.

Other fundamentalist women, however, actively transform the patriarchal gender roles of their community. There are evangelical feminists who assert that the Bible is inerrant, that its rules apply today just as they did in the first century. Yet they insist that submission applies not just to the wife but is mutual and that a woman's calling may include not only motherhood but being a teacher or a lawyer. There are conservative Catholic women who argue that a good Catholic must obey all the rules of the church, including those on contraception and abortion. Yet they believe that this is a profeminist position because it challenges society to acknowledge women's reproductive nature. There are Orthodox Jewish women who live their lives by Halakhah (Jewish law), including the family purity laws that ban a woman from the synagogue during and for seven days after her menstrual period. Yet these women also study the Talmud so they can understand and question some of the laws that restrict them—for example, by demanding equal religious education and bat mitzvah ceremonies for their daughters. To understand fundamentalist women we must distinguish between feminist values (for example, the right to equal pay), which they embrace, and the feminist movement (such as, political organizations like NOW), which they usually reject. We must distinguish between official norms (for example, a prohibition against women pastors) and those that are actually operative in the community (for example, charismatic fundamentalist women preachers who establish their own following). Most important, we must listen to the women themselves. If they do not call themselves fundamentalist (and most fundamentalists do not), perhaps we should not either. If they do not feel oppressed, perhaps they are not.

See Also

ETHNOCENTRISM; FAMILY: RELIGIOUS AND LEGAL SYSTEMS; FUNDAMENTALISM AND PUBLIC POLICY

References and Further Reading

Bendroth, Margaret. 1993. *Fundamentalism and gender: 1875 to the present*. New Haven, Conn.: Yale University Press.

Brasher, Brenda. 1998. *Godly women: Fundamentalism and female power*. New Brunswick, N.J.: Rutgers University Press.

Brown, Karen. 1994. Fundamentalism and the control of women. In John S. Hawley, ed., *Fundamentalism and gender*, 175–201. Oxford: Oxford University Press.

Gilliam, Angela. 1991. Women's equality and national liberation. In Chandra Mohanty, Ann Russo, and Lourdes Torres, eds., *Third world women and the politics of feminism*, 215–236. Bloomington: Indiana University Press.

Harris, Jay. 1994. Fundamentalism: Objections from a modern Jewish historian. In John S. Hawley, ed., *Fundamentalism and gender*, 137–173. Oxford: Oxford University Press.

Kaufman, Debra. 1991. *Rachel's daughters: Newly Orthodox Jewish women*. New Brunswick, N. J.: Rutgers University Press.

Manning, Christel. 1999. *God gave us the right: Conservative Catholic, evangelical Protestant, and Orthodox Jewish women grapple with feminism*. New Brunswick, N. J.: Rutgers University Press.

Marty, Martin, and R. Scott Appleby, eds. 1991–1995. *The fundamentalism project*. 5 vols. Chicago: University of Chicago Press.

Riesebrodt, Martin. 1990. *Fundamentalismus als Patriarchalische Protestbewegung*. Tübingen: Mohr.

Tohidi, Nayereh. 1991. Gender and Islamic fundamentalism: Feminist politics in Iran. In *Third world women and the politics of feminism*, 251–265. Bloomington: Indiana University Press.

Christel Manning

FUNDAMENTALISM AND PUBLIC POLICY

Fundamentalism is a religious movement found mainly among the Abrahamic faiths that has broad political, cultural, and social implications, especially for women. Whether Protestant, Islamic, or Jewish, fundamentalist movements seek to influence the state and ensure that laws and policies conform to religious precepts. Reacting to social changes brought about by modernization and secularization, fundamentalist movements are primarily concerned with identity, morality, and the family. This preoccupation places a heavy burden on women, who are seen as the bearers of tradition, religiosity, and morality, and as the reproducers of the faithful. Such views have profound effects on women's legal status and social position, especially when fundamentalist views are successfully inscribed in constitutions, family laws, penal codes, and other public policies.

Examples of Fundamentalism in the Middle East

In the Islamic Republic of Iran, following the populist revolution that overthrew the pro-West Pahlavi monarchy and installed Ayatollah Khomeini and his associates in power in February 1979, a process of Islamization began. Existing civil laws and policies were abrogated, and new ones enacted in order to institutionalize the *Shari'a* (Islamic canon law) and enforce cultural integrity, family values, and public morality. The *Shari'a* found its way into the new constitution, the family law, and the penal code. Article 4 of the Islamic Constitution stated, "All civil, penal, financial, economics, cultural, military, political, and other laws and regulations must be based on Islamic criteria." In fact, Islamization occurred less in the financial, economic, and military realms than in the cultural, political, civil, and penal domains.

In addition to the bans on the production, distribution, or consumption of alcohol and the prohibition of singing, dancing, and parties—which affected men and women alike—the Islamic government imposed compulsory veiling for women and the segregation of schools, workplaces, and public transportation. The new family law reinstalled Islamic principles pertaining to marriage, divorce, child custody, and inheritance; these principles favor men and disadvantage women. For example, the age of marriage for girls was lowered from 16 to puberty. Restrictions were removed on men's right to polygyny, unilateral divorce, and temporary marriage (muta'a, or sigheh). Abortion, which previously had been illegal but was offered by doctors nonetheless, was outlawed. To encourage female domesticity and the traditional Muslim family, contraception was discouraged and made difficult to obtain.

The penal code revived the ancient principle of "an eye for an eye" while also discriminating between citizens on the basis of gender and religion. For example, the "blood money" given to a male victim or his family (or to the family of a man condemned to death) is twice as high as that given to a women or her family. The reasoning is that the man is the breadwinner. The punishment for killing a Muslim man is more severe than for killing a woman, a non-Muslim, an apostate, or an infidel. Indeed, apostasy is prohibited, and Muslims may not convert to another religion. Sons inherit twice as much as daughters, again on the principle that men are the breadwinners. New policies also banned women from fields of study, such as engineering, agronomy, and veterinary sciences, that were said to be contrary to feminine nature. Certain occupations and professions were also closed to women. For example, women could not become judges (because women are said to be less rational than men), and only a Muslim man could become president of the Islamic Republic. On the other hand, gynecology (though not obstetrics) became a field of study exclusively for women.

These new laws and policies were enacted and enforced by the parliament, which between 1980 and 2000 was dominated by conservative clerics. They were also made possible by the new Islamic political institutions, such as the Velayat-e Faqich (the rule of the supreme jurisconsult, who was first Ayatollah Khomeini and after his death Ayatollah Khamene'i), the Council of Guardians, the Assembly of Experts, the High Council of the Cultural Revolution, and the Expediency Council. During the 1990s some of the early discriminatory legislation regarding women's education and employment was overturned, mainly owing to agitation by "Islamic feminists" in parliament and in the media. Family planning was reinstated as government policy. In May 1997 the reform-minded new president, Mohammad Khatami, encouraged a more open environment and a freer press, leading women to make new demands regarding the modernization of family law and an end to discrimination against women in the Islamic penal code. However, in 1998 the parliament enacted two new restrictive laws, one to segregate health facilities, and the other to ban media images of women.

In Pakistan, the constitution of 1973 stated that there would be no discrimination on the basis of sex. But the rule of General Zia ul-Haq (1977–1988), the domination of the Jamaat-e Islami party, and the creation of the Council of Islamic Ideology led to laws and policies that discriminated against women or penalized them severely in the case of infractions. These included the Hudood Ordinances (which established harsh punishments for adultery) and the Law of Evidence (which limited women's juridical testimony). Other Pakistani laws enacted during the 1980s and early 1990s that further institutionalized fundamentalism were the Shariat Act, the Qisas and Diyat Ordinance, and the Law against Blasphemy (Shaheed, Zia, and Warraich, 1998). A dress code was established, and women government employees were forbidden to wear Indian-style saris to work. Pakistani feminists have called for a repeal of all these laws and policies, and for the implementation of the UN's Convention on the Elimination of All Forms of Discrimination Against Women.

In Afghanistan, the assumption of power by the U.S.-supported Mujahidin in April 1992 ended the previous leftist regime's experiment with women's equality. Clerical leaders in the refugee camps of Peshawar, Pakistan, where the Mujahidin were based, had already issued religious edicts banning women from wearing western dress, perfume, bangles, or cloth that rustled. The Mujahidin government's first announcement was that women were to wear the burqa, the traditional Afghan coverture, at all times. However, renewed civil conflict precluded implementation and enforcement of public policies, and in an environment of anarchy and lawlessness, thousands of women were kidnapped and raped by warlords. The Taliban, or Taleban, arose mainly in response to such lawlessness and violence, but their brand of Islamic law and order proved to be extremely orthodox and brutal, especially for women. After the Taliban came to power in 1996, they swiftly enforced compulsory veiling and female seclusion, all but banishing women from public space. Moreover, education and employment were banned for females until sex-segregated schools and workplaces could be established (Moghadam, 1999).

In at least one case, fundamentalists in power have argued that their laws and policies are superior to traditional and customary laws. Sudan passed a law recognizing marriage as *de jure* in order to secure the wife's Islamically given rights in inheritance and maintenance if she is widowed, divorced, or abandoned. The marriage certificate is supposed to be done by the *mazoon,* a man who draws up marriage contracts, but custom prevails and certificates are rarely kept, especially in remote rural areas. The Islamic marriage contract also allows a wife to insert stipulations, such as her right to work, to continue education after marriage, to own household property, and to agree on the amount of the *mahr* (dower), but it is not customary to put these down on paper (Hale, 1996: 195).

In other countries where fundamentalists have not come to power, they have still exerted pressure on states and governments to revise existing public policies thought to be unduly western, or to introduce new laws that are more in keeping with Islamic precepts. In Egypt, for example, the family law was revisited in the 1980s to make it conform to strict interpretations of the *Shari'a.* This allowed a man to decide unilaterally to alter the form of the family by adding another wife or by divorcing his wife. He is required to inform his first wife about his remarriage, and the first wife has the right to ask for a divorce if she does not accept the additional marriage. However, should she seek divorce, she is required to go to court and prove that adding another wife will cause harm to her. In contrast, Egypt's family law gives the husband the right to divorce without the consent of his wife and without recourse to the court (Badran, 1997:35). In Egypt, women do not serve as judges.

In Algeria, women do serve as judges, but the turn away from socialism after the death of Colonel Boumedienne in 1979 and the growing strength of a fundamentalist movement led to the introduction of a personal status code (family law) that discriminated against women and rendered them minors. Responsibility for the contracting of marriage was removed from the women through the institution of guardianship. Although a woman's guardian may not force her to marry or prevent a marriage, he may oppose the marriage if it is not, by his standards, in her best interest. The husband is deemed the head of the household and the wife must obey him. Divorce by repudiation is allowed, and the Personal Status Code sets forth very limited grounds enabling a woman to seek a divorce. Polygyny is permitted, and the wife's consent is not required, although her husband must inform her of his decision to take a new wife (Ziai,

1997). Not surprisingly, this Personal Status Code met with strong opposition. Indeed, the unintended outcome of the patriarchal family code, and of the growing power of the fundamentalists, was the emergence of a new feminist movement in Algeria.

Of all the countries in the Middle East (Israel included). Turkey is the only one with a secular political-juridical system. Secularism has been the hallmark of the Turkish republic since its beginnings in the late 1920s, and it is mandated by the Turkish constitution. And yet there, too, a growing Islamic movement, along with a growing number of fundamentalist women wearing the Islamic head scarf, presented a dilemma for public policy. In the interests of unity and secularism, Islamic dress was not permitted in universities or in government offices. But Islamists insisted that such a policy infringed on their human rights and personal freedoms. This public policy dilemma confronted the French government as well, when in the late 1980s Muslim immigrant families began to send their daughters to school wearing the head scarf. Public opinion on the subject was divided.

Contemporary fundamentalist movements arose in the 1970s and became especially vocal and visible in the 1980s. In at least two cases, public policies based on religious laws predate the rise of fundamentalism proper, but have similar implications for women and gender relations. Saudi Arabia's political-juridical system is shaped by an orthodox Islamic ideology (Wahhabi) that places a high premium on public religiosity, public morality, sex segregation, female domesticity, and the guardianship of women by men. Thus women are veiled, do not drive, do not mix with men, and do not vote (Doumato, 1995). Saudis must heed the daily calls to prayer, and they are forbidden to drink alcohol. In Israel, the Women's Equal Rights Law (1951) recognizes the equality of women and men before the law, but Article 5 of the law excludes its application to questions of marriage and divorce, which remain within the domain of the religious authorities. In orthodox Judaism, it is only the man who can grant a divorce, and a childless widow must go through a certain ceremony before she can remarry. The Israeli penal code, as amended in 1978, permits the performance of an abortion only after an authorized committee has approved it. Approval may be obtained if the woman is under marrying age or over age 40; if the pregnancy is the result of rape or incest; if there is sufficient reason to believe that the child will be physically or mentally deformed; or if the continuation of the pregnancy could endanger the women's life, or cause her physical or mental damage (State of Israel, 1995: 17).

Fundamentalism in the United States

The Protestant fundamentalist movement in the United States of the late nineteenth and early twentieth centuries eschewed engagement with national policy and preferred a separate existence far from the secularism of the surrounding culture. But the more recent American fundamentalist movement—sometimes known as the Christian right—has taken a vocal and visible role in public affairs, especially on matters pertaining to the family, abortion, and public morality. The rise of the Reverend Jerry Falwell's Moral Majority and the election of Ronald Reagan in 1980 helped establish a vast profamily and antiabortion movement (Bendroth, 1999). In the 1990s, the Christian Coalition spearheaded this movement, also taking part in electoral campaigns. Opposition to abortion, sex education in schools, teenage pregnancy, divorce, and homosexuality unites Protestant fundamentalists, the Catholic church, and like-minded members of Congress. The politicization of abortion rights, the introduction of "family values" on the political agenda, and debates on civil rights for gays are U.S. manifestations of the implications of fundamentalism for public policy.

Women and Fundamentalism

Because fundamentalist movements are rarely concerned with economic, military, or foreign policy matters, they do not offer an economic plan, an alternative program for defense, or perspectives on international relations. Nor do social justice issues, tied as they are to economics, appear to interest them. Thus fundamentalists in the countries mentioned above, as well as elsewhere, have had almost no effect on labor law, economic policy, military expenditures, or foreign policy. By contrast, their influence has been greatest in public policies pertaining to women, family, and morality.

Their preoccupation with legislating women's behavior notwithstanding, fundamentalist movements do have the support of many women, whether in Israel, the United States, Iran, Egypt, Algeria, or Turkey. Indeed, women's active participation in fundamentalist movements has been a source of much debate and discussion among feminist scholars (see contributions in Moghadam, 1993a). For many women, being designated as the carrier of culture and tradition is an onerous burden, one they might prefer not to assume, especially as it is predicated on control and conformity. But for other women, especially those who are economically dependent and anxious about modernity, it is an honor and a privilege to be elevated to such a lofty and responsible position. Such women seem to find value and purpose in the movement's endorsement and exaltation of their domestic activities and their maternal attributes. This is especially the case for women from lower-middle-class, conservative, and traditional families. As the Turkish feminist scholar Feride Acar notes: "Women have been exposed to contradictory, dissonant messages and practices, filled with false expectations and aspirations. This has rendered them vulnerable and receptive to an ideology that simplifies reality and promises escape from role conflict and ambiguity" (cited in Moghadam, 1993b: 147–148).

At the opposite extreme, feminists have formed a bulwark against fundamentalism. In Algeria, Turkey, Pakistan, Bangladesh, Egypt, Jordan, Malaysia, Yemen, Israel, the United States, and elsewhere, feminists have taken a strong public stand against fundamentalist intrusions on their civil, political, and social rights. They insist on reproductive rights, the right to education in their field of choice, the right to seek employment and be paid equally and fairly, the introduction of egalitarian family laws, the criminalization of domestic violence, the right to retain their own nationality after marriage and to pass it on to their children, and the right to attain political office. Feminists in north Africa have drawn up an alternative egalitarian family law that they have publicized through the media, conferences, and translation and publication of the text in French, Arabic, English, and other languages (Ziai, 1997). There and elsewhere, feminists also insist that their governments adopt the Convention on the Elimination of All Forms of Discrimination Against Women and implement the Beijing Platform for Action. These documents make wide-ranging recommendations on women's access to education, health, contraception, employment, and political participation; on social policies to harmonize employment and family life; on active labor market policies to prevent poverty and unemployment among women; and on the allocation of government resources toward these ends.

Religious women who are neither fundamentalist nor secular feminists also contribute to contemporary discussions and policy formulations concerning women. They seek to enhance education, family planning, and economic participation among women, insisting that women have a right to participate fully in the religious or national community. Some engage in a woman-centered reinterpretation of religious texts. For example Muslim feminists in Malaysia have developed serious perspectives on Islam, women's rights, the modern nation-state, and globalization (see Othman, 1994). Similarly, Christian and Jewish feminists have reclaimed their religions from patriarchal and orthodox interpretations. Secular and religious feminists alike represent a shield against patriarchy and fundamentalism.

See Also

CHRISTIANITY: STATUS OF WOMEN IN THE CHURCH; FUNDAMENTALISM: RELIGIOUS; ISLAM; POLITICS AND THE STATE: OVERVIEW; POLITICS AND THE STATE: MIDDLE EAST AND NORTH AFRICA; POLITICS AND THE STATE: NORTH AMERICA; RELIGION: OVERVIEW; REVOLUTIONS

References and Further Reading

Badran, Hoda. 1997. *The road from Beijing.* Cairo: UNDP.

Bendroth, Margaret Lamberts. 1999. Fundamentalism and the family: Gender, culture, and the America pro-family movement. *Journal of Women's History* 10 (1, Winter): 35–54.

Doumato, Eleanor Abdella. 1995. The ambiguity of *Shari'a* and the politics of "rights" in Saudi Arabia. In Mahnaz Afkhami, ed., *Faith and freedom: Women's human rights in the Muslim world.* Syracuse, N.Y.: Syracuse University Press.

Hale, Sondra. 1996. *Gender politics in Sudan: Islamism, socialism, and the state.* Boulder, Col.: Westview.

Moghadam, Valentine M., ed. 1993a. *Identity politics and women: Cultural reassertions and feminisms in international perspective.* Boulder, Col.: Westview.

———. 1993b. *Modernizing women: Gender and social change in the Middle East.* Boulder, Col.: Lynne Rienner.

———. 1999. Revolution, religion, and gender politics: Iran and Afghanistan compared. *Journal of Women's History* 10(4, Winter): 172–195.

Othman, Norani, ed. 1994. *Shari'a law and the modern nation-state: A Malaysian symposium.* Kuala Lumpur: Sisters in Islam and the Friedrich-Naumann Stiftung.

Shaheed, Farida, Asma Zia, and Sohail Warraich. 1998. *Women in politics: Participation and representation in Pakistan 1993–1997.* Lahore: Shirkat Gah.

State of Israel. 1995. *A decade of progress: The Israeli national report to the Fourth World Conference on Women, Beijing.*

Ziai, Fati. 1997. Personal status codes and women's rights in the Maghreb. In Mahnaz Afkhami and Erika Friedl, eds., *Muslim women and the politics of participation.* Syracuse, N.Y.: Syracuse University Press.

Valentine M. Moghadam

FURS

Since sumptuary legislation in the Middle Ages attempted to legislate who could and could not wear fur, fur has always been associated with wealth and attributed to an aristocratic or bourgeois class. It is only during the late nineteenth century and throughout the twentieth century that fur became increasingly identified as a feminine fashion commodity, as well as a sexual fetish, worn predominantly by European and North American women. The history of the fur-clad, white, bourgeois women can be traced to many European artistic and literary sources including seventeenth-century etchings by Wenceslaus Hollar and portrait paintings by Rembrandt, Holbein, Titian, and Rubens, whose works have become representative examples of women's and men's fur fashions. A major literary source for the emergence of the figure of the fur-clad woman and sexual fetishism is Leopold von Sacher-Masoch's novel *Venus in Furs.*

In the twentieth century, films ranging from G. W. Pabst's *The Joyless Street* (*Die Freudlose Gasse*, 1925) to Jennie Livingston's *Paris Is Burning* (1991) contributed to fur's association with feminity, the female consumer, and her symbolic power. In the late twentieth century, the fur-clad women was perhaps best known in Europe, North America, and Japan, as an icon of consumer decadence and violence toward animals, owing in large part to the images produced by the antifur movement of the 1980s. Organizations such as People for the Ethical Treatment of Animals (PETA) in the United States and Lynx in England launched media campaigns during the 1980s and 1990s that made use of various "fashion" industry techniques to engineer and popularize a successful antifur movement. A major consequence of the antifur campaign was the devastating effect it had on the economies of many Aboriginal communities in northern Canada, Greenland, and Alaska. Aboriginal women who produce fur garments for personal use and the fashion market were dramatically affected.

See Also

ANIMAL RIGHTS; DRESS; FASHION; FEMININITY; HUNTING; IMAGES OF WOMEN: OVERVIEW; SEX AND CULTURE

References and Further Reading

Emberley, Julia V. 1998. *The cultural politics of fur.* Ithaca, N.Y.: Cornell University Press.

Seager, Joni. 1996. *Earth follies: Coming to feminist terms with the global environmental crisis.* New York: Oxford University Press.

Steele, Valerie. 1996. *Fetish: Fashion, sex and power.* New York: Oxford University Press.

Julia V. Emberley

FUTURE STUDIES

Future studies—the systematic study of preferred, possible, and probable versions of the future—is a relatively new field. In its modern history it has moved from being focused on uptoianism to making empirical predictions. Currently, future studies in government and business is dominated by strategic planning, technology impact assessment, and risk analysis. In academia, following the social sciences in general, future studies has taken a more critical perspective, focused less on what the future will be like, or even on the range of alternative futures, to what is missing in particular visions of the future. The quest for a more balanced study of the future is being driven by futurists who are far less committed to corporate and scientific interests and far more sympathetic to multicultural concerns as to who is likely to be excluded if a certain future comes about. There is thus a slow but significant shift from future studies as a management tool for controling the future to future studies as a framework for social emancipation.

Still, future studies remains largely male-dominated in terms of practitioners and in terms of the epistemological assumptions that underlie theory, methodology, and content. Women remain excluded from both the history and the future of the future. At the same time, the evidence of women's one-time importance when it comes to understanding and creating the future can be easily found in the realm of old and long memories, for example, as expressed in Slav, Greek, Roman, Nordic, Saxon, and Indian mythology. In most archaic traditions, one of the important functions of a goddess was deciding men's fates. In Slav tradition, *sudjenice* are three women in charge of deciding everyone's personal destiny. One of the rare deities, and possibly the only deity, specifically in charge of the future was in fact not a male deity but a female deity, *Skuld,* one of the *Norns* from the Nordic tradition.

Even during times when patriarchy was at its peak, there were always individual women who challenged perscribed gender relationships and gender roles. But in most societies, men have been in charge of controlling the public future and women have had little say about it. Women's encounter with the future was confined to better care for future generations and present households.

Elise Boulding, a peace theorist and futurist, explains this ambiguity—that is, women's simultaneously being and not being "in charge" of the future. According to Boulding, one important historical role of women was as conservers of resources and as nurturers to fend off "the effects of change as much as possible in order to preserve a space of tranquility for those in their care." At the same time, "every woman with responsibility for a household is a practicing futurist," and women have always been the "womb of the future in every society" (Boulding, 1983:9).

The appearance of the feminist movement was crucial in redefining what issues are "important" and "global." The feminist dictum that the personal is political gave women long-needed legitimization to bring what they considered extremely important to the discussion about the creation of the future. The old and traditional women's activities directed toward influencing the future (for example, through the roles of witches or fates), which were primarily local, personal, family- and community-oriented, got legitimization to be brought to the societal level. Even more important, the legitimization of "women's issues" has created the possibility for many women futurists to write about both local and (redefined) global directions for the future.

Many women futurists have envisioned radically different future societies and suggested feminist alternatives to patriarchy. As a movement for social change, feminism is concerned with offering alternative visions of the future. Women futurists concentrate particularly on the study of the future in order to both redefine the present and articulate an alternative vision.

Women's Visions

Women's visions of the future are usually somewhat different from those of men. While both genders are concerned with the betterment of humankind in the future, most men tend to concentrate on "grand" historical analyses and issues, concentrating especially on realist discussions of emerging political powers as well as on new technologies. The predominance of power-oriented forecasting is evidenced by the focus on nation-oriented "Year 2000" or "Year 2020" studies (strategic in orientation) and the predominance of technological forecasting is evident in the images of the future that are circulated—for example, production of babies in factories and other types of mediation of human relationships through genetic and other new technologies. The methodologies used still rely heavily on "expert" opinion and on development of powerful mathematics "formulas" to forecast and develop accurate trend analysis. Most women futurists do not reject new technologies, nor do they refuse to acknowledge the obvious impact of technology on the lives of present and future generations. But the focus is often rather on human relationships and is more inclusive of the perspective of the powerless.

In terms of methodology, trend analysis is not a preferred method of future studies, as many trends are quite discouraging for the future of women or the speed of change is extremely slow. While this method is useful in revealing the likely future if current trends do not change, it offers no alternatives. On the other hand, methods such as visioning, in which preferred futures are articulated, and backcasting, in which the preferable future is developed and then the path toward it is "remembered," are more relevant for women, and for other similarly disadvantaged members of (global) society.

Visions of future societies are developed everywhere, but those developed in the West are the best known and most influential. Examples include the "win-win world" in which the escape route from the prison of gender as well as economism is through the path of cooperation, community, and caring (Hazel Henderson, 1996); the "gentle (androgynous) society" (Boulding, 1977); and the "partnership society, gylany (Eisler, 1996). In south Asia, Nandini Joshi envisions the future of the world community "not in the huge, crowded, cumbersome, crime-threatened cities, overridden with unemployment and inflation" but in "lustrous, flourishing, free villages overflowing with useful goods, professions, intelligence and arts" (1992: 935). Many other women as well imagine preferable futures, for example, through feminist fiction and through global grassroots movements. There preferable futures are usually decentralized, nonhierarchical, ecologically and economically sustainable societies where communal life, family life, parenting, and education are highly valued, institutions are human-scaled, and diversity is celebrated.

Futurists also develop scenarios for the future. Scenarios are useful in that they can empower individuals and communities, as a range of preferable futures can be chosen and actions developed in order to achieve them. They are also important because they articulate futures that can help women develop strategies to try to avoid certain futures or at least diminish their impact. Scenarios also distance us from the present, creating alternatives that contest traditional gender roles.

Scenarios for women's futures usually include (1) continued female-male polarity (in the form of male backlash, continued growth, patriarchy, or the status quo); (2) (lesbian) separatism; and (3) partnership or a golden age of equality (imagined in the form of unisex androgyny or in the form of multiple gender diversities). In the "continued female-male polarity" scenario, gender is fixed and there is little escape from socially constructed gender roles. Societies either stay the same, with patriarchy changing only form and not substance; or the patriarchy increases, either through slow growth or dramatically in the form of male backlash against recent women's gains in the society. Women's separatism is one response to such futures, as women form women-only groupings. The "partnership" scenario imagines societies where there is equal cooperation of genders, where women increasingly adopt virtues traditionally seen as masculine and vice versa, or where gender becomes even more fluid and essentialist categories such as "man" or "woman" are abandoned altogether.

No mater which scenario dominates, it is imperative that women continue to address the future in public, private, and epistemological spaces.

See also

GLOBALIZATION; INTERNATIONAL RELATIONS; SCIENCE FICTION; TECHNOLOGY; UTOPIANISM

References and Further Reading

Aburdene, Patricia, and Naisbitt, John. 1992. *Megatrends for women.* New York: Villard.
Boulding, Elise. 1977. *The underside of history: A view of women through time.* Boulder, Col.: Westview.
———. 1983. Women's visions of the future. In Eleonora Masini, ed., *Visions of desirable societies.* Pergamon.
Eisler, Riane. 1987. *The chalice and the blade: Our history, our future.* San Francisco: HarperCollins.
———. 1996. *Sacred pleasure.* San Francisco: HarperCollins.
Gender and change. 1989. *Futures* 21(1).
Henderson, Hazel. 1996. *Building a win-win world: Life beyond global economic warfare.* San Francisco: Berret-Koehler.
Jones, Christopher. 1996. Women of the future: Alternative scenarios. *Futurist* 30 (3: May–June).
Joshi, Nandini. 1992. Women can change the future. *Futures* (9: November).
Special report on women's preferred futures. *Futurist.* 1997. (3: May–June).
Women and the future. 1994. *The Manoa journal of fried and half-fried ideas.* Hawaii Research Center for Futures Studies. Honolulu: University of Hawaii.
McCorduck, Pamela, and Ramsey, Nancy. 1996. *The Futures of Women: Scenarios for the 21st Century.* New York: Warner.
Milojevic, Ivana. Feminising futures studies. 1999. In Sardar Ziauddin, ed., *Rescuing all our futures: The future of futures studies.* Twickenham, U.K.: Adamantine.

Ivana Milojevic

G

GAIA HYPOTHESIS

The *Gaia hypothesis* proposes that the Earth behaves like a living organism, actively maintaining the life-supporting chemical composition of its atmosphere by self-regulating the quantity of marine algae and other living organisms in its biomass. Amid the disequilibrium of the Earth's atmosphere, the Earth maintains an improbable constancy of life-support conditions in the biosphere. The dynamics of this self-regulation can be understood as cybernetic feedback: the temperature, oxidation state, acidity, and other characteristics of the rocks and waters are kept constant by the responding levels of biota (living organisms).

The Gaia hypothesis was first proposed in 1972 by James Lovelock, an atmospheric chemist in England. Two years later he expanded the argument in an article written with Lynn Margulis, a microbiologist in the United States. Lovelock credits Margulis with adding the flesh to his skeletal theory, originally drawn from thermodynamics and systems science, by contributing knowledge of rich microbial communities and a biologist's view of how organisms evolve. The name "Gaia" was suggested to Lovelock by the novelist William Golding because Gaia was the classical Greek name for the Earth goddess. (Actually, Gaia was a pre-Greek goddess of the Earth, dating from the pre-Olympian symbol systems of neolithic cultures on the Greek peninsula and islands.) After more than 20 years of accumulating field evidence and developing mathematical models, Lovelock and Margulis noted that their discovery should more properly be called the "Gaia theory," although it is known worldwide by its original label. Lovelock refers to Gaia theory as the catalyst for a new branch of science called "geophysiology."

Initial objections to the Gaia hypothesis from other scientists centered on skepticism regarding the planning and foresight necessary for any sort of regulation. Lovelock, however, has argued, using mathematical computer models such as "Daisyworld," that the dynamics of cybernetic feedback linking organisms with their environment are simply a matter of responses to changes in conditions, which achieve homeostasis without benefit of oversight committees or other direction. In addition, subsequent atmospheric research supports the premise of the Gaia hypothesis by showing that marine algae in remote regions of the oceans, for instance, are the sole source of cloud condensation nuclei over those regions.

The Gaia hypothesis has several significant implications. First, it suggests that life is a phenomenon of planetary scale. Living organisms, nested in communities within their ecosystems all over the world, regulate the planet's atmosphere. That is, Gaian homeostasis originates in the local activity of individual organisms.

Second, the Gaia hypothesis adds further justification for the contemporary correction of Darwin's one-way view of evolutionary adaptation. It is now apparent that organisms not only adapt to but affect their physical and chemical environment. Evolution is much more creatively interactive than scientists previously thought.

Third, the Gaia hypothesis enlarges theoretical ecology. Understanding species and their physical environment as a single system yields new models that shed light on the emergence of diversity.

Fourth, culturally and spiritually the Gaia hypothesis revives the idea—which has been virtually banished in modern times—of life on Earth as a great whole, an enormously complex communion of being. The sense of humans as embedded in a larger and coherent context was a wellspring of art, poetry, and religion in premodern cultures. It survives today in eastern philosophy and the worldview of traditional native peoples. During the twentieth century, it was put forth in the West by such philosophers as Alfred North Whitehead, Mary Daly, and Thomas Berry. It is also a central element in some versions of feminist spirituality, which draw on a religious heritage that located divinity (creativity in the cosmos) in various female symbols and metaphors. In the West one of the earliest expressions of the sacred whole was the bountiful Earth goddess, Gaia.

See Also

EARTH; ECOFEMINISM; ECOSYSTEM; ENVIRONMENT: OVERVIEW; GYN/ECOLOGY; WOMANSPIRIT

References and Further Reading

Lovelock, James. 1979. *Gaia: A new look at life on earth*. Oxford: Oxford University Press.

———. 1988. *The ages of Gaia: A biography of our living earth*. New York: Norton.

Charlene Spretnak

GATEKEEPING

As a general concept, *gatekeeping* refers to the action of any person, institution, or mechanism that selects some information out of a larger body of information for transmission to others. Most gatekeeping studies examine the process by which material is selected or transformed for redistribution through mass media. However, gatekeeping was originally conceived in the context of communication flows in small groups. As metaphors, "gatekeeping" and "gatekeeper" are found in literature ranging from medicine to law, business, and social services, where the connotations include any process by which, for example, patients or managerial decisions or benefits are distributed or circulated through or among organizational systems. In communication studies, the concept of gatekeeping arose within the tradition of mainstream empirical social science research. As a result, its usefulness to feminist and other critical approaches is relatively unexamined.

Most research on gatekeeping in the mass media has focused on decision-making processes that determine which of the large volume of news stories available are selected for inclusion in newspapers and news broadcasts. In news research, the term *gatekeeping* was first used in a study of how a single wire service editor from one newspaper ("Mr. Gates") selected stories to include in a local newspaper. Personal characteristics of Mr. Gates and his perceptions of news values were two of the main factors determining his choice of the 10 percent of wire stories that he decided to include in the local newspaper (White, 1950). Since that early research, the study of individual gatekeepers has emphasized whether they have common characteristics that affect their selection processes: personal values and preferences, implementation of news values they subscribe to, and perceptions of the preferences and interests of intended audiences. Studies of large pools of gatekeepers found consistency in their news values and homogeneity in their demographics. For the most part, individual gatekeepers have tended to be white, middle-class, Euro-American males in news organization in North America and Europe. When the gatekeepers' position within a news organization is taken into account, the preferences and norms of the organization and its leaders (for example, publishers) have been found to be an important influence on their decisions. The nature of the products of the gatekeeping process has also been explored. The most important aspects of news gatekeeping are inclusion or exclusion, length of the story, and its placement within the particular news format. The focus on conventional news values has reflected the normative concerns of journalism educators and scholars.

Gatekeeping has been an important concept in understanding the selection of international or foreign news for wide distribution. A related issue has been how translations from one language to another function as a form of gatekeeping in the course of transmitting, selecting, or circulating international news.

With respect to women's issues or women as gatekeepers, one study of "Ms. Gates" found that the individual gatekeeper's news values were consistent with the norms of the mainstream news organization she worked in. In other words, her gender apparently made no difference in her news decisions. The role of gatekeepers in including or excluding women's issues and the role of male dominance in perpetuating news values that systematically exclude women and their issues from the major news agendas are extremely important. Many analysts have argued that women are "symbolically annihilated" in the news, and that news routines and journalistic practices subtly but systematically exclude women from a kind of institutional level of gatekeeping, and thus from mainstream news agendas.

While some studies use gatekeeping to examine the inclusion of foreign news in U.S. media, but probably fewer studies consider how international news about women and their concerns is systematically excluded. Recent examples—such as how women's issues like female genital mutilation are circulated by the U.S. media when there are tie-ins with domestic stories and are ignored or neglected when they occur outside North America—may suggest that gatekeeping contributes to distortion and appropriation of these issues in news practices that continue to disadvantage women. That these media institutions are gaining increasing control of global news agendas seems to make such studies urgent.

See Also

JOURNALISM; MEDIA: OVERVIEW; MEDIA: MAINSTREAM; PUBLISHING

References and Further Reading

Bleske, Glen L. 1991. Ms. Gates takes over: An updated version of a 1949 case study. *Newspaper Research Journal* 12(4): 88.

DeVito, Joseph A. 1986. *The communication handbook: A dictionary*. New York: Harper and Row.

Galtung, Johan, and Mari Ruge. 1973. Structuring and selecting news. In S. Cohen and J. Young, eds., *The manufacture of news*. London: Constable.

Jacobson, Howard B. 1961. *A mass communications dictionary*. New York: Philosophical Library.

Shoemaker, Pamela, and Stephen Reese. 1991. *Mediating the message: Theories of influence on media content*. White Plains, N.Y.: Longman.

Watson, James, and Anne Hill. 1989. *A dictionary of communication and media studies*. 2nd ed. London: Edward Arnold.

Tuchman, Gaye. 1973. The symbolic annihilation of women by the mass media. In Stanley Cohen and Jock Young, eds., *The manufacture of news*. London: Constable.

White, David M. 1950. The gatekeeper: A case study in the selection of news. *Journalism Quarterly* 27: 383–390.

M. Kathryn Cirksena

GAY PRIDE

Gay pride is a term that derives from the mixed (though male-dominated) gay movement of the 1970s and 1980s, and its concern with "coming out" as a political process involving self-acceptance, integration in some kind of gay community, and public openness about one's sexuality: being "out and proud." In the gay movement, "coming out" in this complex and political sense (rather than in a more recent sense that signifies simply contact with a gay community) was crucial and involved an analysis of heterosexism as a basis of oppression. The depoliticization of the term has gone hand in hand with a more general depoliticization, so that a recognizable "gay movement" in its earlier sense perhaps no longer exists. Using the term *gay* (rather than clinical or pejorative terms) was related to notions of pride replacing shame and openness replacing secrecy; this has been retained in public gay demonstrations taking the more festival-like form of gay pride but otherwise has often been displaced by "queer." Thus Katherine Forrest's detective Kate Delafield moves from a covert lifestyle, through the lesbian Nightwood Bar and friendship with its openly lesbian owner, Maggie Schaffer, to feeling able to be present at the gay pride march in Los Angeles in 1985. In many parts of the world, the term *gay* has been increasingly "colonized" by gay men, obscuring the history of militant lesbian women in the mixed gay movements of the 1970s and 1980s.

See Also

HETEROSEXISM; LESBIANISM; QUEER THEORY

References and Further Reading

Beemyn, Brett, and Eliason, Mickey, eds. 1996. *Queer studies*. New York: New York University Press.

Forrest, Katherine. 1987. *Murder at the Nightwood Bar*. Tallahassee, Fla.: Naiad.

Jay, Karla, and Alan Young, eds. 1972. *Out of the closets: Voices of gay liberation*. New York: Pyramid/Jove (reprinted 1993).

Liz Stanley

GAZE

The first wave of feminist criticism was based on a sociological approach and examined images of women in imaginative works from high art to mass entertainment. Feminist film criticism, which began to take shape in the mid-1970s, opposed this early emphasis on "content" and focused instead on artistic form as a medium of expression, in order to address the question of how meaning is produced. In her article, "Visual Pleasure and Narrative Cinema," which marked the beginnings of feminist film criticism when it was first published in 1975, Laura Mulvey considered patriarchy in cinema by examining the workings of film as an intricate network of "looks." Mulvey identified three types of looks that constitute the filmic (and, one might add, televisual) organization of the gaze: the camera's look at the filmic event, the protagonist's look at other characters, and the spectator's look at the screen.

Mulvey applied preoedipal and oedipal concepts of Freudian psychoanalysis and directly related the film apparatus to the patriarchal unconscious, and she concluded that the filmic gaze is decidedly male. That is, all three types of looks are organized to construe the spectator as male and are in accordance with the needs of his unconscious. The psychic mechanisms instrumental here are voyeurism and fetishism. Thus, the viewing situation in the darkened movie theater is linked to the voyeuristic scenario of the primal scene with the little boy peeping through a keyhole, a scenario in which looking is related closely to notions of domination and submission, not only in sex scenes but in all screen images in which women are sexualized. Fetishism, by contrast, meets the male need to alleviate the threat of castration posed by women by transforming the female body into that which it lacks, a phallus. (Particularly striking examples of the representation of women as fetish may be found, it is often argued, in the Sternberg/Dietrich films.) While in the first mode of looking the gaze of the camera may be technically neutral, the fact that filmmaking is usually restricted to men seems to make it inherently voyeuristic and male. In the second mode of looking, the gaze of the male characters is mostly organized in fetishistic terms in order to make women its objects of the gaze. The look of the male spectator seems to combine voyeuristic and fetishistic modes of looking.

Despite its impact on feminist film and media studies, Mulvey's conceptualization of the cinematic gaze as inherently gender-specific has posed many problems and questions. These have been addressed by feminist critics over the past twenty-five years, yet crucial issues still remain. If classical Hollywood cinema construes its spectator as male despite the actual gender, what are the options for female spectators beyond a masochistic identification with the objectified woman on the screen or a transvestite's identification with the male look (Doane, 1982)? If voyeurism, with its patterns of domination and subordination, may also be pleasurable for women, does the fact that the male look is invested with power (whereas the female gaze is not) prohibit an appropriation of the gaze by women (Kaplan, 1983)? How can we account for the pleasure many women experience when watching Hollywood films (Koch, 1989)? How is the gaze modified in films addressed to a female audience, such as the women's film of the 1940s (Doane, 1987)? How can we conceptualize a feminist countercinema based on a different organization of the gaze (Johnston, 1973)? These questions have posed a challenge to feminist theory and have led to a broadening and diversification of the theoretical spectrum. But the notion of a gendered specular regime first applied to cinema by Mulvey, which differentiates between the bearer of the gaze as male and its recipient, the women defined as the object to be looked at, is still at the core of feminist media criticism.

See Also

CRITICAL AND CULTURAL THEORY; CULTURAL CRITICISM; FILM CRITICISM; FILM THEORY; REPRESENTATION; VIDEO

References and Further Reading

Cowie, Elizabeth. 1997. *Representing the woman: Cinema and psychoanalysis*. Minneapolis: University of Minnesota Press.

Doane, Mary Ann. 1987. *The desire to desire: The woman's film of the 1940s*. Bloomington: Indiana University Press.

———. 1982. Film and masquerade: Theorizing the female spectator. *Screen* 23(3/4): 74–89.

Johnston, Claire. 1973. Women's cinema as countercinema. In Claire Johnston, ed., *Notes on women's cinema*. London: Society for Education in Film and Television.

Kaplan, E. Ann. 1983. Is the gaze male? *Women and film: Both sides of the camera*, 23–35. New York: Methuen.

———. 1997. *Looking for the other: Feminism, film, and the imperial gaze*. London: Routledge.

Koch, Gertrud. 1989. Warum Frauen ins Männerkino gehen—Weibliche Aneignungsweisen und enige ihres Voraussetzungen. In *"Was ich erbeute, sind Bilder": Zum Diskurs der Geschlechter im Film*, 125–136. Frankfurt/M: Stroemfold.

Mulvey, Laura. 1975. Visual pleasure and narrative cinema. *Screen* 16(3): 6–18.

Eva Warth

GENDER

Gender, as the term is used by many scholars and activists, refers to the socially constructed and socially expected differences between men and women, as opposed to *sex*, which refers to the biological distinction between females and males. Humans are socially differentiated into two distinct categories—"men" and "women." Those who do not conform to their gender role may be seen as innately deviant or inadequately socialized.

Many feminists have challenged the view that sex determines gender and, in arguing that gender is socially constructed, have highlighted the cultural relativity of gender—the ways it changes over time and across cultures and shifts from one social context to another (see, for example, Oakley, 1972). Furthermore, gender is seen not just as a "binary" difference, but as a hierarchy. Men and women stand in a power relationship in which men as a class are dominant and women subordinate (Delphy, 1984). By arguing that biological explanations are inadequate to explain gender differentiation, feminists are able to challenge the view that women are "naturally" inferior to men.

Postmodernist feminists, however, have questioned the view inherent in the debate over sex and gender that mind and body can be separated. They argue that we all share the experience of inhabiting a body, and that each body possesses a sex, but female "embodiment" differs from male "embodiment." They conclude that although sex does not uniquely determine gender, neither is it irrelevant to gender.

See Also

BIOLOGICAL DETERMINISM; BIOLOGY; ESSENTIALISM; MASCULINITY; FEMININITY; NATURE-NURTURE DEBATE; IMAGES OF WOMEN: OVERVIEW; REPRESENTATION; SEX AND CULTURE; TRANSGENDER

References and Further Reading

Delphy, Christine. 1984. *Close to home: A materialist analysis of women's oppression.* London: Hutchinson.
Oakley, Ann. 1972. *Sex, gender and society.* London: Temple Smith.

Pamela Abbott

GENDER CONSTRUCTIONS IN THE FAMILY

Families vary in size and composition over time and between cultures. From a macro perspective, families constitute social entities within which cultural values, norms, and traditions are reproduced and practiced. From a micro perspective, families can be seen as units of individuals who share physical and material conditions as well as social and emotional experiences over time. In general, social scientists study families as societal institutions embedded in historical, political, and economical structures. Behavioral scientists focus more on how the family influences its members' development and learning.

Gender, as often used, refers to images, representations, expectations, norms, values, beliefs, and conventions attributed to the biological sexes. Every society has commonly

held ideas of what it means to be a woman or a man, a mother or a father, a girl or a boy. These ideas give rise to principles for organizing behavior, interests, work, appearance, child rearing practices, and other aspects of life, and are initiated, learned, and confirmed in cultural practices and traditions. The family constitutes one of the most important social arenas in which this takes place.

Both family and gender are socially constructed phenomena, created and re-created by people who share sociocultural contexts. This means that neither *family* nor *gender* has a universal meaning; rather, meanings vary with time and place. For example, the modern western nuclear family, a small unit consisting of man, woman, and child, represents ideas based on a limited sample of cultural traditions. The specific historical, political, religious, and economic circumstances during which this version of family has developed differ from conditions that produced alternative versions. Families constructed in other ways include extended families with more than one generation living and working together, or other forms of collective cohabiting; single-parent families; families without children; and families with homosexual adults.

Regardless of type of family, gender construction in families can be seen in daily interactions between family members over time. Certain domains of family activities are particularly relevant. Negotiations about divisions of household tasks, establishment of communication styles, distribution of responsibilities, and patterns of dominance are examples of issues in families' internal daily life, and these all are likely to be gendered. Social constructions of gender in family settings need, in one way or another, to be agreed on by the family members, not through explicit verbal agreements but through daily actions and routines that, taken together, suggest a coconstructed "theory" about the meaning of gender in a shared family context. For example, when children cry in the middle of the night, it is most likely that the mother will comfort them rather than the father. When the car breaks down, the father is more likely to fix it than the mother.

The content in these "local theories of gender" is solely influenced not only by an isolated family and its members but also by the family's ecology—that is, systems of beliefs and norms regarding women and men, femininity and masculinity, child care and work that are embedded in the family's social and cultural environment. Norms and values—gender-specific—present in this environment are "translated" into family routines and habits. Culturally rooted ideas of gender are understood, applied, and acted out within a specific family context. By participating in and influencing activities of various kinds, adults as well as children become involved in their own family's construction of gender.

It is often agreed that principles for organizing activities, responsibilities, social communication, and power structures in families are based on cultural norms for gender differentiation and gendered distribution of power. Such principles are part of our collective social knowledge and have normative and prescriptive implications for behavior and interaction. Embedded in societal structure and policy, gender systems—particularly as revealed in economical, religious, and legal contexts—become a framework for the development of gendered family practices and social interactions.

Marriage, Work, and Economy

In various societies, today as well as throughout history, parents and other family members have been involved in arranging the formation of new families (for example, by marriage). In order to accumulate or keep wealth and property in the family, appropriate partners have been chosen. In some cultures, for example in ancient Rome, the man bought his wife and she became part of his property. By contrast, romantic love is highly valued in contemporary western societies as a way of bringing adults together in family units.

The kind of relationship adults develop within a family is reflected in the distribution of tasks and responsibilities in and around their home. Although tasks and responsibilities can be exchangeable, gender differentiated patterns in which women predominantly perform certain tasks while men predominantly perform others are generally taken for granted. Feminists and others have argued, however, that such gendered distributions of tasks within the family do not originate in the biological nature of women and men—as most patriarchal discourse asserts—but are socially constructed according to organizing principles following contemporary gender systems, in turn related to economical and legal circumstances.

Historical events show evidence of a relationship between gender constructions in the family on the one hand and societal gender systems and economies on the other. Before industrialization, work inside the home and work outside the home were interrelated. Although women and men performed different tasks, their contributions to the survival of the family were equally important. Families were organized largely as economic units, with one major task being to provide their members with material and physical support. With the shifting economy and the rise of the modern industrial society, women's and men's roles changed. Labor became divided into work outside versus work inside the family household. Men were seen as related to labor outside the home, whereas women were related to labor inside the home, and this implied that women stayed at home. Although married white middle- and upper-class women usually did stay at home, unmarried, nonwhite, working-class women generally did not—they also entered wage labor, and so a class-related pattern of women working outside the family emerged.

During the last three decades of the twentieth century married white middle- and upper-class women with children increasingly entered the labor market, in particular in western societies. This was largely because of an increase in jobs and in women's education and an increased political and ideological awareness among women of their right to make their own choices. With the entrance of women into the labor market, a new discussion concerning the distribution of household tasks and responsibilities between women and men was initiated, influencing concepts of gender in the family.

The job market that women entered had gendered job segregation and unequal payment for women and men. Some occupations were predominantly filled by women and others by men, and this reflected and confirmed existent systems prescribing gender differentiation. In addition, men often earned more than women, and this confirmed ideas of male hegemony. When a wife earns less than her husband, it is likely that together they will decide that the woman should spend more hours at home than the father. Studies from Europe and the United States (Björnberg and Sass, 1997; Risman and Johnson-Sumerford 1998) have reported that mothers still have the primary responsibility for household chores and child-related activities. Although men do contribute to a larger extent in these societies, in particular in child- and food-related activities (for example, child care, cooking, and shopping), there still are great differences in the number of hours women and men spend in family work. Deep-rooted ideas about gender may also be revealed when previously childless people become parents. Although equality may be more common before a child is born, families tend to have more conventional gender patterns afterward. Children seem to mean more housework for women and more wage labor for men.

Although economic shifts have stimulated a rethinking of distribution of labor between women and men, the impact on traditional gender patterns for distribution of household tasks seems to be limited.

Political and Legal Conditions

National family policies and family law vary across nations and constitute important conditions for the organization of daily routines in families and the family members' position and rights. It is important to note that "family policy" is a vague term, because it often refers to formal policies and programs and does not always include the indirect ways states shape families (for example, laws concerning birth control and abortion, mandating minimum wages, and regulating health care). In general, family policies range from "no state interventions" to "full state interventions." For example, countries such as Poland, Russia, and the Czech Republic have a history of large-scale state involvement and general use of public child care services, which supported both women and men in their work outside the home. Since the fall of the communist regimes in these countries, different reactions to state involvement have been reported. Whereas Russian women and men often express negative opinions about public child care, studies from other eastern European countries have reported that women in particular view the decrease in public child care negatively (Björnberg and Sass 1997; Zdravomyslova, 1996). Sweden, Norway, and Denmark are well known for high levels of state intervention and a legal system that gives a high priority to gender equity. Historically, the women's rights' movement, initiated in the United States and western Europe, contributed to making women's political, civil, and social position visible; this in turn has influenced formal legislation regarding relationships within families (for example, the right to vote, share economical capital in a marriage, obtain an education, and to work).

Child Rearing and Parental Styles

Child rearing patterns and parental styles have been investigated in studies across cultures and subcultures, by means of ethnographic approaches, and daily patterns of family life have been described. This field of research has contributed to our knowledge about what role parents' and children's sex plays in child rearing practice. It has also provided information about how gendered patterns of interaction between parents and children reflect economical and cultural circumstances.

In general, the birth of a child means an increasing differentiation of the female and male roles—the mother's tasks increase while the father's tasks remain static. In most cultures, mothers have the primary role of caring for the children, whereas fathers provide material conditions (such as food and housing) for the family members. This differentiation corresponds to gender stereotypes reported in a large number of cross-cultural studies, in which females are generally described as being more socially responsive and males as more achievement-oriented (Berry et al., 1992), although the difference is not always very large. It is important to note, however, that although there are similarities across cultures when it comes to beliefs about who is the most appropriate parent to care for a child, an immediate, concrete familial situation may lead to another solution. It is also worth noting that in subcultures with a larger kin orientation, and in working-class traditions, families tend to differentiate less with regard to child care. To explain the mother's role as caregiver, some feminist writers describe the symbolic image of "the good mother" as particularly resistant to change (Haste, 1993). A caring mother, the ideal, is contrasted with a noncaring, self-centered mother who does not fulfil her "natural" duties. Such symbolic images, linked with views of femininity and masculinity, are deeply embedded in cultural theories of gender, and serve as guides for family members in their organization of daily life, including child care.

When observers look more closely for concrete examples of interactions between mothers and fathers and children, they report that fathers generally interact less with their children, that fathers are less available for their children, and that the responsibility of leaving work when the child needs parental care is taken much more often by mothers. Overall, mothers spend more time with children than fathers do, particularly when the children are young. It also has been observed that, although mothers in western families are increasingly employed outside the home, this does not seem to influence the distribution of time spent in child care. These patterns are primarily found in studies of white, middle-class western families, but in working-class and nonwhite families the overall picture seems to be similar. Although fathers in working-class families with both parents employed outside the home for practical or economical reasons tend to spend more time on child care than middle-class fathers, the main responsibility rests with the mother (Björnberg and Sass, 1997).

Parents tend to display interactional styles typical for their sex. Thus, fathers' interactions with children involve more roughness and physical activities, while mothers seem to be more sensitive to the child's emotional state and are more verbal. These styles are commonly linked with toys and activities at hand (a football game requires more physical activity than dollhouse play). Although it was thought at one time that parents behaved differently toward girls and boys, recent findings question this (Maccoby, 1998). It has been reported, however, that fathers are more concerned than mothers to preserve gender differentiated patterns in their children's activities, interests, and social styles; this is particularly true of boys' masculine traits. Maccoby (1998), discussing these findings, suggests that fathers induce their boys "...into male peer culture" (p. 143), but that this does not seems to be the case in mother-child relationships.

Children's Gender Socialization in the Family

For children, the family—a primary agent of socialization—generally is the first encounter with a gendered context. Children's social development is influenced, to a large extent, by daily interaction with parents and siblings, although recent research on gender socialization has stressed the peer groups. "Making sense" of the social world, including understanding what it means to be a girl or a boy, takes place within many social contexts. Gender constructions in the family, however, do involve children. And children adopt their families' interpretation of gender in their emerging understanding of differences and similarities between the sexes. By active participation in family routines—for example, when girls care for younger siblings and do household work—children actively contribute to the construction of gender.

In most cultures, parents generally respond to girls and boys in similar ways as regards to love, warmth, and affection. Boys tend to get more punishment and disciplinary control from their parents, however, than girls do. Girls, by contrast, tend to be more involved in emotional talk, particularly with their mothers. When a child causes a conflict or a problem of any kind, parents tend to approach girls by pointing out negative consequences for others, whereas boys are more often told directly to stop. This kind of gender-differentiated response reinforces the family's construction of gender, and also invites children to participate in it.

When children grow older, peers become more important. Transitions between home and peer groups enable notions regarding gender differences and values to be elaborated and tested in new social contexts. Although a peer group's social construction of gender does not always correspond with familial ideas, similarities in fundamental, culturally based, views of women and men and their relationships are likely to be found.

Concluding Remarks

The construction of gender in the family takes place daily. The dynamics of family life make demands on family members to organize and reorganize practicalities. Separation, altered employment conditions, reduced or increased income, moving, and health have to be dealt with. Conditions for construction of gender thus alter over time for each family and its members.

Fundamental cultural beliefs and norms regarding relationships between women and men will be reflected, however, in the organization of family life and practice. Although the magnitude of differences may vary, the direction is likely to be similar across families in a society. When daily performances of tasks and their distribution among family members confirm beliefs, this contributes to the ongoing construction and reconstruction of gender within families, as well as in society at large.

See Also

DIVISION OF LABOR; FAMILY LIFE CYCLE AND WORK; FAMILY: POWER RELATIONS AND POWER STRUCTURES; FAMILY STRUCTURES; GENDER; GENDER STUDIES; GENDERED PLAY; HOUSEHOLD AND FAMILIES, *specific entries;* SOCIALIZATION FOR INEQUALITY

References and Further Reading

Berry, J. W., Y. P. Poortinga, M. H. Segall, and P. R. Dasen. 1992. *Cross-cultural psychology: Research and implications.* Cambridge: Cambridge University Press.

Björnberg, U., and T. Sass, eds. 1997. *Families with small children in eastern and western Europe.* Aldershot: Ashgate.

Coltrane, S. 1998. *Gender and families.* Gender Lens. Thousand Oaks, Calif.: Pine Forge.

Conway-Turner, K., and S. Cherrin. 1998. *Women, families, and feminist politics: A global exploration.* New York: Harrington Park.

Ferree, M. M., J. Lorber, and B. B. Hess. 1999. *Revisioning gender.* Gender Lens. Thousand Oaks, Calif.: Pine Forge.

Haste, H. 1993. *The sexual metaphor.* New York: Harvester Wheatsheaf.

Komarovsky, M. 1992. The concept of social role revisited. *Gender and Society* 6(2): 301–313.

Maccoby, E. E. 1998. *The two sexes: Growing up apart, coming together.* Cambridge, Mass.: Harvard University Press.

Renzetti, C. M., and D. J. Curran. 1999. *Women, men, and society.* 4th ed. Boston: Allyn and Bacon.

Risman, B. J., and D. Johnson-Sumerford. 1998. Doing fairly: a study of postgender marriages. *Journal of Marriage and the Family* 60(1):23–40.

Zdramomyslova, O. 1996. Reflections on the transition of the breadwinner model in Russia. In U. Björnberg and A.-K.

Kollind, eds., *Men's family relations*, 33–42. Stockholm: Almqvist and Wiksell.

Solveig Hägglund
Ilse Hakvoort

GENDER DIFFERENCE

See DIFFERENCE and SEXUAL DIFFERENCE.

GENDER DYSPHORIA

See TRANSGENDER.

GENDER STUDIES

Gender studies is an interdisciplinary academic field that emerged in the last two decades of the twentieth century and is located mainly in English-speaking academia and its associated publishing industry. Its emergence is a direct result of the particular definition of "gender" that has developed in English-speaking universities under the influence of feminist thought.

The establishment of gender studies in educational institutions is confirmed by the existence of professorial chairs and undergraduate and postgraduate courses in this field and the steady publication of journals (such as *Journal of Gender Studies* and *Genders*) and books presenting research and criticism. Gender studies has links to other interdisciplinary fields, such as gay and lesbian studies and queer theory, and a rather troubled relationship with women's studies, which, in some institutions, it has replaced. Although gender studies is unquestionably indebted to feminist theory, not all feminists are happy with the way this particular offspring has grown up.

One form of gender studies retains a clear political focus, using the concept of gender as an analytic tool for social change, especially extension of the political agenda. *The Polity Reader in Gender Studies* (1994) exemplifies this position, hailing gender studies as a progressive development from women's studies and arguing that feminism has been so successful in introducing gender consciousness to the disciplines that gender now constitutes a field of study in its own right. Those who take this position see gender studies as more inclusive, less likely to be marginalized, and thus able to carry more political weight than women's studies, which they allege has become bland and ghettoized. It is a claim refuted by many feminists. This idea of gender studies emphasizes the gendered relations of men and women within social structures and incorporates concepts such as Connell's "gender order" (1987) to analyze the cultural constructions of hegemonic (dominant) masculinity and femininity rather than focusing solely on women and femininity.

More problematic for some feminists is the development of men's studies as a subset of gender studies, and what this means for women's studies. One concern is that a move from women's studies to gender studies will erode some of the academic career opportunities for women that women's studies introduced. For example, the first chair of gender studies was Harry Brod, editor of *The Making of Masculinities: The New Men's Studies* (1987). Although scholars in men's studies to varying degrees acknowledge this debt to feminist thought and, as in Connell's analysis, seek to deconstruct hegemonic masculinities, their work has the potential to dominate gender studies and eliminate the gains that scholarship in women's studies obtained for women. There are similar concerns that in gender studies, issues of lesbian subjectivity and experience will be subordinated to those of male gays. These concerns are related not only to academia but also to the academic publishing industry as it redefines its marketing categories (Robinson and Richardson, 1996). At issue is the specificity of women and fear that the overarching category "gender studies" will return women to invisibility once again. As numerous critics have commented, the diverse lives of individual women and groups of women are not reducible to the category "gender."

An additional development within gender studies is a move away from sociological to discursive interpretations of gender, following the influence of the French theorist Michel Foucault. A key theorist in this development is Judith Butler, whom Gayle Rubin calls the "reigning 'Queen' of Gender" (1998). Butler's often-cited *Gender Trouble* (1990) moves away from social constructionist interpretation to argue for an interpretation of gender as reiterative performance. When gender studies moves into this area of theory, with its links to queer theory and the implication that gender identity is voluntarily assumed, it tends to attract strong criticism from feminists committed to retaining a field designated as women's studies.

Much of this criticism reflects the increasing pressure faced by women's studies. Since the 1980s, when women's studies became more established in the universities of many countries, its political aims and its focus on "woman" as a subject have been called into question. The editors of an Australian feminist collection, tellingly entitled *Transitions,* hesitatingly introduce their text as follows: "We are in the strange position of offering an introductory text to a subject [women's studies] whose very existence is being challenged and redefined" (Caine and Pringle, 1995: x). Ironically, feminists' success in introducing the concept of gender to academia started to make an emphasis on women seem old-fashioned (Evans, 1990). Some view the development of gender studies as heralding the premature evacuation of women's political issues from academia, rendering passé the notions of "women," "oppression," and "patriarchy" (Modleski, 1991). For socialist-feminist critics, this move is linked to a broader depoliticizing that renders invisible lived inequality, most importantly inequality related to class. They see gender studies as reducing material inequality to a play of difference, "a dressing-up box version of reality" (Evans, 1990:461).

A recurrent theme of critics of some trends in women's studies throughout the 1980s was the increasing divorce of feminist theory from grassroots feminism, particularly through a turn of postmodernism. While theorists such as Denise Riley were depreciating the usefulness or validity of "women" as a unified subject and thus opening up possibilities for gender studies, others were suggesting that women's studies should retain its name, because "the identity of women is not the matter of negotiation and personal choice that some enthusiasts of deconstruction insist" (Evans, 1990:457). Radical feminists identify gender studies with postmodernist elitism and a dilution of feminism's political raison d'être (Bell and Klein, 1996).

At the heart of feminists' concerns about the proliferation of gender studies at the expense of women's studies is a fear that it prematurely forecloses feminist projects for social change by retreating into apolitical theorizing whereby differences are viewed as individual choice detached from material power relations and structures. Gender thereby becomes no more than one among many cultural positions and identities and loses its power to explain and redress some of the inequity experienced by women. In response, proponents of gender studies argue that contemporary theories of subjectivity have rendered the subject "woman" an impossible site for unified political action or argue that gender studies in fact will further feminist projects by scrutinizing masculinity and thus reintegrating feminist issues into the more widely relevant arena of gender relations.

See Also

EDUCATORS: HIGHER EDUCATION; FEMINISM: POSTMODERN; FEMINISM: RADICAL; FEMINISM: THIRD WAVE; GENDER; MEN'S STUDIES; POSTMODERNISM: FEMINIST CRITIQUES; QUEER THEORY; WOMEN'S STUDIES: OVERVIEW

References and Further Reading

Aaron, Jane, and Sylvia Walby, eds. 1991. *Out of the margins: Women's studies in the nineties.* London: Falmer.

Bell, Diane, and Renate Klein, eds. 1996. *Radically speaking: Feminism reclaimed.* North Melbourne, Australia: Spinifex.

Brod, Harry, ed. 1987. *The making of masculinities: The new men's studies.* London: Routledge.

Butler, Judith. 1990. *Gender trouble: Feminism and the subversion of identity.* New York: Routledge.

Caine, Barbara, and Rosemary Pringle, eds. 1995. *Transitions: New Australian feminisms.* St. Leonards, Australia: Allen and Unwin.

Connell, R.W. 1987. *Gender and power.* Oxford: Polity.

Evans, Mary. 1990. The problem of gender for women's studies. *Women's Studies International Forum* 13 (5): 457–462.

Modleski, Tania. 1991. *Feminism without women:Culture and criticism in a "postfeminist" age.* New York: Routledge.

The polity reader in gender studies. 1994. Cambridge: Polity.

Riley, Denise. 1988. *Am I that name? Feminism and the category of women in history.* Minneapolis: University of Minnesota Press.

Robinson, Victoria, and Diane Richardson. 1996. Repackaging women and feminism: Taking the heat off patriarchy. In Diane Bell and Renate Klein, eds., *Radically speaking: Feminism reclaimed,* North Melbourne, Australia: Spinifex.

Rubin, Gayle, and Judith Butler. 1998. Sexual traffic. In Mandy Merck, Naomi Segal, and Elizabeth Wright, eds., *Coming out of feminism?* Oxford: Blackwell.

Barbara Brook

GENDERED PLAY

Gendered play refers to the ways in which girls and boys organize their activities and play to construct ways of being masculine and feminine.

Gendered play is often unnoticed because it happens in the ordinary, everyday activities of young boys and girls. Because children are seen as acting *naturally* in their male and female categories, gendered play appears natural. A close examination of play shows girls and boys working actively to understand themselves as gendered players through social interactions with others. Play provides opportunities for girls and boys to learn about and practice the serious work of getting their gendered behavior right in order to be seen by others (such as other children and teachers) as competent (Danby and Baker, 1998a, 1998b; Davies, 1989).

Gendered play can be examined from a number of theoretical perspectives, including feminist (Jordan and Cowan, 1995; Thorne, 1993), feminist poststructuralist (Davies, 1989; Kamler et al., 1994; MacNaughton, 1997), sociolinguistic (Sheldon, 1996), and conversation analysis (Danby and Baker, 1998a, 1998b; Goodwin, 1990).

Aspects of Gendered Play

Research on gendered play appears to have focused on boys and girls aged 3 years and older. Children playing have been studied in preschool settings (Danby and Baker, 1998a, 1998b; Davies, 1989; Jordan and Cowan, 1995; Sheldon, 1996), elementary-school settings (Clark, 1989; Kamler et al., 1994; Thorne, 1993), and urban neighborhoods (Goodwin, 1990). These studies address various aspects of play, including the ways that girls and boys use talk and manage conflict differently and the ways that boys and girls engage in cross-gender play.

Goodwin's study (1990) of urban black neighborhood children in the United States found that girls were more likely to give attention to shared participation and decision making, whereas boys used more *directives* to get others to do things for them. Similar findings by Thorne (1993) and Danby and Baker (1998b) suggest that girls focus on nurturing and caring, while boys tend to establish and use hierarchies of *social organization* (such as size and age).

Girls seem to deal with conflict in less physical ways than boys. Instead, girls skillfully use language to hide and disguise disagreement (Sheldon, 1996). Jordan and Cowan (1995) found young boys beginning preschool acting as "warriors." Boys' play seems to have more physical action and contact than that of girls. Danby and Baker (1998b) have argued that boys' play can be analyzed as an orderly ritual of *masculinity*. Such a ritual might initiate entry into the masculine play world of older boys. This type of activity protects boys' play spaces as masculine spaces. Similarly, Thorne (1993) found that boys dominated the play spaces of the playground.

Girls and boys tend to play in single-gender groups. However, on occasion, girls and boys cross this gender "bor-

der" to play with the members of the opposite sex. Groups of boys and girls tease one another, invade one another's activities, and chase one another in playground games. Known as *borderwork*, this type of play is charged with excitement and anger (Thorne, 1993). Borderwork is often very public and heightens the sense of difference between girls and boys.

Teacher's Responses to Gendered Play

Where gendered play has been recognized as an *equity* problem, two approaches dominate the ways teachers might respond. In the United States in the 1980s, an *antibias approach* (Derman-Sparks, 1989) proposed that children be exposed to nonsexist toys and activities and to adults in nontraditional roles. At the same time, the *feminist* approach of Davies (1989) in Australia led to the conclusion that children themselves took up gendered positions in their play. MacNaughton (1997) contends that it is not enough for teachers to think that children will soak up nonsexist messages. She asks teachers to actively intervene to challenge traditional notions of gender. For example, she encourages teachers to provide alternative story lines. She, like Davies, suggests that boys should be shown ways of acting other than being aggressive, and girls should be shown how to be assertive.

Young girls and boys may act on teachers' messages differently. For instance, in one study, young girls accepted a female teacher's moral lessons on how to act in caring and nurturing ways, whereas the boys rejected the teacher's version, replacing it instead with their own masculine version (Danby and Baker, 1998b).

Young children seem to have a strong sense of gender difference and play to enforce that difference (Clark, 1989). This is a significant challenge for early childhood education. There is a growing body of research literature on gendered play, but it has yet to influence teachers' interactions with young girls and boys in any substantial way.

See Also

CHILD DEVELOPMENT; COMMUNICATIONS: CONTENT AND DISCOURSE ANALYSIS; EDUCATION: PRESCHOOL; GENDER; GENDER CONSTRUCTIONS IN THE FAMILY; GIRL CHILD

References and Further Reading

Clark, M. 1989. *The great divide: The construction of gender in the primary school.* Canberra, Australia: Curriculum Development Centre.

Danby, S., and C. Baker. 1998a. How to be masculine in block area. *Childhood* 5(2): 151–175.

————. 1998b. "What's the problem?" Restoring social order in the preschool classroom. In I. Hutchby and J. Moran-Ellis, eds., *Children and social competence: Arenas of actions*, 157–186. London: Falmer.

Davies, B. 1989. *Frogs and snails and feminist tales: Preschool children and gender.* Sydney: Allen and Unwin.

Derman-Sparks, L. 1989. *Anti-bias curriculum: Tools for empowering young children.* Washington, D.C.: National Association for the Education of Young Children.

Goodwin, M. H. 1990. *He-said-she-said: Talk as social organization among black children.* Bloomington: Indiana University Press.

Jordan, E., and A. Cowan. 1995. Warrior narratives in the kindergarten classroom. *Gender and Society* 9(6): 727–743.

Kamler, B., R. Maclean, J.-A. Reid, and A. Simpson. 1994. *Shaping up nicely: The formation of schoolgirls and schoolboys in the first month of school.* (A Report to the Gender Equity and Curriculum Reform Project, Department of Employment, Education, and Training.) Canberra: Australian Government Publishing Service.

MacNaughton, G. 1997. Who's got the power? Rethinking gender equity strategies in early childhood. *International Journal of Early Years Education* 5(1): 57–66.

Sheldon, A. 1996. You can be the baby brother, but you aren't born yet: Preschool girls' negotiation for power and access in pretend play. *Research on Language and Social Interaction* 29(1): 57–80.

Thorne, B. 1993. *Gender play: Girls and boys in school.* New Brunswick, N.J.: Rutgers University Press.

Susan Danby

GENETICS AND GENETIC TECHNOLOGIES

Genetics is the science that studies deoxyribonucleic acid (DNA), ribonucleic acid (RNA), genes, chromosomes, and their expression in plants and animals, including humans. On an individual level, genetics allows us to define females as those who possess two X chromosomes and males as those who possess one X chromosome and one Y chromosome. On a global level, genetics is the science underlying cultural conversations about such important topics as biological determinism, evolution, eugenics, the "nature" portion of the nature-nurture debate, and the ethical uses of reproductive technologies, biotechnologies, and genetic screening.

History of Genetics

In 1865, the Austrian monk and botanist Gregor Mendel (1822–1884) articulated the basic principles of genetic inheri-

tance of dominant and recessive single-gene traits by observing their expression in successive generations of pea plants (MendelWeb, 1997). In 1905, the British zoologist William Bateson introduced the term *genetics* when he was seeking a more elegant word for his study of "heredity and variation," which combined principles of Mendelian heredity with Darwin's theories about evolution of species and population change as a result of transmission of hereditary traits and mutations from one generation to the next (Schwartz, 1999).

By the mid-twentieth century, the pace of scientific discovery in genetics had become breathtaking (Chambers, 1995). In 1953, the molecular structure of the DNA double helix was identified. In 1983, the polymerase chain reaction method of reproducing DNA for scientific study was introduced. In 1984, DNA "fingerprinting" came into practice to identify individuals, and in 1990, the Human Genome Project began. Nineteen of the Nobel Prizes for Physiology or Medicine awarded during the twentieth century have gone to scientists studying genetics, among them Thomas Hunt Morgan (1933) for identifying the chromosome's role in heredity; Francis Crick, James Watson, and Maurice Wilkins (1692) for identifying the molecular structure of nucleic acids; Barbara McClintock (1983) for identifying mobility in genes and the possibility of recombinant DNA (Keller, 1983); and J. Michael Bishop and Harold Varmus (1989) for identifying retroviral oncogenes. The omission of Rosalind Franklin from the 1962 Nobel Prize awarded to Crick, Watson, and Wilkins is considered one of the most egregious examples of sexist discrimination in modern science (Sayre, 1975)

The accelerating pace of genetic discovery is likely to quicken in the twenty-first century as research institutes, governments, and corporations compete to meet or improve the many target dates set for the years 2000 through 2005 for releasing decoded genome sequences to the public. Corporations that turn genetic discoveries into patented applications for medicine, agriculture, and industry are growing segments of the world economy and affect global financial markets in important ways.

Genetic Technologies and Genome Projects

The human genome is estimated to contain some three billion units of DNA. The DNA double helix is made up of nucleotides, molecules that include two pairs of nitrogenous bases (adenine paired with thymine and guanine paired with cytosine) linked together by hydrogen bonds. The complete set of base pairs constitutes the genome, and decoding and mapping the specific sequence of bases in each organism is the work of the genome projects now under way. Most genetic technologies are based on recombinant DNA, a form of engineered gene mutation in which original DNA sequences are broken and the fragments are rejoined in new configurations. Applications of recombinant DNA technologies include cloning; gene therapies; transgenic mice predisposed to develop cancer, AIDS, or obesity for the purpose of scientific research; transgenic pigs designed as factories to grow insulin, tissue plasminogen activator, and organs for transplant to humans (xenotransplants); and genetically engineered crops.

After close to a decade of planning, the Human Genome Project began officially in 1990. The Human Genome Project is an international collaboration involving the Sanger Center in Great Britain; Généthon and the Fondation Jean Dausset-CEPH in France; the Genome Sequence Centre in Vancouver, Canada; and a group of research institutes in the United States that includes the National Institutes of Health, the Department of Energy, Los Alamos National Laboratory, Stanford University, and the University of Washington. All of the international partners maintain Web sites that post genomic data. The genomes for the *Caenorhabditis elegans* roundworm, the fruit fly *Drosophila melanogaster,* and several other model organisms favored by scientists for animal experiments have been fully decoded already. In the year 2000, mapping of the human genome, based on genetic material from six men and women of varying ethnicities, had been virtually completed by the combined efforts of Celera Genomics and an international consortium (Celera, 2000).

Genetics, Ethics, and Androcentrism

The scientific disciplines are often said to be androcentric in their organization and contaminated by sexism and racism. Two decades of research about the problem by such feminist scholars as Ruth Bleier, Anne Fausto-Sterling, Evelyn Fox Keller, Sandra Harding, and Sue Rosser seems to have made little difference (Condit, 1999). Scientific "objectivity" still is constructed by white males with PhDs and laboratory funding, while health care and agricultural applications of genome research are chosen by white males with MDs, MBAs, and JDs. A frontier mythos pervades genetic science (Sloan, 2000), with James Watson's memoir *The Double Helix* (1981) portraying DNA research in the 1950s as a gladiatorial competition between Linus Pauling and the Watson-Crick group. Francis Collins of the Human Genome Project consortium and Craig Venter of its corporate competitor Celera Genomics appeared to be playing the same heroic roles in the 1998–2003 phase of the race to decode the human genome. It is possible that the science of population genetics may prove useful in dismantling the antifemale myths of

biological determinism and antifemale constructs in sociobiology (Hrdy, 1999; Morbeck et al., 1997). By tracing matrilineal descent, mitochondrial DNA studies in particular can be expected to offer important new information about female sexuality and reproductive strategies.

Close to 5 percent of the budget for the Human Genome Project was dedicated to studying its ethical and social implications (Sloan, 2000; University of Pennsylvania Center for Bioethics, 1995; U.S. National Human Genome Research Institute, undated). The ethical problems that merit study have been defined by white males, however, and do not include animal rights. In general, bioethics policy has been unable to keep pace with scientific discoveries or with technological advances in reproductive and genetic technologies in particular. The human genome itself (the database of sequenced base pairs) will be in the public domain, but individual genes, gene fragments, and gene sequences are being patented at astonishing rates. Decoded gene sequences that do not offer the possibility of for-profit applications in the agricultural and pharmaceutical industries may be classified as "junk DNA," and new medications and gene therapies unlikely to return sufficient profit to justify clinical trials may become "orphan drugs" that are never brought to market.

Assessing change in genetics and genetic technologies at a time when progress comes in quantum leaps and paradigm shifts requires equivalent leaps of creative imagination. For synthesis of ideas and forecasts of the future, the reader is referred to Andrew Niccol's film *Gattaca* (1997).

See Also

ANIMAL RIGHTS; BIOETHICS: FEMINIST; BIOLOGICAL DETERMINISM; CLONING; EUGENICS; GENETIC SCREENING; NATURE-NUTURE DEBATE; PHARMACEUTICALS; REPRODUCTIVE TECHNOLOGIES; SCIENCE: TWENTIETH CENTURY

References and Further Reading

Celera. 2000. *Celera genomics completes sequencing phase of the genome from one human being.* <http://www.celera. com>

Chambers, Donald A., ed. 1995. DNA, the double helix: Perspective and prospective at forty years. *Annals of the New York Academy of Sciences.* New York: New York Academy of Sciences.

Condit, Celeste Michelle. 1999. *The meanings of the gene.* Madison, Wis.: University of Wisconsin Press.

Harding, Sandra. 1991. *Whose science? Whose knowledge?* Ithaca, N.Y.: Cornell University Press.

Hrdy, Sarah Blaffer. 1999. *The woman that never evolved.* Cambridge: Harvard University Press.

MendelWeb. 1997. *Genetics, botany, and general biology resources.* <http://www.netspace.org/MendelWeb/>

Morbeck, Mary Ellen, Alison Galoway, and Adrienne L. Zihlman, eds. 1997. *The evolving female: A life-history perspective.* Princeton, N.J.: Princeton University Press.

Sayre, Anne. 1975. *Rosalind Franklin and DNA.* New York: Norton.

Schwartz, Jeffrey H. 1999. *Sudden origins: Fossils, genes, and the emergence of species.* New York: Wiley.

Sloan, Phillip R., ed. 2000. *Controlling our destinies: Historical, philosophical, ethical and theological perspectives on the Human Genome Project.* Notre Dame, Ind.: University of Notre Dame Press.

University of Pennsylvania Center for Bioethics. 1995. *Ethics and genetics: A global conversation.* <http://www.med. upenn.edu/~bioethics/genetics/>

U.S. National Human Genome Research Institute (no date). *Ethical, legal and social implications of the human genome project.* <http://www.nhgri.nih.gov>

Faye Zucker

GENETIC SCREENING

Genetic screening for inherited disorders, congenital disorders, and inherited traits that may predispose people to develop major diseases is one of the oldest and most widespread applications of medical genetics and genetic technologies (U.S. Office of Genetics and Disease Prevention, 2000; World Health Organization, 1999). At its best, genetic screening allows for informed decision making about pregnancy, family planning, risks and benefits of medical interventions, and targeted gene therapies that improve survival and quality of life for people with genetic diseases. At its worst, genetic screening leads to discrimination against individuals and populations identified as having "bad" genes, abortion of female fetuses in cultures that practice sex selection and infanticide of girls, coerced abortion of fetuses with genetic disorders, and projects in cloning, genetic engineering, and eugenics that cross the ethical line dividing medicine from murder and genocide.

Genetic Disorders

The human body has 46 chromosomes in 23 pairs (22 pairs of autosomes and 1 pair of sex chromosomes), estimated to contain approximately 80,000 genes and 3 billion units of deoxyribonucleic acid (DNA). Each gene occupies a specific locus on its chromosome, with each half of the chromosome pair referred to as an allele. Identical alleles on paired chromosomes result in homozygous traits (AA or aa), while pairs of different alleles cause heterozygous traits (Aa or aA). Symptoms of genetic disease occur when a fetus inherits two alleles for a dominant disorder (AA) or two alleles for a recessive disorder (aa). Inheriting one allele for a dominant disorder (Aa) also will cause symptoms, but inheriting one allele for a recessive disorder (aA) may not if the dormant gene is healthy. Asymptomatic carriers of recessive alleles can pass them along to offspring, however; hence the importance of genetic screening in families with a history of genetic disorders. The two sex chromosomes determine gender, with females (XX) inheriting X chromosomes from both mother and father, and males (XY) inheriting one X chromosome from the mother and one Y chromosome from the father. Recessive traits linked to the X chromosome often do not cause symptoms in females because of the protective presence of the second X chromosome. Males inherit only one X chromosome, however, putting them at greater risk of such X-linked disorders as hemophilia, Duchenne muscular dystrophy, and color blindness.

Genetic disorders and birth defects may result from inheritance of one or more genes that code for a disorder (for example, hemophilia, sickle-cell anemia, and cystic fibrosis); from extra chromosomes or missing chromosomes (for example, Down syndrome, Turner syndrome, and Klinefelter syndrome); from new or spontaneous genetic mutations, or as a result of genetic damage caused by environmental toxins (for example, lead paint, pesticides, and radiation); from maternal malnutrition (for example, lack of folate); from maternal drug or alcohol use, or from maternal infections (for example, rubella, syphilis, HIV) (Jorde et al., 1998).

Patterns of genetic inheritance were first identified by the Austrian botanist Gregor Mendel (1822-1884), who focused on heterozygous and homozygous dominant and recessive single-gene traits in pea plants. In humans, genetic disorders are classified as autosomal dominant, sex-linked, and multifactorial. Many disorders are involved:

- Autosomal dominant disorders include achondroplasia, familial hypercholesterolemia, Huntington's disease, retinoblastoma, polydactyly, and neurofibromatosis.
- Autosomal recessive disorders include cystic fibrosis, Tay-Sachs disease, galactosemia, phenylketonuria (PKU), sickle-cell anemia, thalassemia, and albinism.
- Multiple gene disorders include rheumatoid arthritis, gout, diabetes mellitus, Alzheimer's disease, and some forms of cancer.
- Sex-linked chromosomal disorders include color blindness, hemophilia, and Duchenne muscular dystrophy. Sex-linked chromosomal abnormalities include fragile X

syndrome, Turner syndrome (XO instead of XX or XY), and Klinefelter syndrome (XXY instead of XY).
- Congenital anomalies resulting from maternal malnutrition, illness, or other causes include cerebral palsy, neural tube defects (spina bifida, meningocele, and myelonengocele), hydrocephalus, clubfoot, hip dysplasia, and structural defects of the heart, lungs, circulatory system, digestive system, and genitourinary system.

Perhaps the best known chromosomal disorder is Down syndrome; it occurs most often when a fetus has three copies of chromosome 21 (trisomy 21) instead of the usual two, for a total of 47 chromosomes instead of 46. Breast cancer, when linked to the susceptibility genes BRCA1 and BRCA2, is considered a multiple-gene disorder involving multiple mutations (Breast Cancer Information Core, 2000). As mapping of the human genome proceeds, knowledge about genetic disorders, genetic testing, and targeted gene therapies will grow.

Genetic Tests

Genetic screening as currently practiced is a medical process that comprises an analysis of family medical history, laboratory tests of blood and body tissue, and genetic counseling to guide decisions about medical care when tests return a positive finding. Tests may screen for genes that cannot code correctly for enzymes or other proteins required to carry out cellular functions; for abnormalities in chromosome number or structure; and for congenital anomalies (birth defects) caused by nongenetic problems during embryonic development. Pregnant women, women planning pregnancy, and newborns are the population most often screened, but adults also may request screening for genes now identified as significant risk factors in the development of such complex diseases as breast and ovarian cancer (BRCA1 and BRCA2), hereditary nonpolyposis, colorectal cancer, and Alzheimer's disease (apolipoprotein E).

Newborns may be screened for phenylketonuria, hypothyroidism, sickle-cell anemia, cystic fibrosis, and HIV. Pregnant women may be screened to detect Down syndrome or neural tube defects in utero or if maternal-child incompatibility of RH factors is suspected. Genetic tests currently in widespread use for pregnant women are blood screening, amniocentesis, and chorionic villus sampling, with ultrasound (sonograms) used to guide testing and to confirm results. The triple screen test and the maternal serum alphafetoprotein (MSAFP) test screen the mother's blood for MSAFP, estriol, human chorionic gonadotropin (HCG), and RH factors. Amniocentesis screens samples of amniotic fluids, chorionic villus sampling screens tissue samples from the uterine wall, and percutaneous umbilical blood sampling screens fetal blood from the umbilical cord. Optimally, genetic counselors should assist women in assessing the risks and benefits of genetic screening before testing, in interpreting test results, in planning medical interventions when test results are positive, and in planning future pregnancies (Baker et al., 1998). In actuality, genetic counselors often are not available or are not correctly trained, and the entire process of screening and counseling may follow a patriarchal paradigm, with ethical issues increasing as more tests and more treatments become available.

Sexism and Racism in Genetic Screening

Feminist scholars have been studying patriarchal paradigms, ethical conflicts, sexism, and racism in genetic screening and other reproductive technologies for decades (Corea, 1987; Spallone and Steinberg, 1987). Traditional misuses of genetic screening have included immigration restrictions against populations with "bad genes," and enforced sterilization of "feebleminded women" in mental institutions and prisons (Gallagher, 1999; Pence, 1995). Perhaps the most serious misuse of genetic screening in the service of sexism occurred during the 1970s and 1980s in India, when amniocentesis was offered for the purpose of detecting and aborting female fetuses (Balakrishnan, 1994; Carson and Rothstein, 1999; Klein, 1992). In the United States during the 1970s and 1980s, genetic screening and genetic counseling for sickle-cell anemia reflected racism against people of African ancestry. Genetic screening also led to the "XYY defense" in criminal trials, when geneticists and epidemiologists linked the extra Y chromosome in XYY men to an increased risk of violent behavior (Carson and Rothstein, 1999). The gene for Huntington's disease also was identified in criminal trials as leading to violent behavior (Pence, 1995).

New developments in genetic screening and in prevention and treatment of genetic diseases will improve quality of life for millions of people. However, ethical questions will accompany those advances and are likely to involve equal access to genetic screening, informed consent for genetic screening, availability of nonsexist and nonracist information from genetic counselors, safeguarding privacy and confidentiality of screening results, and prevention of discrimination against people with genetic disorders and women with BRCA1 and BRCA2 in particular.

See Also

ABORTION; CANCER; DISABILITY: QUALITY OF LIFE; ETHICS: SCIENTIFIC; FAMILY PLANNING; FETUS; GENETICS AND GENETIC TECHNOLOGIES; MEDICAL CONTROL OF WOMEN; SEX SELECTION; STERILIZATION

References and Further Reading

Baker, Diane L., Jane L. Schuette, and Wendy R. Uhlmann, eds. 1998. *A guide to genetic counseling.* New York: Wiley.

Balakrishnan, Radhika. 1994. *The social context of sex selection and the politics of abortion in India. Power and decision: The social control of reproduction.* Cambridge, Mass.: Harvard School of Public Health.

Breast Cancer Information Core. 2000. An open access on-line breast cancer mutation data base.

Carson, Ronald A., and Mark A. Rothstein, eds. 1999. *Behavioral genetics: The clash of culture and biology.* Baltimore, Md.: Johns Hopkins University Press.

Corea, Gena, ed. 1987. *Man-made women: How new reproductive technologies affect women.* Bloomington: Indiana University Press.

Gallagher, Nancy L. 1999. *Breeding better Vermonters: The eugenics project in the Green Mountain state.* Hanover, N.H.: University Press of New England.

Jorde, Lynn B., John C. Carey, Michael J. Barnshad, and Raymond L. White. 1998. *Medical genetics.* St. Louis, Mo.: Mosby-Yearbook.

Klein, Renate. 1992. Reproductive technology, genetic engineering, and woman hating. In Cheris Kramarae and Dale Spender, eds., *The knowledge explosion: Generations of feminist scholarship.* New York: Teachers College Press.

Pence, Gregory. 1995. Presymptomatic testing for genetic disease: Nancy Wexler. In *Classic cases in medical ethics: Accounts of cases that have shaped medical ethics, with philosophical, legal, and historical backgrounds.* 2nd ed. New York: McGraw-Hill.

Spallone, Patricia, and Deborah Lynn Steinberg, eds. 1987. *Made to order: The myth of reproductive and genetic progress.* New York: Teachers College Press.

U.S Office of Genetics and Disease Prvention. 2000. *Human Genome Epidemiology (HuGE).* <http://www.cdc.gov.genetics>

World Health Organization (WHO) 1999. *Human Genetics.* <http://www.who.org/ncd/hgn>

Faye Zucker

GENITAL MUTILATION

See FEMALE CIRCUMCISION AND GENITAL MUTILATION.

GENOCIDE

Although genocide is an ancient phenomenon, the actual term *genocide* was first coined in 1944 by the Polish jurist Raphael Lemkin, later a lobbyist for the United Nations Convention on the Prevention and Punishment of Genocide (UNGC) in 1948. The UNGC defined genocide as (1) the biological destruction or serious injury of a group and (2) indirect destruction by political measures intended to prevent births within the group and by forcibly transferring its children to another group. The major issue in the definition of genocide is intent. Ethnocide (destruction of culture) and failure to protect indigenous peoples from famine and disease are sometimes intended as genocide. However, defining an act as genocide is an issue of perception and ideology.

Genocide can be classified as cultural, violent-latent (where genocide is a by-product of other operations), retributive, utilitarian, or optimal (aiming at obliteration). It can be an aspect of international war or "domestic." Although few peoples have been annihilated through colonization, there are cases, such as the Aborigines of Tasmania and the indigenous people of some Caribbean islands, where colonization led to genocide. Other groups, such as the Aztecs and Incas, were greatly reduced, but their descendants are still large populations, and their original languages are still spoken. "Domestic" genocide affected groups held hostage to the fortunes of the host society, such as the Jews in Europe and the Baháis in Iran, in situations of struggle for power or self-determination or against discrimination, and in the course of war. In an act of genocide during World War I the post-Ottoman Turkish regime massacred much of the Armenian male population, while the women and children were deported to Syria and Mesopotamia; this eliminated an entire national collectivity from its homeland of several millenia.

The first definition of genocide as "the destruction of a nation or an ethnic group" (Lemkin, 1944: 79) was broadened by Helen Fein to include "sustained purposeful action by a perpetrator to physically destroy a collectivity directly or indirectly, through interdiction of the biological and social reproduction of group members, sustained regardless of the surrender or lack of threat offered by the victim" (1993: 24). The ultimate "logic" of racism often entails genocide. Because women bear children, they are, in a sense, uniquely at risk when they are members of a group targeted as racially or ethnically inferior. Taking into account the construction of women as "ethnic subjects," the definition of genocide must include political projects involving mass rape or mass sterilization, aimed, through women, at "ethnic cleansing" and at the elimination of a future ethnic group.

Contemporary international media and political scrutiny do not seem able to prevent genocidal acts. By making states—the main perpetrators of genocide—responsible for punishing their own crime, the UN in effect defends the right of sovereign territorial states to commit genocide (Fein, 1993: 3-4), although the UN does sponsor international conventions and treaties and war crimes tribunals aimed at punishing genocide, including mass rape (as in the former Yugoslavia).

Genocide in History

Much of the theory about genocide is derived from the Holocaust, which occurred in a modern western Christian and post-Christian society. Ethnic collectivities who were victims of the Nazi extermination included the Jews as well as Roma and Sinti (Gypsies), who were murdered to fulfil a declining state's design for a new order "to correspond to the ruling elite's formula by eliminating the groups conceived of as alien" (Fein, 1979: 29-30).

The Nazi regime systematically murdered more than 6 million Jews, condemned to death as a people. They were concentrated in ghettos, starved, tortured, and killed. Many who did not die in the ghettos were taken to the woods and shot or deported to labor and extermination camps in Germany and Poland. There, the able-bodied were selected for slave labor. Others were killed in gas chambers, their bodies cremated or buried in mass graves. The Holocaust was based not merely on anti-Semitism but on state racism—there was a direct ideological and organizational link between the Nazis' killing of the retarded and mentally ill, the *Lebensborn* program (which entailed kidnapping children of "Aryan" appearance in Poland and inducing Aryans to propagate), and the "final solution." The Nazis also murdered between a quarter and a half of the Roma and Sinti (estimates vary between 200,000 and 500,000); they murdered homosexual men (between 500,000 and 600,000) (Laska, 1993: 261-262); they murdered Poles; and they interned, starved, and killed Russians, POWs, the handicapped, Jehovah's Witnesses, communists, socialists and "asocials."

There is a difference between genocide aimed at ethnic, racial, and national collectivities, where membership is reproduced genealogically, and systematic extermination of ideological and sexual minorities, in which people become members on an individual basis, even if their numbers reach millions. For example, the labeling of Stalin's victims as "enemies of the people" was used to legitimize the communist regime. Soviet and communist genocide and mass state killings, sometimes termed *politicide,* occurred in the Soviet Union, Cambodia, and the People's Republic of China. In Cambodia, Marxism served as an ideological justification for the massacre of one-third of

the Cambodians by the Khmer Rouge between 1975 and 1979. Other examples of genocide include the decimation of native peoples in continents and states settled by Europeans: North and South America, Australia and New Zealand, and South Africa. The settlement of Australia is sometimes seen as an act of genocide against the native people through violence accompanying the appropriation of land, diseases imported by the settlers, alcoholism, wars, and slaughter by the colonists. Many leading intellectuals have accused the United States of genocide in Vietnam, and events surrounding the Irish famine have led some to interpret it as genocide.

Genocide and Gender

Genocidal projects are, among other things, sometimes seen as a consequence of the construction of masculinity and femininity. Gender has been offered as the explanation of genocidal massacres resulting from the positioning of women as the reproducers of the next generation and as a symbol of national and ethnic collectivities (Lentin, 1997; Yuval-Davis, 1997). Arguably, without the systematic murder of women and children, mass killing cannot be considered genocide: when men are the only victims, it is called "war," because the continued existence of future generations is not jeopardized.

Some feminist scholars (for example, Bock, 1993; Ringelheim, 1997) link racism, sexism, and genocide, although women can, and sometime do (see, for example, African Rights, 1995, in relation to the role of women as perpetrators of genocide in Rwanda) play an active part in perpetrating genocide. Rape is often cited as evidence of this link. At times of war, mass rape been used as a political instrument and a genocidal strategy of "ethnic cleansing" (Hague, 1997; Lentin, 1999). During the West Pakistanis' occupation of Bangladesh in 1970–1971, for example, between 200,000 and 400,000 Bangladeshi women were raped by the Pakistani army (Rozario, 1997), and it was claimed that this was a conscious military policy by West Pakistan, intended to create a new ethnicity and dilute the Bangladeshi nation. Similarly, it is argued that the Serbs and Bosnian Serbs had a policy of genocidal rape, particularly the version that uses forced pregnancy as a kind of biological warfare (Allen, 1996; Hague, 1997). During the Serb war in Kosovo in 1999, media reports on "missing men" accompanied reports of mass rapes of women.

There are no clear-cut statistics from the Nazi era, but there is some evidence that more Jewish women were deported and killed than Jewish men. As the skills the Nazis needed were those of men, women were often killed first. At the end of the war, more men than women could be found among the Jewish survivors. The same was true of other "racially inferior" groups such as Slavs and Roma (Ringelheim, 1997). However, strategies of survival seem, in certain instances, different for women and men—women tend to form alternative "familial" and communal groupings, seen by some Holocaust survivors as assisting survival (Baumel, 1999).

Women as Mothers

Nazi ideology, based on a belief in German racial supremacy, discriminated against women as childbearers. The Nazis legalized "hygiencic" sterilization as early as the 1930s, when 400,000 people with varying degrees of mental illness were sterilized because they were considered unworthy to reproduce (Burleigh, 1995). At the same time, the Nazis encouraged German women to bear children—even illegitimate children—fathered by SS men and other "racially valuable" Germans. Jewish women of childbearing age, although useful as workers, were considered a menace because they could bear children and ensure the continuity of Jewish life (Rittner and Roth, 1993).

As surgical sterilization was slow and expensive, German doctors, serving genocidal interests, experimented with X-rays, injections, and drugs as faster and more easily applicable procedures to control reproduction by "racially inferior" women. Roma women married to Germans were sterilized, as were their children after the age of 12. Jewish and Roma women were forced to become guinea pigs in Nazi medical experiments (Laska, 1993).

Women As Sex Objects

Women survivors of the Holocaust reported sexual humiliation, rape, sexual exchange, pregnancy, abortion, and vulnerability through their children—experiences that male survivors tend not to describe. Female survivors of concentration camps speak of the humiliation surrounding the entrance to the camp: being nude; being shaved all over; for some being shaved in a sexual stance, straddling two stools, while observed by men. Women often survived through sex, which was used as a commodity in some ghettos and camps (Ringelheim, 1997). Sex with the rulers can become a means of survival under occupation. In some concentration camps there were brothels reserved for the SS and privileged male inmates.

In the past, genocide was studied as gender-neutral, obscuring women's expreinces and sexist oppression. Ringelheim (1985; 1997), among others, makes a case for studying racism and genocide in the context of societal sexism. Lentin (1997; 1999) also argues for studying genocide as a gendered

phenomenon. Laska (1993) notes, too, that women play an invaluable part in resisting genocide.

See Also

ANTI-SEMITISM; APARTHEID, SEGREGATION, AND GHETTOIZATION; ETHNIC CLEANSING; EUGENICS; FASCISM AND NAZISM; HUMAN RIGHTS; RACISM AND XENOPHOBIA; VIOLENCE AND PEACE: OVERVIEW; WAR

References and Further Reading:

African Rights. 1995. *Rwanda. Not so innocent: When women become killers.* London: African Rights.

Allen, Beverly. 1996. *Rape warfare: The hidden genocide in Bosnia-Herzegovina and Croatia.* Minneapolis: University of Minnesota Press.

Baumel, Judith T. 1999. Women's agency and survival strategies during the Holocaust. *Women's Studies International Forum* 22(3): 329–348.

Bock, Gisela. 1993. Racism and sexism in Nazi Germany: Motherhood, compulsory sterilization, and the state, In Carol Rittner and John K. Roth, eds., *Women and the Holocaust: Different voices.* New York: Paragon House.

Burleigh, Michael. 1995. *Death and deliverance: Euthanasia in Germany 1900-1945.* Cambridge: Cambridge University Press.

Fein, Helen. 1979. *Accounting for genocide: National responses and Jewish victimization during the Holocaust.* New York: Free Press.

Fein, Helen. 1993. *Genocide: A sociological perspective.* London: Sage.

Hague, Euan. 1997. Rape, power and masculinity: The construction of gender and national identities in the war in Bosnia-Herzegovina. In Ronit Lentin, ed., 1997, *Gender and catastrophe.* London: Zed.

Laska, Vera. 1993. Women in the resistance and in the Holocaust. In Carol Rittner and John K. Roth, eds., *Women and the Holocaust: Different voices.* New York: Paragon House.

Lemkin, Raphael. 1944. *Axis rule in occupied Europe.* Washington D.C.: Carnegie Endowment for International Peace.

Lentin, Ronit. 1999. The rape of the nation: Women narrativizing genocide. *Sociological Research Online* 4(2).

———, ed., 1997. *Gender and catastrophe.* London: Zed.

Ringelheim, Joan M. 1985. Women and the Holocaust: A reconsideration of research. *Signs* 10: 741-761.

Ringelheim, Joan M. 1997. Gender and genocide: A split memory. In Ronit Lentin, ed., 1997. *Gender and catastrophe.* London: Zed.

Rittner, Carol, and John K. Roth, eds. 1993. *Women and the Holocaust: Different voices.* New York: Paragon House.

Rozario, Santi. 1997. "Disasters" and Bangladesh. In Ronit Lentin, ed., 1997. *Gender and catastrophe.* London: Zed.

Yuval-Davis, Nira. 1997. *Gender and nation.* London: Sage.

Ronit Lentin

GENRES: Gendered

The term *genre* originally referred to a hierarchy of different kinds of subject matter, codified in the eighteenth century in western Europe, but it began in theories associated with the founders of the sixteenth-century Italian academies of design. Academic theory arranged pictorial subject matter in order, ascending from lowly still life through landscape to portraiture, and finally to narratives of historical or religious events and allegories.

The humble genres were considered to require only imitation of surface visual phenomena, while narrative and allegorical painting was supposed to be more intellectually taxing. Rather than imitating reality directly, the narrative and allegorical painter was thought to create a new pictorial nature, imagining actors to convey an idea or instant, and generalizing from years of studying nature and especially the human figure, to produce a dramatically convincing composition. Such paintings—called history or narrative painting—were supposed to have a moral force, teaching good action to the viewer, through relating the lessons of history or the tenets of religious belief. In addition, modest genres like still life were likely to be relatively small and made for private, domestic use, whereas narratives and allegories could be on a grand scale, for important public locations. According to scholars like Germaine Greer (1979) and Deborah Cherry (1993), women painters in the western tradition were usually confined to the humble, imitative, private genres. Women painters were largely prevented from studying the nude, which was part of the training for creating impressive historical and allegorical paintings, until the end of the nineteenth century—that is, until the modernist (male) mainstream was shifting away from naturalistic representation.

From the late nineteenth century, in the West, men dominated the various forms of abstract art and claimed the lofty cerebral and imaginative positions that had been held earlier by male artists making history or narrative paintings.

It was argued that the purest and noblest images referred viewers back to the images themselves and out to the problems of design. In this new system of the arts, the highest genre was considered to take as its subject matter the exploration of art itself.

Only in the 1960s, with the development of feminist art, did a critical mass of women artists turn from varieties of abstraction to exploring different subject matter. This often entailed new media and techniques, to communicate a complex critique of male-dominated societies to undermine the monolithic status of modernism, and to develop postmodernist approaches.

Several avenues have been explored by women who want to destroy the "gendering" of genres of art. Women may, for instance, reject the gender hierarchy by competing for high status in modernist styles, especially styles conventionally associated with men, like large-scale public sculpture in stone or metal.

Women artists have also returned to genres that were assigned to women as appropriate for feminine weakness and have "rewritten" them as resistant and powerful. For example, through changes of scale or the use of unexpected media or unconventional techniques, the traditionally pretty and attractive subjects of still life, or the safe domestic interior, can represent the subordination of women through the institutions of the family. Similarly, the traditions of the genre of landscape have been turned around to explore the associations between women and nature in a critical way, and thus to disclose abuse of women, women's fertility, and the Earth by patriarchal cultures.

Portraiture, especially self-portraiture, has been important in feminist critiques of the gendering of the genres, because women have used portraits to create new images of the woman artist, and in general to suggest the infinite flexibility of identities that women might wish to assume. In representations of women's bodies, new art forms like performance and installations are sometimes used, since these resist masculine "rereading."

Women have also transformed history and narrative painting, seeking events, ideas, or myths from modern life, legend, or the past to depict women's powers or men's fears of them; subjects include abortion, rape, childbirth, menstruation, and women's sexual pleasure, which male artists have ignored.

If modernism asserted the neutrality of shaping and looking at images, feminist artists, in contrast, draw attention to issues of who represents what, for whom, with special reference to issue of gender.

See Also

FINE ARTS, *specific topics*

References and Further Reading

Cherry, Deborah. 1993. *Painting women: Victorian women artists.* London: Routledge.

Deepwell, Katya, ed. 1998. *Women artists and modernism.* Manchester: Manchester University Press.

Green, Germaine. 1979. *The obstacle race: The fortunes of women painters and their work.* London: Secker and Warburg.

Catherine King

GEOGRAPHY

Geography is the study of spatial relationships. The spatial context within which societies operate consists in part of the physical and locational geography that we all learned about in primary school, but it also consists of the "man-made" geography—housing, streets, cities, agricultural systems, workplaces—that is *created* to fit social needs. Thus, geographers study the interplay of culture with its built environment, as well as human relationships to the physical world. Geography often overlaps with anthropology, architecture, political science, economics, and environmental studies; but the geographers' core interest in spatial analysis remains distinctive. Given that virtually all human events occur in a spatial dimension, geography is also distinguished by a mandate of broad curiosity: while some geographers ponder "sense of place," others may study the culture of shopping malls, or the flow of information through urban systems, or global refugee and migration patterns, or the changing structure of the sugar-plantation economy in the Caribbean. Through its disparate interests, geography is unified by its core concern with the dynamics of place, space, landscape, and environment.

Over the centuries, knowledge of—and curiosity about —geography has expanded and contracted with armed forces and empires. From the Romans to the Dutch, geographers and cartographers have been central to colonization, to nation building, and to bringing "other" places into the orbit of the known. Geography is still important to dominant economic and military interests.

The contemporary history of geography as an academic discipline resembles that of most social sciences. Everywhere in the world, geography has been (and remains) a male-dominated academic enterprise. Until the late twentieth century, male-universalizing and positivist paradigms structured the representation of geographical knowledge and the development of geographical theory. Interest in the geography of women and the spatial aspects of gender relations first appeared in the geographical literature in North America and Britain in the 1970s. It wasn't until the 1980s, however, that feminist geography became more than an occasional curiosity and took its place as a firm part of the geographic curriculum (McDowell, 1993: 157).

The feminist contribution to geography starts from a series of linked observations. If we understand that the "geography" of a place is, in part, a cultural creation, then it stands to reason that geography will bear the imprint of that culture. If the culture is patriarchal, so will be its geography. If a society is based on gender divisions of work and play, its geography will be one which protects and facilitates that social organization (Seager, 1985). From this (much-simplified) understanding, four key concepts underpin feminist geography: (1) Space is gendered; the design and use of space are determined in part by ideological assumptions about gender roles and relations. The virtually ubiquitous spatial dichotomies such as public versus private, "work" versus "home," and city versus suburb reflect gendered predispositions. (2) In turn, spatial relations help to shape and maintain culturally specific notions of gender behavior. Geography is not just a neutral backdrop to the human drama; once in place, spatial systems and the built environment have great normative power. (3) Gender is an interpretive lens influencing our relationship to environment; men and women often have markedly different perceptions and experiences of environment, landscape, and place. (4) There are particular disadvantages for women who navigate their daily lives through spaces and places designed by men, often for the purpose of maintaining patriarchal relations; these disadvantages are affected by class, race, age, ethnicity, and sexuality.

One of the core concerns in feminist geography is to simply make the world of women visible. In the broadest sense, the "geography" of women is not encompassed by that of men, nor is the latter substitutable for the former. A considerable (and still expanding) corpus of work in feminist geography details the spatial differences in status and behavior between men and women, and among women themselves: mapping, literally or metaphorically, the contours of the geography of women's poverty, legislative power, family status, mobility, participation in workforce, health, exposure to violence, and access to housing (see, for example, Hanson and Johnston, 1985; Holcomb and Jones, 1990; Seager and Olson, 1986).

Moving beyond these studies, which tend to be descriptive and indicative, feminist geographers are also forging far-reaching theoretical analyses, which cluster around three axes of concern: the ways in which gender is constituted in particular places; the saliency of gender as a category of analysis, at least as powerful as other social and economic factors, in explaining transformation in society and space; the differences in the construction of gender and gender relations across races, nationalities, and sexualities. Studies of urban structure have been especially prominent in feminist geography, including examinations of the development of particular housing forms, the shifting terrain of relations between "work" and "home," differences in mens' and womens' access to urban spaces and services, and particularly revealing microscale studies of the ways in which gender is constituted inside the landscape of the home.

Feminist geographers have made significant contributions to analyses of industrial location, economic restructuring, and regional economies, all of which are shaped by gender relations and the fashioning and refashioning of gender norms. Feminist geographers are also prominent in the study of international development issues, colonialism, postcolonial international relations, and theoretical and contextual studies of underdevelopment processes (see, for example, Momsen and Kinnaird, 1993). Examinations of "difference" among women, in sexuality, age, race, and class, are increasingly featured in studies of the gendered nature of spaces (Bondi, 1993; Kobayashi, 1994; Monk and Katz, 1993; Valentine, 1989).

See Also

ARCHITECTURE; DEMOGRAPHY; ENVIRONMENT: OVERVIEW; NATURAL RESOURCES

References and Further Reading

Bondi, Liz. 1993. Gender and geography: Crossing boundaries. *Progress in Human Geography* 17(2):241–46.

Gender, Place, and Culture: A Journal of Feminist Geography. Biannual journal. London: Carfax.

Hanson, Susan, and Ibipo Johnston. 1985. Gender differences in work length trip: Explanation and implications. *Urban Geography* 6: 193–219.

Holcomb, Briavel, and J. P. Jones. 1990. Work, welfare, and poverty among black female-headed families. In J. Kodras and J.P. Jones, eds. *Geographic dimensions of United States social policy,* 178–199. London: Edward Arnold.

Kobayashi, Audrey. 1994. Colouring the field: Gender, "race," and the politics of fieldwork. *Professional Geographer* 46(1): 73–80.

McDowell, Linda. 1993. Space, place, and gender relations: Part I. Feminist empiricism and the geography of social relations. *Progress in Human Geography* 17(2): 157–79.

Momsen, Janet, and Vivian Kinnaird. 1993. *Different places, different voices.* London and New York: Routledge.

Monk, Janice, and Cindi Katz. 1993. *Full circles: Geographies of women over the life course.* London and New York: Routledge.

Monk, Janice, and Susan Hanson. 1982. On not excluding half of the human in human geography. *Professional Geographer* 34(1): 11–23.

Seager, Joni. 1985. How to put women on the map. *Women's Review of Books* 2(5): 9–10.

———, and Ann Olson. 1986. *Women in the world: An international atlas.* New York: Simon and Schuster.

Spain, Daphne. 1992. *Gendered spaces.* Chapel Hill: University of North Carolina Press.

Valentine, Gillian. 1989. The geography of women's fear. *Area* 21: 4385–4390.

Joni Seager

GIRL CHILD

It is difficult to consider the girl child without considering the woman she is to become. It is not surprising, therefore, that very little has been written about her per se. Even in books where the girl child appears in the title, the discussion often focuses on that status of women. As a more recent subject of study, the girl child is often subsumed in the general rubric either of children or of gender. She is often invisible.

"Gendering" begins at home, where the beliefs of the larger society are often reflected and reproduced. The fate of girls and women is closely intertwined; indeed, what a girl can expect in her later life shapes aspects of her girlhood. In cultures where women are lawyers and doctors, electricians and astronauts, choosing freely to marry or to live alone, the girl child has possibilities of which girls of the past only dreamed. On the other hand, in cultures where women are seen as mere objects of beauty or of sexual pleasure, girls' feet are bound or their sexual organs altered; they become girl brides and girl mothers or girl prostitutes; or they feel impelled to starve themselves to look more pleasing to men. In societies that consider women's productive role to be nonexistent, girls are uneducated and barely fed. Where sons are preferred to daughters, girls may be killed, often in the womb. It is a vicious circle: women get married or take low-paying jobs because they are not educated; girls are not educated because it is expected that they will get married or take low-paying jobs. Therefore, some families see girls as having no value, as they bring neither wealth nor status. Being considered "tomorrow's woman"—a person in the making, rather than a person in her own right—is often burdensome to "today's girl" (Sohoni 1995).

In the developed world, childhood as a differentiated age has been in and out of vogue. Ariès (1962) argues that the concept of childhood has changed over the years: the child is overworked and maligned in one era but overprotected and worshiped in the next. Now, at the dawn of the twenty-first century, children are back in the public consciousness. In business, in politics, and especially in advertising and marketing, children are everywhere. Yet while some children are enjoying unprecedented freedom and power, child abuse plagues even the most developed countries.

Winn (1984) suggests that there is no longer a childhood; Clinton (1996) believes that childhood has been magical in the past and, with the effort of the "village," can become magical again. Although the child may be largely better off in the developed "North" than in the developing "South," the divide is not as great as it may seem. For example, in both developed and developing worlds, the focus is more on preparing the child for adulthood than on protection, children give birth to children in both.

If the notion of childhood is problematic because it deeply contextualized, historically, socially, and culturally, the notion of girlhood is even more so. Where women are powerless because they are female, girls are powerless because they are both female and children. With the onset of puberty and the possibility of pregnancy or even sexual activity, the girl child is feared worldwide as a potential source of shame. Rape is a widespread menace to both girls and women, but incest generally threatens only the girl. It is still hazardous to be a child and female.

In 1975, when International Women's Year was declared by the United Nations and the first global conference was held in Mexico City, it was assumed that improved status for women would naturally lead to improved status for girls. Yet mothers seeking to better their lives, or sometimes just to survive, often had to do so on the backs of their daughters, whose housework and child care duties increased. Now development practitioners are taking the opposite view: improved life chances for girls lead to improved life chances for women. This has led in particular to a focus on girls' education. After the United Nations Decade for Women ended in 1985, the South Asian Association for Regional Cooperation (SAARC) declared 1990 the Year of the Girl Child; this eventually became the Decade of the Girl Child: 1991–2000. Since 1989 the United Nations Children's Fund

(UNICEF), the world advocate for children, has increasingly focused on the girl child, especially in health and education.

In many societies, the girl child has come a long way from the days when her fate was sealed at birth, when she could not inherit her father's property, and her mother had no property. In some societies, however, the girl child herself is still viewed as property, objectified, and abused. If a girl is born in the West, her life chances are better than they have ever been, even while affected by race, class, and social status. In many parts of the developing world, a girl's life chances remain quite limited. Her life course may be one of subservience; her life expectancy may be shortened by minimal access to health care or good nutrition. For one girl child, therefore, becoming a good servant to those around her may be all the status she can ever hope to attain; for another, the sky may be the limit.

See Also

ABUSE; ADOLESCENCE; CHILD DEVELOPMENT; GENDER CONSTRUCTIONS IN THE FAMILY; GIRL STUDIES; GIRLS' SUBCULTURES.

References and Further Reading

Ariès, Philippe. 1962. *Centuries of childhood: A social history of family life*. Trans. Robert Baldick. New York: Random House.

Clinton, Hilary Rodman. 1996. *It takes a village and other lessons children teach us*. New York: Touchstone.

New Internationalist. 1993. 240:Special issues on girls and girlhood.

Rutter, Virginia. 1996. *Celebrating girls: Nurturing and empowering our daughters*. Berkeley, Calif.: Conari.

Shahar, Shulamith. 1990. *Childhood in the middle ages*. Trans. Chaya Galai. London and New York: Routledge.

Sohoni, Neera. 1995. *The burden of girlhood: A global inquiry into the status of girls*. Oakland, Calif.: Third Party.

Winn, Marie. 1984. *Children without childhood: Growing up too fast in the world of sex and drugs*. New York: Penguin.

Zelizer, Vivian A. 1985. *Pricing the priceless child: The changing social value of children*. New York: Basic Books.

Elaine Douglas-Noel

GIRL STUDIES

Girl studies is a very new field, one that has been facilitated by changing demographics both inside and outside of academia. According to statistics reported by the U.S. Bureau of the Census in 1998, women constitute 51 percent of the U.S. population and 46 percent of the U.S. labor force. In 1996, the U.S. Department of Labor projected that the number of women and minorities in the workforce would continue rising, so much so that by the year 2000, only 15 percent of the incoming workforce is expected to consist of white men. More women in the workforce and in public life in general also mean more women in academia, where concerns of girls and about girls have come to be seen as a serious subject for study.

Origins of Girl Studies

Girl studies, which is largely based in the United States, arose from two very different sources. The first was girls themselves: in the early 1990s many girls decided they were tired of scholars, the mass media, and their male peers speaking for them (if they were spoken of at all) and tired of passively accepting the world around them. Beginning with two close-knit communities in Olympia, Washington, and Washington, D.C., the "riot grrl" movement focused on the music scene. Adopting the do-it-yourself ethos of punk, riot grrl argued that it did not matter how girls played, just that they played. On the east and west coasts, riot grrl preached empowerment, urging girls to overcome their traditional position as passive spectators—the cliché of the girl who is the girlfriend (or groupie) of the boys in the band—and take the stage themselves. Riot grrl relied on irony and appropriation, taking symbols of traditional girlhood and turning them on their heads. A key to this movement was the reappropriation and redefinition of the word *girl,* a word that second-wave feminism tended to condemn as symbolic of the female gender's secondary status, operating with an effect similar to that when a white person called a black person *boy.* Comments such as "You throw (or play) like a girl" were questioned. Like the gay culture's appropriation and redefinition of the word *queer* as a rallying point and a term of empowerment, *girl* was transformed from a pejorative to a term of pride.

Names of bands associated with riot grrl reflected irony and deconstruction. Bands like Bikini Kill, Babes in Toyland, Lunachicks, and Hole (initially affiliated with riot grrl, but later cutting ties with the movement) took symbols of traditional femininity and rewrote them with an aggressive edge. We may be girls, these band names proclaimed, but we are not just sugar and spice. Riot grrl played with archetypes of the Amazon, and

these found expression in other forms of popular culture, such as television. *Xena: Warrior Princess* and *Buffy the Vampire Slayer* became icons of the new femininity, a sensibility that combined physical power with more traditional beauty. Riot grrl culture also used fashion for irony and deconstruction. In the early 1990s, girl culture in the United States was characterized by wearing traditionally feminine dresses with combat boots, skirts over pants, makeup such as Courtney Love's signature smudged mascara, and bleached-blond hair with dark roots—calling attention to the degree to which appearance is constructed. Female rappers and hip-hop stars such as Queen Latifah, TLC, and Lauryn Hill were creating their own style, challenging white cultural definitions of beauty, and asserting that black female culture was part of emerging forms of identity within youth culture.

In the late 1990s, girl culture in the music scene seemed less bold. Nonconfrontational pop icons like Britney Spears replaced hard-core girls like Ani Difranco (whose Righteous Babe record label and successful do-it-yourself marketing had served as an example of female success in a different style). The "girl power" marketed by the Spice Girls seemed a power based more on physical appearance and seduction than on anything new. Although performers like Tori Amos, who sang about rape, male bias in religion, and female self-definition, continued to have a dedicated following, there was a definite shift toward more traditionally feminine glamour, embodied in "divas" such as Celine Dion, Jewel, or Shania Twain, who stress looks and pretty melodies. The all-woman Lilith Fair offered a venue for women in music but tended to reinforce feminine stereotypes. At least two hip-hop performers, Even and Lauryn Hill, seemed to be exceptions, however; and hip-hop, rather than alternative rock, had the largest audience.

In sharp contrast to the masculine self-questioning apparent in the early 1990s in grunge (for example, Kurt Cobain and Eddie Vedder), the rap-metal fusion of the late 1990s highlighted traditional sexism. Groups such as Limp Bizkit, Kid Rock, and Korn made the groupie scene popular again, and the "Show us your tits!" relationship of male performer to female groupie—who is, in industry parlance, "mean"—had returned. In 1999, at the Woodstock festival, there were sexual assaults, indicating that this ethos could be literal as well as figurative. There were more women performers in the mainstream than ever before, but many of them presented a fairly traditional feminine image, and the range of acceptable roles seemed limited. Scholars of popular culture assert that it can be used as a resource for self-definition and empowerment, but some observers are troubled by the cyclical trends characteristic of mass culture, by the return of traditional sexism, and by other indicators that mass culture can be reactionary.

Riot grrl initially used the mass media but later went underground when media attention distorted its views and compromised its aims. The political energies that began in riot grrl then found other outlets. One of these was zines: girls pasted together drawings and journal entries that expressed the otherwise inexpressible story of what was happening to their bodies. The zines were frank, creative expressions that told of sexual violence, which, according to some research, may affect as many as one in three girls. Eating disorders and other "female perversions" like self-cutting have been linked to this kind of violence, but it was the autobiographical girl zine culture of the early 1990s that first made these connections. Zine culture has since moved to online communities, with thousands of sites dedicated to girls and their self-representations. Books such as Ophira Edut's *Adios Barbie: Young Women Write about Body Image and Identity* (1998) and Sara Schandler's *Ophelia Speaks* (1999) present young women's own analyses and ideas and indicate girls' reluctance to have their lives dictated to them.

The second source of girl studies came from within academia and from activists devoted to girls in the larger culture. As a result of anecdotal reports in the early 1990s about the decline of self-esteem in young women, the American Association of University Women (AAUW) commissioned a study to find out whether the reports were accurate. The study, "Shortchanging Girls, Shortchanging America," was published in 1992 and gained national attention, serving as a wake-up call for parents and educators who had been assuming steady progress for girls in terms of gender equality and opportunity. The study showed a precipitous drop in self-esteem and confidence for girls as they progress through secondary school, as well as the loss of what Carol Gilligan, a leading theorist of female adolescence, has called their "voices." The survey showed an environment where girls are still consistently perceived as less than their male counterparts: teachers called on girls less in class, challenging them less; and schools still provided fewer opportunities for activities that require self-assertion, such as sports, and assigned less value to girls' participation. As a result, the study concluded, girls were less self-confident overall.

Girls and Low Self-Esteem

The results of AAUW study were repeatedly confirmed throughout the 1990s. The Commonwealth Fund's Survey of the Health of Adolescent Girls, conducted in 1996–1997 by Louis Harris and Associates, found that girls are at much higher risk of depression than boys and that they lose self-confidence as they progress through adolescence—unlike boys, who gain confidence. One of the best-selling books of the 1990s was written by the clinical psychologist Mary Pipher: *Reviving Ophelia: Saving the Selves of Adolescent Girls*. In more than a decade of work with adolescents, Pipher found low self-esteem in many girls and a correlation between low self-esteem and frequent suicide attempts, depression, dropping out of school, high rates of pregnancy, and an epidemic of eating disorders. She concluded such crises were the result not of "dysfunctional families" but rather of a media-obsessed, appearance-oriented, "girl-destroying" culture. Scholars such as Susan Bordo and Joan Jacobs Brumberg have further documented the cultural and historical factors informing these trends. In 1998 surveys commissioned by the makers of Secret antiperspirant and the *Ladies Home Journal* reported that teenage girls had high rates of depression, were uncomfortable about their bodies and appearance, and felt intellectually inadequate. Fifty percent of teenage girls said they felt depressed at least once a week, 29 percent said they felt somewhat or very uncomfortable with their body image, 50 percent said they were unhappy with their appearance, 40 percent said they were struggling in school, 21 percent said they were "not smart enough," and 30 percent said they lacked a strong adult role model.

Girls' Low Self-Esteem and Sports

In conjunction with this research, and with further research showing that sports can allieviate problems associated with low self-esteem, women in athletics have become a national public health issue. A landmark report written under the auspices of the President's Council of Physical Fitness and Sports, *Physical Activity and Sport in the Lives of Young Girls,* was the first interdisciplinary study to consider the effects of participating in sports and other physical activity; it concluded that such activity improved girls' mental health and reduced their risk of many chronic adult diseases, and that female athletes did better academically.

In 1998, a major study expanded on these findings, documenting a link between participation in athletics and lower rates of teen pregnancy. *Sport and Teen Pregnancy,* a report sponsored by the Women's Sports Foundation, found that female athletes were less than half as likely to get pregnant as female nonathletes. "Our results," wrote the project director, Professor Donald F. Sabo, "strongly suggest that, for girls, sport may be used as a developmental strategy in programs intended to reduce teen pregnancy."

Such research suggests that sports are a largely untapped resource for mitigating the problems associated with girls' low self-esteem. In the decades since Title IX—federal legislation passed in 1972 that prohibited sex discrimination in education—women's participation in athletics has grown nationally from 300,000 to roughly 2.4 million participants, disproving the myth that girls do not want to play sports. The rise of women's athletics in the late 1990s, especially women's professional basketball and women's soccer, provided girls with powerful role models. But inequities within the sports would persist, and athletics, though offering one positive avenue for girls' lives, is certainly not the only answer.

Other Resources for Girls

One hopeful outcome of girl studies is collaboration between the academy and the larger community that devotes research to girls. The Girls' Coalition, for instance, is a consortium of organizations in the Boston area working to support girls' healthy development through programs, services, research, and advocacy. The goal of the coalition is to promote education about girls' issues and networking. Members include practitioners, researchers, funders, and policy makers: Big Sister Association of Greater Boston, Boston Women's Commission, Computer Clubhouse Network, Girls Community Centers, G.I.R.L.S. Conference, Girls Inc. of Lynn, Junior League of Boston, KEYS to Empower Youth, LiveSafe, Malden YWCA, Parents United for Child Care, Patriots' Trail Girl Scouts, Title IX Advocacy Project, Wellesley Centers for Women, Women Express/Teen Voices, YWCA Boston, and YWCA Cambridge.

Collaboration like the Girls' Coalition bring a wide range of people and resources together, and the success of girl studies may depend on their work.

Although scholars who focus on girl studies still suffer to some extent from the notion that the study of girls could not be about anything "serious," this attitude is changing rapidly. Despite some reactionary trends in the mass media, girls—who are increasingly important demographically and have more resources—have assumed new cultural power in the new millennium.

See Also:

ADOLESCENCE; BODY; CULTURAL STUDIES; EDUCATION: CURRICULUM IN SCHOOLS; EDUCATION: PHYSICAL EDUCATION; GRRLS; MUSIC: ROCK AND POP; SPORT; YOUTH CULTURE; ZINES

References and Further Reading

Brumberg, Joan. 1996. *The body project.* New York: Random House.
Pipher, Mary. 1995. *Reviving Ophelia: Saving the selves of adolescent girls.* New York: Ballantine.

Web Resources

Cyber Sisters: <http://world kids.net/clubs/CSIS>
Femina: <http://www.femina.com>
Girl Power: <http://www.health.org/gpower/index.htm>
The Girls' Coalition: <http://www.girlscoalition.com>
A Girl's World Online Clubhouse:
      <http://www.agrilsworld.com>
GirlTech: <http://www.girltech.com>
Go, Girl magazine: <http://www.gogirlmag.com>
New Moon publishers: <http://www.newmoon.org>

Leslie Heywood

GIRLS' SCHOOLS

See EDUCATION: SINGLE-SEX AND COEDUCATION.

GIRLS' SUBCULTURES

Young people around the world have often tried to define themselves in ways that will separate them from adults and adults' value systems. Youth subcultures have been one way that young people have developed their own distinct cultures. When examining these subcultures, researchers frequently have focused on boys. The best known of such works is perhaps Dick Hebdige's *Subculture: The Meaning of Style* (1979), an important study of British punks. The author focuses primarily on young working-class men. In more recent years, an increasing number of scholars have turned their attention to girls and the rich variety of subcultures girls have developed. There are subcultures that revolve around fashion, music, religions, and sports. Subcultures include skinheads, "spice babies" (that is, followers of a popular music group, the Spice Girls), and others who try to dress and behave like their idols. There has been an explosion of girls' subcultures, a tremendous growth in the variety and number of such groups, unlike anything seen in earlier decades.

One reason for this phenomenon is the wide availability of inexpensive technology, which has helped to spread the credos of different girls' subcultures. With the use of photocopiers and the Internet, anyone from a "riot grrl" to a "gothic girl" can spread her message far and wide. Such technologies also have made it possible for many girls to take an active role in contesting and challenging the dominant culture's notions about what it means to be a girl. What has resulted from girls' challenging the status quo is a burgeoning of subcultures around the globe, which provide a cultural space where girls can take an active part in calling into question and redesigning what it means to be a girl in a new millennium. For instance, the "gothic" subculture is one of many subcultures for girls that have used modern technology, including the Internet, to spread their philosophy. By searching the Internet, girls can find out about gothic fashions, music, ideals, role models, and even popular gothic movies.

Young people have often formed subcultures based on music. The Grateful Dead, for instance, had their youthful Deadhead followers, who sought to remove themselves from the dominant culture; and the early punk movement of the 1970s was centered on music as a form of rebellion against mainstream society. Today, girls also use music as a form of expression and design subculture groups based on musical preferences. Some girls follow rap and punk. Other girls, involved with rave culture, base their subculture on the driving beats of techno; they travel from rave to rave (that is, all-night dances and parties, which often occur at different locations in order to avoid the control of the authorities). Girls go further than only listening to music in building a subculture based on musical preferences. They also dress like and try to mimic their favorite singers. Girls have, for example, imitated Madonna and Britney Spears. Music offers girls a way to redesign their lives and their self-image.

The influence of music on riot grrl, gothic, rave, and even fashion subcultures is undeniable. Often in society, musicians are very high-profile figures whom girls can easily learn about, and then take as role models. The band Bikini Kill is credited with starting the riot grrl subculture, and the song "Bela Lugosi's Dead" had a profound impact on the beginnings of the gothic subculture. The Spice Girls' phrase "girl power" appears on T-shirts, notebooks, purses, jeans, and bookbags.

Girls who follow rap music and rhythm and blues have a harder time finding role models in music, because often in rap women are portrayed negatively. But positive role models exist in the rap community, and girls often form subcultures based on the messages these role models try to give. The "sistahood" subculture in black communities has had significant influence on many girls; without it, some would not have the support and affirmation they need to grow up in a perhaps difficult and challenging environment. Through their association with other girls, these young women can fight the negative stereotyping of women both in their own race and in other races. Girls realize that there is power in numbers, and use this to their advantage.

Fashion, too, plays a central part in girls' subcultures, and a subculture is frequently defined by specific fashion rules. For instance, in the gothic subculture, fashion is central, and national-chain stores such as Hot Topic sell popular gothic wear such as fishnet stockings, vinyl dresses, and combat boots, along with a variety of jewelry. Riot grrls and gothic girls have adopted an outfit featuring a short dress and combat boots. Followers of Wicca, a subculture that is defined by its adherence to pagan religious ideals and was popularized for girls by the movie *The Craft*, often wear black clothing and jewelry bearing the ankh, pentagram, or "eye of Ra." Girls use the fashion trends of their subcultures to identify themselves and to express their willingness to challenge the dominant ideals of mainstream culture.

The media, too, have offered girls' subcultures a way to subvert dominant notions about what it means to be female. An elaborate subculture has developed around girls who publish zines. These self-produced magazines often help their writers to rebel against the dominant culture's ideals. Whether one is a queer punk or a straight riot grrl, zines offer a space to express one's views.

The Internet also has helped to expand how girls' subcultures express themselves. Now, girls can share their views with an audience of millions. The Internet also has been a powerful way to connect girls across the world who share similar subcultures. Mods, skinheads, punks, and rappers are a few of the subcultures in which the Internet is used for meeting like-minded girls and women.

Subculture groups are a way for girls to form alternative identities opposed to the mainstream images in the pages of glossy fashion and lifestyle magazines such as *Seventeen*, *YM*, *Vogue*, and *Mademoiselle*. Young lesbians develop subcultural groups that provide support and affirmation in a hostile world; such groups also provide them with greater visibility in fighting for social and political issues that affect lesbians and gay men. Girls who are interested in tattoos and piercings form an entire subculture based on such alterations to their bodies—alterations that allow their wearers to express new ideals about femininity and to question traditional notions of beauty. Girls from minority ethnicities and races also use affiliation with a subculture to express different ideals about what it means to be young and female. Whether lesbian, adorned with a multitude of piercings and tattoos, or black or Hispanic, a wide variety of girls find subcultures that enable them to express alternative visions. Such subcultures also offer girls a way to demonstrate that modern girlhood is not only the dominant images that appear in the mainstream media; modern girlhood is composed of an infinite number of dress codes, musical preferences, and personal images.

Literature catering to girls' subcultures can be found widely. Books about piercings and tattoos can be found at many bookstores and libraries. The gothic subculture has particular affection for Anne Rice novels and science fiction-fantasy books. Readers interested in subcultures based on religious ideologies, such as paganism or Wicca, can find numerous books that give detailed information about them.

See Also

FASHION; GIRL STUDIES; MAGAZINES; MUSIC: ROCK AND POP; POPULAR CULTURE; ZINES

References and Further Reading

Austin, Joe, and Michael Willard, eds. 1998. *Generations of youth: Youth cultures and history in twentieth-century America* New York: New York University Press.

Duncombe, Stephen. 1997. *Notes from underground: Zines and politics of alternative culture.* London: Verso.

Gottlieb, Joanne, and Gayle Wald. 1994. Smells like teen spirit: Riot grrls, revolution, and women in independent rock. In Andrew Ross and Tricia Rose, eds., *Microphone fiends: Youth music and youth culture,* 250–274. New York: Routledge.

Jennings, Carol. 1999. Girls make music: Polyphony and identity in teenage rock bands. In Sharon R. Mazzarella and Norma Odom Pecora, eds., *Growing up girls: Popular culture and the construction of identity,* 175–192. New York: Lang.

Kearney, Mary Celeste. 1998. Producing girls: Rethinking the study of female youth culture. In Sherrie A. Inness, ed., *Delinquents and debutantes: Twentieth-century American girls' cultures,* 285–310. New York: New York University Press.

McRobbie, Angela. 1993. Shut up and dance: Youth culture and changing modes of femininity. *Cultural Studies* 7(3): 406–426.

———, and Jenny Garber. 1975. Girls and subcultures. In Stuart Hall and Tony Jefferson, eds., *Resistance through rituals,* 209–229. London: Hutchinson.

Redhead, Steve, ed. 1997. *The clubcultures reader: Readings in popular cultural studies.* Oxford: Blackwell.

Sikes, Gini. 1997. *8-ball chicks: A year in the violent world of girl gangsters.* New York: Doubleday.

Suzuki, Kazuko. 1998. Pornography or therapy? Japanese girls creating the *Yaoi* phenomenon. In Sherrie A. Inness, ed., *Millennium girls: Today's girls around the world,* 243–267. Lanham, Md.: Rowman and Littlefield.

Sherrie A Inness
Julie Hucke

GLOBAL FEMINISM

The term *global feminism* is best understood as a reference to the links between a variety of feminist organizations around the world or, as Alison Jaggar (1998) refers to it, an emerging global discourse community among feminists. Historically, the recognition of the commonalities among women and women's potential as a global political force has been the driving force behind the feminist movement around the world. That is to say, women have long organized "across state boundaries." Global feminism, however, has only recently been recognized as a new phase in feminism. Whereas this development has been facilitated by the growth of alliances among feminist movements around the world, there are a number of factors that also have contributed. Terms related to global feminism include *planetary feminism* (Morgan, 1984), *transnational feminisms* (Caine, 1998), and feminist alliances, coalitions, solidarity, and networks.

One important factor has been a growing acceptance among many western feminists that the interests of women of color and feminists from the developing world have been excluded from dominant feminist thought, insofar as it has represented white middle-class women's interests to the exclusion of the interests of the latter groups. Nonwestern feminists (and, since the 1980s particularly, western feminists) have written and spoken extensively against the assumption underlying much western feminism—that gender identity exists in isolation from race and class identity. This growing awareness, along with the advent of globalization, has opened the way for an emerging global feminist discourse.

Globalization generally refers to the development of the world economy—particularly since the early 1980s—to its present stage of integration and interdependence across national boundaries, along with shifts in relations of power, wealth, and identity. This profound transformation has had far-reaching cultural and ecological effects across the globe. Not only has globalization brought with it new problems and the exacerbation of existing problems for women worldwide—particularly for women in the developing world—it also has provided some useful tools for a global discourse community among feminists, particularly through the development of worldwide information and communication networks. Globalization raises two main questions: (1) What does globalization mean for women across the world?—that is, the issue of the gendered impact of globalization. (2) What does globalization mean for the feminist movement?—that is, how it affects, alters, or can assist resistance to women's oppression.

With regard to the first issue, the gendered impact of globalization, one of the most visible areas in which women are affected is the increasing casualization of the global labor force. Issues of citizenship and immigration are also areas of concern, especially with regard to women (and their children) living outside their state of citizenship, who are, as a result, extremely vulnerable because they lack legal representation and protection; women and their children constitute 80 percent of the world's refugees (Jaggar, 1998). Other problems affecting women and exacerbated by the forces of globalization include the worldwide traffic in women in the prostitution trade; technological interventions in both the promotion and the control of fertility; and the particular danger in emerging exclusivist and nationalist movements reacting against globalization by attempting to reassert cultural integrity, as signs of community boundaries, as reproducers, and as cultural transmitters of the group. Such movements often involve systematic attacks on women's rights and, thus, reinforce the oppression of women, as well as oppression of various minorities, for example, migrants and racialized "others."

Although these issues could be considered explicitly gendered, global feminist discourse also investigates the nature and forces of development and, in particular, issues such as the developing world's debt to the West, the exploitation by multinational corporations from the West of the developing world's natural and labor resources, as well as patterns of western consumption, in order to contextualize discussions on global issues. For example, debates over population control dominate most mainstream environmental agendas and typically put the onus on women in the developing world to reduce—or cease—reproducing, because the Earth cannot sustain the increasing population. Meanwhile, the fact that the consumption rate of the so-called developed world far exceeds that of the developing world is not acknowledged. Although it is predominantly feminists in the developing world who have emphasized these issues, a number of western feminists have insisted that the injustice of the global system itself should be a matter of concern for all western feminists (for example, Jaggar, 1998; Salleh, 1997).

With regard to the question of what globalization has meant for the feminist movement, the development of worldwide information and communication networks has enabled the formation of networks among women in different regions of the world to address global women's issues. For example, there are several Internet sites listed under the heading "Global Feminism," which provide links to women activists all over the world; explain how to assist particular causes concerning women; inform about the status of women in various nations; provide access to global feminist news; give opportunities to take part in on-line discussions; provide access to research, referrals, and bibliographies; and monitor electronic and print media for developments in various arenas, such as economics and development, health, law, science, and technology. The rhetoric of these sites typically promotes "the empowerment of women through direct action on a global level"; a focus on the "politics of diversity and inclusion"; and women as a "worldwide constituency." Whereas the development of telecommunications and information networks has offered new and promising possibilities for the feminist movement, the question of whether it is simply another guise of colonization will be a matter of who stands to gain and who loses or is marginalized by such developments. In particular, access to technology is a key factor in so-called global networks. In any case, it should not be assumed that global feminist activity occurs only in such arenas. For instance, women's global presence has become visible through the United Nations Conferences on women (since 1975) and regional forums leading up to international conferences; international campaigns such as the United Nations Declaration against Violence against Women (1993); and ongoing engagement among regional and global grassroots and activist groups, feminist circles, and complex women's networks (not all of them feminist).

Specific challenges for global feminism include the need to rethink *difference* by taking seriously the experiences of women in different regions of the world, while remaining aware of the powerful appeal, under globalization, of exclusivist identity politics to many women and investigating how links might be established across these borders. In other words, a global feminist discourse needs to address questions such as: How useful is the concept of "global sisterhood?" Are there any issues which should not be open for discussion or criticism in a global discourse? (In particular, women in the developing world might more appropriately discuss some issues without the interventions of western feminists). How might western feminists genuinely take responsibility for their part in the oppression of the developing world, while maintaining alliances with women in the developing world?

See Also

CLASS; DIFFERENCE *I and II*; ESSENTIALISM; FEMINISM: OVERVIEW; GLOBALIZATION; INFORMATION REVOLUTION; NETWORKING; NETWORKS: ELECTRONIC; RACE; SISTERHOOD

References and Further Reading

Caine, Barbara, ed. 1998. *Australian feminism: A companion.* Melbourne: Oxford University Press.

Code, Lorraine. 1998. How to think globally: Stretching the limits of imagination. *Hypatia: A Journal of Feminist Philosophy.* Border crossings, part I. 13(2: Spring): 73–86.

Ferguson, Ann. 1998. Resisting the veil of privilege: Building bridge identities as an ethico-politics of global feminisms. *Hypatia: A Journal of Feminist Philosophy.* Border crossings, part II. 13(3: Summer): 95–114.

Jaggar, Alison M. 1998. Globalizing feminist ethics. *Hypatia* 13(2): Spring, 7–32.

Mies, Maria, and Vandana Shiva. 1993. *Ecofeminism.* London: Zed.

Mohanty, Chandra Talpade, Ann Russo, and Lourdes Torres. 1991. *Third world women and the politics of feminism.* Bloomington: Indiana University Press.

Morgan, Robin, ed. 1984. *Sisterhood is global: The international women's movement anthology.* New York: Anchor.

Narayan, Uma. 1997. *Dislocating cultures: Identities, traditions, and third world feminism.* New York: Routledge.

Salleh, Arie. 1997. *Ecofeminism as politics: Nature, Marx, and the postmodern.* London: Zed.

Shiva, Vandana. 1988. *Staying alive: Women, ecology, and development.* London: Zed.

Terri Field

GLOBAL HEALTH MOVEMENT

The international, or global, women's health movement (GWHM) developed informally in the early 1970s as part of second-wave feminism. Several national women's health movements (WHMs) emerged, at first focusing on sexuality, reproductive rights, and the power of organized medicine.

These early movements had several unifying themes, held to be true (if to differing degrees) worldwide: Women had little control over their own bodies—their health, sexuality, and reproduction. Power was held by male-dominated establishments: medicine, population policymakers, the pharmaceutical industry, and other interlocking, patriarchal political, legal, religious, and cultural institutions. Governments, scientists, corporations, and the media were virtually unaccountable to women. Women were the overwhelming majority of underpaid and unpaid health workers and caregivers. Sexism and misogyny were pervasive in health and medicine. Concepts like medicalization of healthy women, self-help alternatives, and iatrogenesis (harm caused by medicine) were important starting points for feminist political analysis—although in the developing world, women's lack of access to health care or birth control was often the main issue.

Activists demanded more control over women's health care: more knowledge about health products and services, less discriminatory and less punitive services, more alternatives to mainstream medical care, respect for women's human rights by health and medical systems, and a voice for nonprofessional women in the development of health policies, technologies, and services. They also called for a reorientation away from dominant western biomedical and liberal models of health and medicine, which tended to focus on technology and ignored racism, sexism, and socioeconomics; their agenda expanded to include issues like unnecessary surgery, persecution of midwives, violence against women, and population control (BWHBC, 1970, 1973).

Today, GWHM is a complex of formal nongovernmental organizations (NGOs), informal networks, grassroots campaigns, and individual activists, with a common commitment to challenge the institutions controlling women's health policies and women's sexuality worldwide. Its leadership is primarily nonprofessional women—often volunteers—backed up by men and professionals. GWHM evaluates and questions the science and justice underlying health policies and illuminates power relations and the degree to which policies may have as their underlying purpose social or economic control over women and punishment of female sexuality. Thus its political agenda and strategies are broad and varied, including reproductive rights and health, technologies used mainly by healthy women throughout the life cycle, sexuality, violence, the environment, economics and quality of health services, abuses of human rights, and femininst bioethics (Rodriguez-Trias, 1999).

Formation and Expansion: The First Decade

In the West, WHMs began as early as 1969. Small "consciousness-raising" (CR) groups, made up mostly of white, middle-class women, discussed sexuality, treatment by male gynecologists, contraceptives, childbirth, sexually transmitted diseases (STDs), and abortion—in fact, abortion was the earliest focus of some feminist health activism. Public speakouts, marches, rallies, and national conferences followed. The Brussels Tribunal "Crimes Against Women" brought third world women into the debate over control of women's bodies (Russell, 1976, 1984).

In 1970, feminists in the United States demonstrated at Congressional hearings on "the Pill"—the oral contraceptive that had been approved by the Food and Drug Administration (FDA) in 1960—charging that American women were not being informed of its risks and that the Searle Company had covered up the deaths of Puerto Rican women who were subjects in the original clinical trials. This protest highlighted issues of race and class in the testing and marketing of contraceptives and set off a nationwide debate on contraceptive safety; eventually, the FDA established a Patient Package Insert (PPI) program of warnings about medication, including "the Pill" (BWHBC, 1979; Seaman, 1995). Moreover, these activists paved the way for further feminist critiques of the pharmaceutical industry, contraception, population policy, and the FDA. Because many poor countries depended on the FDA's pharmaceutical safety standards, and the United States played a dominant role in other nations' family planning programs, these initiatives had implications for women worldwide.

Another movement, gynecological "self-help," promoted vaginal self-examination with a plastic speculum and "menstrual extraction," a simple technology using a flexible cannula that later became an improved outpatient method of early abortion and was adopted by doctors and paraprofessionals in several developing countries as menstrual regulation (MR). The movement also modeled community health centers controlled by women and encouraged mainstream abortion rights movements to increase women's access to demedicalized gynecological and abortion procedures (BWHBC, 1976).

Feminist health researchers produced books, pamphlets, newsletters, and information packages exposing medical prejudice and incompetence, corporate malfeasance, governmental neglect, and spurious science. Feminists from developing countries published accounts of women's abuse by punitive legal, religious, and social systems. Many of these works were widely translated, and several became best-sellers (Ehrenreich and English, 1979; BWHBC, 1970–1984).

By the late 1970s, WHMs were becoming global. Activists from many countries exposed scandals involving contraceptive methods and sterilization in publicly funded family planning programs for poor and minority women. One notorious example was the sterilization of thousands of poor Native American, African-American, and Latina women in the United States. Feminists led the fight to change sterilization regulations (BWHBC, 1984).

Another issue was an injectable contraceptive, Depo-Provera (depotmedroxyprogesterone acetate, DMPA). Before its safety had been established, and although it would not be approved in most western nations until 1992, DMPA was distributed by a U.S. company, Upjohn, through its Belgian subsidiary, international family planning agencies, and the U.S. Agency for International Development (USAID), to more than eighty other countries. Women from Thailand, India, New Zealand, Bangladesh, Zimbabwe, the United States, and elsewhere participated in this feminist investigation, supporting the FDA in delaying approval (BWHBC, 1984).

Another controversial contraceptive was a popular, profitable intrauterine device (IUD), the Dalkon shield. In 1975, the FDA asked the manufacturer, A. H. Robbins, to withdraw the Dalkon shield, which was linked to unintended sterility and twenty deaths from pelvic inflammatory disease (PID). Robbins then "dumped" the leftover shields (often unsterilized) overseas at bargain prices and without warning labels. GWHM activists attempted to alert women overseas, and their demands for accountability contributed to the FDA's instituting regulations for medical devices (BWHBC, 1984).

A related issue involved foreign-funded population control programs. GWHM criticized population policies that viewed women instrumentally and risked individual women's health for "the good of mankind" (BWHBC, 1976). GWHM also opposed the contraceptive methods of the "population establishment," which often were provider-dependent, stressed effectiveness over safety, and posed greater health risks to women than barrier methods. The movement also documented abuse and coercion—such as sterilization for compensation—resulting from aggressive population control campaigns in Latin America, South Asia, and Namibia, and helped stop some of these programs (BWHBC, 1976, 1984; Hartmann, 1987, 1995; Mass, 1976). In third world countries, health activists—women and men—mobilized against western-funded population programs, which they denounced as racist and as reflecting a deliberate development strategy. U.S. foreign aid was often conditional on population reduction using profitable western-manufactured contraception. Activists' studies found that such policies were ineffective, even counterproductive; these findings challenged the population paradigm (Hartmann, 1987, 1995).

As GWHM expanded, triennial International Women and Health Meetings were held, first in Rome in 1977, and then in Geneva and Amsterdam. They were initially dominated by their western organizers but soon became more inclusive and diverse as Costa Rica, the Philippines, Uganda, and Brazil joined. These meetings focus on health problems that are marginalized or ignored by governments, international agencies, funders, and family planning programs (Berer, 1997)

The Development Decade (1965–1975) and the Decade for Women (1975–1985), sponsored by the United States, were a force behind early activism in developing regions. Three women's conferences gave GWHM activists an opportunity to exchange information and devise strategies for change (ISIS and BWHBC, 1980).

Challenges of the 1980s

The political environment of the 1980s was significantly altered by a religious backlash against feminism around the world and by the conservative administrations of presidents Reagan and Bush in the United States. GWHM welcomed the conservatives' restrictions on some aggressive U.S.-sponsored population control programs, but not the conservatives' chilling effect on birth control and abortion rights. Within GWHM, new factions fought for abortion rights in the third world, and new entities were formed: New Women of Color and Third World Women's organizations (Basu, 1995; BWHBC, 1984, 1992; Sen and Grown, 1987).

In 1986 the International Women's Health Coalition (IWHC) and the Population Council initiated a series of "dialogues" between contraceptive developers (mainly western white males) and feminist health activists. These dialogues culminated in 1991 with "Creating Common Ground," the first of several meetings between scientists and activists, jointly sponsored by IWHC and the Human Reproductive Program of the World Health Organization (WHO), which led to the formation of WHO's Gender Advisory group.

The Population Council also launched Quality of Care in family planning programs, drawing on WHM philosophy and shifting the focus from reducing population growth to improving services. Quality of Care was designed to influence policies and programs at USAID (the single largest foreign donor for family planning programs); the council

stressed the "user's perspective" and "informed choice" of contraceptive methods. The Ford Foundation, a pioneer in international population efforts, began transforming its forty-year-old program into a new strategy: "reproductive health" (RH), a social science perspective on women's reproductive needs.

Quality of Care and RH offered new concepts of population policy: some populationists' goals were potentially compatible with women's health and empowerment; and RH became the centerpiece of several prominent, well-connected, policy-oriented women's health organizations based in the United States.

By the end of the 1980s, GWHM was using new, inexpensive communications technologies, particularly fax transmission and the Internet. Women's Health Documentation Centers expanded, disseminating information and mobilizing global support for local struggles. New issues emerged: female circumcision, Norplant (a contraceptive implant), HIV/AIDS, environmental population policies, migration, and occupational safety (BWHBC, 1984, 1992; Hartmann, 1995). The term *gender analysis* began to replace *women's health*.

Recent Developments and Future Issues: The 1990s and Beyond

GWHM groups took part in five major UN intergovernmental conferences in the 1990s: the Conference on the Environment and Development (Rio, 1992); Human Rights Conference (Vienna, 1993); International Conference on Population and Development (Cairo, 1994); World Summit for Social and Economic Development (Copenhagen, 1995); and World Women's Conference (Beijing, 1995). There have also been ongoing "Plus Five" follow-up meetings.

In preparing policy for UN meetings, GWHM's broader "women and health" agenda was virtually indistinguishable from RH. Moderates argue that focusing on RH is the most efficacious way to maintain public funding for women's health. However, more progressive and analytical GWHM groups reject separation of RH, arguing that women's overall health is linked to their economic, social, and political circumstances (Petchesky and Judd, 1998; Silliman and King, 1999). Some strategists focus on the threat to women's health from traditional and fundamentalist religious groups.

As participants in NGOs, some women's health groups gained unprecedented access to intergovernmental conferences, entering into policy negotiations and holding private meetings with government leaders. These groups have influenced the UN's policy discourse on population, human rights, and the environment and have to some extent changed official rhetoric and standards regarding governmental and institutional accountability.

UN conferences also shaped the internal politics of GWHM by influencing the role of funders. Throughout the 1990s, most foundation funding for women's health went to elite U.S. policy-oriented RH organizations, which channeled funds to overseas groups of their own choosing and also influenced appointments to key posts in international foundations and health agencies. Many outsiders—such as funders of women's health NGOs—see these leading groups as representing the interests of the entire GWHM and as having the greatest potential to influence RH policy at UN conferences. No comparable funding exists for GWHM groups that focus on women's health and economic development, human rights in health, community organizing, and local organizational empowerment.

Thus there is some distance between grassroots activists and moderate insiders, especially since actual funding for RH programs has been negligible. This raises important questions: What is the GWHM today? What are its priority issues and its short- and long-term goals? Who (if anyone) should represent it in policymaking? What have its investments in UN meetings yielded? In the future, who will fund the monitoring of implementation of agreements made at distant meetings? These questions have exacerbated existing class, racial, geographical, and philosophical divisions within GWHM. Some activists argue for more internal accountability, more democratic representation, and closer attention to human rights and to economic and social determinants of health.

Finally, "cooptation" by international institutions has become an issue. RH policy agencies have hired GWHM activists or invited them to join their boards, so that activists have become inside advocates for women's concerns. However, GWHM is wary about the appropriation and manipulation of feminist discourse by the population control, development, and scientific communities; progressive GWHM groups are highly selective regarding dialogues with policy elites and feel that "insider" strategies are more likely to sustain existing top-down institutional arrangements than transform them into entities that could truly empower women. Observers speculate that well-known feminists in the establishment may apparently legitimize those organizations while actually blunting or diluting GWHM challenges to international policies, marginalizing alternative agendas and frameworks, slowing the rate of change, and reordering priorities.

In the future, GWHM is likely to become more involved in governmental implementation of the Cairo and Beijing commitments and the UN Convention on Elimination of Discrimination Against Women (CEDAW); in monitoring the use of new contraceptives (such as antifertility vaccines and quinacrine) that have harmful side effects and could be abused but are often promoted or tolerated by the population establishment; STDs; HIV/AIDS; new establishment strategies for reducing maternal mortality; and violations of women's health rights.

See Also

ABORTION; AIDS AND HIV; CONTRACEPTION; FAMILY PLANNING; FEMALE CIRCUMCISION AND GENITAL MUTILATION; GLOBAL FEMINISM; GLOBAL HEALTH MOVEMENT: RESOURCES; HEALTH: OVERVIEW; NORPLANT; THE PILL; POPULATION CONTROL; REPRODUCTIVE HEALTH; REPRODUCTIVE RIGHTS

References and Further Reading

Basu, Amrita, ed. 1995. *The challenge of local feminisms: Women's movements in global perspective.* Boulder, Col.: Westview.

Berer, M., et al. 1997. The international women's health movement. *Reproductive Health Matters,* no. 10 (issue theme). London: London: Blackwell Science.

Boston Women's Health Book Collective (BWHBC). 1970. *Women and their bodies: A course by and for women.* Boston: New England Free Press.

———. 1971. *Our bodies, ourselves.* Boston: New England Free Press.

———. 1973, 1976, 1979. *Our bodies, ourselves: A book by and for women.* New York: Simon and Schuster.

———. 1984, 1992. *The new our bodies, ourselves: Our bodies, ourselves for the new century.* New York: Simon and Schuster.

Ehrenreich B., and D. English. 1979. *For her own good: 150 years of the experts' advice to women.* Garden City, N.Y.: Anchor.

Ford Foundation. 1991. *Reproductive health: A strategy for the 1990s.* Program Paper (June). New York: Author.

Hartmann, Betsy. 1995. *Reproductive rights and wrongs: The global politics of population control.* Cambridge, Mass.: South End. Previously published 1987, Harper and Row, New York.

ISIS and BWHBC. 1980. *International women and health resource guide.* Somerville, Mass: BWHBC.

Mass, Bonnie. 1976. *Population target: The political economy of population control in Latin America.* Ontario: Charters.

Petchesky, Ros, and Karen Judd, eds. 1998. *Negotiating reproductive rights: Women's perspectives across countries and cultures.* London and New York: Zed.

Rodrigues-Trias, Helen, et al. 1999. Women's health movements today (special issue). *Journal of the American Medical Women's Association* 54(1: Winter).

Russell, Diana E. H., and Nicole Van de Van, eds. 1984. *Crimes against women: Proceedings of the International Tribunal (Brussels, 1976).* East Palo Alto, Calif.: Frog in the Well. Previously published 1976, Millbrae, Calif.: Les Femmes.

Seaman, Barbara. 1995. *The doctors' case against the Pill.* Alameda, Calif.: Hunter House. First published 1969.

Sen, Gita, and Caren Grown. 1987. *Development, crises, and alternative visions: Third world women's perspectives.* New York: Monthly Review Press.

Silliman, Yael, and Ynestra King, eds. 1999. *Dangerous intersections: Feminist perspectives on population, environment, and development.* Cambridge, Mass.: South End.

Norma Swenson
with Amy J. Higer

GLOBAL HEALTH MOVEMENT: Resources

Generally global women's health movement (GWMH) groups fall into three categories: those that adopt a more expansive concept of women's health, including reproductive health; those that focus primarily or exclusively on reproductive rights or health; and those that approach women's health primarily in terms of conventional human rights and feminist and social justice critiques of international development strategies. Activists and scholars sometimes disagree about which groups belong where at any given time; in part, this reflects the fluidity of the movement. This list of prominent GWHM groups and networks (excluding several strong national groups also active internationally) comprises those most often cited in the media and in interviews and publications by activists themselves.

Both cooperatively and on their own, these networks link women's groups working strategically on health and reproductive rights at the global, national, regional, and grassroots levels. All are nonprofit NGOs that welcome donations; none provide direct clinical health or medical services to women. Each group expends a portion of its resources on international networking, usually including travel and conferences. Some are primarily documentation centers that may also undertake programmatic and advocacy activities. All, reformist and radical alike, maintain and disseminate some type of critique of international institutions from a feminist perspective. Most also have their own print or online publications and Web sites. Some also have UN NGO consultative status.

Women's Health Groups

Boston Women's Health Book Collective (BWHBC). P.O. Box 192, Somerville MA 02144. Telephone (617) 625-9277; Fax (617) 625-0294; E-mail office@bwhbc.org; Web www.ourbodiesourselves.org.

National Asian Women's Health Organization. 250 Montgomery Street, Suite 1500, San Francisco CA 94104. Telephone (415) 989-9747; Fax (415) 989-9758 E-mail nawho@nawho.org; Web http://www.nawho.org.

National Black Women's Health Project (NBWHP). 600 Pennsylvania Ave SE, Suite 310, Washington, DC 20003. Telephone (292) 543-9311; Fax (202) 543-9743; E-mail nbwhp@nbwhp.org; Web www.blackfamilies.com/community/groups/Womenshealth.

National Latina Health Organization. P.O. Box 7567, Oakland, CA 94601. Telephone (510) 534-1362; Fax (510) 534-1362; Web http://clnet.ucr.edu/women/nlho.

North American Women's Health Education Resource Center. P.O. Box 572, Lake Andes SD 57356-0572. Telephone (605) 487-7072; Fax (605) 487-7964; Web http://www.nativeshop.org/nawherc.html.

La Red de la Salud de Mujeres de Latinoamérican y del Caribe, Latin American and Caribbean Women's Health Network (LACHWHN), Casilla 50610, Santiago 1, Chile. Telephone (56-2) 634-9827; Fax (56-2) 634-7101; E-mail rsmlac@mail.bellsouth.cl; Web www.infoera.cl/red_de_salud/ingles.html.

Reproductive Rights–Reproductive Health Groups

Catholics for a Free Choice (CFFC). 1436 U Street NW, Suite 301, Washington, DC 20009-3997. Telephone (292) 986-6093; Fax (292) 332-7005; E-mail cffc@catholicsforchoice.org; Web www.cath4choice.org.

Center for Reproductive Law and Policy. 120 Wall Street, New York, NY 10005. Telephone (212) 514-5534; Fax (212) 514-5538. Or 1146 19th Street NW, Washington, DC 20036. E-mail info@crlp.org; Web www.crlp.org/searchworld.html.

International Reproductive Rights Research Action Group (IRRAG). Hunter College, 695 Park Ave, W1726, New York, NY 10021. E-mail irrag@igc.org.

International Women's Health Coalition (IWHC). 24 East 21 Street, New York, NY 10010. Telephone (212) 979 500; Fax (212) 979-9009; E-mail info@iwhc.org; Web www.iwhc.org.

Research, Action, Information for the Bodily Integrity of Women (RAINBOW). 915 Broadway, Suite 1109, New York, NY 10010. Telephone (212) 477 3318; E-mail w.rainbo.org.

Women's Global Network for Reproductive Rights (WGNRR). NZ Voorburgwal 32, Amsterdam 1012 RZ, Netherlands. Telephone (31-20) 620-9672; Fax (31-20) 622-2450; E-mail offfice@wgnrr.nl.

Women' Health Project. PO Box 1038, Johannesburg 2000 South Africa. Telephone (27-11) 489-9917; Fax (27-11) 489 9922; E-mail womenhp@sn.apc.org.

Development Groups

Asian-Pacific Resource and Research Center for Women (ARROW). 2nd floor, Block F, Anjung Felda, Jalan Maktab, Kuala Lumpur 54000 Malaysia. Telephone (60-3) 292-9913; Fax (603) 292-9958; E-mail arrow@arrow.po.my.

Committee on Women, Population, and the Environment (CWPE). c/o Population and Development Program, Hampshire College, P.O. Box 5001, Amherst MA 01002. Telephone (413) 582-5506; Fax (413) 582-5620; E-mail cwpe@hamp.hampshire.edu; Web www.cwpe.org.

Development Alternatives for Women in a New Era (DAWN) [Rotating Secretariat]. University of the South Pacific, Suva, Fiji. Telephone (679) 313-900; Fax 386-403; E-mail dawn@is.com.fj; Web www.dawn.org.fj.

Gender and Development (GAD) Program, Asian and Pacific Development Center. P.O. Box 12224, Pesiaran Duta, 50770 Kuala Lumpur, Malaysia. Telephone and Fax (60-3) 6519-209; E-mail gad@pc.jaring.my; Web www.jaring.my/apdc/programme/default.html.

ISIS Internacional-Santiago, Casilla 2067, Correo Central, Santiago, Chile. Telephone (56-2) 633 4582; Fax (56-2) 638 3142; E-mail isis@reuna.cl; Web www.isis.cl.

ISIS International-Manila, PO Box 1837, Quezon City Main, Philippines. Telephone (63-2) 435-3405; 435-3408; 436-0312; 436-7863; Fax (63-2) 924-1065; E-mail isis@isiswomen.org; Web www.isiswomen.org.

ISIS-Women's International Cross-Cultural Exchange (ISIS-WICCE). Plot 32, Bukoto Street, Kamwokya, P.O. Box 4934, Kampala, Uganda. Telephone (256-41) 543953; Fax (256-41) 543954; E-mail isis@starcom.co.ug; Web www.isis.or.ug.

Women and Development Unit (WAND). University of the West Indies, School of Continuing Studies, Pinelands, Saint Michael, Barbados, West Indies. Telephone (246) 430-1130; Fax (246) 425-1327; E-mail wand@uwichill.edu.bb.

Women's Human Rights Organizations

Center for Women's Global Leadership. Douglass College, Rutgers, State University of New Jersey, 160 Ryders Lane, New Brunswick, NJ 08901-8555. Telephone (732)932-8782; Fax (732)932-1180; E-mail cwgl@igc.org; Web http://www.cwgl.rutgers.edu.

International Women's Rights Action Watch. Hubert Humphrey Institute of Public Affairs, University of Minnesota, 301 19th Avenue, South Minneapolis, MN 55455. Telephone (612) 625-5093; Fax (612) 624-0068; E-mail iwraw@hhh.umn.edu iwraw@hhh.umn.edu; Web www.igc.org/iwraw.

Women Living Under Muslim Laws (WLUML). International Coordination Office, BP 200 23, 34791 Grabels Cedex, France. E-mail run@gn.apc.org; Web wluml.org.

See Also

GLOBAL HEALTH MOVEMENT

Norma Swenson

GLOBAL RESTRUCTURING

See ECONOMY: GLOBAL RESTRUCTURING and GLOBALIZATION.

GLOBALIZATION

Descriptions of globalization tend to use hyperbole, either painting the world as an ever-gloomier arena of centralized economic power and market-driven rationality or as a wonderful people's democracy of new technologies and multiple voices. Its complexity needs to be taken seriously, and its impact considered not as "either-or" but as "both-and." Globalization offers possibilities but also poses some threats.

Also, most agents of globalization and most of the people who write about it are men—predominantly affluent white men—and its theory is written at such a general and abstract level of analysis that differences in experience are rarely addressed. This tends to make gender—or, more precisely, women—invisible; and the same is true of many others who feel its impact, including the old, the poor, and working people. It is vital to keep in mind what Massey (1944) calls the "power geometry" of globalization: whereas more and more people are caught up in globalization, these people have very different positions with regard to power, and different ability to use or control the positive or negative effects of globalization.

Globalization: A Set of Concepts

What is globalization? Not surprisingly, there is no single theory of globalization, and it is probably more useful to think of globalization as a set of concepts.

One element of the contemporary understanding of globalization is that distance no longer has the significance that it once did and that more of many people's lives are affected by processes and events happening far away. Giddens describes this as "the intensification of world-wide social relations which link distant localities in such a way that local happenings are shaped by events occurring many miles away and vice versa" (1990: 64). We are connected in many and varied ways to people we do not and will never know.

Second, this interconnectivity is happening in and across different spheres of life. The major modern social institutions that frame life in the West have global extensions: the nation-state system, military alliances, world markets, and global infrastructures of communications. Increasing mobility—of people, products, politics, and pictures—connect people unknown to each other in ways that were unimaginable a few decades ago.

Third, there is increased awareness of the world as a "single place," a shared idea and a lived experience for more and more people (Robertson, 1992). There is an increasingly shared understanding that many contemporary problems, including how to care for the environment and how to prevent the spread of nuclear weapons, cannot be solved by single nation-states but require global solutions. Much of that awareness is a product of cross-cultural encounters, through daily newscasts, through the immediacy of information on the Web, and through events like the celebration of the twenty-first century, which was tracked by the media in culture after culture around the world.

Fourth, and perhaps most important, global processes are mediated through local institutions, practices, political structures, and ideologies; existing economic, social and sexual divisions of labor; prevailing cultural values; and so on. Globalization will look and feel different depending on how you, your family, your locality, and your nation are inserted in its matrix, and this applies to women as much as to other groups.

Some of this understanding is not altogether new. In 1848, Marx and Engels (1962: 32–36) could discern the emerging dynamics of international capital: "Modern industry has established the world market.... The bourgeoisie has through its exploitation of the world market given a cosmopolitan character to production and consumption in every country.... It has drawn from under the feet of industry the national ground on which it stood.... In place of the old wants, satisfied by the productions of the country, we find new wants requiring for their satisfaction the products of distant lands and climes. In place of the old local and national self-sufficiency, we have intercourse in every direction, universal inter-dependence of nations. And as in material, so in intellectual production. The intellectual creations of individual nations become common property. National one-sidedness and narrowmindedness become more and more impossible.... The bourgeoisie, by the rapid improvement of all instruments of production, draws all ... nations into civilization. It compels all nations, on pain of extinction, to adopt the bourgeois mode of production.... It creates a world after its own image."

Between 1870 and the 1920s came global communication, the standardization of world time, and global competitions and prizes such as the Olympics and the Nobel Prize. Then came global hostilities in two "world" wars, the Holocaust and the use of atomic weapons, and the need to extend the international system of states, the United Nations to include more issues, such as social and cultural concerns; the growth of nongovernmental organizations (NGOs); the rise of new social movements, some focused on women, the environment, and human rights, transcending national boundaries; and the spread of new communication and information technologies, such as satellites and the Internet. At the start of the twenty-first century, there were new, more flexible modes of capitalist production; increases in the number and size of transnational corporations, in the power of global financial markets, and in the significance of service and information sectors; historical events such as the end of the cold war and the breakup of the Soviet Union; and structural adjustment policies, deregulation, and liberalization in the developing "South."

Globalization and Women

What does this all mean for women? The impact of globalization can be felt not only in women's economic lives but also in political and sociocultural spheres. Global debates and standards have developed that can benefit women, some framed by the Nairobi (1985) and Beijing (1995) conferences. The expansion of international law in UN and regional conventions and charters includes definitions of human rights and women's rights as part. International legislation aimed at preventing discrimination against women

(UN Convention on the Elimination of all Forms of Discrimination Against Women, 1979) has many national signatories, although the United States and some Islamic nations still have not signed. Not all movement is uncoerced and not all labor is willingly entered into; the trafficking of women and children in bonded sweatshop labor, forced marriage, forced prostitution, and domestic servitude is a global phenomenon, and there are global campaigns against such trafficking

Economic Globalization

The impact of the world economy and global markets on national economies, including patterns and rates of employment, exchange and interest rates, inflationary pressures, and recession, has implications for women. Perhaps the greatest significance of globalization and its impact on development lies in the widening and deepening of international flows of trade, finance, and information into a single, integrated global market. Deregulation facilitated the rapid internationalization of the global market economy so that over 20,000 multinational corporations now account for one-quarter to one-third of world output and about 70 percent of world trade (Held, 1998). In the deregulated financial markets, new information technologies have facilitated foreign exchange markets and allow the rapid transmission of currencies, stocks, futures, and new international information and knowledge economy. Although most public faces and names are male—Bill Gates, Rupert Murdoch, presidents Clinton and Mahattir, for example—it is women who, behind the doors of factories, are quietly serving the information economy, producing the microchips and circuit boards that link the global networks (Fuentes and Ehrenreich, 1984; Women Working World-Wide, 1991).

Gender has slowly entered our understanding and our ways of conceptualizing development. The concept of human development, expressed in the reports published yearly by the UNDP since 1990, helped to change a vision of development equated solely with economic growth to a focus on people, including social indicators of education, literacy, health, extent of media, and so on. From 1995, the Human Development Index (HDI) was further refined to include a Gender-Related Development Index (GDI) and also a Gender Empowerment Measure (GEM), which in turn includes indexes of participation in economic and political life.

Slowly, a notion of people-centered development is catching on. It encompasses measures of participation and deprivation, criteria equally relevant for industrial countries, suggesting that development is an ongoing process everywhere. Such indexes also reveal the actual scope of national policy making and the setting of social priorities. For example, in the late 1990s Costa Rica, which had given up its standing army in the 1950s, achieved an adult literacy rate of 95 percent and an HDI value of 0.889, which was higher than that of many industrial countries and the same as Brunei, whose real per capita GDP was five times as great: $31,165 compared with $5,969; real per capita GDP rank minus HDI rank give Costa Rica a score of plus 28, Brunei a score of minus 33 (UNDP, 1998). The indexes also help to distinguish inequalities within nations, by class, gender, urban-rural divisions, regions, and ethnicity, although these factors often overlap. They also document the possibilities of economic regression and decline; the Human Development Report for 1998 focused on the dramatic impact of HIV/AIDS in reversing social investment, and of military conflict in absorbing huge proportions of national budgets. Income growth can help the rich more than the poor (as in Honduras and New Zealand). For 27 heavily indebted poor countries, debt is greater than GNP, and Mozambique, for example, has an external debt burden nine times the value of its annual exports and allocates four times what it spends on health to servicing its debt; the floods of spring 2000 wiped away a decade of development policy and planning. Although international organizations are slowly accepting the logic of debt cancellation, structural adjustment programs that cut social welfare put considerable pressure on households to absorb the effects of unemployment, ill health, and old age. More women now work in the formal sectors, but women's work in the informal sector and in the home also expanded—though it remains invisible in measures of economic activity and growth (UN, 1999). Solutions that alleviate poverty—such as microcredit facilities for poor women like those initiated by the Grameen Bank in Bangladesh—suggest a model of empowerment and self-help that is more effective and ethical than the misleading concept of trickle-down wealth. Still, there is concern that such measures help women entrepreneurs but leave many others trapped as an invisible feminized labor force. The necessity of "writing women into" the development process is being recognized, and the World Bank has begun to accept the maxim that by educating a woman you educate the family and the nation.

At the same time, the instability of an unfettered and unregulated global market is increasingly evident; when southeast Asian economies sneeze, the entire world may catch cold. Neoliberal market economics now seem to require better financial regulation, revamped institutions, and increased monitoring, suggesting that the global economy has not replaced the world of states, political power, and policies but rather that states and markets must coexist in mutual negotiation.

Political Globalization

Globalization has precipitated intense speculation over the future role of the nation-state. There is mounting evidence that the Westphalian international order of nation-states is evolving into a far more complex multilevel environment of political-economic actors. These include macroregions (such as the European Community, ASEAN nations, and an emergent Islamic world); existing states with limited sovereignty, including the single global superpower, the United States; the disintegration of some states into microregions (Quebec, Catalonia); and the growing power of transnational corporations, often economically more powerful and employing more personnel than small states.

Yet, although there is much talk of a multipolar, post-hegemonic world, and the change in the nature of actors is important, there is little evidence that the nation-state is coming to an end. If anything, the numbers of claims to nationhood is growing, leading to projections of an international system with far more states than at present. There remain real possibilities for national policy to make a difference: state investment in the development of Malaysia's "super information corridor" and Costa Rica's national development strategy are good examples. Furthermore, although the letter of international law extends, the reality of action within states often eludes it, whether in regard to ethnic cleansing in Kosovo, monitoring nuclear weapons in Iraq, or intensifying gender inequality in Afghanistan. Nowhere is "international intervention" a simple matter.

For women—who still struggle for full involvement in national political structures—transnational organization often provides a better platform and greater solidarity. New social movements are examples of what Falk (1994) describes as "globalization from below" or Castells (1996) describes as the "network society," a global civil society whose lines of solidarity and activism cut across national boundaries. Women have been particularly adept at recognizing and utilizing the power of new technologies, including the Internet, E-mail, and fax, to build networks concerning events and issues, potentially connecting grassroots women's organizations to centers of decision making (Harcourt, 1999; Sreberny-Moham-

madi, 1998). Such developments allow ordinary people to participate not only in local and national civic politics but also in global issues, as members of transnational social movements.

Cultural Globalization

Global cultural homogenization elicits a fear that western capitalist—indeed, U.S.—images will spread everywhere and produce sameness. The main carriers of such images are supposedly the "electronic empires" run by Murdoch, Berlusconi, and Black; the image machine of Hollywood; and the news power of Reuters (Herman and McChesney, 1997).

Reactions have included the banning of satellite dishes in parts of the Middle East, and legislation in Europe to control the amount of imported television programs. There is, however, evidence that, when available, local cultural production is preferred over transnational, and that home production is the best counterbalance to globalized consumption. More and more, social theorists look to hybridization evident in emerging locations of cultural production (Bollywood, the Nile delta); in popular cultural genres (Asian pop music; Latin American *telenovelas*; third world cinema), and in personal experiences and collective narratives of multicultural and diasporic identity. Tension between homogeneity and heterogeneity makes identity an issue in globalization.

But the Internet, the World Wide Web, and the spread of the information society also offer new possibilities for expression and organization to nations, groups, and sectors not noticeably empowered by the old formations. The Web has been taken up by women's movements around the world. Women of both the "North" and the "South" are also actively involved in local radio (as in Tanzania and South Africa), publishing, and cable television, using communications technologies to educate, participate in decision making, and let multiple voices be heard. However, networks designed for solidarity and support also have to address the differences between women in power and resources, and to ask whether "western feminism" pushes the rest of the world's women into a cultural and political conformity that not all find desirable.

As noted earlier, globalization represents opportunities as well as threats. The twenty-first century is likely to see further development in processes of democratization and the empowerment of women everywhere, with transnational networks of technologies facilitating women in imagining different lives and different worlds and offering each other support.

See Also

ECONOMICS: FEMINIST CRITIQUES; ECONOMY AND DEVELOPMENT: OVERVIEW; ECONOMY: GLOBAL RESTRUCTURING; GLOBAL FEMINISM; GLOBALIZATION OF EDUCATION

References and Further Reading

Castells, M. 1996. *The rise of the network society*. Oxford: Blackwell.

Falk, R. 1994. The making of global citizenship. In B. van Steenbergen, ed., *The conditions of citizenship*. London: Sage.

Fuentes, A., and B. Ehrenreich. 1984. *Women in the global factory*. Boston: South End.

Giddens, A. 1990. *The consequences of modernity*. Stanford, Calif.: Stanford University Press.

Harcourt, W. 1999. *Women@Internet*. Zed Books.

Held, D. 1998. Globalization. *Marxism Today* (Nov.–Dec.): 24–27.

Herman, E., and R. McChesney. 1997. *The global media*. London: Cassell.

Marx, K., and F. Engels. 1965. *Manifesto of the communist party*. Peking: Foreign Languages. (Originally published 1848.)

Massey, D. 1994. *Space, place, and gender*. Cambridge: Polity.

Robertson, R. 1992. *Globalization*. London: Sage.

Sreberny-Mohammadi, A. 1998. Feminist internationalism: Imagining and building global civil society. In Daya Thussu, ed., *Electronic empires*. London: Arnold.

UN. 1999. *World survey on the role of women in development*. New York: United Nations.

UNDP. *Human Development Report 1998*. New York: Oxford University Press.

Women Working World-Wide. 1991. *Common interests: Women organizing in local electronics*. London: Author.

Annabelle Sreberny

GLOBALIZATION OF EDUCATION

"Globalization" became one of the defining characteristics of the late twentieth century. The process of globalization is generally associated with an increase in the density and depth of economic interdependency and international interactions, the rapid expansion of information technology, and increasing and newly emerging social interconnections. Additionally, there is a proliferation of nongovernmental and international organizations such as the United Nations, Greenpeace, and the World Bank.

The impact of globalization on the lives of women, and on education, can be best understood in relation to the potential of technology for the development and delivery of global studies and curricula and for changing access. The expansion of technological capability has been the most significant factor in the impact of globalization on education and on implications for women as teachers and as students. The availability of the World Wide Web, E-mail, and real-time interactions across the globe have the potential to alter the ways in which educators design and implement courses. There is the potential for women from diverse cultures and locations to participate in shared learning by using these new technologies. In a global classroom it is possible to have interactive contact between students and teachers in multiple locations by E-mail or by shared Web-based activities. And, while the impact of globalization on education has been generally confined to tertiary-level institutions (in terms of aggressive marketing and privatization), the impact of the technologies of globalization has reached to all levels—students of all ages at all educational levels participate in Web-based activities, which transcend national boundaries and gender differences.

Web-based technologies on which the globalization of education is based provide the potential for greater access for women to education at all levels. Because there is no longer the same need for physical, real-time presence in a classroom, education is more readily available to women and girls who are housebound, disabled, or geographically isolated. Web-based technologies join students and educators from diverse cultural and racial backgrounds, bringing the promise of increased sharing of experiences and the development of worldwide networks of women working together. One aspect of this enhanced access is that the expertise and knowledge of educators can be disseminated beyond the limited spatial constraints of location-bound classrooms and courses—women in different parts of the world can develop shared knowledge and basic skills. In this way, globalization of education provides women with an opportunity to create global awareness of issues and to build networks with other women without the constraints of time or space. Global education, in its capacity to link students and educators from a number of diverse physical and cultural position, has the potential to minimize the hegemony of western male perspectives. However, to turn this potential into a reality, women around the world must continue to work toward increasing access to education in general and to the technologies of globalization in particular.

See Also

ECONOMICS: GLOBAL RESTRUCTURING; EDUCATION: DISTANCE EDUCATION; EDUCATION: ON-LINE; GLOBALIZATION; NETWORKS, ELECTRONIC

References and Further Reading

Ainley, Rosa, ed. 1998. *New frontiers of space, bodies, and gender.* London: Routledge.

Webster, Juliet. 1996. *Shaping women's work: Gender, employment, and information technology.* New York: Longman Group.

Vicki Carrington

GOD

See DEITY.

GODDESS

The concept of deity or deities as female is a controversial but powerful symbol in contemporary feminism. It introduces a spiritual dimension at variance with perceived ideas in both secular and religious thought, and it raises a problem. "Goddess feminists" claim that much of the rationale for the subordination of women is linked to a tradition that expressed God in the masculine gender only (denying women spiritual equality in the image of God), but others point to women's oppression in societies that have long-established nonmonotheistic religions whose pantheons include goddesses.

For modern spiritual feminists, the concept *Goddess* is a symbol of self-worth. It involves rediscovering female divinities and reclaiming characteristics that affirm female abilities, thoughts, achievements, and spirituality. Thus, texts concerning a female deity such as Isis of Egypt may show her as creator of the universe, as immanent in the world, and as an expression of morality and judgment (Engelsman, 1979). This last attribute applies not only to deities in the past. Wotogebe-Weneka (1988:50) reports that goddesses worshiped by African peoples today have played a significant part in the ethical rules of society. He notes that all over Ikwerre land there is a common saying, *Nye Krakwatru, Eli chekwetaa* ("The Earth Goddess protects the just"). *Eli*, Earth Goddess, also means land. If evil is done, it is felt that the Earth itself is violated. In other societies, goddesses are usually understood as sustaining the universe, keeping the forces of nature in harmony, and helping human beings understand the world.

Goddesses in antiquity were also venerated as teachers of humankind, introducing and expounding the arts and sciences. Demeter, of the Hellenistic world, is credited with the introduction of agriculture, and medicine was the province of many ancient goddesses. Perhaps the most famous of these is Gula, of the Babylonians, called the Great Physician. Her temples were hospitals as well as places of worship, and her country, also known as Chaldea, was famous for its medicine throughout the ancient world. It is recorded that priestesses were doctors here and also in the temples of healing in Egypt. A recent study of the female figure of Wisdom (Hochma or Sophia) in the biblical tradition found some evidence that she is an alternative divine figure with God and functions as creator, sustainer, teacher, healer, and even savior (Long, 1992–1993). Inclusion of the female in divinity was combined with an overarching theme of the Goddess as Nature herself, and Lady of its various parts. In contrast to traditional monotheism, there appeared to be no need for a dualist split between the spiritual and the material. Gaia, or Ge, the Greek goddess of the sacred earth, was addressed by Homer as the mother of all, who feeds all creatures that are in the world. Pele, goddess of Hawaii's volcanos, is in modern times, as in the past, portrayed as a fire deity, who is both friendly and dangerous to humankind, and whose fiery talent and fiery rage are both replicated in the female human being. Rivers, springs, and fountains have been revered for their powers of refreshment and healing. The moon and the planets were among the major female divinities: Ishtar or Astarte, of the ancient Near East, became the Roman Venus, giving her name to the morning and evening stars.

Phases of the moon—new, full, and declining—are today often understood as being a paradigm for three phases of women's lives: maiden, mother, and crone. Connections of this kind are made with the many depictions throughout the ancient world, from the Indus Valley through Asia Minor to the Celtic lands, of triple goddess figures. The association of the moon with deity and also with menstruation leads to a new appreciation of the sacredness of women's bodies and their functions; the concept of uncleanness is reversed.

The belief that a nature goddess can provide or destroy the prosperity of the land and of human beings appears as a theme in both ancient and extant goddess-oriented cultures. From prehistoric times Mother Earth has been pic-

tured as a fecund female, and rites were established to pro-
pitiate her and to ensure prosperity, which meant good harvests from land and sea and thriving youngsters, both
human and animal. Such rituals often had overtly sexual features, which were denounced in the Bible and also became
an object of hostile comment from later religious thinkers.
Thus, traditional scholars have referred to goddess figures as
merely "fertility idols," focusing only on their sexual aspects.
Consequently, the female aspects of deity became lost, as did
their association with care for nature and an appreciation of
the ethics this entailed. Ecofeminism is regaining some of
this understanding in the interests of ecology; it is a widely
growing insight in the modern goddess movement.

However, there is room for debate concerning the
worship of goddesses and its connection with the status of
women in society. India, for example, is a country where,
according to a survey by Ajit Mookerjee, the Goddess is
still widely worshiped today, in a tradition that dates to
3000 B.C.E. or earlier. Mookerjee (1988: 16) writes: "Evidence of feminine ultimacy is widely prevalent in India—
whether venerated as Nature or the life-force, as Mother
or Virgin, as the Great Goddess or as Ultimate Reality." In
particular, he describes the worship of Kali the Mother,
who is responsible for both creation and destruction and
who ultimately preserves the universe. Throughout his
work Mookerjee discusses female energy, Shakti, the ener-
gizing force of all divinity and of the universe, and suggests
that female strength or power is the real moving force in
society. Many Indian women challenge rules and customs
that are especially hard on women; the same women will
often declare that it is only Shakti that gives them the
strength to help one another and carry out life's onerous
commands.

Obviously there is no simple formula to connect ven-
eration and acknowledgment of female divinities with
women's place in secular society. Attempts to link such
divinities with ancient matriarchies have been generally discredited, although there is a school of thought, led by Marija Gimbutas (1991), which suggests that there was a
goddess-centered civilization in "old Europe" before the sixth
millennium B.C.E. that was more peaceful and certainly less
androcentric than later societies, reaching down to those of
modern times.

This is a matter of dispute among archaeologists. While
it is of interest, it does not affect the fundamental challenges
and insights of the "Goddess movement." These lie in the
contribution they make to the widespread current struggle
toward gender egalitarianism and thus toward a more just
world.

See Also

DEITY; ECOFEMINISM; EARTH; GAIA HYPOTHESIS;
MATRIARCHY; MOTHER EARTH; SHAKTI; SPIRITUALITY:
OVERVIEW; THEOLOGIES: FEMINIST; WOMANSPIRIT

References and Further Reading

Engelsman, Joan C. 1979. *The feminine dimension of the divine.*
Philadelphia: Westminster. For a full English translation of
the Isis hymn of self-praise dated to the second century
C.E., see pp. 64–66.
Gimbutas, Marija. 1991. *The civilization of the Goddess.* San Fran-
cisco: HarperCollins.
Goodison, Lucy, and Christine Morris, eds. 1998. *Ancient god-
desses.* London: British Museum.
Husain, Shahrakh. 1997. *The goddess.* Boston, Mass.: Little, Brown.
Long, Asphodel P. 1992–93. *In a chariot drawn by lions: The search
for the female in deity.* London: Women's Press; Freedom,
Calif.: Crossing.
Mookerjee, Ajit. 1988. *Kali: The feminine force.* London: Thames
and Hudson.
Wotogbe-Weneka, Wellington O. 1988. Eli (Earth Goddess) as
a guardian of social morality among the traditional Ikwerre
of Rivers State, Nigeria. *King's Theological Review* 11(2):
50–54. Kings College, London.

Asphodel Long

GOVERNMENT

Within each society, governments are the institutions that
make, implement, and adjudicate decisions concerning the
direction and quality of collective life. Comprising the official intuitions of state, governments have responsibility for
the provision of order and the protection of the individual;
for the defense of the nation and the conduct of foreign policy; for establishing laws pertaining to property, labor, marriage, family, sexuality, civil rights and liberties; and for
making policies that affect virtually every aspect of life (for
instance, agriculture, arts, culture, education, health, environment, social welfare, trade, transportation, banking and
finance, patents and copyrights, public utilities, and technology). Governments are often classified according to type
of regime (who rules), electoral system (how rulers are
selected), and the nature of public policy (whose interests
served). Under this classification scheme, contemporary governments include liberal democracies, socialist and post
communist states, authoritarian regimes, and military dictatorships.

GOVERNMENT

A common feature of these various forms of government is the dramatic underrepresentation of women. Although women constitute the majority of the population in every nation that does not practice female infanticide, women do not constitute the majority of decision makers in any contemporary political system or in any political system in the historical record. This article will provide a statistical profile of women in governance at the beginning of the twenty-first century, an overview of the factors that contribute to women's exclusion from governmental offices, the policy consequences of that exclusion, and a discussion of recent efforts to increase women's participation in decision making.

Women in Governance

Of the 190 independent states in the world, less than 1 percent have a woman as president or prime minister. Fewer than 35 women have been elected to the highest national office and more than half of these women have been elected since 1990. By far the most women chief executives have been elected in nations in the developing "South." Women have served as president of Argentina, Bolivia, Ecuador, Haiti, Iceland, Ireland, Liberia, Malta, Nicaragua, Panama, Philippines, Sri Lanka, and Yugoslavia. Women have served as prime minister of Bangladesh, Burundi, Canada, Central African Republic, Dominica, France, Haiti, India, Israel, Lithuania, Netherlands Antilles, New Zealand, Norway, Pakistan, Poland, Portugal, Rwanda, Sri Lanka, Turkey, and the United Kingdom. Around the globe, women hold only 7 percent of national cabinet posts. In the last decade of the twentieth century, women held 15 percent of the ministerial positions in only 8 countries and 15 percent of the subministerial positions in only 23 countries; and in 59 nations, women held no cabinet positions (Peterson and Runyon, 1999).

Data gathered by the Inter-Parliamentary Union indicated that in January 2000 women constituted 12.8 percent of the members of national legislatures, 2 percent less than the record world average (14.8 percent) achieved in 1988. The proportion of women in national parliaments varies significantly from one region of the world to another. Women have made the greatest gains in the Nordic countries, where they currently hold 38.9 percent of the seats in parliament. Women hold 14.9 percent of the legislative seats in Asia, 14.7 percent in the Americas, 13.1 percent in European nations excluding Nordic countries, 10.9 percent in sub-Saharan Africa, 8.7 percent in Pacific states, and 3.8 percent in Arab states. Although women made small but steady gains in legislative chambers from 1975 to 1987, they suf-

fered serious setbacks under "democratization," the transition from various types of state socialist or authoritarian regimes to liberal democracy. Political restructuring in central and eastern Europe and in the former Soviet Union produced the worst setbacks for women. From an average of 29 percent in the mid-1980s, women's representation dropped to 7 percent in 1994 (Jaquette and Wolchik, 1998). By the end of 1999, women had regained some ground, holding 10.9 percent of the seats in these national legislatures.

Women's Underrepresentation: Contributing Factors

For most of human history, men have reserved to themselves the right to rule. By linking political power with war and conquest, men effectively excluded women from participation premised on military service. In most traditional societies, ascription standards restricted governance to a small circle of property-owning families that adopted the norm of primogeniture, passing entitlement to rule along with other rights of inheritance to the firstborn son. Hierarchical belief systems, religious and philosophical, legitimated such inequitable power distributions with claims about "natural superiority" and "divine ordination." As traditional modes of governance slowly gave way to more representative political systems and the rule of law, men in power passed laws restricting the right to vote and hold public office on the basis of gender, class, race, and place of birth. Although a handful of states accorded women voting rights between 1869 and 1900, women's struggle to win rights of citizenship, including the right to vote and to hold elective office, was widely concluded only in the twentieth century.

Women's historic exclusion from the institutions of governance is often discussed in the context of a gendered division of labor in which "women's sphere"—alternatively described as the "private sphere"—was restricted to the realm of biological necessity. Women were assigned primary responsibility for the subsistence needs, as well as the emotional and physical needs, of their families and their communities. Possessing the capacity to bear children, women in most cultures were also given primary responsibility for rearing children. Since the skills required to reproduce and nurture the species and to meet subsistence needs were expected to be passed from mother to daughter, women were often denied educational and professional opportunities. At the close of the twentieth century, women in most of the world continued to receive not only a different education from men, but a good deal less education than men. Most professions remained remarkably sex-segregated.

937

Traditional gender roles and restricted educational and professional opportunities affect women's participation in governance in multiple ways. Lack of education, lack of professional experience, lack of financial resources, and lack of extensive political networks constitute formidible barriers to any woman's pursuit of a political career. Such *individual barriers* not only reduce women's chance of electoral success; they curb women's political aspirations. For many women, rearing children, caring for other family members, and providing the labor necessary to keep a household fed and functioning leave little time to devote to political work. Women's "double duty" in the workforce and at home is one example of a *structural barrier* to participation in governance. Traditional norms suggest that the political world is a man's world, that men are inherently better suited to leadership and governance, and that it is inappropriate for a women to pursue a career in public life; these norms remain effective *cultural barriers* to women's full participation in government.

Within the political world, women also confront *institutional barriers* to equal participation, such as incumbency advantages, political parties' recruitment practices, and, in many places, the nature of the electoral system. To achieve gender parity in governance would require a radical redistribution of political power. Many male political officials would have to be replaced. Although some political opportunities are routinely created through retirements, resignations, and term limits, most women candidates seeking elective office must unseat an incumbent, a notoriously difficult thing to do. Incumbents possess an array of advantages, such as name recognition, an established record of policy accomplishments, access to the media, patronage power, party support, and, often, large campaign coffers. Running as a challenger, a woman candidate must devise strategies to overcome such incumbency advantages if she is to win election.

In most nations, political parties play a crucial role in recruiting candidates for elective and appointive offices. Like government offices, political party hierarchies are dominated by males to a remarkabe extent. According to the Inter-Parliamentary Union, in 1997 women served as party leaders in 10.8 percent of 418 parties in 86 nations. Yet 585 political parties in another 80 nations had no women serving in the party hierarchy. With some notable exceptions, political parties have treated women as voters and party workers, but have not recruited them as candidates for elective offices. In the exceptional cases, in the aftermath of the death or assassination of a president, prime minister, or party leader, party elites have recruited the widow or daughter of the former leader to succeed him.

For example, following the assassination of her husband in 1959, Sirimavo Bandaranaike served as prime minister of Sri Lanka from 1960 to 1965 and again from 1970 to 1977. Corazon Aquino (Philippines), Benazir Bhutto (Pakistan), Violeta Chamorro (Nicaragua), Indira Ghandi (India), Chandrika Bandaranike Kumaratunga (Sri Lanka), Isabel Peron (Argentina), and Khaleda Zia Rahman (Bangladesh) have followed similar paths to political power (Hodson, 1997). Beyond such exceptional cases, party elites have tended to be more hostile to the candidacies of women than have voters. In many parts of Africa and Latin America, parties have created separate women's branches. Although these organizations can provide crucial political education for women, they can also marginalize women's talents and abilities by restricting women's activities to the sphere of "women's issues" narrowly construed, rather than serving as a vehicle for women's movement into public office (Corrin, 1999).

Political parties' tendencies to conceive viable candidates as male candidates is exacerbated by a particular form of electoral system, characterized by single-member districts (one individual represents the population) and "winner-take-all" outcomes (the candidate with the most votes wins the office). Given the scarcity of elective positions in such a system, bias in favor of males leads parties to consider male candidates more worthy of the opportunity to run for office. In contrast, women have experienced far greater electoral success in systems based on multimember districts (multiple individuals represent the population) and proportional representation (offices are assigned on the basis of the percentage of votes won by the party). Under proportional representation, parties offer a slate of candidates in each district and seem less reluctant to add some women's names to their slates. Proportional representation in concert with a commitment to gender equality has been correlated with women's most impressive electoral gains. In the Nordic countries, for example, women have won 42.7 percent of the parliamentary seats in Sweden, 37.4 percent in Denmark, 37 percent in Finland, and 36.4 percent in Norway. In nonproportional representation systems, by contrast, women's share of the legislative seats has not yet reached 20 percent.

Policy Consequences of Women's Underrepresentation

It is often argued that gender is and ought to be irrelevant in the selection of government officials. Voters should cast their ballots for the most talented leader, or on the basis of political ideology, partisan loyalties, or stances on critical political issues. Moreover, since women within each political system differ in their political views on the basis of class, ethnicity, race, religion, and a host of other factors, there is no reason to believe that any particular woman leader could represent women any better than any particular man. While empirical studies document a wide range of political differences among women citizens and great variation among women's leadership styles, they also demonstrate that women elected officials tend to have some different policy priorities from their male counterparts. Women legislators report that they have an obligation to represent "women's interests" and they devote more time to securing passage of legislation beneficial to women, children, and families, such as improved education and health care, child care, and poverty alleviation programs. In the absence of women policy makers, certain issues (such as rape, domestic violence, women's health, and pregnancy discrimination) never make it onto the policy agenda. Indeed, the issue of women's political equality confronts serious opposition in a nation such as Kuwait, where the all-male parliament still refuses to accord women the right to vote and hold public office. As long as women have barely token representation in government, it is difficult for them to initiate systemic policy change. Yet even under such restrictive conditions, women in government have attempted to place women's issues on the agenda, arguing for "gender impact" analyses of pending legislation and for gender-equitable budgets (expenditure of public funds to benefit women in proportion to women's presence in the population). Even when vastly underrepresented, women in government are more likely than their male counterparts to support mechanisms that make governments more open and accountable to citizens (Goetz, 1997; Leijenaar, 1998).

Several scholars have argued that the real impact of women in governance can be measured only when women achieve "critical mass," for instance, when they hold 30 percent to 35 percent of the positions in the government. Sweden provides interesting insights into the possibilities when women achieve a critical mass in government. With women holding 42.7 percent of the seats in the legislature, Sweden currently ranks first in the world in the proportion of women in government. According to two indexes created by the United Nations to measure the quality of life for women, the Gender-Related Development Index and the Gender Empowerment Measure, Sweden also ranks as the best country in the world for women. Although women in Sweden remain mobilized to promote democratic and anti-sexist processes, their gains since the 1970s are impressive. Women in Sweden experience the least pay inequity in the industrialized world; women's issues are included in the mainstream political agenda; over 80 percent of women are in the paid labor force; parental leave benefits are generous; child care of good quality is available at reasonable cost; abortion is available through the National Health Service; and the rate of poverty among elderly women is lower than in other industrialized nations (Gustafsson, Eduards, and Ronnblom, 1997).

Strategies for Change

Women have mobilized around the globe to eliminate individual, cultural, structural, and institutional barriers to their full participation in governance. Although tactics and priorities vary from nation to nation, several common strands are evident. In the aftermath of the Fourth World Conference on Women in Beijing (1995), transnational feminist networks have mobilized to pressure governments to recognize that women's rights are human rights. Women's nongovernmental organizations (NGOs) have renewed efforts to press governments to ratify and implement the Convention on the Elimination of All Forms of Discrimination Against Women (CEDAW) and to fulfill the Beijing Platform for Action, both of which include commitments to gender balance in governmental bodies, committees, and administrative entities. The United Nations has assumed a role in monitoring governments' compliance with the Beijing Accord, convening a special session in June 2000 to review each nation's progress in ending discrimination against women.

In several nations, women have secured constitutional and statutory mandates to increase women's participation in governance. Reservation policies or quotas have been created setting aside a certain percentage of government offices for women, for example, 30 percent in Argentina and Bolivia, 20 percent in Brazil and the Democratic Republic of Korea, 50 percent in France, 33 percent in India, and 5 percent in Nepal. Beyond legislative mandates to increase the number of women in government offices, more than 70 political parties in 30 nations have adopted internal rules to increase the umber of women candidates in each election cycle. In 1993, for example, women in the African National Congress (ANC) after an intensive struggle, persuaded the ANC to adopt a quota requiring 30 percent women on the party slate of candidates. In the elections of 1994, the first in which blacks in South Africa were allowed to vote, 109 women were elected, constituting 27 percent of the members of parliament. Working as equal members of the government, ANC women also secured the creation of the National Gender Commission, a governmental agency responsible for overseeing all branches of government to ensure the promotion of gender equality (Karam, 1998).

Many governments have created official agencies devoted to women's issues. Some of these agencies concentrate on women's economic status and social welfare, but some have made efforts to enhance women's political participation, including developing leadership training programs. Research suggests that these ministries are most effective when they work with grassroots women's organizations and feminist policy networks (Stetson and Mazur, 1995).

In most of the world, women's political mobilization is far more evident at the local than at the national level. In the "South," women are active in political issues such as structural adjustment policies, poverty programs, and access to means of subsistence—land, water, firewood. In the "North" and "South," women's NGOs press for education and employment opportunities, pay equity, decent working conditions, and an end to violence against women. Increasingly, women's organizations are blending service provision, grassroots lobbying, recruitment, training, voter education, and mobilization in support of women's candidates. Their goal is to increase the number of women in governance and create mechanisms of accountability, to ensure that women in office respond to the pressing needs of women, the majority of the voters.

See Also

COMMUNITY POLITICS; EMPOWERMENT; POLITICAL LEADERSHIP; POLITICAL PARTICIPATION; POLITICAL REPRESENTATION; POLITICS AND THE STATE, *specific entries*

References and Further Reading

Afshar, Haleh. 1996. *Women and politics in the Third World.* London: Routledge.

Basu, Amrita. 1995. *The challenge of local feminisms: Women's movement in global perspective.* Boulder, Col.: Westview.

Corrin, Chris. 1999. *Feminism perspectives on politics.* London and New York: Longman.

Goetz, Anne-Marie. 1997. *Getting institutions right for women in development.* London: Zed.

Gustafsson, Gunnell, M. Eduards, and M. Ronnblom. 1997. *Toward a new democratic order? Women's organizing in Sweden in the 1990s.* Stockholm: Publica.

Hodson, Piper. 1997. Routes to power: An examination of political change, rulership and women's access to executive office. In MaryAnne Borelli and Janet Martin, eds., *The other elites.* Boulder, Col.: Lynne Reinner.

Inter-Parliamentary Union. 1997. *Men and women in politics: Democracy still in the making, a world comparative survey.* Geneva: IPU. For the latest statistics: <http://www.ipu.org/wmn-e/world.htm>.

Jaquette, Jane, and Wolchik, Jaquette. 1998. *Women and democracy: Latin America and Central and Eastern Europe.* Baltimore, Md.: Johns Hopkins University Press.

Karam, Azza. 1998. *Women in Parliament: Beyond numbers.* Varberg, Sweden: Institute for Democracy and Electoral Assistance.

Leijenaar, Monique. 1998. *Gender and good governance.* Netherlands: P&D Analytics.

Nelson, Barbara, and Najima Chowdhury. 1994. *Women and politics worldwide.* New Haven, Conn.: Yale University Press.

Peterson, V. Spike, and Anne Sisson Runyon. 1999. *Global gender issues.* Boulder, Col.: Westview.

Rai, Shirin, and G. Lievesley. 1996. *Women and the state: International perspectives.* London: Taylor and Francis.

Randall, Vicky, and Georgina Waylen. 1998. *Gender politics and the state.* London and New York: Routledge.

Stetson, Dorothy, and Amy Mazur. 1995. *Comparative state feminism.* London: Sage.

Mary Hawkesworth

GRANDMOTHER

The term *grandmother* refers to a woman whose children have produced offspring of their own. As female progenitors, grandmothers are generally accorded a high degree of respect cross-culturally, and as they age, they gain seniority and jural and social rights over others. In accordance with their status as elders, grandmothers are often perceived as bearers of wisdom, whose memories of the past and of genealogical links are often important assets, especially in nonliterate societies. Their importance is accentuated by the fact that they have already passed through the major life stages. Many societies elevate a woman's status once her own childbearing years have passed, often because a women's sexual reputation is thought secure only when she can no longer physically produce children.

In patrilineal and patrilocal societies, where a new bride enters her husband's lineage and his ancestral home, as in traditional India and China, a woman has few allies until her children are grown. Once she herself becomes a grandmother, she is accorded the deference and respect of her grandchildren and her grown sons which she did not have in her earlier years. One justification of the abysmal treatment of female children relative to male children in many patrilocal societies is the simple reason that a mother without sons will one day be alone.

According to Victor Turner's classic study of Ndembu life in Zambia, *The Drums of Affliction* (1968), grandmothers play a major role in the household. In this matrilineal and matrilocal society, children are raised in the household of their maternal grandmother for most of their childhood. Grandmothers also play an important part in Ndembu religious rituals and are central figures in a girl's puberty rites. As among many other matrilineal peoples, including the Hopi, the Iroquois, and the Seneca, a maternal grandmother runs the extended family's household and its occupants. Ethnographic evidence suggests that grandmothers may be important in other ways too: when parents' workloads are unduly heavy, a grandparent's assistance often means the difference between a well-adjusted child and a hostile one. A cross-cultural study by Rohner (1975) found that grandparents' and fathers' roles in child care are important for relieving overworked mothers; without such caretakers, children were more likely to feel rejected by authority figures and to suffer psychologically.

Grandmothers can also exert symbolic influence and authority. In traditional Indian communities in Guatemala, for example, a daughter's umbilical cord is buried under the hearthstone known as the "grandmother stone" to ensure that the girl will stay at home when she is grown (Paul, 1974). Among the Hua, a society in New Guinea, a postmenopausal woman who has given birth at least three times loses the dangerous polluting substances perceived to be present in women of childbearing years. These feminine substances, or *nu,* are drained from the woman's body during the natural processes of parturition, menstruation, and even cooking. By the time a women is a grandmother, she is perceived as being "like men," able to live in the men's house and to be a repository of "male" knowledge. In other words, she becomes a woman who is no longer dangerous, her potency nullified by experience (Meigs, 1990).

See Also

AGING; FAMILY: POWER STRUCTURES AND POWER RELATIONS; KINSHIP; MATRILINEAL SYSTEMS; MOTHER

References and Further Reading

Meigs, Anna S. 1990. Multiple gender ideologies and statuses. In Peggy Reeves Sanday and Ruth Gallagher Goodenough, eds., *Beyond the second sex.* Philadelphia: University of Pennsylvania Press.

Paul, Lois. 1974. The mastery of work and the mystery of sex in a Guatemalan village. In Michelle Zimbalist Roasaldo and Louise Lamphere, eds., *Woman, culture, and society.* Stanford, Calif.: Sanford University Press.

Rohner, Ronald. P. 1975. *They love me, they love me not: A worldwide study of the effects of parental acceptance and rejection.* New Haven, Conn.: HRAF.

Turner, Victor. 1968. *The drums of affliction: A study of religious processes among the Ndembu of Zambia.* Oxford: Clarendon.

Maria Ramona Hart

GRASSROOTS MEDIA
See MEDIA: GRASSROOTS.

GREEN MOVEMENT

The term *green* is applied to a wide range of environmental and political positions. Similar conceptual elasticity surrounds the term *green movement* to refer to mobilization concerned with the environment. Thus, distinguishing the green movement from other social movements and from other, more formal, social and political actions is problematic. Given that many environmental activists wish to distance themselves from formal politics, there is merit in identifying the movement as activism that is independent of party politics, but this leaves green political parties in rather awkward and unsatisfactory isolation. The green movement is, therefore, best understood as a culturally and organizationally diverse range of social and political critiques and of environmental activism. Despite its diversity, it has a core of common positions, and its members are involved in new forms of political and social action. Organizationally, at one end of the spectrum the green movement comprises formally structured and constituted groups, including political parties, such as the German Die Grünen, and environmental nongovernmental organizations (NGOs), such as Friends of the Earth. At the other end can be found loose collectives and ad hoc single-issue groups such as the Women's Environmental Network and the Chipko forest protection movement.

Women's Participation in Green Movements

Women have participated in and contributed to the development of these different forms of green critiques and activism. The publication by Rachel Carson of *Silent*

Spring (1962) was important in the evolution of the modern green consciousness. Women were strongly represented in the antinuclear movement of the 1970s, as a precursor of the more general green movement. The murder of Karen Silkwood, an antinuclear activist in the United States, was particularly important in galvanizing action. Gro Harland Brundtland, chair of the UN World Commission for Environment and Development (WCED), drew on the concept of sustainable development to provide the world with an alternative development model in her highly influential report *Our Common Future* (WCED, 1987). Since that time, the goal of sustainable development has become a norm in global environmental politics.

Women's contribution to international green politics has also been facilitated by their activities during the UN International Decade for Women (1976–1985), through the UN International Research and Training Institute for the Advancement of Women (INSTRAW) and, more recently, through the UN Conference on Environment and Development 1992 (the Rio Earth Summit). Through this engagement, a link has been forged between women, environment, and development (WED), facilitating in turn new green activism at the local level, particularly in the developing world.

Women have also contributed at the national level. In many countries, more women than men belong to environmental and conservation groups. The Peruvian journalist Barbara d'Achille did much to raise awareness about the environment, particularly about the Amazon forest. Across the United States, women have established numerous environmental groups, such as the Greenbelt Alliance (1958), the Save the Bay Association (1961), the California Women in Timber (1975), and Women of All Red Nations, a Native American women's protest against uranium mining. The women's movement provided a social base for the formation of the German green party, with Petra Kelly as a founding member. Women also played a key role in the formation of the Swedish Friends of the Earth and in the green party in Tasmania, Australia. Despite this formative role, however, women are not highly represented among the leadership of the green parties they helped form (Seager, 1993; Zirakzadeh, 1997).

Similarly, women took the lead in environmental protection and in the formation of green groups in the last days of the communist regimes in eastern and central Europe. One of the founders of the Polish Ecology Club was the biochemist Maria Guminska. Anna Varkonyi played a similar role in the formation of the Danube Circle, which mobilized opposition to the Gabcikovo-Nagymaros dams

(Pearce, 1991). In the face of high levels of air pollution, mothers in the town of Ruse on the Bulgarian–Romanian border mobilized environmental opposition, becoming a touchstone of the nation's conscience (Baker, 1996). Independent of the party state, green movements went on to play a key role in the collapse of the communist system, particularly in Bulgaria.

Women have also brought an environmental dimension to groups not primarily concerned with green issues. This has contributed to making the green movement diverse, multifaceted, and located in numerous sites of activism. The historic contribution of women conservationists to the environmental movement should also be acknowledged, including, for example, the work of Mrs. Lovell White, founder and president of the women's California Club, who took up the cause of forest protection in the United States. Another example is found in the formation of the Environment Conservation Programme within the Maendeleo Ya Wanaake women's organization in Kenya (Dankelman and Davidson, 1988).

As a result of women's activism, the green movement has become concerned with the challenges that environmental degradation poses for women. In the first world, this involves addressing environmental problems caused by industry, such as the effects of toxic manufacturing processes on the reproductive system, and also leisure and lifestyle issues, such as household consumption and recycling. The Women's Environmental Network (WEN) is an example. In the third world, women's green activism reflects competition over resources. This includes addressing women's role in natural resource management, environmental hazards encountered by women agricultural workers, and women's reproductive health, where a link is seen between population size and environmental degradation (this supposed link is controversial).

Green Movements and Ecofeminism

Women who participate in the green movement do not necessarily see themselves or their cause as feminist (Merchant, 1995). In contrast, ecofeminism is consciously feminist in its environmental critique and action. Introduced by Françoise d'Eaubonne in 1974, the term *ecofeminism* refers to a range of women's actions and ideological positions, linking male domination in the exploitation of women to male domination in the exploitation of nature. Many ecofeminists, especially in the third world, aim simultaneously at liberating nature from ceaseless exploitation and themselves from marginalization. The goal is to protect traditional ways of life, reverse ecological damage from multinational corporations and the extraction industry, and undertake ecological regeneration projects. India's Chipko, or tree hugging movement, formed in the 1970s, is among the most famous green movements. It developed a feminist forest paradigm that has been influential across the Himalayas and beyond (Shiva, 1989). Similarly, the crisis in women's access to wood and water motivated Wangari Maathai (1988) to found the women's greenbelt movement. The environmental movement of Nicaragua explicitly deals with women's issues, in particular the exposure of women agricultural workers to high levels of pesticides. An explicit ecofeminist is Gizelda Castro, of Friends of the Earth Brazil, who says that women should take the lead in environmental regeneration because "men have separated themselves from the ecosystem" (Merchant, 1995).

Ecofeminism has been criticized for presenting an essentialist view of women. Furthermore, feminists have severely criticized the argument that women should provide the moral and the practical efforts necessary to reverse environmental deterioration. Although promoting sustainable development can be seen as progressive, "cleaning up" after men is not—it is what women have always done and conforms to existing stereotypes about women (Johnson and Johnson, 1994). For example, women's involvement in primary environmental care (PEC), promoted by agencies in developing countries, is seen as adding to women's daily burden. Participatory and community-based, it equates "community" work with voluntary, unpaid work by women. This form of participation is not seen as ultimately liberating for women (Jackson, 1994).

Despite these criticisms, ecofeminism has made important contributions to green consciousness. It has stimulated women's involvement in local actions and widened the agenda of the green movement to include the effects of technology and toxic substances on reproductive health. More significantly, it has developed a process-oriented, relational image of nature, which seeks to establish social and ecological relationships based on recognition of the interconnection, interdependence, and diversity of all life (Eckersley, 1992). As such, it makes an important contribution to the post-Enlightenment political philosophy and practice.

More generally, women's green activism has widened the agenda of the environmental movement and has made links between different forms of oppression. Through involvement in the green movement, women are contributing to a steady increase in the capacity of new social movements to exercise autonomy through the use of "techniques of self," such as nonviolent direct action (Welsh, 2000). This is contributing to a new model of politics, where political action is no longer defined only by participation in formal politics and democratic practice is no longer limited to voting. Women's participation in the green movement has contributed to the evolution of flatter, less hierarchical organizational forms, widened the view of what constitutes political action, and expanded the sites available for political engagement. Through this participation women have found new routes to political participation, helping construct a new understanding of the active, female citizen.

See Also

ECOFEMINISM; ENVIRONMENT, *regional entries*

References and Further Reading

Baker, S. 1996, The scope for east–west co-operation. In A. Blowers and P. Glasbergen, *Environmental policy in an international context*, Vol. 3, 135–166. London: Arnold.

Braidotti, R. E. Charkiewicz, S. Hausler, and S. Wieringa. 1994. *Women, the environment, and sustainable development.* London: Zed.

Carson, R. 1962. *Silent spring.* Boston: Houghton Mifflin.

Dankelman, I., and J. Davidson. 1988. *Women and environment in the third world: Alliance for the future.* London: Earthscan.

D'Daubonne, F. 1974. *Le féminisime ou la mort.* Paris: Pierre Horay.

Eckersley, R. 1992. *Environmentalism and political theory: Towards an ecocentric approach.* London: UCL.

Jackson, C. 1994. Gender analysis and environmentalism. In M. Redclift and T. Benton, eds., *Social theory and the global environment.* London: Routledge.

Johnson, D. K., and K. R. Johnson. 1994. The limits of partiality: Ecofeminism, animal rights and environmental concern. In K. J. Warren, ed., *Ecological feminism,* 106–119. New York: Routledge.

Merchant, C. 1995. *Earthcare: Women and the environment.* New York: Routledge.

Pearce, F. 1991. *Green warriors: The people and the politics behind the environmental revolution.* London: Bodley Head.

Plumwood, V. 1993. *Feminism and the mastery of nature.* London: Routledge.

Rodda, A. 1993. *Women and the environment.* London: Zed.

Seager, J. 1993. *Earth follies.* London: Earthscan.

Shiva, V. 1989. *Staying alive: Women, ecology, and development.* London: Zed.

UN WCED. 1987. *Our common future.* Oxford: Oxford University Press.

Wangari Maathi. 1988. *Greenbelt Movement: Sharing the approach and the experience.* Nairobi, Kenya: Environment Liaison Centre International.

Welsh, I. 2000. *Mobilising modernity: The nuclear moment.* London: Routledge.

Zirakzadeh, C. E. 1997. *Social movements in politics: A comparative study.* New York: Longman.

Susan Baker

GRRLS

The grrl movement is a decentralized Web-based movement with a seemingly focused purpose of female empowerment. This empowerment comes through feminist articles, messages, or "rants" posted on personal Web sites or zines. Grrls first appeared on the World Wide Web in January 1995, when zines and sites such as geekgirl.com and cybergrrl.com first appeared. These gender-specific sites were created by women for women at a time when female users were a minority on-line—an often unwelcome minority. Geekgirl's founder, RosieX, noted in an interview with *Computer-Mediated Communication Magazine,* "I've been using computer-mediated communications for six years and for the first few years I was appalled at the Internet 'boys club.' I experienced all the negatives about the Net: the cowardly bullying and flaming that anonymity permits; overt sexism and harassment; plus some pretty unpleasant cyberstalking and taunts online" (DeLoach, 1996a).

When grrl sites emerged on the Web, their feminist developers used terms such as *grrl, geek,* and *herd.* These terms indicated to users that the site was *for* women and not *about* women. These code words were either terms with negative connotations such as *geek,* or terms such as *grrl,* that were altered to connote far more empowerment than the original word, as with *girl.* Aliza Sherman, who founded cybergrrl.com, has said "I just wanted to create an online version of myself and thought Cybergirl sounded too young, so I replaced the i with an r, and thought it sounded perfect—the strong version of girl, as I say when people ask (DeLoach, 1996b).

Sherman's site was (and remained at the time of this writing) positive and upbeat. But many of the grrl sites are more acrimonious. For instance, RosieX's site, geekgirl.com, has an assertive tone and stylized images that ridicule women who only fill traditional mother and wife roles. Many sites also use images that glorify women who appear strong and self-reliant. On grrl sites, in general, the approved female persona is the inverse of the traditional role many women are taught to adopt. As one grrl noted, "If you're going to be damned for something anyway, why not embrace it? Being proud of having technical skills instead of embarrassed by it, being glad to be strong, to be smart.... Why are these things attributes that women are taught to hide?" (DeLoach, 1996b).

Unwillingness to bend to a role defined by society is typical of feminists who consider themselves grrls. The Web is not the only place such feminists articulate their frustration and anger. For example, "riot grrls" articulate their feelings and beliefs through music and the "guerrilla girls" use posters as their medium. In fact, the on-line grrls movement took its name from the riot grrls. While the mediums differ, the musical and on-line movements are similar in that neither has a neatly defined central purpose. This lack of central purpose explains why one grrl can turn her site into a business that serves as a mentor for Web developers, another establishes a zine that pokes fun at the traditional female role, and another establishes a site that objectifies *men.* There are many sites established by students lashing out against the *"Seventeen Magazine babe."*

Even though the movement is diffuse, feminists who identify with it do share some characteristics. First, they are active Internet users who typically live in North America, Australia, and Europe. Second, they have become frustrated with traditional female roles, the objectification of females in on-line or print media, and male dominance on-line. Third, they take action, which often results in the posting of a Web site that is very personal in nature and expresses both feminist and geek values.

But even with their similarities, grrls, on the whole, remain an independent group. As RosieX puts it, "I think this idea of a movement is based on an older style feminist rhetoric [that] tends homogenize all women with the same wants/needs/desires to embrace each other.... Heh, a bunch of us girls really like each other but we certainly don't pizz in each others pockets for ideas and strengths. Oh well, I can't speak for everyone." (De Loach, 1996c).

See Also

FASHION; GIRL STUDIES; GIRLS' SUBCULTURES; MAGAZINES; MUSIC: ROCK AND POP; POPULAR CULTURE; ZINES

References and Further Reading

DeLoach, Amelia. 1996a. RosieX explains. From Grrls exude attitude. *Computer-Mediated Communication Magazine* (March 1). <http://www.december.com/cmc/mag/1996/mar/delros.html>.

———. 1996b. Making two negatives a positive. From Grrls exude attitude. *Computer-Mediated Communication Magazine* (March 1). <http://www.december.com/cmc/mag/1996/mar/delrec.html>.

———. 1996c. Grrls exude attitude. *Computer-Mediated Communication Magazine* (March 1). <http://www.december.com/cmc/mag/1996/mar/deloach.html>.

<http://www.geekgirl.com>.

<http://www.nrrdgrrl.com>.

<http://www.december.com/cmc/mag/1996/mar>.

Amelia DeLoach

GUILT

Guilt as a concept and an experience has a number of meanings and dimensions.

1. Guilt is a legal term meaning violation of a legal code. Guilt in this sense carries a punishment presumably commensurate with the seriousness of the crime and the degree to which the guilty party is considered responsible for it.

2. Guilt is also a moral concept meaning immorality—wrongdoing that is not necessarily a violation of law. A wrongdoer may be considered morally or ethically blameworthy even when no legal sanctions apply.

3. Guilt is a theological concept meaning sin, a violation of God's will or law. The will or law of the deity is endorsed by the self and may be understood as codified in absolute terms (such as the Ten Commandments in the Judaic and Christian tradition) or in general principles (such as "Love your neighbor as yourself"). Each religious tradition has its own moral precepts, often set forth in sacred texts and teachings.

4. Guilt is a psychological concept describing a felt experience, associated with the conscience and often expressed as anxiety or depression. In the western world, Sigmund Freud's analysis of psychological guilt has been very influential. Freud held that people with a strong or harsh superego—a term that corresponds more or less to "conscience"—may experience distressing guilt not attached to any objective violation of a moral code; he described such guilt as neurotic. Neurotic or false guilt can become attached to normal constituents of human life such as sexuality and self-love.

The phenomenon diametrically opposite to overproduction of nonobjective guilt is absence of guilt when an objective moral code has been broken (for example, when someone else has been harmed). A person who lacks objective guilt may be seen as evil, as psychologically disturbed, or as simply outside the realm of morality ("amoral"; an infant is one example of an amoral being).

These different concepts of guilt are often present in various combinations, so that, for instance, it may be difficult to separate theological guilt from neurotic guilt. In fact, theology and psychology often conflict over the issue of guilt: psychologists have often criticized religion for producing unnecessary, inappropriate guilt in the interest of social control; and theologians have often criticized psychology for disregarding or rationalizing genuine ethical concerns.

Women and Guilt

Guilt (which is often gender-specific) plays an important but ambiguous and sometimes destructive role in women's lives. Like pride and shame, guilt can be seen as an emotion involving self-assessment (Taylor, 1985); through experiencing guilt, humans assess their own behavior and moral character. Guilt experienced as alienation resulting from wrongdoing that has harmed others can lead to remorse and reparation. Religions, for example, may offer rituals and other means for healing alienation through confession, penance, purification, forgiveness, and reconciliation.

If a woman's self-assessment is harsh, lacking in self-charity, she will inevitably experience a great deal of guilt—she will perceive herself as breaking or violating a whole range of moral codes. However, it may not be necessary or particularly useful to label this experience "neurotic guilt"; that label defines the woman as "sick" rather than as unhappy or distressed.

A major source of guilt for women is a perceived failure to fulfill the traditional roles of wife and mother—roles that may be defined not only socially but also theologically and may thus carry religious as well as societal sanctions. Many religions see the ideal woman as submissive, protected, and nurturing: Islam is one notable example; Roman Catholics regard Mary, the mother of Jesus, as a powerful role model of the self-sacrificing, other-oriented woman; Protestant women are often socialized to see themselves as helpmeets, supporting their husbands, caring for their children, and never daring to assume control, although in the domestic, private domain they may have some supposed or derived authority. In the developing world, traditional concepts of womanhood may become linked not only to religion but also to concepts of nationalism and statehood; thus women who depart from traditional roles may feel guilty for betraying the nationalistic struggle.

Women must often struggle to overcome guilt and renegotiate their roles (Lowry, 1980). Some continue to function in traditional female roles while others define new roles based on equality and shared power—but both may experience guilt. The strength of such guilt is directly related to the strength of a woman's own internalized messages, images, ideologies, values, and beliefs. In renegotiating roles, however, a woman is challenging more than her internal world, because that internal world is, of course, reinforced by social, cultural, religious, and legal structures in the external world. In western culture, to take just one example, the ideal woman tends to be seen as feminine, modest but decorative, reed-thin, young, and committed primarily to the private domain. For many women, guilt produced by challenging these external structures is costly, and assessing its nature demands both individual and collective efforts. Is this genuine ethical or moral guilt, or is it a creation of a social or religious system with an interest in keeping women inferior and powerless?

The relationship between shame and guilt is an important consideration. Some researchers and writers suggest that shaming experineces and subsequent feelings of shame have been misidentified as "guilt." Shame has to do with the total self and the presentation of that self, whereas guilt, essentially, has to do with harm to others. It has been argued (Capps, 1993; Lewis, 1971) that women are actually more vulnerable to feelings of personal shame and self-contempt than to feelings of guilt.

See Also

CHRISTIANITY; COLONIALISM AND POSTCOLONIALISM; CRIME AND PUNISHMENT; JUDAISM; PSYCHOANALYSIS

References and Further Reading

Capps, Donald. 1993. *The depleted self.* Minneapolis, Minn.: Fortress.

Lewis, Helen Block. 1973. *Shame and guilt in neurosis.* New York: International Universities Press.

Lowry, Suzanne. 1980. *The guilt cage.* London: Elm Tree.

Taylor, Gabrielle. 1985. *Pride, shame, and guilt: Emotions of self-assessment.* Oxford: Clarendon.

Gerda Johanna Olafsen

GYN/ECOLOGY

Gyn/ecology is a term coined by the U.S. radical feminist philosopher and theologian Mary Daly, in her book *Gyn/Ecology: The Metaethics of Radical Feminism* (1978).

The term is, of course, a pun on *gynecology,* the medical discipline that specializes in the female reproductive system and that, according to Daly, is patriarchal and objectifies and fragments women. (Daly's work on the level of language is intended to reveal the hidden patriarchal meanings of words. For example, she has divided the word *therapist* into *the/rapist.*) Gyn/ecology connotes a "metapatriarchal," female space-time and spirit-body energy field or continuum. This holistic, *gynergic* (female-energy) ecosystem has, from Daly's perspective, been polluted by all of patriarchal history, myth, religion, language, ideology, institutions, and scholarship.

Gyn/ecology is conceived of not statically, as a noun, but rather as a verb, as a vital life force, and as a movement in two parts. The first part of this gyn/ecological movement consists of exorcising the demons of patriarchy (for patriarchy is, according to Daly, the religion of the planet) from the entire gyn/ecosystem by exposing the dismemberment of the prepatriarchal goddess religion and civilization by Christian and post-Christian myth. Daly, a professor of theology at Boston College, a Catholic institution, has written numerous feminist critiques of Christianity and considers herself a post-Christian. The gyn/ecological journey consists of reclaiming lost, originally positive meanings of words that are commonly used to denigrate women. Thus, she reclaims *hag* in her neologism *hagography* (based on *hagiography,* the history of saints) and *crone* in her neologism *croneology,* both connoting the story of wise elder women.

Daly examines numerous customs—such as suttee (sati) in India, foot binding in China, witch-hunts in Europe, and gynecology in the United States—that she describes as "gynocidal." She concludes that they represent a vast pattern of interrelated crimes against women. This too is part of the first stage of women's gyn/ecological journey: unmasking the lies, the sado-ritual syndromes in patriarchal religions, and the fundamental matricidal intent of all misogynist systems and propaganda that have been normalized by patriarchal institutions.

Once the demons have been exorcised and the "eight deadly sins of patriarchy" (which include assimilation, elimination, and fragmentation of women and aggression against women) have been identified and expelled, then women can begin the second part of their gyn/ecological journey. This is a journey toward ecstasy, a journey away from the distracting foreground of patriarchally contaminated principles and practices toward the "gynergically" enspiriting background from which women will reclaim, rediscover, and ultimately re-create the true knowledge of their "wild" (undomesticated) selves. This new cultural creation outside patriarchal space-time parameters will make manifest the radiant diversity of women from all races, cultures, and classes who engage in what Daly has termed biophilic bondings to spark the "fire of female friendship" and create true community.

Following the "call of the wild," women who have now dispelled (exorcized the spell of) the alienation caused by the erasure of all memory of a gynocentric world will move away from femicide (the murder of women just because they are female) toward a new authentic being, and, as Daly puts it, will whirl and spin out and away from un-creation toward and into creation.

Gyn/ecology is not synonymous with ecofeminism: gyn/ecology is basically gynocentric, whereas ecofeminism places both women and men within an interconnected web of life but not at its center. However, gyn/ecology is sometimes said to be a precursor and a source of inspiration for the ecofeminist movement that developed during the 1980s.

It should be noted that this article has not attempted to follow Daly's unconventional use of capital letters; readers interested in her system of usages are referred to her own book.

See Also

ECOFEMINISM; FEMINISM: RADICAL; WOMAN: CENTEREDNESS

References and Further Reading

Daly, Mary. 1978, 1980. *Gyn/Ecology: The metaethics of radical feminism.* Boston: Beacon.
2000. *Off Our Backs: The Feminist Newsjournal.* 30(2): issue devoted to Mary Daly.
Hoagland, Sarah Lucia, and Marilyn Frye, eds. 2000. *Feminist interpretations of Mary Daly.* Philadelphia: Pennsylvania State Press.

Gloria Feman Orenstein

GYNECOLOGY

Gynecology is a branch of medicine that deals with the reproductive system of women. Often a gynecologist serves as a woman's primary-care physician in addition to focusing on her sexual, reproductive, and postmenopausal health. Feminists and others have criticized the dependency that the gynecological profession has traditionally encouraged in women—and the resulting power that gynecologists have wielded in women's lives—pointing out that many women in developed countries regularly visit a gynecologist even though they have no complaints or health problems.

Modern Gynecological Practice

General gynecological care usually includes regular examinations to monitor breast health and cervical health. Gynecologists provide screening for and treatment of reproductive tract infections and sexually transmitted diseases. During her fertile years, a woman might visit a gynecologist for birth control, infertility treatment, or care during pregnancy, during delivery, and postpartum. At the onset of menopause, gynecologists may prescribe treatment for symptoms such as hot flashes, irregular bleeding, vaginal dryness, and mood swings.

In the late twentieth century, the profession faced growing criticism because, it was argued, gynecologists routinely prescribed hormone replacement therapy (HRT) to menopausal and postmenopausal women, without regard to whether their clients had physical complaints. The wholesale marketing of HRT has been described as a practice that needlessly turns healthy women into "patients" and treats a normal physiological transition as a deficiency syndrome.

Likewise, critics of traditional gynecology are concerned about the tendency of its practitioners to treat the uterus only as an organ for childbearing, ignoring the significance of the uterus in female sexuality. Pregnancy and delivery in uncomplicated cases are often treated by gynecologists as pathological conditions rather than as normal physiological changes.

Power in Doctor-Patient Roles

Men have dominated the profession of gynecology for most of its history, and entrenched patterns of gender inequality may be magnified at the gynecologist's office when the physician is a man. Predictable roles may unfold, in which the physician acts as the male authority figure and the patient, a woman, surrenders her power and defers to his expertise. Although growing numbers of women were training for and entering the field at the beginning of the twenty-first century, most professors of gynecology were men; this was true even in the former Soviet-aligned countries of eastern Europe, where medicine has been dominated by women and considered a low-status job. Owing to the competitive and strenuous working conditions typical of a medical residency, female gynecologists have little opportunity to challenge or even question the ideas and behavior of their male supervisors. Furthermore, supportive contacts between activists in the women's health movement and gynecologists—contacts that would provide a chance for exchanging ideas and airing constructive criticism about appropriate care for women's health—are rare. The gynecological community tends to be a well-protected group, relatively immune from criticism.

The power imbalance that has traditionally existed between gynecologists and their clients also stems from the embarrassment or anxiety many patients have about discussing sensitive issues such as sexuality or the prospect of illness or abnormality in the most intimate parts of the body. The gynecological examination itself can contribute to a woman's sense of vulnerability and unease: the woman is asked to lie on her back on the examining table with her legs spread so that her naked genitalia are exposed, while the fully dressed (usually male) gynecologist stands and vaginally penetrates her with instruments or fingers. Possibilities for making the examination more pleasant—by explaining the procedure in advance, discussing a woman's previous experiences (especially negative ones) with examinations, or offering a mirror and encouraging the woman to take an active role in the examination—are often neglected.

The power imbalance between gynecologists and their clients emerges in numerous other ways. For example, the use of in vitro fertilization is advantageous for women with occluded tubes, but this form of reproductive technology is often inappropriately recommended in situations where the women is fertile but has a subfertile partner. The gynecologist may offer such suggestions without discussion, disregarding a woman's bodily integrity and abusing a situation that is emotionally fraught for the woman who wants a child. During pregnancy, a woman may, in a sense, become dependent on the physician's "approval" because of screening techniques such as nuchal translucency measurement and ultrasound examinations. This too implies an imbalance of power.

The disparity in power between physician and patient also enables gynecologists to remain unaware of social circumstances that affect a women's health. For instance, complaints such as abdominal pain and dyspareunia (pain during intercourse) are often not recognized by the gynecologist as possible consequences of sexual violence and may be mistakenly "treated" with hysterectomy.

The Right Gynecologist

A woman choosing a gynecologist should look for someone who not only is an expert practitioner of medicine but also has a compatible practice style—for instance, a responsive physician who is easy to talk to and who makes an effort to hear her concerns. A gynecologist should be willing to ensure that patients have objective and comprehensive information about the expected results of a proposed treatment: not only beneficial effects but also long-term and short-term side effects. The physician should be aware of the social factors that affect women's lives (including the possibility of violence or sexual violence), avoid unnecessary medication, and support women in making their own choices by listening and making an effort to understand women's real needs.

See Also

CHILDBIRTH; CONTRACEPTION; FERTILITY AND FERTILITY TREATMENT; HORMONE REPLACEMENT THERAPY; INFERTILITY; MATERNAL HEALTH AND MORBIDITY; MEDICAL CONTROL OF WOMEN; MIDWIVES; PREGNANCY AND BIRTH; REPRODUCTION: OVERVIEW; REPRODUCTIVE HEALTH

References and Further Reading

Foster, Peggy, 1995. *Women and the health care industry: An unhealthy relationship?* Philadelphia, Pa.: Open University Press.

Kolk, Annemarie, Marrie Bekker, and Katja van Vliet. 1999. *Advances in women and health research.* Tilburg, Netherlands: Tilburg University Press.

Sargent, Carolyn F., and Caroline B. Brettell. 1996. *Gender and health: An international perspective.* Englewood Cliffs, N.J.: Prentice Hall.

Showalter, Elaine. 1985. *The female malady: Women, madness, and English culture, 1830–1980.* London: Virago (Reprinted 1988, 1991, 1993, 1995.)

Gunilla Kleiverda

H

HARASSMENT

See SEXUAL HARASSMENT and STREET HARASSMENT.

HEALERS

Women have been healers from ancient times. They have used gentle, natural ways to treat illness in both themselves and their children, often applying plant-based products, salves, and ointments. They learned the application and effect of these remedies from other healers and through their own experience. In primitive times, society valued these women as healers, midwives, and even surgeons and bonesetters (Kane-Berman, 1997). This heritage is a global one and can be found in most cultures. What has changed through history and in various cultures is the way in which the healing and the healers have been viewed, their freedom to practice what they knew, and the practices and products that they used to promote healing. The unchanging essence of women as healers is the thread that connects past, present, and future healers. This thread is a consciousness that mind, body, and spirit are all interrelated and that one's healing can involve the state of health within and among all three domains.

Although many men possess qualities similar to those of women healers, it is females who are more often associated with the qualities of empathy, nurturing, touch, connectedness between patient and healer (partnership), and attention to and acceptance of patients and their stories (Achterberg, 1990; Perrone et al., 1989). Women, more often than men, address the effect that illness has on one's life, emotions, family, spirituality, and mental well-being (Bennett, 1993). These qualities are invaluable to the environment of healing.

History of Women as Healers

To understand the role of women as healers, one must first understand the history of women's roles in health care. From ancient times, women have been associated with qualities of nurturing, intuition, compassion, spirituality, and caring. Others have viewed them as connected to the earth and in tune with natural events (Achterberg, 1990; Kane-Berman, 1997). Although women have served as midwives and nursed the sick through the centuries, acceptance of women as primary, independent healers has been sporadic throughout history. Women were permitted to assume positions of leadership and honor only in those cultures that honored nature or the "earth mother" as positive and good forces and in those cultures in which the main deity either was female or had feminine qualities (Achterberg, 1990).

Feminine qualities supported the ideal of healing in both traditional and early western cultures, which fostered women as primary caregivers, midwives, and herbalists. Treating the sick was considered a natural extension of skills and abilities gained through experience of caring for children and relatives. Although women seldom were political leaders, some women became well known as healers, priestesses, or wise women, and their knowledge was revered (Kane-Berman, 1997). In Sumerian culture, until 2000 B.C., women not only functioned as healers and physicians but also participated fully in sacred events and owned property (Achterberg, 1990).

Helen of Troy, a healer who lived about 2000 B.C., was trained by Polydamna, physician and queen of Egypt (Achterberg, 1990). As the culture changed around 1000 B.C., women no longer were permitted to have formal education or responsibilities outside the home. By around 400 B.C., the status of a woman in western culture had been reduced to little more than that of a slave (Achterberg, 1990).

A famous and beloved healer, Fabiola, founded the first public civilian hospital in Europe in 394 A.D., a time when women healers were accepted. Another healer, Hildegard of Bingen (1098–1179), claimed to have the gift of prophecy and purportedly also could heal by divine prayer. She was a mystic and spiritualist, and her writings, which included a medical text in addition to two theological texts, made a great contribution to the healing traditions (Achterberg, 1990).

The emergence of science and a more rigid church doctrine in about 1300 A.D. led to the view that anything having to do with nature was suspicious or shady. Consequently, women's association with nature led to their persecution by powerful men in both the church and in science. As wars and plagues spread across Europe, medical guilds began to form. Consisting of men educated as physicians, these medical guilds began fining and imprisoning women who practiced traditional illness care or healing methods (Achterberg, 1990).

Women who practiced medicine in the thirteenth century were called physicians, while those who practiced in the fourteenth and fifteenth centuries were identified as witches or charlatans. It was postulated that these women gained their healing knowledge from the devil since they were not permitted formal education (Minkowski, 1992). Witch-hunts that lasted through 1684 led to the sacrifice of countless women on suspicion of black magic or their collusion with the devil. They were burned or hanged, most without evidence of wrongdoing. Some historians have viewed the witch-hunts as an attempt to rid the world of women who did not act as men believed they should act. Other historians have viewed it as an attempt to place blame for the life-threatening disasters that plagued the times (Achterberg, 1990; Minkowski, 1992; Perrone et al., 1989). The witch-hunts revealed the masculine fear of powerful women and resulted in the lessening of women's position, power, and trustworthiness.

The scientific age brought about separation of mind, body, and spirit. Whatever was invisible became strictly defined and trivialized. Caring was separated from curing, and compassion and intuition were eliminated from the discipline of medicine, because of its alignment with science. Women were relegated to nursing and midwifery roles—jobs men did not want (Achterberg, 1990).

Florence Nightingale (1820–1910), founder of the modern profession of nursing, viewed every woman as a nurse. She worked hard during her three years as a practicing nurse and ruled with a heavy hand and a sharp tongue. She became the superintendent of a woman's institution in 1853 and later assumed charge of a hospital in Turkey. Her many patients romanticized her deeds, although she worked hard to improve the appalling conditions and learned a great deal about staffing and building requirements for hospitals. She was consulted worldwide on new hospital construction and founded a training school for nurses before becoming bedridden in her later life (Achterberg, 1990).

During the early nineteenth century, women were educated and viewed as morally and spiritually superior to men. Males, however, thought woman's place was in the home. Harriot Hunt (1805–1875), Elizabeth Blackwell (1821–1910), and Mary Putnam Jacobi (1842–1906) in the United States, the German-born Marie Elizabeth Zakrzewska (1829–1902), and the Briton Elizabeth Garrett Anderson (1836–1917) wanted more. These women physicians, mostly educated in the United States, struggled to survive in a male-dominated medical profession. They were rejected, spurned, and denied access to internships in America (Achterberg, 1990). Elizabeth Blackwell and Elizabeth Anderson opened women's medical training schools in America and England to foster high-quality professional training denied to them by men-only institutions. They made great strides in helping women who followed in their footsteps (Kane-Berman, 1997). By 1897, 75 percent of medical schools were coeducational, with some top schools enrolling up to 42 percent women, causing closure of all but one women's medical school by 1900. Then, as physicians experienced financial problems over the next few years, medical schools again limited women's enrollment. Male physicians accused female physicians of having lowered the status and salary of their occupation, and, thus, women were once more shut out of medical schools (Achterberg, 1990).

From 1900 until the 1970s, few women entered the medical profession. In 1914, for example, only 4 percent of U.S. medical students were women. Female enrollment remained low during World War I and World War II. As recently as the late 1960s, many U.S. medical school administrators had quota systems to limit the number of women admitted. Until the 1960s, women themselves could not agree on whether to compete directly with men for top positions or fill a niche that was not being addressed by men's medicine (Achterberg, 1990). Most women did not want to fight for their place, and so positions were lost (Kane-Berman, 1997). During the 1970s the feminist movement's goal of achieving equality in the United States fostered an environment more conducive to women in medicine. The proportion of American women in medicine increased 310 percent from 1970, when women represented only one in five physicians (Braus, 1994).

At the beginning of the twenty-first century, enrollment of women in U.S. medical schools equaled or exceeded that of men, and by 2010 women in medicine will probably represent a third of all practicing physicians (Braus, 1994). Yet women are underrepresented in specialty fields and are more likely to enter family-practice settings. Women's natural nurturing tendencies, as well as lingering prejudice against women practitioners in some specialties, may well explain these circumstances (Kane-Berman, 1997).

Modern Women as Healers

Modern-day women healers assume many roles. Representative women healers are nurses, doctors, nuns, midwives, body workers, energy healers, ministers, spiritualists, herbalists, and acupuncturists. The categories are numerous, but the essence of these practitioners is the same. They are persistent and dedicated, hardworking, gentle, and kind. They hold strong convictions about the importance and contribution of spirit and mind to the body's state of health. They are committed to focusing on the whole person and enter into partnership with each individual toward the goal of healing. They foster the further development of a new paradigm of healing in western health care where mind, body, and spirit are interrelated.

A unified healing paradigm has always existed in Native American and other traditional cultures. According to Dhyani Ywahoo, priestcraft holder of the Ani Gadoah Tsalagi (Cherokee) Nation and founder of Sun Ray Meditation Society, all disease manifestations, whether occurring in individuals or nations, are based in the mind. Native American healers guide those who come to them for healing to take responsibility for their own healing process. Native American women healers speak and think from the heart, believing that wholeness is inherent in everyone (Perrone et al., 1989).

Mother Teresa (1910–1997), an Albanian-born Roman Catholic nun, Nobel Peace laureate, and founder of the Missionaries of Charity, cared for the poor and indigent in India (Microsoft Encarta, 1995). Her presence, strong spiritual convictions, and unconditional love enriched and comforted those she assisted through the healing process.

Other modern women healers have incorporated the unified healing paradigm with western medical training. Josette Mondanaro, M.D., a general practitioner in California, believes that the process of medical schooling often screens out compassion. In her training, medical students were taught to react to the problem, rather than the person with the problem. She states that the difference in viewpoints is significant and stresses the importance of spirituality and faith in healing work. She believes that a patient's faith in traditional healers is what makes them able to heal and that there is much more to healing than what is known to western medicine (Perrone et al., 1989).

In summary, the common thread among women healers from various times, backgrounds, and experiences is their great capacity for caring, empathy, and creating a healing partnership with the person seeking healing. A person's partnership with and faith in their healer adds significantly to the outcome of healing. With the passage of time, healing practices and products have improved with increasing knowledge, but the essence of a true healing relationship between healer and patient endures. First, the health of the healer's own body, mind, and spirit is a prerequisite before attempting to heal another (Bennett, 1993). Then each healer supports those who seek help by showing them a view of themselves that is whole and complete rather than ill and insufficient. Holding this view of wellness permits persons to focus on the solution rather than the problem, and they become active participants in their own healing process. Thus, they acquire empowerment, strength, and balance, which promote healing.

The healer's focus is on nourishment of the person's whole being—the body, mind, heart, and soul. Women healers help others to view illness as a call to strengthen a part of oneself and sometimes as a catalyst for self-transformation. All persons have the capacity to be healed and whole, and it is the true healer who gives people the "vision" to see themselves in this light.

See Also

HEALTH: OVERVIEW; HOLISTIC HEALTH I; HOLISTIC HEALTH II; NURSING; TRADITIONAL HEALING: HERBALISTS; TRADITIONAL HEALING: NATIVE NORTH AMERICA; WITCHES: ASIA; WITCHES: WESTERN WORLD

References and Further Reading

Achterberg, J. 1990. *Woman as healer.* Boston: Shambhala.

Bennett, R. 1993. Compassionate health care in the wise woman tradition. *American Association of Occupational Health Nurses Journal* 41(7): 327–328.

Braus, P. 1994. How women will change medicine. *American Demographics* 16: 40–47.

Kane-Berman, J. 1997. Women in medicine—priestesses and healers or second-class doctors? *South African Medical Journal* 87(11): 1495–1496.

Minkowski, W. L. 1992. Women healers of the Middle Ages: Selected aspects of their history. *American Journal of Public Health* 82(2): 288–295.

Perrone, B., H. H. Stockel, and V. Krueger. 1989. *Medicine women, curanderas, and women doctors.* Norman: University of Oklahoma Press.

Microsoft Encarta. 1995. *Mother Teresa of Calcutta*. Microsoft Corporation. Accessed on-line May 30, 2000.

Ann Gill Taylor
Pamela A. Foresman

HEALTH: Overview

Challenges to women's health come from various sources. Internal conditions can create vulnerability in women due to their poor social and economic position in society. External pressures such as structural inadequacies and political repression also challenge women's health. Finally, culture invariably impacts women's health and health care globally.

Internal Conditions: Vulnerability

National indices are often compared in terms of life expectancy and prevalence of disease. Neither declining mortality rates (where they exist), however, nor cause-of-death data adequately measure the state of health. Like the notion of quality of life itself, health is political. In this context the question and definition of vulnerability is key. For example, *Women's World Atlas* (Seager, 1997) cites fatigue as the most common chronic health problem for women in developing countries. Several recent studies reveal a similar problem among women in industrialized countries, where autoimmune diseases such as fibromyalgia and chronic fatigue syndrome (CFS) are increasing and disproportionally affecting women. Women traditionally have been treated like children medically, and the scientific basis of women's health concerns are diminished when physical ills are dismissed as psychosomatic and therefore ignored and undertreated.

In nonindustrialized countries obvious stresses such as constant childbearing, neglect of infant girls in favor of boys, and low protein intake (a result of the traditions of eating last, least, and worst), as well as working longer and harder, all contribute to women's vulnerability. Half of all women and two-thirds of all pregnant women in poor countries (except China) suffer from iron-deficiency anemia. According to the World Health Organization, contaminated water causes approximately 80 percent of all diseases in the third world. As the chief water bearers, as well as those who work most constantly with water, women in less industrialized countries are often directly at risk for waterborne parasites. In addition, women are constantly exposed to job-related injuries and physical stress as they fill the lowest-paid rapid-repetition jobs in both more and less industrialized nations.

Less obvious is the physiological impact of emotional distress that creates the predisposition toward disease. This distress is born of continuously living with violence and without nurturance. Apart from biological reproduction, women's work tends to be valued by most societies primarily on what they are able to produce for the agricultural, industrial, and war machines. Even then the reality of women's adulthood (and often of their very existence) may be denied. Some see gender discrimination as global and systemic. Many societies believe that women exist to sacrifice themselves. In addition, an attitude of blaming the victim may be propagated with the simplistic message "if you think better, you will feel better," without any validation of women's experiences or of the relationship between biochemistry and feeling. Since good health is rooted in self-awareness, balance, and wholeness, a socialization of inferiority may undermine women's visualization of completeness and confidence in asserting a right to health.

External Pressures: Structural Inadequacies

For over fifty years, access to health care has been regarded as a fundamental human right in many countries. At Alma Ata in 1978, the World Health Organization adopted Health for All by Year 2000 objectives, which became the goal of public-health and community-health campaigns in most developing countries. In the 1970s and 1980s the implementation of these goals became tied to International Monetary Fund and World Bank conditions through structural adjustment programs. Such conditions devastated any potential for structural improvement that would enhance the quality of care and enable greater access to health services. Women's health care globally is met predominantly at the primary-health-care level, yet at the start of the twenty-first century, primary health care expenditures globally still averaged 15 percent of national health care budgets and was shrinking. The majority of women used government health programs for themselves and their children. Privatization of public health care has become a new field for commercial activity, creating high-tech medicine to meet "effective demand" instead of human needs.

Researchers around the world are increasingly naming poverty as women's leading health problem. Because women and children constitute the majority of the world's poor, they are most seriously affected by so-called western or northern-devised policies. In developing countries, this privatization of health care is increasingly managed through the World Trade Organization. In many countries women's continued vulnerability can be explained by poverty, discriminatory access to education and information, unresponsive health care systems, and research that focuses primarily on reproductive technology (when it focuses on women at all). These conditions also prevail in some communities in developed countries.

The intersections of health, race, class, and gender are seldom analyzed and incorporated into health research or practice. For example, most medical studies continue to target white, middle-class men. Yet data show that in the United States, large numbers of unexplained deaths still occur among women and children of color from preventable health challenges such as hypertension. In New York City, for example, where the U.S. maternal mortality goal was 3.3 per 100,000 births in 1999, it was 28.7 per 100,000 for black women and 5.3 per 100,000 for white women. The gap has not been closed even with thirty years of improvement in health care in the United States. Many elements of illness and disease will remain obscured until the variables of race, class, and gender are incorporated in medical understanding and approaches.

Decades of research have indicated that the most significant indicator of high mortality and morbidity within a population is income level. Poverty constrains women all over the world from taking steps that would improve their health and well-being. The constraints of poverty are fundamental yet are often ignored when researchers explore the health-care-seeking patterns of the socioeconomically disadvantaged. Ignoring these constraints implies that poor women make decisions within a vacuum and subjects poor women to unfair and uninformed criticism. For example, the fairly common phenomenon in many nonindustrialized countries of removing girl children from school either to have them married or prepare them for marriage may appear to be an uncaring or uninformed choice. But for many mothers, marriage is the single most effective means to ensure a daughter's financial security. Many women still face cultural norms in isolation even when they know that better choices are available. With support from other women, resources, and information, women can change policies and promote the cultural dynamism that will produce an environment in which they can make those choices.

The Role of Culture

Globally, the focus of women's health activists has shifted from issues of local concern to the international sphere, resulting in the consideration of complicated and controversial new issues such as the relationship, if any, between women's rights and cultural norms. For perhaps the first time, northern feminists must consider whether women's rights previously viewed as "universal" are truly representative of the views, perspectives, and priorities of women worldwide.

The issue of women's rights and a possible universal standard of women's rights is problematic for many activists. Participation is a central tenet of feminism—listening to different voices and avoiding the imposition of one set of beliefs. But a movement away from universal standards of women's rights in deference to culture may entail accepting culturally, politically, and religiously sanctioned edicts that classify women as minors or deny their right to own or inherit property. Some cultural practices (such as child marriage) violate women's bodily integrity in ways that can cause pain, infection, and even death because of requirements of customs.

Recognizing the myriad views that exist within any culture, activists can begin to build bridges between organizations, communities, and countries. For example, a group in the United States interested in addressing the issue of female genital mutilation (FGM) could identify and then collaborate with activists in Sudan who share the group's view on FGM rather than assume that all Sudanese support the practice of FGM.

Women's Health Movements around the World

Global women's health movements' contributions to the improvement of health options and policy are many. They include requiring governments and international organizations to take a more gender-sensitive approach to health programs, raising awareness about social and cultural practices that result in poor health outcomes for women, teaching women basic body knowledge, and creating safe spaces for women to question harmful or inadequate traditional practices. Women's rights groups in the developed North have called attention to the disfiguring of women's bodies through cosmetic surgery, and the self-mutilation implicit in crash diets, which are used to make women more closely resemble society's standards of beauty. In parts of Africa and the Middle East, local women are concerned about female genital mutilation and the spread of AIDS.

With the growing emphasis on women's health at world conferences and among nongovernmental organizations and government agencies, it is clear that women's health activists and feminists have succeeded in making discourse about women's health an international concern. Additionally, mainstream public health professionals and researchers are beginning to accept that women, without having professional degrees or advanced training, can be "experts" on their own health. Increasing support for grassroots movements and the trend toward involving "target" populations in program development and implementation bear witness to this acceptance, as does increasing reliance on women's nongovernmental organizations.

The growing integration of a grassroots perspective into the definition of women's health has resulted in a more holistic view of women's health and well-being. Contrary to the "one cause, one cure" approach of mainstream western medicine, this new outlook requires an understanding of the complex web of social, economic, and cultural factors that influence women's health.

Family planning programs' evolution in approach and philosophy over the last decade has had an impact on the lives of women worldwide. The rationale of such programs in the past was explicit: the lower the population growth rate, the more successful the program. Thus many programs were evaluated based on "couple years protection," a methodology that judged family planning programs by how many sterilizations were performed and how many long-term contraceptives were distributed within a population. But the impact, both negative and positive, that family planning programs had on the reproductive health and overall well-being of women was not measured.

Due to the long-term activism of women's health groups, however, the approach taken by family planning programs has shifted noticeably. The UN International Conferences at the close of the twentieth century and especially the Vienna Conference on Human Rights in 1993 and the Cairo Conference on Population and Development in 1994 demonstrated the changing attitude toward the issue of population control and the role of women. In Cairo, activists from developing and industrialized nations alike argued that if women were to make reproductive decisions, they must be empowered through programs that include educating women, lessening women's domestic burdens, and providing work opportunities for women outside the home. The Cairo conference strengthened the growing perspective among women that the term *reproductive health needs* must go beyond just contraceptive or gynecological services to women's freedom to express their sexuality without fear of recrimination and to linking population growth to variables such as economic development. It no longer seemed reasonable to believe that poverty could be eliminated primarily by family planning.

Other Avenues of Empowerment

Around the world there is continual tension between western medical practices that focus on curing disease and traditional practices that focus on the whole person. The rapidly growing field of complementary medicine, a holistic approach in which a variety of traditional practices combine with western medical practices, is an encouraging trend. It incorporates the principles of Chinese, Ayurvedic, homeopathic, and other naturopathic and holistic systems. In this approach, mental phenomena are considered, not separate or distinct from physical ailments, but rather part of a whole.

Researchers are now beginning to study traditional remedies to quantify their effectiveness against illness. Some western insurance companies now pay for some alternative therapies. In developing nations, extraordinary model projects have brought together the best of traditional and modern medical and diagnostic systems. In these examples, care is used to bring men and women healers together across class, religion, and ethnicity in a system that serves unmet needs more effectively.

Traditional systems and related new approaches to health focus on wellness. In these systems, healing is defined as a return to a state of balance among body, mind, environment, and spirit. The vital energy of the healthy is reflected in their capacity to adapt, maintain equilibrium and integrity, and perpetuate life on its highest level, continuously. Unfortunately, however, most traditional systems do no more to empower women than western, high-tech, and cure-specific-to-disease medicine. Even where health is proclaimed a right, the means to secure that right are rarely provided. Women's belief in their entitlement to health care continues to be limited by the negotiation between pain, exhaustion and isolation, and cultural norms. Common knowledge and acceptance of the body and its biochemistry and the care of the whole woman, her mind, her emotions, and her physical well-being, even in today's age of continued enlightenment, remain inaccessible to all but a very few.

Particularly in the developing world, health care is synonymous with the use of traditional medicine. In these countries, traditional treatments can range from herbal remedies to specific religious or spiritual rituals. For many, traditional health care systems are the first and often the only alternative, especially in rural areas. For many countries in Africa, for example, up to 90 percent of the population depend primarily on traditional systems for meeting their health care needs. While in some cases traditional treatments are used because there are no other options, in many others biomedical treatments are considered less effective than traditional methods against diseases believed to be caused by evil spirits. For many in the developed world who have varied health care options, the decision to use traditional remedies results from the fact that biomedical treatments are expensive, have many unwanted side effects, and are sometimes ineffective.

There are other lessons to be learned from traditional medicine. For example, traditional practitioners are usually members of the same community as their patients. They are aware, both on a personal and a professional level, of various local environmental factors that can affect the health of community members. They are also usually aware of the social, cultural, and economic constraints that prevent their patients from following a certain treatment plan, and thus can suggest an alternative therapy. Such information could enable researchers, foundations, and policy makers to develop health-promoting strategies that are sensitive to the local social and economic constraints the community faces.

Conclusion

The systematic and thorough identification of obstacles to improved women's health care is vital. As the twentieth century came to a close, women's health movements around the world critically examined concepts of the individual, nature, nurture, and society. Paradigms that reflected this holism incorporated the political economy of justice and a celebration of women's power. Furthermore, UN international conventions are slowly ratifying women's reproductive, sexual, and economic rights. The preamble to the charter of the World Health Organization, as well as the International Convention on Economic, Social, and Cultural Rights Article 12 (1) and the Convention to Eliminate All Forms of Discrimination against Women (CEDAW), affirms that "the enjoyment of the highest attainable standards of health is the fundamental right of every human being." On the national level, more policies should be guided by constitutional language; the French constitution states its "guarantee to all and notably to the child, the mother, and the aged worker, health protection, maternal security, rest and leisure."

In very real terms, the health of the most marginalized women in any nation is an important measure of human development and overall prosperity within that nation. Throughout the world, the trend toward governmental affirmation of women's rights as human rights and of health itself as a human right is growing.

See Also

HEALERS; HEALTH CHALLENGES; HEALTH EDUCATION; HOLISTIC HEALTH I; HOLISTIC HEALTH II

References and Further Reading

Akidi Lore, C. 1995. Consequences of the global economy on women's health: African women's response to the economic crisis. *Political Environments* 2(Summer): 18–21.

Avery, B. 1990. Breathing life into ourselves: The evolution of the national black women's health project. In Evelyn C. White, ed. *The black women's health book: Speaking for ourselves.* Seattle, Wash.: Seal.

Barker-Benfield, G. J. 1988. Sexual surgery in late nineteenth-century America. In *Seizing our bodies: The politics of women's health.* New York: Vintage.

Bass, E., and Davis, L. 1988. *The courage to heal: A guide for women survivors of child sexual abuse.* New York: Harper and Row.

Bhardwaj, S., and Paul B. K. 1986. Medical pluralism and infant mortality in a rural area of Bangladesh. *Social Science and Medicine.* 23(10).

Borysenko, J. 1996. *Woman's book of life.* New York: Riverhead.

Borremans, V. 1977. Inverse of managed health. Contribution to the 1977 Dag Hammaskjold Seminar: Another Development in Health, Uppsala, Sweden, June.

Bradley, C. 1994. Women's empowerment and fertility decline in western Kenya. In S. Greenhalgh ed., *Situating fertility: Anthropology and demographic inquiry.*

Cook, R. Human rights in relation to women's health, The promotion and protection of women's health through international human rights law. Geneva: WHO/DHG/93.1.

Corea, G. 1977. *The hidden malpractice: How American medicine mistreats women.* New York: Jove-HBJ.

Fee, E. 1983. Women and health care: A comparison of theories. In Elizabeth Fee, ed., *Women and health: The politics of sex in medicine.* Famingdale, N.Y.: Baywood.

Forte, D., and K. Judd 1998. The South within the North. In R. Petchesky and K. Judd, eds., *Negotiation reproductive rights: Women's perspectives across countries and cultures.* New York and London. Zed. International Reproductive Rights Research Action Group (IRRRAG).

Fuenzalida-Puelma, H., and Scholle S. Connor, eds. The right to health in the Americas. *Scientific Publication.* 509: 596–607, Washington, D.C.: PAHO.

Higgins, T. 1996. Anti-essentialism, relativism, and human rights. *Harvard Women's Law Journal* 89.

Hodfar, H. 1995. State policy and gender equality in post-revolutionary Iran. In C. M. Obermeyer, ed., *Family, gender, and population in the Middle East: Policies in context.* Cairo: American University.

Kieskka, M. 1990. Gender and mental health in Africa. In E. Rothlum and E. Cole, eds., *Women's mental health in Africa.* Harrington Park Press.

Leary, V. A. The right to health in international human rights law. *Health and Human Rights* 1(1).

Martin, T. C. 1995. Women's education and fertility: Results from twenty-six demographic and health surveys. *Studies in Family Planning* 26(4: Jul.–Aug.).

Northrup, C. 1998. *Women's bodies, women's wisdom.* New York: Bantam.

Pert, C. 1997. Molecules of emotion. New York: Scribner.

Seager, Joni. 1997. *Women's world atlas.* London: Penguin.

Singh, S., and R. Samara. 1996. Early marriage among women in developing countries. *International Family Planning Perspectives* 22(4).

Schoepf, B., and W. Engundu. 1991. Women and structural adjustment in Zaire. In Christina Gladwin, ed., *Structural adjustment and African women farmers*. Gainesville: University of Florida Press.

Thomas, H. 1998. *Chronic fatigue, fibromyalgia and environmental illness*. Ed., B. Golberg et al. Scottsdale, Ariz.: Future Medicine.

Yanco, J. 1995. *Macro-economics policies and women's reproductive health: The case of the Sahel*. Working Paper no. 204, Boston University African Studies Center.

World Health Organization. 1981. *Development of indicators for monitoring progress towards health for all by the year 2000*. Geneva: World Health Organization.

Dianne Forte
Saminaz Akhter
Mary Norris

HEALTH CARE: Australia, New Zealand, and the Pacific Islands

Oceania incorporates hundreds of island populations in the Pacific, inhabited by indigenous peoples who are usually divided into Melanesians, Micronesians, and Polynesians, as well as the larger land masses of New Zealand and Australia, where the majority of the population are descendants of European immigrants who have arrived over the last two centuries. The ethnic diversity and the variant economic systems within this broad region mean that women's health status and the health care services available to women are equally variable.

The intrusion by Europeans into the Pacific countries had profound impacts on the health of original inhabitants, both male and female. New infectious diseases were introduced, and mortality was often high. Initially colonial concern about women's health was generated mainly by the depopulation that ensued. European observers often attributed low birthrates and high infant mortality to women's traditional beliefs and practices, although it is certain that introduced sexually transmitted diseases contributed to female infertility. Mission hospitals were established throughout the Pacific and often provided the basis for the introduction of medical care. In Australia and New Zealand, where white settlers brought with them the ideas of health and medicine prevailing in nineteenth-century Great Britain, the impetus for health services to women often came from pronatalist and racist ideologies derived from imperialism. Provision of maternal and child health care by the state was well established in the early twentieth century in both countries.

Throughout the contemporary Pacific nations western health care is often combined with traditional practices—partly because many rural people do not have access to modern services but also because in the area of women's health, customary ideas of well-being and appropriate care for women remain strong. In Polynesia and Melanesia women remain the main carers of the sick in village communities, and they are often repositories of knowledge about the use of herbal medicines as treatments for common ailments. Traditionally, female fertility was central to ideas of social order and prosperity. In some cultures women's reproductive functions were subject to taboos. Menstruation and childbirth were considered polluting to men, and so the practices surrounding them tended to be female-centered; in some cases women were sequestered from men when their bodies were considered to be in dangerously potent or sacred states. Birth practices vary greatly, but women were usually exclusively assisted by women. Difficult births were often attributed to a moral failure on the mother's part, and in some areas men with special magical knowledge would be called in to assist delivery.

Practices such as prolonged postpartum taboos and ritual sexual abstinence for men were common throughout the Pacific. These traditions, more than any other factor, limited births and probably ensured infant survival as well as maternal health. Although herbal medicines were used for contraception, there is little evidence that they were effective except those that were toxic and produced abortion. Changes introduced by colonial agents and missionaries have eroded many of the customs that regulated fertility, and in many Pacific nations the burgeoning birthrate is seen as a major social and economic issue that also has implications for women's health. In Australia and New Zealand the fertility rates have been declining—in 1999 at 1.9 and 2.0, respectively—and are similar to those in industrialized western Europe and North America. In the Pacific island nations the health transitions associated with improved diet and obstetric care have resulted in fertility rates as high as 4.9 (Solomon Islands) and 4.6 (Papua New Guinea), although the trend at the end of the twentieth century appeared to be turning downward. In all countries in the region, family planning, ready availability of information, contraception, and maternal and child health services are government priorities in health policy. However, the lack of funding in poorer nations means that these programs are not available to all women.

The emphasis on maternal health resulted in a decline in maternal mortality over the last twenty years of the twentieth century in almost all countries. In Australia in the early twenty-first century it was low—9 per 100,000, even though there was still relatively high mortality in the small indigenous aboriginal population. In Papua New Guinea it was very high—at 930 per 100,000—in spite of improvements in female literacy and overall economic development, factors usually associated with improved women's health and mortality. The majority of these deaths are attributed to obstetric complications in unsupervised deliveries. In most other Pacific countries the provision of obstetric services has reduced maternal mortality to below 100 per 100,000, and in a few places, such as the Marshall Islands, where the U.S. government has assisted with service provision, maternal mortality has been nil for years.

Western medicine and medical services in each country follow the patterns established initially by the colonial power. So in New Caledonia and Tahiti the system is similar to that in France, in the Cook Islands it is modeled on the New Zealand system, and in Papua New Guinea the service provision still reflects the influence of Australia. Public hospital provision and specialized programs in women's health exist in all countries, but access to them varies greatly. In New Zealand and Australia, where the majority of people live in cities, most women have easy access, and both public and private care is available. In these countries social welfare services also ensure that poor women have medical services provided. In many developing Pacific countries, where the majority of women live in rural villages and there is no social welfare provided by the state, access is limited by economic and geographical factors.

The range of life expectancy for women across the region indicates the disparities and variance in socioeconomic standards and health care provision. In Australia and New Zealand female life expectancy was 81 and 79 years in 1999. In the Polynesian countries it was gradually improving over the last twenty years of the twentieth century and varies between 64 (Kiribati) and 74 (Fiji). But in Melanesia the range is greater: 77 years in New Caledonia, 73 years in the Solomon Islands, and 56 years in Papua New Guinea. Papua New Guinea is the only country in the region where female life expectancy is lower than male life expectancy. Papua New Guinea is in many ways a richer country than any other in Melanesia, with much of its wealth drawn from mineral development, and women in Papua New Guinea have generally higher literacy rates than other Melanesian women. Therefore, women's low life expectancy (in both relative and absolute terms) appears to involve cultural factors and not just material conditions. Traditional gender ideologies in many areas of Papua New Guinea limit female participation in the modern economy and limit women's access to health care.

Differences in the health status of women vary similarly. Infectious diseases remain the major causes of morbidity and mortality in many of the Pacific islands. In the 1990s tuberculosis increased in prevalence, and respiratory diseases and malaria continue to be major health problems. Malaria is a significant factor in women's health in Melanesia, particularly where it is linked to high rates of anemia and other problems in pregnancy. As economic development and urbanization increase across the region, changes in nutrition and everyday work patterns are reflected in changing disease profiles. Diabetes, hypertension, heart disease, and cancer—diseases associated with industrial societies and common in the populations of Australia and New Zealand—are increasing in incidence, especially in urban communities. Obesity as a health problem for women is becoming common in Polynesian populations, especially urban and immigrant groups, and there is evidence that there is a genetic propensity that is exacerbated by the dietary changes (increased consumption of refined and high fat foods) that come with modernity and a more sedentary life. Public education programs on nutrition directed at women exist in all Pacific countries. While these are often implemented in the context of infant and child health programs, they also include information aimed at improving women's health.

Many sexually transmitted diseases were introduced to the indigenous populations of the region during the period of colonization. They are very common still and increasing in some countries, although precise information is lacking for many countries where limited access to health services and cultural attitudes stressing female shame inhibit women from presenting with symptoms. HIV/AIDS cases are declining in Australia and New Zealand, and in these countries the female incidence of infection was relatively low for the 1990s. In the developing countries of the Pacific region, however, public awareness campaigns have been mounted in an attempt by health departments and international agencies to limit the spread of disease, which is predicted to follow patterns similar to those in many African countries, with heterosexual transmission predominating. Because of the lack of diagnostic facilities in many places and because of established infectious diseases such as pneumonia, malaria, and tuberculosis, detection and diagnosis of HIV/AIDS is difficult in many places. The low figures for the disease in many countries are considered by many health analysts to be unrealistic.

Throughout the Pacific, domestic violence against women is recognized as a factor that negatively affects women's health. In countries such as Fiji, Vanuatu, and Papua New Guinea substantial national campaigns have been undertaken by government departments and NGOs to eradicate the problem and to raise consciousness of women's human rights. Organizations aimed at improving women's health tend to be mainly self-help and lobby groups in the industrialized countries of Australia and New Zealand. In the Pacific nations the political campaigns for women's health issues are integrated into more general programs that include social justice, human rights, and education.

See Also

DEVELOPMENT: AUSTRALIA AND NEW ZEALAND; DISEASE; HEALERS; HEALTH: OVERVIEW

References and Further Reading

Bayne-Smith, Marcia, ed. 1996. *Race, gender and health*. Thousand Oaks, Calif.: Sage.

Bunnell, Julie. 1987. *Women's health in New Zealand*. Wellington, N.Z.: Department of Health.

Kelly, Elizabeth. 1994. *Australian women's health handbook*. Rushcutter's Bay, Australia: Gore and Osment.

Lukere, Vicki, and Margaret Jolly. 2000. *Birthing in the Pacific: Mothers, wives and midwives*. Honolulu: University of Hawaii Press.

Osteria, Trinidad S., ed. 1991. *Women in health development*. Singapore: Institute of South East Asian Studies.

Ram, Kalpana, and Margaret Jolly. 1998. *Maternities and modernities: Colonial and postcolonial experiences in Asia and the Pacific*. Cambridge: Cambridge University Press.

The World Health Organization publishes information on women's health in the region in many forms, and information can be obtained from <http://www.who.org.ph>.

Martha MacIntyre

HEALTH CARE: Canada

Health care in Canada is provided primarily through a national health insurance program funded and administered by the Canadian provincial governments, although some funding comes from the federal government. The national health insurance program is based on five principles: (1) insured health care services such as hospitals and physicians' services must be publicly administered; (2) these services must be comprehensively insured; (3) services must be universally available to all people in Canada, no matter where they live in the country; (4) services must be portable between the provinces; and (5) services must be accessible to all, unimpeded by charges or in any other way. These five principles form the core of Canada's health care system.

Health care in Canada is premised on the idea that health is affected not only by biological factors but also by gender and by social, economic, and environmental factors. These factors are termed determinants of health. One health determinant, gender, highlights several important aspects of women's health and health care in Canada. First, gender is conceptualized as a social construct that is rooted more in culture than in biological differences. Second, it is recognized that in Canada, women will, on average, live longer than men, endure more chronic disease, have less access to health insurance that covers care (such as alternative health services) not covered by national health insurance, be more likely to be single parents, and be more susceptible to health risks and threats such as smoking, substance abuse, and violence. Third, and most important, gender is recognized as the most significant determinant of women's health in Canada, over and above other determinants such as culture, income, education, and environment.

In recent years, reforms have sought to streamline Canada's health care system to meet the requirements of the five basic principles more effectively while still containing escalating costs and meeting changing needs. These reforms have emphasized enhancing health promotion and preventive care, using other health care providers such as nurses and midwives more extensively, and restructuring the health care system to incorporate other types of care delivery such as community health centers and primary health care.

Women's Health Issues

Several issues exist for women's health in Canada (Federal, Provincial, and Territorial Advisory Committee on Population Health [FPTACPH], 1999; Health Canada, 1996, 1997). Health care systems and practitioners in Canada have tended to view women's health primarily in terms of women's reproductive functions and their status and role in society. In addition, women's life processes such as menopause and childbirth have been treated as issues that require medical intervention rather than as normal, healthy developments. Women in Canada are at greater risk of poverty than men. Among the industrialized countries, Canada is second only to Japan in the incidence of low-paid employment for women (Canadian Labor Congress, 1997). A low income limits a woman's access to conditions that contribute to a healthy life, such as health care, child care, education, and adequate housing and nutrition.

In Canada, half of women over 16 years of age have experienced violence by an intimate partner (Health Canada, 1997). Girls, elderly women, aboriginal (Native)

women, and women who live in isolated circumstances are particularly vulnerable to violence (Health Canada, 1996, 1997; Leipert and Reutter, 1998). Violence in women's lives has implications for their psychological, social, and physical health, as well as for the long-term health of their families and communities.

Certain populations of women in Canada are especially vulnerable and experience particular health challenges. Aboriginal women in Canada rank lowest in health and economic well-being (Statistics Canada, 1995), and they experience extremely high rates of violence and suicide, as well as chronic health conditions such as diabetes, cardiovascular and respiratory diseases, cervical cancer, and sexually transmitted diseases (National Forum on Health, 1997). These health issues create an urgent need for health care services, but often such services are unavailable or unused—in particular, available services tend not to be used by aboriginal women in Canada because of prejudice or because the care offered is culturally inappropriate or is being provided by male personnel (FPTACPH, 1999; Health Canada, 1996; Royal Commission on Aboriginal Peoples, 1997).

Other vulnerable populations include single-parent families headed by women, immigrant women, women who are members of racial minorities, women who live in geographically isolated circumstances, disabled women, and lesbians. For these women, access to appropriate—or any—health care is especially problematic because they may either not receive health care that meets their needs or not receive care at all. As a result, these and other vulnerable populations of women across Canada are at risk.

Recommendations

From a feminist perspective, women's health research in Canada needs to expand to become more gender-sensitive, more inclusive, more context-specific, more interdisciplinary, more methodologically diverse, and more meaningful to women; it also needs to exert more influence on health care policy (Health Canada, 1996; Leipert and Reutter, 1998). In addition, research initiatives need to focus more on women's strengths and on their ability to obtain appropriate health care and to promote their own health. In 1996 the federal government created five Centers of Excellence for Women's Health across Canada to redress shortcomings in women's health research across the country.

Additional recommendations for promoting women's health include reducing societal power inequities that lead to violence, supporting women in leadership roles, supporting changes that address poverty and cultural issues, increasing health promotion and preventive care as well as

primary care, guarding against the view that women's normal life events such as pregnancy and menopause require medical intervention, and attending to the effects of health care reform on women's health (National Forum on Health, 1997). Other recommendations include the establishment of national health objectives for women's health, with special attention to women who are in vulnerable circumstances, and the establishment of a yearly report card on the status of women's health in Canada (Liepert and Reutter, 1998). Regular review of the national objectives and the yearly report card could form the basis for more gender-appropriate health care policies and programs in Canada.

Health care in Canada is diverse and multifaceted. Although a national health service does increase access to health care for some, compared with what is available in countries where health care is privatized, several issues remain regarding the advancement of women's health in this country. Nevertheless, with further gender-specific health research, policy, and program development, health care for women in Canada will be strengthened.

See Also

DEVELOPMENT: NORTH AMERICA; GLOBAL HEALTH MOVEMENT; HEALTH: OVERVIEW; HEALTH CHALLENGES

References and Further Reading

Canadian Labor Congress. 1997. *Women's work: A report.* Ottawa: Canadian Labor Congress.

Federal, Provincial, and Territorial Advisory Committee on Population Health (FPTACPH). 1999. *Toward a healthy future: Second report on the health of Canadians.* Ottawa: Health Canada.

Health Canada. 1996. *Canada–U.S.A.* Women's Health Forum commissioned papers. Ottawa: Health Canada.

———. 1997. *National forum on health: An overview of women's health.* Ottawa: Health Canada.

Leipert, B., and L. Reutter. 1998. Women's health and community health nursing practice in geographically isolated settings: A Canadian perspective. *Health Care for Women International* 19: 575–588.

National Forum on Health. 1997. *An overview of women's health.* Ottawa: National Forum on Health.

Royal Commission on Aboriginal Peoples. 1997. *Report of the Royal Commission on Aboriginal Peoples.* Ottawa: Canada Communications Group.

Statistics Canada. 1995. *Women in Canada: A statistical report.* Catalog #89–503E. Ottawa: Ministry of Industry.

Beverly Leipert

HEALTH CARE: Central and South America and the Caribbean

Despite efforts in the last decades of the twentieth century to address the unique problems of women's health care needs, health care for women in Latin (Central and South) America and the Caribbean has been and continues to be characterized by insufficient access and lack of information.

In 1981 the Pan American Health Organizations of the World Health Organization and member governments developed a regional five-year action plan whose objective was "to integrate satisfactorily women of the Americas in new and ongoing health and development activities." According to the plan, "women must be considered not only as active beneficiaries of health care, but also as promoters of health services, both for themselves and for their children and families." However, the plan recommended against designing programs exclusively for women.

In the years following the development of the plan, more women moved into paid work and into primary and secondary education. Fertility and maternal mortality declined in most Latin American and Caribbean countries, with the exception of Haiti, Bolivia, Guatemala, and Honduras. However, other serious health problems of women continued or increased. For example, violence against women remained or increased as a health concern. An increase in low-birth-weight babies in Central America and the Caribbean indicated declining nutrition for pregnant women. Some pharmaceutical corporations experimented with birth control methods among poor, black, and indigenous women.

Health services remained inaccessible for large groups of rural and poor women. Illegal abortion became a major source of death and infertility for adult and adolescent women. Not one country in the region recognizes birth control choice or abortion as an individual right of women. In addition to the problem of lack of access to safe, effective birth control, poor women in Peru are at increased risk for involuntary sterilization. Programs to aggressively sterilize women violate their human rights and also divert resources from other health needs.

The wealthier urban centers in Latin America present many similar health concerns to those in the United States. Anorexia and bulimia are of increasing concern among young women. Poverty drives many young women to the dangerous streets and to harmful drugs at a very young age. The incidence of HIV/AIDS has increased in women amid a lack of education, prevention, and care in the region. Cervical cancer causes a high incidence of death because of limited access to Pap smear tests and early treatment. Occupational health conditions are more hazardous, and governments do little to reform unhealthful working conditions.

The rate of cesarean-section childbirth, with its accompanying increase in maternal risks, has grown at a dramatic rate. Cesarean section increases the cost of child care, placing a greater burden on health systems with limited budgets.

With advances in reproductive technology now enabling women to bear children produced by the union of another woman's egg with sperm, it is feared that women in Latin America will be exploited for their reproductive capacities as "surrogate mothers" to produce children for wealthy infertile couples in the United States and other industrialized nations. Again, poverty drives these concerns.

In 1984 an organization of feminists formed the Latin American and Caribbean Women's Health Network to unite women in nation-states throughout the region in advocacy for women's health. The network publishes two magazines and contains databases and the Isis International Documentation Center. In addition, the network speaks on behalf of women and educates them about health issues including occupational health, contraception, domestic violence, menopause, and other health topics of concern.

The Pan American Health Organization emphasized health care as critical to development of the region in its 1991 report *Orientaciones estratégicas y prioridades programaticas: 1991–1994.* Its subsequent 1994 report, produced jointly with the United Nations Economic Commission of Latin America, *Salud, equilidad y transformación productiva en America Latina y el Caribe,* also cited health care as a major factor in the maintenance and improvement of human life. The report stated that one in every five Latin Americans is too poor to get basic nutritional requirements. Poverty continues to be a significant hurdle to meeting basic health needs. Since women are overrepresented among the poorest people in Latin America, this barrier is especially significant for women and their children.

International women's groups and other nongovernmental organizations have worked to implement the women's health care consensus reached at the International Conference on Population and Development held in Cairo (1994) and the Fourth World Conference on Women (1995) held in Beijing. These advocacy groups continue to work with women's groups and health care providers in Latin America and the Caribbean to improve women's health.

Women's movements in Latin America continue to be advocates for reproductive rights and changes in attitudes toward sexual orientation and sexuality. Their advocacy seeks to change cultural norms. The widespread allegiance to the

Catholic Church makes such advocacy challenging. However, the Catholic Church is addressing the poverty issues that result in such poor health outcomes. Nevertheless, insufficient attention has been paid to other important women's health issues, such as HIV/AIDS, cancer, violence (including rape and domestic violence), and occupational health.

Poverty, lack of education, lack of health care services, and governmental and societal attitudes all contribute to poor health care outcomes for women in Latin America and the Caribbean, especially with regard to women's unique health care issues. Although the international community has recognized these problems, insufficient governmental and nongovernmental resources have been used to address them. Because of women's role as bearers and nurturers of children, these health care problems affect the children who inherit their own health care problems from their mothers or lose their mothers because of inadequate prenatal and maternal health care.

See Also

DEVELOPMENT: CENTRAL AND SOUTH AMERICA AND THE CARIBBEAN; EDUCATION: CENTRAL AND SOUTH AMERICA AND THE CARIBBEAN; ENVIRONMENT: CENTRAL AND SOUTH AMERICA; HEALTH: OVERVIEW; TRADITIONAL HEALING: CENTRAL AND SOUTH AMERICA AND THE CARRIBEAN; WOMEN'S STUDIES: CARIBBEAN; WOMEN'S STUDIES: CENTRAL AND SOUTH AMERICA

References and Further Reading

Belizan, José, and Fernando Althabo. 1999. Rates and implications of cesarean sections in Latin America: Ecological Study. *British Medical Journal.* 27 November, 1397.

ECLA/PAHO. 1994. *Salud, equilidad y transformación productiva en America Latina y el Caribe.* 25th Session. Cartagena, Columbia, 20–27 April.

Gender, health and sustainable development: A Latin American perspective. Proceedings of a workshop held in Montevideo, Uruguay, April 1994, International Development Research Center.

International Women's Health Coalition. http://www.iwhc.og/publications.html.

Key, Sandra. 1997. Cervical cancer kills 25,000 Latin American women each year. *Cancer Weekly Plus,* 26 May, 13.

Lopez, Antoinette Sedillo. 1990. La privacidad y la regulación de las nuevas tecnologías de la reproducción: Un plantamiento para tomar decisiones. *Investigaciones Juridicas* 37: 442.

———. Two legal constructs of motherhood: "Protective" legislation in Mexico and the United States. 1 University of Southern California. *Review of Law & Women's Studies* 239.

———. A comparative analysis of women's issues: Toward a contextualized approach. *Womens Law Journal* 343.

Nothing personal: Latin American and Caribbean Committee for the Defense of Human Rights: Sterilization (Birth Control). 1999. *World Press Review* 46(3): 43.

PAHO/WHO. 1983. *La Mujer en la salud y el desarrollo: Una guia para el Plan Quinquenal Regional de Acción sobre la mujer en la salud y el desarrollo en las Américas.* Washington, D.C.: PAHO/WHO.

———. 1991. *Orientaciones estratégicas y prioridades programaticas, 1991–1994.* Washington, D.C.: PAHO/WHO.

Sanchez, Olga Amparao. 1994. Latin America: Women's health in context. *Women's Health Journal* 3 February, 47–54.

Servicios de Noticias de la Mujer. http://www.sem.or.cr/I-index.shtml.

Antoinette Sedillo Lopez

HEALTH CARE:
Commonwealth of Independent States

After the collapse of the Soviet Union in 1991, the new association of its former constituent republics, the Commonwealth of Independent States (CIS), experienced a deep shock as traditional political and economic links were destroyed, ideological stereotypes were broken, and dramatic changes occurred in the life of the people. These changes affected the health care system in the newly emerged countries as well: the low share allotted to health care in state budgets resulted in growing nonpayment of wages to medical personnel, difficulties in accessing health care, and worsening of the quality of care. The social transformation experienced in CIS countries dramatically affected the status of health services for women and more generally the status of women's health.

Health Status

The health status of women directly reflects the health status of the nation. The clearest indicator of the negative changes in the health status of women in CIS members appears in patterns of morbidity. During the 1990s there was dramatic growth in the rates of so-called social diseases, caused to a large extent by the low living standards and quality of women's life. In Russia, between 1991 and 1998 the number of syphilis cases among women increased by a factor of 36, alcoholism by a factor of 1.6, and drug abuse by 6.6 and tuberculosis rose by 55 percent. The number of women newly diagnosed with syphilis increased by 57 percent in Belorussia and by 82 percent in Kazakhstan, during the same period.

Women's health, especially during pregnancy, is very sensitive to the influences of environmental factors, among which poor working conditions are foremost. Many women in CIS countries still work in an unfriendly environment, and the level of occupational diseases and trauma among women is quite high. In 1998 women amounted to 33 percent of the six million people in Russia working in conditions harmful for health.

Low-quality food is another important factor that can be detrimental to women's health. A study done in 1994 in St. Petersburg, Russia, found that 28 percent of pregnant women had a diet lacking in vitamins and calcium and had other nutritional deficiencies, which in turn negatively affected the health of their babies.

Demographics

The level of population grown in all CIS countries decreased in the 1990s. The aggregate birthrate in Russia in 1999 was only 1.12, one of the lowest in the world. This reflects a major trend in the reproductive behavior of Russian people: having small families has become a characteristic feature and basic orientation for women. For example, in 1992 only 8 percent of families without children said they did not want to have a child; in 1994 about one-quarter of women aged 18 to 44 without children did not want to have them. The total rate of birth in Kazakhstan decreased for the period from 1990 to 1997 by a factor of 1.4, and 71.6 percent of Kazakh women held the opinion that women should have not more than one or two children. During the same period mortality rates in Kazakhstan increased by one-third, and as a result the rate of population growth decreased by a factor of 2.6. In Belorussia the indicators were a bit better: in 1996 the birthrate amounted to 9.3 per 1000. The mortality rate was 13.0, and the rate of population growth was 3.7. These rates are still much worse than the rates in 1990 (which were 13.9, 10.7, and 3.2, respectively). A similar situation held in the Ukraine, where during the period from 1990 to 1995 the birthrate fell from 12.1 to 9.6 per 1,000, the mortality rate increased from 13.9 to 14.7, and the growth rate decreased from 1.7 to negative 4.6.

Reform of the Health System

Health sector reforms and the provision of medical services to improve the health status of the population in general and of women in particular have become central policy issues in CIS countries. But although the principal problem on national agendas is the same—the role of the state in organizing and financing the nation's health care system—the concrete ways that health systems have been reformed during the 1990s have varied to a great extent within the CIS.

The new states can be broadly divided into two groups, in terms of their strategic objectives and the scale of the reform they are making in health care. Countries of the first group have preserved the Soviet-style budget health care system, encompassing universal coverage; delivery of a comprehensive range of medical services; absence of financial barriers; free provision of medical services by the state-owned health services; a unified system of health services: primary, secondary, and tertiary as well as prevention; high-quality medical education and highly qualified medical personnel. They are very cautious in planning and carrying out any reforms. In Belorussia in 2000, the state-financed system practically remained intact. The constitution of Ukraine provided for a state-owned health care system, but notably Ukraine is one of the few CIS countries that allocates a relatively high share of its budget—5.9 percent of GDP in 1996—for health care. Armenia made two attempts in the 1990s to introduce health insurance, but they were not successful, and in 2000 that country still had a budget system for dispensing medical care. Azerbaijan kept the old Soviet system but tried to introduce some changes, such as fees for service. In 1998, 25 percent of the funds for health care in Azerbaijan were raised through fees for service with plans to increase the patient share up to 40 percent.

Countries in the second group started structural reforms of their health systems, with Russia being the acknowledged leader. The strategic aim of such reforms is the introduction of compulsory health insurance. Compulsory health insurance legislation was adopted in Russia as early as 1991. Under the new system, insurance contributions were collected from organizations and local authorities and were used to fund provision, health services. As of 2000 the new developments had failed to bring any positive changes into the health system, and intense debates were under way to decide whether the future of the health system in Russia would move in the direction of budget or insurance medicine. Other CIS countries that introduced compulsory health insurance as the strategic aim of health care reforms took a more balanced approach. For example, in Kyrgyzstan in 1994 a special program of health care reforms was adopted for implementation in the period from 1996 to 2006, with that period to be further divided into three stages. During the first stage, the emphasis was to be on analyzing the existing system and identifying national priorities. Development of primary care and maternity care and control over infectious diseases were named as the program's most important objectives. The second stage aimed to find additional sources of health care financing, for instance, through extra levies on tobacco and alcohol. At the third stage, after the potential of the already existing infrastructure is fully used, the plan calls for introducing compulsory health insurance.

In 1997, the republic of Kazakhstan adopted a law that provides legal, economic, and social foundation for the protection of public health. It regulates the activities of state bodies, individuals, and organizations, regardless of the form of ownership, to secure the constitutional right of citizens for health care. In Kazakhstan compulsory health insurance is viewed as a socially fair means of ensuring that the entire population has access to basic health services.

Protection of Women's Health

Protection of women's health is an important aspect of any health care system because it influences the health status not only of women but of the whole population. Choosing women as a special target group can promote substantial improvement in the health status of the entire population at a relatively low cost. For example, better health care for pregnant women leads to dramatic decreases in the number of babies born with health problems, and healthy babies are also likely to have fewer health problems during their lifetime.

In order to protect women's health, a number of CIS countries including Belorussia and Ukraine adopted various targeted programs. Such programs as "Safe Motherhood" and "Children of Russia" are now being implemented in Russia. Despite their limitations, targeted programs still fulfill two main tasks: in the face of difficult financial and organizational conditions they provide a framework that concentrates administrative efforts on developing health services for women and assures that the funds allocated for women's health care are not spent elsewhere.

See Also

ECONOMY: GLOBAL RESTRUCTURING; EDUCATION: COMMONWEALTH OF INDEPENDENT STATES; FEMINISM: COMMONWEALTH OF INDEPENDENT STATES; HEALTH: OVERVIEW; HOUSEHOLDS AND FAMILIES: COMMONWEALTH OF INDEPENDENT STATES; POLITICS AND THE STATE: COMMONWEALTH OF INDEPENDENT STATES; WOMEN'S STUDIES: COMMONWEALTH OF INDEPENDENT STATES

References and Further Reading

David, Henry P., ed. 1999. *From abortion to contraception: A resource to public policies and reproductive behavior in cen-tral and eastern Europe from 1917 to the present.* Westport, Conn.: Greenwood.

Grigorieva, N., and T. Tchoubarova. 1997. Health status in Russia: The need for a new approach. *Eurohealth* 3(3).

Lazreg, Marina, ed. 2000. *Making the transition work for women in Europe and central Asia.* World Bank discussion paper no. 411. Washington, D.C.: World Bank.

World Bank. 1998. *Improving women's health services in the Russian Federation: Social challenges of transition.* World Bank technical paper no 411. Washington, D.C.: World Bank.

World Health Organization. 1995. *Investing in women's health: central and eastern Europe.* Denmark: World Health Organization Publications.

Natalia Grigorieva

HEALTH CARE: East Asia

State health care for women in east Asian countries is generally incorporated within the wider framework of maternal and child health (MCH). This article first gives an overview of the current state of MCH-based health care and then examines contraception, abortion, and family planning programs. In each case, an introductory outline of the topic is followed by a more specific description of the situations in Japan, Korea, and China. Naturally, health policy and medical systems differ from country to country, in both general structure and specific details. Moreover, east Asia as a region includes developed countries like Japan, developing countries such as China and Mongolia, and countries undergoing rapid economic growth, such as Korea. This article, therefore, can only offer a brief survey of the field; for further information, please consult the materials in the reading list.

MCH-Based Health Care

In Japan, Korea, and China, the government takes the initiative in providing MCH services, and health services for pregnant women are fairly well developed. Compared with developed countries, east Asian countries have a low extramarital birthrate largely because the link between marriage and reproduction is strongly enforced as a social norm. In Japan, for example, there is legal discrimination against children born out of wedlock, and extramarital birth is socially stigmatized, making it difficult for unwed mothers to take advantage of MCH services.

The rates of maternal mortality in east Asian countries are 7 (per 100,000) in Hong Kong, 8 in Japan, 30 in Korean, and 115 in China (up from 94.7 in 1990). The infant mortality rate is 6 in Hong Kong, 4 in Japan, 10 in Korea, and 41 in China (estimated mean levels, 1990–1995) (United Nations Population Division World Population Prospects, 1998). Hong Kong has a low rate of both infant and maternal mortality. Japan has a relatively low rate of infant mortality, but maternal mortality is still high compared with other developed countries.

MCH in Japan. MCH policy in Japan, set forth in the Maternal and Child Welfare Law enacted in 1965, covers the period from before marriage until the birth of children. MCH policy largely consists of health examinations, guidance, medical assistance, and the distribution of information concerning maternal health. Pregnant women can take two cost-free medical examinations at an approved medical organization, once in early pregnancy and once in the third trimester. Pregnant women must register their pregnancy at a local public health center, and they are then supplied with a maternal care handbook, in which they record health-related details about their pregnancy, delivery, and the newborn. This system in turn provides the administration with useful information about pregnant women and newborns, for the purpose of shaping health and child care policy.

Since 1960, when the number of hospital births exceeded home births for the first time, institutional births have increased continuously. In 1990, 99.9 percent of all births in Japan took place in hospitals and clinics. Accordingly, safety of delivery has improved and infant mortality rates have dropped. On the other hand, women have lost some of their autonomy in the birth process, becoming instead objects of medical attention, so that the day and even the time of birth are often adjusted to suit the working time of doctors or hospitals. In the 1990s, hospitals encountered stronger criticism and were reevaluating such inhumane birth methods.

MCH in Korea. In the late 1980s Korea began to place increased emphasis on MCH policy with the aim of controlling population increase and reducing the infant mortality rate. As a result, infant mortality, which was 32.5 (per 100,000 live births) in 1985, dropped to 10 in 1998 (UN Population Division, 1998). The revision in 1985 of Korea's Maternal and Child Welfare Law provided improved health care for pregnant women and infants, including basic health examinations, vaccinations, metabolic tests, prenatal and postnatal care, and free dietary supplements for pregnant women suffering from anemia. These services are provided from the time of the registration of pregnancy, and the health of pregnant women and their children is managed and recorded by means of the system of MCH in Korea, which is very similar to that in Japan.

MCH in China. In China, legislation once known as the Eugenic Protection Law was revised in 1994 as the Maternal and Child Welfare Law and implemented in 1995. A nationwide MCH network was established in late 1992, before this new law took effect: 346 MCH care centers, 2,841 clinics, and 34 pediatric hospitals were affiliated with the network. As a result, 98 percent of pregnant Chinese women in urban areas and 70 percent in rural areas get up to five prenatal medical examinations; 84.1 percent give birth in a hospital or clinic. But, the network has mostly served urban women; the number of rural women having prenatal medical exams has remained low, and in the 1990s fewer than half of them gave birth in hospitals.

Contraception, Abortion, and Family Planning

In the 1990s, the level of contraception in Japan was 59 percent, in China 83 percent, in Korea 79 percent, and in Hong Kong 86 percent. While Japan has a lower rate than other east Asian countries, it is still relatively high on a world level. Japan is very different from the other east Asian countries in that the contraceptive pill had not been approved as a legal form of birth control until 1999.

Abortion is legal in almost all east Asian countries, but the rate of abortion differs markedly from country to country. In Japan, there were 337,799 legal abortions in 1997 (Health and Welfare Statistics Association, 1999), and most of them were for married women, whereas in Korea, which had a rate of abortions similar to Japan's, most were for unmarried women. Despite the high rate of contraception practiced in both countries, Japan and Korea have remarkably high rates of abortions, possibly because of contraceptive failure or insufficient education about contraceptive methods.

In Japan, China, and Korea, especially, family planning programs are run by the government, and the contraceptive acceptance rate is quite high. However, sex education in east Asia clearly lags behind that in developed countries. The taboo regarding talking about sex is still strong, especially in the arena of public education.

Japan. In Japan, under the Eugenic Protection Act (1948; a third version took effect in 1989), abortion can be legally performed up to the twenty-second week of pregnancy in cases where the mother's health is endangered, the pregnancy results from rape or incest, or there are hereditary reasons. The first revision of the act in 1949 added "economic hardship" to the list of grounds for abortion. Currently, 99 percent of abortions in Japan are requested under the economic hardship clause. However, despite the apparent freedom of access, abortion remains illegal in principle under a criminal law enacted in 1880, which is still on the books. This act was revised in 1996, as the Protection of Mother's Body Law, and all activities related to eugenic protection were stopped.

The condom is the main form of contraception in Japan, used by more than 70 percent of married couples: condoms are readily available in neighborhood shops and vending machines. Until recently, the pill had not been approved for use as a contraceptive although doctors occasionally prescribe high-dose pills for a variety of medical conditions. Low-dose pills were scheduled to be approved in 1992, but approval was withheld on the grounds that wide availability of low-dose pills would hamper AIDS prevention programs. In June 1999, low-dose contraceptive pills were approved. In the 1990s discussion of AIDS became an element of sex education programs in schools, but many adults had not been exposed to systematic sex education.

Korea. In Korea, abortion is legal in cases where there is danger to the mother's health, for hereditary reasons (including fetal abnormalities), and in cases of rape or incest. Married couples using contraceptives favor tubal ligation (28.7 percent), followed by vasectomy (11.6), IUD (10.5), and the condom (14.3) (Korean Institute for Health and Social Affairs, 1995).

China. China has pursued a strong family planning program since 1979, with a basic policy that encourages one child per family. In China, unlike Japan and Korea, legal abortion is not restricted according to various conditions; it is freely available on demand. There are no regulations regarding the stage of pregnancy up to which abortion may take place, but most are conducted within the first trimester. The primary methods of contraception in China are the IUD (41.1 percent) and tubal ligation (36.0 percent). The use of condoms is only 4.0 percent (Ministry of Public Health, 1990).

Reproductive Health in East Asia: Some Conclusions

MCH and family planning are addressed in markedly different ways in east Asian countries. Two striking features of health care for women in this region emerge: the strong correlation between the level of economic development and the rates of infant and maternal mortality; and the widespread employment of various methods of birth control, which can be attributed to the dissemination of information on birth control techniques. It goes without saying that health care in east Asia, especially where women are concerned, is greatly affected by each country's social, cultural, and legal discourses regarding the family system and women's place in it.

See Also

AGING: JAPANESE CASE STUDY; EDUCATION: EAST ASIA; FEMINISM: JAPAN; FEMINISM: KOREA; HEALTH: OVERVIEW; POLITICS AND THE STATE: EAST ASIA; POPULATION CONTROL; TRADITIONAL HEALING: EAST AND SOUTHEAST ASIA; WOMEN'S STUDIES: EAST ASIA

References and Further Reading
Health and Welfare Statistics Association. 1999. Trend of health in Japan. *Japanese Health and Welfare Statistics* 46.

Hemshaw, K. Stanley. 1992. Induced abortion: A world review, 1990. In J. Douglas Butler and David F. Walbert, eds. *Abortion, medicine, and the law,* 406–436. 4th ed., rev. New York: Facts on File.

Mason, Karen Oppenheim. 1994. Asian Pacific Issues: Do population programs violate women's human rights? *Analysis from the East-West Centre,* no. 15 (Aug.).

Ministry of Public Health. 1990. *People's Republic of China: Chinese health statistical digest.* In Chinese.

Tsubuku, Masaka. 1993. Not hers to make: Abortion, birth control, and choice in Japan. *Japan International Journal* 38–41.

World Bank. 1994. *World development report 1994.* New York: Oxford University Press.

World Health Organization. 1993. *1993 World Health Organization statistics annual.* Geneva: World Health Organization.

United Nations Population Division. 1998 *World population prospect: The 1998 revision.* New York: United Nations.

Korean Institute for Health and Social Affairs. 1995. *National fertility and family health survey.* Seoul: Korean Institute for Health and Social Affairs.

<http://www.china.org.cn/English/White Papers>
<http://www.mhw.go.jp/English/index.html>
Korean Women's Development Institute, Republic of Korea. 1994. *Korean women now.* Seoul: Korea Women's Development Institute.

Ryoko Yanagibori
Chika Hyodo

HEALTH CARE: Eastern Europe

Women in the countries of central and eastern Europe and the former Soviet Union are in a peculiar position. Unlike their counterparts in developing countries, they enjoy high levels of education and literacy and constitute fully half of the labor force. Since the fall of communism in the late 1980s and early 1990s, however, the position of women has deteriorated. Although part of their worsening situation appears to be due to the loss of real benefits under the former regime, one consequence of the transition to a market economy has been the unmasking of gender inequities inherited from the past. This combination of factors is deleterious to the health of women in these countries.

Under the socialist health care system, the countries of central and eastern Europe provided universal and comprehensive coverage of almost all health services to their citizens. Although problems were inevitable and inefficiencies well documented, the success of the system was evidenced by significant health indicators, for example, infant mortality rates, which decreased, and life expectancies, which increased dramatically from 1950 to 1990.

Some of these trends have continued. Across central and eastern Europe, both infant mortality rates and maternal mortality rates are still decreasing. But in other countries such as Albania, Romania, and most of the countries of the western Commonwealth of Independent States, maternal mortality rates remain above the targets set for Europe by the World Health Organization. Life expectancies have turned downward. Although the drop is greater for men, in 16 of 23 countries for which data are available, life expectancies for women have decreased by several years.

Life in these transitional countries is hard. Although 26 million jobs have been lost in the last decade, women have generally managed to stay employed. But they tend to be clustered in low-paying professions. Moreover, the disappearance of many of the social and family benefits provided under the old regime has increased women's functions. They now must bear the double burden of full-time work and caretaker.

New health threats have appeared in the form of drug and alcohol abuse, particularly among young women, HIV (the virus that causes AIDS) infection, and trafficking in women for sexual exploitation. Although the number of cases of AIDS is still small, it is rapidly increasing. From 1993 to 1998, the number of cases of HIV in eastern Europe and central Asia increased from 30,000 to 270,000. Other sexually transmitted diseases are also increasing. In Russia and other countries, 1 in 100 girls is infected with syphilis. Prostitution leaves a woman particularly vulnerable to contracting HIV and other sexually transmitted diseases and exposes her to violence and psychological abuse by men.

The rising incidence of communicable diseases such as tuberculosis, diarrhea, scabies, diptheria, and cholera is linked to a drop in immunization levels, lax surveillance, and migration of marginalized groups to urban centers.

Population growth in these countries is low, and family planning is not promoted, which limits a woman's repro-

ductive choices. In the absence of family planning programs, abortions have become the de facto form of birth control. Contraceptives are not readily available, and when they are, they are costly. In contrast, women have easy access to free abortion services (except in Poland, where abortion is illegal). In Armenia, women over the age of 40 reported a median of eight induced abortions during their lifetime, and throughout the region abortion is a leading cause of maternal death.

Environmental problems inherited from past years have also become a major threat to women's health and well-being. The increasing incidence of cancer in women of all ages, particularly those aged 20 to 39, is attributed to contaminated air, water, and soil, as is a decline in women's reproductive health. The explosion of the Chernobyl nuclear reactor in 1986 affected the lives and health of millions of people; its long-term effects are still unknown. Stress and depression brought on by socioeconomic difficulties have contributed to rising rates of depression and other mental problems, particularly among elderly women. Rates of suicide among women in countries of the ECE and the former Soviet republics are higher than among women in the European Union. Legal protection against violence to women is minimal. As a result of war conditions in the former Yugoslavia, displaced women have witnessed or experienced killings, torture, sexual harassment, and rape.

Under the insurance-based, fee-for-service health care models that have replaced the socialist models in these countries in transition, poor women have arguably less access to health care. The poor are sicker than the wealthy, and they wait longer to seek care owing to the cost. They also bear more of the burden of hazardous work conditions, and the effective abandoning of preventive checkups (which were a feature of the old system) puts them at additional disadvantage. Women in rural areas must contend with services that are remote, understaffed, and poorly equipped.

Health care services are essentially provided by women, yet women have little impact on the structure and organization of health services. Health curricula do not adequately cover the health needs of women. Sex education in schools is limited or nonexistent, as is apparent in the number of undesired pregnancies and in the growing incidence of HIV infection. Insufficient funds, poor data collection, and the insensitivity of policy makers to human rights and the needs of women all contribute to inequalities in the status of women's health and the care they receive.

The problems of this well-educated, literate vast population of women are exacerbated by their low representation in parliaments. Nor are they inclined to be activist. The strain of long hours at work, minding a family, and being perpetually short of cash take a toll: they are too tired to help themselves. In some cases, nongovernmental organizations are playing a much-needed role as advocates.

The economy and politics of the region are complex and not easily resolved. But some countries, such as Poland and the Czech Republic, are thriving. To the extent that equality can be made part of the transition, women and their health will benefit.

See Also

ABORTION; AIDS AND HIV; CONTRACEPTIVES: DEVELOPMENT; DISEASE; ENVIRONMENT: CENTRAL AND EASTERN EUROPE; HEALTH: OVERVIEW; HEALTH CARE: COMMONWEALTH OF INDEPENDENT STATES; HEALTH CHALLENGES; HEALTH EDUCATION

References and Further Reading

Chen, Meei-shia, and Miroslave Mastilica. 1998. Health care reform in Croatia: For better or for worse? *American Journal of Public Health* 88: 1156–1160.

Dolian, Gayanne, Frank Lüdicke, Naira Katchatrian, and Alfredo Morabia. 1998. Contraception and induced abortion in Armenia: A critical need for family planning programs in eastern Europe. *American Journal of Public Health* 88: 803–805.

Hunt, Swanee. Women's vital voices. *Foreign Affairs* 76: 2–7.

MONEE Project. 1999. *Women in transition.* Regional Monitoring Reports. Florence: UNICEF ICDC.

Nowicka, Wanda. Factors affecting women's health in eastern and central Europe with particular emphasis on infectious diseases, mental, environmental, and reproductive health. Draft paper, United Nations, Division for the Advancement of Women. <http://www.un.org/womenwatch/daw/csw/factor.htm>

Giselle Weiss

HEALTH CARE:
North Africa and the Middle East

Unlike the countries of sub-Saharan Africa, which present broadly similar problems with respect to health and health care delivery, it is very difficult to make generalizations regarding the predominantly Muslim countries of North Africa and the Middle East. Economies vary from very poor to very rich, oil-producing nations, although most are mid-

dle income. In a context where health problems more closely resemble those of developed countries than of developing ones, the status of women's health and the conduct of their lives would appear to be more immediately influenced by the rulings of Qur'an and Islamic law. But the interpretation of these rulings can vary.

In the most traditional Islamic countries, for example, a woman must have the written permission of her husband or male guardian to work outside the home or to travel. In the turmoil of the late 1990s, Afghani women were entirely forced out of the public sphere. It is culturally unacceptable for women in many Islamic countries to drive cars, a fact that severely limits their mobility. Yet in modern, liberal countries such as Turkey and Tunisia, women are encouraged to work and to participate in public life. The perpetual political instability of the region, with the displacement and the erosion of social infrastructure it engenders, further confuses the status of women. These countries vary widely in their commitment to health care for women and in their ability and willingness to organize and to pay for it.

North Africa and the Middle East are largely a desert. In rural areas, poor sanitation caused by water scarcity, malnutrition, and infectious diseases are significant problems. Nomadic groups present a particular challenge in terms of health care delivery, but these groups are increasingly diminishing. In more developed areas, chronic diseases come to the fore. In 1999, ischemic heart disease was the major cause of death among adults in these countries, just as it is in the West. In contrast to sub-Saharan Africa, AIDS cases represented less than 1 percent of deaths for the region reported to the World Health Organization (WHO). Environmental pollution presents significant health risks.

The most telling health indicator for the region is its massive population growth. Fertility rates range from 2.9 children per woman in Lebanon to 7.4 in the Republic of Yemen. High fertility means short birth intervals, and the repeating cycles of pregnancy and childbirth take a toll on a woman's health and reinforce her idealized role as a mother. In many high-fertility countries, family planning programs are weak or nonexistent. According to a 1985 survey, although 56 percent of Egyptian women wanted no more children, only 30 percent were using contraceptives, whereas the prevalence of contraceptive use in Tunisia, which began a family planning program in 1964, is 61.2 percent.

Women in many Middle Eastern countries have little if any control over their own bodies and decisions that affect their lives. For example, arranged marriage at a young age, a man's right to easy divorce, and the pressure to bear children all affect a woman's health and freedom to choose. Decisions about whether to seek care may be made not by the woman herself but by family members or members of the community. The needs of sons may take precedence over those of daughters. The belief that after puberty a woman should not be seen by any male other than a close relative further restricts her access to care, owing to a lack of women health care professionals.

This lack is due in large measure to disparities in education between women and men that stem from the cultural emphasis on protecting women from the outside world. Although education in many north African and Middle Eastern countries is compulsory, many children drop out before completing it, and female dropouts sometimes outstrip male dropouts. In Yemen, by the sixth grade, girls constitute only 25 percent of enrollment. This gender gap is also present, though less marked, in Morocco and Egypt. The problem of dropouts affects poor and rural children disproportionately. By age 15, over 90 percent of girls are still in school in Jordan and Lebanon. In Morocco and Yemen, however, less than 50 percent are still enrolled. Illiteracy rates reflect this reality: in Jordan, 30 percent of women are illiterate compared with 74 percent in Yemen.

The types of health care available throughout north Africa and the Middle East depend in large measure on the economic level and political ideology of the country. Most of the Gulf countries, where a combination of high oil income and the tenets of Muslim culture have resulted in a generous welfare system, provide free medical service to all. In many of these countries, the majority of births take place at health care facilities. In contrast, in Afghanistan 90 percent of deliveries take place at home with traditional birth attendants. Women have no access to emergency obstetric care. There is no organized family planning. Throughout the Middle East, even in more affluent countries, the health reporting and information system is weak, particularly with respect to women. Women at the margins—the disabled, the elderly, and prostitutes—are poorly served. Moreover, structural adjustments in external funding are affecting the role of the public sector and government expenditures on services.

Some countries are able more or less to successfully integrate the dictates of Islam and the needs of women. In Oman, for example, antenatal coverage has increased to 98 percent, and over 92 percent of deliveries take place at a health facility. A national policy on birth spacing is made part of maternal and child health services wherever a trained female physician is available. In contrast, although Yemen offers free delivery at health facilities, there are no maternal or perinatal surveillance systems, and motivation among health personnel is low. Maternal mortality is high, at 351 per 100,000 live births. Maternal and family planning services are beginning to be available through nongovernmental organizations.

Improvements to health care for women are less likely to come from a wholesale attempt at cultural reform than through attempts to remove tractable obstacles to access, insofar as that tactic is possible.

See Also

CONTRACEPTIVES: DEVELOPMENT; HEALTH CARE: OVERVIEW; HEALTH CHALLENGES; HOUSEHOLDS AND FAMILIES: MIDDLE EAST AND NORTH AFRICA; ISLAM; POLITICS AND THE STATE: MIDDLE EAST AND NORTH AFRICA

References and Further Reading

Akhtar, Rais. 1991. *Health care patterns and planning in developing countries.* New York: Greenwood Press.

Stromquist, Nelly P., Edith H. Altbach, and Eva Rathgeber, ed. 1998. *Women in the third world: An encyclopedia of contemporary issues.* New York: Garland.

United Nations, Commission on the Status of Women, Preparations for the Fourth World Conference on Women: Action for Equality, Development, and Peace, "Arab Plan of Action for the Advancement of Women to the Year 2000 Adopted at the Arab Regional Preparatory Meeting, held at Amman on 9 and 10 November 1994."
<gopher://gopher.un.org:70/00/esc/cn6/1995/1995—5.en5>

Wallace, Helen M., and Kanti Giri. 1990. *Health care of women and children in developing countries.* Oakland, Calif.: Third Party.

Education in the Middle East and North Africa: A Strategy Towards Learning for Development. Washington, D.C.: World Bank. <http://wbln0018.worldbank.org/mna/ mena.nef>

World Bank. 1993. *World development report 1993: Investing in health.* Washington, D.C.: Oxford University Press.

Giselle Weiss

HEALTH CARE: South Asia

South Asia represents a textbook case of women's complicated and usually poor access to and use of health care. This region also illustrates well the multiplicity of meanings behind seemingly simple words and terms.

What does the term *health care* include? At its most obvious level it encompasses the use of public or private health services to treat illness. But it should also include the use of services for preventive care, particularly for pregnancy and childbirth, as well as types of domestic behavior conducive to health maintenance: nutrition, environmental and personal hygiene, rest, and leisure.

Access is another word with multiple meanings. Even the purely physical measure of the availability of good, affordable services within easily reachable distance is conditioned by cultural and economic factors. For example, most primary (that is, non-hospital-based) health centers in south Asia (and probably in other parts of the developing world as well) follow rigid hours except when dealing with medical emergencies. How does a working woman seek care for herself or her family without losing a day's wages? In this example, women without time-bound employment are at a seeming advantage.

Impediments to Seeking Health Care

It appears from all studies in south Asia, however, that women who are culturally constrained from seeking outside work are also likely to be culturally constrained from visiting a health center, especially one that is staffed by male doctors. These are also the cultures in which it is the most difficult to train and keep female medical and paramedical staffs, especially in rural areas, where they are acutely needed. The majority of poor, culturally traditional women in many parts of South Asia delay seeking medical care when their symptoms are embarrassing, as they are usually perceived to be in any illness connected with the reproductive system, for example. By the time medical care is sought, it is usually too late.

Before finally seeking medical care, many ill women and girls in south Asia typically follow a similar course. First, they ignore their symptoms. Then they try, in succession, home remedies, traditional healers, prescriptions from pharmacies (it is astonishing how many south Asian pharmacists are, in a sense, primary care providers), and finally, if the symptoms persist, western-style medical centers. Inadequacy of medical care, in terms of timing or quality, seems to be the factor most responsible for gender differentials in morbidity and mortality; it is evidently more significant than other kinds of discrimination—in food, attention, and affection, in particular—that girls and women are believed to suffer commonly in south Asian cultures.

To understand the potential for changing this cycle, one needs to examine differences in behaviors associated with seeking health care. The most obvious are economic differences, which tend to be overlooked in attempts to focus on issues of women's autonomy and empowerment. South Asia is a poor region, chronically short of medical personnel, supplies, and infrastructure. Households lack the money, time, and information needed to seek better care. When, despite these obstacles, medical care is finally sought, it is usually

obtained from private practitioners. Yet south Asia is a region notoriously lacking in medical insurance to cover some of the costs of private care.

Consequently, the poor—and poor women in particular—are the losers. However, it is worth noting that boys' and men's health also suffers the ravages of poverty. Young boys are much more likely than young girls to die from accidents such as drowning and to contract and die from tuberculosis. (Why this is so is not entirely clear; very likely it is an occupational hazard of the kind of work to which poor men are relegated.)

Cultural differences also affect attitudes toward seeking health care. The south Asian region is culturally diverse. Women in the southern parts of the region (and, to a lesser extent, the southeastern parts as well) seem to enjoy much greater freedom of movement, autonomy in decision making, continued access to the parental home after marriage, economic productivity, and relatively more equal conjugal relations than women in the north and northwest. Not surprisingly, the latter are also particularly handicapped in the matter of gender differences in health status and outcomes. In north India, in particular, females experience the worst sex differentials in child health and mortality, and sex-selective abortions are used to reduce the number of girls being born.

Possible Solutions

How is this situation to be addressed? One cannot easily change kinship and marriage systems, but there are women-centered solutions that can increase the empowerment of women even in traditional societies. For example, investments to increase the education of girls and women and to increase the economic independence of women would enable women to have greater control over resources and would increase their voice in household decision making. Equally important, women would learn to recognize illness, to be aware of treatment options, and to demand services from providers. The ability to recognize an illness is crucial. In many poor societies, chronic ailments are common; thus it is easy to regard symptoms of ill health as "normal" and to delay seeking medical help until the symptoms worsen considerably. Again, this dismissal of symptoms is most acute for conditions that cannot be discussed openly—a heavy vaginal discharge, for example.

There is much that the state can do to provide more women-friendly health care. Projects using female paramedical workers have succeeded in many parts of the region, especially in Bangladesh. The results are particularly encouraging when these paramedical workers pay home visits instead of waiting for clients to come to them at health centers. However, there is some resistance to such innovations, and an important part of this resistance in south Asia comes from the medical establishment. Unwilling to relinquish authority, physicians' associations have often blocked attempts to train paramedical workers to provide the most basic services and refer only the more complicated cases to the nearest hospital.

Providing health education (and perhaps some basic health services as well) to women and children through community associations such as mothers' clubs is another way to circumvent the impersonality and inefficiency of standard health centers. Preventive programs that stress nutritional supplementation, micronutrient fortification, and immunization at mobile clinics should be encouraged.

What is ultimately needed in south Asia at the state level is a firmer commitment to good health as a basic human right that cannot be eroded by income or gender.

See Also

DEVELOPMENT: SOUTH ASIA; EDUCATION: SOUTH ASIA; ENVIRONMENT: SOUTH ASIA; HEALTH: OVERVIEW; HOUSEHOLDS AND FAMILIES: SOUTH ASIA; POLITICS AND THE STATE: SOUTH ASIA, *I and II*; TRADITIONAL HEALING: INDIA; WOMEN'S STUDIES: SOUTH ASIA

References and Further Reading

Basu, A. M. 1992. *Culture, the status of women and demographic behavior.* Oxford: Clarendon.

———. 1997. Underinvestment in children: A reorganization of the evidence on the determinants of child mortality. In G. W. Jones, R. M. Douglas, J. C. Caldwell, and R. M. D'Souza, eds., *The continuing demographic transition,* 307–331. Oxford: Clarendon.

Caldwell, J. C., I. Gajanayake, P. Caldwell, and I. Pieris. 1989. Sensitization to illness and the risk of death: An explanation of Sri Lanka's approach to good health for all. *Social Science and Medicine* 28(4): 365–381.

Caldwell, J. C., P. H. Reddy, and P. Caldwell. 1983. The social component of mortality decline: An investigation in south India employing alternative methodologies. *Population Studies* 37(2): 185–205.

Chatterjee, M. 1991. *Indian women: Their health and productivity.* Discussion Paper 109. Washington, D.C.: World Bank.

Chen, L. C., E. Huq, and S. D'Souza. 1981. Sex bias in the family allocation of food and health care in rural Bangladesh. *Population and Development Review* 7(1): 55–70.

Leslie, J., and M. Paolisso, eds. 1989. *Women, work and child welfare in the third world.* Boulder, Colo.: Westview.

National Research Council. 1997. *Reproductive health in developing countries: Expanding dimensions, building solutions.* Washington, D.C.: National Academy Press.

Santow, G. 1996. Gender differences in health risks and use of services. In United Nations, *Population and women.* New York: United Nations, Population Division.

Alaka Malwade Basu

HEALTH CARE: Southeast Asia

Southeast Asia is a vast region with a complicated history. Its social, cultural, and economic diversity probably is unmatched anywhere else on earth. It encompasses countries such as Brunei and Singapore, whose health and developmental profiles rival those of the industrialized West, and Cambodia, Lao PDR, Myanmar, and Vietnam, which are among the poorest nations in the world. A few countries—Thailand, for example—occupy a middle ground: these are countries in transition.

The health status of women in southeast Asia and of women in other regions is similar in that some diseases are unique to women and others have different effects on women than they have on men. Moreover, poverty, birthrates, aging, discrimination, and violence affect the health of women everywhere. But the health of women in southeast Asia also is affected by life in a tropical climate and by the combined legacies of colonialism and of strong traditional cultures. Despite considerable gains in some parts of the region, views of gender, family structure, and social hierarchy underlie the overall struggle of southeast Asian women to survive.

A historical focus on family planning has neglected other issues of women's health. Poliovirus, a disease of poverty and crowding that is no longer feared in the West, has yet to be eradicated in southeast Asia. Anemia, malnutrition, and malaria contribute to complications from birth, abortion, and delivery, which are frequent causes of hospital admission. One-fifth of maternal deaths in Cambodia are due to malaria. Limited access to clean drinking water and latrines cause typhoid and cholera. Female genital mutilation, which is practiced in parts of Indonesia and Malaysia, has both short- and long-term psychological and health consequences.

Although total fertility rates have declined throughout the region, they are still high at an average of 3.37 children per woman. In Cambodia, the figure for 1991 was five births per woman, and in Lao PDR it was six. The number of unwanted pregnancies suggests that even though contraceptive services are widely available, women are not being educated about reproductive choices and family planning. In Myanmar, for example, abortion is illegal, and contraception and sterilization are not actively promoted. In contrast, Vietnam has a national reproductive goal of two children per family with five years between them. Abortion is legal during the first three months and done free in almost all district and provincial hospitals. Between 1990 and 1997, the total fertility rate in Vietnam decreased from 5.0 to 2.4 per woman. Maternal mortality for the same period was at 105 per 100,000 live births, dramatically lower than in Lao PDR, where it is 660. With some exceptions (Vietnam is one), reliance is high throughout southeast Asia on traditional birth attendants, who are often cursorily trained. From 1983 to 1987, only 43 percent of Indonesian childbirths were attended by a trained midwife or doctor.

Southeast Asia is poised to become the next epicenter of HIV (the virus that causes AIDS) infection, and rates in Thailand are the highest in the world. National and international sex tourism, women migrating within countries and across borders as refugees or in search of work, and a growing international sex and drug trade have all contributed to the spread of HIV and other sexually transmitted diseases. In some areas of Cambodia, more than 50 percent of commercial sex workers were infected with HIV.

Natural and man-made disasters also affect the health of women. A series of forest fires in 1997 produced a haze that blanketed the region from Thailand to Irian Jaya. In some locations, the air pollution index far exceeded levels considered to be extremely dangerous to human health. Because women bear the burden of fetching water and firewood, and of certain other kinds of work, they are more exposed to environmental pollution and environmental degradation than are men. In the Philippines, one-fifth of regular smokers are women, and there is concern that American tobacco companies seeking to avoid a hostile market at home might dump cigarettes on a vulnerable population.

Southeast Asian health care systems are primarily entrepreneurial or welfare or socialist oriented, with a growing trend toward privatization. The type of health system seems to matter less than whether it is adequately funded and services are informally distributed. Although Vietnam is extremely poor and overwhelmingly rural, with all the difficulties that description implies, the vast majority of its people have some kind of access to its socialist health system. Indonesia, another very poor country, has an entrepreneurial health system in keeping with the nation's free-market ideology. But the supply of physicians throughout the nation's 10 main islands and 13,500 small ones is badly distributed. In 1979, a UN agency reported that fewer than 10

percent of rural Indonesians had ever been examined by a doctor. In the Philippines and elsewhere, privatization has affected public hospital services in critical areas such as mental health, leprosy, and tuberculosis. In addition, massive migration of physicians and nurses out of the country forces people to depend on volunteer local village health workers. All such changes have an impact on women, who place their health needs before those of their husbands and children, and who come last when cost is an issue. In Thailand, where all services cost something, overall use of hospitals and health care centers is predictably low.

In some countries, delivery of health care has been disrupted by long-standing civil disturbances. For example, 30 years of war in the Socialist Republic of Vietnam from 1945 to 1975 destroyed the physical infrastructure for health services and for training health personnel. Until the early 1990s, the country was isolated from the West. Essential drugs and medical equipment are in short supply, and doctors and patients alike must travel by bus, bicycle, or pedicab. Still, since 1980, almost all childbirths have taken place in a hospital or other health facility.

Similarly, Cambodia under Pol Pot saw its public health system wrecked and the number of doctors and other health care workers decimated. Unlike Vietnam, however, Cambodia's national services are disorganized. A two-tier system has emerged: a public sector that is underfunded and in disrepair and that consequently few patients use and a private sector that is thriving but unregulated. The maternal mortality rate in Cambodia is 900 per 100,000 live births, nearly nine times that of Vietnam.

In southeast Asia, as in other developing areas, women tend to work informally—from home, as subcontractors, or in part-time positions. This sector is often poorly paid and unregulated, and it puts women at risk for a variety of occupational health hazards. The east Asian economic crisis of 1997 had a disproportionate effect on girls and women, because economic cutbacks affected industries that mainly employ women, such as electronics, textiles, and clothing. In response to the crisis, governments cut back spending for health care and education for women. Thailand reduced the budget for its AIDS programs by 25 percent. In Indonesia, women turned to the sex industry to make money, with a concomitant increase in the incidence of sexually transmitted diseases.

As elsewhere, in southeast Asia questions of health are inextricably bound up with ideas about the roles men and women play in society and about who has power. Women may be physically, sexually, and psychologically abused inside and outside of the family, especially during times of conflict. In Cambodia, so many men have been killed in hostilities that over a fifth of the households are headed by women. Indigenous women, the elderly, and the handicapped bear a double burden of discrimination. A lack of available and reliable data is a further barrier to improving health care for women. Governments continue to rely on indicators such as contraceptive prevalence rates, life expectancy, and maternal mortality rates in identifying and prioritizing women's health needs. But a comprehensive program of health care for women obviously requires a more complex data set.

Although profound inequalities persist, the constitutional declarations of almost all the countries in the southeast Asia include concepts of gender equality under equal rights and obligations of all citizens. In most countries—Lao PDR is a notable exception—women have made strong gains in literacy, but they are still largely excluded from decision making. Women have the right to vote throughout the region, but their representation in legislatures is poor. International standards and conventions relevant for women workers have been slow to find signatories among the countries of the region. Much hope is being placed in new technologies to boost development and the condition of women. But, paradoxically, new technologies are most likely to be advantageous to women with better skills and education. In keeping with new directions in development thinking, any plan that seeks to increase opportunities for women to participate in public life must also seek to reduce poverty, expand health services, and increase education.

See Also

AIDS AND HIV; DEVELOPMENT: OVERVIEW; EDUCATION: SOUTHEAST ASIA; HEALTH: OVERVIEW; REPRODUCTIVE HEALTH

References and Further Reading

Craft, Naomi. 1997. Women's health: Women's health is a global issue. *British Medical Journal* 315: 1154–1157.

Heng, Mam Bun, and P. J. Key. 1995. Cambodian health in transition. *British Medical Journal* 311: 435–437.

Roemer, Milton I. 1991. *National health systems of the world*. Vol. 1, *The countries*. New York: Oxford University Press.

———. 1993. *National health systems of the world*. Vol. 2. *The issues*. New York: Oxford University Press.

Stromquist, Nelly P., Edith H. Altbach, and Eva Rathgeber. 1998. *Women in the third world: An encyclopedia of contemporary issues*. New York: Garland.

United Nations, Commission on the Status of Women, Preparations for the Fourth World Conference on Women: Action for Equality, Development, and Peace. 1995. "Jakarta Dec-
laration and Plan of Action for the Advancement of Women in Asia and the Pacific adopted by the Second Asian and Pacific Ministerial Conference on Women in Development, held at Jakarta from 7 to 14 June 1994." <gopher://gopher.un.org:70/00/esc/cn6/1995/1995—5.en1>

World Bank. 1993. *World development report 1993: Investing in health*. Washington, D.C.: Oxford University Press.

World Bank. 2000. *World development report 1999/2000: Entering the 21st century—The changing development landscape*. New York: Oxford University Press.

Giselle Weiss

HEALTH CARE: Southern Africa

Southern Africa shares a number of health problems with the rest of the continent, including female genital mutilation (FGM); violence directed against females, such as wife beating and rape; a high incidence of AIDS, including AIDS and HIV infection among pregnant women; other sexually transmitted diseases (STDs); occupational and environmental hazards; and diseases of poverty. South Africa experiences many of the same issues, but health care in South Africa has had certain distinct features and so will be discussed separately.

Southern African Countries

An important part of health care in southern Africa is the work of the World Health Organization (WHO), which has addressed each of the problems noted above in similar ways. WHO has set up regional headquarters, studies, and pilot programs, involving women in every aspect of program planning and implementation. Women have educated other women about these programs, administered to women's needs on all levels, and called attention to aspects of the problems often hidden from men. One example is WHO's project on the interface between AIDS and family planning, which seeks to ascertain attitudes toward STDs (including AIDS/HIV) and unwanted pregnancy, identify preventive strategies that sexually active individuals consider practical, and explore the possibilities and limits of changing individuals' behavior.

In parts of southern Africa, such as Zimbabwe and Botswana, up to 40 percent of pregnant women in towns are HIV positive. In Zimbabwe at the end of the 1990s, the situation was so bad that coffin makers were plying their trade on the streets outside of hospitals. As in some other parts of Africa, a major difficulty in ending the spread of HIV is cultural—denial of the disease coupled with certain traditional practices and inadequate treatment of women. For instance, although several prominent figures, including government ministers, have died of AIDS, the cause of death was not revealed; polygyny is still practiced, so active heterosexual males can spread HIV to numerous women; and black women report that they have difficulty convincing men that using a condom or adopting monogamy does not compromise masculinity (*Economist*, 1997).

Ironically, the end of apartheid in South Africa since 1991 has intensified health problems in the region because many black doctors are being lost to South Africa. For example, about 80 doctors per year leave Zimbabwe for other nations, especially South Africa and Botswana—this is about the same as the number of doctors graduating in Zimbabwe. Although Zimbabwe, Tanzania, Zambia, and Malawi have signed agreements limiting the number of doctors who can leave one country in the region to work in another, South Africa has not joined them.

Southern African governments have recommended several preventive measures aimed especially at women. One focus is occupational health. Legislation regarding occupational health and safety has often been ignored; moreover, much of this legislation regulates mines, where women have worked rarely, if ever. Changes needed to protect women include legislation covering both physical and mental health; maternity leave; representation of women at all levels of health care and on all health-related committees; workers' compensation for injuries (men too need this); protection against toxic and otherwise harmful substances; preventive and educational health services; rehabilitative services; and child care in the workplace.

South Africa

Because of the long history of apartheid—legalized, institutionalized racial discrimination—in South Africa, its health care system must be seen in a political and economic context. Apartheid fragmented the health system, leaving blacks with inadequate care. Moreover, South Africa combines with discrimination the consequences of industrialization, poverty, and social instability: a high incidence of heart disease and cancer, mainly among whites, and endemic patterns of preventable diseases among the majority black population. The leading cause of ill health is a lack of basic requirements such as adequate housing, safe water, and sanitation. In South Africa, then, health care has features characteristic of the developed world side by side with features typical of the third world. Among white South Africans we find patterns like those in developed countries: low infant mortality and high life expectancy. Among black South Africans we see patterns like those in developing countries:

high infant mortality and low life expectancy. All these generalizations, of course, affect women.

Under apartheid, health services were limited, and for the disadvantaged they were basic and primitive. Overall, the health system has been biased in favor of curative care and the private sector, and even these services were generally inefficient and inequitable. There has been little or no emphasis on how to achieve and maintain health; the emphasis has been on medical care. The postapartheid government has found it expensive and difficult to reverse these trends.

As regards women, diseases related to poverty have the greatest impact on blacks: cholera, typhoid, kwashiorkor, tuberculosis, pneumonia, bilharzias, trachoma, and rheumatic heart disease. Sexually transmitted diseases (STDs, including AIDS), substance abuse, and related diseases are most prevalent in black communities. Black women are affected by the migrant labor system because husbands who are migrant workers are away for most of the year and then bring back diseases from urban centers—particularly STDs and tuberculosis. By contrast, diseases related to industrialization affect all classes but mainly whites: cardiovascular diseases, cancers, and psychiatric conditions. For whites, the major causes of death are chronic degenerative diseases, especially cancer, and circulatory diseases.

South Africa's health service structure was desegregated in May 1990 but is still geared toward the disease patterns of whites: the bulk of the resources are spent on expensive high-technology diagnostic and curative procedures. Health services for industrial workers are often designed to prevent them from taking time off the job rather than to improve their well-being. The medical aid programs that do exist are limited to the 20 percent of the population who have private health insurance.

Statistics are of course informative, but it is important to be aware of their terminology and limitations. Until relatively recently, South Africans were categorized, under the Population Registration Act, as white, African, colored, or Indian. Before 1978, there were no national birth or death statistics for blacks; since then, deaths but not births have been reported for blacks. Also, the omission of the former black homelands from national statistics has affected epidemiological data, especially with regard to women's health, because women constituted the majority of the homeland populations (many men having gone to the cities as migrant laborers). With these reservations in mind, we can consider some representative figures.

- Cervical cancer per 100,000 (crude rate, 1987): African, 21.5; colored, 15.8; white, 9.5; Indian, 5.7

- Cervical cancer per 100,000 (age-adjusted rate, 1987): African, 31.6; colored, 22.1; white, 8.6; Indian, 7.1
- Maternal mortality per 100,000 in 1989: Africans, 58; colored, 22, whites, 8, Indians, 5

Statistics such as these reflect a stark fact: South Africa is not meeting the health needs of disadvantaged women. To achieve health, basic needs such as food, safe shelter, and cost-effective energy must be supplied; but in the townships and rural areas where most black women live, both infrastructure and support systems are lacking. Following are a few examples.

The homes of disadvantaged South African women are, in general, poorly ventilated, poorly insulated, and increasingly overcrowded. These women's health cannot be isolated from their living conditions, since most of them are at home most of the time.

The nutritional level of black women is appalling; poverty, poor housing facilities, and lack of education compel black women to eat—and to feed their families—food that supplies very little nutritional value. A paradoxical result is overweight, which is one of the main causes of hypertension.

Problems with water and sanitation are pervasive. Not only must women (and others) drink polluted water, but women—who are mainly responsible for fetching water in rural areas—must work very hard to get that water, often traveling a mile or more. In areas where houses do not have water taps, outside taps must be used, and there may be nearly 200 people using a single tap. The provision of safe water is a crucial health measure: a supply of clean water dramatically decreases the incidence of disorders such as typhoid, trichinosis, and skin diseases.

South Africa provides most of the electricity for the subcontinent, but as of the 1990s, 84 percent of its own population was without electricity (Kaiser Foundation, 1991). This too is a health hazard to women, especially in rural areas, where they must walk longer and longer distances, often at some risk to themselves, to gather firewood.

There is a striking difference in maternal mortality rates among white women and black women—and that difference is probably understated, since (as noted above) the figures for black women were underreported until recent years. In fact, maternal mortality has almost been eliminated among white women, while the main causes of maternal mortality among black women remain the same as the causes for white women fifty years ago: hemorrhage, infection, and toxemia.

Lack of education is an important factor: black women, especially rural women, as a result of their low educational levels, have significantly less access to vital information regarding health care—and these women have an increased need for such information because their household duties, such as hoeing, building houses, and cutting and carrying wood, put them at a higher risk of injury, disease, and premature death. Another effect of low education is that many women cannot fulfill certain predominantly female roles in health care: they cannot serve as health educators, cannot teach and model sound health practices, cannot limit family size, and cannot take their children to formal health services.

Lack of health care services is an obvious detriment to health. Often, health care services are inaccessible to disadvantaged women because they are far away: the major hospitals are all in urban areas; rural and semirural areas have few readily available, adequate facilities. White women, not surprisingly, have the best and most plentiful health services—which tend to be underutilized while the services for black women are overcrowded and understaffed. For a black woman, going to a hospital is likely to be a test of endurance requiring endless patience and fortitude; and these demands are made on women who may be very ill.

The Reconstruction and Development Program, recognizing the inefficiency of the system in addressing women's health, has made a number of recommendations (African National Congress, 1994):

- Development of comprehensive women's health care services, including contraceptive services, aimed at the needs of all women throughout the life span.
- Giving priority to women's economic and social status.
- Giving priority to cost-effective screening programs for diseases that affect women, such as carcinoma of the cervix.
- Development of regulations to ensure safe and appropriate termination of pregnancy.
- Legal protection and support and counseling services for women who are victims of violence.

South Africa is a highly industrialized and wealthy country, but the ill health of its black women—who suffer from diseases of poverty, malnutrition, and deprivation—is an urgent issue. Now that national liberation has been achieved, the liberation of women is a goal, and South African women have begun to work to change the system.

See Also

AIDS AND HIV; AIDS AND HIV: CASE STUDY—AFRICA; APARTHEID, SEGREGATION, AND GHETTOIZATION; DEVELOPMENT: SUB-SAHARAN AND SOUTHERN AFRICA;

ENVIRONMENT: SUB-SAHARAN AND SOUTHERN AFRICA; GLOBAL HEALTH MOVEMENT; VIOLENCE: SUB-SAHARAN AND SOUTHERN AFRICA

References and Further Reading

African National Congress. 1994. *A national health plan for South Africa.* Johannesburg (May): ANC.

Burdette, Marcia M. 1988. The role of women. In *Zambia: Between two worlds.* Boulder, Col.: Westview.

Kaiser Foundation. 1991.*Changing health in South Africa: Towards new perspectives in research.* Menlo Park, Calif.: Henry J. Kaiser Family Foundation, November.

Harris, Betty J. 1992. *The political economy of the South African periphery: Cottage industries, factories, and female wage labor in Swaziland compared.* New York: St. Martin's.

Kelly, J. 1990. *Finding a cure: The politics of health in South Africa.* Braamfontein: South African Institute of Race Relations.

Machipisa, Lewis. 1995. Southern Africa: Zimbabwe tries in vain to keep doctors home. *InterPress Service English Newswire.*

Southern Africa's unmentionable curse. 1997. *Economist,* 7 July.

Seedat, A. 1984. *Crippling a nation: Health in apartheid South Africa.* London: International Defense and Aid Fund, April.

Matshediso Rankoe

HEALTH CARE: Sub-Saharan Africa

Women make up nearly 67 percent of the total population of Africa south of the Sahara, and they produce 80 percent of its food. In a country where the majority of the population is young, rural, and poor, health cannot be separated out from poverty and questions of development. Large numbers of women in Africa have no proper sanitation and no access to safe water. Forty-four percent of the African population does not take in enough calories for an active working life. Women can become ill from malnutrition, anemia, intestinal parasites, repeated bouts of malaria, and complications from pregnancy. Domestic violence and household accidents can cause severe injuries, and women's exposure to occupational and environmental health risks is greater than men's. Life expectancy at birth for females is low throughout Africa. In Kenya and Senegal, it is 49 years. Moreover, widespread illiteracy, the social role of women, and their dependency on men have serious consequences for women's health and their patterns of seeking health care.

The simple fact of her sex is disadvantageous to a woman's health, because of the depletion of her resources that results from repeated pregnancy and childbirth. Fertility rates in Africa are high (more than six children per woman), and maternal mortality rates dwarf those of other nations, in some cases reaching 700 women per 100,000 live births. Many women begin to bear children while still in their teens, often before they marry, which increases the toll on their bodies and health. Malnutrition and a variety of mineral deficiencies are common.

Tropical diseases are diseases of poverty. Not only do they cause a high level of disability in a context where rehabilitative care is lacking, but disfiguring diseases such as leprosy, lymphatic filariasis, and onchocerciasis may affect a woman's or adolescent female's prospects for marriage, her chances for education, and her self-esteem.

In 1999, AIDS was the number one cause of mortality in sub-Saharan Africa. Infection with HIV (the virus that causes AIDS) is distributed roughly equally between women and men, but women contract the disease more easily and die of it more quickly. Pregnant women account for 10 percent of AIDS cases. Because antiretroviral therapy is lacking, babies born to HIV-infected women suffer the effects of their mother's ill health. The ravages of AIDS have long-term implications for family and social structure in Africa. Tuberculosis has increased with the increasing incidence of HIV, and is now the single biggest infectious killer among women.

African women have more frequent histories of sexually transmitted diseases than women in other countries, and more frequent complications of abortions or childbirth. Syphilis is implicated in high rates of stillbirths, and gonococcal eye infections among newborns are 50 times as common in Africa as in industrialized countries. Female circumcision (also called female genital mutilation), which is commonly practiced throughout most of Africa, is a cause of birth complications and has other serious consequences for a woman's health.

Women's health also is affected by their social role in African society. Although sub-Saharan African countries do not register a preference for boy children over girls, as do south and east Asian countries, in some parts of Africa sick sons are treated differently from sick daughters. Almost all decisions having to do with family size, sexual life, and reproduction are made by men. African women tend to their husbands and children before they will request medical care for themselves. And a woman may require her husband's permission to seek medical help, which is believed to be one reason why cases of tropical diseases—which are disabling but largely preventable—are underreported at health facilities.

One of the realities of African life is that men may have many sexual partners and that women sometimes turn to prostitution to supplement their household incomes. Because women have little bargaining power in insisting on the use of condoms or in refusing sex, the culture contributes to putting them at increased risk of contracting HIV and other sexually transmitted diseases.

Despite Africa's high fertility rate, family planning programs are weak or nonexistent. Until recently, African governments opposed contraception on economic grounds. As a result, contraceptive use is lower in sub-Saharan Africa than anywhere else. Many women have never heard of modern methods of birth control. Even when they are familiar with them, they may not know where to get them, or getting them may mean they have to travel far on foot. Still, women desire to space and limit births, particularly educated women and those living in urban areas. Where commitment has been strong, for example, in Zimbabwe, contraceptive use has improved markedly. Here, too, culture shows its influence. Barrenness, subfecundity, and child death may each lead to social ostracism or isolation.

Dissemination of information in rural areas is hindered by insufficient funds and poor delivery systems. In some places, limited funds mean that mental health care must be integrated into primary health care, so health care workers must be trained to recognize mental illnesses. Cultural practices and attitudes can impede health services, for example, women's reasons for choosing or refusing treatment for malaria depend on cost, access to health facilities, attitudes of providers, and cultural beliefs about the cause of malaria. Even when services are available, people may be unaware of them. Monitoring and evaluation systems are substandard.

Given the variety of local health needs and the income level of most African countries, health systems have tended to depend for funding on a mix of governments, donor agencies, nongovernmental organizations, patient contributions, and, increasingly, the private sector. But who pays is only one piece of the puzzle. The major problem of health systems in Africa is their inefficiency. Clinical and outreach programs and services, as well as government services, are plagued by shortages of drugs, transport, and inadequate maintenance. In situations where communications and roads are unreliable, decentralizing services offers solutions for getting appropriate health care to people.

In the spirit of the Bamako Initiative of 1988, women are being recognized as key to a bottom-up approach to restructuring health services. In Kenya, for example, a woman's self-help group receives funds from the government, foundations, corporations, the United Nations, and other countries to develop a number of projects focusing on maternal and child health and clean water. Wholesale reform, however, will depend on balancing inequalities long entrenched in Africa's educational system and in beliefs about the roles of men and women in society.

See Also

AIDS AND HIV; CONTRACEPTIVES: DEVELOPMENT; FEMALE CIRCUMCISION AND GENITAL MUTILATION; HEALTH: OVERVIEW; HEALTH CHALLENGES; HOUSEHOLDS AND FAMILIES: SUB-SAHARAN AFRICA; POLITICS AND THE STATE: SUB-SAHARAN AFRICA; TRADITIONAL HEALING: AFRICA, *I and II*

References and Further Reading

Akhtar, Rais, ed. 1991. *Health care patterns and planning in developing countries.* New York: Greenwood.

Amazigo, Uche. Women's health and tropical diseases: A focus on Africa. Draft Paper, United Nations, Division for the Advancement of Women. <http://www.un.org/womenwatch/daw/csw/tropical.htm>.

Howson, Christopher P., Polly F. Harrison, and Maureen Law, ed. 1996. *In her lifetime: Female morbidity and mortality in sub-Saharan Africa.* Committee to Study Female Morbidity and Mortality in Sub-Saharan Africa, Institute of Medicine. Washington, D.C.: National Academy Press.

Stromquist, Nelly P., Edith H. Althbach, and Eva Rathgeber, eds. 1998. *Women in the third world: An encyclopedia of contemporary issues.* New York: Garland.

United Nations, Commission on the Status of Women, Preparations for the Fourth World Conference on Women: Action for Equality, Development, and Peace, "African Platform for Action Adopted by the Fifth Regional Conference on Women, held at Dakar from 16 to 23 November 1994," <gopher://gopher.un.org:70/00/esc/cn6/1995/1995—5.en2>.

Wallace, Helen M., and Kanti Giri. 1990. *Health care of women and children in developing countries.* Oakland, Calif.: Third Party.

World Bank. 1993. *World development report 1993: Investing in health.* Washington, D.C.: World Bank.

Giselle Weiss

HEALTH CARE: United States

The United States spends more per person on medical care than any other country, yet women are dissatisfied with many aspects of health care. Quality of care varies widely in urban, suburban, and rural areas. Social class and racial inequalities in access to care are well documented. Wide disparities in health status both between and within racial and ethnic groups reflect the health consequences of social class variations in working and living conditions as well as access to medical services. Widespread dissatisfaction with medical care is reflected in the diversity of women's groups involved in the women's health movement and other women's health organizations.

Organization of Health Care

Medical care is provided through loosely organized networks that are composed mostly of private providers. These systems are costly to administer and difficult to monitor for quality. Without a coordinated national health information system, health services research findings on the efficacy and cost-benefit ratio of medical technologies are not disseminated effectively. There is no national or state health service, except for that available to military personnel and their dependents (through CHAMPUS) and to Native Americans (through Public Health Service).

Most women pay for all or part of their medical services through private or publicly financed insurance plans. Many private plans are tied to women's own or a husband's full-time employment; few employers offer part-time workers any coverage. Private insurance outside of employer's group plans is very expensive and generally unavailable to cover preexisting medical conditions. Employer-provided insurance is actually paid for, in part, by employees through monthly premiums, copayments for medical services, and annual deductibles. Lower-income employees pay a much larger proportion of their incomes for insurance and medical care than do higher-income employees.

Overall, 75 percent of the 78.3 million women aged 18 to 64 have some type of private health insurance. Among the 10.1 million women who have income at or below the federally defined poverty level, 42 percent are covered by Medicaid, a federally mandated public insurance program that is administered and paid for largely by the states. Another 2 percent of women have other forms of public coverage; 15 percent have no insurance. All but 1 percent of the 17.6 million women aged 65 and older are covered by Medicare, the federally financed and administered health plan for older Americans and persons with disabilities (Bureau of the Census, 1991).

There are over seventeen hundred private health plans that vary widely in cost and amount of coverage for hospitalization, out-patient visits and preventative services. Eligibility requirements and benefits under Medicaid vary widely in each of the fifty states. Because Medicare has many restric-

tions, many older women purchase supplementary private coverage.

Most public and private insurance plans reimburse on a fee-for-service basis, in which health providers bill for each service rendered. Women increasingly choose—or are forced by employers or state Medicaid agencies—to enroll in health maintenance organizations (HMOs) that provide a comprehensive range of services for a fixed annual fee. To compete with HMOs, networks of doctors and hospitals have formed or joined preferred provider organizations (PPOs) that discount charges for patients who use services within the PPO. The quality and services of HMOs and PPOs vary, so women must investigate plans carefully before joining (see especially the Editors of *Consumer Reports,* 1993).

Health Status

Women in the United States do not enjoy favorable health status compared with women in other industrialized nations. In terms of life expectancy, the United States now ranks in the bottom fourth of 24 industrialized countries, and it has the highest percentage of babies born at dangerously low birth weights (Schieber, Poullier, and Greenwald, 1994: 108). Within the United States, there are wide disparities in health status. As shown in the table on page 978, black women have the highest mortality for all causes except suicide and motor vehicle accidents. Asians or Pacific islanders have the lowest mortality rates, except for deaths due to cerebrovascular diseases. HIV/AIDS disproportionately affects black and Hispanic women, while Native Americans have the highest rates of death from motor vehicle accidents and suicide. Violence has profound effects on all women's physical and emotional health.

Concerns of Diverse Women

Women in different life circumstances have varied priorities for improving access and quality of care. While middle-class white feminists tend to view health from an individualist perspective, women of color tend to view it as inextricably linked to the health of their racial and ethnic communities. Many middle- and upper-income women express concerns about personal choices of physicians, access to emerging medical technologies (for example, new reproductive technologies, experimental cancer treatments), and difficulty with communication with health providers; some are concerned with inadequate scientific evidence of the safety and efficacy of medical technologies. Many middle- and lower-income women who do not have adequate insurance see access to affordable primary care, including reproductive health services, as their primary concern. Women of color,

Age- and cause-specific mortality rates* for selected leading causes of death among women by race: United States, 1989–1991

Age/ Cause	White	Black	Hispanic	Asian or Pacific Islander	Native American
Heart disease [†]					
45 [†]	376	597	271	205	274
Cancer [†]					
45 [†]	380	457	238	215	239
Cerebrovascular [†]					
45 [†]	84	148	69	81	63
Motor Vehicle					
All ages [†]	11	9	10	8	19
Suicide					
15–24	4	2	3	4	8
65 [†]	7	2	3	9	3
Homicide					
15–24	4	19	7	3	8
25–44	4	21	6	4	9
45–64	2	8	3	3	5
HIV					
25–44	2	24	9	1	2
45–64	1	8	4	1	0

*per 100,000 population

[†]age-adjusted

Source: National Center for Health Statistics (1994).

women with disabilities, lesbians, rural women, and other groups experience many deficiencies in existing care systems.

Health activism organizations encompass diverse constituencies of both professionals and lay groups, apparent in the composition of the Campaign for Women's Health (CWH), a coalition of over one hundred groups representing some eight million women. At the state and national levels, members of the CWH are committed to the principles of universal coverage, equal access, mandated comprehensive benefits, accountability and civil rights protections, and provision of services by a wide range of providers in varied settings (Campaign for Women's Health, 1993).

Will Access and Quality Be Widened?

To achieve greater equity in health services will require that women clarify which factors contribute significantly to health and well-being. Widening access also will require setting priorities, because choices will have to be made about services that should be provided universally at various stages of the life cycle. To establish reimbursement priorities, principles such as those set forth by the CWH need to be shared by the population at large.

The need to find common ground among women to establish priorities poses many challenges. Feminist ideologies, theories, and practices are not yet adequate to mediate long-standing but often unacknowledged strains that are rooted in socioeconomic and cultural diversities among women who live in many different states. Societal resistance to addressing rationing directly—on grounds that rationing is socially or morally unacceptable—denies the reality of how health care is currently rationed, that is, on the ability to pay. If women's groups fail to address the issue of rationing directly, they will succumb to maintaining the current inequitable but highly profitable system of acute-care medicine.

See Also

ETHICS: MEDICAL; GLOBAL HEALTH MOVEMENT; HEALTH: OVERVIEW; HEALTH CHALLENGES; HEALTH EDUCATION; LONG-TERM CARE SERVICES; MATERNAL HEALTH AND MORBIDITY; MEDICINE: INTERNAL, *I and II*; NURSING HOMES

References and Further Reading

Boston Women's Health Book Collective. 1992. *The new our bodies, ourselves.* New York: Simon and Schuster.

Bushy, Angeline. 1990. Rural U.S. women: Traditions and transitions affecting health care. *Health Care for Women International* 11: 503–513.

Bair, Barbara, and Susan E. Cayleff, eds. 1993. *Wings of gauze: Women of color and the experience of health and illness.* Detroit, Mich.: Wayne State University Press.

Bureau of the Census. March 1991. *Current population survey.* Washington, D.C.: Bureau of the Census. (Cited in Karen Scott Collins, Diane Rowland, Alina Salganicoff, and Elizabeth Chiat. 1994. *Assessing and improving women's health,* 34–36. New York: Women's Research and Education Institute.)

Campaign for Women's Health. 1993. A model benefits package for women in health care reform. Washington, D.C.: Older Women's League.

Editors of *Consumer Reports.* 1993. *How to resolve the health care crisis: Affordable protection for all Americans.* Yonkers, N.Y.: Consumer Reports Books.

Fee, Elizabeth, and Nancy Krieger, eds. 1994. *Womens' health, politics, and power: Essays on sex/gender, medicine, and public health.* Amityville, N.Y.: Baywood.

Fine, Michelle, and Adrienne Asch, eds. 1988. *Women with disabilities: Essays in psychology, culture, and politics.* Philadelphia, Penn.: Temple University Press.

Muller, Charlotte F. 1990. *Health care and gender.* New York: Russell Sage Foundation.

Ruzek, Sheryl, Virginia Olefin, and Adele Clarke, eds. 1995. *Women's health: Exploring diversities.* Athens: Ohio State University Press.

Schieber, George J., Jean-Pierre Poullier, and Leslie M. Greenwald. 1994. Health system performance in OECD countries 1980–1992. *Health Affairs* (Fall): 100–112.

Stevens, P. E. 1992. Lesbian health care research. *Health Care for Women International* (13): 81–120.

Villarosa, Linda, ed. 1994. *Body and soul: The black women's guide to physical health and emotional well-being.* New York: HarperCollins.

White, Evelyn C., ed. 1994. *The black women's health book: Speaking for ourselves.* Rev. ed. Seattle: Seal.

Sheryl Burt Ruzek

HEALTH CARE: Western Europe

Women in western Europe enjoy a high quality of health care that is reflected in their health status. Compared with women in low-income countries of Africa and Asia, western European women are more literate and have fewer children, and living in an industrialized society frees most of them from routine backbreaking physical labor. Nevertheless, like anywhere else in the world, European women and men are unequal partners: women earn less, hold far fewer managerial and administrative jobs, and they typically have limited political or decision-making power. European women also report more illness than men, and they use medical services more often.

The overall picture of western European women painted by development indicators is that of a well-educated, healthy group with good access to affordable health care. The literacy rate in most of western Europe is close to 100 percent. Life expectancy at birth for women has increased in all countries since 1970. Nowhere does it go below 75 years.

Relatively low fertility rates reach a maximum of 1.9 in Ireland (for 1997), compared with 5.5 in sub-Saharan Africa and 3.5 in south Asia. Maternal mortality (which reflects a woman's overall health) in the period from 1990 to 1997 ranged from 6 per 100,000 live births in Norway and Switzerland to a high of 22 in Germany. These rates are low compared with those in developing countries, such as Indonesia, where poor health and the poverty of health care contribute to maternal mortality rates of 450 per 100,000 live births, or Ghana, where they reach 1,000.

With the exception of Greece and Portugal, all the countries of western Europe are considered affluent and industrialized. In many countries, a person's access to health care is explicitly defined by law or formulated as part of a constitutional right. Health care systems in western Europe support the cost of medical care for all or most of the population.

Welfare-oriented systems, which provide medical protection for a high proportion but not 100 percent of the population, exist in Belgium, France, Germany, Ireland, the Netherlands, and Switzerland. Comprehensive health systems, by contrast, such as those in Britain and Norway, may cover 100 percent of the resident population. With rare exceptions, such as Greece, geographic distribution of doctors in western Europe is equitable, and hospitals are plentiful. Denmark, Finland, Iceland, and Sweden provide a variation of comprehensive health systems.

In western Europe, since the early nineteenth century, expectant mothers, infants, and small children have been accorded special attention as a matter of course. Depending on the type of health system, pregnant women receive care for prenatal clinics, general practitioners, or obstetricians. In Germany, local public health authorities may provide additional services to pregnant women, such as counseling to prevent mental health problems and education to promote general health. Throughout Europe, midwives provide antenatal care and perform most deliveries in hospitals.

Similar to prenatal care, maternal and child health is covered by law in virtually every western European country. In Italy, a regional law requires health services for mothers and children to prevent illness, along with health promotional measures such as encouraging breast-feeding. In France, despite the predominance of the Catholic religion, both contraception and abortion are legal and supported by public funds.

Countries such as France, Belgium, and Italy set high standards for occupational health. In Belgium, laws require employers to make an industrial physician available. Periodic health examinations are more frequent for special groups such as young workers and women and those who must work in particularly hazardous conditions.

Specific needs of women in Europe include programs for family planning, gynecology, maternal and child health, mental health, HIV (the virus that causes AIDS) and other sexually transmitted diseases, and substance use and abuse.

As in other industrialized countries, heart disease and cancer are the leading causes of death among women, and the risk for both can be lessened by changes in lifestyle. Tobacco is responsible for 30 percent of all cancer deaths in developed countries and overwhelmingly the cause of lung cancer, the most deadly cancer for women. Adolescent pregnancy is high in almost all European countries and contributes to complications from abortions.

Although men have higher rates of completed suicide, women make more attempts; they also seek treatment for depression more often than men. The sameness of domestic life, lack of supports, and multiple burdens of working and caring for children and aging parents all contribute to feelings of hopelessness in women. Signs of clinically significant depression, however, may go unnoticed, because it may seem that for women such symptoms are inevitable. Studies in the United Kingdom and in Norway show that one in four women suffers injuries resulting from battering or coercive sex, and domestic violence is underreported, as it is in other parts of the world.

Inequalities in Health Care in Europe

Health in Europe is linked to social circumstances. The poor have shorter life expectancies than wealthier people, and they are more likely to become ill and to die of their illnesses. In the United Kingdom, for example, studies show that women in the lowest social class experience more chronic illness than women in higher socioeconomic groups. In Sweden, life expectancy has been shown to be higher for men and women in nonmanual than in manual occupations. Marginalized groups, such as immigrant workers and the unemployed, are also more likely to suffer from ill health. In the United Kingdom, non-English-speaking immigrants are more likely to die of complications from childbirth, and they may be less likely to benefit from maternity services, which seem uncaring or hostile, even though they have access to these services. Women with diabetes, epilepsy, and cardiac disease are at particular risk for complications of childbirth that may result when care is substandard.

Even in countries where health care coverage is universal, the quality of care and access to it may vary according to gender, and among women it also may vary according to social class and ethnicity. Studies in the United Kingdom have shown women to be less likely than men to receive renal transplants, and they are more likely to die during operations for cardiac bypass surgery. People in lower socioeconomic groups are more likely to work in physical environments that are hazardous. Some major causes of death among women, such as breast cancer, receive relatively little funding for research. Women's use and perception of health care is affected by their experience of poverty, economic dependence, violence, and negative attitudes.

Western Europe is undergoing a profound demographic shift. The fastest growing segment of the population is the very old: in 1998, the proportion of older people in Europe was 20 percent. For the same year, Italy was the oldest country in the world. Although women outlive men, the time they gain may be time spent suffering from chronic illness. Moreover, women have fewer earnings and savings than men and may live out their old age in poverty. Although transport in western Europe is often held up as a model to other industrialized nations, it is frequently inaccessible to the elderly and the handicapped. A lack of rehabilitative services makes very old age that much more difficult. Health systems in the United Kingdom, the Netherlands, and Denmark recognize the needs of the elderly more than those in Greece, Spain, and Portugal, where the burden of care still rests largely with the family.

Feminism and Health Care

Feminist health care politics began in the West, including western Europe, although a feminist agenda now also has been established in many developing nations. In Europe, as in North America, concerns have evolved from reproductive health to reproductive rights, acknowledging the desire of women to have a greater say in priorities for their own health care. Still, the concept of patient participation has not developed in Europe to the same extent as in the United States.

Despite its best efforts, conventional medicine may ultimately be powerless in the face of long-standing intractable problems such as cancer and multiple sclerosis. Patients' recognition of these limitations appears to be fueling the trend toward use of complementary medicine—for example, acupuncture and homeopathy—in countries such as Belgium, France, Germany, Netherlands, and the United Kingdom. Women consult complementary practitioners more than men. Increasingly, complementary medicine is being incorporated into conventional general practice.

As women join the workforce in increasing numbers, the question of who will care for children and older people takes on weight. In the United Kingdom, 15 percent of women in their working years provide full-time care for someone who is sick, elderly, or disabled. To the extent that women assume the triple burden of work for income, household management, and care of children and adults, these responsibilities interfere with health-promoting behavior. Government support of parental leave, part-time work, and job sharing seeks to counterbalance these social changes and, thereby, improve the health of women and families.

See Also

CANCER; DEVELOPMENT: WESTERN EUROPE; DISABILITY AND FEMINISM; ELDERLY CARE: WESTERN WORLD;

HEALTH: OVERVIEW; HEALTH CHALLENGES; HOLISTIC
HEALTH, *I and II;* REPRODUCTIVE HEALTH

References and Further Reading

Craft, Naomi. 1997. Women's health: Women's health is a global
    issue. *British Medical Journal* 315:1154–1157.

Doyal, Lesley. 1995. *What makes women sick: Gender and the
    political economy of health.* Houndsmills, U.K.: Mac-
    millan.

Power, Chris. 1994. Health and social inequality. *British Medical
    Journal* 308: 1153–1156.

Roemer, Milton I. 1991. *National health systems of the world.* Vol.
    1, *The countries.* New York: Oxford University Press.

———. 1993. *National health systems of the world.* Vol. 2, *The
    issues.* New York: Oxford University Press.

World Bank. 1993. *World development report 1993: Investing in
    health.* Washington, D.C.: Oxford University Press.

———. 2000. *World Development Report 1999/2000: Entering the
    21st Century: The changing development landscape.* New
    York: Oxford University Press.

World Health Organization. 1999. *Health 21: The health for all
    policy framework for the WHO European region.* Copen-
    hagen: WHO Regional Office.

Giselle Weiss

HEALTH OF THE WOMEN OF RASTAFARI:
Case Study

Rastafari is a spiritual, cultural, pan-African movement that
emerged out of Jamaica, West Indies, after the era of Gar-
veyism and Ethiopianism. In 1930, the crown prince of
Ethiopia, Rastafari (Prince of Peace), was crowned Emperor
Haile Selassie (Power of Trinity) and King of Kings, Lord of
Lords, Conquering Lion of the Tribe of Judah. A wave of
black consciousness swept the island and created a worldwide
ripple effect—thus the Rastafari movement.

The foundation of Rastafari is the idea of the African
race's redemption by repatriation to Africa. Rastafari advocate self-reliance, economic independence, theocratic governance, African pride and power, and solidarity of all
oppressed peoples.

The Rastafari way of life is patriarchal; its structure and
philosophy are drawn from the Old Testament. A natural,
healthful, holistic lifestyle is an integral component of the
Rastafari doctrine. This is expressed through the wearing of
uncombed locked hair, the use of herbal remedies, and distinctive arts and crafts and in vegetarian eating practices.

Despite the promotion of a holistic approach to healthful living, Rastafari women are increasingly being lured into
the vices of a declining society. An alarming rise in the incidence of sexually transmitted diseases (STDS), the use of
processed foods, and environmental pollution has raised
concerns about all aspects of health.

Relationships between Rastafari men and women are
defined primarily by each couple and are dependent on the
male's concept of the relationship. Some women live within
a polygynist family system in which the "wife" usually
remains monogamous. Issues of STDs and reproductive disorders directly affect their lives, placing Rastafari women in
the same high-risk situations as many other women of
African descent throughout the United States and the
Caribbean.

Vaginitis, human papilloma virus (HPV), ovarian, cervical, and breast cancers, and human immunodeficiency
virus (HIV) are all prevalent. Rastafarian women's
approaches to these illnesses include fasting, prayer, herbs,
diet, and visits to naturopathic and herbal doctors and at
times a conventional health care provider. Prenatal and
neonatal risks, teenage pregnancy, access to labor and delivery services, and hazards related to smoking of the ritual herb
(cannabis sativa—"ganja"—marijuana) during pregnancy
are other significant medical factors that affect the Rasta
women.

Artificial contraceptives, including condoms, have not
been openly accepted by Rastafari women. They are more
receptive to the use of abstention, withdrawal, rhythm, and
herbs to discourage conception. Adequate nutrition is also a
relevant health issue. Even though most Rastafari women are
vegetarians, the young and elder generations may be susceptible to vitamin and mineral deficiencies and malnutrition.

Specific statistics that relate to the health status of Rastafari women, as well as documentation whether the use of
natural and herbal remedies improved health status for
Rastafari, are unavailable. There are several probable reasons
why these data are not readily obtainable, including financial constraints, lack of access in rural areas to medical facilities, lack of routine and annual physician visits, home
deliveries, rejection of medical experimentation on women,
the general distrust of prescribed drugs and the medical
health care system, and a cultural value of isolation from
mainstream society.

Accumulation of these data would promote support for
funding and provide a knowledge base to identify, prevent,
and cure diseases that may be endemic to the Rastafarian
environment. To begin this data process, a collaborative
effort from the naturopath physicians, herbal healers, mid-

wives, and surveyors from the Rasta community would be needed.

See Also

References and Further Reading

Barrett, Leonard E., Sr. 1990. *The Rastafarians 1990.* Boston: Beacon.

Rowe, Maureen. The Woman in Rastafari. *Caribbean Quarterly* 26(4): 13–18.

Ibigail Reid
Yaa Abofraa

HEALTH CAREERS

At the dawn of the twenty-first century, health care underwent a paradigm shift from a disease- and treatment-centered approach to one of prevention and holistic practice. Despite the change in the focus of western medicine, the stereotypes and barriers for women in the health care profession remain intact and are sometimes insurmountable.

Viewing Women as Nurturers

One stereotype is that women are best suited for roles in health care that emphasize their nurturing ability. Whether it is women's desire to nurture or their response to social pressure that gears them to choose nurturing roles in medicine and health, some clear patterns emerge. For example, in the United States 97 percent of nurses are women, while only 36 percent of medical students are women, compared with 3 percent of men who are nurses and 64 percent of medical students who are men. In 2000 U.S. women made up only 19 percent of social scientists, 5 percent of life scientists, and 1 percent of environmental scientists. The relative numbers of women in health-related careers and in policy-oriented and academic science careers is a pattern repeated globally. Some highlighted figures of college enrollment in the sciences are as follows: in Africa 30 percent of those in medicine and health are women, 25 percent in behavioral sciences, and 20 percent in natural

sciences; in Asia 40 percent of those in medicine and health are women, 35 percent in social and behavioral sciences, and 30 percent in natural sciences. Therefore, although the participation of women in science and medicine runs the gamut of careers, women predominantly choose those in the social sciences and in medicine that involve nurturing roles.

The same patterns prevail as one looks below the level of academic discipline to subspecialties of disciplines and professions. In fact, when women become physicians, they tend to select a specialty that requires concentrated nurturing. For example, a study of Saudi Arabian medical students shows a tendency for males to choose general medicine and surgery and for females to choose obstetrics and primary care medicine.

Should women be encouraged to enter the more traditionally male areas within the fields of science, medicine, and health? Or should the focus be upon redefining the caring profession in ways that add value to the roles most often held by women?

One writer suggests, "In our society, the very project of human caring has become compromised. Aside from those important transformative feminists who value and act upon the caring imperative, women's caregiving has become a negative standard against which we measure our progress" (Gordon, 1991). Others fear that exalting the caregiving roles held by women may perpetuate the view that compassion is an integral part of a woman's makeup or even inherently female. This view suggests that the caregiving assignment may not only end up further limiting women's role in science and medicine but keep them involved in direct patient care and absent from decision making and policy positions associated with academic and administration appointments.

Other Obstacles Facing Women in Health

A 1993 study that explored gender bias and the structure of medicine reported that where the hierarchy governs (that is, where males, being at the top, make decisions), many stereotypes of women physicians persist, several forms of which have been observed. Stereotypes often applied to women physicians include

1. The mother—a woman who is not vulnerable to sexual pursuit but isn't rewarded for her job performance. She is valued for nurturing people but is not permitted to have aspirations or to be critical or objective regarding others.

2. The seductress—this woman is highly desirable and the focus of considerable tension. She bears the brunt of unwanted sexual pursuits; her objective job capabilities are distorted.

3. Token pet—this woman is expected to absorb much humor and is devalued but accepted.

4. The iron maiden—this woman avoids and resists other stereotypes and insists on equity. She is regarded as tougher and more militant than she really is; she is respected by the group, but no one helps her (Lenhart, 1993).

These stereotypes clearly limit a woman's ability to be an effective physician, nurse, or medical professor. But stereotypes, although clearly a barrier, are not the only challenge facing women in science and medicine. In fact, the main challenge seems to precede even the choice of a health career: only a third of U.S. women choose science when they enter college. Over the years many reasons have been put forth for women's underrepresentation in science, including lack of ability, innate proclivities, overt discrimination, absence of role models, lack of access to male corridors of power, doubts as to women's abilities, and female socialization that does not encourage assertiveness. A report by Margaret Eisenhart and Elizabeth Finkel (1998) suggested that women demonstrate considerable success when science is transformed, organized, and defined in ways that encourage participation in immediate socially relevant applications. Women have indeed survived in science in nonacademic settings. A major factor seems to be the lack of career advancement when women choose academic medicine or science. For instance, in academia men achieve the rank of full professor in twelve years, whereas women take an average of twenty years. In fact, although 50 percent of academic professionals in U.S. medical schools are female, only 14 percent have risen to the level of professor, compared with a 42 percent professorship rate for men. In terms of salary discrepancy, U.S. women at the doctoral level earned 79 percent of the salaries of their male colleagues. Outside of the external barriers that have kept women from the academy, other personal barriers are evident.

Women's career advancement in science and medicine requires time. It may thus conflict with the time needed for taking care of family responsibilities. A Canadian study elaborates on many barriers confronting women in academic psychiatry, detailing hardships that women face in combining career, marriage, and motherhood (Penfold, 1987). Half of all U.S. medical programs still have no written maternity leave policy or child care facilities for physicians and staff. A U.S. study of women in academic medicine shows that although motherhood could be successfully combined with a career in medicine, it did slow the progress of their careers. In Japan, both women physicians and nurses agree that their roles as wife and mother took first priority. Thus, for women, the largest barriers to professional success are the personal roles that also require a significant time allotment.

The Future

The factors that will affect women in health and medicine in the twenty-first century may be regional. For example, the Philippines had lost 89,000 nurses by 1982 to the United States. Recruiting foreign nurses is a method used by hospitals in the nation's inner cities to replenish the periodic and cyclic shortages of registered nurses. These nurses have higher retention rates, a fact that supports the efficacy of such a strategy. This constant shift in womanpower from the developing nations will ultimately cause shortages that will have an impact on the career choices of women left behind. Widening opportunities will require a replenishing of womanpower.

In the third world, as communities continue to assume considerable responsibility for their health, a large proportion of newly trained health care workers are women. A demand for midwifery, a health profession dominated by women, is on the increase in some places, while in other places this demand is diminishing. The number of midwives in India appears to be shrinking, although this phenomenon may be a reflection of lower birthrates. In Denmark, Sweden, and the Netherlands midwifery is a highly respected and major component of obstetric care, with 34 percent of Dutch women giving birth with the help of midwives (McKay, 1993).

As the twenty-first century continues, the worldwide trend should be for women finally to take their rightful place in providing care to underserved populations, in research centers, in traditionally male fields of medicine, in community health positions, in managerial leadership, and in positions where their expertise and compassion can be valued and respected.

See Also

CAREGIVERS; EDUCATION: GENDER EQUITY; HEALTH: OVERVIEW; HEALTH EDUCATION; HOLISTIC HEALTH, *I and II;* MANAGEMENT; MEDICINE: INTERNAL, *I and II;* MIDWIVES; NURSING; SCIENCE: TECHNOLOGICAL AND SCIENTIFIC RESEARCH; WORK: FEMINIST THEORIES

References and Further Reading

Affonso, D. D., L. J. Mayberry, J. Shibuya, J. Kunimoto, K. Young Graham, and S. Sheptak. 1993. Themes of stressors for childbearing women on the island of Hawaii. *Family Community Health* 16(2): 9–19.

Eisenhart, M., and E. Finkel. 1998. *Women's science.* Chicago: University of Chicago Press.

Gordon, S. 1991. Fear of caring: The feminist paradox. *American Journal of Nursing* 9(2): 44–46.

Henderson, M., and J. A. King. 1992. Morbidity and mortality in women. Department of Health and Human Services, National Institutes of Health Publication no. 92(3457): 51–62.

Lenhart, S. 1993. Gender discrimination: A health and career development problem for women physicians. *Journal of the American Medical Women's Association* 48(5): 155–159.

Levinson, W. 1989. Women in academic medicine: Combining career and medicine. *New England Journal of Medicine* 321(22): 1511–1517.

Long, S. O. 1986. Roles, careers, and femininity in biomedicine: Women physicians and nurses in Japan. *Social Science and Medicine* 22(1): 81–90.

McKay, S. 1993. Models of midwifery. Denmark, Sweden, and the Netherlands. *Journal of Nurse Midwifery* 38(2): 114–120.

National Institutes of Health. 1992. *Women in biomedical careers: Dynamics of change—Strategies for the 21st century.* 1992. National Institutes of Health Publication on Women's Health (NIH Publication no. 94–630).

Perfold, P. S. 1987. Women in academic psychiatry in Canada. *Canadian Journal of Psychiatry* 32(8): 660–665.

Pizer, C. M., A. F. Collard, C. E. Bishop, S. M. James, and B. Bonaparte. 1994. Recruiting and employing foreign nurse graduates in a large public hospital system. *Hospital Health Service Administration* 39(1): 31–46.

Schmittroth, L. 1991. *Statistical record of women worldwide.* Detroit, Mich.: Gale (2nd ed. 1995).

Wilson, M. P. 1987. Making a difference—Women, medicine, and the twenty-first century. *Yale Journal of Biology and Medicine* 60(3): 273–88.

Jean King

HEALTH CHALLENGES

Around the world, women usually live longer than men in the same socioeconomic circumstances. In most of the developed countries, the gap between male and female life expectancy is as high as 6.5 years (United Nations, 1991: 55). Only in a few countries in Asia do women have a lower life expectancy than men. Yet despite their generally greater longevity, women in most communities report more illness and distress.

Studies in a number of developed countries have found that women's own assessment of their health is consistently worse than that of men (Blaxter, 1990; Rodin and Ickovics, 1990). U.S. women are 25 percent more likely than men to report that their activities are restricted by health problems, and they are bedridden for 35 percent more days than men because of acute conditions (U.S. National Institutes of Health, 1992: 9). In community surveys throughout the developed world, women report about twice as much anxiety and depression as men.

Because of their relative longevity, women also use most medical services more often. Deteriorating health and increasing disability are a frequent—though not inevitable—accompaniment of the aging process, and women make up a large proportion of the elderly—especially the "old old" (Doty, 1987). In the United States, 72 percent of those over 85 are female (U.S. National Institutes of Health, 1992: 8). Older women appear to receive less assistance from relatives and friends than older men of the same age, despite the fact that they suffer higher rates of certain disabling diseases, including arthritis, Alzheimer's disease, osteoporosis, and diabetes (Heikkinen et al., 1983).

Evidence from across the developed world also suggests that more women than men bring psychological and emotional distress to their doctors. In the United Kingdom, female consultation rates with general practitioners for depression and anxiety are three and nearly two and a half times, respectively, those of males. There is also evidence from a range of countries that women are at least twice as likely as men to be prescribed minor tranquilizers (Ashton, 1991).

Broadly speaking, then, the picture in the developed countries is one of women living longer than men but appearing "sicker" and suffering more disability. Women are ill more often than men and use more medical services. There are major variations, however, in the health of women in different social groups. In the United States, strokes occur twice as often in black women as in white women, and black women have the highest incidence of gonorrhea and syphilis (U.S. National Institutes of Health, 1992: 13). Although black women have a lower incidence of breast cancer than white women, it is significant that they also are more likely to die from it (U.S. National Institutes of Health, 1992: 13). In the United Kingdom, women in the lowest social classes are much more likely to experience chronic illness than their more affluent counterparts. In a national survey, 46 percent of unskilled and semiskilled women between the ages of 45 and 64 reported a long-standing illness, compared with 34 percent of professional and managerial women (Bridgewood and Savage, 1993).

Of course, it is in the poorest countries that the state of women's health is at its worst, with millions living in a state of chronic debility, afflicted by the diseases of underdevelopment and the hazards of childbearing (Jacobson, 1992; Smyke, 1991). Estimates suggest that for every one of the half-million women who die of pregnancy-related causes each year, at least 16 more suffer long-term damage to their health—an annual total of about eight million (Royston and Armstrong, 1989: 187). Reproductive tract infections are also extremely common (International Women's Health Coalition, 1991). These diseases are not just distressing and disabling themselves but often result in chronic infection with serious effects on women's overall well-being.

Millions of women in the developing world have to cope with the broader health consequences of poverty: communicable diseases and undernutrition. Although women are at risk from the same endemic diseases as men, both biological and social factors may increase women's exposure or worsen the effects. Malaria, hepatitis, and leprosy, for example, can be especially dangerous during pregnancy, while women's responsibility for domestic tasks increases their chances of contracting waterborne diseases.

The extent of undernutrition in girls and women is dramatically documented in the incidence of anemia. Estimates suggest that at least 44 percent of all women in the developing world are anemic, compared with about 12 percent in the developed countries (World Health Organization, 1992: 62). This is an important indicator of general health status, suggesting that many women are chronically debilitated, never reaching the levels of good health that most women in the developed world take for granted.

In conditions of poverty, deprivation, and disruption, mental distress is clearly a major risk. Although there is little statistical evidence of its prevalence, most community surveys in the developing world show a pattern similar to that in the developed countries, with more women than men reporting feelings of anxiety and depression. The pattern of treatment is very different, however, with many more men than women receiving psychiatric help (Paltiel, 1987). Indeed, evidence from many developing countries suggests that women receive less medical treatment of all kinds than men, despite their greater need. Rural women, in particular, often are unable to get access to modern services, even for obstetric care. Around 75 percent of all births in south Asia and 62 percent in Africa still take place without a trained health worker, compared with about 1 percent in the developed countries (United Nations, 1991: 58). While this statistic reflects very low levels of health spending overall, it also suggests a particular reluctance to invest in the health of women and girls.

Although female life expectancy continues to rise in most parts of the world, the "harsh decade of the 1980s and the economic rigors of structural adjustment policies have meant deteriorating health for many women" (Smyke, 1991). The number of women who are malnourished has risen, resulting in an increased incidence of high-risk pregnancies and low-birth-weight babies. Diseases of poverty, such as tuberculosis, are reemerging, while diseases of affluence, such as cancer and heart disease, proliferate. Environmental degradation has made many women's lives harder, and millions are without access to clean water or sanitation. Yet fewer resources are available to care for them. In recent years, a real decline in per capita health spending has been documented in three-quarters of the nations in Africa and Latin America, and women appear to have been the major losers (UNICEF, 1990).

See Also

AGING; DISEASE; GLOBAL HEALTH MOVEMENT; HEALTH: OVERVIEW; HEALTH CARE, *specific entries;* HEALTH EDUCATION; HEALTH OF THE WOMEN OF RASTAFARI: CASE STUDY; LIFE EXPECTANCY; MEDICAL CONTROL OF WOMEN; POVERTY

References and Further Reading

Ashton, H. 1991. Psychotropic drug prescribed for women. *British Journal of Psychiatry* 158 (supp. 10): 30–35.

Blaxter, M. 1990. *Health and lifestyles.* London: Routledge.

Bridgewood, A., and D. Savage. 1993. *General Household Survey 1991.* UK Office of Population Censuses and Surveys.

Doty, P. 1987. Health status and health services among older women: an international perspective. *World Health Statistics Quarterly* 40: 279–290.

Heikkinen, E., W. Waters, and Z. Brzezinski, eds. 1983. *The elderly in eleven countries: A sociomedical survey.* Public Health in Europe no. 21. Copenhagen: WHO Regional Office for Europe.

International Women's Health Coalition. 1991. *Reproductive tract infections in women in the third world: National and international policy implications.* New York: IWHC.

Jacobson, J. 1992. Women's health, the price of poverty. In M. Koblinsky, J. Timyan, and J. Gay, eds. *The health of women: A global perspective.* Boulder, Col.: Westview.

Paltiel, F. 1987. Women and mental health: A post-Nairobi perspective. *World Health Statistics Quarterly* 40: 233–266.

Rodin, J., and J. Ickovics. 1990. Women's health: Review and research agenda as we approach the 21st century. *American Psychologist* 45(9): 1018–1034.

Royston, E., and S. Armstrong. 1989. *Preventing maternal deaths.* Geneva: World Health Organization.

Smyke, P. 1991. *Women and health.* London: Zed.

United Nations. 1991. *The world's women 1970–1990: Trends and statistics. Social Statistics and Indicators,* Series K, no. 8. New York: United Nations.

UNICEF. 1990. *The state of the world's children 1989.* Oxford: Oxford University Press.

U.S. National Institutes of Health. 1992. *Opportunities for research on women's health.* NIH Publication no. 92–3457. U.S. Department of Health and Human Services.

World Health Organization. 1992. *Women's health: Across age and frontier.* Geneva: World Health Organization.

Lesley Doyal

HEALTH EDUCATION

Health education, also known as health promotion, is education about health—a discipline that focuses on the health and well-being of people across the life span, including different developmental stages and ages, genders, cultures, socioeconomic status, and abilities. Health education has its roots in both public education and public health but also draws heavily on the fields of psychology, sociology, biology, and epidemiology. It relies on the biological sciences for much of its content; on the behavioral sciences for its philosophy, program development, and implementation strategies; and on education for its methodology (Rubinson and Alles, 1984; Gilbert and Sawyer, 2000). As a discipline, health education is defined as any combination of learning experiences designed to facilitate voluntary actions conducive to the health of individuals, groups, or communities (Green, 1990).

Historical Perspective

The term *health education* was first proposed about 1919 at a Child Health Organization conference of health and education leaders in New York. The director of the organization, Sally Lucas Jean, suggested that the term *hygiene education* should be replaced by *health education* (Means, 1975). Sixty years later, the National Task Force on the Preparation and Practice of Health Educators was formed to establish a credentialing system for the health education profession. This work, completed over a decade, determined that there were more commonalities than differences in the roles of school health educators and community health educators (Taub, 1994). In 1988, the National Task Force on the Preparation and Practice of Health Educators became the National Commission for Health Education Credentialing (NCHEC). As an independent, not-for-profit agency, NCHEC has three purposes: (1) to certify health education specialists, known as

CHES; (2) to promote professional development of health educators through continuing education; and (3) to strengthen the professional preparation of health educators at colleges and universities.

Health educators practice in a variety of settings using the basic skills or competencies defined by NCHEC. Work settings include schools and universities; governmental agencies and community organizations; work sites and corporations; and hospitals and clinics. Regardless of work or practice settings, entry-level health educators share competence in seven processes: (1) assessing individual and community needs for health education; (2) planning effective health education programs; (3) implementing health education programs; (4) evaluating effectiveness of health education programs; (5) coordinating provision of health education services; (6) acting as a resource person in health education; and (7) communicating health and health education needs, concerns, and resources.

Health Promotion, Disease Prevention, and Behavioral Risks

Health promotion and disease prevention are important concepts in health education. Prevention efforts include primary prevention, secondary prevention, and tertiary prevention. Each of these three levels of prevention requires a different set of objectives and interventions. Primary prevention, also known as health promotion, emphasizes personal choices, behavior, and lifestyle. Education is crucial to health promotion efforts. Reeducation is important during interventions in which individuals experience secondary or tertiary levels of disease prevention. Secondary prevention relies on a medical model for early detection and screening of a disease or disorder, followed by clinical intervention if needed. Tertiary prevention also relies on the medical model by focusing on rehabilitation and treatment.

Since about 1980, the U.S. Public Health Service has tracked and reported on the health status of Americans through a series of national health objectives known as *1990 Objectives to the Nation, Healthy People 2000,* and *Healthy People 2010.* Health educators in all work settings now derive their content from *Healthy People 2010,* which contains health promotion and disease prevention objectives for the nation.

Effective health promotion activities focus on reducing behavioral health risks that begin in early adolescence. The Centers for Disease Control and Prevention (CDC) of the U.S. Department of Health and Human Services has identified six priority risk behaviors that endanger adolescents. These high-risk behaviors include unhealthy dietary patterns; inadequate physical activity; tobacco use; alcohol and other drugs; sexual behaviors that can result in HIV infection, other sexually transmitted diseases, and unintended pregnancies; and behaviors that can result in intentional and unintentional injuries. Reducing the prevalence of these risk factors is essential to reducing the chronic disease burden facing Americans.

Adolescent morbidity and mortality are rooted in health-risk behaviors. Educational interventions that focus on the development of personal and social skill competence (Drolet and Fetro, 2000) show promise for reducing high risks to health. Personal and social skill competence includes communication skills, decision-making skills, goal-setting skills, and stress management skills.

Program Planning

Health educators are recognized for their competencies in program planning (Simons-Morton, Greene, and Gottlieb, 1995; Office of Disease Prevention and Health Promotion, 1993). One public health program with national support includes the Coordinated School Health Program (CSHP) model (Allensworth and Kolbe, 1987; Marx, Wooley, and Northrop, 1998). The CSHP model promotes intraprofessional collaboration for improving the health status of children and youth on the local level. The model consists of eight interactive school-community components, including health education; physical education; health services; nutrition services; health promotion for staff; counseling, psychological, and social services; healthy school environment; and parent and community involvement. Because CSHP can have a positive impact on health-risk behaviors, many national, state, and local health and education organizations have supported this program model.

Disciplinary Challenges

Health education's relationship to the field of education is still developing. Educational principles and methodologies are important in the design of educational interventions in health education. Currently, many conceptual frameworks and curriculum models exist, but the field still needs to establish a more theoretical foundation for the development of educational programs and curricula. A related challenge includes balancing the uniqueness and contributions of public health theories (Glanz, Lewis, and Rimer, 1997) with more public education theories (Ubbes, Black, and Ausherman, 1999) in order to integrate and advance the profession of health education. In preK–12 (prekindergarten through twelfth grade) education, health education needs to align itself further with other school disciplines such as science, social studies, mathematics, language arts, music, art, and physical education. Shared interests in curriculum, instruc-

tion, and assessment among these disciplines will help learners "to know and be able to do" certain facts and skills called performance indicators.

Curriculum Frameworks and Structures

The National Health Education Standards (Joint Committee on National Health Education Standards, 1995) are used as a framework for K–12 curriculum development. The standards seek health outcomes that will support learners to (1) comprehend concepts related to health promotion and disease prevention; (2) demonstrate the ability to access valid health information and health-producing products and services; (3) demonstrate the ability to practice health-enhancing behaviors and reduce health risks; (4) analyze the influence of culture, media, technology, and other factors on health; (5) demonstrate the ability to use interpersonal communication skills to enhance health; (6) demonstrate the ability to use goal-setting and decision-making skills to enhance health; and (7) demonstrate the ability to speak out for personal, family, and community health.

Health education curricula in schools have three structures: comprehensive, categorical, and integrated. Comprehensive curricula include a documented, planned, and sequential program of health instruction for students in preschool through grade twelve. Comprehensive health education curricula are more successful if they are behaviorally focused and skill based and are developmentally appropriate and culturally sensitive; involve families and the community; are supported by school policy; and involve peers in program decisions (Marx and Northrop, 1995). Comprehensive curricula include a scope and sequence framework of ten traditional health topics that are developmentally appropriate for children throughout the elementary, middle school, and high school years.

Categorical curricula help young people to develop personal and social skills in order to avoid health problems associated with high-risk behaviors. Effective categorical health curricula are named *Programs That Work* from the CDC. Key elements of successful prevention programs require that they are theory based and research driven; examine perceived risks, internal influences, and external influences; focus on developmental needs; emphasize short-term consequences; and focus on personal and social skills.

Integrated curricula are suggested as one strategy for increasing instructional time in health education, building and extending from comprehensive and categorical curricula that should be the main focus of health instruction. Integrated curricula are especially promising in elementary schools where health literacy can be connected to other academic areas, for example, science literacy.

Maximizing time for health instruction in schools is important because research from the School Health Education Evaluation in 1985 found that benefits in behavioral and attitudinal outcomes were achieved at about fifty classroom hours per year but that knowledge outcomes were possible within twenty classroom hours of instruction. Since knowledge gains are not enough in health education, instructional programs need to focus on health behavioral outcomes.

Health Education As It Pertains to Women

The first nationwide movement for health instruction in public schools was initiated by the Women's Christian Temperance Union, founded in 1874. The temperance organizations promoted legislation that would require teaching about the effects of alcohol, tobacco, and narcotics (Means, 1975). Health instruction over the years has expanded into consumer health, community health, nutrition, sexuality education, growth and development, safety and accident prevention, disease prevention, physical activity, and mental health.

Traditionally, health education is taught as a personal health course to a coeducational audience. Occasionally, boys and girls are separated into different classes when discussing topics of sexuality during prepubescence; however, there are many reasons to include both boys and girls in the educational discussions about the opposite sex—namely, to avoid the misconceptions that evolve from gender-specific lessons about reproduction, sexuality, and growth and development.

Health instruction should address the different responses to illness of men and women. Gender differences in disease presentation, progression, and response to therapies must be determined through more clinical studies that are also inclusive of women. Women have unique health needs even apart from breast and gynecological cancers, including menstruation, reproductive health, unwanted pregnancies, and sexually transmitted diseases. Women have a higher incidence of eating disorders—obesity, anorexia nervosa, bulimia—due to increased concerns about body image. Unfortunately, adolescent women have increased their use of cigarettes as a form of weight control despite the fact that tobacco use is the number one preventable cause of death. Skin cancer rates have increased among young women; they too are related to issues of body image and stereotypical media messages.

Women have higher rates of osteoporosis, iron-deficiency anemia, and diabetes because of their unique biological, physiological, and psychological profiles. Heart disease is the number one killer of American women.

Although it is typically viewed as a man's disease, more women than men actually die of heart disease each year. The most common disabling condition reported by women is arthritis. Half of all people affected by arthritis are under the age of 65, but by age 65, about 80 percent of all women report some problem with arthritis.

The U.S. Department of Health and Human Services has an Office of Women's Health that promotes the National Women's Health Information Center. The challenge it is trying to meet is to establish a scientific knowledge base that will permit reliable diagnoses and effective prevention and treatment strategies for all women, whatever their cultural and ethnic origins, geographic locations, and economic status may be (Pinn, 1995). Its Health Information for Minority Women Web site (http://www.4woman.org/minority/index.htm) features unique resources for African-American women, American Indian and Alaskan Native women, Asian and Pacific islander women, and Hispanic and Latina women.

Global Perspectives about Health Behavior

From a global perspective, various types of health behavior during the educational process must be investigated from multiple points of view. Health educators ultimately investigate the health behavior of individuals and groups as they assess, plan, implement, and evaluate educational programs and resources. For example, in the health-related behavior of eating, health educators raise the following issues: What is positive eating? What are the barriers to healthful eating? With whom do people eat, and what are the psychosocial and sociocultural effects of eating? Why do people eat, and what are the physiological effects of food on physical, social, intellectual, emotional, and spiritual health? What are the effects of media, technology, and consumerism on eating behaviors?

Some other types of health behavior that are important to health educators involve physical activity, safety, sexuality, drug use, and disease prevention. People of all backgrounds need to be supported as they try to understand why individuals and groups differ about various health topics, including how physical health, social health, emotional health, spiritual health, and intellectual health are integrated for wellness (Greenberg, 1985). In particular, health education needs to accommodate the developmental needs, preferences, and intentions of the learners. Similarly, health education should take into account gender and cultural differences and adapt interventions to the special needs of people with disabling conditions, limited language proficiencies, and inadequate finances (Bogden, 2000).

"Health and social problems are now recognized as being highly interconnected. Relatedly, many chronic health problems have proven themselves largely to be the product of lifestyle, modifiable only through changes in the environment and the social norms of the population" (Simons-Morton, Greene, and Gottlieb, 1995). Hence, prevention efforts in health education are frequently more cost effective than curative approaches in medicine.

See Also

GLOBAL HEALTH MOVEMENT; HEALTH CHALLENGES

References and Further Reading

Allenworth, Diane D., and Lloyd J. Kolbe. 1987. The comprehensive school health program: Exploring an expanded concept. *Journal of School Health* 57: 409–412.

Bogden, James F. 2000. *Fit, healthy, and ready to learn: A school health policy guide. Part I: Physical activity, healthy eating, and tobacco-use prevention.* Alexandria, Va.: National Association of State Boards of Education.

Drolet, Judy C., and Joyce V. Fetro. 2000. *Applications for personal and social competence.* Santa Cruz, Calif.: ETR Associates.

Gilbert, Glen G., and Robin G. Sawyer. 2000. *Health education: Creating strategies for school and community health* (2nd ed.). Boston: Jones and Bartlett.

Glanz, Karen, Frances Marcus Lewis, and Barbara K. Rimer. 1997. *Health behavior and health education: Theory, research, and practice.* 2nd ed. San Francisco: Jossey-Bass.

Green, Lawrence W. 1990. *Community health.* St. Louis, Mo.: Times Mirror/Mosby College Publishing.

Greenburg, Jerrold S. 1985. Health and wellness: A conceptual differentiation. *Journal of School Health* 55(10): 403–406.

Joint Committee on National Health Education Standards. 1995. *National health education standards: Achieving health literacy.* American Cancer Society.

Marx, Eva, and Daphne Northrop. 1995. *Educating for health: A guide to implementing a comprehensive approach to school health education.* Newton, Mass.: Education Development Center.

Marx, Eva, Susan Frelick Wooley, and Daphne Northrup. 1998. *Health is academic: A guide to coordinated school health programs.* New York: Teachers College Press.

Means, Richard K. 1975. *Historical perspectives on school health.* Thorofare, N.J.: Slack.

National Commission for Health Education Credentialing, I. 1996. *The competency-based framework for professional development of certified health education specialist.* Allentown, Penn.: NCHEC.

Office of Disease Prevention and Health Promotion. 1993. *School health: Findings from evaluated programs.* Washington, D.C.: U.S. Department of Health and Human Services.

Pinn, V. W. 1995. Equity in biomedical research. *Science* 269.

Rubinson, Laura, and W. F. Alles, eds. 1984. *Heath education: Foundations for the future.* St. Louis, Mo.: Times Mirror/Mosby.

Simons-Morton, Bruce G., Walter H. Greene, and Nell H. Gottlieb. 1995. *Introduction to health education and health promotion.* 2nd ed. Prospect Heights, Ill.: Waveland.

Taub, Allison. 1994. *Credentialing: Assuring quality in school health education.* In Peter Cortese and Kathleen Middleton, eds., *The comprehensive school health challenge: Promoting health through education,* Vol. 2, 835–858. Santa Cruz, Calif.: ETR Associates.

Ubbes, Valerie A., Jill M. Black, and Judith A. Ausherman. 1999. Teaching for understanding in health education: The role of critical and creative thinking skills within constructivism theory. *Journal of Health Education* 30(2): 67–72, 135.

Windsor, Richard, Tom Baranowski, Noreen Clark, and Gary Cutter. 1994. *Evaluation of health promotion, health education, and disease prevention programs.* 2nd ed. Mountain View, Calif.: Mayfield.

Valerie Ubbes

HERBALISM

See TRADITIONAL HEALING: HERBALISTS.

HEREDITY AND ENVIRONMENT

See NATURE-NUTURE DEBATE.

HERESY

The word *heresy* comes from the Greek *haerens,* meaning "an act of free choice." This meaning is far removed from the understanding that has more popularly been applied to the word. The history of virtually all religions is littered with the hounding of heretics that led to their deaths or banishment. Any person who chose to believe something that was not sanctioned by an institutional church was considered a heretic. The hierarchical church has historically prescribed doctrine and set the penalties for diversion from that "norm." Church leaders have also, for the most part, been the writers of history. Those who have been described as heretics, therefore, have either been written out of history or represented through the eyes of those who are their detractors. In either case, heretics have had little chance to explain their act of free choice and are instead portrayed as evil and antisocial.

Many view the church as the guardian of absolute truth and as an institution dedicated to disseminating the truth through love and faith. In this light, the church is seen as safe and powerful. Heretics, therefore, are seen as unholy people who are trying to pervert the course of holy history. They are considered maliciously misguided, or deluded fools; some have been thought to be in league with the devil. It is interesting to note that many so-called Christian heresies were either led by women or involved what feminists see as a positive view of women in society and the church. Indeed, the positive position of women was often seen as the heresy itself. It is surprising then that heresy has not been a major area of feminist research.

Some recent research suggests that the Jesus Movement was more concerned with conduct than with orthodoxy. These early followers of Jesus, it is alleged, focused on action and not belief, since they understood the kingdom of God to be one of equality and justice, not simply some orthodoxy. In the early centuries of Christianity, popular, supported ideas were often later declared heretical, while others that were not given much credence later became accepted doctrine. Two such examples are Arianism and Patripassianism. The former was at one time seen as quite orthodox, while the latter was for centuries viewed as heretical and has recently grown in acceptance. Arianism was the doctrine proposed by Arius that Jesus had not always been divine; it was condemned at the Council of Nicaea in A.D. 325. Patripassianism was a third-century view that God the Creator became fully human and therefore suffered. While some believe that doctrine should be subject to change because the nature of truth is so difficult to define, others believe the definition and redefinition of doctrine is as much a political as a religious activity.

This phenomenon is evident in Christianity itself. In the early fourth century, under the Emperor Constantine, the Christian wish to become accepted by the Roman Empire became a reality. As a result, the church also reassessed its role and began to understand itself in a more legalistic light. Rule keeping and conforming to norms replaced charism and prophecy. Tolerance of free spirits who, through their belief, questioned assumptions and pushed societal religious boundaries, rapidly diminished, and the church, instead of influencing the state, became influenced by it, taking on many characteristics of a political body. One of the most noticeable such characteristics was the wielding of power to gain more hierarchical control. Ever since, the

concept of heresy has helped the church to exert the same legalistic and hierarchical power for over a thousand years. The power to define what others should believe and then to punish the transgressors is power indeed. To mold certain ways of thinking by promoting certain beliefs is a very powerful form of social control. With the rise of Jewish, Christian, and Islamic fundamentalism, one may see many examples of how societies can be molded by belief and how dire the consequences can be for transgression from that norm.

Those religions that have the strongest notions of absolute truth are those that also have the most clearly defined ideas of heresy; Christianity, Judaism, and Islam are the obvious examples. Each religion has elaborate ideas about how its faithful should act. A claim of heresy, therefore, can be a powerful political tool, a notion through which society can be molded and controlled.

No longer the idea of acting with free choice, heresy has moved into the realm of absolutes and power over others. It has, over the years, made those religions that employ it religions of ortho*doxy* rather than ortho*praxis*.

Feminist theologies take as their starting point the experience of women in creating theology. By placing female experience at the center of the creation of theology, a revolution is effected, and the traditional concept of heresy is called into question. The power of the few to define matters of religion for the many is challenged, raising the possibility that there may not be an absolute truth after all but rather a number of ways of viewing reality. For this reason feminist theology is itself viewed as heresy by its opponents on the religious right, the forces of societal and religious conservatism. In declaring that there is an act of free choice in reflecting upon and defining one's way of believing, feminist theology sees itself as championing the original meaning of the word *heresy*. It furthermore suggests that politics are involved in the definitions of religious belief and tries to redress the balance by challenging dominant power. Feminist theology, however, acknowledges its own political stance, in which it views the personal as political.

Feminist theologies have not developed their own notion of heresy and probably will not develop one. There is, however, a tendency to declare as outdated many of the foresisters of the movement. The movement acknowledges that change is necessary if theology is to speak to the reality of people's lives. The very diversity of experience within feminist theology makes a definition of heresy almost impossible. The concept of heresy has held people in religious infancy for fear of transgression; the vision of feminist theology is that people will become empowered and debilitating doctrine eliminated. Once considered heretics, people unafraid to push the boundaries of patriarchal thinking to the limits and beyond in search of a more inclusive and whole way of being are embraced in feminist theology.

See Also

CHRISTIANITY: FEMINIST CHRISTOLOGY; CHRISTIANITY: STATUS OF WOMEN IN THE CHURCH; RELIGION: OVERVIEW; THEOLOGIES: FEMINIST; WITCHES: WESTERN WORLD

References and Further Reading

Lambert, Malcolm. 1998. *The Cathers.* Oxford: Blackwell.
———. 1992. *Medieval heresy.* Oxford: Blackwell.
Logan, Alastair H. B. 1996. *Gnostic truth and Christian heresy: A study in the history of Gnosticism.* Edinburgh: T. and T. Clark.
Ludemann, Gerd. 1996. *Heretics: The other side of early Christianity.* London: SCM.
Wakefield, Walter. 1991. *Heresies of the Middle Ages: Selected sources.* New York: Columbia University Press.

Lisa Isherwood

HEROINE

The word *heroine* is taken directly from classical Greek, where it is one of several occurring feminine forms of *heros* ("hero"). Heroes and heroines were entities who occupied a special place in the ritual life of the Greeks during the first millennium B.C. and probably before that. Although modern readers think of them as characters in myth and legend, for the ancient Greeks they were real people who had lived and died in specific places. The events of their lives became celebrated in oral tradition, and their real or purported burial sites became the locations of regular observances, a cultural phenomenon now known as heroine and hero cults. The appellation *heroine* was not given to living women; heroines were by definition deceased persons—spirits existing in the afterworld or semidivine entities. In later classical and Hellenistic Greece, tomb inscriptions indicate that the title was more widely appropriated on behalf of dead women, whom the epitaphs call heroines, or the deceased are said to "become Hekate" (a goddess of the underworld), much as deceased ancient Egyptians "became Osiris" (an underworld god).

Evidence for heroine cults comes from literary and archaeological sources. Contemporary documentation is given primarily by Pausanias, a traveler and geographer of the second century A.D., whose *Description of Greece* includes many notes on local hero and heroine cult observances and monuments. (The Roman poet Ovid's *Heroines* uses the sto-

ries of notable women of mythology to develop themes of romantic love in epistolary verse.) Other information comes from inscriptions and from depictions on reliefs and ceramics.

Scholars studying hero cults once theorized that heroines had been the goddesses of small regional populations but had "decayed" in the public mind as they were replaced by the deities of other peoples during the many waves of migration that swept through the eastern Mediterranean between 5000 and 1000 B.C. Jennifer Larson (1995), in a careful and fascinating study, contradicts this view and demonstrates that cult heroines probably originated in a variety of ways. The largest category she identifies includes mothers, wives, lovers, and daughters of male heroes, who were usually worshipped together with their male kin but might have separate observances. Those who do not have narrative relationships with male figures are anomalous women in their social context: virgins who die by sacrifice, suicide, or some other sudden, violent act; priestesses, huntresses, or warrior women like the Amazons, who assume typically male roles; exotic wanderers from afar; etiological heroines, the protagonists of narratives created to explain the origin of some place or institution; women believed to have become divine, often through sexual relationships with gods; and historical figures who achieved some notable deed, such as saving a city from attackers.

Communities apparently chose as their heroines women whose fame lent significance and importance to the sites with which they were associated—an impulse apparent today where people visit the home of George Eliot or the grave of Princess Diana. Classical heroines were honored by offerings of animal sacrifices and other foods at shrines, particularly on annual dates specified in local ritual calendars. After being symbolically given to the honoree, the offerings were usually consumed by the celebrants (in a few cases, women are specified as the recipients) or distributed in the community. In addition, individuals dedicated votive offerings including libations (portions of wine and food), miniature objects, and sculpted or ceramic depictions; specific dedications were associated with life cycle events, as when women about to marry offered tresses or women who survived childbirth donated clothing. There are obvious parallels between hero and heroine cults and the later saints' cults of Christian and Islamic societies, both in the local appropriation of famous persons (sometimes in places they never visited historically) and in the dedication of annual festivals and specifically symbolic votive offerings to them.

The term *culture hero* is used by ethnographers and folklorists to designate mythic or legendary personages, often semidivine, who are said to have founded a society, protected it from deadly dangers, or provided it with technology or rules of conduct. Familiar examples are Cadmus, founder of Thebes and introducer of writing to Greece, and the Old Testament figure Moses, who led his people out of servitude into their own land and gave them sacred laws. One does not encounter the term *culture heroine* in the literature, however; an anthropologist describing Native American myths calls the man who invents the canoe a culture hero, but no equivalent phrase distinguishes the woman who invents weaving.

The written use of *heroine* is first recorded in English in 1659; in 1662 it was applied to the late Queen Elizabeth I. By 1715 it was used in the sense of "female protagonist." The melodramatic excesses of the gothic literary genre, which often featured female protagonists facing horrible fates, lent the word a pejorative connotation in the late eighteenth century, and by the turn of the nineteenth, Jane Austen was satirizing the concept at length in *Northanger Abbey.* Today it has been semantically somewhat rehabilitated and is used more judiciously to denote women of courage, determination, and achievement.

See Also

ANCIENT NATION-STATES: WOMEN'S ROLES; GODDESS; MYTH; ORAL TRADITION

References and Further Reading

Edwards, Lee R. 1984. *Psyche as hero: Female heroism and fictional form.* Middletown, Conn.: Wesleyan University Press.

Fontenrose, Joseph. 1981. *Orion: The myth of the hunter and the huntress.* University of California Publications in Classical Studies, 23. Berkeley: University of California Press.

Larson, Jennifer. 1995. *Greek heroine cults.* Madison: University of Wisconsin Press.

Rohde, Erwin. 1972. *Psyche: The cult of souls and belief in immortality among the Greeks.* Trans. W. B. Hillis. Repr., New York: Arno.

Jane McGary

HETEROPHOBIA AND HOMOPHOBIA

Hetero—[f. Gk *heteros*, the other of two, other] **homo**—[f. Gk *homo*, same] **phobia**—[Fr. f. L *phobus* f. Gk *phobus*, fearing] (*Shorter Oxford Dictionary*, 1993)

A phobia is an irrational fear, aversion, or hatred. Heterophobia and homophobia, in common usage, describe sexual discrimination, prejudice, and often violence toward heterosexuality and homosexuality. Heterosexuality and homosexuality are nineteenth-century terms derived from the analogy between heterogeneous (composed of different kinds) and homogeneous (composed of the same kind). *Heterosexuality* was first used in 1868 by Karoly Maria Kertbeny, and *homosexuality* was first used in 1893 in Krafft-Ebing's *Psychopathia Sexualis*. *Heterophobia* and *homophobia* are twentieth-century terms and, like *heterosexuality* and *homosexuality*, are binary contrasts. The description of prejudice as a form of phobia has been criticized because it defines discrimination as a disease or pathology, while in fact prejudice is a social problem. In the twentieth century heterophobia was not as prevalent as homophobia. Heterosexuality was socially and culturally sanctioned, while homosexuality was stigmatized, ostracized, and often criminalized.

Heterophobia

Heterophobia predominantly takes place as a reaction to homophobia and compulsory heterosexuality. Forms of separatism, or spaces that discourage or ban heterosexual behavior or specific genders, were generated as a survival tactic, a political response to the violence and hostility of homophobia. All-male or all-female nightclubs generally refuse entry to heterosexual couples. Like the accusations of reverse sexism leveled at women's-only spaces, the accusations of heterophobia are too simplistic an analysis of the situation. Homophobia and sexism are not universally manifested and vary greatly in different historical and geographical contexts. In the twentieth century it was the assumed norm of heterosexuality and the fear of harassment for displaying homosexual affection in the majority of nightclubs that effectively excluded homosexuals from them. Unfortunately, bisexuals can face exclusion from both gender-segregated spaces and from heterosexual clubs.

Lesbian separatists, like the Amazons of antiquity, have been criticized for being heterophobic or man-hating femmo-Nazis. Lesbian separatists argue, however, that they do not hate men at all. What they are opposed to are stereotypical masculine behaviors such as domination and aggression. From a feminist standpoint, heterosexual relations can be seen as problematic because they must take place within a social structure where women are still underrepresented in positions of power. Lesbian separatism is therefore a political action to boycott the channels of power in a patriarchal structure that privileges men.

The notion of a gay mafia, queer subculture, or sisterhood or brotherhood that excludes heterosexuals was a twentieth-century description for the long practice of concealment and deception that homosexuals were forced to adopt to avoid persecution. Queer-friendly spaces ("queer" being an umbrella term for gays, lesbians, bisexuals, transsexuals, and transgenderists), instead of being a forced ghettoization of the community, are a form of proaction by the queer community to create and maintain their own safety and community ties. Dress codes, or uniforms, such as rainbows, pink triangles, camp dressing for men, and butch dressing for women, have allowed members of the queer community to identify one another in the context of a hostile homophobic environment. The close of the twentieth century saw segregated venues become less popular as club goers opted for sexually ambiguous spaces in which they could adopt or discard myriad sexual identities.

Homophobia

Homophobia exists in structures such as the law, public education, the military, health care, language, and religious law, as well as public ignorance. Although in the twentieth century most western countries introduced antidiscrimination policies, they often proved ineffective within a violently homophobic and heterosexist society. Homosexuals occasionally still faced exclusion from leadership roles such as schoolteachers or members of the military—or at least the assumption of exclusion, as in the "don't ask, don't tell" policy of the U.S. military. Repressed male homosexuality, internalized homophobia, and heterosexual men's jealousy of the availability and ease of getting sex in the male homosexual community have also been suggested as factors contributing to homophobic hate crimes.

The privileging and normalization of heterosexuality alongside the invisibility and depreciation of homosexuality began to be called heterosexism by gay activists in the 1970s. Heterosexism is a mechanism of homophobia, an example of prejudice and discrimination in action. During the late twentieth century most western countries decriminalized homosexuality, but institutional homophobia in the legal system still exists in varying degrees in different countries and states. Generally the main areas of entrenched heterosexism are

1. Succession: wills, property division, and inheritance
2. Marriage: the ability to marry one's partner and to receive tax benefits and retirement savings
3. Parenting: in vitro fertilization, custody, visitation rights, and adoption
4. Identity: the pressure to deny or withhold one's homosexuality for fear of being stigmatized or, for transsexuals, the ability to change their sex on passports and other documentation

5. Criminalization: of homosexuals and homosexual practices or the distribution of literature that concerns or promotes a homosexual lifestyle

Discrimination toward homosexuals and people with AIDS became conflated and confused in the late twentieth century, although, by the end of the century, AIDS was evidently predominantly spread by heterosexual contact. AIDS began to be described by the media in 1984 as an epidemic in the gay male community. Feminists have argued that homosexual men's political activism in the 1980s and 1990s, in response to the AIDS epidemic and institutional homophobia, bespoke a notion of male entitlement in a patriarchal society. Health care reforms became necessary because AIDS patients often had visitors who were not relatives or legal spouses.

Homophobia and sexism are fundamentally linked because heterosexuality presupposes certain gender roles. Stereotypical images of homosexuals depict them as displaying an incongruous gender performance: for example, the butch lesbian and the effeminate gay man. The majority of terms to describe homosexuals (such as *poofter, queen, fairy, nancy boy, lemon, pervert, deviant, butch,* and *fruit*) also suggest deviation from traditional gender roles. Since the 1970s many of these terms have been reclaimed by the queer community as positive modes of identification. Symbols of oppression and extermination of queers, such as Hitler's pink and black triangles used to identify homosexuals, have also been reclaimed.

In America during the 1980s and 1990s right-wing Christian fundamentalists became involved in public policy to censor arts and popular culture that alluded to or presented homosexuals or homosexuality. They based their position on Judaic law, in the book of Leviticus, which is commonly interpreted as condemning sexual acts between individuals of the same gender. In 1979 Gore Vidal challenged this translation by pointing out that the Hebrew word, *to'ebah,* which is commonly translated as "abomination," more precisely meant "idolatrous." Idolatry refers to the practice of temple prostitution, which was a socially acceptable aspect of worship in Babylon. Retold in Plato's treatise on love, the *Symposium,* the Babylonian myth states that humans were once joined: man to man, woman to woman, and woman to man. The gods halved them so that now humans seek their female or male other half.

See Also

BISEXUALITY; DISCRIMINATION; GAY PRIDE; HETEROSEXISM; HETEROSEXUALITY; IDENTITY POLITICS; LESBIANISM; QUEER THEORY; SEXISM

References and Further Reading

Butler, Judith. 1990. *Gender trouble.* New York: Routledge, Chapman and Hall.

Foucault, Michel. 1984. *The history of sexuality: An introduction.* London: Peregrine.

Herdt, Gilbert. 1997. *Same sex, different cultures: Exploring gay and lesbian lives.* Oxford: Westview/HarperCollins.

Johnson, Richard. 1997. Contested borders, contingent lives: An introduction. In Deborah Lynn Steinberg, Debbie Epstein, and Richard Johnson, eds., *Border patrols: Policing the boundaries of heterosexuality.* London: Cassel.

Katz, Jonathan Ned. 1996. *The invention of heterosexuality.* New York: Plume/Penguin.

Plato. 1998. *Symposium.* Oxford: Oxford University Press.

Plummer, Ken, ed. 1992. *Modern homosexualities.* London: Routledge.

Vidal, Gore. 1983. Sex is politics. In *Pink triangle, yellow star and other essays 1976–82.* London: Granada.

Weeks, Jeffrey. 1985. *Sexuality and its discontents: Meanings, myths and modern sexualities.* London: Routledge.

Evelyn Hartogh

seen as a metaphor for "normal life" more generally, as in Wittig's (1992) theorizing of "the straight mind." Heterosexism was a key term within the 1970s and 1980s gay movement, and its analysis underpinned ideas about gay pride by conceptually linking the oppression of women, lesbian women, and gay men. However, later lesbian feminist theorizing in response to gay male sexism (toward other men, as well as toward women) argued that the oppression of gay men and of lesbian women was in fact structurally different in its origin and day-to-day expression.

See Also

GAY PRIDE; HETEROSEXUALITY; HETEROPHOBIA AND HOMOPHOBIA; PHALLOCENTRISM; SEX AND CULTURE; SEXISM

References and Further Reading

Johnson, Jill. 1973. *Lesbian nation.* New York: Simon and Schuster.

Wittig, Monique. 1992. *The straight mind.* London and New York: Harvester Wheatsheaf.

Liz Stanley

HETEROSEXISM

The belief that heterosexuality is the only "normal" form of sexuality and lifestyle—heterosexism—has been consistently analyzed and critiqued by feminism. The critique of heterosexism, like that of phallocentrism, builds on ideas associated with the feminist analysis of sexism. It uses these ideas to argue that sexism is not simply grounded in binary gender distinctions (the assumption that males are totally masculine and females totally feminine and that femininity and masculinity are polar opposites). Sexism also depends on the conceptual and practical links that are commonsensically made between gender, "sex" in the sense of being biologically male or female, and "sexual conduct" in the colloquial sense of "having sex" with someone—that "sex" is the penetrational activity that properly masculine men and properly feminine women engage in with each other. This view is known as the correspondence theory and argues that "biological sex" can explain and legitimize women's social subordination by linking hierarchical gender relations and women's sexual subordination to men within institutional heterosexuality. Thus, heterosexism is a stance that assumes heterosexuality to be both innate, "normal," hierarchical, penetrational, and essential to social order and the "biological" legitimator of binary gender relations. Here heterosexuality in its conjunction with gender is

HETEROSEXUALITY

Heterosexual behavior, defined as sexual activity with someone of the opposite sex, is an intrinsic part of all social groups that rely on procreation for their membership. Heterosexual behavior is accepted and widely practiced even in societies with powerful normative institutions that promote homosexual behavior and strict sexual segregation, such as the Kaluli, Etoro, and Sambia of New Guinea and the Azande of the Sudan. Only in exceptional cases of celibate religious or warrior castes, such as the Roman Catholic priesthood and the Ottoman royal home guard, is heterosexual behavior completely prohibited.

Heterosexuality and the Industrial Revolution

Despite the presence of heterosexual behavior throughout human history, the term *heterosexual* and the identity and social norm that it represents are surprisingly recent. The first mention of *heterosexual* in the English language is found in the 1892 translation of the German sexologist Krafft-Ebing's *Psychopathia Sexualis.* Krafft-Ebing presents an explicitly normative vision of heterosexuality as a medical prescription "to remove the impulse to masturbation and homosexual feelings." Krafft-Ebing's use of the term *heterosexual* to describe an identity and practice that excluded all sexual behavior outside male-female relations reflected growing concerns about social place and sexual identity in late-nineteenth-century industrialized countries.

A popular work on both side of the Atlantic, *Psychopathia Sexualis* gave a scientific and scholarly voice to the sexual insecurities of a world in transition. Revolutions in Europe and Latin America, agrarian crises, the spread of wage labor, declining birth rates, the recomposition of the European family, and continued attenuation of religious belief posed terrors and opportunities previously unknown to most people. Out of this social stew of economic growth and change, heterosexual activity came to be less important for its economic and reproductive functions and more important for its role in social identity and what has come to be called "lifestyle."

Like all aspects of human social life, this new lifestyle approach to sexual relations developed an etiquette and a set of rewards for compliance and punishments for transgression. Although the social etiquette changed and developed during the twentieth century, the heterosexual ideal remains at the core of the sexual code of most of the world. Despite much research suggesting that exclusively heterosexual individuals who have never had any same-sex desire or experience are rare, the heterosexual ideal remains so naturalized that all other behaviors and identities are generally viewed as deviations from and adjuncts to heterosexuality.

Many gay and lesbian historians and theorists have noted that the ubiquity of the heterosexual ideal has made the study of other sexualities highly problematic. What has rarely been mentioned, however, is that the ideological dominance of the heterosexual ideal has also severely narrowed the study of heterosexuality itself. One example is the long-standing attempt to estimate the percentage of the population that is gay. The traditional statistic has been 10 percent. However, there has been little interest in estimating the percentage of the population that is "straight." Because sexual preference is usually posed as a nature rather than a behavior and there is little recognition of bisexuality as a nature, one would expect the other 90 percent of the population to be straight. Yet as early as 1948, prior to the advent of the gay rights movement, the famous Kinsey Report on sexuality in the United States found that 37 percent of the men surveyed admitted having had at least one homosexual experience leading to orgasm.

Heterosexuality and Colonialism

Like racial typology, heterosexuality became one of the central normative scientistic discourses of modernity, spreading to every corner of the world in which North Atlantic and Japanese capitalism established hegemony. Anthropologists have observed dramatic social dissonances in places where the western heterosexual ideal exists side by side with the greater tolerance for nonheterosexual activity that generally has been observed in the former colonial world. As with the scientific ideology of race, which has implanted itself around the globe in extremely uneven and often contradictory ways, local sexual systems in the third world have evolved intricate sets of social rules and behaviors to accommodate and accept the heterosexual ideal while continuing previous practices.

The integration of nonwestern sexual norms with the sexual code of the modernizing West was seen by both colonizer and colonized as problematic. The identification of missionaries with the male superior–female inferior sexual position and notorious anthropological discussions about kinship and sexuality among Trobriand Islanders who did not recognize a legal connection between sexual contact and paternity testify to the chasm of fantasy and alterity that separated Europeans and their preindustrial subject populations. Early western colonists clearly engaged in much sexual experimentation with and exploitation of "natives," and there are many examples of the unevenness of sexual modernity in eighteenth-, nineteenth-, and twentieth-century western countries (for example, D'Emilio, 1983, discusses Massachusetts Puritans' greater tolerance of same-sex behavior over opposite-sex adultery). However, the colonial encounter has generally been constructed as a confrontation between a heterosexual West and a polymorphously perverse non-West.

Contemporary Heterosexuality

The centrifugal forces of modernity and industrialization that differentiated and defined heterosexuality and homosexuality now blur many of the classic boundaries. The expansion of civil rights for women and homosexuals in the Soviet Union during the early 1920s and the rise of a women's movement and the gay liberation movement in the capitalist world during the 1960s and 1970s created a tradition of militant and critical self-consciousness and self-identity, yielding queer theory, feminist theory, and a social history of subordinate peoples not previously believed to have a history. This expansion of political rights and social voice for nonheterosexuals in the advanced industrial world has actually had the effect of inverting the trope of the third world as sexually sloppy and the western world as neat, tidy, and heterosexual. In the contemporary period, tolerance for other sexualities has become as much a marker of modernity as intolerance was in the colonial period.

Although heterosexuals, as bearers of the dominant and normative sexual identity, still lag far behind in developing a history and a consciousness, the search for a heterosexual history has been greatly aided by the rigorous theorizing, organizing, and writing done by feminists and sexual minorities. An excellent example of this is a famous article by Adrienne Rich, entitled "Compulsory Heterosexuality and Lesbian Existence" (1985). In an attempt to expand the right to be both female and homosexual, Rich argued that heterosexuality was part of a politics of social control in which the more subordinate the social position, the less power that person had to freely discover and define a sexuality. As a group that has been sexually, socially, politically, and economically subordinate for thousands of years, women were, in Rich's vision, the primary victims of "compulsory heterosexuality." Radical feminists, such as Andrea Dworkin and Catherine MacKinnon, have taken this argument further by claiming that because of the patriarchal environment in which modern heterosexuality exists, it is impossible for heterosexual sex to be fully consensual and equal. Therefore, some feminists have stressed the relationship between all forms of heterosexual sex and rape.

Rich's work, along with that of other gay and lesbian theorists of the 1970s and 1980s and of writers such as Alexandra Kollontai and Emma Goldman in the Marxist and anarchist traditions of the early twentieth century, denaturalized the normality of heterosexuality and the abnormality of homosexuality and provided a key to separating sexual behavior from sexual identity. This crucial separation between the various combinations of sexual organs that meet for pleasure and the social context within which they meet provides the foundation for a greater understanding of human sexuality.

The last decade of the twentieth century witnessed a worldwide "renaturalizing" of social phenomena, including heterosexuality. This process has occurred even among some gay intellectuals who claim that there is a "gay gene" and, presumably, also a "straight gene." This renaturalization may or may not prove positive for the political future of strongly self-identified sexual minorities. For most women, however, this greatly narrows the vision of what is possible in life, making "compulsory heterosexuality" more compulsory along with the normative gender roles that usually accompany it.

See Also

FEMINISM: RADICAL; HETEROPHOBIA AND HOMOPHOBIA; HETEROSEXISM; SEXUAL ORIENTATION; SEXUALITY: OVERVIEW

References and Further Reading

D'Emilio, John. 1983. Capitalism and gay identity. In A. Snitow, C. Stansell, and S. Thompson, eds., *Powers of desire: The politics of sexuality*. New York: Monthly Review.

Dworkin, Andrea. 1987. *Intercourse*. New York: Free Press.

Foucault, Michel. 1978. *History of sexuality*, vol. 1. New York: Random House.

Katz, Jonathon. 1995. *The invention of heterosexuality*. New York: Dutton.

Krafft-Ebing, Richard von. 1998 [1892]. *Psychopathia sexualis*. New York: Arcade.

McKinnon, Catherine. 1989. *Toward a feminist theory of the state*. Cambridge, Mass.: Harvard University Press.

Rich, Adrienne. 1983. Compulsory heterosexuality and lesbian existence. In A. Snitow, C. Stansell, and S. Thompson, eds., *Powers of desire: The politics of sexuality*. New York: Monthly Review.

Richardson, Diane, ed. 1996. *Theorising heterosexuality: Telling it straight*. Buckingham, U.K.: Open University Press.

Segal, Lynne. 1994. *Straight sex: Rethinking the politics of pleasure*. Berkeley: University of California Press.

Jo Sanson

HIERARCHY AND BUREAUCRACY

Although organizational theory, and specifically the concepts of bureaucracy and hierarchy, have been accepted and examined in the social sciences as if they were gender neutral, in the late 1990s a number of feminist scholars critiqued this assumption, showing that bureaucracy and hierarchy are surely not immune from gender and cultural influence. Overall, this newer body of work has endeavored to extend our understanding of the many ways in which gender influences the structures and processes of bureaucratic life.

Toward this end, four streams of research and scholarship have been advanced. The first, and probably the most developed, has focused on occupational segregation by sex. This research has identified the magnitudes of job segregation, industry by industry, the extent of its persistence cross-nationally, and the many gender-based inequities of treatment that have resulted (Kanter, 1977; Leidner, 1991; Roos, 1985; Tomaskovic-Devey, 1993; Walby, 1988).

Following the documentation of gender inequalities that are produced through hierarchical work relations, research has developed to document various grassroots movements that aim to achieve greater gender equality. In this vein, Cockburn (1991) has analyzed equal opportunity campaigns in four U.K. work organizations, and Blum (1992) has examined two pay-equity movements based in California. Taylor and Whittier (1990) have discussed lesbian feminist mobilization efforts whose reach includes workplace equity issues as well as other domains of social life.

A third direction of scholarship in this field has sought to show how bureaucracy theory itself is gendered (Acker, 1990). Acker has ably argued that workers and managers cannot be disembodied, that they cannot be studied as genderless entities, even for purposes of organizational theory, and this point has been key in the development of a feminist critique of bureaucracy theory. Following Acker, Martin (1990) has addressed the issue of definition and concludes by defining feminist organizations as "organizations with a feminist ideology, values, goals, outcomes or founded as part of the women's movement" (184–185). While this definition surely permits a broad variety of organizations to call themselves "feminist," this broad umbrella has raised as many questions as it has answered, and it has suggested the need for a fourth avenue of empirical research that would examine the actual functioning grassroots organizations that have come out of the women's movement.

The women's movement over the past 20 years has produced thousands of enterprises that are organized along nonhierarchical, participatory lines. These include rape crisis centers, battered women's shelters, feminist health centers, and a wide variety of businesses targeted at women. Indeed, the feminist movement, at least in the United States, has been extremely prolific and successful in creating vital, functioning organizations along self-managed democratic lines, suggesting that there are important theoretical and empirical connections between feminism and more participatory organizational structures.

Most persuasive are the scores of studies that have documented relatively flat organizational structures and participatory organizational processes in these "new wave" female-oriented enterprises. Taken together, these studies describe four basic characteristics that link these female-oriented organizations to the other cooperative or collectivist worker self-managed organizations that historically preceded them (Rothschild-Whitt, 1979; Rothschild and Whitt, 1986). First, authority in the collectivist organization resides in the collectivity as a unit, not in any individual incumbent. This is the essential characteristic that separates collectives from bureaucracies. Second, collectivist organizations seek to eliminate hierarchies and to demystify the knowledge needed to perform the organization's tasks by teaching people to share skills, rotate jobs, and work as teams. Third, collectives seek to equalize rewards wherever possible. Finally, collectivists value personal relationships in and of themselves, not just, as in the bureaucratic model, for instrumental purposes. Feminists express these same four core values in the practices of the organizations they have created and studied (Ahrens, 1980; Ian-

nello, 1992; Schlesinger and Bart, 1982; Taylor and Whittier, 1990).

In sum, feminist scholars have taken the lead in conceptually critiquing the masculine biases implicit in hierarchy and bureaucracy (see especially Acker, 1990; Fergusson, 1984). However, most impressive are the efforts of the thousands of grassroots women-centered enterprises. They have found ways to build real-life organizations along self-managed, participatory lines, and they have found ways to accomplish their purposes without recourse to hierarchical bureaucracy. The edited volumes by Ferree and Martin (1995), Rothschild and Davies (1994), and Mills and Tancred (1992) contain analyses of dozens of these grassroots female-centered organizations, detailing their achievements with respect to their development and use of democratized practices within their organizations, as well as the environmental pressures on them to return to more conventional, hierarchical practices. Only time will tell the staying power and influence that these pioneers in building alternative organizational forms will have on the more mainstream organizations in our society.

See Also

BUREAUCRACY; COMMUNITY; EQUAL OPPORTUNITIES; ORGANIZATIONAL THEORY; POWER; WORK: OCCUPATIONAL EXPERIENCES; WORK: OCCUPATIONAL SEGREGATION

References and Further Reading

Acker, J. 1990. Hierarchies, jobs, bodies: A theory of gendered organizations. *Gender and Society*: 139–158.

Ahrens, I. 1980. Battered women's refuges: Feminist cooperatives vs. service institutions. *Radical America* 14: 41–47.

Blum, L. 1992. *Between feminism and labor: The significance of the comparable worth movement.* Berkeley: University of California Press.

Cockburn, C. 1991. *In the way of women.* London: Macmillan.

Fergusson, K. E. 1984. *The feminist case against bureaucracy.* Philadelphia: Temple University Press.

Ferree, M., and P. Y. Martin. 1995. *Feminist organizations: Harvest of the new women's movement.* Philadelphia: Temple University Press.

Iannello, K. 1992. *Decisions without hierarchy: Feminist intervention in organizational theory and practice.* London: Routledge.

Kanter, R. M. 1977. *Men and women of the corporation.* New York: Basic.

Leidner, R. 1991. Serving hamburgers and selling insurance: Gender, work and identity in interactive service jobs. *Gender and Society* 5: 154–177.

Martin, P. Y. 1990. Rethinking feminist organizations. *Gender and Society* 4(2): 182–206.

Mills, A. J., and P. Tancred. 1992. *Gendering organisational analysis.* London: Sage.

Roos, P. 1985. *Gender and work: A comparative analysis of industrial societies.* Albany: State University of New York Press.

Rothschild, J., and C. Davies. 1994. Organizations through the lens of gender: Introduction to the special issue. *Human Relations* 47(6): 585–590.

Rothschild, J., and A. Whitt. 1986. *The cooperative workplace: Potentials and dilemmas of organizational democracy and participation.* New York: Cambridge University Press.

Rothschild-Whitt, J. 1979. The collectivist organization: An alternative to rational-bureaucratic models. *American Sociological Review* 44: 509–527.

Schlesinger, M., and P. Bart. 1982. Collective work and self-identity: Working in a feminist illegal abortion collective. In E. Lindenfield and J. Rothschild-Whitt, eds., *Workplace democracy and social change,* 139–153. Boston: Porter Sargent.

Taylor, V., and N. Whittier. 1990. Collective identity in social movement communities: Lesbian feminist mobilization. In C. Mueller and A. Morris, eds., *Frontiers in social movement theory.* New Haven, Conn.: Yale University Press.

Tomaskovic-Devey, D. 1993. *Gender and racial inequality at work.* Ithaca, N.Y.: ILR Press.

Walby, S. 1988. *Gender segregation at work.* Milton Keynes, Eng.: Open University Press.

Joyce Rothschild

HIGHER EDUCATION

See EDUCATION: HIGHER EDUCATION.

HINDUISM

Defining Hinduism is a very difficult exercise facing both scholars and adherents. What exactly is Hinduism and what does it encompass? Answers to these questions cannot easily result in any unanimous understanding among scholars. There has to be some way, however, in which one could fruitfully use the term *Hinduism* to convey certain general meanings. The term *Hindu* itself comes from a relatively recent history of India and, hence, the uncertainty among scholars as to whether or not it really captures the essence of the range of beliefs and practices of the people in the subcontinent. Although scholars have begun to question its usefulness in understanding the religious vista of the vast region that we know as India, more traditional pundits began to proffer the use of a native term, Sanatana Dharma. But this also has presented problems, in the sense that the people from the south of India—especially the Tamil-speaking communities—could not identify with such a term, as it was seen to be too north Indian or Sanskritic and did not represent the south and the millions of tribal and other peripheral communities. While the debate continues about a common term that can capture the vast range of religious and cultural heritage of India, most people—scholars as well as laypeople—continue to use the term *Hinduism* for practical purposes of general identification.

The term was first used by the Persians and later the Greeks to identify a people in the region of the Indus (Sindhu) river situated in the northwest of India. The native word, *Sindhu,* was corrupted to become *Hindu* in the course of its long history. The Moguls are probably the first ones who used it to refer to the religious beliefs of the majority of the natives and to distinguish it from Islam. Subsequently, the British colonial usage of the term fixed its meaning as the religion of the majority of the natives. Thus came the term *Hinduism* in its more reified sense as a closed system of beliefs. Scholars such as Wilfred Cantwell Smith questioned the use of such reified terms to refer to the continuously growing and changing traditions of people. In that sense, what we now call Hinduism is something that has grown through several centuries and perhaps many millennia and includes a vast range of beliefs, customs, and practices that have been part of the subcontinent.

The known history of India dates back to the Indus valley civilization (c. 3000–2500 B.C.). This civilization, which witnessed a fairly urbanized condition of life, suddenly disappeared after lasting approximately one thousand years. Very little is known about its religion, although a few figurines have been found. In the absence of our knowledge of their script, interpretation of most of what is found on these figurines remains contested. It may be worth noting, however, that some scholars have identified this culture as being the proto-Dravidian. The present form of Shiva worship is, according to this line of interpretation, supposed to have had its origins in the Indus culture. It was succeed by a major cultural force that became known as the Aryan culture. The origin of this culture is a contested one, with most western scholars proffering the theory of Aryan immigration from the European continent (the region around the Black Sea, Lithuania, and so on) and some Indian scholars arguing in favor of the theory that locates Aryans within the subcontinent. Whatever the origins might be, the Aryan culture with its mythology, ritual, and philosophy has contributed to Hinduism enormously. Sanskrit as its primary language became the main medium of spreading this culture. In the course of its spread—initially from the Ganges plain to most of the present Indian subcontinent—it had assimilated many beliefs, customs, and practices from the tribal communities and the other peripheral communities known today as "scheduled castes." One of the most notable features of this culture is its social stratification through the institution of caste.

Although the Aryan culture became the dominant force in shaping the present Hindu religion, the so-called peripheral communities that were held at the bottom of the caste ladder contributed no less to the enrichment of present-day Hinduism. The goddess worship is certainly one such phenomenon that is, perhaps, more prominent in Hinduism than in most other religions. Whereas the Sanskrit-based Aryan form of Hinduism perpetuated mainly a patriarchal form of religious system, the popular and folk beliefs, rituals, and practices have certainly balanced it with their propensity toward a female form of the divine. Thus, present-day Hinduism is able to integrate, both in its philosophy and in its rituals and myths, a whole range of feminist ideas of the divine.

Hindu Theologies

There are fundamentally three types of theologies that have become integrated into the Hindu worldview. These can be identified as (1) patriarchal, (2) matriarchal, and (3) androgynous theologies. The patriarchal theologies are represented by a male dominant deity, such as Vishnu or Shiva, and is associated with his divine consort as a subordinate deity. In the case of Vishnu, it is Lakshmi, and in the case of Shiva, it is Parvati. The matriarchal theologies are represented by a female goddess as the dominant deity with the male deities, such as Vishnu Shiva and Brahma, in a subordinate role. Mythological texts, such as *Devimahatmyam,* depict the goddess as the supreme power from whom all creation, including that of the gods, emanates. In her capacity as the mother goddess or the most sovereign power, she always stands alone and does not have a male partner, as in the case of the male dominant gods. The androgynous theologies are represented mostly by the god Shiva in his dual form of man-woman or half man and half woman (*arthanarisvara*). There are instances when Vishnu also played the role of male and female simultaneously. When the gods and the demons fought for the nectar that was churned out of the ocean, Vishnu made the gods and the demons line up and distributed the real nectar to the gods and the fake nectar to the

demons by appearing to them (that is, the demons) as the enchantress.

Although the patriarchal and the androgynous theologies are primarily documented in the classical Sanskritic texts, the matriarchal theology is quite pervasive within the Sanskritic materials as well as in the popular or folk traditions of village Hinduism. These theological representations depict, at a deeper level, the social reality of the Hindus. Although Hindu society is by and large patriarchal through its caste-based stratification, there are, nonetheless, matriarchal societies present in some tribal societies and also in the mainstream Hindu society. For instance, in Kerala (a south Indian state) matriarchal rule was common in the precolonial era. Even the androgynous representation of the society is quite easily accommodated within Hindu society. The presence of eunuchs in the Hindu royal courts and their specific role in certain Hindu festivals (for example, Shivaratri) even at the start of the twenty-first century enabled the Hindu society to integrate not only a diverse theological outlook but also a highly variegated social reality. These social realities are deeply entrenched in the Hindu ritual. There are temples that depict these different representations: there are temples solely dedicated to either Vishnu or Shiva as male dominant deities; and temples such as the Meenakshi temple in Madurai, the Kamakshi temple in Kanchi, and the Goddess temple in Kanyakumariall in Tamilnadu, a southern state of India. In some Shiva temples, he is often depicted in his half-man and half-woman form.

Issues of Women

In spite of the above-mentioned multifaceted theological outlook of the Hindu worldview, the role assigned to Hindu women in traditional society is very much on the fringe. Hindu society, throughout its history, most certainly witnessed many women saints and poets. Nevertheless, in orthodox Hindu belief, women depend on men for their salvation (until marriage, a woman depends on her father, after marriage on her husband, and in old age on her son). Religious reformers, such as Ramanuja in medieval Hindu society, could send their wives away to the parental home in the name of pursuing celibacy in order to become deeply involved in their religious work. Even in modern Hindu society, Gandhi saw sexual contact with his wife as an impediment to his spiritual growth.

These contradictions in Hindu society have raised some very fundamental issues not only in the context of gender equality but also in the broader context of human rights. Modern Hindu society has to come to terms with these contradictions. Some feminist scholars have utilized the available resources in Hindu society, such as its mythological texts and the like, to reorient the social consciousness in a way that would lead to more opportunities and challenges for women. In spite of the fact that Hindu society witnessed, in the last decades of the twentieth century, an upsurge in the number of women taking up leadership roles in various contemporary institutions such as politics, economics, science and technology, medicine, bureaucracy, and many others, the many age-old practices of Hindu society—such as the dowry and bride burning—still haunt its social consciousness. Many women artists, singers, poets, and literary scholars still have to fight their way through the strongholds of male dominant stereotypes.

Some of the most critical issues that have dogged feminist scholars for years and still continue to do so have to do with the stereotypical roles assigned to women in spite of their achievements in many specialized fields in which men traditionally held prominence. One such issue that is of critical importance is marriage and motherhood. Women in traditional Hindu society consider marriage and motherhood to be the most important aspects of being a woman. This attitude has become a snare in their attempt to overcome male-generated prejudices. Hindu women continue to have a lesser say in the determination of vital issues of abortion, birth control, and family assets.

Another issue that feminist scholars on India have raised in recent years has to do with sexuality. Many subtle issues are intertwined in the larger issue of sexuality. Generally speaking, Hindu society does not openly discuss matters of sexuality, and this silence often results in women being subordinated to male prejudices about sexual matters. Different phases of life of a woman are clearly demarcated by means of rituals. A young girl reaching puberty and experiencing her first menstrual cycle is set apart and ritually purified at the end of that period. At marriage, her chastity is tested by older women. Young girls are more closely guarded in society than boys of the same age. Traditional Hindu society continues to uphold the chastity of woman as the most important factor in the consideration of marriage. In very conservative families, older women check out the bedsheets of the newly married couple to find blood stains on them, so as to confirm the chastity of the bride. Blood in association with menstruation is seen as polluting and, hence, even at the start of the twenty-first century, traditional women followed certain rules that include not participating in family activities, such as cooking, and communal activities, such as staying away from temples and rituals during the period of menstruation. As such, menstruating women become taboo in the society. Such menstruation taboos are embedded in the Hindu ritual texts, the *Rig Veda Samhita* for instance.

Women who are widowed are considered ritually impure and, hence, should not be present at auspicious ceremonies. They are considered to be messengers of bad luck. Besides, a widow cannot attain her liberation without a husband. There exist in Hindu literature hundreds of examples that bewail the misfortune of a widow (for example, the cries of the wife of Manmatha, the love god, when he was destroyed by the fire of Shiva's third eye and the debate of Sati Savitri with Yama, the god of death, when her husband died prematurely are all-too-familiar instances of the plight of the widow without children). To this day, the practice of consigning widows to a shelter attached to a temple can still be seen in sacred cities, such as Benares, where they simply while away what remains of their valuable life. Although the practice of widow burning (*sati*—the practice of burning the widow on the pyre of the dead husband) is banned in India and is considered a crime, there are occasionally cases reported in the media. Women without children also are considered inauspicious people and are unwelcome at certain family functions, such as marriage. A widowed mother cannot give away her daughter in marriage (her auspicious married sister or relative has to step in to perform that function), and the sight of a woman without children is avoided in marriage.

Despite the assignment of such subordinate roles to women in both Hindu literature and Hindu society, there are a number of examples where women asserted a great deal of independence. Such instances can be seen in the devotional literature of the Hindus. One of the most common themes in the devotional literature associated with women is their longing to marry the deity. Feminist scholars often have seen this as an important act of denial of marriage, which indicates not only their self-affirmation but also a radical rejection of the male-centered conception of marriage. Similarly, there are instances of women devotional singers who left their husbands and families to follow an ascetic form of life. In some of these cases, such women had difficult marriages, and devotional life is seen as a form of liberation (for example, Lallesvari of Kashmir in the fourteenth century C.E.). It is interesting to note, however, that even when women sought freedom from the male dominant social practices, they seem to have done so within the framework of the Hindu value system. Feminist scholars have seen this response as a serious limitation in the struggle of Hindu women to achieve their independence in society. Nevertheless, such attempts need to be seen as significant achievements toward progress of Hindu women. In the meantime, these women continue to challenge androcentric Hindu values and attempt to reinterpret their own roles in continually changing Hindu society. No social system is carved in stone.

References and Further Reading

Caldwell, Sarah. 1999. *Oh terrifying mother: Sexuality, violence and worship of the goddess Kali.* Oxford: Oxford University Press.

Chawla, Janet. 1992. The Rig Vedic slaying of Vritra: Menstruation taboos in mythology. In *Manushi*, edited by Madhu Kishwar, no. 68, April 1992.

Doniger O'Flaherty, Wendy. 1980. *Women, androgynes and other mythical beasts.* Chicago: University of Chicago Press.

Douglas, Mary. 1992. *Purity and danger: An analysis of concepts of pollution and taboo.* London: Routledge and Kegan Paul.

Harman, W. 1989. *The sacred marriage of a Hindu goddess.* Indianapolis: Indiana University Press.

Hawley, J., and D. Wulff, eds. 1996. *Devi: Goddesses of India.* Berkeley: University of California Press.

Kinsley, David R. 1986. *Hindu goddesses: Visions of the divine feminine in the Hindu religious tradition.* Delhi: Motilal Banarasidass.

———. 1993. *Hinduism: A cultural perspective.* Englewood Cliffs, N. J.: Prentice Hall.

Kumar, P. P. 1997. *The goddess Lakshmi: The divine consort in south Indian Vaishnavism.* Atlanta, Ga.: Scholars.

Leslie, Julia. Some traditional Indian views on menstruation and female sexuality. In Roy Porter and Mikula Teich, eds. *Sexual knowledge, sexual science: The history of attitudes to sexuality,* 63–81. Cambridge: Cambridge University Press.

Sastri, A. M. 1988. *The Vedic law of marriage, or the emancipation of women.* New Delhi: Asian Educational Services.

Winslow, Deborah. 1980. Rituals of first menstruation in Sri Lanka. *Man* 15(4: Dec.): 603–625.

P. Pratap Kumar

HISTORY

Though constituting half of humankind, women were until the latter part of the twentieth century nearly invisible in history texts and courses, marginalized along with the poor, the working class, and minorities. Because women's contributions have occurred mainly in the home, they often have been devalued and gone unrecognized as remarkable in their own right and in facilitating men's achievements. The global study of women's history began in earnest in the 1970s, coinciding with a feminist movement that created a thirst for knowledge about women's experiences. "Women's history is an assertion that women have a history," says the historian Apama Basu of the University of Delhi in India.

While it is valid to ask how events and experiences affect men and women differently, critics of traditional texts charge that women have for the most part not been integrated into the general arena of study, with only a few names familiar to a mass audience, such as the French martyr Joan of Arc, England's great queens Elizabeth I and Victoria, the American patriot Betsy Ross, the black American abolitionist Harriet Tubman, and the wives of famous men. Because history has been defined mostly in male terms, research historians have failed to ask questions pertinent to women's lives, leaving a chasm within mainstream studies. In placing more importance on traditional male activities, such as military and political events, historians dismissed traditional women's activities, such as child rearing and the building of communities and culture. Because women have been historically on the fringes of the power structure, they have been reduced to a subtopic in the eyes of male historians. Only when women began to report on women was some degree of equity achieved.

One of the first women to write a history of women was Christine de Pizan (1364–1430), an Italian-born aristocrat who lived in France. Widowed at age 25, Pizan supported herself and three children with her writings, including biographies and *The Book of the City of Ladies* (1405), a work that chronicled the lives of heroic women.

In 1792, Mary Wollstonecraft, a British writer and social activist, became a powerful voice for the recognition of women when she published *A Vindication of the Rights of Woman,* which attacked social conventions oppressing women, promoted equal partnerships between men and women, and called for gender equity in education. She recognized that women had come to depend on men for their survival but supposed that if women had their own businesses and means of income, they "would not then marry for a support...nor would an attempt to own their own substance, a most laudable one! sink them almost to the level of those poor abandoned creatures who live by prostitution." Wollstonecraft also became a leading biographer of women; this profession was generally considered safer for female writers of her time than championing women's rights.

Margaret Fuller, a leader in the transcendentalist movement, wrote *Women in the Nineteenth Century,* which was published in 1845 and greatly influenced the Seneca Falls women's rights convention held three years later. In its time, it was extolled as one of the major documents in the history of American feminism.

Mary Ritter Beard is considered the "materfamilias" of American women's history, as she assailed the traditional view that women existed only as adjuncts to history with no achievements of their own except as helpmates to men. Beard, born in 1876, entered DePauw University at age 16, graduated in 1897, and joined the suffrage movement as editor of *The Woman Voter* for the Woman Suffrage Party of New York. She and her husband, Charles Beard, collaborated on several texts on history, which integrated women's experience. She also published several important works including *Women's Work in Municipalities* (1915), *A Short History of the American Labor Movement* (1920), *On Understanding Women* (1931), and *America through Women's Eyes* (1933). Beard's *Women as Force in History*, published in 1946 when she was 70 years old, is considered her most significant contribution to women's history. It disputed the idea that women's influence on society and civilization has been minimal and inconsequential. Ten years later, she published *The Force of Women in Japanese History*. Beard most often addressed the issues of a husband's legal "ownership" of his wife and the tradition of matriarchy in ancient and contemporary cultures.

Gerda Lerner, an Austrian, a very prominent international historian, turned the study of women's history into a scholarly discipline. Courses in women's history, she has noted, often serve as introductory programs that lead students into more generalized studies in history. Skepticism about women's history as a legitimate discipline dissipated with endorsements by the American Historical Association and other academic organizations.

In *The Creation of Patriarchy*, Lerner declared that even brief exposure to historical accomplishments of women has an intensely positive impact on female students. Alternatively, failure to acknowledge women as full participants in history diminishes women's sense of self-worth. One of the purposes of emphasizing women's history is to validate female heroines and role models and thus to redefine the world. Recognizing that the field of women's history has perhaps been wrongly labeled, Lerner asserts that the deeds of men and women can not be separated. But she acknowledges that, as written by men and constructed by male values, history has been overwhelmingly biased toward men and therefore must be reordered to become inclusive.

By the middle of the twentieth century, interest in the history of women was revitalized by the nascent second wave of feminism. The two fields of study would overlap without being mutually inclusive. The historiography of the first was reflected in the postsuffrage era, in which women sought to break from their traditional gender-assigned functions in society and assume roles equal to men's. The textbooks of women's history were now being written as tracts of social activism and calls for revolution in the structure of society, not merely examining women's roles but advocating their metamorphosis in ways that Mary Wollstonecraft and other pioneers had boldly anticipated a century before. Finally, women's history was being recorded even as it was being made.

Women historians vigorously began uncovering their own countries' heritage, disinterring women's places in history as the passion to know more about the past spread internationally, where once it had been centered in France, Great Britain, and the United States. What emerged were, not stories of war and conquest, but stories of family, work, domesticity, and children, topics specifically and intentionally divided by gender. Gender, historians concluded, may appropriately indicate an emphasis on women's subordination in a social, cultural, political, and historical context rather than as an aspect of sexuality.

Voices once unheard were recovered. In Canada, Sylvia Van Kirk discussed the role of women in the western Canadian fur trade in *Many Tender Ties: Women in Fur-Trade Society, 1670–1870*, disclosing female participation in what had been assumed to be an all-male industry. Believing women had been left out of the historical accounts of the Canadian socialist movement, Joan Sangster published *Dreams of Equality: Women on the Canadian Left, 1920–1950*. Canadian historians strove to write inclusively, acknowledging the nation's vast immigrant population and its great regional diversity, while fostering a rapprochement between English speakers and Francophones.

As in most countries, women's historians in Australia have found themselves struggling to gain entrance into the larger debate on history. The women's liberation movement arrived in Sydney and Melbourne around 1969 and sparked interest in exploring women's history and the relations of Australian men and women in a country with an entrenched male myth of "mateship," or male bonding. Before the 1970s, little was written about women's contributions to the national heritage. In fact, Australian historian Patricia Grimshaw states, "it would be difficult to point to a national historical tradition which more clearly represented a celebration of white male achievement." Grimshaw published accounts of women's history and politics in such books as *Women's Suffrage in New Zealand* and *Families in Colonial Australia*. Other important history texts include Anne Summers's *Damned Whores and God's Police: The Colonisation of Women in Australia*, and Miriam

Dixon's *The Real Matilda: Women and Identity in Australia, 1788 to 1975.*

Postwar Japan began to reflect on the history of its women between 1945 and the early 1960s. In 1948, Inoue Kiyoshi published *Nippon no Joseishi* (Women's History in Japan), which traced the history of Japanese women back to ancient times in terms of class struggle. Though written by a man, the book decried the absence of women from histories in which the assumption of women's subordination was prevalent. Takamure Itsue, a woman, published a three-volume history, *Josei no Rekishi* (Women's History in Japan), over a four-year period beginning in 1954. Since the 1970s, the field of women's history has grown in Japan, nurturing research projects conducted not only by scholars but also by nonacademic women.

Social customs, religious practices, and the status of women have captured the attention of women's historians in India, who have been inspired by what Aparmu Basu has identified as the maturation of social history and the growth of the women's movement. Significant works include the *Position of Women in Hindu Civilization: From Pre-History to the Present Day* by A. S. Altekar, *Social Status of North Indian Women* by Ila Mukherji, and Neera Desai's *Indian Women, Change and Challenge in the International Decade, 1975–1985.* Basu is the author of *Growth of Education and Political Development in India.*

African nations have only recently begun to address women's history, reflecting the belated account of African history as a whole. Scholarly works on women's history have focused largely on biography and studies of female institutions. Till 1950, writing about African women was done primarily by missionaries and anthropologists. Texts since then have used such sources as missionary reports, archaeological excavations, and oral histories. In Nigeria and elsewhere, research projects on women's issues are being created to foster networks and promote the study of the roles and concerns of women, to found work centers for scholars, and to seek sources of funding. In 1992, the Nigerian historian Bolanle Awe published *Nigerian Women in Historical Perspective.*

In the Nordic countries, contemporary studies in women's history began during the 1970s. One of the leading figures of women's history in Norway is Ida Blom, professor of women's history at the University of Bergen. She has authored anthologized essays on women's history and published such books as *Gendered Nations: Nationalisms and Gender Order in the Nineteenth Century,* which she edited in March 2000. In Sweden, 1883, Ellen Fries became the first woman in Scandinavia to defend a doctoral thesis in history. Nevertheless, the concept of women's history remained

obscure until the 1970s. One notable work was Anita Goransson's *Fran familj till fabrik. Teknik, arbetsdelning och skiktning i svenska fabriker 1830–1877* (From Family to Factory: Technology, Division of Labor, and Stratification in Swedish Factories), published in 1988. In 1990, Yvonne Hirdman published *Att laggalivet tillratta. Studieri svensk folkhemspolitik,* (The Making of Everyday Life: Studies in Swedish Reform Policy 1930–1950), which discusses the restructuring of everyday life, including issues of welfare. In Denmark, Anne Magrete Berg's book *Kvindfolk* (Womenfolk, 1984), was a pioneering work that helped to rekindle interest in women's history in the country.

Vicki Ruiz, chair of the Arizona State University Department of Chicana and Chicano Studies, is one of the leading historians of Hispanic women. Her comprehensive work, *From Out of the Shadows: Mexican Women in Twentieth-Century America,* addresses the contributions of Latinas to the American Southwest after four centuries of helping to shape culture in North America. Virginia Sanchez Korrol wrote of the Puerto Rican woman's experience in *From Colonia to Community: The History of Puerto Ricans in New York City* (1983).

Much of the work on women historians in Central and South America began in the 1960s when educated women looked into history texts and saw no reflection of their own lives. Latinas had been aware of their place in history since the nineteenth century but were not trained historians. Instead, they communicated through women's magazines.

In the twentieth century, Latin American women living in the United States became the most frequent chroniclers of the Latin American woman's experience. Prominent writers include Asuncion Lavrin, a Cuban-American, the author of *Sexuality and Marriage in Colonial Latin America* (1989), and *Women, Feminism and Social Change in Argentina, Chile, and Uruguay, 1890–1940* (1995).

Donna Guy, a history professor at the University of Arizona, wrote *Sex and Danger: Prostitution, Family and Nation in Argentina* (1991) and, with Daniel Balderston, *Sex and Sexuality in Latin America* (1997). She has investigated the history of state policies toward street children in Argentina and how governments invented new definitions of mothers, fathers and families.

Vicki Ruiz and Virginia Sanchez Korrol are coauthors of a forthcoming two-volume reference work, *Latinas in the United States: An Historical Encyclopedia.* Its entries cover prominent Latina women from the sixteenth century to the present and include essays on such topics as religion, arts, politics, labor, and marriage.

The history of African-American women followed a course similar to general women's history, awakened in the

1970s when Rosalyn Terborg-Penn and Sharon Harley published *The Afro-American Woman: Struggles and Images*, a collection of essays about black women's rights. African-American women's history gained momentum in the 1980s when other significant works were published, including Deborah Gray White's *"Ar'n't I a Woman?": Female Slaves in the Plantation South*. With a conceptual framework that put black women at the center of their historical accounts, it is considered a classic that examined slave society as a discrete culture with its own hierarchy.

Gray White remains one of the most prominent historians of black women. In 1999, she published *Too Heavy a Load: Black Women in Defense of Themselves, 1894–1994*. In 1994, Terborg-Penn and Darlene Clark Hine published *Black Women in America: An Historical Encyclopedia*. Hine also edited *We Specialize in the Wholly Impossible: A Reader in Black Women's History; Black Women in American History: From Colonial Times through the Nineteenth Century;* and *Black Women in American History: The Twentieth Century*. Nell Irvin Painter, Edwards Professor of American history at Princeton University, published *Sojourner Truth, A Life, A Symbol*, in 1996, and edited two nineteenth-century texts, *Narrative of Sojourner Truth* and *Incidents in the Life of a Slave Girl*.

As women's history became a distinct discipline in the 1960s and 1970s, zeal engendered a new lexicon. The word "herstory" was coined to indicate a fresh approach to history that would encompass the lives of women as well as men. Though it was rejected as frivolous and unscholarly by some, others found it useful for emphasizing the need to tell history from a female perspective. The American historian Natalie Zemon Davis rescued forgotten luminaries with her term "women worthies" to recognize laudable women of the past. It was a phrase savored by other historians.

At the century's end, historians had progressed beyond treatises that simply acknowledged forgotten women and began addressing fresh issues. These included human relationships, sexuality, childbirth, and domestic work. Historians were asking different questions, even about traditionally male topics, such as war. The questions were no longer merely of battles lost and won but of how war affected civilians. For example, what roles did race and gender play in war? How is rape manifested as a war crime?

In 1998, the historian Linda Kerber of the University of Iowa analyzed women and politics in *No Constitutional Right to Be Ladies: Women and the Obligations of Citizenship*. Eileen Boris and Nupur Chaudhuri collected personal reminiscences in their book *Voices of Women Historians: The Personal, the Political, the Professional* (1999), a compendium of essays in which each writer recounted her entry into the field, celebrating activism and scholarship over three decades to enrich the historiography.

In the encyclopedic *Reader's Companion to U.S. Women's History*, editors Wilma Mankiller, Gwendolyn Mink, Maryso Navarro, Barbara Smith, and Gloria Steinem compiled more than four hundred entries covering women's experiences from America's colonial times to the present. Contributors included historians and legal scholars, anthropologists and public servants.

Nancy F. Cott, who had explored the women's movement in the early twentieth century in *The Grounding of Modern Feminism* (1987) and addressed postcolonial women's lives in *The Bonds of Womanhood: Woman's Sphere in New England, 1780–1835* (1977), was working in 2001 on a history of marriage in America. Women's history was finally linked to every larger theme in human society, integrally connected, as Kerber terms it, to "how the world works."

Some historians think men's and women's history will one day be integrated as "people's" history, although courses in women's history and studies are increasingly popular on college campuses and are among the fastest growing fields of history. While most universities try to integrate their curricula, elementary and secondary schools still fail to foster an "omnitext" that would bring women into history curricula as fundamentally as men.

The American historian Berenice Carroll believes it will be many years before all histories—including those of women and ethnic minorities—can be incorporated into one discipline. Women are often still neglected in textbooks of general history. Change has been significant but not as monumental as women historians would like. They nevertheless emphasize the need to retain specialties, just as the topic of banking, for instance, remains a subset of the study of economics. The study of history requires a varied set of lenses, each of which has a unique focus.

Fully integrating women into universal history requires exhaustive work in reconstructing a heritage for women and incorporating women into all disciplines while retaining discrete specialty areas. Its proponents consider this work vital. When women are omitted from the historical record, they become invisible and appear not to have existed at all, leaving vaporous half the world's population.

See Also

EDUCATION: HIGHER EDUCATION; KNOWLEDGE; WOMEN'S STUDIES: OVERVIEW

References and Further Reading

Awe, Bolanle. 1992. *Nigerian women in historical perspective.* Lagos: Sankore.

Beard, Mary Ritter. 1987. *Woman as force in history: A study in traditions and realities.* New York: Persea.

Blom, Ida. 1999. *Gendered nations: Nationalisms and gender order in the nineteenth century.* Berg.

Falco, Maria, ed. 1996. *Feminist interpretations of Mary Wollstonecraft.* University Park: Pennsylvania State University.

Itekar, A.S. 1987. *The position of women in Hindu civilization.* New Delhi: Anmol.

Itsui, Takamure. 1954–1958. *Josei no Rekishi* (Women's History in Japan). 3 vols. Tokyo: Kodansha.

Jones, Constance. 2000. *1001 things everyone should know about women's history.* New York: Doubleday.

Kerber, Linda K. 1998. *No constitutional right to be ladies: Women and the obligations of citizenship.* New York: Hill and Wang.

Laurin, Asuncion. 1995. *Women, feminism and social change in Argentina, Chile, and Uruguay, 1890–1940.* Lincoln: University of Nebraska Press.

Lerner, Gerda. 1986. *Creation of patriarchy.* New York: Oxford University Press.

Offen, Karen, Ruth Roach Pierson, and Jane Rendall, eds. 1991. *Writing women's history: International perspectives.* Bloomington and Indianapolis: Indiana University Press.

Peteet, Julie. 1991. *Gender in crisis: Women and the Palestinian resistance movement.* New York: Columbia University Press.

Sangster, Joan. *Dreams of equality: Women on the Canadian left.* Toronto: McClelland and Stewart.

Summers, Ann. 1994. *Damned whores and God's police: The colonisation of women in Australia.* New York: Penguin.

White, Deborah Gray. 1999. *Too heavy a load: Black women in defense of themselves, 1894–1994.* New York: Norton.

Barbara Yost

HIV (Human Immunodeficiency Virus)

See AIDS AND HIV and LESBIANS: HIV PREVALENCE AND TRANSMISSION.

HOLISTIC HEALTH I

Holistic health assumes the unity of all life and the essential interconnectedness or oneness of mind, body, and spirit. The term *holistic* is derived from the Greek word *hale,* meaning whole. Thus, the goal of holistic health care is to help the total person rather than to treat only a disease, condition, or symptom.

While the practice of holistic health care is a recent development in western health systems, the concept has been practiced in traditional health systems around the world for centuries. More than two hundred years before Christianity, Chinese philosophers believed in treating the mind first. They held that there were no diseases—only persons who happened to have diseases. Also, ayurveda, the Indian Hindu system of healing, emphasized the trinity of life—body, mind, and spiritual awareness more than two thousand years ago. Among the approaches used in ayurveda is yoga, which helps one achieve longevity, rejuvenation, and self-realization (Chopra, 1991). As in ancient China and India, holistic care calls for more than a particular treatment; holism involves an "approach" to healing and maintaining health (Griffin, 1980) that uses the body, mind and spirit to control disease, promote a sense of well-being, and enhance one's quality of life.

Women have long been fascinated with the healing process and the creative forces therein. The earliest of healers were individuals selected to serve as masters of a tribe's healing traditions. These individuals came to be known as medicine men and women and shamans. The shamans held that the purpose of life was to advance into the visionary realms of the spirit and to achieve balance in all things (Achterberg, 1985). While much of the shamans' lore had been dismissed by the twenty-first century, a few practices persisted alongside conventional thought, perhaps reflecting the need for a more humanistic and spiritual component to twenty-first-century health care.

During the seventeenth century—the period of the scientific revolution—the philosopher Réné Descartes published *Principles of Philosophy* (1644), which reflected his duality of thinking that led to the mind-body split (Berman, 1981). Other scholars continued to build upon Descartes's philosophy of the separation of mind and body during the eighteenth century. The Cartesian approach to the healing arts prevailed into the nineteenth century as well, except within religious communities that educated many women as nurses, who, unlike other healers of the time, embodied a spiritual approach in their practices. Florence Nightingale (1820–1910), the first nurse to have a scientific education, retained her holistic orientation despite her scientific background. She emphasized the importance of the total environment to patients' recovery and believed that the laws of health were the same for the well and the sick (Nightingale, 1859). In the late nineteenth and early twentieth centuries, the medical profession embraced the concept of holistic health care less and less, fearing that it would impede the scientific process (Achterberg, 1985).

In the 1940s Flanders Dunbar, a psychiatrist at Columbia Presbyterian Medical Center, revived the whole-person concept through her pioneering work in psychosomatic medicine. Dr. Dunbar's research revealed that certain personality characteristics were typical of persons experiencing particular disorders (Dunbar, 1945). In the 1960s Holmes and Rahe expanded on her work through their development of a questionnaire used to assess the impact of life changes on an individual and the corresponding potential for onset of illness. Their research established a strong relationship between lifestyles and health (Holmes and Rahe, 1967).

In the early 1960s, women witnessed the introduction of the concept of "high-level wellness" which emphasized that individuals should direct efforts to live as healthy a lifestyle as possible to promote a state of wellness (Dunn, 1961). Nurses, primarily women, identified closely with this concept, integrating it into nursing curricula across America. In 1974, the Canadian Ministry of Health and Welfare published *A New Perspective on the Health of Canadians*, which presented epidemiological evidence of the importance of lifestyle and environment to health and illness (LaLonde, 1974). Two years later in the United States, the Senate Select Committee released a report on the relationship between nutrition and health that paved the way for changes in the American diet (U.S. Senate Select Committee 1976).

During the 1970s the number of holistic health care practitioners increased, as did their influence. Large numbers of women advocated a wellness lifestyle that emphasized nutrition, physical awareness, stress reduction, and self-care responsibilities. This new focus in health care practice and, later, health care research influenced the way North Americans conceptualized health and healing and included an increased awareness of the mind-body-spirit connection, leading to further emphasis on holism and illness prevention. In 1980, a group of nurses formed the American Holistic Nurses' Association—recognized today as the first professional organization to bring "whole-person healing" back into mainstream nursing (Dossey et al., 1988).

Although the nursing profession has a long history of focusing on the whole person, conventional medicine has only recently moved beyond its reductionist medical model of treating disease toward a system closer to holistic health care. The founding of the American Holistic Medical Association in 1978 fostered a movement toward a broader and more holistic approach to the medical management many physicians provide.

An increasing number of practitioners in medicine, dentistry, pharmacy care, and nursing have sought education and training in total health care, with a specific focus on lifestyle, diet and nutrition, self-responsibility and accountability, caring and stress management, and collaboration and teamwork within the health care system. The twenty-first century began with some leading physicians—Andrew Weil, James Gordon, Larry Dossey, and others—shedding the idea of an exclusive medical model and moving toward one that emphasized achieving maximum wellness. Persons around the world spend billions of dollars annually on complementary practices and products that they believe will foster this goal.

Healing practices and health care perspectives have evolved in many different cultures over time. Many women strive to integrate the best of traditional medicine (complementary and alternative practices and products) with the best of western medicine. Those who espouse a holistic approach recognize that many diseases and disorders come about in response to a disturbance in physical, mental, and spiritual environments. Consequently, they seek to find holistic health care professionals who can guide them in ways that will bring balance in all three areas.

See Also

HEALTH: OVERVIEW; HEALTH CARE, *specific entries*; HEALTH CHALLENGES; HEALTH EDUCATION; HOLISTIC HEALTH II; NURSING; NUTRITION, *I and II*; SCIENCE: TRADITIONAL AND INDIGENOUS KNOWLEDGE

References and Further Reading

Achterberg, J. 1985. *Imagery in healing.* Boston: New Science Library.

Berman, M. 1981. *The reenchantment of the world.* Ithaca, N.Y.: Cornell University Press.

Chopra, D. 1991. *Perfect health: The complete mind/body guide.* New York: Harmony.

Dossey, B. M., L. Keegan, C. E. Guzzetta, and L. G. Kolkmeier. 1988. *Holistic nursing: A handbook for practice.* Rockville, Md.: Aspen.

Dunbar, F. 1945. *Psychomatic diagnosis.* New York: Haeber.

Dunn, H. 1961. *High level wellness.* Arlington, Va.: Beatty.

Griffin, M. M. 1980. A holistic approach to the health care of the elderly client. *Journal of Gerontological Nursing* 6: 193–196.

Holmes, T. H., and R. Rahe. 1967. The social readjustment rating scale. *Journal of Psychosomatic Research* 11: 213–218.

LaLonde, M. 1974. *A new perspective on the health of Canadians.* Ottawa: Government of Canada.

Nightingale, F. 1969. *Notes on nursing: What it is and what it is not.* New York: Dover. (First published in 1859.)

U.S. Senate Select Committee Report. 1976. *Dietary goals for the United States*. Washington, D.C.: U.S. Government Printing Office.

Ann Gill Taylor

HOLISTIC HEALTH II

The increasingly popular type of medicine currently known as holistic health has its roots in prehistory, when humans had to rely on their religion, common sense, and knowledge of plant and food medicines for their health and lives. Of course, ancient peoples were as different in their personalities and spiritual inclinations as those now living. There must have been at least a few wise women of yore who looked at plants the way modern allopathic physicians look at a pharmacy—with a purely utilitarian view. However, most saw the plants as gifts from the earth, part of the cycle of life, involving the sun, the moon, the stars, the rain, the seasons, and the animals and humans who were living in the middle of it all. Hundreds of healer women were killed in Europe during the witch-hunts of the fourteenth century and for the next three hundred years because they practiced herbalism. The healing uses of botanical medicines, relaxation therapy (to add to or extend a sense of spirituality), and foods, now with the backing of scientific research, continue this ancient tradition. More recent additions are acupuncture (as part of Chinese medicine, twenty-five hundred years old), hydrotherapy, homeopathy (both about two centuries old as formal systems of medicine), and a wide variety of other techniques.

What most westerners know as conventional medicine (that is, that practiced by M.D.s in hospitals or clinics) is a relatively recent form of medical treatment. Its rational and logical approach to the ailments of the human body—as flaws in a machine—probably has its basis in the scientific revolution of the seventeenth century. With the advent of technologies that enable even closer examination of the chemical workings of the body, this system of belief has only grown more entrenched and validated. This analytical approach to health does have its benefits. Over the years, funded by grants not made available to those outside the predominant system, research in allopathic medicine has been responsible for innumerable advances in knowledge of the human body and the treatment of its ills. In so doing it has attained a respectability not presently shared by most alternative systems of medicine, in large part because natural medicine relies so much more on anecdotal evidence and physicians' clinical instincts than on research studies.

A vicious circle is operating here. Few, if any, peer-reviewed articles on, for example, the physiological effects of oat straw as a treatment for insomnia exist because oat straw, as a natural substance, cannot be patented. There are no financial incentives for any multinational corporation to invest in research on botanical or homeopathic medicines; the paucity of scientific research in this area is due not to natural medicine's being second best but to economics. People living in societies in which less emphasis is put on the findings of scientific research, whether because the information was not disseminated to them or because of a cultural background that promoted a different view of medicine, have always believed in more than a reductionist approach to health and disease—that disease is due to evil spirits, susceptibilities, or pernicious influences in the environment. However, even people with a solid working knowledge of chemistry and biology have lately begun to accept the idea that the body is more than its physical self and that lifestyle factors such as stress levels, spirituality, and personality have major effects on health.

Nevertheless, the allopathic model of medicine is pervasive. Most people have been brought up to use antibiotics for infections and pills for symptoms. Often, when they switch to natural medicine, they bring the allopathic model with them; for example, there is little difference in taking cramp bark tincture for menstrual cramps and taking a couple of aspirins. There are fewer side effects to the cramp bark, but the thinking behind the treatment is still allopathic. Holistic medicine, to be truly holistic, involves treating the root cause. Is a woman with menstrual cramps not eating a diet that provides all her nutritional needs, leading to heavy bleeding or muscle spasms? Was she brought up to believe that menstruation is shameful and to hate her periods? Are there any benefits, such as having to do less work around the house, that she subconsciously would miss if the cramps were gone? There is nothing wrong with treating the symptom of cramps on the day they appear, but a practitioner of holistic medicine would also examine the possible causes in the hopes of eventually preventing them altogether.

The treatments—botanical, homeopathic, manipulative (physical manipulation of the skin, fascia, muscles, or joints)—are generally, though not necessarily, gentler than the pharmaceuticals of today. It is true that a few botanical medicines in particular can be dangerous if used inappropriately; however, pharmaceutical medicines can be even more so. In the case of botanical medicines, the whole leaf, flower, or root is used, and the myriad constituents tend to modulate one another's effects, whereas pharmaceuticals are generally administered one or two active ingredients at a time, resulting in a greater likelihood of side effects. Another reason natural treatments are often better for a patient is that holistic practitioners are interested in the whole body, not just the system being treated. For example, a pharmaceutical drug used to reduce the production of stomach acid may seem to relieve the problem of heartburn, in which the acidic contents of the stomach wash backwards up the esophagus, causing pain. However, the decrease in stomach acidity can dramatically impair the digestion and absorption of essential nutrients, and the maldigestion of food in the stomach may end up leading to other symptoms of indigestion or abdominal discomfort. Despite the side effects, if a pharmaceutical drug relieves the specific symptom it is supposed to relieve—in this case, heartburn—it is thought to be effective. This is not to say that allopathic practitioners are indifferent to the side effects of the medicines they prescribe, but most are likelier than a holistic physician to add another medication to relieve the secondary symptom than to reassess the prescription of the original drug (after all, it did relieve the heartburn). A practitioner of holistic medicine might ask a patient with heartburn about the conditions under which she eats, her feelings about food, and so on, and focus on changing the causes thus unearthed rather than (or in addition to) prescribing a botanical or homeopathic medicine, digestive enzymes, or a new diet to relieve the symptoms. An allopathic physician might do the same, in which case she too would be practicing, at least to some extent, holistic medicine.

Many people think that the use of holistic medicine is dangerous if conditions are misdiagnosed or treatments given that are ineffective. Certainly the possibility exists that an untrained practitioner could provide poor medical care. However, there are many fields of natural medicine in which a license is required or extensive training is available. In India there are hundreds of medical colleges that focus on homeopathy. In China the same is true for traditional and classical Chinese medicine and acupuncture. In western societies allopathic physicians have access to training in systems of holistic medicine, and there are dozens of colleges where others can be trained in massage, Oriental medicine, and homeopathy. These schools turn out students who are well educated about the limits of their training and when they should refer patients to licensed physicians. In the United States there are four-year colleges of natural medicine with programs of study modeled on those of allopathic medical schools, with the same training in anatomy, physiology, pathology, and so on, although different systems of healing are taught. The physicians who graduate from these colleges are licensed

to practice in several states, most choosing to focus on general family medicine.

Women, the majority of health care consumers, may find that holistic medicine is well suited to their needs. Its practitioners are concerned with their patients' entire emotional, spiritual, and physical lives, an outlook many women like (especially when the doctor "prescribes" that a woman insist on having time to herself or reducing her stress in other ways). Women's bodies, in many ways, are more interesting and more meaningful to them than men's are to men. Women's bodies have the ability to reproduce; or if they do not, that may in itself sometimes complicate the relationship between a woman and her body. Women's bodies have noticeable cycles throughout the month and a pattern that changes with the seasons of their lives. Women may simultaneously have a child on one hip and a grocery sack or a bundle of wood on the other. Their bodies may cause anxiety and self-hate sometimes and tremendous admiration and self-love at other times. These things can be true of men's bodies as well, but thanks to differences in either anatomy or culture, most women have a more intimate relationship with their bodies than men do; they know, deep down, that there is more to them than proteins and fats and bones and blood. For this reason, and perhaps because of a distant memory of women ancestors who harvested medicinal plants by the light of the moon, holistic medicine and holistic health seem particularly suited to the needs and instincts of women today.

See Also

HEALERS; HEALTH: OVERVIEW; HEALTH CHALLENGES; TRADITIONAL HEALING, *specific entries*

References and Further Reading

Beinfeld, Harriet, and Efrem Korngold. 1991. *Between heaven and earth: A guide to Chinese medicine.* New York: Random House.
Domar, Alice, and Henry Dreher. 1996. *Healing mind, healthy woman: Using the mind-body connection to manage stress and take control of your life.* New York: Dell.
Gladstar, Rosemary. 1993. *Herbal healing for women.* New York: Simon and Schuster.
Maciocia, Giovanni. 1989. *The foundations of Chinese medicine.* Singapore: Churchill Livingstone.
Weed, Susan. 1986. *Wise woman herbal for the childbearing year.* Woodstock, N.Y.: Ash Tree.

Brinlee Kramer

HOLY SPIRIT

Virtually all religions envision the origin of the cosmos and human beings in terms of birthing, hatching, or speaking the world into being. The rise of patriarchal monotheism in Judaism, however, brought to world culture a concept of the paternity of God as a single, male, transcendent deity. Christianity inherited and developed this father metaphor as the dominant concept of God, but feminist theologians find that the Christian doctrine of the Trinity offers a vision of a maternal feminine aspect of God that challenges its traditional patriarchal monotheism. In the Christian tradition, the one God is expressed through the trinitarian symbol, a communion of three divine personages within one godhead: the Father, the Son, and the Holy Spirit. It is within this figure of the Holy Spirit that feminist theologians trace a feminine maternal imagery, inherited from Jewish mysticism (and perhaps dating back to the matricentric religions that Judaism supplanted), that offers a female metaphor for the Divine, correcting an exclusively male vision of God.

The Holy Spirit is understood as the life-giving "holy breath." The Latin word *spiritus* comes from the Hebrew *ruah*, a feminine noun meaning "breath in motion" or "life-animating principle." This holy "breath of life" is figured in biblical texts as a life-giving, liberating power that animates all creation and inspires prophecy (the Latin *inspirare* shares the *spiritus* root); it is also repeatedly associated with feminine maternal imagery. For example, the Divine Spirit energizes the creation of the world in Genesis 1:1: "In the beginning she hovers like a great mother bird over her egg, to hatch the living order of the world out of primordial chaos." The Holy Breath is also described as exercising a vital role in Israel's liberation in Exodus and enacts a transforming capacity when she is said to turn the wilderness into a fruitful field in Isaiah and Ezekiel.

As a force that inspires prophecy, the Holy Spirit is associated with Sophia (wisdom) in the Jewish wisdom tradition and Gnostic Christianity. As the Spirit of Wisdom, Sophia's creative and saving involvement in the world is interpreted as "fashion[ing] all that exists and pervad[ing] it with her pure and people-loving spirit, and work[ing] in history to save [her people] through the vicissitudes of liberating struggle" (Johnson, 1993: 91). The idea of the Holy Spirit as mother, seen in scriptural imagery of mother birds (especially eagles and doves), and reflected in metaphors of pregnancy, birthing, and suckling, expresses God's compassionate maternal care.

To acknowledge the symbolization of the divine as feminine in the Holy Spirit is not necessarily to imagine the Christian Trinity as a sort of divine nuclear family. Some feminist theologians, such as Mary Daly (1978), distrust the supposed femininity of the Holy Spirit as a "transsexual male mother" that reflects the "ideal all-male world of Christian myth" (75–79, 229). Other feminist theologians who have recovered the maternal aspect of God, which has been all but erased in the Christian tradition, have been more interested in acknowledging the significance of the mother metaphor's contribution to a more integral image of God. From this perspective, to be empowered by the Holy Spirit is to participate in the Spirit's task of liberating the universe, an important way that feminist theologians have worked to make Christianity more of a spirituality of empowerment for women.

See Also

DEITY; SHAKTI; THEOLOGIES: FEMINIST

References and Further Reading

Daly, Mary. 1978. *Gyn/ecology: The metaethics of radical feminism.* Boston: Beacon.

Jacob, P. J. 1980. The motherhood of the Holy Spirit. *Journal of Dharma* 5 (2): 160–174.

Johnson, Elizabeth. 1993. *She who is: The mystery of God in feminist theological discourse.* New York: Crossroads.

Rayan, Samuel. 1979. *Breath of fire, the Holy Spirit: Heart of the Christian Gospel.* London: Geoffrey Chapman.

Ruether, Rosemary. 1993. *Sexism and God talk: Toward a feminist theology.* Boston: Beacon.

Margaret Shanthi Stephens

HOME ECONOMICS

See EDUCATION: DOMESTIC SCIENCE AND HOME ECONOMICS; NUTRITION AND HOME ECONOMICS.

HOMELESSNESS

As of the year 2000, many households in both the developed and the developing worlds fail to realize one of the basic elements of human adaptation: maintaining stable shelter. Women may experience homelessness alone, with partners, or with children whose fathers may or may not be with them at the time.

HOMELESSNESS

Homelessness has two principal causes: a society's shortage of affordable housing and an individual household's lack of the economic and social resources its members require to meet their health and social needs. When all of a culture's members do not realize its norms for living in aggregated rather than isolated, atomistic groups, that culture has failed.

Women almost always bear the heaviest physical and emotional burdens of supporting homeless households, whatever their demographic makeup may be: the lack of help in caring for children, the shattering of health-related behavior patterns and the inability to maintain family food supplies and to cook and serve regular meals, the impossibility of keeping household members and their belongings clean and securing the privacy and protection needed to sleep. Because the instability of homelessness also fractures their social networks, most homeless women cannot work, and their children do not go to school and thereby lose out on enculturation in the society's mainstream norms.

Despite these commonalities in the experiences of homeless women everywhere, those of women living in the developed world differ, quantitatively and qualitatively, from those of women living in the developing world.

Women's Homelessness in the Developed World

The numbers of homeless women in the wealthy social democracies of Canada, western Europe, and the United States are much lower than in poor countries of the developing world. However, as economic growth slowed worldwide in the early 1970s and the Middle East oil embargo in 1973 led to higher rates of inflation, the United States—the world's wealthiest, most advanced nation—all but stopped building subsidized housing for the poor, and its numbers of homeless increased substantially (Dehavenon, 1995). Later, some U.S. cities began razing their older subsidized housing as it deteriorated; examples included the dynamiting of some of the projects in Newark, New Jersey, and of Pruitt-Igoe in St. Louis, Missouri. As heating oil costs mounted, private landlords also abandoned their properties in poor neighborhoods through tax default or renovated them as "gentrified" housing for middle- and upper-class households. As the shortage of affordable housing mounted in the United States during the 1970s and 1980s, so did homelessness (Dehavenon, 1996); even when the economy boomed in the 1990s, the housing crisis continued to mount (Molotsky, 2000: A20).

The estimated number of New York City families at risk of homelessness in 1999 was 781,000, or more than two million people (Dehavenon, 1999). Based on city statistics (Department of City Planning, City of New York 1996–

1999), this estimate includes families with incomes below the median who pay half or more of their income for rent and those who live in unsafe housing or in the overcrowded apartments of relatives or friends.

By contrast, the social democracies of Canada and western Europe continue to build new and renovate older subsidized housing, and their homelessness rates remain lower than those in the United States. For example, in the 1990s homelessness was 10 times higher in Hartford, Connecticut, than in Quebec City, Canada (Glasser, Fournier, and Costopoulos, 1999).

Social supports other than subsidized housing are also more generous in the social democracies than in the United States. In the social democracies, subsidized family allowances enable households to pay rent and other expenses, and the minimum wage is much higher than the U.S. minimum. Universal health care is provided, as is child care for children of working parents. In France, for example, where domestic conflict is the principal cause of family homelessness, wives whose husbands have thrown them out go to a "foyer," where there is a nursery for children under age 3, or to a shelter with older children. These mothers continue to work, and their families receive comprehensive social services that help them prepare to move into an apartment within a reasonable period of time.

By comparison, the minimum wage and public assistance payments in the United States are not adjusted for changes in the consumer price index. Since the mid-1970s, both have been so eroded by inflation that their purchasing power is about half what households need to maintain sufficient food supplies and pay rent. Meanwhile rents for privately owned housing have risen dramatically; in New York City tens of thousands of households are on the waiting list for public housing, and it can take years for them to get an apartment.

Homeless Women in the Developing World

Poverty is much more severe and widespread in Asia and Africa than in nations of the developed world. India's official poverty rate is 40 percent in rural areas and about 35 percent in cities. The primary causes of women's homelessness are extreme poverty, lack of employment opportunities, violence by husbands, being abandoned by their husbands for other women, being thrown out of their husbands' homes on account of dowry demands, being unable to bear sons and so refused shelter by their husbands and in-laws, being refused shelter by their families on account of social stigma, illiteracy and lack of access to information, and government and legal policies that are insensitive to women's issues (Mangalagiri, 2000).

1010

There is some subsidized housing in India for families below the poverty line, but the district collectors must identify these families at the district level. The system of identification is replete with corruption, and families allotted housing often lack money and therefore fall into the trap of middlemen who buy the housing from them for a certain amount, these back in the slums and homeless.

Except for the Destitute Women's Homes, which are inadequate, India has no systematic policy on housing homeless women. In urban areas, women without housing are constantly in transit on the streets; most who live on their own or with their children set up shacks in slum areas. They also live on the pavement and in railway stations and support themselves by begging and prostitution. In rural areas, they may return to their natal families if they are accepted there or may keep shifting residence from relative to relative. Given the strength of the Indian family system, this practice is still possible but is always a temporary arrangement. The most destitute women turn to prostitution and are picked up by the police and sent to the Destitute Women's Homes (Mangalagiri, 2000).

In Africa there are no family allowances and very little subsidized housing for the poor. The traditional homelessness of women—moving from one relative to another all their lives, with or without children—has been overshadowed by the displacement associated with war and AIDS. AIDS widows and orphans try to escape the grinding poverty exacerbated by the disease by going to the city to beg for food and look for work in the informal sector. There is no housing for them or for the other poverty-stricken women and the young children who also live and beg on the streets. Prostitution and other forms of exploitation are rife. Most of the women eventually create some form of self-employment and construct makeshift housing for themselves in slums. Housing originally built for the poor is located far away from women's trade networks and usually winds up in the hands of the middle class because of corruption (Obbo, 2000).

The experiences of these women and their families in India and Africa are similar to those of poor homeless women in other developing nations, where extreme poverty and the forces of urbanization draw women into cities to try to escape destitution through cash employment.

See Also

HOUSING; POVERTY

References and Further Reading

Dehavenon, Anna Lou, 1995. The cultural materialist approach and the causes of hunger and homelessness. In Maxine Margolis and Martin Murphy, eds., *Science, materialism and the study of culture.* Gainesville: University of Florida Press.

———. 1999. An estimate of families at risk of homelessness in New York City in 1999.

———. 1996. *There's no place like home: Anthropological perspectives on housing and homelessness in the U.S.* Westport, Conn.: Bergin and Garvey.

Glasser, Irene, Louise Fournier, and Andre Costopoulos. 1999. Homelessness in Quebec City, Quebec and Hartford, Connecticut: A cross-national and cross-cultural analysis. *Urban Anthropology* 2 (20).

Molotsky, Irvin. 2000. Robust economy is contributing to a loss of affordable housing. *New York Times* (20 March): A20.

Mangalagiri, Anjana. 2000. Personal communication. Program Officer in UNICEF for Education and Child Development, responsible for the states of Tamil Nadu and Kerala, located in the state office in Chennai.

Department of City Planning, City of New York. 1996–1999. *Consolidated plans for 1996 and 1999.* New York: Department of City Planning.

Obbo, Christine. 2000. Personal communication. Africanist specializing in gender, AIDS and urbanization.

Anna Lou Dehavenon

HOMOPHOBIA

See HETEROPHOBIA AND HOMOPHOBIA.

HOMOSEXUALITY

See LESBIANISM; SEXUALITY: OVERVIEW.

HORMONES

It is now impossible to imagine a world without hormones. Women all over the world take hormonal pills to control their fertility. Hormones have become part of our day-to-day language as a way to explain our bodies and behavior. This was not the case a century ago. The concept of hormones was first introduced in 1905, two decades before pharmaceutical companies began the mass production of hormones. Hormones are defined by biologists as chemical substances that circulate in the blood and regulate specific bodily processes. Although there are different categories of hormones, the term is often used to refer to sex hormones. Sex hormones are considered the "chemical messengers" of femininity and masculinity. They control the sexual differentiation and the reproductive functions of the body. Initially, scientists suggested that there existed just two sex hormones, male and female. Nowadays, sex hormones are known not to be exclusive to either sex. Nevertheless, the distinction between "male" and "female" sex hormones still persists in our culture. Although the hormonal model of the body can be applied to both sexes, more attention has been given to women. Throughout the twentieth century the female body became increasingly portrayed as a body completely controlled by hormones (Oudshoorn, 1994; Vines, 1993).

Hormones As Woman's Destiny?

In the 1970s feminist biologists began to criticize the belief that hormones have the power to control what women are. They showed how the science of hormones reflects cultural notions about the roles of women and men in western society, rather than mirroring nature. During the last four decades many types of behavior, roles, and characteristics considered typically male or female have been ascribed to sex hormones. Male sex hormones are invoked to explain why boys play football or why there are more male than female mathematicians, composers, and so on. Female sex hormones are invoked to explain why girls play with dolls and women prefer mothering or nursing (Fausto Sterling, 1985). Feminists have also pointed to the distinctly different ways in which hormonal explanations have been applied to both sexes. Men's actions are usually related to hormones to explain deviant behavior such as excessive aggression and criminality, while female hormones are often used to explain the essence of a woman's whole being (Vines, 1993). In the science of hormones, the female body became characterized by cyclic hormonal regulations and the male body by stable hormonal regulations. Sex differences thus became conceptualized in terms of cyclicity and stability. This association of femininity with cyclicity was not entirely new. In the latter half of the nineteenth century, psychiatrists ascribed the "periodic madnesses" of their female patients to the cyclic nature of their menstruation. Psychiatrists even questioned the "mental integrity" of menstruating women (Fausto Sterling, 1985; Oudshoorn, 1994). The science of hormones transformed this notion of cyclicity into a basic model for understanding the specific nature of the psychology and the physical features of the female body. Feminists have emphasized that this association of femininity with cyclicity depicted women as limited by their "biological nature" in ways that men, in general, are not.

Most feminists reject the idea that hormones are a woman's destiny. They emphasize that sex differences in behavior are caused by education and other social factors. As against the idea that behavior is socially constructed, a minority of feminists suggest that hormones, and biology in general, are not irrelevant to our understanding of the differences between women and men (Birke, 1986).

Women's Health

Hormones play yet another important role for women in contemporary culture. Since the 1960s hormone therapy for menstrual irregularities, premenstrual syndrome (PMS), and menopausal symptoms has become very popular, particularly in the United States. In addition, women all over the world now use hormonal contraceptives (the pill). Estrogens and progesterone have become the most widely used drugs in the history of medicine.

Many women appreciate the benefits of hormonal drugs. They consider hormone replacement therapy an acknowledgment of their problems by the medical profession. Yet the awareness of health hazards has turned the faith in hormones as problem solvers into a reality of growing ambivalence and severe criticism. Since 1960, the women's health movement has signaled the health risks of taking hormonal drugs. In the late 1960s feminist and health advocates campaigned against the side effects of the pill. They accused the medical profession and the pharmaceutical industry of not taking seriously the many complaints of pill users (Seaman and Seaman, 1978). Since the 1960s there have been recurrent debates about the risks of cancer and the other serious side effects of hormones. Feminists have also demanded the development of a "male pill" to equalize the sharing of health risks and family responsibilities between women and men.

In the 1970s the medical world acknowledged the health risks of hormones and reduced and modified the hormonal compounds in the pill. However, uncertainty about the long-term effects of the use of hormones still persists. Moreover, the reductionist view of hormonal explanations for menopause and PMS continues to be criticized. Feminists have argued that hormonal explanations reduce menstruation and menopause to disease entities (Fausto Sterling, 1985; Greer, 1991). In summary, sex hormones may best be portrayed as a mixed blessing for women.

See Also

BIOLOGICAL DETERMINISM; BIOLOGY; CANCER; CONTRACEPTIVES: DEVELOPMENT; ENDOCRINE DISRUPTION; ESTROGEN; FEMININITY; HORMONE REPLACEMENT THERAPY; MASCULINITY; MEDICAL CONTROL OF WOMEN; MENOPAUSE;

MENSTRUATION; NATURE-NURTURE DEBATE; PHYSIOLOGY; THE PILL; PREMENSTRUAL SYNDROME (PMS); REPRODUCTIVE PHYSIOLOGY; SCIENCE: FEMINIST CRITIQUES

References and Further Reading

Birke, Linda. 1986. *Women, feminism and biology: The feminist challenge*. Brighton, U.K.: Harvester.

Fausto Sterling, Anne. 1985. *Myths of gender: Biological theories about women and men*. New York: Basic Books.

Greer, Germaine. 1991. *The change: Women, ageing and the menopause*. London: Hamish Hamilton.

Oudshoorn, Nelly. 1994. *Beyond the natural body: An archeology of sex hormones*. London: Routledge.

Seaman, Barbara, and Gideon Seaman. 1978. *Women and the crisis in sex hormones: An investigation of the dangerous uses of hormones from birth control to menopause and the safe alternatives*. Brighton, U.K.: Harvester.

Vines, Gail. 1993. *Raging hormones: Do they rule our lives?* London: Virago.

Nelly Oudshoorn

HORMONE REPLACEMENT THERAPY

Hormone replacement therapy (HRT) is a controversial drug treatment given to women at menopause. It consists of the hormone estrogen, sometimes given with progestogen as well, and is available as pills, transdermal patches, implants, gels, and creams. HRT has been vigorously marketed to doctors and to women in midlife .

Estrogen was first isolated in 1923 but it was not until 1943, when Ayerst Laboratories developed a cheap, easy-to-administer product (called Premarin because it was made from pregnant mares' urine), that postmenopausal hormone treatment became a commercially viable proposition.

HRT was popularized among doctors and promoted to the wider public by the efforts of Dr. Robert Wilson, a gynecologist in New York who formed a trust, funded by pharmaceutical companies, to promote estrogen. In the 10-year period between 1963 (when Wilson published his first medical paper on estrogen) and 1973, dollar sales of estrogen quadrupled in America. His book for women, *Feminine Forever*, published in 1966, was marketed in most western countries and sold more than 100,000 copies in its first seven months.

Wilson succeeded in defining menopause as a state of estrogen deprivation (he called it "living decay"), and he argued that women needed estrogen therapy from "puberty to grave" to ward off the supposed physical, sexual, and emotional deterioration that would overtake them at menopause.

By the mid-1970s, postmenopausal estrogen was a multi-million-dollar industry. But the publication in 1975 of studies demonstrating that women who used estrogen had a greatly increased risk of endometrial cancer led to a dramatic decline in prescribing. Then, in the mid-1980s, HRT was aggressively remarketed as a prevention for osteoporosis, or bone thinning, and later, in the 1990s, as a way to prevent heart disease. For these purposes, healthy women were supposed to use HRT for long periods—for 20 or 30 years or even for life. By the year 2000, however, nonhormonal drugs were available for osteoporosis, and new research findings had cast serious doubt on the efficacy of HRT in preventing heart disease.

HRT came on the market at a time when drug approval processes were rudimentary, and there has been a lack of randomized, controlled trials to prove the effectiveness and safety of HRT, especially in the case of long-term use. A growing number of studies since 1989 have suggested that users run an increased risk of breast cancer, but this claim is disputed or underplayed by medical advocates of HRT.

Feminists have responded ambivalently to HRT. Some women's health organizations, such as the Washington-based National Women's Health Network, have taken a critical position on HRT, and a feminist critique of HRT is provided in books such as Sandra Coney's *The Menopause Industry* (1991) and Germaine Greer's *The Change* (1991), but other feminists have regarded use of HRT as a matter of choice for women, a position also expounded by many doctors.

The principal users of HRT are white women of high socioeconomic status. The promise of HRT—of perpetual youthfulness and prolonged sexual attractiveness—has proved persuasive in societies which devalue women as they age.

Use rates of HRT vary between countries. They are highest in the United States, where, in some states, up to 40 percent of early menopausal women are using the therapy. In almost all western countries, the use of HRT is increasing.

See Also

ESTROGEN; ETHICS: MEDICAL; GYNECOLOGY; HEALTH: OVERVIEW; HORMONES; MEDICINE: INTERNAL, *I and II*; MENOPAUSE; PHARMACEUTICALS

References and Further Reading

Coney, Sandra. 1991. *The menopause industry: A guide to medicine's "discovery" of the mid-life woman*. Auckland: Penguin (U.K. ed. 1995; U.S. ed. 1994).

Greer, Germaine. 1991. *The change: Women, aging, and the menopause.* London: Hamish Hamilton.

Rinzler, Carol Ann. 1993. *Estrogen and breast cancer: A warning to women.* New York: Macmillan.

Seaman, Barbara, and Gideon Seaman. 1977. *Women and the crisis in sex hormones.* New York: Bantam.

Wilson, Robert. 1966. *Feminine forever.* London: Allen.

Sandra Coney

HOUSEHOLDS: Division of Labor

See DIVISION OF LABOR.

HOUSEHOLDS: Domestic Labor

See DOMESTIC LABOR.

HOUSEHOLD WORKERS

Female Household Workers: Who Are They?

Female household workers (domestics, servants, helpers, maids, girls) are women, often of a different class and race than their employers, who work in private homes for pay. In many countries they are a familiar sight: hurrying to market, hanging out the wash, taking their employers' children to school or playground. Household workers have been mostly invisible to researchers and to the feminist movement.

In the industrialized countries and in Latin America, household workers are most often female: men are gardeners, butlers, and chauffeurs, and women are cooks, laundresses, and baby minders. In much of Asia and Africa, however, "boys" of all ages were traditionally servants; now female workers are increasing in these countries. In many regions of the United States, there is a notable resurgence of domestic work, and Latinas, both foreign- and native-born, have largely replaced black women, who have moved into other occupations. (For Asia and the Pacific, see Heyzer et al., 1994; Asia and Africa, Sanjek and Colen, 1990; Latin America, Asia, and Africa, Hosmer Martens and Mitter, 1994; Latin America and the Caribbean, Chaney and Garcia Castro, 1989, and the United States, Hondagneu-Sotelo, 1997, 2001, and Mary Romero, 1992.)

Household workers form a large percentage of the female labor force in many world areas. In South and Central America and the Caribbean, for example, about 20 percent of the *counted* female labor force works in domestic service.

A large proportion of female household workers are rural migrants drawn to metropolitan centers in search of jobs, education, and cash to send to their children and rel-

atives. With little education or training, they find domestic service one of the few urban occupations immediately available and one that offers bed and board.

Poor women also cross international boundaries, hoping to find better working conditions and pay in richer countries. For example, Caribbean islanders go to London, Toronto, the U.S. Virgin Islands, and New York City; Mexicans to California and Texas; Bolivians to Brazil and Argentina; Salvadoreans to Washington, D.C.; Colombians to Venezuela; Nicaraguans to Costa Rica; Dominicans to Madrid; and Filipinas to Hong Kong, Singapore, and Italy.

Not all migration is voluntary; trafficking in women includes not only prostitutes, hostesses, dancers, and mail-order brides but also household workers. Many are undocumented, eluding border patrols or overstaying tourist visas (Azize and Kempadoo, 1996; Chaney and Garcia Castro, 1989; Foner, 1986; Hosmer Martens, 1994).

In some countries, little girls get their first job as early as 10 or 12 years of age. While most household workers are in the 15–35-year age group, many remain in domestic service for their entire working lives. But others may be considered "too old" to do a full day's work at 40 years of age. With limited access to other employment, without pensions, and cut off from their rural origins, they find themselves abandoned and alone.

In sum, those who engage in housework for pay are almost always poor, uneducated, and unskilled; they may be noncitizens and often are of a different race than their employers. Research makes clear that this is a recipe for exploitation, with the "servile elements" in the employer-worker relation "clearly delineating the limited value of housework in the eyes of society and the low esteem for the maid as a person" (Gálvez and Todaro, 1989: 316).

Conditions of Work

Household workers may "live in" or "live out." The former receive their salaries in cash and in kind. The latter may work for the same family or divide their week among several households. Laundresses typically are dayworkers, washing and ironing for different employers. Worldwide, the tendency is toward "live out" work with fixed hours; more workers are seeking escape from the watchful eyes of employers monitoring their private lives and the semislavery of being on call day and night.

In many countries professionals, academics, feminists, and other workers cannot conduct their careers and contribute to their country's development without domestic help. Yet housework, whether carried out by the employer or by hired hands, is depreciated. Essential domestic tasks are noted only when they remain undone, and household workers may themselves be ashamed of what they do. Working conditions and compensation are almost uniformly substandard. Household workers tell of long hours (16–18-hour days are not uncommon), low pay, lack of days off or paid vacations, disrespect and inconsiderate treatment from family members, and often aggressive sexual advances from the male members of the household. Even where there is protective legislation for household workers, it is rarely enforced. If household workers are undocumented, then they have no rights at all.

Personal Lives

Most migrants arrive in the cities with only two or three years of schooling and an almost universal desire for education. In some countries younger household workers have a legal right to time off for school in the afternoon or evening. But there is no way to guarantee that employers will respect the law.

Some household workers go on to study for "short careers" such as dental assistant, laboratory assistant, or clerical worker but afterward have a difficult time finding jobs. In Peru, for example, many ads specify that the job seeker must have *buena presencia* (good appearance; shorthand for "not lower class" and "not indigenous").

Many household workers become single mothers; this is an obstacle to education and better jobs. They may have several children by different fathers and often are solely responsible for them. Sometimes an employer will permit her servant to bring one small child to the workplace or even to live in with a child. With the birth of a second child, the worker almost certainly needs to seek day work, giving up her dreams of education and a better future.

Toward Organization

After they get to know the city, some household workers learn how to negotiate better conditions; in other cases— for example, among West Indian migrants to New York, Toronto and London—they are able to move out of housework altogether (Foner, 1986: 144–145).

Bargaining for their rights—even when favorable legislation exists—can be a formidable task in the face of an unlimited supply of labor. Moreover, there is evidence that the economic crisis brought on by global restructuring has increased competition by propelling lower-middle-class women into domestic service.

A few women join household worker associations or unions. But household workers are a notoriously difficult group to organize: they lack a common workplace, a common management with which to bargain, and the same day off. If they live out, they must devote their free time to their own families. Often their employers look with disfavor on union activity.

Nevertheless, from South Africa to Hong Kong, from Singapore to Paraguay, from Los Angeles to New York City, and among immigrants to various European countries, household workers are organizing. In some cases, they have been struggling to organize for decades (see part II in Hosmer Martens and Mitter, 1994, and part IV in Chaney and Garcia Castro, 1989).

In Latin America household worker unions first appeared in Mexico, Chile, and Bolivia. Initiatives in Mexico began in the early 1920s; by 1940, *sindicatos* (unions) existed in eight cities (Goldsmith, 1992: 82–83); sadly, these have all disappeared. In Chile the first union was founded in 1926 during the period of fervent organizing fostered by "labor priests" inspired by the encyclicals of Leo XIII and Pius XI. The first Chilean union disappeared, reinvented itself, and reappeared again; as the Union of Household Workers in Private Homes, it has had a continuous life since 1943. In Bolivia a feisty union of *culinarias* (cooks) existed from 1935 to 1958 (Gill, 1994; Wadsworth and Dibbits, 1989). Today there are organizations in almost every country of the region, many fostered by the Young Catholic Workers movement (imported from France in the 1950s). There are national federations in Argentina, Bolivia, and Brazil. As yet, few organizations exist in the United States, but there are some positive initiatives on the east and west coasts (Hondagneu-Sotelo and Riegos, 1997).

In 1988 household workers from 12 countries, meeting in Bogotá, Colombia, founded the Confederation of Latin American and Caribbean Household Workers. The conference has held several congresses, has sponsored many training workshops, publishes a newsletter, and funds studies of household workers in seven countries of Latin America; members of the associations do most of the work. The conference sponsored a session during the NGO (nongovernmental organization) Forum 1995 in Beijing, and made plans with household worker organizations from Asia, Africa, and Europe to form an international network.

See Also

DOMESTIC LABOR; ECONOMY: INFORMAL; HOUSEWORK; MIGRATION; TRAFFICKING; WORK, *specific entries*

References and Further Reading

Azize Vargas, Yamila, with Kamala Kempadoo. 1996. *Tráfico de mujeres para prostitución, trabajo doméstico y matrimonio: América Latina y el Caribe.* Utrecht: Foundation Against Trafficking in Women: Bangkok: Global Alliance Against Trafficking in Women.

Bunster, B., Ximea, and Elsa M. Chaney. 1985. *Sellers and servants: Working women in Lima, Peru.* New York: Praeger Special Studies.

Chaney, Elsa M., and Mary Garcia Castro, eds. 1989. *Muchachas no more: Household workers in Latin America and the Caribbean.* Philadelphia: Temple University Press.

Foner, Nancy. 1986. Sex roles and sensibilities: Jamaican women in New York and London. In Rita James Simon and Carolina B. Brettell, eds., *International migration: The female experience.* Totowa, N.J.: Rowan and Allanheld.

Gálvez, Thelma, and Rosalba Todaro. 1989. Housework for pay in Chile: Not just another job. In Elsa M. Chaney and Mary Garcia Castro, eds., *Muchachas no more: Household workers in Latin America and the Caribbean,* 307–321. Philadelphia: Temple University Press.

Gill, Lesley. 1994. *Precarious dependencies: Gender, class and domestic service in Bolivia.* New York: Columbia University Press.

Goldsmith Connelly, Mary. 1992. Sindicato de trabajadoras domésticas en México. *Mujeres y Política* 1: 57–89.

Heyzer, Noeleen, Geertje Lycklama à Nijeholt, and Nedra Weerakoon, eds. 1994. *The trade in domestic workers: Causes, mechanisms and consequences of international migration.* London: Zed.

Hondagneu-Sotelo, Pierretta. 1997. Affluent players in the informal economy: Employers of paid domestic workers. *International Journal of Sociology* 17(3/4): 130–158.

———. 2001. *Maid to work in L.A.* Los Angeles: University of California Press.

———, and Cristina Riegos. 1997. Sin organización, no hay solución: Latina domestic workers and non-traditional labor organizing. *Latino Studies Journal* 8 (3): 54–81.

Hosmer Martens, Margaret. 1994. Migrant women as domestic workers. In Margaret Hosmer Martens and Swasti Mitter, eds., *Women in trade unions: Organizing the unorganized,* 49–52. Geneva: International Labour Office.

———, and Swasti Mitter, eds. 1994. *Women in trade unions: Organizing the unorganized.* Geneva: International Labour Office.

Romero, Mary. 1992. *Maid in the U.S.A.* New York: Routledge.

———. 1996. Who takes care of the maid's children? Exploring the costs of domestic service. In Hilde Lindemann Nelson, ed., *Feminism and families,* 151–690. New York: Routledge.

Sanjek, Roger, and Shellee Colen, eds. 1990. *At work in homes: Household workers in world perspective.* Monograph Series, no. 3. Washington, D.C.: American Ethnological Society.

Wadsworth, Ana Cecilia, and Ineke Dibbits. 1989. *Agitoras de buen gusto: Historia del Sindicato de Culinarias (1935–1958).* La Paz: Tahipamu-Hisbol.

Elsa Chaney

HOUSEHOLDS AND FAMILIES: Overview

The distinction between families and households is crucial, as is the importance of exploring the activities and experiences of women, men, and children within these socially constructed entities. Increasingly researchers have explored the cross-cultural variations in the principles of social organization that inform the composition of families and households and the roles and activities carried out by members of each. The results of these comparative studies have led most social scientists to believe that families and households are fundamentally different entities.

Definition of Terms

The term *family* is defined as a social institution made up of people related by blood or marriage and rooted in systems of descent, kinship, and marriage. In addition, these kinship relations are encoded with culturally (and sometimes legally) determined sets of rights and obligations (see Sanjek, 1996). Recognition is usually given to the wide cross-cultural and intracultural variation in the organizational and residential patterns of families, as well as to the rights and obligations of particular family members.

The term *household* is generally conceptualized as the physical space in which people live. These spaces may or may not contain family members. Cross-culturally the central criteria used for determining household membership are coresidence and sharing in the carrying out of a set of domestic activities (Yanagisako, 1979).

Although these are the central defining characteristics of households, researchers have been shifting their focus from the structure of these units to the processes of production, reproduction, and consumption carried out within them. This has raised critical concerns about the hidden, often Eurocentric assumptions embedded in the concept of a household (Harris, 1981; Oppong, 1982; Ekejuba, 1995).

Variations on the Definitions

These concerns stem from the emergence of a large body of feminist literature that examines how women as members of families and households participate in production and reproduction across cultures. This literature shows the wide variety in the organization of households or residential units as well as the way in which their members are integrated into different activities. It also shows how important it is to not to generalize the experiences of women, children, and men within households and to note the diverse ways in which resources are generated and distributed and how productive and reproductive activities are carried out in specific contexts (see Sage, 1993, for an interesting example).

The impact of both local and global forces, as well as class, race, ethnicity, and gender, on the composition and organization of households has been the focus of much research on women and their lives. Numerous assumptions embedded in the concept of the household have been made by social scientists, policy planners, and others. Normatively, in the United States, such residential units are defined as people who live together, share a common kitchen, and share in the domestic activities necessary for maintaining the household. However, members of other residential units, such as extended family members or friends, may play major roles in a household, including economic support, child care, food preparation, and a wide variety of smaller but essential day-to-day chores.

Among the middle class in Brazil, different segments of a large extended family often own small apartments in the same apartment building and share many day-to-day activities. The same is true of some ethnic and racial groups in the United States. Women living in close proximity to their relatives and women living in isolated nuclear households have different life experiences. In some instances, living close to relatives may be restrictive; however, most of the time women enjoy greater freedom, including being able to take jobs outside the home, if relatives look after their children.

In rural west Africa, the compound, composed of a few or numerous dwellings located near each other within a bounded geographical space, constitutes the usual form of residential organization. Each coresidential unit has its own sleeping and food processing facilities. However, the compound, rather than the coresidential unit, is the more appropriate unit of analysis for comparative examinations of the productive, reproductive, and consumption domestic activities.

Ekejuba suggests the term *hearth-hold* as "a more gender sensitive analytical framework" to be used instead of *household*. In her conceptualization, hearth-holds are units composed of women and their dependents within the compound—those whose food security they are partially or fully responsible for. These units may be either independent or subsets within the larger context of the household which is composed of these smaller coresidential units (Ekejuba, 1995).

Expanding the Definitions

These examples raise the question of whether it is appropriate to treat households as bounded residential places of reproduction, production, and consumption. It might be more useful to conceptualize a household in terms of a living space or series of spaces, with links based on various types of social relations and transfers that shape the nature of household composition, functioning, and boundaries (see Oppong, 1982).

In addition to links at the local level, the functioning of these coresidential units is also influenced by macroeconomic, political, and social forces that inform the productive, reproductive, and consumption activities of members. For example, one of the central features of Namibia during the period of South African control was the degree to which sectors of the economy were linked to the outside world rather than being internally integrated. During this period the apartheid system included a two-tier reserve-area structure and short-term migrant labor system for the lucrative mining industries and export-oriented agriculture. The work done by women in the reserve areas subsidized the capitalist sectors of the economy. Survival for Ovambo families, who represent about 50 percent of the population, was dependent on subsistence agriculture grown on reserve area plots and migrant contract labor. The lack of sufficient food in these areas and the need for cash for essential family expenses forced high levels of Ovambo men into the contract labor system. Most of the women remained in Ovamboland, forced to assume responsibility for all productive and reproductive activities when male members were absent and struggling to survive on poor yields from subsistence agriculture and low irregular remittances from migrant men. This situation resulted in high levels of female-headed or supported households and serious disruptions in family life. The legacy of this history is reflected in the current high level of revolving male labor migration in many regions of contemporary Namibia.

In an attempt to capture the essential link between migration for wages and subsistence agriculture in the organization of kinship groups and residential units, households in the Namibian context have been defined as "supporting units with one or more sources of income. This includes all family members who belong to the same homestead, be they present or absent, and who live on and contribute to the same income" (Centre for Advanced Training in Agricultural Development, 1994: 11). This definition is designed to capture the reality of the temporary or permanent absence of adult members from the household and of children who are fostered or who are living in school-based hostels away from home.

This example demonstrates various factors that affect the composition and functioning of households:

1017

1. The influence of the state, and the effect of the global economy on female and male roles as they relate to both production and reproduction of the workforce

2. The importance of exploring the impact of economic, political, and social forces in household composition, women's roles in the household and the ways in which production and reproduction are organized in specific contexts

3. The diverse survival strategies needed by women and men in different societies

4. The internationalization of production and capital accumulation that can segment different regions and household members so that they may be working at cross-purposes

5. The processes and activities necessary for women to maintain their household that depend on different sectors of the national and global economy

For example, if a household is dependent on a daughter working in Singapore in the export-processing zone, the security of that household, which might contain her parents and younger siblings, is affected by the demand in New York City for a particular kind of shoe.

New Research Leads to a New Approach

New research in the 1990s raised new questions regarding what kinds of households are found. Are they solely coresidential units? Do people from outside also share resources? Does the main daytime childcare activity take place in this residence? Many more questions could be asked. This approach has the advantage of forcing a movement in the analysis away from structure to process and explaining the composition and organization of the groups of people involved in carrying out domestic activities. It allows researchers to (1) explore the ways the state, region, and local economy are integrated into the global economy; (2) see how these processes shape the contours, functioning, and actual experiences of members of coresidential units; and (3) explore the content of male and female roles by class, race, ethnicity, gender, and age.

This new perspective shows the wide range of cross-cultural variation in the formation, composition, organization, and functioning of coresidential units. It also yields information on the activities carried out by women, men, and children involved in the domestic functions and the processes necessary to maintaining these units. Moreover, a better understanding of the link between these activities and the local, regional, national, and global economy can be gained.

Attention to these issues may provide useful data on the relations governing the distribution and consumption of household unit resources, decision making, and consequences for individual members. It might also provide a lens through which to view the relationships that are formed and used to carry out domestic activities, such as acquiring material resources and providing life-sustaining activities essential for the maintenance of these groups and the movement of members of the household within the community and across regional and national borders.

Conclusion

The term *coresidential unit* may be a better alternative than *household*, because it avoids many assumptions embedded in the later term. However, it is important to approach this concept with a series of questions: (1) Who are the people who ideally constitute coresidential units? (2) What are the common processes for the formation of these units? (3) What types of activities are necessary for the maintenance and production of these units? (4) How are these activities carried out and by whom? (5) How are the resources that belong to these units produced, distributed, and consumed? (6) To what degree and in which way does the state penetrate these units and inform domestic activities carried out by the members of these units? (7) How are the various productive and reproductive activities of these units integrated into the local, regional, national, and global economy? (8) How do these outside factors inform male-female and child-adult relations and the nature of relationships between those involved in carrying out domestic functions? (9) How do these sets of relationships vary by ethnicity, race, class, and gender?

Answers to these questions will help show the gendered content of male and female roles and activities in different contexts and the strategies involved in essential domestic activities. It also shows the cross-cultural similarities and differences in the experiences of women and the consequences of these arrangements for women. Within this larger framework, it is important to explore the culturally determined sex-gender system and the ways that it informs the roles of women, girls, men, and boys. This is not a static system: it is undergoing rapid change and increasing penetration by the global capitalist system and international finance agencies such as the World Bank and International Monetary Fund. In many instances these forces have radically changed the composition of coresidential units and the processes involved in carrying out essential productive and reproductive activities.

See Also

EDUCATION: DOMESTIC SCIENCE AND HOME ECONOMICS; FAMILY: RELIGIOUS AND LEGAL SYSTEMS, *all entries*; FAMILY STRUCTURES; HOUSEHOLDS: FEMALE-HEADED AND FEMALE-SUPPORTED; HOUSEHOLDS: POLITICAL ECONOMY; HOUSEHOLDS: RESOURCES; HOUSEHOLDS AND FAMILIES: *regional entries*; MIGRATION; POLITICS AND THE STATE: OVERVIEW; SECTS AND CULTS

References and Further Reading

Basch, Linda, Nina Glick Schiller, and Cristina Szantou Blanc. 1994. *Nations unbound: Transnational projects, post-colonial predicaments and deterritorialized nation-states.* U.S.A., Switzerland: Gordon and Breach.

Bruce, Judith. 1995. The economics of motherhood. In Judith Bruce, Cynthia Lloyd, and Ann Leonard with Patrice Duffy, *Families in focus: New perspectives on mothers, fathers, and children.* New York: Population Council.

Centre for Advanced Training in Agricultural Development. 1994. *Participatory methods for situation analysis and planning of project activities: Experiences with women and youth in the communal areas of Namibia.* Berlin: Humboldt University.

Ekejuba, Felicia. 1995. Down to fundamentals: Women-centered hearth-holds in rural West Africa. In Deborah Bryceson, ed., *Women wielding the hoe: Lessons from rural Africa for feminist theory and development practices,* 25–45. Washington, D.C.: Berg.

Emeagwali, Gloria. 1995. *Women pay the price: Structural adjustment in Africa and the Caribbean.* Africa World.

Folbre, Nancy. 1991. Women on their own: Global patterns of female headship. In Rita Gallin and Anne Ferguson, eds., *The women and international development annual,* Vol. 2. Boulder, Col.: Westview.

Harris, Olivia. 1981. Households as natural units. In Kate Young, Carol Wolkowitz, and Roslyn McCullah, eds., *Of marriage and the market: Women's subordination in international perspective,* 49–67. London: C.S.E.

Oppong, Christine. 1982. Family structure and women's reproductive and productive roles: Some conceptual and methodological issues. In Richard Anker et al., eds., *Women's roles and population trends in the third world,* 133–149. London: Croom Helm.

Osirim, Mary Johnson. 1997. We toil all the livelong day: Women in the English-speaking Caribbean. In Consuelo Lopez, ed., *Daughters of Caliban: Caribbean in the twentieth century,* 41–67. Springfield: Indiana University Press.

Sage, Colin. 1993. Deconstructing the household: Women's roles under commodity relations in highland Bolivia. In Janet

Momsen and Vivian Kinnaird, eds., *Different places, different voices: gender and development in Africa, Asia and Latin America,* 243–255. London: Routledge.

Sanjek, Roger. 1996. Households. In Alan Baruand and Johnathan Spenser, eds., *Encyclopedia of social and cultural anthropology,* 280–288. London: Routledge.

Yanagisako, Sylvia Junko. 1979. Family and household: The analysis of domestic groups. *Annual Review of Anthropology* 8: 161–205.

Anne Francis-Okongwu

HOUSEHOLDS AND FAMILIES: Caribbean

The subject of households and family has been a favorite one for sociologists, social workers, demographers, and moralists in the Caribbean for many decades. One of the main concerns has been with the problem of definition. Some have argued that the established European definition of family is not true for the Caribbean, or at least a part of its population, while others argue that what is often described as the "Caribbean family" should really be seen as "disorganized" deviation from acceptable norms.

The Caribbean is a complex region. There are many similarities but also many differences. Among the similarities that characterize this region are the history of decimation of the indigenous populations; colonization by European powers; large-scale importation of Africans as slaves; smaller-scale importation of other groups—for example, from India, Madeira, China, and Indonesia as bonded labor; the establishment of plantation agriculture for export to Europe; and the continued tradition of migration both within the region and to metropolitan countries.

All of these factors have affected the development of families and households in the Caribbean. Caribbean family and household forms can be seen therefore as adaptations of cultural practices indigenous to a particular group on its arrival to the Caribbean, where it faced the exigencies of life in situations of forced labor and colonial control of economy, values, institutions, and so on.

But differences in family and household forms within the Caribbean have also been influenced by the rigid hierarchical class, color, and ethnic structures established for all the reasons stated above. As a result, forms may vary within a particular ethnic or cultural group according to class or income. In spite of these variations, social researchers have usually concentrated their research on two main groups: the African

Caribbean majority and the Indian Caribbean minority. More recently, studies of the European and Jewish elite have begun to appear.

From very early on, demographers working in this region found it necessary for purposes of quantification to differentiate between households and families. This tack was taken largely because family forms in this region did not conform to accepted European norms of marriage, family composition, residence, and division of labor.

African Caribbean families were found to be particularly deviant, characterized as they were by a large proportion of nonlegal unions, a significant proportion of children born outside of legal unions, and a large number of households "headed" by women. Efforts to change these patterns through the work of Christian missionaries, middle-class do-gooders such as governors' wives, or social welfare agencies had little success because these patterns have proved resistant to change and indeed have often been assumed by other groups.

Indian Caribbean families have also warranted some attention. These families were—and in rural areas still are—characterized by joint or extended households, early marriage, strong patriarchal authority, patrilocal residence, and the subordination of daughters-in-law in the patriarchal residence. These families, however, received far less attention from authorities, possibly because within them, patriarchal control was never in question.

There has been a continued resistance to referring to these various forms as "families," and in particular to seeing households of women with their children and maybe a grandmother as bona fide families. So the word *household* has been the preferred one in a situation where many Caribbean families do not conform to Peter Murdock's "universal" definition. Murdock, in his study of 250 societies entitled *Social Structure,* defined the family as "a social group characterized by common residence, economic cooperation and reproduction. It includes adults of both sexes, at least two of whom maintain a socially approved sexual relationship, and one or more children, own or adopted of sexually co-habiting adults" (Murdock, 1949: 1).

Scholars of the Caribbean family find that the concept of family cannot be encapsulated within one household. Families often span more than one household and sometimes more than one country. But in addition, specific characteristics have been identified that need to be explained in detail. These include a range of union types, the structure and composition of households, and the issue of female-headed households.

Marriage or Union Types

The term *union type* was developed among family scholars in the region because legal marriage was only one of the forms of sexual and residential unions in existence. It was necessary to differentiate between marital status as a legal state and union status, which was the lived reality. For example, although data on marital status may show marriage to be a dominant form, persons who are legally married to one person, are divorced, or are widowed may at the same time be involved in other forms of union with other individuals.

As early as the 1960s scholars noted that after taking into account the basic difference of early and compulsory marriage for Indians and later marriage or no compulsion to marry for African Caribbeans, many similarities were emerging. After the dissolution of an early marriage or widowhood, for example, Indians may enter visiting or common-law unions, especially because for Hindu widows, remarriage has been an unacceptable alternative.

Different typologies have been developed by various scholars to describe these types of unions. In addition to *marriage,* the terms most commonly used in the early twenty-first century were the following:

Casual relationship. This term was developed by Roberts and Sinclair (1978) to describe unions, usually among sexually active teenagers, that usually ended after the first pregnancy. These can be seen as a subset of visiting relationships, which are discussed below.

Visiting unions. This term refers to situations where a man and woman have a recognized or unrecognized sexual relationship but do not live in the same household. They may have one or more children and the man may contribute to the upkeep of the woman, the children, or both. By the same token, she may also provide for his upkeep and may perform domestic duties such as preparing meals or doing laundry.

Some researchers see visiting unions as a first stage to a more stable coresidential union. This is sometimes the case, but visiting unions may end even after the birth of one or more children or may continue for a number of years.

Common-law union or companionate union. This is a coresidential relationship that is not legally sanctioned. These relationships are usually entered into at later ages than visiting relationships and may or may not end in marriage. Many common-law unions, however, last for a number of years, often resulting in children.

In spite of the strong moral, religious, and legal sanction against such unions, they continue to exist. Researchers have identified reasons for this state of affairs, including societal assumptions about the economic responsibilities of women and men in a "real" marriage that many low-income people find difficult to implement. Women apparently would accept deficiencies in a common-law union that they would not accept in a marriage.

At the same time, there are within the society women who resent the hold that marriage is perceived to place on women. Thus they see a common-law relationship, referred to as a "friending" relationship in some countries, as a more comfortable option.

For many people in society, however, a common-law union is a marriage without the legal trimmings, so often the terms *husband* and *wife* are used, and similar obligations and responsibilities are expected. Unfortunately, no acceptable alternative terminology exists for partners in these unions.

In a belated and half-hearted effort to come to terms with the realities of Caribbean unions, some governments are slowly beginning to put in place legislation to recognize common-law unions. In most countries of the English-speaking Caribbean, children of common-law and visiting unions have equal legal status with children of legal unions.

Household Composition and Structure

A 1980s study of 1,600 households and families in three Caribbean countries found that one-third comprised a woman, her partner, and their children. The rest comprised a range of forms: a woman and children (10–11 percent); multiple or extended relationships, laterally or vertically (36–45 percent) (Women in the Caribbean Project, 1982). Household composition is also not always the same. Members may leave—go to the household of a relative, godmother, or friend or migrate and return while another goes abroad. Other individuals live in more than one household.

This situation is compounded when Caribbean women and men migrate to northern metropoles and leave children with grandmothers, fathers, female relatives, godparents, and even friends. These persons, although they may be scattered, still consider themselves "family," although they do not live in the same household. Mothers and, to a lesser extent, fathers continue to play an important role in providing essentials, paying school fees, counseling, and making important life decisions even from a distance. In some instances children may join their mothers or parents in these countries when their parents' legal or economic status has improved.

Mothers may send their children back to the Caribbean because they are unable to cope single-handedly or because they prefer their children to receive a Caribbean education

or upbringing. One Caribbean scholar, Rosina Wiltshire (1987), has coined the term *transnational family* to describe this phenomenon.

Indian Caribbean families, especially in rural areas, have adapted to the new situation by shifting from a joint family ideal to a patrilocal extended family pattern. In this situation, older women subordinated in their youth in the home of in-laws exercise greater power and influence over daughters-in-law and sons later in life. As early as the 1950s scholars noted a trend toward greater collaboration and cooperation between Indian Caribbean daughters and mothers even after marriage, a pattern more characteristic of African Caribbean families.

As the societies and groups grow together, however, practices are borrowed from one another, and the middle and upper classes of all ethnic and cultural groups increasingly adopt the patterns of the dominant western Euro-American culture.

Household Headship

Another contentious issue related to Caribbean family has been that of "headship." Headship in a social sense has had to do with control over the family, importance in decision making, and so on. For demographers a main concern has been with economic responsibility for maintaining the household. In the more patriarchal Indian family system, headship was not seen as a problem; however, with the African Caribbean families it was a major concern. This concern is reflected in the range of terms that were developed mainly by metropolitan scholars to describe a family system where they found that women—often, mothers—had "inordinate" power and centrality.

Thus, this family form has been described as matrifocal, matrilineal, matriarchal, mother- or grandmother-centered, and even denuded. In more recent times the literature has tended to use the term *female-headed households*. This term is obviously derived from the view that male headship of households is normal, while the opposite is deviant and cause for concern. The significance of the concept of head of household can be traced to sixteenth-century western Europe, where the male head of the post-Reformation middle-class household assumed from the clergy some of the religious authority for his economic dependents.

Caribbean demography is still in many ways tied to the ideal of the male as familial head and breadwinner and the female as dependent housewife. And many statistics on income distribution and social mobility are still structured around this understanding. As a result, most households defined as female-headed are households without adult male partners. Indeed, studies show that the majority of women in female-headed households were never married. But the possibility of women heading households where adult male partners are present is increasingly being accepted. This usually occurs, however, where "he is unable to function as household head for health or economic reasons" (Massiah, 1982: 67). What is still not accepted is the possibility of shared responsibility of partners in a relationship or household. It is assumed that every household must have a head. This notion is being continuously challenged by feminist scholars.

Statistics for the region show the proportion of female-headed households ranging form 22 percent to 43.9 percent in 1992. The higher ranges are in countries with a larger African Caribbean and mixed population, a fact that suggests that this phenomenon is linked with adaptations from matrilineal sub-Saharan African family forms and the slave experience, in addition to the other economic factors shared with other cultural and ethnic groups.

In the Caribbean region the concept of family extends much further than the household. Indeed, family has much more to do with being related either biologically or socially than with common residence. The universal definition of the basic family unit may not be as Murdock (1949) defined it, characterized by two adults of both sexes in a socially approved sexual relationship. Rather, the basic family unit may comprise a woman—who may have a sexual relationship with an adult male—and her children or grandchildren. By that token, the large number of female-headed households in this region and other parts of the world could be redefined as families, because this is, to a large extent, how the people involved experience them.

See Also

DEVELOPMENT: CENTRAL AND SOUTH AMERICA AND THE CARIBBEAN; FAMILY STRUCTURES; HOUSEHOLDS AND FAMILIES: OVERVIEW; HOUSEHOLDS: FEMALE-HEADED AND FEMALE-SUPPORTED; MARRIAGE: REGIONAL TRADITIONS AND PRACTICES

References and Further Reading

Abraham-van der Mark, Eva. 1993. Marriage and concubinage among the Sephardic merchant elite of Curaco. In Janet Momsen, ed., *Women and change in the Caribbean*. Kingston, Jamaica: Ian Randle; Oxford: James Currey; Bloomington: Indiana University Press.

Barrow Lisa. 1988. Anthropology, the family and women in the Caribbean. In P. Mohammed and C. Shepherd, eds., *Gender in Caribbean development*, 156–169. St. Michael, Barbados: University of the West Indies.

———.1998. Caribbean masculinity and family: Revisiting "marginality" and "reputation." In Christine Barrow, ed., *Caribbean portraits: Essays on gender ideologies and identities*. Kingston, Jamaica: Ian Randle; St. Michael, Barbados: University of the West Indies Centre for Gender and Development Studies.

Dann, Graham. 1987. *The Barbadian male: Sexual attitudes and practices*. Cambridge: Cambridge University Press.

Douglass, Lisa. 1992. *The power of sentiment: Love, hierarchy and the Jamaican family elite*. Boulder, Col.: Westview.

Garrison, Vivian, and Carol I. Weiss. 1987. Dominican family networks and United States immigration policy: A case study. In Constance Sutton and Elsa M. Chaney, eds., *Caribbean life in New York City: Sociocultural dimensions*, 235–254. New York: Center for Migration Studies of New York.

Lazarus-Black, Mindie. 1995. My mother never fathered me: Rethinking kinship and the governing of families. *Social and Economic Studies* 44(1): 49–71.

Massiah, Joyceline. 1982. Women who head households. In *Women and the family*, 62–130. St. Michael, Barbados: Institute of Social and Economic Research, University of the West Indies.

Morrissey, Marietta. 1998. Explaining Caribbean family: Gender ideologies and identities. In Christine Barrow, ed., *Caribbean portraits: Essays on gender ideologies and identities*. Kingston, Jamaica: Ian Randle; St. Michael, Barbados: University of the West Indies Centre for Gender and Development Studies.

Murdock, George. 1949. *Social structure*. New York: Macmillan.

Rawlins, Joan. 1986. *Recent research on the family in the Caribbean: An annotated bibliography*. St. Michael, Barbados: Institute of Social and Economic Research, University of the West Indies.

Roberts, George, and Lloyd Braithwaite. 1962. Mating among East Indian and non-Indian women in Trinidad. *Social and Economic Studies* 11(3).

Roberts, George, and Sonia Sinclair. 1987. *Women in Jamaica: Patterns of reproduction and family*. Millwood, N.Y.: KTO.

Senior, Olive. 1991. *Working miracles: Women's lives in the English-speaking Caribbean*. Bloomington: Indiana University Press.

Smith, Raymond T. 1996. *The matrifocal family: Power, pluralism and politics*. New York: Routledge.

———, and Chandra Jayawardena. 1959. Marriage and the family amongst East Indians in British Guiana. *Social and Economic Studies* 8: 321–76.

Wiltshire, Rosina. 1987. The Caribbean transnational family. Paper prepared for UNESCO Institute of Social and Economic Research seminar, Changing Family Patterns and

Women's Role in the Caribbean, University of the West Indies, St. Michael, Barbados.

Women in the Caribbean Project. 1982. *Women and the family.* St. Michael, Barbados: Institute of Social and Economic Research, University of the West Indies.

Rhoda Reddock

HOUSEHOLDS AND FAMILIES:
Central and Eastern Europe

Throughout eastern and central Europe there are many regional and cultural variations, which make any generalizations about the region problematic at best. The common features of the peoples inhabiting the region are the feudal and imperial past, the heritage of two world wars, and the experience of different variations of socialism. The social roles within the family have been defined by both tradition and social policy. Eastern and central Europe encompasses Poland, the Czech Republic, Slovakia, Bulgaria, Hungary, Romania, Albania, and the countries of the former Yugoslavia. The fall of the Soviet Union brought to life many independent states in the area that is geographically in the east of Europe, but they will not be included here.

Some of the most important differences within the area result from the variety of religious traditions. The region houses large populations of Catholics, Eastern Orthodox, and Muslims. Some areas, such as Poland, are dominated by one major religion, Catholicism in this case. But the region of the former Yugoslavia encompasses Macedonia, Serbia, Bosnia-Herzegovina, Croatia, and Slovenia, all of them with mixed populations of different religious allegiances. Religious and cultural traditions play an important role in determining women's role within the household, the family, and thus the larger society. All three above-mentioned religions hold a traditional and conservative outlook on women's roles, tying them to household duties and childbearing. There are some variations to this pattern in Protestant communities, and some countries are more homogeneous (like Poland), while others, such as Hungary with its ties to Asia and the Ottoman Empire, are less so. Heterosexuality is the official norm in eastern Europe, and homosexuality has been unmentioned or prohibited, at least until the later years of the twentieth century. When homosexuality was mentioned, it refered to gay men and left lesbians invisible in the public domain.

Eastern European regions have been subject to different feudal and imperial authorities and thus to different policies regarding women. For example, in Slovenia, formerly part of Austrian crown lands, there was a considerable amount of opportunity for both young men and women. The families were patriarchal but not patrilocal, and women were not perceived as invaders in the close knit society of lineally related men. In the areas formerly under Ottoman control, there was a long-standing tradition of the peasant, Christian family unit being in opposition to the imperial administration and exercising some autonomy in the tight, self-sufficient communities. The family patterns that evolved thus incorporated the code of honor and the blood feud, a strict hierarchy, and an emphasis on women's fertility, as large families offered greater protection and the family had to surrender one male child to the state. Catholicism, as practiced in Poland, also dictated that families be large and advocated strict antiabortion rules. The Polish population, although overwhelmingly claiming allegiance to the church, was nevertheless independent-minded when it came to family planning, and the average Polish family has never been large, except in rural regions. In the former Yugoslavia, as in many eastern European countries, adult identity for most women was inseparable from marriage and hence family. This case was especially true in the rural areas. Throughout the war period, the rural regions of eastern Europe followed a pattern characteristic of "bride wealth societies," in which families were organized on patriarchal and patrilocal principles. But in countries such as Poland and the Czech Republic, there also were some different patterns present. In all, however, it can be generalized that women's role in the family was perceived as one of strength, as opposed to her minimal impact on the larger society.

The creation of the Soviet bloc redefined the role of women in the family and society. Under the communist system, the governments in eastern and central Europe were officially committed to a policy of women's emancipation, to be achieved through legislation and social policy. Women's responsibilities were to be eased by government-sponsored school and workplace canteens, communal laundries, and improved shopping and service facilities. These promises were only partially fulfilled, because of economic problems, severe social dislocation after World War II, and the fast pace of industrialization. The drive to collectivize agriculture, in order to abolish that stronghold of private property, was made into a state priority and drained financial resources of the government. In effect, most Soviet bloc countries had inadequate child care facilities and severe food shortages; thus the women in families thus bore the burden not only of motherhood, but also of work outside the home. The social roles within the family have been defined by both tradition and social policy. The new socialist society had a greater effect on the relationship and responsibilities of the family toward society than on intrafamily relationships and roles.

The official doctrine of state socialism treated the family as being responsible for duties toward the society and the state. Women were responsible for fulfilling their obligations as both mother and worker. The traditional gender divisions within the family still persisted from the early twentieth century and the traditional peasant culture. The equality of men and women was constitutionally affirmed and made subordinate to the obligation to work. The end of World War II brought the entry of large numbers of women into the labor force. Women have generally entered the job market, however, to fulfill their financial needs, not for self-liberation. Paid employment did not replace their household work—child care, provision of goods and clothing, and housekeeping. The conception of women's and men's domestic tasks did not change with women at work outside of the household.

As in western Europe, the occupations in which women have made greatest advances are those that offered small financial rewards and minimal social prestige. Women moved mostly toward unskilled manual labor, while men pursued intellectual occupations and skilled labor. Furthermore, despite the large number of women entering the labor force in all sectors, they have played a very small role in economic decision making. As in many western countries, the poor in many eastern and central European countries are also disproportionately female.

Women's reproductive and sexual lives have been closely linked to state prerogatives. Whereas in Poland, Czechoslovakia, and Hungary there was relative reproductive freedom during the socialist years, with free availability of abortion (although scarce supplies of contraceptives, such as the pill), in Romania contraception was outlawed in the 1960s and divorce was extremely difficult to obtain. In countries like Poland, state measures relating to demographic concerns were a balancing act between the official dogma of women's emancipation, labor force requirements, and the moral dictates of the very powerful Catholic church. Several countries introduced material incentives to boost the birthrate. In spite of state policies and church pressures, however, there is evidence of a very high rate of divorce throughout eastern Europe and a preference for smaller families. This phenomenon certainly had to do with women's double burdens and with chronic shortages of apartments and basic supplies

but it also was an expression of their ability to make choices regarding their own lives.

During most of the twentieth century, urban women in Hungary generally spent half as much time on housework as rural women. The leisure time of all women across eastern Europe, however, is generally less than that of men. In Poland and Bulgaria, women became increasingly frustrated in the struggle to obtain basic goods, shelter, food, and clothing during the crises of the socialist period. The early 1970s were a fairly prosperous time in Czechoslovakia, but the country slid into economic crisis after 1975. Hungarian families were doing relatively well economically, and women could take advantage of affirmative action: mothers with young children spent up to 50 percent of their total annual work time away owing to maternity leave or sick leave or taking the "household day" once a month to "catch up on domestic labor." Although these measures eased the burden of housework, they also further reinforced the gender-based division of domestic labor. Although Albanian women suffered the same effects of double burden, for many of them the communist years brought an opportunity to gain education and enjoy some freedoms unattainable under the legacy of the Ottoman Empire and the Islamic world.

Farm women constitute a very heterogeneous population; their positions differ depending on region, household, and farm structure, and personal characteristics such as level of education, age, and marital status. But throughout eastern Europe, their lives and circumstances are changing fairly radically since the fall of the Soviet bloc. Change is occurring in gender relations manifest at a macrosocial level (for example, in the composition of the labor force, in educational systems, and in policies oriented toward equality or emancipation) as well as within farm households, although there the gender division of labor appears relatively impermeable to change and continues to have substantial effects on women's position both on and off the farm.

The fall of the Soviet bloc had a major impact on public policy regarding women's rights and their place in the family. Many societies experienced a backlash. Women used to live in regimes that at least theoretically guaranteed them the legal right to equality and basic family planning practices but are now subjugated to right wing parties' rejection of state socialist policies on women's emancipation and feminism. The Catholic church's growing influence on political life has facilitated the passage of the most recent antiabortion law (as of this writing) in Poland. The fact that women's emancipation was connected to their double burden of housework and paid work played an important role in the renewal of traditional values after the collapse of communism. For example, it is commonly believed that eastern European women value marriage and a happy family life above all else. This assumption is often used to argue that women should stay at home and take care of the family, because it is natural for them and in accordance with their values.

Most women still work outside the home, but unemployment has disproportionately affected women. Institutionalized child care has increasingly become out of reach for women, and it has been stigmatized as the worst possible alternative. Privatization of child care facilities and subsequent increases in fees make most facilities less accessible to poor and middle-class women. Because of unemployment, most women are afraid to take parental leave. It seems that the social group that best adjusted to Polish capitalism is young, professional men with business experience and an interest in computer science. Many women are trying to take advantage of the opening markets, but household burdens limit their opportunities.

Since the fall of the Soviet Union, eastern and central European societies have been trying to redefine themselves. Poland is an example of how difficult the new reality can be. The symbolic meaning of the Polish mother has not significantly changed over the last century. Women are still expected to sacrifice their personal aspirations and needs and give priority to their husband's professional careers and their children's needs. The centuries-old image of the Polish mother has been transformed to one in which women are expected to undertake, heroically and eagerly, the double burden of professional life and primary household duties. Heroism and martyrdom are considered Polish national features, but the expectations resulting from this national mythology are not gender neutral: men are expected to prove themselves heroes in the event of war or other difficult periods of history; women are to be heroines in everyday life.

See Also

DEVELOPMENT: CENTRAL AND EASTERN EUROPE; HOUSEHOLDS AND FAMILIES: COMMONWEALTH OF INDEPENDENT STATES

References and Further Reading

Einhorn, Barbara. 1993. *Cinderella goes to market: Citizenship, gender and women's movements in east central Europe.* London: Verso.

Lobodzinska, Barbara. 1995. *Family, women and employment in central-eastern Europe.* New York: Greenwood.

Moghadam, Valentine, ed. 1993. *Democratic reform and the position of women in transitional economies.* Oxford: Oxford University Press.

Renne, Tanya. 1996. *Ana's land—sisterhood in eastern Europe.* New York: HarperCollins.

Scott, Hilda. 1976. *Women and socialism: Experiences from eastern Europe.* London: Allison and Busby.

Temida, Polish Women's Organization: <www.temida.pl> (posted in June 1998).

Wolchik, Sharon L., and Alfred G. Meyer, eds. 1985. *Women, state, and party in eastern Europe.* Durham, N.C.: Duke University Press.

Agnieszka Kajrukszto

HOUSEHOLDS AND FAMILIES:
Central and South America

Family Composition and Household Organization

Any single definition of *family* and *household* in the context of Central and South America is problematic, first, because of regional variations in what "counts" as a household or family and, second, because a genuine understanding of these terms must encompass many different definitions (for example, social, historical, and economic interpretations). Despite these difficulties in defining the features that characterize the institution of the family in South and Central America, certain trends and patterns can be observed.

The emergence of alternatives to the traditional extended model is one important feature. In the extended model the family includes other relatives living in the home, with the husband being the sole member to engage in waged work while his wife takes responsibility for domestic duties and child care. It is a common misconception to assume that the extended family model is the norm since, in reality, there is no single structure that typifies family composition or household organization in Central and South America. There is a huge variety of arrangements, including nuclear or extended families, male-headed or female-headed households, and complex arrangements of stepfamilies and housing units comprising lodgers and unrelated individuals. It is the broadness of these exceptions to the traditional extended family model that characterizes Latin American societies.

An example of alternative family structures becoming more widespread is the increase in female-headed households. In Argentina the number rose from 16.5 percent to 19.2 percent between 1970 and 1980, and in Puerto Rico female-headed households rose from 16 percent to 23.2 percent between 1970 and 1990 (Chant, 1997). In a study of a low-income community in Guayaquil, Ecuador, it was observed that female-headed units rose from 12 to 19 percent between 1978 and 1988.

One explanation for these changes is male migration to the cities in search of work, leaving women as the sole breadwinner. Other reasons include increases in divorce rates and in the feminization of labor, meaning that out of financial necessity, combined with more opportunity in the workplace, women are increasingly working outside the home. Economic changes such as these are accompanied by gradual changes in attitude, whereby it is becoming more acceptable for women to build careers. Changes in women's economic role indirectly affect household composition. Recent studies suggest that the added number of burdens women face in working inside and outside the home and the injustice felt by women at men's limited help in housework and child care can lead women to reject the traditional family model (Benería, 1992).

In addition to the differences stated above, variation among households is influenced by such factors as class and wealth. Income distribution in Latin America is very unequal. Middle-class families often employ domestic servants, whose plight has been well documented. These servants are often exploited and have to neglect their own families. In poorer families who cannot afford to employ domestic servants, domestic responsibilities generally still fall to women. Only in exceptional cases does women's incorporation into the labor market lead to male family members taking responsibility for child care and domestic work. Indeed, if the mother is forced to work outside the home, the burden of child care and domestic work tends to fall to her daughter, who will have to miss schooling as a result and whose opportunities for later advancement will be curtailed.

There are also regional differences that affect household composition. The populations of South and Central America are a rich fusion, with different cultural histories. In simple terms there are indigenous populations, mestizo (literally, "mixed race"), and Hispanic populations (though there is much variation within these categories). Thus, the composition of a wealthy household of predominantly Hispanic origin living in a prosperous district such as Miraflores in Lima, Peru, will differ greatly from that of a Shipibo Indian living in the Peruvian Amazon. Interestingly, the Mundurucu Indians of Brazil are not organized into family units or households at all since they are patrilineal (recognizing clans) and matrilocal (husbands live in the wives' villages). As Jelin (1991) notes, "in the case of these Indians, the group formed by a man, his wife, and his children is not a domestic unit nor a household, but constitutes a basic reference for the organization and mutual distribution of the products of male and female labor."

As well as ethnic differences affecting cultural and familial norms, there are differences between rural and urban areas that have a direct bearing on women's lives within the family unit. For example, in rural areas such as Acatlán, Mexico, where wages are low and there are few opportunities for advancement, men migrate to the cities, leaving women to manage their farms alone. This situation might suggest that it is tougher for women in rural areas than in towns. However, by contrast, in urban areas of Mexico such as Zapopan, where the cost of living is higher, low-income women may be even worse off, having no farmlands of their own from which to feed their families.

The sexual division of labor within and outside the family unit determines patterns of behavior, control, and authority within it. The "head" of the household is generally understood to be either the person earning the major income or the person who exerts the most influence over decisions affecting the household (Chant, 1997: 7). However, increases in a woman's income do not necessarily translate into greater power and control in the family. In many countries in the region, laws and social convention reinforce male authority as household heads. For example, in Peru a woman cannot prove ownership of property without the formal consent of her husband. Research on women living in the poorest districts of Lima (the *barriadas*) suggests that when women apply for credit in order to set up small businesses—"microenterprises"—they are often unable to meet collateral requirements because of discriminatory laws and practices that deny them the right to hold land titles and property (Wright, 1997). For example, women applying for credit to start a business are often required to obtain their husband's signature on the loan application. In effect, discrimination of this kind means that although a woman may provide the major income in the family, thus constituting a female "head," she is not recognized as such in formal legal terms or socially.

Sexual Division of Labor

The traditional model of sexual division of labor in Latin America determines that waged labor is the function of the husband, who as household head provides for household maintenance. His wife is assigned domestic work, child rearing, and socialization of the children. Women increasingly feel obliged to work for profitable activities outside the home to supplement the family income. It is often argued that this outside work does not alter the traditional model since men maintain their economic power and authority (Jelin, 1991).

In Central and South America women tend to perform a dual role. On the one hand, women's lives are circumscribed by their domestic chores and child care. Yet at the same time, women are forced by financial necessity to engage in waged work. This reformulation of the division of labor may be perceived as a threat to the institution of the family itself. As women become financially independent and more self-reliant, they are less likely to depend on marriage for survival and may even question the sexual division of labor. Marriage breakdown is one of the most common results of female-headed households in Latin America. (In Africa, by contrast, marriage breakdown is mostly due to male migration, and in Asia, it is principally due to widowhood; Willis, 1993.)

In a study of the relationship between labor mobility and the household in Central America (Pérez and Larín, 1984), it was argued that women's choices in the labor market are restricted by the domestic role that they are forced to assume. In Guatemala, Honduras, and Nicaragua more women were engaged in subsistence activities (such as selling foodstuffs) while men predominated in small enterprises. It was observed that labor mobility is conditioned by the individual's position in the family and that women and children are the most constrained because of the demands placed on them in the household. Lack of basic services causes much time to be wasted completing unnecessarily arduous household tasks. In this way men living in Central America gain better positions in the informal sector by making few or no concessions to domestic life. By contrast, domestic considerations determine women's possibilities and confine them in most cases to subsistence activity rather than more lucrative income generation. This situation is often reinforced by cultural norms: "To be a mother includes a predestination to sacrifice, a concept that is not only accepted, but also made a priority in deciding amongst labor alternatives" (Portés and Benton, 1989: 85). The importance of motherhood in Central and South America, perpetuated by the Catholic ideology of the *marianismo* tradition, defined by Evelyn Stevens as "the cult of feminine spiritual superiority," which teaches that women are semi-divine, morally superior to and spiritually stronger than men (Stevens, 1973: 90–91), and the assumption that this "natural" vocation is accepted socially as a "fact of life." The spheres of production and reproduction overlap. Low-income women are exploited as a cheap, flexible source of labor and are subordinated to patriarchical relations within the household.

Domestic Violence

Domestic violence is one such manifestation of patriarchal control. Alcoholism is a real concern for impoverished families. In Chile 60 percent of women who live with their partners suffer domestic violence, and in Ecuador 60 percent of female residents in Quito's poorest districts have been beaten by their partners. Even in Brazil, where the women's movement has been particularly progressive and has served as a model for the rest of the region, the courts did not regard domestic violence such as rape and murder as a crime if motivated by *emoção violenta* (violent emotion) until 1991. The related *defensa de honra* (defense of honor) was also used to condone violence in cases of alleged unfaithfulness (Nelson, 1996).

Studies of domestic violence by the Inter-American Development Bank in Nicaragua in 1997 suggest that women in family units who assumed control of small enterprises and manage resources were less likely to be victims of domestic violence. The study revealed that 41 percent of non-wage-earning women were victims of physical violence, while only 10 percent of women who held paid work outside the home suffered in this way. Results of this study showed that in Central America women with no income of their own—especially those who worked in a family business but were not paid—were more frequently the victims of cruelty. However, other evidence suggests that women who engaged in waged work might be perceived as a threat to a man's traditional function as breadwinner. Thus, women's microenterprise activity may actually be causing domestic violence, not preventing it.

Household Networks

The existence or absence of social networks (used for help with child care, housework, job information, and financial assistance) influences women's employment opportunities. Researchers working in Central and South America suggest that there is much interhousehold exchange and that it is an essential self-help strategy for low-income families. Yet, conflicting research indicates that there is little evidence of interhousehold exchange or social networks in Oaxaca City, in one of Mexico's poorest states (Willis, 1993), or similar areas. Where interhousehold exchange is absent and public provision is inadequate, poor households have to look inward to protect the family economy from total collapse. The "moral economy" of the household (that is, balancing needs and earning power) depends on ingenious management. For low-income families lacking access to support from state or private institutions, management entails personal sacrifice and putting the interests of the family above those of individual members. However, women often bear the brunt of this sacrifice.

See Also

DIVISION OF LABOR; FAMILY: RELIGIOUS AND LEGAL SYSTEMS—CATHOLIC AND ORTHODOX; HOUSEHOLDS: FEMALE-HEADED AND FEMALE-SUPPORTED; HOUSEHOLD WORKERS

References and Further Reading

Benería, L. 1992. *Unequal burden: Economic crises, persistent poverty and women's work.* Boulder, Colo.: Westview.

Chant, S. 1997. *Women-headed households: Diversity and dynamics in the developing world.* London: Macmillan.

Jelin, E., ed. 1991. *Family, household, and gender relations in Latin America.* New York: UNESCO.

Martin, C. J. 1996. Economic strategies and moral principles in the survival of poor households in Mexico: An urban and rural comparison. *Bulletin of Latin American Research* 15 (2): 193–210.

Nelson, S. 1996. Constructing and negotiating gender in women's police stations in Brazil. *Latin American Perspectives* 23 (1:Winter): 131–148.

Pérez Sáinz, J. P., and R. J. Larín. 1984. Central American men and women in the urban informal sector. *Journal of Latin American Studies* 26 (2): 431–447.

Portés, A., M. Castells, and L. A. Benton. 1989. *The informal economy: Studies in advanced and less developed countries.* Baltimore: John Hopkins University Press.

Stevens, Evelyn. 1973. Marianismo: The other face of machismo in Latin America. In Ann Pescatello, ed., *Female and male in Latin America*, 89–101. Pittsburgh, Pa.: University of Pittsburgh Press.

Willis, K. 1993. Women's work and social network use in Oaxaca City, Mexico. *Bulletin of Latin American Research* 12 (1): 65–82.

Wright, K. 1997. Enterprising women: Microenterprise activity in the *barriadas* of Lima, Peru. Master's thesis, University of Liverpool.

Katharine Wright

HOUSEHOLDS AND FAMILIES:
Commonwealth of Independent States

Households and Family Life in the Commonwealth: Then and Now

With the demise of the former Soviet Union, precipitated by the fall of the Berlin Wall in 1989, rapid changes in the politics and economy of the Soviet state resulted in the cre-

ation of the Commonwealth of Independent States (CIS) in 1991. Currently, the CIS is a fragile union of fifteen self-ruled states: Russia, Byelorussia, Ukraine, and Moldova (the "Western States"); Armenia, Georgia, and Azerbaijan (the "Transcaucasian States"); Kyrgyzstan, Kazakhstan, Turkmenistan, Tadzhikistan, and Uzbekistan (the "Central Asian States"); and Lithuania, Latvia, and Estonia (the "Baltic States"). These states, formerly republics of the Soviet Union, are today asserting varying degrees of national identity, cultural autonomy, and religious independence, changes that challenge women throughout the commonwealth. Diversity and multiculturalism have a long history in this heterogeneous commonwealth and are reflected in the material, social, and spiritual aspirations of their peoples. Women have both informal and formal influence, especially in household and family life.

Greater Russia, a region covering a vast geographical area (8.6 million square miles, about 2 1/2 times the size of the United States), might be considered prototypical for household and family life in its fourteen associated commonwealth states. Akheiser (1993) writes of Russia at the turn of the millennium as being at the "crisis point" in world history, and he relates the current situation to previous crises in the country's past. Historically, the household and family have provided an anchoring institution in times of economic and political turmoil. Despite changes in the political (r)evolution of the entity known as the state, the family remains for those in the CIS the unit on which people rely in periods of rapid social change. However, throughout the CIS, the family continues to identify its members with the patronymic, that is, "son of" or "daughter of" the father. Surnames indicate the gender of the individual, but the lineage of the father dominates. For example, the authors of this article are identified as "daughter of Vladimir" and "daughter of Lev," and this patriarchal usage remains deeply ingrained in the national cultures of the CIS.

The Concept of *Byt* in Russian Household Life

Byt, a word that refers to the burdensome aspects of daily existence, typifies family life in the CIS. Boym (1994) compares Russian and American cultural mythology, contrasting American emphasis on individual self-sufficiency with Russian resistance to the ordinary and banal aspects of everyday life conveyed by the unique notion of *byt* (264). The experience of *byt* has been exacerbated by the scarcity of basic necessities that are taken for granted in the more affluent societies of the developed world. In Russia, for example, one in three people lives in poverty, while the top 10 percent on the income scale are estimated to be in possession of about

50 percent of the nation's overall wealth (Nichols, 1999). This figure will vary throughout the CIS but is indicative of the general failure of prosperity to replace poverty in the past decade. Meeting the demands of *byt* remains the central issue for women in day-to-day life in the CIS, and this task places heavy responsibilities on them to maintain or improve their families' well-being.

Women and the Household in Three Historical Periods

Three distinct historical periods have shaped the Russian household and family and the role of women: (1) imperial Russia, or Russia under the local grand dukes and the czars in the period of territorial expansion; (2) the "command economy" of the Soviet era; and (3) the emergence of a so-called postcommunist "market economy," now barely a decade old. The historical continuity of certain basic "family values" throughout these periods is apparent among the differentiated peoples of the present-day CIS.

Imperial or Czarist Russia

The impact of centuries of Mongol invasion remains in the psyche and social organization of the national cultures of the CIS (especially the central Asian republics). In a sense, the family in Russia has always been multicultural—shaped both by the circumstances of conquest and the influence of three monotheistic religions, primarily Russian Orthodox Christianity. Russia was Christianized in the tenth century. The Christian faith is represented today by other national orthodox churches, the Ukrainian and Georgian churches for example. Significant also are Judaism and Islam, as well as remaining animistic faiths. In imperial Russia, the practice of *domostroi,* or household authority, made the husband the absolute ruler of his family. Under this practice, a husband was prohibited from striking his wife with a stick thicker than his ring finger. *Domostroi* continues in the Russian psyche—not always in direct practice—but popular songs still say, "The weather in the household is much more important than the weather outside," implying that the family "climate" remains the wife's responsibility.

The last czar—Nicholas II, known as a family man—was referred to as *batuskha,* or little father. Much like Victorian families in England, Russian families (at least of the aristocratic and propertied classes) emulated the royal family. The different classes—from peasant to noble—were joined in the overall belief in *Mat Russia,* or Mother Russia. The Russian idealization of woman and motherhood remains closely associated in the "Russian soul" with the *bogoroditsa*—the Mother of Christ. Under the czars, education for "young ladies" was provided by the Smolny Institute in St. Petersburg, which established a precedent for women's higher education in subsequent eras.

Household Life in Soviet Russia

The ideology of Marxism-Leninism anticipated the "withering away" of the state and the elimination of the "bourgeois" family in favor of the worker's (proletarian) family. However, the newly privileged communist *apparatchiks* (functionaries) were able to provide amenities for their families not available to the vast majority of workers in the society. While the old class system under the czars was abolished, a new class evolved in which some women, by virtue of their association with those in power (status by ascription), enjoyed privileges and luxuries unknown to those in the ranks of workers. This impeded any likelihood of true solidarity among women and explains many Russian women's resistance to western notions of feminism.

Village life continued to shape household and family life in the vast areas of the Soviet Union. Lands expropriated from the nobility and the propertied classes were incorporated into *kholkhozy,* or collective farms, under government control. Nevertheless, small patches of land—*ogorody,* or vegetable gardens—provided basic staples for the family, and surplus produce could be exchanged or sold by individuals for their own benefit. This practice provided many rural women with small amounts of cash for their own family's use. The *ogorody* continue, in the postcommunist era, to provide important staples for urban Russian households through an informal economy. Since land remains the property of the state, formal inheritance of real property then and now is not permitted. Land today is "leased" from the state, but farmers have more control over their farming operations.

The housing crisis in Russia and elsewhere in the CIS dates back to precommunist times. The persistence of a housing shortage and the shortage of consumer goods during the communist era resulted in most urban families living in communal apartments that typically accommodated one or more extended (three-generation) families who shared common facilities with other families. Each family had its own space for sleeping and dining but shared cooking and lavatory facilities with other families. The sense of privacy and ownership so familiar to other societies remains a foreign concept to many of the older generation (Zamoshkin, 1992). For average families in the cities of the CIS, such "doubling up" continues to be the norm. While private property was technically not of concern under communist rule, privileged families expanded their living space to *dachas,* or country houses, that also provided food from their gardens, which they preserved for consumption in winter.

A "classless" society gave women and men from previously disadvantaged sectors opportunities for technical and professional education. With such educational opportunities, women enjoyed wider employment opportunities in such fields as engineering and medicine, and "working mothers" became the norm under communism. Because women were expected to work, the Soviet regime promoted universal day care attached to factories and offices. The extended family also offered working women support in household and family management through the presence of *babushki* (grandmothers) and *dedushki* (grandfathers) as added sources of emotional attachment.

The Post-Soviet Era and the CIS

Beginning with the policies of *perestroika* (reconstruction) and *glasnost* (openness) in the late 1980s and early 1990s, the West had increasing influence on events leading to the dissolution and reorganization of the Soviet Union and the establishment of the CIS. The introduction of a "new" economy supporting market competition in Russia and the CIS brought into existence a "new" new class—entrepreneurs and businessmen (and even a few successful women). For a privileged few, conspicuous consumption has replaced unremitting deprivation, and a new privileged class now receives the benefits once enjoyed by the old *intelligentsia* (educated elite) and *nomenklatura* (former party officials and those in charge of government agencies).

Despite seventy years of a regime that promoted atheism and secularism, religious affiliation colors household and family life in the postcommunist CIS, especially among the older generation. As in other countries, women are frequently the carriers—often the unrecognized carriers—of religious tradition, and the resurgence of religious identity has influenced migration to more accepting nations such as Israel and the United States. The prevalence of Muslim family values in the central Asian republics and in the "breakaway" regions of the Transcaucasian republics reflects a general preference among Muslims for large families. Attempts to secularize the peoples of the CIS under the Soviet regime appeared to have failed at the close of the millennium, as was evident in Chechnya, where Muslim militants in the Republic of Georgia challenged Russian hegemony. In such conflicts, women have a central complaint with state regimes, namely the military risks to which their sons are exposed for political gains.

With imported foreign media and greater access to western ideas, consumerism and materialism have begun to influence "family values" in the CIS. The impact of consumer materialism after a period of deprivation intensifies the contrast between the privileged "new Russians" (the haves) and others (the have nots) in the new market economy. It creates tension between the older and the younger generation with challenges to traditional norms and gender roles. As noted by Novikova (1994), the switch to a market economy exacerbated preexisting problems of labor and everyday life for women, who, in addition to their traditional responsibility for household work, often take on a "second shift" of employment in dangerous and harmful occupations such as highway and building construction, the textile industry, nuclear facilities, and chemical factories. Although some women have moved up the economic ladder, male competition for the better positions in the new economy has resulted in an increase in the trend the West calls the feminization of poverty. As elsewhere, the prevailing view of household and family life is that it provides the nucleus of the state.

Although women represent the majority of the population and an almost equal number of those employed in social production (Novikova, 1994: 3), their complex social and political identity makes women of the CIS resistant to western feminism, especially American feminism as a social movement. As one Russian woman said to an American feminist, "What you American feminists call 'oppression' would be an improvement in our situation." The Russian extended, multigenerational household and family unit continues as the normative family type. The division of labor in most CIS households was and remains "traditional." Household duties to maintain the family's standard of living remain largely gendered, with women mainly responsible for the day-to-day tasks of household management and emotional caretaking. Because of continuing shortages of consumer goods, much time and energy continues to be expended by ordinary families on shopping for the barest household necessities, let alone the luxuries available to the "new Russians."

The greatest tension and dislocation in households and families is the sudden relaxation of old norms in the conduct of everyday life. Freedom and a market economy have had a variable impact on the women of the CIS, and today's youth have but the dimmest recollection of a time when medical care was state supported and housing, though scarce, was allocated to workers' families. The explosion of a "consumer culture" in the CIS promises to create an even more serious chasm between the haves and the have nots than existed in previous eras. The fate of democratic ideals may well rest with evaluations of the quality of life and standard of living enjoyed by the majority of households and families in the CIS in the new millennium.

The Exodus of Russian Women as Brides of Americans

The desperate post-Soviet economic situation and the dream of a better life for women has prompted a major industry in dating and marriage services that act as matchmakers between American men and women from the CIS (Visson, 1998: ix). Newspapers have featured stories of American men "hunting" for Russian wives. Explaining the quest, one man said that Russian women were more "family oriented" (Schillinger, 1993: 16). To Russian women, American women's "emancipation" makes them less marriageable and less domestic than themselves. Russian women often express the feeling that the family is primary and a "career" secondary, since family life is the true source of happiness (16–17). To some, Russian society was the last vestige of a prefeminist society; thus *byt* remains an obstacle to a meeting of the minds between many American and Russian women.

See Also

DEVELOPMENT: COMMONWEALTH OF INDEPENDENT STATES; POLITICS AND THE STATE: COMMONWEALTH OF INDEPENDENT STATES

References and Further Reading

Akheiser, A. 1993. Russia enters a new development cycle. *Social Science Quarterly Review* 24 (4):66–88.

Boym, Svetlana. 1994. The archeology of banality: The Soviet home. *Public Culture* 6(2):263–292.

Eisenstein, Zillah R. 1994. Eastern European male democracies: A problem of unequal equality. In Zillah R. Eisenstein, *The color of gender: Reimaging democracy*, 15–35. Berkeley: University of California Press.

Gray, Francine Du Plessix. 1990. *Soviet women*. New York: Doubleday.

Gryaznova, Ljudmila. 1994. Women's entrepreneurship in Belarus. Minsk: Independent Institute of Socio-Economic and Political Studies.

Kotlyar, Z. 1994. Demographic changes in east European countries and Russia. *Social Sciences Quarterly Review* 25(1): 86–96.

McClellan, David. 1975. *Karl Marx*. New York: Viking.

Nichols, Bill. 1999. Doubts riddle optimism of young Russians. *USA Today* (15 Nov): 22-A.

Novikova, Elvira. 1994. Women in the political life of Russia. Paper presented at a Workshop "Social Changes in East and West: The Public of Women—Women's Research—Women's Policies II." Academic Frankenwarte: Friedrich Ebert Stiftung, Würzburg, Germany, July 9–16.

Schillinger, Liesel. 1993. Bride and seek. *New Republic* (June 17): 15–17.

Sinyavsky, Andrei. 1990. *Soviet civilization: A cultural history.* New York: Arcade.

Thompson, Patricia J. [Yelena Vladimirovna Mayakovskya]. 1994. The question of *byt* in the daily lives of Russian and American women. Paper presented at a Workshop "Social Changes in East and West: The Public of Women—Women's Research—Women's Policies II." Academic Frankenwarte: Friedrich Ebert Stiftung, Würzburg, Germany, July 9–16.

Visson, Lynn. 1998. *Wedded strangers. The challenges of Russian-American marriages.* New York: Hippocrene.

Zamoshkin, Yuri. 1992. Private life, private interest, private property. *Russian Studies in Philosophy* 31(1):49–86.

Yelena Vladimirovna Mayakovskya (Patricia J. Thomson)
Tatiana Eidinova

HOUSEHOLDS AND FAMILIES: East Asia

In spite of their individual variations, the family systems in east Asian societies are greatly influenced by Confucian values, which emphasize a hierarchical social order based on generational seniority, age, and gender. Young people are filial and obedient to the elderly, and women are compliant and respectful to men in the family. These values are particularly prevalent in Taiwan, China, and Korea, where the family is patrilineal (that is, descent is traced through male lines, with the family name passed from father to sons) and marriage is generally patrilocal (that is, a woman leaves her natal family to join that of her husband at marriage). Male offspring are therefore essential for the continuation of the family line, whereas daughters are comparably dispensable. It is also the cultural expectation in these societies that a son will look after his parents in their old age whenever the need arises. Japan presents a slightly different case in these matters. In Japan, the family is not entirely patrilineal. Bilaterally symmetrical kinship terminology (that is, equal weight given to the kin of father's side and mother's side) and bilateral inheritance are part of the Japanese family system.

Ancestor Worship

The importance of having male heirs is reinforced by the custom of ancestor worship. Ancestor worship refers to the benefits and rituals surrounding the interactions of the living and their departed relatives. In Taiwan, China, and Korea, people believe that ancestors continue to live in the afterlife and watch over their descendants. An ancestor is presumed to be endowed with supernatural power that he or she may use to help the offspring. Ancestors, however, must be taken care of by living relatives through worship; otherwise, they will become homeless and be forced to wander in the world as ghosts. This is what happens to those who have no descendants. The practice of ancestor worship gives Taiwanese, Chinese, and Korean parents an additional incentive to have sons to perform the rituals and, thus, secure an eternal life for themselves and their ancestors.

The patrilineal and patrilocal principles result in a sharp contrast in attitudes toward males and females both among people in the living world and in the perceptions of life beyond. In Taiwan and south China, a man naturally becomes a member of the family he was born into, and his name is ensured to be listed on the ancestral tablet after death. A woman, by contrast, is not expected to stay with her natal family for all her life, nor can her name be listed along with her father's ancestors. Only when she is married can she have a permanent belonging and can her soul rest in peace.

Inheritance

The inheritance of family wealth in east Asia also tends to favor male descendants. In Taiwan, although the law has granted all children equal rights of inheritance, customarily family property is divided only among sons. Daughters are given a dowry as a form of inheritance at marriage. Korea acknowledges the primacy of the firstborn son, who inherits the house and the lion's share of the family's property, whereas secondary sons and their wives leave the family to establish independent households. In Japan, male primogeniture (that is, succession by the eldest son) is preferred but not exclusively followed.

The difference in inheritance patterns has great impact on the family dynamics in each of these societies. In Taiwan, as equal inheritance among sons is the rule, individual families constantly face tension and conflicts of interest between the two male roles: as sons they have to keep their father's family intact, and as brothers they may wish to establish independent households. Married sons' diverse calculations often affect the timing of division of family property (Cohen, 1976). That is, married brothers may be more likely to stay together if they see it as beneficial to the economic well-being of their own individual households, and they may push for family division when they feel they will be better off going separate ways.

Although brothers may be the actual initiators of family division, their wives are often blamed for instigating the division. It has been a cultural stereotype in Taiwan and China that women are by nature quarrelsome, jealous, petty-minded, and preoccupied with the interests of their own husbands and children at the expense of the larger family. They frequently are alleged to be the ones who come between parents and sons and between brothers, and, thus, women are deemed to be the agitator of family quarrels and the cause of family division. By contrast, in Korea where family inheritance is not partable, women are not blamed for pulling families apart (Kendall, 1985).

Structural Dilemma of Women

East Asian women also face difficulties built into their structural positions in the households under the patrilocal rule. A woman who goes to live with her husband's family often finds that she is surrounded by strangers in an unfamiliar or even hostile environment. The initial stage of married life is especially hard for a daughter-in-law, not only because it is her duty to assume most of the domestic responsibilities but also because she has to learn to do them according to the ways of her new family. She is under the constant supervision of her mother-in-law, who at some level may resent this newcomer and act as a demanding overseer. The daughter-in-law–mother-in-law relationship is particularly difficult. A daughter-in-law presents a threat to the mother-in-law as a competitor for domestic authority and for the son's support and affection.

Because the son's loyalty is likely to be split between his wife and his mother and there is always a possibility that he may be closer to his mother than to the new bride, a woman who goes to live with her husband's family is left with little or no emotional support save for her children. In east Asian societies, men depend on institutionalized authority and rights for power and influence, whereas women are forced to make what they can of their relationships with their children. Taking advantage of their roles as mothers, they forge solidarity between themselves and their children, particularly with sons. The creation of "uterine family" (Wolf, 1972) by married Taiwanese women indicates their efforts to secure their positions in the family. This very behavior is also submissive to the patrilineal principle, however, and contributes to the reproduction of a social system within which males are privileged.

Family as a Corporate Unit

Observers of east Asian cultures have highlighted the importance of the household as a social, ritual, and economic unit. Taiwanese and Chinese families have traditionally acted as a corporate unit to which family members contribute labor and incomes, under the authority of the household head (usually the eldest male or the father). The household head's job entails a careful calculation of the household division of labor in order to maximize family prosperity. Diversification of economic activities—with sons, daughters-in-law, and unmarried daughters performing different tasks or occupations—is a usual strategy to accomplish this goal. The ideal Japanese stem family, the *ie,* is best understood as a corporate group that holds property in perpetuity (Kondo, 1990: 119–198). An *ie* is a unit of production and consumption, encompassing the roles of corporation and household, especially for families engaged in a family enterprise. As opposed to the patrilineal systems in Taiwan and China, however, where the ideal is an extended family of parents, several brothers, and their wives and children living under one roof, the *ie* is limited to only two successors (the heir and his or her spouse) in each generation. The overriding concern in Japanese culture is to ensure the continuity and integrity of the *ie* over time. This culture is thus in striking contrast to the Taiwanese and Chinese, where partition of family property is natural and inevitable. Despite male primogeniture's being the preferred form of succession, the Japanese system holds merit to be of considerable importance. In order to ensure the continued prosperity of the *ie,* an incompetent firstborn son may be passed over for a more able secondary son, a daughter, or even someone unrelated by blood. This *ie* ideal remains a strong vector in the lives of Japanese, even though the postwar civil code has made equal inheritance the law and, thus, legally abolished the preference of male primogeniture.

As most of the east Asian societies undergo rapid industrialization and urbanization and wage earning becomes the primary source of income, individual families also have become a site of consumption rather than production. Nevertheless, in Taiwan and Japan, where small enterprises remain prevalent in the economy, the family continues to be an important economic unit. Recent studies of Taiwan's industrialization highlight the lasting importance of family in this regard. Family labor has been crucial to the success of Taiwan's small-scale industry. It provides a cheap, steady, flexible, and efficient workforce that enables Taiwanese manufacturers to produce commodities at a low price while ensuring reliable, on-time delivery. Taiwanese families engaged in industrial production have prospered accordingly.

Hidden in the emphasis on collaborative family welfare, however, are the generational and gender inequalities that arise under the name of a "common good" (Greenhalgh, 1994; Hsiung, 1996). The success of Taiwanese small producers depends heavily on the sometimes unwilling participation of unpaid or underpaid family members. Unmarried daughters are in an especially difficult position. They often work hard—or are pushed to work hard by their parents—to advance the family wealth, yet they are frequently denied inheritance rights as all is left to their brothers.

State and Family in the People's Republic of China (PRC)

After its victory in 1949, the Chinese communist regime became actively involved in creating a new institutional and moral environment for Chinese families. The Maoist era witnessed a swift elimination of child betrothals, concubinage, sales of children into servitude, elaborate weddings, and early marriages. The Chinese government declared that children were able to choose their own spouses, and women were given the right to pursue divorce, which had previously been denied to them. Under collectivization (1956–1980), the state became the primary agency of economic production and distribution. In both urban and rural areas, the Chinese family ceased to be a unit of economic planning and cooperation, for every able-bodied person was mobilized by the state, assigned a task, and rewarded for it. Women benefited by having their work points calculated separately and by beginning to get at least local recognition (Davin, 1976). Nevertheless, patriliny and patrilocal postmarital residence continued to guide Chinese social life, despite state intervention, particularly in the countryside, where the team and brigade affiliations in the collective production system were passed from father to son. Women were still left to marry strangers who had to prove themselves worthy or temporary residents who would soon depart. As a result, there was little incentive for the work unit to recommend girls over boys for higher education or special training or to prepare them for leadership and responsibilities (Diamond, 1975).

The economic reform (and decollectivization) beginning in the late 1970s saw the revitalization of the household as an economic unit. Under the household responsibility system, the state relegated land and other agricultural resources to individual families for management. Each contracting household had to turn in a certain amount of product but could retain the surplus beyond the contracted levels. This policy was designed in the hope that direct material incentive would motivate higher yield and more efficient use of resources (Judd, 1994). Rural households in the PRC have regained some autonomy in planning their own economic welfare since then. Diversification of household economy, by entrusting family members to different economic activities, has once again become a common strategy to maximize family prosperity.

In spite of reducing its control of economic affairs, the Chinese state remains intrusive and coercive, especially in the domain of reproduction. The one-child policy (also launched in the late 1970s) indicated the Chinese government's conviction to control population growth in order to retain its hard-won economic gains. Despite the initial vehemence, the implementation of one-child policy was soon moderated and its effect appears complex and heterogeneous (Davis and Harrell, 1993). The one-child policy particularly works against the interests of rural families, to whom the value of child labor has been increased since decollectivization and the dismantling of the collective welfare system. The lack of cooperation from rural families has forced local cadres to renegotiate their strategies and goals.

See Also

AGING: JAPANESE CASE STUDY; CONFUCIANISM; FAMILY: RELIGIOUS AND LEGAL SYSTEMS—BUDDHIST TRADITIONS

References and Further Reading

Cohen, Myron L. 1976. *House united, house divided: The Chinese family in Taiwan.* New York: Columbia University Press.

Davin, Delia. 1976. Women in the countryside of China. In *Woman-work: Women and the party in revolutionary China,* 243–273. Oxford: Clarendon.

Davis, Deborah, and Steven Harrell, eds. 1993. *Chinese families in the post-Mao era.* Berkeley: University of California Press.

Diamond, Norma. 1975. Collectivization, kinship, and the status of women in rural China. In Rayna R. Reiter, ed., *Toward an anthropology of women,* 372–395. New York: Monthly Review.

Greenhalgh, Susan. 1994. De-Orientalizing the Chinese family firm. *American Ethnologist* 21(4):746–1775.

Hsiung, Ping-chun. 1996. *Living rooms as factories: Class, gender, and the satellite factory system in Taiwan.* Philadelphia: Temple University Press.

Judd, Ellen R. 1994. *Gender and power in rural north China.* Stanford, Calif.: Stanford University Press.

Kendall, Laurel. 1985. *Shamans, housewives, and other restless spirits: Women in Korean ritual life.* Honolulu: University of Hawaii Press.

Kondo, Dorinne K. 1990. *Crafting selves: Power, gender and discourses of identity in a Japanese workplace.* Chicago: University of Chicago Press.

Perry, Elizabeth. 1996. *Putting class in its place.* Berkeley, Calif.: Institute of East Asian Studies.

Rofel, Lisa. 1999. *Other modernities: Gendered yearnings in China after socialism.* Berkeley: University of California Press.

Wolf, Margery. 1972. *Women and the family in Taiwan.* Stanford, Calif.: Stanford University Press.

Anru Lee

HOUSEHOLDS AND FAMILIES:
Melanesia and Aboriginal Australia

Households of Aboriginal Australia and of the Melanesian islands to the north (from the Australian territory of the Torres Straits islands to Papua New Guinea, PNG, the Solomon Islands, Vanuatu, New Caledonia, and Fiji) have structures and functions that vary by region and with history. There are, however, some commonalities. Before European colonization, both culture areas had clearly separate and respected gendered spheres of action and considerable reliance on the subsistence activities of women. Having decentralized, "stateless" political organizations, the household unit was central. Exchange, trade, and regular warfare drew small groups of households into wider entities. Neither Melanesia nor Aboriginal Australia clearly differentiated the natural and supernatural and so to comprehend the significance of family requires recognition of ancestor spirits and ancestral culture heroes as continuing players in the affairs of the living. Existing at opposite extremes, however, the sedentary horticultural base of Melanesia, crowned by intensive irrigation systems in the central highlands of PNG, contrasts strongly with the fully hunting and gathering nomadic lifestyle of desert indigenous Aboriginal Australians.

With the introduction of the pig and southeast Asian plants such as yam and taro 6,000 to 9,000 years ago, Melanesians established a variety of sedentary, swidden (slash and burn) subsistence economies, many using pigs and other valuables such as shells and feathers for ceremonial exchange. Although these ceremonies were preeminently built on the domestic labor of women, they were organized by men and had wider political and economic implications. Daily subsistence production was generally carried out by the nuclear family unit, but feast and exchange preparations and house building required the cooperative labor of a clan or a network of kin.

Polygyny was common in Melanesia. Most communities had preferred kin groups into which a woman could marry but which allowed considerable scope for choice as well. Women were highly valued as reproducers of new clan or lineage members; as producers in the day-to-day planting, maintenance, and harvesting of root crops, raising of pigs, or collecting of shellfish; and as links in potential political alliances. Their value was reflected in the institution of bridewealth, wherein a woman's family was compensated for her loss upon marriage with a considerable collection of produce and valuables. A marriage thus brought a wide group of kin into a transaction, and many had a continuing interest in the stability and fertility of the marriage. A woman wishing to leave her marriage might find opposition from her father and brothers, who would not want to return the bridewealth. A woman in an infertile marriage might be sent home and demands made for the return of the bridewealth. In many Melanesian communities a wife who failed to fulfill culturally appropriate roles for a wife, such as harvesting and preparing the evening meal, might be subject to physical violence from her husband.

Household arrangements in many Melanesian village communities included small domestic houses for women, young girls, and children and a men's house. This was often the sleeping house for all men and a holding place for secret, powerful artifacts and ritual paraphernalia. Brothers, cousins, fathers, and uncles linked through patrilineal ties cooperated in garden and exchange negotiations, slept, and ate together.

Children were suckled for up to three years or until replaced by a younger sibling and generally had a happy, free life playing with their peers until age 6 or 7 for a girl and until puberty for a boy. Firstborn children were given preferential treatment, but other children were sometimes given in adoption to balance out a domestic unit lacking male or female members or to cement exchange relations.

Most Melanesian societies were patrilineal, in that descent and land ownership were traced through the father's line and a young woman, when married, moved to her husband's village. In practice, the systems were flexible and pragmatic, so much so that it has been argued that exchange is a more important structuring principle than kinship.

In the minority of matrilineal communities, ownership and title were traced from mother's brother to sister's son. The status of women in such societies may have been higher than in patrilineal communities. It has been argued that symmetrical and complementary gender oppositions were basic to the Trobriand Island social order and that the role of women in death exchanges was central (Weiner, 1977).

In most of Melanesia the separate spheres of men and women were associated with a gender tension linked to a belief system that women are potentially dangerous, because of their capacity to menstruate. Women thus gained an informal form of power through their perceived ability to harm. The debate over whether the gendered spheres can be seen as equal or symmetrical depends to a large extent on point of view and which aspects of society are seen as central: political, economic, or ritual-religious.

Colonization brought enforced peace to warring clans and tribes, Christian missions, and larger conglomerations of households in many areas. Women's labor was less affected than men's by the cessation of warfare and the transition from stone to steel tools. While freed from the need to be constantly prepared for warfare, men were constrained by head taxes to seek work in towns, on plantations, and later on cash crops, while women successfully bore the brunt of village subsistence. Government development schemes focused on men, but some nongovernment organizations have nurtured separate development programs initiated by groups of women.

Christianity in general disapproved of separate family residence and highlighted the importance of the marital relationship, and so in many areas polygyny ceased and families began to reside together; men's houses were abandoned or left for young single men. Coresidence and European medical aid influenced the rise in fertility rates.

Gender tension persists, particularly in Papua New Guinea, which has the highest rape rate in the world. Legislative beginnings have been made throughout Melanesia to end wife beating.

Most Melanesian families live in rural villages. The most urbanized island, Fiji (41 percent), has the lowest fertility rate (2.7), and the least urbanized, PNG (17 percent) and the Solomon Islands (18 percent), have the highest fertility rates (4.6 and 4.9 percent, respectively). The 1990 PNG national census found 58 percent nuclear family households and 37 percent extended families, most households overall having more than eight members. PNG has a high maternal mortality rate and a low life expectancy of 51.4 years for females, 52.2 years for males.

In general, the eras of colonization and independence saw the entrenchment of male power in the public arena. Local law courts appear to operate with wide power differences, but some Melanesian women contest and challenge this power. Gewertz and Errington (1997) describe a PNG woman who called on the police, the magistrate, and God to successfully avert a miscarriage of justice in relation to a paternity case.

Precolonial Aboriginal Australians were nomadic hunter-gatherers for at least 6,000 years, but in the 2,000 years before colonization, specialized food gathering and processing in relation to, for example, eel harvesting developed, and in the southeast, near-sedentary life in villages of stone-based houses developed, making the accepted understanding of nomadism problematic. In seasons of water shortage or abundance, Aboriginal bands could successfully break up into small family units: one man and one woman had all the skills needed to survive.

The main regional variation that is widely recognized in Australian ethnography is that between the desert and the rest of Australia. Inhabitants of the desert regions had less defined boundaries, more choice, more flexibility in defining links to land through mother or father, greater gender balance, and sophisticated secret rituals belonging to women as well as men. Most of the rest of the more densely populated Australia reserved links through the patriline for estate land ownership, with links through the mother often providing the role of manager for such land. The group making use of a particular range of land consisted of those with links through a man and his wife, the size of the group altering according to seasonal and ceremonial requirements and the makeup altering according to life cycle.

Aboriginal Australia developed a complex system of prescribed marriage and standardized social behavior and obligations through a system of 4, 8, 16 or more kinship sections. Children were assigned a section according to the section of their mother. Kin with ties through the mother often had significant roles in death and initiation rituals. Child rearing was indulgent, with a long period of breast feeding, no physical punishment, and efforts made to accede to a child's wish, but the need for reciprocity and sharing with some kin sections and "avoidance" behavior—such as no eye, verbal, or physical contact with other sections—was inculcated through example, gesture, and persuasion.

Girls were often promised in marriage at birth and could be married at or before puberty to a man much older than themselves. Polygyny was practiced. As a girl got older, she could marry several times, ending up with a husband younger than herself. The age difference in marriage partners may have accounted for the frequent tension over elopements, "wrong marriages," and adultery, for which harsh punishments (spearing) could be meted out to men or women.

As a settler colony, Australia had a colonial policy that greatly affected indigenous families. Most lost their means of subsistence, populations were ravaged by sickness and violence, and, under the auspices of assimilationist social policy, many children were separated from their families, first in mission dormitories, then in children's homes, and finally, by the 1960s, through adoption into white families. In the coastal, heavily populated regions of Australia, the majority of indigenous people have changed to recognizing kin groups traced through mother or father from a known ancestor (nonunilineal, cognatic systems).

Today, families tend to be slightly larger than the Australian average and consist of younger mothers. Prescribed marriage into kinship sections has evolved in urban areas to broadened taboos regarding distant relatives. Eckerman's research (1988) in Queensland and New South Wales found that the contemporary indigenous family was most likely to be a compound family: a family wherein the household head

(male or female) has taken a boarder or fosters a child. The national survey in 1994 revealed that 80 percent of Aboriginal and Torres Strait households consisted of a single family. If the man fulfils his role as breadwinner, he is accepted as the patriarch, but because of unemployment, illness, and accident, many men do not fulfill this role (29 percent of families have only one parent).

There is considerable debate over whether colonization has improved or decreased the status and power of Aboriginal women. Barwick (in Gale, 1978) argued from historical evidence that the mission at Coranderrk, Victoria (southeastern Australia), changed the gender balance by taking away much of the men's power and enabling greater literacy among women. This view is compatible with the evolution of flexible kinship reckoning and the acknowledged centrality of senior Aboriginal women in provincial and urban communities. For the less-settled, more classical indigenous communities, Bell (1993), on the basis of ethnographic research in a desert community, argued the inverse. From a near egalitarian base, government development and land rights schemes have entrenched patriarchal models and male power.

Colonialism has diversely affected Aboriginal households. More are headed by a female, and dozens of such women have made their mark as community leaders, but, in contrast to the past and to mainstream Australia, contemporary Aboriginal women experience more domestic violence and greater dependence on social security for household survival.

See Also

ADOPTION; COLONIALISM AND POSTCOLONIALISM; DOWRY AND BRIDEPRICE; FOSTERING: CASE STUDY—OCEANIA HOUSEHOLDS AND FAMILIES: MICRONESIA AND POLYNESIA; INDIGENOUS WOMEN'S RIGHTS; MATRILINEAL SYSTEMS; POLYGYNY AND POLYANDRY

References and Further Reading

Bell, Dianna. 1993. *Daughters of the dreaming.* St. Leonards, New South Wales: Allen and Unwin.

Bourke, Collin, and Eleanor Bourke. 1995. Aboriginal families in Australia. In Robyn Hartley, ed., *Families and cultural diversity in Australia.* St. Leonards, New South Wales: Allen and Unwin.

Eckerman, Annette. 1988. Culture vacuum or cultural vitality? *Australian Aboriginal Studies* 1: 31–39.

Gale, Fay, ed. 1978. *Women's role in aboriginal society.* 3rd ed. Canberra: Australian Institute of Aboriginal Studies.

Gewertz, Deborah, and Frederick Errington. 1997. Why we return to Papua New Guinea. *Anthropological Quarterly* 70(3): 127–137.

Hamilton, Annette 1981. *Nature and nurture: Aboriginal child-rearing in north-central Arnhem Land.* Canberra: Australian Institute of Aboriginal Studies.

Jolly, Margaret, and Martha Macintyre. 1989. *Family and gender in the Pacific.* Sydney: Cambridge University Press.

Langton, Marcia. 1997. Grandmothers' law, company business and succession in changing aboriginal land tenure systems. In G. Yunupingu, ed., *Our land is our life: Land rights—past, present, future,* 84–116. Brisbane: University of Queensland Press.

Reay, Marie. 1963. Aboriginal and white Australian family structure: an enquiry into assimilation trends. In *Sociological Review.* 11: 19–47.

Stathern, Marilyn. 1972. *Women in between, female roles in a male world: Mount Hagen, New Guinea.* New York: Seminar.

Sutton, Peter. 1998. *Native title and the descent of rights.* Perth, Western Australia: Commonwealth of Australia, Native Title Tribunal.

Weiner, Annette. 1977. *Women of value, men of renown.* St. Lucia, Queensland: University of Queensland Press.

Janice Newton

HOUSEHOLDS AND FAMILIES:
Micronesia and Polynesia

Micronesia and Polynesia are geographical terms used to refer to thousands of Pacific islands, atolls, and reefs and their surrounding oceanic reaches. Micronesia includes the Northern Mariana Islands, Guam, the Federated States of Micronesia, the Marshall Islands, Nauru, Kirbati, Tuvalu, and Tokelau; Polynesia comprises the Wallis and Futuna Islands, Samoa (formerly Western Samoa), American Samoa, the Kingdom of Tonga, Niue, the Cook Islands, French Polynesia, Hawaii, Rapanui (or Easter Island), and New Zealand. Fiji is sometimes considered Melanesian, sometimes Polynesian. Polynesia extends from Hawaii, in the north, located on the Tropic of Cancer, to the southern tip of New Zealand, 53 degrees south of the equator. The east-to-west dimensions of Micronesia and Polynesia are similarly extensive. When it is 3:00 P.M. on a Monday afternoon in Rapanui, further west in Palau it is 6:00 A.M. on a Tuesday morning.

The geographic extent means that there is considerable variation in climate, resources, and landscapes in the region. This physical variation is mirrored by the variety of people living throughout these islands. Thus, the diversity among the region's original inhabitants, their languages, and their social customs is tremendous. Also, early interactions resulted in shared patterns in some areas within the region, while European exploration, colonization, missionization, and modernization have further altered the fabric of life in the islands. Because of this diversity, it is difficult to generalize about households and families, although the following features do apply to women living in much of Micronesia and Polynesia.

Geographic Extent of Family Connections

The prehistories and histories of Polynesia and Micronesia are replete with accounts of voyages, migrations, and territorial incursions. Travels at the turn of the twenty-first century, whether temporary or permanent, fit comfortably within this long tradition of voyaging. Family members or groups may move their households to find work, to visit other family members, to seek better educational or economic opportunities, or for a variety of other reasons. However, the cumulative result of this tradition of population movement is that contemporary families often span several islands or even several nations, and some may be widely dispersed across the Pacific.

Extended Family Networks

"Family" in Micronesia and Polynesia includes a variety of kin who may not be included in European and American conceptions of the nuclear family. Households are typically larger and include a greater range of relatives living together than might be typical in a western context.

Household members often eat from the same food source, although they may not eat together, depending on beliefs relating to gender, status, or other concerns. Symbolically, this reliance on and sharing of the same food or the same style of preparation, often a cooking oven, are evidence of the close ties and dependence on one another within families.

Living arrangements are usually flexible, and household composition can alter dramatically within the memory of any one family member. At times, a household may have temporary visitors who stay for several months at a time. These visitors may include children who are sent to live with relatives in the larger urban areas while they attend school. Sometimes such arrangements are later formalized as adoptions; at other times, the arrangement remains informal.

Informal "borrowing" of children has been misunderstood by both missionaries and colonial authorities. Traditional adoptions have been used as evidence that Polynesians or Micronesians had little interest in or concern for the welfare of their children. However, more accurate is Linnekin and Poyer's "Oceanic theory of cultural identity that privileges environment, behavior, and situational flexibility over descent, innate characteristics, and unchanging boundaries," to which they add the qualification that the "contrast is to some extent a matter of emphasis rather than an either/or distinction" (Linnekin and Poyer, 1990: 6).

Gender Socialization

In both Polynesia and Micronesia, gender roles are more flexible than is typical in Euro-American societies. Gender transformation by men who take on the dress, attributes, and roles of women, however, is more common than women changing their gender. Many Pacific languages have a word for the transformation of men into women; for example, in Samoan it is *fa'afafine*. This transformation may last for a short period of time or may hold for most of the individual's lifetime.

At times, gender transformation is initiated by the individual; on other occasions, the family encourages the process. Morton describes the situation in Tonga, where "there appears to be a great deal of variation in the way in which individual families react to boys behaving as *fakaleiti* [like a lady]" (Morton, 1996: 110). Variation is the norm for many of the islands; however, there is less acceptance of transformative gender roles if the family migrates to non-island locations, such as to the United States or Australia.

Awareness and Documentation of Women's Experiences

Polynesian and Micronesian peoples maintained oral histories but did not have writing systems prior to the arrival of the Europeans beginning in 1520. With missionization and colonization, written accounts were produced that provide some information concerning the family structures and household organization of the early historic period. However, such accounts have typically been recorded by men, and usually they concentrated on only selected female attributes, often related to sex. Generally men were not privy to the other events and activities that concerned women. The result is that the early histories overemphasize the importance of men and provide limited data for understanding the lives of women. In the 1990s, feminist scholars have tried to find traces of women's activities in the early accounts and to rewrite these histories accordingly, but the task is far from complete.

For example, in the case of French Polynesia, the earliest European accounts date to 1767, and they portray Tahiti as an earthly paradise whose women occupied an ambiguous status ranging from practitioners of free love to prosti-

tutes. The European voyagers displayed much interest in the sexuality and pursuit of Tahitian women and correspondingly decreased attention to the other industries of island women. The historic documents briefly mention women's involvement in rulership, shell fishing, mat fabrication, and *ahu,* or bark cloth, production, among other activities. In the case of *ahu,* women produced this textile and often ceremonially presented gifts of the fiber. Using their bark cloth resources, they clothed their families, bedecked their elite, and materially identified the social transformations of their kin. Indeed, understanding the role of *ahu* and its manufacture is an essential step in interpreting the role and behavior of women in Tahitian society.

There are additional challenges that contribute to the difficulty of understanding Oceanic practices relating to women. Interpretations of many female activities are based on accounts by men, and these narratives are further complicated by religious prohibitions imported by the missionaries. Contemporary religious beliefs and conceptions of honor in the islands further confuse an understanding of the past. An example of such a case is the debate unleashed by the works of Margaret Mead and Derek Freeman in Samoa.

Scholarly interest in the specific history of women in the region has been accompanied by better attempts to record the present lives of island women at the beginning of the twenty-first century. Local women have taken a strong lead in this work. More accurate accounts of women's family and household commitments and their work translates into the development and completion of more women-friendly community development and foreign aid projects.

Increased awareness concerning the lives of contemporary women in the region has focused attention on the difficult issues of family violence and child abuse. These practices were exacerbated by the processes of colonization but were also a characteristic of the societies before European contact.

Discussion of family violence in these communities is considered both taboo and shameful. Additional difficulties come from the fact that illness of an individual has often been considered to be the result of family disharmony. This belief exemplifies further how an individual is typically placed in the context of her or his family relationships and is seldom considered in isolation.

These issues all contribute to the greater difficulties in both ascertaining the prevalence of domestic violence and in intervening against it than is the case in the Euro-American world. However, Micronesian and Polynesian women are improving the range of options for women and children in the Pacific nations, including programs for the development of legal literacy among women and agitation to change the laws to better enable women to support themselves economically by owning or inheriting land.

Because of legal and social changes in the islands in the 1990s, the status of Polynesian and Micronesian women living in the larger towns has been directly affected. Educational and employment opportunities are also located in the population centers, again favoring urban women. However, despite many improvements, gender inequities still exist throughout the region, and Oceanic women have many different opinions regarding both the appropriateness and the methods of promoting change. Nonetheless, all women in the region have the means of effecting some shifts in the worldview of the next generation through their interactions with children, whether their own or those of others.

Socialization of Children

Also in the 1990s, there has been increased interest in the experiences of children (the "ethnography of childhood") and how they are socialized and develop into adults with their own sense of personhood. This work has highlighted both the development of culturally appropriate values and the assumption of roles that are specific to gender, age, and status or rank of the individual and the family.

Generally, Polynesian and Micronesian children are socialized to a more communal maturity than Euro-American children, who learn to value the individual over their family and social connectedness. Typically, Micronesians and Polynesians conduct their social interactions within a complicated sphere of commitment and responsibility to family, household, village, and sometimes broader social structures. Children learn their place or places within these relationships through watching others and by performing activities with others; seldom are they instructed specifically on how to act. By the time they grow into adulthood, Polynesians and Micronesians have learned when to defer to other family members concerning decisions affecting themselves or their children. This deference to the broader family or community with regard to decision-making powers is often not understood and may be derided by outsiders.

Custom and Tradition

Any discussion of households and families in Micronesia and Polynesia must take into account the notion of custom or tradition. Typically, people draw on their understanding of what is customary or traditional in order to explain contemporary family and household structures. However, the notion of custom is not without its own ambiguities and

politics. As Malama Meleisea writes, "[b]ecause every matia [community leader or elder] has his or her own carefully constructed version of the past, a version designed to enhance his or her family's claims to land and social status, Samoa's past is still contentious" (Huntsman, 1995: 35).

While general patterns concerning the households and families in Polynesia and Micronesia can be considered, it is important to emphasize the variety of arrangements that have been subsumed in these norms.

See Also

ANCIENT INDIGENOUS CULTURES; ENVIRONMENT: PACIFIC ISLANDS; FOSTERING: CASE STUDY—OCEANIA; GENDER CONSTRUCTIONS IN THE FAMILY; HEALTH CARE: AUSTRALIA, NEW ZEALAND, AND THE PACIFIC ISLANDS; LITERATURE: AUSTRALIA, NEW ZEALAND, AND THE PACIFIC ISLANDS; HOUSEHOLDS AND FAMILIES: OVERVIEW; MIGRATION; VIOLENCE: AUSTRALIA, NEW ZEALAND, AND THE PACIFIC ISLANDS

References and Further Reading

Adair, Vivienne, and Robyn Dixon, eds. 1998. *The family in Aotearoa New Zealand.* Auckland: Addison Wesley Longman.

Crocombe, Ron. 1983. *The South Pacific: An introduction.* Auckland: Longman Paul.

Freeman, Derek. 1983. *Margaret Mead and Samoa: The making and unmaking of an anthropological myth.* Cambridge, Mass.: Harvard University Press.

Huntsman, Judith, ed. 1995. *Tonga and Samoa: Images of gender and polity.* Christchurch: Macmillan Brown Centre for Pacific Studies, University of Canterbury.

Linnekin, Jocelyn, and Lin Poyer, eds. 1990. *Cultural identity and ethnicity in the Pacific.* Honolulu: University of Hawaii Press.

Lockwood, Victoria. 1993. *Tahitian transformation.* Boulder, Col.: Lynne Rienner.

Mead, Margaret. 1928. *Coming of age in Samoa: A study of adolescence and sex in primitive society.* New York: Morrow.

Morton, Helen. 1996. *Becoming Tongan: An ethnography of childhood.* Honolulu: University of Hawaii Press.

Rensel, Jan, and Margaret Rodman, eds. 1997. *Home in the Islands: Housing and social change in the Pacific.* Honolulu: University of Hawaii Press.

Ritchie, Jane, and James Ritchie. 1979. *Growing up in Polynesia.* Sydney: Allen and Unwin.

Small, Cathy A. 1997. *Voyages: From Tongan villages to American suburbs.* Ithaca, N.Y.: Cornell University Press.

Susan J. Wurtzburg

HOUSEHOLDS AND FAMILIES:
Middle East and North Africa

Family and kinship are important organizing principles in the Middle East and north Africa. The predominant form of kinship and family is patrilineal and patriarchal, but ties with maternal kin are also strong in many parts of the region. Households are organized around a core of parents and children, with daughters marrying out and sons bringing wives in, but the composition of a household changes over one's lifetime and varies by region, rural and urban area, and class. Though men are officially and culturally considered the family heads, women have varying degrees of influence in practice, again depending on regional, rural-urban, and class variations.

The Middle East and north Africa as a region cover a vast expanse of territory (from Morocco to Iran; from Turkey to the Sudan) encompassing some 5.7 million square miles, twenty states, three major religions (Islam, Christianity, and Judaism, and their various offshoots), and several languages: Arabic, Turkish, Persian, Kurdish, Hebrew, and Berber as major languages, plus many minor languages spoken by particular tribal or ethnic groups. While most of the population today is urban (68 percent in southwest Asia; 51 percent in north Africa), there are still significant rural populations, particularly in north Africa. Furthermore, in some areas, such as Turkey and Iran, there are still groups that practice nomadic pastoralism, though most have become sedentary. Despite shared historical experience and commonalities of culture, there is much diversity and variation that must be taken into account.

Family and Family-Centeredness

Middle Eastern and north African societies are in general very family centered, and this is expressed in a number of ways. The family is considered the basic building block of society. People are not considered fully adult until they are married with children, and the percentage of people never married is one of the lowest among the world's regions, ranging from 1.1 percent to 4.3 percent for women and 1.6 percent to 5 percent for men (United Nations, 1995). There is also a strong desire to have children as soon as possible. Even where family planning programs have taken hold and reduced the number of children per family, it is still the goal of almost every married couple to have a child within the first year of marriage. Family planning is used to space children or stop having children after the desired number of children is reached. It is rarely used to delay the start of a family.

The details of the definition, shape, and organization of families vary across the region, but everywhere families share certain common themes. The basic idiom of kinship is patrilineal and patriarchal. That is, descent and naming patterns are primarily traced through males, and a senior male of the household or kin group is generally considered the head of the unit or group, though de facto decision-making power may in exceptional circumstances rest with a son or a widowed woman. This patrilineal and patriarchal focus is supported both by custom and by the ideologies and doctrines of the three major religions in the area—Islam, Christianity, and Judaism. There are, however, a few exceptions. Among the Tuaregs of the Sahara, descent is traced matrilineally, and among religious Jews descent from a Jewish mother is necessary to prove one's status as a Jew, despite the overall patriarchal bias of the religion. In practice, kin ties through maternal relatives are equally important in many parts of the region, and because marriages within the larger kin groups are encouraged, people are often related simultaneously through both paternal and maternal ties.

The terms for "family" are often elastic, the same term referring either to immediate family (household members or family of origin) or to a larger extended family, lineage, or tribal segment. The precise meaning, therefore, must be inferred from the context in which the term is employed. Neighbors also may acquire the status of honorary kin or be treated and referred to as if they were kin.

Households

Actual household composition varies within the region according to wealth, urban or rural domicile, and stage in the domestic cycle. Compared with all other regions of the world, households are relatively large (an average of 5.6 to 5.7 persons), and north Africa is the only region where average household size increased between 1970 and 1990, from 5.4 to 5.7 (United Nations, 1995).

A typical pattern of household composition consists of a husband and wife and their children. As the children reach marriageable age, daughters marry out, and sons, unless they have the means to establish an independent household, bring their wives to live in their paternal household. As time goes on and the extended family grows, putting pressure on family resources and increasing the likelihood of family conflicts, the household may divide, with some of the junior generation moving out to establish independent households. Old people generally live with their sons. Hence, whether a household is nuclear or extended in composition depends on the stage of the domestic cycle, and most households experience both forms of organization in the course of their lifetime.

However, even when an extended family breaks up or the sons move out, the family is likely to remain tied together by close proximity. Often the new households are established in the same neighborhood or building, and wealthier families may build houses or apartments in advance for their children to move into upon marriage in order to keep the family close. If such proximity is not possible, family members usually keep in close contact in a number of ways: by frequent visiting, telephone calls, reciprocal exchanges of family members and resources, and so on.

A number of variables affects how closely and in what way particular families correspond to this pattern at any given time, though nuclear families are becoming increasingly more common. Generally, the extended-family variant is more likely to be found among wealthier families, who have significant assets to manage and protect, and among rural families who are still connected to the land. However, much also depends on the availability of resources and of housing. In crowded urban areas, the difficulty of finding affordable housing may make it hard for young marrieds to establish independent residences of their own. Changes in education and employment opportunities have also affected the de facto patterning of household composition, with educated young people often having a strong desire to establish a nuclear household upon marriage and the means to do so through urban technical or professional employment. Labor migration is also a factor, since most wives or labor migrants remain in their husband's household while their husbands are gone.

Single person households are extremely rare. Young persons are expected to live with their parents until marriage; divorced individuals generally live with parents, siblings, or children, depending on their age. While polygyny is permissible within Islam, polygynous marriages are the exception rather than the rule. Morocco has the highest incidence of polygynous marriage at 5 percent of currently married females (United Nations, 1995). At the other end of the spectrum, Turkey, Tunisia, and Israel have all banned polygyny. When polygynous marriages do occur, the husband provides separate rooms for each of his wives or sets them up in separate dwellings.

Household composition may also be temporarily affected by exchanges of family members between households for varying lengths of time. It is not uncommon for students to live with aunts or uncles in town, to give them access to higher education or secondary school, or for a household with young children and much housework to borrow a sibling or niece to live in and help out with chores. This exchange of people is also a way that dispersed families stay in touch and helps to bridge the urban-rural gap experienced by so many families as young people go off to the cities to seek education or employment.

Marriage Patterns

Marriage is a significant stage in a person's life cycle and is the first step to becoming recognized as fully adult. Marriages are generally arranged or semiarranged (with Israel being a significant exception), though today the prior consent of the couple is usually obtained. Young people, particularly those with secondary or higher education who have had opportunities to meet people outside the family or neighborhood circle, are often ingenious in bringing about the marriages they prefer. However, considerable deference continues to be shown to the parents' wishes. While formal negotiations about the marriage are carried out by male parents or guardians, it is usually women who make the preliminary inquiries about prospective brides for their sons and are in the best position to know the background and character of potential brides. Since a young bride generally lives with her husband's family for the first several years of marriage (except in Israel), it is also to the mother's advantage to select a daughter-in-law whom she will find compatible. Since kinship connections are important in many aspects of economic and political life outside the domestic sphere, women's roles in arranging marriages must be seen as a significant source of informal influence and power (Al-Torki, 1986).

Generally the preferred marriage is with someone of approximately equal status (based on considerations of family origins, class, wealth, and special attributes), and there is a strong preference for marriage with relatives (or quasi-kin neighbors) rather than strangers. In some areas, particularly where tribal identities are still strong (such as Saudi Arabia and Jordan), the preferred marriage is with patrilineal kin (known as marriage with the father's brother's daughter or son, though the term is extended to a wider range of kin); in other areas (such as among the urban poor in Cairo), marriage may be equally frequent with maternal kin, and men and women may have different views as to which is preferable from a personal standpoint (Rugh, 1984). But the actual incidence of kin marriage varies from one group or segment of the population to another.

Marriage, divorce, and inheritance are generally governed by religious law, though some states in the area (notably Turkey and Tunisia) have modified this tradition in certain ways (by prohibiting polygyny, restricting unilateral divorce, modifying inheritance laws, and so on).

According to Islamic law, a man may take up to four wives (though few do in practice), marry outside his faith (though only to a Christian or a Jew), unilaterally repudiate a wife, and gain custody of older children (though the age at which this occurs varies from state to state). Women can initiate divorce only for a cause, marry only within their faith, and have custody only of younger children. Inheritances are divided equally among sons, with only half shares going to daughters, though in most cases daughters forfeit their rights of inheritance in return for a claim on the brother's protection and care in case of divorce or early widowhood. Men are expected to be responsible for the economic support of their wives and children, but women have control over the property they bring with them into the marriage, including whatever gold and gifts were negotiated as part of the initial marriage contract. In some places, women may not work without their husband's consent. Personal status law in Judaism and Christianity is similar in its overall patriarchal thrust, but with differences in the details. In Christian sects, marriage is monogamous, and in most sects divorce is forbidden. Among Israeli Jews, only Orthodox marriages are religiously recognized; a woman may not get a divorce without her husband's consent; and polygyny, though religiously permissible, is outlawed by the Israeli state.

Family Dynamics

As for general dynamics within the family, among all religious groups, the husband is recognized as the head of the family and is considered to have authority over his wife. There is generally a clear division of labor within the family by gender: the husband is generally expected to be the economic support of the family, while the wife has primary responsibility for managing the household and raising the children.

While the status of mother and homemaker still confers the highest prestige for women in most parts of the region, attitudes toward work outside the household vary considerably from place to place. If a woman works outside the home for pay, she is still expected to put home and family first, and working outside the home is generally justified only if it is for the family and can be done without neglecting her primary responsibilities. Hence, she must assume the "double burden" (of home and outside work) so characteristic of working women in most parts of the industrialized world. Women take pride in their ability to manage home and family, and most men feel little responsibility for helping out with domestic chores (though that situation is beginning to change slightly among some younger, educated couples). These patterns are also echoed in the relations between siblings, where daughters are generally expected to help with household chores and wait on their brothers and

brothers are expected to exercise authority over their sisters in the absence of their fathers.

Within extended family households, there is considerable variation in status and authority among the women who compose it. The senior woman (with grown children) is in the most powerful position, as she manages the labor of the daughters and daughters-in-law brought into the household. By contrast, a new daughter-in-law brought into the household is in the most vulnerable position, and the mother-in-law–daughter-in-law relationship is often fraught with tension (Mernissi, 1987; White, 1994). The new bride is expected to do much of the work and expend every effort to please her mother-in-law. In the early years of a marriage, before having children, she has little status and little security (since barrenness is one of the most frequent causes for divorce or polygyny). She may also have little emotional support from her husband, since mother-son bonds are generally strong and she may not know her husband well before marriage. It is for this reason that women generally prefer to marry close relatives or neighbors, in order to marry into a family which is already known and in which her own kin are close enough to ease any initial strains in the marriage. As time goes on, however, a young wife will become more firmly established and emotionally integrated in her new household, and when she acquires daughters-in-law of her own will in turn become the most powerful woman in the household.

Decision Making within the Family

Despite the patriarchal skewing of family dynamics outlined above, in actual practice there is considerable variation in how particular households operate. While men have the formal authority in the family, women often have many informal resources that give them considerable clout within the family setting, and many play an influential role in family decision making. In addition to their role in arranging marriages, mothers' cultivation of strong emotional relations with their sons gives them influence over sons' decisions and helps ensure that sons will provide for them in their old age. In those societies where many activities are gender segregated, women often cultivate strong relationships with other women, giving them some leverage in the court of public opinion and gossip, which may subtly be used to reign in errant husbands. In addition, the rather clear distinction between women's and men's spheres of activity and responsibility gives women considerable prestige and managerial authority within their own domain.

Income-generating activities within the home and work outside the home often give women greater leverage in family decision making and provide them with independent income that they control, but the overall incidence of women working is the lowest of all world regions: 30 percent of adult women in western Asia and 21 percent in north Africa are economically active, according to 1994 UN projections (United Nations, 1995), though actual women's work is often underrepresented in the statistics. Such employment or income-generating opportunities as exist vary considerably from state to state. The number of economically active women varies from 9 to 11 percent in the oil-rich countries of the Arabian Peninsula to 37 to 45 percent in Israel and Turkey, respectively (United Nations, 1995), from rural to urban settings, and by class (Moghadem, 1993). Educated women most frequently find employment as professionals or bureaucrats; this work is seen as respectable and provides benefits. Lower-class women may work as factory workers, vendors, craftspeople, or seamstresses. In rural areas women may generate income through poultry and dairy activity or work as unpaid or family labor, as is frequently the case. Their activities, though essential, do little to enhance their authority within the family setting (White, 1994).

External Political and Economic Factors

External political and economic factors often have significant impact on family and gender dynamics. The 1970s and 1980s saw a strong flow of mostly male migrant labor from poorer countries of the region to the oil-rich states of the Persian Gulf. For some women left behind, greater subordination within their husband's natal household was the result; for others, it was greater independence in managing family resources and decisions, which often continued after their husband returned home. In Jordan, the flow of migrants to the Gulf created an economic opportunity that, combined with need and skilled training provided by the government, pulled Jordanian women into the workforce in large numbers, with consequent increases in their independence, influence, and autonomy (Hijab, 1988).

The continuing Palestinian-Israeli conflict, particularly after the outbreak of the intifada (Palestinian uprising against Israeli occupation) in 1987, mobilized many Palestinian women to assume political, economic, or social roles outside the household, which in turn led to revisions of gender roles both within and outside the family (Peteet, 1991).

Economics and politics also have strong effects on fertility and family size, which in turn have an impact on gender roles within the family. Many states or governments in the area have strong pronatalist policies, whether to replen-

ish population sacrificed in wars (Israel, Iran, Palestine), to carry out perceived religious mandates (Iran, Israel), to correct for perceived underpopulation (the Arabian Peninsula), or to stake out political claims to territory by creating "facts" on the ground (Israel; Palestine). Such policies accentuate women's primary roles as bearers and nurturers of children. In other areas, the rapid increase of urbanization (Turkey), or of women in the workforce (Morocco), or migration abroad (Morocco) and the rising cost of raising children, particularly in urban areas, have contributed to a decrease in fertility (Obermeyer, 1995).

The rise of Islamist movements in many parts of the region since the 1970s has had a mixed and often bipolar effect on gender roles within and outside of the family (Dwyer, 1991; Moghadem, 1993). Some Islamists call for women's return to home and family and advocate greater gender segregation and male authority. Still others are active in redefining and developing an Islamic feminism and seek to involve women further in the public sphere while protecting their modesty and fundamental religious values.

Access to schooling and media increased substantially over the last twenty or thirty years of the twentieth century. Between 1970 and 1990, girls' primary and secondary school enrollment increased from 50 percent to 67 percent in western Asia and from 71 percent to 84 percent in north Africa (United Nations, 1995). As more girls go to school, the workload of mothers increases, as their daughters become less available to help with family chores. On the other hand, education for girls is increasingly seen as a desirable asset for upwardly mobile girls: it gives a woman something to fall back on should she become divorced; it may prepare her for a respectable white collar job that provides income and benefits; and it may be perceived as an asset in contracting a middle-class marriage. While there is greater motivation and opportunity for wealthier and urban girls to pursue education beyond the elementary school level, the availability of free education in rural and provincial areas (provided the labor of girls can be spared) puts this opportunity within reach of many rural girls as well. The education of girls has one other advantage worth noting: it contributes to a later age at marriage and thus contributes to a decline in fertility by delaying the age of first childbirth.

Access to media, even in remote villages, gives women greater exposure to national influences and cultures, particularly with regard to a new awareness of orthodox religious practices in the many areas that have religious programming and to discussions of shifting or contested family roles and issues as portrayed in highly popular soap operas, which regularly deal with issues of marriage, generational conflict, and the like. The result of exposure to these influences is only just beginning to be felt.

Israel

Israel is something of an exception to many of the generalizations in the preceding sections, with the smallest average household size (3.8 persons), the lowest fertility rate (3.8 children), and one of the higher rates of economically active women (37 percent) and of woman-headed households (18 percent) (United Nations, 1995). But these statistics obscure the bipolar nature of the population. Those Israelis of Ashkenazi (western European) origin more closely conform to the European patterns of smaller family size, nuclear families, independent living for young people, and freedom of marital choice. With the Orthodox Jews and Israelis of Middle Eastern and north African origin, there is a closer approximation to the fertility and family patterns described for the rest of the region. Sabras (native-born Israelis) combine elements of both. Israeli Arabs show a similar bipolar pattern concerning aspects of family and gender organization. Christian Arabs are close to Jews of European origin in terms of education, women's participation in the labor force, family size, and levels of fertility, while the Arab Muslim population generally has the highest levels of family size and fertility and the lowest levels of female education and employment of any group save the ultra-Orthodox Jews (Goldscheider, 1996).

See Also

DEVELOPMENT: MIDDLE EAST AND THE ARAB REGION; FAMILY: RELIGIOUS AND LEGAL SYSTEMS—ISLAMIC TRADITIONS; FAMILY: RELIGIOUS AND LEGAL SYSTEMS—JUDAIC TRADITIONS; FAMILY LAW; KINSHIP

References and Further Reading

Al-Torki, Soraya. 1986. *Women in Saudi Arabia: Ideology and behavior among the elite.* New York: Columbia University Press.

Dwyer, Kevin. 1991. *Arab voices: The human rights debate in the Middle East.* Berkeley: University of California Press.

Fernea, Elizabeth Warnock, ed. 1985. *Women and the family in the Middle East.* Austin: University of Texas Press.

Goldscheider, Calvin. 1996. *Israel's changing society: Population, ethnicity and development.* Boulder, Col.: Westview.

Hijab, Nadia. 1988. *Womanpower: The Arab debate on women at work.* New York: Cambridge University Press.

Kagitcibasi, Cigdem, ed. 1986. *Sex roles, family and community in Turkey.* Bloomington: Indiana University Press.

Maher, Vanessa. 1974. *Women and property in Morocco.* New York: Cambridge University Press.

Mernissi, Fatima. 1987. *Beyond the veil.* Bloomington: Indiana University Press.

Moghadem, Valentine M., ed. 1993. *Modernizing women: Women and social change in the Middle East.* Boulder, Col.: Lynne Rienner.

Obermeyer, Carla Makhlouf, ed. 1995. *Family, gender, and population in the Middle East.* Cairo: American University in Cairo Press.

Peteet, Julie M. 1991. *Gender in crisis: Women and the Palestinian resistance movement.* New York: Columbia University Press.

Rugh, Andrea. 1984. *Family in contemporary Egypt.* Syracuse, N.Y.: Syracuse University Press.

Shaaban, Bouthaina. 1988. *Both right and left handed: Arab women talk about their lives.* London: Women's Press.

United Nations. 1995. *The world's women 1995: Trends and statistics.* New York: United Nations.

White, Jenny B. 1994. *Money makes us relatives: Women's labor in urban Turkey.* Austin: University of Texas Press.

Barbara Larson

HOUSEHOLDS AND FAMILIES: Native North America

Matrilineal Societies

In most tribal societies of aboriginal North America, household units assumed different meanings in different tribal contexts. Social organizational factors predicated the structure and function of these family clusters. Among groups such as the matrilineal, matrifocal family units of the Iroquois in the northeast, women owned the houses and fields. Men marrying into the group assumed residency in the multifamily longhouse. In most cases, these families were part of the larger social structure of clans. Clans, such as those in the matrilineal Pueblo sedentary groups of the southwest, were given names like Squash or Turquoise. Clans regulated marriage choices and economic enterprises, such as cleaning the irrigation ditches, and they functioned in the ritual systems of the kiva (ceremonial chamber) events. In addition, overarching social units (moieties) were present, for example, among the Haida of the northwest coast. These larger clans often usurped the allegiances of individuals in ritual to ensure that the pueblo operated in equilibrium. Family members were obligated to dance in summer rituals to restore harmony. Social control also was exerted through the clan and religious leaders in this highly structured social system. In this arrangement, the mother's brother was most significant in the socialization of his sister's offspring. His primary loyalty was to this matrilineal configuration. Often heard is that "divorce was easy, as all the wife did was put his possessions out the door." Moreover, the children remained in the mother's home.

Matrilineal groups guaranteed the continuity of inheritance of the abode from mother to daughter and a prescribed residence pattern for males. These factors resulted from a structured social organization and from a stable economic horticultural base among both Iroquois and Pueblo groups. The strictly patriarchal mode that characterized the Euro-American model was not common among pre-Columbian native nations. Thus, the Martinez case in the Santa Clara pueblo illustrates the impact of external control of inheritance. The secular tribal council—a federally imposed governing body—ruled (buttressed by a Supreme Court decision) that a house could not be inherited by a daughter whose mother was married to a Navajo. Significantly, this ruling may have further repercussions on tribal sovereignty, which controls indigenous identity in enrollment. It also contravenes individual decision making.

Bilateral Societies

By contrast, societies that are identified as band-type or hunting and gathering societies are often bilateral in descent. Equal emphasis on male and female affiliation lends a more egalitarian domestic unit. Contrary to the "man the hunter" myth, reevaluations of these societies have evidenced a balanced economic equilibrium between men and women, in which "woman the gatherer" was as important in the production and provisioning of items. Tanned skins, dried meat, and the collection of fruits and vegetal materials were as important parts of household maintenance as the initial trophies of large mammals.

Bands were usually composed of households extended by native terms that were descriptive, as among the Lakota. The kinship term *tiospaye* can be translated as *ti* = lodge, home; *ospaye* = part of. These congeries were very flexible in composition. Family units or nuclear families were free to associate themselves with other extended families for purposes of hunting or ritual activities and for temporary living arrangements. If tensions arose in these social units, a family often aligned itself with another kin unit. This flexibility allowed for group harmony that, in a way, was self-determined. Individual autonomy was a strong point, and kinship was a binding force that held smaller groups together by such alliances of bilaterality.

In most of the native societies of North America, kinship was a major binding mechanism in small, face-to-face communities. Women's ability to add to a kin unit was an important asset, as was their participation in ritual and economic endeavors. In clan-based groups, such as the Navajo, sexual intercourse—no matter how distant the clan—was considered to be incestuous.

In the Plains culture area, because of the bilaterality of traditional kinship rules and residence patterns, greater degrees of relatedness could be activated at certain times for hunting, warfare, or gathering. Social and economic reciprocity was maintained. Gender equity diminished, however, during the era of colonization and forced placement in reservations.

Colonization and Patrilineal Models

Colonization by European immigrants did irreparable damage to these indigenous social units. Efforts to "civilize" by means of Christianization and education imposed a patriarchal model with patrilineal descent and patrilocal residence. This process was not as detrimental to ecologically stable societies as it was to the wide-ranging band organizations. Placement on an enclosed land base and the placing of nuclear families on allotted tracts introduced concepts of individual land ownership, land use, and mercantilism. Contained family units were forbidden to speak native languages and to practice traditional value systems that stressed sharing and group welfare.

At present, such government agencies as the Department of Housing and Urban Development (HUD) have reversed earlier federal policies by gathering families in clustered communities on the Great Plains. In addition, governmental church policies and hiring practices often have favored women's development in such occupations as nursing, social work, and education. Men's economic roles, already eroded, were neglected. Since the 1960s and the War on Poverty, there have been many single-parent, female-headed families in native enclaves in both urban and rural native communities. Forced culture change and assimilationist policy have had a lasting effect on family life in native North America.

See Also

FAMILY: RELIGIOUS AND LEGAL SYSTEMS—NATIVE NORTH AMERICA; KINSHIP; MATRILINEAL SYSTEMS; SOCIALIZATION FOR COMPLEMENTARITY

References and Further Reading

Hassrick, Royal B. 1964. *The Sioux: Life and customs of a warrior society.* Norman: University of Oklahoma Press.

Ortiz, Alphonso. 1969. Dozier, Edward P. 1970. *The Pueblo World.* New York: Holt, Rinehart and Winston.

Lee, Richard B., and Richard Daly, eds. 1999. *The Cambridge encyclopedia of hunters and gatherers.* Cambridge: Cambridge University Press.

Beatrice Medicine

HOUSEHOLDS AND FAMILIES:
North America

This article focuses primarily on findings for households and families in the United States from the 1970s to the end of the twentieth century, and some comparisons are made with those in Canada during the same period. An overview of changes in family life throughout the industrialized world shows delayed marriage and declining rates of marriage, deferred childbearing, fewer children and more out-of-wedlock births, high rates of divorce, increasing rates of cohabitation outside of marriage, and single parenthood, overwhelmingly by women (Kamerman, 1995).

Deindustrialization and the rise of information and service economies in both the United States and Canada coincided with changes in the labor force and a rise in the cost of raising children. Two out of three jobs after World War II were filled by married women (Harris, 1991). Partly because of the premium these economies placed on education for upward mobility, it became increasingly difficult for middle-income families with one wage earner to rear even one or two children.

These infrastructural changes affected marriage patterns, the organization of family life, and the behavioral and ideological aspects of gender roles and sexuality. Rates of marriage and fertility declined, divorce rates rose, and new gender roles and forms of family structure and sexuality emerged (Harris, 1991). Lugaila (1992) employs U.S. census data to show that between 1960 and 1990, the average size of households and families declined, because there were fewer children per family, more single-parent families, and a growing number of people who lived alone. By 1990, there were on average 1.63 persons per household and 3.17 persons per family, compared with 3.3 and 3.67, respectively, in 1960 (Lugaila, 1992).

An overview of household composition shows that it also changed between 1960 and 1990. Married-couple households declined from 75 percent of all households in 1960 to 56 percent in 1990, because of a drop in the proportion of married couples with children under 18 and an increase in the number of single-parent family households. This trend appeared to have leveled off in the 1990s, even as those changes became embedded in the culture (Kilborn, 1996). The trend toward fewer married couple households was strongest among blacks (64 percent to 39 percent), less strong among Hispanics (74 percent to 67 percent), and least strong among whites (87 percent to 72 percent). Nonfamily households of one or more persons increased from 15 percent to 29 percent. Among families with children, those with only one or two children increased from 64 percent in 1960 to 80 percent in 1990 (Lugaila, 1992).

Mother-child families increased dramatically because of the rise in divorce and births outside marriage. In both mother-child and father-child families, a grandparent, the other biological parent in an unmarried couple, or someone with whom the parent has a close personal relationship also may live in the household. There were important differences by race in the 32 percent of all one-parent families with a never-married parent: 22 percent of whites, 53 percent of blacks, and 37 percent of Hispanic origin (Lugaila, 1992).

Parents' educational attainment increased significantly between 1960 and 1990, when only 25 percent of all single-parents had less than a high school education, as compared with 62 percent in 1960. Also in 1990, 20 percent of both married-couple and mother-child families completed one to three years of college. A larger proportion of married couples, however, completed four or more years. Family income rose with level of education, but within particular levels, poverty rates for blacks and Hispanics were much higher than for whites (Lugaila, 1992).

The proportion of married women in the labor force nearly doubled to 58 percent in 1990 (Lugaila, 1992). By 1993 half of working women in married-couple households brought home half the income, and 23 percent of women earned more than their husbands, whose jobs, however, offered more financial security than their own (Lewin, 1995). By 1990, almost three-fourths of married women with children of school age were in the labor force, compared with just over half of childless wives (Lugaila, 1992). The proportion of mothers with infants under age 1 in the labor force increased from 31 percent in 1976 to 53 percent in 1990. Despite wives' increased participation in the labor force, the median income for all families was only 6 percent higher in 1990 than in 1973. In 1990, the incomes of female-headed families were 58 percent smaller than those of married-couple families (Lugaila, 1992). By 1990, both parents worked in the paid workforce in 70 percent of families with children. A majority of female-headed family households with children also included others who worked. A significant proportion of female-headed family households, however, had no one at home who had worked at all during the previous year (24 percent) (Lugaila, 1992).

After 1969, income inequality began to increase among families with children. The proportion with a low relative income rose from 15 percent to 24 percent, while the proportion with a high relative income increased from 8 to 10 percent. The proportion with incomes in the middle range declined from 74 percent to 66 percent. Poverty rates for all married-couple families have been much lower than for female-headed family households. Within the two family types, however, the poverty rates for blacks and Hispanics have been substantially higher than for whites (Lugaila, 1992).

The living arrangements of children also changed after 1960. The proportion of children living with only their mother increased from 8 percent to 21.6 percent. In 1990, the majority of white and Hispanic children lived with both parents, whereas the majority of black children lived in single-parent situations (see Dehavenon, 1993, for a discussion of the low sex ratios that remove many black males from the marriage market during the years when their children are socialized). The proportion of both white and black children living with a single parent, however, more than doubled between 1960 and 1990 (Lugaila, 1992).

Between 1960 and 1980, the number of unmarried heterosexual couples who said they were living together increased almost as quickly as the number of female-headed families. Although this trend seemed to slow between 1980 and 1985, the increase in the number of young adults, aged 25 to 34, who said they were living alone continued during the same period (Herbers, 1985). It seems likely that people in this age group living alone were not, however, sleeping alone (Harris, 1991).

Parents' work experience varied across married-couple families, from full-time year-round to less than full-time and from less than year-round to no work. Family income of two-parent families varied with the work experience of the parents. The younger children of most working mothers were cared for in a private home. Almost three-fourths of employed mothers with 1- and 2-year-olds or a child under 1 used care provided at the child's home or the provider's home (Harris, 1991).

Children's poverty rates fluctuated over time, whereas parents' work experience affected family poverty. While it dropped sharply during the War on Poverty between 1959 and 1969, it fluctuated from 14.4 to 17.1 percent in the 1970s. By 1990, it was 20.6 percent and much higher for black and Hispanic than for white children (Harris, 1991). Despite an economic boom, these rates continued to increase throughout the 1990s.

Children's poverty rates also varied by family structure. It was much lower for children in married-couples than in single-parent families (10 percent as compared with 53 percent), and in both family structures they were made much higher for black and Hispanic than for white children. These rates also continued to increase throughout the economic boom in the 1990s.

Income inequality among children increased with the rise in single-parent families after 1969, the end of the War on Poverty, and slow economic growth worldwide. Children's health care varied by poverty level and family status, and in 1995, at least 37 million individual Americans were without any form of health insurance. After 1980, homelessness among children rose to levels unheard of since the Great Depression of the 1930s. Poverty and homelessness have varied by region in the United States, depending on local economic conditions, rates of unemployment, and the severity of the periodic recessions associated with market-driven capitalism. Fitchen (1991) has shown that all the above changes affect rural as well as urban and suburban households and families.

Unlike Canada and all other western industrialized nations, the United States does not have a coherent set of explicit family policies but, rather, has a series of policy initiatives designed to achieve different objectives and directed toward different aspects of child and family functioning. Sixty-three other nations provide a universal family allowance in a modest income supplement, whereby society shares as a whole in the costs of rearing children, regardless of family income, employment, or structure. A few countries, including Canada, have introduced income-testing as a way of targeting expenditures (Kamerman, 1995).

In the United States and many other countries, social or public assistance programs provide for low-income families in need of child support owing to an absent parent. In the United States, public assistance payments are not indexed to the consumer price index, and their purchasing power declined by about half between 1969 and 2000. This decline, the low level of the minimum wage, and the congressional overhaul of the public assistance program in 1996 contributed substantially to the ongoing rise in hunger conditions and homelessness since the early 1980s. By 1999, millions faced homelessness in spite of a booming economy (Burt et al., 1999), and the boom itself contributed to a loss of affordable housing (Molotsky, 2000).

In addition, many countries—not including the United States and Canada however—supply housing allowances that supplement family income to reduce the need to use their public assistance payments to pay excess rent. Cash maternity benefits that offset some of the cost of a new baby and replace wages forgone at the time of childbirth are payable in more than a hundred countries, including Canada (Kamerman, 1995). In 1992, a maternity leave without pay was granted to mothers in the United States for the first time.

Analyses of the effects of child-conditioned income transfers in several countries show that they redistribute income from those with more to those with less and from those with no children to those with children (Kamerman, 1995). One result, attributable largely to these and other child-related income transfers, is significantly lower rates of child poverty than in the United States.

In the 1970s, job-protected parental leaves developed largely in countries with low fertility or very high rates of labor-force participation among women. In addition to the mother's right to an extended job-protected, paid leave at childbirth, these leaves included paid time off to care for a sick child or visit a child's school and a leave for fathers at the time of a child's birth. In many countries, including Canada, fathers can share in some portion of all these leaves (Kamerman, 1995).

Unlike the United States, Canada and most European nations provide free public preschool for children aged 3 to 6 during the normal school day. Children can participate in these programs regardless of the employment status of their mothers, and they are viewed to be as important for child development as for providing childcare for working parents. Infant and toddler care is not as extensive as care for children aged 2 or 3 and up. In Europe, day care is largely defined as a service for children under 3 who have mothers in the labor force (Kamerman, 1995).

Despite the economic boom in the United States in the 1990s, the gap between rich and poor families widened substantially, and families in the middle-class were just getting by (Uchitelle, 1999). As of 1995, poor American children who had already borne the brunt of economic inequality ranked sixteenth in a study of children in 18 industrialized nations (Bradsher, 1995). Furthermore, as a result of the public assistance overhaul in 1996, one million parents lost their health insurance under Medicaid (Pear, 2000), and three million welfare recipients were expected to find jobs to support themselves (Burtless, 1998). While the majority of welfare recipients do find work, especially in times when unemployment is low, unskilled single parents usually find jobs that pay low wages, are temporary, and do not provide medical coverage (Burtless, 1998). These trends do not bode well for middle- and low-income families who, without the social protections that exist in other industrialized countries, have already suffered the effects of tax and budget cuts. They also threaten to jeopardize the

nation's human and social capital and its competitiveness in the global economy.

See Also

DIVORCE; HOUSEHOLDS: FEMALE-HEADED AND FEMALE-SUPPORTED; SINGLE PEOPLE

References and Further Reading

Bernstein, Nina. 2000. Poverty found to be rising in families considered safe. *New York Times* (April 20): B1.

Bradsher, Keith. 1995. Low ranking for poor American children. *New York Times* (August 14): A9.

Burt, Martha, L. Y. Aron, T. Douglas, J. Valenti, E. Lee, and B. Iwen. 1999. *Homelessness: Programs and the people they serve.* Washington, D.C.: Urban Institute.

Burtless, Gary. 1998. Can the labor market absorb three million welfare recipients? *Focus* 19 (3, Summer-Fall): 1–6. Madison: University of Wisconsin.

Dehavenon, Anna Lou. 1993. Not enough to go around: An etic model for the scientific study of the causes of matrifocality. In J. Mencher and Anne Okongwu, eds., *Where did all the men go? Female-headed/female-supported households in cross-cultural perspective.* Boulder, Col.: Westview.

Fitchen, Janet M. 1991. *Endangered spaces, enduring places: Change, identity, and survival in rural America.* Boulder, Col.: Westview.

Harris, Marvin. 1991. *Cultural anthropology.* 3rd ed. New York: HarperCollins.

Herbers, John. 1985. Non-relatives and solitary people make up half of new households. *New York Times* (November 10): 1. Cited in Harris, 1991.

Hilts, Phillip. 2000. Europeans perform highest in ranking of world health. *New York Times* (June 21): A12.

Kamerman, Sheila B. 1995. Child and family policies: An international overview. In Edward F. Zigler, Sharon Lynn Kagan, and Nancy W. Hall, eds., *Children, families and government: preparing for the 21st century.* New York: Cambridge University Press.

Kilborn, Peter T. 1996. Shift in families reaches a plateau, study says. *New York Times* (November 27): A18.

Lewin, Tamar. 1995. Women are becoming equal providers: Half of working women bring home half the household income. *New York Times* (May 1): 27.

Lugaila, Terry. 1992. U.S. Bureau of the Census. Households, families, and children: A 30-year perspective. *Current Population Reports*, 23–181. Washington, D.C.: U.S. Government Printing Office.

Molotsky, Irvin. 2000. Robust economy is contributing to a loss of affordable housing. *New York Times* (March 28): A20.

Pear, Robert. 2000. A million parents lost Medicaid, study says. *New York Times* (June 20): A14.

Uchitelle, Louis. 1999. The American middle, just getting by. *New York Times* (August 1): B1.

University of Wisconsin–Madison Institute for Research on Poverty. 1999. Women in the labor market, part 2: Welfare mothers. *Focus* 20 (2, Spring): 14–37.

Anna Lou Dehavenon

HOUSEHOLDS AND FAMILIES: South Asia

Throughout south Asia the basic structure of intrafamilial roles, rights, and responsibilities reflects the kinship norms within which it is located. In addition, religion, regional culture, caste, and the shifts in the salience and scope of the domain of kinship interweave and constitute specific familial milieus within which women shape their lives. State policy and intervention have been major sources of change. Macroprocesses like industrialization and urbanization have also been sources of change. It is, however, important to recognize the distinction between change in size and composition of the household and change in its ideological underpinnings.

Diversities and Pluralism

Although most of the south Asian region follows patrilineal kinship, there are specific regions and communities that operate on other principles. In southwest India several caste communities (for example, the Nair) followed matrilineal kinship until it was superseded by legal reform in the early twentieth century. In northeast India some tribal communities are matrilineal (for example, the Khasi and the Garo). Sri Lanka had a marked bilateral leaning, making it in some ways closer to the southeast Asian pattern. These systems differ from one another in line of property devolution, rights to living space, formation of group identity, and so on, all of which have definite psychological and material outcomes for women.

In the south Asian region patrilineality has several faces. The compulsions of boundary maintenance within caste structure, associated as they are with female sexual purity, gave patriliny among upper-caste Hindus certain distinct features, which have not fully disappeared even though nineteenth- and twentieth-century reform legislation modified Hindu family law extensively. These features include the overwhelming stress on female virginity, absence of remarriage among widows (suttee is an extreme example of the problematic status of widows), early (child) marriage for girls, and segregation (veiling). Purdah in Islamic communities in south

Asia has to do largely with ideas of female modesty in the public sphere, in contrast with Hindu communities in north India where the veiling of women is restricted to their affinal homes, in the presence of senior, especially male, affines (that is, in-laws). It has been suggested that purdah in Islamic communities derives from the notion of protecting women from the predatory external world and that the veiling of women in Hindu communities derives from the notion of female sexuality as inherently disruptive of social (and familial) order. In the sphere of family relations, Muslim communities in south Asia are governed by Shari'a (Muslim law), which, although based on patrilineal assumptions, has special features with both positive and negative implications for women. Both men and women, for example, are recognized as individuals equally capable of inheriting, holding, and disposing of property in absolute terms, though the woman's share is half that of the equivalent male. On the other hand, legal recognition of polygamy has, with rare exceptions, negative outcomes for women. Buddhist-influenced ideas about woman as a source of temptation and evil, combined with preexisting kinship structures, produce quite different familial milieus in Bhutan, Nepal, and Sri Lanka.

In India southern and northern regional cultures have brought different nuances to family life. In much of southern India there seems to have been a historical base of bilateral kinship. Given the widely prevalent norm of cross-cousin marriage and the absence of the rule of village exogamy, there is greater reciprocity between bride givers and bride takers, as well as continuing and close contact between a woman and her natal kin, all of which factors provide security and support for women, as compared with their counterparts in northern India. Patriliny is evinced differently in tribal communities. Their intrafamilial relations have been excluded from the scope of codified law and are extremely heterogeneous. Given the relatively localized and small-scale functioning of tribal communities, with their high degree of influence on the domain of kinship, patrilineal rules are there applied with greater flexibility, with tighter mechanisms of community control to ensure pragmatic justice for men and women.

Dominant Pattern

Despite the diversity of kinship systems in south Asia, the dominant system—covering a contiguous region across Afghanistan, Pakistan, North India, Bangladesh, and Nepal—is patrilineal, and it is increasing in scope and influence. The three major religions—Hinduism, Islam, and Buddhism—have for the most part reinforced this dominance. Both the colonial and postcolonial states have had significant roles in strengthening it.

The typical household within this dominant patrilineal pattern is internally stratified on the basis of age, kinship, and gender, with the young incoming female affine representing the lowest point of authority and influence. The hypergamous (socially upward) context of marriage is reflected in a gap between the status of bride givers and bride takers, the gifts and marriage payments moving only in one direction, from the bride givers to the bride takers. The absence of married daughters' rights of inheritance to immovable assets (primarily land and house) of the natal family stems from the central notion of temporary membership of women in their natal home and lineage and the transfer of control over their sexuality, fertility, and labor to another lineage. Despite partial legal reform, practice lags far behind. The jewels, clothing, vessels, and other movable assets that a woman receives on marriage are considered, in one view, to be an alternative form of inheritance. In another, these assets are seen as compensation for the absence of real inheritance. In any case, marriage is seen as an avenue to better one's material prospects. The ambivalent position of women in patriliny explodes into the modern social problem of dowry, or payment of huge amounts in cash and kind to the groom and his family by the bride's family. The woman herself rarely has control over her dowry, at least not for some years. Dowry is widespread across south Asia, cutting across strata, regions, and religions, pushing many families into debt and impoverishment by the time they marry off daughters. There is some evidence that even communities traditionally practicing bride-price switch to dowry as they gain prosperity, which they hope to convert to social status. "Dowry death," a phenomenon much written about, involves harassment of a young married woman over the issues of inadequate dowry, culminating in her suicide or murder. Although such drastic outcomes are less frequent than the publicity suggests, the underlying notion of women's inherent transferability and the lack of rights of her natal family to her is widespread. The heavy burden of dowry seems to be a strong reason for devaluation of girl children by the natal family. Preference for sons is pervasive throughout the region, manifested by an increasing use of technology (sex-detection tests) for selectively aborting female fetuses and discrimination toward girl children in access to food, health care, and education, especially (but not exclusively) in poorer families. Studies that document the imbalanced sex ratio, lower nutritional and health status, and literacy levels of women give tangible and measurable evidence of discrimination, though regional and temporal variations need careful consideration. In general, Sri Lanka, the state of Kerala in India, and to some extent the southern states of India present less extreme gender-

based disparities in the household, though even there trends suggest some reversals.

The family socializes children to accept and internalize gender biases as inherent and natural. Household rituals, customs, and family lore often reinforce the secondary status of women.

Women's Work

In the south Asian region, the social security function of the family has not been supplanted by the state, whose welfare measures are thin and patchy. Within the household the prime responsibility for caretaking lies with women, across regions and strata. Sharing of domestic work by males is virtually nonexistent. Moreover, the formally articulated role of males as breadwinner is not sustained consistently. Women contribute to household income in a variety of ways, even among those families where considerations of "status" and "honor" forbid wage labor outside the home. Women assist or share in the family occupation or undertake home-based production. In most socioeconomic levels of society, however, a large section of women have to enter the arena of economic activity outside the home through self-employment or wage labor. There is some evidence that the earlier-held notions of women not working in certain kinds of occupations are eroding. But the male-as-breadwinner ideology undermines womens' economic contribution or treats their income as additional pocket money, even though in many cases it is the main or only income for the family. The emphasis on the male as breadwinner also prevents the recognition of de facto female-headed households due to death, desertion, or migration of the male spouse. Although scholars and activists have brought gender issues to the attention of policy makers, their concrete and effective implementation remains a promise. In urban areas, it is not uncommon to find women in various kinds and levels of occupations, but their "outside work" is absorbed into the larger interests of the family. The nature of the work women engage in, the time and energy they invest in it, and the timing of their entering and withdrawing from the workforce are determined by the family's overriding concerns about how to use women's work to ensure the family's survival, augment its resources, enhance its status and mobility, and amass symbolic capital.

Family Form: "Jointness" and "Nuclearity"

The long-standing discussion of the south Asian extended, or "joint," family and its transformation into nuclearity has somewhat obscured issues of gender disparity by focusing attention on form and composition. Part of the confusion arises from failing to distinguish between *household* and *fam-*

ily. In examining changes in household composition, the assumed shift from jointness to nuclearity has been found by researchers to be nonlinear—that is, not a necessary or inevitable concomitant of industrialization and urbanization. Research suggests that the form of the household at a given moment, whether nuclear or extended, can give only a limited picture of interpersonal relationships. Family is an entity that goes beyond the residential dimension denoted by the household. The retaliations of households with one another and with the larger structures in which they are embedded, the location of a household in the domestic developmental cycle, and the nature and significance of kinship in a given society are germane to understanding women's position. Nuclear households in south Asia and the position of women in them cannot be directly equated with nuclear households in other cultures and societies. Although there does appear to be a weakening of classical patrilineal restrictions on women and a move toward a bilateral ethos among the more urbanized and educated levels of society, overall sociopolitical developments, notably the growth of identity politics, sometimes seem to be strengthening restrictive concepts of woman and family.

See Also

CASTE; DOWRY AND BRIDEPRICE; ELDERLY CARE: CASE STUDY—INDIA; FAMILY: RELIGIOUS AND LEGAL SYSTEMS—BUDDHIST TRADITIONS; FAMILY: RELIGIOUS AND LEGAL SYSTEMS—ISLAMIC TRADITIONS; FAMILY LAW: CASE STUDY—INDIA; SUTTEE (SATI)

References and Further Reading

Aziz, K. M. 1979. *Kinship in Bangla Desh.* Dacca: Institute for Diarrhoeal Disease Research.

Bennett, Lynn. 1983. *Dangerous wives and sacred sisters: Social and symbolic roles of high caste women in Nepal.* New York: Columbia University Press.

Donna, Hastings. 1988. *Marriage and Muslims: Preference and choice in northern Pakistan.* Delhi: Hindustan.

Dube, Leela. 1993. Kinship and family in south and southeast Asia. Report prepared for the United Nations University and the project Women's Work and Family Strategies.

Gray, John N., and David J. Mearns, eds. 1989. *Society from the inside out: Anthropological perspectives on the south Asian household.* New Delhi: Sage.

Kolenda, Pauline. 1987. *Regional differences in family structure in India.* Jaipur: Rawat.

Sen, Amaartya. 1988. Family and food: Sex bias in poverty. In T. Srinivasan and P. Bardhan, eds. *Rural poverty in south Asia,* 453–472. Delhi: Oxford University Press.

Shah, A. M. 1973. *The household dimension of the family in India.* Berkeley: University of California Press.

Srinivas, M. N. 1984. *Some reflections on dowry.* Delhi: Oxford University Press.

Kamala Ganesh

HOUSEHOLDS AND FAMILIES: Southeast Asia

Southeast Asia is a diverse region of many countries, languages, and cultural traditions. Yet across this vast area, which includes the countries of Brunei, Cambodia, Indonesia, Laos, Malaysia, Myanmar (formerly Burma), the Philippines, Singapore, Thailand, and Vietnam, women are perceived as having relatively high status. There are common patterns of family organization and living arrangements across the region among the lowland, plains-dwelling, wet-rice cultivators. Distinctive cultural features of the region "emphasize complementarity rather than opposition, and authority based on rank rather than gender" (Ong, 1989). These features, combined with the fact that rank is most often related to achieved rather than ascribed status in southeast Asia, create the possibility that women can attain high status in society.

The assessment that southeast Asian women are "relatively equal" is often made specifically in contrast to the perceived position of their sisters in neighboring China and India. There are several reasons for this positive assessment. First, the rice cultivators of the plains have bilateral kinship systems, meaning that people related through either the mother or the father are considered relatives and ancestors. In addition, many societies have a stated preference for residence after marriage with the family of the wife, known as uxorilocal residence. Such residence may be only short term and largely symbolic, as in Java (Geertz, 1961), or it may be essentially permanent, as in northern Thailand (Potter, 1977). This practice is seen as a way of providing protection for the young woman, who is surrounded by her own kinspeople.

The practice of giving bride wealth, money offered by the family of the groom to that of the bride, is common in southeast Asia. In previous times some of the peoples of the region practiced bride service, whereby the prospective groom worked for the family of the bride for a period of time in order to prove himself worthy. This custom, of course, stands in sharp contrast to a dowry system, whereby a daughter must take wealth into a marriage.

The central role of the mother in the kinship network and, in practice, in the day-to-day running of the household, has been described as "matrifocal" (Geertz, 1961; Potter, 1977; Tanner, 1974). The importance of the mother-child bond, the mother's role as the key link in the larger network of kinspeople, and her role as financial manager of the family's resources give her significant influence on household decision making. In-marrying sons-in-law are in a tenuous position in relation to the wife's family, most especially with the father-in-law.

Women traditionally have the right both to own and to inherit property. Land is often divided among both male and female children, although there are some variations across the region. For example, in northern Thailand it is the youngest daughter who usually inherits the parental home, whereas in Java it is generally the eldest male. Although Islam has changed inheritance patterns in Malaysia and Indonesia to an extent, Islamic law is often bypassed in favor of local custom, and land is divided equally between male and female children. Only in patrilineal Vietnam, particularly northern Vietnam, is land passed only from fathers to sons (Luong, 1992).

Divorce is relatively common and easy to obtain throughout the region. In Java it is so common that some people have come to see the first marriage as only transitory (Geertz, 1961). Women who bring property into a marriage have the right to an equal division of property upon divorce. If children are old enough, they may be allowed to choose the parent with whom they prefer to live. Young children usually stay with their mothers.

Residences are single-family dwellings, occupied by a husband, wife, and children. There are commonly other related individuals in the household, including elderly parents and unmarried younger siblings, often from the wife's side of the family. These arrangements are fluid, with household composition changing over time. The couple's place of residence often changes as well; they may initially choose to reside with the parents of the bride or in some cases with the parents of the groom, but the ultimate goal is to establish their own neolocal residence.

Another main reason for the perceived equality of women in southeast Asia is the complementarity in the sexual division of labor. Although certain tasks in the cycle of rice cultivation are seen as predominantly women's work or men's work, in practice men and women engage in a wide range of tasks in cultivation. Men plow, although with the shortages of male labor after the devastation of war in Vietnam and Cambodia, women have been known to do so. Women transplant the rice seedlings, although men may help with this task. Both men and women work in the har-vest. A range of other tasks from animal husbandry to market gardening and carrying daily supplies of water and wood may be taken on by either males or females, depending on who is available. This sharing of labor creates a cooperative production unit in which the work of all members of the group is valued.

Women are responsible for the control of the family finances. Women keep the money, and any accumulation is usually stored in the form of jewelry, which they wear. Control of finances extends beyond the household and into the local marketplace. Women are the sellers and buyers in local markets throughout southeast Asia. They are also the ones who borrow money if necessary. It is this control of finances that, perhaps more than any other characteristic, led early visitors from China and Europe to remark on the astonishing power of women in the region.

This interpretation is, however, at least partly erroneous, in that it applies a foreign rather than local system of value and morality. While southeast Asia includes the Theravada Buddhist countries of Myanmar, Thailand, Laos, and Cambodia, the Muslim nations of Malaysia, Indonesia, and Brunei, Mahayana Buddhist and Catholic Vietnam, and the Catholic and Muslim Philippines, there are limitations on the spiritual status of women that are common across the region. The association of women with the marketplace, perceived by outsiders as a mark of high status, is in fact devalued in southeast Asia. In Buddhist terms, the goal of one's existence is to gain detachment form this world and to focus on the spiritual, but a rigid sex division prevents women's participation. Only men can become monks. Women, through their attachment to their family and to the search for profit in their marketing activities, can never attain this spiritual focus (Kirsch, 1984). Only in Burma does it seem that female religious mendicants are accorded respect in any way similar to that accorded monks (Khaing, 1984).

A very high value is placed on the virginity of young girls before marriage. Women must therefore be protected and controlled when they are young. A woman gains in status after she marries and produces children, as well as when she is of advanced age, because great respect is accorded to the elderly. But a young woman is constantly under suspicion, and a woman who is thought not to be a virgin or who lacks adequate male protection can be the target of sexual advances and assaults. The devaluation of women through association with money and loss of virginity is part of the complex of notions that has led to southeast Asia's becoming a major sex-tourism destination.

Exceptions to the patterns described above, including unilineal descent, varying household composition, and gender relations are found among the upland populations in peninsular southeast Asia. The upland and forest dwellers practice swidden agriculture or hunting and gathering or some combination thereof. There is also significant variation among the islands of the Indonesian archipelago, where one of the best-documented societies is that of the Minangkabau. The Minangkabau are an interesting case of a matrilineal society in a Muslim nation-state where the complementary roles of men and women have allowed women to retain their high status in a changing world (Sanday and Goodenough, 1990).

While the bulk of the population of southeast Asia remains in rural areas, rapid urbanization has changed patterns of daily life. The lives of the wealthy upper classes and a growing urban middle class vary drastically from those of rural farmers and the urban poor. Thorbek (1987) has described the lives of residents of a slum area of Bangkok and notes several changes in family interactions. While women remain the central focus of the family, men are more likely to keep the money they earn, and since they are more likely to earn a living wage, women become more dependent on them.

The establishment of world-market factories in southeast Asia has drawn large numbers of young female workers into the global economy. Ong (1987) has written about such factories in Malaysia and about the reaction to the role of these women as productive wage earners by their families and by society. The perceived freedom that comes with being a factory worker is threatening to male members of the workers' families and to some Islamic organizations, which move to restrict the young women's actions and movements. Ong argues that modern factories manipulate traditional gender imagery to appropriate the control of young women's lives that previously belonged to the males of their family.

In Vietnam, Cambodia, and Laos, the people are still struggling to overcome the traumatic effects of years of warfare. In Vietnam and Cambodia there is still a shortage of men; and some women, especially older and more educated women, must face the difficulties of living without a family. Hy Van Luong (1992) has written about the changes in family life in a particular village in northern Vietnam. Unlike much of southeast Asia, northern Vietnam has a patrilineal and patrilocal kinship system. But before the revolution, neighborhood groups called *giap* served as crosslinkages, binding the community with ties through both men and women. Although patrilineages remained a central focus of social organization after the war, the crosscutting linkages through women did not retain their former importance. In Cambodia, the shortage of males was related

to the high death toll during the Khmer Rouge period and the civil war, which ended only in 1998. Thus, women in the 1980s and 1990s engaged in many forms of "male" labor, including government service. Some women without marriage prospects became "second" wives (although polygamy is illegal) or created households with other women by adopting children.

See Also

DOWRY AND BRIDEPRICE; FAMILY: RELIGIOUS AND LEGAL SYSTEMS—BUDDHIST TRADITIONS; FAMILY: RELIGIOUS AND LEGAL SYSTEMS—ISLAMIC TRADITIONS; HOUSEHOLDS: RESOURCES; VIRGINITY

References and Further Reading

Atkinson, Jane Monnig, and Shelly Errington. 1990. *Power and difference: Gender in island southeast Asia.* Stanford, Calif.: Stanford University Press.

Ebihara, May M. 1968. *Svay: A Khmer village in Cambodia.* Ph.D. diss., Columbia University.

Ebihara, May M., Carol A. Mortland, and Judy Ledgerwood. 1994. *Cambodian culture since 1975: Homeland and exile.* Ithaca, N.Y.: Cornell University Press.

Geertz, Hildred. 1961. *The Javanese family.* Glencoe, Ill.: Free Press of Glencoe.

Khaing, Mi Mi. 1984. *The world of Burmese women.* London: Zed.

Kirsch, A. Thomas. 1984. Text and context: Buddhist sex roles/culture of gender revisited. *American Ethnologist* 12 (2): 302–320.

Luong, Hy Van. 1992. *Revolution in the village: Tradition and transformation in North Vietnam, 1925–1988.* Honolulu: University of Hawaii Press.

Mills, Mary Beth. 1999. *Thai women in the global labor force.* New Brunswick, N.J.: Rutgers University Press.

Ong, Aihwa. 1989. Center and periphery, and hierarchy: Gender in southeast Asia. In Sandra Morgen, ed., *Gender and anthropology.* Washington, D.C.: American Anthropological Association.

———. 1987. *Spirits of resistance and capitalist discipline: Factory women in Malaysia.* Albany: State University of New York Press.

Peletz, Michael G. 1996. *Reason and passion: Representations of gender in Malay society.* Berkeley, Calif.: University of California Press.

Potter, Sulamith Heins. 1977. *Family life in a northern Thai village.* Berkeley: University of California Press.

Sanday, Peggy Reeves, and Ruth Gallagher Goodenough. 1990. *Beyond the second sex: New directions in the anthropology of gender.* Philadelphia: University of Pennsylvania Press.

Tanner, Nancy. 1974. Matrifocality in Indonesia and Africa and among black Americans. In Michelle Rosaldo and Louise Lamphere, eds., *Women, culture, and society*, 129–156. Stanford, Calif.: Stanford University Press.

Thorbek, Susanne. 1987. *Voices from the city: Women of Bangkok*. London: Zed.

Van Esterik, Penny, ed. 1982. *Women of southeast Asia*. Occasional Paper no. 9. De Kalb: Northern Illinois University, Center for Southeast Asian Studies.

Judy Ledgerwood

HOUSEHOLDS AND FAMILIES:
Southern Africa

The nations of Botswana, Lesotho, Mozambique, South Africa, Namibia, Swaziland, Zimbabwe, and Comoros (Madagascan and Mauritian islands off the east coast of South Africa) make up the southern African region. People in the region exhibit a historical and cultural richness as diverse as the varied landscapes that characterize the southern African escarpment. Khoisan people are the earliest known inhabitants of southern Africa; however, the vast majority of southern Africans are black African descendants of Bantu-speaking peoples who arrived in present-day eastern Nigeria around A.D. 200 (Giles et al., 1997). Today more than 17 major ethnic groups exist, each with its own language and social culture.

Although most of the households in southern Africa are in rural areas, urbanization is increasing. This situation is largely attributable to racially oppressive apartheid policies meted out by a white minority South African government. Apartheid policies represented an extreme form of racism that subordinated the lives of all others to those of white South Africans. Not only did apartheid cause the systematic division of families with the recruitment of young men for contract wage work on south African mines, it also increased the hardships for women who were left behind to farm in rural areas and neighboring countries. In a rural household, which represents the smallest unit of an extended family structure, women are the least powerful adult participants. The typical hierarchical and patrilineal social order, where a family's lineage is traced through its sons, is undergirded by value systems that help perpetuate unequal gender contrasts. The Ovambo people from southern Angola are the exception with family lineages traced through daughters. The collapse of apartheid laws in 1991 meant that South African women were granted full enfranchisement and legal equality; however, a continuum of societal norms, taboos, traditions, and customs continues to deny southern Africa rural women, in particular, a status equal to that of men.

Effect of Colonialism and Apartheid on Household and Family Structure

Nineteenth-century colonialism affected all of southern Africa in similar ways. The discovery of gold and the arrival of European traders led to British predominance in and occupation of the region. By 1910, all of southern Africa was under British or Boer (white Afrikaner) rule. Christian missionaries arrived to propagate Christianity, and—despite resistance by the Ndebele in southern Rhodesia, the Ovambo peoples of Namibia, the Zulu and Xhosa in South Africa, and others—the region was colonized. The ensuing colonial displacement of indigenous families onto unfertile land began an agricultural underdevelopment trend that continues in most of southern Africa. The imposition of colonial employment practices, the eradication of legal rights, and discriminatory social welfare programs prohibited women from ensuring the adequate survival of their families, while men migrated to the goldfields and mining towns (Makoa, 1997). When migrant labor was institutionalized under apartheid's influx control laws in the 1970s, it was associated with rural poverty, a breakdown in traditional family life, and a high incidence of women-headed households, as high as 70 percent in Lesotho (Ferguson, 1994). The workings of the migrant labor system posed similar structural problems for most southern Africa countries, such as a decline in agrarian production, the progressive destruction of family cohesion, and loss of social support from close kin and communities.

Female-headed rural households were highly dependent on wage remittances from men working in the cities, and women were denied legal access to resources in patriarchal systems of local authority. When disposable income was not consistently forthcoming, the burden of care for women, who were responsible for food production and the care of the young and old, was immensely heightened. The political regulation of labor in Mozambique and elsewhere restricted the migration of women to South Africa, whereas women from the former Bantustans (that is, independent reserves set up for black South Africans within the country's boundaries), Lesotho, Botswana, and Swaziland could find work as domestic workers or in the informal sector of sprawling shantytowns of South Africa. The widespread oppression and its ensuing poverty in rural households led them to function as collective economic units. All members of the household, including children, were utilized to maximize food production. Children herded cattle and collected firewood, while the elderly cared for younger children. In order to overcome some of the hardships of rural (and urban) life, families looked to social and cultural practices for support and kinship and to neighborhood networks to assist with the numerous tasks of daily living.

Marriage, Religious Beliefs and the Role of Cultural Practices in Southern African Families

Traditionally, marriage constitutes the entry point into a family for most ethnic groups in southern Africa. Although marriage customs vary from one group to another, certain practices, such as polygyny, are generally accepted for men but not women. Certain southern Africans of Indian descent may favor arranged marriages within extended family groups; however, this practice is not the norm. In urban areas in southern African societies, marriages occur with the consent of the bride and groom. In contrast, during the period of apartheid in South Africa, the Immorality and Mixed Marriages Act prevented members of different racial groups from having sexual relations or intermarrying.

Prerequisites to marriage in almost all nonwhite southern African ethnic groups are bride wealth (lobola) and gifts. The payment of bride wealth in cattle or money by the family of the husband to the family of the wife continues to be a key part of the marriage process in rural areas. It is deemed necessary for the affiliation of children to the husband's lineage and is representative of the household's place in the community. In other words, the act of giving bride wealth can be viewed as a link between marriage and wider political processes within patrilineal systems (O'Laughlin, 1998). Bride wealth, along with cattle wealth, offspring, and polygyny, is illustrative of the social status of men. Consequently, a newly married bride experiences considerable pressure to bear children soon after marriage; in fact, in Swaziland, men are encouraged to replace infertile wives who have not borne children with more fertile partners. The status of a new wife in a patrilocal rural household (one where a woman joins her new husband's household) is inferior to that of all other adults until the point of childbearing. A new daughter-in-law is expected to assume numerous domestic responsibilities, while subordinating herself to the authority of her mother-in-law and senior wives. A young bride's position in the hierarchy of a homestead is determined by how well she is able to interact with her new mother-in-law and other wives in the village. The importance of extended family networks and in particular membership in a clan (a group that tracks its origin to a revered ancestor) is illustrated by the practice of ancestral reverence.

Ancestor and spirit reverence is a well-established custom practiced by all black southern African groups. Common beliefs that the souls of the dead have the power to influence the lives of the living are held in conjunction with Christian, Muslim, and other religious beliefs. Offerings are regularly made to the spiritual or ancestral guardians as part of ritual worship or when they are asked to intercede on behalf of the living. The Sotho people from South Africa make offerings to *badimo* (spirits) to show gratitude, while the Shona people of Zimbabwe believe that the living also possess mediums enabling them to intercede on behalf of others. The Xhosa people of South Africa lost some of their ancestral beliefs following the "cattle killings" of 1856 and 1857 (Giles et al., 1997). A young girl called Nogwqawuse prophesied that white settlers would be swept into the sea and that the Xhosa would rise again if all existing cattle and food supplies were destroyed. The unfulfilled prophecy resulted in widespread poverty and death, contributing to the defeat of the Xhosa people in 1878. Although women and men have been known to invoke their ancestors to request intercession, men are more likely to request assistance in reinforcing their superior social status within both the household and the clan.

A related and widespread practice among the peoples of southern Africa is the use of traditional healers to cure diseases and maladies. *Sangomas* (diviners) are more likely to be women, as with the Xhosa people of South Africa, whereas *nyangas* (medicine people) are more likely to be men, as with the Ndebele. Women practitioners of healing abound but do not enjoy the same status as male practitioners, who monopolize the representation of healers in national and international forums. In rural areas, experienced older women practice midwifery, a tradition supported by clan members. The entire village celebrates the birth of children, who are traditionally regarded as symbols of joy and economic assets in the village. Multiple offspring may give men superior social standing and may give women, who often have to depend on their children in the absence of their partners, emotional support and household assistance.

The Evolving Position of Women, Households, and Family Structure

In southern Africa, hardships caused by sociopolitical and economic changes, growing family insecurity, and house-

HOUSEHOLDS AND FAMILIES: SOUTHERN AFRICA

hold tensions have affected social relationships within families. Many of the socioeconomic problems of women are traceable to unbalanced gender relations, supported by repressive laws. Apartheid, for example, was instrumental in robbing women of fundamental human, legal, and land rights. Southern African black men and women were reduced to third-class status through the creations of Bantustans and systems of authority invested in puppet structures such as homeland governments and traditional chief hierarchies. These laws contributed to the triple oppression suffered by black southern African women, by virtue of their gender, race, and class (poor rural women suffered greater hardships than wealthy urban women). Not only were the lives of South Africans disrupted by a legacy of inequality and oppression through apartheid, but neighboring countries were destabilized so as to coerce governments into repressing democratic forces that resisted the upkeep of apartheid. Some think that the demise of apartheid in 1991 constituted the single most significant event for the region. Southern African men and women of conscience played a critical role in catalyzing the events that led to liberations. Women's domestic struggles intersected with their struggle for national emancipation. A postapartheid democratic South African constitution guaranteed fundamental human rights and equality for all and provided a baseline from which the corridors of power for South African women may be opened to abolish oppressive institutions. Unfortunately, political liberation has brought little or no significant improvement to the social status of most women in other southern African countries. In Lesotho and Zimbabwe, for example, married women are still considered legal minors (Makoa, 1997) in all decisions regarding property inheritances.

A high priority for the postapartheid government of South Africa has been to combat poverty among its indigenous black African population by increasing employment opportunities for its citizens. As a result, neighboring southern African states, which are highly reliant on migrant work opportunities in South Africa, have suffered. The ongoing marginalization of small-scale subsistence production and increasing urbanization of men and women have caused a deepening rupture between marriage and the traditional approaches to the bearing and raising of children. As extended family networks disintegrate and women continue to experience gender-specific constraints, such as lack of child care support, women still remain saddled with numerous tasks of daily living. Within households the status of poor women remains unchanged, exacerbated by rising costs of living and the failure of international development initiatives to take note of women's reproductive and produc-

tive roles. Additional scourges in the form of AIDS affect women, who are the predominant caregivers of those afflicted with the disease.

In spite of new opportunities, households in southern Africa seem no longer able to hold onto the traditional solidarity that comes from an extended family structure but must negotiate a different set of hardships associated with urbanization.

See Also

APARTHEID, SEGREGATION, AND GHETTOIZATION; FAMILY: RELIGIOUS AND LEGAL SYSTEMS—SOUTHERN AFRICA; HOUSEHOLDS AND FAMILIES: SUB-SAHARAN AFRICA; MARRIAGE: INTERRACIAL AND INTERRELIGIOUS; POLITICS AND THE STATE: SOUTHERN AFRICA

References and Further Reading

Ferguson, James. 1994. *The anti-politics machine: Development, depoliticization and bureaucratic power in Lesotho.* Minneapolis: University of Minnesota Press.
Giles, B., et al., 1997. *Peoples of southern Africa.* Diagram Group.
Grove, M. J. 1991 The urban population of southern Africa: A regional profile 1980–1990. *Urban Forum* 2(1): 113–153.
Leliveld, A. 1997. *World Development* 25(11): 1839–1849.
Makoa, F. 1997. Gender and politics: A note on gender inequality in Lesotho. *Journal of Social Development in Africa* 12(1): 5–14.
Manana, T. 1992. In Meena R., ed., *Gender in southern Africa: Conceptual and theoretical issues,* 126–156. Harare, Zimbabwe: Sapes.
O'Laughlin, B. 1998. Missing men: The debate over rural poverty and women-headed households in southern Africa. *Journal of Peasant Studies* 25(2): 1–48.
Ross, F. 1995. *Umntu ngummtu ngabanye abantu: The support networks of black families in southern Africa.* Pretoria: HSRC.
Schlyter, A., and A. Zhou. 1995. *Gender research on urbanization, planning, housing and everyday life.* Harare, Zimbabwe: Sithole-Fundire.
Timaeus, I., and W. Graham. 1989. Labor circulation, marriage and fertility in southern Africa. In J. Lesthaghe, ed., *Reproduction and social organization in sub-Saharan Africa,* 365–400. Berkeley: University of California Press.
Walker, C. 1990. *Women and gender in southern Africa to 1945.* London: James Currey.
Wolfe, D. 1990. Daughters, decisions and dominations: An empirical and conceptual critique of household strategies. *Development and Change* 21(1): 43–74.

Shehnaaz Suliman

HOUSEHOLDS AND FAMILIES:
Sub-Saharan Africa

Households and families are two separate but linked concepts that should not be confused. A household has a specific spatial connotation: it is coresidential and physically discrete. The residents of a household are usually but not necessarily related, and these relations may be biological (blood relations), conjugal (through marriage), or fictive (socially created, such as "town brothers or sisters" or foster children). A family is a group of persons related by blood, marriage, or both who may or may not live together in a household. There is no specific African household or African family but, rather, a wide range of different household and family structures and compositions, changing in relation to social, cultural, political, and economic considerations. Household membership ranges from 1 person to 20 or more. Farming households in areas with sufficient available land and households of wealthier persons or traditional leaders are often larger than others in the area. Members of three or more generations may live together in a household.

Feminist researchers have done important work in the analysis and deconstruction of the household, particularly in relation to access to, control over, and ownership of household resources and in relation to the rights, obligations, and responsibilities of household members. A household's size, composition, and activities will vary, depending, for example, on the availability of and access to land and labor, the class and wealth of the household members, the state of the household unit or units in the developmental cycle, whether the household is rural or urban, and the availability and type of housing.

Land and Labor

Women are the mainstay of African economies, inasmuch as they are the primary food producers in most African countries and are generally responsible for subsistence production for themselves and their children in both rural and urban areas. It is within and from the base of the household that women carry out much of their labor. In agricultural households women's labor includes farming, processing of agricultural produce for home and market, seasonal nonfarm occupations, childbearing and child care, and domestic labor and maintenance. Bryceson (1993) uses the term *homestead* rather than *household* to reflect and to integrate the extensive spatial and social context within which women

work, including agricultural as well as residential land, labor, and obligations.

Access to land and labor are differentially available within a household according to, for example, gender, age, and relationship to household head. Where land is traditionally owned by clan or lineage, ownership is deemed to pertain to and be allocated primarily by and to men (brothers and sons in patrilineal societies, mother's brothers and sister's sons in matrilineal societies). Women living with their husband in their husband's home are usually allocated access to land but not land ownership. Such land may be reclaimed on the husband's death, particularly if there are no children from the marriage, and land so allocated is certainly reclaimed by the kin group on divorce. When women return to their own kin, they may then seek land as sisters and daughters. Husbands and male household heads generally expect wives' labor on household farms and may be able to claim wives' labor on husbands' own plots, as Whitehead (1981) shows for the Kusasi in Ghana. There is generally no equivalent claim possible from women for husbands' labor on wives' own plots. Differential access to labor and land is of growing concern, given the increasing involvement of men in cash-crop rather than subsistence production. Cash tends to be treated as a personal rather than a household resource, and so the agricultural labor of men becomes more personalized and the proceeds alienable by the man himself. As land becomes more privatized, it is also less accessible to women, who often lack the cash resources and credit to buy it and are less likely than men to inherit. The ideology of complementarity and joint maintenance of the household obscures what is often great inequality between men and women and particularly between husband and wife in a household, as Geisler (1993) notes for Zambia, for example.

Income and Expenses

The household is a site of sought-after but finite resources that are owned and allocated according to culturally specific rules, subject to negotiation and sometimes conflict. Husbands and wives in west Africa, in particular, even when living in the same household, tend to have distinct income from nonfarm occupations and from "own-account," as opposed to household, farms (Roberts, 1991). Some ethnic groups, such as the Yoruba, Nupe, and Akan in Nigeria and Ghana, are known for the trading skills of the women. However, even secluded Muslim women remaining within the confines of the household have income-earning occupations. The products are often sold by their children, and the proceeds belong to the women themselves (Pittin, 1984).

The household head in many ethnic groups in Africa is often assumed to be male and is generally expected or said to provide financially for the household that he heads. In practice, in a large and increasing number of households, up to possibly a third of all households, a woman is the sole breadwinner (Snyder and Tadesse, 1995). Where there are both men and women in the household, there are also divided responsibilities toward children and other kin. Besides providing for or assisting in the provision of food, clothing, and household goods, women also often contribute to or may wholly provide for major expenses such as school fees (Robertson, 1990). The need to share household expenses is more obvious with the effects of structural adjustment, including the loss of formal-sector jobs and freezing of wages, reduction and privatization of social services, and spiraling inflation.

In cities, both women and men work in the informal sector, and some work in both formal and informal sectors, where they take on a series of occupations to support household members. With the growth of urban farming, agriculture has become yet another subsistence occupation carried out by women and men to eke out household resources even in urban areas. A study of households in Kampala, Uganda, for example, demonstrates that income diversification, including wages and allowances, farming, business income, and remittances, is a necessary and widespread response to the uncertain economic environment (Bigsten and Kayizzi-Mugerwa, 1991). In any analysis of household income and labor, the unremunerated expenditure by women of time and labor in domestic work, services, child care, and other areas of subsistence production must be taken into account in terms of their opportunities to earn income and undertake other activities.

Households are important as social entities also because they are used as primary social units in censuses and surveys. They are often treated as coherent single units of production and consumption. However, as shown earlier, a household may include several producers, each with his or her own earnings, which are used for household or other expenses, depending on the authority and control of individual household members, the requirements and bargaining power of those members (these differ also in relation to gender, age, and positioning in the kin group), and societal expectations. The members of the household may "share the same pot," or for example, cowives may cook for themselves and their children (the mother-children cooking and social unit is sometimes called a hearth-hold), with some of the ingredients provided by the wife and others (often the staple grain) expected to be provided by the husband or the senior male in the household, although such provi-

sion is not always forthcoming. Both men and women in the household also may send food daily as a matter of course to relatives living elsewhere. With respect to both production and consumption, therefore, the household may be both narrower and broader than the physical structure of the unit suggests.

Families and Kin

Family is a less specific concept than household because it lacks even the spatial criterion of the household. Michele Barrett suggests that "'the family' does not exist other than as ideological construct, since the structure of the household, definition and meaning of kinship, and the ideology of 'family' itself...var[y] enormously in different types of society" (1980: 199). It is certainly thus in sub-Saharan Africa. The meaning of *family* must be contextualized within both the broader kinship structures and the specific occasion or event in which "family" ties are evoked. The meaning is generally broader and more complex than spouse (or spouses) and biological children living together.

Kinship structures in Africa traditionally may be based on lineages (matrilineal, patrilineal, double unilineal) and clans or may be cognatic (nonlineal). Kin structures have been the basis of land and other resource allocation and of political authority. With increasing commoditization and the creation and imposition of alternative political organization, the functions of the broader kinship groupings have been greatly reduced. The mother-children unit is important, particularly in polygynous situations, although with patriarchal control and ease of divorce, resulting children often remaining with their father or father's kin.

Fostering is common, and a child may well be raised by kin other than her or his father and mother as a matter of parental choice, even if the father and mother remain together. Children may be raised, for example, by a grandparent or a favorite sister or brother of one of their parents. A child may be sent to kin in the city to enhance educational opportunities or, as in southern Africa, to kin in the rural areas so the child is not spoiled by city life and behavior. Seasonal and long-term labor migration by adults is also common, so that a father or mother, for example, may be away for long periods of time. Cash remittances from family members working in urban areas or outside the country or agricultural inputs from kin in rural areas to sisters, brothers, children, or other kin in the city are a significant component of income for many households. Migration, limited urban housing facilities, and increased polarization of wealth and education have tended to reduce extended kin accessibility and involvement. There appears to be increasing focus on immediate maternal and paternal kin.

Education for girls has been limited in the past, in part on the basis of the idea that this training is then lost to the girl's kin or her marriage and is gained by the husband and his kin. However, it becomes more evident that women prioritize their assistance to close kin, such as parents and brothers and sisters and their children, when they have resources beyond those immediately required by themselves and their own children. Because men may spend money seeking other women (as wives or girlfriends) if resources become available, parents are beginning to recognize daughters' efforts and interest in supporting or assisting their kin, in spite of women's generally more limited access to high-paying jobs or income-earning opportunities. High levels of separation and divorce also ensure that women maintain close ties with their own kin, to whose home they may at some point return.

See Also

AGRICULTURE; DEVELOPMENT: SUB-SAHARAN AND SOUTHERN AFRICA; FAMILY: RELIGIOUS AND LEGAL SYSTEMS—EAST AFRICA *and* WEST AFRICA; HOUSEHOLDS AND FAMILIES: SOUTHERN AFRICA; POLYGYNY AND POLYANDRY

References and Further Reading

Barrett, Michele. 1980. *Women's oppression today: Problems in Marxist feminist analysis.* London: Verso.

Bigsten, Arne, and Steve Kayizzi-Mugerwa. 1991. Adaption and distress in the urban economy: A study of Kampala households. *World Development* 20(10): 1323–1341.

Bryceson, Deboray Fahy. 1993. Easing rural women's working day in sub-Saharan Africa. Working Paper no. 16. Leiden: African Studies Centre.

Geisler, Gisela. 1993. Silences speak louder than claims: Gender, household, and agricultural development in southern Africa. *World Development* 21(2): 1965–1980.

Kuiper, Marja. 1991. Women entrepreneurs in Africa. Training Discussion Paper no 68. Geneva: International Labor Office, Training Policies Branch.

Pittin, Renée. 1984. Documentation and analysis of the invisible work of invisible women: A Nigerian case-study. *International Labour Review* 123 (4, July–Aug.): 473–490.

Roberts, Penelope. 1991. Rural women's access to labour in west Africa. In Sharon B. Stichter and Jane L. Parpart, eds., *Patriarchy and class: African women in the home and the workforce,* 97–114. Boulder, Col.: Westview.

Robertson, Claire C. 1990. *Sharing the same bowl: A socioeconomic history of women and class in Accra, Ghana.* Ann Arbor: University of Michigan Press.

Snyder, Margaret C., and Mary Tadesse. 1995. *African women and development: A history.* Johannesburg: Witwatersrand University Press and Zed.

Whitehead, Ann. 1981. "I'm hungry, Mum": The politics of domestic budgeting. In Kate Young et al., eds., *Of marriage and market,* 88–111. London: SCE.

Renée Ilene Pittin

HOUSEHOLDS AND FAMILIES:
Western Europe

The most striking feature of households and families in western Europe is their diversity. Household and family forms vary by region, culture, and class, and this heterogeneity reflects the diversity of western Europe itself, which includes countries of the European Union, as well as Switzerland. Some countries, such as Germany, Britain, and France, are highly industrialized, though the agricultural sector of their economies continues to make a significant contribution to the gross national product. Other nations—Portugal, Spain, Greece, Denmark, and Sweden—are predominantly agrarian, and a good part of the population operates small-scale family farming, fishing, and rural manufacturing enterprises. Western Europe is also divided by countries that have a strong Catholic tradition, for example, Belgium and Italy, and those that are rooted in Protestantism, for example, Scotland and the Netherlands. To some extent this coincides with a division between northern and southern Europe and between those regions in which customary law prevailed and those in which Roman laws prevailed (Goody, 2000).

In contemporary western Europe, over half of consensual unions formed result in nuclear family arrangements and they exist in both the countryside and the city, in northern as well as southern Europe. Nuclear families consisting of a married man and a woman and their offspring represent the highest proportion of any particular family arrangement in Catholic Europe, in such countries as Ireland, Spain, Italy, and Portugal. In those countries, roughly half of all family configurations are nuclear. While the nuclear family is the most common of all domestic structures, it must be noted that this form of organization exists as one of many different family structures in modern western Europe. Indeed, western European households are formed by multigenerational cohabiting kin, individuals, cohabiting heterosexual couples (as well as same-sex couples), single parents, reconstituted as well as blended families, and stepfamilies containing children of previous unions.

In western Europe in the last decades of the twentieth century there was a decrease in the proportion of domestic arrangements representing the classic nuclear family pattern. In Britain, for example, in 1961, 48 percent of all households conformed to the conventional nuclear pattern; in 1981, 40 percent of all households had conformed to the pattern. Many other countries in western Europe have followed this trend as well (Rapoport, 1989). There has been a shift away from the conventional nuclear family and an increase in the number of nontraditional family forms. This growing diversity is associated with demographic change and, especially, with changes in the social position of women as they have entered the paid labor force in increasing numbers.

Demographic Change

Demographically, western Europe has experienced an overall trend of declining fertility from the end of the eighteenth century (with the exception of the period from 1945 to 1960). There has also been a reduction in infant mortality and an increase in life expectancy. For women, not only have the numbers of births (particularly third and subsequent births) been reduced, but there has been a postponement of first and subsequent births, as well as a rise in childlessness. Although the rates of fertility vary from region to region, the countries of the European Union have the lowest rates of fertility in the world, with an overall average of 1.45 children per woman in 1991. This has also been accompanied by low mortality rates. Observers of these trends have suggested that this decline can be traced to such factors as the availability of contraceptive technology, higher levels of education, and rising living standards. Contraceptive practices have enabled women to plan their families and decide whether and when they will have children. Moreover, the substantial increase in life expectancy has had many positive effects as it has lightened the burden of maternity on women and enabled them to participate more freely in the labor market. Women have entered into paid employment in increasing numbers and the increased participation of women in the paid labor market has in turn also influenced demographic patterns and family structures.

The Participation of Women in Paid Labor

Women are engaged in forms of paid work on an unprecedented scale in western European history. In countries such as Germany, Great Britain, and Italy, for example, more than 40 to 50 percent of the contemporary labor force consists of women. The greater economic independence of women who engage in paid work as well as the practical challenges of combining domestic work with work outside the home has had a significant impact on both the form and organization of domestic arrangements as well as the basis upon which families are formed. Not only is childbearing delayed and sometimes avoided, but marriage itself is postponed and often rejected. The mean age at first marriage of women has been creeping upward in the European Union. In 1960 it was 23.2. In 1970 it was 24.2. In 1993 it was 26.1. Accompanying this rise has been a change in the choices available to individuals and couples in the organization of domestic life. There seems to be less adherence to permanent monogamous family units as the basis for family life in western Europe. The trend, therefore, has been toward lower marriage rates, higher levels of cohabitation, and increased divorce and remarriage rates, as well as births outside marriage. These changes have resulted in the pluralization of family forms and changing functions of domestic groups and roles of their members.

Cohabitation

The postponement of marriage—and in some cases the replacement of it—is related to the increased popularity of cohabitation, or consensual union. As more and more women have become economically independent, marriage has decreased in importance as the main criterion in the formation of families or for defining family relationships or duties. A couple starting a family is as likely to be cohabiting as to be married. This pattern tends to be more frequent in northern countries as well—the Netherlands, France, and the United Kingdom. It is less common in countries with a tradition of Catholicism, such as Belgium and Ireland or southern European countries such as Italy and Spain. In many countries, consensual unions have been formally accepted, although the degree of acceptance in law varies from country to country. The rights of unmarried cohabiting couples were first recognized formally in the 1970s in Denmark and Sweden; France soon followed. There, unmarried couples could officially register their partnership, implying that they could be considered living together for such purposes as opening joint bank accounts. Legal systems are also coming to recognize these unions as de facto marriages that are accompanied by certain rights in property, in inheritance, and over children. The institutional recognition of consensual unions has been formally opposed in Italy by the Catholic church, as it continues to hold up its conception of the family as a heterosexual union founded on marriage. Still, unmarried couples in Italy can register their union and enjoy certain limited rights. In other countries, such as Germany, Greece, and Ireland, consensual unions have not been formally accepted. Throughout western Europe, marriage is defined as a heterosexual union in which a man and a woman are joined in a conjugal relationship.

Same-sex marriage has been prohibited by law. Same-sex couples must therefore form a family through cohabitation. While most western European countries have made some provisions for heterosexual consensual unions, law reform to recognize homosexual cohabitation has encountered much greater resistance. However, some countries, such as Denmark and Sweden, acknowledge a form of de facto marriage between same-sex partners through domestic partnership contracts. In many countries, measures are being taken by activists to promote the legal recognition of the rights of homosexual couples to health benefits and property, as well as in inheritance (in many contexts, the privileging of males prevails in inheritance; Lem, 1999).

Divorce

Since the 1960s, the divorce rates of western European countries have risen. It has been estimated, for example, that in the United Kingdom, 40 percent of marriages will end in divorce. This trend is reflected in a number of other European countries, particularly in northern Europe. The increase in divorce has been linked to the liberalization of divorce legislation. There has been a move away from a system based on matrimonial offence, guilt, and punishment, to one based on irreparable breakdown, mutual responsibility, and need. The rise in rates of divorce has also been linked to the increased material independence of women who have entered the paid workforce. Marriage for women is no longer an economic necessity. Certain other factors are also cited as linked to the dissolution of marriage. For example, the individualization and the privatization of marriage is a growing tendency, where the idea of conjugality has shifted from a public union joining families to one in which individuals seek personal happiness and fulfillment. This idea represents a break from the traditional adherence to conformity, obligation, and duty.

Lone Parenting

The higher rates of divorce have also contributed toward increasing the diversity of family arrangements. They have contributed to the rise in the number of lone-parent families, consisting of one parent, usually a woman, and children. Observers have noted that, far from being unusual, the one-parent family has become a widespread and permanent way of life for many women, stemming from the breakdown of the "conjugal" family or an alternative consensual union. Lone-parent families result not only from divorce, separation, and births outside marriage but also from widowhood and emigration. During the postwar period and particularly in southern European countries, lone parenthood resulted from the permanent, temporary, and intermittent separation of family members through national and international emigration.

Reconstituted Families

The rise in divorce rates in western Europe has also been accompanied by a rise in the number of remarriages and instances of cohabitation and the emergence of what has variously been called the reconstituted family, multiparental family, stepfamily, blended family, and reordered family. These complex structures arise when households are composed of one biological parent and a stepparent living with children from more than one marriage or nonmarital relationship. The boundaries of this unit are more difficult to define, particularly when the children share their time between more than one family or more than one household. Through these processes, household and family structures are becoming increasingly diverse in all countries of western Europe. The demographic and related social changes that have characterized the countries of western Europe have fostered increasing gender symmetry in work patterns, more freedom in conjugal choice, higher degrees of marital instability, a greater degree of freedom in lifestyle choices (that is, whether to live alone or in unions of some sort), and changing patterns of parenting. One of the consequences of this increasing diversity is a trend toward smaller household sizes. In 1960, approximately 21.4 percent of the households in the current European Union had five or more family members. By 1991, this number had dropped to 9.3 percent. While much of the diversity of family arrangements that has emerged in western Europe can be seen as a form of liberation from the constraints of tradition and convention, it must be noted that such forms can be subjected to other difficulties. For example, the levels of poverty, particularly for lone parents and individuals who live outside consensual unions, may be exacerbated, particularly where the state, as in the United Kingdom, still bases its family and welfare policies on the normative expectation that an individual—usually male—breadwinner will be the provider in the family. In other words, new family forms have generated new political, social, and economic challenges both to those living within them and to states that formulate and execute policies to regulate domestic life within western Europe.

See Also

FAMILY: RELIGIOUS AND LEGAL SYSTEMS—PROTESTANT; FAMILY: RELIGIOUS AND LEGAL SYSTEMS—CATHOLIC AND ORTHODOX; HOUSEHOLDS AND FAMILIES: OVERVIEW; HOUSEHOLDS AND FAMILIES: EASTERN EUROPE

References and Further Reading

Boh, Katja. 1989. European family life patterns—A reappraisal. In Katja Boh et al., eds. *Changing patterns of European family life: A comparative analysis of 14 European countries*, 265–298. London: Routledge.

Commaille, Jacques, and Françis de Singly, eds. 1997. *The European family: The family question in the European community.* Dordrecht, Netherlands: Kluwer Academic.

Drew, Eileen, Ruth Emerek, and Evelyn Mahon, ed. 1998. *Women, work and the family in Europe.* London: Routledge.

Goody, Jack. 1983. *The development of the family and marriage in Europe.* Cambridge: Cambridge University Press.

———. 2000. *The European family.* Oxford: Blackwell.

Gullestad, Marianne, and Martine Segalen, eds. 1995. *La famille en Europe: Parenté et perpétuation familiale.* Paris: Editions la Decou.

Hantrais, Linda, and Marie-Thérèse Letablier. 1996. *Families and family policies in europe.* London: Longman.

Laslett, Peter. 1972. *Household and family in past time.* Cambridge: Cambridge University Press.

Lem, Winnie. 1999. *Cultivating dissent: Work, identity and praxis in rural Languedoc.* Albany: State University of New York Press.

Rapoport, Rhona. 1989. Ideologies about family forms: Toward diversity. In Katja Boj et al., eds., *Changing patterns of European family life: A comparative analysis of fourteen European countries*, 53–69. London: Routledge.

Winnie Lem

HOUSEHOLDS: Domestic Consumption

Social scientists and government statisticians have traditionally treated family-based households as "units of consumption" on the assumption that families pool resources on an equitable basis. Feminist research challenging this assumption has revealed that members of a single family do not necessarily share the same standard of living. Because this inequality is closely associated with male power and privilege, it is most marked in heterosexual households headed by men. The conditions governing the distribution of resources within households vary from one society to another as a result of local economic conditions and cultural practices, but in most of the world women contribute more labor to their households than men and receive fewer rewards (Mitter, 1986; United Nations, 1995).

Most of the research on everyday domestic consumption has been done within the wealthy postindustrial nations, where men's financial power has historically derived from the ideal of the male breadwinner supporting his family. Although this ideal may no longer seem tenable, the patterns of domestic consumption associated with it persist. In Britain, for example, numerous studies have analyzed the practices and ideologies through which the importance of women's earnings are played down, confirming men as the "real" breadwinners (even when they are unemployed). Yet when women are earning, they generally contribute a higher proportion of their wages to collective expenditure than do men and keep relatively little money for themselves (Pahl, 1989). Men, whether they are employed or not, almost always have personal spending money. The inequities that result are such that, among poorer households, women and children are sometimes better off within lone-parent families than in male-headed households (Brannen and Wilson, 1987; Jackson and Moores, 1995). Recent research suggests that a more equitable distribution of resources is achieved within lesbian and gay households (Dunne, 1999; Heaphy et al., 1999).

Women's relationship to domestic consumption is mediated through an ethic of altruism and self-sacrifice, associated with their work of caring for others. Hence, patterns of domestic consumption are related to the domestic division of labor. Food consumption, which depends on women planning, shopping, and cooking for their families, is a good example (Charles and Kerr, 1988; DeVault, 1991). Within the constraints of family income, a woman typically cooks to please her husband (if she has one) first and then to please her children. Her own preferences come last, and if food is short, it is she who will go without. Sometimes men directly influence the meals cooked by demanding that their tastes be catered to. More frequently, however, men get what they want simply because wives routinely defer to their likes and dislikes. Women do not necessarily experience their lack of choice as a constraint: providing food that others enjoy can be experienced as creative and satisfying, especially when the food is appreciated. Yet it is clear that even when family members are engaged in collective consumption, eating the same meal, they are not all consuming in the same manner. She who cooks and serves does not experience the same meal as those who are cooked for and served (Delphy and Leonard, 1992).

See Also

DOMESTIC LABOR; ECONOMY: HISTORY OF WOMEN'S PARTICIPATION; FOOD AND CULTURE; HOUSEHOLDS: POLITICAL ECONOMY; HOUSEHOLDS: RESOURCES; NUTRITION AND HOME ECONOMICS

References and Further Reading

Brannen, Julia, and Gail Wilson, eds. 1987. *Give and take in families*. London: Allen and Unwin.

Charles, Nickie, and Marion Kerr. 1988. *Women, food and families*. Manchester, U.K.: Manchester University Press.

Delphy, Christine, and Diana Leonard. 1992. *Familiar exploitation*. Cambridge: Polity.

DeVault, Marjorie L. 1991. *Feeding the family: The social organization of caring as gendered work*. Chicago: University of Chicago Press.

Dunne, Gillian. 1999. What difference does "difference" make? Lesbian experiences of work and family life. In Julie Seymour and Paul Bagguley, eds., *Relating intimacies: Power and resistance*. Basingstoke, U.K.: Macmillan.

Heaphy, Brian, Catherine Donovan, and Jeffrey Weeks. 1999. Sex, money and the kitchen sink: Power in same-sex couple relationships. In Julie Seymour and Paul Bagguley, eds., *Relating intimacies: Power and resistance*. Basingstoke, U.K.: Macmillan.

Jackson, Stevi, and Shaun Moores, eds. 1995. *The politics of domestic consumption*. Hemel Hempstead, U.K.: Prentice Hall/Harvester Wheatsheaf.

Mitter, Swasti. 1986. *Common fate, common bond: Women in the global economy*. London: Pluto.

Pahl, Jan. 1989. *Money and marriage*. Basingstoke, U.K.: Macmillan.

United Nations. 1995. *The world's women 1995: Trends and statistics*. New York: United Nations.

Stevi Jackson

HOUSEHOLDS:
Female-Headed and Female-Supported

Female-headed and female-supported households are found worldwide, frequently correlated with poverty, yet they differ significantly in different parts of the world. The importance of culture and the ways in which culture interacts with race, caste, class, and gender in defining the experience of women who have the responsibility of supporting their households cannot be underestimated. There are a wide variety of situations, across cultural, national, class, racial, and ethnic boundaries, in which women provide the main source of economic support for their households and often, though not always, function as the "head of the household." Female-headed and female-supported households can be understood only in terms of their link to wider economic, social, and political processes (see Mencher and Okongwu, 1993).

There is a great deal of baggage associated with the concept of headship that needs to be broken down because it includes a number of sometimes overlapping and sometimes discrete elements. The same individual may not necessarily fulfill all of the functions traditionally associated with headship in the West and in Asia, nor is the same pattern found in all households within a given population, even in the West or in parts of Asia, such as India, although general patterns may be observable. In the past traditional societies tended to be less diversified in patterns than colonial and contemporary societies. Nonetheless, where data exist, even the traditional societies exhibited some degree of variation.

Four major aspects of headship include (1) authority of power, (2) decision making, (3) sources of economic support, and in some instances (4) control over and possession of children (for example, in the case of divorce or death). These aspects present a multidimensional picture derived from explorations of "female-headed" households and of women in a wide variety of "male-headed" households.

A household primarily supported by women can, for example, have a formal male head who is (1) too old or too infirm to work, (2) unemployed, (3) living away from the household because of migration and not sending much money home because of low wages or unwillingness, (4) a polygamous husband who expects each wife to provide for herself, (5) a man who simply refuses to support the household, (6) a farmer who produces only cash crops that provide for occasional luxury items and for the man's status-producing activities but do not feed the family, (7) a man who is primarily involved in political or religious activities for which he receives little compensation, or (8) a man whose major obligations are to his sister's children rather than to his own (such as among the Ashanti in Ghana). Female-supported households also include families supported by an unmarried or widowed daughter.

The factors responsible for women assuming prime responsibility for the economic support of households include (1) death of a spouse, father, or other responsible male; (2) migration of the male for employment; (3) high male unemployment; (4) divorce, abandonment, or separation; (5) residence with another wife in another location—for example, a man living with one wife in an urban area and another in a rural area and refusing to give economic support to the rural wife apart from her access to the land; (6) culturally prescribed role behavior; (7) drug abuse; (8) other problems connected with urbanization or female choice and with the stages of women's lives at which these problems occur.

Globally, there has been a rise in female-headed households, and this increase has been accompanied by international concern. Why the increase? Why the concern? Gender, race, class, and ethnic dimensions of the contemporary global economy and the vulnerability of women and households are intimately related to shifts in economic, social, political, and military policies. These policies force changes in the amounts of money women need to feed households, the possible sources of income generation that exist, and availability of opportunities for housing and education. The size, shape, and activities of households and their members need to be seen against this larger backdrop. Researchers working in a broad range of societies have illustrated the importance of analyzing contemporary families both within national and international contexts.

These worldwide data suggest the following:

1. The particular ways in which a nation is incorporated into the world economic system shape the contours of the opportunity structure within a particular social context.
2. The level of development and internal structure of the state, including the range and types of subsidies to citizens, importantly condition the strategies employed by families to gain access to the essentials of life.
3. Within each social context, it is necessary to give careful attention to the historically and culturally specific ways in which structures of inequality manifest themselves at a given point in time and to the impact of these structures of inequality on differential incorporation into the opportunity structure, access to life-sustaining resources, and the current and future life chances of family members.

In considering the genesis of female-headed households, it is important to include what is happening to men along with women in the discussion. Some important differences that emerge cross-culturally include beliefs and practices concerning the generation, disposal, and control of income and resources in the following three different types of societies: (1) those in which women generate but do not control resources or income; (2) those in which women generate, dispose of, and control resources or income; and (3) those in which women control household expenditure but do not generate income.

Beliefs about sexuality and control over women's sexuality also shape the kinds of households that are formed in response to external conditions. For example, in Bangladesh, the combination of war and gender ideology created female-headed households where they did not exist before (M. Islam in Mencher and Okongwu, 1993). There are also significant differences in attitudes toward women bearing children out of wedlock in various parts of the world. In the Middle East and Asia this occurrence is extremely rare. In Brazil, by contrast, it is the main reason for the rapid increase in the number of female-headed households in recent years, with teenage pregnancies, married men having more than one family, and a higher average age for marriage all playing a role in household formation. In Asia and most of Africa there is a tendency for females to marry soon after puberty.

The effect of migration in promoting the existence of female-headed and female-supported households is also an important consideration. Yet processes like migration are affected by different types of employment structures for men and women, both within the nation and internationally. These employment structures determine who migrates and the amount of remittances to the household. In some cases the amount might be of major significance for daily life, but in other instances the remittances might provide only for the rare purchase of a luxury or the reproofing of a house, not for day-to-day maintenance.

A cross-cultural examination of female-headed and female-supported households highlights the need for researchers to do the following:

1. Explore the range of factors leading to the emergence of female-headed households.
2. Examine the impact of variations in religious, ideological, and cultural traditions in defining the content of male, female, and children's roles and family organization.
3. Examine the impact of socioeconomic factors and the particular ways in which structures of inequality manifest themselves at a given point in time.
4. Examine the critical role of class or differential access to income in a wide variety of societies and circumstances as they condition the life chances of children, women, and even some of the men in these households.

5. Examine the role of race or caste as it impinges on the lives of young women and men during their formative years.

6. Examine differences in the role of the state in providing supplemental support for some female-headed and female-supported households.

7. Examine how each nation is integrated into the world economic system, which in turn influences the resources held by the state and available to female-headed and male-headed households and the possible strategies available to each for survival.

Factors Leading to the Emergence of Female-Headed Households

1. *Early marriage of girls to men considerably older than they* (noted in Bangladesh, India, and Egypt). One of the obvious consequences of such marriages is that women with young children are more likely to be widowed. Although widows and divorced women in Islamic countries such as Egypt and Bangladesh may have more control than married women over their own lives and the lives of their children, they may be too poor to afford education for their children because of the lack of any male income unless education is not only free but also includes such state subsidies as noon feeding, uniforms, and books. The long-term implications for the future of these children should be noted by policy makers.

2. *War or political unrest* (among refugees, for example, in Africa). It may be easier for women who have lost husbands to function alone in some settings than in others. What most women suffering from the effects of war or political unrest share is the loss of male income and male sociopsychological and physical support. In addition, these women have often lost their own traditional modes of generating income and have become ever more dependent both on the state where they currently reside and on international agencies.

3. *Differential mortality rates among males in some sectors of the society resulting from the intersection of several structures of inequality, creating greater vulnerability to unemployment, involvement in illegal activities, and incarceration.* This factor is particularly striking in the United States, where poor black males have disproportionately high rates of unemployment, incarceration, and death. The kinds of services, job training, and education available to inner-city males are so grossly inadequate that these men are in effect often structured out of formal-sector employment.

4. *Desire to escape from oppressive structures emanating from the sex-gender system in particular contexts.* Mary Castro (in Mencher and Okongwu, 1993) has noted that some poor women in São Paulo may be heads of households because of choice and not simply because of economic constraints.

5. *The way that the state's eligibility criteria for welfare acts to separate poor men from poor mothers and children in order for the latter to gain access to life-sustaining goods and services.* The presence of men who earn incomes too low to support a family can deny welfare payments to the women and children.

6. *Cultural attitudes toward marriage and consensual unions and the processes involved.* Cultural attitudes that do not totally disown a female for bearing a child out of wedlock are prevalent in a wide variety of places (most of South America and the Caribbean, most western countries, and some parts of Africa). In contrast, in many parts of rural Africa and most parts of Asia, girls tend to marry soon after reaching childbearing age.

7. *The effect of the general economic climate.* For example, the ways in which the oil boom and bust affected Curaçao (see E. Abraham in Mencher and Okongwu, 1993) or the effect of the recession of the early 1990s in the United States.

8. *The effect of migration.* Migration sometimes involves males, sometimes couples or families, and sometimes women alone. Often male migration has had the effect of creating large numbers of de facto female-headed households. In some of these cases the women may be left alone for years to manage their households as best they can. Migration also sometimes involves women migrating without males to urban areas. Sometimes women leave children at home with relatives or friends; in other instances they migrate before they bear children.

9. *Polygamy* (in parts of Africa). In many parts of Africa, polygamous households represent a significant part of the population. For certain purposes, polygamous, non-coresidential unions, where women provide the basic subsistence needed for themselves and their children, have been considered female headed (in terms of some but not all of the criteria for headship).

Cultural Factors

1. *Religion* is one of the powerful forces influencing the extent of female-headed households and the autonomy of women who find themselves without husbands. Wherever fundamentalist religions are strong (and this

includes at least some sects in all of the world's major religions—Islam, Hinduism, Buddhism, Christianity, and Judaism), women tend to be expected to be under the power of some male, and female-headed households tend to be stigmatized. Under such circumstances, divorce on the part of women is rare, and a divorced woman must be subject to the authority of her father or brother. Bearing children out of wedlock is severely sanctioned. Even among the less orthodox sects of the traditional religions, there is considerable variation in the extent to which female-headed households are accepted.

2. *Traditional patterns of sex-role allocation* also play a part in the incidence of female-headed households, as well as in the extent to which they suffer disabilities. The functioning of female-headed households is affected by cultural definitions of what women should and should not do as well as by cultural attitudes toward female sexuality and control over children. Mahumuda Islam (in Mencher and Okongwu, 1993) points out for Bangladesh that while poor landless (or practically landless) female-headed households may be found in villages, if a woman is left land by her husband, then his relatives are likely to incorporate her and her children into their household in order to control the use of the land. In the case of India, this practice tends to vary by region, as well as by the age of the woman, her caste, and her socioeconomic class.

3. *Socioeconomic factors.* Another factor influencing the formation of female-headed households is the number of workers needed to generate subsistence for a given household. This number is determined by the dependency ratio (the ratio of dependents, including all household members, to wage earners), as well as by the income of each working person—that is, the relationship between each working person's income and what it can buy in the market. The more people working, the greater the income coming into the household. Culturally defined spending priorities play an important role in the viability of female-headed households.

4. *Other cultural factors.* The proportion of female-headed households in any given society is mediated by both cultural and socioeconomic factors. For example, in Taiwan the only female-headed households are single-person households. Taiwan is at the extreme, where women can live in female-headed households only if they never marry or have children. Other cultural factors relate to these questions: Are men expected to spend a significant proportion of their incomes on male status-producing activities such as drink, dress, gambling, or other women? Does each household have to spend money on religious activities? Does a man or a woman have to support other dependents, such as parents? Are men expected to make major economic contributions to public rituals or to political activities? The ability to mobilize networks both for day-to-day living and in times of emergency is more important in female-headed households than in households with two parents. How homogeneous or heterogeneous the networks may be varies from society to society, and this variability relates to the degree of rigidity of class location within the society. The kinds of assets that flow through the networks in which female-headed households are embedded come from family, friends, and state agencies.

Concerns about female-headed households are expected to increase in importance over the coming decades in so-called developed societies as well as in third world societies. Any understanding of survival patterns of female-headed households must include an awareness and understanding of both cultural and economic factors and must take into account both national and international policies, all of which point to the need to avoid the kinds of stereotyping of female-headed households that have clouded rather than clarified policy planning.

See Also

FAMILY STRUCTURES; GRANDMOTHER; HOUSEHOLDS: POLITICAL ECONOMY; MATRILINEAL SYSTEMS; MIGRATION; POVERTY; SINGLE PEOPLE

References and Further Reading

Ariea, E., and A. Palloni. 1999. Prevalence of poverty of female-headed households in Latin America, 1970–1990. *Journal of Comparative Family Structures* 30(2): 257–279.

Buvinic, M., and Geeta Gupta. 1997. Female-headed households and female-maintained families: Are they worth targeting to reduce poverty in developing countries? *Economic Development and Cultural Change* 45 (Jan.): 259–280.

Chant, Sylvia, ed., and Jo Campling, consulting ed. 1997. *Women-headed household: Diversity and dynamics in the developing world.* New York: St. Martin's.

Mencher, Joan, and Anne Okongwu, eds., 1993. *Female-headed/female-supported households: A cross-cultural comparison.* Boulder, Col.: Westview.

Mies, Maria. 1982. The dynamics of the sexual division of labor and integration of rural women into the world market. In Lourdes Beneria, ed., *Women and development: The sexual division of labor in rural societies,* 1–28. New York: Praeger.

Moynihan, Daniel P. 1965. *The Negro family: A case for national action.* Washington, D.C.: Office of Policy Planning and Research, U.S. Department of Labor.

Nash, June, and M. P. Fernandez-Kelly, eds. 1983. *Women, men and the international division of labor.* Albany: State University of New York Press.

Vecchio, M., and K. C. Roy. 1998. *Poverty, female-headed households and sustainable economic development.* Westport, Conn.: Greenwood.

Joan Mencher
Anne Okongwu

HOUSEHOLDS: Political Economy

A household can be defined as a social unit that shares and organizes consumption. It is fundamentally an economic concept; in fact, the English word "economy" derives from *oikonomos,* the Greek word for "managing households."

Whereas economists analyze households as units of consumption, abstract actors that exchange with firms as units of production on the market, sociologists view households as concrete units. They ask how their structure differs in different types of society and analyze their internal structural characteristics, including political conflicts, cultural patterns, and the division of labor in the household.

Households may be said to have various components, including a place or location, a physical structure, the material goods that make up its equipment and furnishings, the people who are its members, and the norms or culture that govern their relationships among household members. The actual form of these may be highly varied. For instance, the household of a Paraiya untouchable family in south India consists of little more than an open hut, some cooking utensils, and a few rough sacks to sit or sleep on; it is very quickly constructed and its members are a small nuclear family. Nevertheless, it is "home" for these people, the place where they come back to, their "base," and where limited choices or decisions about consumption are made. In contrast, the household of a British aristocrat included a large, multiroom mansion, storage places, stables, fields, a wide variety of furnishings, vehicles, and other possessions, a large or small family and many servants (some might live and eat in the lord's household, others separately in their own households) and related or unrelated dependents and guests. In the case of the untouchable family, there might be relatively little sharing of income, with husband and wife both economically independent; the British lord in contrast might oversee the finances of his small empire with an iron hand. Yet, the division of labor and economic decision making of the two have many factors in common.

The importance of households for women lies in the fact that these common factors include a gender division of labor and rights connected with households. Households are usually patriarchal, though to varying degrees. The classic concept of patriarchy was taken from the agrarian-based large male-headed households in which women, children and servants were included. But even in smaller households in industrial societies, men are normally "household heads" and have final decision-making power over the household economy. For this reason "female-headed households" are treated as an abnormality. Women are "housewives," and even though they have been managers of households and their working life has been generally within the framework of households and they are often considered to have little life outside of households (exemplified by the English saying "women's place is in the home" or the way in which Indian women speak of being confined to "the four walls") their place in households is subordinate. Women are uniquely identified with—but do not normally control—households.

Household and Family

Households and families are the smallest formal collectivities in posttribal societies. They are closely related but not synonymous. Statistics on households currently include family and "nonfamily" households, meaning either one person living alone or two or more unrelated persons. Sociologically, such a nonfamily group is a household only if its members share consumption to a significant degree. For instance, when two women share an apartment and are clearly not a family, they are called "roommates" or "housemates" but they are not said to constitute a "household" unless there is significant sharing of consumption and household chores. Nonfamily households constituted 30 percent of all U.S. households in 1990, up from 15 percent in 1960.

"Family" is a kinship unit; it is defined in terms of parentage and marriage and carries with it the emotional sentiment that provides bonding. "Household," in contrast, is an economic unit. Families inhabit and control "households," and the existence of a family is the most important way to provide the social bonds that hold households together. In contrast to states that represent the means of violence and are held together by a combination of force and consent or religious communities that are integrated by a common worldview, the household is bound together by the fact that its core family shares strong emotional bonds based on real or presumed kinship. The household may, however, include more or less than the family, while the family, even the nuclear family, may stretch beyond the household (for example, it would include the student away at school).

Family and household can be separated, and are today; but in hierarchical precapitalist societies where wife and sons were dependent on the household head in a way similar to, though to a lesser degree than, servants or even slaves, all were considered part of the larger "family" of the household head. The Roman word *familia* referred to households in this sense.

Households in Agrarian Society

Households typically emerge with agrarian societies. Hunting and gathering and pastoral societies generally have a much larger clan or extended kinship unit around which economic life is organized. One does not usually speak of "households" in such societies, largely because they are difficult to separate from the larger unit. For instance, where hunting is a collective activity and the product of the hunt is collectively consumed or where there is a systematic sharing between kin who live apart, the "household" as such is not so relevant. Similarly, it may be difficult to say which is the "household" in an African society in which a chief has many wives, each with her own hut and cooking facilities and carrying on some independent agriculture, but where income and consumption also derive from cattle owned by the chief.

Settled agricultural production gives rise to family-centered households for several reasons. Production requires stable groups, with year-round supervision and management of the land, and flexible allocation of labor between changing tasks. The smallholding family is most efficient at doing this. Labor is flexible (a wide variety of tasks can be performed without supervision at varying times), intelligent, and more or less willingly applied. Household producers who are workers, managers, and consumers, and who pass on skills sometimes developed over generations, are thus the typical unit in agrarian society (Netting, 1993).

Traditionally, agrarian households, whether rich or poor, shared several characteristics. They were nearly all patriarchal, headed by a "father" on an authoritarian basis; they frequently included not only women and children but also servants, slaves, and various other dependents, and they were all regulated by the states that emerged in agrarian societies. Finally, and perhaps most significantly, they were units of both consumption and production.

Households, not families, produced the word "patriarch." The oldest male in the family that controlled the property of the household was its head. His position was politically enforced and seen as religiously ordained. Even in agrarian societies that retained many matrilineal or matricentric elements (such as in Thailand, where women had significant control of land and property), the male represented the household to the state. In more patrilineal societies, patriarchal authority in the household was even more pronounced. Although women played a major role in household management, the decision-making power rested with men.

Households included family dependents, slaves, servants, apprentices, and poor relatives. This was the case not only in the huge households of the aristocrats but also in poorer families, where it was normal for children to grow up in households not their own, serving as apprentices and gaining a particular education. Very poor families would often send their children to slightly better-off relatives for upbringing.

State regulation of households included not only "taxation" and other forms of resource extraction but also laws on property, inheritance, and almost all aspects of the relations between husbands and their wives and children and between householders and their slaves and servants. Religious doctrines justified these relationships: "Slaves, obey your masters; wives, obey your husbands." For example, India's brahmanical legal texts normally forbade adult men to forsake their families for religious renunciation, whereas other texts, such as Kautilya's Arthashastra, were concerned to regulate marriage relations and provide opportunities for low-caste women of childbearing age to remarry. The concern here was for the provision of laborers.

Finally, households were units of production. They could include the huge estates of the nobility that produced not only crops but woven textiles, clothes, furnishings, and most of the subsistence for the home. They also could mean the households of craftsmen, whose production might have been sold or turned over to the lord. Although "household production" is normally thought of as subsistence production, distinguished by economists from market production, labor in the household was rarely entirely for subsistence. Goods for trade and other exchange were produced, and there were numerous mechanisms by which the products of household labor, as well as services, were extracted for circulation and appropriation by an elite.

Households in Industrial Societies

Industrialism brought crucial changes that economists usually identify as the change from subsistence household to market production. The rise of factories led to the breakdown of the household as a unit of production and the separation of home and workplace. No longer were members under the authority of the patriarch for both work and consumption; now they sold their labor power to a capitalist. With manufacturing removed from the household and consumption goods increasingly purchased on the market, the household became limited to the site where the nurturing and feeding of workers went on, where children grew up, where income earners found refuge and recovery, and where the major work carried on was "housework" (meaning the nonmarket reproductive labor of child care, cooking, cleaning, and maintaining the home). Industrialization inaugurated a new division of labor in which the man became the typical income-earning "worker" and the woman the "homemaker" responsible for the household, now identified with family and emotional life. Yet women have always worked outside the home, and as industrialism advances are increasingly doing so.

Thus, the process of marketization also transforms the typical work of reproduction. This transformation involves two aspects, the purchase of goods and services increasingly provided by unpaid labor in the household and the increasing use of capital-intensive equipment in the home. Prepared foods and "ready-made clothes" replace home processing and sewing, and at the same time, vacuum cleaners, pressure cookers, mixers, and microwaves become increasingly indispensable tools for housework.

Hiring of service exists in varying forms for industrial households. It includes both services provided from outside, from day care service and baby-sitting to marriage counseling; it also includes full-time live-in servants, as typified by au pairs. Maid service may increase, not decrease, with industrialization, spreading from the nobility and upper bourgeoisie to the middle classes.

The increase of women's work also requires and gives a basis for state intervention. As women's wage rates and work opportunities rise outside the home, there is a demand for provision of child care, education, and old-age services. Although part of this demand is met by the market, education and social security (noted by early sociologists as representing "a revolution in the family") become a public responsibility. As market production is more easily taxable than household production, the basis for state intervention also grows. Thus, where the state in agrarian societies regulates households, its growth in industrial societies is related to the decline in subsistence production.

Yet there are limits to marketization. Estimates today are that nonmarket household production probably accounts for more than half of economic production, whereas care for the elderly and child raising are as important to "standard of living" as material goods (Rosen and Weinberg, 1998).

Households Today:
Home Production in Postindustrial Societies

The new information economy has profound implications for forms of production. Computers, telephones, and other forms of communication are dissolving the structure of the hierarchical factory and the workplace as flexible specialization, small-batch manufacturing, and just-in-time production replace the assembly line. Some argue that the "job" itself as a lifetime income-earning occupation in one slot in the production system is disappearing: workers may shift from task to task and company to company and move in and out of the workplace. This change means, in part, movement in and out of the household. An extreme form of the flexible workplace is what the popular theorist Alvin Toffler calls the "electronic cottage," the return of production to the home on the basis of high technology. Advanced computer equipment and modern communication make it possible to do many tasks in the home itself. Designers, engineers, writers, and consultants in a wide variety of fields can work out of their homes and often do so in husband-wife teams and other family-based units.

Toffler's other notion, the "prosumer," represents the reunification of producer and consumer. As the cost of purchasing goods and services from the market grows and as both information and tools for home work and maintenance become more available, many tasks return to the home. Home gardening, carpentry, many forms of food processing, sewing, knitting, and repair of household equipment are now often done by the household members themselves, although again with the help of expensive equipment, as well as raw materials, purchased on the market, along with manuals for production and maintenance. Telephoned instructions replace the home visit of plumbers, computer servicers, and doctors, and so on. This new "prosumer" is clearly not a subsistence producer but has intensified and complex links with the market.

Households Today:
Home-Based Production in the "South"

Developing countries have only partly undergone industrialization and marketization. With a large farming population, they include significant numbers of smaller households that unite work in agriculture, fishing, animal husbandry, and artisanship for market production and for home consumption, as well as processes of housework that are more laborious and less capital intensive than in industrialized societies and are supported by fewer state-provided services.

Home-based production in the developing South is significantly different from that in preindustrial societies. It is much more likely to be linked to wider, even global, markets through sales, purchases of inputs, training, and credit. Even in rural areas it can be part of a global economy. For example, whereas care of goats and sheep was traditionally the work of women in the pastoral areas of India, Africa and elsewhere, now such women may seek to form a cooperative that manages a modern slaughterhouse, sells meat from animals that include hybrid varieties for export to Arab countries, and develops leather and wool processing. Their work remains part of the household, carried on in cooperation with husbands and children; however, they become part of a worldwide network. The proliferation of rural credit institutions, with the Grameen Bank of Bangladesh as a model, illustrates the role of finance, and the increasing concern of nongovernmental organizations (NGOs) to support "microenterprises" of the rural and urban poor shows the importance of the phenomenon. These enterprises, like small procedure agriculture, are embedded in kinship-based household units.

Contemporary Households: Globalization

The globalization of communication has profound effects on the relationship between households and society, both in industrial and developing countries. In agrarian societies the household was the major unit of a territorial state: it was through the household that people were members of the state, even though often only the household head was represented. This situation prevailed in industrial society until women got the vote, but although the nation-state is now formally composed of citizens and not households, the household has provided the basic socialization that has given identity to the nation.

Now that telecommunications and rapid travel make mobility of information and people possible over long distances, nations no longer remain limited to territorial boundaries. "Diasporas" emerge as major social configurations, and their base by and large remains households. The boundary between "England" and "India" may no longer be simply a geographical fact but a household one: "Step into their house and it's just like going to India." The household continues to be a unit giving identity to the nation, helping to constitute its cultural being, but the nation is reaching beyond the borders of the state.

Conceptualizing the Household within Society

Although the household seems to be a relatively simple concept, there have been important variations in how cultures conceive of households and their relations to other social institutions. Cultures have contrasted households with political life, religious life, and, most recently, economic life.

For the ancient Greeks the main contrast was between the household, or *oikos,* as the realm of necessity and the city-state, or *polis,* as the realm of freedom and human action. Citizenship and political life required economic subsistence and family support, but this was dull, deadening work, oriented to nature and survival. Economic work was carried on in the household and was the province of women and slaves, who created the material base that made it possible for the head of household, the citizen, to participate in public affairs. This general distinction in many ways was the origin of the "public-private" dichotomy (Elshtain, 1981).

In ancient India, by contrast, at about the same time, the life of a householder was contrasted with the life of a renouncer, who rejected the duties of married life and economic survival for a life of wandering and religious-philosophical quest. The two clashing trends of Brahmanism and shamanic or ascetic traditions (Buddhism, Jainism, and so on) gave opposing interpretations of the relationship between household and economic life. For Buddhism, it was almost an absolute contrast: the symbol of Siddhartha leaving his wife and responsibilities as a prince stands at the beginning of religious life. Buddhism prescribed a simple and moral life for householders but few rituals, and its main concern was for the life of the renouncer, or Buddhist monk, who could be of any age, man or woman. In contrast, brahmanic Hinduism sought to reconcile the two by making the household the second of the "four stages of life" and by forbidding men to take up the life of renouncer until they had completed the duties of this stage. There was an elaborate, caste-linked ritual life for the household, which was the center of society. There was no concept of the political sphere as separate from economic household life; artha, one of the four "ends" of human life, included both economics and politics. And whereas the primary division in Greece was between slave and citizen, in brahmanic India the role people had in political-social as well as household life was mediated through the caste system, where the primary division was between those who had rights to go beyond the household stage and seek religious salvation (the "twice-born" castes) and those who had to remain as servants (the "shudras"). However, just as in Greece women's place in the household deprived them of the prerequisites of religious life; in brahmanic India women's place in the household meant their religious subordination. Renunciation was not for them, salvation was found through devotion and service to husbands.

Economic Conceptualizations

The new political economy that arose with industrial society made a different division: instead of the contrast between household and polity or household and religious life, it focused almost solely on the economy and saw the family-household unit as the basic noneconomic structure of society. In Hegel's famous conceptualization, "civil society" refers to or includes the economy, but it contrasts not only with the state but also with the family. Indeed, with the separation of production from consumption, with the growth of factory labor outside the home, the "family," or kinship unit, as a center of emotional life arises as a conceptually separate unit for the first time and is assumed to coincide with the household.

This family-household—an arena of domestic and emotional life, removed from the economy and production—was ignored by the new economic theory. Neither Adam Smith nor Karl Marx saw the need to discuss the household, housework, or the organization of consumption in their magnum opera. Smith's worker, with his "propensity to truck, barter, and consume," was assumed to be a male coming out of nowhere. To Marx, consumption was a result of production and insignificant. In a memorable account in *The German Ideology*, he and Engels referred to the "production of new life" as one form of production, along with the production of goods, but this production-reproduction and the human relations involved in it were seen as a natural rather than a social phenomenon. Thus, Marx could make a brief mention of the fact that the value of labor power had "material and moral" aspects that varied historically, but he saw no need for any sociological investigation of how this situation came to pass in terms of households and families. Similarly, Engels's major work, *The Origin of the Family, Private Property, and the State*, discussed the family only in terms of reproduction and inheritance, seeing household work only as something women must escape from.

Contemporary economic theory assumes as its base rational actors or agents making decisions in terms of utility maximization. Yet in fact, people engage in action in the market as well as in other aspects of social life through social units. Microeconomics thus takes "households" and "firms" as the two basic social units. Households are units of consumption that supply the basic factors of production, labor, capital, and land, selling these on the market for income that is used for consumption. Firms or enterprises, in turn, buy the factors of production and use them to produce commodities to sell to households or to other firms. These core concepts of conventional economic theory represent a division that builds the separation between home and factor in

industrial society into an ahistorical abstraction: a farm household, for instance, will be defined as both "household" and "enterprise" depending on which activity is looked at. This abstraction sees no necessity to investigate social relations and processes internal to the household.

Feminist Critiques

Since the late 1960s, a profound feminist critique has directed itself against both Marxist and conventional economics. This critique looks at the household as an economic and political unit. It begins with a simple fact: if labor is divided into four major types—waged work, production of commodities for the market, production of goods for subsistence, and "housework" or services carried on in the household—one can see that whereas the first is nonhousehold labor, the last three are forms of "household production." The fourth type is never counted in national income statistics, and the third type is normally counted if it is done by men and not if it is done by women. In reality, however, there is no material type of work that is in principle only household production. Any type of product or service, from clothes and food to sex and reproduction, can be provided through the market. Thus, the initial and unexceptionally valid point of the feminist critique is that household work is *productive*.

This critique had different forms. Marxist feminists emphasized that domestic labor had as its primary result the production of a "commodity" crucial to capitalism—labor power. It was not recognized as economically productive or valuable, then, owing to patriarchal structures that ensured that such work was primarily the domain of women and that it was unpaid. Non-Marxist feminists raised the question of household labor and its measurement (Folbre, 1986; Waring, 1988) and critiqued national income statistics. Why should the gross national product (GNP) go down if a man marries his housekeeper and quits paying her a salary? Why is it that farmwork for subsistence is counted in the GNP especially if it is done by men, while the processing work women do with the same crops is not counted?

Regarding the process of development or marketization, the feminist critique has been more complex and less obviously clear. One trend—ecofeminism—tends to see marketization as unambiguously harmful to women. This view has had a wider impact. For instance, the feminist critique of "structural adjustment" in developing countries has centered on three points. First, it is argued that declining social spending burdens women in households who have to spend increased time on child rearing, food preparation, and the like. Second, the overall effects of lower income due to economic crisis or recession force a reversal of marketization with the same impact. Third, it is argued that a shift from policies favoring heavy industry to those favoring agriculture and agro-industries (from "nontradables" to "tradables" in economists' terms) also increases the burden of women's work time, because they spend more time in agriculture or other, possibly paid work, without being compensated by reduced housework. Here, economic growth is said to occur without benefiting women, and marketization itself can be harmful.

The first two points are uncontested. All economists seem to agree on the need for "social safety nets" and "social spending" and stress the importance of "human capital resources" (education, health, and so on) in economic development. It is also undeniable that crises and cutbacks—the most recent coming with the Asian financial crisis—affect women badly. What is disputed are the causes and remedies of such crises. The last point is a critique of marketization itself. If the economy is growing, the increase in women's work and income should lead to an increase in their bargaining power, in their ability to "marketize" household work and to demand services from the government. Important intervening variables may be cultural factors and governmental policies that support women—education, access to credit, control over land and other resources. If, for instance, liberalization makes agriculture more profitable, women agricultural laborers may not benefit so much as women who can control land themselves and have access to credit and training.

Inside the Household:
Allocation of Work, Resources, and Income

Charged with neglecting to examine the internal structure of the household and with assuming either internally unified structures or simple control by the "head of household," economists have generalized the model of utility maximization. They have analyzed the allocation of time and labor within the household, the degree of control over income and other resources, and the final decisions made about economic action as emerging from the coming together of actions of individuals who act to maximize the benefits in terms of their scale of preferences under the situation they face, including costs of achieving them. These costs—that is, the conditions under which the household operates—are taken as external and given. This analysis gives the "new household economics" of Becker (1981) and others, which looks at shifts and relationships between household production and wage work. In addition, women's position in the family or household is analyzed as linked to their position outside it (Sen, 1990). Though useful, this perspective does not analyze the social structures and norms that set the terms of action.

These debates have given rise to a plethora of studies on the structure, division of labor, allocation of work, and income within households. The household remains patriarchal, that is, there is an unequal gender-based division of labor and income in which women perform most of the labor but men control most of the income and decision making. But studies seek to find out to what degree this view is true, how much variation there is between cultures, how much women continue to bear the burden of the "second shift" as they go out to work, and how much an economic recession or crisis affects household structures. Some studies have seen a "domestic labor revolution," with men increasingly subject to unemployment or intermittent jobs and women working outside the home; a British study showing husbands performing significantly more household work in 1987 argued for a process of "lagged adaption" (Anderson et al., 1994). A similar Marxist argument says that the earlier pattern was functional only for the early stage of capitalism and that the movement is toward its reversal (Kotz, 1994). Most studies, however, show that the total amount of work done by women remains higher; men do take more part in domestic labor with growing employment of women but not enough to compensate, and the percentage of total work done by women seems to be rising. Thus, the incorporation of women into the labor force in industrial societies remains within the context of patriarchal household control, although it is shaking that control to some extent.

This statement also appears true of developing countries, where women perform an even higher share of total work. A United Nations Development Program (UNDP) survey in 1994 showed that women did 51 percent of total (market and nonmarket) work in industrialized countries, 53 percent in developing countries, and 55 percent in the rural areas of developing countries. The surveyed rural areas included Bangladesh (women, 52 percent), Guatemala (59 percent), Kenya (56 percent), Nepal (56 percent) and Philippines (73 percent) (UNDP, 1995).

Allocation and management of household finances is another important variable. Pahl (1989) identified five systems for Britain: the male whole-wage system (male management), the female whole-wage system (male turns over salary minus personal expenses to the wife for household management), the household allowance system; the pool; and independent management of separate incomes. Female management, either of the whole wage or of a household allowance, seems to have been the classical pattern for working-class families and is asso-

HOUSEHOLDS: RESOURCES

ciated with control by men. The contemporary period sees a shift toward pooling, which may be more or less male-dominated, especially among higher-income and middle-class families with more women's employment. The overall trend, like the shift in household division of labor, moves in the direction of equality but primarily among better-off couples, and male dominance remains.

The Future of the Household

Where will these trends lead? Feminism and the increasing market participation of women are challenging traditional patterns of male dominance and the gender division of labor. With a more egalitarian, companionate marriage no single person may be "head" of the future household. With the salaried, lifetime job coming into question in postindustrialism, home production may increase and is hailed by some "green" thinkers as a more ecologically sustainable "third way in economics" (Kaufman, 1995). With increasing computerization and globalization, with economic linkages as well as emotional ones extending worldwide, this changing household becomes linked in changing ways to state and nation as well as the economy. Finally, as the family itself drastically changes and there is a question as to whether its emotional and spiritual core will survive, one can wonder if the household will exist at all. But these are all questions; the future, indeed, seems open.

See Also

DIVISION OF LABOR; DOMESTIC LABOR; ECONOMICS: FEMINIST CRITIQUES; HOUSEHOLDS: DOMESTIC CONSUMPTION; HOUSEHOLDS: RESOURCES; POLITICAL ECONOMY

References and Further Reading

Anderson, Michael, Frank Bechhofer, and Jonathan Gershuny, eds., 1994. *The social and political economy of the household.* Oxford: Oxford University Press.

Becker, Gary. 1981. *A treatise on the family.* Cambridge, Mass.: Harvard University Press.

———. 1995. Housework: The missing piece of the economic pie. *Business Week* (Oct. 16).

Elshtain, Jean Bethke. 1981. *Public man, private women: women in social and political thought.* Princeton, N.J.: Princeton University Press.

Folbre, Nancy. 1996. Engendering economics: New perspectives on women, work and demographic change. In Michael Bruno and Boris Peskovic, eds., *Annual World Bank Conference on Developmental Economics 1995.* Washington, D.C.: World Bank.

———. 1986. Hearts and spades: Paradigms of household economics. *World Development* 14(2).

Kaufman, Maynard. 1995. The need for a third way in economics. *Synapse* 31(Spring).

Kotz, David. 1994. Household labor, wage labor and the transformation of the family. *Review of Radical Political Economics* 16(2).

Netting, Robert. 1993. *Smallholders, householders: Farm families and the economy of intensive, sustainable agriculture.* Stanford: University of California Press.

Pahl, Jan. 1989. *Money and marriage.* London: Macmillan.

Quah, Euston. 1993. *Economics and home production: Theory and measurement.* Alderston, U.K.: Avebury.

Rosen, Sherwin, and Bruce Weinberg. 1998. Incentives, efficiency and government provision of public services. In Joseph Stigler, ed., *Annual World Bank conference on developmental economics 1997.* Washington, D.C.: World Bank.

Sen, Amartya. 1990. Gender and cooperative conflicts. In Irene Tinker, ed., *Persistent inequalities: Women and world development.* Oxford: Oxford University Press.

Singh, Andrea Menefee, and Anita Kelles-Viitanen, eds., 1987. *Invisible hands: Women in home-based production.* New Delhi: Sage.

Toffler Alvin. 1981. *The third wave.* New York: Bantam.

United Nations Development Program (UNDP). 1995. *Human Development Report.* Oxford: Oxford University Press.

Waring, Marilyn. 1988. *If women counted: A new feminist economics.* San Francisco: Harper San Francisco.

Gail Omvedt

HOUSEHOLDS: Resources

The household is the locus of both productive and reproductive activity. That is, a household's resources encompass both the items a household produces or uses for the sake of production (for example, land, agricultural products) and the items a household uses in order to reproduce human beings as productive members of society (for example, food, clothing, and education). What resources are regarded as valuable in the household, who has authority over decision making, and how resources are distributed within the household vary significantly. Women are frequently disadvantaged in their access to and control over household resources.

Writing about household resources has suffered from a western male bias. Many authors have assumed that households are male-headed nuclear families, that decisions are made by the group as a whole, and that resources are shared equally by all members. Feminist researchers, focusing on women's roles and participation in the household, have pointed to the complexity of household arrangements. Frequently, households are governed not by shared interests but by a hierarchy in which sex, rank, and age determine decision-making power and access to and control over resources. Women and children, especially young girls, often suffer from relations of inequality. Maher's (1984: 128–129) study of Berber-speaking households in Morocco, for example, shows that men eat before women and children. When meat is available, it is considered the prerogative of men, even though a woman's caloric needs (especially if she is pregnant or lactating) may be greater. If food is in short supply, little girls learn to go to bed hungry. In India, Pakistan, and Nepal, poverty and a hierarchical distribution of food within households result in a markedly higher death rate among young girls (Nash, 1988).

Households are frequently characterized by a sexual division of responsibility in which women are seen as more directly responsible than men for the sustenance of children. Studies have shown that the best predictor of child nutritional status is not the total household income but the income of the mother. A study among poor households in rural Kerala (India) demonstrated that increases in a mother's income caused a marked improvement in child nutrition. In contrast, in areas where women did not work for wages, increases in a father's income were not matched by an improvement in children's nutrition (Charlton, 1984: 50). In general, women's earnings tend to go toward collective family needs, whereas men keep more of their earnings for personal use. For example, a study of households in Mexico City showed that 100 percent of women's earnings were contributed to a common household fund but that men divided their earnings between household needs and personal expenditures (Roldan, 1988).

Considerable debate has centered on the determinants of women's authority and control over household resources. Charlton (1984) suggests that the value attached to women's productive activities may play an important role in determining their power within the household. She argues that in highly stratified, patriarchal societies, such as north Africa, the Middle East, and much of south Asia, women have few opportunities to earn significant income and inherit property. Even when women are able to earn money, wages do not necessarily translate into power within the household, because husbands take control of the income that women earn. As a result, women tend to rely on their reproductive abilities, especially the ability to bear sons, to gain power within the household.

In contrast, Charlton (1984: 49) points to sub-Saharan Africa, where societies are frequently matrilineal and where women play important and valued roles in agricultural production. Women traditionally control and cultivate a piece of land that they use to feed their family, and they have rights to sell any surplus crops from that land and to make decisions about the income. Women also contribute important labor to men's land. Women's recognized roles as producers and partners with men translate into power within the household decision-making process.

One area of great concern has been the role that rural development projects and the introduction of commercial agriculture have played in undermining important female roles in agriculture in the third world, particularly in sub-Saharan Africa. The erosion of female power has serious consequences for the stability of households. Numerous studies have suggested that "cash-cropping" has reduced land tilled for subsistence, decreased women's income-earning capabilities, and increased women's workload (see Charlton, 1984; Moore, 1992; Nash, 1988; and Whitehead, 1984). These social changes not only erode women's status but also threaten the stability of households that rely on women's food-related activities for survival.

See Also

ECONOMIC STATUS: COMPARATIVE ANALYSIS; HOUSEHOLDS AND FAMILIES: OVERVIEW; HOUSEHOLDS: DOMESTIC CONSUMPTION; HOUSEHOLDS: POLITICAL ECONOMY; NUTRITION AND HOME ECONOMICS

References and Further Reading

Charlton, Sue Ellen M. 1984. *Women in third world development*. Boulder, Col.: Westview.

Hart, Gillian. 1992. Imagined unities: Constructions of "the household" in economic theory. In Sutti Ortiz and Susan Lees, eds., *Understanding economic process*, 111–129. Monographs in Economic Anthropology, no. 10. Lanham, Md.: University Press of America.

Klasen, Stephan. 1998. Marriage, bargaining, and intrahousehold resource allocation: Excess female mortality among adults during early German development, 1740–1860. *Journal of Economic History* 58 (2): 432–467.

Maher, Vanessa. 1984. Work, consumption and authority within the household: A Moroccan case. In Kate Young, Carol Wolkowitz, and Roslyn McCullagh, eds., *Of marriage and the market*, 117–135. London: Routledge and Kegan Paul.

Meeker, Jeffrey, and Dominique Meeker. 1997. The precarious socio-economic position of women in rural Africa: The case of the Kaguru of Tanzania. *African Studies Review* 40: 35–58.

Moore, H. L. 1992. Households and gender relations: The modelling of the economy. In Sutti Ortiz and Susan Lees, eds., *Understanding economic process*, 131–148. Monographs in Economic Anthropology, no. 10. Lanham, Md.: University Press of America.

Mullins, G., L. Wahome, and P. Tsangari. 1996. Impact of intensive dairy production on smallholder farm women in coastal Kenya. *Human Ecology* 24: 231–253.

Nash, June. 1988. Implications of technological change for household and rural development: Some Latin American cases. In Connie Weil, ed., *Lucha: The struggles of Latin American women*, 37–71, Minnesota Latin American Series, no. 2. Minneapolis: Prisma Institute.

Rogers, Beatrice Lorge. 1996. The implications of female household headship for food consumption and nutritional status in the Dominican Republic. *World Development* 24: 113–128.

Roldan, M. 1988. Renegotiating the marital contract: Intrahousehold patterns of money allocation and women's subordination among domestic outworkers in Mexico City. In D. Dwyer and J. Bruce, eds., *A home divided*. Stanford, Calif.: Stanford University Press.

Whitehead, Ann. 1984. "I'm hungry, Mum": The politics of domestic budgeting. In Kate Young, Carol Wolkowitz, and Roslyn McCullagh, eds., *Of marriage and the market*, 93–116. London: Routledge and Kegan Paul.

Katherine T. McCaffrey

HOUSEWORK

Housework refers to activities that are performed and coordinated to serve household members, including cooking, cleaning, and washing. As work, it is isolated, repetitive, monotonous, and fragmented in nature. The term *housewife* reflects women's total or primary responsibility for housework (Oakley, 1981).

In poor countries, the focus of housework is on the daily production of food. Women may spend the bulk of their domestic workday fetching water or collecting wood for household use. In the relative affluence of western industrial capitalist societies, some production for family use has been converted into consumption because there are more commodities available in the market. The use of modern domestic technology has raised the standards of housework and added to the household workload. For example, clothes are changed more frequently, meals are more elaborate, and individual possessions need cleaning and maintenance. Women of the upper classes are traditionally freed from housework by hired domestic servants.

The increase in dual-earner households has created a "double day of work" for women, also called a "second shift" by Arlie Hochschild and Anne Machung (1989). These terms refer to the additional work that wage-earning women perform in their homes. Married women do more housework than unmarried cohabiting women, and the amount of housework increases with the number of children (Lero, 1996).

Women's participation in the labor force has not equalized men's and women's share of housework. Nevertheless, North American husbands of housewives have increased their contributions to housework nearly as much as husbands of wage-earning women. But in general, men have more leisure time than women. Furthermore, those men who do participate in housework tend to choose the more pleasant and creative tasks, such as cooking.

Surveys of married women in South Korea, Indonesia, Taiwan, the Philippines, and the United States show that wives' economic resources have no consistently significant effect on husbands' participation in housework (Sanchez, 1993). Hochschild and Machung's research (1989) suggests that men who rely on women for economic support still tend to do less housework. Among couples who share modern norms or have advanced academic degrees and professional careers, men do tend to participate more.

Although women do not necessarily think it is unfair for them to do more household labor, women with alternatives to marriage or with economic resources are more likely to consider their share of housework unfair. These women are also more likely to report less psychological well-being (Lennon and Rosenfield, 1994).

There have been worldwide calls for recognition of the value of unpaid work in official calculations of national wealth. In the West estimates range somewhere between one-sixth and one-quarter of the gross national product (GNP). Estimates are even higher worldwide, reflecting the greater proportion contributed in the poor countries of the world. Occasionally there have been proposals for homemakers' pensions and wages for housework as a way to recognize women's contributions in the household. Opponents argue that his practice would only reinforce the domestic division of labor and perpetuate the undervaluation of women's work, because no society would be willing to pay anywhere close to the real value of housework (Malos, 1980).

See Also

COOKING; DIVISION OF LABOR; DOMESTIC LABOR; DOMESTIC
TECHNOLOGY; ECONOMY: FEMINIST CRITIQUES; HOUSEHOLD
WORKERS; NUTRITION AND HOME ECONOMICS

References and Further Reading

Hochschild, Arlie, with Anne Machung. 1989. *The second shift.*
New York: Avon Books.

Lennon, Mary Clare, and Sarah Rosenfield. 1994. Relative fairness and the division of housework. *American Journal of
Sociology* 100(2): 506–531.

Lero, Donna. 1996. Dual-earner families. In Marion Lynn, ed.,
Voices: Essays on Canadian families, 19–54. Toronto: Nelson.

Malos, Ellen, ed. 1980. *The politics of housework.* London: Allison and Busby.

Oakley, Ann. 1974. *The sociology of housework.* London: Martin
Robertson.

————. 1981. *Subject women.* London: Fontana.

Sanchez, Laura. 1993. Women's power and the gendered division
of domestic labor in the third world. *Gender and Society*
7(3): 434–459.

Vappu Tyyska

HOUSING

A woman is wrapped around a house, her enlarged arms
enveloping the facade, her face peering around and over
the roof. This sketch, by the artist and humorist James
Thurber, appeared in an American magazine in 1943. In
the 1990s, in another American journal, the illustration for
an article on the cost of living was a row of houses whose
facades were huge dollar signs. These pictures typify the
continuum of research issues about women and housing.
The first image represents women's identity entwined with
a house; the second, housing's identity as a capital investment and the largest outlay in the household budget.
Housing research and related literature in developed countries is likely to examine the topic in terms of personal
meanings as well as poverty, affordability, women's roles,
and the housing industry. In comparison, research on
housing in developing countries usually emphasizes
women's integration into society and shelter as part of the
development process.

The housing industry contributes to countries'
economies and also to the creation of ideology about
women. Housing research divides markets into private and
public sectors, but many countries have a third stream that
receives government encouragement. Various kinds of non-
profits dominate the third stream: building societies in England and Sweden; unions in Germany; and cooperatives
and self-help enterprises in Canada, Central and Latin
America, Africa, and Asia. Countries that support a third
stream are likelier to assume societal responsibility for the
general welfare in contrast to nations that expect all citizens
to fend for themselves. Tenure forms of housing, by race and
ethnicity, also reflect social systems. Discriminatory lending
practices prevent homeownership from expanding, while
segregation concentrates owners and renters into enclaves.
Taxation policies and rising house prices, as in the United
States, favor homeownership and influence household formation; nuclear families with two adults working are more
likely to own than rent.

Ideological concerns relate to the privileged position of
property owners, who tend to be men, in housing delivery
systems and to society's general subordination of women. In
the United States, for example, banks consider renters second-class citizens, although most owners make monthly
mortgage payments to financial institutions for 20 years or
more. In countries where women lack representation, political bodies and societal restrictions reinforce their second-
class status. Whether women are or are not property owners,
their place or sphere is considered to be within the house.
This identification with the house and homemaking
enforces the cult of domesticity. Low status, whether in
developed or developing societies, is further enforced by the
devaluing of domestic work. Gender, class, race, and ethnicity interact and decrease women's chances for securing
housing equity with men. Additionally, certain types of gov-
ernment-assisted housing are disparaged. For example, in
the United States, public housing residents are typically low-
income women of color, whose identity is preassigned by
their address; negative attitudes toward public housing
become attached to its residents.

The housing industry in all societies involves a range of
participants: land surveyors, builders, developers, designers,
financiers, mortgage bankers, lawyers, credit unions, officials and bureaucrats at all levels of government, material
suppliers, real estate brokers, appraisers, contractors, interior
decorators, gardeners, landscape architects, and consumers.
Supply-side studies relate to production, construction, management and maintenance, rehabilitation, and design;
demand-side studies include issues that focus on consumers,
such as gaps between incomes and affordability and impacts
created by discrimination. These studies do not tend to dis-
aggregate by gender.

Rendering the Invisible Visible

Early research on housing focused on women's invisibility as a category for analysis and also on women as both producers of housing and consumers with particular needs that derive from their multiple roles. Many scholars in the United States found omissions about women in their planning and design education, which led them to inquiries about training of women in related fields, such as at the Cambridge School that existed from 1915 to World War II in Massachusetts (Berkeley and McQuaid, 1989). Depending on the historical period and the society, references to women and housing may be found under community builders, municipal housekeepers, or developers, as well as architects or government officials. In the mid-1990s, literature on women and housing in English-speaking countries included diverse emphases by location, regulatory mechanisms, residential types, theory, and roles: for example, the city, land use, zoning, and safety (Peake and Little, 1988); neighborhoods (Leavitt and Saegert, 1990); theory and design (Franck and Ahrentzen, 1989); and women in suburbia, in public housing, as activists, and as housewives.

Studies in the United States, Canada, England, Australia, and New Zealand clarify the ways in which neighborhoods can ameliorate or create barriers for women. Historians have reformulated the public-private split, particularly for poor and working-class women; research about women and housing in developing nations is also exploring the acts that occur in the boundaries between public and private space. Critical theorists have identified examples where marginal space, whether in the home or at the cities' edges, provides sites of resistance for women of color (hooks, 1990).

Homelessness studies are uneven for different racial and ethnic subgroups, such as Latinas in the United States. Material on Australian homelessness from a feminist perspective provides a useful comparative and theoretical framework (Watson and Austerberry, 1986).

The Difference Gender Makes in Housing Research

Gender research reinterprets existing data, emphasizes different issues, includes feminist scholarship from other disciplines, and involves original studies. The house is a starting point for a variety of studies.

As a physical structure, the house is a site for housework, homemaking, child rearing, and wage labor (Hayden, 1989). The house layout influences and affects gender roles among household members, and therefore mirrors change in society's concept of the family (Clark, 1986; Dandekar, 1992). For example, colonial families in the United States explicitly organized as economic household, with blood relatives, kin, and boarders struggling for survival; little room for differentiation existed. In the postwar era of the 1950s, companionate families gazed inward at each other, with activities organized and centered within the home, which now included a specifically designated family room.

Finance and tenure studies include women's roles in the labor force, difficulties in securing loans for purchase, and quality and affordability of rental housing. Research shows that single female parents, for example, move more frequently than single male parents, and housing quality becomes worse with each move. Gender and housing studies that focus on demographics, household structure, and housing stock analyze fit with available supply, such as satisfying single parents' needs (Franck and Ahrentzen, 1989); the match with finance, such as alternative institutions for women in rural agricultural communities (Moser and Peake, 1987); contrasts between women's lives in their country of origin, for example, Mexico, and the country in which they are working (Pader, 1991); and differences by age, race, and ethnicity in reclaiming landlord-abandoned buildings and forming limited equity co-ops in New York City (Leavitt and Saegert, 1990).

See Also

ARCHITECTURE; BUILT ENVIRONMENT; GEOGRAPHY; HOMELESSNESS; HOUSEHOLDS AND FAMILIES: OVERVIEW

References and Further Reading

Berkeley, Ellen Perry, and Matilda McQuaid, eds. 1989. *Architecture: A place for women,* Washington, D.C.: Smithsonian Institution.

Clark, Clifford, Jr. 1986. *The American family home: 1800–1960.* Chapel Hill and London: University of North Carolina Press.

Dandekar, Hemaleta, ed. 1992. Shelter, women and development: First and third world perspectives. Proceedings of an international conference, College of Architecture and Urban Planning, University of Michigan, May 7–9.

Ferguson, Gael. 1994. *Building the New Zealand dream.* Palmerston North, New Zealand: Dunmore.

Franck, Karen A., and Sherry Ahrentzen, eds. 1989. *New households, new housing.* New York: Van Nostrand Reinhold.

Hayden, Dolores. 1989. *The grand domestic revolution: A history of feminist designs for American homes, neighbourhoods, and cities.* Cambridge, Mass.: MIT Press.

hooks, bell. 1990. *Yearning: Race, gender, and cultural politics.* Boston: South End.

Leavitt, Jacqueline, and Susan Saegert, 1990. *From abandonment to hope: Community-households in Harlem.* New York: Columbia University Press.

Moser, Caroline O. N., and Linda Peake. 1987. *Women, human settlements, and housing.* New York: Tavistock.

Pader, Ellen J. 1991. "Spatiality and social change: Domestic space use in Mexico and the United States." *American Ethnologist* 114–137.

Peake, Linda, and Jo Little, eds. 1988. *Women in cities: Gender and the urban environment.* London: Macmillan.

Watson, Sophie, with Helen Austerberry. 1986. *Housing and homelessness: A feminist perspective.* London: Routledge and Kegan Paul.

Jacqueline Leavitt

HUMAN RIGHTS

The term *women's human rights* and the set of practices that accompanies its use are the continuously evolving product of an international movement to improve the status of women. In the 1980s and 1990s women's movements around the world formed networks and coalitions to give greater visibility both to the problems that women face every day and to the centrality of women's experiences in economic, social, political, and environmental issues. In the evolution of what is becoming a global women's movement, the term *women's human rights* has served as a locus for praxis, that is, for the development of political strategies shaped by the interaction between analytical insights and concrete political practices. Furthermore, the critical tools, the concerted activism, and the broad-based international networks that have grown up around movements for women's human rights have become a vehicle for women to develop the political skills necessary for the twenty-first century.

The concept of women's human rights owes its success and the proliferation of its use to the fact that it is simultaneously prosaic and revolutionary. On the one hand, the idea of women's human rights makes common sense. It declares, quite simply, that as human beings women have human rights. Anyone would find herself or himself hard-pressed to publicly make and defend the contrary argument that women are not human. So in many ways, the claim that women have human rights seems quite ordinary. On the other hand, women's human rights is a revolutionary notion. This radical reclamation of humanity and the corollary insistence that women's rights are human rights have profound transformative potential. The incorporation of women's perspectives and

lives into human rights standards and practice forces recognition of the dismal failure of countries worldwide to accord women the human dignity and respect that they deserve simply as human beings. A women's human rights framework equips women with a way to define, analyze, and articulate their experiences of violence, degradation, and marginality. Finally, and very important, the idea of women's human rights provides a common framework for developing a vast array of visions and concrete strategies for change.

A Short History of Human Rights

The Universal Declaration of Human Rights adopted by the United Nations General Assembly in 1948 outlines what is now considered to be the fundamental consensus on the human rights of all people in relation to such matters as security of person; slavery; torture; protection of the law; freedom of movement, speech, religion, and assembly; and rights to social security, work, health, education, culture, and citizenship. It clearly stipulates that these human rights apply to all equally "without distinction of any kind such as race, colour, sex, language...or other status" (Art. 2). Obviously, then, the human rights delineated by the declaration are to be understood as applying to women. However, tradition, prejudice, and social, economic, and political interests have combined to exclude women from prevailing definitions of "general" human rights and to relegate women to secondary or "special interest" status within human rights considerations. This marginalization of women in the world of human rights has been a reflection of gender inequity in the world at large and also has had a formidable impact on women's lives. It has contributed to the perpetuation and indeed the condoning of women's subordinate status. It has limited the scope of what was seen as governmental responsibility and thus has made the process of seeking redress for human rights violations disproportionately difficult for women and in many cases outright impossible.

The difficulties posed by women's peripheral status within international human rights mechanisms and organizations have been compounded by the division between the so-called public and private spheres prevalent in so many societies. The pervasive division of life into public and private spheres has its roots in the desire to limit the jurisdiction of the government. In many countries, this notion has meant that what individuals do in the public sphere is subject to regulation, while activities taking place in the private sphere are thought to be exempt from governmental scrutiny. Since this public sphere is seen as the focus of interaction between state actors and citizens, abuses of that relationship have been the focus of international human rights advocacy. Of course, the status of citizen has often been exclusionary, formally or informally entailing gender, racial, and socioeconomic bias and privileges. Thus, for those citizens, primarily men, who predominate in public and governmental realms and who enjoy gender, racial, and economic privilege, the issues of primary concern have tended to be those abuses to which they are most vulnerable—abuses of civil and political aspects of human rights, such as the violation of the right to speech, arbitrary detention, torture during imprisonment, and summary execution.

While women have been able to invoke international human rights machinery when they have found themselves in such situations, some of their specifically gendered experiences of such human rights abuse—for example, rape in detention—have not been visible within the prevailing definitions of abuse. This is the case because women traditionally have been relegated to the private sphere of the home and family; the typical citizen has been portrayed as male, and thus the dominant notions of human rights abuse implicitly have had a man as their archetype. A major effect of the gendered nature of the public-private split is that human rights violations of women that occur between private individuals have been made invisible and deemed to be beyond the purview of the state. It is particularly important to note that gender is a significant factor in the decisions of governments to intervene in the so-called private sphere to prosecute human rights violations. For example, many activities that take place in the private sphere, such as murder between siblings or the systematic enslavement of African peoples in the Americas, are subject to government censure internationally. However, much of what happens to women at the hands of men and male family members—for example, domestic violence or confinement—is overlooked by governments even when there are laws against such abuse. Thus, abuse of women in the name of family, religion, and culture has been hidden by the sanctity of the so-called private sphere, and perpetrators of such human rights violations have enjoyed immunity from accountability for their actions.

The historical emphasis on human rights abuses in the public sphere and the concomitant neglect of the human rights of women were exacerbated by the politics of the Cold War. The United Nations human rights treaties and mechanisms developed after the horrors of World War II and were consolidated during the cold war. The purpose of many human rights organizations that developed along with them was to monitor the treatment of citizens by their governments and to ensure respect for citizens' human

rights as they worked for democratic governance. As positions polarized during the cold war, western governments attributed priority to civil and political rights, which they believed were integral to a prosperous free market economy. Meanwhile, the socioeconomic rights to work, shelter, and health, for example, became identified with the socialist bloc and were thus suspect to many in the West. Thus, human rights bodies, dominated by western conceptions of human rights priorities, focused on violations within the civil and political realm—the public sphere. So, in addition to the obstacles for women posed by the split between so-called public and private spheres, the predominance of civil and political rights within human rights organizations eclipsed the ways in which women often do not enjoy the social and economic conditions that make possible the exercise of civil and political rights and participation in public life.

The Concept of Women's Human Rights

During the United Nations Decade for Women (1975–1985), women from many geographical, racial, religious, cultural, and class backgrounds organized to improve the status of women. The UN-sponsored women's conferences, which took place in Mexico City in 1975, in Copenhagen in 1980, and in Nairobi in 1985, were convened to evaluate the status of women and to formulate strategies for women's advancement. These conferences were critical venues at which women came together, debated their differences and discovered their commonalities, and gradually began learning to bridge differences to create a global movement. In the late 1980s and early 1990s women in diverse countries took up the human rights framework and began developing the analytic and political tools that together constitute the ideas and practices of women's human rights.

Taking up the human rights framework has involved a double shift in thinking about human rights and talking about women's lives. Put quite simply, it has entailed examining the human rights framework through a gendered lens and describing women's lives through a human rights framework. In looking at the human rights framework from women's perspectives, women have shown how current human rights definitions and practices fail to account for the ways in which already recognized human rights abuses often affect women differently because of their gender. This approach acknowledges the importance of the existing concepts and activities but also points out that there are dimensions within these received definitions that are gender specific and that need to be addressed if the mechanisms, the programs, and the human rights framework itself are to include and reflect the experiences of the female half of the world's population.

When people utilize the human rights framework to articulate the array of human rights abuses that women face, they bring clarifying analyses and powerful tools to bear on women's experiences. This strategy has been pivotal in efforts to draw attention to human rights that are specific to women, which heretofore have been seen as women's rights but not recognized as "human" rights. Take, for example, the issue of violence against women. The Universal Declaration states: "No one shall be subject to torture or to cruel, inhuman or degrading treatment or punishment." This formulation provides a vocabulary for women to define and articulate experiences of violence such as rape, sexual terrorism, and domestic violence as violations of the human right not to be subject to torture or to cruel, inhuman, or degrading treatment or punishment. The recognition of such issues as human rights abuses raises the level of expectation about what can and should be done about them. This definition of violence against women (in terms of human rights) establishes unequivocally that states are responsible for such abuse. It also raises questions about how to hold governments accountable for their indifference in such situations and what sorts of mechanisms are needed to expedite the process of redress.

Applying the Human Rights Framework to Women

The Universal Declaration of Human Rights defines human rights as universal, inalienable, and indivisible. In unison, these defining characteristics are tremendously important for women's human rights. The universality of human rights means that human rights apply to every single person by virtue of his or her humanity; this also means that human rights apply to everyone equally, for everyone is equal in simply being human. In many ways, this theme may seem patently obvious, but its egalitarian premise has a radical edge. By invoking the universality of human rights, women have demanded that their very humanity be acknowledged. That acknowledgment—and the concomitant recognition of women as bearers of human rights—mandates the incorporation of women and gendered perspectives into all of the ideas and institutions that are already committed to the promotion and protection of human rights. The idea that human rights are universal also challenges the contention that the human rights of women can be limited by culturally specific definitions of what counts as human rights and of women's role in society.

The idea of human rights as inalienable means that it is impossible for anyone to abdicate her human rights, even if she wanted to, as every person is accorded those rights by virtue of being human. It also means that no person or group of persons can deprive another individual of her or his human rights. Thus, for example, debts incurred by migrant workers or by women caught up in sex trafficking can never justify indentured servitude (slavery) or the deprivation of food, of freedom of movement, or of compensation. The idea of inalienable rights means that human rights cannot be sold, ransomed, or forfeited for any reason. The idea of inalienability also has been important in negotiations over the priority given to social, religious, and cultural practices in relation to human rights. For decades, work to transform practices that are physically or psychologically damaging to women and that often have been "protected" under the rubric of religion, tradition, or culture has been particularly difficult, given both the integrity of culture guaranteed by the Universal Declaration and the history of northern domination in much of the world. Thus, it was important that both the Vienna Declaration and Programme of Action, from the World Conference on Human Rights held in Vienna in 1993, and the United Nations Declaration against Violence against Women, passed by the General Assembly the same year, affirmed that in cases of conflict between women's human rights and cultural or religious practices, the human rights of women must prevail.

The indivisibility of human rights means that none of the rights that are considered fundamental human rights is more important than any of the others and, more specifically, that they are interrelated. Human rights encompass civil, political, social, economic, and cultural facets of human existence; the indivisibility premise highlights that the ability of people to live their lives in dignity and to exercise their human rights fully depends on the recognition that these aspects are all interdependent. The fact that human rights are indivisible is important for women because their civil and political rights historically have been compromised by their economic status, by social and cultural limitations placed on their activities, and by the ever present threat of violence that often constitutes an insurmountable obstacle to women's participation in public and political life. The idea of indivisibility has provided women with a common framework through which the complexity of the challenges they face can be emphasized and in which the necessity of including women and gender-conscious perspectives in the development and implementation of policy is highlighted. By calling on the indivisibility of women's human rights, women have rejected a human rights hierarchy that places either political and civil rights or socioeconomic rights as primary. Instead, women have charged that political stability cannot be realized unless women's social and economic rights are also addressed; that sustainable development is impossible without the simultaneous respect for and incorporation into the policy process of women's cultural and social roles in the daily reproduction of life; and that social equity cannot be generated without economic justice and women's participation in all levels of political decision making.

The Movement for Women's Human Rights

The term *women's human rights* does not refer simply to the theoretical approaches that women have used to transform human rights concepts, programs, and agendas. In addition to being instrumental in the formulation of the conceptual challenges and demands levied by women, the idea of women's human rights has had immense impact as a tool for political activism. The concept of women's human rights has enabled women around the world to ask hard questions about the official inattention and general indifference to the widespread discrimination and violence that women experience every day. Whether used in political lobbying, in legal cases, in grassroots mobilization, or in broad-based educational efforts, the idea of women's human rights has been a rallying point for women across many boundaries and has facilitated the creation of collaborative strategies for promoting and protecting the human rights of women.

While women have raised questions for a long time about why their rights are seen as ancillary to human rights, a coordinated effort to change this attitude using a human rights framework gained particular momentum in the early 1990s. The opening of new debates afforded by the end of the cold war facilitated the exchange of ideas and experiences among women around the world and led to strategizing about how to make women's human rights perspectives more visible. As women's activities developed globally during and following the United Nations Decade for Women, more and more women raised the question of why "women's rights" and women's lives have been deemed secondary to the "human rights" and lives of men. During the 1990s, a movement around women's human rights emerged to challenge limited notions of human rights, and it focused particularly on violence against women as a prime example of the bias against women in human rights practice and theory.

The United Nations World Conference on Human Rights, held in Vienna in 1993, was the first such meeting since 1968, and it became a natural vehicle to highlight the new visions of human rights thinking and practice being developed by women. Its initial call did not mention women, nor did it recognize any gender-specific aspects of human rights in its proposed agenda. As the conference represented a historic reassessment of the status of human rights, it became the unifying public focus of a worldwide global campaign for women's human rights—a broad and loose international collaborative effort to advance women's human rights. The campaign launched a petition calling on the world conference "to comprehensively address women's human rights at every level of its proceedings" and to recognize "gender violence, a universal phenomenon which takes many forms across culture, race, and class...as a violation of human rights requiring immediate action." The petition was eventually translated into 23 languages and was used by more than a thousand sponsoring groups that gathered a half million signatures from 124 countries. The petition and its demands instigated discussions about why women's rights, and gender-based violence in particular, were left out of human rights considerations and served to mobilize women around the world conference. Women acted to inject issues of women's human rights into the entire preconference preparatory process: women from all regions demanded that women's human rights be discussed at the preparatory meetings held in Tunis, San Jose, and Bangkok, as well as at other nongovernmental and national preparatory events. The idea of women's human rights was a framework for women to articulate and collaborate around broad and similar concerns about the status of women. It also provided women with a way to elaborate on the most pressing human rights issues specific to particular political, geographic, economic, and cultural contexts.

By the time the world conference convened, the idea that "women's rights are human rights" had become the rallying call of thousands of people all over the world and one of the most discussed "new" human rights debates. The Vienna Declaration and Programme of Action (1993), which was the product of the conference and was meant to signal the agreement of the international community on the status of human rights, states unequivocally: "The human rights of women and of the girl-child are an inalienable, integral and indivisible part of universal human rights" (I, 18).

Women continued to lobby for and gain wider recognition of women's human rights at subsequent UN conferences. So, for example, at the International Conference on Population and Development in Cairo in 1994, women's reproductive rights were explicitly recognized as human rights. A particularly significant development was the way in which the Platform for Action at the Fourth World Conference on Women in Beijing in 1995 became virtually an agenda about the human rights of women. This platform signaled the successful mainstreaming of women's rights as human rights.

The agreements that are produced by such conferences are not legally binding; however, they do have ethical and political weight and can be used to pursue regional, national, or local objectives. Conference documents also can be used to reinforce and interpret international treaties, such as the Covenant of Social, Economic, and Cultural Rights. These covenants, when signed by a country, do have the status of international law and have been used in courts by lawyers seeking redress for human rights violations. The most important international treaty specifically addressing women's human rights is the Convention on the Elimination of All Forms of Discrimination against Women (CEDAW), which was initiated during the United Nations Decade for Women and has been ratified by more than 130 countries. Furthermore, local women's groups have integrated the women's human rights framework into their legal literacy programs and legal strategies.

Although the framework of women's human rights has been tremendously useful in efforts to lobby for legislative and policy changes at local, national, and international levels, it has been an equally important tool for grassroots organizing. The concept of women's human rights not only teaches women about the range of rights that their governments must honor; it also functions as a kind of integrated structure by which to organize analyses of their experiences and plan action for change. The human rights framework creates a space in which the possibility for a different account of women's lives can be developed. It provides women with principles by which to develop alternative visions of their lives without suggesting the substance of those visions. The fundamental principles of human rights that accord to each and every person the entitlement to human dignity give women a vocabulary for describing both violations and impediments to the exercise of their human rights. The large body of international covenants, agreements, and commitments about human rights gives women political leverage and a tenable point of reference. And, finally, the idea of women's human rights enables women to define and articulate the specificity of the experiences in their lives as it provides a vocabulary for women to share the experiences of other women around the world and work collaboratively for change.

See Also

ACTIVISM; GLOBAL FEMINISM; INDIGENOUS WOMEN'S RIGHTS; INTERNATIONAL ORGANIZATIONS AND AGENCIES; JUSTICE AND RIGHTS; POLITICS AND THE STATE: OVERVIEW; REPRODUCTIVE RIGHTS; VIOLENCE AND PEACE: OVERVIEW

References and Further Reading

Bunch, Charlotte, and Roxanna Carrillo. 1991. *Gender violence: A development and human rights issue.* New Brunswick, N.J.: Center for Women's Global Leadership. Contact: Center for Women's Global Leadership, 160 Ryders Lane, New Brunswick, N.J. 08903.

Bunch, Charlotte, and Niamh Reilly. 1994. *Demanding accountability: The global campaign and Vienna tribunal for women's human rights.* New York: United Nations Development Fund for Women (UNIFEM). Contact: Women Ink, 777 UN Plaza, 3rd Floor, New York, N.Y. 10017.

Butegwa, Florence, Stella N. Mukasa, and Susan Mogere. 1995. *Human rights of women in conflict situations.* Harare, Zimbabwe: Women in Law and Development in Africa (WiLDAF). Contact: WiLDAF, P.O. Box 4622, Harare, Zimbabwe.

Center for the Study of Human Rights. 1996. *Women and human rights: The basic documents.* New York: Center for the Study of Human Rights. Contact: Center for the Study of Human Rights, Columbia University, 420 West 118th Street, 1108 International Affairs Building, Mail Code: 3365, New York, N.Y. 10027.

Cook, Rebecca J., ed. 1994. *Human rights of women: National and international perspectives.* Philadelphia: University of Pennsylvania Press. Contact: Women Ink, 777 UN Plaza, 3rd floor, New York. N.Y. 10017.

Human Rights Watch Women's Rights Project. 1995. *The Human Rights Watch global report on women's human rights.* New York: Human Rights Watch. Contact: Human Rights Watch, 485 Fifth Ave., New York, N.Y. 10017–6104.

International Gay and Lesbian Human Rights Commission. 1995. *Unspoken rules: Sexual orientation and women's human rights.* San Francisco: International Gay and Lesbian Human Rights Commission. Contact: International Gay and Lesbian Human Rights Commission, 1360 Mission St. 200, San Francisco, Calif. 94103 USA.

International Women's Tribune Center (IWTC). 1998. *Rights of women: A guide to the most important UN treaties on women's human rights.* New York: International Women's Tribune Center. Contact: Women Ink, 777 UN Plaza, 3rd floor, New York, N.Y. 10017.

ISIS Internacional. 1991. *La mujer ausente: Derechos humanos en el mundo* (2nd ed. 1996). Santiago, Chile: ISIS Internacional. Contact: Isis Internacional, Casilla 2067, Correo Central, Santiago, Chile.

Kerr, Joanna, ed. 1993. *Ours by right*. Ottawa, Canada: The North-South Institute and Zed Books. Contact: The North-South Institute, Institut Nord-Sud, 200–55 Murray, Ottawa, Ontario, Canada K1N 5M3; Zed Books Ltd., 57 Caledonian Road, London N1 9BU, U.K., or 165 First Ave., Atlantic Highlands, N.J. 07716.

Maramba, Petronella, Bisi Olateru-Olagbegi, and Rosalie Tiani Webanenou. 1995. *Structural adjustment programs and the human rights of African women*. Harare, Zimbabwe: Women in Law and Development in Africa (WiLDAF). Contact: WiLDAF; P.O. Box 4622, Harure, Zimbabwe.

Mertus, Julie, with Mallika Dutt and Nancy Flowers. 1999. *Local action/Global change: Learning/About the human rights of women and girls*. New Brunswick, N.J. Center for Women's Global Leadership, and New York: UNIFEM. Contact: Center for Women's Global Leadership, 160 Ryders Lane, New Brunswick, NJ.

Petchesky, Rosalind, and Karen Judd, eds. 1998. *Negotiating reproductive rights: Women's perspectives across countries and cultures*. New York: International Reproductive Rights Research and Action Group. Contact: Women, Ink, 777 UN Plaza, 3rd floor, New York. N.Y. 10017.

Sajor. ed. 1998. *Common grounds: Violence against women in war and armed conflict situations*. Philippines: Asian Centre for Women's Human Rights. Contact: Women, Ink, 777 UN Plaza, 3rd floor, New York. N.Y. 10017

Schuler, Margaret, ed. 1995. *From basic needs to basic rights: Women's claim to human rights*. Washington, D.C.: Women, Law, and Development International. Contact: Institute for Women, Law and Development, 1736 Columbia Rd., NW, #311, Washington, D.C. 20009.

United Nations. 18 Dec. 1979. Convention on the elimination of all forms of discrimination against women. RES34/180. Contact: Center for Human Rights, United Nations, New York, NY 10017; or Center for Human Rights, United Nations, 1211 Geneva 10, Switzerland.

———. 23 Feb. 1994. Declaration on the elimination of violence against women. A/RES/48/104.

———. 25 June 1993. World conference on human rights: The Vienna declaration and programme of action. A/CONF.157/ 23.25.

Watts, Charlotte, Susanna Osam, and Everjoice Win, eds. 1995. *The private is public: A study of violence against women in southern Africa*. Harare, Zimbabwe: Women in Law and Development in Africa (WiLDAF). Contact: WiLDAF; P.O. Box 4622, Harare, Zimbabwe.

Wolper, Andrea, and Julie S. Peters. 1995. *Women's rights, human rights: International feminist perspectives*. New York: Routledge. Contact: Women, Ink; see above.

Women, Law and Development International and Human Rights Watch. 1997. *Women's human rights step by step: A practical guide to using international human rights law and mechanisms to defend women's human rights*. Washington, D.C.: Women, Law and Development International. Contact: Women, Law and Development International, see above.

Media References

The Vienna Tribunal: Women's rights are human rights. 1994. Augusta Productions, with the Canadian National Film Board, in association with the Center for Women's Global Leadership. Director: Gerry Rogers. *The Vienna Tribunal* highlights the testimonies given by women around the world at the Global Tribunal on Violations of Women's Human Rights at the United Nations World Conference on Human Rights at the United Nations World Conference on Human Rights in Vienna in 1993.

Charlotte Bunch
Samantha Frost

HUMANITIES AND SOCIAL SCIENCES: Feminist Critiques

Feminist critique of the humanities and social sciences has all but revolutionized the way we make sense of disciplines such as literature, history, and philosophy, as well as specific areas in social sciences such as education, sociology, psychology, and even geography. As Sandra Harding (1986: 9) has noted, "Feminist thinkers have challenged the intellectual and social orders at their very foundations." Not only has this critique put the issue of gender in the spotlight, but feminist interest in and criticisms of and within these disciplines have also led to a critical view of the way in which scholarship in these areas is undertaken. As a way of thinking, being, and doing, feminism has opened people's eyes to a whole other way of looking at the world and human endeavor. Thus, women's efforts and voices no longer go unnoticed or unacknowledged.

At the heart of feminist critique lie two particular issues. First, feminist critique of both the humanities and social sciences has meant that a series of "claims to truth" have been exposed as myth. For example, in recent decades, feminist critique of psychology has meant that some theories have not only been challenged but have actually needed to be rewritten in order for women to be brought into the picture.

This development has led to much of what was previously accepted as "the norm" being revealed as masculinist or male-oriented. This has been the case both in terms of what is focused on and whose interests are represented. Feminists have argued that it has been men's rather than women's concerns and experiences that have been traditionally represented.

Feminist critique has, therefore, been responsible for an extension of what is focused on in various areas of scholarship. For example, whereas a discipline such as history would have relied primarily upon official, public documents (for example, Parliament Hansards) to understand a particular event or time period, feminist critique has led historians to look to other documents (for example, personal letters between women) in order to understand where women fit into the picture. Given that the public world of politics is predominantly a man's world, in order to understand women's lives and experiences other sources of information are needed. Feminist critique of history has meant that women have been able to be included in the big picture. This type of critique also has led to what counts as genuine historical material being expanded.

Second, in the social sciences more broadly, feminist critique has led to methods of inquiry being extended and, in some cases, made more personable. For example, feminism has played an important role in introducing and legitimating qualitative methods such as individual and group interviewing. Unlike impersonal large scale surveys, interviewing methods have been seen by some to be *the* feminist method, because they allow women researchers to connect with their research participants at a very personal level rather than treating participants as merely numbers or uninvolved research subjects.

Finally, feminist critique has led to a questioning of what is actually investigated and, therefore, to what a research program can look like. In this final respect, feminism has led to entire research programs being revamped; a move that often has as its aim a sort of equal representation of, and investment in, the lives of women *and* men. In all these ways, feminist critics have worked alongside other critics for whom the issues of race, sexuality, and class are the key foci to reveal and challenge the neutrality of the standpoint of white, middle-class, heterosexual men and to include the diversity of women's lives and voices in all respects.

See Also

EDUCATION: NONSEXIST; ETHICS: FEMINIST; FEMINISM: OVERVIEW; FINE ARTS: CRITICISM AND ART HISTORY; LITERARY THEORY AND CRITICISM; LITERATURE: OVERVIEW; PEDAGOGY: FEMINIST; POSTMODERNISM: FEMINIST CRITIQUES; SOCIAL SCIENCES: FEMINIST METHODS

References and Further Reading

ClicNet: Etudes Féministes. <http://clicnet.swarthmore.edu/etudes.feministes.html>

Fraser, N., and L. Nicholson. 1995. Social criticism without philosophy: An encounter between feminism and postmodernism. In Steven Seidman, ed., *The postmodern turn: New perspectives on social theory,* 242–261. Cambridge: Cambridge University Press.

Harding, S. 1986. *The science question in feminism.* Ithaca, N.Y.: Cornell University Press.

I am not a feminist but… <http://www.asahi-net.or.jp/~RF6T-TYFK/feminism.html>

Lorber, J. 2000. Using gender to undo gender. *Feminist Theory: An International Interdisciplinary Journal* 1(1).

Masini, B. E. 1999. Futures studies and sociology: A debate, a critical approach and a hope. *International Review of Sociology / Revue International de Sociologie* 9(3): 325–332.

O'Loughlin, P., N. Converse, and H. Hoechst, 1998. Listening to women's voices: Toward a comparative politics of women's difference. *Advances in Gender Research* 3: 103–137.

Fiona Stewart

HUMOR

Humor empowers people. Oppressed groups deliberately use humor (as they do music) to lighten their burdens. Women's studies has brought a newly conceived political analysis to humor theory. It has also demonstrated the existence of feminist humor, which was barely acknowledged before 1980.

Feminist humor arises from the conviction that assigning power on the basis of genitalia is both ludicrous and unacceptable. Unlike mainstream humor, feminist humor is not content merely to ridicule an inherently fatuous status quo. Rather, it grows out of informed visions of better worlds. Feminist humor, unlike survival humor of other oppressed groups, is hopeful and transformative. It participates in and inspires changes for the better. Sometimes it conveys immediate insight into complex problems, eliminating the need for extended analysis.

The first collection of feminist humor, *Pulling Our Own Strings,* edited by Gloria Kaufman and Mary Kay Blakely, was published in 1980, and it stimulated many subsequent publications. Also in the 1980s, several new feminist performers substantially supplemented the rarer feminist comic artists of the 1960s and 1970s. Taken in sum, their practice celebrated modes of power vastly different from masculine societal norms. They regularly ridiculed the equation of force and power. In the feminist view, the physical brute and the man with the gun lack persuasive power, imagination, and essential rhetorical skills, and such people are thus insecure and weak, not strong. They are power deficient, not powerful. In the 1990s, feminist comedians continued to ridicule the use of force as puerile, illogical, historically unjustified, or just plain foolish.

Women's studies scholarship has modified the popular Freudian view of hostility humor as cathartic for the performer or teller. Viewing people from inclusive rather than exclusive perspectives, feminism questions the advisability of creating new victims through the release of repressed hostilities. Where cathartic humor for one leads to trauma for another, is there (ask feminists) a significant gain? Partially in response to such arguments, aggressive attack humor in Anglo-American cultures substantially decreased in the 1980s—although it did not disappear, nor does it seem to be dying. In contrast to mainstream put-down humor, feminist theory and practice has placed new emphasis on constructive laughter. Feminist humor favors pickups over put-downs.

Stereotypes have been the bread and butter of mainstream humor. By A.D. 101 Juvenal's "Sixth Satire" firmly defined the female for most western cultures as stereotypically nasty, lying, vicious, pretentious, emasculating, garrulous, aggressive, vulgar, nymphomaniacal, gluttonous, dishonest, shameless, quarrelsome, greedy, impertinent, and disgusting. Notably absent were "stupid" and "ineffectual," added in subsequent centuries. Although this article is mainly concerned with occidental humor, varying cultures produce varied stereotypes.

In the West, the pernicious and ugly female stereotype persuaded women to bond with men (not with each other), as they sought to establish their difference from the stereotypically obnoxious women whose existence they did not question. For example, reacting to the profusion of unsavory mother-in-law jokes, even married women were disposed to bond with their husbands against stereotypically oppressive mothers and mothers-in-law.

Conventions of joke telling do not allow listeners to question the stereotypes and the values upon which the jokes are based. One can respond to the joke as good or bad merely on the basis of its artfulness. Feminist humor, however, has given people tools for questioning values underlying humor. People can now comment that a clever joke is socially pernicious.

The values of society are reflected in its humor. Feminist analysis reveals negative stereotypes of women as a mainstay of patriarchal culture. It further demonstrates that patriarchal humor assists in maintaining the rule of "superior" white males over stereotypically conceived women, children, minorities, and even majorities arbitrarily defined as inferior.

Feminist humor, in contrast, avoids stereotypes. It has not responded in kind to mainstream hostility humor by creating a stereotypical male or father-in-law or patriarch. While it does attack harmful, stereotypical *actions*, it rarely attacks specific persons. Feminist humor seeks more often to convert than to scoff at or to destroy its enemies.

The aim of feminist humor is to celebrate and promote political equity and social difference. It invites people to cherish and to enjoy the rich varieties we find in nature, in ethnic groups, and in societies.

People generally and mistakenly have valued humor only for the pleasure it gives. Feminist humorists, however, consciously appreciate and exploit humor's classically important power to convey knowledge and to inspire understanding. Enjoyment alone, although a requirement, is not a sufficient motivating value for the feminist. The joys of insight and of bonding for a common good are pleasures consistently sought in feminist humor.

Feminist humor emphasizes the healthy aspects of humor for everyone. Humor (in addition to improving physical health) is effective in promoting balanced perspectives, in affording insights, and in encouraging playfulness. Feminist humor seeks to touch the hugely positive potential of human beings and, in a world darkened by excessive reporting of destructive events, to remind everyone of rejuvenating choices.

See Also

CARTOONS AND COMICS; HUMOR: CASE STUDY—COMEDY, UNITED STATES

References and Further Reading

Bilger, Audrey. 1998. *Laughing feminism: Subversive comedy in Frances Burney, Maria Edgeworth, and Jane Austen*. Detroit, Mich.: Wayne State University Press.

Clinton, Kate. 1982. Making light: Another dimension. *Trivia: A Journal of Ideas* I (1: Fall).

Horowitz, Susan. 1997. *Queens of comedy*. Amsterdam: Gordon and Breach.

Kaufman, Gloria, ed. 1991. *In stitches: A patchwork of feminist humor and satire*. Bloomington: Indiana University Press.

Kaufman, Gloria, and Mary Kay Blakely, eds. 1980. *Pulling our own strings: Feminist humor and satire.* Bloomington: Indiana University Press.

Killer, M. Alison. 1999. Gender conflict and coercion on A&E's "An Evening at the Improv." *Journal of Popular Culture* 32 (4) 45–57. Online: EBSCOhost Academic Elite.

Morris, Linda A., ed. 1994. *American women humorists.* New York and London: Garland.

Stannard, Una. 1977. *Mrs (sic) Man.* San Francisco: Germainbooks.

Walker, Nancy A. 1988. *A very serious thing: Women's humor and American culture.* Minneapolis: University of Minnesota Press.

Gloria Kaufman

HUMOR:
Case Study—Comedy, United States

For years, comedy was a male-dominated profession, aided by the myth that women had no sense of humor and the perception that to deliberately provoke laughter was "unfeminine." With the influence of the women's movement, however, women comics overcame this cultural resistance to the "funny woman" and are no longer a marginalized or alternative voice but have begun to shape mainstream culture.

Lotta Crabtree is credited with being the first female comedian. Crabtree began performing humorous songs and dances, physical bits, parodies, characters, and improvisation in mid-nineteenth-century variety halls and went on to become the highest-paid actress of her day. In vaudeville's early days, performers such as Marie Dressler, May Irwin, Trixie Friganza, and Irene Franklin achieved success with acts made up of comic songs and dances, impersonations, skits, character sketches, and self-depreciating stage patter (including fat jokes). Women comics were a vaudeville rarity, and their comedy was crafted so as not to offend or challenge predominantly male audiences. Self-depreciating humor served to downplay the power a performer held over her audience, as did the comic stereotype of the desperate man-chaser, which emerged at this time. The custom of adult women performing in the personas of nonthreatening "kid characters" also emerged during these years.

After the turn of the twentieth century, vaudeville performers such as Eva Tanguay, Sophie Tucker, and Mae West created comedy that was more aggressive and uninhibited and often overtly sexual. Tanguay, one of vaudeville's biggest stars, took the stage in scanty, attention-grabbing costumes, performing provocative dances and comic songs loaded with sexual innuendo. Tucker, whose trademark song was "I'm the Last of the Red Hot Mamas," was a large, bold woman who, dressed in sequined gowns and furs, sang bawdy songs filled with double entendres. Yet both, like most women comics of this era, continued to rely on self-mockery and fat jokes to disarm audiences. Mae West was a true groundbreaker in that she shunned self-depreciating humor. Her comic persona was strong, witty, and aggressively sexual. While frankly interested in men, she consistently rejected the limitations of the domestic sphere with lines such as "Marriage is a great institution. But I'm not ready for an institution yet." Another strong, aggressive performer whose career began in vaudeville was Jackie "Moms" Mabley, who performed as an elderly housedress-clad mother figure and addressed her audience as "children," but whose material was raunchy, assertive, and laced with political and social satire.

Although women silent comedy stars participated as fully as their male counterparts in the slapstick physical humor that was silent movie comedy (Mabel Normand, the most popular female comic of the silent era, is credited with originating—in 1913—the custard-pie-in-the-face gag), when it came to spoken comedy, women in radio, the movies, and eventually television, during the decades of the 1920s through the 1960s, were limited to nonthreatening comic roles such as the desperate man-chaser, the ugly-but-funny wisecracking dame, the precocious kid, and the "Dumb Dora." Fanny Brice achieved radio stardom in the 1930s as Baby Snooks, a kid character. Carol Channing and Judy Holliday both built careers on portraying adorable dimwits. Judy Canova and Eve Arden played wisecracking man-chasers. Minnie Pearl's smart-mouthed hillbilly constantly joked about her unattractiveness to men. Joan Davis and Jane Ace played scatterbrained housewives.

Gracie Allen was the most popular and most beloved of the Dumb Doras. Although Allen's comedy arguably contained a subversive element, in that her dizzy "illogic" was actually a form of verbal cleverness that continuously undermined her partner's more stolid "male logic," it was Lucille Ball, the most popular 1950s-era television star, who first truly subverted the prevailing sitcom convention of the contented homemaker. A basic premise of *I Love Lucy* was the housewife Lucy Ricardo's desire to be a star just like her husband Ricky. Although she always failed to achieve this goal, Lucy continued to rebel against the traditional domestic role. Other performers whose comedy challenged the compliant housewife stereotype at this time were Imogene Coca (who performed brilliant comic sketches and physical comedy on *Your Show of Shows),* Elaine May (who, with her partner Mike Nichols, presented intelligent social satire), and Carol

Burnett (whose popular comedy and variety show ran from 1967 to 1978).

The Mary Tyler Moore Show made the definitive break from the repressiveness of domestic comedy by basing a sitcom on a single career woman who, rather than getting herself into scrapes from which a man had to rescue her, was happily self-sufficient and independent. At the same time, the stand-up comics Joan Rivers and Phyllis Diller, while continuing to use self-depreciation to disarm audiences, firmly rejected the limitations of the domestic sphere, reveling in aggressive, often hostile, wit, telling jokes mocking both husbands and housekeeping.

These developments were grounded in the women's movement, which helped transform the content of women's comedy, enabling material to move from the personal to the political and allowing women comedians to define real problems while mocking or subverting prevailing cultural stereotypes. A male audience was no longer assumed, nor was material limited to what wouldn't offend or challenge men. Lily Tomlin, who first became famous in the early 1970s for the characters she created on *Laugh-In,* went on to star in one-woman shows grounded in feminist values. A former welfare mother, Whoopi Goldberg, came to prominence in 1984 with a one-woman Broadway show that brilliantly critiqued the racism and sexism of the dominant culture. Roseanne Barr based a successful long-running television series on her large, loudmouthed, working-class, and outspokenly feminist stand-up persona.

As the women's movement freed the content of women's comedy, the proliferation of comedy clubs, cable comedy shows, and other "alternative" performing venues increased the ability of diverse comic voices to reach an audience. Sandra Bernhard, Marsha Warfield, and Elayne Boosler began comedy careers in the clubs. Bette Midler developed her "Divine Miss M" persona while performing at gay bathhouses. And years before Ellen Degeneres "came out" on national prime-time television, lesbian comedians such as Robin Tyler and Kate Clinton developed successful careers by performing for all-women audiences.

See Also

HUMOR; THEATER: OVERVIEW; THEATER: WOMEN IN THEATER

References and Further Reading

Martin, Linda, and Seagrave, Kerry. 1986. *Women in comedy.* N.J.: Citadel.

Warren, Roz. 1995. *Revolutionary laughter: The world of women comics.* Freedom, Calif.: Crossing.

Roz Warren

HUNGER

See FOOD, HUNGER, AND FAMINE.

HUNTING

Hunting, most broadly defined, is the armed pursuit of wild animals, with the specific intention of killing them, for food, hides, fur, or other goods for human use. Whether for trophies, sport, or subsistence (categories that frequently overlap), hunting has been in most historically recorded times and places a predominantly, sometimes exclusively, male activity. Involving a complex aggregate of skills and lore passed from one generation of males to the next, hunting has served both in primordial hunter-forager societies and in developed western societies as a masculine rite of passage. The apparent link between hunting and a culture of male violence against both women and nonhuman nature has led radical feminists and vegetarian ecofeminists to be sharply critical of hunting in all its forms, with the possible exception of pure subsistence hunting.

The too-ready identification of hunting with "manhood" is called into question, however, by the fact that in many cultures, both ancient and modern, women have always hunted, either alongside the men or by themselves. The Tiwi Aborigines, the Mbuti Pygmies, the Philippine Agta, and several Native American groups provide models of female hunting that, along with a growing body of archaeological evidence, throws into question the conventional image of "man the hunter." So, too, does the fact that North American women are hunting in increasing numbers. When surveyed as to why they hunt, these women tend to cite the same motivations male hunters do: to put food on the table, get into closer touch with nature, demonstrate skills, get exercise. As a group, women are more likely than men to seek instruction in firearms use and safety, less likely to cite "trophyism" as a prime motivating factor for hunting, and less likely to violate game laws. Women are also (proponents and critics of hunting agree) playing an increasingly visible role in the hunting community.

See Also

ANIMAL RIGHTS; ECOFEMINISM; FOOD AND CULTURE; FOOD, HUNGER, AND FAMINE; FURS; VEGETARIANISM

References and Further Reading

Dahlberg, Frances. 1981. *Woman the gatherer.* New Haven, Conn.: Yale University Press.

Morrow, Laurie, and Steve Smith. 1996. *Shooting sports for women.* New York: St. Martin's.

Stange, Mary Zeiss. 1997. *Woman the hunter.* Boston: Beacon.

Mary Zeiss Stange

HYBRIDITY AND MISCEGENATION

The double-edged terms *hybridity* and *miscegenation* suggest the interbreeding of species, varieties, races, or other heterogeneous sources and have been a focus in two areas of feminist scholarship, both of which concern female embodiment and women's particular relationship to processes of both biological and sociocultural reproduction. On the one hand, feminist historians and social, political, and cultural critics in both western and postcolonial contexts have explored the impact on specific groups of women of the policies and discourses of colonialism, slavery, racism, ethnocentrism, and narrow nationalism, which have linked personal and community identities to notions of purity of race, stock, or heredity. In both historical and contemporary contexts, the fear of miscegenation, of a degeneracy rooted in racial impurity, "tainted blood," and the production of hybrid, "bastard" races, has been evoked to justify a range of specific strategies of surveillance and control over women's reproductive activities. At their most extreme, these have included the repeated use of rape and sexual violence as a weapon of ethnic and racialized conflict and the lynching of men identified as real or potential rapists in the name of "protecting" women (Stoler, 1996; Hurtado, 1989; Butalia, 1995). More generally, when the female body and women's reproductive activities are appropriated as a boundary marker safeguarding the purity of national, racial, religious, and ethnic community identities, then exercising the power to define those identities involves taking women's bodies as both a symbolic and material target of conflict and contestation (Kandiyoti, 1993). The focus in this first area of feminist scholarship is, therefore, on the ways in which racist and colonial "antimiscegenation" discourses and practices have contributed to producing women's identities and social positioning through specific intersections of unequal power relations structured by gender, race, ethnicity, and sexuality.

A second area of scholarship and debate, which has emerged particularly in the work of black, postcolonial, and diasporic feminist theorists, has concerned the usefulness of reclaiming and redefining the concept of hybridity, together with related concepts such as creolization, *mestizaje,* in-betweenness, and diaspora. Different notions of hybridity have been evoked as a basis for alternative feminist models of identity that challenge both the racist and imperial discourses of antimiscegenation discussed earlier and the limitations of feminist resistance based on narrow versions of identity politics. Avtar Brah (1996) uses the concepts of diaspora and "diaspora space" to critique discourses of fixed, pure origins, while also seeking to reconstruct a space of identity from which a different kind of feminist subject might speak and act. The concept of diaspora space, in which both "native" and "migrant" are implicated, problematizes the question of pure origins by stressing the "entanglement of genealogies of dispersion with those of 'staying put'" (Brah, 1996: 181). Brah's diaspora space, like Gloria Anzaldúa's "borderlands" (1987) or Trinh T. Minh-ha's "inappropriate/d others" (1989), all suggest models of personal and collective identity in which hybrid bodies inhabit and act in impure spaces and where multiple positionings of identity are the norm rather than a dangerous deviation.

Feminist critics of hybridity models have argued that, when used in a decontextualized and universalizing way, they can work to cover over the specificities of gender, class, caste, and other differences. For some, they also misrepresent the dynamics of both anticolonial and postcolonial struggles that aimed, not to celebrate the mobility and intermingling of ideas and identities, but rather to recover an authentic cultural identity debased and dismissed by colonialism (see Loomba, 1998). However, others argue that, when specifically situated and contextualized, hybridity concepts offer a way of both acknowledging and reworking the injuries of colonialism and of thinking about identities that "survive, not on the basis of original innocence, but on the basis of seizing the tools to mark the world that marked them as other" (Haraway, 1991: 175). Chicana feminist retellings of the story of Malinche, the indigenous woman who, as Cortez's first interpreter and mistress, is seen as the shamed mother of the mestizo "bastard" race, provide one example of this reworking of the injuries of conquest to positively rethink identity (Moraga, 1986). Malinche's mastery of the conqueror's language is seen as an "illegitimate production that allows survival" of both self and community in a model of identity that does not depend on access to pure origins (Haraway, 1991: 175). Moraga and Anzaldua's hybrid—"borderlands" writing that shifts between English and Spanish, poetry and prose—is a further working out of the modalities of survival "without the founding myth of original wholeness" (176).

Drawing on this and other work by feminists of color and postcolonial feminists, as well as her own explorations of the paradigm shifts emerging from late-twentieth-century science and technology, the white U.S. theorist Donna Haraway (1991) offers feminism another hybrid figure—the cyborg, or cybernetic organism, a hybrid of machine and organism. The cyborg is Haraway's ironic, monstrous challenge to prevailing models of identity based on subject-object, nature-culture dualisms. Rejecting identity narratives based on pure, unified origins and confounding categorical distinctions, the cyborg's identity story always begins "in the middle" and can never be taken as an organic, "in the blood" basis for identity politics. For Haraway, a cyborg feminist politics would be based on affinity rather than identity. Affinity groups come together, not because of an assumed, preexistent and "natural" wholeness, but because they are "imperfectly stitched together" as partial, differently situated, and hybrid selves. Haraway's vision of women as cyborgs has been taken up as a critical focus of debate within a variety of feminisms over humans' (and particularly women's) relationship with nature, machines, and new technologies, including questions of new reproductive technologies and technologies of body modification. It has also been the focus of debate over the pertinence to feminism of a model of a "disassembled and reassembled, postmodern collective and personal self" (Haraway, 1991: 163) and of the effectiveness of a vision of coalition politics based on learning to read "geometries of difference and contradiction crucial to women's cyborg identities" (170). Hybridity models such as diaspora space, borderlands, and the cyborg are therefore also interventions into the ongoing debate within feminist political theory over strategies of resistance to women's subordination. Drawing both from models of resistance as emancipatory identity politics and from postmodern strategies of destabilizing identity, hybridity models argue for strategies that simultaneously problemize and reconstruct a space of identity and agency.

See Also

BLACKNESS AND WHITENESS; BODY; COLONIALISM AND POST-COLONIALISM; DIFFERENCE, *I and II*; IDENTITY POLITICS; POSTCOLONIALISM: THEORY AND CRITICISM; POSTMODERNISM: FEMINIST CRITIQUES

References and Further Reading

Anzaldúa, Gloria. 1987. *Borderlands/La frontera.* San Francisco: Aunt Lute.

Brah, Avtar. 1996. *Cartographies of diaspora: Contesting identities.* London and New York: Routledge.

Butalia, Urvashi. 1995. Muslims and Hindus, men and women. In T. Sarkar and U. Butalia, eds., *Women and the Hindu right,* 58–81. Delhi: Kali for Women.

Haraway, Donna. 1991. *Simians, cyborgs and women: The reinvention of nature.* London: Free Association.

Hurtado, Aida. 1989. Relating to privilege: Seduction and rejection in the subordination of white women and women of colour. *Signs* 14(4): 833–855.

Kandiyoti, Deniz. 1993. Identity and its discontents. In L. Chrisman and P. Williams, eds., *Colonial discourse and post-colonial theory,* 376–392. London: Harvester Wheatsheaf.

Loomba, Ania. 1998. *Colonialism/postcolonialism.* New York and London: Routledge.

Moraga, Cherrie. 1986. From a long line of Vendidas: Chicanas and feminism. In T. de Lauretis, ed., *Feminist studies/critical studies,* 173–190. Basingstoke: Macmillan.

Stoler, Ann Laura. 1996. *Race and the education of desire.* Durham, N.C.: Duke University Press.

Trinh T. Minh-ha. 1989. *Woman, native, other.* Bloomington: Indiana University Press.

Irene Gedalof

HYPERMASCULINITY

The term *hypermasculinity* has entered the popular lexicon of feminist writers to refer to a glorification of those traits conventionally identified with men or masculinity. As such, hypermasculinity recalls a related concept, hegemonic masculinity. The latter, as first defined by R. W. Connell, stems from the Gramscian understanding of the concept of hegemony where "a social ascendancy achieved in a play of social forces…extends beyond contests of brute power into the organization of private life and cultural processes" (Connell, 1987: 184). As such, hegemonic masculinity propagates a certain ideology of being for both men and women, one that may, in fact, have little to do with their daily lives. But herein lies the major difference between these two concepts. While hypermasculinity also comes to assume ideological pretensions, it affects actual lives and bodies all too intimately. This effect stems from the primarily reactionary nature of hypermasculinity. Where hegemonic masculinity serves as an ideal, hypermasculinity arises when that ideal is threatened or jeopardized.

This shift from masculinity to hypermasculinity, according to Cynthia Weber (2000: 11), indicates "an oversaturation of signs of the masculine." She cites U.S. foreign policy toward Cuba as an example. Whereas Cuba had been "feminized" into a gambling-and-whoring playground for North American and European *turistas,* it achieved a "hypermasculinized" aspect with Castro's revolution. Castro himself embodied such hypermasculinity, with his "unmanicured beard…olive fatigues and cap." But the Cuban revolution also upturned the hegemonic power of (masculine, white) Uncle Sam. For this reason, according to Weber, U.S. foreign policy has sought consistently to *re-hegemonize* itself by emasculating Cuba and Castro through such hypermasculine tactics as cutting off (assassinations), penetration (invasions), and withdrawal (embargoes). Yet Uncle Sam has remained unsuccessful in dethroning Castro Rex and taking feminized Cuba to bed, so to speak. Cuba mirrors for the United States a sense of national castration.

This gendered context provides special insight for some into the custody battle over a 6-year-old Cuban refugee boy, Elián González, that captured public attention in 1999 and 2000. Elián (read: male progeny) was found floating in the open sea, gripping for life onto a rubber tire. His mother and stepfather had drowned in their attempt to cross from Cuba (read: Castro's socialist patriarchy) to Miami (read: Uncle Sam's capitalist patriarchy). Elián's biological father (read: Cuban patriarch), who had remained in Cuba, wanted him back. But Elián's relatives in Miami (read: subaltern Cuban patriarchs in white-male America) refused to return the boy, claiming that to do so would sentence him to a lifetime of tyranny under Castro. Meanwhile, the Immigration and Naturalization Service (INS) (read: white Uncle Sam), ruled that Elián should be returned to his father. As the dissenting relatives lobbied to get Elián U.S. citizenship so that he could remain in the country, the boy's two grandmothers (read: Cuban matriarchs) flew first to New York, then to Washington, D.C., then to Miami and back again to persuade the "American people" (read: white patriarchs and matriarchs) to let him "go home." Fidel Castro himself (read: the ultimate *patron*) spoke on the issue, declaring that the Cuban people were willing to fight for Elián's return even if it took 10 years.

Two patriarchal camps claimed this little boy: his biological father, his grandmothers, and the Cuban nation on one side and his Miami relatives with some U.S. politicians on the other. Overlying this communal struggle was the larger context of U.S.–Cuban interstate relations for the past forty years. In a historic twist, Elián's Miami relatives sought to avenge Uncle Sam's previous "emasculation" by aggressively possessing the boy as *their* rightful progeny or heritage. To counter this hypermasculine tactic, Elián's biological father and, by extension, Castro himself turned to a potent mix in Latin culture: religion and matriarchy. With the help of Christian groups, Elián's grandmothers built on their cultural cachet to achieve a masterful double move. First, they subverted the hypermasculine impasse between Cuba and the United States by internalizing it, with the Cuban émigré community in Miami taking up the hypermasculine stance against Cuba and Castro. Elián's Miami relatives, however, had little cultural recourse to deflect the grand-

mothers' powerful rhetoric of family and love in comparison with their cold, abstract arguments of ideology and politics. In Anglo America, moreover, the grandmothers reestablished a familiar, comforting discourse of feminized Cuba, one that rendered them more sympathetic precisely because they helped to remasculinize Uncle Sam.

For adherents of this theory, this case highlights the significance of hypermasculinity in constructing identities and scripts in world affairs. Not only do people need to pay attention to the cultural underpinnings of race, gender, and sexuality to understand strategies of power and resistance, but they must also trace their intimate linkage with a larger context of imperialism and colonialism.

Ashis Nandy initially developed the concept of hypermasculinity to explain the impact of British rule on India. Hypermasculinity, according to Nandy (1988: 35), rationalized all those "magical feelings of omnipotence and permanence" that colonialism and imperialism projected onto men, especially if they were white. In turn, hypermasculinity conformed to colonialism's denigration of anything smacking of the feminine, including women, the household, homosexuality, intellectual activity, and social welfare. Colonizers and colonized alike embraced hypermasculinity because it allowed each to claim a right to manly mastery over various feminized "others." Where the British colonizers could feminize all Indians as "ineffectual" or "subordinate," elite Indian men, in turn, could feminize lower-caste men and all women as "unworthy" or "submissive."

Nandy (1988: 32–33) found that hypermasculinity also incurred an "underdeveloped heart." It eroded the master self as much as the slave other with four pervasive social pathologies: (1) a denigration of the feminine that justified "a limited role for women—and femininity—by holding that the softer side of human nature is irrelevant to the public sphere," (2) a false cultural homogeneity that "blurred the lines of social divisions by opening up alternative channels of social mobility in the colonies... through colonial wars of expansion," (3) an "underdeveloped heart" that "triggered 'banal' violence" due to an "isolation of cognition from affect," and (4) an empty potency that "promised to liberate man from his daily drudgery" but that, with the decline of empire, unleashed a "racist underside" and "wholesale Westernisation."

Some critics extend this notion of hypermasculine pathology to capitalist economic development—most recently identified as globalization. In this context hypermasculinity reconstructs social subjects, spaces, and activities into economic agents that "valorize" a masculinized, global competitiveness associated with men, entrepreneurs, the upwardly mobile, cities, and industrialization. It assigns a feminized, local stagnancy to women, peasants, the poor, and agrarian production. Hypermasculine development induces an "underdeveloped heart" through a seemingly objective, economistic rhetoric that, nevertheless, corrodes with an alienating, materialistic malaise. As with colonialism, hypermasculine capitalism confounds the self even while glorifying it against a "backward," "envious" other.

Elsewhere, for example, it has been argued that hypermasculinity accounts for east Asia's drive for "miracle" economies (Ling, 2001). This developmental ideology sought to reverse the West's historical feminization of east Asia through colonization (Singapore, Hong Kong, China) occupation (Japan, Korea, Taiwan). Certain leaders—notably Singapore's Lee Kuan Yew, Malaysia's Mohamad Mahathir, Korea's Kim Dae Jung, and the author of *The Japan That Can Say No* (Shintaro, 1991)—have attributed the region's "miracle" growth to newly masculinized "Asian values" such as hard work, tenacity, and virtue in contrast to "western" ones like sloth, decadence, and deceit. Those with a less racist rhetoric, nevertheless, also envisioned a new type of Asian capitalism that would challenge the supremacy of the West (Commission for a New Asia, 1994).

These Asian values, however, included a systematic exploitation of women and their labor, whether in households, factories, offices, or brothels (Truong, 1999). In 1997 and 1998, the financial crisis in Asia arguably demonstrated the hollow, self-defeating boasts of "miracle" economies and the like, as well as a complicit submission of certain governments to their international financial overlords. South Korea's Kim Dae Jung, for example, declared in 1997 that his country would not deviate from the International Monetary Fund's (IMF) reforms even "by one percent" (S. Young, 1998). Such conformity in light of western denunciations of Asian "crony capitalism," "macro mismanagement," and "poor governance" invariably recalls previous conditions of colonial subservience.

Hypermasculinity, however, cuts both ways. It corrodes the western self as much as the Asian other. Internal dissent against the IMF and its handling of the Asian financial crisis, particularly in violence-ridden Indonesia (Glassman, 1997; Radelet and Sachs, 1998; Wolf, 1997) has led to what many believe is a breakdown in the "Washington consensus" (Bullard, 1998). At the same time, the neocolonial rhetoric of western institutions has incited a revival of reactionary hypermasculinity from the region. Mohamad Mahathir may be alone in accusing the West outright of a currency neoimperialism, but the sentiment remains potent, especially in those areas racked by unemployment, strikes, protests, riots, and violence while western companies buy bankrupt companies and banks at bargain prices.

These two cases—the custody battle over Elián González and Asia's financial crisis—argue for the impact and relevance of hypermasculinity in today's world. A reactionary distortion of hegemonic masculinity, hypermasculinity may destabilize the world into ever greater, more expansive spirals of attack and counterattack.

See Also

COLONIALISM AND POSTCOLONIALISM; FEMININITY; GLOBALIZATION; IMPERIALISM; MASCULINITY; MISOGYNY; OTHER; PATRIARCHY: FEMINIST THEORY; PHALLOCENTRISM; SEXISM

References and Further Reading

Berger, M. 1996. Yellow mythologies: The east Asian miracle and post–cold war capitalism. *Positions* 4(1): 90–126.

Bullard, N. 1998. Taming the IMF: How the Asian crisis cracked the Washington consensus. Paper presented at the international conference on "The Economic Crisis in East Asia and the Impact on Local Populations," Roskilde University (29–30 October).

Commission for a New Asia. 1994. *Towards a new Asia: A report*. Tokyo: Sakasawa Foundation.

Connel, R.W. 1987. *Gender and power: Society, the person, and sexual politics*. Cambridge: Polity.

Glassman, J. K. 1997. IMF doing more harm than good. *Straits Times* (11 December).

Ling, L. H. M. 2001. *Conquest and desire: Postcolonial learning between Asia and the West*. London: Macmillan.

Nandy, A. 1988. *The intimate enemy*. Delhi: Oxford University Press.

Radelet, S., and J. Sachs. 1998. The onset of the east Asian financial crisis. *Straits Times* (10 February).

Rao, V. V. B. 1998. East Asian economies: The crisis of 1997–1998. *Economic and Political Weekly* (6 June): 1397–1416.

Shintaro, I. 1991. *The Japan that can say no: Why Japan will be first among equals*. New York: Simon and Schuster.

Truong, T. D. 1999. The underbelly of the tiger: Gender and the demystification of the Asian miracle. *Review of International Political Economy* 6(2): 133–65.

Weber, C. 2000. *Faking it: U.S. hegemony in a "post-phallic" era*. Minneapolis: University of Minnesota Press.

Wolf, M. 1997. Same old harsh medicine being doled out to help ailing economies. *Financial Times* (16 December).

Young, R. 1990. *White mythologies*. London: Routledge.

Young, S. 1998. Korea's financial crisis: Causes and prospects. *BAD-OECD Forum on Asian Perspectives*, Paris (3 June).

L. H. M. Ling

HYPERTENSION:
Case Study—Class, Race, and Gender

In any study pertaining to women, it is critical to remember that they are not a single group, defined chiefly by biological sex or through membership in the abstract, "universal" (and often implicitly "white") category of "woman." Instead, women are a mixed lot, with gender roles and options shaped by history, culture, and deep divisions that fall along the jagged lines of class, race, and ethnicity. Because population patterns of hypertension among women in the United States parallel not only these class and race divisions but also pose important tests of current etiologic theories, it is important to consider how knowing the effects of sexism, racism, and social class may improve understanding of the causes of hypertension.

Hypertension is a term given to chronically elevated blood pressure. Typically, a person is considered to have hypertension if her or his systolic blood pressure is measured as being greater than 140 mm Hg, if diastolic blood pressure is greater than 90 mm Hg, or both.

Hypertension matters because it is an important risk factor for heart disease and stroke, which currently are the first and third leading cause of death in the United States. In 2001, hypertension occured among one in four adults age 20 and older in the United States, affecting approximately 25 percent of men and 20 percent of women. Globally, hypertension is the fourth leading cause of morbidity, affecting nearly 700 million people annually.

Evidence suggests that working-class, poor, and poorly educated women currently are at greater risk of being hypertensive than more affluent women. For example, from 1988 to 1994, among U.S. women aged 20 and older, 31 percent of women living below the poverty line had hypertension, compared with 20 percent of middle-high-income women living in households whose income was at least two times higher than the poverty line (for a family of four in 1995, the poverty line was $15,569). At each income level, however, the prevalence of hypertension was higher among black, non-Hispanic women then among white, non-Hispanic women: 40 percent versus 30 percent among poor women, and 30 percent versus 20 percent among middle-high-income women. Among Mexican-American women, rates did not vary by income level: among poor women, the prevalence of hypertension (25 percent) was lower than that of black and white women, whereas among middle-high-income women, the prevalence of hypertension among Mexican-American women (25 percent) was intermediate between that of black and white women. As of the early

twenty-first century, accepted risk factors (obesity, diet, alcohol, and exercise) do not fully account for these patterns or the prevalence of hypertension among women as a whole.

Explanations of hypertension that focus only on biological mechanisms and that fail to account for class and race-based differences in risk among women may be, at best, incomplete and, at worst, misguided. As Geoffrey Rose (1985) argued in his essay "Sick Individuals and Sick Populations," the causes of individual cases are not necessarily the same as the determinants of the incidence in populations. At issue are two different questions: Why do some individuals have hypertension? and Why do some populations have much hypertension, while in others it is rare? The former question emphasizes individual susceptibility, while the latter shifts the focus to population exposures. Consequently, to understand the epidemiology of hypertension, one needs to explore the social patterning of both exposure and susceptibility in women's everyday lives as shaped by their intertwined histories as members of a particular society and as biological organisms who grow, develop, interact, and age.

What is known about social class and hypertension among women in the United States is limited, in part because the literature is slim and in part because what does exist mainly "controls" or "adjusts" for social class rather than directly analyze its effects. Few studies employ comparable measures. The profusion (or confusion) of measures, as well as the disregard for the different meaning of social class measured at the individual versus household level, is not unique to the literature on women and hypertension and reflects the state of epidemiologic research in the United States today.

Before considering the relationship between race or ethnicity and hypertension among women, it is important to stress that "race" is fundamentally a social and ideological—and not a biological—construct. Considerable research has established that nearly 95 percent of known human genetic variation occurs within the so-called racial groups and extremely little occurs across these groups. Starting with slavery and the conquest of the New World, the category of race has been inextricably linked to division based on property and wealth. Despite recent growth in what has been termed the black middle class, in 1993 fully 26 percent of black households and 24 percent of Hispanic households either had no assets or were in debt, compared with 10 percent of white households. Moreover, the median wealth of white households was 10 times that of black and Hispanic households: in 1993, the net worth of white households was $45,740, compared with $4,418 for black households and $4,656 for Hispanic households. Thus, even though the vast majority of poor women in the United States are white (because the white population is numerically the largest), women of color nonetheless are two to three times more likely than white women to be poor.

Substantial evidence indicates that, despite comparable blood pressure during childhood and adolescence, in young adulthood blood pressure rates start to rise more quickly among the black population than among the white population. As of 2001, among adults age 20 and over, 19 percent of white non-Hispanic women, 34 percent of black non-Hispanic women, and 22 percent of Mexican-American women have hypertension. National data on hypertension rates among subpopulations of black non-Hispanic and Hispanic women are difficult to obtain, although specific studies suggest that rates vary by country of birth and length of time lived in the United States. Data regarding hypertension among different groups of Asian and Pacific island women in the United States are even more varied and sparse. They also usually combine results for women born in the United States and abroad. Two studies conducted in California indicate that hypertension is much less common among Japanese and Chinese than white women, whereas the prevalence among Filipinas almost equals that among black women. Although factors associated with immigration and acculturation have been hypothesized to contribute to these differences, research on these topics has focused chiefly on Asian men, not women. Even fewer data exist for women among the diverse tribes and peoples labeled American Indian and Alaska Native. Risk may be higher, however, among Native Americans in the northern Great Plains then in the Southwest. Countering the view that Native Americans are at low risk of hypertension, recent surveys have found comparable levels among the Zunis and whites in New Mexico and among the Penobscot and whites in Maine. Once again, these patterns remain unexplained.

To address these gaps in our knowledge, researchers have begun to look at issues such as anger and the diverse ways people respond. Research, for example, has examined whether there is relationship between risk of hypertension and whether people hold anger in, let it out, or deal with it in a reflective manner. Along these lines, one study conducted among women reported that "anger-in" was associated with higher blood pressure among blacks but not whites living in areas of high socioeconomic stress and among whites but not blacks in areas of low socioeconomic stress.

Until recently, studies of women and hypertension have failed to consider explicitly whether risk of elevated blood pressure is influenced by experiences of discrimination and other forms of subordination or oppression. Countering or buffering negative effects might be the various ways in which women in diverse groups have been able to garner relevant social support as well as develop and maintain affirming identities at the individual and group level. Moreover, evidence shows that subjective appraisal of stressors may be inversely associated with the risk of hypertension; people who can name the source of their problems may be better off than those who are uncomprehending or silent. Nor can all kinds of discrimination be equated in terms of how people are treated by others and interpret the treatment of others. Some women may share the beliefs linking women's superiority in the domestic sphere with their lesser presence in public life and may not find such an arrangement oppressive. In contrast, no such favorable superior role has ever been granted to black Americans by the dominant culture, except perhaps as musicians, performers, and athletes.

Studying effects of gender discrimination on women is rendered difficult by ways in which, for women, the dualism of inferiority and superiority runs deep: allegedly inferior to men in the public sphere of work, intellect, and civic life but allegedly superior and cherished in the domestic sphere of caregiving, emotional nurturance, and raising children. This framework, however, has always been rife with contradiction. Many women are socialized to take care of others before taking care of themselves. Women routinely are treated as sex objects and on a daily basis may face the harassment of street remarks, the fear of rape, and—for some—the threat or memories of sexual abuse and domestic violence. In work, the route to both professional success and menial, low-paid, dead-end, insecure jobs can be stressful.

Add to this mix the realities of racism for women of color. As Harold Freeman (1991) remarked in an editorial in the *Journal of the National Cancer Institute* regarding differences in cancer among blacks and whites, "Black Americans have been legally free in this country for 25 years, having prior to that experienced 250 years of slavery and 100 years of legalized segregation." Little attention has been paid to the effects of ongoing, often daily insults, in which black women (regardless of class) are marginalized and patronized by their white coworkers or classmates. Black women are constantly aware that they may be suspected of shoplifting when they enter stores to purchase goods. Disproportionately, they suffer rude service at public accommodations and restaurants, and with their Hispanic sisters, they live more with the impact of violence and linguistic barriers. Self-doubt and a sense of inferiority permeate the lives of many working-class women, constituting part of what some term "the hidden injuries of class."

A new body of literature, accordingly, is beginning to study explicitly whether experiences or awareness of racial and gender discrimination are risk factors for hypertension, in conjunction with social class. Beginning in the late 1980s, both experimental and observational studies on this topic began to appear in the published literature. One early experimental study involving black and predominately female college students discovered that their blood pressure rose when shown movie excerpts displaying racist incidents but not when shown clips featuring angry, nonracial events. In 1990, the first small study was published explicitly addressing women's experiences of racial and gender discrimination in relation to risk of hypertension and found that black women who state that they usually accept and keep quiet about what they perceive as unfair treatment are over four times more likely to report hypertension than those who say they take action and talk to others. The study also reported no clear association between gender discrimination and hypertension in white women. Subsequent studies, in larger populations, have documented important associations between self-reported experiences of racial discrimination. Other studies continue to investigate associations between blood pressure and self-reported experiences of gender discrimination, with newer studies focusing on discrimination based on sexual identity or orientation. New work, bringing together epidemiologists, sociologists, social psychologists, and others, is tackling ways in which to study the multiple effects of racism, sexism, and class on hypertension and other outcomes, in both their interpersonal and structural or institutional manifestations.

It is possible that new, interdisciplinary work is necessary to find answers. At issue is how to frame both the questions and the solutions. For example, instead of studying "suppressed hostility" or people's "failure" to "cope" or "adapt"—as if the fault were located within individuals—researchers may need to consider the best ways people can express what they deem righteous anger at being treated unfairly on account of gender, race, and class. From the standpoint of disease prevention, there is a need to generate ideas and build coalitions to change the conditions that perpetuate these inequalities. For those who fear that these suggestions pollute science with politics, it is critical to stress that it is as political to ignore these issues as to raise them.

While pursuing promising leads regarding people's experiences and perceptions of interpersonal manifestations of discrimination, one also must not forget that the social relations of class, race, and gender shape not only people's patterns of interactions but also their exposure to other potentially important noxious agents. Lead, for example, recently has been linked to hypertension and is especially a problem among the poor and people of color. Bringing together all of these concerns without reducing issues of race to class or ignoring the role of gender remains a major challenge.

The strongest clues to etiology arise out of variation in disease patterns, not out of uniformity. To understand and ultimately prevent hypertension and other health problems, researchers must be guided by the "why" questions of explaining population patterns of disease and not only the "how" questions of disease causation.

See Also

HEALTH CHALLENGES; HEALTH: OVERVIEW; HEALTH CARE: UNITED STATES; POVERTY; RACE; RACISM AND XENOPHOBIA; SIMULATNEOUS OPPERSSIONS; STRESS

References and Further Reading

Armstead, C. A., K. A. Lawler, G. Gorden, J. Cross, and J. Gibbons. 1998. Relationship of racial stressors to blood pressure responses and anger expression in black college students. *Health Psychology* 8: 541–556.

Cavalli-Sforza, L. L., P. Menozzi, and A. Piazza. 1996. *The history and geography of human genes.* Princeton, N.J.: Princeton University Press.

Clark, R., N. B. Anderson, V. R. Clark, and D. R. Williams. 1999. Racism as a stressor for African Americans: A biopsychosocial mode. *American Psychology* 54: 805–816.

Fee, E., and N. Krieger, eds. 1994. *Women's health, politics, and power: Essays on sex/gender, medicine, and public health.* Amityville, N.Y.: Baywood.

Freeman, H. 1991. Race, poverty and cancer. *Journal of the National Cancer Institute* 83: 526–527.

Krieger, N. 2000. Discrimination and health. In L. Berkman and I. Kawachi, eds., *Social epidemiology,* 36–75. Oxford: Oxford University Press.

———. 1999. Racial and gender discrimination: Risk factors for high blood pressure? *Social Science and Medicine* 39: 1273–1281.

———, D. Rowley, A. A. Hermann, B. Avery, and M. T. Phillips. 1993. Racism, sexism, and social class: Implications for studies of health, disease, and well-being. *American Journal of Preventive Medicine* 9(Suppl. 2): 82–122.

Krieger, N., and S. Sidney. 1996. Racial discrimination and blood pressure: The CARDIA study of young black and white adults. *American Journal of Public Health* 86: 1370–1378.

Marmot, M., and P. Elliott, eds. 1992. *Coronary heart disease epidemiology: From aetiology to public health.* Oxford: Oxford University Press.

Martinez-Maldonado, M. 1991. Hypertension in Hispanics, Asians and Pacific Islanders, and Native Americans. *Circulation* 83: 1467–1469.

National Center for Health Statistics. 1998. *Health, United States, 1998, with socioeconomic status and health chartbook.* Hyattsville, Md.: National Center for Health Statistics.

Rose, G. 1985. Sick individuals and sick populations. *International Journal of Epidemiology* 14:32–38.

Sole, J. E., G. Heiss, H. A. Tyroler, W. B. Davis, S. B. Wing, and D. R. Ragland. 1991. Black-white differences in blood pressure among participants in NHANES II: The contribution of blood lead. *Epidemiology* 2: 348–352.

U.S. Census Bureau. Asset ownership of households: 1993 highlights. <www.census.gov/hhes/www/wealth/highlite.html>.

Wenger, N. K. 1995. Hypertension and other cardiovascular risk factors in women. *American Journal of Hypertension* 8: 94S–99S.

World Health Organization. 1998. *The world health report 1998. Life in the 21st century: A vision for all.* Geneva: World Health Organization.

Nancy Krieger